EXPERIMENTAL PSYCHOLOGY

VOLUME I: SENSATION AND PERCEPTION

WOODWORTH & SCHLOSBERG'S
EXPERIMENTAL PSYCHOLOGY
Third Edition

J. W. KLING & LORRIN A. RIGGS
Brown University

and
seventeen contributors

HOLT, RINEHART AND WINSTON, Inc.

New York   Chicago   San Francisco   Atlanta   Dallas   Montreal   Toronto

Contributors

MATHEW ALPERN   University of Michigan
ALEXANDER K. BARTOSHUK   University of Western Ontario
LINDA BARTOSHUK   John B. Pierce Foundation Laboratory
DONALD S. BLOUGH   Brown University
ROBERT M. BOYNTON   University of Rochester
RUSSELL M. CHURCH   Brown University
CHARLES N. COFER   The Pennsylvania State University
TRYGG ENGEN   Brown University
JULIAN HOCHBERG   Columbia University
DAN R. KENSHALO   Florida State University
J. W. KLING   Brown University
LEWIS P. LIPSITT   Brown University
RICHARD B. MILLWARD   Brown University
MAXWELL M. MOZELL   State University of New York, Upstate Medical Center
LEO POSTMAN   University of California, Berkeley
LORRIN A. RIGGS   Brown University
ALLAN M. SCHRIER   Brown University
CHARLES F. STEVENS   University of Washington
WILLARD R. THURLOW   University of Wisconsin

Copyright 1938, 1954, © 1971 by Holt, Rinehart and Winston, Inc.
Volume I, *Sensation and Perception,* copyright © 1972 by Holt, Rinehart and Winston, Inc.
All rights reserved
Library of Congress Catalog Card Number: 72-82602
ISBN: 0-03-002801-9
Printed in the United States of America
3 4 5 6   0 7 1   9 8 7 6 5 4 3 2

This is Volume I of a two-volume printing issued in 1972. Volume I will serve as a textbook in undergraduate and graduate courses dealing with sensory and perceptual problems, while Volume II will serve courses in learning, motivation, and memory. The original one-volume printing (1971) will still be available for the traditional courses that include all of the principal topics of experimental psychology. The index and reference matter have been included in both volumes of the 1972 printing.

PREFACE

TO THE THIRD EDITION

In 1938, Robert S. Woodworth brought out the first edition of his *Experimental Psychology*. In his preface he remarked on the "youth and immaturity of experimental psychology" in which "the student can rather quickly penetrate the zone of unsettled problems in original investigation." Woodworth traces the beginning of his work on the book to 1910 and states that a preliminary mimeographed edition of the book came out in 1920 with the collaboration of A. T. Poffenburger.

Surely no other psychologist could have made so lucid and comprehensive a presentation of the field as did Woodworth in 1938. He had had experience as a teacher and student in the basic fields of mathematics, philosophy, and physiology. He had also done research in collaboration with the great Sir Charles Sherrington in the study of expressions of anger and defense in the decerebrate cat. He later worked with Thorndike in the more traditionally psychological area of transfer of training and did his own research on voluntary movement, imageless thought, psychophysics, motivation, and tests of emotional stability. All this had brought Woodworth to the age of 70 by the time *Experimental Psychology* first appeared. Prior to that he had written several other books, including a revision of Ladd's *Physiological Psychology,* the widely used *Contemporary Schools of Psychology,* and the best-selling elementary textbook, *Psychology,* of which there were five editions from 1921 to 1947.

vii

The second edition of *Experimental Psychology* appeared in 1954 as a collaborative effort by Woodworth, then 85 years of age, and Harold Schlosberg. Schlosberg, like Woodworth, was known for the breadth of his interests in psychology, his eclectic position with regard to the various schools of psychological thought, and a strong concern for the intellectual development of students. In their preface, Woodworth and Schlosberg expressed the conviction that a book such as theirs should be revised at least once every decade. They did, in fact, start the revision of the first edition in 1949, but found as they went along that a new book was required, rather than a mere updating of the old one. Thus the second edition emphasized American psychology while the old one had been concerned to a large degree with European, especially German psychology, and much of the old material was omitted to make room for a greatly expanded coverage of topics of current interest. The new bibliography was larger by forty percent than the old, and over half of the 2,480 items cited had not been used in the old edition.

It is remarkable that two men could achieve in five years the enormous task of bringing out the second edition. With all this, they managed to preserve the easy informality and clarity of the earlier work despite the increasing complexity of the material covered. Both first and second editions were thus able to serve three rather different groups: advanced undergraduates, taking courses in experimental psychology, learning, motivation, sensory psychology or perception; graduate students, seeking a review of selected research areas to complement their study of primary source materials; and instructors, selecting illustrative materials directly within their own areas of specialization.

Before his death in 1964, Harold Schlosberg conceived the idea of bringing out a third edition of *Experimental Psychology* as a collaborative work with his colleagues in the Psychology Department at Brown University. The present edition is an outgrowth of that idea in which the two present editors and seven of the other authors are, indeed, members of that department. Of the remaining ten authors, five studied with Schlosberg and have degrees in psychology from Brown. Obviously, these authors could not aim their chapters equally at undergraduate, graduate, and professional psychologists. We have, instead, concentrated on the needs of the advanced undergraduate students; but we hope that this edition, like its predecessors, will also be found useful by the more advanced readers. Appraisal of the degree to which this edition fills these needs will have to come from our readers.

A good part of the success of the previous editions can be attributed to the avoidance of any preoccupation with jargon and narrowly defined experimentation. Especially to the student making his first explorations of an area, this is an important characteristic. We hope that we have achieved authenticity by having the chapters prepared by persons actively engaged in research in these areas; but we trust that the experience each author has had as a student and a teacher has been reflected in the organization he has given to his materials.

The present editors have found, as did Woodworth and Schlosberg in 1954, that great changes have occurred in the field of psychology since the previous edition. In fact, we estimate that only ten to fifteen percent of the figures, examples, and descriptive material contained in the earlier editions are retained in this one. While many of the chapter headings are carried over, some entirely new ones have been included, namely those on basic mechanisms of neural function, color vision, positive reinforcement, and aversive behavior. To make way for these new chapters and the mass of new material in others, we have necessarily dropped some previous chapters on reaction time, attention, emotion, conditioning, maze learning, and problem solving. In most cases, the experiments in these areas are covered within the other chapters to the extent that they are still active subjects for investigation. But the earlier editions of this work will have to be consulted by those particularly interested in such topics as reaction time and maze learning. We must similarly admit that most of the chapters present an unbalanced sample of species used as experimental subjects, but that is only a reflection of the research in those areas. Most of psychophysics and sensory psychology is based on data gathered with adult human subjects, while many problems in learning and motivation have been studied almost exclusively with the laboratory rat or pigeon. For some problems, of course, the unique characteristics of the octopus or the tree shrew may make it the species of choice, and wherever possible, the authors have tried to include such information. But a textbook, however large, must sacrifice breadth of coverage for depth, and therefore the emphasis in each chapter has been on the problems that have been most thoroughly studied. In that sense, it seems fair to say that the biases shown in the chapters are the biases of experimental psychology in the 1960s.

We make no claim for completeness of coverage of this book. In the sensory chapters, for example, there is a heavy emphasis on vision and only scanty coverage of kinesthesis, static sensitivity, or the common chemical sense. In some measure we reflect a proportionate amount of experimental work in these areas at the present time, and we choose to cover in depth the topics most thoroughly explored with the idea that the methods and principles involved will be found common to areas remaining for future exploration.

We wish to acknowledge most humbly our indebtedness to Woodworth and Schlosberg for defining the area of experimental psychology and bringing it through its years of "youth and immaturity." Our hope is that this multi-author book has not lost the cohesive and elucidative qualities brought to the field by the previous authors.

To the present authors we wish to express

our gratitude for undertaking the task and willingness to take on rather extensive revision where recommended by the editors or by the many readers of early versions of the separate chapters. These readers, colleagues and students, have helped immeasurably by pointing to gaps or errors of coverage.

To our publisher we wish to express our appreciation of tolerance for the repeated delays and changes in plan that have occurred over the years since this undertaking was first begun. We particularly value the cooperation of Mr. Brian Heald in securing the reviews of the chapters by competent experts in each area and in bringing each author to the achievement of a manuscript of quality and attractiveness.

Mrs. Lynn Sullivan and Mrs. Kathryn Huntington have typed—and retyped—the many versions of the manuscript, and Mrs. Dody Giletti has constructed our index. They all have our admiration, affection, and appreciation.

Finally we wish to acknowledge our debt to the following book publishers for permitting us to use illustrations: Academic Press, Inc.; Allyn and Bacon, Inc.; Almqvist & Wiksell Foerlag AB; Appleton-Century-Crofts; Chapman and Hall, Ltd.; Charles C Thomas, Publisher; Clark University Press; Cranbrook Institute of Science; D. C. Heath & Company; Doubleday and Company, Inc.; Dover Publications, Inc.; D. Van Nostrand Co., Inc.; Elsevier Publishing Company; Gyldendalske Bodhandel, Nordisk Forlag A/S; Henry Kimpton, Ltd.; John Wiley & Sons, Inc.; Holden-Day, Inc.; Holt, Rinehart and Winston, Inc.; Houghton Mifflin Company; Institute supérière de Philosophie; McGraw-Hill Book Company; Pergamon Press, Inc.; Psychological Institute, University of Helsinki; Stanford University Press; The Clarendon Press, Oxford; The Johns Hopkins Press; The Macmillan Company; University of Chicago Press; W. B. Saunders Company; Yale University Press.

We are also indebted to the following journals, proceedings, and other periodical publications: Acta Physiologica Scandinavica; Acta Psychologica Scandinavica; American Journal of Ophthalmology; American Journal of Physics; American Journal of Physiology; American Journal of Psychology; American Psychologist; Annals of Otolaryngology; Annals of the New York Academy of Science; Archiv fur die Gesamte Psychologie; Archives of Philosophy, Psychology, and Scientific Methods; Archives of Psychology, New York; AV Communication Review; Biological Review; British Journal of Applied Physics; British Journal of Psychology; British Medical Bulletin; Canadian Journal of Psychology; Cold Spring Harbor Symposia on Quantitative Biology; Education Monographs; Illuminating Engineering; Journal of Biophysics, Biochemistry, and Cytology; Journal of Cellular and Comparative Physiology; Journal of Clinical Investigation; Journal of Comparative Psychology; Journal of Comparative and Physiological Psychology; Journal of Experimental Psychology; Journal of General Physiology; Journal of General Psychology; Journal of Neurophysiology; Journal of Physiology; Journal of Psychology; Journal of the Acoustical Society of America; Journal of the Experimental Analysis of Behavior; Journal of the Optical Society of America; Journal of

Verbal Learning and Verbal Behavior: L'Année Psychologique; Optica Acta; Perception and Psychophysics; Perceptual and Motor Skills; Physiological Review; Physiology and Behavior; Proceedings of the National Academy of Science; Proceedings of the Royal Society, London, Series B; Psychological Bulletin; Psychological Monographs; Psychological Reports; Psychological Review; Psychologische Forschung; Psychonomic Science; Quarterly Journal of Experimental Psychology; Scandinavian Journal of Psychology; Science; Scientific American; Vision Research; Zeitschrift fur Psychologie; Zeitschrift fur Sinnesphysiologie.

We have tried to make this a useful book, both for independent study and for help in connection with actual laboratory exercises. Accordingly we have emphasized the headings and subheadings within each chapter, the wide use of cross-references from one chapter to another, and a list of tables and formulas likely to be used by the student and easily available to him at the end of the book.

J.W.K. and L.A.R.
Providence, Rhode Island

CONTENTS

    II. Space and Movement
                       Julian Hochberg

    Formulating the Problems of Visual Depth   475
    Nonvisual Cues of Depth and Distance   477
    Binocular Visual Cues   480
    Stereoscopic Vision   482
    Monocular Visual Cues of Depth and Distance   494
    Objects in Space   505
    Perception of Visual Movement   519
    Perceiving a Stationary World   529
    On the Nature-Nurture Question in Space Perception   546

VOLUME II

14. **LEARNING: INTRODUCTORY SURVEY**   551
                       J. W. Kling

    Definition of Learning   551
    Paradigms of Learning   554
    Conditioning   554
    Extinction   569
    Sensitization, Pseudoconditioning   577
    Exposure Learning, Imprinting, Habituation   579
    Concepts of Inhibition, Excitation, Response Strength
        and Habit Strength   595
    The General Scheme of a Learning Experiment   598

15. **POSITIVE REINFORCEMENT**   615
                 J. W. Kling and Allan M. Schrier

    Quantitative Variation in Reinforcers: The "Amount" Problem 616
    Shifts in Amount of Reinforcer   631
    Reinforcing Brain Stimulation   642
    Secondary Reinforcement   660
    Delay of Reinforcement   677
    Summary Statement: The Concept of Reinforcement   689

16. **AVERSIVE BEHAVIOR**   703
                     Russell M. Church

    Methods for Administering Electric Shock   704
    Correlations of Aversive Events with Stimuli and Responses 706
    Conditioned Fear   709
    Escape   720
    Avoidance   725
    Punishment   733
    Requirements for a General Theory of Aversive Behavior   740

Lorrin A. Riggs and J. W. Kling

INTRODUCTION

1

Experimental psychology, as a separate field of scientific inquiry, is only a hundred years old. But it did not burst forth, fully formed, when Wundt "founded" the first laboratory at the University of Leipzig in 1879. Much earlier, experimental investigations of distinctly psychological problems had been undertaken by astronomers, physicists, and philosophers. These men were indeed the first to be confronted with the major question of whether psychological processes could ever be studied by experimental methods. Sensory physiology and psychology had already proved to be fertile fields for the experimentalist, but whether the "higher mental processes" (such as learning and memory, judgment, thinking) and such complex phenomena as motivation and emotion could also be probed by these techniques was doubted by many.

The ingenuity of the nineteenth century experimentalists soon provided techniques suitable for the investigation of many of these problems, and it is now possible to claim that it was the success of the experimental part of psychology that finally established the field as a separate discipline, just as it had been the success of the experimentalists in physics, chemistry and biology that validated their claims to independence from the older philosophical inquiries. Experimental psychology gained much needed prestige at the time from the active involvement of such intellectual giants as Helmholtz, Darwin, and Galton,

1

each of whom opened up important fields of psychological inquiry. Then came a succession of men, starting with Wundt, who were self-acknowledged practitioners of experimental psychology, interested in psychological problems per se rather than as adjuncts or incidentals to the investigation of philosophical or physiological questions. Brentano, Ebbinghaus, Binet, James, Titchener, Watson, Skinner—these are some of the best known shapers of the course of experimental psychology, for they have occupied pivotal positions in the evolution of our basic concepts, our methods, and our self-image.

A science, of course, is not just a haphazard collection of experimental observations; early attempts to systematize and theorize gave birth to what we now know as "schools" of psychology: Structuralism, Functionalism, Gestalt Psychology, and Behaviorism. Each had its ardent champions and each left its contributions to method and emphasis on special problems. Today it probably is correct to say that the majority of experimental psychologists have adopted the eclectic viewpoint of Woodworth and Schlosberg: few of us are Behaviorists; rather we are all behaviorists who have accepted the best (the surviving) ideas and methods of the earlier schools of psychology. Whether we deal with programmed learning, perceptual constancy, or payoff matrices, few of us feel called upon to wave the flag for a single basic approach to all the problems of our science.

We find that just as the global schools have disappeared, so also have the broad theories gone from psychology. For example, learning in all its forms is no longer regarded as reducible to the formation of conditioned reflexes according to the models of Pavlov, Guthrie, or Hull. Instead, we have more restricted paradigms for human verbal learning, discrimination learning, or schedule-generated behavior. Similarly, the seemingly contradictory theories of Helmholtz and Hering in color vision are now shown to account for particular stages in the visual process and so have their individual contributions to offer,

just as the quantum and wave theories of light are both fruitful concepts for the contemporary experimental physicist. In short, the present complexity of our field seems to leave little possibility for all-embracing explanations. Instead, the trend of theorizing and systematization in the 1960s has been toward the development of more restricted (and hence more realistic) models or paradigms, and toward the utilization of a greater variety of experimental techniques, many adapted from other laboratory sciences.

Definition of Experimental Psychology

All psychology is based upon observation, but not all observation occurs in experimental settings. For some problems, such nonexperimental techniques as the case history method or observation in naturalistic settings may be the methods of choice. But the pages of any contemporary introductory textbook will attest to the fact that the great majority of the facts of modern psychology are derived from formal experimentation.

Much excellent experimental investigation is being carried on in such fields as social psychology, child psychology, and personality, but these are not ordinarily included within "Experimental Psychology." In part, the restricted application of this label is an historical accident: sensing and perceiving, learning and remembering—these were the earliest problems to be attacked with success by laboratory experimentation; these formed the core of such influential textbooks as Woodworth's 1938 edition of *Experimental Psychology*; these were the topics around which the basic theories grew and for which the most fundamental experimental techniques were developed.

In this edition, we continue to treat Experimental Psychology in its rather narrow sense, but we need not look further back into our history than to the 1954 edition to see that there are continual changes in even so restricted a field. The most noticeable trend seems to be toward an amalgamation of physiological psychology and experimental psychology, with the physiological and anatomical contributions to behavioral phenomena becoming a natural part of the body of psychological knowledge. Another trend is toward a rapid increase in the number of psychological problems in relation to which significant quantitative theorizing can be carried out.

The Experimental Method

Can we define the experimental method in psychology? If we try to do so, we soon find that contemporary methodology has become so highly specific that it is difficult to lay down general rules applicable to all experiments. However, a few characteristics of the experimental method may be mentioned.

1. The experimenter starts with some purpose in mind. Whether he has a rather general question or some quite specific hypothesis to test, he will at the least know what selected aspects of behavior to observe, and when to observe them. Thus, he starts with an immediate advantage of having defined just what it is he will try to study.

2. The experimenter creates his own opportunities and can initiate the procedure for observation when he is fully ready to measure and record the behavior. Thus he is prepared to observe under the best possible conditions. By controlling the occurrence of events, he can also repeat the events under controlled conditions, and thus obtain some idea of how consistent is the phenomenon he is studying.

3. Since the experimenter has established the conditions for observation, he can specify his procedure so that both he and others can repeat the process.

4. Having control of the conditions, the experimenter can usually manipulate them systematically, to the end that he can specify the effects on behavior of making certain changes in the conditions.

Independent and Dependent Variables

In designing an experiment, one attempts to control the situation in such a way that meaningful relationships can be established between antecedents and consequences. Among the antecedents are conditions present in the environment and in the organism, as well as the so-called independent variables, such as stimuli deliberately imposed upon the organism at the time of the experiment. Among the consequences are the so-called dependent variables, in particular the responses of the organism and physiological changes following upon the stimuli. In the simplest case one can distinguish between constants and variables in the situation. Constants are defined as those aspects of the experiment that are not under primary study, typical of which are the immediate environment and the characteristics of the subject such as age, alertness, familiarity with the task, and motivation. Environmental constants may typically include the conditions of lighting, quietness, temperature, and specific provisions for the experiment, such as comfortable seating and adequate communication between subject and experimenter.

In the majority of experiments, it is still possible to follow the old standard "rule of one variable," where the experimenter holds constant all aspects of the situation except the one factor which he makes his "experimental variable." In such cases, it is tempting to conclude that changes in the dependent variable are attributable to manipulations of the independent variable, and while we are all aware that correlation does not prove causation, many an experimenter has discovered to his sorrow that some previously unsuspected factor has really had the immediate controlling influence in his experiment. For example, the "stimulus discriminations" of laboratory animals sometimes prove to be controlled by factors which the unwary investigator may overlook: the noises of programming equipment, or the presence and absence of reinforcement are two common sources of such stimulation. After eliminating all possible stimuli correlated with the independent variable, the cautious experimenter frequently will see what happens if he completely removes the stimulus which he thinks is controlling the behavior of his subject. As Blough (1966, page 370) has pointed out, there is no more convincing argument for such empirical evaluations of experimental conditions than "seeing a pigeon continue to make a difficult 'visual' discrimination after the stimulus lamp has been turned off."

A still more complex task of control and evaluation faces the experimenter who would manipulate two or more antecedent conditions in the same experiment. Statistical techniques by which the effects of each variable and their interactions may be evaluated can be very valuable adjuncts to experimentation, but these techniques assume that the experimenter does indeed know what the true antecedent factors were. Unfortunately, it sometimes seems that the more complex and obscure the experimental problem, the more variables the experimenter decides to include in a single study!

Independent variables are those imposed on the subject by the experimenter, and are all those aspects of the experiment which the experimenter varies systematically. In studying the effects of intensity of light on speed of reaction, for example, light intensity would be the independent variable. By convention, the independent variable is marked off in units of intensity, time, trials, and so forth, and scaled accordingly on the baseline or abscissa of any graph displaying the results of the experiment.

Sometimes what is the independent variable in one experiment will be merely one of many antecedent conditions to be held as nearly constant as possible in another experiment. For example, a great many species show cyclic changes in their responsivity. Sometimes these changes are correlated with the day–night cycle and so are called "circadian rhythms." The experimenter who is not studying such rhythms usually will schedule each subject to be run at the same time every day. Thus, while the state of the organism remains one of the antecedent conditions influencing his behavior, the influence will be relatively constant for each subject throughout the experiment. On the other hand, an experimenter may be primarily interested in such

rhythms, and he may therefore try to hold constant other environmental conditions (such as temperature) and vary the time of day at which his observations are taken.

Typical dependent variables are measures of the response of the organism, whether these be enumerations of errors or correct performance, magnitude or speed of reaction to the stimulus, or physiological changes such as contraction of the pupil, electrophysiological changes evoked by the stimuli, or changes in heart rate. Thus we may consider the observed changes in a dependent variable to be the main result of the experiment and we conventionally plot our data on a graph in which the ordinate is used for an appropriate scaling of the dependent variable.

Having outlined typical or traditional procedures, we must now recognize their limitations for some types of experimental work. Sometimes, for example, one cannot distinguish clearly between independent and dependent variables, and sometimes there may be many of each, rather than a single one, so that the process of graphical description may become much more complex. As one example, the critical frequency of fusion may be observed as a function of intensity of flashes delivered to the eye. In this case, both frequency and intensity are manipulated by the experimenter so that it is only for convenience that we consider frequency of fusion as a dependent variable to be plotted on the ordinate as we see it on page 311 in the chapter on vision. The true dependent variable, of course, is not plotted at all. This is the verbal response of the subject indicating whether the light appears to be steady or flickering at any given time. Similarly, one may cite an operant conditioning paradigm in which the animal is given bits of food when it presses a bar. The schedule of reinforcement in this case is partly an independent variable, since it is set up in advance by the experimenter. Moreover, selection of the reinforcement schedule determines, more than does any other single factor, the rate and pattern of responses emitted. But the reinforcement schedule is also related, as a dependent variable, to the responses of the animal; it is those responses that determine whether any reinforcements will occur. The point is that even seemingly straightforward procedures may include many factors, not all of which can be classified simply as independent or dependent variables. These situations impose special problems for graphical or tabular presentation of results, and the elementary rules do not always apply.

Every field of experimentation has now, of necessity, developed special tricks and precautions to avoid artifacts and spurious conclusions. No living organism remains the same throughout the day, or even during a few minutes of experimentation. Apprehension and excitement at the beginning of the run may give way to boredom and fatigue at the end. Dark adaptation can only be tested by the use of light, and certain perceptual phenomena can only be reported if the subject learns and remembers the appropriate words with which to describe them. Similarly, an overly cooperative subject may report detecting an odor when none is present, while a less alert subject may overlook test stimuli even when they approach moderate strength. The basic remedy in all these situations is so to design the experimental procedure that the uncontrolled variations in performance have a minimal effect on the final conclusions drawn from the experiment. Counterbalancing the order of presentation is one of the most valuable features of experimental design. The comparison of Condition A with Condition B for learning lists of nonsense syllables (see Chapter 21) sometimes may best be made by following an ABBA order to balance out the factors of inexperience at the beginning and boredom at the end of the experiment. Similarly, sensory experiments may be designed in such a way that progressive changes in adaptation or alertness are also counterbalanced. This may often be done by randomizing the order of presentation of stimuli of different strengths.

Single and Repeated Observations

In theory, it would seem that the experimenter's job would be least complicated if he could always work with the same subjects, thus coming to know their characteristics and controlling for their past experiences. While this often proves to be possible, there are some experiments which, by their very nature, can only be carried out once on a given subject. For example, in his studies of double-alternation behavior, Hunter found that once the human subject came upon the solution to the problem, the experiment was over and the subject could not be used again.[1]

If it is the case that a subject can be tested but once, the experimenter is then forced into the use of different subjects for each value of his independent variable. If a great many subjects can be included in each such group, random assignment of subjects to groups may balance individual differences and the groups may be directly compared. Where such large numbers are not feasible, subjects may be matched on the basis of a significant variable, and then so assigned that the groups are balanced before the crucial phase of the procedure is introduced. Finally, there are even some statistical techniques (such as analysis of covariance) that allow the experimenter to estimate the significance of his procedure in spite of having nonmatched groups with which to work. These techniques are discussed in many textbooks of statistics and experimental design.

Performance Criteria

When the experimenter sets out to study the effects of X on Y, he not only must decide which subjects to use, and what antecedent

---

[1]Hunter referred to such experiments as ones in which "you can only skin a fox once." Whether the experimental problem does indeed have but one pelt must always be determined by experimentation. (See Hunter, W. S., & Bartlett, S. C. Double alternation in young children, *J. exper. Psychol.,* 1948, *38,* 558–567). Other examples of "one-shot" experiments can be found in the study of hidden figures in perceptual patterns. Still others are in several types of experiment on memory where the mere testing of retention may facilitate future performance on retention tests (for example, Brown, 1923).

and consequent conditions to employ, but he must also determine just how he will relate antecedent to consequent in his procedure. In this regard, particular mention should be made of the use of a "constant effect" as the performance criterion. The alternative procedure is to measure the subject's response under a constant set of stimulating conditions. A few examples may make the distinction clear. Suppose first that the problem is to study the learning of nonsense syllables. A constant-effect procedure might require that each subject attempt to recall the nonsense syllables immediately after each reading of the list of syllables, and to keep at this practice until it had produced some constant effect, such as the errorless recall of the list on two successive trials of practice. The subject would then be scored on the number of trials taken to achieve this constant effect, and this number of trials would be the basis for comparing him with other subjects, or comparing the mean performance of subjects using one method with a similar mean of subjects using another method of learning. This is basically the method introduced by Ebbinghaus in his pioneering studies in 1885.

As opposed to the constant-effect procedure, the "constant-treatment" method would allow each subject a fixed number of practice trials in which to learn as many of the correct responses as he could. His score would then be the number of nonsense syllables mastered in that many trials. The chief weakness of the constant-treatment procedure is our ignorance of the characteristics of the units in which the dependent variable is measured. What does it mean to say that a subject has learned eight of twelve words in a list when using one practice procedure, but only six of twelve when using another procedure? At most, we can conclude that the first method is the more efficient, but we cannot carry out such manipulations of the data as are involved when we attempt to say how much better is one method than the other. By way of contrast, the dependent variables in the constant-effect procedure usually are

measured in units whose characteristics are well known, and the experimenter does have some confidence that his manipulations of the data (adding, dividing, and so forth) are valid ones. Of course, many problems in psychology are still at the stage of development where it is necessary to discover whether Treatment A produces any effect at all, or whether A has a greater or lesser effect than Treatment B; in such cases, the constant-treatment procedure will continue to find applications.

The advantages of the "constant-effect" procedure are perhaps even more clear in sensory experiments. In a typical experiment on visual dark adaptation the subject's eyes are first exposed to light for a preliminary interval of time. Then the light is cut off and the increase in visual sensitivity is measured by determining the intensity of a test flash that the subject is just able to see at various intervals of time after the light is cut off. In this case, we assume that when a test light can barely be detected, it is producing a relatively constant level of responding on the part of the visual system, and accordingly we express the visual sensitivity of the organism as the reciprocal of that amount of light. Much less satisfactory would be the "constant-treatment" procedure of using a fixed intensity of test flash throughout the process of dark adaptation and asking the subject to give repeated estimates of its apparent brightness.

Intervening Variables

The design of experiments requires decisions about independent and dependent variables, but the interpretation of results and their implications almost always involves the experimenter with "intervening variables." A few comments about them may help to define this term.

First, it is essential that we recognize that an intervening variable is a concept: it is a product of the experimenter's consideration of his observations and his comparisons of other sets of information. The visual sensitivity mentioned above is such a concept, as is memory or retention. They are called "intervening variables" because they are not directly observed independent or dependent variables of an experiment, but they frequently do help the experimenter think about the relations between such antecedents and consequences, and thus "intervene" between them. They are, to this extent, hypothetical entities and for this reason we must be especially careful in the use of them in drawing conclusions from the experiments. Retention, for example, may turn out to be zero as tested by the method of recall, or 50 percent as measured by a recognition procedure. Similarly, visual sensitivity may seem to reach a maximum value after 15 minutes in the dark as judged by the subject himself, while other more careful psychophysical procedures may show increasing sensitivity out to an hour or longer of dark adaptation. Yet retention and sensitivity are useful concepts and need to be kept in our working vocabulary along with others such as set, bias, deficiency, or preference.

The constant hazard to the experimenter from such concepts as that of the intervening variable is the temptation we all have to reify them. Thus, the beginning student may ask which is the "true" measure of retention or the "best" index of visual sensitivity. Such questions imply that retention or visual sensitivity really is somewhere, if only we could get at it, or that the concepts have some meaning other than that which we abstract from the observed relations of independent and dependent variables. Unfortunately, being verbal creatures with a rich history of associations among words, we frequently compound the situation by letting additional meanings accrue to such concepts, so that a commonly used term such as "preference" may begin to imply desire, pleasure or conscious choice. Properly employed, however, this term simply designates the relative frequency with which a subject approaches or avoids each stimulus among several that are made equally available to him.

Analysis of Results

We have outlined some of the general problems involved in the design and conduct of psychological experiments. We must now say a few words about the way in which results can be analyzed so as to yield valid conclusions. It is customary here to distinguish between descriptive statistics or data processing on the one hand, and the testing of hypotheses, estimating the significance of a given effect for the entire population of subjects, or the establishment of functional relationships, on the other hand. These topics may well form the subject matter of separate courses in quantitative methods in psychology. We may simply mention here that on the descriptive side one needs to have available in the laboratory standard statistical books, various sorts of graph paper, a slide rule, and preferably access to calculators or modern computers for reducing the drudgery and increasing the accuracy of numerical work. The numerical tables and formulae to be found at the end of this book may provide a sort of bare minimum of help to the student in the experimental laboratory.

On the analytical side, the guiding principle would be that of a healthy scientific skepticism. In a very real sense it is true that the body of knowledge in any scientific subject consists of those generalizations and hypotheses that have survived repeated experimental attempts at rejection. The scientist, in fact, does not set out to prove a pet theory of his or to agitate for its acceptance by the rest of the scientific community. Instead he sets himself the task of stating his theory as explicitly and objectively as possible so that it will be testable by those undertaking experiments in his field. It is generally true that no one experiment is ever able to establish the validity of a scientific theory or hypothesis. A single well-conducted experiment, on the other hand, may sometimes yield results that lead to the rejection of an hypothesis at a high level of confidence. The natural history of theories seems to be that ad hoc adjustments in them are made as required by such well-designed disproving experiments, until the burden of these qualifying adjustments becomes so great that the advantages of a simpler explanation become apparent.

Of course, some generally accepted guidelines are needed to help us decide when an experimental effect can be considered of sufficient importance to warrant our serious consideration. This introduces the concepts of *reliability, validity,* and *relevance.* An effect is reliable to the extent that it is repeatable. In many experiments, we actually repeat the procedure dozens or hundreds of times, and observe the degree to which the results vary around some average value. In other cases, where we can only expose each subject to the treatment one time, we use large numbers of subjects and estimate reliability from the variability in the group results.

Validity refers to the degree to which our dependent variable is really measuring that with which we are concerned. Suppose, for example, that we wish to find a valid measure of animal motivation. We may start by training an animal to press a bar in a Skinner box situation (see p. 752). We observe that the animal will not respond very much unless it is well motivated, and we decide to find out whether rate of responding is a suitable dependent variable, that is, whether it is a *valid* measure of motivation.

To answer such questions of validity, we must first agree on a criterion. For example, suppose the motivation in question is "thirst." To find out if response rate measures thirst, we must pick some criterion that defines thirst. Suppose we agree that an animal is thirsty if he drinks water, and that the thirstier he is the more water he will drink. The amount of water consumed is now our *criterion* of thirst. To get different degrees of thirst, we may deprive the animal of water for varying lengths of time. We then give him free access to water for a testing period of, say, ten minutes, and measure the amount he drinks during that interval. Now we can see if rate of bar pressing is a valid measure of

thirst by doing a separate experiment in which we again deprive the animal of water and measure the rate at which he presses the bar (reinforced by drops of water) at various levels of deprivation. The correlation of response rate with the criterion, water consumption, at the same levels of deprivation, indicates the *validity* of the rate measure of thirst motivation.

Much of the work in psychology laboratories is devoted to efforts to obtain "good" measures, by which we mean performance measures that are highly reliable and that vary in a meaningful way as we manipulate conditions in which we are interested. The term "meaningful" introduces the concept of relevance, which obviously is based on value judgments that must be made by the experimenter when he considers how he will spend his time in the laboratory, and by the teacher or writer when he decides which experiments he will cite in a lecture or in a chapter. Fads and fashions exist in science as well as in everyday life, and judgments of relevance are no doubt influenced by them. For the most part, however, we can use as a working criterion, against which to judge the relevance of an experiment, our judgment of whether it makes a contribution to our understanding of behavior. In the broadest sense, we may ask, "would another 10 years of this type of experimentation give us a better appreciation of the factors governing the behavior of organisms?" Unfortunately, every psychologist sometimes completes an experiment that is technically adequate and that meets objective standards of reliability, but that is relegated to the rear of a file drawer because it does not meet his own subjective standards of relevancy. This, of course, is a matter of personal style, and no textbook can provide rules for such judgments!

The Challenge to the Student

We have summarized some of the guidelines and a few of the common precautions which have governed the behavior of the experimenters whose work is cited in the following chapters. Their standards probably are the best basis against which the student may judge his own work. This emphasizing of precautions should not lead the student to conclude that all the fun has gone out of experimental psychology or that one must be an experienced researcher to make a contribution to the field. Far from it! Probably in no other laboratory science are so many undergraduates participating in, and making significant contributions to, the experimental literature. As you study the following chapters, jot down on the back page of your notebook the ideas that come to you for experiments that may fill gaps in our knowledge, or help us evaluate an hypothesis. Don't be too self-critical at this stage of the process; do include the page number so later you can reread the material and see how your idea sounds; if you don't jot down a few key phrases and a page number when the idea strikes you, it may be lost forever! Discussion with your colleagues and instructors will help you sharpen your judgments; some of your ideas may be developed into your own research problem. There is plenty of room in experimental psychology for fresh viewpoints, bright ideas, and clever experimentation.

Trygg Engen

PSYCHOPHYSICS

I. DISCRIMINATION AND DETECTION

2

When Fechner, one of the chief precursors of experimental psychology, published in 1860 a voluminous treatise on "Psychophysics," he was trying to work out in a scientific manner the relations between mind and body, or between the psychical and physical worlds. Being a scientist with strong interests in mathematics and philosophy, he hoped to discover some definite quantitative relation between the physical stimulus and the resulting conscious sensation. The basic philosophical notion of Fechner's psychophysics was that mind and body actually are identical, or merely different sides of one reality, but appear to be separate entities depending on whether the observer takes an introspective and internal (mind), or an objective and external (body) viewpoint. To solve this problem he had to develop suitable methods of experimentation. A large share of his book was devoted to these psychophysical methods, although they have lost the philosophical significance attached to them by Fechner. However, it should be noted in passing that on the basis of research with these methods Fechner proposed as scientific evidence in support of his philosophy what is now called Fechner's Law, that sensation intensity is proportional to the logarithm of the stimulus intensity. The next chapter will take up this problem of *scaling*. The present chapter is devoted to the problem of *threshold*, beginning with what might be called classical psychophysics based on Fechner's methods and the statistical treatment of the data they yield.

Since the time of Fechner the term "psy-chophysics" has been used to describe the relationship between sensation and stimula-tion. It is not necessary to delve into the metaphysics or even into the long and ani-mated debate about "sensation" and whether it can be measured. Operationally the experi-ments are really straightforward and fit easily into the familiar formula $R = f(S)$. Here R is a *response*, typically the observer's verbal report regarding S, and S is a particular *stimu-lus* of a defined value or magnitude. The observer is instructed in advance to make a certain kind of report regarding the stimulus. For example, S may be one of a number of tones which differ in physical wave amplitude or wavelength, and the instructions specify the dimension to be observed, as by saying, "This tone is louder than the standard tone," or, "This tone is higher in pitch than the stand-ard tone." Loudness is the psychological at-tribute that corresponds to wave amplitude, and pitch is the psychological attribute that corresponds to wavelength, but the relation-ships are by no means simple and linear. They are examples of what "sensation" means in a psychophysical experiment.

The response, R, is not always a verbal report. The instructions may require the ob-server to adjust one tone to match another in pitch, or to react with his hand as soon as a tone changes its pitch. Pavlov found a way to conduct psychophysical experiments on animals by the conditioning method, and a great deal of progress has been made in this field in recent years (see Chapter 17). In the early days of behaviorism, Watson (1916) sug-gested that conditioning might well be em-ployed in the human laboratory, for it seemed to him that such terms as "louder" or "yel-lower" were tainted with subjectivism. He wanted to get rid of the instructions. How-ever, until recently it was the general opinion of psychophysicists that the conditioning procedure would be a waste of time with human subjects who can, they believe, be told what they have to do and if necessary be given

a little preliminary training in responding objectively to such attributes as pitch. The idea is that the observer is merely observing stimuli, just as in a physical experiment, al-though the data are used for the investigation of the observer's power of discrimination.

The problem of classical psychophysics as first formulated by Fechner was the relation between stimulus and response, but the stim-ulus variable received most of the emphasis. The basic purpose of the classical method was to determine a threshold, measured as a tran-sition point on the physical dimension. Direct measurements were not made of the response variable in the $R = f(S)$ formula, and classical psychophysics may be said to have been lim-ited to this extent. Contemporary psycho-physics differs from classical psychophysics in two *basic* ways: (1) It makes a more detailed psychological analysis of the observer's hon-esty and objectivity and attempts to correct the threshold values by adjusting them in terms of measures of his response biases. One might say modern psychophysics puts more emphasis on R–R laws than S–R laws. We shall come back to this problem at the end of the chapter. (2) Contemporary psychophysics has made a new attack on the original purpose of psychophysics, as exemplified by Fechner's Law, by devising methods for measuring re-sponse magnitude (R), and is thus a more complete psychophysics. These measures will be considered in the next chapter.

As has been noted, the classical methods have an application beyond Fechner's philo-sophical problem. His methods are devoted to various kinds of threshold, or minimum discriminable physical value, which will now be considered.

Threshold, Uncertainty, and Equality

The word *threshold* and its Latin equiva-lent, *limen*, mean essentially what one would guess: a boundary value on the stimulus di-mension (continuum) separating the stimuli that elicit one response from the stimuli that elicit a different response or no response. For example, let a very light weight be placed gently on the observer's palm. If the weight is below a certain value, his report may be, "No, I don't feel it," but if the weight is increased trial by trial, it eventually reaches a value which gets the positive response, "Yes, now I feel it." The value of the weight has crossed the *absolute threshold*—often called *stimulus threshold* and abbreviated *RL* from the German *Reiz Limen,* psychophysics having begun as a German enterprise. Typically the value of *RL* is defined as that value that can be detected 50 percent of the time.

If the weight in our experiment is increased after crossing the absolute threshold, the observer will report that it feels heavier and heavier. For such supra-threshold weights one can determine a *difference threshold,* abbreviated *DL* for *Differenz Limen,* which is also known as *just noticeable difference* (*jnd*). A *DL* is usually measured by presenting the observer with a constant *standard stimulus* (*St*) and, for comparison, a variable stimulus. Suppose in our weight example that the experimenter begins by presenting the *comparison stimulus* (*Co*) at a much lower value than *St* and then he increases *Co* in small steps until it can no longer be distinguished from *St.* The value of the weight has crossed the lower difference threshold. If the same experiment is performed by starting with a *Co* of greater value than *St* one can similarly determine the upper threshold by decreasing the *Co* until it is indistinguishable from *St.* The upper and lower thresholds so determined mark the upper and lower limits of the *interval of uncertainty* (*IU*). Because this *IU* runs from a *Co* that is just noticeably lighter to one that is just noticeably heavier than *St, IU* includes two jnd units; that is, $DL = IU/2$.

These examples of measuring threshold are typical for the classical psychophysical methods and answer the classical questions about boundary values on the physical stimulus continuum. Only a few more concepts need be considered to complete the list. What is the value of that comparison stimulus which on the average is judged equal to a specified *St?* This value is usually called the *point of* *subjective equality* (*PSE*) and is used particularly in the study of perceptual illusions, for example, the Müller-Lyer illusion (see Chapter 12). The extent of the illusion may be defined as the difference between *point of objective equality* (*POE*), defined as the exact value of *St,* and the *PSE* established by pair comparisons of stimuli. In other words, the *constant error* (*CE*) is, for this example, an index of illusion that is defined by the expression $CE = PSE - St$. Finally, the observer's judgments vary from moment to moment as his sensitivity, motivation, or attention to the task varies from moment to moment. Because of this variation, the sources of which will be considered more closely later, a threshold is always a computed average based on a large number of individual judgments. The *variable error* is given by some measure of the variability of the distribution of judgments; for example, the standard deviation of the weights judged equal to the standard in determining the *PSE* above.

THE BASIC PSYCHOPHYSICAL METHODS

Fechner himself contributed three psychophysical methods, and these are the so-called basic methods. Many other methods are reported in the literature, but they are usually modifications of one or another of these three methods. These three methods are alike in certain respects but quite different in others. All of them may be used to define the concepts described above, and a choice of one of them in this respect usually depends on two technical and practical considerations: (1) The nature of the stimulus continuum, that is, whether the stimuli can be varied continuously (or at least in *very* small steps) or can be presented only in discrete steps. The use of discrete steps is often required, for example in the study of taste and smell. (2) The nature of the stimulus configuration as, for example, whether simultaneous or only successive presentation of pairs of stimuli is possible. In this respect more flexibility is possible in vision than hearing. The basic psychophysical methods will first be described briefly and then in detail.

1. *The method of limits* (just noticeable difference, minimal change, or serial exploration). This is the most direct method of locating a threshold. For *DL* the experimenter varies the *Co* in small steps in ascending and descending series, and the observer reports for each step whether the *Co* is smaller, equal, or larger in comparison with the *St*. The data are the physical values of the *Co* where the observer's response shifts from one of these response categories to another. For *RL* there is no *St* and the observer's task is to report whether he does or does not detect the presence of the stimulus.

2. *The method of adjustment* (average error, reproduction, or the equation method). For *DL* the observer himself usually adjusts the value of the *Co,* which can be varied continuously, and sets it to apparent equality with the *St*. He does so repeatedly, and the central tendency and variability of his settings are computed. His average setting is a direct indication of *PSE* and his variability can be used to calculate a *DL*. For *RL* the observer repeatedly sets the variable stimulus to a value that he judges to be the lowest that he can detect; the average of these settings is taken to be the *RL*.

3. *The method of constant stimuli* (right and wrong cases, or frequency method). For *DL,* each of several fixed, discrete values of the *Co* is compared with the *St* many times, and the relative frequency of the different responses, for example, "smaller" and "larger," are counted for each of these fixed values. When only two response categories are used the observer will be right half of the time by just guessing, and his *DL* is therefore usually defined as that increment or decrement he judged correctly 75 percent of the time, that is, halfway between 50 percent (chance performance) and 100 percent. This percentage is located by interpolation or by one of several alternative statistical treatments. If a third response category is added, permitting a response of "equal," "doubtful,"

and the like, the method of constant stimuli becomes very similar to the method of limits. The method of constant stimuli can also be used to find *RL*. In this case no *St* is used, and *RL* is usually specified as the value of the variable stimulus for which there are equal numbers of "Yes" and "No" judgments of detection.

Our aim in the following pages is to enable the student, given suitable apparatus, to conduct an experiment by each basic method and to handle the data statistically. The work of Luce, Bush, and Galanter (1963) may be consulted for a fuller mathematical treatment of the problem.

THE METHOD OF LIMITS

The Absolute Threshold (*RL*)

The procedure and computations for determining the lower pitch threshold by the method of limits are shown in Table 2.1 (taken from Titchener, 1905, II, p. 6). The observer has been instructed to report "Yes" when he hears a tone and "No" when he hears no tone during a certain interval indicated by the experimenter. There should be practice trials preceding the collection of data to ensure that the observer understands the procedure, for verbal instructions are difficult to write briefly and clearly and are often inferior to the preliminary training in the task itself.

The first column of Table 2.1, reading downward, records the observer's responses in a descending series. The experimenter starts the *Co* at 24 cycles per second (Hz) and the observer reports "Yes." The experimenter lowers the *Co* by 1 cycle per trial, and the observer continues to report "Yes" until he reaches 14 cycles when he reports "No." Thus, the threshold lies somewhere between 15 and 14 cycles; it is taken as the midpoint, 14.5, and this *T* (for Threshold) value is entered below this column as one estimate of *RL*.

Next the experimenter starts an ascending series at 10 cycles, well below the observer's threshold as indicated so far, and the report is "No." The experimenter again increases the

TABLE 2.1 DETERMINATION OF STIMULUS THRESHOLD BY THE METHOD OF LIMITS: LOWER LIMIT OF AUDIBLE PITCH

Frequency (Hz)	Alternate descending and ascending series									
24	Y									
23	Y									
22	Y		Y							
21	Y		Y							
20	Y		Y						Y	
19	Y		Y				Y		Y	
18	Y		Y		Y		Y		Y	
17	Y		Y		Y		Y		Y	
16	Y	Y	Y		Y		Y		Y	
15	Y	N	Y	Y	Y	Y	Y		Y	Y
14	N	N	N	N	a?	N	?	Y	?	N
13		N		N		N		N		N
12		N		N		N		N		N
11		N		N		N		N		
10		N		N				N		
9				N				N		
8				N				N		
7				N				N		

(1)	T =	14.5	15.5	14.5	14.5	14.5	14.5	14.5	13.5	14.5	14.5
	M =	14.5;		SD =	.45						

(2)	AvT =	15.0	14.5	14.5	14.0	14.5
	M =	14.5; SD = .32				

a? = "Doubtful," and counts as a shift in sign from the previous judgment. See text.
Data from Titchener, 1905, II, p. 6

Co 1 cycle per trial. This time the response shifts from "No" to "Yes" at 16 cycles, yielding a T of 15.5 cycles. As many alternating descending and ascending series are run as are feasible or until the experimenter is satisfied with the relative uniformity of the T values. He varies the starting point of the successive series to prevent the observer from falling into a routine. Near-threshold judgments are difficult, and even a conscientious observer may fall into the habit of utilizing some incidental cue that seems to facilitate his task.

The following procedure is used for the computation of RL from these data. The T values can be averaged (arithmetic mean) in any one of three ways, two of which are shown at the bottom of the table. (1) Below the upper line all the single values of T are added across the page and averaged; the mean, 14.5 Hz, is the RL. The standard devia-

tion of this distribution measures the variability of the observer's performance. (2) Below the second line each pair of T values (one from a descending and one from the following ascending series) is averaged to give a neutral T value, and then these averages are averaged. The final RL remains the same, of course, but the SD is smaller because the variation associated with separate ascending and descending series is reduced. (3) All the descending Ts may be averaged to give a descending RL, and all the ascending Ts similarly. The final neutral RL is the average of these two averages and will be the same, of course, as obtained above. But the ascending and descending RL values may be different because of certain "constant errors." The *error of habituation* is the tendency to keep on reporting "Yes" in a descending series, or "No" in an ascending series; the *error of anticipa-*

TABLE 2.2 DETERMINATION OF THE DIFFERENCE THRESHOLD BY THE METHOD OF LIMITS

Values of Co	Responses in alternate descending and ascending series							
8	+	+		+	+	+		
7	+	+	+	+	+	+	+	+
6	+	+	+	=	=	=	+	+
St = 5	=	=	−	+	+	+	=	=
4	=	−	−	−	−	=	+	+
3	−	−		−	−	−	=	=
2	−	−					−	−
1	−						−	−
T(+) =	5.5	5.5	5.5	4.5	6.5	4.5	5.5	3.5 Mean T(+) = 5.125
T(−) =	3.5	4.5	5.5	4.5	4.5	3.5	2.5	2.5 Mean T(−) = 3.875

IU = Interval of Uncertainty = $T(+) - T(-) = 5.125 - 3.875 = 1.25$

DL = Difference Threshold = 1/2 Interval of Uncertainty = 0.625

PSE = Point of Subjective Equality = $\dfrac{T(+) + T(-)}{2} = \dfrac{5.125 + 3.875}{2} = 4.5$

CE = Constant Error = $PSE - ST = 4.5 - 5.0 = -.5$

tion (or expectation) is just the opposite, a tendency to expect a change and thus change from "Yes to "No" in descending trials and "No" to "Yes" in ascending trials. The primary purpose of alternate ascending and descending series is to balance out either of these constant errors when it is present. Habituation would be indicated by overlap of the T values on the stimulus scale from ascending and descending trials; anticipation would be indicated by a gap on the stimulus scales of the T values from ascending and descending series. Practice and fatigue affect the data in opposite ways; their effects can easily be evaluated by comparing the first and second halves of the total number of series run. Such effects may be studied in a more refined way by analysis of variance (see Guilford, 1954). One can get an estimate of reliability of the RL by calculating the standard error of the mean by the usual formula

$$\sigma_M = \frac{SD}{\sqrt{N - 1}}$$

where SD = the standard deviation of the distribution of T values and N = the number of ascending and descending series. Regarding the observer's task in determining RL with the method of limits, it is well to limit him to two response categories, "Yes" and "No," and to instruct him to guess when not certain in order to avoid the response of "doubtful" which suddenly appeared in Titchener's data in Table 2.1, especially since less practiced observers are likely to be used in contemporary psychophysics.

The Difference Threshold (*DL*)

The same general procedure is followed as for RL but now three rather than two response categories are used. Fictitious data are given in Table 2.2. On each trial two stimuli are presented for comparison, the St and one Co. Three response categories suitable for the sense modality are prescribed for judging the comparison stimulus in relation to St, such as, "larger" (+), "smaller" (−), and "equal" (=), with the instructions for the observer to guess which category when he is not certain. The recommended procedure for locating the T values in this case is as follows: in a descending series, consider only the first shift from plus to equal, and the first shift from equal to minus; and, similarly, in ascending series, locate the first shift from minus to equal and the first shift from equal to plus.

The experimenter starts with the comparison stimulus well above St, as in the preceding example, and runs a descending series. The observer shifts from plus to equal when the comparison stimulus is 5. The experimenter continues the descending series and the first minus judgment occurs at the value of 3. Splitting the step intervals where the two shifts occur, $T(+) = 5.5$ and $T(-) = 3.5$ for this series. The scoring in the other columns shows how the rule applies to different series.

In order to reduce this table to average values, the means for $T(+)$ and $T(-)$ are determined. These will divide the whole range of comparison values into two parts: an upper part where plus judgments predominate, a lower part where minus judgments predominate, and a middle *interval of uncertainty* (IU) where the equal judgments are most frequent. The IU obviously covers a range of two DLs or jnd's from minus to equal and from equal to plus. A DL measured by this method is therefore defined as $IU/2$, which is $1.25/2 = .625$. If there were no constant error this would be the physical difference which must be added to or subtracted from St for the observer to notice it. The midpoint of IU (that is, $[T(+) + T(-)]/2$, or $(5.125 + 3.875)/2 = 4.5$) is taken as the best estimate of the *point of subjective equality* (PSE). PSE is theoretically the point where the comparison stimulus is most likely to appear equal to St, or where plus and minus judgments balance. Strangely enough, PSE is rarely identical with St. If it lies above St, there is what is called a positive *constant error* (CE); if below, a negative constant error, as in the present illustration where $St = 5$ and $PSE = 4.5$. Note that these constant errors are balanced out in computing a DL, but sometimes the constant errors are of interest in themselves in the study of perception (Chapter 12).

Weber's Law

The physical value corresponding to the DL is called ΔS or ΔI. Often one is interested in *relative discriminability*, defined as $\Delta S/S$, or the ratio of the minimum noticeable differ-

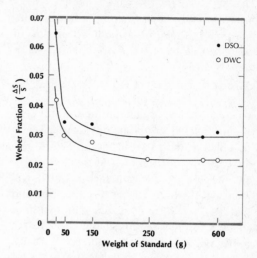

Figure 2.1. Tests of Weber's Law with lifted weights. The weights were lifted successively with one hand. ΔS was determined by using the standard deviation in connection with the method of constant stimuli. See text. The point here is that the Weber fraction may appear to be constant over most of the stimulus range used, but it increases (Weber's Law breaks down) as RL is approached.

ence to the stimulus intensity. With the values in our example we obtain $\Delta S/S = 0.625/4.5 = 0.139$. This fraction is called the Weber fraction and should be constant for different values of S according to Weber's Law:

$$\Delta S/S = k, \text{ or } \Delta S = kS$$

$\Delta S/S$ is different for different sense modalities but it tends to be constant within a sense modality for moderate stimulus values. However, it usually increases greatly when S (stimulus magnitude) approaches the observer's stimulus threshold, or RL. Note that in calculating the Weber fraction PSE is used rather than St, because judgments tend to be distributed more symmetrically about PSE than St. In practice it usually makes only a little difference. According to Weber's Law, as S decreases, ΔS decreases and at RL, therefore, ΔS would be minute, but the data in Figure 2.1 show that this is not what happens, for ΔS actually increases as one approaches RL. Psychophysicists since Fechner (see Stevens, 1951, p. 36) have been aware of this inadequacy and have recognized that it is related to the problem of *RL*. Therefore a modified version of Weber's Law has been proposed that states

$$\frac{\Delta S}{S + a} = k, \text{ or } \Delta S = k(S + a)$$

where *a* is a small value on the stimulus continuum related to *RL* but not identical with it, which added to *S* will make $\Delta S/(S + a)$ a straight-line function of *S*. At small values of *S*, *a* will be a significant factor, but it will decrease in significance as *S* is increased and may be omitted for high values of *S* without influencing the data appreciably. The constant *a* may be considered the value of ΔS at *RL*. It may also be considered as the value of "sensory noise"—a notion of great interest in contemporary detection theory discussed below—which is always present and which is added to the value of *S* presented by the experimenter. Ekman (1959) has shown how the constant *a* may be estimated algebraically and with *a* as the unit "how absolute and differential sensitivity, as well as the relation between stimulus magnitude and subjective magnitude, might be treated within a com-

mon theoretical framework" (p. 350). This is theory rather than fact, but the new form of Weber's Law seems to be a valid description of discrimination data for all sense modalities, and of course lawful relations are desirable. For this reason further empirical work on this problem could prove very useful and particularly in relation to neurophysiological studies of noise (see Chapters 4 and 9).

First of all Weber's Law states that relativity is the principle of sensory intensity according to which *DL* increases with stimulus magnitude. Secondly, the Weber fraction $\Delta S/S$ differs widely from sense to sense and furnishes an important index of power of discrimination. Depending on psychophysical methodology and state of adaptation (McBurney, Kasschau, & Bogart, 1962) the Weber fraction will range from about 1/333 or 0.3 percent for the pitch of pure tones (Shower & Biddulph, 1931) to 1/4 or 25 percent for odor intensity (Stone, 1964). In Table 2.2 above the Weber fraction was 0.139. (The unmodified Weber fraction is used for this illustration.) According to Weber's Law a change in the *St* of 13.9 percent would be

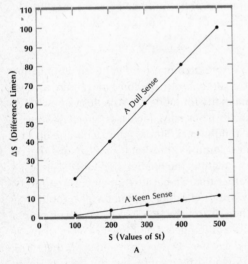

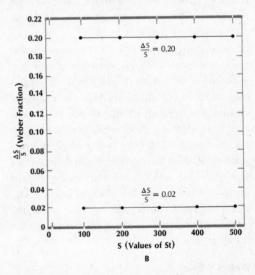

Figure 2.2. Fictitious data illustrating the operation of Weber's Law on two sense modalities, one "dull" (ΔS is relatively large) and the other "keen" (ΔS is relatively small). The figure shows two ways of plotting *DLs* obtained over a wide range of stimulus values. The abscissa represents values of the *St* in both cases. The ordinate in Figure 2.2A is ΔS or the *absolute* change in the physical value of each *St* required for *DL* or jnd. In Figure 2.2B the ordinate is $\Delta S/S$, Weber's fraction, or the *relative* change that is just noticeable.

required for a jnd (*DL*); for example, since ΔS = kS, for St = 10, ΔS would equal 139 × 10.00 = 1.39, which of course is 13.9 percent of 10.00. In other words, a test of Weber's Law means determining ΔS or *DL* or jnd—all are names for the same physical quantity—with at least several values of *St* spread over as wide a range of the stimulus continuum as possible. Graphically the data should yield a function as the one shown in Figure 2.2A or Figure 2.2B, depending on whether one plots ΔS or $\Delta S/S$ as a function of *S*. The smaller the Weber fraction the keener the sense, and thus vision and hearing are the keenest senses and taste and smell the dullest, with the other senses ordered in between.

Variations on the Method of Limits

Sometimes, as in measuring *RL* for luminance in the dark-adapted state, a long descending series of stimuli would raise the observer's adaptation level (Chapter 3, p. 59). This difficulty is minimized if the experimenter makes a rough preliminary determination of *IU* and then uses relatively short series extending only a little beyond *IU*. This device is what writers mean when they speak of the "modified method of limits." An alternative in this situation is to use the method of constant stimuli described below.

Another common and useful variation of the method of limits is the so-called *ascending method of limits*, which simply means omitting all descending series. This is used when it is especially desirable to keep the observer's state of adaptation as constant as possible, for example, *RL* for olfactory intensity. Starting with a strong stimulus in a descending series could possibly raise the *RL* considerably.

The forced-choice method is in turn a variation of the ascending method of limits suggested by Blackwell (1953) in research on vision and Jones (1956) for research in taste and smell. The stimulus is presented in small discrete steps as in the regular method, but at each level the observer is forced to choose which of several alternative presentations

actually contains the stimulus when the remaining samples are "blanks." Depending on sense modality and apparatus, one may have *temporal forced-choice*, where the observer must judge which of several marked time intervals contained the stimulus; or *spatial forced-choice*, where he must judge in which of several alternative locations (for example, top, bottom, left, right) the stimulus was presented on a trial. For example, in an *RL* experiment on olfaction (Engen, 1960) the observer was presented four test tubes which were all alike in every respect, but only one of them contained the odorant and diluent while the other three contained only the odorless diluent. The four test tubes were presented side by side on a rack with the position of the tube containing the odorant varied at random as the stimulus series was ascended in small steps. In other respects the *RL* procedure for the ascending method of limits was followed. One can also determine *DL* with this method by using one comparison value and three identical values of *St* for each trial. Threshold is simply defined in terms of probability of correct choice. The observer's probability of being correct from pure guessing is 1/4 on each trial, 1/16 for two successive trials, 1/64 for three successive trials, and so forth. In the experiment just described it was decided that correct judgments on two successive concentrations of the ascending series would suffice to specify the *RL*; preliminary work had shown that errors on the following (higher) concentrations were unlikely. The size of the step used on the stimulus continuum would of course be one important consideration in such a decision.

It was hoped that this method would tend to produce a more stable judgmental criterion in the observer than do the classical procedures, reduce the effects of errors of expectation and habituation, and thereby yield more valid thresholds. However, our olfactory thresholds are influenced by practice and especially by changes in the observer's criterion; for example, the observer may attempt to detect amyl acetate by attending to the smell of "bananas," which is a typical association to amyl acetate at relatively high concentrations, or he may ignore this psychological attribute and attempt to select by some lower criterion or attribute that is less easily named or popular but by which, nevertheless, he can distinguish better than chance between the odorant and diluent. This criterion problem is similar to the distinction between recognition and detection thresholds. One of the important psychophysical problems is how the experimenter can get control of the observer's criterion. The present forced-choice method is semantically superior to the more phenomenological classical methods where it is difficult to determine the observer's criterion (Blackwell, 1953), but apparently it does not eliminate the problem.

Still another variation of the method of limits is the *up-and-down* or *staircase* method (Dixon & Massey, 1956; Cornsweet, 1962). Only two categories of response are used: Yes or No; and Greater or Smaller. One begins as in the usual method of limits but changes direction (that is, from ascending to descending series or vice versa) each time the observer changes his response. For example, in a RL experiment in an ascending series, when the observer changes from saying "No" to "Yes" the experimenter will decrease the stimulus value for the next value and continue in a descending series until the observer says "No", whereupon he will start ascending again. This method saves work and time and is therefore of clinical value. Besides, the regular method of limits may disregard a great many, perhaps most, of the observer's responses and use one or two transition points in each series. However, Dallenbach (1966) reminds us that accuracy in estimating both the observer's biases and other possible constant and variable errors requires the classical approach with as many paired ascending and descending series as necessary. He states that to classical psychophysicists, "Accuracy, not time, was the essence. Researches were continued over days, weeks, months, and even years. Errorless techniques were sought that

facts would be obtained" (p. 654).

The staircase method resembles von Békésy's method of "tracking," the main difference being that in tracking, the stimulus is varied continuously, and in this respect resembles the method of adjustment below. For example, as long as the observer presses a key in von Békésy's audiometer the intensity of the tone decreases until he can no longer hear it, but when the key is released the intensity of the tone increases again. In this manner the observer "tracks" his RL (see also Oldfield, 1949). This is a method adapted to animal psychophysics. For example, Blough (1958) first trained pigeons to peck one key when a target was visible and another when it was too dim, and thereafter they tracked their own dark-adaptation curves.

From what has been said, the method of limits is obviously a very flexible one. It can be used with a variety of stimuli and for a wide variety of purposes. It has one final merit; it is the one method that shows clearly what is meant by "threshold." That is, it shows directly where the stimulus passes the boundary separating one response category from another. It is thus the reference experiment for basic psychophysical concepts including the Weber fraction.

THE METHOD OF ADJUSTMENT

As suggested by the name of the method, the observer himself manipulates a continuously variable comparison stimulus. Sometimes it may be better for the experimenter to manipulate the comparison stimulus, but in its most typical form the observer is instructed to adjust the stimulus until it appears equal to a given St. He does so repeatedly. The main application of the method is to measure PSE, although it can be used to determine DL. The method will be illustrated with the use of data from an experiment on the Müller-Lyer illusion with the apparatus shown in Figure 2.3. The lines are equally long but the one on the left, the comparison stimulus, looks longer than the one on the right,

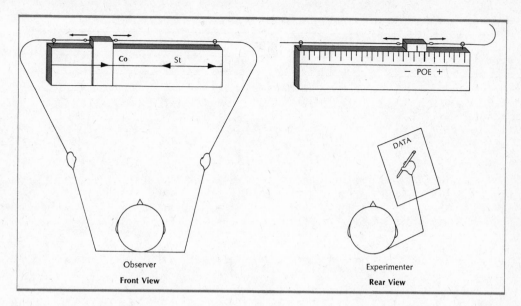

Figure 2.3. Schematic drawing of a simple apparatus for study of the Müller-Lyer illusion.

the *St*. The extent of the illusion can be measured as a constant error (*CE*) in a physical unit of length. The observer was seated about 2 m from the apparatus where he viewed the lines at eye level and was allowed to adjust the length of the variable line and move it back and forth ("bracket") before making a final adjustment. The experimenter sat immediately behind the board where he arranged the presentation of 60 trials and recorded the observer's adjustment to the nearest millimeter. The observer was not informed about his actual settings since the purpose in this experiment is only to determine whether he agrees with or deviates from the physical measure of the line. Half of the adjustments were done with the variable set smaller than the standard line (*St*) and requiring outward movement ("Out" or ascending trial); for the other half, the variable was set larger than the standard so that an inward movement was required ("In" or descending trial). A further necessary variation is to set the variable at different distances from apparent equality at the beginning of each trial. The In and Out trials were balanced for possible effect of practice and fatigue by presenting the first 15 Out, the next 30 In, and the last 15 Out. Other

variables of potential significance might likewise be considered in the design of the adjustment experiment, depending on the generality required of the psychophysical results.

The results are presented in Table 2.3. First it is determined whether the difference between *St* (230.0 mm) and the average adjustment (177.2 mm) is reliable. The *St* is constant and the standard error of only one mean, the average adjustment, need be considered in order to test the difference with a *t* test. *t* = 29.3, which for 59 *df* (degrees of freedom) indicates a reliable difference (*p* < .01). In a similar manner one might test for the effect of trials, direction of movement, orientation of the line, and so forth with a *t* test of more complex design, depending on the number of potentially significant variables and the generality of results desired.

It should of course be realized that with only a few observations one cannot report the size of the illusion very exactly, although in principle any degree of accuracy may be obtained for the individual observer. In order to illustrate the method, the present numerical results will be treated as though they included a much greater number of judgments. Figure 2.4 illustrates the variables in an adjustment

TABLE 2.3 DETERMINATION OF PSE, CE, AND VE[a] BY THE METHOD OF ADJUSTMENT

				Trials				
OUT	mm	IN	mm	IN	mm	OUT	mm
1	181	16	189	31	177	46	166
2	162	17	183	32	180	47	178
3	168	18	194	33	180	48	177
4	168	19	192	34	179	49	184
5	162	20	197	35	181	50	198
6	159	21	180	36	162	51	195
7	168	22	177	37	170	52	191
8	150	23	188	38	164	53	193
9	159	24	179	39	170	54	194
10	152	25	197	40	162	55	196
11	169	26	192	41	154	56	192
12	179	27	188	42	154	57	196
13	176	28	179	43	162	58	187
14	178	29	178	44	148	59	188
15	181	30	185	45	158	60	191

	OUT	IN	TOTAL
M	177.9	176.6	177.2 mm
SD	13.9	13.3	13.6 mm
σ_M	2.6	2.5	1.8 mm

$$PSE = M_{Co} = 177.2 \text{ mm}$$
$$VE = \sigma = 13.6 \text{ mm}$$
$$\sigma_M = 1.8 \text{ mm}$$
$$St = 230.0 \text{ mm}$$
$$CE = PSE - St = 177.2 - 230.0 = -52.8 \text{ mm}$$

$$t = \frac{230.0 - 177.2}{1.8} = 29.3$$

[a] VE = variable error.
Data obtained in an unpublished undergraduate laboratory exercise.

experiment in which it is assumed that a normal distribution of adjustments would be obtained and that the mean and standard deviation would be proper statistics. The mean of the observer's adjustment, M_{Co}, was 177.2 and that is the PSE. The difference between M_{Co}, or point of subjective equality (PSE), and St defines a constant error, CE = PSE − St, which is 177.2 − 230 = −52.8. In other words, on the average the observer systematically underestimated the standard line length by over 52 mm.

The difference between PSE and the observer's setting at any one specific trial is called a *variable error*, or VE, and varies in magnitude and direction from M_{Co} over trials. VE is thus measured by the standard deviation,

as illustrated in Figure 2.4; since both St and CE are constant and leave the standard deviation unchanged, the distribution of the observer's judgments directly reflects the VE. The standard deviation (13.6 mm) of this distribution could also be used as an index of DL. The ΔS corresponding to the DL thus measured is usually of a different magnitude but linearly related to one obtained by the method of limits. The standard deviation, if used consistently throughout an investigation, serves well as a measure of discrimination or in a test of Weber's Law. For the interval of uncertainty (IU) one might use the interval between the first (Q_1) and third (Q_3) quartiles of the distribution.

This method has several advantages. One

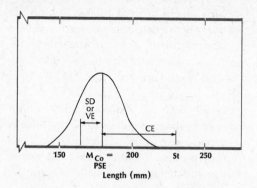

Figure 2.4. Hypothetical distribution of adjustments obtained in study of the Müller-Lyer illusion.

that has been indicated is the conventional statistical treatment of the data. Another is that the experimental procedure is somewhat more appealing to the typical observer as natural and direct, though he would perhaps have preferred to be informed of his performance on each trial. His interest is maintained because he himself manipulates the stimulus, but he may overshoot what seems to him at the moment the equality point, and so motor skills may play an important role in the judgments, as might the amount of time the observer devotes to each judgment. These factors are likely to affect the variability of judgments and hence the DL rather than the PSE. In general, when the observer is manipulating the stimulus it is somewhat more difficult to maintain constant experimental conditions, as compared with the other two basic psychophysical methods. Finally, as mentioned, many stimuli cannot be varied continuously or in small steps, and the method does not give a direct measure of DL, but a measure of the same sort. The essential advantage of the method of adjustment is its simplicity and speed when the proper apparatus is available. The method is difficult to apply in sense modalities where the pair of stimuli to be compared must be presented successively (for example, weights or sounds). At best one would always have to present the comparison stimulus after St and would neither be able to counterbalance nor to measure

series effects such as adaptation. (See Kellogg, 1929, for a comparison of the methods of adjustment and of constant stimuli.)

THE METHOD OF CONSTANT STIMULI

This method is concerned with determining stimuli that lie in the transition zone between those that can almost always be perceived and those that can almost never be perceived. When the stimulus or stimulus difference is perceived 50 percent of the time it locates the RL and DL, respectively. In order to map the whole transition zone, from five to nine stimulus magnitudes increasing by equal small steps are usually chosen over the range from the rarely noticed to the almost always noticed. When measuring RL one selects stimuli spanning the stimulus or absolute threshold. See, for example, the "frequency-of-seeing curves" in Figure 2.22. The only response categories are usually "Yes" and "No." "Catch" trials or "blanks" should be included unbeknownst to the observer. The responses to the blanks provide additional data whereby individual RLs can be evaluated for guessing and other response biases. RL is usually taken as the stimulus value perceived 50 percent of the time, although other arbitrary p values can be used.

When the constant stimulus method is used to determine the DL, stimulus values decidedly above RL are selected and difference judgments relative to a St in the middle of the series of comparison stimuli are required. Note that the 50 percent value in the RL transition zone corresponds to the PSE in the transition zone in the experiment on DL, which is based on the value judged greater than PSE (as in the method of limits) 75 percent of the time. Since the same stimuli are used throughout the experiment, the method is called the method of constant stimuli or sometimes, when a St is used, the method of constant stimulus differences. A trial in the latter case consists of a comparison of a St and one of the comparison stimuli. To balance out series effects, for example adaptation, the comparison stimulus is presented first on half of the trials and second on the other half of the trials (or on left versus right, and so on). The comparison stimuli are presented in random order as above and as often as possible, and at least 20 comparisons are made for each stimulus value. The observer's task is to state whether the first or the second stimulus is greater in some attribute of the stimulus; for example, "is the second weight heavier or lighter?" The results are tabulated with respect to the frequency with which the observer perceived it in the *RL* case (50 percent level) or the frequency with which each comparison stimulus was judged larger than *St* (75 percent level). As mentioned, there are usually only two response categories available to the observer, although one variation of this method that will be discussed a little later uses three response categories, for example, larger, smaller, and equal.

Because the raw data are frequencies with which the observer applies the response categories to each comparison stimulus, the term frequency method is another name often used in connection with these procedures. Fechner called it the method of right and wrong cases.

Why is this additional method needed? The method of adjustment is impracticable in some fields because many stimuli are not continuously adjustable. The method of limits brings in problems of habituation and anticipation that are avoided in the method of constant stimuli because the stimuli are given in a random order. It may demand a large number of trials, but each trial takes very little time. However, the method of constant stimuli may demand more careful planning; at least one preliminary tryout (and often more) is necessary to show that a series of equally spaced stimuli will adequately cover the observer's transition zone. The method of constant stimuli is flexible, although it is usually applied to the problem of *DL*, Weber's Law, and related problems. In a sense it typifies classical psychophysics with its emphasis on a statistical and indirect approach to psychological quantities.

Our concern in what follows is with the treatment of the data obtained by the method of constant stimuli. Fuller mathematical discussion of treatments may be found in Guilford (1954) and Luce et al. (Vol. 1, 1963). Here the purpose is merely to provide simple and reasonable ways of handling the data. Unfortunately, perhaps, a great deal of the history of classical psychophysics concerned itself with the problem of what is the best way to treat such data rather than with the problem of perception.

Typical data are shown in Table 2.4, which was taken from an unpublished study of the effect of time and space variables on differential sensitivity for length of lines. The apparatus utilized two commercial projection units with specially designed adapters in place of slide carriers. The function of the adapter was to produce a line of variable length through a projection screen for individual viewing. The change in length of line was accomplished by rotating a cam in desired steps across a pair of parallel knife edges, thus allowing a slit of light to be projected through the system. The line-lengths used in the present study were selected on the basis of preliminary work and were 61, 62, 63, 64, and 65 mm, with a standard of 63 mm (the same as the middle comparison stimulus) viewed at a distance of approximately 2.3 m. The projection systems could be adjusted by a positioning device whereby one projector could be placed in any one of several vertical positions, and the other projector be placed in any one of several horizontal positions. Both the se-

TABLE 2.4 DATA FOR *DL* FOR APPARENT LENGTH OF LINES WITH METHOD OF CONSTANT STIMULI. *St* = 63 mm.

Co	Frequency "longer"	P	z
61 mm	22	.22	−0.77
62 mm	34	.34	−0.41
63 mm	59	.59	0.23
64 mm	83	.83	0.95
65 mm	93	.93	1.48

Engen, Unpublished data

lection of line length of each projector and the vertical-horizontal relationship between the two projectors could be made from a remote station and displayed for selected presentation durations. The data presented in Table 2.4 were obtained on one observer who judged the lines according to the method of constant stimuli with forced choice for two response categories,—that is, whether the second line was longer or shorter than the first. One of the lines was the *St,* which was presented first on half of the comparisons and second on the other half. The order of presentation of the five comparison stimuli was random. A total of 500 judgments was made, 100 on each of the five comparison stimuli. Table 2.4 gives the number of times each comparison stimulus was judged longer than the standard. (The values in the column under *z* will be discussed later.) Each experiment required 2–3 days for completion, with several sessions each day and a rest period after each block of 50 trials. Fifty practice trials were given before the start of the experiment; during the practice trials the experimenter indicated whether or not the observer's judgment was correct. During the experiment the experimenter signaled the start of a trial by saying "ready," but gave no information about the observer's performance. Whether or not correction or reinforcement is given depends on the purpose of the experiment.

The data shown in the table are all the results obtained with the method using two response categories, and obviously no further information can be provided by tabulating the "shorter" judgments.

Simple Graphic Interpolation of Median and Q

In Figure 2.5 the *p* values from Table 2.4 have been plotted as a function of the length of the comparison lines. Assuming a reasonably large sample of responses the data usually suggest an *s*-shaped function. The lower values of the comparison stimulus are judged longer than the standard only occasionally and the higher almost always. The point plot-

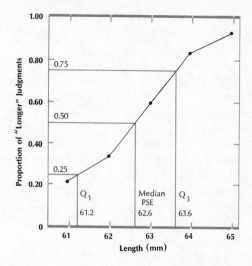

Figure 2.5. Proportion of "longer" judgments as a function of line length obtained with the method of constant stimuli. The standard stimulus (*St*) was 63 mm. See text for further details.

ted for 63 mm (the value of *St*) is the proportion of times this length was judged longer as the second member of the pair of identical values. This is a typical result showing socalled "negative time-order error," a problem of considerable interest in perception. Having connected the data points by straight lines one simply draws horizontal lines from the ordinate at the 25-, 50-, and 75-percent levels, and notices where these cross the data lines. Then one draws vertical lines from those intersections to obtain the physical values corresponding to Q_1, the Median (Q_2), and Q_3 respectively, as shown in Figure 2.5.

The *median* (*mdn*) is the value that would theoretically be judged longer half of the time and shorter half of the time. In this case this is the point of subjective equality (*PSE*), to be compared with the physical value of the *St.* In locating the value of *PSE* it is assumed that the curve is linear between values corresponding to 62 and 63 mm, which is at best only approximately correct. However, depending on the application of the results, the error associated with this may not be of any serious consequence. In the present example the *PSE* or 50 percent level is approximately 62.6 mm.

Algebraic determination of the median is also possible, of course, and gives the following results:

$$Mdn = PSE = 62 + (63 - 62)\ \frac{.50 - .34}{.59 - .34}$$

$$= 62 + \frac{.16}{.25} = 62.64$$

where .34 is the obtained p value for 62 mm just below and .59 for 63 mm just above the desired p value of .50.

Note that the obtained stimulus value which corresponds to a p value of .50 is almost the same as the one obtained from graphic interpolation. This is not surprising, for both are only approximations subject to the assumption of linearity noted above. As one might expect from such judgments, the value of PSE obtained by either method is close to St. However, the 50 percent level is not usually of great interest here; it is only in experiments on the absolute threshold that this point, defining the RL, is of major importance. The measure of variability or uncertainty is what is desired in the present DL experiment, and the semi-interquartile range, Q, is of primary significance for the present method of analysis.

$$Q = \tfrac{1}{2}\ (Q_3 - Q_1)$$

where Q_3 and Q_1 are line lengths corresponding to p values of .75 and .25, respectively, obtained from interpolation in the same way as the median in Figure 2.5. With these values

$$Q = \tfrac{1}{2}\ (63.6 - 61.2) = 1.2$$

This measure of variability is used as an index of differential sensitivity or DL, although it is not numerically identical with DL, as for example measured by the method of limits, but similar to $DL = IU/2$. Assuming the frequency distribution of judgments is normal one could use the standard deviation as a measure of DL by use of the relation

$$\sigma = 1.483\ Q$$

According to the data in Table 2.4

$$\sigma = 1.483 \times 1.2 = 1.8$$

The standard deviation has well-known and desirable characteristics, and direct determination of it would obviously be a better method. The mean is also more reliable and desirable than the median, assuming the judgmental distribution is normal.

Mean and Standard Deviation of an Unaccumulated Frequency Distribution

The last consideration is the basis of Spearman's (1908) distribution method which computes the mean (as PSE or RL) and the standard deviation (used either as index of DL or simple variability of judgments respectively) from the distribution of judgments. It does this, one should note, by making use of the classical psychophysical assumption that threshold varies from moment to moment. Summation of values (for example, momentary threshold values) will transform a normal distribution into an ogive similar to Figure 2.5 (p. 25). By subtraction therefore one can reverse this and transform the ogive into a normal or symmetrical distribution. In other words, by subtraction one can find the frequency of the observer's thresholds (not only judgments of "longer" or "shorter") which would theoretically fall within each step on our physical scale of length. For example, when the observer gives a response of "longer" to a certain comparison stimulus on a certain trial, Spearman's procedure assumes that his momentary threshold, PSE in our experiment, lies somewhere below the value of the stimulus on that particular trial. In our Table 2.4, the momentary PSE fell below 61 mm on 22 trials and below 62 mm on 34 trials; therefore PSE fell in the 61–62 mm interval $34 - 22 = 12$ times. One would similarly obtain the frequency with which PSE fell in the remaining intervals by subtraction. These frequencies should be symmetrically distributed. Note the different meaning of N, which now refers to the sum of the various frequencies with which PSE falls within the various class intervals. Table 2.5 shows all the computation necessary to determine the mean and standard deviation for the same data used for Table

TABLE 2.5 MEAN AND STANDARD DEVIATION (SPEARMAN'S METHOD)

Co	f "longer"	Co class	Class interval X	f*	fX	d= X-M	d²	fd²
		60-61	60.5	22	1331.0	−2.09	4.3681	96.0982
61	22	61-62	61.5	12	738.0	−1.09	1.1881	14.2572
62	34	62-63	62.5	25	1562.5	− .09	.0081	.2025
63	59	63-64	63.5	24	1524.0	+ .91	.8281	19.8744
64	83	64-65	64.5	10	645.0	+1.91	3.6481	36.4810
65	93	65-66	65.5	7	458.5	+2.91	8.4681	59.2767
				100=N	6259.0			226.1900

$$M = PSE = \frac{6259.0}{100} = 62.59$$

$$\sigma = \sqrt{\frac{226.1900}{100}} = 1.50$$

$$DL = Q = .67\sigma = 1.01$$

f* is frequency with which *PSE* falls in a certain class interval and $N = \Sigma f$

2.4 (p. 24). The problem with Spearman's method, well illustrated with our data, is that there is some uncertainty at each tail of the distribution. Twenty-two of these momentary *PSE*s would be below 61 mm, but is it reasonable to assume that all of them lie in the 60–61 mm interval? At the other tail, is it reasonable to assume that by adding a stimulus of 66 mm 100 percent "longer" judgments would be obtained? The limitation of the method is that it is fully justified only when the experimenter has extended his stimulus series far enough down to approach closely the 0 percent level, and far enough up to approach the 100 percent level. The analysis itself after converting to the unaccumulated frequency distribution of judgments consists of the simple computation of the mean and standard deviation from grouped data where N is the total number of judgments. When the distribution is normal one would of course prefer to compute the mean, unless one is only interested in the p value of .50 for *PSE* or *RL*, and especially if the measure of variability is of interest. Fortunately, there is a straightforward method for computing the mean and standard deviation without the limitation of the Spearman method.

The Normal-Graphic and Least-Squares Solution of Mean and Standard Deviation

Experiments with the method of constant stimuli indicate that the ogive describes the results well. Classical psychophysical theory also agrees with the general assumption that whenever a biological function or structure varies, it tends to show an approximately normal distribution of values, as pictured in

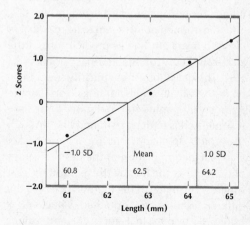

Figure 2.6. Proportion of judgments "longer" expressed as *z* scores as a function of line length. These data are the same as those plotted in Figure 2.5.

the familiar normal distribution curve. As indicated above, the ogive is simply the summated or cumulative form of this curve. In this case, one can use a third method that, in keeping with the assumption of normality, converts the experimentally obtained p values to z scores, and this transformation will simplify our graphic representation of the data. If the normality assumption is correct, z scores, unlike p values, will mark off equal steps on our physical continuum, and a linear plot is obtained depending on sampling error as shown in Figure 2.6. Instead of adjusting the spacing on the ordinate of the graph paper by converting p values to z scores, one may accomplish the same by two methods. One method is to draw a good ogive and interpolate from that, but this is relatively difficult. Therefore it is better to transform the ordinate so that a straight line would be the proper curve to draw. Normal-probability paper with the ordinate divided into proportions according to the normal curve and the abscissa divided into the usual arithmetic steps accomplishes this. Figure 2.6 shows how the same goal is achieved on ordinary graph paper by transforming p values into z scores by use of the normal distribution table, a part of which is reproduced in the reference tables at the end of the book.

The z scores corresponding to our experimental proportions are also listed in Table 2.4. The transformed points seem to lie reasonably close to a straight line as predicted from the classical theory of the normal variation of PSEs. The deviations from linearity seem to be no more than random sampling errors. For the purpose of graphic interpolation, a satisfactory method is to draw a straight line through the points freehand, but for a more exact algebraic determination of the desired values one should fit the line by the method of least squares. The name of the method refers to the differences between obtained values of Y (plotted z scores in Figure 2.6) and values predicted from X (line length) according to the straight line. It is assumed that *the line of*

best fit is the one for which the sum of the squares of these differences is a minimum (see Lewis, 1960).

The normal graphic method involves z scores rather than empirical p values, and therefore PSE corresponds to the p value of .50 and can be read off as the arithmetic mean corresponding to the z score of 0 on the ordinate and the corresponding values on the stimulus dimensions can be read off on the abscissa, as shown in Figure 2.6. The standard deviation is also shown and it is obtained by first following the same procedure for a z score of 1.0 or -1.0, which are associated with stimulus values located one standard deviation above and below the mean, and then simple subtraction.

Due to sampling errors the results from this method will not necessarily agree perfectly with those obtained with other methods, for example Spearman's method above, but if the assumption of normality is appropriate the various methods usually agree quite well. The normal graphic method is useful particularly in the case of the present results which render assumptions about the proportions in the tails

TABLE 2.6 METHOD OF CONSTANT STIMULI—LEAST SQUARES

X (Co)	Y (z)	X^2	XY
61	$-.77$	3721	-46.97
62	$-.41$	3844	-25.42
63	.23	3969	14.49
64	.95	4096	60.80
65	1.48	4225	96.20
$\Sigma315.00$	1.48	19855	99.10

$$a = \frac{(\Sigma X^2)(\Sigma Y) - (\Sigma X)(\Sigma XY)}{N(\Sigma X^2) - (\Sigma X)^2}$$

$$= \frac{(19855)(1.48) - (315.00)(99.10)}{5(19855) - (315.00)^2} = -36.622$$

$$b = \frac{N(\Sigma XY) - (\Sigma X)(\Sigma Y)}{N(\Sigma X^2) - (\Sigma X)^2}$$

$$= \frac{5(99.10) - (315.00)(1.48)}{5(19855) - (315.00)^2} = \frac{29.3}{50.0} = .586$$

of the distribution debatable. Also, of course, the data obtained with the method of constant stimuli come in the form of cumulative frequencies.

The method of least squares provides a more exact treatment of these data, analogous to graphic or algebraic determination of the median and Q above. In this case, fit a function to the data and determine the values of the constants, and then determine the mean and standard deviation with these constants rather than fitting a straight line by eye and then interpolating. Thus one needs the constants in the equation

$$y = a + bx$$

which describes the regression of y on x. Columns for X^2 and XY have been included in Table 2.6 to compute the parameters of this function, where X represents stimulus values and Y represents z scores, that is, response proportions to different stimulus values (Co) expressed as z scores. Now the equation for the desired function with the constants a and b can be written

$$z = a + b\,(Co)$$
$$= -36.622 + 0.586\,(Co)$$

From this it follows that the mean which corresponds to PSE is obtained by solving the equation for Co when $z = 0$:

$$Co = \frac{z - a}{b}$$

$$M = PSE = \frac{36.622}{0.586} = 62.495$$

The standard deviation which could be used as an index of DL of the data is equal to the distance from $z = 0$ to $z = 1$ (or -1) and is therefore obtained by first solving the equation for Co when $z = 1$:

$$Co = \frac{1.000 + 36.622}{0.586} = 64.201$$

$$\sigma = 64.201 - 62.495 = 1.706$$

This value agrees well with those obtained by other methods above. Assuming a normal distribution, $Q = .674\sigma$, or $.674 \times 1.706$, which gives a value of 1.1 compared to 1.2 obtained with the graphic interpolation from Figure 2.5. If many judgments are made with great care by a few observers for individual analysis, one should probably use the normal-graphic approach or solution of values by the method of least squares. This approach uses all the data in determining the desired values rather than just two adjacent points as in the normal-graphic method. If a few judgments are made by many observers for group analysis, linear interpolation of the median may be refined enough.

Variations on the Method of Constant Stimuli

As mentioned above, the two thresholds RL and DL can be defined in almost the same terms, for in both cases the observer is instructed to respond by using certain prescribed categories. Typically he would be instructed to use only two categories, such as "Yes" and "No," but experimental conditions may demand other alternatives.

Two categories: plus and equal The standard may be a light of steady luminance to which the observer's retina becomes adapted, and the comparison stimulus may be a momentary increment (ΔL) of the light in the center of the field preceded by a signal. If the observer perceives the increase, he says "Yes" (plus); otherwise "No" (equal). The result of interest here is the mean or median transition point between one category and the other, or the DL corresponding to ΔL. Mueller (1951) used this method to determine Weber's fraction over a wide range of light intensities. The "warble" technique in auditory DL determinations is similar (Harris, 1952).

Three categories: plus, equal, minus Suppose the experimenter in a weight-lifting experiment prescribes or allows the three categories: heavier, equal, and lighter. His purpose is probably to determine two transition points,

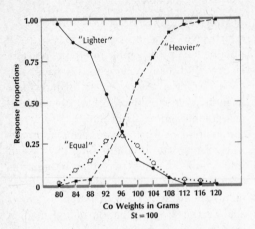

Figure 2.7. Results from weight-lifting experiments with the method of constant stimuli with three response categories, "heavier," "equal," and "lighter." There were 500 trials for each of the five central comparison stimuli from 92–108, with smaller frequencies tapering to 100 trials at each extreme. (In general, constant numbers of trials are desirable.) The curves are regular enough to give almost the same values of the mean and standard deviation by the methods we have described.

			PSE $\frac{(T+) + (T-)}{2}$	DL $\frac{(T+) - (T-)}{2}$
Method	T+	T−		
Simple interpolation	98.0	92.9	95.4	2.6
Spearman	98.4	93.3	95.8	2.5
Least squares	98.4	93.7	96.0	2.4

PSE as determined by the intersection of the plus and minus curves is 95.5 and the same when taken as the mean of the distribution of "equal" judgments. $CE = PSE - St$, is about -4.5 g, a negative time error since the comparison stimulus was lifted after St. (Data from Bressler, 1933, p. 65.)

as in the method of limits, one separating the minus from the equal, and the other the equal from the plus. In using this variation the purpose might merely be to accommodate an observer who insisted on being allowed to say "Equal" or "Doubtful" in certain cases. The experimenter would then have the task of dividing the equals somehow between the plus and minus frequencies to reduce the three categories to two, and he would then handle the data just as in a two-category experiment. He might follow Fechner and divide the equals equally between plus and minus at each separate value of the comparison stimulus, or he might follow another early suggestion and divide them in proportion to the plus and minus frequencies for each value. For example, if for a certain stimulus value there were 45 judgments of plus, 15 of minus, and 40 of equal, these 40 would be divided 3 to 1, and 30 of them assigned to plus and 10 to minus, so that the corrected percentages would be 75 for plus and 25 for minus. Neither of these schemes is perfect, for if the observer is instructed to guess plus or minus instead of using the equal category, he usually guesses right more often than wrong (Fullerton & Cattell, 1892, p. 132).

If the experimenter wishes to use data from three categories as in Figure 2.7, he will now have two thresholds, $T+$ and $T-$, as in the method of limits used to determine the DL above (see p. 16). The difference between the two methods is mainly the order of presentation of stimuli, serial versus random. In this case one takes the plus frequencies alone and determines central tendency and variability by any of the methods already described. For example, the mean for the plus judgments would be an index of $T+$. Between $T+$ and $T-$ is the interval of uncertainty (IU) where neither plus nor minus judgments have a clear majority. One half of IU is the DL. PSE is usually taken as the midpoint of IU, halfway between $T+$ and $T-$:

$$IU = (T+) - (T-)$$
$$DL = \tfrac{1}{2}\left[(T+) - (T-)\right]$$
$$PSE = \tfrac{1}{2}\left[(T+) + (T-)\right]$$

The mean and standard deviation of the equal judgments would provide other estimates of PSE and DL, as in the method of adjustment. Various determinations of PSE and DL agree closely in the experiment shown in Figure 2.7, which is based on careful selection of stimulus values and on a large number of trials in the tradition of classical psychophysics.

Instability of the *IU* and the Attitude of the Observer

Whether *IU* shall be large or small is correlated with the total frequency of "equal" judgments. If the observer gives many of them, his *IU* will be relatively large; if few, relatively small. Since *DL* may be defined as half of *IU*, it is similarly related to the number of "equal" judgments; this may produce misleading results. If the observer happens to be a very confident individual, he may use only the plus and minus categories and avoid the equal category as a sign of indecision. This kind of response will probably yield a small *DL* and suggest keen discrimination. At the other extreme is the cautious person who does not give a plus or minus judgment unless he is perfectly sure; he gives a large *DL,* which again reflects his attitude as much as his perceptual ability to discriminate the stimuli. Moreover, the observer's attitude toward the equal category might change in the course of a long experiment and from one experimental condition to another. If discrimination becomes more difficult he may drop the equal category because he feels that guessing between two categories is all he can manage. His *DL* will thus become smaller, and difficult conditions may appear to favor or improve ability to discriminate.

Obviously such results run counter to the purpose of classical psychophysics, discussed above, and make questionable the *validity* of the method of constant stimuli with three categories. One would on the whole do well to limit the observer to two categories, because it gives all the usable results with economy of time and effort. But there is still one unsolved problem.

The Instability of PSE

The *PSE* and thereby *CEs* such as illusions and time errors may be controlled by the observer's response biases rather than his sensory system. Figure 2.8 illustrates this problem by comparing the psychometric functions

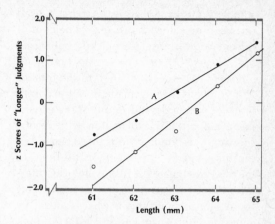

Figure 2.8. Psychometric functions obtained by two observers under the same experimental conditions with the method of constant stimuli. z score equivalents of proportions of judgments "longer" are plotted against line length. The standard was 63 mm. The data for the observer plotted as filled circles (●) are also shown in Figures 2.5 and 2.6.

obtained by the method of constant stimuli with two response categories from two paid observers, one of whom produced the results shown in Table 2.4. The observers were students with previous experience in psychophysics who worked in the laboratory during the summer on the same project of discrimination. They were exposed to the same experimental conditions throughout, and their results were similar, with one important exception as shown in Figure 2.8. Observer A has a *PSE* of about 62.5 mm and thus a negative *CE* (*PSE* − *St* = − .5), while observer B has a *PSE* of about 63.5 mm and a positive *CE* (*PSE* − *St* = + .5). The question is whether this difference represents their perception of the lines and thus different modes of operation of the underlying sensory system, perhaps "fading traces" versus "adaptation" (Chapter 9), or is a simpler explanation based on response biases possible? Figure 2.8 indicates that the answer probably is that observer A simply was more likely to say "longer" than was B. Analysis of all 500 judgments of all the values of comparison stimuli in this experiment shows that A used the response category "longer" 58 percent of the time (and "shorter" 42 percent) but B used the "longer" 40 percent of the time (and "shorter" 60 percent). Analysis of the total of 7000 comparisons they made in all the conditions (of standards, and so on) of the experiment support this explanation with results showing A responding "longer" 48 percent of the time and B, 33 percent of the time. In other words, regardless of the physical difference between *St* and *Co,* A was more likely to say "longer" and this is what is meant by a response bias, an important factor in a psychophysical experiment although often irrelevant and even detrimental to its purpose. Of course it may turn out that the desired *DLs,* which are 1.7 mm for A and 1.3 mm for B, are unaffected by this problem, but since the method does not control this response bias one must at least add a cautionary note to our psychophysical conclusions.

Classical psychophysics worked hard to eliminate response biases by carefully training observers, by proper experimental designs, and the like, but the opinion among contemporary psychophysicists grows steadily stronger that the bias is an inherent psychological problem. The most important recent contributions to psychophysics have involved attempts to devise means whereby the experimenter can manipulate and measure the bias, and such research has been successful enough to suggest to some (for example, Swets, 1961) that psychophysical results may be understood better in terms of the psychology of judgments than in terms of the psychophysics of sensory systems.

CLASSICAL CONCEPTS OF THE THRESHOLD

All of the classical methods discussed thus far are based on the following general theory of the nature of the threshold. A stimulus falling on a receptor initiates a train of impulses which produce an effect in brain centers. The size of this central effect will vary with the strength of the stimulus, the sensitivity of the receptor, the efficiency of the connecting paths, and the background level of activity of the center. If the effect on a given trial is greater than a certain minimum, the center will discharge and lead to a response, for example, "Yes, I perceive it." The stimulus which produces that effect represents the *momentary threshold.* The complex of factors listed above will produce random variation from trial to trial, yielding a more or less random distribution of momentary thresholds. The *phi-gamma* hypothesis assumes that the normal cumulative distribution will fit the function obtained when the probability of detection is plotted against stimulus magnitude in linear coordinates. (This curve is similar to Figure 2.5 above, and according to Guilford [1954] the terms *phi* and *gamma* refer to the stimulus and response variables respectively as used in classical psychophysics.) Thurstone (1928) has pointed out that since ΔS increases as a function of S as in Weber's Law or a similar function, the psychometric function would be positively skewed and the skewness would be inversely proportional to the $\Delta S/S$ ratio. Plotting the probability of detection as a function of the logarithm of the stimulus magnitude would normalize the psychometric function, and this is known as the *phi–log gamma hypothesis.* Because there is such a short range of stimuli for these experiments, it is consequently difficult to distinguish between the two hypotheses empirically, although the evidence indicates that Thurstone is correct. In other words, almost the same ogives will result from plotting p as a function of S and of log S.

To return to the general theory, the mean of the distribution of momentary thresholds corresponds to the value of the stimulus threshold. The various psychophysical methods described above were simply different ways of obtaining and treating the data to measure the typical value and its variation. The same line of reasoning was applied to the difference threshold, which was assumed to be related to the distribution of differences in excitation from two stimuli, *St* and comparison stimulus. This variability theory of threshold has been accepted in one form or another since the time of the classical psychophysicists (see Fullerton & Cattell, 1892; Boring, 1917; Guilford, 1927). Apparently it offered no theoretical problems as long as it was believed that the nerve impulse worked like an ordinary current in a circuit, increasing or decreasing its intensity to reflect stimulus changes.

The Quantum Hypothesis

Because neurophysiological research demonstrated that the nerve impulse is all-or-none, the question, "Is discrimination really stepwise?" seemed an obvious one to ask (Stevens, Morgan, & Volkmann, 1941). For example, assume that a brief tactual stimulus is just strong enough to set up a burst of 10 impulses; gradual increase in strength of the stimulus would not increase the strength of the sensation until the stimulus was strong enough to elicit 11 impulses, whereupon the observer would feel a certain finite increase in tactual sensation. (This theory applies to discrimination and *DL*, but not to detection and *RL*, since overall sensitivity of the receptor system is assumed to be continuous.) It

could be assumed that these relatively small discrete steps were not readily evident because of the variability of the receptive system and lack of experimental control of conditions affecting the observer. In 1930, however, von Békésy showed evidence for such steps in auditory thresholds when he minimized variability by giving the observer practice in the observation of a particular stimulus change of short duration. Likewise, each stimulus was judged several times in succession rather than in a random sequence, as in the method of constant stimuli above, in order to prevent temporal variations within the observer that might affect the psychometric function. The resulting quantal psychometric function has three distinguishing characteristics: the probability of detection is a linear function of stimulus magnitude; the slope of this function is inversely proportional to its intercept; and the stimulus increment that is barely sufficient to reach a detection probability of 1.0 is twice as large as the stimulus that is just low enough to yield a detection probability of 0.

Figure 2.9 schematizes the phi–gamma, the phi–log gamma, and the quantal hypotheses and illustrates why it has been difficult to obtain data that would clearly support one hypothesis and reject the other two. The pre-

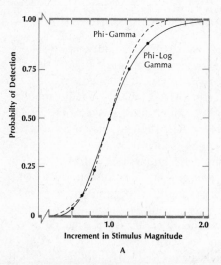

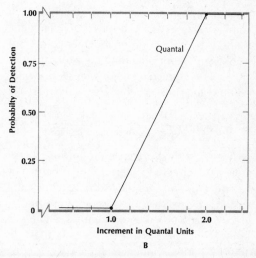

Figure 2.9. Schematic representation of results expected under various hypotheses about the form of the psychometric function. Probability of detection is plotted as a function of *stimulus differences*.

dictions made on the basis of these hypotheses are similar and the proper statistical technique for testing the goodness of fit of the psychometric function is not yet available (Corso, 1956).

It is evident that the quantal hypothesis, even more than the other hypotheses mentioned, demands that the observer in the study of such sensory psychological problems is just another valid and reliable part of the measuring apparatus. However, as Stevens (1961, p. 813) states, "The difference between a human observer and an electron is that the human observer is human. At any moment he may not keep his mind on his work—and thereby spoil the experiment."

General Comments on Classical Psychophysics

A great deal of useful information has been obtained with the classical methods in the study of sensation and perception. However, psychophysicists have long been aware of certain biasing factors (see Guilford, 1954), that must be reckoned with when threshold is used to evaluate the keenness of perception. Classical psychophysics attempted to deal with biases by (1) eliminating them by experimental design—for example, by counterbalancing; (2) by assumption, for example, that fatigue and practice will balance each other in a series of psychophysical judgments; and (3) by correction of judgments. A common formula for obtaining the proportion of judgments corrected for guessing (P_c), or what is now generally called "false alarms" is:

$$P_c = \frac{\text{proportion of hits} - \text{proportion of false alarms}}{1 - \text{proportion of false alarms}}$$

where P_c is the corrected proportion; "hits" refers to correct judgment of the presence of a stimulus or stimulus difference; "false alarms" means that the observer states incorrectly that a stimulus or stimulus difference is present on a so-called "catch trial" or "blank." This formula assumes, as can be shown by rearranging it, that the proportion of hits is a linear function of the proportion

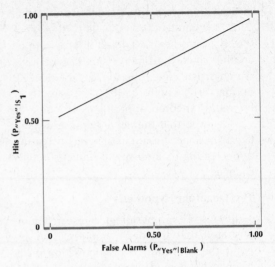

Figure 2.10. Hypothetical relation between the proportion of hits (correct detection) and false alarm (false positives) in classical psychophysical theory. The probability that the observer would respond "Yes" when a certain stimulus, s_1, is actually presented $(p_{\text{"Yes"}}|s_1)$ is plotted against the probability that he would respond "Yes" on a blank or catch trial $(p_{\text{"Yes"}}|\text{blank})$.

of false alarms obtained, for example, in an experiment with the method of constant stimuli (see Figure 2.10).

DECISION ANALYSIS MODEL OF PSYCHOPHYSICAL THRESHOLD

The main empirical contribution to psychophysics by the theory of signal detectability, which was developed originally in connection with problems in radio and telephone communication and radar (see Swets, Tanner, & Birdsall, 1961) has been that the assumption shown in Figure 2.10 is false. Classical psychophysics, with its carefully trained observers, did not usually obtain large enough proportions of false alarms to make a good test of this assumption. Modern detection theory criticizes this training of observers on two counts, (1) that it forces the observer to make the assumption that there is a real sensory threshold, and (2) that accordingly the observer tends to set high criteria for saying "Yes" and thus high values of *RL*. The modern theory assumes no fixed cutoff for "Yes, I perceive" and "No, I do not perceive," and hence no fixed criterion. For example, the observer's criterion for saying "No" rather than "Yes" may vary depending on whether or not he expects a stimulus to be presented. To obtain a higher proportion of hits the observer must more or less deliberately lower his criterion for saying "Yes," and this means that he is also likely to increase his proportion of false alarms. By comparison, classical psychophysics assumed that increasing proportions of hits and false alarms depended on the observer responding "Yes" on a greater number of trials which he somehow selected at random or by guessing, but that there was nevertheless a real sensory threshold. Detection theory does not assume a sensory threshold and puts the emphasis on judgmental rather than sensory aspects of the psychophysical experiment. It therefore emphasizes the relationship between two kinds of response, hits and false alarms, rather than the relationship between stimulus and response. The sensory effect of a stimulus is continuous, not discrete; and whether or not a response of "Yes" results depends on (1) the effect of the stimulus relative to the effect of noise on the very same sensory continuum, (2) what the observer expects in the situation, and (3) the potential consequence of his decision.

A consequence of this view is the tendency in psychophysical detection theory to deal with only a few, and often with only one stimulus value rather than a series of stimuli. It is not that the stimulus magnitude is unimportant but rather that the effect of the stimulus must be evaluated in relation to the two kinds of response bias. Table 2.7 shows the various stimulus and response alternatives in a typical so-called *"Yes-No" experiment* with one stimulus. It is similar to a trial in the method of limits or constant stimuli in that the observer must judge the effect of *S* or Δ*S*, but blanks and identical pairs are used frequently. *S* or Δ*S* is presented on some trials and not on others according to a predetermined random schedule and the observer is required to judge whether indeed the stimulus was On or Off during each trial, a time interval that is indicated by a signal (for example, a light in an experiment on hearing).

TABLE 2.8

| | | RESPONSE | |
		YES	NO
STIMULUS	ON	.50	.50
	OFF	.00	1.00

Table 2.7 shows the four possible events in this experiment. Let us assume that a threshold value has been obtained with the method of limits and that one physical value is used in our detection experiment. One would present this stimulus a large number of times interspersed with an equal number of blanks in a random sequence—at least several hundred trials may be required to obtain stable results. According to classical theory one would expect something close to the probabilities shown in Table 2.8.

TABLE 2.7

| | | RESPONSE | |
		YES	NO
STIMULUS	ON	Hit	Miss
	OFF	False Alarm	Correct Rejection

TABLE 2.9

| | | RESPONSE | |
		YES	NO
STIMULUS	ON	.66	.34
	OFF	.36	.64

However, results shown in Table 2.9 were actually obtained in such an experiment where the observer's task was to judge "sugar" (Yes) or "water" (No) (Engen, Barto-shuk, & McBurney, 1964, unpublished). The stimulus was a .225 percent (weight/volume) solution of sucrose in distilled water inter-spersed at random with distilled water, and both were tasted from cups following proce-dures similar to those used by Linker, Moore, and Galanter (1964). The proportions are based on 60 trials with a water rinse and 30-sec intertrial interval. (Further details of the experiment will be given later). These results indicate that the stimulus was above the ob-server's 50 percent threshold and the con-centration would have to be reduced to ob-tain equal proportions of "Yes" and "No" but that is a minor problem. What is unexpected is the relatively high false-alarm proportion (.36) of "Yes" when the stimulus was OFF, that is, a strong tendency by the observer to call water "sugar." Such results were hardly ob-tained in classical psychophysics and probably for the reason that it did not use nearly as many blanks as were used in this detection experiment and therefore did a poor job of sampling the response bias. Of course, the present data were obtained from an experi-ment in which a difficult judgment was re-quired and the observer was inexperienced in psychophysics, while an important part of classical psychophysics was the training of observers. However, by whatever means such biases are reduced, it may be argued that it is accomplished by manipulation of the ob-server's criterion for saying "Yes" versus saying "No" and that classical psychophysical theory implicitly promoted a high criterion and thereby high threshold values. False alarms can be reduced by increasing the stimulus magnitude required before the observer is certain enough to say "Yes," but the problem is that it is difficult to change the proportions of false alarms independently of the propor-tion of hits. Indeed, experiments tend to show that the proportion of hits is a function of the proportion of false alarms. Basically the con-tribution of detection theory in psychophysics is the determination of the psychophysical

S–R relation in a theoretical frame of reference based on a function called a *receiver-operat-ing-characteristic* (ROC) curve or an *isosensi-tivity function*. These terms will become clearer as the theory is developed. Only two of the values in our four-fold stimulus re-sponse matrix for this function are needed, because when hits and false alarms are known in this binary situation, misses and correct rejections are determined. The treatment of response biases will be considered first.

Bias Related to the Observer's Expectation Regarding the Probability of S

Two kinds of bias form the empirical basis for detection theory in psychophysics. One of these concerns the observer's expectancy that the stimulus will be ON at a particular trial, and this expectancy will be developed by the instructions given by the experimenter, the observer's prior knowledge of the experi-ment, and his experience during the experi-ment.

A simple example will demonstrate the effect of expectancy regarding the stimulus presentation probability. Suppose that instead of presenting the stimulus on 50 percent and blanks on 50 percent of the trials as above, the experimenter presents the stimulus on 90 percent and blanks on 10 percent of the trials. After some experience with this condition the observer tends to expect the stimulus on many trials and so is inclined to say "Yes" more often than in the 50-50 condition above. This situation is very similar to the procedures used in classical psychophysics with few if any blanks. The results obtained by Linker et al. (1964) in just this experiment show a high proportion of hits, about .94, *and* a high pro-portion of false alarms, about .77, as shown in

TABLE 2.10

		RESPONSE	
		YES	NO
STIMULUS	ON	.94	.06
	OFF	.77	.23

Table 2.10. In other words, the tendency to say "Yes" depends at least partly on the probability that a stimulus will be presented, and in addition there is the important fact that the proportions of hits and false alarms are related; this relation defines an isosensitivity curve.

TABLE 2.11

		RESPONSE	
		YES	NO
STIMULUS	ON	.24	.76
	OFF	.06	.94

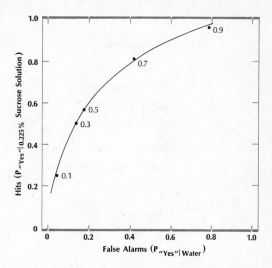

Figure 2.11. The isosensitivity function. Proportion of hits plotted against the proportion of false alarms in an experiment where the observer's task was to detect the presence of sucrose in water. The numbers in the graph show the stimulus presentation probabilities yielding the observed point. These data were adopted from Linker et al. (1964). See text.

One more example from Linker et al. may suffice to make this clear. In this case the stimulus was presented only on 10 percent and blanks on 90 percent of the trials. As shown in Table 2.11, this results in low proportions for both hits and false alarms, because under this condition the observer is likely to expect a blank, or water in this case, on each trial. It is not true that the stimulus plays no role, but the problem is that this stimulus is very weak and it is not unusual in psychology that response biases or "sets" (Chapter 12) will be most evident when the situation is ambiguous. In other words, the most reliable S–R relation will begin to falter if the stimulus is reduced to a level where the observer is unable to detect it (at least occasionally). Linker et al. (1964) explored this problem of expectancy systematically with many different probabilities of stimulus presentation, and the results shown in Figure 2.11 have been taken from their paper. The curve drawn by eye through the data represents one isosensitivity function, which means that different points on the curve reflect the same sensitivity, for the experimental points were obtained with the same stimulus but under different conditions of response bias. It is important to realize that this is not at all a standard psychophysical S–R relation but an R–R relation with two dependent variables plotted on the axes and to that extent more

purely psychological than psychophysical. For this reason sensitivity cannot be defined in simple terms as, for instance, by locating some point on a stimulus dimension, but instead a less direct and more theoretical approach will be required.

Bias Related to the Effects of Rewards and Punishments

Before discussing this theory, the effect of the consequences of the observer's decision will be illustrated in terms of losses or gains, outcome structure, payoff matrix, or what might more generally be called the effect of motivation on psychophysical judgments. It seems reasonable to assume that a person is more likely to make certain errors of judgment or mistakes, rather than others, depending on the consequences involved; for example, in attempting to detect an enemy one wants most of all to maximize the number of hits and minimize the number of misses, while false alarms and correct rejections are

TABLE 2.12

RESPONSE

		YES	NO
	ON	+1¢	−1¢
STIMULUS			
	OFF	−1¢	+1¢

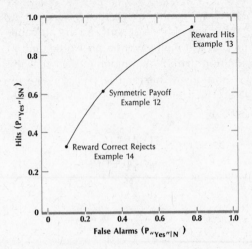

of minor consequence. Such situations might be imitated by payoff matrices of losses and gains in our "Yes–No" experiment. Table 2.12

TABLE 2.13

RESPONSE

		YES	NO
	ON	+25¢	−1¢
STIMULUS			
	OFF	−1¢	+1¢

shows a symmetrical payoff matrix where the observer must pay 1¢ for each error and where he gets paid 1¢ for each correct judgment. As far as the biases are concerned, this situation would be somewhat analogous to a stimulus presentation probability of .50. Table 2.13 is

TABLE 2.14

RESPONSE

		YES	NO
	ON	+1¢	−1¢
STIMULUS			
	OFF	−1¢	+25¢

an asymmetrical matrix that pays the observer handsomely (25¢) for hits relative to correct rejections as well as to misses and false alarms. One would expect such payoffs would lead to a tendency to say "Yes" with very high conditional probabilities for both hits and false alarms, analogous to a stimulus presentation probability of .90. Table 2.14 shows another asymmetrical payoff matrix that rewards correct rejections relative to hits, misses, and false alarms and would be expected to encourage the observer to say "No" rather than "Yes," with a relatively low pro-

Figure 2.12. Fictitious data on payoff matrices and the isosensitivity function. Proportion of hits are plotted against false alarms under conditions which rewarded responses of "Yes," or "No," differentially or equally (symmetrically).

portion of hits and false alarms, analogous to a low-stimulus presentation probability. If the same stimulus as above is used with a stimulus presentation probability of .50 and applied to the three payoff matrices shown, one should obtain an isosensitivity function as schematized in Figure 2.12. Again the observer's proportion of hits has been manipulated in a psychophysical experiment without varying stimulus magnitude.

Thus far two general ways have been shown in which this might be done and it has been stressed that with stimulus magnitude kept constant the results will fall on the same isosensitivity function whether the results came from experiments on stimulus probabilities or payoffs. Figure 2.13 shows part of the results of an experiment by Galanter and Holman (1967) for one observer whose task was to observe the difference in loudness in a pair of tones. The presentation probabilities were .1, .3, .5, .7, and .9, and the payoff matrices involved losses or gains of 1¢, 1.5¢, or 2.5¢, accumulated over a total of about 10,000 trials following careful preliminary practice of the observer. Different instructions given to instill various biases also produced results

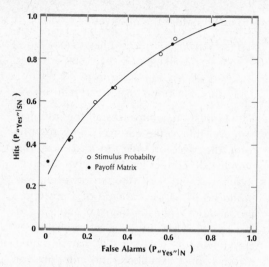

Figure 2.13. The effects of stimulus presentation probabilities and pay-off matrices in an auditory detection experiment involving one stimulus magnitude. All the data seem to be described by the same isosensitivity function. See text.

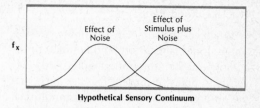

Figure 2.14. Hypothetical effect of noise and stimulation on a sensory continuum in the theory. The distributions are assumed to be density functions.

consistent with this isosensitivity function.

It is against this background of psychological biases that the effect of the stimulus must be evaluated. How this is accomplished in the theory of signal detectability will now be considered. In general, it should be noted that this theory is part of a more general statistical decision theory and conceives the observer's task as one of testing hypotheses.

The Hypothetical Distribution of Sensory Events

It is usually, although not necessarily, assumed that the sensory events resulting from repeated presentation of the same stimulus are normally distributed, an assumption similar to Thurstone's "discriminal dispersion." This underlying hypothetical sensory dimension cannot be observed directly and yet it is there that one must locate our measure of sensitivity and relate it to stimulus magnitude. Furthermore, the theory also assumes that "noise" is ever present as an inherent part of a psychophysical experiment because of external events, variability of the stimulus

source, spontaneous neural firing, or because it has been deliberately introduced by the experimenter. This noise may have an effect on the same hypothetical sensory continuum and, whatever the source, its sensory effect cannot be distinguished from the stimulus effect. It is a problem of signal-to-noise ratio. The sensory effects of noise and stimulus-plus-noise are assumed to produce a normal or Gaussian density function as shown in Figure 2.14. The theory assumes that the observer knows in some sense (possibly from experience with a constant stimulus) that the sensory effect is influenced by noise and thus will vary. His observation is considered analogous to a statistical sample and his "Yes" and "No" therefore do not mean really that he did or did not perceive the stimulus but that he prefers or does not prefer the decision that the stimulus was presented on the basis of the information received from the trial. In other words, there is a sensory event on each trial either due to stimulus-plus-noise (SN) or from noise alone (N), and the observer must decide which produced it, N or SN. Although it has been noted that response biases will influence his decision, the effect of the stimulus is to displace the sensory effect away from that produced by N alone in proportion to its magnitude as shown in Figure 2.14. Both N and SN yield a continuously variable effect on the underlying sensory continuum and produce density functions, where the height of the curve indicates the relative frequency of a certain sensory magnitude on the abscissa.

The Likelihood Ratio

Whatever the subjective attributes (tastes, smells, tones, and so on) and no matter how complex the stimulus (for example, pure tones versus samples of music), it is assumed that the observer can and does assign conditional probabilities to each sensory effect (that is, the probability that the effect arose from SN, and the probability that it arose from N), and, thus, that each observation can be treated as an event in probability theory. Assuming the distributions shown in Figure 2.14, the likelihood ratio is the probability that a particular sensory effect, s_1, was produced by stimulus-plus-noise, Ps_1/SN, to the probability that it was produced by noise alone, Ps_1/N. Theoretically, therefore, the underlying sensory continuum shown in Figure 2.14 is translated into a likelihood ratio continuum where the observer's criterion is represented by a particular likelihood ratio that is a point on this axis and that divides it in two. It is assumed that the observer will, on the average, respond "Yes" when his observation on the trial is to the right of this point and "No" when his observation is to the left of this point. That the observer's criterion is influenced by stimulus presentation probabilities and pay-offs has been shown, but how does the observer combine into a decision rule the information available to him before a trial with the information obtained on a particular trial? According to the theory, given a sensory event, s_1, the observer can compute the odds in favor of that event arising from SN (that is, the a posteriori probability) according to the following ratio:

$$\frac{P(SN/s_1)}{P(N/s_1)} = \frac{P(SN)}{P(N)} \cdot \frac{P(s_1/SN)}{P(s_1/N)}$$

$P(SN/s_1)/P(N/s_1)$ = the ratio of the a posteriori probabilities and represents the probability that s_1 arose from SN, after observing s_1 and knowing the probability of receiving an SN trial

$P(SN)/P(N)$ = the ratio of a priori probabilities of presentation of SN and N, known before the observation s_1

$P(s_1/SN)/P(s_1/N)$ = the likelihood ratio, that is, the likelihood that the particular sensory event, s_1, arose from SN relative to the likelihood that it arose from N.

This expression summarizes all the information available to the observer and is used to form the decision rule. To maximize the number of correct decisions the observer should respond "Yes" (the sensory event was produced by SN) if the ratio of a posteriori probabilities is greater than 1.0, and "No" if it is less than 1.0. If the a priori probabilities are known, the decision rule may be stated in terms of a likelihood-ratio criterion. For example, if $P(SN)$, the stimulus presentation probability, is .50, then the ratio of a priori probabilities is $P(SN)/P(N) = .50/.50 = 1.0$ and the likelihood ratio is the same as the ratio of a posteriori probabilities. The criterion value of the likelihood ratio is also 1.0. However, if $P(SN) = .80$, the a priori ratio is $.80/.20 = 4.0$. In this case, the a posteriori ratio is $P(SN/s_1)/P(N/s_1) = .80/.20 \cdot P(s_1/SN)/P(s_1/N)$, the latter term being the likelihood ratio. If the likelihood ratio exceeds .25 it is clear that the a posteriori ratio will exceed unity; thus the observer responds "Yes" when the likelihood ratio is greater than .25 and "No" when it is less than .25. The likelihood ratio thus has a nonzero numerical value represented on the decision axis, which in turn is a transformation of the sensory axis schematized in Figure 2.14.

The criterion or decision rule is thus determined by the stimulus presentation probability, the values of the observer's decision outcomes, and the stimulus magnitude. The observer might attempt to achieve any number of different goals in a detection situation, but a likelihood-ratio criterion may be calculated to maximize any goal. In theory, the observer's criterion can be compared with that of an *ideal observer*, which is a mathematical abstraction referring to maximal performance computed for the experimental conditions by determining the likelihood criterion that will

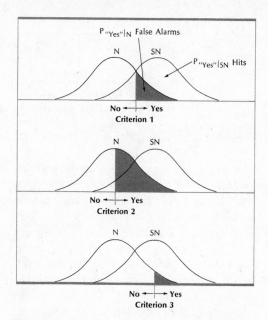

Figure 2.15. The schematic representation of sensory information in the theory of signal detectability. Probability density is plotted against the value of the sensory information expressed as a likelihood ratio on the decision axis. The hypothetical effects of three different criteria are illustrated. The distributions for *N* and *SN* are not affected, for it is assumed the stimulus is constant, but the proportions of hits and false alarms do change as the criterion is moved along the decision axis plotted on the abscissa.

maximize payoffs for average or known values of the payoff matrix weighted by known or expected stimulus presentation probabilities. As far as the real observer is concerned this could be a difficult, perhaps impossible task requiring a great deal of practice and understanding. This problem shows signs of bringing psychophysics and the psychology of learning closer together (Atkinson, 1961). Although usually there is the general goal of reporting "Yes" on trials during which the stimulus is presented and "No" otherwise, there is also the notion in detection theory of performing in an optimum manner with respect to the particular payoff matrix and the stimulus presentation probability. Presumably the observer translates the sensory response into a likelihood ratio and then compares this

ratio with the criterion established on this continuum, but no general statement can be made as to how this is done. However, a comparison can be made between the optimal criterion determined theoretically and the observer's criterion as determined by his performance. Three such criteria are illustrated in Figure 2.15. These three pairs of distributions might conceivably have been generated by the *same* stimulus magnitude for the presentation probabilities of .10, .50, and .90 or the three payoff matrices illustrated in Tables 2.12, 2.13, and 2.14. They would yield points that would fall on the same isosensitivity curve, for example, Figure 2.12, which is generated by different criteria as represented theoretically by the cutoffs in Figure 2.15. The curves also show the proportions corresponding to hits and false alarms, which, of course, are empirically determined and define the values on the coordinates of the isosensitivity curve.

The Effect of Stimulus Magnitude

The effect of a constant stimulus is to displace the total sensory effect away from the noise distribution, thus generating two theoretical distributions, *N* and *SN*. Assuming that both these distributions are normal and have equal variances, the difference between their means divided by the standard deviation of the distribution for *N* would provide a parameter *d'* or

$$d' = \frac{M_{SN} - M_N}{\sigma_N}$$

This is an index of the observer's sensitivity which is independent of the criterion, and hence independent also of payoffs, stimulus presentation probabilities, and instructions. The value of *d'* may be estimated by converting the experimentally obtained proportions to *z* scores and subtracting the *z* score corresponding to false alarms (as an index of the observer's criterion) from the *z* score corresponding to hits. In the theoretical "ideal observer," *d'* relates linearly to the common measure of stimulus and noise intensity and

TABLE 2.15   STIMULUS PRESENTATION PROBABILITIES

	.10		.50		.90	
	P	z	P	z	P	z
Hits	.24	−0.71	.66	+0.41	.94	+1.55
False Alarms	.06	−(−1.55)	.36	−(−0.36)	.77	−(+0.74)
$d' =$		.84		.77		.81

"real" and "ideal" observers may be compared (see Green & Swets, 1966, ch. 6). Elliot (1964) has provided tables for the detection experiment considered here so that d' can be looked up directly by means of the probability values of hits and false alarms.

The procedure is illustrated in Table 2.15 for the data on stimulus presentation probabilities presented in Tables 2.9, 2.10, and 2.11. These values of d' are very similar and indi-

cate about the same sensitivity by the observers, which is reasonable since the same stimulus was used in all three cases. Yet the p values listed for hits are of course very different, and classical psychophysics might therefore have concluded that they were produced by individual differences or variability in sensitivity when the source of the problem may be the observer's criterion. In a similar manner the theory of signal detectability has been able to show agreement in results from different psychophysical methods, such as the present method, forced-choice, and rating (see Green & Swets, 1966).

If d' really measures sensitivity, it should vary as a function of stimulus magnitude as shown in Figure 2.16. Figure 2.17 shows the experimentally expected data, namely that

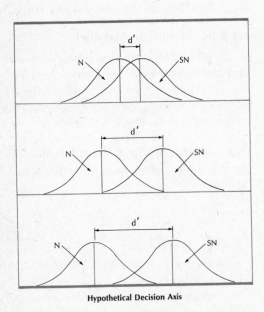

Hypothetical Decision Axis

Figure 2.16. Schematic representation of the effect of stimulus magnitude with other factors constant. Probability density is plotted against likelihood ratio as in Figure 2.15. As stimulus magnitude is increased, the *SN* distribution is displaced away from the *N* distribution. We assume the variances remain equal, and the displacement can be expressed as a difference between means or ds.

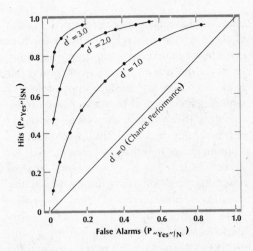

Figure 2.17. Different isosensitivity functions associated with different stimulus magnitudes as indicated by different response criteria with stimulus magnitude constant.

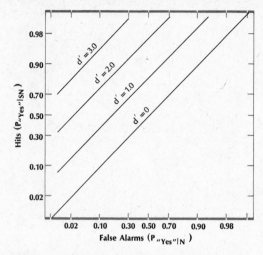

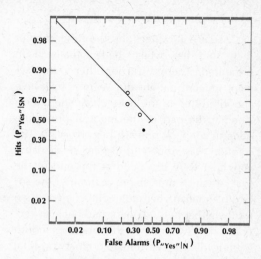

Figure 2.18. Different isosensitivity functions associated with different stimulus magnitudes. This graph is the same as Figure 17 except that the values on both axes have been converted to z scores.

Figure 2.19. The results of a detection experiment in taste measured in terms of d' along the curve drawn along the diagonal in a plot of false alarm as a function of hits. See text for experimental details.

different stimulus magnitudes should be associated with different isosensitivity curves (for example, $d' = 0, 1, 2,$ and 3). The points on each curve represent various possible criteria as discussed above. Note that the d' value of 0 (the straight diagonal line) represents chance performance, while performance worse than chance (as, for example, from confusing the response categories) would be located below this diagonal. Increase in d' is associated with increase in the curvature of the isosensitivity curve as is consistent with the normal curve model. One can make these functions linear with a slope of 1.0 by converting the probability axes to z scores or by plotting the probabilities on normal-normal paper in the first place as in Figure 2.18. The values of d' in Figure 2.16 are located on a scale extending from the diagonal (chance performance) toward the upper left-hand corner of the graph (stimulus magnitudes which are detected all of the time). In this manner d' simply indicates the difficulty of the detection task. Figure 2.19 illustrates this with previously unpublished data in taste referred to above (Engen et al., 1964). The research was concerned with the effect of

deprivation on taste sensitivity, and it has already been shown that the data obtained on the first day agreed with the experiment published by Linker et al. (1964). The observer was an 18-year-old obese woman hospitalized in order to keep her on a strict diet; she did not really eat at all for ten days but received approximately 20 calories per day from liquids such as tea with lemon and dietary colas. Her task was to discriminate between a small (ca. 1 cc) sip of distilled water and a small sip of sucrose dissolved in distilled water (weight/ volume). There were two concentrations, .125 percent and .225 percent, which were run in separate sessions each day. The so-called "sip and spit method" was used, meaning that she tasted a liquid and then expectorated. The stimulus presentation probability was always .50. Because of the difficulty of discrimination and shortness of time the .125 percent solution was omitted about halfway into her fast. It was possible to make observations under the same conditions each day, and data on three consecutive days were combined to obtain a more stable performance. There were 70 trials each day of water and sucrose in a random order, but the first 10 trials were used for practice only. The observer responded by saying "sugar" or "water" and the experimenter then told her which had actually been presented. There was no other reinforcement but the patient did seem cooperative and interested in the test, which she understood to be part of the medical procedure done in cooperation with her physician. The solution was sipped from very small paper cups that were discarded at the end of the trial, at which time she expectorated the solution and made her judgment. She was then told whether her judgment had been correct or incorrect, whereupon she rinsed her mouth with distilled water from an ordinary hospital glass, and then waited 30 seconds for the next trial. The results show that as expected the stronger sucrose solution yields the larger d' and also that d' increased over the test period for the .225 percent sucrose solution, and this indicates an increase in sensitivity. In the present case there is relatively little variation in false alarms for the four points plotted, but in another situation there could be, and the point is that d' provides the possibility of measuring sensitivity independently of variations in such factors. Response bias is probably not of primary interest to the sensory psychologist, but the effect of deprivation on sensitivity is. The present data of course are based on only one subject, and the increase in sensitivity in this patient as measured by d' might have resulted from practice rather than sensory physiological effects of deprivation. Further experiments could produce this information in a clearer manner than is possible with classical methods. The effect of practice on sensitivity as well as response bias is another problem of interest to learning psychologists (see Gibson, 1953) and can be studied anew within the theory of signal detectability (Atkinson, 1961).

As expected, d', as defined here, also increases as a function of stimulus magnitude. In a number of "Yes–No" experiments on contrast in brightness, Wuest (1961) found that d' is an approximate power function of luminance, as shown for two observers in the

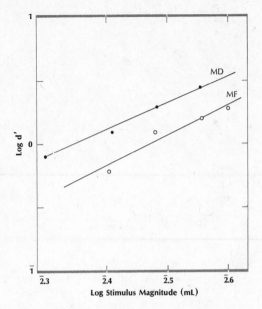

Figure 2.20. The logarithmic values of d' plotted against the logarithm of luminance in a forced choice brightness detection task at a background intensity of .8881 mL and with stimulus duration at 32 msec. Data are shown for two observers. Lines are fitted by the method of least squares. (Wuest, 1961.)

example in Figure 2.20, but more research needs to be done on the form of this type of psychometric function. Recall that in the "ideal observer" d' is a linear function of stimulus magnitude.

Detection theory in psychophysics has been developed to a sophisticated level and has stimulated new interest in the field. The present chapter has only shown how the basic principles relate to classical psychophysics in a simple detection situation and it has made only occasional references to the so-called "ideal observer" and possible applications to problems of sensory physiology. However, two problems appear crucial to the development of the theory in this direction: (1) the nature and empirical determination of noise and (2) the development of tests of the goodness of fit of experimentally obtained data to theoretical isosensitivity curves. The latter has been a continual problem in psychophysics; for example, the attempts to ob-

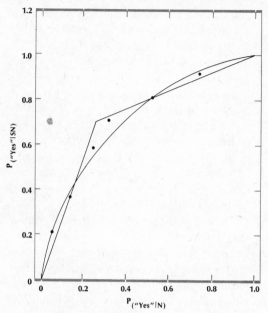

Figure 2.21. Schematic representation and comparison of the isosensitivity function of the multi-state theory of signal detectability and Luce's (1963) two-state threshold theory. Curves fitted by eye.

tain data reliable enough to decide whether the psychometric function would be better described by the phi–gamma or by the quantal hypothesis. Similarly, the classical notion of a threshold, which is a two-state theory in contemporary terms, has not yet been disproven by the data on isosensitivity curves but it has certainly been weakened. Luce (1963) has proposed a threshold theory which assumes that the presentation of the stimulus will place the observer in either a detection state or a nondetection state. The observation he makes *in either state* may be biased by nonsensory factors in such a way that a random portion of the observations are falsified in two mutually exclusive ways, namely, saying "No" when he is in the detection state and "Yes" when he is in the nondetection state. When correct detections, or hits, are plotted as a function of false alarms, this refined threshold theory yields two straight line segments as in Figure 2.21. As can be seen,

the prediction from this theory yields a function very similar to that of the theory of signal detectability. Presently available data and curve fitting methods do not make possible a clear-cut choice between these models, which is reminiscent of the situation with the form of the psychometric function discussed above. Interestingly enough, the sensory criterion proposed by Luce is the number of quantal units required by the observer to define the detection state. However, there is agreement on the very important point that careful measurement must be made of false

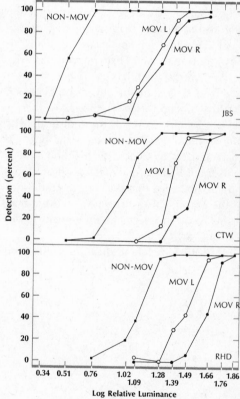

Figure 2.22. Data of Volkmann (1962) for the detection of visual targets during a voluntary saccadic eye movement to the left (MOV L) or to the right (MOV R) as compared with a control condition of no movement (NON-MOV). Method of constant stimuli in which percentage of targets seen is plotted as a function of log relative luminance of the target.

alarms in order to distinguish between the response criterion and sensitivity.

While it is well to be mindful of the limitations of psychophysical thresholds, it would be deceptive to end this methodological chapter without a reminder of some of the more "beautiful" and precise data obtained by classical psychophysical procedures. Figure 2.22 presents one of many possible examples of that kind of data.

The experiment from which the data of Figure 2.22 were obtained is one in which flashes of light were presented to the observer. Flash intensity is displayed on a logarithmic scale on the abscissa. Intensities range over a sufficiently wide domain so that the brightest flashes are nearly always reported as "seen" and the dimmest ones are nearly always "not seen" by an experienced observer. In other words, the brightest flashes are characterized by a stimulus-plus-noise Gaussian density function (see Figure 2.14) that is almost wholly beyond the noise density function; while the dimmest flashes are characterized by a density function that is indistinguishable from that of noise alone. Notice, however, that the various conditions of the experiment with respect to eye movements result in systematic differences in detection.

Thus it is possible to draw the conclusion that these experimental conditions have produced significant changes in the detectability of visual stimuli. In particular, it is clear that for each observer a luminance can be designated such that the stimulus is reported as almost always seen by the nonmoving eye and as almost never seen by the moving eye. This fact, along with appropriate statistical analysis of the data for all subjects, justified the use in this experiment of the traditional method of constant stimuli, and warranted the conclusion that vision is significantly depressed during an eye movement.

Detection theory is one of the few important contributions made to psychophysics since Fechner, and is at least partly responsible for the new interest in psychophysics that led to the translation of Fechner's *Elemente* into English over 100 years after its publication. Another reason for the revival of psychophysics is the effort of S. S. Stevens in psychophysical scaling. As was noted at the outset, Fechner was primarily interested in this problem. Detection and discrimination are important and interesting topics in their own right, but to Fechner they represented a means to solve the more important problem of the law governing the relation between psychological magnitude and stimulus magnitudes over the whole range of values. This is the problem considered in the next chapter.

Trygg Engen

PSYCHOPHYSICS

II. SCALING METHODS

3

Chapter 2 was concerned with methods for determining the acuteness of our senses. It dealt with the smallest perceptible stimuli, that is, absolute and differential thresholds. The present task is to measure the whole range of sensory magnitudes so that one can determine, for example, which gray is halfway between black and white or, more generally, how much visual brightness increases as luminance is increased. Of course, there are physical scales for measuring stimuli, but something else is needed, namely, a psychological scale for measuring the magnitude or intensity of sensation. Suppose a radio engineer wants to design a set that sounds twice as loud as a competing brand. If he merely doubles the physical output, he will be disappointed to find that he has increased loudness by only a trifle. How much will he have to step up the physical output to double the loudness? Questions like this have considerable theoretical and practical importance and involve scaling for the purpose of measuring psychological variables.

Experimental psychologists prefer to work with quantitative data for the basic reason that a thorough study of a dependent variable as a function of an independent variable is possible only when both variables have been measured. Many measurements made by psychologists are not intrinsically psychological or behavioral; for example, latency of response is a behavioral variable, but the measure involved is physical. Such physical measures dominated experimental psychology until about three decades ago.

There are two reasons why physical measures alone are not sufficient, even though they will continue to play an important role in psychological research. One obvious reason is that human and animal subjects are not always able to detect the physical stimuli or stimulus differences that the experimenter presents. A second reason is that, even when the stimulus exceeds the subject's threshold, equal increments or decrements in the physical value of the stimulus are not usually perceived as equal by the subject. Therefore, in order to understand behavior in relation to physical energies which may elicit or control that behavior, it is valuable to know the relationship between perceived (or response) magnitude and physical stimulus magnitude. This is the problem of psychophysical scaling and measuring.

Before going on to outline the actual methods of scaling and measuring, it is necessary to describe four types of scale. In general, measuring means assigning one or more properties of the number scale to attributes of objects. Scaling refers to the methods whereby one determines which properties of the number scale apply to the dimensions of the objects and which transformations leave these properties invariant (Stevens, 1951). Four properties are usually considered, and for each one there is a rule for permissible transformations.

1. *Nominal scales* refer to classifications such as bird–fish–mammal, pleasant and unpleasant odors, and men and women. Because the principle of classification is usually nonquantitative, one cannot properly use the term "measurement" in connection with nominal scales. Although numbers may be used as names for categories of classification or identification, all objects having the same attribute and only those being given the same number, names could be used instead. The transformation rule involves maintaining the identification of the objects and any direct substitution of names which perserves it is permissible; for example, one could call all the men "males" and women "females," or one could substitute the symbols "1" and "2" for "male" and "female" respectively.

2. *Ordinal scales* arrange things in order of magnitude. An example from common experience is found in a foot race; the man who took second place was slower than the winner but faster than the man who took third place. The ranks do not tell how much difference there was in the running times of the three contestants, although it is a rank order and to that extent a quantitative dimension. One can use the rank order of the number system and call the three contestants "1," "2," and "3." This entails more than the arbitrary naming in nominal scaling.

The ordinal scale makes possible comparisons of objects of the type "greater than" and "less than" and mathematically satisfies the condition $1 < 2 < 3$ in time, or $1 > 2 > 3$ in speed. Any transformation that preserves the order is permissible, such as calling the contestants "13," "57," and "148" or just plain "first," "second," and "third," because the size of the steps between the categories is not specified.

3. *Equal-interval scales* go one step further than the ordinal scales and allow statements about how much difference there is between two objects or individuals; they are based on a constant unit and satisfy the condition $2 - 1 = 3 - 2 = n - (n - 1)$. To some scientists this is the first level of quantification where one really talks about measurement, for variables measured on interval scales can be plotted as functions of other variables; for example, average temperature may be plotted as a function of the time of year. However, such numerical values are not absolute magnitudes of the attribute of interest but correspond only to the differences in their values. For example, on the Fahrenheit thermometer there is as much difference between 60° and 70° as there is between 70° and 80°, but because this scale lacks a true zero it is not permissible to say that 80° F is twice as high a temperature as 40° F.

4. *A ratio scale* has a true zero as well as a constant unit. For example, on the physical dimension of length an 8-inch stick has twice the value of a 4-inch stick. Another example of a ratio scale is the Kelvin scale of temperature. With a ratio scale all the operations of arithmetic may be performed, with the numerical values representing absolute values of the object. Only a linear transformation of these values of the form $y = ax$ is permissible. An equal-interval scale permits the use of an additive constant. Thus, $y = ax + b$. In other words, for an interval scale, b may be zero or some other value, but for the ratio scale it must be zero.

How is a psychological scale developed that will have equal intervals and a true zero? Perhaps one can get some hints from physical scales. Consider the problem of measuring the length of some small objects when there is no ruler handy. Find the midpoint of a sheet of paper by folding it in half and continue to divide it into quarters, eighths, and so on, to produce a scale of equal units. After measuring the objects with this arbitrary scale, the lengths can be compared as if a ruler had been used, and these measures in our arbitrary unit can be transformed into inches by the formula $y = ax$. To do so let x = length as measured, y = length in inches, and a = the ratio of the two measures, that is, the number of inches contained in one arbitrary unit.

Can the experiment described above be done with sensations? One can certainly ask the observer to judge whether one sound is twice as loud, or half as loud, as another. The observer can also be asked to choose a series of gray cards that seem to represent equal steps of increasing brightness. This *direct approach* to constructing psychological scales seems plausible, but until recently psychologists viewed it with doubt, and many still consider it too "subjective." Because of such doubts, most psychophysicists resorted to indirect methods of scaling sensory response. Several have been used, such as the *DL*, reaction time, and confidence of judgment methods, but the validity of such indirect

measurement has also been questioned. The current tendency seems to be to accept the direct method as the ultimate check, but the issue is by no means dead (see Garner & Creelman, 1967).

INDIRECT SCALING

Scales Based on DL and Fechner's Law

The *DL* and Fechner method for scaling sensation go back to Fechner (1860) who thought that Weber's Law (see pp. 17–19) furnished the key to the measurement of mind. It is an indirect method that uses the *DL* as the unit for an equal-interval scale. Because Weber's law states that the *DL*

TABLE 3.1 EXAMPLE OF WEBER'S LAW

Psychological steps	Stimulus value	Log stimulus	Increment of log
0 (RL)	8.0	0.903	
1	12.0	1.079	0.176
2	18.0	1.255	0.176
3	27.0	1.431	0.176
4	40.5	1.607	0.176
5	60.75	1.784	0.177

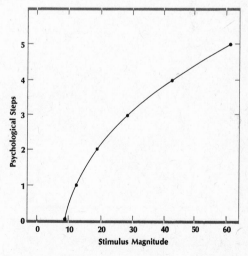

Figure 3.1. An illustration of Fechner's Law. The number of psychological steps (sensory magnitude) as a function of stimulus magnitude in linear coordinates.

is a constant fraction of the standard, $(DL/St) = (\Delta S/S) = k$, the physical steps must be increased as the scale of intensity is ascended, in order that the corresponding subjective increment remain constant or "just noticeably different." Thus, in a hypothetical sense, with an RL of 8.0 physical units and a Weber fraction of $\frac{1}{2}$, the stimulus value required for each successive unit or psychological step would be $1\frac{1}{2}$ times the preceding one; for example, $8.0 \times \frac{1}{2} + 8.0 = 12$, which is the physical intensity that gives us the second step on the psychological scale, as is shown in Table 3.1.

These data are plotted in Figure 3.1, which shows that successive steps require larger and larger increments in stimulus value for equal increments in sensation value. The increase in psychological sensation as a function of stimulus magnitude is described more conveniently with logarithmic than with arithmetic steps because it entails multiplication by a constant. This is accomplished simply by adding the logarithmic value of this constant (0.176) to obtain each successive step on our scale. The log values have been entered in the third column of Table 3.1, and the constancy of the increment in logarithmic value is en-

tered in the fourth column. When the sensation values are plotted as a function of the logarithm of the stimulus values, as in Figure 3.2, a straight line instead of a curve is obtained.

Assuming that Fechner's reasoning is correct, it is obvious that the logarithms are especially convenient when only the relative magnitude of a sensation is of interest. Without going through intermediate steps, one can calculate the log of the intensity of stimulation required to produce any level of sensation (see Reference Tables at the back of this book). Multiply the number of the step by the increment in logarithmic value (which then will be one plus Weber's fraction); add the logarithm of the RL; the result is the logarithm of the desired stimulus. Fechner wrote several formulas for carrying out this operation, but the most familiar is

$$R = k \log S$$

where S is measured in terms of the detection threshold (RL), so that $R = 0$ for $S = 1$. This is Fechner's Law, which states that the magnitude of sensation or response (R) varies directly with the logarithm of the stimulus magnitude (S). Remember that Fechner assumed (1) that jnd or DL was an equal increment in sensation, regardless of the absolute level at which it is taken, and (2) that a sensation is the sum of all the jnd steps that come before it in the scale. Both of these assumptions have been questioned, and they are discussed more fully below. Nevertheless, Fechner's contribution should be recognized, for he gave psychology a way of constructing sensory scales.

The instabilities of classically determined thresholds have been noted in Chapter 2, pages 31–34, but the DL is at least a defined unit. It is ultimately a measure of variability, and because the amount of variability in many biological and psychological processes is a constant fraction of the intensity of the process, many scales in psychology have been based on variability. Examples are the standard or z scores used in psychological testing.

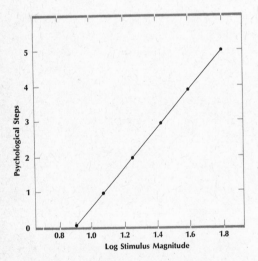

Figure 3.2. Data in Figure 3.1 replotted. The number of psychological steps (sensory magnitude) as a function of the logarithmic value of stimulus magnitude.

A scale based on the *DL* can be obtained either by adding the individual *DL* steps that are obtained by actual measurement or by assuming the validity of the more convenient logarithmic type of formula. The additive method is the more accurate if either extremely weak or strong stimuli are involved, where Weber's Law (unmodified, see p. 17) does not hold well, but the logarithmic transformation may be satisfactory for the middle ranges, which are often of greatest interest. (See Helson's modified Fechnerian function and the comparison of direct and indirect scales below.)

Pair Comparison and the Discriminal Dispersion

The scaling principle used by Fechner was the hypothesis that, regardless of the physical values involved, stimulus differences which are detected equally often are subjectively equal. Thurstone (1927a) started with this principle to promote psychology as a "quantitative and rational science." First, he provided a mathematical model, the Law of Comparative Judgment, which states explicitly the theoretical assumption about the distribution of the effect of stimulation. Second, he devised methodology applicable to the scaling of attributes, such as beauty, for which there are no specifiable physical correlates.

The method of pair comparison was first introduced by Cohn (1894) in his study of color preferences and then developed further by Thurstone. It is often regarded as the most appropriate way of securing value judgments. The observer's task is simplified by giving him only two stimuli to compare. Usually every stimulus is paired with every other stimulus in a randomly presented matrix of pairs. This results in $N(N-1)/2$ pairs; for example, 45 pairs for 10 stimuli. The number of pairs increases rapidly as stimuli are added, but the task can sometimes be shortened by breaking up a series of stimuli into two or more overlapping series.

In Chapter 2 the general psychophysical assumption is stated that repeated presenta-

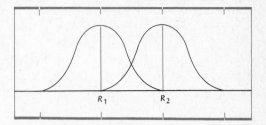

Figure 3.3. Two hypothetical normal frequency distributions of mean response values (R_1 and R_2) corresponding to two stimuli, S_1 and S_2, for a group of observers.

tion of the same stimulus does not produce an identical response each time but rather a distribution of responses that may be described in terms of central tendency and dispersion. In that case, means and standard deviations of physical stimulus values producing the responses were calculated. However, in the present case, calculations will be made on the basis of Thurstone's theory that the sensory or perceptual distribution is a nonobservable and hypothetical continuum. (See the theory of signal detectability in Chapter 2.) Although the discussion is limited to individual differences, which represent the more common application of pair comparisons, Thurstone applied the theory to both individual differences and differences from moment to moment in the same individual.

Theoretically, when the same stimulus S_1 is presented to each member of a group of observers, a distribution of perceptions will result with a mean of R_1. Likewise S_2, which it is assumed is similar to S_1, produces a distribution with a mean of R_2. Figure 3.3 shows the two resulting hypothetical normal distributions where the frequency of different magnitudes of R results from S_1 and S_2. Although both stimuli belong on the same continuum, R_2 (the mean response to S_2) is larger than R_1 (the mean response to S_1). However, some individuals would judge S_1 larger than S_2. The effect of S_1, for example, on observer A can be described as $R_{1A} = R_1 + d_{1A}$, where R_{1A} refers to A's re-

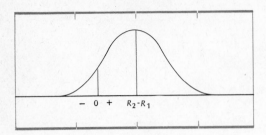

Figure 3.4. Hypothetical normal frequency distribution of differences in response values associated with a pair of stimuli.

sponse to S_1 and d_{1A} to his deviation from R_1, the mean response to S_1 for the group. Likewise, $R_{2A} = R_2 + d_{2A}$ describes observer A's perception of S_2. The important point to note here is that Thurstone's Law of Comparative Judgment made it possible to obtain perceptual scale values associated with the *single* stimulus, S_1 and S_2 in the present example, by starting quantitatively with these individual differences, namely, $D_A = (R_{2A} - R_{1A}) + (d_{2A} - d_{1A})$. By summing the value of D for the N individuals in the group, one obtains the mean $D = R_2 - R_1$ because, by definition, the sum of the individual deviations is zero. The sum of these individual Ds squared and divided by N gives the standard deviation of the differences between the distributions shown in Figure 3.3.

$$\sigma_D = \sqrt{\sigma_2{}^2 + \sigma_1{}^2 - 2r_{21}\sigma_2\sigma_1}$$

where σ_2 and σ_1 are standard deviations for the distributions of R_2 and R_1, the responses associated with stimuli S_2 and S_1, and r_{21} is the correlation between the individual observers' deviations from the means, R_2 and R_1, of the distribution. Figure 3.4 shows the hypothetical distribution of differences and the mean of $R_2 - R_1$. This is Thurstone's theory.

The problem now is to relate Thurstone's theory to actual data. Here Thurstone made use of the known relationship between proportions under the normal curve and the z scores discussed in the previous chapter (*see* Table 2.4). The proportions are simply the number of individual observers, divided by N,

who choose one stimulus over another: this would be S_1 over S_2 in the present example.

Assuming the distributions are normal, as in Figure 3.4, this proportion will correspond to a z score that defines the psychological distance between stimuli S_1 and S_2. Therefore, the experimentally obtained proportions are converted to z scores with the aid of tables of the normal curve (the Reference Table at the back of this book will do for most cases).

In other words, the proportion $R_2 - R_1$ is the only kind of datum obtained, and the rest is theory as is shown in Figure 3.4, in which the zero on the abscissa represents the point at which S_1 is judged equal to S_2. Negative values of $R_2 - R_1$ represent differences for individuals by whom S_1 is judged greater than S_2, but on the average S_2 is judged greater than S_1. The standard deviation of this distribution is σ_D, as defined above.

If we convert the obtained proportion, $R_2 - R_1$, the mean of the distribution of differences, to a z score, z_{21}, and express its value using the standard deviation, σ_D, as the unit of measurement, one then obtains

$$R_2 - R_1 = z_{21} \sqrt{\sigma_2{}^2 + \sigma_1{}^2 - 2r_{21}\sigma_1\sigma_2}$$

This is Thurstone's so-called *"Law of Comparative Judgment'"* of the *psychological* distance between stimuli. Because experimental data on any of the values under the radical are usually not available, this equation cannot be tested directly. However, Thurstone (1927), proposed several simplifying assumptions or "cases," as he called them. One assumption is that the underlying, hypothetical distribution of responses resulting from a given stimulus is the same whether it was obtained from different individuals on one trial or from one individual on different trials. The standard deviation, σ, of this distribution is called the *discriminal dispersion*. The other value under the radical sign, r, refers to the potential correlation between perceptual values of different stimuli. If it is assumed that $\sigma_1 = \sigma_2$ and that $r = 0$, then we obtain $R_2 - R_1 = z_{21}k\sqrt{2}$ where k is a

TABLE 3.2 PROPORTION OF CHOICE OF COMPOSERS BY 308 MUSICIANS IN PAIR COMPARISON

	Bach	Beethoven	Mendelssohn	Mozart	Schumann
Bach	—	.38	.82	.52	.78
Beethoven	.62	—	.94	.79	.94
Mendelssohn	.18	.06	—	.03	.71
Mozart	.48	.21	.97	—	.83
Schumann	.22	.06	.29	.17	—

Each entry is the proportion of musicians preferring the composer listed in the column at the left to the corresponding composer in the row at the top. Data from Folgemann, 1933.

constant corresponding to the value of the discriminal dispersion. If $k\sqrt{2}$ is used as the arbitrary unit of measurement, one can define

$$R_2 - R_1 = z_{21}$$

This is a simplified form ("Case V") of Thurstone's Law of Comparative Judgment. It is theoretically an equal-interval scale.

Much has been written about testing the assumptions that have been made about the form of the distributions and the size of the correlations and dispersions (see Thurstone, 1927b; Guilford, 1954; Torgerson, 1958).

Some data in a large study by Folgemann (1933) of the preference of musicians for the music of different composers illustrate scaling based on pair comparison. The judges were 308 members of the Philadelphia, Boston, Minneapolis, and New York Philharmonic orchestras. For the study, the composers' names were presented in pairs, each name being paired with every other one. The instructions were as follows:

This is an experimental study of preferences of the music of different composers. You are asked to underline the name of the one composer of each pair whose *music you prefer* in general, *not* taking the personality or greatness of the composer into consideration.

For example, take the pair:

Puccini—Gounod.

If in general you prefer the music of Puccini to that of Gounod, underline *Puccini,* if on the other hand you prefer Gounod, underline *Gounod.* To make this experiment valid, it is absolutely necessary not to omit any pair, even if it is difficult to make a choice. It is also of the greatest importance not to discuss the experiment with anyone before its completion.

Folgemann used 19 different composers. He published tables showing the proportion of the 308 judges who chose each composer when compared with every other one in a total of 190 comparisons, which included 19 control trials. (A smaller sample of five composers has been selected to simplify the illustration of computations which begins with the matrix of proportions in Table 3.2.)

The proportions are obtained by dividing the number of the musicians who preferred Bach to Beethoven, for example, by the total number of judges. This value (118/308 = .38) is entered in the second column of the first row. The proportion who preferred Beethoven over Bach (190/308 = .62) is shown in the first

TABLE 3.3 z-SCORES (PSYCHOLOGICAL DISTANCE) BETWEEN FIVE COMPOSERS AS JUDGED BY 308 MUSICIANS BASED ON PAIR COMPARISON DATA IN TABLE 3.2

	Bach	Beethoven	Mendelssohn	Mozart	Schumann	Σ	Mean R	Linearly transformed R
Bach	—	−0.31	+0.92	+0.05	+0.77	+1.43	+0.38	1.34
Beethoven	+0.31	—	+1.55	+0.81	+1.55	+4.22	+1.06	2.02
Mendelssohn	−0.92	−1.55	—	−1.88	+0.55	−3.80	−0.95	0.01
Mozart	−0.05	−0.81	+1.88	—	+0.95	+1.97	+0.48	1.44
Schumann	−0.77	−1.55	−0.55	−0.95	—	−3.82	−0.96	0.00

column of the second row. Cells in the diagonal, which should theoretically yield proportions of .50, are empty because pairs of identical composers were not used.

The next step in the analysis is to convert the proportion to z scores. Note that a proportion of .50 would yield a psychological distance of zero. The larger the distance between the stimuli, the greater is the z score, as is shown in Table 3.3.

The sign of the z score indicates whether the composer listed in the row or column received a majority $(+)$ of the votes. Note that the part above the diagonal is otherwise a mirror image of the part below the diagonal.

Table 3.3 is a matrix of all the distances between the R values (preference) corresponding to the S value (composers), but it does not yet reveal the psychological continuum, where single R values can be located. The question now is how best to accomplish that. Each column or row of the matrix represents a continuum that includes such scale values, but they are relative to only one of the five composers. There are actually four estimates of each distance, one direct one, $A - B$, and three indirect ones, $(A - C) - (B - C) = A - B$, and so on. Therefore, the best estimate of each R value is obtained by taking the mean of the values in each row, for this gives the estimate containing *all* the information about each stimulus in the matrix. These then are scale values with $k\sqrt{2}$ as the arbitrary unit according to Case V.

However, it is awkward to deal with positive and negative values, and because the unit is arbitrary anyway, one can get rid of the sign by adding 0.96 to each R value, as is shown in the last column of Table 3.3. Accordingly, the composers are ordered and the psychological (preferential) distances between them are as follows:

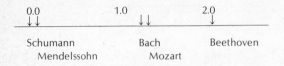

This scale should not be interpreted to imply that Beethoven was judged three times better than Schumann. The numbers only serve to mark off distances along a psychological continuum and show that Schumann and Mendelssohn were located almost in the same place on this continuum, more than a unit below Bach and Mozart, who were placed about a half unit below Beethoven, and so on. Only an arbitrary zero has been defined on this scale.

The method of pair comparison can be applied to any stimulus material for which pairs can be presented. The inclusion of too many pairs may make the task tedious for the observer, and stimulus differences that lead to proportions of 0 or 1.0 only make the computation of scale values more complicated for the experimenter. One usually can overcome such practical problems by using overlapping ranges and making careful preparations.

A more serious problem than the one above is theoretical; that is, will the data actually conform to the model and its strict assumptions? Two checks can be made easily. First, one should compare the mean scale values with each of the scale values in the columns of the matrix of z scores, for these should agree within experimental error. There are such discrepancies, for example, in our matrix between the Mendelssohn and the Beethoven column. Second, one can attempt to reproduce the experimentally obtained proportions by going backwards from our mean scale values. The difference between any two scale values corresponds to a score, and by making the proper subtractions and converting these differences into p values by using Reference Table 1, it should be possible to generate the obtained matrix of proportions in Table 3.2 with only chance variation.

The two sets of data can be evaluated by a chi-square test. Significant differences would indicate that the data do not fit the model and that one or more of its assumptions must be rejected. (See Torgerson, 1958; Bock & Jones, 1968).

Stimulus Rating and Successive Categories

Some of the experiments discussed are called *psychophysical* because they are concerned with the psychological scaling of attributes which can be measured on a physical continuum. The fact the stimuli can be specified in physical terms is a great help in studying various problems in sensation and perception. The last example showed, however, that psychological scales can be constructed even when there is no physical continuum for comparison. Such scales are often called *psychometric*, and perhaps the most familiar example of this type is the rating scale. Rating, pair comparison, and ranking (discussed below) can be applied to both psychophysical and psychometric problems.

Galton (1883) may have been the first to develop rating scales. His purpose was to quantify a strictly psychological attribute, the vividness of memory images. Since then, the rating scale has been used for various purposes in experimental psychology. Most people are familiar with these scales for description of academic achievement, personality characteristics, and the like. Probably no students get through high school without being rated, and the method is widely used in industry, the armed forces, and whenever some simple quantitative description of people is desired. The task of the observer is to judge one attribute of the stimuli by placing it in one of about seven categories reflecting different quantities of the attribute. (Do not confuse rating with methods of interval judgment, partitioning, or the method of equal sense distances, which are considered below.)

The interpretation of facial expression, which is an important aspect of interactions among people, giving clues to feeling or motivations, has been studied seriously with the rating method since the time of Darwin (1872). The typical procedure is to use photographs posed by actors portraying various emotions. The early studies asked the observer to interpret or identify which emotion the

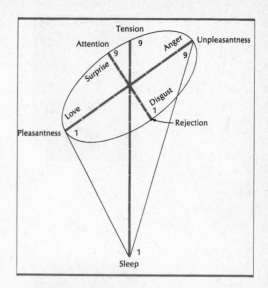

Figure 3.5. Schlosberg's model of the relationship between three dimensions of facial expression: sleep-tension, attention-rejection, and pleasantness–unpleasantness. Each dimension is represented as a nine-point rating scale. The figure illustrates where in this special representation certain emotions, for example, love, would fall.

actor was portraying. The results indicated many confusions in the typical observer, for example, between fear and anger, and seemed to show that emotions are identified in the total situational context rather than in terms of facial expressions alone. However, largely due to Schlosberg (1952, 1954) it came to be realized that the confusion was due to actual similarity in the facial expression associated with different emotions. These similarities, Schlosberg proposed, are the operating psychological dimensions used in judging facial expression, and he showed how these dimensions may be related theoretically by the model shown in Figure 3.5. Rating data along these dimensions are reliable and provide the empirical support for the model (Schlosberg, 1952, 1954).

One procedure employed in Schlosberg's experiments was to present pictures of various emotions, portrayed by the same actress, to a group of observers. Each observer judged

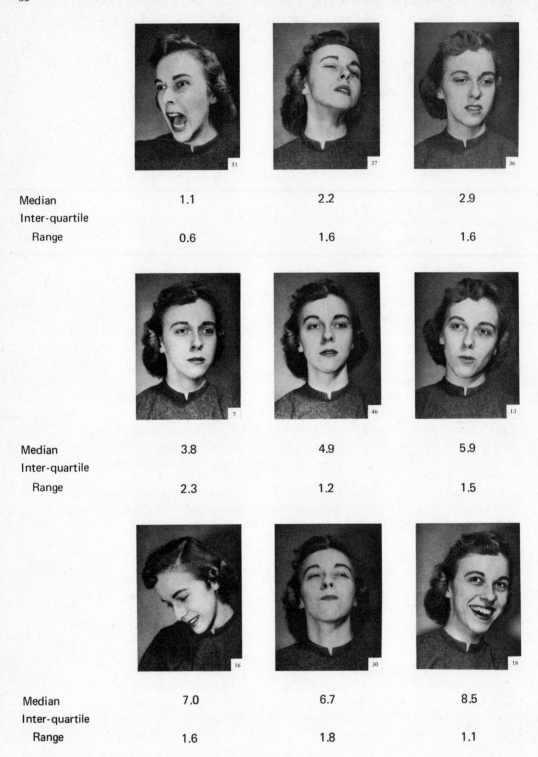

Median	1.1	2.2	2.9
Inter-quartile			
Range	0.6	1.6	1.6

Median	3.8	4.9	5.9
Inter-quartile			
Range	2.3	1.2	1.5

Median	7.0	6.7	8.5
Inter-quartile			
Range	1.6	1.8	1.1

Figure 3.6. Rating scale values for Lightfoot pictures on the Schlosberg dimension of pleasantness–unpleasantness obtained with 96 observers. (Numbers in lower right-hand corner were not visible to the observers and serve only to identify the pictures. See Engen, Schlosberg, & Levy, 1958.)

the pictures along the three Schlosberg dimensions defined by the experimenter and clarified by illustrations. The following instructions were given for the dimension of pleasantness.

> The purpose of this experiment is to see how accurately you can judge the degree of pleasantness in a series of photographs posed by the same actress. Note that you are *not* to judge whether *you* like the picture or not, but the pleasantness *she* is trying to represent. The pictures are arranged in an irregular order. You are to rate each picture on a 9-point scale, where 1 indicates that the actress feels very unpleasant and 9 indicates she feels very pleasant. The facial expressions you will see may fall anywhere on this scale. Your task is to assign a whole number which reflects this degree. Don't worry about whether or not you have seen a picture before—some of them are similar—but judge each picture as independently as you can. There is no right or wrong answer. We want to know how *you* judge the pictures. Any questions?

The instructions quoted above were presented to each observer, along with a table for recording his judgments, and were also read aloud by the experimenter. Usually about 50 pictures representing as varied a sample of the dimensions as possible were presented in one session, but for the present purpose just a few of the so-called "Lightfoot pictures" (Engen, Schlosberg, & Levy, 1958) are shown in Figure 3.6. As can be seen, rating-scale values are simply the measure of the central tendency plus dispersion of the judgment for each stimulus.

Medians are often used, as in the present case, because these distributions are often skewed for stimuli falling at the extremes of the rating scales, that is, extremely pleasant and unpleasant expressions in the present case. (Consult Abelson and Sermat [1962] for a multidimensional analysis of Schlosberg's model.)

The ideal rating scale is one with equal intervals, but the data obtained from the observers are only ordinal. Thus, the problem is how to obtain a possible *latent* equal-interval scale from such *manifestly* ordinal data. If this could be accomplished, one could, for exam-

ple, test Fechner's Law very conveniently with rating data, for ratings can be obtained very quickly for a large number of stimuli as compared with *DL*s and discriminal dispersions.

Those who have been concerned with the construction of interval scales from rating data have usually started with the assumption that the judgments of any object are normally distributed on an interval scale. (See Guilford, 1954, p. 226.) Torgerson (1959) has shown how the theoretical principles of the Law of Comparative Judgment can be applied to rating data and he has thus proposed a *Law of Categorical Judgment*.

The Law of Comparative Judgment assumes that each stimulus of a pair produces a response distribution with certain quantitative attributes. While applying the Law of Categorical Judgment, the same assumption is made about this response distribution, but, in addition, it is assumed that the boundaries between categories on the scale have an effect and a distribution like the one obtained for the stimulus. According to Torgerson (p. 206):

> 1. The psychological continuum of the subject can be divided into a specified number of ordered categories or steps.
> 2. Owing to various and sundry factors, a given *category boundary* is not necessarily always located at a particular point on the continuum. Rather, it also projects a normal distribution of positions on the continuum. Again, different category boundaries may have different mean locations and different dispersions.
> 3. The subject judges a given stimulus to be below a given category boundary whenever the value of the stimulus on the continuum is less

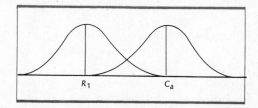

Figure 3.7. Two hypothetical frequency distributions of response values; R_1 corresponds to a stimulus, S_1, and C_a, to the boundary between two categories on the response scale.

than that of the category boundary. Essentially, this amounts to the assumption that the boundaries between adjacent categories behave like stimuli.

To make pair comparisons, the scaling entails converting proportions to z scores that theoretically represent psychological distances between stimuli. In Torgerson's category scaling, the proportion of the time a certain stimulus is placed in a certain category is converted to a z score, which in this case represents the psychological distance between the stimulus and the category boundary. Figure 3.7 is thus analogous to Figure 3.3 except that a category boundary has been substituted for one of the stimuli in a pair. The first and last categories are limited on one side and open on the other.

The experimenter obtains proportions of individuals who put a stimulus S_1 in a certain category. The category scale may be 1 2 3 4 5, specific examples, or adjectives, which would then be converted to numerals before scaling. The problem is to determine the numerical values of category boundaries on a hypothetical psychological dimension. For n categories there are $n - 1$ upper category boundaries $(C_a, C_b, \ldots C_{n-1})$. The proportions of raters for whom a certain category boundary lies above a certain stimulus, or P_{co}, where O is an individual rater and C a certain category boundary are obtained in the experiment. If these proportions are converted to z scores, we may write Torgerson's Law of Categorical Judgment,

$$C_a - R_1 = z_{a1} \sqrt{\sigma_a^2 + \sigma_1^2 - 2r_{a1}\sigma_a\sigma_1}$$

which is directly comparable to Thurstone's Law of Comparative Judgment (p. 51) except that the category boundary has been substituted for one of the stimuli in the pair. Simplifying assumptions must again be considered because the formula contains parameters that are not easily evaluated.

The elegant theory described above ideally should provide a scale with equal intervals for psychological measurement. Unfortunately, great difficulty has been encountered in obtaining stable, useful, and valid ratings at even this ordinal level due to various biases in the observers and variability in the objects or persons rated (see Guilford, 1954). It is apparently almost always necessary to provide the raters with a common anchor or reference point, in order to obtain reliable data.

Another attempt to improve the reliability of the data has involved the use of descriptive adjectives, such as: Very poor—Poor—Fair—Good—Excellent. The rater makes a check on the line above the phrase which best describes the person or object rated. The trouble is that most of the checks seem to land in the central category, unless the rater is consistently optimistic or pessimistic. To spread out and stabilize the ratings, the descriptive phrases are made more specific still, even to the extent of listing typical items of behavior.

In another variation of the method the rater may be told to let each of five successive categories represent 20 percent of the college population. Still another attempt to anchor the scale and prevent context effects uses specific individuals or objects known to all raters as anchors for each category. In spite of all these devices, the raters will tend to produce approximately normal distributions of ratings. One cannot always be sure whether this represents a bias in the rater or the fact that most traits are normally distributed. Unfortunately for both psychophysical and psychometric scaling, there is no *external check* or independent evidence of this kind.

Guilford (1938), Attneave (1949), and Garner and Hake (1951) have developed procedures similar to those described above for equal-interval scaling. The same normality assumption is made, but different data are used to start the procedure. For example, the *method of "absolute" judgments,* which involves essentially the same procedure as the *method of single stimuli,* may be used instead of rating. The latter method was proposed by Wever and Zener (1928) and is in turn similar to the method of constant stimuli

(p. 23), except that no standard stimulus is used; instead each comparison stimulus is to be judged in absolute categories appropriate to the attribute being judged, such as "high," "medium," "low," or on the basis of the observer's previous experience. The first comparison stimulus is judged almost at random, but the observer soon adjusts himself to the range of stimuli encountered and uses the categories consistently and in fair correspondence with the stimuli presented. If the experimenter then shifts the range of the stimuli, by removing the lowest and adding some higher tones for example, the observer soon follows suit by readjusting the category values. This latter observation illustrates the context effect which is of interest in studies of judgment, for example by social psychologists, but which is a nuisance in psychophysical scaling.

Helson (1964) relied on the effect of context on judgments as the starting point for developing a psychological relativity theory much more general than the one suggested above in connection with Weber's Law (p. 17). The basic point in Helson's theory is that there are no absolute quantities in psychology as there are, for example, in physics. Psychology is restricted to relative quantities because the effect of any stimulus is related to the *adaptation level* of the organism, which is determined by all past as well as present stimulation. The value of this neutral point is the mean of the stimuli weighted in terms of their hypothetical psychological effect. To determine the physical value corresponding to this mean in a psychophysical experiment, one needs to know the psychophysical function relating response magnitude to stimulus magnitude, and Helson has assumed that a modified Fechnerian Law is correct. Because this is a logarithmic function, the stimulus distribution corresponding to the hypothetical normal response distribution will be geometric, and the geometric mean is the proper measure of central tendency. In the simple case, adaptation level is determined by taking the mean of the logarithmic values of the

comparison stimuli, and this mean is the psychological origin for the observer's scale.

Helson predicts that ratings can be expressed as differences between the adaptation level and the comparison stimuli weighted in terms of their values, which are determined by curve-fitting methods. Assuming that Fechner's Law is valid, it would provide a more general and powerful statement of the theory.

Fechner's Law (see p. 50) may also be written as $R = k \log (S/S_0)$ where S_0 is the value of S at threshold or RL. Helson obtains a modified logarithmic function by substituting the stimulus value corresponding to the adaptation level for that corresponding to RL.

The formula is compact and the actual calculations can be specified more conveniently in a pair of general formulas. Let $S =$ any value of the stimulus. $S_0 =$ that particular value of the stimulus that is selected as the arbitrary origin or zero. Helson uses the adaptation level (AL) or the geometric mean of the comparison stimuli. This would be the logical measure of central tendency in view of the Fechnerian assumption that the sensory effect of stimuli is proportional to the logarithm of their physical intensity. $d =$ the constant stimulus ratio by which each value of S must be multiplied in order to give the value lying one sensation step or unit higher up the scale. That is, $d =$ the Weber fraction plus 1.0. This sensation unit is defined in terms of the observer's responses and could be defined in some other way as, for example, by rating scale values. If $n =$ the number of psychological units from S_0 to S, then

$$S = S_0 d^n$$
$$\log S = \log S_0 + n \log d$$
$$n = \frac{1}{\log d} (\log S - \log S_0)$$

To adapt this general formula for use in any particular sense modality, one needs a well-defined sensation unit, DL or the numerical value of d, and the arbitrary value of the stimulus, S_0 or AL. For example, to locate in the musical scale any assigned vibration frequency, A of 440 cycles may be defined as S_0 and the octave ($d = 2$) as the sensation unit. The last equation then reduces to

$$n = 3.322 \ (\log S - 2.644)$$

If $S = 10,000$ cycles, the equation gives us $n = 4.505$; in other words, the tone of 10,000 cycles is 4.5 psychological units above A (see Michels & Helson, 1949; Helson, 1964, p. 197).

TABLE 3.4 ABSOLUTE JUDGMENTS OF SINGLE STIMULUS

Very very light	1
Very light	2
Light	3
Medium-light	4
Medium	5
Medium-heavy	6
Heavy	7
Very heavy	8
Very very heavy	9

Helson actually uses a rating method instead of one of the classical methods for determining DL and RL. An example of the kind of rating scale for judgments of weights used by Helson is shown in Table 3.4.

After practicing weight lifting, for example, and becoming familiar with these response categories, the observer may be instructed to lift one weight at a time and apply one of the verbal descriptions to it. These rating categories are considered to have the numerical equivalents shown in Table 3.4 that are used by Helson for numerical computation of scale values. This presupposes that the observer uses the verbal rating scale as though the psychological distance between what he calls "very very light" to "very light" (1 to 2) is the same as the distance from "very light" to "light" (3 to 4) and so on. Furthermore, whatever the range of weights that has been presented, it is assumed that the observer will divide it up into nine psychologically equal intervals. In other words, Helson assumes that the rating scale is a manifest equal-interval scale, as compared with the latent equal-interval scale assumed in Torgerson's Law of Categorical Judgment.

Two related criticisms have been made of the adaptation level theory. The first, as noted previously, is that ratings are unstable measures. Of special interest here is the observation that rating categories, such as those in Table 3.4, are semantically arbitrary, as well as restricted in number (see Campbell, Lewis, & Hunt, 1958). For example, "very large" can be applied independently to both a flea and an elephant without any link to a common psychological dimension. In using this kind of rating scale the observer might bias his judgments by responding in terms of his expectation of the proper use of the categories in the context. Another criticism of Helson's theory involves the Fechnerian function assumed to govern relations between psychological and physical magnitude. Does a rating scale yield psychologically equal intervals? Can the observer judge only relative magnitude, or is he capable of stating in absolute terms the magnitude of a sensation? These are really problems of direct scaling which we shall consider further after the discussion of indirect scaling has been completed.

The Ranking Method

An older name for the ranking method is *Order of Merit*. The observer arranges a number of stimuli or objects in an ordinal series along a given dimension. The same objects then are either ranked many times by the same observers or once by many observers; the mean rank is computed as a psychological scale value for each object. It is a very convenient method for developing (manifest) ordinal scales directly in psychophysical and psychometric studies. Furthermore, it is an easy procedure for the observer except when the number of objects is very large.

Usually the whole set of objects is presented together, and the observer is allowed to proceed as he wishes as long as he comes through with a single rank order along the dimension specified by the experimenter. If many objects are presented, he may be asked to sort them roughly into grades before he attempts the final ranking. The development of the ranking method was mainly the work of Cattell (1903) and Spearman (1904) who made an important contribution by showing how to use rank order in the measurement of correlation.

Cattell used the ranking method to identify the leaders in each natural science on the basis of judgment by their colleagues. For example, he asked 10 psychologists to rank the 200 people (a very large number) in the United States who were considered psychologists at that time. The 10 judges worked separately and independently. Cattell computed the mean of the 10 ranks assigned by the judges to the psychologists and eventually revealed the names in 1933. The 10 highest ranking men and their mean ranks were:

William James	(1.0)
J. McKeen Cattell	(3.7)
Hugo Munsterberg	(4.0)
G. Stanley Hall	(4.4)
J. Mark Baldwin	(7.5)
Edward B. Titchener	(7.5)
Josiah Royce	(7.6)
George T. Ladd	(9.2)
Joseph Jastrow	(11.6)

In the list of psychologists, numbers 2, 3, and 4 were nearly equal; the same is true for the next three men, and so on. Some of the men on the list were philosophers and the "order of merit" would probably be different if established by a contemporary sample of judges. Cattell's original statement (1903) is clear about the significance of such a list:

It should be distinctly noted that these figures give only what they profess to give, namely, the resultant opinion of ten competent judges. They show the reputation of the men among experts, but not necessarily their ability or performance. Constant errors, such as may arise from a man's being better or less known then he deserves, are not eliminated. There is, however, no other criterion of a man's work than the estimation in which it is held by those competent to judge.

Why are the mean ranks so close together for the 10 top people listed above? Suppose a group of observers were asked to rank 10 weights differing very noticeably from each other. The chances are good that every observer would rank them in the same order and that the mean ranks would be simply 1, 2, 3, ..., 10. However, if one tried the same experiment with 10 equal weights, the chances are each observer would rank them in a different order, and the mean ranks would all be nearly the same. Finally, let the weights differ by small amounts so that every observer would be likely to make a few errors. The results would lie between the two extremes mentioned, that is, not perfectly ordered according to weight but closely correlated with it. The principle here is that, given competent judges, the mean ranks probably will agree with both the order and the spacing of the objects. In addition, it is possible, of course, to measure the amount of disagreement among the judges (see Siegel, 1956; Hayes, 1963). As a result it can be shown once more that, given variability in the judgments, the same kind of scale can be derived from ranking as from pair comparison by converting rank orders to choice frequencies and then to p values and finally to z scores.

If a judge ranks a certain object No. 1, he obviously prefers it to the others. If he ranks it No. 2, he prefers it to the remaining, and so on. In this manner each rank (r) can be converted into a choice score (c). In general, with n objects, $c = n - r$, and because this equation holds for all the ranks assigned by the judges to the same object, it holds for the mean choice score (M_c) and the mean rank (M_r) of that object. Therefore,

$$M_c = n - M_r$$

The values of M_r are converted into p values according to the formula

$$p = \frac{M_c}{n - 1}$$

TABLE 3.5 RANKS REDUCED TO CHOICE SCORES AND z SCORES

	Astronomers									
	A	B	C	D	E	F	G	H	I	J
Judges										
1	1	2	4	3	9	6	5	8	7	10
2	1	4	2	5	6	7	3	10	8	9
3	1	3	4	5	2	8	9	6	10	7
4	1	3	4	5	2	6	10	8	7	9
5	1	9	2	5	6	3	4	8	10	7
6	1	4	9	2	5	6	7	3	10	8
7	1	3	5	10	2	6	9	7	8	4
8	1	3	5	7	6	4	8	10	2	9
9	1	2	8	4	9	6	3	7	5	10
10	1	2	4	5	9	8	6	3	7	10
Sum of ranks	10	35	47	51	56	60	64	70	74	83
M_r	1.0	3.5	4.7	5.1	5.6	6.0	6.4	7.0	7.4	8.3
$M_c = n - M_r$	9.0	6.5	5.3	4.9	4.4	4.0	3.6	3.0	2.6	1.7
$p = M_c/(n - 1)$	1.00	.72	.59	.54	.49	.44	.40	.33	.29	.19
z	?	+.58	+.23	+.10	−.03	−.15	−.25	−.44	−.55	−.88
$R = 5z + 6$		8.90	7.15	6.50	5.85	5.25	4.75	3.80	3.25	1.60

The following are used as checks: the average M_r must $= (n + 1)/2$; the average M_c must $= (n - 1)/2$; the average p must $= 1/2$.

That is, if there are 10 objects in the set, each is compared with the remaining 9. There

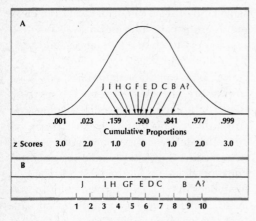

Figure 3.8. *Top.* Psychological scale values (cumulative proportions) for astronomers based on rank ordering of their eminence and an illustration of the assumption of the normal distribution of the psychological distances between them (z scores). *Bottom.* Linearly transformed z scores from data above, with the formula $y = ax + b$, where y is the desired scale value and x the z score. The scale shown here was obtained with $a = 5$ and $b = 6$. See also Table 3.6.

are certain checks on these computations, as is indicated in Table 3.5. The data are taken from Cattell's 1906 study of the 10 leading astronomers of that time; these data were used also in the first edition of this book (p. 373).

The p values have been converted into z scores using Table 3.5. These z scores represent scale values for the astronomers on a psychological scale with equal intervals on the assumption that the rankings are normally distributed, as is illustrated in Figure 3.8A. The reasoning here follows the same general theory discussed in connection with obtaining interval scales from pair comparisons or ratings (also see Guilford, 1954). Unfortunately, astronomer A was invariably ranked No. 1, which means that the scale value for him cannot be determined, which is a limitation of indirect methods.

There must be less than perfect agreement among the judges to obtain an equal-interval scale. The size of the arbitrary unit may be changed, and the negative values may be eliminated by arbitrarily multiplying the z scores by a constant value and then adding a constant, respectively. In the present example $R = 5z + 6$ as is shown in Figure 3.8B. It must be borne in mind that these are at best interval data and that they limit our interpretation to differences between the scale values, for absolute values have no meaning on this scale. Just adding a constant would be enough (see Table 3.3).

Of course, one might object to scale values on the basis that the empirical (manifest) data are merely ordinal numbers, because the judge says nothing about the spacing or distance between them on a psychological interval scale. Yet the theory claims that mean ranks represent something more than ordinal scale positions. One sample of data from an individual judge reflects nothing about the spacing of the objects, for although some may be close together and others far apart, the observer has been asked only to arrange them so that each object has more of a particular quality than those ranked below it. However, mean ranks are not the output of a single judge but of a group of judges. Although the single individual is limited to the ordinal numbers, the group may have a finer (latent) fractional scale of mean ranks at its disposal.

A basic point claimed to support the theory proposed above is that the frequencies of objective (physical) measures of an attribute of different individuals, for example, height measured in inches, are normally distributed, and z scores therefore mark off equal distances on the physical dimension above and below the value corresponding to the mean. It is assumed that the psychological attributes, for example, preferences, would also be normally distributed if they could be measured objectively. A normal distribution of judgments along an arbitrary (subjective) dimension is taken as consistent with this assumption and presumptive evidence supporting the use of z scores as measures on the psychological continuum.

On this basis mean ranks are converted and handled as proportions are handled in the methods of pair comparison and constant stimuli. Even the method of constant stimuli, where the stimuli are measured objectively, relies on the psychological data of ordinal numbers because each comparison stimulus is only judged larger or smaller than the standard stimulus rather than how much larger or smaller. If one comparison stimulus is judged larger than the standard 60 percent of the time, while another is judged larger 90 percent of the time, the latter lies above the standard on the psychological continuum by a distance defined in terms of the relationship between z scores and proportions under the normal curve. Thus, this whole group of methods is based on an assumed normal distribution, and the statement of the normality assumption takes different forms depending on the observer's task. The response, whether it be a statement of preference or intensity of sensation, is only considered to be an indirect index of a mechanism mediating between these hypothetical psychological quantities and the stimuli. Guttman's *scalogram analysis* (1950) and Coombs's *unfolding technique* (1964) are methods which emphasize the internal consistency of the judges in ordering the objects in a more direct evaluation of the numerical properties of the scale. Coombs's book, *A Theory of Data,* should be consulted for further study of this topic.

In any case, many investigators are willing to make stronger (equal-interval) assumptions regarding a hypothetical psychological dimension than they are regarding the observer's ability to describe his preference or sensation. They prefer to obtain the equal intervals indirectly or theoretically in the tradition established by Fechner and rationalized by Thurstone. Direct scaling, on the other hand, involves methods which ask the observer for more than ordinal judgments.

DIRECT SCALING

Direct scaling refers to methods for obtaining direct judgments of psychological quantities on an interval or ratio scale. The methods described under the section above on indirect scaling, for example, rank ordering, are direct methods of obtaining psychological ordinal scales and indirect methods of obtaining equal-interval scales. This distinction entails the so-called "latent" versus "manifest" numerical properties of the data. In direct scaling methods the quantitative property desired is stated in the instructions the experimenter gives the observer at the beginning of the experiment, for example, "I want you to tell me for each comparison light *how much* brighter or dimmer it looks than the standard light." Another reason for describing them as direct methods is that the step between the raw data and the final scale is as short as possible. There is really only one assumption involved, namely, that the observer is able to describe his observations at the quantitative level demanded by the instructions. Presumably therefore the data obtained are such that, unlike those obtained with the indirect methods, they need not be supplemented by further theoretical assumptions in order to construct a scale from them.

Operationally the indirect scales may be defined as *confusion scales* (equal intervals obtained from proportions), and direct scales may be defined as *partition scales* (equal intervals based on direct judgment of intervals), or *magnitude scales* (ratio scales based on direct judgment of ratios). Using direct scaling methods, which yield partition scales or magnitude scales, one can distinguish between *estimation methods,* in which the experimenter manipulates the stimuli and the observer judges them, and *production methods,* where the observer manipulates the stimuli so that they reflect a defined subjective relation.

Partition scales involve procedures where the observer works with subjective intervals. These scales are often called *category scales* because the observer works with numerical categories. They should not be confused with rating scales because the instruction given the observer is different—although it is not always clear that the outcome is different.

To use the *category estimation method,*

also called the method of equal-appearing intervals, the observer is usually given one low and one high stimulus as anchors to define the ends of the psychological continuum. The anchors may be included among the comparison stimuli, but usually they are not. Preventing the observer from using a higher or lower category in the event he judges some stimuli more extreme than the anchors, tends to produce skewed response distributions at the extremes of the category scales. The following instructions were used in one study of scaling odor pleasantness (Engen & McBurney, 1964):

> We should like you to judge the pleasantness of odor. The odors will be presented in a random order. In each case your task is to place the odor on a scale by assigning it a whole number. Here is an odor most people find very unpleasant (pyridine). We shall call the odor 2. Here is an odor most people find very pleasant (safrole). We call that 8. The odors we will present next will probably lie somewhere between these two odors in degrees of pleasantness—your task is to assign it a whole number which reflects this degree. Smell number 2 and 8 again and try to remember their relative pleasantness. If you should find an odor even less pleasant than

TABLE 3.6 CATEGORY ESTIMATION SCALE VALUES FOR PLEASANTNESS OF ODORANTS

S (Odorant)	R (Mean judgment)
Safrole	8.0 (as anchor)
Ambre	7.7
Anethol	7.2
Iso-amyl acetate	6.9
Rose double	6.4
Benzaldehyde	6.2
Jasmin	6.0
Citronellol	5.4
Flavor arome chocolate	5.1
Oil of camphor	4.8
Ethyl acetate	4.2
Essence cardamone	4.1
N-Caprylic acid	4.0
Guaiacol	3.7
Heptanal	2.9
Asafoetida	2.8
Pyridine	2.0 (as anchor)
Iso-butyric acid	1.8

number 2, call it 1. And if you should find an odor even more pleasant than number 8 call it 9.

The anchors had been selected as extreme on the basis of preliminary work but were not identified as such or by name to the observer. Many of the 20 observers used in the present experiment actually used both categories 1 and 9. Categories 2 and 8 rather than 1 and 9 were defined in an attempt to avoid the so-called "end effect." This effect refers to the skew of judgmental distributions of stimuli at the extremes of the continuum (Guilford & Dingman, 1955).

The category scale values are obtained by determining the central tendency of the judgments for each stimulus (see Stevens, 1955). The results shown in Table 3.6 are based on the mean. (Note that these scale values depend on the samples of compounds used, and that pleasantness depends on concentration. The present concentrations were matched for psychological intensity, but no attempt was made to maximize the pleasantness or unpleasantness of each odor.)

Except for the instructions, the category estimation method is operationally very similar to the rating scale method discussed above, and it is subject to the same problems noted in that connection and in relation to Helson's work (see p. 59). A particularly important problem is that the observer's results might be influenced by his *expectation* that all the numerical categories should be used equally often regardless of the actual distribution of stimulus values presented. It would have dramatic effects on the form of the psychophysical function if, for example, category scale values for heaviness are plotted as a function of the stimulus weights in grams. (See Johnson, 1944, for a similar experiment.)

Stevens and Galanter (1957) have suggested an *iterative procedure* for eliminating response bias. Their prescription for a "pure" category scale is as follows:

> We will assume that the observer expects the series of stimuli to be so arranged that all categories appear equally often. Since at the outset

we know nothing about the form of the observer's category scale, we present to the first group of observers a series of stimuli spaced in some arbitrary manner along the continuum. The results of this test give us a first approximation to the category scale. For the second group of observers we space the stimuli so that they reflect equal intervals on the scale obtained from the first group of observers. This is a new curve—a second approximation to the "pure" scale. Using this better approximation we respace the stimuli and repeat the procedure with a third group of observers. We repeat this process until stability is reached, i.e., until the results of a test are such that no further changes in spacing are called for.

> With enough homogeneous groups of observers, this iterative procedure could in principle reveal the unadulterated form of the category scale—the form in which the effects of expectation have been neutralized, and discrimination is the only first-order factor left to interact with the observer's intent. (p. 381)

This would eliminate the effect of expectation on the rating scale, but whether it would reveal a valid psychophysical law is still debatable, as will be seen when we compare the results from various direct scaling methods.

The category production method is a much older procedure known as the method of equal sense distances for direct interval scaling and is in a sense estimation in reverse. The observer is now instructed to adjust a continuously variable stimulus, or select one value from a range presented in small steps, to correspond with category scale values of 1, 2, 3, and so on. There are a number of variations of this method but the observer's task is always to adjust or select stimuli so that they mark off subjectively equal distances. *Bisection* was already used by Plateau in the 1850s (see Titchener, 1905, II, ii, pp. 210–214; Boring, 1942). Plateau had eight artists mix a gray which was midway between white and black, so that there was as great a psychological distance between the white and gray as between the gray and black. Plateau's purpose was to test Fechner's logarithmic law, which predicts that the midpoint selected by the artists should correspond to the geometric mean rather than the arithmetic mean. Plateau's results did not verify Fechner's Law.

Instead Plateau found that the relative reflectance of the gray (see Chapter 9) remained approximately constant even with change in illumination. On the basis of these results Plateau suggested that visual brightness grows as the cubic root of the photometric intensity of the stimuli, or $R = cS^{1/3}$ where R is sensation intensity, c a constant, and S the photometric value of the stimulus. This appears to be the first mention of a power function, that is, that sensation intensity is a function of stimulus intensity raised to a power. Plateau's contribution was buried in the methodological and semantic arguments typical of classical psychophysics (see Titchener, 1905, II), but it has been revived as the main alternative to Fechner's Law in contemporary psychophysics.

There is no reason to limit judgments to

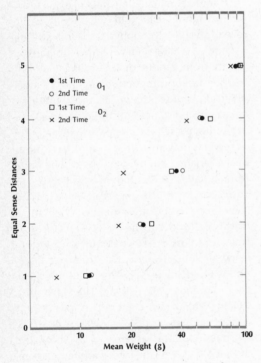

Figure 3.9. Data from an experiment by Titchener (1905). Mean weight in grams assigned to each of five categories representing equal sense distances. It appears that a straight line would describe these data well. Because the coordinate system is semilogarithmic this is consistent with Fechner's law.

bisection, for one can break up a subjective distance into as many equal intervals as desired. This variation of category production also has a long history and is known as the method of *equal-appearing intervals*. In a weight experiment recommended by Sanford for the experimental psychology course of an earlier day (Titchener, 1905, I, p. 33; II, p. 82) the observer was instructed to sort 108 envelopes, ranging in weight from 5 to 100 g, into five piles while keeping the "sense distances" between the piles equal. The average weight placed in each category then defines the psychological scale value of each pile. According to Fechner's Law, if the equal sense distances are plotted against the logarithmic value of these mean weights, one should obtain a linear function. According to Titchener (1905, II, p. 82) results plotted in Figure 3.9 are typical of results obtained from "entirely unpracticed observers." The functions appear linear and represent the kind of results which kept Fechner's Law alive, and for this reason there is still great interest in category scaling in contemporary psychophysics.

However, there is a serious problem with category scaling, namely the problem of the sorter's expectation, which was mentioned above. The distribution of Sanford's weights could also easily have set the stage for this kind of bias. For example, the 26 smallest weights differed from each other by only 0.2 g, whereas the heaviest 25 differed in 2 g steps. In commenting about the data plotted in Figure 3.9 Titchener states that

> . . . the choice of differences recommended by Sanford brings with it a source of error. There is a marked tendency, as well with the observers who are ignorant of the purposes of the experiment, as with those who knew it, to make the piles equal, if possible. Many of the envelopes are so weighted that it is difficult to decide whether they shall be assigned, e.g., to pile 2 or pile 3. Almost invariably, the observer will tend to put them on the pile which contains the smaller number of envelopes. The error cannot be eliminated; it may, in some degree, be counteracted by requiring the observer to revise his first grouping before the measurements are made. The requirement suggests that the in-

structor does not like the look of the piles, as they stand, and so leads to a more objective estimation of the weight of the envelopes.

In other words, the results might have been influenced as much by limiting the observer to a small number of response categories as by the law governing the relation between sensory magnitude and stimulus magnitude. This difficulty was not peculiar to the present method; it is a common problem of response bias. Later, as we have seen, Stevens and Galanter (p. 65) suggested that despite Titchener's pessimism the response bias due to expectancy can be eliminated. In any case, this kind of data and the electrophysiological recording data mentioned below (p. 81) constitute the support for Fechner's Law, which continues to be cited and therefore demands explanation.

There has been a tendency in psychophysics since about the 1950s to develop more and more direct methods in an attempt to maximize the possible variation in the response. The most direct of all would of course be to ask the observer to match numbers to his sensation and eliminate all categories, orderings, or comparisons. This approach to scaling usually requires the observer to make ratio judgments, on the assumption that he is capable of such sophisticated performance.

Direct scaling was derived from production methods which, as is noted above, may only be used when the stimuli can be varied continuously or in very small steps. In direct scaling, the observer is instructed to adjust or select stimuli so that they stand in a prescribed subjective relation to a standard stimulus. One can eliminate the standard and instruct the observer to produce a stimulus which corresponds to various (subjective) numerical values. For example, Ekman, Eisler, and Künnapas (1960) required observers to adjust the visual brightness of a light so that it would correspond to 4, 6, 8, 12, 14, or 16, with a standard designated as 10, and plotted these numbers as a function of the average physical intensity chosen by the observers.

However, the more common method has been *fractionation,* typically halving, with occasional determination of internal consistency of the judgments by doubling. This method received little attention until the 1930s when Stevens (1936) pointed out its value for building a ratio scale for loudness, the well-known *sone scale.* This early work was very successful, and for some time the fractionation method was considered the fundamental method for scaling subjective magnitude. The sone scale was followed by the *mel scale* for pitch (Stevens & Volkmann, 1940), the *veg scale* for heaviness (Harper & Stevens, 1948), the *bril scale* for visual brightness (Hanes, 1949a and b), and others. Some data from an experiment in halving heaviness (Engen & Tulunay, 1956) will be used as an illustration of how psychological scale values are developed.

Thirty-two observers (elementary psychology students) were divided at random into four groups and asked to lift weights, cylinders containing shot, from behind a screen so that the observer could not see them. Each group had a different standard stimulus, 150, 300, 550, or 900 g. The following instructions were given:

> You will be given a container which you will lift with your preferred hand—like this. You will first be given the standard weight. Then you will be given another container which will feel either more or less than half as heavy as the standard. What I want you to do is to tell me to add more weight or to subtract some from this weight until it feels half as heavy as the standard. You may subtract or add to the comparison weight as often as you want before you make your final half-heaviness judgment. We will repeat the procedure several times.

TABLE 3.7 STANDARD WEIGHTS AND MEAN HALF-HEAVINESS VALUES SELECTED BY 8 OBSERVERS

S	$S_{1/2}$
900 g	541.6 g
550 g	325.3 g
300 g	159.0 g
150 g	93.5 g

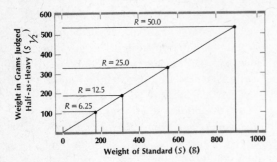

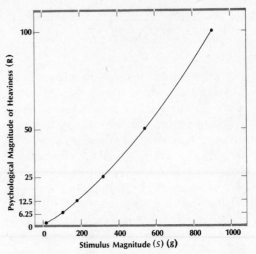

Figure 3.10. Mean half-heaviness judgments in grams plotted as a function of the weight of the standards in grams. The graph illustrates the determination of psychological (R) values by interpolation by defining arbitrarily $R = 100$ when $S = 900$ g on an S-S relation.

The experimenter used a measuring spoon to add and subtract an amount of shot which varied from more than 1 percent to less than 10 percent of the standard weight. Each observer made eight half-heaviness judgments in counter-balanced ascending and descending trials. The weights judged half as heavy ($S_{1/2}$) as each of the standards (S) are shown in Table 3.7, and these average half-heaviness values have been plotted in Figure 3.10 as the first step in obtaining psychological values.

Figure 3.10 shows a linear fit which simplifies the problems of curve fitting (see Harper & Stevens, 1948, and Ekman, 1958, 1961). This is, of course, only a stimulus-stimulus function and not a psychophysical function. The next step is to arbitrarily select a starting point. The highest standard, 900 g, is defined as corresponding to a response value of 100. The response value of 50 will therefore correspond to 541.6 which was judged half as heavy as 900 g. These values have been entered in Table

Figure 3.11. Psychological magnitude (R) obtained by interpolation in Figure 3.10 as a function of stimulus magnitude (S) in grams.

3.8 (rounded to the nearest integers, which is precise enough for the present purpose). From now on one must interpolate on the data

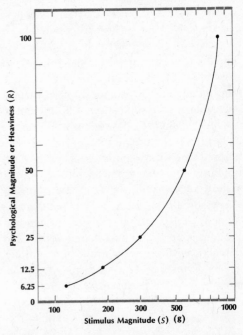

TABLE 3.8

R	S
100	900 g
50	542 g
25	320 g
12.5	185 g
6.25	110 g

Figure 3.12. Data in Figure 3.11 replotted in semilog-arithmic coordinates, that is, psychological (R) values as a function of the stimulus magnitude (S) on a logarithmic scale.

plotted in Figure 3.10 to determine other pairs of stimulus and response values. Therefore, 542 g (for which $R = 50$) is located on the abscissa and used to find its corresponding response value on the ordinate, namely, 320 g, which corresponds to the response value of 25. *Half of 25 is 12.5 and thus with 320 g, 185 g is located in Figure 3.10.* One proceeds in this manner toward the lower left corner of Figure 3.10 without going too far beyond actual data points.

The data for the positively accelerated psychophysical function plotted in Figure 3.11 were obtained with this procedure. In accordance with Fechner's Law, psychological magnitude should be a linear function of the physical values of stimuli plotted on a logarithmic scale. Data plotted on such coordinates, however, turn out not to be linear. As shown in Figure 3.12, for example, such data are curved even more upwards—and do not confirm Fechner's Law.

Stevens' Power Law

The present results are in agreement with the veg scale and other results obtained from direct scaling mentioned above. It is clear that in ratio production the observer does not behave as though logarithmic steps are psychologically equal. The fact that Figure 3.10 shows that $S_{1/2}$ is a linear function of S suggests a constancy in the ratios of stimuli judged to be in the subjective relation of 2:1 and that physically equal ratios are psychologically equal. The ratios of the obtained values in Table 3.7 are actually very similar; for example, 900/541.6 is almost identical to 541.6/325.3. This is in agreement with the power law proposed by Stevens that equal physical ratios are psychologically equal (Stevens, 1957). According to Fechner's Law the stimuli should be converted to logarithms in order to provide equal distances on a psychological interval scale and thus produce a linear function in semilogarithmic coordinates.

To test the power law in the manner described above, the stimulus values are con-

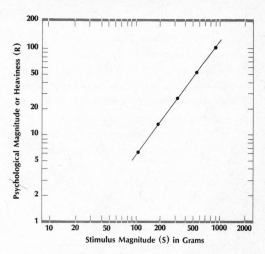

Figure 3.13. Data in Figure 3.12 replotted in double logarithmic coordinates, that is, psychological magnitudes in logarithmic steps as a function of stimulus magnitude in logarithmic steps.

verted to logarithms in order to mark off equal stimulus ratios, but because equal physical ratios should be psychologically equal, one should also mark off the psychological continuum on the ordinate in logarithmic steps in order to obtain a linear plot of the psychophysical function. Thus the arithmetic spacing of our ordinate in Figure 3.11 is converted to logarithmic spacing and we obtain the results shown in Figure 3.13. The latter is obviously a linear function of the form $y = ax + b$ where x and y are logarithmic values of the stimuli and responses. As determined by the method of least squares the line drawn through the data, shown in Figure 3.13, can be stated as

$$\log R = 1.33 \log S - 2.10$$

The line shown will intercept the ordinate at a value (-2.10), which depends on the arbitrary starting point of 100 for the psychological values. The slope of the function (1.33) is the interesting parameter which indicates how heaviness varies as a function of weight. Note that the goodness of the fit of the straight line drawn in Figure 3.13 cannot be evaluated because the values of R were derived from Figure 3.10, which implied a power function. However, psychological magnitude is typically a power function of stimulus magnitude specified by the value of the exponent (slope) in a log-log plot. The value of the exponent varies widely from one sense modality to another. (The determination of the parameters of the power function and goodness of fit are considered in detail in connection with estimation procedures below.)

As mentioned above, one limitation of fractionation is that it is limited to stimuli which can be readily manipulated. In contrast, one possible advantage of this method, compared with other direct methods, is that it may simplify the task of the observer by limiting him to one ratio, and it can readily be checked by plotting halving judgments against doubling judgments on reversed co-ordinates (see Torgerson, 1958). The main problem with the method seems to involve the danger that the observer's selection of a half-value may be determined by the stimulus context and not the sensory system. For example, Garner (1954) questioned the validity of fractionation judgments because his unpracticed observers made half-loudness judgments that seemed to depend entirely on the range of comparison stimuli presented. With the same standard (90 dB) but with different ranges of comparison stimuli (55–65, 65–75, 75–85 dB) three different groups produced half-loudness values which corresponded closely to the midpoint of the range of comparison stimuli, that is, approximately 60, 70, and 80 dB. However, to the contrary, Stevens and Poulton (1956) argue that Garner's conclusions are of limited generality because he *restricted* the observer to fixed comparison stimuli. In other words, Garner used a method that is analogous to the method of constant stimuli rather than adjustment and that deliberately limits variation of response— contrary to the spirit of direct scaling. By allowing the observer to adjust the loudness of a comparison tone himself, Stevens and Poulton obtained results in agreement with the sone scale.

In other experiments it has also been shown that by allowing the observer to adjust the comparison stimulus himself the effect of context is reduced, which may be inevitable with fixed comparison stimuli. Even when the observer makes the adjustments, context effects analogous to "anticipation error" (see p. 15) may be observed. In the weight-lifting experiment described in Table 3.7 the observers tended to select a lower half-heaviness value in the relatively light stimulus context of an ascending series than in the relatively heavy stimulus context of a descending trial. However, practiced psychophysical observers (for example, graduate students in psychology) are decidedly less affected by context than are inexperienced ones (see Engen & Tulunay, 1956).

The fact that psychological scaling rarely works perfectly is often taken as evidence against the validity of psychological scales in general. It seems more probable, however, that such imperfections simply reflect the effect of specific factors in the experimental situation, such as the biases noted, or difficulties in imagining a specific fraction like $\frac{1}{2}$ in specific situations. Hanes (1949a, b) found $\frac{3}{4}$ particularly bad to use in scaling brightness.

It is perhaps more appropriate to conclude that sensory scales based on fractionation are somewhat crude, like the folded paper rule described above, but that the concept of sones, mels, brils, and so on is basically sound. The problem is to eliminate the factors which distort or invalidate the scales; this can best be done by using the most appropriate methods and preferably with a variety of different methods. The restriction of the observer to one ratio is apparently not the best general approach. For example, it became evident during a fractionation experiment ($\frac{1}{2}$) in olfaction (Engen, 1961) that the subjective range of odor intensity is relatively short. The method had been selected because of its successful application in audition and vision, but in olfaction the observers were unable to produce internally consistent half-intensity judgments with different standards, although a wide range of concentrations was provided. Scaling, using estimation methods, indicated that the reason for the problem was that the whole subjective range is only about two or three to one for these odorants. In other words, for many of the standards of lower concentration value, the determination of half-intensity was an unreasonably difficult task. For this and other reasons estimation methods are generally preferred over production methods in direct scaling.

The method for ratio estimation was first suggested by Metfessel (1947), and a procedure for treating the data by Comrey (1950), under the name of the *constant-sum method*. The most popular variation of this method was developed by Ekman (1958). The data analysis suggested by Torgerson (1958) is presented here. Metfessel suggested that the observer be instructed to make "a direct estimate of the ratio between psychological magnitudes" corresponding to each of the $n(n-1)$ pairs of stimuli in a set by dividing 100 points between the members of each pair. For example, a division of 75 to 25 would indicate that one member of the pair had three times more of the psychological attribute than the other member. However, division of points makes it difficult for the observer to report large ratios as accurately as small ratios. For example, 94 to 6, 95 to 5, and 96 to 4 correspond to ratios of 15.67:1, 19:1, and 24:1, while 54 to 46, 55 to 45, and 56 to 44 correspond to ratios of 1.17:1, 1.22:1 and 1.27:1 respectively. Ekman's variation of this method reduces this difficulty of judgment by allowing the observer to report the ratio directly as a percentage, for example, "The second weight appears 75 percent as heavy as the first one." This method follows a procedure very similar to that for pair comparison and is subject to some of its advantages and disadvantages. For example, not too many stimuli can be compared in one session; for $n(n-1)$

TABLE 3.9

Matrix A. Mean ratio estimates of apparent length of pairs of lines are listed above the diagonal and their reciprocals below the diagonal.[a]

Length in inches

	3.00	4.00	6.00	9.00	12.00
3.00		.756	.531	.326	.240
4.00	1.323		.717	.445	.328
6.00	1.884	1.455		.669	.527
9.00	3.069	2.249	1.495		.775
12.00	4.162	3.044	1.893	1.291	

[a] Engen, T., Unpublished data.

Matrix B. Determination of scale values from logarithmic values of the ratio estimates in Matrix A.

Length in inches

	3.00	4.00	6.00	9.00	12.00	Σ	Mean	Antilog of Mean
3.00		−.121	−.274	−.487	−.619	−1.501	−.375	.42
4.00	.121		−.164	−.352	−.483	− .878	−.220	.60
6.00	.274	.164		−.176	−.276	− .014	−.004	.99
9.00	.487	.352	.176		−.111	+ .901	+.226	1.68
12.00	.619	.483	.276	.111		+1.489	+.376	2.36
						00*		

*Check the values in the matrix. They should add to zero.

grows geometrically with *n*. In contrast, it is a very flexible method, and overlapping ranges can be used to advantage. According to Ekman, "It is possible to obtain two separate scales for stimuli, whether identical or not, which are compared under two different conditions. The two groups may include stimuli presented simultaneously to various parts of the body—weights lifted by the right hand and left hand or pain stimuli applied to one normal and one anesthetized area" (Ekman, 1958, p. 291). Guilford and Dingman (1954) obtained the same results in ratio estimation and fractionation for weights judged to be in ratio of 2/1.

Data from a simple unpublished experiment in judging apparent length of lines with this method are presented in Table 3.9. Pairs of lines were presented horizontally with one line 3 inches above the other but not aligned at the ends. The observer sat 7 feet from the screen and viewed the lines at eye-level. The instructions were as follows:

> Each of a series of slides will project two lines of various lengths just like this one [Example]. In each case tell me which is the longer of the two lines and then report the apparent length of the shorter as a percentage of the longer one. For example, if it is half as long, say 50. Use any number you feel is appropriate and be as accurate as you can. Any questions?

The results are shown in Table 3.9, which shows the mean judgments for a group of observers each of whom judged the 10 pairs of lines twice. The experimentally obtained ratio estimates are presented as proportions above the diagonal in matrix A. The cells in the diagonal are empty because identical pairs were not used. The reciprocals are entered below the diagonal. Following Torgerson's procedure (1958) for computing scale values, the values in matrix A are converted to logarithms, which are entered in matrix B, for equal logarithmic differences correspond to equal ratios. Psychological values are then obtained by computing the mean of each row of matrix B and converting to the antilogarithm of this mean. The psychological scale

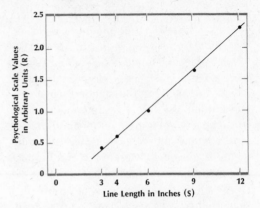

Figure 3.14. Psychological scale values for apparent length (*R*) obtained by the method of ratio estimation plotted as a function of the length of lines (*S*) in inches.

value for each stimulus therefore is the geometric mean of the response to each stimulus in comparison with each of the other stimuli in the set. (Note that if identical pairs were used, their ratios would be 1.00, the logarithm of which is 0.) The psychophysical function obtained when these scale values are plotted as a function of the physical values of the stimuli is shown in Figure 3.14. The unit of the

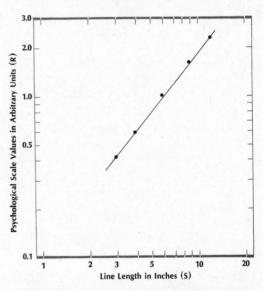

Figure 3.15. Data in Figure 3.14 replotted in double logarithmic coordinates, that is, psychological magnitude in logarithmic steps as a function of line length in logarithmic steps.

psychological scale is arbitrary, and one can multiply the scale values with a constant to obtain any convenient range or magnitude of numbers. However, the actual subjective unit used by each observer is not and cannot be known. This problem will be discussed further in connection with magnitude estimation.

Because the function is linear in arithmetic coordinates, it is obvious that the present psychophysical function does not conform to Fechner's Law, which would require that the function in Figure 3.14 be curved concavely downward or be linear in a semilogarithmic plot. If the data are plotted in such a coordinate system, the function will in fact look like the one in Figure 3.12. Transformation of both axes to logarithmic values in Figure 3.15 results in a linear plot, as required by Stevens' Power Law. Reese et al. (1953) obtained very similar data with the method of fractionation.

The main problem with ratio estimation is that psychophysically naive observers may tend to use a constant range of numbers regardless of the range of stimulus values presented. The results of Table 3.9 illustrate this problem. The psychophysical function obtained has a slope (exponent) greater than 1.00, indicating that the apparent length increases faster than the physical length. Table 3.9 covers a relatively short stimulus range. With a very long range of stimuli, or very large ratios, the results would probably have shown a slope less than unity because of the tendency of the observer to use a constant range of numbers. One can counteract this tendency by training and experience (see Engen & Levy, 1958) or by making the observer's task even more direct.

The Method of Magnitude Estimation

The most direct approach of all would be to ask the observer to match a number directly to the perceived magnitude of each stimulus and eliminate all intervening categories, orderings, comparisons, and theories about the same. This is done in magnitude estimation. Although the so-called "method of sense-ratios" may be traced to Merkel around

1890 (Titchener, 1905, II), the chief contributions to such methodology have been made since the 1950s. As Stevens puts it, "It all started from a friendly argument with a colleague who said, 'You seem to maintain that each loudness has a number and that if someone sounded a tone I should be able to tell him the number.' I replied, 'That's an interesting idea. Let's try it'" (Stevens, 1956, p. 2).

As mentioned above, the basic assumption of direct scaling is that the observer is able to match numbers to his perceptions. The direct methods discussed so far have restricted him to equal intervals, ratios, and pair comparisons, but in magnitude estimation one attempts to avoid all restrictions and encourage the observer to assign the numbers *he* feels are appropriate without any of the biases which may be associated with a response system devised by the experimenter— as has been illustrated amply in this and the previous chapter. Any defined attribute of any set of stimuli may be scaled; for example, visual brightness, intensity of odors, the saltiness of solutions, or the beauty of works of art. It is not a requirement that a corresponding physical continuum be known, although this is necessary in studying the form of the psychophysical law. Usually a fixed set of suprathreshold stimuli covering a wide range of a certain attribute is presented to the observer.

There are two forms of the method. When it was first used it was typical for the experimenter to present the observer with a standard stimulus first and define the subjective value of that as the observer's *modulus*. For example, he might present a weight and tell the observer that it corresponded to a psychological value of 10 and that his task was to judge each of the other weights (presented in an irregular order) in relation to that value. In an experiment on the intensity of odors the observers were given the following instructions, which will define the task in a magnitude estimation experiment with a modulus:

We want you to estimate the intensity of odors. This stimulus defines the standard intensity. The other odors will be presented in an irregular order. They will all be the same quality of smell but the strength will vary.

Call the standard odor before you 10. Your task is then to estimate the intensity or strength of each of the other odors in relation to the standard odor. In other words, the question is: The standard is called 10, what will you call the comparison odor?

Use whatever numbers seem appropriate to you—fractions or whole numbers. For example, if the comparison stimulus smells 7 times as strong as the standard, say 70. If it smells one-fifth as strong, say 2; if a twentieth, say 0.5, etc.

There is no right or wrong answer. We want to know how *you* judge the intensity of odors. Any questions?

TABLE 3.10 GEOMETRIC MEANS (PSYCHOLOGICAL SCALE VALUES) OF 8 CONCENTRATIONS OF AMYL ACETATE DILUTED IN DIETHYL PHTHALATE.[a]

Response value (geometric mean)	Stimulus (concentration)
2.86	1.56
3.81	3.12
5.74	6.25
8.19	12.50
11.57	25.00
15.92	50.00
24.67	100.

[a]The observer was told to assign a scale value of 10 to the modular concentration of 12.5 percent.

Twelve observers were presented each of 7 concentrations twice. The concentration values of the stimuli, obtained by diluting 100 percent amyl acetate in diethyl phthalate, and the geometric means of the observers' judgments are presented in Table 3.10.

One reason for calling the methods "direct" is that there is but a short step between the raw data and the final scale. In this case the step consists of computing the *central tendency judgment* for a group of observers. The appropriate central tendency is usually the geometric mean or the median because occasionally a few unusually high numbers are obtained. For example, while most of the observers described the

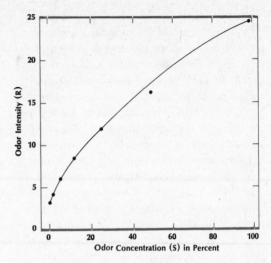

Figure 3.16. Odor intensity (*R*) obtained by the method of magnitude estimation as a function of the concentration of amyl acetate (*S*).

weakest stimulus with numbers between 1 and 5, two observers called it 10. In addition, theoretically the distributions of judgments may be assumed to be log normal for reasons discussed further below. (Note also that the value of the standard stimulus was included in the series of comparison stimuli, but it obtained a scale value of less than 10 for

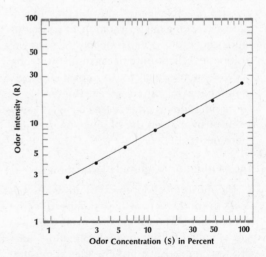

Figure 3.17. Data in Figure 3.16 replotted in double logarithmic coordinates, that is, another so-called "log-log" plot of odor intensity versus odorant concentration.

reasons which will not be considered here.) The data are plotted in linear coordinates, as shown in Figure 3.16, which shows that odor intensity is one of many psychophysical functions exhibiting a negatively accelerated form. Some functions of this kind are linear, and some yield positively accelerated functions in linear coordinates like the one for weight in Figure 3.11 above. This means that in log-log coordinates the slopes (exponents) of many psychophysical functions are less than 1.00, such as for the present data which are replotted in log-log coordinates in Figure 3.17. In other words, all psychological continua scaled by such direct methods seem to be power functions of their respective stimulus continua, and usually stimulus magnitude increases faster than response magnitude.

The main shortcoming of the method of magnitude estimation with a prescribed modulus is that the slope is somewhat influenced by the choice of standard. The highest slope is likely to be obtained for standards in the middle of the series of comparison stimuli, but it decreases as the standard is moved toward either extreme. For example, scaling the odor intensity of the same concentrations as in Table 3.7 using standards of 3.25, 12.5, (as in the present case), and 50 percent concentrations gave the results shown in Figure

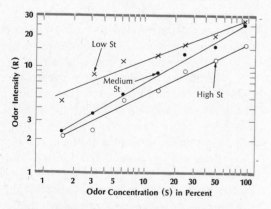

Figure 3.18. Odor intensity obtained by the method of magnitude estimation plotted as a function of log odorant concentration on logarithmic scales of low (3.12%), medium (12.5%), and high (50%) standards.

3.18 (Engen & Lindström, 1963). The value of the intercept on the ordinate reflects the arbitrary choice of modulus, but what is of interest is the slope, which should remain relatively invariant for a perceptual continuum. It is as though the observer spaces the stimuli farther apart when the standard is in the middle of the series than when it is out toward the extreme.

Although this bias appears to be small on a log-log plot and may not change the form of the function, it must at least be considered as a possible contaminating factor when results for the same series of stimuli are being compared and when the slope for a particular perceptual continuum is being specified. The most effective method for reducing this bias seems to be *the free-modulus variation of the method of magnitude estimation.* No standard is presented, and no number is prescribed by the experimenter; instead the observer himself is instructed to select the number he finds appropriate for the first and every subsequent stimulus. Usually the experimenter presents the stimuli in a different random order for each observer in the group. Usually there are about three practice trials although they are often not identified as such for the observer. The instructions may read as follows:

> I am going to present you, in irregular order, a series of test tubes containing the same odor at different intensities. Your task is to tell me how intense or strong they are by assigning numbers to them.
>
> When you have smelled the first stimulus, give its intensity a number—any number you think appropriate. I will then present another to which you will also give a number, and a third, etc.
>
> Try to make the ratios between the numbers you assign to the different odors correspond to the ratios between the intensity of the odors. In other words, try to make the numbers proportional to the intensity of the odor, as you smell it. Remember, you may assign any number and there is no limit on the number that you assign.
>
> There is no right or wrong answer. I want to know how you judge the intensity of the odors. Any questions?

The free-modulus experiment will be illustrated with data obtained by Cain (1968). The

TABLE 3.11A INDIVIDUAL JUDGMENTS OF PENTANOL CONCENTRATIONS

Observer	Percent concentration						
	100.	50.00	25.00	12.50	6.25	3.12	1.56
1	20.0	10.0	4.00	10.0	2.5	1.0	.5
1	50.0	7.5	20.0	7.5	5.0	1.5	.5
2	10.0	5.0	5.0	1.0	2.0	3.0	.5
2	8.0	3.0	5.0	1.0	2.0	2.0	2.0
3	30.0	25.0	10.0	5.0	10.0	2.0	5.0
3	50.0	30.0	20.0	5.0	1.0	10.0	1.0
4	140.0	30.0	70.0	85.0	15.0	20.0	8.0
4	70.0	45.0	50.0	10.0	3.0	2.0	3.0
5	20.0	12.0	8.0	2.0	1.0	1.0	1.0
5	25.0	10.0	15.0	4.0	3.0	1.0	2.0
6	20.0	15.0	10.0	12.0	12.0	10.0	7.0
6	30.0	25.0	10.0	25.0	17.0	7.0	5.0
7	25.0	13.0	10.0	10.0	3.0	6.0	3.0
7	20.0	18.0	15.0	4.0	8.0	7.0	5.0
8	40.0	20.0	20.0	15.0	12.0	7.0	10.0
8	60.0	25.0	18.0	10.0	15.0	5.0	15.0
9	30.0	25.0	28.0	15.0	10.0	4.0	2.0
9	35.0	35.0	40.0	25.0	18.0	3.0	1.0
10	10.0	5.0	3.3	5.0	10.0	1.0	1.0
10	7.5	2.0	3.3	2.0	2.0	1.0	1.0
11	150.0	200.0	250.0	100.0	50.0	25.0	10.0
11	125.0	150.0	100.0	80.0	130.0	90.0	75.0
12	30.0	12.0	7.0	15.0	12.0	9.0	2.0
12	25.0	10.0	10.0	5.0	5.0	7.0	10.0
13	80.0	65.0	30.0	20.0	10.0	5.0	1.0
13	85.0	70.0	35.0	10.0	5.0	4.8	1.0
14	20.0	16.0	10.0	6.0	3.0	7.0	2.0
14	18.0	15.0	8.0	5.0	9.0	3.0	1.0
15	60.0	50.0	45.0	40.0	20.0	15.0	15.0
15	85.0	45.0	25.0	30.0	25.0	10.0	10.0

stimuli were presented by an olfactometer in which the odorant (pentanol) was diluted with air and sniffed from a nose piece. Fifteen observers judged each of 7 concentrations twice following the instructions above, and the responses are entered in Table 3.11A.

Geometric means of the responses in each column of the matrix in Table 3.11A may again be used to define scale values, as is done in Table 3.10 above. However, there are two sources of variance which may be eliminated from these data. The first is associated with differences in the modulus chosen by each observer; the overall magnitude of numbers he assigns in the second presentation of the stimuli may be different from that of the first. In that event, the intercepts of the two psy-

chophysical functions will differ and add to the variance of the response distribution, even though the exponents of the functions may be similar. The second source of variance relates to the fact that different observers may prefer to work in different number ranges; this again results in different intercepts. (Such variance is perhaps particularly high in olfaction, and one must take the present data as illustrative only of the kind and not the size of the variance.)

The basic interest in a magnitude scaling experiment is the exponent of the function, and what is needed is a transformation of the data which leaves invariant the individual slopes as well as the average of the individual intercepts, while partialing out the

TABLE 3.11B LOGARITHMIC VALUES OF JUDGMENTS AFTER TRANSFORMATION OF JUDGMENTS IN TABLE 3-11A

Observer	Log percent concentration						
	2.00	1.70	1.40	1.10	0.80	0.50	0.20
1	1.84	1.27	1.29	1.27	0.89	0.43	0.04
2	1.54	1.17	1.28	0.59	0.89	0.97	0.59
3	1.68	1.53	1.24	0.79	0.59	0.74	0.44
4	1.70	1.27	1.47	1.17	0.53	0.50	0.39
5	1.74	1.43	1.43	0.85	0.63	0.39	0.54
6	1.28	1.18	0.89	1.13	1.04	0.82	0.66
7	1.42	1.26	1.16	0.87	0.76	0.88	0.66
8	1.50	1.15	1.08	0.89	0.93	0.58	0.89
9	1.43	1.39	1.44	1.20	1.04	0.46	0.07
10	1.42	0.98	1.00	0.98	1.13	0.68	0.83
11	1.20	1.31	1.26	1.02	0.97	0.74	0.50
12	1.47	1.07	0.96	0.97	0.92	0.94	0.69
13	1.78	1.70	1.38	1.02	0.72	0.56	−0.13
14	1.47	1.38	1.14	0.93	0.91	0.85	0.34
15	1.41	1.23	1.08	1.10	0.91	0.65	0.65
Σ	22.88	19.32	18.10	14.78	12.86	10.19	7.15
Mean log	1.53	1.29	1.21	0.99	0.86	0.68	0.47
Antilog (geometric mean)	33.5	19.4	16.2	9.7	7.2	4.8	3.0

variability due to intra- or inter-individual sources of inconsistency. A procedure originated by Lane, Catania, and Stevens (1961) eliminates interobserver variance caused by differing choice of moduli; additional steps are necessary to eliminate intra-observer variability (Kalikow, 1967). The following procedure may be used to accomplish both.

  1. Convert each response value to its logarithm.
  2. Determine the mean of the logarithms of the two responses made by each observer to each stimulus. This value is the logarithm of the geometric mean of the observer's responses to each stimulus.
  3. Determine the mean value of each row. This is the logarithm of the geometric mean of each observer's responses to all the stimuli.
  4. Determine the mean of all the values obtained in step 3. This is the logarithmic value of the grand mean of all the responses for all observers to all stimuli in the original data matrix.
  5. Subtract each of the individual mean log responses in step 3 from the grand mean log response determined in step 4.
  6. Add the value obtained in step 5 to the

TABLE 3.12 THE METHOD OF LEAST SQUARES APPLIED TO MAGNITUDE ESTIMATION DATA

X (log S)	Y (log R)	X^2	XY
.20	.47	.04	.09
.50	.68	.25	.34
.80	.86	.64	.69
1.10	.99	1.21	1.09
1.40	1.21	1.96	1.69
1.70	1.29	2.89	2.19
2.00	1.53	4.00	3.06
Σ 7.70	7.03	10.99	9.15

$$a = \frac{N(\Sigma XY) - (\Sigma X)(\Sigma Y)}{N(\Sigma X^2) - (\Sigma X)^2}$$

$$= \frac{7(9.15) - (7.70)(7.03)}{7(10.99) - (7.70)^2}$$

$$= .56$$

$$b = \frac{(\Sigma X^2)(\Sigma Y) - (\Sigma X)(\Sigma XY)}{N(\Sigma X^2) - (\Sigma X)^2}$$

$$= \frac{(10.99)(7.03) - (7.70)(9.15)}{7(10.99) - (7.70)^2}$$

$$= .39$$

Note that $N = 7$, the number of stimuli in the experiment.

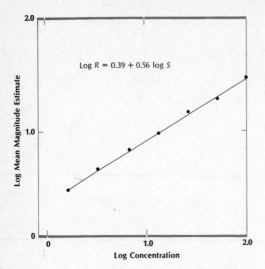

Figure 3.19. Log mean magnitude estimate plotted as a function of log concentration of pentanol.

row of values obtained for each observer in step 2.

These six steps result in a logarithmic matrix, shown in Table 3.11B. The transformation of the data affects only the variability around the main function because none of the six steps affects its exponent or intercept. This problem will be discussed further in deriving the power function from the data, which requires a logarithmic *matrix*. This transformation results in Table 3.12.

The data in Table 3.11 conform to the power function, as can be seen in Figure 3.19, where the mean logarithmic judgments are plotted on Cartesian coordinates as a function of the logarithmic values of the concentrations. The important parameters of the power function have been mentioned occasionally, and now they will be determined more precisely by fitting a function to the data in Table 3.11B. The same procedure will apply to the *R-S* data in Tables 3.8, 3.9 (Matrix B), and 3.10. The curve fitting is simplest when the data are in logarithmic form. Actually, for many purposes the parameters can be estimated from a straight line drawn through the points by eye, but the method of least squares is more precise (see Lewis,

1960). A power function can be described mathematically as

$$R = cS^n \qquad [Eq. 1]$$

where R is the geometric mean judgment of a stimulus, S the corresponding stimulus magnitude, c a constant reflecting the (arbitrary) unit of measurement used by the observers, and n is the exponent of the function.

If Equation 1 is expressed in logarithmic terms,

$$\log R = n (\log S) + \log c \qquad [Eq. 2]$$

which is a simple linear equation of the form

$$y = ax + b$$

This equation can be written in this form with $y = \log R$, $a = n$, $x = \log S$, and $b = \log c$. In the coordinates of Equation 2, the exponent n in Equation 1 becomes the slope of the function, and the multiplicative constant c yields the intercept term $\log c$.

The parameters of the power function may be determined graphically, but more precise values are obtained from the computations shown in Table 3.12. The simplest formulas for the method of least squares require that the data approximate a straight line, and Equation 2 satisfies this condition with logarithmic scaling of stimulus and response. Except for the special case where $n = 1$, the power function is nonlinear in Cartesian coordinates. Table 3.12 shows how to determine the values of a and b, which are then converted into a form compatible with Equation 1.

The value of a, .56, is the value of parameter n in Equation 2 and is therefore the slope of the function in logarithmic coordinates. The value b, .39, is the value of parameter ($\log c$) in Equation 2 and is the intercept of the function which states

$$\log R = .56 (\log S) + .39$$

This function describes the line drawn through the data plotted in Figure 3.19. In translating into Equation 1 the value of n is unchanged, and the value of c becomes the antilog of .39, or 2.45. In linear coordinates the function plotted through the data may then be stated as

$$R = 2.45S^{.56}$$

This is a power function because it states that response magnitude is proportional to stimulus magnitude raised to a power. In the present case that power or exponent is .56, which means that if the stimulus magnitude were increased by a factor of 10:1, or one logarithmic unit, the corresponding increase in response magnitude would only be .56 expressed in these logarithmic units, or a factor of 3.6:1. This conclusion follows, of course, from our previous observation that sensory intensity grows more slowly than does stimulus intensity in olfaction. Exponents have been found to vary from about .33 for visual brightness (in agreement with Plateau's early work mentioned above) to more than 3.00 for electric shock (Stevens, 1961). See also Figure 3.26.

In the six steps outlined above two main operations were made. First, in step 2 each observer's responses to each of the 7 stimuli were averaged. This has no effect on the values derived in Table 3.12. Second, in step 5 factors were added to the values obtained in step 2 to produce a new response matrix. The factors added sum to zero, and therefore the sums of columns used in Table 3.12 are unaffected. It is only necessary to minimize variability associated with the modulus in case of a more detailed analysis of the data. For example, in stating the variance of the original data one might compute the deviations of each observer's responses from that least-squares line. However, this variance would be spuriously high and would obscure the judgmental variance, which is often of interest. Step 5 moves the different observers' functions up or down in the double logarithmic coordinates to minimize the variance around the least-square line without changing the average intercept and slope. This transforma-

tion may present a clearer picture of how well a group of observers approximate the power function despite large differences in the numbers they used. This variability is an index of the goodness of fit and could be useful in comparing sense modalities.

PROBLEMS IN PSYCHOPHYSICAL SCALING

Individual Functions

It should not be assumed that the functions are perfectly stable; for besides effects of specific experimental conditions such as the standard and range used, there are the inevitable individual differences in exponent, as can be observed by inspecting the individual data in Table 3.11B (see also Marks & Stevens, 1966). Keep in mind that the individual slopes are based on few judgments and again that odor judgment is not a psychophysical model for reliability! However, differences in the form of the function are apparently negligible. In a linear plot, for example, all the individual functions for odor intensity are almost invariably negatively accelerated, and those for heaviness positively accelerated. The mean slope in the present odor example is .56 with a standard deviation of .22. Individual exponents (constant a in our example) and the parameter represented by the constant c, the coefficient of the individual function, can easily be determined. However, the perceptual (subjective) value associated with the latter constant cannot be known. It can be determined that one observer agrees with another in judging the ratio of stimuli 1 and 2, but whether or not observer A's response to stimulus 1 (or 2) is less than, equal to, or greater than observer B's response cannot be revealed. Problems of this sort can only be considered by indirect scaling theory of the kind developed by Thurstone (Björkman & Ekman, 1962). This missing link is the reason for a great deal of criticism and debate about the power function.

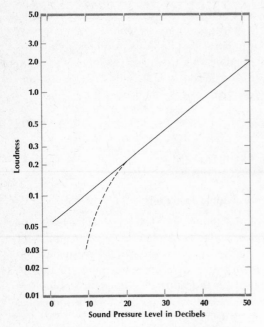

Figure 3.20. Loudness measured by magnitude estimation and ratio production as a function of sound pressure level in decibels. The graph shows how the loudness function becomes steeper near threshold. By correcting for threshold the curvature is eliminated and the obtained data fall along the straight line in a log-log plot. See text. (Data adopted from Scharf & Stevens, 1961.)

Threshold Connection

The most important deviation from the simple power function has been observed for weaker stimulus magnitudes near threshold. Figure 3.20 illustrates this with a psychophysical function for loudness obtained by Scharf and J. C. Stevens (1961). The dotted line represents the obtained function, which seems to be approaching the stimulus threshold value and may therefore reflect a rapidly decreasing effectiveness of stimulus magnitudes at this level. This would suggest a slight modification of the power function, that is,

$$R = c(S - S_0)^n$$

where S_0 is a value roughly corresponding to threshold for the conditions of the particular experiment and may be estimated from scaling

data. Of course, threshold could be measured with any of the methods discussed in the previous chapter, but it must be recalled that such threshold values are also variable and depend on specific experimental procedures. Replotting the response values as a function of each stimulus value minus this threshold value will straighten the function as indicated by the solid line in Figure 3.20. To fit a curve to the data with the method of least squares one would use $\log (S - S_0)$ instead of $\log S$ for X. This "threshold" usually represents a very small quantity; thus it will mostly affect very low stimulus values and may often be excluded. Nevertheless, it cannot be ignored; for example, if Scharf and Stevens (Figure 3.20) had used only the softer stimuli, the loudness function would have appeared steeper and curved. Furthermore, sometimes S_0 is a large quantity compared with S, as in the case of the so-called "physiological zero," which must be considered in scaling warmth (Stevens & Stevens, 1960). Occasionally a more complicated situation arises. In developing a method for estimating the value of S_0, Ekman (1959) discovered that at times its value turned out

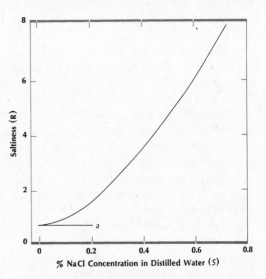

Figure 3.21. Saltiness (R) as measured by magnitude estimation and ratio estimation as a function of NaCl concentration. The constant a represents a positive value of R at $S = 0$. See text. (Data from Ekman, 1961.)

to be negative, which could mean that response magnitude may be greater than zero when S equals zero. Ekman therefore suggested the modified form of the power function be written as

$$R = c(S - a)^n$$

where a was tentatively considered "sensory noise," resulting from spontaneous nervous activity (see the discussion of Weber's Modified Law in Chapter 2, p. 17). For smell and taste one is quite likely to obtain $R > 0$ when $S = 0$. For example, water may be reported as salty because the saliva contains NaCl (Bartoshuk, McBurney, & Pfaffmann, 1964; see Chapter 6). Figure 3.21 illustrates this effect in a psychophysical function estimated from an experiment on taste (Ekman, 1961). Actually, functions of this type may best be described as $R = a + cS^n$, which suggests more complex curve-fitting problems (see Ekman, 1959, 1961; and Fagot & Stewart, 1968).

The constant a may be of considerable interest when weak stimuli or the effect of adaptation on psychophysical functions are being studied (Stevens & Stevens, 1963). The constant c may likewise be of interest when comparing two sets of stimuli in a free-modulus experiment, for it will indicate the overall psychological magnitude involved. In this way the parameters of the power function have begun to define problems of interest to sensory psychologists and appear to be taking over the role which was dominated by Fechner's logarithmic function for over 100 years.

The Usefulness of Fechner's Law

Fechner's psychophysical function is based on Weber's Law, $\Delta S = kS$ (see p. 17), that ΔS tends to increase linearly with stimulus intensity, S. Weber was concerned exclusively with the stimulus dimension, but Fechner assumed that there was a ΔR, a difference in the sensory magnitude associated with the ΔS (the physical value of the DL) and that the value of ΔR was the same size regardless of where ΔS had been determined on the stimulus continuum. Fechner's Law was thus based on an assumption that could not be tested directly because direct scaling methods were not available to classical psychophysics (p. 49).

Taking a direct scaling approach, Fechner's Law can be tested simply by plotting R as a function of the logarithm of the S value, but, as has been shown, when this is done in practice, Fechner's Law almost never holds. Research in vision and hearing has tended to support Weber's Law and by implication Fechner's Law. When these modalities are scaled by direct scaling methods, their power functions have exponents about $\frac{1}{3}$, which means that in linear coordinates the functions are negatively accelerated and similar to an exponential (semilogarithmic) function. Both the exponential function and the power function will provide a better approximation to the changes in psychological magnitude in these two modalities with logarithmic rather than arithmetic spacing of the stimuli. However, results from other modalities where the exponent is greater than 1 support the generality of the power law. (The telephone engineers have found it convenient to use the *decibel,* a logarithmic unit, in specifying the intensity of auditory stimuli [see Chapter 8]; the dB is 1/10 of a log unit of energy and corresponds very roughly to the DL. Those who work in photography and optics may use filters calibrated in density, again using a logarithmic scale [see Chapter 9].)

The sensory physiologists also were uncovering relevant facts through the use of electrical recording of the frequency of impulses obtained from sense organs as a function of stimulus intensity. In 1946 Ruch summarized the data by saying that ". . . Fechner's equation appears to express a fundamental feature of sense organ behavior. Over a certain range of intensities, the frequency of discharge is a linear function of the logarithm of the stimulus. This has been shown for the muscle spindle by Matthews, and for the Limulus eye by Hartline and Graham" (p. 314; see also R. Granit, 1955). However, Rosner and Goff have reviewed this, along with more recent evidence, and came to the conclusion that while the Fechnerian logarithmic function may fit the data, a power function fits the data as well. The relationship between peripheral physiological events and central sensory events is still unsettled. Take note of their warning: "Beware of psychophysicists bearing gifts" (Rosner & Goff, 1967, p. 216). The problem is basically a psychophysical one.

Fechner (1860) considered psychophysics a theory about the relation between the psychological and the physical. He divided this problem into *outer* and *inner psychophysics*. Inner psychophysics was concerned with the indirect relationship between sensory physiology and anatomy and sensation, and outer psychophysics is psychophysics in the contemporary sense of the term, that is, the concern with the more direct relationship between sensation and an external stimulus. Fechner acknowledged the importance of inner psychophysics but argued that, "The basic knowledge for all of psychophysics can only be sought in the realm of outer psychophysics since only this is susceptible to direct experience, and therefore, the point of departure must be outer psychophysics" (Fechner, 1860, vol I).

Comparison of Direct and Indirect Scales

Category and magnitude scales are often compared because category scales have provided evidence for Fechner's Law, whereas magnitude scales are power functions. It is assumed then that category scales are equal-interval scales and that magnitude scales are ratio scales.

It was noted in the beginning of this chapter that the formal difference between an interval scale and a ratio scale is essentially the origin of the scales and therefore category scale values should plot as a linear function of magnitude scale values for a set of stimuli, with the slope and intercept of the linear function determined by difference in unit and origin of the two scales. However, the results in a great many experiments on numerous

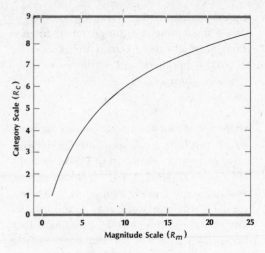

Figure 3.22. Category scale values plotted as a function of magnitude estimation scale values. (Fictitious data.)

continua are almost invariably curved downward, as is shown in Figure 3.22 (see, for example, Stevens, 1957; Stevens & Galanter, 1957; Ekman, 1962; Ekman & Künnapas, 1960, 1962a and b, 1963a and b). Although this is one of the most reliable findings in experimental psychology, the possible reason for the curvature in this function has produced considerable debate and speculation without any

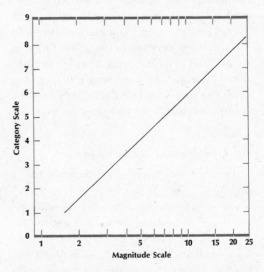

Figure 3.23. Data in Figure 3.22 replotted in semilogarithmic coordinates, that is, category scale values as a function of log magnitude scale values.

definite conclusions (see Eisler, 1962a). Ekman and Künnapas suggest that the category scale (as well as the pair-comparison scale) is closely approximated by a logarithmic transformation of the magnitude scale, shown in Figure 3.23. This transformation can be described mathematically as

$$R_c = a + b \log R_m$$

where R_c is a category scale value and R_m the corresponding magnitude scale value. A theoretical explanation according to what has been called *Ekman's Law* involves traditional and by now familiar psychophysical relations and assumptions. The curvature in Figure 3.22, it is suggested, is caused by the inability of the observer to discriminate constant physical differences equally well along the scale. For example, the difference between lines of 1 and 1.5 inches presented successively will be quite noticeable, and the observer will put these two stimuli in different categories. However, the difference between 20.0 and 20.5 inches often is not detected, and, on these occasions, the observer puts them in the same response category. This is consistent with Weber's Law, $\Delta S = k_s(S + a)$, where k_s and a are constants (see p. 18). Ekman has produced evidence that an analogous relation

seems to apply to the psychological continuum, that is,

$$\Delta R = k_R(R + a),$$

where ΔR is a value on the psychological continuum, for example a magnitude estimation scale, and a and k_R are constants analogous to the Weber fraction and the "threshold" or "noise" factor. The important point is that this contradicts the assumption made by Fechner—whose proposed law is supported by the category scale, which in turn is nonlinear with the magnitude scale—that the discriminal dispersion is constant over the whole psychological continuum. Ekman's relation states that the discriminal dispersion is proportional to stimulus magnitude. In Figure 3.24, Ekman (1956, 1959) has provided evidence for this proportionality on the psychological continuum. The function relates two psychological variables and was obtained by comparing Harper and Stevens' veg scale (1948) with Oberlin's (1936) data on DL for heaviness. ΔR in the present case is estimated, but it may be defined more directly as the intra-individual variance of a certain R value as follows: (1) Obtain several (for example, 10) judgments from each observer for a set of stimuli with the method of magnitude estimation without a prescribed modulus. (2) Multiply the numerical judgments (Rs) for each stimulus magnitude by a factor which renders the sum of the numerical judgments for each stimulus constant (for example, 1.0). (3) The standard deviation of these transformed Rs, or σ_R, will be analogous to ΔR above (see Eisler, 1962b). Alternative definitions of ΔS are likewise considered in Chapter 2.

The power function implies that both Ekman's Law and Weber's Law should be correct. Fechner apparently considered the power function, and Brentano anticipated Ekman's relation, but it seems that the development of direct methods was required to crystallize the ideas. With respect to the observer's task in category scaling, (Figure 3.21), this means that his categories, or "equal ap-

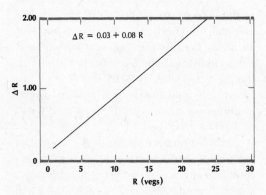

Figure 3.24. Discriminal disperson (ΔR) on the psychological continuum (heaviness measured in vegs) as a function of psychological magnitude. The plot relates two psychological variables and is an R-R rather than the more familiar S-R relation. (Data adapted from Ekman, 1956.)

pearing intervals," are not equal; rather, they are relatively narrow at the low end of the scale and wide at the high end. Therefore, the category scale is steeper at the low end and flatter at the high when plotted against either stimulus magnitude or magnitude estimates. This argues that the bias is in the category scale, which imposes a discrimination that is neither required in magnitude estimation, nor basic to the question concerning the relation between R and S. Consistent with this is the evidence that the spacing of stimuli has a dramatic effect on category scale values while the magnitude scale remains almost invariant. According to Galanter (1962), "In consequence, many psychophysicists have come to believe that the magnitude scale reveals more about the sensory effects of stimuli, and therefore more about the bases of the judgmental process of people when they are called upon to act with respect to stimuli in their environment" (p. 153).

Empirically, the power function is probably as well established as is possible for any quantitative relation involving the whole man, and better than any other in psychology.

The virtue of direct scaling is its simplicity: It makes but one assumption, namely that the observer is able to carry out the instructions to quantify his perceptions. All the criticisms leveled at the power function seem to involve this necessary assumption. Are the numerical judgments valid indicators of perceptual magnitudes? Some think not (for example, Garner, 1954a and b; Graham, 1965), while others propose different interpretations of what the numerical estimates might mean (for example, Warren & Warren, 1963; Treisman, 1964a and b; Savage, 1966). Although the available indirect (or necessary) evidence is undeniably impressive, sufficient evidence of validity can only come from further experience with the practical usefulness of such scales.

Cross-modality Matching

In order to eliminate potential problems with the use of numbers, Stevens has proposed that "cross-modality matching" be used to test the form of the psychophysical function (Stevens, 1959, 1966). These matching experiments follow the general procedure for determining the point of subjective equality (PSE) with the method of adjustment discussed in Chapter 2 (p. 20). The observers are presented several standards, for example, five weights, well spaced, and in irregular order, under the instruction to adjust the value on the second continuum, for example, loudness, to match the psychological value of each of these standards. If both psychological continua are power functions of their respective stimulus continua, for example, $R_h = W^m$ and $R_l = P^n$, where R_h is heaviness; W physical weight; R_l loudness, P sound pressure; and m and n are exponents. The proportionality constants are not important to the argument. Matching implies that $R_l = R_h$, and the function relating the average sound pressure to the weights of the standards should conform to the function

$$P^n = W^m$$

which in logarithms is

$$\log P = (\log W)\, m/n$$

Therefore the results of the cross-matching should show a linear equal-sensation function in log-log coordinates with an exponent equal to the ratio of the exponents of the psychophysical functions for heaviness and for loudness. Because the exponent for loudness (in decibels) is about .6 and for heaviness 1.5, the predicted slope is $.6/1.5 = .4$. To test further one would match heaviness to several loudness standards with the predicted result of $1.5/6 = 2.5$.

Equal-sensation functions have borne out the power functions because cross-matching functions are well fitted by straight lines in log-log coordinates, and the obtained and predicted slopes have been almost identical. The predicted slopes are sometimes slightly lower due to a possible "regression tendency" (Stevens & Greenbaum, 1966). In general the observer tends to shrink the continuum he adjusts; this has the effect of reducing the slope in estimation experiments and increas-

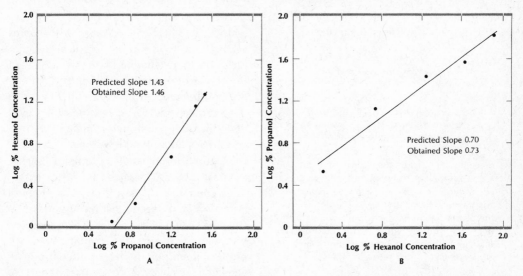

Figure 3.25. Equal sensation function for the odor intensity of hexanol and propanol when (A) hexanol concentration was adjusted to match the intensity of 5 propanol standards and when (B) propanol concentration was adjusted to match the intensity of 5 hexanol standards. The values plotted on the ordinate are median concentrations chosen by 12 observers from a concentration range of .59 to 100 percent in 24 dilution steps. The odors were sniffed from cotton wrapped on a glass rod. When propanol and hexanol had been scaled earlier with the method of magnitude estimation, psychophysical power functions were obtained with a slope of .20 for propanol and .14 for hexanol. From the ratio of these slopes one would predict that the equal-sensation functions obtained when one of these alcohols is matched to the other should be power functions with slopes of .20/.14 = 1.43 and .14/.20 = .70, depending on whether propanol or hexanol is the standard odorant. The lines shown represent the slope obtained as determined by the method of least squares. (From Cain, 1966.)

ing the slope in production experiments. It is necessary therefore to perform a counter-

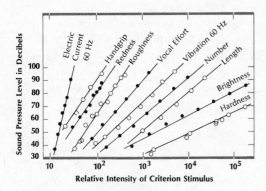

Figure 3.26. Equal-sensation functions obtained by matching 10 other stimuli to loudness. The relative position of each equal-sensation function is arbitrary, but its slope conforms to the prediction made from the ratio of the slopes for psychophysical functions of loudness, electric current, force of handgrip, and so on. (Data by Stevens, 1965.)

balanced cross-matching experiment for the most precise determination of the slope of an equal-sensation function. Examples of a cross-matching experiment are shown in Figures 3.25 and 3.26.

In connection with the problem of matching Ekman (1964) has made the following suggestion.

Let us assume, for the purposes of the present discussion, that Fechner's law is generally valid, so that

$$R_s = a + b \log S, \qquad (1)$$

where R_s is a subjective magnitude corresponding to the stimulus magnitude S. Let us further assume that a subject reacts also to *number stimulation* according to Fechner's law. Then

$$R_n = c + d \log N, \qquad (2)$$

where R_n is the subjective magnitude corresponding to the stimulus magnitude, i.e., the number N, to which the subject is exposed.

In a typical scaling experiment with a direct method, the subject is instructed to respond to a stimulus S with a number N chosen so that $R_n = R_s$. On this condition the relation

$$\log N = \alpha + n \log S, \qquad (3)$$

where $\alpha = (a - c/d$ and $n = b/d$, or

$$N = \beta S^n,$$

where $\beta = $ antilog α. This is the well-known power law in its simplest form, which has now been derived from Fechner's Law.

The essential feature of the response model presented here is the assumption that a subject reacts to number stimulation in the same way, i.e., according to Fechner's law, as he reacts to any stimulation. In this sense the derivation of the power function is based on a generalization of Fechner's law. According to the model, a direct scaling method is a procedure in which *the subject matches two sets of stimuli*.[1]

Ekman's suggestion highlights the problems associated with the assumption of direct scaling. No clear-cut experiments suggest themselves, but alternative assumptions can always be made about what the observer's numerical responses really mean. On the other hand, there is indirect evidence of the validity of equal-sensation functions and the flexibility of the cross-matching procedure. Abbey (1962) has shown that both linear and nonlinear equal-sensation functions will be obtained in cross-matching experiments, as is predicted from the two contributing individual psychophysical functions. That is, a linear plot of the equal-sensation function is not a necessary consequence of the Fechnerian assumption discussed by Ekman (see also Luce & Galanter, 1963, pp. 278 ff).

[1] G. Ekman. The power law: A specialized case of Fechner's Law? *Perceptual and Motor Skills,* 1964, *19,* 730. Reprinted with permission of author and publisher.

"Methodology can easily become methodolatry," says Stevens (1958), who warns against the tendency of classical psychophysicists to treat methods as ends rather than the means of learning how men and animals respond to stimulation. Psychophysics is evidently still characterized as a "necessary evil" of methodology, although contemporary psychophysics undoubtedly will make contributions to this substantive problem. Psychophysical progress has been made in two almost contradictory ways. The psychology of detection and discrimination discussed in Chapter 2 has attempted to deal with response bias by maximizing the conditions which produce them, and this has resulted in a more general as well as more abstract theory of detection. This in turn has brought psychology into closer contact with the study of learning and animal behavior. Psychophysical scaling, in contrast, in an attempt to eliminate or reduce response bias, has produced simpler and more direct methods for dealing with problems of perception that could not be considered as long as only measurement on the physical continuum was considered. This has widened the applicability of psychophysical scaling, so that it is no longer limited to sensory problems for which the relevant physical correlates are well understood. These two approaches to contemporary psychophysics have in common a greater emphasis on the relationship between psychological variables than was the case with classical psychophysics. We may therefore anticipate an increasing influence of modern psychophysics on psychology as a whole.

Charles F. Stevens

BASIC MECHANISMS
OF NEURAL FUNCTION

4

Chapter 4 presents the basic information necessary for a preliminary understanding of the electrophysiological method as an analytic tool for studying the mechanism of neural function, and as a procedure for enlarging the classes of behavior that can be observed. Experimental psychologists have come to depend more and more heavily upon the concepts and tools of neurophysiology. Thus a chapter on neurophysiology not only serves the practical purpose of indicating to the student of psychology how these tools are applied but also acquaints him with the concepts necessary for the interpretation of results obtained with them. Along with the chapters on psychophysics, then, this chapter provides a background for the later chapters on sensation, perception, and the more complex topics of experimental psychology.

Associated with the activity of nerve and muscle are certain voltage changes that may often be recorded without great difficulty. Because these voltage changes are so intimately involved with the functioning of nerve and muscle, the physiologist studies electrical concomitants of function in an effort to unravel the mechanisms that ultimately underlie behavior. For the psychologist, however, recording voltage changes associated with the operation of the nervous and in particular muscular systems has the additional advantage of extending the range of "behavior" that can be observed and studied (for example, see Hefferline, Keenan, & Harford, 1959).

ANATOMICAL SUBSTRATE FOR BEHAVIOR

The analysis of behavior often proceeds by identifying stimuli and responses and then by discovering orderly relations between them. When we are dealing with the structural basis for behavior, it is useful to follow an analogous system by considering organs for gathering information about the environment, organs for acting on the environment, and the neural machinery responsible for relations between stimulus and response. This section introduces the anatomical concepts necessary for understanding the function of the neural and muscular elements underlying gross behavior. We first develop certain notions about the structure of the nervous sys-

tem proper—the central organization responsible for relations between stimulus and response—and then briefly consider in turn structures that gather information from the environment and those that act upon the environment.

The natural functional and anatomical unit of the nervous system is the nerve cell. Although neurons may be classified into a considerable number of structural types, virtually all of these types share certain anatomical properties which have proved to be of significance for the physiologist. We therefore describe a typical neuron in order to illustrate the most important of these common features and then present some of the frequent variations in structure.

The typical neuron may be described as

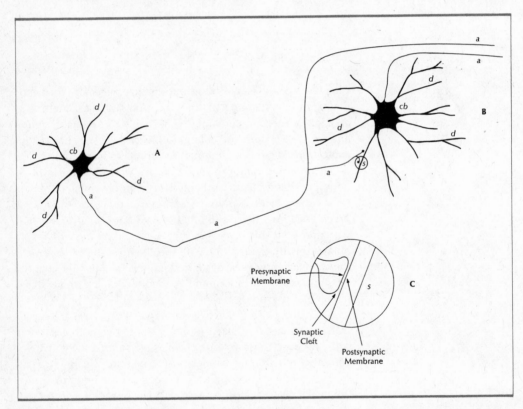

Figure 4.1. Two neurons, A and B, are illustrated schematically. The soma is labeled *cb,* some dendrites are labeled *d,* and the axon is labeled *a.* Neuron A sends its axon to synapse with neuron B, and one of the synapses is marked with *s.* C gives a much magnified and highly schematic view of synapse *s.* The synaptic cleft is about 200 Å in diameter, and the axon terminal may be from half to 10 μ in diameter.

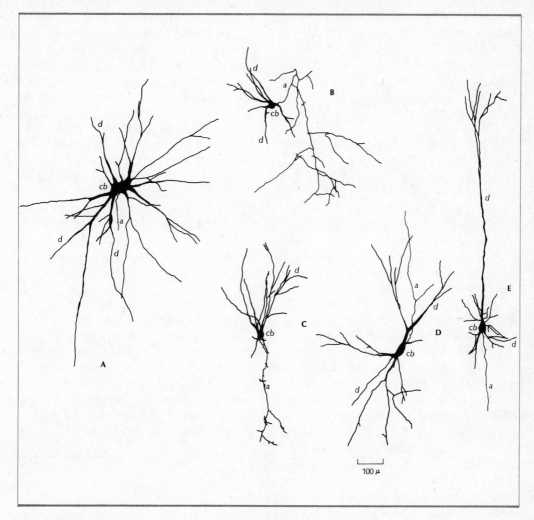

Figure 4.2. Five neurons from various areas of the brain are illustrated. These nerve cells were drawn from ones stained by a special technique, the Golgi method; it should be noted that the actual neuron processes were not all in one plane, but rather they radiated from the cell body in all directions. Neuron A is a motoneuron from the spinal cord and is the type of cell involved in the reflex behavior to be described later. Most of the axons have not been included in the drawings from cells A, C, D, and E, but much of cell B's axon has been drawn to illustrate the complicated branching pattern typical of axons. Cell E is termed a pyramidal cell and is the type of neuron characteristically found in the cortex; because so much of the human brain is taken up by the cortex, this particular type of neuron may be the most common. As in Figure 4.1, *cb* denotes cell body, *d* dendrite, and *a* axon.

having an approximately spherical cell body (or soma, *cb* in Figure 4.1A) with numerous protrusions known as the axon (*a*) and dendrites (*d*). A thin (100 Å)[1] membrane, .called the *plasma membrane,* defines the boundary

[1]See index for definition of Å (Ångstrom), μ (micron), and other units.

of the neuron and forms a sharp separation between the cell and its surroundings. The main dendrites, of which there may be a half dozen, divide into smaller branches; these in turn divide again, so that the immediate vicinity of the cell (within a sphere with a radius of perhaps several hundred microns) contains a delicate network of dendritic branches. While a neuron usually has many dendrites, it typically gives rise to a single axon only. Often this axon may branch along its course, and generally does divide repeatedly into a number of fine twigs near its end. At the end of the axon branches, the axon terminals come into contact with the dendrites or cell body—or occasionally with other axon terminals—of another neuron.

The component structures at this point of contact between one nerve cell and another are collectively called the *synapse* (see Figure 4.1B, *s*). Specifically, under the higher magnification provided by the electron microscope, we may see that the synapse consists of a *presynaptic membrane*, a *postsynaptic membrane*, a *synaptic cleft*, and certain membrane specializations and other structural details that need not be considered here (see Stevens, 1968, for more extensive references). In the case of an axo-dendritic synapse, as illustrated schematically in Figure 4.1C, for example, the presynaptic membrane is simply a membrane of the axon terminal, the postsynaptic membrane is the adjacent membrane of the dendrite, and the synaptic cleft is the gap, 200–400 Å wide, that separates pre- and postsynaptic membranes. The synapse is a particularly important structure because it forms the channel of communication by which information is passed from one neuron to the next.

The approximately 10 billion neurons of the human brain are interconnected in fantastically complicated networks. Thus, each neuron receives thousands of synaptic contacts from perhaps hundreds of other neurons, and in turn sends its axon to synapse with many different nerve cells. These interconnecting networks form the anatomical substrate for behavior. Standard neuroanatomy books (Crosby, Humphrey, & Lauer, 1962, for example) summarize our knowledge about brain structure and the principal connections between neurons in different areas.

The neurons that have been described thus far have been ones with "typical" structure.

In fact, probably the majority of neurons do not have the typical structure illustrated above, but rather they have some modification of this structure, often a rather drastic modification. Some of the varieties in neuron size and shape are illustrated in Figure 4.2. In each case, although it is still possible to identify a soma, an axon, and dendrites, the form taken by these structures is quite different from that of the typical cell.

The organs responsible for gathering information from the environment are structures containing neurons with special features that permit stimuli to be translated into neural messages of a type described later (see p. 99). The detailed structure of sensory neurons is extremely varied, and specific examples are considered in the appropriate chapters. In general, however, much as for other nerve cells, it is possible to identify dendrites, a cell body, and axons in sensory neurons. Rather than receiving their input primarily through synapses, the dendrites of sensory neurons are specialized to respond to some particular aspect of the environment. A specific example is a stretch receptor neuron, whose role is to report the state of muscle

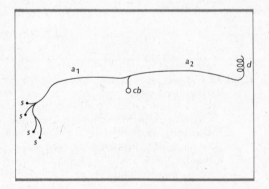

Figure 4.3. The neuron illustrated schematically is a bipolar receptor neuron. *cb* denotes the cell body, *s* denotes axon terminals, which form synapses within the animal's nervous system, a_1 and a_2 are the two branches of the axon, and *d* is a sensory dendrite that is located in muscle. The segment of axon a_2 would in general be much longer than has been illustrated here; in fact it could be a meter in length.

stretch to the central nervous system (see Figure 4.3). The dendrites of this neuron, which are responsive to deformation in a way to be described later (see p. 96), intertwine among special muscle cells; furthermore, the cell body is not in its normal position in proximity to the dendrite. Nerve cells of this general type, known as *bipolar neurons* because the axon divides into two branches after leaving the cell body, are quite commonly employed by the nervous system to receive and transmit sensory information.

The most important effector system (that is, a system which has an effect on the environment) from the point of view of gross behavior is the skeletal musculature. Although the details of muscle structure are beyond the scope of this chapter (see articles in Bourne, 1960), information about certain basic anatomic features is required for the discussion in the following chapters. A muscle is constructed of many small muscle cells arranged in parallel. Each muscle cell may be thought of as a long tube, on the order of 100 μ in diameter, running for the length of the muscle. These muscle cells attach at both ends to strong tendons which in turn usually fasten onto bone. The muscle cell is, like nerve cells, bounded by a very thin (100 Å) plasma membrane and has an internal structure consisting of fibers which are responsible for the ability of these cells to shorten or exert force on their attachments. Just as one neuron forms a synapse with other neurons, so do neurons synapse with muscle cells; the neuron which sends its axon to synapse with a muscle cell is called a *motoneuron,* and the synapse between motoneuron and muscle cell is known as the *myoneural junction.*

Although the most readily observed effects of nervous system operation are mediated through the skeletal musculature, neuronal signals can also produce glandular secretion. Glandular secretions are, of course, sometimes viewed as behavior, but more frequently this effector system is studied in the separate field of neuroendocrinology (see Martini & Ganong, 1966).

NEURON FUNCTION

The properties of neurons and their interconnections ultimately underlie all behavior, and so the most natural context for a discussion of neuron function is as the substrate for behavior. Even a simple behavior is characteristically quite complicated in its own right, however, and in only relatively few

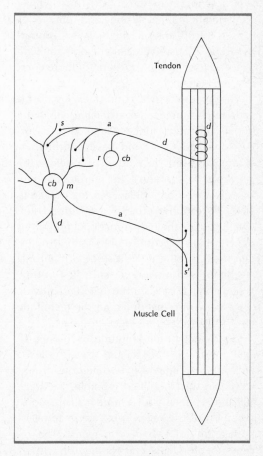

Figure 4.4. This figure presents a schematic representation of the neuronal network responsible for a stretch reflex that operates on a hypothetical three-muscle cell muscle. The bipolar receptor neuron *r* has its stretch-sensitive dendrite wrapped around a special muscle cell and sends its axon to synapse *s* with the motoneuron *m*. The motoneuron *m* sends its axon *a* to form a myoneural junction *s'* with one of the two remaining muscle cells. The innervation of the third muscle cell is not illustrated.

instances can the orderliness of behavior be traced in great detail to the underlying neural function. To minimize complications, then, neuron function is described in the context of a particularly simple form of behavior, the *reflex*. Although more complicated behavior can seldom, if ever, be analyzed into simple component reflexes, it is true that most of the properties of neurons now known do appear in a description of the reflex. Thus it must be remembered that although a simple reflex is used for illustration, the neuronal properties to be discussed are general ones, and are believed to form the substrate for more complicated behavior.

The knee jerk is a familiar example of a particularly simple reflex; when muscles in the upper leg (the quadriceps, a knee extensor) are subjected to a rapid passive stretch by tapping the muscle tendon just below the knee cap (the stimulus)[2], the muscles contract actively after a brief delay, causing the leg to kick (the response). The following discussion will introduce the basic functional properties of neurons in the context of this simple reflex. Before embarking upon a study of neuronal mechanisms, however, we must first outline the anatomical basis for the reflex and provide some basic information about the technique used for recording bioelectric signals.

A schematic representation of the neuro-anatomical substrate for the stretch reflex is presented in Figure 4.4. Two neurons are involved in this simplified example (see page 103 and Figure 4.14 for a more realistic representation of the reflex substrate in terms of populations of two neuron types). The receptor neuron (*r*) is a bipolar neuron with its dendrites intertwined with certain special muscle cells and its axon traveling to form a synapse (*s*) with the second neuron (*m*). This second neuron, a motoneuron, in turn sends its axon back to the same muscle, where it forms a neuromuscular junction (*s'*). The task now is to understand the operation

of each link in the chain of events between the stimulus (passive stretch of the muscle) and the response (active contraction of the muscle). Because the neural activity is associated with voltage changes within the neurons, an understanding of nerve-cell properties requires some knowledge of the technique for measuring each of these voltage changes.

Basic Recording Techniques

The general experimental arrangement used for measuring nerve and muscle voltages is illustrated in Figure 4.5. An electrode that makes contact with the tissues being studied is held in a micromanipulator which, because nerve and muscle cells are small, must permit movements of the electrode tip to an accuracy that is on the order of 1 to 10 μ. For reasons to be described later, signals from the electrode are usually led through a special input circuit and then into a preamplifier, which provides output voltages of convenient amplitude. The signals are then usually displayed by making a graph of voltage as a function of time; this is done either with a special ink writing device, or more frequently with an oscilloscope. Whitfield (1959) has provided a readable and more detailed account of the electronic apparatus used in electrophysiology, and the book edited by Nastuk (1964) contains excellent articles on electrodes, micromanipulators, and electronic equipment and its use.

A variety of different electrode types are used for recording the electrical activity of nerve and muscle. In some instances, for recording the EEG (see p. 114) cardiac (see p. 834) and other potentials from the body surface, the recording electrodes are simply silver, platinum, or stainless steel buttons or bands taped or glued to the skin. Stainless steel needles, insulated except for the tip, are inserted into muscles to monitor the electrical activity associated with muscle movements. For recording gross electrical activity from within the brain (see p. 113, for example), satisfactory electrodes may be constructed

---

[2] By tapping the muscle tendon, the tendon is briefly indented and the attached muscle quickly stretched by a small amount.

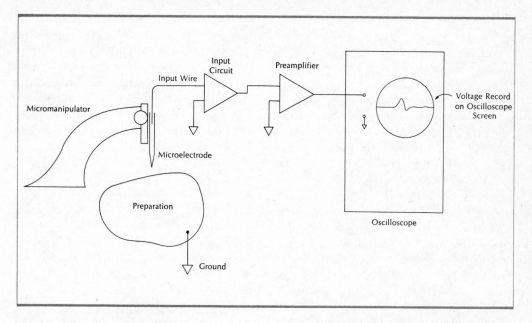

Figure 4.5. The basic arrangement for recording signals from neural tissues involves a micromanipulator to position an electrode on the preparation, a microelectrode to connect the recording apparatus to the preparation, and appropriate equipment for amplifying and displaying the voltages originating in the neural tissue.

from stainless steel, platinum-iridium, or tungsten wire about 200–400 μ in diameter, coated, except for the tip, with varnish or some other insulating material; also, fine insect pins similarly insulated are often used.

The electrodes described in the preceding paragraph are all used for recording the activity of simultaneous active groups of cells; for recording from a single cell, electrodes with particularly small tips, known as *microelectrodes,* are required. Although there is a variety of types of microelectrode, it is convenient to divide them into two classes, the metal microelectrodes and fluid-filled glass micropipettes. Metal microelectrodes are most commonly constructed by electrolytically sharpening stainless steel insect pins or fine tungsten wire which is then coated with insulating varnish. Metal microelectrodes are frequently employed for recording extracellular signs of activity in single cells (see p. 112).

Glass micropipettes used for intracellular recording (that is, for recording potential differences between the inside of the cell and the bathing solution; see p. 95) are made by drawing out glass capillary tubing (with a 1 mm outside diameter, for example) to an extremely fine tip and filling it with a concentrated salt solution. Such electrodes are drawn by heating a short stretch of the capillary tubing until the glass becomes soft, and then pulling rapidly. With this technique it is possible to construct hollow microneedles with an external tip diameter of 0.25 μ or less. The electrodes are then filled by boiling them in concentrated salt solution, 2.8 molar KCl for example, under reduced pressure. The construction of various types of electrode is well described in Nastuk (1964).

Several general principles govern the design and manufacture of electrodes used for recording bioelectric potentials. These principles pertain to the electrical, mechanical, and biological properties of the electrodes. Because different voltages occur in neighboring regions of the brain at the same time, there is a danger that an electrode will record the sum of two adjacent potentials. To avoid such summing, an electrode tip must be no larger than the size of the region over which a voltage is approximately constant. Thus, if a certain potential variation in time were widespread over the surface of the tissue, a large electrode would suffice, whereas if the potential to be recorded occurs only in a small, circumscribed region, an electrode with a small tip is required.

The smaller electrodes are made, the more their resistance increases, and high resistance electrodes require special circuits (see later discussion). For reasons which cannot be discussed here, metal microelectrodes are often superior for recording small, rapidly changing potentials, and glass micropipettes are required for recording steady or more slowly changing voltages.

An essential property of electrodes is that they do not damage the tissue in which they are being used. When recording is to be made from the depth of the brain, one uses an electrode with as small a diameter as possible in order to minimize trauma to the surrounding tissues. If a cell is to survive penetration by an electrode, the electrode tip must be very small indeed; this is why microelectrodes are required for intracellular recording. Although any metal will do for recording electrical activity in the brain, the ions from certain materials tend to be toxic to the tissues. Thus, stainless steel, silver, platinum, or other relatively inert metals are preferred, and metals such as copper and zinc are avoided. If fluid-filled electrodes are used, either electrodes are manufactured with a tip so small that diffusion of the contained salt solution is minimal, or, if a larger tip diameter is used, the electrode is filled with a physiological salt solution.

As is stated above, to obtain finely localized recordings, and to minimize damage to the tissues, it is generally desirable to use an electrode with as small a diameter as possible. However, one often wishes to insert these electrodes through tough material, or into the depth of the brain. Thus, large, or at least

strong, electrodes are required. Altogether then, one must have electrodes with a small diameter but with great rigidity and mechanical stability. These requirements also limit the number of materials that can be used for electrode construction. For example, soft materials such as copper, zinc, and pure platinum generally are not strong enough, so that stainless steel, platinum-iridium alloy, or glass—which is surprisingly strong—must usually be used.

Microelectrodes have a very high resistance, on the order of 10 megohms, because of their small tip diameter. This very high resistance necessitates the use of a special input circuit such as a *cathode follower,* or, of more recent development, a *field effect transistor* amplifier. A cathode follower or

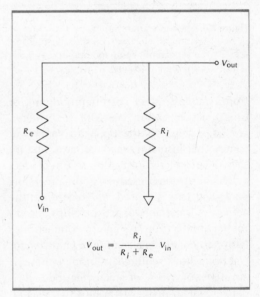

Figure 4.6. The recording situation established after a microelectrode is employed may be represented by the circuit containing an electrode resistance R_e and an input resistance for the amplifier R_i. If the V_{in} is the voltage measured at some point in the neural tissue with respect to some neutral point outside the tissue and V_{out} is the voltage measured with respect to the same neutral point, the relation between these two voltages is given by the equation above. If R_i is very large compared to R_e, the output voltage will be very nearly equal to the input voltage.

$$V_{out} = \frac{R_i}{R_i + R_e} V_{in}$$

some similar device is necessary because any amplifier has a resistance between input and ground, known as the *input resistance.* The resistance may be 1 megohm, although in special amplifiers it may be thousands of megohms. If an electrode with a resistance of say 9 megohms were used with an amplifier with an input resistance of 1 megohm (see Figure 4.6), the electrode and input resistances would form a voltage divider that would attenuate the input signal to one tenth of its true value. Thus, it is clear that the input resistance of the input amplifier must be very high compared to the electrode resistance. For example, if a special circuit with an input resistance of 1000 megohms (such as a cathode follower) were used, the input signal would be attenuated by only 1 percent.

There is another reason why a special input circuit must be employed. In an ordinary amplifier, a certain amount of current flows out of the amplifier through the input. This input circuit current is very low by ordinary standards, on the order of 10^{-9} amps, but it is sufficient to have a marked effect on the nerve cells from which the signals are being recorded. Therefore an appropriate amplifier for electrophysiological investigations must have input current (or *grid current,* as it is often called) that remains much less than 10^{-9} amps.

Elementary Neuron Properties

With the background of the preceding discussion, we may now follow information through the neural circuit subserving the stretch reflex by presenting the schematic intracellular recordings that might be obtained at a number of points along the way. Because the neural mechanisms of the stretch reflex are thought to be typical of nervous system operation in general, tracing information through this neural circuit will serve to introduce important functional properties of nerve cells.

After outlining the sequence of events that starts with muscle stretch (the stimulus) and ends with the muscle contraction (the re-

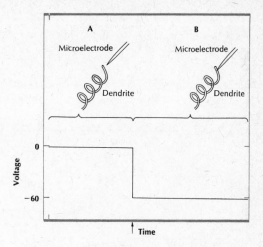

Figure 4.7. A. A microelectrode tip is placed in the bathing solution outside of the bipolar neuron dendrite, and the voltage measured is 0 volts (the bathing solution is grounded). B. The microelectrode is inserted into the sensory neuron dendrite at the time indicated by the arrow, and at once a potential of −60 millivolts is recorded; this is the resting potential.

sponse), we return to several reflex properties for a more detailed consideration. It must be emphasized that the approach here is primarily descriptive and does not deal with the mechanism of the events described. Certain points about mechanism are discussed later in the chapter, but for more detail the reader may refer—in order of increasing difficulty—to Stevens (1966), Ochs (1965), and Ruch and Patton (1965). Further, a number of simplifications will be made for the sake of convenience; some of these simplifications will also be discussed at a later point.

If a microelectrode were advanced toward the dendrite of a bipolar neuron (see Figure 4.7) until the cell is penetrated, that is until the microelectrode tip entered the interior of the dendrite, the recording apparatus would register a steady voltage difference relative to the bathing fluid of approximately −60 millivolts. This constant voltage or inside-outside *polarization* of the cell is known as the *resting potential,* and it is a characteristic of all inactive neurons as well as of other cells. During any activity of the neuron, the voltage re-

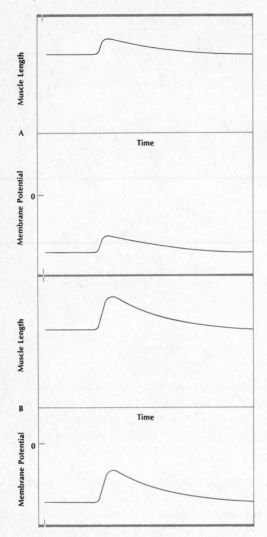

Figure 4.8. Graphs of muscle length as a function of time are presented here with corresponding graphs of membrane potential as a function of time. In A, a slight stretch was applied to the muscle resulting in the lower membrane potential recording. In B a larger muscle stretch produced a larger depolarization.

corded with the microelectrode varies, rather than remaining constant, and for this reason it is useful as well as traditional to have a general term for the voltage inside the cell relative to the outside solution. Because voltage differences exist across the cell membrane, the inside-outside potential difference

is called the *membrane potential.* The resting potential, then, is the particular membrane potential that is recorded in the resting cell. The remainder of this section describes variations in membrane potential that are observed during neuron function.

When the muscle is subjected to a brief stretch, the receptor neuron dendrite is deformed and a change in membrane potential is produced within the dendrite. This voltage change, called the *generator potential,* is the characteristic response of the dendrites to deformation (see Figure 4.8A). If the muscle is stretched more intensely, the generator potential is of greater magnitude (see Figure 4.8B). Altogether, then, by a mechanism which is considered later, the dendrites contain an electrical representation of the muscle stretch within the neuron; the magnitude of the stretch is represented by the magnitude of the membrane potential change.

At this point, it will be convenient to introduce some descriptive terminology widely used in discussions of neuron function. In the resting neuron, the membrane potential is approximately −60 millivolts, that is, the inside is 60 millivolts negative with respect to the outside of the neuron. In the case of the dendrites just described, stretching the muscle caused dendritic deformation and produced a change in the membrane potential toward zero volts. Specifically, the membrane potential changed from −60 millivolts in the resting state to −20 millivolts at the peak of the stretch. Such a change is called a *depolarization.* More generally, any change in the membrane potential that causes the interior of the neuron to become less negative than the resting potential is a depolarization, so that the effect of the stimulation of sensory neuron dendrites can be described by saying that stretch causes a dendritic depolarization the magnitude of which reflects the magnitude of the stimulus. Similarly, changes in the membrane potential that cause the inside of the neuron to become more negative than the resting potential are termed *hyperpolarizations.* The terms *de-* and *hyperpolarization*

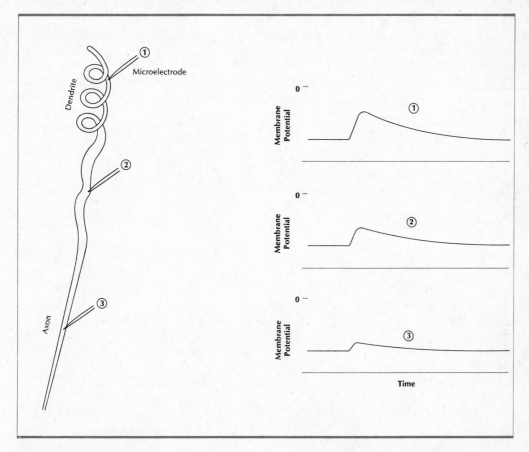

Figure 4.9. Three microelectrodes inserted into the dendrite are indicated by the numbers 1, 2, and 3. When a small stretch is applied to the muscle, the depolarizations that might hypothetically be recorded from each electrode are indicated in the graphs numbered 1, 2, and 3, corresponding to the electrodes with the same number. All three graphs have the same time axis.

arise, of course, because they describe changes in the cell's natural polarization.

With muscle stretch represented as dendritic depolarization, the next problem facing the nervous system is the transmission of this information about stretch to other nerve cells. If a second microelectrode ([2] in Figure 4.9) is inserted into the dendrite at a greater distance from the muscle than the first microelectrode, the generator potential at this more distant point is observed to be smaller than at the closer recording site (see Figure 4.9). If a third microelectrode ([3] in Figure 4.9) is inserted still further away from the muscle, the generator potential at this point is still smaller. A more detailed examination reveals

that the generator potential magnitude falls off quite rapidly with distance from the region of the dendrites where the dendritic membrane is deformed, that is, where the generator potential originates. If a larger stretch is applied to the muscle, thus producing a larger generator potential, this larger generator potential is also seen to decay in magnitude from its site of origin in the dendrite. The phenomenon of a depolarization in one region of a dendrite spreading to neighboring regions is termed *passive spread*. Passive spread of a depolarization along a dendrite is quite analogous to the spread of heat along an iron bar when one region of the bar is heated. Similarly, just as cold will spread

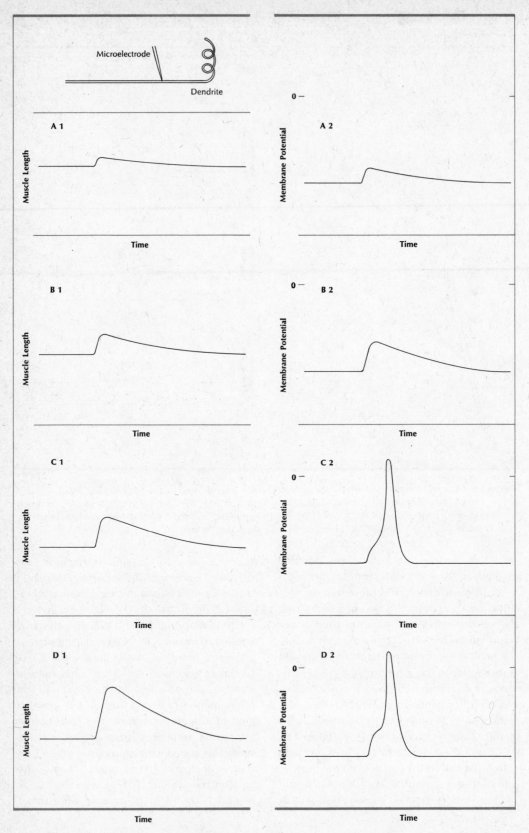

Figure 4.10. Pairs of graphs plotting muscle length and membrane potential as a function of time are presented for muscle stretches of various magnitudes. The recordings are hypothetical ones obtained from a stretch receptor axon near the dendrites.

along an iron bar from a cooled region, so will a hyperpolarization spread passively along a dendrite. In summary, then, a generator potential influences neighboring regions of the dendrite by a process called passive spread, and through this mechanism information about stretch of the muscle is transmitted over several millimeters.

Although the generator potential spreads passively for several millimeters, it is apparent that some further mechanism must be responsible for the transmission of information over the relatively long distances spanned by neuron axons; if passive spread were the only mechanism, the depolarization would decrease to undetectable levels long before the signal reached the axon terminal. Indeed, axons exhibit a particular type of response, the *action potential,* that permits transfer of information over the entire axon length; to see how axons can transmit information we must consider the action potential in detail. Figure 4.10 shows intracellular recordings from a site in the axon near its junction with the dendrite. The magnitude of the stretch applied to the muscle was increased for each of the succeeding records A through D. Only the generator potential, which has spread passively from its site of origin in the dendrite, appears in A and B. In C, the slightly larger stretch has produced not only a somewhat larger generator potential at the site of

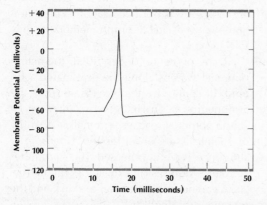

Figure 4.11. A tracing from an oscilloscope record from an experiment illustrates the form of the nerve action potential.

recording, but, in addition, a new response of the axon consisting of a 90 millivolt depolarization lasting approximately 1 millisecond. This brief explosive depolarization, the characteristic response of axons, is the action potential. The graphs in Figure 4.10 are hypothetical results of the experiment described; Figure 4.11 is taken from a photograph of the oscilloscope trace of the action potential in an actual experiment.

It is important to emphasize a fundamental difference in the properties of the generator potential and the action potential. The generator potential was caused by an external stimulus—deformation of the dendritic membrane in the example above—whereas the action potential was caused by a depolarization. Thus, in one case a mechanical stimulus produced a neuronal voltage change (the generator potential), and in the other case one voltage change (the generator potential) produced another (the action potential). The adequate stimulus for an action potential, then, is a depolarization.

Two additional differences in the properties of generator potentials and action potentials deserve special mention. It will be recalled that no threshold was apparent in the production of the generator potential; the very slightest stretch produced some detectable generator potential. In contrast, threshold behavior was apparent in the case of the action potential discussed in the preceding paragraph. The two smaller generator potentials A and B in Figure 4.10 produced no action potential, whereas both of the larger generator potentials in that figure gave rise to an action potential. The existence of a threshold, then, is a conspicuous property of action potentials not exhibited by generator potentials. A second difference between generator potentials and action potentials is that while increasing stimulus magnitude produced increasingly larger responses in the case of the generator potential, as is illustrated in C and D in Figure 4.10, an increase in the size of the generator potential did not cause larger action potentials. (Increasing the size of a generator potential does have an effect on the *rate* at which action potentials occur, however. See page 108.) This property of action potentials is usually referred to as the *all-or-none law* which states that no action potential results from a below-threshold stimulus (that is, generator potential), whereas the action potentials produced by above-threshold depolarizations are all identical in size regardless of the magnitude of the depolarization.

It is now possible to describe how action potentials permit the transmission of information over long distances in the nervous system. Axons, like dendrites, exhibit the phenomenon of passive spread, so that an action potential will spread to neighboring regions of the axons much as the generator potential spreads to neighboring regions of the dendrite. Thus the action potential will cause a large, brief depolarization of the axon region immediately adjacent to the site of origin of the action potential. This depolarization will itself give rise to an action potential, which will in turn spread to the neighboring region of the axon where again it will cause a depolarization, and still another action potential. Much as the flame sweeps along a firecracker fuse, the action potential sweeps along the axon.

One might ask why an action potential does not spread backwards and re-excite the region which was just previously active. Re-excitation is prevented from occurring because of another property of axons termed the *refractory period*. An axon which has just generated an action potential is temporarily inexcitable, that is, it will not produce another action potential until there has been adequate time for recovery. Thus depolarizations that spread passively back into a previously active region of the axon cannot stimulate this region to produce an action potential. Passive spread of depolarization, the all-or-none phenomenon, and the refractory period thus combine to permit the nervous system to transmit information over long distances.

For the reasons described in the preceding paragraph, action potentials normally travel in only one direction along an axon, from the axon's origin toward the axon terminals which form synapses with the next cell. The impressive term *orthodromic* is used to describe this normal direction of action potential propagation; thus one would say, "Normal action potentials are orthodromic" which would simply mean that normal action potentials conduct in the normal direction. For a variety of reasons, it is often useful in experiments to excite an axon near the terminal end and cause an action potential to travel in the reverse of the normal direction. This reverse direction is called *antidromic*, and one would say, for example, "Exciting an axon near its terminal causes an antidromic action potential."

A modification of the transmission process just described occurs in many axons in the vertebrate nervous system. Although some axons may be considered to be a long cylinder with uniform properties, other axons, termed *myelinated axons*, have small patches of membrane capable of generating action potentials. These patches are separated by long stretches of axon over which the excitable membrane is covered by an insulating *myelin sheath*. The excitable patches are termed *nodes of Ranvier*. In these myelinated axons, the action potential does not spread continuously along as previously discussed, but rather hops from node to node. This specialization of the axon saves energy for the organism. It also serves to speed up the conduction process, for it is not necessary for the action potential to excite all of the membrane, only selected parts.

By the process just described, the action potential sweeps along the myelinated axon until it comes to the synapses upon the motoneuron (*s'* in Figure 4.4). Whenever an action potential reaches terminals, a quantity of chemical substance, termed a *transmitter substance*, is rapidly released. This transmitter substance diffuses quickly across the narrow 200 Å gap between the axon terminal and the motoneuron dendrite, where it is broken down to an inactive form, often in less than

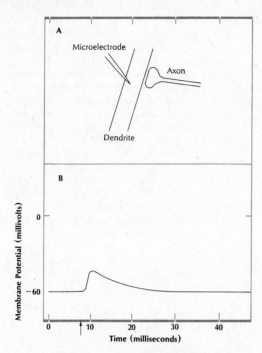

Figure 4.12. A illustrates the recording situation with the microelectrode inserted into the motoneuron dendrite. The result of an action potential invading the axon terminal, an EPSP, is shown in B. Note that the duration of the EPSP is 10 or more times that of an action potential. The action potential reached the axon terminal at the time indicated by the arrow.

a millisecond. During the period before its inactivation, however, the transmitter substance has a very marked effect upon the dendrite of the motoneuron. This effect is illustrated in Figure 4.12. A microelectrode inserted into the dendrite near the axon terminal would record a depolarization which rises rapidly and lasts for approximately 10 milliseconds or more. Further investigation would reveal that this rapid depolarization, called the *excitatory postsynaptic potential* or EPSP, shares many properties with the generator potential. It has no threshold, for even the smallest amount of transmitter produces an effect; the size of the EPSP reflects the concentration of transmitter applied to the dendritic membrane. Furthermore, the EPSP

is transmitted over the motoneuron's dendrites by passive spread and decreases in amplitude with distance from its origin.

Just as the generator potential spreads down the receptor neuron's dendrites to the axon, where it generates an action potential, so does the EPSP spread along the motoneuron's dendrites, through the soma, and into the axon where, as in the receptor neuron, an action potential is generated, provided the EPSP is above threshold. This action potential then sweeps along the motoneuron axon until it reaches the axon terminals on the muscle, the myoneural junction (s' in Figure 4.4).

The synaptic contact between motoneuron axons and the muscle, the myoneural junction, is essentially like the synapse already

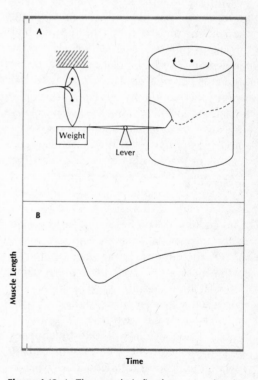

Figure 4.13. A. The muscle is fixed at one end and is provided with a weight to lift at the other end. When an action potential is produced by the muscle cell membrane, the muscle lifts the weight and contracts, as is illustrated in the graph in B.

described. When an action potential reaches the axon terminal, transmitter substance is released and a depolarization with the appearance of an EPSP occurs within the muscle. Although this depolarization has the same general appearance as an EPSP, it has been called, for historical reasons, an *end-plate potential,* abbreviated EPP. The muscle membrane is much like the axon membrane; it also generates action potentials when depolarized. Thus when the EPP occurs, an action potential is generated within the muscle cell. Muscle cells are specialized to contract, and the event which triggers their contraction is a large depolarization. Then when an action potential occurs in a muscle cell, a brief contraction results. This is termed a *muscle twitch* (see Figure 4.13).

We have now traced the chain of events between the stimulus (muscle stretch) and the response (muscle contraction). Stretching the muscle produces a generator potential in the dendrites of the bipolar neuron, and this generator potential spreads passively to the axon of the neuron. In the axon, action potentials are generated, and these sweep along the axon to the terminals upon a motoneuron. An EPSP is produced in the motoneuron as a result of the transmitter release from the axon terminal of the bipolar neuron, and this EPSP causes the motoneuron in turn to generate an action potential. The motoneuron's action potential is propagated along the axon to the myoneural junction, where it causes an EPP; the EPP triggers an action potential in the muscle cell, and this muscle action potential in turn results in contraction of the muscle. It must be emphasized that the properties of nerve cells which have been described in connection with the stretch reflex are not peculiar to this reflex, but indeed are common to neurons throughout the nervous system.

Before returning to a more thorough consideration of certain aspects of the stretch reflex, it is well to make explicit a distinction between the properties of axons and dendrites that has only been implied in the preceding discussion. Note that axons have been described as giving action potentials, whereas dendrites have been described as producing graded depolarizations, generator potentials, or EPSPs. Although there is still controversy regarding the extent to which action potentials can invade dendrites, we shall continue to maintain a sharp distinction between the properties of axons and dendrites. Specifically, it is assumed that a response typical of axons is the action potential and that action potentials do not occur in dendrites. Similarly, EPSPs, or generator potentials, are considered the sole property of dendrites. Although such a sharp distinction between axon and dendrite properties breaks down in fact, a less dogmatic version of the same distinction is generally accepted, and for our present purposes we may therefore continue to maintain a clear separation between characteristics of the axonal and dendritic membranes.

THE REFLEX

Behavioral Properties

Viewed as a simple form of behavior, the reflex has a number of characteristic properties, most of which now have a reasonably satisfactory neurophysiological explanation. Because the neural correlates of many of these properties serve to elucidate general mechanisms operating in the nervous system, an abbreviated listing of reflex properties is presented here preliminary to a discussion of their neuronal basis. Our classification of reflex properties follows Skinner's (1938) discussion of what he termed the static and dynamic laws of reflex behavior.

A conspicuous property of reflexes is the existence of threshold, or, in Skinner's terminology, the Law of Threshold. This law refers to the fact that the stimulus must reach a certain critical amplitude before the response is elicited; in the case of the stretch reflex, then, a passive stretch of the muscle of a certain critical size would be required in order to produce an active contraction of that muscle, and smaller passive stretches would be without effect. A second characteristic of reflexes is that they have a nonzero, and usually quite noticeable, latency (the Law of

Latency). For example, a delay of approximately 25 milliseconds is observed between the stretch of the muscle (the stimulus) and the active contraction of that muscle (the response), and in other reflexes the latency can be quite long, up to a number of seconds. A third property of reflexes relates to the reflex magnitude; this is Skinner's Law of the Magnitude of the Response. As one presents stronger and stronger stimuli—larger muscle stretches in the case of the stretch reflex—a parallel increase in the response magnitude— the muscle contraction—is typically observed.

Stimuli that do not themselves elicit a particular reflex can, however, affect the size of the response when they are paired with stimuli which do elicit the response. Thus, certain stimuli make themselves felt only indirectly, but not directly. If an indirectly effective stimulus causes a larger response, that stimulus is said to *facilitate* the reflex; in contrast, if an indirectly effective stimulus causes the response magnitude to diminish, or causes the response to be absent, that stimulus is said to cause *inhibition*. Skinner referred to these reflex properties as the "Laws of Facilitation and Inhibition." These fourth and fifth properties of reflex action, namely the properties of inhibition and facilitation, are illustrated by the stretch reflex: A muscle that has the same action as the particular test muscle is termed a *synergist*, or synergistic muscle, while a muscle which has an opposing action to the test muscle is called an *antagonist,* or antagonistic muscle. For example, if the test muscle bends the elbow, another muscle which also bends the elbow is a synergist, and one which straightens the elbow is an antagonist. A brief stretch of a synergistic muscle or of an antagonistic muscle does not cause a contraction of the test muscle. However, if a brief stretch of a synergist is paired with a subthreshold stretch of the test muscle, an active contraction of the test muscle may result; the stretch reflex has been facilitated by a simultaneous stretch of a synergist. Alternatively, if a brief stretch of an antagonistic muscle is paired with a suprathreshold stretch

of the test muscle, the contraction of the test muscle may be absent or diminished; stretch of an antagonist causes reflex inhibition.

The five laws just described identify important behavioral properties of the reflex; we now outline the current neurophysiological explanations for these laws, and in doing so we discuss mechanisms of neural interaction thought to be central to much of neuronal function.

Neural Integration

Although a complete analysis of the factors responsible for reflex latency is beyond the scope of the present discussion, it is important to identify several neuronal properties

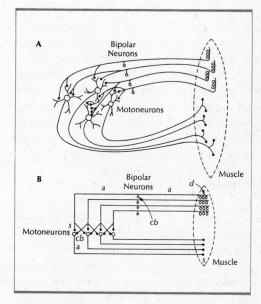

Figure 4.14. The dotted lines indicate the boundaries of the muscle (the individual muscle cells are not illustrated). In A, a group of four bipolar sensory neurons sense the stretch of the muscle and send their axons to a group of four motoneurons. These motoneurons in turn send their axons back to muscle cells within the muscle body. Part B shows the same type of circuit in a still more schematic form. The degree of simplification in this figure can be appreciated from the fact that an actual muscle would be supplied by perhaps 1000 motoneurons rather than 4.

which set the minimum latency of such a reflex. An action potential does not spread instantaneously from one end of an axon to another, but rather is conducted at velocities between 0.1 and 100 m/sec depending on the axon. Furthermore, there is a delay, called the *synaptic delay,* of approximately 0.5 millisecond between the time when the action potential reaches the axon terminals and the appearance of the EPSP in the motoneuron. The conduction delay over axons and the synaptic delay thus establish the minimum latency for a reflex because they determine the minimum time required for information to travel from the sense organ back to the muscle responsible for the response.

An obvious explanation for the minimum threshold of a reflex is contained in earlier parts of this discussion: If a stimulus is so weak that the resulting generator potential is too small to produce an action potential in the axon, information about the stretch cannot reach the central nervous system and no response can result. In actuality, however, the factors determining threshold are rather more complicated, and an understanding of them requires a somewhat more detailed picture of the neuronal interconnections underlying the stretch reflex.

Figure 4.14 presents a more realistic, but still highly schematic circuit diagram of a stretch reflex. Rather than there being a single bipolar sensory neuron, there is a large population of these neurons (represented by only four in the figure), and a pool of perhaps a thousand motoneurons replaces the single motoneuron of the earlier description (Figure 4.4). Each sensory neuron sends its axon to synapse with a number of different motoneurons, and each motoneuron receives synaptic contacts from a number of different sensory neurons. To see how reflex threshold is determined by this interconnecting neural circuit, it is necessary to investigate the effect of several simultaneously active axons on a single motoneuron.

When separate synapses on a motoneuron are simultaneously active, the total effect is,

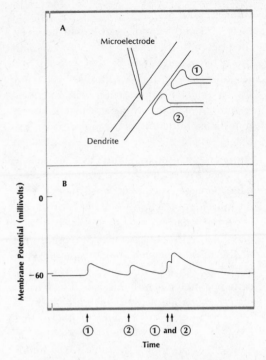

Figure 4.15. A. The microelectrode is inserted into a dendrite near two synapses, 1 and 2. B. Recordings from the dendrite reveal the EPSPs produced by stimulating the axons leading to synapses 1 and 2. The numbers below the arrows indicate which synapses were responsible for production of the EPSP. Note that the size of the EPSP is not the same for both synapses; this illustrates the natural variation that occurs between the effects of different synapses. Spatial summation results when both synapses are simultaneously active (arrows denote 1 and 2).

to a first approximation, simply the sum of the separate effects. The interaction of synchronously occurring EPSPs is illustrated in Figure 4.15; the first EPSP is the result of an action potential arriving at synapse No. 1, the second EPSP is the effect of an action potential arriving at synapse No. 2, and the third EPSP is the result of simultaneous activity of both synapses 1 and 2. This phenomenon of summation of effects from separate synapses is termed *spatial summation*. Note that the designation *EPSP* applies both to the effect of a single synapse, and to the sum effect of a number of synchronously active synapses.

The magnitude of an EPSP produced by a single axon is on the order of .1 to .2 millivolt, and, because approximately a 10 millivolt depolarization is required to produce an action potential in a motoneuron, we may estimate that some 50 or more receptors must be stimulated in order to activate motoneurons. The stretch receptors in a muscle generally have a range of thresholds, and the magnitude of a stimulus adequate to excite a number of these receptors is therefore considerably above the minimum required to excite the most sensitive receptor. Because a response can result only if at least one motoneuron is activated, the reflex threshold requires stimulation of a number of muscle stretch receptors. The precise number required will depend on details of the distribution of axon synapses among the motoneuron population, and on the distribution of receptor thresholds. It should be noted that whereas a single EPSP generally has a peak amplitude of only .1 to .2 millivolt, a single EPP is much larger. In fact, one EPP is sufficiently large to be above threshold for the muscle cell. Once a motoneuron sends an action potential to a muscle cell, that muscle cell will give a twitch contraction.

Just as individual EPSPs can add together to produce a larger depolarization, so can the twitch contraction of individual muscle cells sum to give a larger muscle contraction. This summation of contractions occurs because the individual muscle fibers exert their effect through a common attachment to bone, so that the total force exerted is the sum of the individual forces. Each motoneuron sends its axon to form myoneural junctions with a limited number of muscle cells, and thus the amplitude of a response depends upon the number of motoneurons activated.

It is now possible to see why increasing the stimulus magnitude causes an increased response magnitude. Consider the stretch reflex: As we apply larger brief stretches to the muscle, we increase the stimulus above the threshold for greater numbers of receptors, and consequently the motoneuron pool

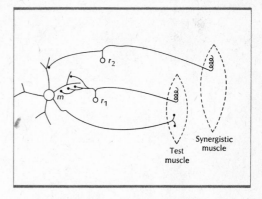

Figure 4.16. The neuroanatomical basis for the effect of synergistic muscle stretch upon the stretch reflex is illustrated by including neuron r_2 in the stretch reflex circuit made up of neurons r_1 and m.

receives a larger number of action potentials. As an increased number of synapses is activated in the motoneuron pool, spatial summation of the individual EPSPs produces an above-threshold depolarization in greater numbers of motoneurons. Therefore, more muscle cells are activated, and the increased number of individual twitches sum to give a larger total contraction. The precise details of the relationship between stimulus intensity and response magnitude, of course, depend on the exact neural circuit arrangement and upon the range of thresholds of the individual elements involved. Nevertheless, the general notion of the cooperative activity of the elements in a pool of neurons is a valid one and illustrates a general principle of nervous system functioning.

Not all axons synapsing with a motoneuron have a single source. Rather many neurons within the nervous system and many different receptors send their axons to form synapses on a given motoneuron. In addition to stretch receptors in the test muscle, stretch receptors in synergistic muscles send their axons to terminate upon the motoneuron, as is illustrated in Figure 4.16. Intracellular recording reveals that stretch of synergistic muscles causes EPSPs in the test motoneuron, but that these EPSPs are generally smaller than those produced by stretch of the receptors in the

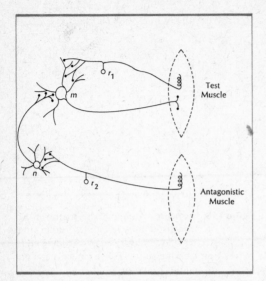

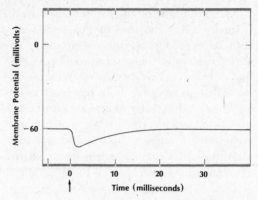

Figure 4.18. At the point indicated by the arrow, an action potential arrives at the axon terminal producing the illustrated IPSP. Note that the form and duration of the IPSP are generally similar to those of the EPSP but that the IPSP is hyperpolarizing, rather than depolarizing.

Figure 4.17. The effects of antagonistic muscle stretch on the stretch reflex are mediated through an interneuron n as illustrated in this figure. The stretch reflex circuit consists of the receptor (r_1) and the motoneuron (m); stretches of the antagonistic muscle are detected by the receptor r_2.

test muscle. In fact, EPSPs produced by stretching synergistic muscles are not sufficiently large to cause the test motoneurons to produce action potentials. However, subthreshold EPSPs arising from slight stretches of the test muscle can sum with EPSPs from the synergistic muscle and produce a depolarization sufficiently large to activate the motoneurons, thus producing a response. This, then, is the explanation for reflex facilitation.

Figure 4.17 presents a schematic neural circuit for a stretch reflex that includes the contributions from antagonistic muscles. Axons from stretch receptors in the antagonistic muscle terminate upon a neuron within the nervous system, which in turn sends its axon to the test motoneuron; this intermediate neuron is termed an *interneuron,* or *internuncial neuron.* Intracellular recording reveals that stretching the antagonistic muscle produces EPSPs in the interneuron and that these EPSPs can be sufficiently large to cause action potentials to be produced.

Recording from the motoneuron, one finds that stretching the antagonistic muscles produces a brief hyperpolarization, which has the same general form as an EPSP but is, of course, inverted (see Figure 4.18). This hyperpolarization is a second type of synaptic event, called an *inhibitory postsynaptic potential,* or IPSP. Generally speaking, IPSPs have the same properties as EPSPs in that they show spatial summation and spread passively along the dendrite. Furthermore, IPSPs and EPSPs occurring simultaneously show a type of spatial interaction in which the IPSP subtracts from the EPSP. If a stretch of the test muscle just to the threshold is paired with a nearly simultaneous stretch of an antagonistic muscle, the sum of the IPSP and EPSP may cause the depolarization to fall below threshold for producing an action potential in the motoneuron and thus prevent a response from occurring. These neural circuits, then, provide an explanation for reflex inhibition.

In the preceding discussion we give what is believed to be an essentially correct explanation for a number of the behavioral properties of reflexes. However, additional behavioral properties that are not discussed here also have generally satisfactory, although less completely understood explanations in terms of the properties of neurons and their inter-actions. It should be said, however, that the neuronal basis for two of the reflex laws—Conditioning and Extinction—is at present completely unknown. In fact, the neural basis for information storage is considered by many as neurophysiology's central problem and is currently coming under intensive investigation.

Furthermore, human behavior seldom can be analyzed into single reflexes or even groups of reflexes. The central neurons are in a continuous state of activity, as are also certain integrating centers of afferent and efferent systems. Stimuli do not so much initiate activity as modify existing activity, and responses are generally as dependent on the alertness, previous experience, and other complex aspects of the central nervous system as on immediate sensory input. Thus another of neurophysiology's central problems is to understand the principle of the neural inter-connections responsible for these more sub-tle phenomena.

Temporal Aspects of Neural Interaction

In order to simplify the preceding descrip-tion of neuron properties, the discussion has been limited to one very special type of stim-ulation, namely the application of very brief stretches to a stretch-receptor neuron. Most stimuli experienced by the organism in real life, however, are of much longer duration, and the nervous system must transmit infor-mation about these longer stimuli. To see how the nervous system handles stimuli of longer duration, we will follow the effects of a long stretch as they proceed around the stretch reflex circuit.

Intracellular recording from the sensory neuron dendrites during a prolonged stretch reveals that, as before, the stretch is repre-sented within the neuron as a depolarization (see Figure 4.19). The duration of the depola-rization reflects the duration of the stretch, and the depolarization amplitude represents the magnitude of the stretch. For many re-ceptors, it appears that the relationship be-tween generator potential magnitude and stimulus intensity (assuming the proper

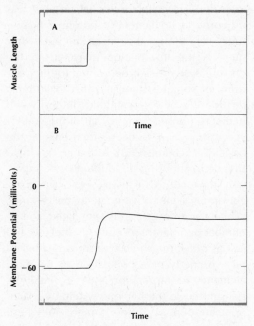

Figure 4.19. The upper graph (A) illustrates muscle length as a function of time during a stretch, and the lower graph (B) shows the generator potential that results from this stretch.

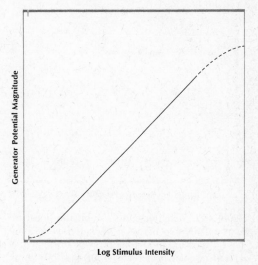

Figure 4.20. Plots of generator potential amplitude as a function of log stimulus intensity are linear over a wide range of stimulus inten-sities for a number of different receptors, as shown here.

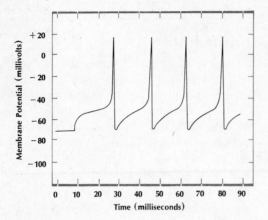

Figure 4.21. This drawing from a photograph of an oscilloscope trace illustrates the repetitive firing produced by a maintained depolarization.

measure of stimulus intensity is used) often is a logarithmic one, as is illustrated in Figure 4.20.

If one compares stretch magnitude with generator potential magnitude, however, some differences may be noted: Most striking is the fact that the generator potential usually

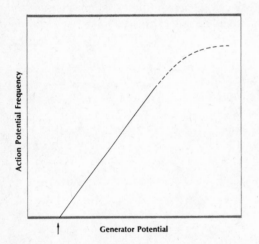

Figure 4.22. Many receptors exhibit the linear relationship between log intensity of stimulus and magnitude of generator potential (as shown in Figure 4.20) and the further linear relationship between magnitude of generator potential and frequency of nerve impulses. The threshold depolarization required to produce an action potential is indicated by the arrow.

declines in the face of a maintained stimulus, a phenomenon known as *adaptation*.

Recording from the axon of a sensory neuron during prolonged stimulation reveals, as might be expected, an action potential at the onset of the generator potential. With a maintained above-threshold generator potential, moreover, a second action potential follows the first after a delay. Furthermore, in many types of neuron, action potentials are produced repeatedly for the duration of an above-threshold depolarization, a phenomenon termed *repetitive discharge* (see Figure 4.21). The frequency of this discharge depends upon the amplitude of the generator potential; for many neurons, action potential frequency (that is, the number of action potentials per second) is proportional to depolarization (see Figure 4.22). Stimulus intensity, then, is first coded logarithmically by the receptor and then transmitted within the nervous system as nerve impulse frequency.

Because generator potential amplitude is proportional to the logarithm of stimulus intensity and action potential frequency is proportional to generator potential magnitude, it follows that nerve impulse frequency—the information delivered to the nervous system—is proportional to the logarithm of stimulus intensity. This logarithmic relationship between stimulus intensity and neural response is reminiscent of the Weber-Fechner Law and has been supposed to be the basis of it (Granit, 1955). Although this logarithmic relationship undoubtedly has important implications for psychology, it is probably premature to assign it a specific role. Whenever an organism is stimulated, a large number of different receptors is affected, and just as reflex threshold was shown earlier to be a property of a population of neuronal elements, so information about a stimulus is transmitted to the nervous system by a large population of receptors. In general, these receptors have a range of thresholds and a variety of proportionality constants by which action potential frequency is related to the logarithm of stimulus intensity. How the sum

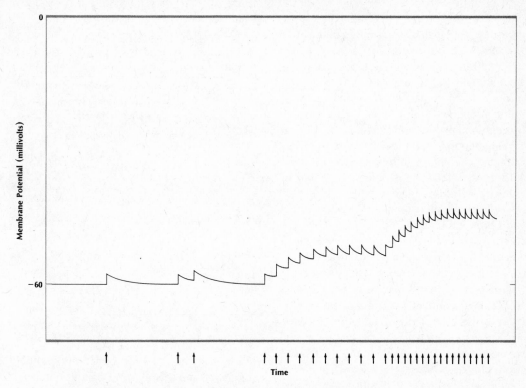

Figure 4.23. This figure illustrates the phenomenon of temporal summation. Each arrow indicates the arrival of an action potential at the axon terminal, and, as can be seen, a steady though rather jagged depolarization is the result of constant frequency of action potential arrivals. It is evident from the figure that a larger average depolarization results from a highter action potential frequency.

total of information carried over all of these receptor channels, with their different properties, is used by the nervous system depends upon the details of the synaptic connections between neurons processing the information. The situation is a very complicated one, then, and it is difficult to assess the significance of any stimulus intensity-action potential frequency relationship without a detailed study of the system under consideration.

Just as EPSPs occurring simultaneously at two separate synapses add together in a neuron, it is reasonable that an EPSP should add to any depolarization remaining from previously occurring EPSPs at the same or other synapses. This phenomenon of an EPSP adding onto the tails of preceding EPSPs is called *temporal summation* (see Figure 4.23) and is extremely important in the functioning of the nervous system. If one records from a moto-

neuron during the stretching of its muscle, the repetitive discharge of the bipolar neuron will cause a rapid sequence of EPSPs to be produced in the motoneuron, and these EPSPs will exhibit temporal summation. Assuming that a second EPSP is produced before the first has died away, the second EPSP will add to what remains of the first; similarly, the third EPSP will sum with the remainder of the first and second, and so on. After an interval equal to the decay time of a single EPSP, this process will reach a steady state, and the mean depolarization will remain constant. This steady (average) depolarization will, by spatial summation, add to the inputs over any other synapses. In this way, then, a replica, although perhaps a distorted one, of the sensory neuron generator potential will have been transmitted to the motoneuron.

The maintained depolarization thus generated by the processes of temporal and spatial summation will be transmitted to the axon by means of passive spread, where, if the depolarization is above threshold, action potentials will be generated repetitively. The process in motoneurons by which a maintained depolarization produces a train of action potentials is strictly analogous to the one already discussed in receptor neurons. Thus, an adequately large muscle stretch will lead first to a maintained generator potential in sensory dendrites, next repetitive firing of sensory axons, then a maintained depolarization of motoneurons, and finally a repetitive discharge over motoneuron axons leading to the muscle cells. In a manner quite analogous to the temporal summation of EPSPs, successive muscle twitches may sum to produce a maintained contraction, the average magnitude of which is approximately proportional to action potential frequency in the motoneuron axons. Thus, in our simplified situation, stretch of a muscle will excite stretch receptors, and these will cause a repetitive discharge of the motoneurons that will result in a maintained contraction of the muscle. Altogether, then, the stretch reflex acts to oppose passive stretches of the muscle by causing active contractions, thus maintaining a constant muscle length in the face of outside disturbances.

Summary of Neuronal Function

The preceding discussion of the stretch reflex has illustrated the types of neural interaction believed to be typical of the function of the nervous system. It is a general rule that receptors act by representing some feature of the environment as a generator potential, and information about this generator potential is, as a rule, transmitted to other neurons in terms of action potential frequency. Furthermore, spatial and temporal summation of EPSPs and IPSPs are of central importance in integrating information within the nervous system. Generator potential magnitude, in general, reflects stimulus intensity, and information about stimulus in-

TABLE 4.1 FREQUENTLY USED EQUIVALENT TERMS*

Term used here	Synonym or approximate equivalent
action potential	spike; spike potential; nerve impulse; impulse; nerve spike
generator potential	receptor potential
myoneural junction	neuromuscular junction; end plate
passive spread	electrotonic spread; electrotonus
electroencephalogram	electrocorticogram (ECG); brain waves
axon terminal	bouton terminal
action potential frequency	nerve impulse frequency; impulse frequency; firing rate

*Although many of the terms are not precisely synonymous, they are frequently used interchangeably.

tensity is carried in terms of action potential frequency and the number of active neurons. Information about the quality of the stimulus, however, as opposed to stimulus magnitude, is represented by the type of neuron or neurons active: Some receptors are maximally sensitive to the deformation of their dendrites, while other neurons respond best, for example, to photic stimulation. Thus by keeping track of which neuron is sending information, the nervous system may know the quality of the stimulus. Finally, although the situation is more complicated, the complex patterns of muscle contractions responsible for gross behavior are produced by mechanisms essentially similar to those involved in the production of a simple stretch reflex.

A number of synonyms for neurophysiological terms are in common use; some of the more important ones appear in Table 4.1.

MECHANISMS OF NERVE ACTIVITY

Although understanding the mechanisms underlying the phenomena described earlier has been a primary concern of students of the nervous system, a detailed presentation of information about these mechanisms is beyond the scope of the present discussion. The following paragraphs deal only briefly with the ionic mechanisms for the action potential and for EPSPs and IPSPs; the reader interested in further details may consult the references cited on page 95.

By the expenditure of metabolic work, nerve cells maintain concentration differences of certain ions across their membranes: Sodium ions are in higher concentration on the outside than on the inside, and potassium ions have a greater concentration inside than outside. The nerve membrane has the ability to increase its permeability to sodium or to potassium independently; and when it does so, sodium, because of its concentration difference, tends to enter the cell, whereas potassium tends to leave the cell. Associated with these ionic flows are changes in membrane potential. The flow of sodium tends to depolarize a neuron while the potassium outflow tends to cause a hyperpolarization.

The event that triggers an increase in sodium permeability is a depolarization, such as that arising from a generator potential. If a nerve cell is depolarized, it rapidly increases its sodium permeability and sodium flows in, causing still further depolarization. This extra depolarization again causes a further increased sodium permeability, increased sodium inflow, additional depolarization, and so on until the cell is quite strongly depolarized. The events just described account for the rising phase of the action potential.

The return of the membrane potential from its peak to the resting potential depends upon two mechanisms. First, after sodium permeability has increased, it then decreases in spite of a depolarization; this phenomenon is termed *sodium inactivation* and is to be contrasted with the increased sodium permeability called *sodium activation*. With the cessation of sodium inflow resulting from sodium inactivation, the membrane potential returns to its resting value. The second mechanism accelerating this return to the resting level is an increase in potassium permeability. Although *potassium activation*, like sodium activation, is a consequence of neuron depoarization, the increase in permeability occurs less rapidly for potassium than for sodium. Thus when the neuron is depolarized by the sodium inflow, potassium permeability increases gradually to a value that is sufficient, when combined with the sodium inactivation, to return the membrane potential to its resting level.

The ionic flows that occur during EPSPs and IPSPs are rather more complicated than those that occur during the action potential in the sense that many different ions may be involved. For our purposes, however, we shall consider the EPSP to be the result of an increase in sodium permeability, and the IPSP to be the result of an increase in potassium permeability. In contrast to the increases in permeability during the action potential, which are triggered solely by a depolarization, the increases in permeability for EPSPs and IPSPs are the result of the transmitter action on the postsynaptic membrane and are independent of the postsynaptic membrane potential. Thus, arrival of an action potential in an axon terminal results in the liberation of a transmitter substance that diffuses to the dendritic membrane; this transmitter then causes an increase in sodium permeability and a consequent depolarization. The transmitter does not continue to act indefinitely, however, because an enzyme transforms it to an inactive form. This destruction occurs very rapidly in many cases, so that the permeability increase producing an EPSP or an IPSP is very short-lived.

OTHER ELECTROPHYSIOLOGICAL TECHNIQUES

Although the intracellular recording technique described in the previous section is in principle the most appropriate one to use for studying the electrical activity of nerve cells, in practice technical difficulties limit its applicability. Fortunately a number of alternative techniques are available for use in situations where intracellular recording is not practicable. Because these techniques involve recording voltages in the fluids surrounding nerve cells, a brief discussion of how voltages arise in a conducting medium is required.

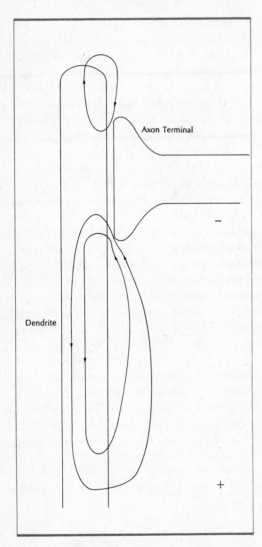

Figure 4.24. Current flows into the dendrite at the site of an EPSP synapse because of the increase of sodium permeability; thus it must flow out through the membrane to make closed loops of current flow of the type illustrated above. Because current flows from + to −, the voltage in the surrounding fluids near the EPSP is negative and is positive at a distance from the synapse.

Nerve cells are surrounded by a fluid that contains, among other things, a relatively high concentration of sodium chloride, and which therefore has a relatively low resistance to the flow of electrical currents. When current flows into a neuron at the site of an EPSP, for example, that current must flow through the neuron interior and out again through the external medium (see Figure 4.24). The activity of nerve cells is therefore associated with currents flowing through the surrounding salt solution, and, because the flow of current through a conductor is associated with voltage differences, the activity of neurons produces voltage differences in the fluid around the cells. Thus by recording the voltage changes in the medium surrounding neurons one can often detect their activity. A detailed explanation of how these extracellular voltages are produced is quite difficult and is beyond the scope of this discussion.

When a neuron discharges action potentials, voltage changes are produced in the surrounding tissue fluids. The amplitude of these voltage changes, which typically ranges from one-tenth to several millivolts, varies inversely with distance from the active soma, and frequently falls to undetectable levels at a distance of several cell-diameters.

Extracellular signs of action potentials are termed, for historical reasons, *extracellular unit potentials*. The term *unit* has its origin in one of the criteria used to identify the activity of one single cell: Often it happens that an extracellular electrode will detect the activity of two adjacent neurons simultaneously, and because the amplitude of the signals recorded from both cells seldom are of the same size, one can distinguish between the responses of the two cells. In contrast if a record reveals signals of a uniform size, it can be concluded that those voltages were generated by a single cell; these "unitary voltages" are now referred to as *unit voltages* or simply *units*. The advantage of extracellular unit recording over the intracellular technique described previously is that extracellular recording is much less difficult, and is even possible in waking, freely moving organisms (see, for example, Evarts, 1968).

Unlike the extracellular signs of a single action potential, the current flows resulting from activation of one or a few synapses are usually too small to produce detectable voltage changes in the fluids surrounding the cell. However, if a large number of synapses are synchronously active and if the shape and orientation of the cells is such that the current from these synapses flows in the same direction and therefore sums, it is possible to record quite large voltage changes. The voltage changes produced by synchronously occurring EPSPs and IPSPs form the basis for an electrophysiological technique termed the *evoked potential method*. Using a brief stimulus, it is possible to produce synchronous action potentials in a bundle of axons that form synapses on cells in a certain region. Because all of the action potentials arrive simultaneously, the postsynaptic potentials are produced simultaneously, and it is possible to record a relatively large voltage change in the region; this voltage change is termed the *evoked potential*. Because evoked potentials are usually the product of a population of cells, it is often quite difficult to infer from them events occurring at the level of the single cell. Nevertheless, simply demonstrating a connection between one brain area and another by demonstrating that stimulation at one location causes an evoked potential to occur at another may be very valuable. Furthermore, even without an understanding of the mechanism of the evoked potential in terms of events occurring in single neurons, increases or decreases in size concomitant with variations in other conditions can in some instances give insight into function.

Although many evoked potentials are sufficiently large to be easily recorded, in some instances—particularly when the stimulus is a weak one—the evoked potential has a small amplitude and is obscured by electrical noise of neural and artifactual origin. Modern developments in data handling have provided a method for detecting such evoked

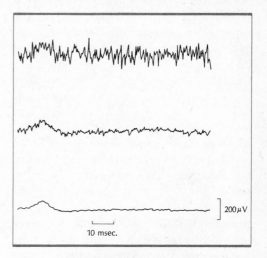

Figure 4.25. Evoked potentials recorded without averaging (top trace), after averaging 10 responses (middle trace) and after averaging 100 responses (bottom trace).

potentials obscured by noise. The basic idea is as follows: Each time a stimulus is presented, it produces a sequence of voltage changes that are always about the same, and these voltage changes are added to the random voltage changes constituting the electrical noise. Whereas the form of the evoked potential is about the same from trial to trial, the noise is constantly changing, so that if a positive noise voltage occurs on one trial, a negative voltage is likely to occur on another. If successive records are added together, the invariant evoked potentials tend to add, while the noise, being out of phase from trial to trial, tends to cancel. The effect of averaging is illustrated by the data presented in Figure 4.25; these data are typical of the type obtained, for example, by recording from the region of cat cortex that receives input from a forepaw that can be stimulated with a weak electrical shock of short duration (0.1 msec). Although the evoked potential is difficult to detect with a single trial, it becomes apparent after 10 responses are averaged and quite clear and noise-free if 100 responses are averaged.

Several difficulties limit the application of the averaging technique described in the preceding paragraph. First, the response must occur with a fixed latency after the stimulus, for otherwise the separate trials will not produce responses which add together. Second, because there is variation in the form of an evoked potential from trial to trial, the sum of many such evoked potentials may bear little resemblance to any of the individual components. Finally, the very power of the technique can be a serious disadvantage; potentials can spread over very large distances, and voltages can be recorded in one area that actually occurred at quite a distant site. It is possible, for example, to record potentials generated by contracting neck muscles over a region which one might expect to record visual potentials, and therefore to mistakenly attribute to the brain evoked potentials which were in fact a result of a gross but not noticeable motor response.

In order to study the function of some brain regions, it is necessary to have a technique that permits the accurate positioning of electrodes within the desired structures. Because brain structure is very similar from animal to animal, brain locations bear a fixed relationship to certain landmarks on the skull, and by using these landmarks for reference, an electrode may be inserted through a small hole in the skull to a predetermined location within the depths of the brain (Horsley & Clarke, 1908). An animal is suspended in a special frame by bars that fit firmly in the ear canals, and by a bite bar that holds the snout in position. When the animal is placed symmetrically in this apparatus, structures within the brain may be located by reference to an arbitrary zero: the most common reference point is the intersection of the line connecting the two ear bars and the animal's midline. For example, to reach the cat hypothalamus, one would move the electrode to a position 11 mm in front of the reference point, 1 mm to the side, and 5 mm down.

The method of locating specific brain areas described above is called the *stereotaxic technique,* and brain maps, known as *stereotaxic atlases* (for example, Jasper & Ajmone-

Marsan, 1955) are available for many of the commonly used species. The stereotaxic technique, combined with microelectrode and evoked potential recording, has proved a very fruitful approach to understanding brain function, for by using the appropriate type of stimulation, it is possible to produce evoked potentials in almost any region of the brain.

The evoked potentials from certain neural tissues have been given special names, both for historical reasons and for the reason that these potentials have been of particular significance. Examples are the electroretinogram (ERG) and the electro-olfactogram (EOG). The ERG is generated by photic stimulation of the retina and arises as a result of neural and photochemical activity in retinal cells, although it may be recorded from the cornea and other locations; it has been used, for example, in investigations of light-receptor mechanisms (see p. 307 in Chapter 9). The EOG is an analogous potential generated in the olfactory system and has been used in the study of receptor processes in olfaction (see p. 221 in Chapter 7).

In some areas of the brain it happens, for reasons that are not entirely clear, that the EPSPs and IPSPs are spontaneously synchronous in a large population of cells. Whatever the reason for the synchronization of activity, its result is that spontaneously occurring potentials from the brain reach sufficiently high voltages that they may often be recorded by the use of gross electrodes applied to the scalp. These potentials are referred to as the brain's *electroencephalogram,* abbreviated EEG. Because there are certain differences between normal EEG records and those seen in some pathological conditions, the EEG has proved very valuable in clinical medicine as a diagnostic tool. As a research technique, analysis of the EEG has depended mainly on demonstrating changes in electrical activity with manipulation of experimental conditions.

Just as the activity of nerve cells produces measurable voltage changes in the fluids surrounding them, so may one record voltage changes produced by muscle cell activity. This technique, called *electromyography,* abbreviated EMG, has been of considerable clinical use and is of particular interest to psychologists because it provides a way for recording muscle activity too small to produce gross movements. By inserting small needles into the muscle, or by placing small disc electrodes on the skin over a muscle to be studied, muscle potential may be quite conveniently measured (see Hefferline, Keenan, & Harford, 1959, and p. 379 in Chapter 11).

The heart is a muscular organ, and, like other muscles, it has voltages which produce a record, called the *electrocardiogram* (EKG), associated with its contraction. From the point of view of the psychologist, recording the electrical signs of heartbeats offers a way to measure heart rate in the waking and freely moving animal. Thus if an investigator wishes to use heart rate as a measure of the animal's "emotional state," or if he is interested in heart rate conditioning, he may conveniently record the electrocardiogram. In the study of autonomic conditioning, for example, EKG has proved to be a useful measure of heart rate (see p. 711 in Chapter 16).

The preceding discussion is primarily concerned with recording the voltage changes within and around nerve cells during their activity. An inverse problem, in a certain sense, is concerned with producing activity in neurons by changing their membrane potential. This may be accomplished, for reasons which are quite complicated, by passing current through the fluids surrounding nerve cells. By placing stimulating electrodes stereotaxically, *electrical stimulation of the brain* (ESB) may be accomplished with considerable precision. This technique may be employed in waking, freely moving animals and has proved useful in a number of areas of psychology. For example, stimulation of certain brain areas can act as a reinforcer, and this stimulation has been relied upon in the study of reinforcement *per se* (see Chapter 15). Despite the usefulness of ESB, a number of

sources of error can make results difficult to interpret in terms of normal brain function: ESB tends to cause synchronous activity in the population of stimulated neurons as opposed to the normal asynchronous activity; neurons with opposing actions may be simultaneously stimulated; larger neurons tend to be more affected than smaller ones; it is difficult to know whether neuron somas or passing axon bundles are stimulated; and it is generally impossible to discover whether the observed effects are mediated through the activation of excitatory neurons (those which produce EPSPs) or inhibitory neurons. Nevertheless, used with care, ESB is a valuable research tool.

NEURAL SOURCES OF VARIABILITY

Although behavior can be very predictable, one of its striking attributes is its randomness. The variability of gross behavior appears at first to contrast sharply with the constancy of neuron properties described in the preceding sections. In fact, however, neuronal properties themselves vary somewhat with time, and even if they did not, a nervous system constructed of elements of the type described would be expected to show con-

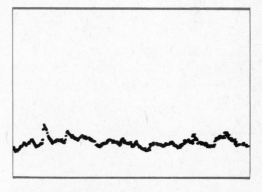

Figure 4.26. The recording of a neuron's membrane potential, photographed from an oscilloscope plot of voltage as a function of time, illustrates the synaptic noise so frequently seen when recording from neurons in the central nervous system. The amplitude of the noise illustrated is approximately 3 mv peak-to-peak.

siderable variability in its behavior. This variability has two main sources. First, even a completely deterministic system that is sufficiently complex can give the appearance of random behavior. If the behavior of a system depends on a sufficiently large number of variables, the inevitable uncontrolled changes in some of these variables can give the appearance of capriciousness to the system. Second, a type of noise can creep into any system, such as the nervous system, in which the individual elements are richly interconnected. In fact, the nervous system is not analogous to a telephone switchboard in which electrical activity is confined to the lines that are busy. Instead, the neurons in the brain are spontaneously active. Stimuli do not serve to initiate activity but to modify existing activity. Responses are governed not only by stimuli but by existing patterns of activity. An individual neuron receives thousands of synaptic contacts, and when large numbers of these synapses are asynchronously activated, the membrane potential exhibits haphazard fluctuations around its mean value. These fluctuations, termed *synaptic noise* by the physiologist (see Figure 4.26), are a ubiquitous property of neurons and can become so large that they dominate the behavior of a nerve cell. (Some implications of noise within the nervous system have already been discussed in relation to signal detection in Chapter 2.)

Dan R. Kenshalo

THE CUTANEOUS SENSES*

5

This chapter is concerned with sensations aroused by stimulation of the skin, *somesthesis*. One of the most remarkable characteristics of the organism is its possession of receptors that are sensitive (or "tuned") only to certain characteristics of various physical and chemical stimuli including those within its body. Most receptors, however, especially those of the skin, are not as specific in their sensitivity to certain aspects of the stimulus as was once thought. It becomes clear how the early impressions of receptor specificity arose when the physiological, anatomical, and psychological data are considered historically.

We experience different sensations, in part because of the selective sensitivity of the receptors. We also experience different sensations in part because the nervous activity initiated by the receptors travels through the nervous pathways to different parts of the brain.

We cannot confine our consideration of the skin senses, or the other senses for that matter, to data obtained by psychophysical methods only. To do so deprives us of the store of information that has been amassed by the physiologists, the anatomists, and the physicists about the characteristics of skin and the other sensory systems. That is, we must be able to describe not only the way in which thresholds and sensations

*Preparation of this chapter was facilitated by USPHS Grant No. NB-02992 and NSF Grant No. GB-2473.

117

change when the conditions of stimulation are changed, but we must also know the mechanical and thermal properties of skin (physics), what structures are available to respond to a particular stimulus (anatomy), and how these structures translate a stimulus into patterns of nerve impulses along relatively specific neural pathways (neurophysiology).

DELIMITATION OF THE SENSES

More than 2000 years ago Aristotle spoke of five senses—sight, hearing, taste, smell, and feeling (as in touch). Then, and in the centuries that followed, the way in which the human organism obtained accurate information about its environment and how the information was conveyed to the brain was of primary concern. In the philosophical period, during the development of the sciences of physiology and psychology, it was generally held that pictures or images—*eidola*—of objects were conveyed to the brain by way of the nerves (Boring, 1942). Thus, red was thought to appear red because a neural image of the color red was directly conveyed to the brain.

The Doctrine of Specific Energies of Nerves

The image theory of sensations persisted to the turn of the nineteenth century. Then in 1826, at the very beginnings of experimental investigations of nervous system functions, the great physiologist Johannes Müller proposed a theory that has become known as the *doctrine of specific nerve energies* (Dennis, 1948). He said that the brain is directly aware of the activity in the sensory nerves, not of the objects that excite them, and that the sensory nerves convey nerve impulses to the brain which are not, in themselves, different in their ability to produce specific sensations. Different sensations arise because each sensory nerve has its characteristic type of activity. Thus, optic nerve activity signals light and color; auditory nerve activity

signals sounds; olfactory nerve activity signals odors; and so on. The theory is vividly expressed by the statement that, if the auditory nerve and visual nerve were crossed, we could see thunder and hear lightning. The experiment is impractical, of course, but there are other ways to identify the source of this specificity. Thus, when the same stimulus, for example, electric current, is applied to the different nerves, or if different stimuli, for example, mechanical, chemical, electrical, and so on, are applied to the same nerve, sensations are produced according to the special properties of the nerve stimulated. Müller thought these special properties might be in the nerves themselves or in the parts of the brain to which they are connected. There is some evidence for the latter view. A blow on the back of the head, over the occipital lobe of the brain where the visual pathways terminate, makes one see a flash of light. This atypical form of stimulation has been called *inadequate stimulation*. Thus, for the sense of sight, the *adequate* stimulus is light, but inadequate ones include an electric current or a beam of x-rays passed through the eyeball.

Sensory Modalities

Why do we say that sight is one sense and hearing is another? There are at least five criteria which set them off as separate or primary sensory modalities (Neff, 1960). They have (1) *markedly different receptive organs* that (2) respond to *characteristic stimuli*. Each set of receptive organs has its (3) *own nerve* that goes to a (4) *different part of the brain*, and the (5) *sensations are different*. With these criteria, we can identify 9 or perhaps 11 different senses: vision, audition, kinesthesis (joint sense), vestibular sense (one or two?), tactile sense, temperature sense (one or two?), pain, taste, and smell. If we insist that all of the criteria for a primary sensory modality be fulfilled in each case, our knowledge of the structure and function of several of the senses disqualifies them as primary sensory modalities. For example, we do not yet know the receptive organs for temperature and pain, nor the specific parts of the brain for them. If we insist that each primary sensory modality has its own nerve pathway, the tactile, pain, and temperature senses fail to qualify as different modalities because their nerves are intermingled, at least in the peripheral nerve bundles. Nor do we have at present a satisfactory account of the chemical characteristics of the stimuli required to stimulate taste and smell.

Within a primary sensory modality, a number of unique sensory experiences can be described. These are classified on a psychological basis according to the different primary qualities of sensation experienced, for example, sweet, bitter, red, blue, cold, warm, and so on. Physiological classifications have also been used in which the number of elementary physiological processes required to account for different psychological qualities of sensation that can be discriminated were determined. Structures that could be morphologically identified were then assigned to each physiological process. For example, Helmholtz knew the physics of light mixing when he accepted Young's trichromatic theory of color vision. He also knew that any pure spectral hue could be matched approximately by blending any three wavelengths of light provided the wavelengths were widely separated in the spectrum. On this basis he suggested that there were red-, green-, and violet-sensitive nerve fibers (receptors) which when differentially stimulated could account for all of the discriminably different hues of the light spectrum. Hering, on the other hand, started with a knowledge of the psychologically primary hues: red, yellow, green, and blue. He proposed that two reversible chemical reactions could account for color vision. A shift in the equilibrium of one reaction toward one side or the other resulted in the sensations of red or green. Shifts in the equilibrium of the other reaction gave yellow or blue sensations.

Unfortunately, these types of classification are as confusing when applied to other sense modalities as they are when used in vision. The confusion is a result of the assumption that there is a one-to-one correlation between elementary psychological qualities of sensation and the elementary physiological and morphological properties of receptors (Melzack & Wall, 1962).

Extension of the "Doctrine"

The doctrine of specific nerve energies is a theory of how an organism can differentiate between the five traditional primary sensory modalities. Müller tried to explain how stimulus objects, which become encoded into nerve impulses, are represented to the brain so that they yield sensations that are clearly different in their essential nature. Müller's theory was effective, for it successfully combatted the earlier notion that pictures of stimulus objects are conveyed to the brain by the nerves.

It is clear, however, that within each of the primary sensory modalities there occur differences in the qualities of sensation, which also must be taken into account. What are the primary qualities in each of the primary sense modalities? That is, if differences between visual and auditory sensations might be accounted for by the part of the brain in which their nerves terminate, how are differences between red and green or between various pitches to be explained? Most researchers think that the peripheral receptor mechanism is responsible for the differentiation of the qualities of sensation within each sensory modality. In order to determine the specific mechanisms within the receptors for such differentiations, the primary qualities of sensations that occur within each primary sensory modality must be defined.

The search for the primary qualities of cutaneous sensations was begun by three physiologists: Blix, a Swede; Goldscheider, a German; and Donaldson, an American, who independently published accounts maintaining that the skin is not uniformly sensitive to tactile, warm, or cold stimuli but shows spots of sensitivity to each of these stimuli.

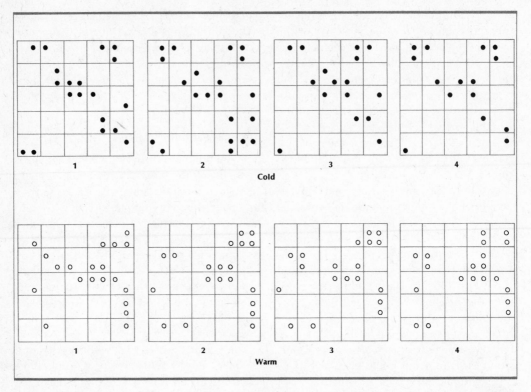

Figure 5.1. Distribution of cold and warm spots found on the upper arm. An area of 1 cm² was mapped four
times for cold spots and four times for warm spots on four days within about a week. Each square
of the grid contains four tested points. Note most spots on the skin are insensitive to either warm
or cold, that cold and warm spots seldom coincide, and that day-to-day reliability is fairly good but
by no means perfect for either the cold spots or the warm. (Data from Plate II of Dallenbach, 1927.)

By stamping a grid of ink lines on the skin
at 2 mm intervals and exploring each square
with appropriate stimuli they found, as have
others since, that some squares gave clear
tactile sensations when prodded with a stiff
hair, for example, but other squares did not.
Similarly, when the grid of squares was explored using warm or cool stimuli (delivered
by the small tip of a brass cylinder heated or
cooled by water) some squares gave rise to
clear sensations of cold. Warm sensations
were also produced by stimulation of some
of the squares with a heated brass cylinder,
but these warm spots usually did not coincide
with the cold spots found in the same grid,
as is shown in Figure 5.1. Sharp, "bright" pain
could also be registered by most of the
squares in the grid when a needle was stuck
into the skin over each square. Thus, the

foundation was laid to establish touch,
warmth, and cold as the primary qualities of
cutaneous sensation. The establishment of
pain as the fourth primary somesthetic quality, however, was not achieved until the work
of von Frey was published in 1895, some seven
years later.

Von Frey extended Müller's theory of specific nerve energies to the periphery by pro-
posing a particular type of receptive structure
for each of the four primary cutaneous sensations. Considering the trends in physiology
and psychology of those times, it is not surprising that von Frey proposed, on meager
evidence, specific "types" of structure within
the skin as receptors for each of the primary
qualities of somesthesis, for Helmholtz had
proposed three and Hering two specific
channels to account for hue discriminations.

Helmholtz had also proposed a large number of specific receptors in the form of resonators in the inner ear to account for the tonal qualities of pitch.

Von Frey's proposition was simple. He proposed that certain histologically identifiable structures associated with the terminals of sensory nerves were responsible for the specificity of response exhibited by the sensory mapping experiments. The correlations between structure and sensation that he drew were that Meissner corpuscles in hairless skin and hair follicle receptors in hairy skin signaled touch, Krause end bulbs signaled cold, and Ruffini cylinders signaled warmth, but only the free nerve endings of the dermal nerve net were widely enough distributed to account for pain. Other cutaneous sensations, such as wetness, oiliness, tickle, and roughness, were held to be blends of these four primary qualities of sensation. It was natural for von Frey to expect to find a particular type of nerve terminal beneath a skin spot that gave a particular quality of sensation. These structures should be different from the nerve terminal structures found beneath other skin spots that gave other qualities of sensation.

Despite its apparent simplicity, von Frey's proposal makes at least three major assumptions (Melzack & Wall, 1962):

1. a physiological assumption that receptors are specific in their responses to a particular stimulus dimension,

2. an anatomical assumption that a morphologically discrete type of receptor lies beneath each sensory spot on the skin,

3. a psychological assumption that an identifiable quality of sensation bears a one-to-one relationship to a single stimulus dimension, and therefore, to a given type of skin receptor.

We next examine each of these assumptions to determine its basis in fact.

1. There can be little doubt that receptive structures have a great deal to do with selecting the characteristics of the stimulus to which their associated nerve fibers will respond. The tendency is so great that the great physiologist Sherrington defined the function of a receptor as increasing the sensitivity of a sensory nerve fiber to one aspect of the stimulus and decreasing it to all others (Sherrington, 1906). This selectivity, as compared to specificity of response, is clearly demonstrated in the spectral light absorption curves of the red-, green-, and blue-sensitive cones of the retina (see Chapter 10). Retinal cones of each type show a selectivity of response in the broad peaks of response at the long, medium, and short wavelengths of visible light. They do not show a specificity of response to particular wavelengths or even narrow bands of wavelengths.

As is discussed later, some cutaneous receptors show a high degree of selectivity by responding either to mechanical or thermal stimuli, but others show considerable activity when stimulated by either. Furthermore, a continuous gradation of intensity of stimulation, from weak to strong enough to cause actual tissue damage, may be required to make the receptors discharge their associated nerve fibers. There is apparently no clear-cut demarcation between the intensity of stimulation required to elicit a mechanical or a thermal sensation and that required to elicit a painful sensation.

These lines of evidence lead to a rejection of the first assumption of von Frey's theory, that receptors of the skin are highly specific in their responses to a particular stimulus dimension. They may be selective, but they are not specific, for there are too many receptor units that fail to fall exclusively into the catagories responding only to tactile, temperature, or pain stimuli.

2. Von Frey's assumption that there are specific types of receptor beneath each characteristically sensitive spot of skin is most in error. The crucial experiment of making histological examinations of the tissue beneath carefully mapped temperature spots has been carried out at least a dozen times (Kenshalo & Nafe, 1962). With one exception (von Frey, 1895), neither Krause end bulbs nor Ruffini cylinders have been found beneath cold or

warm spots. Furthermore, encapsulated endings do not occur in hairy skin except for the Pacinian corpuscles, which lie deep in the dermis. Yet hairy skin shows a sensitivity to mechanical and thermal stimuli at least as high as that of hairless skin (Hagen et al., 1953). Whatever the function of the specialized, encapsulated, nerve endings found in hairless skin, it appears *not* to be that of specific sensitivities to increases or decreases in the temperature of the skin or its mechanical deformation.

3. The psychological assumption that there are four primary qualities to somesthesis, each bearing a one-to-one correlation to a single stimulus characteristic and to a given type of skin receptor, is the most questionable part of von Frey's theory. It proposes a concept of the nervous system in which information is carried from the skin to the brain by a system of nerves that bear a functional resemblance to the differently colored wires of a telephone cable; that is, distinct nerves in separate pathways run from the skin to specific receiving areas of the brain. Although this type of conceptual nervous system was acceptable in von Frey's time, it is totally inconsistent with the modern concepts of neurophysiology. The activity of peripheral sensory nerve fibers passes through several synapses on its way to the brain. At each synapse the patterns of activity undergo temporal and spatial modifications. When they finally arrive at the brain, they bear little resemblance to the patterns of activity that started at the peripheral receptors.

A one-to-one correlation between the physical dimensions of the stimulus and the psychological dimensions of the sensation cannot be assumed for somesthesis. Although skin spots have been described whose stimulation produces one of the four primary qualities of sensation, the variety of somesthetic sensations is much richer than can be accounted for by combinations of these four primary qualities. The data indicate that activity in many sensory fibers supplying the skin shows a high degree of selectivity in response to mechanical or thermal stimulation. However, because there are, for example, warm spots separate from cold spots, it should not be assumed that there are also separate warm and cold receptors or specific warm-sensitive and cold-sensitive, peripheral sensory nerve fibers. If so, it would be the exception rather than the rule in sensory processes.

STRUCTURE OF HUMAN SKIN

The skin is the largest, and, from the standpoint of its diverse functions, the most versatile structure of the body. It has no equal among the other body organs in its regenerative powers. It provides a flexible elastic covering for the body machinery; it provides protection against infrared and ultraviolet radiation, invasions of microorganisms, toxic substances and chemicals; and it prevents the escape of the body's vital juices. The skin contains the mechanisms (cutaneous vascular system and sweat glands) to cool the body effectively when the body core temperature has become too high and to minimize body heat loss when the body core temperature is too low. The cutaneous vascular system also aids in regulating blood pressure (Montagna, 1962).

As a sense organ the skin is the most extensive of the body, and its value to the survival of the individual is clearly demonstrable. For example, the skin serves an important function in the development of affectional systems in lower primates (Harlow & Harlow, 1965) and presumably man. Also, individuals who have no sense of pain usually die early (Sternbach, 1968). In spite of the importance of the skin as an organ of sense, there is little agreement among investigators as to the critical variables of stimulation, the neurological and associated structures that are responsible for its sensitivity, or the nature of the neural code that allows the differentiation of sensations resulting from mechanical, thermal, or painful stimulation.

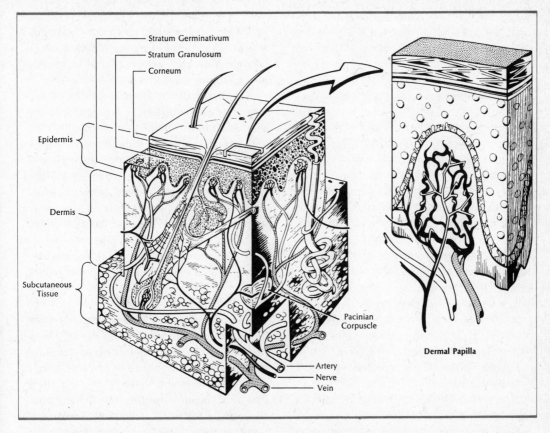

Stratum Germinativum
Stratum Granulosum
Corneum
Epidermis
Dermis
Subcutaneous Tissue
Pacinian Corpuscle
Dermal Papilla
Artery
Nerve
Vein

Figure 5.2. A schematic representation of human hairy skin. Sensory nerve fibers terminate around the hair follicles, close to the border of the dermis and epidermis, and among the smooth muscle fibers of the arterioles and venules, especially in the dermal papillae. Encapsulated sensory nerve terminals of the Pacinian corpuscle type are frequently found in the vicinity of the dermis-subcutis boundary as well as in the subcutis proper.

The Basic Skin Structure

Human skin consists of three main layers: The most superficial layer is called the *epidermis;* the *dermis* is the central layer; and underlying these, but external to the fascia, is the *subcutis,* which is composed of fat and loose connective tissue. As may be seen in Figure 5.2, the epidermis may be subdivided into several more or less distinct layers. The main ones, starting with the most superficial, are the *stratum corneum,* the *stratum granulosum,* and the *stratum germinativum.* Apparently cells that originate in the stratum germinativum are continually displaced upward by newly developed cells. They die in the process and become flat and cornified.

These dead cells form the corneum. The epidermis varies in thickness from 0.07 mm over most of the body to as much as 1.4 mm on the soles of feet.

The line of demarcation between the epidermis and the dermis is distinct. It is marked by a basement cell layer and the stratum germinativum. The demarcation is usually irregular and the dermal hillocks, where the dermis pushes into the epidermis, are called *dermal papillae.*

The distinction between the dermis and the subcutis is much less distinct. Although measurements of the dermal thickness are difficult to make, it averages between 1 to 2 mm in thickness over most of the body; it is thinner on the eyelids and prepuce (less than 0.6 mm), but it may reach a thickness of 3 mm or more on the palms and the soles.

The Cutaneous Vascular System

The cutaneous blood supply is derived from a plexus of small arteries lying in the deepest part of the dermis and in the more superficial layers of the subcutis. This plexus of large arterioles and small arteries is usually referred to as the *deep cutaneous vascular plexus*. From the deep plexus, single more or less straight arterioles ascend to the region of the dermal papillae. They branch throughout their course especially as they approach the dermal papillae, where they form the *superficial vascular plexus*. Papillary arterioles send off branches into the individual papillae, which terminate in a capillary net high in the top of the papillae. From there, venules collect blood and join the venous limbs of the superficial vascular plexus. The blood is then collected in the larger veins of the subcutaneous tissue.

The walls of arterioles extending into the dermal papillae contain encircling layers of smooth muscle cells throughout their length. Arterioles lying deeper in the dermis usually possess several layers of smooth muscle fibers. Venules and veins are also muscularized although not as extensively as the arterioles.

In addition to supplying nutrients to the dermis and the epidermis and assisting in the regulation of the blood pressure, the cutaneous vascular system serves an important role in the regulation of body temperature when the skin temperature is between 30° C and 35° C. Certain areas of the brain adjust the amount of heat that is lost from the skin surface in order to maintain body temperature at a relatively constant 37° C by regulating the caliber of the arterioles in the superficial vascular plexus. When the environmental temperature is low and excessive heat loss threatens to reduce the body temperature below normal, the cutaneous arterioles constrict, forcing the blood away from the surface of the skin. When heat loss is too low and

body temperature might rise above normal, as in a warm environment, the cutaneous arterioles dilate, allowing the blood to circulate close to the surface of the skin, thus increasing the heat loss.

Regulation of the arteriole caliber in this type of heat regulation is accomplished by the sympathetic innervation of the arterioles and venules. However, smooth muscle of the cutaneous vascular system may also respond directly to temperature changes. When warmed the smooth muscle elements relax, allowing more blood to flow in the outer layers of the skin. Thus, the hands become red when held in hot water. The direct effect of cooling constricts the smooth muscle elements and causes the skin to appear pallid.

The Cutaneous Nerve Supply

All skin and visceral organs receive sensory innervation from myelinated nerve fibers (usually 5 to 8 μ in diameter) whose terminations are not encapsulated or of a specialized structure (Weddell & Miller, 1962). The fibers lose their myelin sheaths, and branch until they finally terminate in the *free nerve endings* that are too small to be seen, even under the most high-powered light microscope. They most frequently end among the cells of the superficial layers of the dermis and perhaps also in the lower layers of the epidermis. The endings appear to form a dense network of fine branches—the *dermal nerve network*. Branches and collaterals of a single fiber may innervate an area of from 3 to 800 mm². Branches from many other nerve fibers may end in the same area, so there is a considerable overlap of the terminal branches of fibers that end in this fashion.

Other myelinated fibers (1.5 to 3.0 μ in diameter) follow the course of the cutaneous arterioles, sending collaterals into the vessel walls at intervals to terminate as a dense nerve net among the smooth muscle cells (Weddell & Pallie, 1954).

Recent evidence indicates that unmyelinated fibers also terminate in the dermis. They appear to end for the most part in the upper part of the neural net formed by myelinated fibers, around the hair shaft in hairy skin, on the piloerector muscle elements of the hair shaft, and among the smooth muscle elements of the cutaneous vascular system (Winkelmann, 1958). Some of the terminals of these fibers show a threshold of response to mechanical or to thermal stimulation that is as low or lower than many of the terminals of the larger fibers supplying the skin.

One variety of encapsulated ending, the *Pacinian corpuscle,* is found deep in the dermis and the subcutis of almost all skin. Pacinian corpuscles are also found in the immediate vicinity of the tendons, around joints, and in the mesentery of the viscera.

The innervation of skin, just described, applies to all skin whether hairy or hairless. However, hairy and hairless skin exhibit some differences. These differences are emphasized in the following sections.

In hairy skin each hair follicle is innervated by 5 to 12 sensory nerve fibers whose diameters vary between 8 and 12 μ—some of the largest myelinated sensory fibers. A single fiber may also send branches to several hairs. These fibers form a dense network around the shaft of the hair follicle so they are ideally placed to be stimulated when the hair shaft is moved.

Hairless skin has the same innervation characteristics as hairy skin, except that it lacks hair follicle receptors. In their place are nerve terminals that have a variety of organized epithelial capsules about them, for example, Krause end bulbs, Ruffini cylinders, Golgi-Mazzoni endings, and so on. They are found in the conjunctiva, lips, breast nipple, the plantar surfaces of the hands and feet, and the genitalia.

More than 100 different varieties of encapsulated endings have been described, each named for its discoverer. The profusion of types has led many histologists to suggest that, rather than each being a discrete type, they constitute a continuum of complexity from the simplest to the most complex organization of epithelial investments. The current

trend in histology is to emphasize the similarities among them rather than the differences. Of the numerous end organs described, only a few have morphological features sufficiently constant and distinctive to justify separating them into types. Among them are the dermal nerve network, the hair follicle networks, Pacinian corpuscles, and Meissner corpuscles (Montagna, 1962). All of these have been discussed except the Meissner corpuscles, which are found primarily and in profusion in the dermal ridges of the plantar surfaces of the palms and soles, especially at the tips of the fingers.

One cannot help but wonder what functions are performed by the varieties of encapsulations. Whatever their function, it appears certain that they do not provide nerve terminals with selective devices to permit differentiation of mechanical, thermal, or painful stimuli. Comparisons of the sensitivities of hairless and hairy skin to tactile, thermal, or painful stimuli fail to reveal any differences (Hagen et al., 1953). This fact, considered along with the limited distribution of encapsulated endings, indicates that they cannot function as the sole receptors for any particular primary quality of cutaneous sensation.

SOMATIC SENSORY PATHWAYS

The nervous system of vertebrate animals is composed of two main parts—the *central* and *peripheral* nervous systems. The central nervous system is further subdivided into the brain and the spinal cord. The brain, consisting largely of the cerebral and cerebellar hemispheres, is contained within the skull case. The spinal cord in adult man extends down the vertebral column in the spinal canal for as much as 40 cm (16 in.) and up into the central part of the brain case, where it is known as the brain stem. The upper part of the brain stem is connected to the cerebral and cerebellar hemispheres by large bundles of nerve fibers. These bundles carry to and from the hemispheres impulses that result in

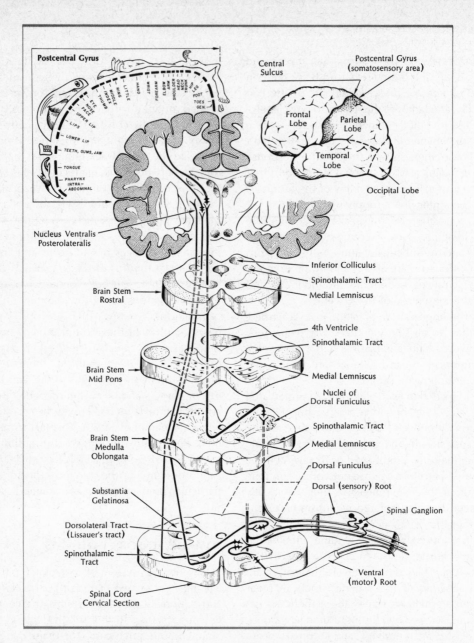

Figure 5.3. The somatosensory neural pathways. Three main pathways exist in the central nervous system for the transmission of impulses from the skin of the body to the upper levels of the central nervous system and the cerebral cortex. Two of these are believed to be involved in conveying impulses to the brain that are aroused by mild mechanical stimulation of the skin. The third pathway is believed to convey impulses that result from thermal and painful skin stimulation. See the text for a detailed description of these pathways.

The nervous system is bilaterally symetrical; thus structures and nerve pathways that exist on one side of the body have a similar representation on the other side of the body. In this figure only those of one side are shown for simplicity.

A uniform dimension scale has not been used throughout this figure. The scale for the section through the cerebral hemispheres is only about one-fourth that used for the sections through the brain stem and spinal cord. (Adapted from Figure 2 of Rasmussen, 1947; and Figure 17 of Penfield & Rasmussen, 1950.)

sensation and also in action (muscular movements) by the organism.

The peripheral nervous system is composed of a large number of bundles of nerve fibers which serve two functions. Some nerves carry *sensory* impulses from receptors located in outlying parts of the body towards the central nervous system. Other nerves carry *motor* impulses from the central nervous system to muscles for movement and, in the *autonomic system,* to internal organs to help regulate the internal environment of the body (heart rate, respiration rate, digestion, glandular secretions, and so on.)

The nerves of the peripheral nervous system enter and leave the spinal cord by 31 pairs of *spinal nerves* and the brain stem by 12 pairs of *cranial nerves.* One member of each pair serves a limited area of one side of the body; the other member of the pair serves a similar area of the opposite side of the body. The area of the body served by a particular spinal nerve is called a *dermatome.* In the human adult each dermatome is irregular in shape; furthermore, the boundaries between dermatomes are not distinct but overlapping.

In general, the cranial nerves serve the olfactory receptors, the eyes and their muscles, the taste buds and muscles of the tongue, the skin and muscles of the face, and the receptors of the ear. Discussion of these pathways will be taken up in the appropriate chapters. Of primary concern here are the nervous pathways between the skin and the cerebral hemispheres.

Spinal Roots

Both the motor and sensory nerves of the peripheral nervous system group together into larger and larger bundles as they approach their connection with the spinal cord. The largest bundle is the spinal nerve. The *sensory* (dorsal root) *ganglion* is composed of the cell bodies of each sensory neuron entering the cord from the dorsal side. The motor fibers leave the cord from the ventral side; their cell bodies are located within the spinal cord itself. The anatomical relationships are shown in Figure 5.3.

Spinal Pathways

The sensory branch of the spinal nerve contains fibers that carry impulses associated with tactile, temperature, and pain sensations from both the skin and the deep structures of the body, as well as those associated with joint movement and muscle stretch. In the peripheral sensory nerve these fibers are intermingled, but once they enter the spinal cord they tend to separate themselves according to function, at least in a gross way. As a result fibers carrying tactile information follow spinal pathways that are separate from that taken by fibers carrying temperature or pain information.

Tactile pathways There are at least two pathways in the spinal cord by which tactile information reaches the brain. In the first pathway, the primary fibers (or first-order neurons—those that enter the spinal cord) turn upward in the *dorsal funiculus* immediately upon entering the spinal cord and continue to the lower margin of the brain stem where they end in the dorsal funiculus *nuclei.* The terminal ends of these primary fibers synapse with the cell bodies of secondary (second-order) fibers that cross to the opposite side of the brain stem and continue in the *medial lemniscus* to the thalamus, at the head of the brain stem. There they end in a specific part of the thalamus—the nucleus *ventralis posterolateralis.* A second synapse is formed here. The axons of the tertiary neurons leave the region of the thalamus and continue on to the cerebral cortex where they end in the *postcentral gyrus* of the parietal lobe.

In the second tactile pathway, primary fibers enter the cord and end in the gray matter of the spinal cord close to their point of entry. The terminals of these primary fibers synapse with the cell bodies of secondary neurons whose axons cross to the opposite side of the spinal cord where they turn toward the brain in the *spinothalamic* tract. In the brain stem, the spinothalamic tract runs close to the medial lemniscus and continues on to the thalamus where these secondary fibers end in the nucleus ventralis posterolateralis, along with the secondary fibers of the dorsal funiculus—this is the medial lemniscus tactile pathway. Terminals of the fibers of the spinothalamic pathways also synapse with the cell bodies of tertiary neurons in the thalamus, whose axons continue on to the postcentral gyrus of the cerebral cortex.

Why two pathways have evolved to carry tactile information to the brain, can only be surmised. There is evidence, however, that the spinothalamic pathway is mainly concerned with general tactile sensibility whereas the dorsal funiculus pathway is concerned with the fine localizing and discriminatory aspects of tactile sensibility (Everett, 1965).

Temperature and pain pathways   The primary fibers that carry information about temperature and pain are supposedly smaller in diameter and less heavily myelinated than those that convey tactile information. As these primary fibers enter the spinal cord, they send branches up and down the spinal cord for three or four segments. The short branches form the *dorsolateral* (Lissauer's) tract. Terminals of these branches and the cell bodies of secondary neurons form an immediately adjacent structure—the *substantia gelatinosa*. Secondary axons cross to the opposite side of the spinal cord where they ascend toward the thalamus in the lateral part of the spinothalamic tract. Where these secondary fibers terminate is not known; it is questionable that tertiary fibers reach the cerebral cortex. Only a few reports have been made of electrical activity in the cortex evoked by thermal or painful skin stimulation. However, Rose and Mountcastle (1959) state that all sensory input to the thalamus is relayed to the cortex.

A word of caution should be injected at this point. The somatic pathways from the skin have been drawn as though they were wires in a cable with fixed connections at each synapse. Actually, the nervous system does not have that functional configuration at all. At each synapse the terminals of many fibers, some exciting and others inhibiting, end on the cell bodies of successive neurons. The pattern of neural activity is not merely relayed but may be drastically changed at each synapse.

Somatic Cortical Projection Area

It should be clear from Figure 5.3 that the entire surface of the body is represented along the postcentral gyrus of the cerebral cortex. The fibers that carry impulses from the skin to the cortex cross from one side of the spinal cord or brain stem to the other so that the left half of the body is represented in the right cerebral hemisphere and the right side of the body in the left hemisphere.

Furthermore, the amount of cortex devoted to a particular site on the skin varies from one part of the body to another. As will be shown later, there is a high correlation between point localization and two-point discrimination on a particular skin site and the amount of cortex devoted to the site.

In general, electrical activity observed in the postcentral gyrus or sensations produced by electrical stimulation of the postcentral gyrus are of a tactile quality. Only rarely have thermal sensations been reported to result from electrical stimulation of the cortex; pain never has been.

TACTILE SENSITIVITY

One of the reasons given for neglect of the study of the cutaneous senses is that the receptors are so readily available for stimulation that their investigation does not carry the challenge afforded by the elaborate receptor machinery of the special senses—vision and audition. However, it is clear from Figure 5.2 that getting the stimulus to the skin receptor involves no fewer problems than stimulation of the eye or the ear. Manipulations carried out at the skin surface will be modified by the mechanical properties of the tissue between the stimulator and the receptors. Pushing a probe into the skin, for example, will cause the tissue to be displaced laterally, as well as downward in front of the probe. Tissue will also be displaced upward around the probe, as when a finger is poked into soft mud. The extent to which these mechanical events influence tactile sensation depends on many factors. Among them are the thickness of the corneum, the plasticity of the tissue of the epidermis and dermis, and the character of the substrate—whether bone, tendon, muscle, or a vascular bed.

Tactile Receptors

The principal receptor organs for arousing tactile sensations are the hair follicle endings in hairy skin and, probably, Meissner corpuscles in hairless skin. One need only move a hair slightly to be satisfied that a tactile sensation is aroused. The evidence that Meissner corpuscles are involved in touch is indirect. Their density in the finger tips agrees with the small two-point limen reported there. Also, Cauna (1968) has described their relationship with the surrounding tissue such that each corpuscle is discretely sensitive to stimuli applied to only one point on the skin.

Stimulation of the dermal nerve network is also perceived as touch. Tactile sensations as well as pain can be elicited from mechanical stimulation of the cornea of the eye (Kenshalo, 1960) and from mucous membranes where the only nerve terminals present are those of the dermal nerve network. There is evidence to suggest that both the dermal nerve network and the Pacinian corpuscles located in the subcutis are the receptive organs involved in sensations of vibration. Whether other endings, especially the other encapsulated ones of hairless skin, are involved in tactile sensations is not known.

Some authors have ascribed deep pressure sensitivity to Pacinian corpuscles or muscle spindle endings (nerve terminals wrapped around striate muscle fibers which discharge when the muscle fiber is stretched). Present evidence does not justify these correlations. The term "pressure sensation" implies a continued sensation in the presence of a maintained pressure on the skin. The Pacinian corpuscle induces activity in its attached axon only while its capsule is being distorted. Neural activity ceases almost as soon as movement of the capsule stops, even though the distortion is maintained (Loewenstein, 1959). Other evidence indicates that the activity from stimulation of the muscle spindle endings does not play a part in the appreciation of limb position (Gardner, 1967) or the sensation of deep pressure sensitivity (Gelfan & Carter, 1967).

Stimulation and Adaptation

During a so-called "mechanical event," force is applied to a substance in order to move it from one position to another. In the case of fluids, or semifluids such as the skin, it is usual to express force in terms of the force per unit dimension, for example, grams per millimeter (tension), grams per unit area (pressure), or simply in terms of the work accomplished, for example, force times distance (the distance a substance has been moved or displaced). These are the static aspects of work. When time is involved, dynamic characteristics of the mechanical event are added. These are velocity or the rate at which the work is accomplished (the first temporal derivative of displacement) and acceleration and deceleration (the second temporal derivative of displacement). The question is, which of these stimulus dimensions best describes the events associated with tactile thresholds and sensations?

Psychophysical studies For many years it was thought that the static aspect (pressure, tension, or displacement) of a force applied to the skin was the stimulus characteristic to which tactile receptors responded. Weber (1846) and his predecessors maintained that the perception of pressure was caused by pressure; thus the sensation could be named for its stimulus. In 1859, Meissner (who first described the capsule in hairless skin) pointed out that pressure itself was imperceptible;

thus when the finger was dipped in a thermally neutral pool of fluid, such as mercury, no sensation was experienced except where the finger emerged from the fluid. For this reason, Meissner contended that tactile receptors responded to a gradient of pressure rather than to pressure per se. The gradient theory was perpetuated by von Frey and Kiesow (1899) when they reported that tactile thresholds appeared to be more closely related to tension than to pressure. They emphasized the tensions that are set up at the edge of the deforming stimulus, where tension gradients are the steepest. Von Frey found further support for his tension hypothesis after he discovered that pulling the skin outward was as good a tactile stimulus as pushing it inward.

In spite of the invention of several devices for the application of tactile stimuli, no one thought to provide a means to record the

response of the skin to the application of mechanical forces. Thus, the question of the nature of the stimulus parameter best suited to elicit tactile sensations is not yet settled, even though the evidence so far implicates

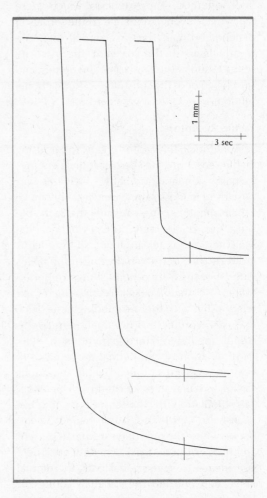

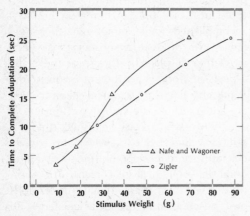

Figure 5.4. Time for complete tactile adaptation as it depends on the weight of the stimulus. Zigler's values (Carleton and Singleton data) were obtained on the hand and forearm using a stimulator surface area of 470 mm[2] whereas Nafe and Wagoner's were taken from 7.5 cm above the knee and with a stimulator surface area of 200 mm[2]. Differences in the surface area of the skin involved in stimulation do not appear to be an important variable in determining adaptation nor, as Nafe and Wagoner showed, the rate of stimulus movement at complete adaptation. (Modified from Figure 11-A from Nafe & Wagoner, 1941b.)

Figure 5.5. Records of the tactile stimuli as they sank into the skin when 35, 17.5, and 8.75 g of weight were applied to 12.5 mm[2] area of the skin of the web between the thumb and index finger. The vertical marks toward the end of each record represent the points where the subject reported that tactile adaptation was complete; he no longer felt the stimulator even though it was still sinking slowly into the skin. This point on each record represents the critical minimum rate of tissue movement required to produce a tactile sensation. (Modified from Figure 14 of Nafe & Wagoner, 1941a.)

movement of the skin tissue rather than maintained pressure or tension.

The tactile sense is subject to adaptation. If you put on a glove and hold the hand still, the strong tactile sensation will diminish rapidly and almost disappear unless the glove pressure becomes intermittent as a result of blood pulsing through the arteries beneath the skin of the hand. The term *adaptation,* used in this way, refers to the reduction in intensity or the disappearance of the sensation when the stimulus is constant. The time necessary for complete adaptation (complete disappearance of a tactile sensation) to the application of various weights when the area of the skin being stimulated is held constant is shown in Figure 5.4. In both experiments, it is clear that the heavier the weight, the longer is the time required for complete adaptation.

Although tactile receptors take a long time to adapt to heavy weights, there is reason to believe that most of the receptors adapt almost instantly to a completely steady stimulus. In other words, most cutaneous receptors apparently respond only to the movement of the stimulator. From some clearcut results, Nafe and Wagoner (1941a, b) concluded that the necessary stimulus for tactile sensations is movement of the tissue. To show this, they obtained simultaneous records of the movement of a weight as it sank into the skin of the web between the thumb and index finger or on the thigh, 7.5 cm above the knee cap, and the tactile sensations experienced by the subject. As may be seen from Figure 5.5, the weight sank rapidly into the tissue but slowed as the tissue began to push back. During this time, the subject experienced a tactile sensation. As the rate of the fall continued to slow, the subject signaled that tactile adaptation was complete. He could no longer detect the presence of a tactile stimulator, even though the stimulator was still sinking slowly into the skin.

The results indicate that adaptation in the tactile sense is a stimulus phenomenon and not a receptor property. The data indicate that

the stimulus characteristic necessary to arouse a tactile sensation is movement of the tissue at a rate greater than a critical minimum. The data also suggest that adaptation of a tactile sensation is the result of a failure of the stimulus to stimulate the tactile receptors rather than failure of the receptors to respond to the stimulus because they have become less sensitive to it. In other words, the stimulus is changing from a dynamic to a static state, and the critical rate of movement represents the transition point as far as the tactile sensation is concerned.

Neurophysiological studies Information obtained from observing neural activity in single peripheral sensory axons provides extremely useful information concerning the functioning of a sense modality, especially when it is used with psychophysical data from the same modality. The usual method involves exposing a peripheral nerve, stripping away the connective tissue surrounding the nerve bundle, and then dissecting out single axons that show activity to stimulation of the area of skin in which they terminate. These are called *single-unit preparations.* Preparations of this type from frogs and higher organisms, including man, provide information about the following: (1) the stimulus dimension(s) to which the units are sensitive; (2) the size of the area of skin to which the unit is responsive—its *receptive field*; (3) differences in the activity of sensory nerves that supply hairy and hairless skin in response to identical stimulations; and (4) different thresholds and patterns of response in different units to mechanical, thermal, and pain stimuli.

Although the technique is powerful, interpretation of the results is difficult, for activity in a peripheral afferent nerve does not necessarily mean that it makes a contribution to the sensory experience. Such activity is used as indirect evidence. Thus, the fact that the stimulus dimension for many of the tactile units is movement of the tissue supports the conclusion of the psychophysical study by

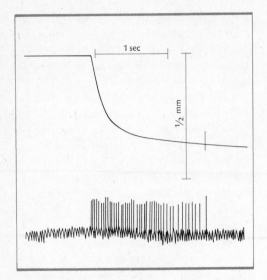

Figure 5.6. A record of a tactile stimulus as it sank into the tongue of a rat. The stimulus weighed 8.75 g and covered 12.5 mm² of the tongue. A simultaneous record of the nerve action potentials from a single tactile fiber terminating in the skin beneath the stimulator was made. Activity in the tactile unit stopped even though the weight was still sinking slowly into the skin. The rate of stimulus movement at the cessation of the nerve activity corresponds roughly to the critical rate of movement shown in Figure 5.5 for the 8.75 g weight. (Modified from Figure 3 of Nafe & Kenshalo, 1958.)

Nafe and Wagoner that tissue movement is the critical stimulus dimension for tactile sensations.

In an effort to extend the Nafe and Wagoner study to animals, peripheral neural activity was relied upon by Nafe and Kenshalo (1958) instead of verbal reports from human subjects. They obtained simultaneous records of various weights (8.75 to 70 g) sinking into the tongues of anesthetized rats or the dorsal skin of frogs and the neural activity in single tactile units supplying the areas. As shown in Figure 5.6, the frequency of neural activity was high at first when the rate of stimulus movement was high, but it decreased as the rate of movement slowed, ceasing altogether as the rate of movement approached zero.

Fibers that show activity only during the time that the stimulus is producing a movement of the tissue are referred to as *rapidly adapting*. Receptors that are rapidly adapting, mechanically sensitive, and presumed to have a relationship with tactile sensations include the Pacinian corpuscles, hair follicle receptors (except those of vibrissae), and the dermal nerve network.

There are also *slowly adapting* receptors found in the skin of some mammals. Not only do the nerve fibers of these receptors show an initial burst of activity while the stimulator is moving, but they continue to discharge at a slow rate for long periods of time (minutes) after the stimulus has apparently stopped moving. It is not definitely known whether slowly adapting receptors exist in human skin.

Both rapidly and slowly adapting mechanoreceptors have receptive fields that range from a single spot of less than 1 mm² on the skin to areas of up to 800 mm². Mechanical stimulation of any part of the receptive field will produce a train of impulses in the fiber, but the sensitivity of the field appears to be greater at its center than toward its margins.

The receptive fields of single fibers innervating the skin overlap considerably. When a point on the skin is stimulated mechanically it is almost inevitable that activity will be produced in a number of individual fibers. The threshold intensity required to activate the fiber varies so that the stronger the stimulus, within limits, the greater the number of fibers that are discharged.

Another relationship exists between the strength of the stimulus and the response of individual fibers; that is, the stronger the stimulus, within limits, the greater is the frequency of impulses in the individual fiber. When these relationships are considered together, a mechanical stimulus of increasing strength will increase the number of nerve fibers responding and will also increase the frequency of activity within each nerve fiber.

The primary difference in the innervation of hairy and hairless skin is that the latter is innervated by Meissner corpuscles rather than hair follicle receptors. Nevertheless, neurophysiological investigations of the mechano-receptors of primate hairy and hairless skin provide no evidence of a difference in the response to identical stimuli applied to the two types of skin that cannot be accounted for by differences in the thickness of the corneum (Iggo, 1963).

There is a marked selectivity of response of most mechanically sensitive units to me-chanical stimuli. Pacinian corpuscles, hair follicle receptors other than vibrissae, and the dermal nerve network terminals, which re-spond to mechanical stimulation, are not

readily excited by even large changes in the temperature of the skin. Slowly adapting mechanoreceptors tend to show responses to changes in skin temperature, but these changes in activity are small compared to their responses to mechanical stimulation.

Touch Thresholds

The sensitivity to touch varies with the mechanical properties of both the skin and the stimulator, as well as the particular site on the skin chosen for stimulation. Touch sensitivity may be demonstrated by use of a

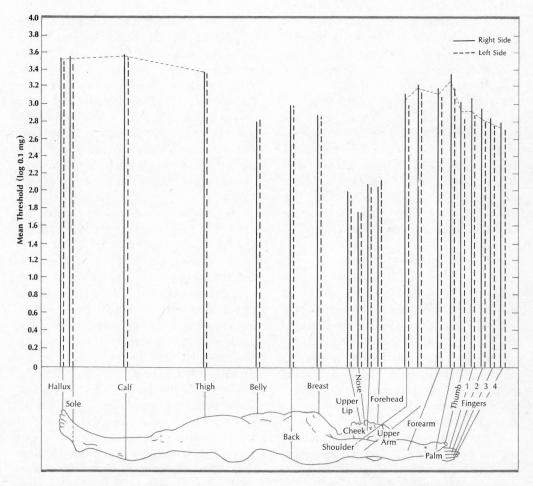

Figure 5.7. Regional variations in the tactile sensitivity of males. Females show a similar distribution of tac-tile sensitivity but were slightly more sensitive than the males. The measurements were made with a set of modified von Frey-type nylon filaments calibrated on a chemical balance for the force exerted. (Figure 10-2 from Weinstein, 1968.)

series of calibrated hairs (von Frey hairs) of varying stiffness fastened perpendicularly to the ends of light wooden handles. The force that will just bend the hair can be measured by pressing the free end of the hair on the pan of a sensitive balance. The diameter of the hair is also measured, with the aid of a microscope, so that thresholds can be expressed in terms of g/mm^2. Von Frey explored an inked grid on the leg and found 15 points within the grid that responded to 33 g/mm^2, or less. An increase in the force did not yield an increase in the number of touch spots, until the force was increased to about 200 g/mm^2. Above this pressure, the subject reported a pricking painful sensation. There were, then, two sets of points within the grid, one set with low thresholds, giving sensations of contact, the other set with high thresholds, giving sensations of pain.

The touch threshold (RL) varies considerably from one body site to another. Part of this variability is attributable to the thickness of the skin and part to the amount of nerve supply. Figure 5.7 shows the touch RLs measured on various parts of the body by calibrated von Frey hairs (Weinstein, 1968). The face was the most sensitive, followed by the trunk, the fingers, and the upper and lower extremities.

Vibratory Sensitivity

Mechanical stimuli applied to the skin have intensive, spatial, and temporal characteristics. Variations in any of these characteristics will produce a change in the quality of the sensation experienced. Changes in the intensity of a mechanical stimulus will lead to a more intense touch sensation. Changes in the location of the stimulator on the skin will cause the touch sensation to be localized at a different point on the body.

Certain qualities of a touch sensation are notable for their temporal features, for example, tickle and vibration. Tickle sensations may be aroused by moving a hair to and fro or by touching adjacent points on the skin in an appropriate temporal sequence (Nafe, 1927). Vibratory sensitivity is a special case of

the tactile sense rather than a sense system in its own right (Geldard, 1940a, b, c, d).

Sensitivity to vibration, like that to touch, is not evenly distributed over the skin surface. If one uses a phonograph needle, inserted in a phonograph cutting head and driven by an oscillator and a powerful amplifier, to explore a small area of skin systematically, some patches of skin will give rise to a lively whirring sensation, whereas others will show little sensation. These spots that are sensitive to vibration usually coincide with spots sensitive to touch (as determined with a von Frey hair).

Frequency limits What, in vibratory sensitivity, corresponds to the 16 to 20,000 Hz sensitivity of the ear? The critical factor in establishing the lower limit of vibratory sensitivity is the frequency at which the sensations of the individual oscillations fuse into a continuous sensation of vibration. The question is not easy to answer experimentally and all experimenters have not meant the same thing by "lower limit." The values reported range from 10 to 80 Hz (Geldard, 1940c).

The question of what is the upper limit of vibratory sensitivity is even more obscure than that of the lower limit. No one really knows what it is. Unlike the lower limit, which depends on the definition of a sensation, the determination of the upper limit is complicated primarily because it is difficult to design the proper apparatus. Mechanical vibrators with sufficient mass (to move the skin at high frequencies) and structural strength (to hold together) are difficult to activate with the necessary amplitudes of vibration at high frequencies.

Values of the upper limit of vibratory sensitivity range from 640 to 8192 Hz, and Geldard (1953) has reported bursts of vibration at frequencies as high as 10,000 Hz. In each instance, however, the upper limit was imposed by the mechanical characteristics of the stimulator and not by the ability of the subject to detect the vibration.

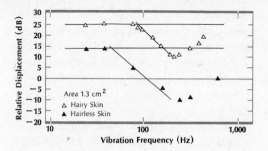

Thresholds, absolute and differential The absolute vibratory threshold (*RL*), as measured by the displacement of the stimulator probe, depends on the frequency of the vibration, the site of the stimulation, and the temperature of the skin. As shown in Figure 5.8, the vibratory *RL* was relatively high at frequencies up to 40 Hz in hairless skin and 90 Hz in hairy skin (Verrillo, 1966). At higher frequencies the *RL* decreased, reached a minimum at about 250 Hz in both types of tissue, then increased at still higher frequencies. The curve is clearly not a monotonic (result of a single continuous variable) function but appears to have at least two components. For hairy skin, it appears that one component operates up to about 90 Hz, followed by the second that takes over at 90 Hz and beyond. The same holds true for hairless skin except that the transition point is at about 40 Hz. Other evidence, given below, shows that the vibratory *RL* is the result of two different types

Figure 5.8. Comparison of vibrotactile absolute thresholds (*RLs*) measured on hairy and hairless skin for a stimulator surface area of 1.3 cm². Hairy skin was less sensitive than hairless skin to all frequencies of vibration, and the frequency at which frequency of vibration became important in determining the *RL* was lower in hairless than in hairy skin. Relative displacement is reported on the vertical axis in decibels. In this instance a decibel is 20 times the logarithm of the ratio of the displacement to a reference displacement of 1 μ. (Figure 3 from Verrillo, 1966.)

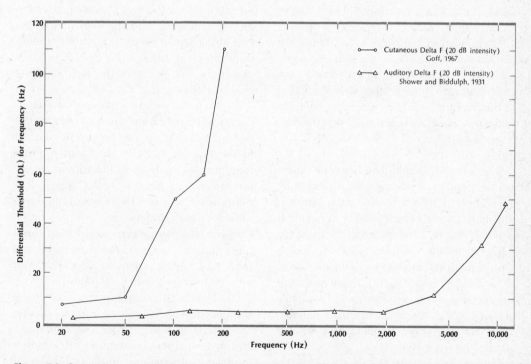

Figure 5.9. Comparison of cutaneous and auditory differential thresholds (*DLs*). The skin and the ear are about equal in their ability to discriminate between frequencies up to 50 Hz. At higher frequencies the ear is vastly superior to the skin. (Modified from Figure 5 of Goff, 1967.)

of receptor—one that functions at a relatively high threshold for low frequencies and a second, of greater sensitivity, that takes over at higher frequencies.

There is an obvious difference between hairy and hairless skin in the vibratory RLs shown in Figure 5.8 (in which the sites of stimulation were the hand and the volar surface of the forearm). The reasons for this difference in the RLs in hairy and hairless skin and the differences in the frequency at which the frequency of vibration became a variable (90 and 50 Hz) are not clear. Comparisons of vibratory RLs with histological and neurophysiological evidence have not yet been done systematically.

Skin temperature is a third variable that affects the vibratory RL. When the skin was maintained at a temperature about 4° C above normal (about 36° to 37° C) the vibratory RL was at a minimum for a 256 Hz vibration. Either a decrease or an increase in skin temperature resulted in an increase in the RL. Perhaps a chemical reaction whose speed is optimal at about this temperature (36° to 37° C) is involved in the process of translating mechanical stimulation of the skin into nerve impulses (Weitz, 1941). Considering the duplex nature of the vibratory RL as a function of the frequency of vibration, what happens to the threshold as a function of skin temperature when frequencies other than 256 Hz are used?

The skin can discriminate between different frequencies of vibration. If, for example, a vibration of 100 Hz is used as a standard, the subject feels one of 150 Hz as having a different "pitch." The differential threshold (DL), when other frequencies were used as the standard, and the auditory DLs are shown in Figure 5.9 (Goff, 1967). Compared to the ear, the skin is a reasonably good frequency discriminator at low frequencies but deteriorates rapidly at high frequencies (see also Figure 8.20, page 249).

Adaptation   During prolonged exposure to a local vibration, adaptation has been found to occur in vibratory sensitivity (Hahn,

1966). In order to measure the amount of adaptation that occurs, vibratory RLs were measured before and immediately after the skin had been exposed for 25 minutes to an adapting stimulus of 60 Hz. After exposure to the adapting stimulus, the vibratory RL was increased by 20 dB (tenfold). Recovery from adaptation was almost complete within 10 minutes after the adapting stimulus ceased. These data are surprising because vibration applied to the skin stimulates the tactile sense and adaptation to tactile stimuli involves stimulus failure (see p. 131). Several considerations may explain this discrepancy. First, the adaptation effect may be purely mechanical. Prolonged vibration may compact the tissue so that it fails to recover promptly to its normal position after each impact. A second possibility, exclusive of or in combination with the first, is that an adaptive process may occur in the central nervous system.

Electrical stimulation of the skin   Electrical currents are the great "inadequate stimuli." When applied to the skin they excite everything. Under carefully controlled conditions, however, they can be used to produce sensations that feel like the taps of a mechanical stimulator.

In the initial experiments sine wave alternating currents were used. Hahn (1958) pointed out that the rise time of the current in the individual cycles varies when either frequency or intensity of the current (measured in milliamperes) is varied. Hence, it is not possible to assess the effect of these two variables, each independent of the other. However, if square electrical pulses of variable duration are used, pulse intensity and frequency may be varied independently. Also a third variable is added—duration.

The temporal properties of an electrical stimulus determine, at least in part, whether it will arouse touch or pain. For example, electrical square pulse stimuli of 100 Hz may produce only painful sensations even at threshold intensities, but when the frequency is raised to 1000 Hz, they may produce tactile sensations even at intensities considerably above threshold. Short pulses (less than 0.5 msec duration) tend to be more painful than longer ones, probably because the shorter pulses require higher intensities to produce a sensation. The pain that occurs with high pulse intensities is associated with a breakdown of the electrical resistance of the skin at a small point, causing a high current density at that point (Gibson, 1968). The lowest electrically induced tactile *RL*, in terms of the pulse duration necessary to arouse a tactile

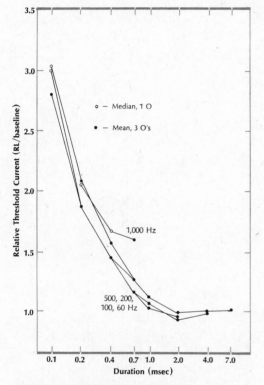

Figure 5.10. The strength and duration of electrical pulses required to produce absolute thresholds (*RLs*) of vibration. The ordinate is the ratio of the intensity of pulses of various durations required to produce *RLs*, to the intensity of a 2.0 msec duration pulse *RL* (baseline). Thus, almost three times the intensity was required to produce an *RL* when the pulse duration was 0.1 msec as when it was 2.0 msec. Unlike the mechanical vibration *RL* shown in Figure 5.8, the electrical vibration *RL* was independent of the frequency but depended on the duration of the individual pulses. (Figure 1 from Hahn, 1958.)

sensation, has been found with pulses of about 2 msec duration, regardless of their frequency, as is shown in Figure 5.10 (Hahn, 1958).

Another interesting aspect of the results appearing in Figure 5.10 is that the electrically aroused vibratory *RL* is not a function of pulse frequency. These results are contrary to those achieved if vibratory sensations are mechanically induced, where frequency markedly influences the mechanical vibratory threshold. This difference suggests an interesting hypothesis: Mechanical stimulation has its principal effect on the tactile receptive structures, whereas the electrical stimulus has its principal effect directly on the sensory nerve fibers. That is, electrical stimulation by-passes the receptive structure.

Receptors The receptors responsible for mechanical vibratory sensitivity have been the subject of both psychophysical and neurophysiological investigations. The mechanical vibratory *RL*, shown in Figure 5.8, appears to be a duplex function of the frequency of vibration. It is as though two receptive elements, each with different sensitivities to mechanical vibration, combine to form the *RL* curve. An analogy is the visual dark-adaptation curve in which cone function determines the early part of the curve and rod function the latter part (see p. 284).

In order to identify the possible nerve terminal configurations responsible for the duplex vibratory *RL* curve, psychophysical measurements of the vibratory *RLs* of skin tissues at various sites of the body were compared (Verrillo, 1968). Verrillo found that tissues gave a duplex curve when the dermal nerve network and Pacinian corpuscles were the sole nerve terminal configurations. When a tissue was used that lacked Pacinian corpuscles (the topside of the tongue tip) the vibration *RL* did not decrease at frequencies between 90 to 300 Hz, as it did in the other tissues.

Neurophysiological studies have also implicated the Pacinian corpuscle with mechanical vibratory sensitivity at the higher frequencies. The Pacinian corpuscle has a high threshold to vibration at frequencies below 60 Hz, a low threshold at 250 Hz, and an elevated threshold at still higher frequencies (Mountcastle et al., 1967).

Localization and Two-point Threshold

We frequently speak of an object touching our hand or coming in contact with our face. How do we know which part of our body has been contacted? How accurate is this localization? As in vision, where each small area of the retina is represented in a particular part of the visual cortex of the brain, so in somesthesis each part of the body surface is represented in a particular part of the somesthetic cortex. There is a topographical arrangement of loci so that the skin is represented in an orderly fashion in the somesthetic cortex (see Figure 5.3). Some areas of skin, such as the fingers, lips, and tongue, are much more densely innervated than others. These areas of denser innervation are represented by larger areas of somesthetic cortex.

A partial answer to the question of what body part has been touched is that the activity in a particular part of the somesthetic cortex resulting from stimulation of a particular body part provides the local sign and makes stimulus localization possible. This is supported by

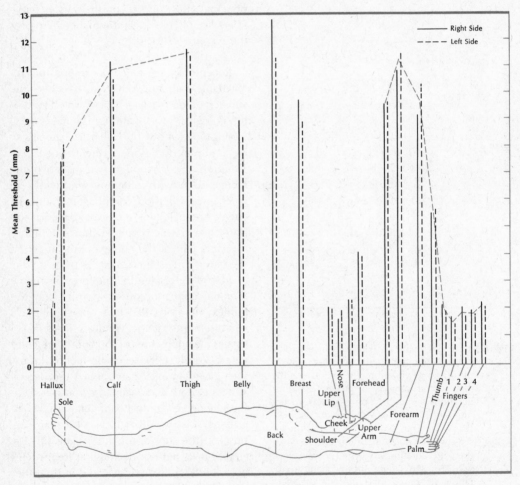

Figure 5.11. Regional variations in point localization of males. The height of each bar represents the size of the difference, in mm, between the reference stimulus and the test stimuli that the subject would accept as located at the reference stimulus. (Figure 10-6 from Weinstein, 1968.)

the fact that mild electrical stimulation of a point on the somesthetic cortex will cause a sensation, usually tingling, which is localized in the body part served by that part of the cortex. If stimulation is applied to the hand area of the cortex, the sensation is localized in the hand, not in the cortex.

The accuracy of point localization is not evenly distributed over the body surface. Figure 5.11 shows that localization is most accurate in the area of the nose and mouth and least accurate on the back. The correlation between accuracy of localization at various skin sites and the amount of area of somesthetic cortex representing that body part is about +0.76 (Weinstein, 1968).

Another kind of tactile acuity, like point localization, is the ability to resolve tactile stimuli separated by very small distances along the skin. The minimum spatial separation of the two points that is judged as two is called the *two-point limen* (threshold). A low two-point limen is essential to such activities as reading Braille, judging fabrics, or determining the texture of objects by feel. Like point localization, the two-point limen varies at different skin sites, and there is a high correlation between two-point sensitivity and the amount of the cortex devoted to the representation of the body part. In contrast to point localization (the nose and mouth yield the smallest errors), the fingers are most acute in two-point discriminations, followed by the areas around the mouth and nose.

Another feature of the two-point discrimination, and somewhat less apparent in point localization, is the proximodistal gradient of two-point sensitivity on all limbs. Thus, the fingers show greater tactile acuity than the forearm, upper arm, and shoulder, and the toes show greater tactile acuity than the calf and thigh.

Interaction of Tactile Stimuli

Tactile stimulation of skin areas adjacent to a main stimulus area produces a variety of modifications in the sensation of the main stimulus. The stimulus may appear to move from one location to another—cutaneous *phi phenomenon;* the sensation of an adjacent stimulus may diminish or completely cancel the sensation produced by the main stimulus—*inhibition;* an adjacent stimulus may enhance the effects of the main stimulus—*summation;* and summation and inhibition may occur simultaneously in the tactile sense—*funneling.* Whether such interactions are phenomena of the peripheral or central nervous system is not clear, although present facts implicate both locations.

Phi phenomenon The cutaneous phi phenomenon is like the visual phi phenomenon (see p. 526) in many respects. It depends upon the interval between the onsets of the stimuli (interstimulus onset interval, ISOI), their duration, and the distance between them. For example, one vibrator can be placed at the wrist and another on the forearm, 15 to 20 cm away. If single pulses with an ISOI of approximately 100 msec are used, a sensation is produced that appears to move from one site of stimulation to the other (Sherrick, 1968). Other combinations of ISOI and dura-

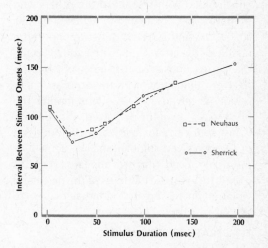

Figure 5.12. The interstimulus interval and stimulus durations required for optimal movement (phi phenomenon). The squares are the data of Neuhaus for visual movement. The circles are the data for tactile movement. (Figure 5 from Sherrick & Rogers, 1966.)

tions that produce good movement are shown in Figure 5.12.

An interesting comparison is made in Figure 5.12 between ISOIs and stimulus duration for tactile and visual movement. The conditions that maximize the visual and tactile apparent movement are similar enough to suggest that they are not specific to a modality, but result from the operation of a common set of neurological principles.

Inhibition, summation, and funneling
When a vibrating needle is brought in contact with the skin of the arm, traveling waves are set up in the skin that involve the whole arm (von Békésy, 1959). However, the sensation is felt only at the point of the stimulator contact. The sensations that should be experienced from the traveling waves in the skin do not occur. Apparently, the effect of the neural activity set up at areas other than the point of contact is somehow blocked (inhibited).

Funneling (simultaneous inhibition and summation) occurs when an array of vibrators placed on the forearm are started simultaneously (von Békésy, 1959). When each is equally loud with respect to the others, and they are set to vibrate in one-octave steps (20, 40, 80, 160, and 320 Hz), only the one in the middle of the array is felt, with a judged pitch that corresponds to its frequency of vibration (80 Hz). Stimulation from the other vibrators is not perceived and does not modify the pitch sensation of the perceived vibrator. This is not so for the intensity aspect (loudness) of the perceived stimulation. The activity of the unperceived vibrators appears to add to (summate with) the loudness of the perceived vibration, increasing its loudness.

TEMPERATURE SENSITIVITY

One of the vital processes of any organism is the regulation of its body temperature. This is particularly true in those organisms that maintain a constant body temperature (homotherms). Two general mechanisms have evolved which help the organism maintain a set body temperature regardless of the environmental temperature conditions. The first, an automatic process, controls processes such as heat production by changes in metabolism, peripheral thermal conductance (regulation of the cutaneous vascular system), shivering and sweating. The second, primarily in man, is the use of external devices such as clothing and air conditioning to help control the demands placed upon the automatic temperature regulating system. The proper operation of both mechanisms depends, to a considerable extent, upon information provided by the cutaneous temperature sensing mechanism. The available evidence seems to indicate that there is one common temperature-sensing mechanism, which contributes both to the process of body temperature regulation and to the awareness of the environmental thermal conditions.

Receptors

In spite of intensive histological examinations of skin over the past one hundred years, there is no evidence that clearly implicates specific structures in the reception of thermal stimuli. Examinations of the tissue beneath warm and cold spots with light microscopes have failed to reveal structures other than the terminals of the dermal nerve network and clusters of arterioles and capillaries.

In spite of the lack of a specific structure to associate with temperature reception, it is possible to locate the depth of thermal receptors beneath the skin surface by either one of two means. Both methods require information about the rate at which temperature changes are transmitted through skin tissue. The depths of the receptive elements for both warm and cool sensations have been calculated to be 150 to 200 μ beneath the skin surface (Hensel, Ström, & Zotterman, 1951; Hendler & Hardy, 1960). The older notion that warm receptors are located deeper within the skin than the cold receptors is in error.

The important variable in thermal stimulation is the temperature of the tissue at the site of the receptor, approximately 150 to 200 μ beneath the surface. This is difficult to measure directly but may be approximated by calculation if the temperature of the skin surface is known (Hensel, 1952). However, uncontrolled factors may affect the calculations, for example, the rate of blood flow through the cutaneous vascular system, which is also about 150 to 200 μ beneath the surface, and the thickness of the corneum.

Physical Considerations in Thermal Stimulation

The reports on the sensitivity of human skin to changes in its temperature have not been even in general agreement. This can be attributed, at least in part, to the diverse methods that have been employed experimentally to manipulate skin temperature and the equally diverse methods of recording and reporting the stimulus temperatures—either of the stimulus object or the skin surface.

Two primary methods for experimentally controlling skin temperature are the application of conducted heat, as when a temperature controlled object is brought in contact with the skin, and radiant heat, as when the infrared wavelengths from a heater or the sun are directed at the skin.

Two techniques using conducted heat to change skin temperature have involved dipping the fingers or arms into thermostatically controlled water baths, and covering various areas of skin (less than 1 mm² to larger than 20 cm²) with a hollow metallic chamber through which temperature controlled water is circulated (a *thermode*). Recently, the Peltier effect has been incorporated in a new type of conducted heat stimulator. Heating or cooling can be produced, relying on the Peltier effect, when direct current is passed through the junctions of two dissimilar electrical conductors. The amount of current determines the rate and extent, and the polarity of the current determines the direction of the temperature change. Kenshalo (1963) has described an electrical circuit which will permit the Peltier device to maintain any skin

temperature within the physiological range, to an accuracy of $\pm 0.012°$ C. The device will also produce changes in skin temperature of as little as 0.05° C up to 20° C at rates up to 2° C/sec.

In many experiments the stimulus temperature reported is that of the water bath, the water circulating through the thermode, or the surface of the thermode, apparently on the assumption that these reflect the temperature of the skin. It is a false assumption. Skin temperature is affected not only by the temperature of the stimulating surface, but also by the *specific heat* and the *thermal conductivity* of the surface material. Specific heat is the heat required to raise a unit volume of a substance by 1° C, and thermal conductivity is the ability of a substance to transfer heat energy through itself. Thus, wood and brass, each at 15° C, do not feel equally cool, and water and air each at 40° C do not feel equally warm.

Radiant heat energy from electric lamps has been used to change skin temperature and to produce warm sensations. Dry ice has been used to absorb heat and produce cool sensations. These methods have the advantage that they can be used to stimulate very large or very small areas of skin. They have the disadvantage that the intensity of the radiation must be reported in cal/sec–cm² and as yet there is no convenient method of measuring skin temperature directly during radiant stimulation. The change in skin temperature (ΔT) produced by a particular intensity of radiation for a specified interval of exposure can be calculated (Lipkin & Hardy, 1954). In order for the calculation to be accurate, factors such as the amount of radiation absorbed by the skin and the thermal inertia of the skin must be taken into account.

Another important variable to consider, in addition to methods of stimulation, when quantitative measurements of temperature sensitivity are sought is the size of the skin surface to which a ΔT is applied. A ΔT applied over a small area (less than 1 cm²) does not produce the same change in the temperature of the subsurface tissue as the same ΔT applied to a larger skin surface area. For example, a brass cylinder tapered at one end so as to contact a skin surface of 2 mm² and heated to 40° C will produce only a slight temperature rise in the tissue 200 μ beneath the surface. Another brass cylinder, at the same temperature, but having a 100 mm² stimulating area, produces a larger temperature rise beneath the surface. Similar effects occur with variations in the surface area to which radiant energy is applied.

Adaptation

Thermal adaptation is the reduction in the intensity of the thermal sensation with continued exposure to a constant temperature. When we first step into a hot bath the sensation of warmth is usually intense. As we sit down in the bath water and remain there quietly, we notice that the warm sensation has diminished. This is, of course, due in part to the cooling of the bath water, but it is also due to adaptation of the temperature receptors. To demonstrate this, slide farther down in the bath. A warmer sensation is experienced in the newly immersed skin than in the adapted area.

Adaptation to mild temperatures may become complete; that is, the warm or cool sensation may disappear completely with continued exposure to that temperature. A number of questions should immediately occur to us about thermal adaptation, such as: (1) What are the limits of skin temperature to which complete adaptation can occur? (2) What is the rate of adaptation? (3) Are the temperature limits for complete adaptation fixed or can they be changed? (4) How does the initial skin temperature affect the rate of adaptation to higher or lower temperatures? Answers to these questions are important in describing one aspect of human temperature sensitivity and the operation of temperature receptors.

The usual method used to investigate thermal adaptation has been to place thermodes on the skin at various extreme temperatures and then to note the time required for the thermal sensations to disappear. Using this method, Holm (1903) found that adaptation was complete to an applied temperature of 45° C after 152 seconds and to 5° C after 210 seconds. Less extreme temperatures required less time. Gertz (1921) has reported a narrower range for complete adaptation, namely from 15° C to 40° C, whereas Hensel (1950) was unable to obtain complete adaptation to temperatures lower than 19° C. Several difficulties are inherent in the procedures used by these investigators. The most important is that subjects have difficulty attending to the stimulus for 1 minute, let alone 30 to 40 minutes.

Kenshalo and Scott (1966) adapted the Peltier stimulator so that the up and down method (see p. 20) might be used to investigate the temporal course of adaptation. Thoroughly trained subjects were instructed to maintain the temperature of the stimulator on the forearm at a "just detectably warm"

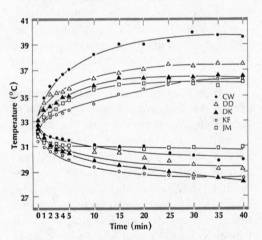

Figure 5.13. The temporal course of thermal adaptation to just perceptably warm and cool stimuli starting from a T_0 of about 32.5° C. The temperature limits of complete adaptation were about 29° to 37° C although some individuals adapted completely to temperatures as high as 40° C. The differences between individuals appear to be due to unique characteristics of the individual rather than variability of the measurements. (Figure 1 from Kenshalo, 1970a.)

or "just detectably cool" sensation by moving a two-way switch. As the subjects adapted to a given temperature, they changed the stimulator to a new temperature, so that the rate of change of the stimulator temperature could be used as an index of the rate of change of adaptation. As shown in Figure 5.13, the subjects started with a normal skin temperature (T_o) of approximately 32.5° C; they changed the temperature of the stimulator rapidly toward either warm or cool during the first 10 minutes or less of adaptation. Beyond that time, the rate of adaptation was slow. After 30 to 40 minutes, the subjects made no further changes in the temperature of the stimulator. The temperature extremes of about 29° and 37° C therefore represent the temperature limits of complete adaptation. Although the range of complete adaptation generally lies between 29° and 37° C, there is evidence, from studying Figure 5.13, that each subject has a different range. For example, the range for CW (filled circles) is 30° to 40° C, but is only 30° to 35° C for JM (open squares). It is not likely that this difference represents different criteria for "just detectably warm" or "just detectably cool" because the warm and cool RLs of these thoroughly trained subjects did not vary by more than 0.1° C.

The data indicate that the range of complete thermal adaptation is from about 29° to about 37° C for most subjects. Outside of this range, persisting cool and warm sensations occur no matter how long the stimulator is left in place on the skin.

Physiological Zero and the Neutral Zone

It should now be apparent that the human thermal receptive system does not respond like a good absolute thermometer. It adapts, and within a narrow range of temperatures, it adapts completely. This leads to another concept, that of *physiological zero* (T_o). As usually defined, T_o is a skin temperature that is thermally indifferent, that is, a temperature to which the subject reports neither warm nor cool. On either side of T_o is a narrow range of temperatures through which the skin temperature may be changed, even rapidly, without evoking a thermal sensation. This is called the *neutral zone*. The size of the neutral zone may be as little as 0.01° C or as large as 8° C depending upon the particular value of T_o, the size and location of the surface stimulated, and the rate of change of the stimulus temperature.

There may be considerable variation in T_o over the body surface at any one time. For example, the ear lobe may have a T_o of 28° C whereas the forehead or cheek may have a T_o of 35° C. In both instances, the subject feels neither warm nor cool at these particular body locations.

On the forearm T_o may be shifted through a narrow range of temperatures, generally 29° C to 37° C. It is not known whether similar limits exist at other locations of the body. The range of skin temperatures within which complete thermal adaptation occurs represents the range of temperatures through which T_o may be shifted provided sufficient time for adaptation is allowed, or the imposed change in temperature is sufficiently slow (less than about 0.007° C/sec on 20 cm² of the forearm).

Thermal Thresholds

No one value suffices as the RL for warm or cool sensations because thermal RLs vary with the conditions under which they are measured. In this section, the effect of three major conditions of measurement are considered: (1) skin temperature; (2) the rate of change of the stimulus temperature; and (3) the size of the area stimulated.

The smallest RL yet reported for warm sensations is an increase in skin temperature ($+\Delta T$) of 0.003° C and for cool sensations, a decrease ($-\Delta T$) of 0.004° C (Hardy & Oppel, 1937, 1938). In both measurements the entire ventral surface of the body above the waist was exposed to the radiant energy. Exposure of smaller areas results in larger RLs because of the powerful spatial summation capabilities of the temperature-receptive system (see p. 146).

Skin temperature The temperature to which the skin is adapted determines the sensation experienced when a ΔT occurs. Within the T_o zone, and after adaptation is complete, a small $+\Delta T$ or $-\Delta T$ in temperature is felt as warm or cool. When the skin has been adapted to temperatures outside the range of T_o, the warm or cool sensation persists indefinitely, although some adaptation occurs. At these adapting temperatures, a small ΔT increases or decreases the persisting sensation. For example, if the skin has been adapted to 40° C, a warm sensation is experienced no matter how long adaptation is allowed. A small $-\Delta T$ (0.5° C) is felt as a decrease in the persisting warm sensation, not as a cool sensation. A small $+\Delta T$ intensifies the persisting warm sensation.

The temperature to which the skin has been adapted has profound influence upon the warm and cool RLs outside of the T_o zone. Both Hensel (1950) and Lele (1954) have reported that the warm RL is increased by adapting the skin to low temperatures whereas the cool RL is increased by adapting it to high temperatures.

Similar results, reported by Kenshalo (1970a), are shown in Figure 5.14. These measurements of the thermal thresholds were obtained after setting the Peltier stimulator at the desired adapting temperature for a specific period of time and then changing its temperature by various amounts for short intervals (10 seconds). For example, when the cool threshold was to be measured at an adapting temperature of 28° C, the subject was seated in a chair and the stimulator, set to maintain 28°, was placed on the skin of his forearm. After a 40-minute adaptation period, measurements of the cool threshold were made according to the psychophysical method of limits (see p. 14). The temperature of the stimulator was decreased by regular amounts at 1-minute intervals. The stimulus temperature was maintained for a period of 10 seconds or until the subject reported a cool sensation, whichever was shorter; after that the stimulator was returned to the adapting temperature. The threshold for a cooler sensation at this adapting temperature was about $-0.15°$ C or a reduction in skin temperature from 28° to 27.85° C.

It is immediately apparent from Figure 5.14 that the thresholds of the thermal sense are indeed unusual when compared to those of the other senses. What are RLs and what are

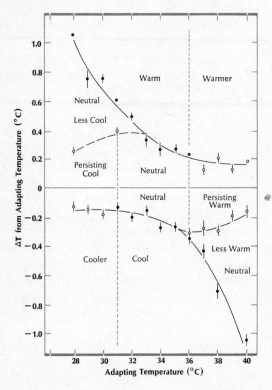

Figure 5.14. The change in the warm and cool RLs and DLs as a function of the temperature to which the skin of the forearm was adapted. Warm and cool RLs are shown by the filled circles. The open circles show DLs. When the adapting temperature of the stimulator was low the subject experienced a persisting cool sensation. A detectably cooler sensation occurred when the temperature of the stimulator was lowered by 0.15° C (DL). When the warm RLs were measured from a low adapting temperature there was first a detectable decrease in the persisting cool sensation, a DL, then thermal neutrality, and finally a warm RL occurred. A similar series of sensations occurred when the skin had been adapted to high temperatures and measurements of the cool RLs were made. (Modified from Figure 3 of Kenshalo, 1970a.)

DLs? Further refinement of the definitions of these terms is required in order to apply them to the thermal sense. As discussed in Chapter 2, a DL is the smallest change in a stimulus dimension that can be detected on an arbitrary percent of the presentations (usually 50 percent). The RL is the limiting case of the DL, for it represents the smallest quantity of a stimulus dimension that can be detected as compared to its absence. If intensity thresholds are viewed from the standpoint of the change in the intensity of the stimulus energy required to excite the receptor, all of the thresholds shown in Figure 5.14 are DLs, for zero thermal energy is about $-273.63°$ C (absolute zero), and there are only increasing amounts of thermal energy from there on up the temperature scale. However, we measure thresholds of sensation, not thresholds of the quantity of the stimulus dimension, and it is a characteristic of the temperature-sensing system that the absence of thermal sensations occurs at skin temperatures between 29° and 37° C. The zero point for the cutaneous thermal sense is T_o, and T_o may assume values between 29° and 37° C. At skin temperatures below the T_o zone a cool sensation persists no matter how much time is allowed for adaptation. After adaptation to these temperatures below T_o a small $-\Delta T$ is detected as being cooler, so this is a DL. A small $+\Delta T$ is detected as less cool, and this also is a DL; however, a $+\Delta T$ that is felt as warm is an RL because of the transition from thermal neutrality to warm. At high adapting temperatures a similar condition exists, except that the persisting sensation is warm and a small $+\Delta T$ is sensed as warmer, a DL. A small $-\Delta T$ is sensed as less warm and is also a DL, but a larger $-\Delta T$ that is felt as cool is an RL, for the sensations were first less warm and then neutral before becoming cool. All thresholds measured in the T_o zone are RLs.

Rate of temperature change The rate at which the temperature is changed during the process of measuring a warm or cool RL has a pronounced effect upon the size of the RL. Hensel (1950), for example, found that the

warm RL at T_o (33.3° C), increased when the rate of warming of the thermode was less than 0.02° C/sec. A further reduction in the rate of warming resulted in a further increase in the RL until, starting from a skin temperature of 33.3° C and using a rate of warming of 0.0083° C/sec, an RL was obtained only after the skin temperature had reached 36° C, close to the upper limit of T_o. The effect of the rate of ΔT on the cool RL is that rates of cooling of 0.007° C/sec become just noticeable only after the skin has been cooled to 29° C, close to the lower limit of T_o.

The effects of the rate of ΔT on warm and cool RLs are shown in Figure 5.15. Warm and cool RLs were measured for skin at normal temperatures ($T_o = 31°$ to 32° C), and the rate of warm or cool ΔT's was varied between 0.01° and 0.3° C/sec. Neither the warm nor

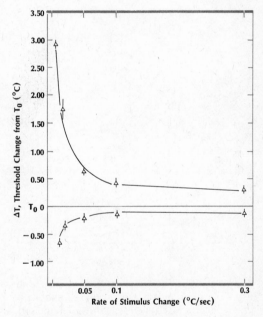

Figure 5.15. The effect of rate of the stimulus temperature change upon the warm and cool RLs measured from a T_o of about 32.5° C on the forearm. The effect of the rate of temperature change on both the warm and cool RLs was small when the rates were greater than 0.1° C/sec. At slower rates of temperature change both the warm and the cool RLs increased, the effect being larger on the warm RL. (Modified from Figure 1 of Kenshalo, Holmes, & Wood, 1968.)

the cool *RL* was markedly affected by rates of ∆*T* of 0.1° C/sec and faster. At rates of ∆*T* slower than 0.1° C/sec, there was a marked increase in the warm *RL*. When a rate of 0.01° C/sec for ∆*T* was used, the *RL* was almost 3° C above normal skin temperature, as is shown in Figure 5.15.

Spatial summation It is a common observation that our sensitivity to ∆*T*s increases with an increase in the size of the exposed surface. For example, it is difficult to determine whether an object is cool, warm, or indifferent if we touch it with a fingertip. However, if the whole hand is placed in contact with the object, we may experience the entire gamut of thermal sensations. Little

work has been done to quantify the relationship between the surface area of stimulation and the thermal *RL*. The implication of the effect of spatial summation on *RL* is that the activity of individual thermal receptors adds together to increase the intensity of the sensation. For example, suppose two adjacent skin areas each have 10 receptive elements. When one area alone is stimulated, the warm *RL* = +0.5° C. When both areas are simultaneously stimulated, the neural activity from the 10 additional receptive elements is somehow added to that of the original 10 and now perhaps *RL* = +0.25° C.

Quantitative functions of spatial summation for both warm and cool stimuli have been described using radiant energy stimulation (Hardy & Oppel, 1937, 1938). The results for the spatial summation of warm stimuli are similar to those shown in Figure 5.16 (Kenshalo, Decker, & Hamilton, 1967). The formula describing these data is

$$I = kA^{-b} + c$$

in which *I* is the threshold intensity of stimulation for warm sensations in cal/sec–cm^2 applied to area *A* in cm^2; *k* is a constant whose values change with the site of stimulation (back, forehead, or forearm); *c* is the warm threshold in cal/sec–cm^2 for very large areas of exposure (greater than 2000 cm^2); and *b* is a constant which represents the degree to which spatial summation takes place. Because *b* ∼ 1 for these data, it indicates that spatial summation is complete and that *A* × *I* = a constant. In other words, as the number of receptive elements doubles, the intensity of stimulation required to produce an *RL* is halved for areas of exposure up to 14 cm^2.

In Figure 5.16, warm *RL*s were also obtained using conducted energy for areas of 1.7, 7.1, and 14.4 cm^2. The *RL*s obtained using conducted energy are related to the *RL*s obtained using radiant energy by calculating the elevation in skin temperature produced by various intensities of infrared radiation (Lipkin & Hardy, 1954). The *RL*s obtained by

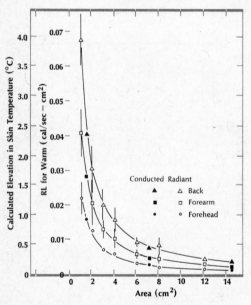

Figure 5.16. Warm *RL*s obtained by nonpenetrating infrared heat (open symbols) and conducted heat (filled symbols) when the surface area of the skin exposed on the back, forearm, and forehead was varied. The elevation in skin temperature produced by various intensities of radiation were computed by the formula given by Lipkin and Hardy (1954). It was possible to compare the thresholds obtained by radiant and conducted energy in this way. (Modified from Figure 1 of Kenshalo, Decker, & Hamilton, 1967.)

using conducted energy agree with those obtained by radiant energy, which demonstrates that there is no unique characteristic in either form of thermal stimulation and that warming of the skin tissue is the necessary factor to produce a warm sensation.

Because the stimulator rests on the skin surface, thermal stimulation by conducted energy involves tactile stimulation as well. Radiant energy, however, involves only thermal stimulation. The close agreement between the RLs from conducted and radiant energy suggests a lack of interaction between tactile and thermal stimulation, a suggestion supported by several investigators (Jones, Singer, & Twelker, 1962; Vendrik & Eijkman, 1968).

A second type of spatial summation, involving widely separated areas of stimulation, has also been shown to occur (Hardy & Oppel, 1937). Simultaneous stimulation of the backs of both hands with radiant energy gave a warm RL with approximately 30 percent less energy than was required to obtain a warm RL from similar stimulation of either hand, individually.

At first glance this type of thermal summation appears similar to the apparent summation encountered in vision when monocular RLs were found to be larger than binocular RLs (see p. 296). The reason for the apparent visual summation is purely statistical. The probability of detecting a flash of light at near-threshold intensity is greater when the flash is presented to both eyes than when it is presented to either eye, individually. However, the evidence suggests that thermal spatial summation involving widely separated areas of skin is of nervous rather than statistical origin. Simultaneous stimulation of the hand and the forehead failed to show the summation effect.

In what part of the nervous system might spatial summation of thermal stimuli take place? Herget, Granath, and Hardy (1941) have suggested that the data could be explained if spatial summation were assumed to occur at two sites in the nervous system. They sup-

posed that the terminal branches of single temperature-sensitive fibers may innervate areas of skin of up to perhaps 6 cm^2. The most peripheral point at which spatial summation could occur is the point at which the terminal branches join to form the stem axon.

In confirmation of Herget's theory, it has been found that a single temperature-sensitive axon (an axon insensitive to other forms of stimulation), in which the activity can be changed by warming or cooling its terminals, may innervate up to 8 individual spots on the skin of rhesus monkeys (Kenshalo & Gallegos, 1967). The spots, each less than 1 mm in diameter, may be separated by as much as 16 mm. When any one of the spots is cooled, an increase in the frequency of nerve impulses is observed in the axon. When several spots are simultaneously cooled by the same amount, the increase in impulse frequency is found to be proportional to the number of spots cooled.

The second locus at which spatial summation of thermal stimuli may occur is at the first or subsequent synapses in the central nervous system. Summation probably occurs at both loci, for warm and cool stimuli may summate over areas of up to about 2000 cm^2 and from widely separated areas, for example, the backs of both hands.

Other variables There are factors other than the three primary ones already discussed that affect thermal RLs (Kenshalo, 1970a). Women show smaller cool RLs during the postovulatory phase of the menstrual cycle than for the period from the onset of menses to ovulation, but only when the skin has been adapted to temperatures above 36° C. No change in the warm RLs has been found at any adapting temperature. Both males and females give smaller cool RLs in the afternoon than in the morning. A change in the warm RLs with a change in the time of day of the measurement has not been demonstrated. Psychological stress, such as the anticipation of a major examination, increased the cool RL, but only when the skin had been adapted to temperatures greater than 36° C. Adrenalin infused into the skin produced cutaneous vasoconstriction, among other things, and caused an increase in the cool RL at adapting temperatures above 35° C and an increase in the warm RL at adapting temperatures below 31° C.

Paradoxical Cold, Warmth, and the Heat Sensation

An interesting phenomenon has been reported in which some cold spots, identified by previous mapping, give a sensation of cold when touched with a hot stimulator (45° C). Von Frey (1895), thinking that arousal of a cold sensation by a hot stimulus represented a paradox, labeled the sensation *paradoxical cold.*

Paradoxical warmth, the arousal of a warm sensation by stimulation of a warm spot with a cold stimulator, would be the opposite of paradoxical cold. The necessary and sufficient conditions for the arousal of this phenomenon have been sought by many investigators with little success. Its existence as a bona fide phenomenon of temperature sensitivity is open to question, although Jenkins and Karr (1957) seem to think that it may occur when the repeated stimulation of a warm spot by a warm stimulus preceeds the application of a cold stimulus.

Paradoxical cold cannot be aroused by applying a hot stimulus to a large area. The closest approximation is a momentary confusion of cold and hot that sometimes occurs when a hand or a foot is plunged into hot water.

Many early investigations of temperature sensitivity sought the necessary conditions for the arousal of the "heat" sensation. This sensation is said to be uniquely different in quality from that of warm and pain. The uniqueness of the heat sensation, as compared with that of intense warm, apparently lies in the addition of a slight stinging sensation, which soon adapts. The threshold of the heat sensation has been reported to range from 40° to 46° C with an average at 42° to

43° C. The threshold for burning heat (pain?) ranges from 43° to 51° C with an average at about 46° to 47° C (Lowenstein & Dallenbach, 1930). These are the temperatures of the water circulating through the stimulator; because perfect heat conduction is never attained, skin temperatures should be expected to be somewhat lower.

Two theories dealing with the mechanism of the heat sensation have been advanced. The older (Alrutz, 1908) suggests that the heat sensation is synthesized by the simultaneous stimulation of warm and cold receptors. The second (Herget & Hardy, 1942) maintains that the unique quality of the heat sensation that differentiates it from warmth—the adapting sting—is mediated by its own receptor type.

The basis of the Alrutz theory is that a hot stimulator arouses a warm sensation and paradoxically arouses a simultaneous cold sensation. The synthesis of heat should therefore be possible by simultaneously stimulating warm and cold spots with mild warm and cool stimuli. One of the clearer demonstrations of synthetic heat is that of the heat grill. Water from two tanks, one at 10° C, the other at 43° C, is circulated through copper tubes so that their temperatures alternate— W C W C W C. The subject places his forearm on the grill; the first sensation reported is usually that of cool, followed by heat, which often disappears after a few seconds and gives way to cold again. Warmth is often experienced at some time during a 10 to 15 second stimulus (Burnett & Dallenbach, 1927). Others have reported that they have synthesized heat by simultaneously applying cold and warm (not hot) stimuli to cold and warm spots on the forearm separated by as much as 15 cm (Alston, 1920). The same effect has also been produced by warm and cold spot stimulation plus mild electric shock (Ferrall & Dallenbach, 1930).

In spite of the impressive evidence presented above, the issue is by no means settled. Others (Jenkins, 1938) have tried to reproduce the results of earlier reports without success. Apparently, the experimental results depend upon the knowledge, attitude, and instructions of the subject, and the conditions of stimulation and the procedures employed. Furthermore, the heat threshold (42° to 43° C) appears to be low compared to the temperature required to stimulate cold spots paradoxically (45° C).

The evidence favoring the second theory of heat—that it is due to its own receptor type—arose primarily from studies of the spatial summation of threshold warm, heat, and cool sensations (Herget & Hardy, 1942.) There was less spatial summation for heat than for either threshold warm or cool sensations. Were cool and warm receptors producing the sensation of heat, as is suggested by the Alrutz theory, the spatial summation rate for threshold heat sensations should have fallen between those of threshold warm and cool sensations. It did not.

Physiological Mechanisms of Temperature Sensitivity

Investigations of temperature sensitivity have taken two different routes in recent years. Psychologists have conducted numerous experiments on the effects of various conditions of thermal stimulation on thermal sensations. Meanwhile physiologists, with the development of neurophysiological methods, have studied changes in peripheral neural activity produced by thermal stimulation. Neither approach can provide a complete picture of the functions of the system. The psychological approach cannot tell us anything about how neural messages of the environmental thermal conditions originate in the nervous system and are conveyed to the brain, and the neurophysiological approach cannot tell us how sensations change when a change occurs in the pattern of neural activity in peripheral afferent fibers. The two methods must be used in close coordination so that a more complete description of the system may be obtained.

How can closer coordination be achieved? The work discussed so far has been concerned with the changes in human temperature sensations that result from changes in the conditions of thermal stimulation. Human subjects cannot, usually, be subjected to the procedures necessary to obtain neurophysiological data. The answer lies in the use of subhuman species to obtain both behavioral measurements of sensation and neurophysiological measures of changes in neural activity.

Behavioral investigations Psychophysical measurements of sensory capacities, conducted on subhuman organisms, involve devising a language, comparable to the human "yes" or "no," by which the animal subject and human experimenter may communicate (see p. 753). The usual method has been to employ an avoidance conditioning method in which the animal is trained to avoid a mild electric shock (UCS) if it detects a stimulus (CS). As the CS becomes less intense, failures to detect it increase until at some arbitrarily determined frequency of failures a threshold is said to be reached.

Investigations of the temperature sense of subhuman species have lagged far behind the investigations of the other senses, perhaps because of the technical difficulties involved in the control of skin temperature. The success of any behavioral technique to measure the thermal sensory capacities of subhuman animals depends on how well the experimenter can present the stimulus without providing simultaneous extraneous cues, a click, a touch, or vibration. The development of the Peltier stimulator (Kenshalo, 1963) has made it possible to maintain and to change the temperature of a patch of skin without extraneous cues.

There is good reason to believe that the temperature sense of cats is not generally distributed over their body surface, yet they can select locations of higher environmental temperature in which to bask, for example. How this discrimination is made is shown in Figure 5.17. The procedure used to measure the cats' sensitivity to warm and cool stimuli was made as nearly like that used to measure human warm and cool RLs as was possible.

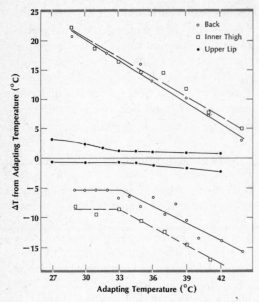

Figure 5.17. The thresholds of a conditioned avoidance response to warm and cool stimuli applied to the shaved skin of the back, inner thigh, and upper lip of cats as a function of the temperature to which the skin was adapted. The cats were insensitive to mild warm stimuli applied to the back and inner thigh. At these sites the skin temperature had to be raised to about 50° C regardless of the adapting temperature before the cats could use skin warming as a cue to avoid electric shock. Somewhat smaller thresholds to cool stimuli were found on the back and inner thigh. These appeared to depend on adapting temperatures above about 33° C. However, they are 40 to 70 times larger than human cool thresholds. Similar measurements, not shown, were obtained from the footpad. In contrast, the upper lip was much more sensitive than either the back or inner thigh to both warm and cool stimuli. Here sensitivity approximates that of the human forearm, considering that the area of skin exposed on the cat's upper lip was smaller than that of the human's forearm. (Modified from Figure 4 of Kenshalo, 1964; Kenshalo, Duncan, & Weymark, 1967; and Brearley & Kenshalo, 1970.)

The stimulator was placed on the shaved skin of different body parts, and the skin was allowed to adapt to temperatures between 27° and 44° C for 40 minutes. After the adaptation period, ΔTs of increasing intensity were presented for 10 second durations at irregular intervals until they were sufficiently intense for the cat to use as a cue to avoid electric shock by lifting its leg (Kenshalo, 1964; Kenshalo, Duncan, & Weymark, 1967).

The upper part of Figure 5.17 shows avoidance conditioned response thresholds to $+\Delta T$s. When the site of temperature stimulation was on the shaved skin of the back, the inner thigh or the footpad, the stimulus temperature had to be raised to almost 50° C, regardless of the adapting temperature (for example, an adapting temperature of 29° C plus an increase in the stimulator temperature of 21° C) before the cats could sense the $+\Delta T$ as a cue to avoid electric shock. (Other evidence also indicates that this 50° C temperature is noxious to cats.) Furthermore, the human pain threshold remains constant at a skin temperature of about 45° C, regardless of the temperature to which the skin has been adapted (Hardy, Goodell, & Wolff, 1951). Given these two facts, it is reasonable to surmise that the cats were responding to pain rather than warmth. The cats could detect much smaller $+\Delta T$s when the stimulator was applied to the shaved upper lip and the measurements of warm sensitivity were repeated (Brearley & Kenshalo, 1970).

Much the same picture of sensitivity to $-\Delta T$s is shown in the lower part of Figure 5.17. When the stimulator was placed on the back, inner thigh, or footpad the thresholds were on the order of $-5°$ to $-9°$ C for low (29° to 33° C) adapting temperatures; larger $-\Delta T$s were required (10° to 18° C) for higher adapting temperatures (35° to 40° C). The upper lip was at least 10 times more sensitive to $-\Delta T$s than the other sites of stimulation.

The sizes of the avoidance thresholds for warm and cool stimuli of the upper lip are sufficiently like those of the human RLs to lead one to believe that these resulted from the stimulation of the feline temperature sense.

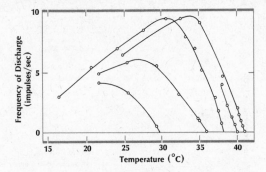

Figure 5.18. The steady-state frequencies of discharge of 5 cold fibers from the lingual nerve of cats measured after 5 minutes of adaptation of the skin of the tongue to temperatures between 16° and 41° C. (Figure 5 from Hensel & Zotterman, 1951.)

The next question concerns the form of the peripheral nerve activity which may account for the behavioral measurements described above.

Thermally sensitive nerves Peripheral afferent nerve fibers that show changes in activity exclusively to changes of skin temperature are referred to here as "warm" or "cold" fibers. It is a short-hand way of referring to the receptor, its attached sensory

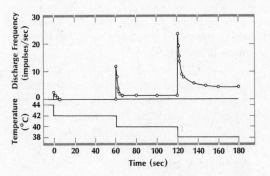

Figure 5.19. The change in discharge frequency of a single cold fiber in the lingual nerve of the cat that resulted from cooling its tongue in 2° C steps from 44° to 38° C. Temperature changes of equal size produced different frequencies of discharge depending on the temperature to which the skin had been adapted. (Figure 9 from Hensel & Zotterman, 1951.)

nerve fiber, and the form of energy specific for its stimulation.

Temperature-sensitive fibers have been found both among the myelinated fibers of 1 to 6 μ in diameter and the very thinly myelinated or unmyelinated fibers.

Myelinated temperature fibers show a regular discharge whose frequency is a function of the static temperature of the skin (the steady-state discharge). Figure 5.18 shows the relationship between skin temperature and the frequency of the steady-state discharge in five different cold fibers. In response to cooling the skin, the myelinated cold fibers show a transient increase in the frequency of their discharge to skin cooling, the amount of which depends on the intensity of cooling and the temperature to which the skin was adapted (Figure 5.19). When the skin is warmed, these fibers show a reduction or complete suppression of their steady-state discharge.

Myelinated cold fibers have been found in the infraorbital and lingual nerves (supplying the face and tongue) of rats, cats, and dogs. They have not been seen in other nerves of these animals, for example, the saphenous, femoral, or clunium nerves of cats (supplying the leg, foot, and inner thigh). Cold fibers have been found, however, in the median and saphenous nerves (supplying the arm, hand, leg, and foot) of rhesus monkeys and the radial nerve (supplying the thumb and back of the hand) of man.

Myelinated warm fibers that show responses opposite to those of cold fibers (that is, an increase in the frequency of activity to warming and a decrease in frequency to cooling) have been found only in specialized areas of skin such as the tongue and bridge of the cat's nose (Hensel & Kenshalo, 1969), and the rat's scrotum (Iggo, 1969).

There are specific temperature fibers among the unmyelinated fiber group as well. In general, these respond like the temperature fibers of the myelinated group. They show a steady-state discharge whose frequency depends on skin temperature, and the cold unmyelinated fibers show an increase in frequency of activity when the skin is cooled and a decrease in frequency when it is warmed. Unmyelinated warm fibers show an increase in frequency when the skin is warmed, and a decrease in frequency when it is cooled. Unmyelinated temperature fibers have been found in the saphenous nerves of cats and the infraorbital nerves of rats, cats, and dogs.

A correlation of behavioral thresholds and neural activities will be made to show how behavioral and neurophysiological methods can be used to complement one another in the interpretation of data. Behavioral evidence shows that responses can be conditioned to mild thermal stimuli applied to the upper lips of cats. The size and form of the threshold curves obtained in these experiments are similar to those found on the human forearm. Responses cannot be conditioned to mild thermal stimuli applied to the inner thigh, footpad, or back of cats. Cold fibers, of the myelinated class, have been found in the nerves supplying the upper lip of cats, but warm fibers have not been found in these nerves. Neither cold nor warm myelinated fibers have been found in the nerves supplying the inner thigh or footpad. Unmyelinated cold and warm fibers have been found in both nerves. Because responses cannot be conditioned to thermal stimuli applied to the inner thigh or footpad and can be conditioned to thermal stimuli of the upper lip and because unmyelinated temperature fibers exist in the nerves supplying both areas of skin, it is doubtful that the unmyelinated fibers contribute in any appreciable way to the experiences of temperature stimulation. Because the upper lip is sensitive to mild temperature changes and the inner thigh and footpad are not, it may be possible that myelinated cold fibers carry the temperature information to which the responses are conditioned. If so, the cold fibers can carry information not only about skin cooling but also about warming. Recall that the steady-

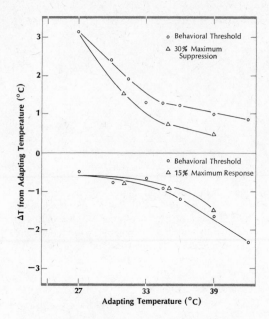

Figure 5.20. Comparison of the behaviorally measured warm and cool thresholds of the cat's upper lip and a constant percent of change in the integrated records of neural activity in small twigs of the infraorbital nerve that innervates the lip. It was assumed that skin warming was signaled to the brain by a reduction in the neural activity (suppression) and that skin cooling was signaled by an increase in neural activity. (Figure 2 from Kenshalo & Brearley, 1970.)

state response of cold fibers is enhanced when the skin is cooled, and suppressed when it is warmed.

In order to test the hypothesis proposed above, measurements were made of the neural response magnitude of fibers supplying the upper lip to warm and cool stimuli of various intensities after the skin had been adapted to temperatures between 27° and 39° C (Kenshalo & Brearley, 1970). The neural code for cooling the skin was assumed to be an increase in neural activity whereas that for warming was assumed to be suppression of activity in the same nerves. Thresholds at each adapting temperature were computed from these response curves to see if they matched the behavioral data shown in Figure 5.17. The result is shown in Figure 5.20. The behavioral warm and cool threshold curves are matched if a 30 percent maximum decrease and 15 percent maximum increase in neural activity, respectively, are assumed to represent the neurophysiological threshold. It is possible that a single temperature-sensing system of cold fibers can convey all of the necessary information to the brain concerning changes in skin temperature.

Because we are at the very edge of scientific progress here, these tentative conclusions may be wrong. More important than the conclusions, however, is the demonstration of the value of using both behavioral and neurophysiological measurements to complement each other in providing answers to common questions.

Specificity of response   The specific temperature-sensitive fibers have come to be looked on as the archetype for cutaneous thermal receptors. However, many fibers are encountered, especially in the saphenous nerves of cats, the median nerves of rhesus monkeys, and the radial nerves of man that show responses to both temperature and tactile stimuli. It is difficult to determine what role these multimodal fibers play in sensation, although there is a tendency to regard them as basically mechanoreceptors that may have their activity altered by changes in temperature (Iggo, 1963).

Theoretical Points of View

Temperature sensitivity and the doctrine of specific nerve energies   Traditionally, the temperature-sensing system is perceived to be composed of two relatively independent systems—one for sensing warm, the other for sensing cold. This point of view arose from the doctrine of specific nerve energies and was given strong support by the discovery of warm and cold spots that exist independent of each other on the skin. However, like the failure of studies using histological methods to demonstrate a morphologically different structure beneath the spots to which temperature-receptive functions could be assigned, studies using neurophysiological methods

have generally failed to demonstrate two functionally different sets of nerve units, one each for warm and cool stimuli (see p. 151). Whether temperature sensitivity is the result of a single or a dual system is still open to debate. The strongest evidence for two systems is still the independent existence of spots sensitive to warm and cool on the skin, but other explanations may account for these.

Stimulation of thermoreceptors   Various theories have been advanced to explain the initiation of thermal sensations. The earliest (Weber, 1846) postulated a temporal thermal gradient to excite thermal sensations; that is, the receptors must be subjected to a changing temperature. However, we have already seen that some thermal sensations may persist indefinitely outside of the range of T_0 and that specific temperature fibers may discharge at a steady rate for several hours even though skin temperature is constant.

Spatial thermal gradients have also been proposed as the necessary requisite to stimulate thermal receptors (Ebbecke, 1917; Bazett, 1941; Lele, Weddell, & Williams, 1954). Each investigation, in a different way, relied on the fact that tissues are at different temperatures at various depths. Thus, if the skin surface is at 32° C, the temperature 300 μ beneath the surface may measure 32.5° C. The receptors were believed to be activated by an alteration in this spatial thermal gradient. Theories which propose that thermal receptor stimulation is made by spatial thermal gradients do not work for the same reasons that the temporal thermal gradient theory will not work. Furthermore, Hensel and Witt (1959) demonstrated that thermal receptors are stimulated by cooling, independent of the intracutaneous temperature gradient. Hensel and Witt used preparations in which a specific temperature fiber innervated a spot on the upper surface of a cat's tongue. Cooling either the upper or lower surfaces of the tongue, or injecting cold saline into the lingual artery, all produced an increase in the activity of the cold fiber. Moreover, Vendrik and Vos (1958) and Hendler and Hardy (1960) have compared threshold warm sensations resulting from nonpenetrating infrared heat with those obtained by heating the skin with radar pulses. Although they do not agree on the effects of the radar stimulation (it is supposed to heat the tissue uniformly throughout its depth), they do agree that spatial thermal gradients could not account for their results.

Another major theory was proposed by Hering (1877). He suggested that the amount of heat conducted to the receptor was the sole stimulus condition necessary to arouse a thermal sensation. He thought of warm and cold as belonging to a single temperature sense and theorized that the receptive organ was capable of a reversible reaction. Heat is always being conducted outward at normal environmental temperatures, and at this rate of heat conduction, the reaction is at equilibrium. Decreasing the outward heat conduction (warming the skin) drives the reaction in one direction whereas increasing outward heat conduction (cooling the skin) drives it in the opposite direction. Both processes adapt so that within a narrow band of skin temperatures the reaction can again achieve equilibrium. A change in heat conduction upsets the equilibrium, and the predominant process engenders a thermal sensation.

Theories of the thermal receptor It is now generally accepted that encapsulated endings of the Krause and Ruffini types play little, if any role in temperature reception. The histological studies of Weddell and his collaborators (Weddell, 1955) leave little doubt that encapsulated endings exist only in hairless skin and cannot be found in hairy skin. Furthermore, Hagen and his coworkers (1953) were convincing in their demonstrations that hairy and hairless skin show no significant differences in comparisons of their warm and cool thresholds.

If not morphologically different nerve terminal structures, then what? Weddell and his coworkers have argued that because a variety of sensations may be aroused by activation of free nerve endings with a variety of stimuli, these are not modality-specific. As evidence for this argument, they report having experienced touch, warm, and cool sensations, as well as pain, from appropriate stimulation of the cornea, which contains only free nerve endings (Lele & Weddell, 1956). Kenshalo (1960) agrees with their reports of producing touch sensations in the cornea but challenges their report of arousing thermal sensations with thermal stimulation of the cornea. Furthermore, the repeated demonstrations of specific temperature-sensitive fibers that innervate either one or a few small spots on the skin argues strongly for specificity of modality, at least for thermal stimulation.

Nonspecificity plus an ill-defined pattern of activity does not appear to be the way to account for the data of temperature reception. Hence the question remains: What are the differences in nerve terminals such that one will discharge when it is distorted by mechanical means and another only when its thermal environment is changed? Two hypotheses seem worthy of consideration, although there is as yet no direct evidence in support of either. The first, the "specific terminal hypothesis," assumes a molecular configuration or other specific feature of the terminal membrane that governs differential responsiveness to thermal and mechanical stimuli. The second, known as the "specific tissue hypothesis," assumes that afferent nerves are essentially alike, but they end in non-neural tissues whose characteristics are responsible for the stimulus specificities observed in the activity of the associated axon. An example of this type of hypothesis is the *vascular theory*, proposed by Nafe (1934) and reviewed by Kenshalo (1970b), in which the smooth muscles of the cutaneous vascular system contract when cooled and relax when warmed. The movement of the vessels initiates activity in the afferent nerves that terminate in the vessel walls.

PAIN

Since the days of von Frey (1895) pain has generally been regarded as a separate sense of the skin, as are those of temperature and touch. However, if it is considered strictly as a sensory system, measurements of the pain sensation behave in unexpected ways. The *RLs*, for example, in the visual and auditory systems or even of temperature and touch are not greatly affected by attitudinal variables of the subject. However, pain thresholds are markedly affected by the attitude of the subject toward the experiment and experimenter, his attention and suggestibility. Obviously some strong influence must be feeding into the pain system from the central nervous system to account for these profound effects.

Two different approaches to the study of pain have done little to clarify the issues. On the one hand are the investigators who induce pain experimentally in normal subjects and attempt to measure the effects of analgesic agents (pain relievers) on thresholds of pain. Generally, they find the analgesic has little or no effect upon the intensity of stimulation required to produce a threshold pain sensation, when carefully controlled procedures are used. On the other hand, the physician is faced daily with the problem of alleviating pain in his patients. It is here that analgesics are known to work. What is the difference between experimentally induced pain and that which accompanies pathological conditions? The answer is not easy, although the difference appears to be the presence of anxiety, a state not readily produced by experimental methods (Beecher, 1966).

Pain varies along a sensory-discrimination and a motivational-affective dimension. The intensity of the pain is influenced by the patient's own evaluation of the seriousness of the damage he has sustained, a cognitive process. If tissue damage does not evoke an aversive drive, it cannot be called pain, and by the same token, anxiety not accompanied by a sensory input is not pain. Pain must,

therefore, be a combination of all three processes: a discriminatory, a motivational, and a cognitive (evaluative) process (Melzack & Casey, 1968; Sternbach, 1968). The importance of these variables is best exemplified by a report of Beecher (1956) of responses of soldiers to war wounds. Of the soldiers who suffered grievous, but not fatal wounds, only about one-third wanted medication to relieve their pain. Two-thirds refused it, yet many of them complained bitterly about the discomfort experienced if an inept corpsman failed to make a successful venous puncture. According to Beecher, the wounded soldier experienced relief, thankfulness to escape alive from the battlefield, and even euphoria (feeling his wound was a good thing).

There appears to be no direct relationship between the extent of the wound and the pain experienced. The intensity of the pain is dependent, to a considerable extent, on how the patient views the wound from the standpoint of the anxiety produced, its seriousness, and what it means in terms of his future existence.

With full knowledge that the motivational and cognitive aspects of pain are being ignored, pain will be considered here as a sensory process. Reference is made to investigators such as Beecher (1959), Melzack and Casey (1968), and Sternbach (1968) to supply information on the processes related to the motivational and cognitive aspects of pain.

The Definition of Pain

The definition of pain may be made in terms of the stimulus, in which case both its intensity and locus are important. It may also be defined in terms of the response to a stimulus, for example, verbal responses, motor reflexes, or changes in cardiovascular responses.

Painful stimuli   Methods to produce pain for experimental purposes may be divided into two categories, according to the locus of stimulus application—cutaneous pain and deep pain. These are not necessarily different pains, although the deep visceral or muscular pains tend to have the long persistent aching quality associated with pathologically induced pain in contrast to the fleeting, sharp quality of cutaneous pain.

The methods of stimulation employed to produce pain are numerous. Almost any violence done to the body, either internally or externally, is likely to produce pain. One cannot conclude, however, that tissue damage and pain are always associated. For example, x-radiation can cause tissue destruction that may not be accompanied by pain, and pain may be felt where no evident tissue damage has occurred, as when an exposed tooth nerve is lightly touched.

Whatever the stimulus used to produce experimental pain, it must be amenable to quantification. Also it should be remembered that most methods of producing experimental pain have a common defect: that repeated exposure to such stimulation usually damages tissue so that succeeding trials fall on tissue that has been altered, at least slightly, by previous exposure.

Experimental production of cutaneous pain was considerably advanced by the introduction of infrared radiation techniques (Hardy, Wolff, & Goodell, 1940). Radiation from a high-intensity lamp was collected by a lens and directed toward the skin through a shutter. The current to the lamp was increased until the subject experienced a sharp stab of pain just before the shutter closed at the end of a 3 second exposure.

Electrical stimulation of the skin has also been used, but the pin-prick sensation experienced usually accompanies the electrical breakdown of the resistance of the skin, and hence, the electrical quantity is associated with the dielectric properties of the skin rather than a threshold of the receptive process (Mueller, Loeffel, & Mead, 1953).

Mechanical methods of producing pain have varied from making gross blows on the fingers (Wells, 1947) and applying pressure on the styloid process of the mastoid bone (Libman, 1934) to driving carefully sharpened needles into the skin with blows of varying intensity (Jones, 1956). However, little success has been attained in producing reliable stimuli.

Arousal of pain with chemical agents has been more successful (Armstrong et al., 1951). A skin blister is produced by cantharidin. After the blister is formed, the top is carefully cut away and chemical solutions, for example, potassium chloride or acetylcholine, of known concentrations are applied to the blister base. The area remains sensitive for about 48 hours during which 50 to 60 applications of the chemicals can be made.

Several methods of producing deep pain have been explored. Distension of the esophagus (Chapman & Jones, 1944) or the bile duct (Gaensler, 1951) with small rubber balloons have been used in studies on the effectiveness of analgesic agents on pain. The results were not generally satisfactory because the methods do not yield clear-cut end-points between the point where there is or is not any pain. Another method, involving muscle ischemia (blocking arterial blood flow to the muscles) induced by the pressure of a blood-pressure cuff, shows considerably more promise. If the subject exercises the muscles below the tourniquet at a regular rate, for example making a fist every second, the onset of pain occurs with a prompt and clear-cut end-point (Harrison & Bigelow, 1943).

Other more radical or drastic procedures employed to induce pain in man include applying electric shocks to the teeth through amalgam fillings (Goetzl, Burrill, & Ivy, 1943), applying shocks to the exposed digital nerve of the index finger (Pattle & Weddell, 1948), to the saphenous nerve, which is sensory to the medial skin of the leg (Heinbecker, Bishop, & O'Leary, 1933), and the sural nerve sensory to the lateral skin of the leg (Collins, Nulsen, & Randt, 1960). Methods of stimulating the gasserian ganglion electrically in awake and active rhesus monkeys have also been developed (Weitzman et al., 1961). (The gasserian ganglion contains the cell bodies of the nerve fibers of the trigeminal nerve which is, in part, sensory to the face.)

Response definitions Methods by which pain is induced are of importance in investigations of this sensory process. Of at least equal importance are the response criteria employed. They may be divided into categories of verbal responses, behavioral responses including reflexes, and physiological indices employed with both man and animals.

Language is rich in adjectives that can be used to describe painful sensations. Dallenbach (1939) catalogued 44 of them, from "achey" to "thrilling" to "vicious." There is obvious overlap in the meaning of many of these adjectives, but their profusion suggests many subtle, qualitative differences in the sensations of pain. Furthermore, a number of them imply a spatial characteristic whereas others suggest a temporal characteristic.

Measurements of the stimulus intensity required to produce changes in behavior or reflex withdrawal in both man and animals have been employed. Thus, the intensity of a stimulus that causes the animal to escape from the situation has been used as one behavioral criterion of pain. Rice and Kenshalo (1962) defined the heat-induced pain of cats as that intensity of heat required to cause the cat consistently to initiate a response to terminate it. Others, such as Weitzman et al. (1961), defined pain as the intensity of electric shock administered to the gasserian ganglion that would cause the rhesus monkey to press a lever to reduce the intensity of the shock.

Two reflexes used extensively to mark a nociceptive (painful) threshold response to radiant stimulation are the tail flick of the rat and the contraction of the *cutaneous maximus* muscle of the rat, guinea pig, and dog. Also, the leg flexor reflex may be used as an index of painful stimulation in both man and animals. For example, the intensity of radiant

stimulation required to produce a flexor reflex in paraplegic man is about the same intensity as that required to produce a pain sensation in normal man (Rice & Kenshalo, 1962).

Physiological indices of pain have consisted mainly of measures of the activity of the sympathetic nervous system. These include changes in systolic and diastolic blood pressure, pulse pressure, heart rate, salivary flow rate, palmar skin resistance (galvanic skin response), finger pulse volume, and respiration rate (Sternbach, 1968).

When we consider the variety of methods that have been used to induce pain, the variety of descriptive adjectives used in the verbal report of pain, as well as the other behavioral and reflex indices, it is not surprising that so little headway has been made in the study of pain as a sensation. This is exclusive of the factors of anxiety and cognition which ultimately must also be considered! A more unified attack on the problems of pain would likely yield more certain knowledge.

Behavioral Analysis

Pain may be aroused in a variety of ways, but it is not easy to find a way that permits quantification of the stimulus intensity. Mechanical devices have been used, but usually they must produce radical deformations of the tissue before pain is aroused. Neither chemical nor electrical stimulation is suitable because it is practically impossible to control the spatial boundaries of their action. Thermally aroused pain appears to be more controllable, and Hardy, Wolff, and Goodell (1940) have made extensive use of it to measure both the *RL*s and *DL*s of pain.

When radiant energy is to be used to cause pain, the energy delivered to the skin surface by the radiant source is measured in millicalories/sec–cm^2. The elevation in the surface temperature of the skin produced by a 3 second exposure to radiation of various intensities may then be calculated. Direct measurements of skin temperature with thermocouples or thermistors during the time of the exposure to radiation do not suffice because their thermal properties differ from those of skin. Thus, the readings may be in error by a degree or more. More recently, however, the development of rapid response radiometers have made possible direct readings of skin temperature immediately following radiation (Hendler & Hardy, 1960). A radiometer detects changes in the temperature of an object by responding to changes in its rate of infrared emission—in this case, the skin. When the mass of the radiation sensing element is large, however, seconds or even minutes are required for it to complete its response to a change in the temperature of the skin. Rapid response to temperature changes (a few milliseconds) has been made possible by the development of extremely small sensing elements that can change temperature rapidly.

Thresholds and scaling   The *RL* of pain produced by thermal stimulation has been reported to be as high as 48.6° C (McKenna, 1958). At skin temperatures as low as 36° C a transient pain may be experienced (Lele, Weddell, & Williams, 1954). Measurements of the pain *RL* show a single individual is fairly consistent in his reports of pain, but the differences between individuals are so great that generalizations of the stimulus intensity required to evoke pain are difficult to make.

The pain *RL* reported at the lower skin temperatures may be synonymous with the slight sting that characterizes the heat threshold (see p. 148), but the sting might be construed as the *RL* by a relatively naive or timorous subject. Trained subjects usually report threshold pain after a 3 second exposure to a radiation intensity of 0.206 gcal/sec-cm² (206 millicalories, for short) (Schumacher et al., 1940). This intensity of radiation produces an elevation in skin temperature of about 12.5° C above normal, so that the pain *RL* is a skin temperature of about 44.5° C. Starting from other skin temperatures, greater or smaller intensities of radiation are required to reach the pain threshold. Unlike the warm

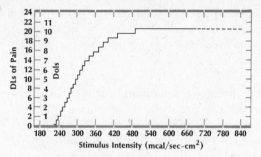

Figure 5.21. The dol scale of pain sensitivity. Although 480 millicalories/sec–cm² may not produce the most intense pain possible, it does represent the approximate practical upper limit for experimental purposes. Higher intensities of radiation produce protracted reddening of the skin and even blistering which makes the effects of repeated applications of the stimulus questionable. (Figure 3 from Hardy, Wolff, & Goodell, 1947.)

threshold, which changes with the adapted skin temperature (see Figure 5.14), a pain *RL* occurs when the skin is heated to 44.5° to 45° C, regardless of the initial skin temperature (Hardy, Goodell, & Wolff, 1951).

The radiant heat method has also permitted measurements of the pain *DL*s. Hardy, Wolff, and Goodell (1947) first determined that the highest intensity of radiation that could be used repeatedly, without inducing hours of long-lasting consequences, was about 480 millicalories during a 3 second exposure (an elevation in skin temperature to about 61° C). Between the limits of 210 and 480 millicalories, they found 21 jnd's (just noticeable differences) of intensity. As shown in Figure 5.21, at intensities up to about 360 millicalories, the *DL* increased, so that the Weber fraction, $\Delta I/I$, was roughly constant at 0.03. The ratio increased at higher intensities. Pain can therefore be scaled, and accordingly Hardy et al. have suggested a unit of pain, the dol, which is equal to 2 jnd's.

Adaptation   There is no general agreement on whether or not pain adapts or ceases to be felt even though the cause of the pain is still present. On the one hand, it is held not to adapt, for to do so would be counter to its important function in the survival of the organism. On the other hand, there is considerable evidence to suggest that it does adapt, and in some circumstances it does adapt completely. Yet, we can all think of pains we have experienced that seemed to last for interminable periods of time, such as severe sunburn, an inflamed appendix, a headache, or a toothache. Those who contend that pain adapts point out that these pains involve constantly changing conditions at the pain site, usually rhythmic ones based on circulatory events. As we mention below, many contend that there is a chemical step between painful stimulation and the arousal of peripheral, afferent, neural activity. The adaptation of pain would then be linked to the amount of the responsible chemical substance present.

Complete adaptation of pain induced by heat, for example after an arm and hand has been dipped into thermostatically controlled water baths, occurs when a large area of skin is exposed to temperatures from 40° C up to 45.5° C and may occur infrequently at temperatures up to 47° C (Hardy, Stolwijk, & Hoffman, 1968). The sensation builds rapidly to a maximum for 5 to 10 seconds after immersion, followed by adaptation and generally a complete disappearance of the pain within 15 to 20 seconds. The sensations experienced at these temperatures may be akin to, or even identical with, the sensation of heat described earlier (see p. 148). At higher temperatures (46° to 48° C), pain occurs with little delay and increases to a peak or temporary plateau 4 to 12 seconds after immersion; this is generally followed by a further increase in the pain sensation during the 30 second immersion period. At temperatures above 47° C, pain is nonadapting. The most intense pain is frequently that experienced at the end of the 30 second exposure period. In one subject, the intensity of the pain continued to increase over a 3 minute period. This agrees with the earlier work of Greene and Hardy (1962) in which subjects were required to

maintain a threshold pain sensation by adjusting the intensity of radiation for periods of up to 60 minutes. Once the pain threshold was reached, the subject made no further increases in the radiation intensity, as would have been expected had adaptation occurred.

Pain, produced by radiant energy, may adapt completely if the energy is applied to small areas of skin. Stone and Dallenbach (1934) reported that pain, aroused by radiant heat applied to a 2 mm² area of the forearm, adapted completely. During the course of adaptation the initial sensation was intense heat, followed by warmth, and finally indifference, all within a span of 20 to 30 seconds following onset of the warming of the skin. These findings do not necessarily invalidate those of Hardy et al. that pain induced in large areas of skin does not adapt. Adaptation of small areas to pain stimuli may indeed be as complete as that of small areas to warm and cold stimuli. It is also possible, in view of the fact that Stone and Dallenbach failed to report the skin temperatures produced by their stimuli, that they were within the temperature range where Hardy et al. also reported adaptation of pain.

Complete adaptation of pain produced by cold stimuli is generally agreed to occur within about 5 minutes, even when the whole hand is immersed in a water bath maintained at 0° C (Wolff & Hardy, 1941). The initial sensation experienced is one of ache that becomes progressively stronger for the first minute of exposure but then diminishes and disappears in 4 to 5 minutes. If smaller areas are exposed to cold, the pain adapts completely in shorter times (Edes & Dallenbach, 1936).

The results of various experiments generally agree that the pain produced by mechanical or cold stimuli adapts completely. It is likely that cold pain adapts because of the physiological consequences of the tissue cooling. Cooling nervous tissue blocks stimulation of receptors and conduction of impulses in the peripheral neurons. Mechanically induced pain is not a fatigue phenomenon, as is shown by the fact that once the pain of a needle jabbed into the skin has adapted, pain is again produced when it is withdrawn. This pain sensation fails because of failure of stimulation rather than because of failure of the ability of the receptor to respond—similar to touch adaptation as suggested by Nafe and Wagoner (see p. 131). The pulsations of pain sensations may have a mechanical basis in tissue movement produced by arterial pulsations. Pain produced by heat may adapt when heating is not intense or is not applied over a large area of skin. However, pain engendered by intense heating of the entire forearm does not adapt but frequently becomes more intense with time. These findings suggest that adaptation of heat-pain, as that of tactile and thermal sensations, is a characteristic of the stimulus conditions rather than a characteristic of the neurological processes involved in the transmission or perception of pain.

Spatial summation There appears to be no clear-cut answer to the question of whether or not spatial summation of the pain sensation exists. In any event, if spatial summation of pain occurs at all, it is much less pronounced than that encountered for warmth, cold, and heat sensations. Pain induced by radiant heat (Greene & Hardy, 1958) or by conducted heat (Benjamin, 1968) applied over areas of 2.5 to 70 cm² shows a slight but reliable summation effect. That is, threshold pain is produced at lower skin temperatures as the area of skin heated is increased. Spatial summation of the aching pain produced by cold does not occur, nor has spatial summation of mechanically induced pain been successfully demonstrated (Bishop, 1949).

Double pain Two kinds of pain arising from a single stimulation may frequently be distinguished. One is bright and sharp like the pain from the prick of a needle, whereas the other is dull like deep bodily aches. In addition to their qualitative differences they are also distinguished by the length of time it takes to arouse each kind of pain to the maximum. The sharp pain is relatively rapidly aroused, whereas the dull pain is more slowly aroused; it is also more persistent.

Two lines of evidence support the existence of "double" pain sensations. The first is provided by sensory dissociation experiments in which the order of disappearance of qualities of cutaneous sensations is noted after various nerve blocking agents are used. Arrest in blood flow to the nerves results in progressive loss of function in the small myelinated fibers, and then in the larger ones. After all the myelinated fibers have failed, the unmyelinated fibers finally become blocked. When the order of sensory loss is recorded as a function of onset of limb asphyxia, the sharp pain disappears first, leaving the delayed, persistent dull pain (Zotterman, 1933). Cocaine, in contrast, blocks activity in unmyelinated fibers first, followed later by a loss of function of the myelinated ones. Cocaine has been found to abolish the second pain response before it affects the first (Lewis & Pochin, 1937).

The second line of evidence in support of the existence of double pain is derived from measurements of the reaction time to painful stimuli applied to different body loci. Lewis and Pochin (1937) showed that the time interval between the occurrence of the first and the second pain was greater when the toe rather than the thigh was pricked.

Several considerations dictate caution in accepting the evidence as proof that double pain results from differences in conduction velocities of the fibers carrying the information or that the phenomenon even exists at all. First, even the protagonists of the double pain sensation advise caution in interpreting evidence obtained by the use of nerve blocks. Gasser (1943) has pointed out "it is misleading to state that asphyxia blocks large fibers first, while cocaine blocks small fibers first." Further, critical evaluations on the use of nerve blocks in support of the reality of double pains has been offered by Sinclair and Hinshaw (1951). Second, Jones (1956) has criticized the techniques used to measure reaction time in previous experiments and has suggested that the second pain may well be an artifact of these methods. Rebuttals have been made by Libet (1957) and Pieron (1959). Third, if two pains occur as the result of transmission of information in two types of nerve fiber, why, then, are there not two touches or two thermal sensations? Certainly, it should be most obvious in the case of touch where the information is conducted over both types of fiber as well as in the case of temperature where both types have also been shown to be active. Perhaps the existence of double pain depends on processes that are more central in the nervous system (see p. 165).

Visceral and referred pain An excellent summary of the problem of visceral and referred pain, from a physiological point of view, is given by Ruch (1965). Pains that arise from deep within the muscles and the viscera show some characteristics different from those pains that arise from the skin stimulation. Surgeons, operating under local anesthesia, have noted that the visceral organs can be crushed, cut, or burned without arousing any sensation. However, a tug on the mesentery (the membranes that hold the gut in place) or stimulation of the lining of the body wall will induce sensations that include pain and nausea. The fact that pathologic states may be accompanied by pain shows that visceral organs are sensitive to stimulation. However, the viscera are not normally exposed to the conditions of stimulation to which the skin is exposed; thus, sensitivity to these conditions may not have evolved. Stimulation of the viscera that results in sensations, usually painful, include (1) spasms or strong muscular contractions, for example, childbirth pains; (2) sudden or extreme distension, for example, a full urinary bladder; (3) chemical irritants, for example, gastric juices in the esophagus, heartburn; (4) mechanical stimulation, especially when the organ is congested with blood. These pains are not often the result of mesentery traction alone. Normal contractions and relaxations of

the viscera are not accompanied by pain, although they may become so when the blood supply is inadequate.

Pains from visceral organs can usually be correctly localized, although at times the pain may appear to arise from the skin surface instead. Such pains are called referred pains. The best known example of a referred pain is from the heart (angina pectoris) in which the pain seems to come from the chest and a narrow strip of skin on the inner surface of the upper arm.

Several theories have been advanced to account for referred pain. One, the convergence-facilitation theory, suggests that afferent impulses from the viscera associated with painful stimulation cannot pass directly to the brain because the visceral afferent fibers have no direct connection with the spinothalamic tract, but they create an "irritable focus" in the part of the spinal cord they enter. Afferent impulses from the skin that enter in the same part of the spinal cord are thereby magnified and cause a pain sensation that is referred to the skin rather than the viscera. A second, the convergence-projection theory, maintains that nerve impulses associated with pain in both the viscera and the afferent fibers of the skin converge on the same cell bodies at some point in the sensory pathways—spinal cord, thalamus, or cortex—so that the origin (whether from the viscera or skin) of the pain is lost. The evidence is conflicting. It indicates that both facilitation and information on the origin are of importance in explaining referred pain.

Physiological Mechanism

Here we consider the evidence for specific pain receptors, a possible chemical link between stimulation and peripheral neural activity, and the evidence that specific types of fiber are involved in the peripheral mediation of pain.

Receptors The search for the end organs of pain has failed to reveal any distinctive structures that might serve that function. Histological examination of abnormal skin, in which pain is the only sensation that can be evoked, has shown that the ubiquitous free-nerve endings (like those of the dermal nerve network) are the only neurological element present (Sweet, 1959).

Most anatomists find that the cornea of the eye is innervated only by free-nerve terminals. Thus, this tiny bit of tissue has become a veritable battleground over what cutaneous sensory qualities can be aroused by its appropriate stimulation. Certainly pain is one of them and many have shown that touch or sensations of contact can also be experienced. Whether thermal sensations are experienced from appropriate stimulation of the cornea is open to question (Lele & Weddell, 1956; Kenshalo, 1960). From such findings, it seems likely, at least, that the free-nerve endings of the cornea are capable of setting up impulses that allow man to distinguish between light touch, and pain.

Research on deep somatic and visceral pain is at an elementary stage. Free-nerve endings occur in the peritoneum, tendon surfaces, periosteum of the bone, and in the intermuscular connective tissue of the viscera. Appropriate stimulation of any of these tissues will evoke pain (White & Sweet, 1955). Furthermore, afferent nerve plexuses develop in the adventitial and muscular walls of arteries, and arterial puncture in man usually results in severe pain, in contrast to venopuncture. Likewise, distention of the cerebral arteries with histamine is a standard method of experimentally inducing a headache. Fine terminal endings have been described in close relation to the capillary walls (Weddell, Palmer, & Pallie, 1955) and may account for the pain Landis (1930) produced in man when his micropipette penetrated these tiny blood vessels. It appears, then, that free-nerve endings are involved in the reception of pain as well as other sensations. Furthermore, the free-nerve endings are the only ones sufficiently generally distributed throughout the body to mediate pain. They must be implicated in pain though that is not their exclusive function.

Chemical link   There is considerable speculation and much research to indicate that there is a chemical step intermediate to the action of a painful stimulus on tissue and the appearances of impulses in afferent nerve fibers. Among the possible chemicals might be (1) intracellular potassium, released by tissue damage (Benjamin, 1968); (2) bradykinin, an enzyme frequently found at the site of tissue injury and inflammation (Lim, 1968); (3) histamine, both because it is found at the site of painful stimulation and because antihistamines have been shown to elevate the pain threshold (Rosenthal, 1968); and (4) a more direct effect, modification of molecular configurations in the receptor membrane by thermal agitation (Hardy et al., 1968).

Specific pain fibers   Correlations between the primary qualities of cutaneous sensation and the diameter of peripheral afferent nerve fibers have been attempted many times through the years. Bishop (1960) has reviewed the literature and concluded that there is no clear separation of the cutaneous senses according to fiber size. However there is abundant evidence, reviewed by Douglas and Ritchie (1962), that the unmyelinated fibers exhibit action potentials when noxious (both mechanical and thermal) as well as mild stimuli are applied to the skin. In studies in which exposed peripheral nerves of awake human patients were stimulated electrically, pain was experienced when the recorded compound action potential included fibers of the finer myelinated group (Heinbecker, Bishop, & O'Leary, 1933; Collins, Nulsen, & Randt, 1960).

In other experiments, many fibers in the cat's saphenous nerve have been examined that respond only to pinching of a skin fold. Characteristically, these fibers have conduction velocities between 6 and 30 m/sec and do not respond to strong heating, acid, or the application of bradykinin to the abraded skin (Burgess & Perl, 1967). The implication is that these fibers, covering the range of conduction velocities of the finer myelinated group, convey impulses signaling only mechanically induced skin injury.

Investigations of the activity in fibers that show a response only to strong stimulation of one type or another lead to another question about which there is very little information. That is, when a strong stimulus is applied to the skin, what happens to the response of fibers that show a vigorous response to less intense stimulation? Cold fibers, for example, cease activity altogether at temperatures above about 42° C, except for the few that show a paradoxical discharge at 45° C and above. Furthermore, recordings may be made from the cell bodies of neurons in the ventral medial nucleus of the thalamus that respond to mild mechanical stimulation. Activity in these neurons ceases altogether when a stimulus, judged to be noxious, is applied to the receptive fields of the skin (Poggio & Mountcastle, 1960). Sketchy as it is, the evidence seems to suggest that neurological elements which show a response to mild stimulation are blocked or inhibited from responding during intense stimulation. Furthermore, there appears to be a degree of specificity of response shown by the fibers in that those responding to intense mechanical stimulation do not respond to other noxious agents.

The Management of Pain

It is not the intention here to present a comprehensive review concerning the clinical management of pain but only to provide a brief overview of some of the research, including the effects of some analgesics on experimentally induced pain.

Analgesics With the development of radiant heat as a stimulus amenable to quantification in the production of experimental pain, the effects of standard analgesics, for example, aspirin, morphine, and so on, came under investigation. Many investigators reported that morphine sulfate, for example, affected the experimentally induced pain threshold in a manner similar to its effects

on clinical pain. The pain threshold, in terms of radiant heat units, increased for 3 hours when the effect of the 30 mg injection of morphine sulfate reached a maximum, after which it decreased and returned to a normal level 4 hours later. Lesser doses had a less pronounced effect on the pain threshold, and for a shorter period of time. A similar effect was reported for acetylsalicylic acid (aspirin), although it was less profound and lasted for a shorter period (Hardy, Wolff, & Goodell, 1940).

In many of the early measurements, both the subject and the experimenter were fully aware of the nature of the experiment and when and what analgesic was administered. When measurements of analgesic effectiveness were repeated, however, using the stringent experimental control of a *double-blind procedure*,[1] the effects of the analgesics on the pain thresholds could not be reproduced (Beecher, 1959).

Another factor of considerable importance in the effect of analgesics on experimental pain has been emphasized by Beecher and his colleagues (Smith et al., 1966). This factor is the presence of anxiety, a state not readily produced by the fleeting pain of skin stimulation at threshold. In their experiment, Smith and his coworkers induced ischemia to produce pain. A blood-pressure cuff was placed around the arm of the subject and inflated to interrupt the blood flow. This was followed by periods of exercise of the hand interrupted by rest periods. Pain was judged in five categories from slight to unbearable. Only for the two most intense pain categories were they able to show dose-effect curves after injections of morphine sulfate using the double-blind procedure. Whatever the rea-

---

[1] In this procedure, neither the experimenter nor the subject knows the treatment condition until after the measurements have all been completed. Furthermore, a placebo (an inert substance like lactose) is also given in random order with the analgesics. Thus, this procedure controls both the subject variables which involve subject attitude and expectation as well as experimenter variables which may induce unintentional biases. This control is perhaps more necessary in this type of experiment because of the profound effects of subjective variables on pain sensation.

sons, whether because of the anxiety involved or something else, they concluded that there are qualitative differences between threshold pain and severe pain.

It has long been known that counterirritants may reduce the intensity of pain already being perceived by a subject. For example, pain induced in a limb by the tourniquet method may act as a counterirritant to reduce the intensity of the pain of a tooth ache (Beecher, 1959). Very loud sounds also may be used to reduce dental pain. Gardner, Licklider, and Weisz (1961) have reported that stereophonic music and white noise served as effective analgesics during more than 65 percent of the dental operations and minor skin surgery in which they were used. The authors note that they allowed the subject to control both the intensity and the choice of music or noise, so that subjective factors associated with a partial control of the situation may play a major role in the effectiveness of the auditory stimulation. Vibratory stimuli applied to the skin also seem to reduce the effects of painful stimulation (Wall & Cronly-Dillon, 1960). Thus, although cross-modality masking (one sense modality interfering with action of another) may be a factor in audio-analgesia, it does not appear likely (Carlin et al., 1962). Rather, its success appears to depend on both distraction and suggestion.

Causalgia and neuralgia Causalgia and neuralgia are general terms applied to abnormal sensations, usually intensely painful, that are associated with injury to the peripheral nerve bundles; for example, from cuts, lacerations, crushing, and puncture wounds. There may be such an identifiable injury associated with the onset of the causalgia (defined as a neurally produced sensation of burning) or neuralgia ("nerve pain") or as in the instance of trigeminal neuralgia (see below), no reason may be apparent for the appearance of the pain.

Peripheral nerve causalgias may be of two general forms: those associated with injury, including the peripheral nerve fiber bundle, and those associated with amputation of a limb. In causalgias that involve injury of a peripheral nerve, a peculiar burning pain is produced by light tactile stimulation. The pain sensation is of long latency, poorly localized, and outlasts the stimulation. It spreads to a wide area and causes vigorous protective movements of the member involved. The skin becomes shiny and glossy smooth and may become discolored. Relief from this type of pain usually involves an exploratory operation to determine and clear the peripheral nerve of its involvement with its surrounding tissues (White & Sweet, 1955).

Phantom limb causalgia is one of the most interesting and baffling sequels to the amputation of a limb. Frequently, but not always, the patient seems to experience phantom sensations that he attributes to the limb in the position that he last remembers it. There are frequently profound psychological experiences associated with the phantom. For example, although a young tank soldier had his arm blown off at the elbow, he tried to re-enlist after recovery and was rejected. When the request was refused he wanted to strike out with the limb, now amputated, and clench his missing fist. At that moment, he became aware of his phantom limb, the fist of which seemed to remain clenched and painful, until finally he was accepted and sent overseas as a Red Cross Field Director (White & Sweet, 1955).

Sensations such as those described above are frequently attributed to stimulation of the regenerating fibers of the nerve stump. However, injections of alcohol or procaine (to kill or block the regenerating nerve fiber tips) usually have no effect on the sensation. Even cutting the nerve farther up in the limb or even at its entry into the spinal cord has no lasting effect. Removal of the area of the cortex that served the phantom is of such questionable value that it is not a recommended procedure (White & Sweet, 1955).

Another variety of pathological pain that is so far of unknown origin is trigeminal neuralgia or *tic douloureux*. Pains of tic douloureux are confined to the area of the face innervated by branches of the trigeminal nerve; they are usually localized on one side of the face. These pains are paroxysmal (lasting only a few seconds or minutes followed by periods of no pain or a dull ache). There is usually a trigger zone, stimulation of which is followed by pain. Triggering stimuli may be a touch, a draft of air, a facial movement, as involved in talking, chewing, swallowing, yawning, or any jarring of the body that moves the face. The paroxysms of pain may occur only briefly and may be separated by days, weeks, months, or even years, but they may occur with such regularity that they seriously impair eating, thus producing a condition of starvation in the patient. Treatment usually involves killing branches of the trigeminal nerve by alcohol injection, which provides up to 24 months of relief, or cutting the trigeminal branch involved. A new technique for the relief of causalgia and tic douloureux is that of electrically stimulating the larger sensory nerve fibers (Shelden, 1966; Wall & Sweet, 1967) (see p. 166).

Theories of Pain

The varying definitions of pain, the indeterminate role of attitudes and perceptions upon its intensity, and the various approaches to its investigation (behavioral, psychophysical, and neurophysiological) have all created a wealth of literature with little in the way of a central theme. This state of affairs makes the task of theory building and testing exceedingly difficult.

Many questions are posed by the literature on the topic of pain. One of the first is whether pain is really a separate skin sense or whether it is merely a result of intense stimulation of other receptive systems. Few follow the intensive theory now, for there is too much evidence opposed to it, including the fact that stimulation of certain areas of skin (the pain spots) causes only pain. Also, intense stimulation of tactile receptors may yield high frequencies of nerve discharge with no evidence of a painful sensation, for example, vibratory stimuli (Geldard, 1953) or puffs of air (Cattell & Hoagland, 1931). Certainly, the fact that pains occur and continue after nerve section to treat causalgia, neuralgia, tic douloureux, and phantom limb, is difficult to explain by an intensity of stimulation theory.

If pain is not simply an extension of normal sensitivity to mechanical and thermal stimuli, then it appears to be a separate sense system. To most investigators, a separate sense system implies a distinct set of receptors, fiber tracts, and brain centers. Whereas many investigators have started with this assumption, it has remained little more than an assumption, and there is little evidence for its support. To contend that the system reporting pain is a separate sense system with its own receptors implies that the skin contains receptors that respond only to intense stimulation; that the receptor is specialized to respond to a particular kind of stimulus—an intense thermal or mechanical stimulus. There is convincing evidence that such receptors exist within the somesthetic system (Maruhashi, Mizuguchi, & Tasaki, 1952; Hunt & McIntyre, 1960a, b; Burgess & Perl, 1967). To maintain that these are pain receptors, however, is a psychological assumption which implies that pain will always be experienced when that receptor, or the nerve to which it is attached, is stimulated. There is no direct evidence to support this implication.

It should be obvious that neither the intensity nor the specificity theories of pain can successfully accommodate the forms of pain and the conditions of stimulation that lead to its experience. A third general theory of pain, the gate control theory, has been proposed by Melzack and Wall (1965). It is, in part, a specificity theory and, in part, a pattern theory in which the frequency of nerve impulses in the small and large axons that arrive at the spinal cord nerve cells is assumed to determine whether pain will be experienced.

In the awake, behaving animal (human or otherwise) a continuous flow of afferent impulses travel from the receptors in the skin, viscera, and elsewhere (*primary* fibers) to the spinal cord. Some of these axons (usually those of a large diameter) continue, uninterrupted, up the spinal cord to specific brain centers where the information that they carry receives further processing. Other peripheral afferent fibers end in the spinal cord, there to synapse with the cell bodies of other neurons. These *secondary* or *transmission* neurons (*T* cells) may have long axons that then convey afferent impulses to other brain centers. It is at this first synapse of the afferent fiber pathways that Melzack and Wall propose a gate. When the gate is open, activity in the endings of the primary neurons induces activity in the *T* cells. *T* cells activate neural mechanisms that are responsible for the pain phenomena. When the gate is closed, however, pain will not be experienced.

Control of the gate comes from at least two sources. The first source of gate control is the relative amounts of activity in the small as compared to the large fibers. If more small fibers are active, the gate is opened and the *T* cells can be stimulated. If the reverse is the case, the gate is shut and activity in the *T* cells is diminished. A second source of gate control is the brain, for impulses in the efferent fibers (those traveling from the brain to the spinal cord) are known to influence the afferent activity at this earliest synapse in the afferent pathway. A mechanism is provided here by which perceptions, attitudes, and so on, may also control the gate.

The sensation of pain, according to the gate theory, is not the responsibility of a single and separate system of receptors and peripheral nerve fibers. Rather pain occurs as a result of interaction at the *T* cells between three sources of neural activity. These are (1) activity in peripheral nerve fibers of a small diameter that are usually activated only by relatively high intensities of stimulation; (2) activity in fibers with large diameters that are activated by mild stimulation; and (3) activity in fibers carrying information from the brain concerned with the affective state of the organism.

In order to be of value, a theory must be testable. Wall and Sweet (1967) have provided one such test of the gate control theory. In patients with chronic cutaneous pain, the sensory nerves or roots supplying the painful area were stimulated by electrical pulses of low intensity. Low intensities of electrical stimulation will produce impulses in only the fibers of large diameter, for these have lower thresholds to electrical stimulation than do the small fibers. During the stimulation, pressure on the previously sensitive areas failed to evoke pain; half of the patients reported relief of their pain for more than half an hour after receiving 2 minutes of electrical stimulation. A similar technique has been used to relieve the pain of tic douloureux (Shelden, 1966). In this instance, a small radio receiving unit was implanted on the skull and platinum wires were connected to the trigeminal nerve. A transistor oscillator was built which, when held close to the receiver, caused electrical stimulation of the nerve and immediate relief of the pain paroxism. A similar device has also been used successfully to relieve chronic heart pains.

THE NATURE OF QUALITY IN SOMESTHESIS

Many different qualities of sensation can be aroused by stimuli that are rough, smooth, wet, dry, oily, ticklish, and itchy, to name but a few. According to the specific receptor theory of the late nineteenth and early twentieth centuries, these qualities result from the simultaneous activity of several different specific receptors blending to form a unitary sensation quality. Thus, wet was analyzed into stimulation of tactile and cold receptors, whereas oily was thought to result from the simultaneous stimulation of tactile and warm receptors (Bershansky, 1922). Itch was held, and still is by many, to result from stimulation of pain receptors (Arthur & Shelley, 1959).

Some of the shortcomings of the specific receptor theory have been discussed earlier in this chapter. The lack of structures in the skin that might serve as receptors for the four primary psychological qualities, the lack of evidence in support of a one-to-one correlation between a physical dimension of a stimulus and a psychological dimension of the sensation, and the inaccurate concept of a nervous system in which neural activity, from specific receptors of one or another type, travels in its own pathway to arrive at its own cortical location have all weakened the specificity theory. Furthermore, were it true, why should cold and touch be expected to blend into a single qualitatively different sensation of wet when we do not expect visual and auditory sensations to blend into a single qualitatively different sensation?

The pendulum of somesthetic theory was driven hard to the opposite extreme when, after an intensive and extensive series of investigations of the morphology and sensitivity of skin, Weddell was unable to find support for the specific receptor theory. He stated, ". . . that sensory experience is now being considered in terms of a spatio-temporal pattern of nervous activity rather than a series of discrete connections within a limited number of modes" (Weddell, 1955, p. 132). Accordingly, there are no specific receptors or specific fibers, but rather spatially and temporally dispersed patterns of activity leaving the skin that are somehow decoded and interpreted by the brain (Sinclair, 1955). No hypothesis is given to explain how the patterns originated or how the brain decoded and interpreted the patterns.

Both theories described above are unacceptable in their present form, yet both have concepts of use to any new theory to be proposed. There must be some degree of specificity or selectivity of response to stimulation at the receptor or fiber terminal because, as is shown above, there is evidence that the terminals of tactually excited fibers do not respond readily to temperature changes and vice versa. Temporal patterns of neural activity must also be part of the neural code, for otherwise how could the smoothness of an object be determined when a finger tip is moved across its surface, or the textures of silk or burlap cloth be discriminated?

Melzack and Wall (1962) have proposed a theory that synthesized some of the concepts from both the specific receptor and pattern theories. Furthermore, they suggest the probable origin of the neural patterns and the manner in which the brain might decode and interpret the patterns. Spatio-temporal patterns of neural activity originate at the receptive structure in the skin. They occur because of variations in the physiological properties of the receptors or nerve terminals themselves. We have already seen that some receptors respond almost exclusively to mild mechanical stimuli and that others respond predominantly to mild thermal stimuli. Hence, two different populations of fibers in a nerve bundle show activity—the one when mechanical stimuli are involved, and the other when thermal stimuli are involved. Painful stimuli apparently involve a third group of fibers in peripheral nerve bundles. Here it is important to know what happens in the receptors or terminals that respond to mild stimuli when a painful stimulus occurs. Is their activity blocked in some way by intense stimulation or do they also respond, even more vigorously, to the painful stimuli? Such considerations are important in the control of the pain gate proposed by Melzack and Wall (1965).

In addition to the peripheral units that specialize in their responsiveness to particular stimulus characteristics, other peripheral units exist that respond to several forms of stimulation, as those that respond to both mechanical and thermal stimuli. This further complicates both the temporal and spatial dimensions of the neural activity pattern.

Variations in both the temporal and spatial dimensions of neural activity are also introduced by variations in sensitivity to stimulation of the individual receptive units within each broad class of specialization. These variations in sensitivity of the individual receptive units include (1) variations in the threshold to mechanical or thermal stimuli; (2) peak sensitivity to temperature change (in Figure 5.18 five cold fibers are shown, each with a different temperature for peak steady-state responses); (3) variations in speed of adaptation; and (4) differences in the magnitude of response (frequency of nerve impulses) to changes in the strength of stimulation.

On the basis of currently available information, it is safe to say that every different cutaneous sensation that can be discrimi-nated is the result of a unique pattern of neural activity arriving at the points in the brain where it is interpreted. It should also be added that the pattern of neural activity that arrives at the brain will not resemble the pattern in the peripheral afferent nerve because of modifications that occur at each synapse in the pathways from the receptors to the brain. This, in the cutaneous and other sensory channels, is a part of the central decoding and interpreting system.

Linda Bartoshuk

THE CHEMICAL SENSES

I. TASTE

6

In order to survive, an organism must avoid substances that are harmful, and must consume necessary nutrient substances. The chemical senses of gustation and olfaction play a major part in allowing the organism to make these responses in an efficient manner, and the taste or smell of an object often leads at once to its acceptance or rejection without appeal to the other senses. The chemical senses, in addition, have strong hedonic overtones and are intimately involved in satisfying the basic drives of hunger, thirst, and sex.

In this chapter on taste, and in the following one on olfaction, we attempt to "break" the sensory code; that is, to determine by what means the organism translates contact with a chemical substance into neural events that ultimately lead to behavioral responses of approach or avoidance of the substance. We find substantial differences in the encoding of taste and smell, even though we must recognize the difficulties, already enumerated in Chapter 5, that lie in the way of sharply distinguishing one sense modality from another. The sense of taste, at least in the higher animals, originates mainly from contact of substances with the specialized gustatory receptors located on the tongue. The sense of smell, on the other hand, arises mainly from the effects of substances on olfactory receptors lying within the nasal passages. Exceptions to these generalizations are considered in the introductory paragraphs of Chapter 7. Thus two channels of

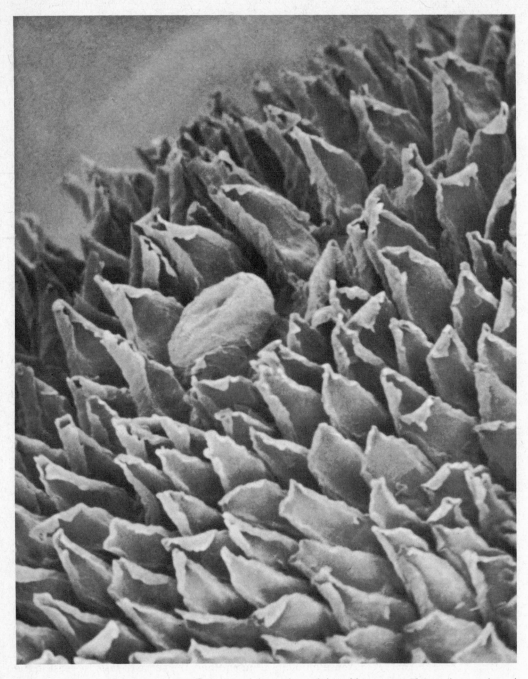

Figure 6.1. Electron scanning microscope picture of the surface of the rabbit tongue. The mushroom shaped structure is a fungiform papilla and the surrounding structures are filiform papillae. (Photograph furnished by L. M. Beidler.)

chemical analysis are open to the organism, and two separate chapters are needed to do justice in this book to the chemical senses.

The study of taste begins with neural responses in the specialized receptor cells at the periphery and continues with responses through the central nervous system. At each point in the nervous system that the investigator studies, he attempts to determine what information is available to the organism. In particular, he looks for properties of the neural message that correlate with intensity and quality as well as more complex taste phenomena such as adaptation and mixture effects. However, the presence of certain correlates does not necessarily mean that a particular organism makes use of them. Psychophysical data, either human or from other species, are necessary to demonstrate that the organism actually uses the information observed in the nervous system.

The latter part of this chapter deals with the hedonic properties of tastes, which Pfaffmann (1960) has described as motivating behavior for the "pleasures of sensation." As an example of hedonic behavior, animals not only can distinguish between such substances as sugar and quinine but they also show a preference for sugar and an aversion to quinine. That is, organisms respond hedonically to the information provided by the taste system. Much of the research directed toward this motivational function of taste has been oriented toward clarifying its exact role in the regulation of food intake and determining whether the hedonic properties of tastes are produced or influenced by learning.

ANATOMY AND PHYSIOLOGY

The Tongue

Four morphologically distinct kinds of projections or papillae are found on the human tongue. The most numerous of these are the *filiform papillae,* which, unlike the other three, contain no taste buds. These filiform papillae are conical in shape and are found over the entire dorsal surface of the tongue.

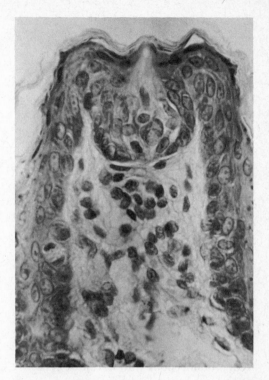

Figure 6.2. Histological cross-section of a fungiform papilla in the rat tongue showing the taste bud near the top surface. (Beidler, 1965.)

In some species, for example the cat, these papillae are somewhat rigid in structure, providing a rough surface which appears to aid in lapping up foods. The other three kinds of papillae differ in appearance and distribution. The *fungiform papillae* are shaped like button mushrooms (see Figure 6.1) and are found mainly on the tip and sides of the tongue. The *foliate papillae* in some mammals consist of a set of folds on the sides near the back of the tongue but are vestigial in man. The *circumvallate papillae* are larger than the others and are shaped like a flat mound surrounded by a trench. They are arranged in an inverted "V" at the back of the tongue.

The taste buds contain the taste receptor cells (see Figure 6.2). In the fungiform papillae the location of the taste buds is still in question. Most sources suggest that the taste buds are on the upper surfaces (Amerine, Pangborn, & Roessler, 1965) but one investigator has suggested that in man taste buds may appear on the sides of fungiform papillae (von Békésy, 1966). Taste buds are found in the folds of the foliate papillae and on both sides of the circular trenches in the circumvallate papillae. Taste buds can occasionally be found in other parts of the mouth, especially in children. Each fungiform papilla contains only a few taste buds, 3 or 4 in man, but the other papillae contain many more, making the total number of taste buds in man about 10,000.

A taste bud is goblet-shaped, with several receptor cells arranged much like the segments of an orange. Slender apical portions of the tops of each cell (microvilli) project into a "taste pore" at the top of the bud and thus are in contact with whatever taste stimuli are present on the tongue. The microvilli presumably contain the sites at which the physicochemical events giving rise to the neural activity take place.

Neural Connections with Receptor Cells

The receptor cells are innervated by nerve fibers which interdigitate to form a plexus beneath the taste bud and extend upward toward the receptor cells. The fibers terminate close to the receptor cell forming a synapse between the cell and the sensory fiber. A single nerve fiber may branch and innervate more than one taste cell. In addition, more than one nerve fiber may send branches to the same taste cell. These taste fibers run from the receptor cells to the brain via three cranial nerves. Fibers from the front of the tongue enter the chorda tympani nerve, which is a branch of the facial or seventh nerve. Fibers from the back of the tongue enter the glossopharyngeal or ninth nerve and fibers from the larynx and pharynx enter the vagus or tenth nerve.

The projections of these fibers to the central nervous system can be studied with several different techniques. Stimulating the taste nerves electrically or the tongue electrically or chemically produces responses that can be recorded from the areas of the brain to which the nerves project. Placing lesions in these areas of the brain causes degeneration along the projections that can be observed histologically. Since lesions also interfere with normal functioning, areas in the brain mediating taste can be located by observing which lesion placements produce impaired taste behavior.

Studies made by using the methods described above have provided the following information about the central projections of the taste nerves. The taste fibers of the seventh, ninth, and tenth cranial nerves meet in the solitary nucleus of the medulla. The taste tract then extends to the thalamus near the area containing tactile input from the face and tongue (Pfaffmann et al., 1961). The localization of taste in the cortex has proved to be most difficult. Benjamin and his coworkers have found two cortical taste projection areas in the squirrel monkey. One of these areas is located in somatosensory area 1 (S1), which contains the cortical projection area for tactile input from the tongue. This area is not exclusively concerned with taste but contains units responsive to tactile and temperature stimulation as well (Landgren, 1961; Benjamin et al., 1968). The other area is located a short distance away in the anterior opercular-insular cortex which is within the sylvian fissure. This area in the sylvian fissure may be responsive only to taste (Benjamin & Burton, 1968).

Taste Cell Replacement

The life span of the taste cells was studied by Beidler (1963). By radioactively "labeling" the chromosomes of newly dividing epithelial cells, he demonstrated that some of these new cells move into the taste bud and become taste cells. These taste cells have an average life span of about 10 days in the rat (Beidler & Smallman, 1965). As the taste cell ages, it moves toward the center of the taste bud and presumably becomes innervated by different fibers. Beidler suggested that the sensitivity of a taste cell to various stimuli may change with the age of the cell. In this case, constancy would be maintained in the taste system because fibers near the edge of the taste bud would always innervate young taste cells while those near the center would innervate old ones.

The maintenance of the taste bud is apparently dependent on the taste nerves because the taste buds degenerate when the taste nerves are cut and regenerate as the nerves grow back. Oakley (1967) has shown, however, that the sensitivity of taste cells to different stimuli does not appear to be determined by the type of taste nerve innervating them. He cut the chorda tympani and glossopharyngeal nerves and crossed them, so that, after growing back, each nerve innervated the part of the tongue normally innervated by the other. These two nerves normally are maximally sensitive to different taste stimuli; for example, the glossopharyngeal nerve is more sensitive to quinine than the chorda tympani. After crossing, the sensitivities of the nerves changed. Thus sensitivity to different tastes appears to be determined by the tongue area that is innervated by the nerve and not the nerve itself.

TASTE PHENOMENA

The following sections are concerned with the kinds of taste phenomena that have been studied in man and other animals. The studies on human subjects were psychophysical for the most part, although some electrophysiological recordings are available. The studies on other animals were both psychophysical and electrophysiological.

Electrophysiological recording methods have made possible the study of the neural correlates of taste-directed behavior in receptor cells, peripheral nerve fibers, and the cells and fibers of central nervous system structures connected with taste. One study involved the recording of receptor potentials through a microelectrode that had been inserted into a single taste cell. After the microelectrode had been placed in the interior of the taste cell, a negative potential change (30 to 50 mV) was produced with respect to the tissues outside the cell (Kimura & Beidler,

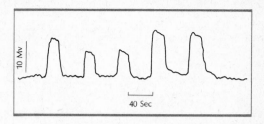

Figure 6.3. Receptor potential of a rat taste cell in response to 0.1 M of NaCl, KCl, NH_4Cl, $CaCl_2$, and $MgCl_2$ applied to tongue surface with water rinses between stimuli. (Kimura & Beidler, 1961.)

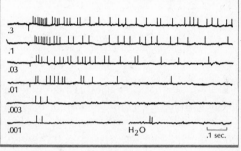

Rat Na Cl Series

Figure 6.4. Responses of a single rat chorda tympani fiber sensitive to NaCl. Responses of this fiber are shown by profile D in Figure 6.7 (Pfaffmann, 1955.)

1961). When taste solutions were flowed over the tongue, slow, positive deflections of this steady potential resulted (see Figure 6.3). The magnitude of these graded deflections depends on the concentration[1] and the solution used.

Another recording technique yields action potentials from single nerve fibers. These potentials consist of a series of "spikes" of negative potential rather than graded potential changes like those of the receptor cell (see Figures 6.4 and 6.11). To apply this technique, the nerve must be dissected, under high visual magnification, into small strands of only one or a few functioning single fibers each. These small strands are then placed on electrodes

[1]A solution has a concentration of 1 mole if the molecular weight of the substance, in grams, is added to enough water to make one liter of solution.

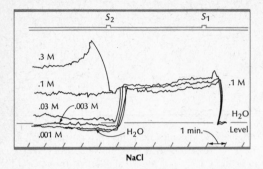

Figure 6.5. (Read from right to left) Several superimposed, averaged whole chorda tympani responses from the rat. 0.1 M NaCl (S_1) was applied for 5 minutes followed by water or one of several other NaCl concentrations (S_2). The magnitude of the whole nerve response is proportional to the average impulse frequency across all fibers. (Pfaffmann & Powers, 1964.)

and the potential changes that take place at the electrodes are amplified so that they can be displayed on an oscilloscope or recorded on magnetic tape for storage. Action potentials vary in frequency with the concentration and the solution used. In general, the frequency is highest when the solution is first applied to the tongue and then it decreases to a steady average value, although some solutions, in particular sugars, produce responses that gradually increase over the first few seconds.

Still another technique involves placing the whole nerve on a relatively large electrode. This provides information about the average responses from a population of fibers. Responses from whole nerves appear on an oscilloscope as a large number of single fiber responses superimposed. For data analysis such responses are usually "averaged" electronically with an "integrator" or summator so that a potential is produced that is proportional to the frequencies of the spikes and the number of fibers stimulated in the whole nerve (see Figure 6.5).

Recordings from the central nervous system are obtained both with microelectrodes that record from one or a few neural units and with larger electrodes that record from populations of units.

In the following section the data on each taste phenomenon will be divided into two sections; the human studies, which are primarily psychophysical, and the animal studies, which are primarily electrophysiological. Ideally, psychophysical and electrophysiological data should be obtained from the same species to allow the best determination of the neural correlates of taste. In a few cases direct comparisons are possible.

Some neural recordings have been made from man during ear surgery. The studies were made during the surgery because the chorda tympani passes across the ear drum, on its way from the tongue to the medulla, and is exposed during the procedure. Consequently it can be readily cut and placed on an electrode, and neural responses to various solutions applied to the tongue can be recorded (Diamant et al., 1963).

In addition, several techniques have provided behavioral measures in species other than man that can be compared to the information available in the nervous system of these species. Even though direct comparisons between the results obtained from psychophysical and electrophysiological studies on the same species are not always available, the similarities in taste mechanisms across species allow many meaningful cross-species comparisons between human psychophysics and animal electrophysiology as long as these comparisons are made with caution.

Intensity

Human data As the concentration of a taste solution is increased above threshold, the intensities of the resulting sensations increase in magnitude. This increase can be measured by both indirect and direct scaling methods. The indirect methods (see Chapter 3) have been used to establish thresholds and to provide jnd scales for some taste solutions (Pfaffmann, 1959). More recently, the direct methods have been used to scale taste intensity Lewis (1948) used the fractionation method (see Chapter 3) to construct intensity scales for sucrose, quinine sulfate, tartaric acid, and sodium chloride (NaCl). Beebe-

Center and Waddell (1948) generalized these scales by having subjects make intensity matches between different concentrations of the four solutions. They arbitrarily defined a unit called a "gust" as the perceived intensity of a 1 percent sucrose solution. Thus the intensity of any of the four solutions used could be expressed in terms of gusts by comparing it with the sucrose standard. Stevens (1960) constructed scales for saccharine, sucrose, and NaCl using a simpler direct method, that of magnitude estimation (see Chapter 3). These taste scales, like the scales he constructed for other modalities, suggest that the mathematical relationship between stimulus intensity and sensation intensity is a power function, although other results suggest limitations for this generalization (Ekman, 1961; Ekman & Akesson, 1964; McBurney, 1966). Deviations from the power law are important to the theory of scaling but do not invalidate the direct methods as a means of investigating a particular sensory system.

The magnitude estimation procedure has proved to be of great utility in taste psychophysics because of the convenience and speed with which data can be collected, which in turn minimizes subject fatigue and boredom that can seriously distort results.

The size of the tongue area stimulated has an effect on taste intensity. Camerer (1870) demonstrated that concentrations of NaCl that are near threshold were identified correctly less often if the concentrations were placed on a small area of the tongue than they were if placed on a larger one. When extremely small areas or single papillae are stimulated, quality itself may be difficult to identify (Öhrwall, 1891; Kiesow, 1898; von Békésy, 1966; Harper, Jay, & Erickson, 1966). Systematic investigations have confirmed that the concentration must be increased as the area stimulated is decreased before the threshold can be reached (Bujas & Ostojčić, 1941; Hara, 1955; McBurney, 1969). One interesting exception to this was reported by von Békésy (1966). He reported optimal concentrations for the stimulation of single papillae which are near threshold for stimulation of

the entire tongue. The techniques used to apply stimuli differed considerably between experiments, and this may explain the different results. Stimulating a single papilla is such a delicate operation that many more data on the anatomy and physiology of the taste papillae as well as on different methods of stimulation are required in order to reconcile the contradictory results.

A few data are available which directly compare human psychophysics and electrophysiology. For the few stimuli tested, the thresholds derived from recording experiments are similar to those derived from psychophysical experiments (Diamant et al., 1963). In addition, the magnitudes of the whole chorda tympani nerve responses were found to be directly proportional to direct magnitude estimates of intensity (Borg et al., 1967). The agreement between electrophysiological responses, which primarily reflect average action potential frequency, and psychophysical estimates of intensity strongly supports the theory that the average frequency of action potentials is the correlate of intensity.

Comparative data on other species
As concentration is increased, the average frequency of the action potentials increases (see Figure 6.4). Just as in the human data, this suggestion, that intensity is coded by the frequency of action potentials, can be tested behaviorally by comparing neural and behavioral thresholds and neural and behavioral suprathreshold responses. If the neural and behavioral thresholds are similar and if the frequency of action potentials varies over the same concentration range as the behavioral responses, average frequency would appear to be the probable correlate of intensity.

The two-bottle preference test has provided threshold data for a number of species. This test consists simply of giving an animal access to two solutions, usually water and a taste solution. The concentration of the taste solution is varied and relative intake of the taste solution above 50 percent indicates preference over water and that below 50 per-

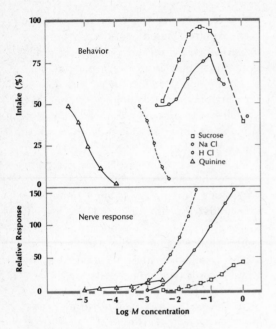

Figure 6.6. Composite graph of preference functions and whole chorda tympani responses from the rat. The upper figure shows the percentage intake of the taste solution as a function of concentration. The lower figure shows chorda tympani responses in arbitrary units. (Pfaffmann, 1960.)

cent indicates aversion in favor of water. Preference functions and whole chorda tympani nerve responses in rats are compared in Figure 6.6. Preference thresholds can be higher than sensory thresholds if the animal has no preference for or if it has an aversion to weak concentrations. For example, for the rat the neural threshold for NaCl appears to be lower than the preference threshold. The rat may simply be indifferent to very weak NaCl solutions even though it can discriminate the solution from water.

Techniques that do not depend on preferences may in some cases determine thresholds more accurately. Carr (1952) and Harriman and MacLeod (1953) used forced taste discrimination methods to obtain NaCl thresholds in rats. Carr presented both water and a NaCl solution to water-deprived rats and shocked them for drinking water. When the rats avoided water the NaCl concentration was

lowered. Threshold was defined as the concentration below which choices did not differ from chance. Harriman and MacLeod used a similar procedure, but they shocked the animals for drinking the salt solution rather than water. The thresholds at which salt in a solution could be detected in both studies were lower than the preference thresholds.

Koh and Teitelbaum (1961) developed a technique based on using taste as a cue for other behavior to obtain thresholds for sucrose, NaCl, hydrochloric acid (HCl), and quinine hydrochloride (QHCl). They trained rats to lick one of two solutions (either water or a taste solution) to obtain food pellets (or in some experiments to avoid shock). If the animal licked the correct solution, the concentration of solute was lowered, and if it licked the incorrect solution the concentration was raised. Under these circumstances the rat's choices varied around a particular concentration, which was defined to be the threshold.

In general, it was found that the levels at which taste can be detected are among the lowest behavioral values and are very similar to those derived from chorda tympani recordings. However, the levels of concentration at which HCl and QHCl can be detected are actually lower than the electrophysiological values. This finding may be explained by referring to the electrophysiological thresholds in the rat glossopharyngeal nerve (Pfaffmann et al., 1967). The HCl and QHCl thresholds are about one log unit lower in the glossopharyngeal than the chorda tympani nerve.

Behavioral and electrophysiological suprathreshold responses cannot be compared as easily as absolute thresholds because a method must be found to enable the animal to display differential responses over a range of concentrations. If an organism uses all the information available to it, the concentration range which produces different frequencies for different concentrations in the taste nerves should also produce differential behavioral responses. Preference functions give us information about the distinctiveness of different concentrations as well as about thresholds. Figure 6.6 shows preference functions and whole chorda tympani nerve responses to four taste solutions in the rat. These two sets of data indicate that the discriminations based on preference take place in the concentration range which produces changes in the average impulse frequency.

Morrison and Norrison (1966) devised a technique to scale suprathreshold concentrations in rats that does not depend on preference behavior. The rats were trained to lick at a tube containing a fairly high concentration of NaCl in water or of water alone. Five licks turned on a tone that signaled that a food reinforcement would be presented if the rat then pressed the correct one of two bars. The rat gradually learned that if he tasted NaCl, he was to press one bar; if he did not taste NaCl, he had to press the other bar for food. After training, the concentration was decreased successively until discrimination just failed. The procedure was then repeated using sucrose, tartaric acid, and quinine sulfate.

The data Morrison and Norrison used for constructing the scales consisted of the probability of a "hit," that is, choosing the taste solution bar when the solution had been in the tube, and a "false alarm," that is, choosing the taste solution bar when water had been in the tube. Morrison and Norrison applied signal detection theory (see pp. 41–46) to combine the two measures to produce an index of detectability, d'. When d' is plotted against concentration, an increasing function results that is a power function. These functions show that detectability increases with concentration over the same range in which average frequency does for NaCl and sucrose. Unfortunately there are no neural data for quinine sulfate and tartaric acid with which the detectability scales can be compared. The concentrations of minimum detectability obtained from the rat agree generally with the absolute thresholds obtained in the experiments reported above. This correspondence

of the animal behavioral and neural response functions agrees with the correspondence found for the human and strongly supports impulse frequency as the peripheral neural correlate of intensity.

Quality

Human data The existence of the four basic tastes (sweet, sour, bitter, and salty) has not been universally accepted throughout the history of taste research and is still very controversial. The very early lists of basic tastes were considerably longer. Linnaeus in 1751, for example, suggested the following list of tastes: sweet, acid, astringent, sharp, viscous, fatty, bitter, dry, aqueous, saline, and nauseous (Hollingworth & Poffenberger, 1917). Suggested lists underwent many changes but by the late nineteenth century tastes which had tactile and olfactory components had been eliminated and the familiar sweet, sour, bitter, and salty were left. For many early taste investigators one of the important questions connected with the four basic tastes was whether or not these should be considered independent modalities. Careful observation demonstrated that different areas of the tongue are differentially sensitive to different tastes. Bitter sensitivity is greatest at the back of the tongue, sweet at the tip, and sour on the sides, while salt sensitivity is more evenly distributed but greatest at the tip.

Additional observation demonstrated that some drugs have differential effects on the four tastes. One of the more prominent effects is the suppression of the sweet taste after chewing on leaves from the plant *Gymnema sylvestre* (Warren & Pfaffmann, 1959; Bartoshuk et al., 1969). Sugar on the tongue has no taste and feels like sand. The fruit of *Synsepalum dulcificum*, more commonly called miracle fruit, appears to change sour to sweet-sour (Inglett et al., 1965; Bartoshuk et al., 1969). Cocaine differentiates between the four tastes by abolishing sensations in a particular order: bitter first, then sweet, salt, and finally sour (Moncrieff, 1967). Since these four tastes appeared to be relatively independent of one another in some ways, they have often been regarded as primary taste qualities, which combine to produce all other tastes.

Observations like those described above have encouraged the search for four types of taste receptor, but the search has been generally unsuccessful. Allen and Weinberg (1925) reported data from electrical stimulation of the human tongue that for many years were considered evidence for the existence of four distinct receptor types (Moncrieff, 1967). Their results, however, were not confirmed by later studies (Jones & Jones, 1952; Ross & Versace, 1953; Pierrel, 1955). Öhrwall (1891) and Kiesow (1898) attempted to stimulate individual papillae by applying small amounts of highly concentrated taste solutions from the tip of a fine brush in order to determine whether each papilla was responsive to only one of the four tastes. Although a few such papillae were indeed found, most of them responded to two or more solutions. These data imply that if sensors specific to the four tastes exist they must consist of smaller units than papillae, for example, taste buds, receptor cells, or even particular sites on receptor cells. However, applying solutions from a brush may allow solutions to spread to adjacent areas and stimulate additional papillae. Von Békésy (1964, 1966) reported data which he felt supported the existence of four different types of papilla. When individual papillae were electrically stimulated with positive current, subjects reported tasting only one of the four tastes although the tastes reported "were a bit different from the tastes produced by chemical substances." Von Békésy reported that his experimenters could visually identify papillae of four different types under 30–60 power magnification and predict quite accurately the taste to be elicited from each. Von Békésy also stimulated single papillae chemically by touching them with small drops of solutions and found that most papillae responded to only one of the four tastes. In two subjects tested with electrical and chemical stimulation the taste qualities were the same. How-

ever, von Békésy concluded that the results do not provide a final answer to the question of whether papillae are specific to one quality partly because of difficulties involved in doing such experiments. Harper and his colleagues (1966) tested the chemical sensitivities of single papillae with a different technique and higher stimulus concentrations than von Békésy used. They used slight suction to elevate individual papillae into a chamber through which solutions could be flowed. The results corroborated those of Öhrwall and Kiesow and contradicted those of von Békésy. Most of the papillae were not specific to one of the four tastes.

In summary, the stimulation techniques and concentrations used by various researchers into taste differ extensively. Furthermore, the fact that the location of taste buds in human fungiform papillae is still uncertain suggests that much more research is needed to determine the sensitivity of single papillae. It would be interesting if human papillae turned out to be highly specific because the data to be discussed below indicate that the individual receptor cells of other mammals respond to several substances and a single papilla contains several taste buds, each one containing several receptor cells.

The adequate stimuli for the four tastes that have in the past been considered basic can be generally grouped. Sourness is primarily due to the hydrogen ion in acids, although this does not entirely account for the sour taste because an organic acid tends to taste more sour than an inorganic acid with an equal hydrogen ion concentration. Saltiness appears to be produced by both chlorides and sulfates (Dzendolet & Meiselman, 1967a). The most typical salty taste is that of NaCl. Other salts tend to have additional tastes, and in some cases the additional taste is predominant, for example, some iodide and bromide salts are bitter, and some inorganic salts of lead and beryllium are sweet. Both sweet and bitter tend to be produced by organic substances. Some of the classes of stimuli producing sweet tastes are aliphatic hydroxy compounds (which include sugars), aldehydes, ketones, amides, esters, amino acids, sulfonic acids, and halogenated hydrocarbons. The best known of the classes that taste bitter are the alkaloids (Pfaffmann, 1959).

The generalizations made above are complicated by the shifts in the quality of the taste that occur when the concentration of some chemicals is changed (Dzendolet & Meiselman, 1967b). Dzendolet (1968) has suggested a common property for substances tasting

sweet to man but no theory available suggests a common property for substances tasting bitter to man.

Comparative data The development of single-fiber recording techniques allowed a new approach to the question of the four basic tastes. If the four tastes that man reports were present in other species and if they were produced by four different types of receptors, this specificity should be observable in the

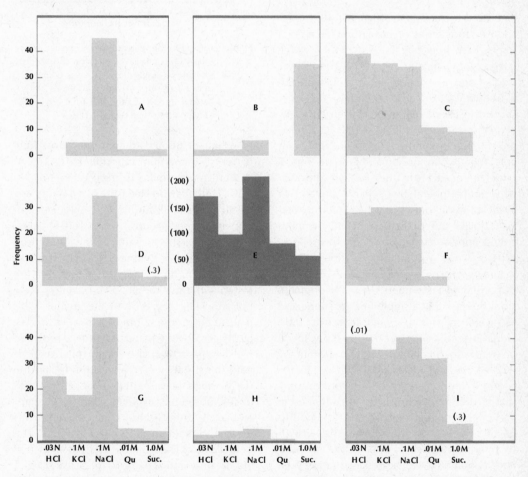

Figure 6.7. Histograms summarizing frequency of impulses during the first second to five standard taste solutions in nine different single fiber preparations in the rat. Sucrose of 0.3 M was used as the test solution in elements D and I, 0.01 M HCl, in element I. In all other cases concentrations are as shown on the abscissa. The darker histogram superimposed on the figure for element E shows the relative magnitude of whole chorda tympani responses for test solutions. Figures in parentheses give magnitudes in arbitrary units. Note that only elements D and G resemble the response of the total nerve. (Pfaffmann, 1955.)

peripheral nervous system. However, Pfaff-mann (1941), by recording action potentials from single fibers in the cat chorda tympani, found that the fibers of the peripheral nervous system were not specifically sensitive to the four basic tastes. Rather, most fibers responded to many different taste stimuli. In addition, Pfaffmann (1955) showed that the fibers cannot even be classified into a few single types, a fact that has been confirmed by subsequent investigations on cats as well as several other species (Oakley & Benjamin, 1966).

Figure 6.7 shows histograms of the responses to a series of taste stimuli for 9 rat fibers. Each fiber has its own profile, which suggests that quality cannot be coded by a single fiber. For example, looking at Figure 6.7, a frequency of action potentials of 30 per second in fiber C could be caused either by HCl, potassium chloride (KCl), or NaCl. Unless information from other fibers were also available, there would not be a unique peripheral correlate for each stimulus. This lack of specificity in peripheral fibers led Pfaffmann to suggest the "across-fiber patterning hypothesis"; quality discrimination in all mammals tested appears to be based on the relative activity across a population of fibers (Pfaffmann, 1955). The lack of specificity observed in peripheral taste fibers does not originate from the fact that a single fiber is connected to several cells because recordings from individual receptor cells also fail to show specificity for a particular taste quality (Kimura & Beidler, 1961; Tateda & Beidler, 1964). In any case the central nervous system receives only that environmental information contained in the peripheral nerves and any attempt to decode the sensory message must deal with this peripheral lack of specificity. We have already noted (p. 166) a similar situation with regard to specificity in cutaneous receptors.

Erickson (1963) elaborated the across-fiber patterning hypothesis and provided behavioral tests. He constructed profiles of fibers responsive to salts in order to determine which salts were electrophysiologically similar

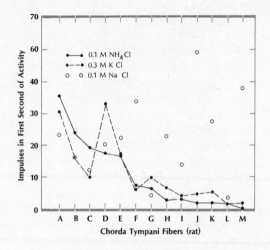

Figure 6.8. Across-fiber patterns of response to three salts in the rat. Each letter on the abscissa indicates a single fiber. Fibers are arranged in order of responsiveness to 0.1 M NH_4Cl. Patterns for NH_4Cl and KCl are more similar to each other than to NaCl. (Erickson, 1963.)

(see Figure 6.8). According to the across-fiber patterns, ammonium chloride (NH_4Cl) and KCl are more similar to each other than to NaCl. His behavioral measure of similarity was based on generalization of the avoidance of drinking. Three groups of rats were shocked for drinking a specific salt solution. One group was shocked for drinking NH_4Cl, a second for KCl, and a third for NaCl. When the rats were tested with the two salts for which they were not shocked, they showed the greatest generalization for the salt most similar according to the across-fiber pattern. Evidence provided by Nachman (1963) also supports across-fiber patterning. Rats were given lithium chloride (LiCl) which, because of its toxic effects, produces subsequent avoidance which will generalize to other salts. Generalization was greater to NaCl than to NH_4Cl or KCl. The neural data of Erickson, Deutsch, and Marshall (1965) show similar patterns for LiCl and NaCl, which differ from those for NH_4Cl and KCl.

Morrison (1967) devised a behavioral technique to measure how similar a variety of salts tasted to the rat, based on using taste as a cue for other behavior. He trained rats to press one of two bars in a Skinner box after a NaCl solution was presented and to respond to the other bar after a second solution was presented. The solution used was sucrose for one group, quinine sulfate for a second, and HCl for a third. When a test salt was introduced, the percentage of responses to the non-salt bar was taken to represent that component of the taste of the test salt. For example, if a rat had been trained to respond to bar 1 after tasting NaCl and bar 2 after tasting quinine, the responses to bar 2 after tasting KCl would represent a component in the taste of KCl similar to quinine. The percentage of responses to the non-NaCl bar across the three groups varied for the different test salts. Similarity of these percentages for test salts is assumed to represent perceptual similarity of these salts. Similarity as measured by this test and similarity determined from the data of Erickson et al. show remarkable agreement.

Evidence for the across-fiber patterning hypothesis also has been obtained, using the opossum, by Marshall (1967). He used a discrimination technique in which the taste of the solution was a cue for the presence of a water reinforcement for water-deprived opossums. In any single trial, three drinking tubes were available. One tube contained a solution of a given taste quality which was defined as correct; that is, licking this tube gave the opossum access to water. Two tubes contained a solution of a different taste quality which was incorrect; that is, licking these tubes did not give the opossum access to water. Successful discrimination was taken to be 5 seconds of licking the correct solution after sampling and rejecting one or both incorrect solutions. Nine solutions were tested and the discriminability of each pair compared to the correlation between these two solutions across all fibers tested. The more similar the solutions, as reflected by low discriminability, the more similar the across-fiber pattern. These behavioral data strongly support the across-fiber pattern as the peripheral neural correlate for quality in mammals.

Experiments on chemoreception in insects have revealed a different sensory code for quality based on highly specific receptors. Dethier and his co-workers investigated the sensory hairs on the mouth parts of the blowfly. A single sensory hair may contain 3 to 5 receptor cells, one of these responding to mechanical stimulation and the remaining cells responding to chemicals. The chemoreceptive cells respond to sugars, cations, anions, and water (Hodgson, 1967).

Von Békésy (1964) has proposed a quality code for man based on specificity. Von Békésy supports the existence of four types of receptor in man, specific to the four basic tastes. He explains the failure to find specificity in the single fibers of other mammals by suggesting that these mammals have different basic tastes so that solutions commonly used in electrophysiological experiments would not be "monogustatory." According to this view, if animals were tested with appropriate monogustatory stimuli, the single fibers would show specificity. Even if this were to be demonstrated (and so far no such stimuli have been found), the pattern across fibers would still be critical for the discrimination of all solutions tested up to now in infrahuman mammals. In von Békésy's theory these solutions would be "mixtures." All solutions other than the basic tastes in human subjects would also be mixtures. Thus even if human papillae were specifically sensitive to four tastes, this would not suggest any alternative for the across-fiber patterning hypothesis for available animal data; or any alternative to across-fiber patterning for the coding of tastes other than these four tastes in man.

The sensory code for quality is complicated by the sensitivity of taste neurons to temperature. Recordings from single chorda tympani fibers in both the rat and cat show that many taste fibers respond to thermal, as well as chemical stimulation (Sato, 1963; Yamashita, Ogaiva, & Sato, 1967). The significance of this in the sensory coding of taste is still unclear.

The way in which taste information is coded may change as that information moves from the periphery to the central nervous system. Multiunit responses from the medulla and thalamus in general appear to be similar to whole chorda tympani recordings, and single units show nonspecificity similar to that found in the periphery (Pfaffmann et al., 1961; Halpern, 1963; Makous et al., 1963). However, there is evidence for some spatial separation of taste centers in both the thalamus and the projection area for the anterior tongue in the medulla; that is, taste areas of the thalamus and the medulla may be organized somewhat chemotopically (Frommer, 1961; Halpern, 1967a; Ishiko, Amatsu, & Sato, 1967). In addition, the posterior tongue area projects to a location in the medulla that is different from that of the anterior tongue and shows sensitivities to taste solutions that differ from those of the anterior tongue area. This suggests an additional spatial separation of tastes that may be important in coding.

Halpern and Nelson (1965) recorded multiunit responses from the medulla while applying taste solutions to the posterior as well as the anterior parts of the tongue in the rat. A quinine hydrochloride solution moving from the front to the back of the tongue produced a small response in one part of the solitary nucleus of the medulla and a larger response slightly later in a different area. A NaCl solution initially produced a large response and later a smaller response. These spatiotemporal patterns of response magnitude could be one means of coding taste information in the nervous stystem.

Taste Variations within and across Species

Human data Some substances taste different to different individuals. Phenylthiocarbamide (PTC) provides a dramatic example of such an effect. Thresholds for the taste of PTC fall in a bimodal distribution so that some individuals can be classified as "tasters" and others as "nontasters." The inability to taste PTC is generally believed to be a simple Mendelian recessive characteristic (Fischer, 1967) and is dependent in part on differences in the saliva of tasters and nontasters (Fischer & Griffin, 1964). Substances more commonly

encountered than PTC also produce different responses in different individuals, although these are not generally reflected by the striking bimodal distribution found for PTC. These individual differences are reflected primarily in variations in the thresholds but secondarily also in quality judgments. Skude (1960), for example, found some subjects who reported that sucrose was bitter.

Fischer (1967) reported some results from a cooperative twin research project on the genetics of taste thresholds. Thresholds for quinine, HCl, and 6-n-phenylthiouracil (PROP), which is an odorless compound similar to PTC, were determined in identical and nonidentical twins. The greatest differences between the two kinds of twins were found for PROP thresholds, indicating a strong genetic influence. Quinine produced a slight difference and HCl produced little difference at all.

Species differences Members of the same species have generally not been studied for individual differences by animal psychophysics or electrophysiology. However, whole nerve recordings are available from more than 20 species. Perhaps the most prominent finding of the study of so many species is the inter-species variation with regard to the most effective stimuli. For example, in some species (hamster, guinea pig, monkey, man) the chorda tympani produces large responses to solutions which taste sweet to man, while in others (cat, rat) the corresponding chorda tympani responses are relatively small.

Contrast Phenomena between Different Tongue Areas

Human data For taste, the term *contrast* has been variously defined. Following von Skramlik (1926) and Dallenbach and Dallenbach (1943) we use the term here to describe the enhancement of tastes on one tongue area produced by exposing another area to various solutions. If the taste is decreased rather than enhanced, the phenomenon is called *suppression*. In general when the two stimuli have different tastes, contrast has been reported (Kiesow, 1894; von Skramlik, 1926; Bujas, 1937). For example, if sucrose is placed in one area of the tongue, this lowers the threshold for NaCl on another area; and enhances the intensity of suprathreshold concentrations of NaCl. However, these effects were dependent on stimulus concentration (Bujas, 1937). Low concentrations of sucrose enhance the sensitivity to NaCl but concentrations over 6 percent actually depress the sensitivity to NaCl. In at least one case, when the two stimuli have the same taste, suppression results. Bujas (1937) showed that if NaCl is put on one area of the tongue, the sensitivity of the tongue to NaCl is decreased in another area, as measured by an elevation in the threshold. Unfortunately, more recent data have not confirmed some of the early results (Pfaffmann et al., 1969). Contrast and suppression phenomena clearly need reexamination, particularly since they may be essential to a thorough understanding of taste mixtures.

Neural interaction An experiment on the frog suggests that the branching of taste fibers to more than one papilla may provide pathways for contrast effects (Rapuzzi & Casella, 1965). When a papilla was stimulated electrically, impulses traveled from the papilla into the nerve fiber branches that innervated that papilla and on into the central nervous system as usual, but the impulses also traveled backward (antidromically) along the other branches of the innervating fibers and on toward the other papillae contacted by those branches. Presumably, when the frog tongue is stimulated chemically the antidromic impulses coming toward a papilla could prevent impulses originating in that papilla from proceeding toward the central nervous system. Mammalian nerve fibers also branch to more than one receptor, but interactions like those in the Rapuzzi and Casella study have not been demonstrated with either electrical or chemical stimulation in mammals.

Adaptation

Human data If the tongue is exposed to a taste solution for around one minute, the taste will decrease in intensity and finally disappear, with the possible exception of stimulation by highly concentrated solutions. This decrement in taste intensity during prolonged stimulation is called *adaptation*. The tastes of foods do not ordinarily disappear when we are eating because chewing and tongue movements cause different receptors to be stimulated at different times and thus prevent prolonged, constant stimulation. The first demonstration of complete adaptation in taste unconfounded with dilution of the solution by saliva was provided by Kiesow (1898) in his investigations of the sensitivity of single papillae. The subsequent research focused on the following:

(1) The time required for the sensation to disappear; (2) The changes in absolute threshold during adaptation; (3) The changes in absolute threshold during recovery, that is, after stimulation has been stopped.

The results were as follows: The intensity

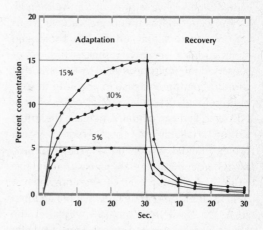

Figure 6.9. Adaptation and recovery curves for NaCl. The ordinate indicates threshold concentrations and the abscissa indicates time of adaptation or recovery. The curves show the temporal course of shifts in the absolute threshold for NaCl during adaptation and recovery for three concentrations of NaCl. The unadapted threshold was 0.24%. (Modified from Hahn, 1934.)

of most taste sensations is greatest when the solution is first applied and begins to decline very rapidly (Abrahams, Krakauer, & Dallenbach, 1937; Krakauer & Dallenbach, 1937). However, for some substances there may be an initial period where the intensity actually increases (Bujas, 1953). During adaptation, the absolute threshold increases until it is at a concentration slightly higher than that of the adapting solution. When the adapting solution is removed, the threshold begins to fall until it returns to its initial value (see Figure 6.9). As concentration increases, the time required for the sensation to disappear increases, the time required for the absolute threshold to arrive at a value slightly above that of the adapting solution increases, and the time required to recover the original threshold increases (Hahn, 1934; Abrahams, Krakauer, & Dallenbach, 1937; Krakauer & Dallenbach, 1937). McBurney and Pfaffmann (1963) demonstrated that the "unadapted" threshold for salt is itself a consequence of adaptation to salt in the saliva. When saliva is removed with a distilled water rinse, the threshold drops to about $\frac{1}{30}$ of the value obtained when saliva is present on the tongue.

The experiments mentioned above focus on the decremental effects of prolonged stimulation on sensitivity, that is, the loss of sensation originally produced by the adapting stimulus and the increase in absolute threshold. Prolonged stimulation has other effects, however, and can actually increase the information available to the nervous system (Keidel, Keidel, & Wigand, 1961). McBurney, Kasschau, and Bogart (1967) measured the size of the jnd near 0.1 M NaCl. The jnd was half as large after the tongue had become adapted to 0.1 M NaCl than the jnd was after the tongue was adapted to water. Thus a smaller change could be detected after adaptation to 0.1 M NaCl.

The association of adaptation with increasing information concerning taste is also supported by experiments on quality shifts. The classic experiments on adaptation mentioned above were concerned with the re-

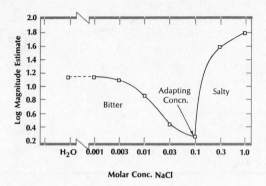

Figure 6.10. Estimated magnitude of sodium chloride solutions after adaptation to sodium chloride. The quality labels reflect the predominant qualities reported for the sub-adapting and supra-adapting concentrations (Modified from Bartoshuk et al., 1964; Bartoshuk, 1968; and McBurney, 1966.)

sponses to concentrations equal to or greater than the adapting concentration (supra-adapting concentrations) and assumed that concentrations lower than the adapting concentration (sub-adapting concentrations) would be ineffective. However, these sub-adapting concentrations undergo quality as well as intensity changes. Bartoshuk, McBurney and Pfaffman (1964) showed that after adaptation to NaCl, sub-adapting concentrations of salt tasted either bitter or sour. Furthermore, McBurney (1966) showed that the magnitude of the sub-adapting bitter or sour taste increased as the concentration decreased, with a maximum at water (see Figure 6.10). In fact, the bitter taste ascribed to distilled water by many investigators is apparently the result of adaptation to salivary salt. The fact that water can take on discriminable taste qualities if it follows exposure to appropriate solutions was noted anecdotally in the early literature about taste research (von Skramlik, 1926). These observations have been substantiated for HCl, QHCl, and sucrose (Bartoshuk, 1968). For most observers, adaptation to QHCl or HCl makes sub-adapting concentrations taste sweet and adaptation to sucrose makes sub-adapting concentrations taste bitter.

In the discussion above, the term "adaptation" was used to refer to the decrement in sensation reported by a human observer during prolonged taste stimulation. Unfortunately, there is no universally accepted definition of "adaptation." The term has been used to refer to changes in sensation measured psychophysically, to refer to the physiological mechanisms underlying these changes in sensation, or both. In addition there are different sensation changes, for example, the disappearance of taste and the increase in absolute threshold. The only feature these definitions share is dependence on prolonged stimulation. (In fact, in some cases the operation of prolonged stimulation itself is called "adaptation.")

The problem of definition is complicated still further in animal work, where behavioral responses paralleling the psychophysical reports of human subjects are extremely difficult to obtain; information about taste depends heavily on studies made using electrophysiology.

The use of the same term in the study of all the senses has also provided some confusion. It has been established that prolonged stimulation of most if not all the senses decreases their sensitivity to the applied stimulus. However, the mechanisms and the significance of this decrease vary considerably in the different senses. Using one term for such varied phenomena has emphasized some interesting similarities between the senses; however, the differences between them may be even more interesting. Occasionally the decrease in sensitivity has been described as "fatiguelike." This is rarely justified not only because "fatigue" itself is usually undefined but also because "fatigue" fails to suggest the shifts in quality and differential sensitivity that result from prolonged stimulation. Thus, restricting the use of "adaptation" to the reported decrease in taste sensation with prolonged stimulation avoids implicitly grouping phenomena which may or may not prove to be closely related. For example, Bujas (1939) showed that the increase in the absolute threshold does not keep exact pace with the decrease in sensation. The different taste phenomena that accompany prolonged stimulation probably are produced by very different mechanisms and may even be mediated by widely separated parts of the nervous system. Hopefully, as the effects of stimulation are studied further, the relations between the various phenomena will suggest a more precise usage for "adaptation" or a better term.

Electrophysiology of adaptation Not all of the taste phenomena described above have been systematically studied with electrophysiological methods; however, some neural activity changes in animals are analogous to human adaptation. When a given taste solution is applied to the tongue, an initial transient increment usually occurs in the activity of the whole nerve. This is followed by a decline to a steady-state rate of activity that is characteristic of the given concentration (see Figure 6.5). If a higher concentration is applied, a new transient increment and subsequent decline to the corresponding steady-state results. If a lower concentration is applied, a transient decrement and subsequent increase to the steady-state level results. This is especially clear in the rat, which tends to have high steady-state rates. Some species, in particular the cat, show much lower steady-state rates so that most of their responses tend to be transients. In the rat, the steady-state responses to most salts continue until the salt is removed. However, in man, taste sensations disappear rapidly during prolonged stimulation. If man's peripheral neural responses were like those of the rat, some additional mechanism would be necessary to account for the rapid disappearance of sensation. However, recordings from the human chorda tympani indicate that a steady-state rate is not maintained (Borg et al., 1967). During continuous stimulation the peripheral neural response appears to decline in much the same way as does the sensation.

The generalizations made above are complicated by responses to water. The "water" response was originally discovered by Zotterman, first in the frog (Zotterman, 1950) and then in the cat and other species (Liljestrand & Zotterman, 1954; Zotterman, 1956). This response was originally thought to result from a type of fiber responsive to water which was present in some species (for example, cat, rabbit, monkey) and absent in others (for example, rat, man). However, if the tongue is rinsed with appropriate solutions, water produces a peripheral neural response even in the rat, analogous to the water tastes produced in man with appropriate adapting solutions. In addition, if different rinsing solutions are used, different fibers respond to water in species supposedly having a unitary "water" response; for example, one cat fiber may respond to water following exposure to a salt solution, but it may not respond to water following exposure to acid; another fiber may do the reverse (Bartoshuk & Pfaffmann, 1965). The responses to water are contingent on the concentration as well as the chemical nature of the preceding stimulus. A fiber responsive to water following salt will also respond to salts weaker than the concentration of the "adapting" salt. Thus, while sub-adapting concentrations produce decreases in some fibers, they produce increments in some others. The role of these positive responses to sub-adapting concentrations and water is still obscure. Presumably if the pattern across fibers produced by water is similar to the pattern produced by some other taste solution, the water would taste similar to that other solution. This may be the explanation of the bitter, sweet, and sour tastes of water reported in man (Bartoshuk, 1968).

Cross-adaptation

Human data *Cross-adaptation,* like "adaptation," has not been precisely defined; in general it refers to the effects on the taste of one substance by previous adaptation to a different substance. The presence of cross-adaptation can be established by demonstrating an increase in threshold or a decrease in intensity for suprathreshold concentrations of the second solution. However, the adapting solution may also enhance the taste of the second stimulus. Experiments have tested for cross-adaptation or enhancement among groups of substances that have different as well as similar tastes. In general, enhancement has been reported for tastes that are not similar (Kiesow, 1894; Mayer, 1927; Dallenbach & Dallenbach, 1943; Meiselman, 1968). When a change in threshold is used as the measure for substances with similar tastes, cross-adaptation is found among many but not all sweet substances and bitter substances but among all acids. Hahn (1949) found no cross-adaptation among 24 salts with a salty taste; however, his subjects responded to total intensity. When Smith and McBurney (1969) instructed subjects to divide total intensity among appropriate qualities they found that adaptation to NaCl removed the salty taste from other salts.

Cross-adaptation phenomena have been considered important for theories of receptor mechanisms. The decreased effectiveness of the second substance is assumed to mean that the two substances stimulate at least in part the same receptor sites. The second substance is less effective presumably because the first substance has already produced some adaptation.

Neural data Few electrophysiological data analogous to human cross-adaptation or enhancement data have been reported. Most of the observations have been on salts. Beidler (1961) made recordings from the rat chorda tympani and found that exposing the tongue to 0.1 M calcium chloride for nearly 4 minutes had only a small effect on the response to 0.1 M NaCl. Halpern (1967b) obtained similar results from the medulla using calcium chloride and NaCl also; however, for some other salt pairs, he found results analogous to the human cross-adaptation results achieved by McBurney and Lucas. Analysis of single unit data at different levels in the nervous system would be particularly interesting.

Andersen, Funakoshi, and Zotterman (1963) demonstrated that NaCl depressed chorda tympani responses to sucrose in the dog. Thus fibers responsive to sucrose after the tongue had been rinsed with water were much less responsive to sucrose after the tongue had been rinsed with NaCl. However, fibers responsive to NaCl were not inhibited by prior rinsing with sucrose. These results are in the opposite direction from the enhancement usually found between NaCl and sucrose in human psychophysical experiments (Kiesow, 1894; Mayer, 1927), although this particular comparison may have little meaning. The early human data, although very interesting, are so sketchily described that a great deal of additional work is necessary to accurately determine the facts about cross-adaptation as well as its role in sensory coding.

Mixtures

Human data   Early opinion held that, in general, a mixture of taste solutions produced "competition." That is, the overall sensation was produced by tasting each component separately at different times and on different parts of the tongue (Luciani, 1917). However, Kiesow (1896) provided one example of a "compensatory" interaction. He mixed weak solutions of sucrose and salt and found that the resulting solution had little taste at all. Later work (Fabian & Blum, 1943) demonstrated that other taste mixtures can also produce compensation as defined by an enhancement or depression of a taste by the addition of another substance. A considerable amount of work has been done on these interactions both with taste substances dissolved in water and other natural mixtures such as fruit nectars and tomato juice (Amerine, Pangborn, & Roessler 1965). In general, when two substances are mixed the intensities of both components appear to be suppressed. However, when one or both components are weak, some are enhanced rather than suppressed.

Neural data   Mixtures applied to tongues of rats, dogs, and cats appear to produce chorda tympani nerve responses that are an algebraic summation of the responses to the components in the mixture if the magnitudes of the component responses are equated (Halpern, 1967b). This holds true, however, only when the responses to the individual components are not near the maximum response. In addition, if a mixture contains components that stimulate the same receptor sites, the response to the mixture will not necessarily be an algebraic sum. For example, 0.1 M NaCl added to 0.1 M LiCl produces a response equivalent to 0.2 M NaCl in the rat (Beidler, 1953). Because the response to 0.2 M NaCl is not twice the response to 0.1 M NaCl, 0.1 M NaCl and 0.1 M LiCl would not sum algebraically.

Halpern (1967b) has compared response magnitudes in the medulla with those in the chorda tympani. Responses to mixtures in the medulla are smaller than the sum of the responses to the components. This suggests the possibility of interactions between responses to different chemicals in the medulla (Halpern, 1967b), which could mean that some of the complex effects of mixtures that have been reported by human subjects may be produced centrally.

Taste Enhancers

Human data   Monosodium glutamate (MSG) is said to enhance whatever other tastes are present. Human subjects are only in partial agreement on this point, but, in general, the enhancement by MSG does not appear to occur with simple test solutions (Amerine, Pangborn, & Roessler, 1965). Foods to which MSG has been added are often reported to be more palatable, but this may be due to the addition of the taste of the salt itself. The 5'-nucleotides are used as taste enhancers in Japan. These substances appear to combine with MSG to produce what is known as a synergistic action, that is, their combined effect is greater than the sum of their separate effects. For example, Yamaguchi (1967) reported a synergistic effect for sodium inosinate (IMP) and MSG by demonstrating that the taste intensity of a mixture of the two was greater than the sum of the intensities of the components.

Neural effects Adachi (1964) studied responses of the cat chorda tympani to solutions formed by adding IMP or MSG to sodium chloride, quinine, sucrose, or acetic acid. IMP and MSG added to solutions of NaCl or acetic acid appeared to have little effect but when added to quinine or sucrose, produced smaller responses than those produced by either quinine or sucrose alone. These data certainly do not support the conclusion that

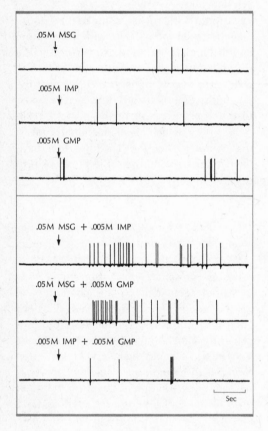

Figure 6.11. Responses of a single chorda tympani fiber from a cat to 0.05M MSG, 0.005M IMP, and 0.005M GMP solutions and to the mixed solutions of 0.05M MSG and 0.005M IMP; 0.05M MSG and 0.005M GMP; and 0.005M IMP and 0.005M GMP. (Adachi, Funakoshi, & Kawamura, 1967.)

MSG enhances the tastes of simple solutions.

Adachi, Funakoshi, and Kawamura (1967) also examined the effects of MSG, IMP, and sodium guanylate (GMP) on the taste system of the cat (see Figure 6.11). MSG, IMP, and GMP alone produced very little response, and IMP added to GMP also produced very little response. However, MSG added to either IMP or GMP produced large responses, demonstrating that the synergistic effect does occur in the cat.

The phenomena of adaptation, contrast, and suppression, and the taste interactions resulting from mixtures, are undoubtedly related. However, they must be carefully distinguished, for the mechanisms of the different effects are very likely to be different. Contrast and suppression are phenomena that involve spatially separated receptors, while adaptation involves temporal effects on the same receptors as well. Interactions in mixtures involve all of these effects as well as the simultaneous presence of two or more substances.

Effects of Bodily Needs

Human deprivation effects Wilkins and Richter (1940) reported that a boy with a tumor of the adrenal gland developed a craving for NaCl. Because the adrenal gland is responsible for salt balance, the boy was presumably in a state of salt deprivation. A correlation of this type between a bodily need and a "specific hunger" for the needed substance led some investigators to suggest that taste sensitivity varies under conditions of need. Several studies with man and other species have examined thresholds as a function of fasting and deprivation of specific substances, such as NaCl. The human experiments have produced conflicting results. Some investigators found that absolute thresholds are elevated after eating while others studying fasting found no changes (Moore et al., 1965). Furthermore, one investigator (Yensen, 1959) found that when the amount of sodium in the blood decreased, the NaCl threshold decreased, while others

(De Wardener & Herxheimer, 1957; Henkin & Solomon, 1962; Pfaffmann, 1964) found no change in the threshold for the detection of salt with changes in blood sodium. In two studies, no relation was found between blood sugar levels and sucrose thresholds (Bartolović, 1964; Yensen, 1964). At this time there is no convincing evidence that large threshold shifts take place following deprivation.

Comparative data Electrophysiological data give a much clearer description of the influence of bodily needs on taste perception than do the human psychophysical data discussed above. Pfaffmann and Bare (1950) showed that neural thresholds for salt are the same both for adrenalectomized and normal rats; Nachman and Pfaffmann (1963) showed that the neural thresholds are the same for normal rats and those deprived of NaCl; Pfaffmann and Hagstrom (1955) showed that the neural thresholds for sucrose are the same for hamsters given an injection of insulin and those that were not. This evidence suggests that the lowered preference thresholds shown for NaCl by adrenalectomized rats and for sucrose by hamsters injected with insulin reflect a change not in peripheral taste sensitivity but rather in an increased preference for weak solutions. Complicating the results, however, the chorda tympani had been cut in order to place it on the recording electrode in these experiments. Thus, any possible sensitivity changes mediated by efferent fibers in this nerve could not have been observed. Sensitivity changes mediated by changes in salivary constituents could not be observed either, because saliva is rinsed from the tongue during electrophysiological experiments, and the possibility certainly exists that changes in salivary constituents could produce threshold variations via changes in the state of adaptation (see the discussion above on the effects of changes in the adaptation level). However, just as with the human data there is no convincing evidence now available that threshold changes do result from deprivation.

THEORIES OF TASTE RECEPTOR MECHANISMS

The complete sequence of events leading from the application of a taste stimulus to the graded potential in the receptor cell and ultimately to the action potentials in the sensory axon is still unknown. The initial interaction between the stimulus and the receptor site has received the most attention. The presence of enzymes in the area of the taste bud led Baradi and Bourne (1951) to suggest an enzyme theory of taste. According to this theory the action of enzymes could lead to ionic changes which would ultimately give rise to action potentials. This enzyme activity would be differentially influenced by taste substances. For example, one taste could inhibit the activity of a specific enzyme, enhance that of another, and leave a third unchanged. A second taste substance might enhance all three. Baradi and Bourne localized enzymes in six main sites in and around the taste papillae of the rabbit. The pattern of enhancement, inhibition, or no change across these six sites was presumed to code taste quality. Beidler (1961) criticized this theory on several points. In particular, he pointed out that the data concerning the enzyme localizations are themselves in question. Furthermore, the theory contradicts some established neurophysiological evidence, for taste neurons do not fire at moderate rates in the absence of stimulation and then vary their rate of fire with stimulation, as Bourne theorized.

Beidler's more recent work on the initial stimulus-receptor interaction establishes the position that the responsive sites are located on the microvilli of the taste cells and that the molecules of the taste stimulus are bound to the outside of the cell membrane by weak physical forces. This hypothesis is consistent with much of the data from mammals as well as insects (Beidler, 1954; Evans & Mellon, 1962).

The nature of the receptor sites responding to sugars has been studied in two species. Dastoli and Price (1966) isolated from cow tongues a protein fraction that formed complexes with substances sweet to man. Although these results are not conclusive, this material may be the component of the taste bud which interacts with sugars. Evans (1963) has suggested some requirements for the sugar sites in the blowfly based on both electrophysiological and behavioral data. At least two different sites are necessary, because the relative sensitivity to two different sugars was differentially affected by rearing the larva in the presence of one sugar or the other. These sites appear to be associated with a single receptor cell. Evans investigated the requirements of the receptor site for D-glucose by testing compounds with small structural changes and was able to determine what part of the glucose molecule interacts with the receptor site. The manner in which the receptor membrane is depolarized by the physical combination of one part of a stimulus molecule and the receptor site is not known.

HEDONIC PROPERTIES OF TASTE STIMULI

The discussion above has dealt mainly with the processing of information by the taste system; however, tastes have hedonic properties also. Some tastes appear to elicit approach or avoidance very generally across species. Substances tasting sweet to man are usually important nutrients in the environments of most organisms, and are readily accepted by most species (Frings, 1951; Maller & Kare, 1967), whereas substances tasting bitter to man, which are often poisonous alkaloids, are rejected (Fisher & Griffin, 1964). These hedonic responses apparently begin to be made very early in the life of an individual organism; furthermore, they are relatively unchanged by subsequent learning. Jacobs (1964) measured the acceptability of saccharine, water, and quinine in neonate rats by rating the acceptance or rejection of drops applied to the tongue. Maximum acceptance of saccharine together with avoidance of

quinine was reached 9 days after birth, which control experiments showed was related to maturation and not to simple trial and error learning (Jacobs & Sharma, 1968). Warren and Pfaffmann (1958) raised newborn guinea pigs on a solution of sucrose octaacetate, which is bitter to man and avoided by guinea pigs, and which served as the only source of water for three weeks. Later these animals showed the typical rejection of sucrose octaacetate.

The NaCl preference displayed by most species is another example of an apparently biologically determined hedonic response. However, preference for NaCl appears to depend on species and concentration. The hamster, for example, shows no preference for NaCl (Carpenter, 1956). The rat, which has been extensively studied, shows a peak preference for salt when it is in a solution of about 0.1 M and begins to avoid it in solutions near 0.3 M. The preference of rats for NaCl was challenged by Deutsch and Jones (1960). They suggested, on the basis of neural data reported by Zotterman (1956), that the intake of weak salts resulted from the similarity of the sensory codes for weak salt and water. Rats would drink more weak salt than water because the neural signal was diluted by the salt. Additional evidence, both neural and behavioral, does not support the diluted water hypothesis (Benjamin et al., 1965; Stearns, 1965).

The preference of rats for NaCl is dramatically demonstrated with the so-called "contingent lick procedure" developed by Fisher (1965). The rat is required to lick at one tube a specified number of times to get access to a second tube. When the first tube contains salt the rat does not shift to the water in the second tube. However, when the first tube contains water, the rat shifts to the salt as soon as it is made available.

Although these taste-directed preferences can be clearly demonstrated when a choice of solutions is offered, taste is obviously not the sole cue controlling food intake. A number of experiments show that rats will adjust their total food intake to maintain a constant caloric intake when the caloric density of the diet is varied. For example, they increase intake when the diet is diluted with cellulose, which contains no calories, and decrease intake when the diet is calorically enriched with corn oil (Jacobs & Sharma, 1969).

Taste may play a role in the regulation of food intake by inducing some of the metabolic changes (in the absence of ingestion) that usually occur postingestionally. Nicolaidis (1969) demonstrated several direct effects of oral stimulation on metabolic events. One of the most striking of these was the rise in blood glucose after either sucrose or saccharine was applied to the tongues of deprived rats.

The neural correlates of the hedonic properties of taste stimuli have not been studied as extensively as those of the informational content. As electrophysiological techniques improve, these very complex hedonic properties will probably receive more attention. Hopefully, the information obtained about taste will be helpful in understanding other sensory experiences, for example, pain, which also possess affective properties.

Maxwell M. Mozell

THE CHEMICAL SENSES

II. OLFACTION

7

Substances give off some of their molecules. These are then transported to the animal through the medium—air or water—in which he lives. Higher organisms are supplied with receptors of several types, each with its own afferent neural pathway, that can respond to at least some chemical molecules. In vertebrates these receptors include the olfactory and gustatory together with many free nerve endings apparently supplied by the trigeminal, glossopharyngeal, and vagus nerves.

Because any or all of the sensory receptors may, under some set of circumstances, respond to the molecules of a particular chemical stimulus it is very difficult to differentiate or define any of the chemical senses precisely by simply referring to the characteristics of their stimuli. For instance, in terrestrial animals one may be able to distinguish smell from taste by saying that the molecules underlying the former are in the form of vapors and are thus transmitted to the animal through the air. However, this does not hold true for aquatic animals, where all the molecules (those affecting both gustatory and olfactory receptors) are in aqueous solutions. Neither, in view of these aquatic forms, can an iron-clad distinction be made on the basis that olfaction involves the detection of molecules emanating from distant sources whereas gustation seems more like a contact sense. Since in these forms the gustatory and olfactory receptors are stimulated with molecules dispersed in an aqueous solution, the source of the molecules for either sense may be either near or far from the animal.

Note, too, that even in the air-breathers one cannot dogmatically say that olfaction is definable as the sense that responds to air-borne vapors, for, as we shall see, the free nerve endings also respond to such stimuli. In addition, it has recently been shown (Tucker & Shibuya, 1965) that the olfactory receptors of an air-breather can respond quite well to odorous molecules in an aqueous solution, provided that the solution is properly intro-duced into the nasal cavity. Thus, in the final analysis, the chemical senses are distinguished from each other not by the stimuli that im-pinge upon them nor by the way the stimulus is presented. Rather they can only be dis-tinguished by their structure. That is, each chemoreceptor has a different morphology and a different afferent neural input to the central nervous system.

The very maintenance of life for many animal species depends upon the olfactory system. On the one hand, the detection of

olfactory cues is essential in foraging for prey, whereas, on the other hand, the detection of such olfactory cues is the first line of defense against the animal's own predators. In many species the finding of a mate depends upon olfaction. A species of moth, for instance, is reputed to be able to find his mate by olfac-tory cues from a distance of up to $2\frac{1}{2}$ miles (Moncrieff, 1967). Many animals use odorous secretions and excretions to mark off terri-tories and to designate places they have been. Among the ants and social insects the whole society appears to communicate through olfactory stimuli called pheromones (Wilson, 1965). The adult salmon, swimming inland from the sea, relies heavily upon olfaction in his quest for the stream in which he was spawned (Wisby & Hasler, 1954).

To civilized man olfaction no longer has the life-or-death significance that it still has for lower species, although it has some im-portance—the smell of smoke signifying fire, for example. Rather, civilized man has taken advantage of the strong affective tone the

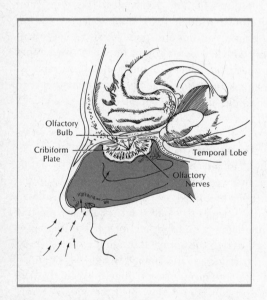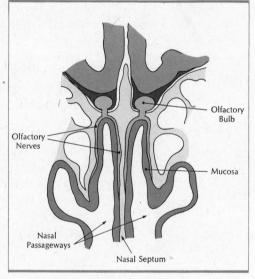

Figure 7.1. The gross anatomy of the olfactory system in man. *Left.* A saggital section through the head showing a lateral view of the position of the olfactory receptive area, the cribiform plate, and the olfactory bulb. The receptor layer of the mucosa has been stripped away showing the underlying bundles of olfactory nerve axons. *Right.* Cross-sectional view of the uppermost nasal passageway lined with the receptor-bearing mucosa. Also shown is the course of the olfactory nerves toward the bulb.

olfactory stimuli can generate by using them for esthetic or hedonic purposes. Thus, rather than merely relying upon odors to forage for a meal, he adds such odors as those of herbs and spices to his food, so that eating is not only a necessity but a pleasurable experience as well. For other hedonic reasons he douses himself with perfumes, grows honeysuckle in his backyard, burns incense in his church, or puts his clothes in a cedar chest.

Not all odors are pleasurable to man, and several large industries have been developed to produce deodorants that protect man from the displeasure generated by certain odors which otherwise are not particularly harmful.

FUNCTIONAL NEUROANATOMY

In man the patch of mucosa that bears olfactory receptor cells lines the lateral, medial, and superior walls of the uppermost passageway of the nasal cavity (Figure 7.1). As the axons of the olfactory receptor cells course centrally they combine into larger and larger nerve bundles and enter the cranium through a series of perforations in the bone (the cribiform plate), which forms the superior wall of the passageway. They then con-

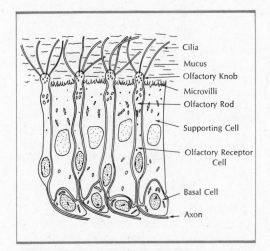

Figure 7.2. Simplified diagram of the olfactory epithelium. (Moulton & Beidler, 1967, slightly modified.)

tinue to the surface of the olfactory bulb.

The olfactory neuron is a bipolar cell which simultaneously serves as the end organ and the primary afferent fiber (Figure 7.2). The distal or dendritic end, called the *olfactory rod,* is 20–90 μ long and 1 μ in diameter (LeGros Clark & Warwick, 1946). For most of its length the olfactory rod is wrapped by supporting cells. However, near the surface of the olfactory epithelium, which is bathed in mucus, the rod ends in an unsheathed swelling called the *olfactory knob* (Bloom, 1954). This swelling supports 6 to 12 cilia, which are believed (without direct evidence) to bear the sites that are stimulated by the odorant molecules. In the frog these cilia are as long as 200 μ; their diameters are 0.25 μ proximally and 0.15 μ distally (Reese, 1965). The distal ends of the supporting cells bear a large number of microvilli which appear to become entangled with some of the cilia (de Lorenzo, 1957). This suggests a possible interrelationship between these two structures.

Of considerable interest in conceptualizing the mechanisms of olfactory stimulation and discrimination is the enormous number of receptors involved. In the rabbit there are about 50,000,000 olfactory cells on one side of the nose; about 150,000/mm² (Le Gros Clark & Warwick, 1946). Perhaps these large numbers reflect the necessity of having selectively tuned receptors for each of the vast number of odorants that can be discriminated. Perhaps the large number of olfactory cells is needed to increase the redundancy in an otherwise noisy system (that is, by replicating the same stimulation process and by increasing the number of channels transmitting the same information, momentary distortions at some points will be offset by the fidelity at other points). Perhaps the large number of receptors is needed to amplify certain aspects of the input by summating their synaptic effects on the succeeding neurons. Perhaps this vast number of closely packed receptors with their many cilia might play a role in the differentiation of vapors by providing a large, very finely divided surface area that can adsorb the incoming molecules of different chemicals in a variety of regional patterns.

Also of much theoretical interest is the mucus bathing the epithelium. In the frog this mucus is 20–35 μ thick (Reese, 1965) and covers the cilia which lie below and parallel to the surface (Reese, 1965). This suggests that odorant solubility may play a key role in determining the distribution of the incoming molecules across the receptor sheet even before the receptors themselves are triggered. Indeed, it appears probable that the number of molecules reaching the receptor and the time it takes them to do so depend upon their interaction with the constituents of the mucus. However, the number of molecules of an odor that usually can be detected is often so small that even compounds classified as insoluble might put a sufficient number of

molecules into solution to be detected. Therefore, perhaps solubility is being over-emphasized as a limiting factor in the access of the molecules to the receptors lying beneath the surface of the mucus.

The thin (0.2 μ diameter) axons of the bipolar olfactory cells are sheathed for their entire length although they themselves are unmyelinated C-fibers. Initially they are surrounded by supporting cells and basal cells (Figure 7.2). Later, where they meet below the epithelium to form a series of longitudinal bundles, groups of them are sheathed by the plasma membranes of Schwann cells, as

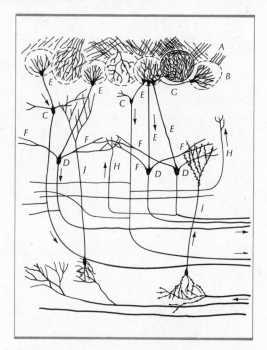

Figure 7.4. Schematic diagram showing how the neural elements of the mammalian olfactory bulb are anatomically related. *A*, primary olfactory nerves; *B*, olfactory glomeruli; *C*, tufted cells; *D*, mitral cells; *E*, primary dendrites; *F*, accessory dendrites; *G*, cells that interconnect nearby glomeruli; *H*, recurrent collateral axons; *I*, fibers passing into the bulb from both the opposite bulb and from more central brain areas; *J*, interneurons which connect the incoming fibers to the mitral and tufted cells. Arrows show the direction of information flow. (Allison, 1953b; the letter designations have been modified.)

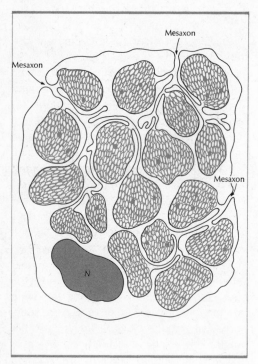

Figure 7.3. Schematic representation of the relationship of the olfactory nerve axons to the Schwann cells. Bundles of olfactory nerve cell axons are enveloped by the invaginations (called mesaxons) of the Schwann cell plasma membrane. The nucleus of the Schwann cell is denoted by *N*. (de Lorenzo, 1957.)

shown in Figure 7.3 (Gasser, 1956; de Lorenzo, 1957). This common sheath raises the possibility that the firing patterns of the axons in a given group influence each other such that the whole group can be considered a type of functional single unit.

In the olfactory bulb the axons of the primary olfactory cells synapse with the dendrites of the secondary olfactory cells, the tufted and mitral cells (Figure 7.4). These synapses are not diffusely scattered but are instead aggregated into very dense packets called the *olfactory glomeruli*. In the rabbit 26,000 primary fibers enter each glomerulus and about 100 secondary fibers leave (Allison, 1953a). Because this 260 to 1 reduction affords an excellent opportunity for summation, the final output of the glomerulus reflects the interplay of a rather large amount of incoming information.

Each receptor in the epithelium is represented directly in only one glomerulus, and, in mammals, each mitral and tufted cell also emanates from only one (Figure 7.4). Thus it might be expected that the group of secondary fibers leaving a given glomerulus carries information from only those receptors which feed into it. However, such an insulated "direct line" from periphery to central nervous system appears unlikely. In the first place "cross-talk" could occur through the cells that connect nearby glomeruli. Second, the mitral cells and the tufted cells of neighboring glomeruli appear to communicate through their accessory dendrites and recurrent axon collaterals. Finally, there are fibers passing into the bulb from more central brain areas as well as from the opposite bulb, which, through interneurons, impinge upon the secondary olfactory cells. Thus, there is an anatomical basis for believing that the output signals of a given secondary olfactory neuron may reflect information gathered from several areas of the ipsilateral olfactory mucosa, from the contralateral olfactory mucosa, and from more central areas of the brain. This last contribution probably represents processed information from other systems as well as from the olfactory system itself.

There is a regional isomorphism in the projection of the epithelium upon the bulb, but its degree of precision differs from region to region. The upper and back parts of the epithelium project quite precisely to the glomeruli on the upper surface of the bulb. Other epithelial regions, although they project to localizable areas of the bulb, do so more diffusely (LeGros Clark, 1951, 1957). Thus, there appears to be an anatomical substrate for a central nervous system analysis of the activity spatially spread across the olfactory mucosa.

Receptors other than olfactory are present in the nasal passageways. First, there are trigeminal nerve fiber endings. Second, in many species, there are the receptors lining the vomeronasal organ. This organ is a sac, tube, or slit lying on the floor of the nasal cavity. Its exact morphology varies widely between species. As we shall see, these two systems can respond to vapors, and their inputs may add further dimensions to olfactory experiences.

In addition, the pharynx also is supplied with receptors that apparently detect at least some odorous molecules. This information seems to be transmitted via the ninth and tenth cranial nerves (Henkin, 1967).

ODOR STIMULATION TECHNIQUES

As is discussed below, the concentration of any given odorant in a carrier medium is one of the primary determinants of the olfactory response. Likewise, the procedures for introducing the odorant to the olfactory mucosa also influence the responses. Unfortunately, perhaps because of the difficulties encountered in trying to control these parameters, they are often either inadequately controlled or overlooked.

Control of Concentration

Several authors have gained at least some knowledge concerning the olfactory effect of stimulus intensity by diluting the odorants with predetermined amounts of inodorous liquid solvents (Beck, Kruger, & Calabresi, 1954). These solutions are kept such that they only partially fill their containers. Although these containers can be anything from a volumetric flask to a pickle jar, they are often referred to as "sniff bottles." The use of liquid dilutions for controlling the odorant intensity coming from a "sniff bottle" is based upon an idealized system described by Raoult's and Henry's Laws. When an ideal liquid solution reaches equilibrium with its vapor in a closed container, the number of molecules of each of the constituent chemicals in that vapor phase can be calculated if two factors are known: (1) the number of molecules of the chemical which would have been in the vapor phase at the existing temperature if, as an undiluted liquid, its molecules were the only ones available for vaporization at the liquid surface; (2) the decrease in the number of these available molecules brought about by their competition with the molecules of the diluent for positions on the surface of the liquid. The first factor can be measured by the chemical's vapor pressure, which is the pressure exerted on the walls of a closed container by its molecules in the vapor phase. The vapor pressure for each chemical at a given temperature must be independently determined, and the greater the value of the vapor pressure, the greater is the concentration of molecules in the vapor phase. The second factor is measured by the mole fraction which represents the fraction of the total number of molecules in the liquid phase of the solution which is contributed by the chemical in question.[1] This is given by the following ratio:

$$\frac{\text{number of moles of the chemical}}{\begin{array}{c}\text{number of moles of the chemical} +\\ \text{number of moles of the diluent}\end{array}}$$

Thus, in the ideal system, dilution in known steps will decrease the mole fraction proportionately, and, therefore, the pressure contributed by the vapor of the odorant (and thus its concentration) will be reduced proportionately.

However, in olfactory research a dilution series is often prepared with no heed either to the vapor pressure of the chemicals or to their molecular weights. Thus, because these are constants for any one chemical (at any given set of conditions) but differ among chemicals, a series of vapor concentrations in known ratios to each other might be prepared for any one chemical by simple dilution ratios but nothing can be said about the relative concentrations between different chemicals. Diluting different chemicals the same amount does not produce the same vapor concentration unless their vapor pressures and molecular weights happen to be the same. That is, chemicals can be compared only when the calculations are based on both the mole fraction and the vapor pressure.

As is noted above the procedure to determine stimulus concentration is actually valid only for ideal solutions. An ideal solution is one in which the molecules all act individually (that is, the molecules of each chemical are attracted neither to each other nor to the molecules of the other chemical in the solution). In the vast majority of solutions, however, the molecules do attract each other; they form molecular structures that, to varying degrees, affect the accuracy with which the actual molecular concentration of the vapor phase can be predicted from the vapor pressure and the mole fraction (Stone, 1963b). Nevertheless, this method of estimating concentration can still be quite useful as an approximation. Indeed, this approximation becomes progressively more accurate as the mole fraction of the odorant is made smaller by dilution because the more dilute the solution is made, the more it approaches the ideal system.

Finally, it should be re-emphasized that even with ideal solutions the calculation of concentration described above can be strictly applied only when the solution and its vapor phase are in equilibrium. The moment the container holding the odorant is opened this

[1] It will be recalled that the number of moles of a chemical is expressed as the ratio of its weight in grams to its molecular weight and that every mole, regardless of the chemical, contains the same number of molecules.

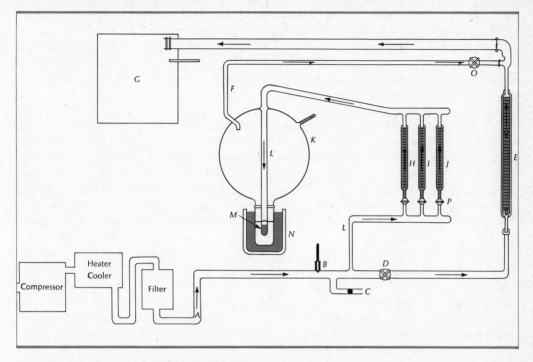

Figure 7.5. An example of a simple but useful flow-dilution olfactometer. Air is supplied by a compressor. It is temperature-regulated and the thermometer, *B*, is used as a monitor. Unwanted odors are removed from the air by filtering it through activated charcoal. This supply of air, *A*, is then split into two streams: one to provide deodorized air and the other to provide odorized air. The latter, *L*, is saturated by bubbling it through the odorant, *M*. The odorant is contained in a diffusion bulb, *K*, which is kept at a known constant temperature by a water bath, *N*. The concentration in the air leaving the diffusion bulb in stream *F* can be calculated from the vapor pressure of the odorant which in turn depends upon its temperature (that is, the temperature maintained by the water bath). This concentration of odorized air can then be diluted to any desired value by recombining it with the pure air in appropriate proportions. The proportion of each stream in the final mixture is controlled by varying its respective flow rate. This is achieved by adjusting valves *C*, *D*, *O*, and *P* in accordance with the flow rates monitored by the flow meters in each stream (*H*, *I*, and *J* allowing fine control through different ranges for the odorized stream and *E* for the deodorized stream). The final mixture reaches the subject whose head is enclosed within a plexiglass hood, *G*. (Stone, 1964, slightly modified.)

requirement is no longer fulfilled. Nevertheless, by using partially closed containers equilibrium may be approached, and the concentration may at least be estimated for each dilution (Moulton & Eayrs, 1960). It is, of course, necessary in this liquid dilution technique to find a diluent which simultaneously is odorless to the animal to be tested and is also a solvent for the odorants to be used (Jones, 1953, 1955; Engen & Pfaffmann, 1959; Moulton & Eayrs, 1960).

In order to gain more precise control of the

stimulus intensity and in order to quantify it more accurately in physical units of concentration, a variety of "olfactometers" have been developed. One widely used type is the flow dilution olfactometer (Figure 7.5), which odorizes a previously purified air stream by passing it at known volume flow rates over or through a given odorant. The concentration of this odorant in the air stream is then given by the volume of air passed through it and its consequent weight loss (Allison & Katz, 1919). An alternative to measuring weight loss directly, is to compute the amount of odorant in the air stream, assuming saturation, from its vapor pressure at the ambient temperature (Woodrow & Karpman, 1917; Ough & Stone, 1961).[2] Lower concentrations can then be obtained by diluting this odorized air stream with another air stream containing only purified air. The ratio of the two flow rates, that of the pure air stream and that of the odorized air stream, defines the final concentration.

Control of the volume flow rates is based on the Poiseulle equation, which describes the flow of a gas through a tube as follows:

$$V = \pi r^4 (P_1 - P_2)/8yL$$

where V is the volume per unit time (that is, the volume flow rate), $P_1 - P_2$ is the pressure difference between the two ends of the tube, y is the viscosity of the carrier gas, L is the length of the tube, and r is the radius of the tube. The Poiseulle equation may be used directly to quantify volume flow rates by passing the air through capillaries of fixed diameters and lengths (Stuiver, 1958; O'Connell, 1967; O'Connell & Mozell, 1969), or the air may be passed through stopcocks which afford continuously varying diameters. Because it is difficult to know the exact diameter of the stopcock apertures, investigators using this latter system generally dispense with calculating the flow rates from the Poiseulle equation and instead read them directly on some type of flow meter (Mozell, 1958; Tucker, 1963a). The flow rate may also be controlled by infusion pumps which act by pushing air out of containers with constant velocity pistons (Mozell, 1966).

Another type of olfactometer incorporates the principle of successive air dilutions. In this method a known amount of odorant is allowed to evaporate in a container of given volume filled with pure air. A small amount of the resulting concentration is then injected into another container of given volume, and the procedure is repeated until the desired concentration is achieved (Goff, 1961).

No matter what the basic design, it is of course important that the olfactometer should be constructed from materials which are themselves odorless. Also these materials should not readily adsorb odors, which could then be given off into the air stream. Thus, rubber tubing and many plastics including Tygon and polyethylene have been found to be inappropriate. Glass and Teflon appear satisfactory but there should be provision for deodorizing or discarding contaminated pieces. Stopcock grease, even the silicone variety, should be used cautiously. Teflon-coated stopcocks are a better choice. Since olfactory sensitivity is so great, any slight contamination is likely to be crucial.

Odorant Presentation

The simplest technique of odorant presentation is normal sniffing, and in man it is often regarded as the only practical technique. Nevertheless, the consistency of the results obtained by this method between subjects and for any given subject has been questioned. In recent years this problem has become particularly troublesome because one of the variables of a sniff is its flow rate, and, as is discussed at length later, the flow rate with which an odorant approaches the mucosa is now known to be one of the primary determinants of the olfactory response.

An attempt has been made to standardize the sniff by Le Magnen (1942–1943) who made constant sniffing a matter of pitch discrimination. He attached a whistle to his olfactometer which changed pitch with the force of the subject's sniff. Thus the subject had to maintain a constant sniff in order to maintain a constant pitch.

However, several authors have found normal sniffing to be quite satisfactory in their experiments, and thus they did not resort to such special procedures (Beck, Kruger, & Calabresi, 1954; Jones, 1955; Engen, 1964).

[2] This calculation depends upon the ideal behavior of gases just as the liquid dilution method, discussed earlier, depends upon the ideal behavior of solutions. Ordinarily, the assumption of "ideal gas" does not introduce much error because it is generally applied to gases with small simple molecules such as oxygen and carbon dioxide. However, we should keep in mind that when the assumption is applied to the large complex molecules of odorants it could, perhaps, introduce an error.

Presumably this is a highly learned motor response which has become quite constant for any given subject. Jones (1955), using "sniff bottles," found that for the determination of thresholds sniffing yielded results with rather high reliability within subjects. On the other hand, between subjects there were large differences. This controversy may have been somewhat resolved by Stone (1963b) who compared the results of sniffing odors from "sniff bottles" to the results of sniffing odors from an olfactometer. He found greater reliability between subjects when they sniffed from the olfactometer. This suggests that any variability observed with sniffing may arise not from the sniffing *per se* but rather from the "sniff bottle" technique of preparing stimulus concentrations which, of course, depends upon the ideality of solutions.

A major problem in normal sniffing is the possible interference of ambient odors. Many authors consider it sufficient merely to ventilate and exhaust the experimental area with the usual commercially available equipment. However, other authors have felt it necessary to go to great lengths in order to enclose either the whole subject or just his head in elaborate odor-controlled compartments (Foster, Scofield, & Dallenbach, 1950; Schneider & Wolf, 1955).

Even though natural sniffing may be an adequate method for presenting stimuli, some investigators have preferred a still more rigid control. This has been especially true in animal experiments where surgical techniques can be used. A glass cannula can be passed into the nasopharynx of an anesthetized, tracheotomized animal (Adrian, 1942). By pulling back on a syringe connected to this cannula the animal is given an artificially produced sniff of controlled flow rate, duration, and volume. An artificially produced sniff for human subjects can be achieved by fitting the subject with two nose pieces: one attached to the olfactometer and the other to a suction pump. During a Valsalva maneuver[3] this pump can draw air in through one nostril and out

the other at any desired flow rate, volume, and duration.

Occasionally the continuous flow method of presentation is still used. In this method, as its name implies, odorized air is made to flow continuously through the nose. The effect of such continuous flow, even when one controls for the possibility of mucosal drying, is still unresolved.

FIRST-ORDER DETERMINANTS OF OLFACTORY EFFICACY

Tucker (1963) has classified three variables as first-order determinants of olfactory efficacy: (1) the particular odorant used, (2) the concentration of the odorant in the carrier gas, (3) the flow rate of the odorant at the mucosa. The measures of efficacy to be discussed will include the absolute threshold, the relative threshold, and the total stimulus-response curve.

The Particular Odorant and Its Concentration

Absolute threshold Allison and Katz (1919), using a flow-dilution olfactometer with human subjects, found the "just detectable" (that is, absolute threshold) concentration for 24 chemicals. The range was quite wide; the highest (5.833 mg/liter) for ether being 100,000 times greater than that for the smallest (4×10^{-5} mg/liter) for artificial musk. Five of these substances were also tested by Bach (1937) who, using the successive-dilution technique, found the absolute thresholds to be about 10,000 times smaller than did Allison and Katz. However, there was some tendency in the two studies for the chemicals to hold about the same rank in their respective ranges. Here we have a difficulty seen all too often in most areas of olfaction, namely, a problem in comparing the data from various laboratories. Comparison is difficult because each uses different odorants, different animal species, different odorant presentation techniques, and different units of concentration.

Occasionally the claim is made that human absolute thresholds are not too different from

---

[3] Forcibly breathing against a closed glottis as when straining to empty the bowels.

the thresholds of other animals. For instance, human thresholds for clove oil and anethole do not appear very different from dog thresholds for the same substances (Becker, King, & Markee, 1962). It has been suggested that the difference in the olfactory prowess between man and lower animals is not due to a difference in the ability to detect minute quantities but rather to a difference in ability to discriminate a large number of qualities (Adrian, 1953). Perhaps then, it is not the sensitivity of the dog's nose that allows it to track a man (Kalmus, 1955), but rather its ability to differentiate that man's body odor from all the other odors that must be on and around the trail. Nevertheless, there are several studies that show that lower mammals, especially dogs, do indeed seem to have greater olfactory sensitivity than humans. For instance, the dog's sensitivity for butyric acid is reported to be 100 times greater than man's (Moulton, Ashton, & Eayrs, 1960).

It is generally agreed that olfaction is very sensitive, but what this assertion actually means is unclear. From Stuiver's data (1958) we can compute that his own absolute threshold for ethyl mercaptan was 1.6×10^{-12} moles/liter. Although this sounds like a minute concentration, it should be emphasized that a single 1-milliliter sniff of this mixture still contains 10^9 molecules of odorant. This is certainly not a small number. Thus, by referring to the great sensitivity of olfaction, one probably refers to the fact that the olfactory system can detect the presence of a smaller number of molecules than can most laboratory methods used for the same purpose. The nose even challenges the great sensitivity of the flame ionization detector, which can detect 10^{-12} grams per second. In 1 ml of a concentration of ethyl mercaptan that a human subject can just detect there is 10^{-13} grams.

According to Stuiver (1958) the nose is even more sensitive than the discussion above suggests because, although these values indicate the number of molecules entering the nares, only a small fraction of these molecules

ever actually reaches the receptors. This is the case because (1) many molecules entering the nose are adsorbed by the mucous lining of the non-olfactory epithelium; (2) many of those molecules not so adsorbed will pass through the nose in air streams that are ventral to the olfactory mucosa; (3) many of those that do reach the level of the olfactory mucosa will continue through the region without striking it. Thus in a normal inspiration only about 2 percent of the odorous molecules entering the nose actually reach the olfactory epithelium. Because the approximate number of receptors is known and because the number of molecules needed to reach threshold is also known, the average number of molecules per receptor can be calculated for a threshold stimulation. The probability of a sense cell receiving more than this average may be computed statistically. By comparing this with the actual probability of detection at this concentration, the number of molecules needed to excite a single receptor may be estimated. This number is at most 9 and perhaps as little as 1 for mercaptans. At least 40 receptors must be excited to reach threshold.

Although the analysis above makes many assumptions which require validation, the approach, reminiscent of a similar approach in vision (see p. 284), does emphasize anew the exquisite sensitivity of the olfactory system when it is compared to physical systems.

Difference thresholds   At long last in recent years there have been a few studies concerning olfactory differential thresholds and Weber fractions (see p. 17), in which modern olfactometers and sophisticated stimulus presentation techniques have been used. In general, the Weber fractions determined by these studies showed only minor variations as a function of concentration (Stone, Ough, & Pangborn, 1962; Stone, 1963a; Stone & Bosley, 1965). However, they did differ to some degree between chemicals. For instance, a Weber fraction of 0.36 was found for propionic acid, 0.26 for acetic acid, 0.31 for ethyl-n-valerate, and about 0.20 for 4 other chemicals. Consequently the Weber Law holds about as well for olfaction as it does for the other senses, but, as can be seen from the size of the fractions, the differential thresholds are relatively poorer in olfaction than in most other senses. This latter observation may just be another manifestation of what may be a basic attribute of the olfactory system, that is, low information capacity concerning stimulus intensity. In the succeeding discussion concerning olfactory stimulus-response curves other manifestations of this attribute will become apparent.

Stimulus response curves Mozell (1958) electrophysiologically recorded the multi-unit discharge strength from the olfactory bulb of rabbits as a function of stimulus concentration. As is true with most of the other senses, equal stimulus increments yielded diminishing response increments as the stimulus intensity was increased. However, the asymptotes of the curves recorded for the 4 chemicals used were reached after a concentration increase of only 10 to 33 times, that is, about 1 to 1.5 log units. This range, over which the stimulus intensity can increase and still yield an increasing electrophysiological response, is considerably smaller for olfaction than that determined for vision (Hartline, 1938) and audition (see p. 230).

It is questionable whether we can legitimately expect support from behavioral experiments for this electrophysiologically determined concept that only a comparatively small increase in olfactory stimulation is necessary to account for the major part of the increase of the olfactory response. First, the electrophysiological recordings only sample, at best, a small percentage of the total number of the receptors the animal has. It is possible then that this electrophysiological sample, especially if the sample were small, would exclude the particularly sensitive or the particularly insensitive receptors. This would reduce the width of the electrophysiologically determined range compared to that of the behaviorally determined range. Second, the

behaving animal has the advantage of using other sensory nerves that also respond to chemical vapors, notably the trigeminal nerve (see later). Thus these extraolfactory inputs would give an apparently wider stimulus range when it is determined behaviorally than when it is determined by recording from the olfactory nerve alone. Notwithstanding these problems, some parallels can still be drawn between results obtained by using the behavioral and the electrophysiological techniques, albeit with several reservations.

Allison and Katz (1919) reported data from studies using behavioral techniques that can be used to support the apparent narrow range of stimulus intensity increase. Their subjects were instructed to rank various concentrations into five categories ranging from (1) "detectable" to (5) "very strong." Assuming that the scale of 1–5 gives a complete stimulus-response curve, one can compute the stimulus increase in log units necessary to go from the least response to the greatest response for each chemical. These ranged from .8 to 2.3 log units for 21 chemicals with 14 of them ranging from .9 to 1.5 log units (Mozell, 1958). Moulton (1960) reported similar results from his studies with rats. The percentage of correct choices made by rats trying to discriminate several acetates increased asymptotically over a range of only 2 to 3 log units of stimulus increase. It has been suggested that perhaps this narrow intensity coordinate is related to the apparent lack of fine intensity discrimination in olfaction.

There is not universal agreement that the range of the stimulus concentration coordinate in olfactory stimulus-response curves is a narrow one. As could be expected from the previous discussion, this is especially true of behavioral experiments. In one study, using an operant discriminative procedure with rats, olfactory discrimination appeared to improve linearly over a concentration increase of 6 or more log units (Goff, 1961). In another study a similar effect was noted with human subjects (Moncrieff, 1957). However, multiunit recordings from the olfactory nerve (Tucker,

1963) suggest, even beyond the behavioral and electrophysiological methodological differences, that this disagreement concerning the width of the stimulus range might be resolved by considering the water solubility of the odorants. At a constant flow rate the responses to increasing concentrations of amyl acetate level off, whereas the responses to benzyl amine over an equally wide concentration range do not. Because amyl acetate is only slightly soluble in water, whereas benzyl amine is infinitely soluble, one may assume that the amyl acetate will saturate the mucus at a lower concentration than will the benzyl amine. Thus, the range of concentrations over which increasing numbers of mole-

cules can be dissolved in the mucus, in order that they can then reach the receptors, is less for the amyl acetate. After scanning the literature it appears that every odorant reported by all the investigators mentioned above (Allison & Katz, 1919; Moncrieff, 1957; Mozell, 1958; Moulton, 1960; Goff, 1961; Tucker, 1963) that has infinite solubility in water also has a wide range of intensity increase. In many but not all cases where the odorant was not very soluble, a narrow range is reported. Direct confirmatory evidence of this solubility relation would have far-reaching theoretical implications for any model of olfactory stimulation.

There is now experimental confirmation of

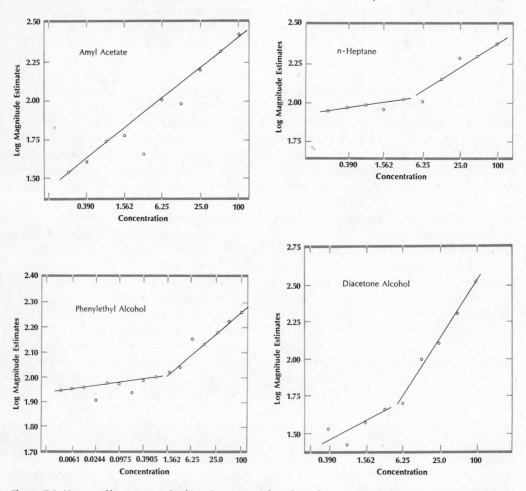

Figure 7.6. Human olfactory magnitude estimates as a function of concentration. The concentration series was prepared by diluting the odorants in benzyl benzoate. Concentration is denoted as the percentage of odorant in the solution. (Engen, 1961.)

the heretofore anecdotal observation that the range of subjective odor magnitude in olfaction is rather short. Engen (1961, 1964) had his subjects estimate the magnitude of the odors given off by chemicals that had been diluted in a geometric series with benzyl benzoate. He found that by raising the concentration of the stimulus from its absolute threshold dilution all the way up to its being completely undiluted, he could increase the perceived magnitude by as little as a factor of 2 (Figure 7.6). With such a narrow range of perceived odor magnitude it is no wonder that his subjects were unable to use fractionation methods as a scaling technique since for many intensities they could not find another that appeared half as intense.

Another type of study also suggests that the salient characteristic of the olfactory system is not its detection or storage of intensity information. Subjects were asked to learn the position of each of five stimulus concentrations ranked according to their intensity, and later the same subjects were asked to identify those ranks when each of those concentrations was presented separately (Engen & Pfaffmann, 1959). They did less well than did subjects in similar studies made of vision and audition (Miller, 1956). Therefore, it may be concluded that intensity in olfaction is somewhat less distinctive than it is in other sensory systems.

Engen's magnitude estimation studies, discussed above, as well as similar studies by other authors (Jones, 1958; Reese & Stevens, 1960) show that the perceived odor magnitude increases as a function of the stimulus intensity raised to some power (Figure 7.6). The power varies considerably around 0.5, depending upon the study quoted and the chemical tested, but in all cases it is considerably less than 1.0. Thus, sensory magnitude in olfaction seems to be "compressed"; that is, successive equal increases in stimulus intensity yield progressively decreasing additions to the perceived sensory magnitude.

Although, as may be expected for power functions, a plot of the log of the estimated magnitude as a function of the log of the stimulus intensity yielded a straight line for amyl acetate, such plots for n-heptane, phenyl ethyl alcohol, and diacetone alcohol did not yield simple straight lines (Figure 7.6). Instead the slopes were smaller at low concentrations and greater at high concentrations. One reason for this change in slope may be the previously discussed difficulty in predicting the vapor phase concentration of an odorant from its percentage in a solution if the solution is not ideal. Thus, the actual stimulus concentration presented to these subjects at each dilution could have been quite different from that expected.

Another reason that the slopes varied with concentration may be that in each graph the two slopes may represent two entirely separate functions. If such is the case, one function, as expected, might depend upon the olfactory input, but the other function, somewhat unexpectedly, might depend upon another input such as that from the trigeminal nerve, for it has been shown electrophysiologically in subhuman species that most odorants can routinely stimulate the trigeminal system as well as the olfactory (Beidler & Tucker, 1956). Previously it had been thought that those odorants yielding a pungent or stinging odor probably stimulated trigeminal receptors; however, it now seems that even mild odorants such as phenyl ethyl alcohol (a rose odor) can likewise do so (Beidler, 1960). In addition, the vomeronasal fibers of the tortoise also respond to vapors. In general, the olfactory and vomeronasal thresholds are lower than the trigeminal threshold for any given odorant. It is therefore possible that the two different slopes in the magnitude estimation curves represent the changing contribution of the olfactory input and the trigeminal input to the subjectively perceived magnitude as the intensity of the stimulus is increased. Of course, it is still to be demonstrated that there is as much overlap between olfactory and trigeminal stimuli in man as in lower animals. That there is at least some overlap has been demonstrated by patients who have lost their olfactory input but have retained their trigeminal, glossopharyn-

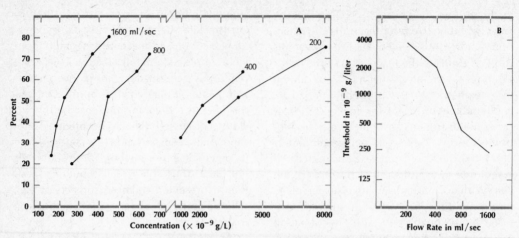

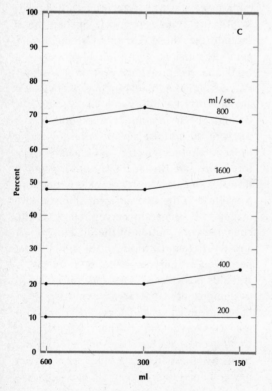

Figure 7.7. A. The effect of concentration and flow rate upon the ability of human subjects to detect the odor of eucalyptol. The ordinate is given as the percentage of stimulus presentations responded to affirmatively. The abscissa gives the concentration in 10^{-9} g/liter. The curves represent the effect of varying the concentration of eucalyptol while the flow rate of the inspiration is held constant at any one of the 4 values designated, in milliliters per second, by the number at the top of the curve to which it refers. The volume of all inspirations was held constant at 600 ml. Note that at any given flow rate the ability to detect an odor increases with concentration. Likewise, where concentrations are equal, the ability to detect an odor increases with the flow rate of the inspiration. B. The human olfactory threshold as a function of the flow rate of inspiration. Threshold is given in 10^{-9} g of eucalyptol per liter of air. The threshold is taken as the concentration at which 50 percent of the presentations are responded to affirmatively. The volume of the inspiration is held constant at 600 ml.

C. The effect of volume upon the ability to detect an odor when the flow rate is held constant. The ordinate is the same as above. Volume is given along the abscissa. The flow rate is indicated by the number, in milliliters per second, near the curve to which it refers. Note that there is no effect of volume upon detection ability; that is, the curves are all essentially horizontal.

It is necessary to point out that this set of curves by itself offers no information concerning the effect of flow rate upon the ability to detect an odor because for each flow rate the author had to use a different concentration (not shown on figure). Consequently, the effect of flow rate is confounded with the effect of concentration. However, the conclusion made above concerning volume is still valid because for any one curve the only variable is the volume. (Le Magnen, 1944–1945; part B has been redrawn.)

geal, and vagal inputs (Henkin, 1967). These patients can still discriminate several vapors, and these discriminations can only be mediated by one or more of the remaining systems.

Volume Flow Rate[4]

Concentration has not been the only variable used to control the strength of olfactory responses. In various studies flow rate and volume also have been varied. It still remains necessary, however, to determine whether flow rate and volume are meaningful, independent measures of olfactory stimuli.

Le Magnen (1944–1945) described a method in which concentration, volume, and volume flow rate could all be varied independently. The frequency with which his human subjects could smell the stimulus was determined for several values of each variable. As expected, the percentages derived from these frequencies increased as a function of concentration at all flow rates (Figure 7.7A). Less expected was the observation that at any given concentration the percentage of affirmative responses varied quite decidedly with the flow rate (Figure 7.7A). In addition threshold decreased as the flow rate increased (Figure 7.7B). In contrast, the percentage of affirmative responses did not appear to vary with the volume when the flow rate and the concentration were held constant (Figure 7.7C).

The importance of flow rate has also been observed electrophysiologically in lower animals (Tucker, 1963 a, b). The summated neural discharges increased with the flow rate when the concentration was held constant. Perhaps the sniffing behavior of lower animals and man, when they suspect the presence of an odor, takes advantage of this enhancement of the olfactory response by increasing the flow rate through the nose.

One of the common explanations for this dependency of olfaction upon flow rate assumes that eddy currents in the nose facilitate the movement of odorous molecules toward

[4]Throughout this chapter the term "flow rate" will often be used to refer to the volume flow rate, that is, the volume of gas moving through a given plane per unit time. It will never refer to the linear flow rate, that is, the distance a gas is moved per unit time.

the olfactory epithelium which is, after all, situated a considerable distance from the main nasal air stream. Presumably, the greater the flow rate the greater the eddy currents and consequently the greater the number of molecules reaching the mucosa. This explanation was tested by placing a plastic tube through the naris directly to the olfactory epithelium (Beidler, 1958) so that odors could be brought into contact with the epithelium without the aid of eddy currents. The responses were still found to depend on the flow rate.

Tucker (1963a, b) gave a better explanation of this flow rate dependency. He suggested that the effectiveness of the stimulus depends upon the number of molecules that can be established at the receptors within a certain period of time depending upon the receptor response properties. Thus, for any given stimulation the number of molecules will be dependent upon both the flow rate and the concentration of the odorant. Both of these variables control the number of molecules available at the receptor in any specified period of time. Therefore, both flow rate and concentration are primary determinants of the olfactory response.

SECONDARY VARIABLES CONCERNING THE OLFACTORY RESPONSE

There are many other variables besides those directly associated with the stimulus that have been shown to affect the subject's olfactory report both qualitatively and quantitatively. Only a few of these can be discussed here.

Instructions

There has been a long-standing controversy concerning the possible existence of two olfactory thresholds, that is, one at which the subject merely detects the presence of an odor and another at which the subject can identify the odor. Engen (1960) demonstrated that such a dual threshold is indeed present in olfaction and that one must specify, in determining the absolute threshold, whether the subjects are to identify an odor or merely detect the presence of one. He presented his subjects with four test tubes only one of which contained an odorant at some given dilution. He asked his subjects either to detect the test tube that smelled different or to identify the test tube containing a given, named odorant. The first set of instructions yielded considerably lower absolute thresholds. In addition, once the subject operated under the "smelled different" instructions, he found it difficult to go back to the "named odorant" criterion.

The fact that there appear to be two thresholds in olfaction (detection and identification) has far-reaching theoretical implications. For example, are there two sets of receptors, or receptor sites, analogous to a similar duality in vision where the low threshold rods detect the presence of a light and the higher threshold cones permit the identification of its color? Or is it simply that a certain amount of summation of the peripheral events is necessary at some central locus for positive identification?

Effect of Food Consumption

The assertion that hunger increases olfactory sensitivity while food ingestion decreases it fits our teleological notions about food foraging by animals and, therefore, is readily accepted. However, in applying the same type of teleological reasoning to the protection of the animal, one should predict that no changes would occur. Why, for instance, should the animal be hindered in his detection of predators because he himself has eaten?

Several groups of investigators, using a variety of different procedures, have attempted to determine whether eating affects olfactory ability, but unfortunately their results do not agree very closely. One group found a decrease in olfactory sensitivity after eating (Schneider & Wolf, 1955). Another group found no statistically significant change after eating, although there was a little tendency (statistically not significant) toward reduced sensitivity (Furchtgott & Friedman,

1960). Still another group actually showed olfactory ability to be greater after eating than before eating (Berg et al., 1963). Thus, although we may like to think that our olfactory thresholds increase after eating, it is not yet agreed that they do so.

The Effects of the Status of the Mucous Membranes

Recording from the olfactory nerve of the rabbit, Tucker (1961) noted that the strength of the discharge for a given concentration of a given chemical could be increased considerably if he simultaneously either pinched a toe, clapped his hands, shined a light in the rabbit's eye, or electrically stimulated the cervical sympathetic nerves. There are no known feedback loops to the receptors themselves to change their sensitivity, so another explanation is needed.

By direct optical observation of the nasal interior Tucker noted that pinching the foot, shining a light, clapping the hands, and electrically stimulating the cervical sympathetic nerves all produced a blanching of the nasal mucosa and an increase in the width of the nasal passageways. Both of these effects are probably related to a reduction in the engorgement of the nasal tissue with blood, which may produce a less obstructed air flow path leading to the receptor areas. This in turn may allow more molecules of any given stimulant to reach the receptor area.

In addition, Tucker noted that electrical stimulation of parasympathetic outflows to the mucosa decreased the response to a given odorant and simultaneously increased the flow of nasal mucus. Such an increase in mucus probably "stuffs" the nose. Therefore, it appears that the accessibility of the molecules to the receptors is significantly impaired in these animals and that the degree of impairment is controlled by the autonomic nervous system.

Human olfactory thresholds have also been observed to depend upon the state of the epithelium, but the effects vary somewhat from those observed with the lower species.

Again, obstruction was the most important reducer of olfactory sensitivity but short of frank obstruction the highest sensitivities in man were attained when the tissues were considerably swollen, red, and wet (Schneider & Wolf, 1960). Given the contour of the human nasal passageways, these conditions probably increase the efficiency with which the olfactory mucosa traps the available molecules as they pass by. This would produce an apparent reduction in threshold because fewer molecules need now enter the naris to achieve the same olfactory effect.

Sex and Olfaction

Anecdotal evidence and the advertisements of the perfume and cosmetic industries testify to a supposed connection between olfaction and sexual arousal. However, only in comparatively recent years has this connection, together with its underlying neurohumoral mechanisms, been clearly demonstrated experimentally.

The usual evidence employed to demonstrate the relationship between sex and olfaction is a change in the olfactory threshold during a period when the levels of the various hormones also are varying. This hormonal variation could be due either to normal events or to outside intervention. The sensitivity for certain substances (especially a lactone called exaltolide) varies in such a way with the course of the human female's menstrual cycle that it suggests that this sensitivity is positively correlated with her estrogen production (Le Magnen, 1953). This involvement of estrogen is also suggested by the raised threshold for exaltolide found in women who have been deprived of estrogen by the removal of their ovaries and by the restoration of the threshold to within a normal range after the administration of exogenous estrogen. In addition, prepubic females and both prepubic and adult males are less sensitive to these odorants than are adult females.

It appears, then, that the level of a hormone may affect the olfactory thresholds but the site of this action is still in doubt. One mechanism may depend upon the state of the olfactory mucosa, as discussed in the previous section. Thus, the administration of estrogen to hypogonadal women increased their sensitivity for citral as it concomitantly tended to decrease their nasal obstruction. On the other hand, androgen decreased the sensitivity in one woman and at the same time tended to increase obstruction (Schneider et al., 1958). Thus the hormonal recipe may not be affecting olfactory thresholds by direct action upon the olfactory system itself, but rather indirectly through systems which in turn affect olfaction. This cannot be the only explanation, since the administration of androgen to men increases the sensitivity to some chemicals while reducing it to others (Le Magnen, 1953).

The discussion thus far has been concerned with the effect of the hormonal status upon olfaction; however, there is a reverse relationship, that is, olfaction has an effect on the hormone recipe. Of course, the olfactory system is not unique in this regard, for it has long been known that other sensory systems can also affect the hormonal balance.

The most dramatic example of the regulation of sex hormones by olfactory stimuli is the pregnancy block brought about in female mice by the odor of strange males as reported by Parkes and Bruce (1961). They showed that if female mice are mated, about 8 percent ordinarily do not become pregnant and go back into estrus. However, if soon after mating these females are confronted with the smell of strange males, about 80 percent of them return to estrus. The mechanism of this pregnancy block by an odor appears to be a reduction in the secretion of prolactin,[5] for if they are fortified with exogenous doses of this hormone, the block is prevented (Parkes, 1961). In the mouse, prolactin maintains the corpus luteum which in turn is necessary for the maintenance of a uterine endometrium suitable to support a fertilized ovum. Thus, by interfering with the secretion of a hormone, the odor forces the mouse to abort.

[5] An adenohypophyseal gonadotropin.

As has been mentioned earlier, olfactory cues are important for some animal species to find their mates. When a male rat is faced with the choice of an estrous or a diestrous female, he makes his choice on the basis of olfactory cues (Le Magnen, 1951). Castrated and prepubic males showed no preference until given an injection of androgen (Le Magnen, 1953). Carr and Caul (1962) investigated whether the differences in the choices of castrated and normal rats depended merely upon their differing preferences or whether their choices depended upon their differing abilities to detect and discriminate the odors given off by receptive females. Because castrated and normal rats showed no difference in learning to discriminate the odors of estrous and diestrous females in a choice box situation, the authors concluded that the hormonal state of these animals affected only their preferences and not their sensitivities.

Another body of evidence also suggests a hormonal effect upon olfaction. Patients with adrenal insufficiency tend to have very low olfactory thresholds for aqueous solutions of NaCl, KCl, and $NaHCO_3$ (Henkin and Powell, 1962).[6] Treating these patients with hydrocortisone brings their thresholds back to normal. Likewise, an increased olfactory sensitivity for the same chemicals occurs in patients with cystic fibrosis.

Adaptation

Olfactory adaptation is an everyday experience. Most people have noticed that after being in an odorous environment for some time the odor seems to disappear.[7] For instance, the odor of your impending evening meal is quite clear when you first enter your home, but soon you no longer smell it. Olfactory adaptation is here defined as a decrease in responsiveness and sensitivity to odorants as a result of being exposed to them. Recovery from adaptation is used here to mean an increased responsiveness and sensitivity after the removal of the odorous stimuli.

There are two major behavioral methods of studying adaptation. The first is to measure the time needed for a continuously presented odor to disappear. The second is to measure the threshold before and after a subject has been exposed to an odor for a given amount of time.

Most of the studies using the first, simpler, method show that as the concentration of the odorant is increased, the time needed for its smell to disappear is also increased. In addition, equal increments in concentration yield

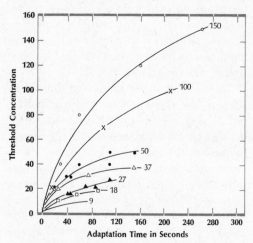

Figure 7.8. Curves showing human adaptation to several different concentrations of d-octanol. Each curve shows the effect of a different concentration (the concentration is noted at the right). Note that at any given concentration the threshold increases as the exposure time increases. Likewise, for any given exposure time the adaptation increases (that is, there are higher thresholds) as the adapting concentration increases.

The notation of concentrations in this figure is a bit unusual. The threshold concentration for the completely unadapted subject was first determined. Then, all other concentrations are given as multiples of this unadapted threshold concentration. (Stuiver, 1958.)

[6]Notwithstanding the obvious importance of these observations from an olfaction-hormone point of view, there is another interesting aspect of these studies, that is, the chemicals used are not typical olfactory stimuli and in the non-aqueous state they may even be classified as non-odorous. Perhaps in the aqueous solution some odorous contaminant is released.

[7]However, it is necessary to note Cain's (1968) recent evidence which suggests that a smell is not likely to disappear unless the subject is told that it will do so.

equal increments in the disappearance time, although in one study this linearity did not occur until after the first 100 seconds (Woodrow & Karpman, 1917; Stuiver, 1958).

The second behavioral method of measuring adaptation is exemplified by a study by Stuiver (1958), who measured thresholds as a function of the intensity and duration of an adapting stimulus (Figure 7.8). His procedure was to present low intensity test concentrations at specified intervals throughout the course of the subject's adaptation and to record whether these interspersed test concentrations were above or below the subject's threshold. Stuiver found that the threshold increases as either the concentration or the exposure time of the adapting stimulus is increased, but, contrary to some earlier work (Zwaardemaker, 1925), he believed that the relationship between threshold and exposure time was not linear. However, for at least the first 100 seconds, his curves are actually not very far from straight lines. Only after 100 seconds, and therefore beyond the exposure times used in the earlier work, does it become quite apparent that the curves are not linear; in fact, the thresholds reach a final constant level after prolonged exposure. An important observation is that prior to reaching this constant threshold value the decrease in sensitivity appears to be a function of the total amount of odorous material inspired (Figure 7.8). For example, 40 seconds of exposure to a concentration 100 times the absolute threshold will decrease the sensitivity about the same amount as 80 seconds of exposure to a concentration 50 times the threshold. It was also noted that recovery from adaptation is at first quite rapid and then quite slow. The rapid phase accounts for most of the recovery.

It is easy to demonstrate the phenomenon of olfactory adaptation; however, to elucidate its physiological mechanism has proved to be difficult. Even the locus of adaptation has proved elusive. One's initial supposition, that adaptation is an olfactory receptor phenomenon, has not been verified by recordings from primary olfactory receptor cell axons. At each inspiration, a burst of activity is recorded from the rabbit's olfactory fibers, but at low stimulus intensities these bursts are all of the same strength (Beidler & Tucker, 1956). Thus, there appears to be no neural effect which parallels the human behavioral effect, at least up to this level of the olfactory nervous system. Beidler (1957) has therefore concluded that the locus of adaptation is more centrally located in the nervous system. Human behavioral data also supported the same conclusion when it was demonstrated that both sides of the nose adapted even though only one side had been exposed to a continuous stream of odorant (Stuiver, 1958). Beidler (1957) also noted that at medium stimulus intensities the bursts of neural activity do decline with successive inspirations, but even here they reach a steady size, and do not decline to zero as one might expect from the behavioral reports. Only at the highest concentrations do the bursts disappear altogether. Note that these medium and high concentrations are within the range necessary to evoke the autonomic nasal reflexes which, as discussed previously, alter the nasal swelling and mucus flow. Therefore, Beidler suggested that the response decrements observed at medium to high concentrations are not due to olfactory receptor mechanisms per se but are rather due to changes in the accessibility of the receptors to the molecules.

There is still some reason to believe that the olfactory receptors do play some part in adaptation. This is based upon observations of a slow potential change (called an electroolfactogram) which can be recorded directly from the mucosa and which is believed by some investigators to be the electrical sign of olfactory receptor activity (Ottoson, 1956). After 15 seconds of a continuous flow of odorous air over the mucosa, the electroolfactogram decreased as much as 60 percent from its initial size at the beginning of stimulation. Thus at least some part of the process of adaptation may be occurring in the mucosa.

In summary, it appears that the greater part of adaptation occurs in central areas; the process includes feedback to nasal accessory organs via the autonomic nervous system. However, it is still too early to discount the part played by peripheral olfactory elements completely.

Odor Mixture

Several types of sensory report are conceivable when two or more odorants are mixed together. First, the subject may be able to discriminate each odor separately. Second, an entirely new odor may develop which resembles the components but does not smell exactly like any of them. Third, one odor may predominate making it impossible to discriminate the others. This effect is generally called *masking*. A fourth possibility, neutralization, was described by Zwaardemaker (1925). He claimed that for a few combinations of odors no sensation at all can be perceived if they are presented simultaneously. However, Henning (Woodworth & Schlosberg, 1954) denied the existence of neutralization as a physiological phenomenon but conceded that it could occur by a chemical or physical interaction between the molecules before they enter the nose (Pfaffmann, 1951).

There is a great lack of modern reliable work concerning odor mixture; indeed, a good deal of the information available borders on being anecdotal evidence. As for the first three possible reactions to odor mixing mentioned above, it is generally accepted that olfaction is analytical like pitch discrimination, where one note in a chord may be singled out from the others. Olfaction is generally not considered synthetic like color vision, where the individual hues in a mixture of hues are seen not separately but rather as a totally new hue. However, this exclusively analytic nature of olfaction may be too readily accepted. Its main support is that some experts, such as perfume chemists, are capable of identifying each of about a dozen chemicals in a mixture. However, perhaps these trained chemists only appear to be discriminating all the individual components, for, when they smell a fragrance, they would

know from experience the ingredients needed to approximate it. In color vision even non-experts give similar apparent analyses, yet color vision is not considered analytical. For instance, most people, believing that orange looks more like yellow and red than like blue and green, would likely suggest that orange is composed of the former pair. However, the important issue in this context would be the ability of subjects to determine whether a given orange light is composed of one narrow band of wavelengths in the orange range of the visual spectrum or whether it is composed of a mixture of several wavelengths, none of which is in the orange range of the visual spectrum. With well controlled conditions subjects cannot do this, and thus color vision is considered synthetic. Whether subjects can perform the analogous task with smells (namely determine which odorants contain more than one type of molecule and which do not) has not yet been given adequate experimental testing.

The things we smell in the course of our daily lives are almost always composed of the molecules of several different chemicals, yet we do not often smell them as several simultaneously presented individual odorants. Likewise, we most often smell chemicals purchased from manufacturers as totalities even though, as gas chromatographic analysis tells us, they contain many contaminants. On the other hand, in some instances olfaction has more in common with the perception of pitch, which is analytical, than it does with the perception of hue, which is synthetic. For instance, the perceived intensity of a mixture of pure odorants is less than the sum of the perceived intensities of the same two odorants taken separately (Jones & Woskow, 1964).

At the present time it is probably safest to say that depending upon the circumstances, odorant mixtures may result in any of the possibilities mentioned above. They may continue to be smelled separately. They may combine to yield a new odor (Johnston, 1963). Finally, one of the odorants may mask the others. This last effect is evidenced by the large number of companies manufacturing "odor destroyers," some of which simply lay down such a strong pine or floral scent that the other odorants present can no longer be appreciated.

Deodorization

Deodorizing techniques have taken several forms (Kulka, 1964). First, they may not really deodorize at all but actually only replace an unpleasant odor with a supposedly more pleasant one. As discussed above, this can be done either by masking or by synthesizing a new odor. True deodorization takes place when the odorous molecules themselves are removed from the environment. This can be accomplished by passing the contaminated air over adsorbants such as activated charcoal. Alternatively, the odorant molecules may be made to react with other chemicals to form odorless products. Still another technique is to prevent the production of odorous molecules in the first place. For example, many under-arm deodorants prevent the bacterial activity that converts essentially odorless sweat into its several highly odorous breakdown products.

There are two other techniques that presumably operate on the olfactory system itself. One is the selective adaptation of the receptors to certain unpleasant odorants so that they are no longer annoying. The other is to render the receptors or their axons inoperative by the introduction of certain vapors. For example, several aldehydes are said to anesthetize the receptors (Kulka, 1964).

QUALITY DISCRIMINATION

Attempts to Understand Quality Discrimination by Behavioral Techniques

There appears to be a countless number of discriminable odors, and, indeed, probably the most salient feature of olfaction is the variety of its quality discriminations. However, there are very few generic terms to describe this vast number of odors. Rather they are generally described by the name of the sub-

stance or the article with which they are associated (for example, rose or gasoline) (Harper, 1966). In order to obtain a concise descriptive vocabulary of odor qualities, many investigators have attempted to categorize odors. Perhaps an even more important motivation for categorization has been the hope that if odors could be properly grouped together into categories or placed side by side along some continuum, an insight into the basic mechanisms of quality discrimination could be gained.

Odor categories The most famous of these category systems is Henning's smell prism (Woodworth & Schlosberg, 1954). The corners of the prism were labeled "putrid," "ethereal," "resinous," "spicy," "fragrant," and "burnt." Although Henning's subjects were able to place each odorant on the prism, depending upon how closely it fulfilled the corner descriptions, other authors have had difficulty reproducing the results.

Another classification scheme described odorants numerically rather than by location on a figure (Crocker, 1947). Four basic odor receptor types presumably corresponding to four basic odor qualities were arbitrarily assumed: (1) fragrant; (2) acidic; (3) burnt; (4) caprylic. Subjects were instructed to decide how much of each quality they could find in any given odorant and to assign numbers from 0 to 8 accordingly. Thus, an acid may finally be designated as 4813 meaning that it smells halfway fragrant (4), very acidic (8), slightly burnt (1), and moderately caprylic (3).

Such classification systems have had only limited success in describing odors and even less success in giving insight into the basic discrimination mechanisms. One of the major problems has been that it is difficult to have all odors conform to such arbitrarily chosen categories.

A more promising categorization scheme, with attendant suggestions for the mechanism of discrimination, has been proposed (Amoore, 1962a, b). First, it was assumed that the terms most frequently used to describe the odors of chemicals with rigid molecular configurations defined the so-called "primary odors." These were ethereal, camphoraceous, musky, floral, minty, pungent, and putrid. Odorants particularly exemplifying each of these categories were chosen and a detailed inspection was made of scale models of their molecules. On the basis of the dimensions of these models Amoore suggested that corresponding to each of these first five primary categories there is a corresponding distinct molecular size or shape. Electrical charges were the common features of the remaining two categories. For each of the first five molecular groups it was hypothesized that there was a receptor site with a shape congruent to that of the molecule. The molecules of those chemicals that have only pure "primary odors" were presumed to fit snugly into only one type of receptor site, whereas the vast majority of molecules were presumed to fit into several types and were said to produce compound odors, that is, odors composed of more than one "primary odor." Although this categorization and theory of discrimination has had some early moderate success in correctly predicting the results of a few simple experiments (Amoore, Johnson, & Rubin, 1964), the results obtained from more recent work have forced a rather drastic revision of some of its major tenets. Amoore himself (1965) was unable to demonstrate that the ability of chemical molecules to fit the prescribed primary sites correlated well with human judgments of their odor similarity. Also to be noted here are the recent electrophysiological recordings from single olfactory receptor units (see p. 217) that show that chemicals drawn from the same category may not stimulate the same units in the same way (Gesteland, Lettvin, & Pitts, 1965). Because of the results of his later work, Amoore (1965) abandoned the concept that odorant molecules with particular shapes fit into correspondingly shaped sites. However, if he did not require the molecules to possess rigidly specified configurations, then the human judgments of odor similarity appeared to

correlate reasonably well with molecular shape. Accordingly, Amoore has still retained the concept that the shape of the molecule determines odor quality, but he no longer requires that the molecule have a given shape or that it conform to a set of prescribed primary receptor sites.

Cross-adaptation Adaptation has been used as a basis to classify olfactory stimuli. The rationale for doing this is that a subject's adaptation to one odorant often will increase the subject's threshold to another odorant (cross-adaptation), and it is assumed that odorants that do cross-adapt have some common characteristic or property for the stimulation of the olfactory receptors. In this way some property of the molecule such as its water solubility, its dipole moment, or its shape, among other characteristics, may eventually be identified as the basic physical correlate of olfaction.

Cheesman and Townsend (1956) measured the change in their subjects' thresholds for several test odorants after they had smelled various concentrations of several adapting odorants. The authors found a linear relation between the log of the intensity of the adapting odorant and the log of the threshold concentration for the test odorant. The slope of these curves differed for different combinations of the test odorant and adapting odorant. The results were interpreted to mean that the greater the slope the more the two chemicals were similar in some property for the stimulation of the olfactory system and the more they could be classified together. So far this approach is more noteworthy for the potential of its general concept than for the information it has produced.

It is also possible to reverse the procedure described above by determing whether chemicals known to be very similar in some property also show more cross-adaptation than those chemicals that are less similar. In this way it may be possible to gauge the importance of any given property of a chemical as a basis for its discrimination by the olfactory receptors. Engen (1963) has made a modest start in this direction. He took advantage of the fact that in an homologous series of odorants many physical properties vary in an orderly fashion with the length of the carbon chains in their molecules. One might therefore expect that the closer members in a homologous series will cross-adapt each other more than will the members that are farther apart. However, Engen found that for a homologous series of aliphatic alcohols the amount of cross-adaptation was not related to the closeness of the members. One cannot immediately conclude from this experiment that none of the physical properties of chemicals which vary within an homologous series play a role in the basic process of discrimination. This reluctance to draw such a conclusion is necessary because, as Engen suggests, several properties may be operating simultaneously. Each of these may affect olfaction in a somewhat different and perhaps opposing manner. On the other hand, one could question whether such cross-adaptation studies could ever materially aid our understanding of olfactory receptor discrimination mechanisms. This skepticism is engendered by the previously discussed findings showing: (1) that adaptation may depend more upon the central nervous system than upon the receptors, and (2) that other sensory systems in addition to the olfactory system also contribute to the subjects' perception of vapors.

Continua of the olfactory impression   It is becoming increasingly apparent that the olfactory sensory impression is so complex that no single stimulus continuum is likely to account for it. Indeed, Engen (1962) has shown that the olfactory subjective response varies along several dimensions at once. He presented his subjects with an homologous series of alcohols and had them estimate the similarity in quality of each odorant to every other odorant. Three factors were then extracted by a multidimensional analysis of the data. One decreased with chain length and appeared by introspective analysis to be related to an "alcohol" smell. Another, increasing with chain length, appeared to be a "musty" smell. The third factor seemed to vary along a "pleasantness" dimension.

As the subjects went from chemical to chemical in the above study, the stimulus intensity as well as the stimulus quality varied because vapor pressures are inversely related to chain lengths in an homologous series. Therefore, it is possible that one of the dimensions, perhaps the "alcohol" dimension, was actually an intensity dimension. However, it is still quite apparent that smells vary along more than one dimensional continuum. One of the several possible physiological bases for this is the trigeminal input which may add one or more subjective dimensions.

Special notice should be taken of the "pleasantness" dimension in Engen's study. It is clear from everyday life that many odors produce a definite affect, and it is, indeed, difficult to feel serenely indifferent to the presence of most of them. Nevertheless, there are very few controlled experimental studies primarily concerned with the hedonic effects of olfaction.

As a start, several authors have asked subjects to rank odors on some sort of pleasantness-unpleasantness scale. There is a fairly high correlation ($r = .80$) for successive rankings of the same odors by the same subjects over a period of months. However, the correlation between different subjects for the same odors is at best only moderate ($r = .42$) (Beebe-Center, 1931). A partial explanation for this lower correlation between subjects may be the finding that subjects are very much affected by their own past experiences when they are ranking odorants (Young, 1923; Kniep, Morgan, & Young, 1931). For example, phenol recalled medical situations for many subjects, and it was, therefore, often classified as unpleasant. In addition, the order in which the odorants are presented plays an important role in their ranking because the affect they engender shows definite contrast; that is, an unpleasant odor is more unpleasant after a series of pleasant odors and vice versa (Kniep,

Morgan, & Young, 1931). The affective tone generated by an odorant appears to be an integral part of its impression (Eysenck, 1944; Hsü, 1946; Yoshida, 1964), although it may play a lesser role for professional expert perfumers (Yoshida, 1964). Even when subjects were asked not to judge odorants on such a dimension, they were apparently unable to refrain from doing so (Engen, 1962). Thus, this hedonic effect may be such an indelible concomitant of smells that it cannot be disregarded.

The importance of affect to olfaction is also demonstrated by the rather wide range over which odors differ in their pleasantness as compared to the narrower ranges of other olfactory subjective dimensions. For instance, odor pleasantness can increase about 125-fold over its whole range (Engen & McBurney, 1964) whereas the range of subjective odor magnitude can show an increase of as little as twofold. Thus, it is quite possible that odors are in part discriminated from each other by the affective tone they engender.

Attempts to Understand Quality Discrimination by Electrophysiological Techniques

On the basis of behavioral odor discriminations alone, it is very difficult either to determine the receptor mechanisms basic to olfactory discrimination or to classify odors according to some stimulus property relevant to the olfactory discrimination mechanism. The difficulty arises because behavioral judgments use information from other systems in addition to the olfactory system. Consequently, these judgments vary along several perceptual dimensions, some of which may not depend solely upon the olfactory input. A method which circumvents these problems is to classify odorants according to the neural discharges that they produce in the peripheral olfactory system. Chemicals yielding similar neural responses are presumed to have similar properties and to be mediated by similar mechanisms.

Single-unit studies   Because of the technical difficulty in recording from the very small single units in the mucosa, the first recordings from single units in the olfactory system were taken from the second-order neurons in the bulb (Adrian, 1953, 1954). On the basis of these recordings chemicals were grouped together according to the units they excited. All those that excited any given unit were placed in the same group. Although within each group there often was one chemical which stimulated only that particular unit, the other chemicals in that group would excite one or more of the other units. Each chemical, therefore, excited different combinations of single units. Although no single bulbar unit could be discharged by only one odorant, the population of single units would be fired in different patterns depending upon the stimulus used. Extrapolation of these findings peripherally to the mucosa suggested to Adrian receptor types corresponding to the bulbar units. Thus, the mechanism of olfactory discrimination at the level of the mucosa was believed to depend upon receptors that are also selectively sensitive to overlapping groups of stimuli and that would consequently respond together in different patterns to encode different odorants.

However, the hope of discovering the stimulus properties basic to olfactory discrimination by classifying together those odorants that stimulate the same neuron was never quite realized by Adrian's single-unit recordings from the bulb. Perhaps, in order to make the trends apparent, a more detailed quantification should have been made of the frequency with which each odorant stimulated a given unit. In a series of more recent papers Döving (1965, 1966a, b) has offered the necessary quantification. Every odorant he used, working with frogs, was classified as to whether it excited, inhibited, or had no effect upon a given bulbar neuron. Each odorant was then compared to every other odorant to determine whether both fell into the same or different classifications. This was repeated on many cells and a statistical analysis allowed

Döving to determine the degree to which both members of any given pair of odorants were alike in the responses they produced. For instance, in a homologous chemical series the chemicals that had nearly the same molecular weights were more likely to be classified together than those with more variant molecular weights. This suggests that it is some physical property of the molecule, rather than the chemical reactions of its functional group per se, that determines its olfactory effect.

Considering the whole spectrum of neural discharge frequencies that can be observed when a unit responds to stimulation, it may appear that Döving's three-category system is a rather gross matrix upon which to measure the similarity of odorant effects. In addition, there is some question about the precision with which the information taken from these secondary olfactory units can be extrapolated back across a rather complex synapse to explain the mechanism of discrimination by the primary receptor cells. Nevertheless, Döving's method holds much promise.

Only recently have investigators been able to record from the single receptor neurons of the olfactory mucosa (Shibuya & Shibuya, 1963; Gesteland, Lettvin, & Pitts, 1965; O´Connell & Mozell, 1969). Gesteland and his co-workers appeared to confirm Adrian's contention concerning the selective sensitivity of the receptors to overlapping groups of stimuli. However, when the chemicals were ordered according to their ability to affect the single receptor neurons, these same investigators (Lettvin & Gesteland, 1965) found that for each neuron there appeared to be a different order. This result prompted the authors to discuss the possibility of "utter chaos" where no two receptors are alike in all of their sensitivities (Gesteland, Lettvin, & Pitts, 1965). Such a system could, of course, still encode the presence of different chemicals by the pattern of activity of all the receptors to-

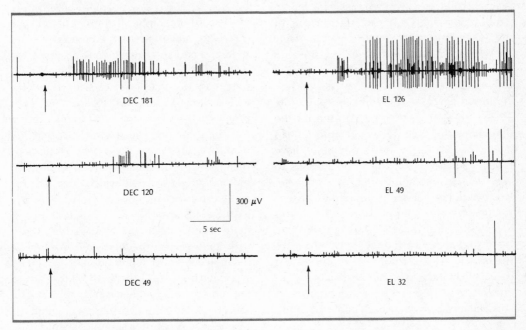

Figure 7.9. The response of a single unit in the olfactory mucosa of a frog to several concentrations of two chemicals, ethyl lactate (EL) and diethyl carbonate (DEC). Because the responses of two different units can be seen on these traces, the reader is asked to concentrate upon the unit giving the larger amplitude action potentials. It will be seen that this unit can respond to both chemicals but at a lower concentration of EL than DEC. Concentration is given in micromoles per liter. (O'Connell & Mozell, 1969.)

gether. However, this finding makes it difficult to predict which molecular properties are basic to olfactory discrimination.

Recent evidence has shown, as Lettvin and Gesteland had earlier suspected (1965), that "utter chaos" is too extreme a term to describe the responses of different units to olfactory stimuli. O'Connell and Mozell (1969) recorded the responses of a large number of single units to the same four chemicals and then ranked the chemicals according to their efficacy in exciting each unit. They found that although the rank orders were not the same for every unit, certain orders were more prevalent than others, and some theoretically possible orders were not observed at all. Thus, although not all units respond in exactly the same way to a battery of odorants, neither are they completely chaotic.

Before leaving this topic a word of caution is necessary. When we are studying the selective sensitivity of the olfactory receptors for different odorants we can easily be led to wrong conclusions if the concentrations of the chemicals are neither quantitatively known nor quantitatively varied. As shown in Figure 7.9, a unit may respond to one chemical at one concentration and may respond to another chemical at a different concentration. Thus, if the only concentration used for the unit giving the large spikes in Figure 7.9 had been 120 μM/liter or less, we might have falsely concluded that this unit responds to ethyl lactate but not to diethyl carbonate. However, as can be seen, raising the concentration of diethyl carbonate to 181 μM/liter excites the unit. Studies that try to determine the degree to which the receptors are selective must be suspect if only one concentration of each chemical is used. In summary, an olfactory unit responds to a variety of odorants, but its sensitivity to each odor may differ.

Multiunit studies Multifiber recordings from the olfactory bulb and olfactory nerve have also suggested mechanisms which, operating at the level of the mucosa, may be basic

to olfactory discrimination. It was observed in the rabbit that some chemicals such as amyl acetate, ethyl acetate, and ether were more efficient in exciting the anterior part of the olfactory bulb than were other chemicals such as pentane, heptane, and coal gas; these, in contrast, were more efficient in exciting the posterior areas of the bulb (Adrian, 1950, 1953; Mozell & Pfaffmann, 1954). In addition to this spatial differentiation of odorants there was also noted a temporal differentiation, namely, the multiunit discharges to esters had shorter durations and were more abrupt in their growth and decay than were responses to hydrocarbons. Thus, in the bulb there appeared to be a spatio-temporal encoding of odorants.

In order to account for this bulbar code, Adrian (1950, 1953) reasoned that it reflects a spatio-temporal encoding of odorants that began at the level of the mucosa. He had a good anatomical basis for this contention because, as is discussed earlier, the olfactory mucosa is topographically represented in the bulb. He suggested that the molecules of different odorants might spread across the olfactory mucosa in different spatial and temporal patterns in accordance with those molecular properties that are able to affect their progress. These include such properties as their diffusion rates in air and their solubility in mucus. Later it was suggested that perhaps their progress is affected by the different binding strengths with which they are adsorbed to the receptors; those with the weakest adsorption may move farther and more rapidly across the mucosa than those with the strongest (Beidler, 1957). As a result the molecules of different odorants would be separated from each other as they move across the mucosa in a manner similar to that of a sorption column in a gas chromatograph.

Evidence supporting such a concept as that described above has been reported (Mozell, 1966). Recordings were taken from the olfactory nerve branches of frogs subserving two widely separated regions of the olfactory

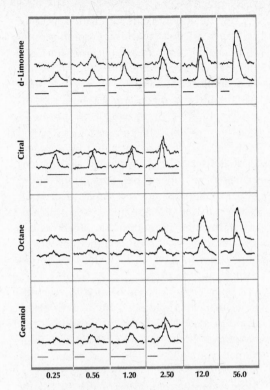

Figure 7.10. These traces are electronically summated multifiber responses taken from two frog olfactory nerve branches; the upper trace in each couplet is the response of the branch supplying the mucosal region near the internal naris and the lower trace is the response of the branch supplying the region of the external naris. The size of the trace reflects the magnitude of the multifiber discharge. This in turn reflects the magnitude of the activity occurring in that region of the mucosa which is supplied by the particular nerve branch in question. Concentration is given along the bottom in terms of the partial pressure ($\times$ 10^{-2} mm Hg). The odorants are noted along the side. The stimulus marker shows only the onset of the stimulus, but in each case the stimulus lasts 3 sec and has a volume of .4 ml. The vertical time lines occur once every 10 seconds. Note that at any given concentration the size of the upper trace relative to the size of the lower trace (that is, their ratio) differs among chemicals. Note also that the magnitude of the time lapse between the onset of the discharges on the two nerve branches likewise differs among chemicals. (Mozell, 1966.)

mucosa, one near the external naris and the other near the internal naris. (If the olfactory mucosa is conceived of as a sorption column, these two regions would be comparable to the areas around its entrance and exit respectively.) The size of the neural discharge recorded from the exit region relative to the size of the neural discharge recorded from the entrance region differed for different odorants and was found to be quite characteristic of each odorant (Figure 7.10). In addition, the time lapse between the onset of the discharges on the two nerve branches also differed for different chemicals.

When the direction of the odorant flow across the mucosa was reversed, the nerve branch that originally gave the larger discharge now gave the smaller. This result would not have been expected if the different activity patterns across the mucosa were merely reflecting a topographical gradient of receptor sensitivity to each chemical. On the other hand, this reversal of activity patterns with the reversal of flow direction is quite consistent with the gas chromatographic model; namely, as a result of their differential attraction to the media of the olfactory mucosa, the molecules of some chemicals progress more rapidly and in greater numbers along the mucosal sheet than do the molecules of other chemicals. The receptors could then simply signal these molecular movements, just as the auditory receptors signal the movements of the basilar membrane, without necessarily having any selective sensitivities of their own. It should be noted that the gas chromatographic concept of olfactory discrimination does not necessarily preclude selective sensitivity of individual receptors as an additional, superimposed mechanism for discrimination; it only precludes such sensitivity as the mechanism basic to the spatio-temporal activity patterns recorded multicellularly.

In summary, evidence is now at hand to support the possibility of two mucosal mechanisms upon which olfactory discrimination may be based: (1) a loose selective sensitivity of the receptors themselves; (2) a spatio-temporal encoding based upon the relative distribution and speed of travel of the molecules across the mucosa.

EXCITATION OF THE OLFACTORY RECEPTOR BY THE ODORANT MOLECULES

At least two tasks emerge as we try to explain how the olfactory receptor is excited: (1) we must identify the molecular property that does the triggering, and (2) we must describe the ensuing depolarization of the receptor.

Identification of the Triggering Property

At the outset one should be warned against confusing some aspects of the previously discussed process of discrimination with some similar aspects of the process of receptor excitation. It is not necessary, for instance, that the property of the molecule that triggers the receptor be the same property that is basic to its discrimination. For example, as an early step in the discrimination process, the shape of the molecule, according to one theory, may allow it to occupy only certain receptor sites, but then some other property of the molecule, which acts at all sites regardless of shape, may actually do the triggering of the receptor.

So far, attempts to identify the triggering property have not been successful. Where evidence is sparse, contradictory theories abound, of course, and this has been all too true in the study of olfaction. With varying amounts of empirical evidence and logical argument a long line of properties have been proposed as the trigger. Almost every property that chemicals possess has at one time or another been implicated. Reviews of olfaction have almost compulsively incorporated a summary of these theories (Gerebtzoff, 1953; Jones & Jones, 1953; Ottoson, 1963; Benjamin et al., 1965; Wenzel & Sieck, 1966; Moncrieff, 1967; Moulton & Beidler, 1967). Because there are so many reviews, it is only necessary here to emphasize a few points.

Theories ascribing the stimulating ability of odorants strictly to chemical properties other than enzyme action have become quite unpopular. Even enzyme theories, in reality neochemical theories, have also lost their earlier glitter. A once-popular theory hypothesized a series of enzymatically catalyzed reactions in the olfactory receptors which were supposed to be inhibited by odorants (Kistiakowsky, 1950). Although several enzymes have indeed been reported in the olfactory area (Baradi & Bourne, 1951), their relation to the olfactory process is problematical, for they are not only in receptors but also in some of the other structures of the epithelium as well; in fact, they are found throughout the body.

Special attention has been paid to intramolecular vibrations as the physical correlates of odors. Both the infrared absorption of the molecules (Beck & Miles, 1947) and their Raman shifts (Dyson, 1938) were proposed as measures of the underlying trigger property. More recently attention has been called to the low-frequency vibrations rather than the high-frequency vibrations (Wright & Michels, 1964). Although these vibrational measures have been used with some success to predict odors, several embarrassing contradictions always arose when chemicals with similar spectra smelled differently and vice versa. In addition, the infrared absorption theory has been refuted by a variety of experimental procedures and by theoretical, thermodynamic considerations (Beets, 1964).

However, Dravnieks (1964) noted that at certain frequencies the Raman spectrum is related to the dipoles of the molecules. The dipole of a molecule is related to its shape. It is also one of the properties of a chemical which would determine its selective adsorption or absorption across the mucosa. Thus, all of these properties may be correlated with each other, and it may be difficult, if not futile, to try to isolate the "basic" trigger. Each of the measures emphasized by the different theories depends upon the fundamental organization of the molecule itself, and this may account for the partial success of each of these theories in predicting the odors of chemicals. One sometimes wonders whether there is a similarity between the factions supporting these different theories and the proverbial six blind men who happened to feel different parts of the same elephant and hence "saw" the same animal in six different ways.

Receptor Depolarization

At some point along the chain of events that begins with the impingement of the necessary molecular property upon the receptor and culminates in the propagation of action potentials along the primary olfactory axon, the molecular energy involved must be transduced into electrical energy. In many other sensory systems this transduction has been shown to involve a sustained depolarization of the receptor, called the *generator potential*. These generator potentials increase in amplitude with increasing stimulus intensity. Their most important attribute is that they provide the immediate drive for the development of action potentials. The generally accepted explanation is that a sustained depolarization of the receptor membrane brings about a potential difference between the receptor and the axon which in turn results in a current flow from the receptor, through the cell, and out through the axon membrane. This outward flowing current depolarizes the axon membrane, and when a certain threshold level of depolarization is reached, an action potential is produced. As the generator potential grows so does the current density depolarizing the axon, and consequently the axon's firing rate increases (see Chapter 4, pp. 95–99).

A potential change, which has many of the characteristics of a classical generator potential, has been recorded with electrodes placed directly upon or in the mucosa (Ottoson, 1956). When odorous air is puffed onto the surface, a slow, negative, potential shift can then be recorded. (The record of this potential shift has been named the electro-olfactogram

[the EOG]. See page 114.) It has been suggested that it is actually the summation of many small generator potentials produced by many single olfactory receptors. However, the work of several authors has cast some doubt upon the role of the EOG as a generator potential. It has been observed that under certain conditions the EOG and the action potentials do not parallel each other as one would expect if the former generated the latter. For example, repeated stimulation reduced the magnitude of the EOG, but the magnitude of the neural discharge was not reduced. More cogent is the observation that by removing a piece of absorbent filter paper which had been placed on the mucosa, one could obliterate the EOG but not the neural response (Shibuya, 1964). This would be quite unexpected if the EOG is really needed to generate the action potentials.

How seriously these studies should be taken as evidence for denying that the EOG is a reflection of olfactory generator potentials is still debatable. Indeed, for the most part, the EOG and neural discharge are well correlated. In addition, because the EOG is recorded extracellularly in volume, changes in the direction of current flow may greatly reduce its magnitude as recorded by the electrodes. Therefore, local damage (caused by removing filter paper, for example) may short-circuit these currents in such a way that the EOG will no longer be detected by the electrodes even though they may still be present.

Gesteland and his coworkers (1965) believe that the EOG does, indeed, represent many generator potentials, but they have shown that the EOG includes positive potential shifts as well as the negative ones. Using the Hodgkin-Huxley formulation of the nature of the nerve impulse, Gesteland suggested that the odorant molecules depolarize the receptor by increasing its permeability to sodium ions. The resulting inward flowing current, recorded as a negative shift, is one side of the circuit which is completed by outward flowing current at the axon. By analogy to the crustacean stretch receptor (Kuffler & Eyza-guirre, 1955) the positive shift in potential was interpreted as an increase in the permeability to outward flow of potassium ions. This shunts the current through the receptor rather than allowing it to pass through the axon, thus, presumably, reducing the production of action potentials.

Although most authors of olfactory theories are quite explicit in designating a particular molecular property as the trigger, they are far less explicit when they try to describe just how this property alters the receptor membrane so that sodium ions can enter the receptor and thus depolarize it. An exception is Davies (1965) who suggested that a molecule adsorbed to the receptor membrane leaves a hole through which ions may flow when it is desorbed. It should be obvious to the reader that our knowledge concerning the excitation of the olfactory receptor by the odorant molecule is abysmally meager.

Willard R. Thurlow

AUDITION

8

The general term "audition" may appear somewhat abstract. To clarify the term, we shall list here some of the questions we shall try to answer in this chapter.

How well can we detect auditory signals?

In what ways does our auditory system fail to be a perfect "high-fidelity" analyzer of signals that are put into it?

How much do loud sounds interfere with our hearing and annoy us?

How are we able to make judgments of musical pitch and of loudness?

What cues are of importance in enabling us to discriminate different speech sounds? Can intelligible speech sounds be synthesized from these cues?

How do we localize sound sources? How well can blind people locate objects by means of echoes? (Bats and porpoises can use echoes. Can people?)

Before we can deal effectively with the questions posed above, we must review the characteristics of auditory stimuli—characteristics you will need to know about (if you do not already) to understand experiments we describe later on in the chapter. Then we will discuss "basic biological mechanisms" of the auditory system. These mechanisms are not only of great interest in themselves, but furnish important clues to how

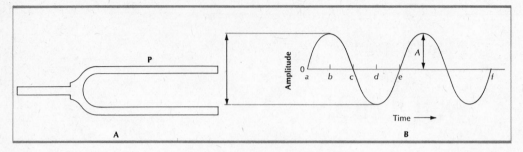

Figure 8.1. A. Tuning fork. B. Limits of the up-and-down vibration of prong P shown, in enlarged view, by vertical arrows. Sine-wave motion of P is also shown as it vibrates in time.

people react to sounds (as you will note in later sections of the chapter).

THE AUDITORY STIMULUS

The auditory stimulus is produced by some vibrating object, which causes vibrations in the surrounding medium (typically air). Finally, the vibrations of the air molecules cause the eardrum of the observer to vibrate.

A simple type of vibration, shown for example by a vibrating tuning fork, is called *simple sine-wave motion.* Figure 8.1 shows a tuning fork, with the limits of the displacement of prong P amplified and indicated by the vertical arrows. If we photographed this motion with a moving-picture camera, we could then plot out how the displacement of the prong varies with time after it is set into vibration. We would obtain a graph as shown in Figure 8.1B. This graph portrays what can be described mathematically as a sine function.

The graph shows that the prong starts from rest (time a), moves in an upward direction until it comes to rest (time b), moves back to the starting position (time c), then moves in a downward direction until it comes to rest (time d), and then moves back to the starting position (time e). By this time it has finished one complete *cycle* of motion and is ready to start another similar cycle. The frequency of vibration is defined as the number of such cycles of vibration per second. (The abbreviation cps is often used for cycles per second; or Hz, an abbreviation for *Hertz.*)

The vibrating tuning fork causes the surrounding air molecules to vibrate, and the amplitude of their vibration can also be shown to be a sine wave. The variation in pressure from moment to moment at any point in the surrounding air is also a sine-wave function, and so the variations in air pressure that push our eardrum back and

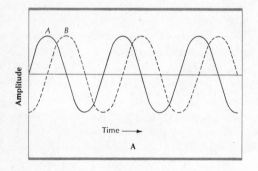

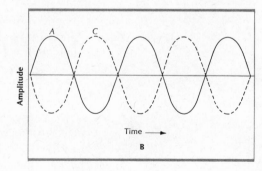

Figure 8.2. A. Diagram of 2 sine waves, *A* and *B,* which differ in phase by a quarter of a cycle. B. Two sine waves that differ in phase by half a cycle.

forth cause the eardrum to move in a simple sinusoidal function. The magnitude of variations in pressure at the eardrum will obviously be related to the amplitude of movement of the prong of the tuning fork back and forth. The letter A in Figure 8.1B designates the amplitude of the displacement of the prong of the tuning fork from its rest position.

In order to specify such a simple auditory stimulus adequately, we need to specify not only the frequency, and amount of sound pressure variation, but also the *phase* of the sound wave. Figure 8.2A portrays 2 sine waves, A and B. Sine wave B starts upward from the baseline a quarter of a cycle later than wave A; it is said to lag by one-quarter cycle. Often, the phase difference is expressed in terms of degrees, where 360 degrees equals one full cycle. A lag of one-quarter cycle then would be $(\frac{1}{4})$ (360), or 90 degrees. In Figure 8.2B, wave C is 180 degrees out of phase with wave A. In this case, wave C is said to have the "reverse" phase of wave A.

The characteristics of a sound-wave stimulus in air can be determined by placing a microphone in the sound field. The *frequency* of the stimulus can be determined by leading the electrical output of the microphone to an electronic counter, which can count the number of cycles per second with great accuracy. If the microphone has been calibrated, it is possible to compute from the voltage of the electrical output from the microphone the sound pressure produced at the location of the microphone in space. The computed sound pressure (actually a measure of amount of pressure change associated with vibrations of the air molecules) is typically expressed as the number of *decibels* above some reference level. The pressure reference level most commonly used is .0002 dynes per square centimeter. The formula for calculating the number of decibels is

$$N_{dB} = 20 \, \log_{10}\frac{p_1}{p_0}$$

where p_1 is the sound pressure we are trying to describe in terms of decibels, p_0 is the reference pressure (such as .0002 dyn/cm^2), and N is the number of decibels. (Decibels are often expressed in the notation, dB re .0002 dyn/cm^2.) From the formula it can be seen that a sound 10 times the reference pressure corresponds to 20 dB [because 20 $\log_{10}$ (10) = 20]. A sound 100 times the reference pressure corresponds to 40 dB [because 20 $\log_{10}$ (100) = 40]. In other words, for each successive multiplication of sound pressure by a factor of 10, we add 20 dB. Because, in a plane sound wave, energy, E, is proportional to the square of pressure, number of decibels can also be calculated from the energy ratio by the formula:

$$N_{dB} = 20 \, \log_{10}\frac{p_1}{p_0} = 10 \, \log_{10}\frac{(p_1)^2}{(p_0)^2}$$

$$= 10 \, \log\frac{E_1}{E_0}$$

E_0 would usually be taken as 10^{-16} watt per square centimeter.

To gain a more concrete idea of the dB scale (when the reference pressure is .0002 dyn/cm^2), note that a tone of 1000 Hz reaches threshold at about zero dB; ordinary conversation averages about 60 dB; and sounds become painful to many listeners when the sound pressure reaches 120 to 130 dB.

Simple sine-wave stimuli used in the laboratory are typically produced as electrical sine-wave stimuli by an instrument known as an oscillator. The electrical sine wave then is led through an attenuator, which can be used to decrease the voltage of the signal in decibel steps. From the attenuator the signal passes through an electrical transformer to the subject's earphone. If the attenuator is properly matched to the oscillator and transformer in its electrical impedance characteristics, then a change of N dB in the voltage of the electrical signal produces a change of N dB in the sound pressure produced by the earphone in the ear canal of the subject. It is thus possible in many experiments to specify the auditory stimulus to be used in terms of the number of dB of sound pressure above the absolute threshold of the subject. This measure is defined as the *sensation level*. For example, if the average threshold setting on the attenuator for the subject is 90 dB for a 1000 Hz stimulus, and we wish to use a 1000 Hz tone at 40 dB above threshold in the experiment, we would set the attenuator at a 50 dB reading (90 minus 40). The stimulus then would be at a sensation level of 40 dB. It is important to note that the attenuator setting gives the ratio, in dB, by which the tone has been weakened (attenuated) in sound pressure. It does not indicate the amount of sound pressure directly.

Specifying the sound pressure produced by the earphone may be preferred unless there is some reason to believe that the phenomenon being investigated is more a function of sensation level than of sound pressure level. With suitable equipment, it is possible to measure the sound pressure level at the eardrum of the subject by means of a probe tube. Alternatively (and with less difficulty) if a specification of pressure produced for an average ear is sufficient, it is possible to measure the output of the earphone in a coupler (or cavity), in which the pressure produced is similar to that produced at the entrance to the ear canal of an average ear. The pressure measured in such a coupler is not exactly the same as that which would be produced at the eardrum of the subject. Pollack (1949) has gathered together data showing relations between pressure measurements made in various ways; he includes data showing the relation between sound pressure produced at the eardrum (for an average ear) by an earphone, and sound pressure produced in a 6 cubic centimeter coupler by that earphone.

You may wonder why we have been talking about using an earphone in laboratory experiments rather than a loudspeaker. It is certainly possible to use a loudspeaker, but in this case the prediction of what sound pressure will reach the ear of the listener is considerably complicated because of reflections of the sound from the walls, floor, and ceiling

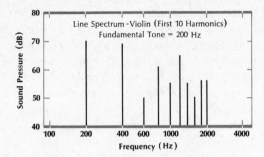

Figure 8.3. First 10 frequency components in a violin tone. (Davis & Silverman, 1960; after Fletcher, 1946.)

of the room. (The term *reverberation* is used to refer to the presence of such reflected sounds in a room.) Furthermore, slight changes in the position of the subject's head may result in sizable changes in sound pressure.

In order to avoid these difficulties, some psychologists use an *anechoic* room, which means a room free of reflection from the walls, floor, and ceiling. These rooms are typically constructed with large wedges of fiberglass mounted on all surfaces in such a way that they absorb practically all of the sound which strikes them. Thus the stimulus used in such a room is not complicated by additional reflected sound waves.

So far we have talked about only simple sine-wave stimuli. Obviously, we can use more complex stimuli. It is possible to analyze complex sounds that have a recurring wave pattern into component frequencies. Instruments for accomplishing this are called wave analyzers.

Figure 8.3 shows the first 10 frequency components in a violin tone. For this complex musical stimulus, the fundamental or lowest tone is 200 Hz, but there are additional frequencies called *harmonics* at multiples of the fundamental (400, 600, 800, and so on).

Not all complex sounds have their frequency components arranged as simple multiples of the lowest frequency.

"Thermal" noise (or "white" noise) is often used in the laboratory as a masking stimulus. To get an idea of what white noise sounds like, say "sh." The "sh" sound is not perfectly "white," that is, certain frequencies have greater energies than others. The thermal noise produced in the laboratory, however, can be thought of as being composed of an infinite number of different frequencies of the same amplitude with no systematic relation between the phases of the components. It is often desirable (as in masking experiments) to produce the thermal noise in restricted frequency regions. Typically we may use low-pass, high-pass, or band-pass noise. For example, we could use 1000 Hz, low-pass noise, that is noise with frequencies only below 1000 Hz, or 1000–2000 band-pass noise with frequencies in the band of 1000–2000 Hz only. It should be noted that the transition from frequencies that do pass the filter to frequencies that do not pass is never perfectly sharp. It is necessary to refer to the description of filters in any given experiment to find what the precise nature of the transition is.

The intensity of noise, in regions of uniform average amplitude, is often expressed in terms of intensity per cycle, or "spectrum level." This figure is obtained by dividing the total intensity measured over a given frequency band by the size of the frequency band in cycles. The resulting intensity can then be expressed in decibels.

For certain complex sounds it may be very important to take into account not only the frequency components and the amplitude of each, but also phase relations. Particularly we should examine the total stimulus to see whether it has a pulselike character. Figure 8.4 shows the wave forms for two complex sounds. Each is composed of 32 component sine waves. The frequencies and the intensities of the components are the same for the two sounds, but the phase relations are different. The sound shown in the upper part of the figure has a pulselike character and is perceived by the listener as harsher, somewhat louder, and of lower pitch than the sound shown in the lower part of the figure.

BASIC BIOLOGICAL MECHANISMS IN HEARING

The Auditory Receptive Apparatus

Figure 8.5 shows a semidiagrammatic representation of the ear structures. Sound enters the external auditory canal and sets the ear drum in motion. The vibrations are transferred by the bones of the middle ear (malleus, incus, and stapes) to the fluid of the inner ear or *cochlea*. Figure 8.6 shows how these three middle ear bones (in black) are displaced as sound pressure pushes the drum membrane in. Figure 8.6 also shows a diagram of the inner ear or cochlea "unrolled." (The fluid-filled ducts of the inner ear are actually arranged in a spiral, like the passages in a snail's shell, but for purposes of visualization it is convenient to portray these ducts as straightened out.) The third of the middle ear bones, the stapes, conducts vibrations into a duct or tube called the *scala vestibuli*. A membrane at the *oval window* to which the stapes is attached, allows the stapes to vibrate. When the stapes is pushed in (see Figure 8.6), pressure is exerted through the *scala media* and *scala tympani*, and pushes out a flexible membrane in another opening to the middle ear, the *round window*.

A cross section of these ducts (scala vestibuli, scala media, and scala tympani) is shown in Figure 8.7. The scala vestibuli and scala tympani are filled with a fluid called *peri-*

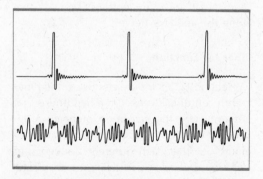

Figure 8.4. Wave forms of 2 sound stimuli with components of the same frequency and amplitude but different phases. (Bergeijk, Pierce, & David, 1960.)

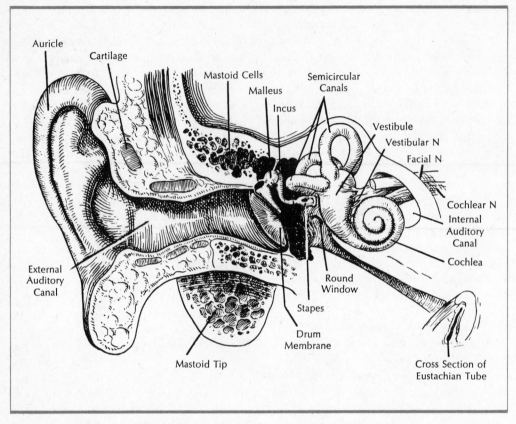

Figure 8.5. A semidiagrammatic drawing of the ear. (Davis & Silverman, 1960.)

lymph, and the scala media is filled with *endolymph.* The inner and outer *hair cells* sit on the *basilar membrane* which is pushed up and down by pressure variations caused by

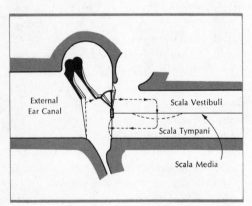

Figure 8.6. Schematic diagram of middle ear bones, and ducts (or scalae) of inner ear. (Modified from Stevens & Davis, 1938.)

the vibrating stapes. The hair cells are the receptors for auditory stimuli and are stimulated by movements of the basilar membrane. Nerve fibers of the spiral ganglion are connected to the hair cells, and when fired off send signals into the central nervous system along the auditory nerve.

Inner Ear Function

Helmholtz, a famous scientist of the nineteenth century, advanced the hypothesis that not only was the sensation of hearing dependent on the vibration of the basilar membrane, but that each different frequency of vibration caused a particular region of the basilar membrane to vibrate. This theory is known as a "place" theory of frequency analysis. (See Wever [1949] for a review of early hearing theories.)

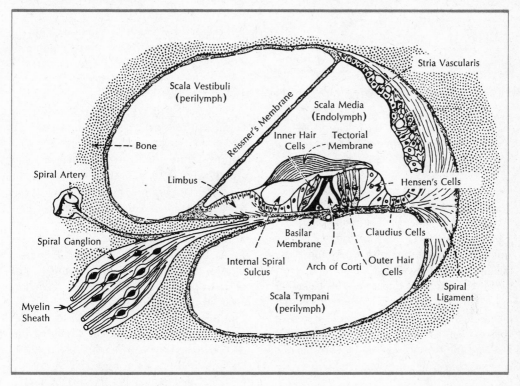

Figure 8.7. Schematic cross section of some details of the ducts of the inner ear. (Flanagan, 1965; adapted from Davis, 1957.)

In more recent years von Békésy (see von Békésy and Rosenblith, 1951) has made direct observations of the displacements of the membranes of the inner ear. These observations had to be made with the aid of a microscope. Measurement of the amplitude of the vibration of the transparent membranes was made possible by scattering tiny light-reflecting crystals of silver over the membranes. Von Békésy was able to show that the basilar membrane was not under tension as Helmholtz had supposed. He showed, however, that it did vary systematically in *stiffness*. (Stiffness is inversely related to the volume of fluid displaced by the membrane when a given pressure difference is exerted across it.) The stiffness was greatest in the portion of the basilar membrane nearest the stapes end of the membrane. Furthermore, he was able to show by means of a model (von Békésy, 1956) that variation in *stiffness* of the membrane and the degree of *coupling* between

adjacent portions of the membrane determined the pattern of vibrations produced by the membrane of the model. (No coupling would correspond in the model to having separate elastic fibers side by side, not connected to each other; the strands in the model could be coupled by applying a thin sheet of rubber over the whole set of fibers. Coupling could be increased by increasing the thickness of the rubber sheet.) When the stiffness and the coupling of the membrane of the model were made the same as that which had been measured on the basilar membrane of animal and human ears, the pattern of vibration to a tone shown by the model was the same as that shown by the basilar membrane: There was a *travelling wave* which proceeded down the basilar membrane from the stapes end. Perhaps most important, the maximum amplitude of this wave occurred at *different places* along the basilar membrane for different frequencies of

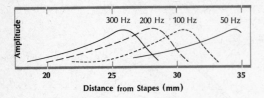

Figure 8.8. Amplitude of displacement of the basilar membrane at various distances from the stapes for several frequencies of stimulation. (von Békésy, 1947.)

tone. Figure 8.8 shows the relative amplitude of displacement of the human basilar membrane for frequencies of stimulation of 50, 100, 200, and 300 Hz as a function of distance along the membrane from the stapes. The higher the frequency of stimulation, the further the location of maximum displacement moves toward the stapes end of the basilar membrane. Thus it is evident that there is a "place" analysis of frequency. (Dr. von Békésy received the Nobel prize in 1961 for his discoveries concerning the dynamics of the inner ear.)

Electrical Potentials of the Inner Ear

Wever and Bray (1930) discovered an electrical potential in the vicinity of the inner ear which followed the input stimulus in frequency. At first this potential ("cochlear microphonic") was thought to be from the auditory nerve, but later work clearly differentiated it from the nerve potentials (Stevens & Davis, 1938). The wave form of the cochlear microphonic tends to be very similar to that of the stimulus, while that of the nerve response is a brief "spike" potential which occurs only at a certain phase of the stimulating wave. The nerve potential is much more affected by anesthetics.

Further experiments, in which potentials were recorded as a microelectrode was pushed slowly up through the basilar membrane, indicated that the principal source of cochlear microphonics was near the boundary between scala media and structures on the basilar membrane (von Békésy, 1952a; Tasaki, Davis, & Eldredge, 1954; Lawrence,

1965). Evidence gathered earlier had associated the hair cells with production of microphonics—for injury to the cells by loud noise or by drugs had been found to lead to depression of cochlear microphonics (Stevens & Davis, 1938; Davis, 1960).

The cochlear microphonic response from the normal internal ear of an animal can be used as an index to study the effect of modifications in the middle ear conduction apparatus (Wever & Lawrence, 1954). Thus variables important in human conduction hearing loss can be studied. The microphonic can also be used as an electrical indicator of mechanical wave motion taking place in the inner ear (Tasaki, Davis, & Legouix, 1952; Teas, Eldredge, & Davis, 1962). It is presumed that the electrical microphonic triggers off the nerve impulses in the auditory nerve. However, there is no direct proof of this hypothesis yet.

Other potentials have been found within the cochlea (see Wever, 1966). A steady positive potential has been observed to exist in the scala media (von Békésy, 1952b; Tasaki, Davis, & Eldredge, 1954). It is as if there were a direct current ("d.c.") battery located in the scala media. The source of this potential has been identified (Davis, 1960) as the *stria vascularis* (see Figure 8.7)—a structure in the scala media. There are also steady negative potentials in and near the cells on the basilar membrane. The relations of the positive and negative steady potentials to the cochlear microphonic and to the nerve impulse are not yet fully worked out.

Potentials Recorded in the Auditory Nervous System

Differential response to stimulus frequency One method of recording electrical activity from nerve fibers and cells of the auditory nervous system involves use of a microelectrode, the tip of which is of the order of 1 μ in diameter. In a pioneering study, Galambos and Davis (1943) recorded from single cells of the *cochlear nucleus* of the cat. The cochlear nucleus is the first nucleus in the brain stem to which fibers of the

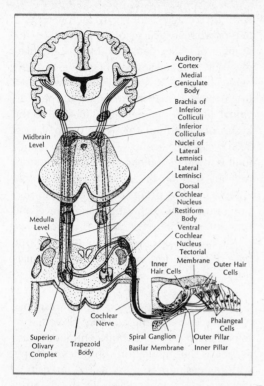

Figure 8.9. A simplified diagram of the ascending auditory pathways. (Flanagan, 1965; adapted from drawings by Netter.)

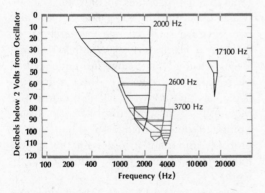

Figure 8.10. The "response areas" obtained from four separate neural units in the cochlear nucleus of the cat. The vertical scale shows how much attenuation was required at each frequency to produce just a threshold response in each unit. Note that a large number on the vertical scale represents a weak intensity tone, and a small number represents a strong intensity tone. (Galambos & Davis, 1943.)

auditory (or cochlear) nerve connect (see Figure 8.9). Galambos and Davis found that each cell was most sensitive to a narrow band of frequencies, though it responded to other frequencies when these were presented at higher intensity. Figure 8.10 shows the triangle-shaped "response areas" they obtained. For instance, in recording from a cell that was most sensitive to tones having frequencies near 2000 Hz, the response area labelled "2000 Hz" on the graph was obtained. The graph shows that it took the least amount of sound pressure (the greatest attenuation of the signal) to produce a threshold response (minimal firing of the cell) when a stimulus of 2000 Hz was used. Frequencies higher and lower than this, however, required more sound pressure in order to produce a threshold response in this cell. The other "response areas" in Figure 8.10 represent cells most sensitive to frequencies in the region of 2600, 3700 and 17,100 Hz. More recent experiments (see Rasmussen & Windle, 1960; Katsuki, 1961) have found cells at various higher levels of the auditory nervous system—inferior colliculus, medial geniculate body, auditory cortex (Figure 8.9)—with response areas for both low and high stimulus frequencies, of the same general shape as those found in the cochlear nucleus. Single nerve fibers in the cochlear nerve also show such "response areas" (Katsuki, 1961). These "response areas" have a much sharper peak than would be expected on the basis of the mechanical analysis of frequencies in the inner ear. The mechanisms by which this "sharpening" is accomplished are not yet fully understood. Von Békésy (1967) and Huggins and Licklider (1951) have discussed several possible mechanisms.

We would infer from the systematic "place" analysis of frequency in the inner ear—where the maximum displacement takes place at a position progressively nearer the stapes as the frequency of stimulation is raised—that there might be a systematic arrangement of cells in the auditory nervous system, so that cells sensitive to progressively higher frequencies would be arranged in

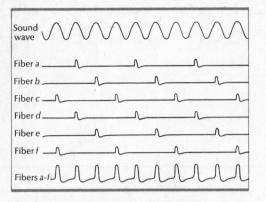

Figure 8.11. Schematic diagram of the volley principle. At this particular stimulus intensity, each nerve fiber is portrayed as firing at every third cycle of the stimulating wave. The combined action of many such fibers produces a summed response (represented at bottom) which is synchronized with the stimulus frequency. (Wever, 1949.)

some linear array from low to high. Evidence has been found for such "tonotopic" organization (Rose, 1960; Tunturi, 1960; Woolsey, 1960; Rose et al., 1963). These results indicate clearly that a possible cue for distinguishing one frequency from another is the difference in the *place* at which the disturbance due to each frequency occurs in the nervous system.

Another *possible* cue for discriminating low frequencies is the rate at which the nerve impulses are discharged (Wever & Bray, 1930). If we make records with a larger size electrode (larger than a microelectrode), from the auditory nerve, the recorded potentials reflect the action of a large number of nerve fibers. It has been found that if a low-frequency stimulating tone is used, nerve impulses occur at a certain phase of the stimulating wave. A volley of nerve impulses occurs once for each cycle of the stimulating wave. As the stimulating frequency is raised, the individual nerve fibers cannot fire at each cycle because of the refractory period of the fiber. However, a given fiber may fire every second cycle, or every third cycle. Figure 8.11 shows schematically how volleys of impulses are produced at each cycle and how they are synchronized

with the stimulus tone. As a result, the number of volleys per second is equal to the number of cycles per second in the stimulating tone. Recent studies of single auditory nerve fibers (see Rose et al., 1967) have shown in great detail that the response of the individual auditory nerve fiber is "locked" to the cycles of the stimulating wave up to at least 5000 cycles per second. (The upper frequency limit is lower in higher centers of the auditory nervous system.) By "locked" we mean that a nerve impulse occurs only at a certain portion of the cycle of the stimulating wave; and time intervals between successive nerve impulses are equal to, or some multiple of, the time necessary for one cycle of the stimulating wave.

Complex influences on neural response

At lower levels in the auditory nervous system, the typical neural unit continues to fire as long as the stimulation continues, and fires with increasing frequency as the intensity is increased. At higher levels in the auditory system, relations of responses to the stimulus may be less simple. For instance, at the cerebral cortex, some units respond when the tonal stimulation comes on, or when it ceases (Galambos, 1960; Hind, 1960). Some units respond to a small *change* in frequency or intensity (Galambos, 1960; Whitfield & Evans, 1965). Sensitivity to change in frequency has been noted at the level of the inferior colliculus also (Thurlow et al., 1951; Grinnell & McCue, 1963; Nelson, Erulkar, & Bryan, 1966). Ability to detect change in stimulation is probably important in order for the animal to respond to sounds in the natural environment.

A good deal of interest has been excited in recent years by experiments showing that attentional variables can modify the magnitude of responses in the nervous system to auditory (and other) stimuli. For example, certain cells in the auditory cortex respond only when the animal's attention is directed to the source of sound (Hubel et al., 1959). Some components in the human cortical response to clicks are greater when the subject pays attention to the clicks (Spong, Haider, & Lindsley, 1965).

What causes the neural response to change in magnitude? We do not know precisely. We do know, however, that the reticular activating system, which is involved in changing states of arousal of the organism, can affect the size of cortical responses to acoustic stimuli (Desmedt, 1960; Bremer, 1961). Some of these effects can be inhibitory. (By an *inhibitory effect,* we mean an effect in which a given response is decreased from what it was originally.)

Another kind of important inhibitory effect occurs very early in the input to the auditory nervous system. One tone can inhibit the firing of an auditory nerve fiber to another tone (Sachs & Kiang, 1967).

A whole system of "efferent" inhibitory mechanisms has been discovered, which may involve control of sensitivity to sound (Rasmussen, 1960; Desmedt, 1962; Rossi & Cortesina, 1965). One of these "efferent" control mechanisms involves nerve connections that come from the cerebral cortex and extend to the cochlear nucleus. When these fibers are stimulated electrically, they inhibit, or block,

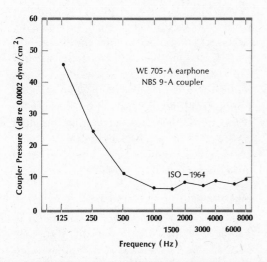

Figure 8.12. Minimum audible pressure for absolute threshold of hearing, as a function of stimulus frequency. (Davis & Krantz, 1964.)

responses in the cochlear nucleus to auditory stimuli. Another set of inhibitory fibers (believed to be part of the same general system) travels from the olivary nucleus back down to the cochlea. Electrical stimulation of these fibers causes a decrease in the response of the auditory nerve to acoustic stimuli. Fex (1962) has shown that the olivo-cochlear nerve fibers can be activated by sound. The role of the stapedius and tensor tympani muscles in decreasing responses to sounds of high intensity is discussed below (page 236).

DETECTABILITY THRESHOLDS

Sensitivity to Stimuli of Different Frequency

Figure 8.12 shows the minimum audible pressure (in dB above .0002 dyn/cm²) necessary for threshold at frequencies from 125 to 8000 Hz. The data combine the results from a number of studies, reviewed by the International Organization for Standardization (ISO), that evaluate the thresholds of normal human hearing. Young adults who showed no signs of disease of the auditory system served as subjects; listening conditions were optimal. The human auditory system is extremely sensitive, for in the most sensitive frequency region, the displacement of the eardrum at threshold is considerably less than the diameter of a hydrogen molecule (Stevens & Davis, 1938).

Many studies show that the pressure required at very high frequencies rises rapidly (Licklider, 1951). Some young people can hear frequencies up to about 24,000 Hz (Wever, 1949; Corso, 1967). Most cannot hear frequencies that high. However, if vibrations with a high intensity are applied to the mastoid bone of the head, subjects can perceive a high-pitch sound at much higher stimulus frequencies (Corso, 1963).

The hearing of low frequencies by humans has been recorded down to a few cycles per second (Corso, 1958). More and more sound pressure is required as frequency is lowered.

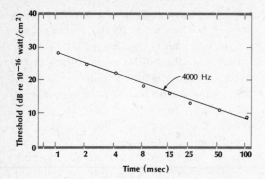

Figure 8.13. Threshold intensity required to hear a 4000 Hz tone as a function of duration of the tone. (Garner, 1947b.)

Summation Effects at Threshold

Numerous studies have shown that, as is the case for other senses (see pp. 136, 303, and 306), the auditory system appears to be capable of temporal summation, in which the effects of a stimulus are added up over short periods of time (Zwislocki, 1960). Figure 8.13 shows that less energy is required for threshold as the duration of a tonal stimulus (4000 Hz) is increased. At longer durations (near .2 seconds) the curve would become parallel with the baseline. The equation $(I - I_0)(t) = K$, a constant, has been found to fit the data (Garner & Miller, 1947; Olsen & Carhart, 1966). I represents the intensity of the stimulus; I_0 represents a constant minimal intensity, and t represents time. (It is of course necessary to specify the largest value for t within which the equation holds.) You can think of I_0 as being the very small stimulus intensity of a tone which, even if continued forever, will not produce an effect beyond the small residual noise present in the auditory system. Any excess in intensity over I_0 will lead to proportionate neural effects that will be summed up over time by the auditory system. A constant total effect is required to reach the subject's criterion for threshold. If the experimenter obtains detection with a stimulus intensity I_1 at duration t_1, and then doubles the stimulus duration (t_1), he only needs to use half as large a value of $(I_1 - I_0)$ to

obtain the same total neural effect required for threshold. The equation above tells us that the product of the intensity and time factors again will be equal to K:

$$\frac{I_1 - I_0}{2}(2t_1) = K$$

The simple type of relation described above is not obtained for all stimuli. The energy in a pure tone spreads out increasingly into other frequency regions as the duration is made shorter (Garner, 1947b). If these regions have markedly different sensitivities, the neural effect will not be so easily predictable. Another complication arises from the fact that maximum summation effects occur only when the frequency components in a complex stimulus are not separated very much from each other (Scharf, 1961). They must be contained within a "critical band" of frequencies. If, at very short durations, the stimulus energy of a tone spreads out beyond the critical band, then it is not integrated perfectly. Thus there may be a *lower* duration limit for perfect integration as well as an upper duration limit (Sheeley, 1964).

Temporal summation can also be shown to take place when a series of bursts of tone or noise is presented (Garner, 1947a; Harris, 1958; Zwislocki, 1960; Small, 1963a). In other words, the auditory system can summate the effects of stimuli even when there are short periods of time between bursts of stimulation. However, the summation effect is less under these conditions than when stimulation is continuous, apparently because of dissipation of neural effects during the silent periods. Theories to explain the various types of observed summation effect have been developed (Zwislocki, 1960).

Measurement of Hearing Loss

A pure-tone *audiometer* is calibrated in such a way that *loss* in sensitivity to each frequency in decibels can be determined with respect to normal hearing. [It has been recommended by the International Organization for Standardization that "normal" hearing be defined in terms of the data of Figure 8.12 (Davis & Krantz, 1964).] Tests of the ability to recognize speech (which we discuss in a later section) are also used to evaluate the degree of hearing loss. They are especially valuable in supplementing the pure-tone threshold tests because threshold tone tests do not always indicate completely the degree of impairment present. For example, some patients do fairly well with tones, but very poorly when asked to discriminate speech sounds at above-threshold levels (Hirsh, 1955; Davis & Silverman, 1960). Patients with cerebral damage may often have trouble in integrating and understanding minimal speech cues presented to both ears simultaneously (Bocca & Calearo, 1963).

In order to test very young children, nonverbal indicators of hearing have been developed (Davis & Silverman, 1960; Jerger, 1963). Some of these depend upon the conditioning of a response to tonal stimuli. At the present time there is considerable research being done to explore the possibilities of utilizing electrical brain potentials, recorded from the scalp and averaged by a computer (Davis & Zerlin, 1966; Ward, 1966; Davis et al., 1967).

SOME HARMFUL EFFECTS OF LOUD SOUNDS

In discussing measurements of auditory threshold, we have just been describing measurement of hearing loss. It seems appropriate now to turn to a discussion of the harmful effects of loud sounds—effects ranging from annoyance to permanent loss of hearing.

Temporary Threshold Shift (TTS)

Although many studies have been carried out to investigate the effects of continued auditory stimulation on various kinds of auditory discrimination (see Small, 1963b), perhaps most interest has centered on the effects of continued stimulation on auditory threshold. Probably this interest has arisen from

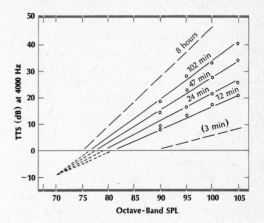

Figure 8.14. Temporary threshold shift (TTS) as a function of sound pressure level and duration of octave-band noise (1200–2400 Hz). (Ward, Glorig, & Sklar, 1959.)

concern with the possibility of permanent hearing loss.

The effects of brief prior stimulation on auditory threshold disappear rapidly; terms such as "residual masking" and "short-duration fatigue" have been used to categorize these effects (Small, 1963b; Ward, 1963). We present some data on residual masking later in the chapter.

Longer durations of exposure with higher intensity stimuli lead to cumulative effects, which have been generally referred to as "temporary threshold shift" (TTS). The amount of TTS produced is a complex function of such variables as the intensity and duration of the stimulation, the duration of intervals between exposures, and stimulus frequency. Despite this complexity, considerable progress has been made in working out predictions of the amount of TTS to be expected as a result of certain types of stimulation. Figure 8.14, for instance, shows the amount of threshold shift measured 2 minutes after a fatiguing noise stimulus was terminated (TTS_2). It is apparent that there is a lawful relation between intensity level of the fatiguing stimulus and TTS_2. The effect produced is also systematically related to the duration of the fatiguing stimulus. TTS_2 is a useful index of fatigue produced because it is possible to predict from TTS_2 the amount of fatigue present (as the ear recovers) at intervals longer than 2 minutes following termination of the fatiguing stimulus. For intervals of time less than 2 minutes following the termination of stimulation, unusual changes in threshold may occur, which have been interpreted as indicating the presence of more than one type of recovery process.

From Figure 8.14 it can be seen that sizeable amounts of temporary hearing loss can be produced by a noisy environment. People who work in such environments may not only suffer large elevations of thresholds after a day's work, but may suffer permanent loss of hearing if exposed daily to high noise levels for long periods of time without protection for their ears. It is possible to predict the amount of permanent hearing loss that would be produced by daily exposure for about 10 years to a sound, from the TTS_2 produced by this sound (Nixon & Glorig, 1961). Making use of this relationship, as well as other data, it has been possible to set up "damage risk contours" for certain noises (Kryter, 1963; Kryter et al., 1966). These contours state the levels of the steady noises which, if exceeded, will lead eventually to significant hearing loss. Much further work remains to be done in improving the accuracy of prediction of hearing loss produced by different types of sound, and different durations of exposure, as well as in predicting individual differences in susceptibility to hearing loss (see Ward, 1969).

Two muscles, which modify the action of the chain of middle-ear bones, are capable of providing significant protection to the ear, particularly against low-frequency sounds: the *stapedius* muscle, attached to the stapes, and the *tensor tympani* muscle, attached to the malleus. High-intensity sounds cause contraction of these muscles, which in turn decreases the intensity of sound transmitted to the inner ear. In man, the stapedius muscle may have the more important protective action (Jepsen, 1963). These muscles have a latency (or reaction time) to sound stimulation of about 10 msec. On a firing range, pro-

tection against shock waves can be given, however, by presenting a tone just prior to the firing of the gun. The tone elicits the muscle reflex and helps to protect the ear from the noise-impact of the gun (Fletcher & Riopelle, 1960).

Annoyance of Noise, "Annoisance"

If the sound pressure level of a tone is high enough, it will produce unpleasant reactions in the listener. It has been found that subjects can reliably judge the degree of "noisiness" of various noises and that the degree of noisiness can be predicted ahead of time from the intensity level of the various frequency components of the noise, and the duration of the noise (Kryter & Pearsons, 1963). Predicted values of noisiness can be used, in turn, to predict what actions people annoyed by noise will take—ranging from complaints to authorities, to legal action (Kryter, 1968).

Noise can cause annoyance in a variety of ways. It can disturb relaxation or sleep; it can startle; it can interfere with conversation. (See Kryter, 1966, for a study of reactions of people in communities exposed to jet aircraft noise.) Will noise interfere with the *performance* of tasks that do not involve speech communication or auditory signals? A number of studies of this problem indicated no difference in the effect of a high noise level as compared to a lower level on performance of a variety of tasks (Kryter, 1950). However, evidence has shown (Broadbent, 1958), that noise does produce a deleterious effect on the performance of tasks that require continuous attention to signals that are difficult to discriminate and unpredictable with respect to their time of occurrence.

LIMITATIONS OF THE EAR AS AN ANALYZING SYSTEM

If the ear were a perfect frequency analyzing system, different frequencies would not interfere with each other, or interact with each other. Obviously, they do. In the next 3 sections, we are going to consider limitations of the ear as a "high-fidelity" analyzing system. We discuss beats, distortion, and masking.

Beats

Beats are heard when 2 tones, which are not too different in frequency, are sounded simultaneously. If the difference in the frequencies of the 2 tones is small, the beats are heard as fluctuations in loudness. For example, with frequencies of 200 and 202 Hz, the loudness fluctuates, and maxima of loudness occur twice a second. If we lead these 2 frequencies to a loudspeaker instead of the ear, then pick up the resulting output of the loudspeaker with a microphone and look at the waveform, it turns out that the amplitude of the resultant wave fluctuates twice a second. So our perception of beats is related to fluctuations in the amplitude of the wave form produced by 2 frequencies simultaneously stimulating the same physical system. If our ear were a perfect analyzer, and each frequency were isolated at a separate place in the inner ear, beats would not occur.

As the difference in frequency between 2 tonal stimuli is made larger, there is a transition to a perception of intermittent pulses, then to a perception of roughness; finally all beat effects vanish (Wever, 1929). The vanishing of beat perception is not simply due to a lack of overlap of the vibrations on the basilar membrane (von Békésy, 1960). Perceptible beats are heard again as the higher frequency approaches simple multiples of the lower (Wever, 1949).

Beats are of importance in music. If the strings for a given note on the piano are not tuned to give the same frequency, beats occur and produce an unpleasant effect. Two beginning violin students playing the same melody together may cause a very dissonant result, for the slightly different tones they produce beat against each other.

Distortion

Those interested in high-fidelity sound equipment are well acquainted with problems of distortion in physical instruments. The ear itself is a complicated mechanical system, and produces some distortion, even if there is no distortion present in the stimulus.

When a mechanical system capable of vibration is displaced by a small force, the displacement is proportional to force. However, when the force becomes much greater, the displacement is no longer proportional to the force applied. This "nonlinearity" can be shown mathematically to lead to the production of additional frequencies of vibration. Thus if a single frequency is applied to the system at high intensity, harmonics arise which are multiples of the original frequency. (If a frequency of 200 Hz is applied, harmonics of 400, 600, and so on may be produced.) If 2 intense frequencies are applied to the system, difference tones and summation tones ("combination tones") will appear in addition to harmonics of each of the frequencies applied. If we represent the lower frequency by L, and the higher frequency by H, the difference tones produced would have frequencies $H - L$, $2L - H$, and so on. Summation tones would have frequencies of $L + H$, $2L + H$, and so on. In general, frequencies of possible "combination tones" would be predicted by the formula $mL \pm nH$, where m and n are any integers. Study of the actual combination tones produced will give information concerning the type of nonlinearity present.

How do we measure the amount of a combination tone present? One method for measuring *audible* distortion is to introduce an additional frequency equal to that of the distortion frequency we wish to evaluate; then the sound pressure and phase of this additional frequency are adjusted until the pitch corresponding to the distortion frequency vanishes, due to cancellation of the distortion frequency (Zwicker, 1955; Goldstein, 1967). (If the basilar membrane is being pushed in one direction, and you introduce a frequency with a phase that pushes the membrane in the opposite direction at the same moment, then the effects will cancel.) Another method is to increase the intensities of the 2 primary frequencies until the distortion frequency (produced by the 2 primary frequencies) can just be detected by the observer (Plomp, 1965). Plomp has recently summarized earlier results and has also discussed experiments of his own. Early investigators found that the combination tones $H - L$, and $2L - H$ were clearly audible. Plomp found that $3L - 2H$, as well as $H - L$ and $2L - H$, was also detectable by all of his observers. $L + H$ was not detected by his observers. It seems quite likely that harmonics and combination tones (such as $L + H$) above the 2 primary frequencies could be masked out by the more intense primaries. (Low tones at a high intensity tend to mask out high tones.) Clack (1968) varied a frequency $2f_1$ (equal to twice the fundamental frequency f_1) in phase and amplitude in such a way that

it added to the distortion harmonic $2f_1$ present in the ear and made it audible. With this method, he was able to study the characteristics of the $2f_1$ harmonic.

Where in the auditory system do these distortion frequencies arise? Helmholtz thought that they arose in the middle ear, in the movements of the eardrum and chain of middle-ear bones (Wever & Lawrence, 1954). In more recent times, von Békésy (1960) was able to show that neither harmonics nor difference tones were generated by the eardrum. However, his experiments showed that difference tones could be produced by non-linearity in the middle ear—most likely in vibrations of the footplate of the stirrup (the small bone which transmits vibrations to the fluids of the inner ear). Harmonics were shown not to arise from middle-ear distortion. Von Békésy supposed that the production of

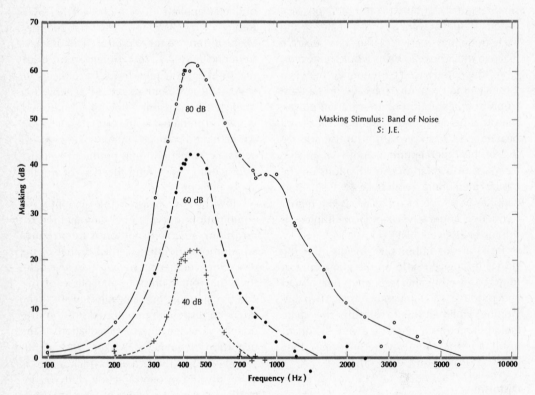

Figure 8.15. Masking produced by three levels (40, 60, 80 dB) of a narrow-band masking noise. Masking is measured by shift in absolute threshold from that measured without noise present. (Egan & Hake, 1950.)

harmonics was related to eddy movements of the fluids of the inner ear. More recently Tonndorf (1958) has been able to show that audible harmonics occur at sound levels at which eddies appear in the fluids of a model of the inner ear. The inner ear has also been implicated in production of combination tones of the type $L - n(H - L)$, where n is a positive integer. The most prominent of these is $2L - H$ (Zwicker, 1955; Goldstein, 1967). In contrast to the combination tone $L - H$, which appears only above a sensation level of about 50 dB, the combination tone $2L - H$ appears at low intensity levels; it is relatively unaffected by changes in the level of the primaries L and H (once it appears) and decreases sharply with frequency separation of the L and H primaries. We would not expect these characteristics if the distortion were produced by a nonlinear system preceding the inner ear.

Masking

Much of our listening in everyday life is done in the presence of various types of noise that interfere with our ability to detect signals. Certain specialized jobs, such as Sonar operator, require detection of a signal in the presence of noise. We shall describe various types of masking situation that have been experimentally investigated and the masking phenomena produced in each of them. (Further information on masking of speech appears later in the chapter.) We should emphasize at the outset that there are undoubtedly a number of different mechanisms operating to produce the masking observed in these various situations.

Masking by tones and bands of noise in the same ear as the signal The most common measure of masking is the threshold shift in the signal (in decibels) caused by the masking sound. That is, we first measure the threshold of the signal by itself; then we remeasure the signal threshold when the masking stimulus is present. The difference in threshold is the amount of masking.

A narrow band of noise was used as a masking stimulus by Egan and Hake (1950), and Ehmer (1959). Figure 8.15 shows one set of results from the study of Egan and Hake. A masking band of noise was used which was 90 Hz wide, and centered at 410 Hz. The amount of masking produced is shown for a number of masked frequencies (horizontal scale). When the noise was at low (40 dB) and medium (60 dB) levels, the amount of masking produced was quite symmetrical. However, at the 80 dB level, the masking noise produced considerably more masking on higher than on lower frequencies.

Some of the earliest experiments on masking were done with tone-on-tone masking (Wegel & Lane, 1924). These indicated clearly that, particularly at high intensity levels, masking was greater on test tones above the frequency of the masking tone than on test tones below it in frequency. Study of tone-on-tone masking is complicated by the presence of beats, and (at higher intensities) by distortion. For instance, if the separations in the frequencies of the masking and masked tones are small, the masked tone can be detected by the presence of beats. The masking effect may involve a neural "inhibition" effect for larger frequency separations between the tones (Galambos & Davis, 1944; Sachs & Kiang, 1967).

"Remote" masking Not only is it possible to obtain a surprising degree of spread in masking effects to frequencies above the band of masking noise, but under special conditions it is possible to obtain masking of *low* frequencies by an intense *high*-frequency noise stimulus. This has been termed "remote" masking (Bilger & Hirsh, 1956; Bilger, 1958). One hypothesis is that the remote masking is caused by distortion processes in the inner ear, which produce interfering vibrations in the low-frequency regions of the inner ear (Deatherage, Bilger, & Eldredge, 1957; Deatherage, Davis, & Eldredge, 1957; Hirsh & Burgeat, 1958). Modulation (variation) of the amplitude of the masking stimulus is an important factor in producing the effect.

Although it was thought that activation of the stapedius muscle reflex might help explain remote masking effects, a recent experiment by Bilger (1966) casts doubt on this hypothesis. Bilger found remote masking even when the stapedius muscle had been removed.

The concept of critical band Fletcher (1940) pointed out that when a masking noise (such as thermal noise) is used that involves a wide band of frequencies of approximately uniform amplitude, masking of a tone signal is caused by components in the noise close to the tone signal in frequency. Components within certain frequency limits on either side of the signal frequency ("critical band") contribute to the masking, whereas components beyond these limits do not add to the masking. The size of the critical band can be measured directly by taking a broad band of thermal noise, with the signal frequency at the center of the band, and gradually narrowing the size of the band of noise, by successively filtering out high and low frequencies. At first the masked threshold for the tone signal does not change. However, when the noise bandwidth is made narrower than the critical band, the masked threshold starts to decrease; it takes less energy for the signal to be detected (Fletcher, 1940; Scharf, 1961; Swets, 1963).

It turns out that when a tone signal is just detectable in wide-band noise, the energy of noise in the critical band is close to 2.5 times the energy of the tone. (See Scharf, 1961.) Thus it is possible to predict the detectability of a tone signal ahead of time from measurement of the noise intensity present in the critical band (Hawkins & Stevens, 1950). One explanation of what the subject is doing when he detects a signal in noise is that he is listening to input in a restricted frequency region surrounding the signal and is making his judgment in terms of whether the average

energy level present in this region exceeds some criterion level (see Green & Swets, 1966). It is assumed that when the signal is present, it adds to the energy level produced by the noise alone. Discrimination between noise alone and signal plus noise becomes more difficult, however, as noise level increases, probably due to increased variability of neural effects. (Recall Weber's Law, which predicts a proportionality between ΔI, the intensity of a just noticeable "signal," and I, the initial stimulus level—in this case noise. See Chapter 2, p. 39.)

A critical band turns out to correspond to a distance of 1 millimeter along the basilar membrane of the inner ear (Greenwood, 1961). Neurally, the critical band may correspond to a spatial region within which neural effects sum with each other because of lateral neural connections. The critical band mechanism is undoubtedly not the only mechanism involved in integration of information from different frequency regions. The judgment of the loudness of complex sounds, for instance, may involve integration of energy over a frequency range much wider than that of a critical band.

Recruitment In our discussion of masking so far we have used the shift in the signal threshold caused by the masking stimulus as the criterion of masking. It is important to note at this point that as the signal is increased in intensity *above* its masked threshold, the loudness grows rapidly, until at 15 to 20 dB above the masked threshold, the loudness of a tonal signal is as great in the presence of the masking stimulus as it is alone without any masking stimulus (Steinberg & Gardner, 1937; Small & Thurlow, 1954). Thus the effect of masking on the processing of signals is not always so devastating as might appear from threshold masking curves. A similar "recruitment" or the "gaining-back" of loudness is found in certain cases of deafness in which sensory cells in the inner ear are damaged (Harris, 1953; Egan, 1954).

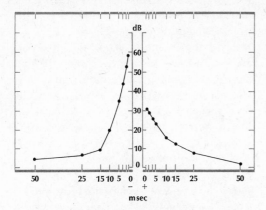

Figure 8.16. The left side of the graph shows backward masking produced by a masking noise burst of 90 dB (re .0002 dyn/cm²) on a probe tone of 5 msec duration and 1000 Hz frequency. The end of the tone burst *preceded* the masking noise burst by intervals of time indicated on the horizontal scale. The right side of the graph shows forward masking produced by this masking noise on the same probe-tone burst when the beginning of the probe tone *followed* the masking burst by intervals of time indicated on the horizontal scale. (Elliott, 1962a.)

Backward masking Although most masking effects involve the simultaneous presence of a masking stimulus and signal, there are some important exceptional situations. It was noted by Miller (1947) in an experiment on the masking effects of short pulses of sound, that a brief sound could be made inaudible by a pulse of sound which *followed* it in time. Since this initial experiment, numerous others have been made on the phenomenon, which is called "backward masking" (Raab, 1963). See also the analogous case of backward visual masking (p. 310).

Figure 8.16 (left side) shows illustrative data from an experiment by Elliott (1962a). A 50 msec burst of thermal noise at 90 dB (re.0002 dyne/cm²) was preceded by a "probe" tone signal of 1000 Hz, 5 msec in duration. Subjects were instructed to indicate whether the addition of the probe tone produced a noticeable change in the sound of

the masking thermal noise burst. The ending of the probe tone was made to *precede* the thermal noise burst by different intervals of time, as is indicated in Figure 8.16. The ordinate of the graph shows the number of decibels that the 5 msec probe tone had to be raised above its unmasked threshold in order to be detected. It is apparent that the amount of backward masking is relatively small when the 5 msec tone precedes the masking burst by more than 10 to 15 msec. The amount of backward masking has been found to be less when lower intensities of noise burst are used.

The apparent paradox of masking "backward" in time can possibly be understood by assuming that an intense stimulus causes a burst of neural activity that reaches the central nervous system quickly and "overtakes" neural activity caused by a less intense stimulus (Miller, 1947). There is evidence that the masking stimulus actually shortens the effective and perceived duration of a preceding stimulus (Gol'dburt, 1961; Wright, 1964). It is as if the masking stimulus has overtaken and masked out the last part of the signal.

In some studies of "backward masking" the subject identifies the signal by a distinctive characteristic, such as its pitch (see Elliott, 1962b). In other experiments, however, subjects appear to use as their criterion (of detection of the signal) a change in the total composite of the signal plus the masker. For example, they may use as their criterion the total duration of the composite of a click and burst of masking noise (Osman & Raab, 1963) or the total loudness of the composite of a click plus another masking click (Chistovitch & Ivanova, 1959). In these latter cases is it necessary to assume that there is any diminution of the neural effect of the signal caused by the masker?

Interaural stimulus relations and masking We now turn to masking effects which involve interrelations between the 2 ears.

Sound in 1 ear, if sufficiently intense, can

be conducted physically to the opposite inner ear and cause masking of a sound in the other ear. If precautions are taken to rule out such cross-conduction effects, it is found that "cross-masking" effects can still be obtained, though they are smaller than when masking and masked stimuli are being heard by the same ear; also, the masking effect is restricted more to frequencies near to the masking frequency than in the monaural masking situation (Ingham, 1959; Sherrick & Mangabeira-Albernaz, 1961; Zwislocki et al., 1967). An exception to the last statement is found when one ear is exposed to an intense high-frequency band of noise; it is observed that masking occurs in the low-frequency regions of the other ear. This effect is called "contralateral remote masking" (CRM). Ward (1967) concludes that CRM is due primarily to masking in the central nervous system, part of which is central masking caused by low-frequency distortion originating in the ear listening to the high-frequency noise. The contribution to CRM by the reaction of the ear muscles to the high-frequency noise is considered to be minor.

Far more research effort has been devoted to investigating variations in masking effectiveness that are related to interaural phase relations of noise compared to those of the tone. Early observations by Langmuir and collaborators (Langmuir et al., 1944) showed that detection of a tone signal in masking noise depended on the apparent spatial direction of the tone in relation to the noise. Other researchers have conducted systematic investigations of the phenomenon (Hirsh, 1948; Jeffress et al., 1956; Jeffress, Blodgett, & Deatherage, 1962; Robinson & Jeffress, 1963). The magnitude of the effects depends on the signal frequency used; effects are obtained primarily at low signal frequencies. The following is a brief description of some of the main effects observed:

(1) Start, for example, with a signal tone of 500 Hz, and with thermal noise at an intensity per cycle of 45 dB. Both stimuli are applied to one ear, say the right ear. Determine the threshold SPL for the 500 Hz tone to be detected.

(2) If the identical signal and noise are applied to the other ear (assuming the ears are not different) the threshold for the tone will not be changed appreciably. This result, however, will hold true only if the phase of the tone is the same in each ear, and if the phase of the noise is the same in each ear. This condition is designated as the "homophasic" condition.

(3) If we now determine the threshold for a condition where the tone has been applied to the right ear, and the noise to each ear (with identical phase), the threshold turns out to be about 9 dB lower than for the homophasic condition. A gain in detection over the homophasic condition is termed a "masking level difference" (MLD).

(4) If we start with the homophasic condition and reverse the phase of the signal in the 2 ears (a 180 degree phase difference) we find an MLD of about 14 dB. (There are slight sampling differences in the magnitude of the MLD in different experiments.) If we start from the homophasic condition and reverse the phase of the noise, we obtain a slightly smaller MLD (see Robinson and Jeffress, 1963).

Several types of theory have been proposed to explain MLD effects (Jeffress et al., 1956; Durlach, 1963; Schenkel, 1967). Earlier theorists (Webster and Jeffress; see Jeffress et al., 1956) had pointed out that we should pay attention to the frequency component of the noise in the immediate vicinity of the signal and see what happens to the phase of the composite wave in each ear produced by adding signal to noise. They calculated that adding enough signal intensity to the noise to make the signal detectable should produce a constant shift in the phase between the wave forms at the 2 ears, in the region of the signal frequency. (Studies of sound localization show that such a phase shift should result in a change in the perceived direction of a sound.) Despite some success, this theory was found not to predict

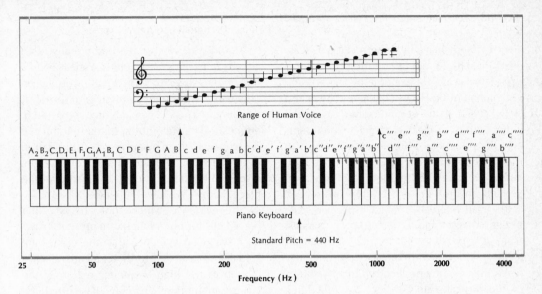

Figure 8.17. Relations between frequency in cycles per second, notes of the piano keyboard, and musical notes that can be sung by the human voice. (Modified from Boring, Langfeld, & Weld, 1948.)

accurately in all cases (Jeffress, Blodgett, & Deatherage, 1962).

The theoretical explanations have become more and more complex as more detailed experiments have been performed on MLD phenomena. For example, investigation of the MLD as a function of differences in the intensity of both signal and noise in each ear have led to elaborations in theory (Colburn & Durlach, 1965; Egan, 1965; Dolan & Robinson, 1967). Green and Henning (1969) have recently reviewed data and theory concerning MLD.

PITCH

Pitch Scales

Psychological pitch is most closely related to the physical dimension of frequency (yet it is by no means identical with physical frequency). Figure 8.17 shows the notes on a piano—with letters corresponding to the musical scale and frequencies in cycles per second below. The note a′ corresponds to 440 Hz. You will notice that the sequence of letters repeats. Each sequence is at an *octave* above the one to the left. Thus, in the series

of c's: C_1, C, c, c′, c″ . . . , each is an octave above the preceding. The fundamental (lowest) frequency for each c is twice that for the preceding c. Put more generally, the musical interval of the octave, defined *physically*, corresponds to a doubling of fundamental frequency. But do octaves, physically defined as a 2-to-1 frequency ratio, always sound like the same *subjective* interval? The answer is no. Even though subjects' judgments of an octave correspond to a 2-to-1 frequency ratio quite closely over a fairly wide frequency range (Ward, 1954), there may be marked departures from this simple relation at very high frequencies. Not all subjects can judge pitch above about 4000 Hz (the upper range of fundamentals on the piano keyboard). However, some subjects with musical training can judge the pitch of these high frequencies in terms of subjective musical intervals. The judged pitch of these very high frequencies has been shown to be a function of variables that appear to depend on the "arousal" state of the subject (Thurlow, 1946; Elfner, 1964; Thurlow, 1965). Thus, loss of sleep tends to lower judged pitch, while administration of a drug which tends to arouse the subject (benzedrine) counteracts the effect of loss of sleep.

Experiments have been performed to scale pitch magnitude independently of the musical interval scale, for example by Stevens and Volkmann (1940), Harris (1960), and Beck and Shaw (1963). However, in some cases, the judgments of subjects in such experiments may be influenced by their experience with the musical scale. Harris (1960) has pointed out that results with the Method of Bisection depend on the size of the interval bisected. With small intervals, the scale derived from bisection resembles the ordinary musical scale. It is possible that in judging small intervals, subjects with musical training may make their judgment according to the notes on the musical scale. Furthermore, in judging larger frequency intervals, some subjects with musical training may use the octave relationship as a basis for giving numerical estimates of pitch relations (Warren, 1958; Beck & Shaw, 1961). For instance, subjects may assign numbers in such a way that a constant increase in number corresponds to each successive octave increase in pitch (Beck & Shaw, 1961). The use of responses learned in musical training, for judgment of pitch, is not unexpected. However, it is well worth discussing because it serves to emphasize the importance of looking into the mechanisms by which subjects are able to assign numbers to relations between stimuli (see Chapter 3).

Psychological pitch is mainly related to the frequency of the stimulus. However, the pitch of a pure tone can also be affected by intensity. Although there are large individual differences, it has been found that the pitch of low tones tends to go down as the intensity is increased, and the pitch of high frequencies tends to go up (Stevens & Davis, 1938; Morgan, Galambos, & Garner, 1951; Cohen, 1961). Stimulation of the opposite ear can cause similar changes in the pitch of pure tones (Thurlow, 1943). The pitch of a complex musical tone, which contains many low and high harmonics, is not much affected by intensity (Fletcher, 1934).

"Place" Theory of Pitch

Theories of pitch have traditionally been aimed at finding basic physiological events that could serve to explain the correlation between psychological pitch and physical frequency. The "classical" theory of pitch, enunciated by Helmholtz, stated that the cue for pitch was given by the *place* of stimulation in the inner ear and auditory nervous system. (Wever, 1949, has discussed the history of the place theory.) We have earlier described some of the evidence which shows clearly that place cues for pitch height are present. However, we need evidence that these cues are actually used. Recently, direct electrical stimulation of the high-frequency region of the basilar membrane in man has produced pitches that are correlated with place of stimulation (Simmons et al., 1965).

Acceptance of a "place" theory for low frequencies has not been by any means unanimous because there appear to be other possible cues for low pitch. Nevertheless, "place" could be *one* of the cues for low pitch. Zwicker (1964) has found tonal "after-images," following stimulation with bands of noise which have a gap (no acoustical energy) in a certain frequency region. The pitch of the after-image corresponds to the frequency location of the gap. The after-images apparently can be explained in terms of neural "after-discharge" in a particular place in the nervous system. The after-images were obtained in both high- and low-frequency regions.

Convincing evidence for a "place" mechanism for pitch (including low pitch) also comes from observations on "diplacusis." A person with diplacusis hears a different pitch when a given tone stimulates the right ear than when it stimulates the left ear. When the tone stimulates both ears simultaneously, he hears a pitch in between the 2 pitches he hears when the 2 ears are stimulated separately. This phenomenon has been known for years and can be explained by a "place" theory (see von Békésy, 1963). (Can you draw a diagram showing how? Represent each "place" disturbance as a distribution of neural effects with a maximum.)

Time Cues for Low Pitch

In discussing the volleys of nerve impulses produced by a pure low tone, we mentioned that the rate of volleys might act as a cue to the pitch of a low-frequency tone. As the frequency of the tone increases, the number of volleys increases, and pitch increases (Wever, 1949). However, we need to have some more direct evidence that such a cue does operate.

One way of separating this type of cue from a place cue is to use bursts of thermal noise. (At a very slow rate, these would sound approximately like: *sh, sh, sh.* . .). The thermal noise stimulates all frequency regions—so there is no differential place cue. The number of bursts per second can be varied, however, and thus the rate of volleys in the auditory nerve will vary accordingly. Under these circumstances, it has been found that many subjects hear a low pitch that corresponds to the rate of noise pulses (Miller & Taylor, 1948; Licklider, 1959). The upper rate limit for perception of pitch by this cue was originally found to be between 200 to 300 pulses per second. Some later experimenters have tended to put the limit higher (Harris, 1963). In these experiments, there may be difficulty in telling whether the subject is perceiving intermittency or pitch; matching the noise bursts with a non-intermittent oscillator tone provides one method for solving this problem.

It is of interest to note that recently the auditory nerve of a human ear was stimulated electrically with pulses (Simmons et al., 1965). The subject heard a low pitch corresponding to the rate of the pulses, up to an upper limit of about 300 pulses per second. Simmons, Mongeon, Lewis, and Huntington (1964) have reviewed some of the experimental difficulties in such research.

Other experimenters have used acoustic stimuli which create pulses in restricted frequency regions (Small, 1955; Licklider, 1959). (See Figure 8.4 for an illustration of a series of pulses.) In these experiments it is important to find out whether the low pitch may be produced within the inner ear by a low-frequency component corresponding to pulse rate (von Békésy, 1963). For if a low physical frequency were produced, the low pitch would be explained as due to the physical stimulus and not due to the pulses of nerve activity produced in another frequency region. Schouten (1940) was the first to show that the low pitch "residue" heard in a series of pulses was not due to the introduction of a low physical frequency equal to the rate of the pulses. (He cancelled out the physical frequency by means of an additional pure tone, varied in phase and intensity.) Several experimenters have used a masking noise in the low-frequency region to mask out any possible low-frequency artifact (Thurlow & Small, 1955; Licklider, 1959; Small & Campbell, 1961; Rosenberg, 1965). They have found that the low pitch remains despite the low-frequency masking.

Further Theoretical Approaches to Low Pitch

In order to take account of the fact that low pitch appears to be related to volleys in the nerve, but also appears to show some "place" characteristics, Licklider (1959) developed a theory of low pitch constructed on the assumption that there is a time-analyzing system in the auditory nervous system that converts the time intervals between volleys of nerve pulses into a "place" cue.

There is another characteristic that might act as a cue to the perception of a low pitch—the pattern of harmonics (Licklider, 1951; de Boer, 1956). It was pointed out earlier in the chapter (see Figure 8.3) that a tone produced by a musical instrument, such as a violin, consists of a fundamental frequency together with many higher frequency harmonics. Fletcher (1934) observed that even when the fundamental was filtered out, his subjects still perceived a low pitch corresponding to the fundamental. Wilson (1969) has recently found a clear correlation between perceived pitch and the pattern of "place" cues in a complex stimulus, analogous to the pattern of harmonics.

If there can be several cues to low pitch, how do these different cues produce a given low pitch perception? We could suppose that a "conditioned pitch perception" might be involved. That is, we suppose that people, especially those with musical training, listen to the pitch produced by a given musical instrument, or singing voice, thousands of times. These stimuli have various cues—which include not only a low fundamental frequency, but also harmonics, and harmonic components which may produce a pulse rate equal to the fundamental frequency. Now, when only one of these cues is presented, it may still be effective in producing the conditioned perception. (Garner, 1952, has spoken of the possibility of a Gestalt "completion" effect in connection with this problem.)

Thurlow and Hartman (1959) noted that subjects often made use of a vocal humming response (or reported they "hummed to themselves" without singing out loud) in matching their perceived pitch to an oscillator tone. Thurlow (1963) has hypothesized that the vocal response may play an important role in perception of the low pitch of complex stimuli. Its role, however, is limited by the vocal range of the subject. Further research is needed on these possibilities.

LOUDNESS

In this section we will look at some of the various ways in which psychological loudness has been measured. When we talk about loudness scales, we will be looking at the data as we look at data from other psychological experiments (Bergman & Spence, 1944). We consider questions such as: How could these responses have been produced? How can different response scales be related?

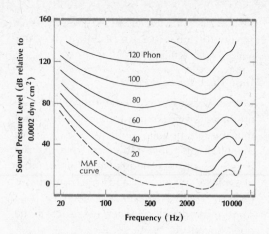

Figure 8.18. Equal-loudness contours. The number associated with each curve represents the loudness in phons for all frequency-intensity combinations of that curve. (Robinson & Dadson, 1956.)

Equal-loudness Contours

Figure 8.18 shows what are called "equal loudness contours" (Robinson & Dadson, 1956). The contour (curve) marked 40, for example, shows the sound pressure level (SPL), in dB at each frequency, that is necessary for a tone of that frequency to sound just as loud as a 1000 Hz tone at 40 dB SPL (SPL with reference to .0002 dynes/cm²). As a more specific example: If you will refer to the graph, you will see that a frequency of 100 Hz must be at an SPL of close to 50 dB in order to sound as loud as a 1000 Hz tone at 40 dB SPL. The loudness of each of the frequencies on the 40 dB contour is said to be 40 "phons."

The contours in Figure 8.18 are called "free-field" contours because of the measuring technique used. The observer faces the source of sound in an anechoic (or "free-field") room, and the sound intensity is adjusted for a given loudness match. The sound intensity is measured after the observer has left, at the position in which the observer's head was located. The curve marked "MAF curve" (meaning "minimum audible field") in Figure 8.18 represents a graph of threshold sensitivity obtained with this same measuring technique. The sensitivity curve shows some differences from that obtained by measuring the minimum audible pressure ("MAP") at the eardrum, due to the influence of the head structures on the sound field.

The technique of measuring the loudness of a sound by equating it to the loudness of a 1000 Hz tone can be applied to various kinds of sounds in addition to pure tones. One disadvantage of the "phon" scale, however, is that it does not tell us anything about psychological loudness relations *between* phon levels. For example, we would be mistaken in believing that the difference between 90 and 100 phons is subjectively the same as the difference between 10 and 20 phons.

Ratio Judgments of Loudness

Stevens (1955) summarized data obtained from estimates of half and double loudness and found that the median value of the change in intensity required for a two-fold change in loudness was close to 10 dB. He defined one *sone* as the loudness of a 1000 Hz tone of 40 phons. A level of loudness judged to be twice as great would then be 2 sones. If a 10 dB increase in intensity is required to double the loudness, an equation can be derived relating sound intensity to the loudness in sones. For a 1000 Hz tone, $L = .06 \, I^{.3}$, where L is the loudness in "sones" and I is intensity. Robinson (1953) proposed a similar equation.

Other data approximating a power law have been found by experimenters who have used methods known as *magnitude estimation* and *magnitude production* (see p. 64). Results obtained vary somewhat depending on the exact procedure followed. For example, if the magnitude estimation method is used, the shape of the function obtained is influenced by the intensity of the stimulus taken as a standard (Stevens, 1956b) and also by the size of the number assigned to the standard stimulus (Hellman & Zwislocki,

1961). Large individual differences in the exponent of the power function have been found by J. C. Stevens, who used the method of magnitude production (Stevens & Guirao, 1964).

Deviations from a simple power law occur at low intensity levels (see Figure 3.19, p. 78). More complex mathematical functions have been proposed in order to describe the loudness judgments at these low intensity levels more adequately. However, it has been difficult to develop a completely satisfactory rationale for these formulations (Ross, 1967).

Why is a power function obtained? Stevens (1961) argues that the power function reflects the neural input into the nervous system from the sense organ. However, other psychologists would worry more about how the numbers get assigned to the neural quantities inside the brain (Attneave, 1962; see also the discussion of cross-modality matching in Chapter 3). Warren has proposed that the

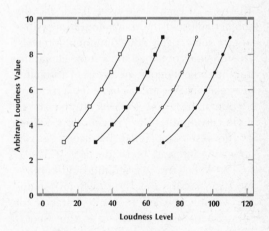

Figure 8.19. A set of data representing equal loudness *intervals* obtained with a 1000 Hz tone. Four different intensity ranges were used: 10 to 50 dB, 30 to 70 dB, 50 to 90 dB, and 70 to 110 dB. On the graph, equal intervals are indicated by 1 unit increase in number on the vertical scale. The horizontal scale is in phons, which in this case is equivalent to decibels with reference to .0002 dyn/cm². (Garner, 1954.)

numbers representing loudness are assigned on the basis of the subject's experience with sound pressure level and physical distance (Warren, Sersen, & Pores, 1958). In free space, the sound pressure level decreases by 6 dB for each doubling of distance. Thus, according to this theory, the number assigned to loudness would double for each 6 dB decrease in the sound pressure level. Most of the data gathered do not agree with this prediction (Stevens, 1963). In the next section we continue our discussion of the question of how numbers are assigned to loudness by the subject.

"Equal-interval" Judgments of Loudness

Figure 8.19 shows results obtained by Garner (1954) when he asked subjects to adjust the intensity of a series of tones (all 1000 Hz) so that the difference in loudness between adjacent tones would be equal. Each curve represents a range of 40 dB—10 to 50, 30 to 70, 50 to 90, and 70 to 110. Seven intensities were presented for each of these ranges. The ends of each range were fixed, and the subject adjusted the remaining 5 intensities to give subjectively equal loudness intervals. The functions obtained show some curvature, but they do not depart greatly from a straight-line relation. Stevens has obtained a function for one of these ranges (55–95 dB) that shows more curvature (Stevens & Guirao, 1962).

The results obtained by using "equal-appearing interval" methods suggest a relation between sensory magnitude and stimulus more of the form $S = k \log I$ where S stands for "sensory" magnitude, and I stands for stimulus intensity. In this case, the "sensation" appears to be increasing by equal units for equal ratio changes in the stimulus. On the other hand, the power law implies that the "sensation" is increasing by equal *ratios* for equal ratio changes in the stimulus. One interpretation to reconcile these results (outlined in the earlier chapter on scaling) is that discriminability of stimuli in the category scaling situation modifies the expected

power-law relation. However, other psychologists have obtained evidence that makes them prefer alternative explanations (Torgerson, 1960; Schneider & Lane, 1963). Torgerson (1961) has suggested that the subject's judgment is based on a single quantitative relation, which is interpreted as a distance or a ratio by the subject, depending on his instructions. Thurlow and Melamed (1967) have tried to indicate what this "quantitative relation" might be, in terms of subject responses in the loudness judgment situation. We might suppose that the subject is using a "measuring response" in both situations involving "equal-interval" and "ratio" scaling—such as that of moving his hand along an imaginary measuring scale in response to a change in stimulus intensity. The increase in the distance he moves his hand would depend on his matching internal kinaesthetic change, associated with hand movement, to an increase in sensory input associated with the change in sound intensity. A given movement along the measuring scale (such as from 1 to 2 inches on the scale) could be interpreted either (1) as an interval—1 to 2—or (2) as a ratio—2/1, depending on the instructions given by the experimenter. The same response would presumably be applied over and over again to enable the subject to make judgments at different intensity levels.

Loudness of Complex Sounds

It would be desirable to be able to predict the loudness of a complex sound from its physical characteristics. Several schemes have been devised which seem to work satisfactorily for certain types of complex sounds (Stevens, 1956a; Zwicker & Scharf, 1965). These schemes involve essentially adding up the contributions to loudness from various frequency regions, making allowance for masking. There are some types of complex stimuli, however, for which the prediction of loudness is difficult. The loudness of impulsive stimuli (produced by typewriters, ham-

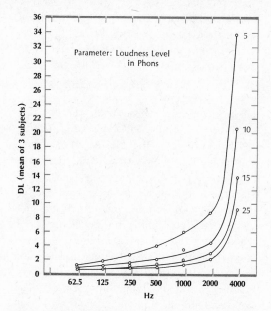

Figure 8.20. Variation of frequency difference threshold as a function of frequency. Vertical and horizontal scales are both in cycles per second. (Harris, 1952.)

mer blows, heel impacts) cannot as yet be predicted satisfactorily (Stevens, 1956a; Corliss & Winzer, 1965).

ACCURACY OF DISCRIMINATIONS OF PURE TONE STIMULI FROM FREQUENCY AND INTENSITY CUES

Frequency Discrimination Threshold

Early studies of frequency discrimination (see Stevens & Davis, 1938) were not completely satisfactory because the frequency was not adequately controlled. It is important in studying frequency discrimination to make sure that the frequency used does not suffer from distortion, and the frequency must be turned on and off slowly enough to avoid introducing transients—which sound like clicks to the subject. The duration of the stimulus also must be controlled (Turnbull, 1944; Sekey, 1963). Figure 8.20 shows data from a more modern study where stimuli were carefully controlled (Harris, 1952). This graph shows how the difference threshold, in

cycles per second, increases as a function of the frequency level at which the difference threshold is measured. The graph also indicates that the difference threshold is higher at low levels of loudness.

In the Harris experiment the subject listened to pairs of tones. He was required to judge whether the second tone was higher or lower in pitch than the first (standard) tone. Systematic changes in the experimental situation lead to different results for threshold measurements. Thus a somewhat different threshold results if a different psychophysical method is used (Rosenblith & Stevens, 1953), or if the stimulus frequency is "warbled" up and down instead of being presented at discrete frequency values (Shower & Biddulph, 1931). These results should serve to remind us that there is no such thing as a simple, single, differential frequency threshold. From the point of view of predicting behavior, this does not cause us any insuperable difficulty. We just have to remember to specify carefully the type of testing situation to which a given set of results applies.

The thresholds shown in Figure 8.20 were obtained with highly trained subjects. These thresholds certainly represent a very fine degree of frequency discrimination. As we might expect from studies of discrimination learning in general, practice produces a lowering of the differential frequency threshold (Campbell & Small, 1963).

Intensity Difference Threshold

If we now consider discrimination of intensity differences, we find that many of the comments in the preceding paragraphs apply. That is: (1) Great care is necessary in the control of the stimulus, especially to prevent transient clicks when the stimulus is turned on and off. (2) Results will vary with the exact nature of the testing method used (Harris, 1963). (3) The degree of training of subjects will be expected to influence the results.

For well-trained subjects, discrimination of

intensity is very acute when a standard is available for comparison. Subjects can detect a change in intensity of the order of .5 dB from a standard intensity under optimal observation conditions.

Frequency and Intensity Discrimination by the Method of Single Stimuli

If the subject is tested for frequency or intensity discrimination by the "Method of Single Stimuli," his ability to discriminate decreases greatly. This loss in discrimination occurs mainly because the subject is not given a standard stimulus on every trial to which to compare the variable stimulus. You will remember that in the Method of Single Stimuli, the subject is given a number of stimuli in succession. Initially each stimulus is labeled with a number. However, on test trials the subject has to recall the number for each stimulus as the stimuli are presented in a random order. Of course, this situation is more like the everyday situation where a stimulus is presented, and a subject classifies it in terms of a scale of numbers or categories he has learned previously. Miller (1956) has pointed out that when a set of stimuli is judged along a single dimension, as in the Method of Single Stimuli, there appears to be an approximate upper limit of 7 stimuli that can be perfectly discriminated. However, we must remember that this conclusion holds only when subjects have had a limited amount of training; also, if more dimensions are introduced, a much greater number of accurate discriminations is possible. Pollack and Ficks (1954) have shown that if auditory stimuli are varied along 6 dimensions—frequency, intensity, rate of interruption, on-time fraction, total duration, and spatial location—about 150 categories can be identified by subjects without error.

Discrimination of Simultaneously Sounding Tones

If 2 or more tones are presented simultaneously, the subject will have very great difficulty in identifying which tones are present,

or even in telling how many tones are present (Thurlow & Rawlings, 1959; Pollack, 1964). It should be emphasized that the inability to detect the components is not due to simple masking. If a component is changed slightly in intensity, then it can be detected (Thurlow & Rawlings, 1959). These results are contrary to the implications of Ohm's Law (Boring, 1942) which states that the ear "hears out" the simple harmonic components in a complex wave.

Some experienced listeners are able to detect a given component if they are first given a cue tone that is in the vicinity of the frequency to be detected (Thurlow & Bernstein, 1957; Plomp, 1964). Other listeners are not assisted by this procedure (Pollack, 1964).

Current signal detection theories (see Chapter 2) are incomplete in that they do not consider this problem. Signal-detection theories deal with situations where there is a change in signal energy, which must be detected. Although the detection of a change in signal energy is more difficult if the subject is not cued as to the frequency region of the signal (Green, 1961), the effects of lack of prior cueing are nowhere near as profound as in the situation of simultaneously sounding tones.

SPEECH

Production of Speech Sounds

The vibration of the vocal folds (or "cords") of the larynx (back of the "Adam's apple"), caused by air pressure from the lungs,

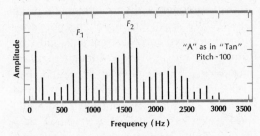

Figure 8.21. Amplitude of the frequency components in the vowel sound *a* as in *tan*. F_1 and F_2 represent first and second formants. (Fletcher, 1953.)

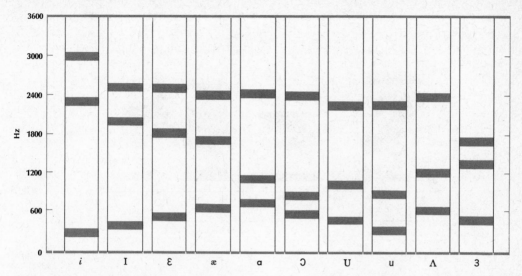

Figure 8.22. Vowel formants. Bars represent frequency regions for formants F_1, F_2, and F_3 of different vowel sounds, produced in an /h — d/ environment. The vowel sounds represented by the symbols are similar to the following vowel sounds: *Eve, (i); it, (I); met, (ε); at, (æ); father, (a); all, (ɔ); foot, (ʊ); boot, (u); up, (ʌ); bird, (ɝ).* (Flanagan, 1965; after Peterson & Barney, 1952, as plotted by Haskins Laboratories.)

produces the basic "noise" of our voice. This noise consists of a series of pulses of sound at a rate of 100 to 200 per second. Analysis of this series of pulses shows that they contain acoustically a fundamental and a great many harmonics. This noise, however, travels through the cavities of the throat and mouth and is modified in a way that depends on the shape and size of these cavities. Figure 8.21 shows the peaks produced in the spectrum of harmonics for the vowel *a*, as in *tan*. Black lines indicate individual harmonics; height indicates the amplitude of each harmonic. The peaks, labeled by the letters F_1 and F_2,

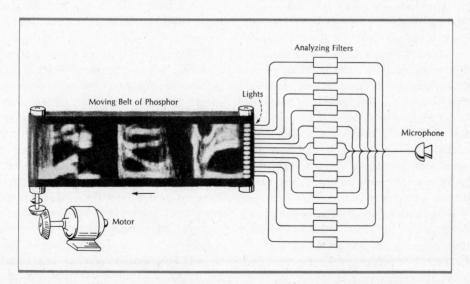

Figure 8.23. Schematic diagram of a sound spectrograph. (Potter, Kopp, & Green, 1947.)

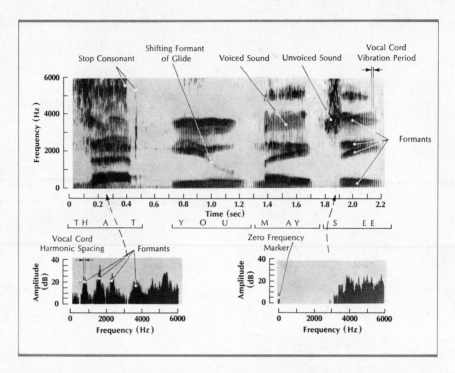

Figure 8.24. A. Sound spectrogram of "That you may see." B. "Amplitude sections": Arrows indicate where the amplitude section was taken from the sound spectrogram. (Flanagan, 1965; after Barney & Dunn, 1957.)

refer to first and second formants, respectively. (A "formant" refers to a concentration of acoustic energy in a restricted frequency region.) The formants of different vowels are at different frequencies; the perceived sound of a vowel depends on the frequency location of the formants. Figure 8.22 shows a chart of the frequency location of the first three formants corresponding to certain English vowels. The lowest bar corresponds to F_1, the next to F_2, the highest to F_3.

Various types of consonant sounds also form an important part of our language. While the vocal tract is left relatively unobstructed when we make the vowel sounds, consonant sounds typically involve narrowing or closing the passageway. For example, the sound of *f* is produced by turbulent air-flow at a constriction between lips and teeth.

A quantitative representation of all the sounds produced can be obtained by using a *sound spectrograph.* A schematic diagram of this machine is given in Figure 8.23. Speech

sounds picked up by the microphone are analyzed by filters. Each filter passes energy in only a narrow frequency band. Bands represented by the filters cover the frequency range from high to low. The output voltage of each filter determines the brightness of a small light, which in turn leaves a trace on a moving belt of phosphor. Thus a graphical representation of the frequency content of a speech sound is produced on the vertical scale, with brightness representing intensity, and time being indicated along the horizontal scale.

In most commonly used sound spectrographs today, intensity is indicated by the darkness of the trace. Figure 8.24 shows the sound spectrogram for the phrase "that you may see." The concentrations of sound energy at the formants are seen as dark bars on the record. Vibrations of the vocal cords (producing pulses of sound) show up as vertical striations in the record.

Because the darkness of the record gives

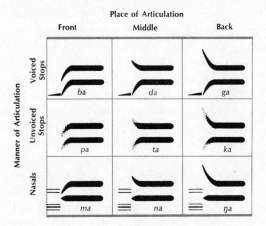

Place of Articulation

Front   Middle   Back

Manner of Articulation

Voiced Stops: ba, da, ga

Unvoiced Stops: pa, ta, ka

Nasals: ma, na, ŋa

Figure 8.25. Pattern playback spectrographic patterns that show the transition cues for the stop and nasal consonants in initial position with the vowel /a/. The dotted portion for unvoiced stops indicates the presence of noise. In each pattern, as in Figure 8.24, the vertical scale represents frequency and the horizontal scale represents time. (Liberman, 1957.)

only a qualitative indication of intensity, other procedures for analysis of intensity are desirable. Figure 8.24 also shows an "amplitude section"—a plot of amplitude in decibels against frequency, which can be obtained at any point in the spectrogram. Arrows show the point in the spectrogram from which the amplitude section was taken. A number of new techniques for analyzing the details of speech signals are currently being investigated (Flanagan, 1965).

Analysis of Cues to Speech Sounds by Synthesis

A machine has been developed that in a sense does the opposite of the sound spectrograph. We start with a visual pattern similar to that produced by a sound spectrograph (see Figure 8.25); the "pattern playback" machine produces speech sounds from it. We can paint patterns of various kinds to see how a modification of the patterns changes the perception of the speech sounds. Thus we can experimentally manipulate determinants of speech sounds. Although other types of speech synthesizers have been developed

(Flanagan, 1965), a great deal of the research on speech sounds up to the present time has been done with the pattern playback machine. In this section we give illustrative findings from research on the synthesis of consonant speech sounds. (See Liberman et al., 1967, for further references.)

Work with the pattern playback has shown that *p, t,* and *k* can be discriminated from each other on the basis of the frequency location of the noise burst for each of these sounds and the transition from the consonant to the second formant of the vowel (Cooper et al., 1952). The transitions of the second formant typical of *p, t,* and *k* preceding an /a/ sound, as in *bah,* are shown in Figure 8.25. The transitions are the "hooks" preceding the formant bars.

Liberman, Delattre, Cooper, and Gerstman (1954) showed that the second formant transitions can be important cues for discriminating *b, d,* and *g* as well as *p, t,* and *k.* The transitions for *b, d, g* preceding /a/ are also diagrammed in Figure 8.25. Third formant transitions (not shown in Figure 8.25), have also been shown to be important in discrimination of *b, d,* and *g* (Harris et al., 1958).

Further research has shown that characteristics of the *first* formant are important in distinguishing *b* from *p, d* from *t,* and *g* from *k.* Cutting off initial portions of the first formant transition was found to cause *b, d,* and *g* to sound like *p, t* and *k* respectively (Liberman, Delattre, & Cooper, 1958).

In the bottom row of illustrations in Figure 8.25 are shown patterns for the nasal consonants *m, n,* and ŋ (the latter having a sound like the *n* in sing). Note how similar the second formant transitions are within each column. In addition, however, there are initial lines indicating a "nasal resonance"; your nasal cavity is used as an additional resonator in the production of these sounds. When the transitions for *p* and *b* were combined with a nasal resonance, subjects perceived *m;* transitions for *t* and *d* plus nasal resonance were perceived as *n;* and transitions for *k* and *g* plus nasal resonance were heard as ŋ (Liberman et al., 1954).

We have not yet mentioned some of the problems that have arisen in trying to find invariant cues for particular speech sounds. For instance, Liberman found that the direction and extent of the second formant transition for g is different when g is followed by different vowels. Yet the sound g is perceived in all these cases. There was no invariance present in these synthesized speech sounds that could account for the perception of g. Liberman suggests that the similarity of sound perception occurs because all of these g sounds were originally produced by the same articulatory movement (in this case, movement of the back of the tongue with respect to the soft palate, which is in the upper back region of the mouth cavity); that perhaps the "motor command" for this articulatory movement is the invariant accompaniment of our perception of g (Liberman et al., 1962). Other psychologists (Lenneberg, 1962; Lane, 1965) have questioned whether such a "motor" theory is necessary or adequate to account for all of the facts of speech learning. Lenneberg (1962) has discussed the case of a patient who learned to understand speech despite his inability to articulate speech sounds. Liberman's theory, however, is based on *perception* of speech sounds (Liberman et al., 1967). It is possible that normal subjects who are trying to judge whether certain speech sounds *sound* alike, utilize articulatory responses—and these responses may have an important effect on perception. To what extent such articulatory responses (or their representations in the central nervous system) function to facilitate communication in normal subjects remains to be worked out.

Intelligibility of Words

There are many practical situations in which it is desirable to obtain a measure of the intelligibility of samples of speech. We may wish to develop such measures in order to evaluate the hearing of individuals with various types of hearing loss (Hudgins et al., 1947; Egan, 1948; Hirsh et al., 1952; Davis & Silverman, 1960); or we may wish to develop

these measures in order to obtain quantitative measures of the hearing of speech as transmitted by different communication systems, which might introduce various kinds of distortion (Licklider & Miller, 1951; Fletcher, 1953).

The development of an intelligibility or articulation test poses interesting problems in measurement. Although it would be possible to have listeners rate the intelligibility of speech, or to have the experimenter count the number of times the message had to be repeated before it is understood, the most precise method for measuring intelligibility is to count the number of words a listener hears correctly.

One of the first problems that arises is the choice of a speaker. Obviously, the number of words a listener hears depends on how clearly the speaker enunciates. Optimally, if only one speaker can be used, the speaker should represent a typical manner of speaking for the situation being tested. However, the usual procedure adopted in the construction of standardized speech tests has been to make use of an individual who enunciates clearly (such as a radio announcer), and who presumably uses "general American" pronunciation. No attempt has been made to take regional differences in pronunciation into account. (No "Southern accent" is represented!)

Another sampling problem arises with re-

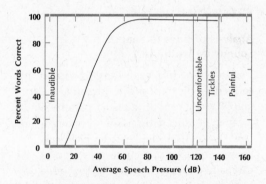

Figure 8.26. Percentage of monosyllabic words that can be recognized correctly as a function of intensity. (Miller, 1951; data from Kryter, 1946, and Silverman, 1947.)

spect to speech materials. Which words should be used? One solution has been to use "phonetically balanced" (PB) monosyllables (Egan, 1948; Hirsh et al., 1952). (Monosyllables are 1-syllable words.) These monosyllables are selected so that the frequency of occurrence of various consonant and vowel sounds is representative of English speech. Figure 8.26 shows how the percentage of monosyllables correctly heard increases as the intensity of the speech sounds is raised. In obtaining data for this graph, a separate list of monosyllables was used at each of a number of intensity levels. A "threshold" value for intelligibility can be taken as the sound pressure level (in decibels) at which 50 percent of the words are correctly received. Although a single threshold value for monosyllables might be useful for subjects considered to hear normally, more extensive information is desirable in the case of subjects with abnormal hearing who may never be able to discriminate between the more difficult words. For these subjects, a useful additional measure is to determine the maximum percentage of words received correctly (Davis & Silverman, 1960).

In constructing syllable lists for practical use, an effort is made to use words that are familiar to the subject population. There is experimental evidence showing precisely how intelligibility is dependent on the frequency with which each word is used. Studies by Rosenzweig and Postman (1957) and Howes (1957) show that threshold for the recognition of a word heard in noise is inversely related to the logarithm of the frequency with which the word occurs. That is, a word that occurs frequently in the English language can be perceived at a lower sound pressure level than one that occurs infrequently; the relationship between frequency and threshold is a simple mathematical function. Similar results have been found for visual recognition (Howes & Solomon, 1951).

Why are frequently used (or more familiar) words more detectable than infrequently used words? A "fragment theory" originally

formulated by Solomon and Postman (1952) has been used by a number of researchers to account for the effects of word frequency on detection (see Neisser, 1967). This theory states that a fragment of the stimulus word perceived at a low stimulus intensity can act as a cue to a limited number of complete word responses. Certain word responses in this set will have a higher response strength because they have been used more frequently before the experiment. The word response with the highest response strength will be given by the subject. A fragment from a low-frequency word will be likely to produce a high-frequency word response—which will be an error. Thus, in general, the number of correct responses to low-frequency words will be lower than to high-frequency words at a given intensity level.

Pollack, Rubinstein, and Decker (1959) have shown that if the subject knows the set of words that are to be used in testing threshold, the effects of word frequency noted above do not occur. (According to the theory above, if the message set is known, subjects will not give high-frequency erroneous words from outside the set.) House, Williams, Hecker, and Kryter (1965) have found, in addition, that using a small "closed set" of response alternatives has definite advantages in certain practical evaluations of voice-communication systems where a trained crew of listeners is to be used over and over (see also Black, 1957; Fairbanks, 1958). They have used an intelligibility test where the subject chooses the correct response from 6 alternatives. (Example: *bat, bad, back, bass, ban, bath.*) The subjects' performance on this test showed great stability over many repetitions of the test. In test situations where the subject is originally uninformed as to the test words, performance tends to show improvement over successive test sessions (see, for example, Egan, 1948; Moser & Dreher, 1955). An extensive training period then is necessary if the listeners are to be used as a "trained crew" for evaluating voice-communication systems.

If subjects know which words are to be used in the test, less intensity is required for correct recognition as number of words in the test vocabulary is decreased (Miller, Heise, & Lichten, 1951; Sumby & Pollack, 1954; Bruner, Miller, & Zimmerman, 1955). In addition, the threshold of recognition is dependent on context: If words are presented in the context of a sentence, they can be perceived more easily (Miller, Heise, & Lichten, 1951; O'Neill, 1957).

Why is recognition of a word presented from a known message set poorer when the message set is larger? One explanation states that the larger the message set, the larger is the number of response alternatives the stimulus must be matched against—with a resulting greater chance for confusion (Pollack, 1959; Garner, 1965). The higher intelligibility of a word presented in the context of a sentence can be understood by supposing that the context reduces the size of the possible set of words from which the correct word must be chosen (Miller, Heise, & Lichten, 1951).

In ordinary conversation visual cues may be given the listener from the speaker's face. Sumby and Pollack (1954) showed that the advantage these visual cues provides is increased as the noise level is increased relative to the speech; O'Neill (1957) showed that the visual cues were more helpful when less auditory information was available. Hard-of-hearing individuals can be trained to make use of these visual cues to aid them in understanding speech (Davis & Silverman, 1960).

Factors Reducing Speech Intelligibility: Single Source

In the preceding section we have discussed primarily cues that will increase the probability that a given word will be perceived correctly when it is spoken. In this section we discuss a number of variables that primarily cause a decrease in intelligibility. These variables have been studied most often by experimenters interested in speech-communication systems. They wished to find how

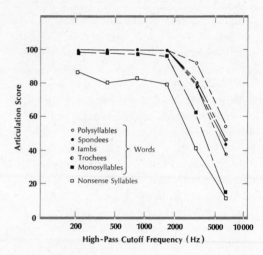

Figure 8.27. Articulation score as a function of low-pass filtering. A *spondee* is a 2-syllable word with an approximately equal accent on each syllable. An *iamb* is a 2-syllable word with accent on the second syllable. A *trochee* is a 2-syllable word with accent on the first syllable. (Hirsh, Reynolds, & Joseph, 1954.)

distortions of various kinds in speech-transmission systems would affect intelligibility of speech (Licklider & Miller, 1951; Fletcher, 1953). Knowledge acquired from these inves-

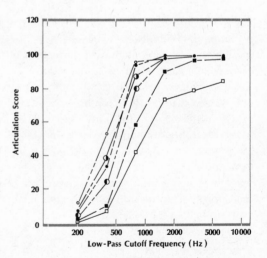

Figure 8.28. Articulation score as a function of high-pass filtering. The different symbols and lines are identified in Fig. 8.27. (Hirsh, Reynolds, & Joseph, 1954.)

tigations can lead to design of speech-communication systems that will meet requirements for efficient speech communication at the least cost.

Filtering   A number of experiments have investigated the effects of eliminating various frequency regions from speech (Licklider & Miller, 1951; Fletcher, 1953). Results from one of these experiments (Hirsh, Reynolds, & Joseph, 1954) are shown in Figures 8.27 and 8.28. Six high-pass filter settings, and 6 low-pass filter settings were used. (Recall that a high-pass cut-off frequency of 200 means that all frequencies above 200 Hz were passed by the filter; a low-pass cut-off frequency of 400 means that all frequencies below 400 Hz were passed by the filter.) The articulation score refers to the percentage of each kind of word heard correctly. From Figures 8.27 and 8.28 it is evident how intelligibility deteriorates as more and more of the high frequencies, or more and more of the low frequencies, are eliminated. Study of individual speech sounds in other experiments shows that eliminating high frequencies affects consonant intelligibility more than vowel intelligibility, while the opposite is true for elimination of low frequencies (Fletcher, 1953).

Another way of going about the filtering is to pass only a band of frequencies. For instance, if a band of frequencies ranging from 500 to 2500 Hz is passed by the filter, an articulation score of about 45 percent is obtained (Egan & Wiener, 1946).

Some temporal variables in speech intelligibility   If speech is interrupted (pieces "chopped" out of it), the resulting intelligibility depends on the rate of the interruption as well as on the percentage of time the speech is actually sounding. For example, with 50% "on" time, intelligibility is poor for very low rates of interruption—where syllables and even words are chopped out; but intelligibility becomes much better at higher rates of interruption. If we take the pieces of interrupted speech, and place them

adjacent to each other, we can achieve a speeded-up communication. Experiments show that words can be made about 2.5 times faster than normal without loss of intelligibility (Garvey, 1953; Fairbanks & Kodman, 1957), provided that the pieces chopped out are not too large. Playing a phonograph record of speech at a higher speed is not a suitable experimental technique for investigating the effects of rate of speech on intelligibility because this procedure also changes the frequencies in the speech sounds by a factor proportional to the change in speed. Shifting the frequencies in speech will in itself cause a decrease in intelligibility (Fletcher, 1929).

Reflection of sound from the walls of a reverberant room causes each sound to persist longer than usual. The sound from one syllable persists and overlaps that of the next syllable, and thus intelligibility is adversely affected (Licklider & Miller, 1951; Lochner & Burger, 1961; Thompson, Webster, & Gales, 1961). Information on the relation between intelligibility and the amount of reverberation is useful in the design of auditoriums.

Noise masking   In practical situations, noise of various kinds often interferes with

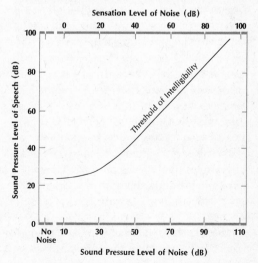

Figure 8.29. Change in threshold for the intelligibility of speech with an increase in the sound pressure level of noise. (Licklider, 1951; after Hawkins & Stevens, 1950.)

speech intelligibility. If noise with a continuous and uniform spectrum is present, the masking effect is reasonably simple to predict. Figure 8.29 shows how the threshold for detectability of speech increases as the level of masking noise increases. It can be seen that at medium and high noise levels a given decibel increase in noise level results in an equal decibel increase in the sound pressure level of the speech required for detectability.

Location of the noise source in space with reference to the location of the speech signal is also an important variable (Hirsh, 1950; Kock, 1950). Speech intelligibility is best when the speech and noise sources are in different locations. The advantage of separating the speech and noise sources is reduced, however, in more reverberant surroundings (Hirsh, 1950; Harvey et al., 1963). Moving the speech source in space leads to changes in the time of arrival (and phase) of the speech signal at both ears, as well as to changes in intensity at both ears. In order to control these variables, analytical studies have been carried out with earphones (Licklider, 1948). These studies are closely related to those on "masking level differences" (MLDs) we discussed earlier in the chapter. Experimenters, however, have not only measured the *detectability* of the speech signal, but also the *intelligibility* (where the subject must recognize words rather than just detect the presence of some sound). Results show that, if we start with noise in-phase and speech in-phase at both ears, a gain in intelligibility of about 6 dB is obtained if we reverse the phase of the speech signal at the 2 ears (Levitt & Rabiner, 1967). The exact amount of gain depends on the stimulus frequencies present that are important in the understanding of the particular speech stimuli used (Carhart, Tilman, & Johnson, 1967).

It has been found possible to predict interference with speech in many practical situations, where the noise spectrum is not uniform, by taking an average of noise levels in certain octave bands, for instance, in bands of 600 to 1200, 1200 to 2400, 2400 to 4800 cycles per second (Beranek, 1956; 1957). Thus it is possible to make recommendations about desirable and permissable noise levels in offices and ships, for example, by knowing how these noises interfere with speech (Beranek, 1957; Kryter et al., 1963; Webster, 1965).

Responding to Speech from Multiple Sources

If the observer has to pay attention to several signal sources and respond to certain relevant messages, a number of new variables enter in to determine performance. For instance, the greater the amount of irrelevant material presented, and the greater the similarity of relevant and irrelevant material, the lower the efficiency of performance (Webster & Thompson, 1954; Poulton, 1956). A control-tower operator at an airport must observe in this type of situation; he may have to pay attention to messages coming from several loudspeakers, and respond to messages from aircraft directed to his control tower only. "Selectivity of attention" was emphasized early in the history of American psychology by William James, but renewed interest in this problem, and especially experimentation, has only occurred in more recent years. Broadbent (1958) has summarized much relevant information and has stressed the conclusion that humans have limited capacities to process information arriving from multiple sources.

A more common type of listening situation in everyday life is one in which the subject is trying to listen to one message and exclude other interfering messages (the "cocktail party" problem). This situation is analogous to those investigated in classical masking experiments, where the subject is trying to detect a particular kind of signal in the presence of an interfering noise. At the same time, listening in the presence of interfering messages is more complex and undoubtedly involves mechanisms beyond those required in the noise-masking situation.

As in the case of noise masking, interference by an irrelevant message is less if this message comes from a loudspeaker or source that is spatially separated from the source of the relevant message to which the subject must listen (Broadbent, 1958). If the irrelevant message is spoken by a different voice, or by a voice that sounds different due to high-pass filtering (removing some of the low frequencies), then reception is improved over the condition where both relevant and irrelevant messages are spoken by the same voice (Broadbent, 1952; Egan, Carterette, & Thwing, 1954).

Further experiments have been performed to find out more about the nature of the attentional mechanisms utilized in rejecting the unwanted material. Cherry (1953) used a technique he called "shadowing," in which the subject was required to repeat aloud a message presented to one ear by earphone. At the same time, irrelevant messages were presented to the other ear by earphone. When subjects were questioned about the irrelevant material, they could report only gross changes from one voice to another, or a change from a voice to a pure tone. They could not report the content of the irrelevant speech or even what language it was in. However, when Moray (1959) included the subject's own name in the "irrelevant" material, he found that this was often noticed by the listener.

Thus, suppression of irrelevant material is by no means complete. The suppressed material can "break through" to the subject's attention under certain special conditions. Treisman (1960) found that if the passages each ear was listening to were suddenly switched to opposite ears, some subjects would repeat 1 or 2 words from the message that was now going to the ear whose word stimuli were not supposed to be repeated.

It has also been found that if messages going to each ear are made the same but the message to the ear *not* attended to is made to lag behind the message to the ear attended to, the subject fails to notice that the messages are the same unless the lag is reduced to

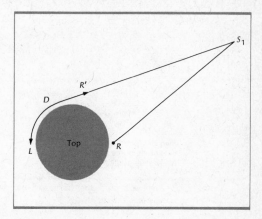

Figure 8.30. Schematic diagram of paths of sound to each ear. Assume that you are looking down from the top at the subject's head and that the source of sound is to the right.

about 4 seconds or less (Cherry, 1953; Treisman, 1964). This effect even occurs with some bilingual subjects when the message to one ear is given in French and the message to the other is given in English, provided that the messages are similar in meaning (Treisman, 1964).

USE OF SOUND CUES IN LOCALIZATION

Available Cues for Localization of Right-Left Direction of a Sound Source

Results of early experiments (Pierce, 1901) which measured the accuracy of sound localization showed that *even if the head was held fixed in position,* discrimination between sources to the left and right of the head was good. Front-back discrimination and up-down discrimination were very poor. What are some possible cues? Let us first consider a source in the horizontal plane—the plane parallel to the ground passing through the ears.

Figure 8.30 indicates schematically the paths of sound from source S to the 2 ears L and R. SR is the distance of the source to the right ear, SL is the distance of the source to the left ear, and $D = SL - SR$, the *difference* in the distance from the source to the left and right ears.

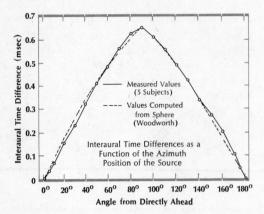

Figure 8.31. Interaural time differences in milliseconds as a function of angular position of source from listener's head. Zero degrees represents a source directly in front of the subject. (Feddersen et al., 1957.)

A sound at S will arrive at the left ear later than it will at the right ear. For each centimeter of difference D in the distance to the 2 ears, there will be a time difference of about .029 msec. The time difference can give a cue to the left-right location of the source. Figure 8.31 shows the difference in the time of the arrival of a click at the 2 ears measured by a small microphone in each ear canal (Feddersen et al., 1957). An angle of zero degrees

represents a click source straight ahead of the subject, and an angle of 180 degrees represents a click source behind the subject. It can be seen that the time difference reaches a maximum (of near .6 msec) when the click source is opposite one ear (90 degrees).

There will also be an intensity difference at the 2 ears, due to the "shadowing" effect of the head, for the head acts as a barrier to attenuate sounds getting to the ear farthest away from the source (ear L in the diagram). Figure 8.32 shows the difference in intensity of sound at the 2 ears for pure tones of various frequencies as the angle of the source is changed. These results, as well as those for time differences, were obtained using a subject placed in an anechoic room, the source being 7 feet from the subject's head. The difference in the intensity of the sound tends to be greatest when the source is nearly opposite one ear. It is greater for high frequencies—reaching 20 dB for frequencies of 5000 and 6000 Hz. However, the variation in the difference in the intensity is such that we would predict—correctly—that determination

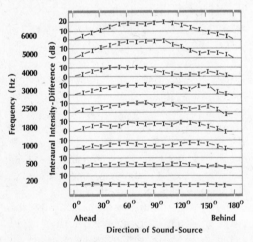

Figure 8.32. Interaural intensity difference in decibels as a function of frequency and direction of sound source. Zero degrees represents a source straight ahead. (Feddersen, et al., 1957.)

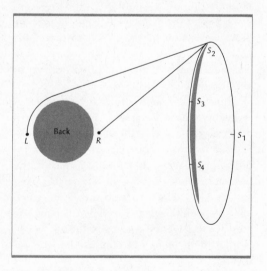

Figure 8.33. S_1, S_2, S_3, S_4, represent sources located so that the differences in the distance to the 2 ears, L and R, are the same. The head is approximated by a sphere, so the diagram applies only as an approximation to the actual human head. Position S_1 corresponds to the source position shown in Figure 8.30.

of the exact location of the source of a pure tone by means of an intensity cue alone would be rather inaccurate when the tone is in a position to the side of the head.

We have so far been considering cues from sources in the horizontal plane. The concern with sources in this plane is understandable because the majority of the sources we have to locate in everyday life (voices, automobiles) occur in approximately this plane. As soon as the possibility arises that sounds may originate from all three dimensions, however, the problem of localization becomes more difficult—because sources in different positions may produce very similar cues. The circle in Figure 8.33 shows the locations of sources that might be expected to produce very similar intensity and time differences at the two ears. The "shadowing" effect of the auricle (Figure 8.5) helps us to differentiate signals coming from these different directions; and head movements are of especial importance in resolving ambiguities in cues. We discuss the role of the auricle and of head movements in more detail in later sections.

Use of Earphones for Investigation of Right–Left Localization in the Horizontal Plane

If we use earphones to present stimuli to subjects, we can vary the time difference at the 2 ears while holding intensity difference constant, and vice versa. Thus the effects of each of these cues can be determined separately.

If pulse stimuli of equal intensity are led to each ear, and each pulse arrives at the same instant, the subject will perceive a sound in the median plane. (This is the plane through the nose dividing the head into left and right halves). If the pulse to the right ear is made to arrive slightly earlier in time, the perceived composite sound will appear to be coming from a direction more to the right. However, if the intensity of the stimulus to the right ear is increased (even when the time of the arrival of pulses is the same at each ear)

the composite sound will again appear to be coming from a direction to the right of the median plane.

When earphones are used in localization studies, the subject encounters certain problems in indicating where he perceives the sound source. Some subjects perceive the source as traveling inside the head. Others perceive the source as traveling in an arc over, in front of, or behind the head (and close to the head) as the intensity or time difference at the 2 ears is changed. Some experimenters have found it possible for experienced subjects to "project" the sound heard with earphones on to an external scale (von Békésy, 1960; Jeffress & Taylor, 1961; Sayers, 1964).

The term "lateralization" is typically used at the present time to refer to the judgment of the location of sounds when stimuli are produced by earphones worn by the subject, while the term "localization" is reserved for situations where the subject judges the location of a sound coming from some external source not mounted on the head.

Early investigators found that a time difference as small as 30 μsec (microseconds—millionths of a second) between clicks presented to the 2 ears resulted in the perception of a change of location from the median plane. Other investigators (Hornbostel & Wertheimer, 1920; Klemm, 1920) found that time and intensity could compensate for each other within limits. This has been designated a "time-intensity trade." For example, if the right ear received the click 100 μsec earlier than the left, the sound would be localized to the right, but if the intensity of the click in the *left* ear was now increased, the perceived location of the sound could be brought back to the median plane.

Early experimenters also used low-frequency pure tones with earphones and varied the phase relations at the 2 ears. When the tones in the two ears were in phase (zero degrees phase difference) the observer localized the resulting sensation in the median plane. As the phase in one ear was made to

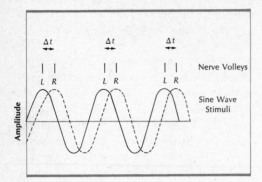

Figure 8.34. Schematic diagram of way in which a *phase* difference in a low-frequency stimulus at the 2 ears gives rise to a *time* difference, Δt in the nerve volleys corresponding to the two waves. Volleys for wave *L* are in the left auditory nerve; for wave *R* they are in the right auditory nerve.

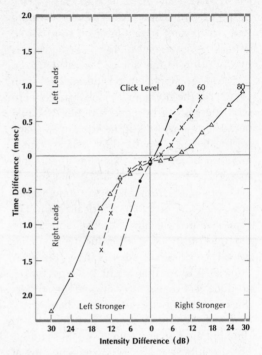

Figure 8.35. Time difference in milliseconds between click stimuli delivered to the 2 ears which will compensate for a given intensity difference between the 2 ears. The parameter is the sound pressure level of a 1000 Hz tone the peak amplitude of which equals the maximum peak of the stronger click. (Deatherage & Hirsh, 1959.)

lead, the tone was localized toward that side. Above about 1500 Hz, no effect of phase shift could be observed (Hughes, 1940). These facts can be understood if we think of the phase difference at both ears as actually presenting a *time* difference to the nervous system. This is possible because of the fact that each cycle of a low pure tone stimulates a volley of nerve impulses (see Figure 8.11). In Figure 8.34 *R* represents schematically a sine-wave stimulus to the right ear, *L* a sine-wave stimulus to the left ear. In this particular example the stimulus to the right ear lags in phase. The volleys sent along each auditory nerve are represented above each wave, and the symbol Δt represents the resulting difference in the time of arrival in the central nervous system of each pair of volleys. Shaxby and Gage (1932) were able to show experimentally that the crucial variable in change of phase was actually a time difference at the 2 ears. They measured the phase difference at the 2 ears necessary to compensate for an opposing intensity difference and to bring the perceived sound image back to center (median plane). They found that the various phase changes necessary at different low frequencies to compensate for a given intensity difference all reduced to a single time differ-

ence (when each phase difference was expressed in terms of a time difference).

Recent Analytic Studies with Earphones

More recent studies have sought to investigate the "time-intensity trade" over a wider range of conditions. Deatherage and Hirsh (1959) set the sound pressure level of a click in one ear at a standard value (40, 60, or 80 dB) and the level of the click in the other ear at a different intensity value. The difference in intensity caused the click image to be perceived toward the ear with the higher intensity click. They found how much the click in this "higher intensity" ear had to be delayed in time in order for the perceived click image to be shifted back to the median plane. Figure 8.35 shows their results. It is evident that the results differ at different click intensity levels (40, 60, or 80 dB). A larger difference in intensity between the ears can be compensated for by a given time difference in the 2 ears at a high intensity level than at a low intensity level.

David, Guttman, and van Bergeijk (1959) have also found that a time difference at the 2 ears was relatively more important at a high intensity level: they found that a much greater time difference (about 5 times) was needed at a low intensity of stimulation than at a high intensity to compensate for a difference in intensity at the 2 ears. Their study, in addition, emphasizes an important point about localization of high-frequency sounds: If high-frequency stimuli come in the form of pulses, the subject can determine the origin of these impulsive, or "transient," high-frequency sounds by utilizing the difference in the time of arrival of the pulses at each ear (David, Guttman, & van Bergeijk, 1958; Leakey, Sayers, & Cherry, 1958; Cherry & Sayers, 1959). A stimulus with sudden onset (with low- or high-frequency content) sets off a large number of nerve impulses that travel as a wave of activity along the auditory nerve into the nervous system. This is similar to the "volley" of impulses caused by a cycle of a sine wave of low frequency.

As more studies were carried out on the time-intensity trade, it became evident that the results depended on frequency content of the signal pulses as well as the intensity level (David, Guttman, & van Bergeijk, 1958; Cherry & Sayers, 1959). A detailed study made by Harris (1960) documented the difference in the trading relation found for low-frequency pulses as compared to high-frequency pulses. The change in time difference between the ears necessary to compensate for each decibel difference in the intensity between the ears was 25 μsec for low-frequency pulses (with a frequency content below 1000 Hz), whereas the figure was 60 μsec for high-frequency pulses (with frequency content above 4000 Hz). In other words, in the operation of the localization system, it requires less time difference at low frequencies to compensate for intensity difference at the 2 ears than at high frequencies.

Further characteristics of the localization system have been revealed by other studies using earphones: Increase in the duration of the stimulation, or in the repetition rate, appears to increase the effectiveness of a stimulus in determining localization (Tobias & Zerlin, 1959; Thurlow & Elfner, 1961; Butler & Naunton, 1964).

Additional experiments have used stimuli of different frequencies in the 2 ears. When 1 pulse is presented to one ear, and 1 to the other, localization interactions may occur even though these pulses are very different in frequency content (Teas, 1962). When 1 pure tone is led to one ear and another pure tone to the other, localization interactions can occur even when these tones do not have the same frequency (Thurlow & Elfner, 1959; Butler, 1962; Butler & Naunton, 1964). The frequency differences for which interaction can be obtained are small, except when the tone in one ear is made much more intense than the tone in the other ear (Thurlow & Elfner, 1959; Butler, 1962; Butler & Naunton, 1964). The interaction observed is a "pulling-over" of the less intense tone toward the perceived location of the other, more intense tone. Low tones will also interact with certain tones in the other ear that are simple multiples in frequency (Thurlow & Elfner, 1959). For example, it has been observed that a tone of 100 Hz in the left ear will cause multiples of 100 Hz up to about 700 Hz to be pulled toward the median plane when the phase relations in the 2 ears are properly adjusted.

Butler (1962) and Butler and Naunton (1964) have found that noise in one ear will cause a pulling over laterally of the perceived location of stimuli in the other ear—including noise, square wave, speech, and tone stimuli. "Pulling over" effects are greater as the intensity of noise used in the opposite ear is increased, and effects are greater when there is an overlap in the frequency content at the 2 ears.

The main purpose of the various analytic

studies we have been discussing is theoretical. The studies seek to find out not only what types of localization effect are possible, but also to understand better what type of system or systems can be responsible for the localization effects.

Physiological and Perceptual Evidence in Relation to Some Theories of Right–Left Sound Localization in the Horizontal Plane

Interaction of neural inputs from the two ears Our understanding of the mechanisms responsible for sound localization, even in the horizontal plane, is far from complete. However, it will be valuable to discuss some of the current theories and evidence.

Rosenzweig (1954) has gathered data in experiments with cats that show that the amplitude of summated electrical response is larger from the auditory area of the right side of the cerebral cortex when the left ear receives a pulse stimulus slightly ahead of the right ear. When the right ear receives the pulse stimulus earlier, the electrical response is larger in the auditory area of the left side of the cerebral cortex. This result led to the hypothesis that localization is determined by the relative amount of neural activity in the right and left auditory cerebral areas. (A similar type of theory, involving a comparison of the amount of activity coming from 2 lower neural centers, was developed for explaining localization due to intensity differences at the 2 ears. See van Bergeijk, 1962.)

For this hypothesis to be correct, there would have to be some mechanism capable of comparing the amount of neural response in the 2 cortical areas. However, there are other experiments, performed with cats, which show that these animals can still localize sounds even when the interconnections between the higher levels of the 2 sides of the brain are severed (Neff, 1961). Thus, section of the *corpus callosum* (which joins the 2 cerebral hemispheres) and of the neural path which joins the left and right *inferior colliculi* (midbrain region), does not affect sound localization. Finally, Walsh (1957) has

reported the case of a man with only 1 cerebral hemisphere who was able to localize on the basis of time differences between clicks. Hodgson (1967) has recently reported that a female patient with only 1 cerebral hemisphere showed no defect in "centering" the location of a tone (by manipulating the intensity at the two ears). It would appear that localization information can be processed in either cerebral hemisphere. Behavioral experiments with cats show that although some reflex behavioral reactions to sound location may be controlled by cells of the inferior colliculus, other adaptive reactions to sound location require that the analysis of time and intensity differences performed at lower neural centers be somehow coded and transmitted all the way to the cerebral cortex (see Neff, 1961; Masterton, Jane, & Diamond, 1968). It must be remembered that the evidence we have been discussing has been obtained with mammals.

Of course, the neural signals from one ear must cross over and interact at some place in the nervous system with signals from the other ear in order to provide the basis for sound localization. Recent evidence, obtained with cats, indicates that an important center for this interaction is the *accessory nucleus* of the *superior olive*. (This is a nucleus well down in the brain stem; see Figure 8.9.) Galambos, Schwartzkopff, and Rupert (1959) discovered neural cells in the accessory nucleus of the superior olive the responses of which were extremely sensitive to difference in time of arrival of stimuli at the 2 ears. However, different reactions occurred in different types of cells when a click stimulus was delivered to each ear within a short interval of time, or was delivered to one ear alone. *Type 1:* Clicks in both ears produced neural discharge from the unit whereas a click in 1 ear did not. *Type 2:* Clicks in both ears produced a marked increase in latency (the time it takes to react to the stimulus) compared to that produced by a click in 1 ear. *Type 3:* Clicks in both ears inhibited the neural discharge produced by a click in 1 ear.

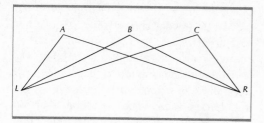

Figure 8.36. Schematic diagram of a "place" theory of sound localization in the horizontal plane. *L* and *R* represent input from left and right auditory nerves respectively. *A, B,* and *C* represent cells where the input from the 2 sides meets. Which cell is fired depends on the time relations between the inputs from *L* and *R*.

Hall (1965) has described a type of cell that responds more to simultaneous stimulation of both ears than to 1 ear alone. This type appears related to type 1 of Galambos, Schwartzkopff, and Rupert. Hall has also made detailed measurements with cells similar to type 3 of Galambos, Schwartzkopff, and Rupert. He found this type much more frequently than other types. The degree to which the firing of these cells was inhibited by binaural stimulation was a function of interaural time difference and interaural intensity difference. A "time-intensity trading relation" was derived from the results which is comparable to that found in experiments with humans.

Other investigators, also using cats, have discovered cells higher up in the nervous system that are sensitive to time differences in stimulation at the 2 ears (Brugge, Dubrovsky, & Rose, 1964; Rose et al., 1966). Cells have also been discovered recently in the inferior colliculus of the cat that are sensitive to small differences in *intensity* at the two ears (Rose et al., 1966).

"Place" theory   Some years ago, Jeffress proposed a "place" theory of sound localization for clicks and low-frequency tones that was based on time of arrival of impulses in the neural localization system (Jeffress, 1948). It can be diagrammed very schemati-

cally, as in Figure 8.36. (See also Licklider, 1959.) It essentially proposed that a neural impulse from *L* (left auditory nerve) would travel over pathways *LA, LB, LC* (and many more) the distances of which would increase from left to right. A neural impulse from *R* (right auditory nerve) would travel paths *RC, RB, RA* (and many more). If the impulses started simultaneously from *L* and *R,* they would meet at *B,* and (it is assumed) their effects would summate to cause a cell at *B* to fire, thus signalling a median plane localization. If the pulse at *R* occurred earlier in time, then the *L* and *R* neural pulses would meet at a place such as *A,* the place depending on the difference in starting time of the two pulses. A cell at *A* would fire, and signal that the sound source was a certain distance to the right. (Note that actual localization space and neural localization space would be reversed—but this would be no problem in cueing appropriate reactions. Recall that the image on the retina is upside down!) The "type 1" neural units Galambos, Schwartzkopff, and Rupert found, act in a manner similar to the postulated units at *A, B, C.*

There is evidence from localization experiments with humans that seems to fit in with a "place" theory of the localization processes. Von Békésy (1960) has reported that when bursts of noise are presented alternately at a low rate from 2 positions in space (not too widely separated) only 1 noise is heard, in between the 2 sources. Thurlow and Marten (1962) observed that a steady noise could be heard in between 2 alternating sources, even if the sources were placed at fairly large angular separations, provided the alternation rate of the sources was as high as 7 to 14 per second. These results can be interpreted in terms of interaction between 2 spatially adjacent distributions of neural activity in the localization system. (See also Thurlow, Marten, and Bhatt, 1965.)

Evidence of a separate system for binaural intensity differences   At one time it seemed that it was only necessary to assume 1 type of localization system operating for low tones and pulse stimuli—a system operating primarily in terms of time differences at the two ears. The effects of intensity, it was supposed, could be understood in terms of the change in the latency of the nerve discharge (David, Guttman, & van Bergeijk, 1958; Deatherage & Hirsh, 1959). For instance, if a click in one ear was made more intense, the nerve fibers would discharge sooner (latency would decrease), and the neural pulse in the nerve corresponding to this more intense click would arrive in the nervous system earlier. Thus an intensity difference would be converted to a *time* difference.

However, there is mounting evidence from perceptual experiments to indicate that the effects of differences in intensity at the 2 ears can operate through a separate system to influence localization. For instance, in studies described earlier (Thurlow & Elfner, 1959; Butler & Naunton, 1964), it was found that a stimulus in one ear could influence localization of a stimulus in the other ear, in the absence of any systematic temporal relations between these stimuli. Even in the older literature there was evidence that when time and intensity cues of a tone were very different, 2 separately localized tones were heard (Halverson, 1922; Banister, 1926). Harris (1960) has noted an analogous effect more recently. Sayers and Toole (1964) emphasize that in their experiments with pulses, a change in the intensity of the sound at one ear produces effects that are not equivalent to a change in time. We have already seen in a previous section that there is physiological evidence indicating that there are cells specialized for responding to small differences in intensity at the 2 ears.

Experiments on Accuracy of Localization of Direction of Sound Sources at Various Locations in Space

Localization with no head movements allowed An experiment which measured the localization in space of tonal stimuli, without interference from wall reflections, was performed by Stevens and Newman (1936). They measured the accuracy with which subjects could localize the source of sound in the horizontal plane, and found that some front-back discrimination was possible for high frequencies even when the subject's head was fixed in position. They concluded that their subjects were utilizing differences in stimulus intensity correlated with the front and back positions of the source. Burger (1958) has also found some front-back discrimination possible for noise stimuli. This discrimination is mainly due to the presence of the external auricle, or pinna, which blocks sounds coming from the rear more effectively than sounds coming from in front. Kietz (1953) showed how perception of a sound as being in front or behind could be changed by modification of the physical characteristics of the pinna.

Familiarity with the stimulus should increase the accuracy with which a subject can make front-back discriminations. If the subject has learned how the stimulus sounded when it was in front of him, he is better able to notice changes in overall loudness and quality (dependent on high frequencies) when the stimulus is presented from behind him.

Mills (1958) has made measurements, in an anechoic room, of the threshold for *change* in the perceived location of a source of sound in the horizontal plane. He was able to show that thresholds at low frequencies (up to 1400 Hz) for the detection of a change in the position of a source from the median plane were related to thresholds obtained by earphones for the detection of a difference in the phase of stimulation at the 2 ears (Klumpp & Eady, 1956; Zwislocki & Feldman, 1956). An upper limit of 1400 to 1500 Hz was also found by Sandel et al. (1955); we have noted previously a similar upper limit found from work carried out with earphones for the effect of the phase on lateralization.

In a later experiment Mills (1960) demonstrated that thresholds for the detection of a change in the position of a source of *high* frequencies from the median plane were related (at 1500 to 6000 Hz) to thresholds obtained with earphones for the detection of change in the lateral position of a tone from the median plane, when only a difference in the *intensity* at the 2 ears was available as a cue. Mills (1958) also presented detailed data showing how the discrimination of a change in the position of pure tones deteriorates if the tones originate from positions at the side of the head (as compared to straight ahead). This deterioration is particularly marked for high frequencies. It is important to remember that in these experiments carried out by Mills, no head movement was allowed.

Fairly accurate discrimination of the direction of thermal noise in the *vertical* ("up-down") direction has been found for angles of elevation up to 30 to 40 degrees above or below the horizontal plane passing through the 2 ears (Thurlow & Runge, 1967; Roffler & Butler, 1968). Because of the shadowing effect of the head and body, the intensity of high-frequency sound reaching the ear opposite the sound source would be expected to increase with the elevation of the sound source. It is possible that the pattern of intensity differences at the 2 ears, in certain high-frequency regions, may be an important cue to elevation.

Role of head movements in sound localization Observation of subjects trying to locate a source of sound in space shows that they make extensive use of head movements. (See, for example, Thurlow, Mangels, & Runge, 1967.) Analytical experiments are necessary, however, to find out which movements are effective as aids to localization.

Some years ago, Klensch (1948) performed demonstrational experiments that showed the crucial role of head movements in front-back discrimination. (See Young, 1931; Koenig, 1950; Jonkhees and Veer, 1958; for related experiments.) He used 2 funnels, 1 connected to each ear by a tube. The funnels were both

oriented toward a source of sound in *front* of the head. Subjects rotated their heads. (You can produce "rotation" of your head by keeping it upright, and turning it to the left or to the right.) If a subject rotated his head to the right at the same time that the left funnel was advanced toward the source of sound (and the right funnel was moved away from the source) he perceived the source to be in front of his head. (Relatively earlier arrival of sound in the left ear, and increasing intensity in the left ear relative to that in the right ear, are ordinary accompaniments of turning the head to the right when the sound source is in *front* of us.) When the subject rotated his head to the *left* under these conditions, however, he perceived the source in *back* of his head. This result is related to the fact that ordinarily when we rotate our head to the left, and the source is in *back* of us, the left ear receives increasingly greater intensity compared to that received in the right ear, and the sound arrives progressively earlier at the left ear than it does at the right ear. Note that utilization of this information for front-back discrimination does not require previous familiarity with a particular sound stimulus.

Burger (1958) has presented quantitative data on front-back discrimination in the horizontal plane, using filtered thermal noise as a stimulus. Performance was best when head movements were allowed. Thurlow and Runge (1967) showed that if the head of the subject was rotated through a controlled angle (by a motor), errors in location of a source of thermal noise in the horizontal plane were substantially reduced.

Movements of the head would also be expected to help discrimination of the *elevation* of a sound source. Differences in time of arrival and intensity at the 2 ears, produced by a sound source in a given location, should change systematically as the head is rotated, or pivoted, and the type of change should be related to the elevation of the sound source. (A "pivot" movement can be produced by starting with your head upright,

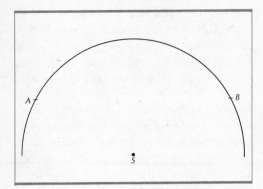

Figure 8.37. Click sources in a "precedence" experiment. One source is indicated at location A, and another at location B. The subject's head is at S.

then tilting your head toward either left or right shoulder.) Wallach (1939, 1940) has emphasized the importance of rotational movements and has pointed out that the changes in time and intensity cues with head rotation are maximal when the source is in the same horizontal plane as the ears, but become less and less as the source elevation is increased until they become zero when the source is directly above the head. Despite these theoretical expectations, Thurlow and Runge (1967) did not find that either induced "rotation" or "pivot" movements aided much in improving elevation discrimination. However, it seems possible that, with special training, subjects might learn to use head movements to obtain more substantial improvements in the discrimination of the elevation of sound sources.

Precedence effects If 2 sounds occur in space, one slightly ahead of the other in time, the first sound appears to dominate in its effects on perception. Figure 8.37 shows schematically a typical location of the subject and click sources A and B. Let us suppose that 2 clicks, 1 from A and 1 from B, at equal intensity, are sounded one after the other, A then B, with a very short time interval between. The following are several of the important phenomena that occur:

For time intervals below 2 msec, only 1 click

is heard, and its location is a compromise between the localizations of A and B. If they arrive simultaneously, the single click is heard midway between A and B. As the interval is lengthened (up to about 2 msec), the click heard moves toward A. Thus, the effect of the first click stimulus is more important in determining localization. Wallach, Newman, and Rosenzweig (1949) and von Békésy (1960) have studied this problem.

When the time interval between the A and B clicks is between about 2 and 6 msec, only 1 click is heard, and that is at position A. When the time interval between A and B is greater than about 6 msec, then click B can be heard also at its proper location (Wallach, Newman, & Rosenzweig, 1949). This time interval is longer if click B is less intense than A (Thurlow & Parks, 1961). Could this be masking? It does not appear to be entirely masking because the effect of increasing rate of presentation of click pairs appears to be different for this situation (Thurlow & Parks, 1961), than when click pairs are presented simply to 1 ear alone (Guttman, Bergeijk, & David, 1960).

For time intervals when click B is not heard, the loudness of the click heard at A is greater than it would be if click A were sounded by itself. This is a further reason for believing that click B is not simply masked out in the inner ear by A. We might describe what is happening as a type of "funneling" in which a stimulus occurring second in time is "funneled" neurally toward the location of the first. Von Békésy has introduced the concept of funneling to describe a number of broadly similar types of interaction in cutaneous as well as in auditory perception (von Békésy, 1959). Thurlow, Marten, and Bhatt (1965) have sketched neural mechanisms that might help to explain several types of precedence effects.

Precedence effects for complex stimuli such as speech and music have been recognized for many years (Haas, 1951; Gardner, 1968). The time intervals over which these precedence effects last are longer than with simple click stimuli. The effects are especially noticeable when we listen to a speaker in an auditorium. The speech appears to be coming from the location of the speaker even though a great deal of sound is being reflected from the walls. The reflected sound enhances the loudness of the speech heard.

In cases where the subject can see the source, there may be an additional effect of vision on auditory localization (a "ventriloquism" effect): If speech sounds from a visible speaker come from a concealed loudspeaker within about 20 degrees of the visible speaker, the sound is perceived as coming from the speaker (Witkin, Wapner, & Leventhal, 1952).

Perception of Source Distance

Perhaps the most obvious cue we can use to determine the source of a sound is sound pressure. In free space, there is a loss of 6 dB in sound pressure for each doubling of distance. Von Békésy (1949) varied the intensity of speech sounds coming from a loudspeaker in an anechoic room and found that the apparent distance of the source increased as the intensity was reduced.

If we are familiar with the source of the sound, pressure magnitude can enable us to estimate the distance of the source. If we are not familiar with the source, we can only make relative judgments of distance on the basis of sound pressure (Coleman, 1962).

Variation in frequency spectrum with distance also can play a role in distance perception (Coleman, 1963). Von Békésy has shown that for distances up to 4 feet, impulsive sounds appear closer as the low-frequency content increases (von Békésy, 1960).

For enclosed spaces there is an additional important factor of reverberation. It has been known for many years in radio broadcasting that a listener can judge the distance of a speaker from the microphone on the basis of amount of reverberation. The greater the distance, the more the reverberation. Von Békésy (1960) reported an experiment in which he systematically varied the amount of reverberation of a speech signal (with an apparatus that kept loudness and frequency spectrum constant). Listeners reported that the speaker was moving farther away as reverberation was increased.

Utilization of Echoes

In the present century man has developed a "sonar" system for detecting underwater targets. In this system (analogous to radar)—a pulse of high-frequency sound is sent out by the source. A target will reflect back sound waves, which then can be picked up at the location of the source, and interpreted to give information about the nature of the target (size, distance, material). Some animals have highly developed sonar or echo-ranging systems. We discuss some of these first before discussing problems of human echo detection.

Bats and porpoises The remarkable ability of bats and porpoises to detect objects at a distance without the aid of vision has been studied extensively.

Spallanzani, before 1800, showed that blinded bats catch as many insects as normal bats. He also showed that plugging the ears of these animals prevented their responding to objects at a distance; they collided with any obstacle in their path. It was not until the twentieth century when equipment was developed to detect and measure frequencies above the range of human hearing, that Griffin discovered that bats were emitting pulses of very high frequencies. If the bats' mouth is covered—thus preventing emission of these high-frequency sounds—the bat is unable to avoid obstacles (Griffin & Galambos, 1941). Thus it is apparent that the bat under normal conditions emits pulses; echoes are then reflected by an obstacle back to the animal's ears, enabling it to detect the obstacle. Frequency, intensity, and duration characteristics of pulses emitted vary with the species of bat. The most studied of the bats— the little brown bat—emits a pulse which lasts for about 2 msec, and sweeps from 90 kilocycles down to 45 kilocycles. Ordinarily these pulses (or chirps) are repeated at rates of 10 to 20 per second. However, if the bat approaches even a small obstacle, the rate of the pulse emission rises greatly. This reaction to an obstacle can be used to measure the distance at which a bat detects an obstacle. When moving pictures of the bat (with sound track) were analyzed, it was found that a wire only 180 μ in diameter was detected at a distance of 110 cm (Griffin, 1959). Wires have to be reduced to a diameter of 70 μ—about the diameter of a human hair—before a bat is unable to detect them. Grinnel has found that the midbrain of the bat has some special neural mechanisms that facilitate the detection of an echo. (See Grinnel, 1963, the first of a consecutive series of articles.)

Kellogg (1961) has described a series of experiments with the porpoise, aimed at demonstrating how this animal utilizes echoes from objects ("echo-ranges") to avoid obstacles and obtain food. Experimentation with these animals is difficult because of their habitat, size, and expense. Consider for example the difficulty of blindfolding a porpoise! C. S. Johnson has found an ingenious solution to this problem by using suction cups, applied over the eyes of the porpoise. (See Stevens and Warshofsky, 1965.)

As a challenge to your ingenuity, try to design a series of experiments which would prove that porpoises make use of echo-ranging in detecting objects. Then refer to Kellogg's account of the experiments he carried out.

Humans Blind people are often able to avoid running into obstacles. There have been numerous theories of how this is accomplished (Hayes, 1935, 1941). One of the most prominent of these theories is the theory of "facial vision," which states that the face is somehow sensitive to stimulation by air currents from obstacles. Supa, Cotzin, and Dallenbach (1944) tested the effectiveness of auditory cues as well as "air-current" cues. They used a Masonite board approximately 4 by 5 feet in size as an obstacle, which could

be moved to various distances from the location of the subject in a large room. The subjects tested were 2 blind people and 2 with normal vision who were blindfolded. The best of the subjects (blind) were able to detect the obstacle when they were 7 to 8 feet from it.

Air currents or pressure waves to the face and hands were ruled out as cues, for it was found that if a heavy felt veil was placed over the head and leather gauntlets on the hands, the detection of the obstacle was only slightly interfered with. In contrast, plugging the ears or interfering with auditory cues by a loud masking tone caused the subjects to fail. Furthermore, when the subject was able to use only auditory cues—when listening with earphones in another room to the experimenter, who walked toward the target with a microphone attached—he did well in detecting the obstacle the experimenter was approaching. It was concluded that auditory cues played a vital role in obstacle detection. It was apparent that noises made by the shoes of the subject interacted with the obstacle to create the cues. Subjects would sometimes try to make additional noises with their feet to provide better cues.

Other similar experiments (Worchel & Dallenbach, 1947) with deaf and blind subjects showed that these subjects could not detect the Masonite obstacle and were not able to learn to detect it. Worchel and Berry (1952) repeated the experiments in an outdoor setting with a group of deaf subjects who were blindfolded, and found that these subjects were incapable of learning to perceive the obstacle. The results of these experiments are of special interest in that they rule out another possible cue—pressure waves on the skin of the external canal of the ear, and on the eardrum.

Ammons, Worchel, and Dallenbach (1953) point out that there are other cues which can conceivably function, but which usually are not present to aid the blind person in detecting obstacles. For instance, odor cues, temperature cues (when the obstacle is between the sun and the subject), and wind pressure cues (if the obstacle intervenes to shield the subject from wind) are possibilities. The limits of effectiveness of these cues remain to be determined.

The experiments so far performed, then, are mainly aimed at showing that auditory cues *can* function importantly in the detection of obstacles by the blind. The next question is: What kinds of auditory cues? Cotzin and Dallenbach (1950) had subjects listen to a sound source approaching the obstacle, and indicate when they detected the obstacle. (Subjects listened with earphones in another room to sound picked up by a microphone which moved on the same carriage as the sound source.) Subjects were not successful in detecting the obstacles if pure tones were used, except when a high frequency of 10,000 Hz was used. Subjects were more successful when they listened to a thermal noise source approaching the obstacle. They reported a rise in pitch as a stimulus approached the obstacle. Bassett and Eastmond (1964) have subsequently shown that when thermal noise is used as a sound source, the pitch heard at a given distance in front of the obstacle is related to the pattern of the sound spectrum at that distance in front of the reflecting obstacle. The pitch is most easily noticed with frequencies from 200 to 2000 Hz; very high frequencies are not required. It cannot be produced with a single pure tone. Thus the cue for obstacle detection with these complex sounds is not the same as that for high frequency pure tones.

Kellogg (1962) has performed experiments with human subjects to find thresholds for the discrimination of the characteristics of objects by means of echoes. His 4 subjects (2 of whom were blind) made various kinds of noise to aid in their discrimination. It was found that the blind subjects were able to do surprisingly well in discriminating depth, size, and the degree of reflectivity of the surface. For example, the better of the blind observers could detect a change in the position of a disc 1 foot in diameter placed 2 feet away when the disc was moved nearer or farther by little more than 4 inches. The blind observers were able to discriminate between hard surfaces (such as sheet metal) and soft, poorly reflecting surfaces of cloth.

Lorrin A. Riggs

VISION

9

This chapter covers some of the main facts about the sense of sight. It starts with the sequence of events that begins when patterns of light enter the eye to act as stimuli for the visual receptors, and goes on to the conduction and integration of information that takes place in the visual pathways. It calls attention to the almost incredible sensitivity and range of the sense of sight. Finally, it describes the evidence, both physiological and psychophysical, that supports our present hypotheses with regard to the visual process. However, because the topic of vision is so important, a broader coverage is needed and therefore the subsequent chapters of this book are designed to present the fields of color vision (Boynton, Chapter 10), the motor aspects of vision (Alpern, Chapter 11) and visual perception (Hochberg, Chapters 12 and 13).

What is the difference between vision, as covered in this chapter, and visual perception? The main difference is in point of view, which a physical analogy may help to clarify. A table may be considered either as a collection of atoms and molecules arranged in certain configurations or as a solid having the more obvious dimensions of length, width, height, and weight. In this chapter we adopt a kind of molecular point of view in trying to understand the basic nature of our responses to light. The perception chapters, in contrast, are concerned with a world of real objects and the way in which we react to them as visual stimuli.

THE VISUAL STIMULUS

The typical visual scene contains stationary or moving objects that are characterized by their ability to transmit to the eye distinctive patterns of visible light. For a basic understanding of such patterns we need to consider the physical nature of light and the degree to which it is capable of stimulating the visual receptors (see Riggs, 1965b).

Light Quanta

Light may be said to consist of individual particles. The particles of light are sometimes known as photons, to distinguish them from the many other elementary particles of matter (protons, electrons, neutrons, and so on). More often, however, the particles of light are called *quanta*. These quanta are emitted or radiated from a variety of sources such as very hot objects (the sun, the wire filament of a light bulb, a glowing candle), ionized gas (a neon or mercury tube), and many special materials that are activated by diverse forms of energy (fluorescent lamps, television screens, electroluminescent panels, fireflies, lasers). Once emitted, a quantum travels in a straight line at very high speed (186,000 miles/sec in air, although it travels more slowly in water, glass, or other substances). If it hits the surface of an object, the quantum may be absorbed, it may be reflected from the surface to resume its travel in a different direction, it may be transmitted through the object, or it may possibly undergo more complex events having to do with refraction, fluorescence, diffraction, and so on.

Light Waves

The quantum concept of light is often supplemented by the wave concept, especially when we speak of its effects upon the eye. According to this view, light belongs to a class of electromagnetic radiation that includes radio waves, x rays, and others, each having its own particular spectrum of wavelengths. Visible light is in an intermediate region between the shorter ultraviolet waves and the longer infrared waves. The eye is most sensitive in the middle part of the visible spectrum, namely over a range of wavelengths from about 400 to 700 nanometers (1 nanometer, nm, = 1 millimicron; mμ is an older equivalent of the same unit).

The quantum and wave concepts of light, though seemingly incompatible, are merged in the theoretical field of quantum mechanics, in which the Einstein equation plays a key role:

$$E = h\nu$$

where E is the energy of a quantum of light, h is Planck's fundamental constant of the theory, and ν is the number of waves per second (that is, frequency) characterizing the particular quantum. The frequency ν is inversely related to the wavelength λ of the light. Thus the equation tells us that a quantum of light having a wavelength of 400 nm, for example, contains more energy than a quantum of 600 nm light. The relative energies are in inverse proportion to the two wavelengths, that is, a 400 nm quantum has 600/400 or 1.5 times as much energy as a 600 nm quantum. Light of shorter wavelengths,

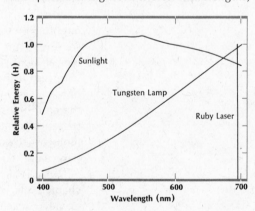

Figure 9.1. Sample energy distributions of sunlight (data of C. G. Abbot in Moon, 1936), a tungsten lamp at a temperature of 2854° K (CIE standard *Illuminant A*), and a ruby laser at various wavelengths of light. Each curve describes the irradiance distribution H of the light source as a function of wavelength λ.

called ultraviolet light, must be very intense to be seen at all. It is absorbed by the cornea or lens of the eye and may damage it if it is present in sufficiently large quantities. Longer waves characterize infrared light, which can also be seen if present in large amounts. These pass more readily through the media of the eye and are therefore potentially harmful to the retina.

Within the 400 to 700 nanometer range over which the eyes operate most efficiently, the wavelength composition of the light is a major determining factor of its hue and saturation (see Chapter 10). Sunlight appears white or achromatic. It has a spectrum that has approximately the same energy overall, that is, the light that it emits contains nearly equal amounts of energy at all wavelengths (see Figure 9.1) within the visible range. Light from a tungsten bulb appears yellowish because it is relatively weak in the short-wave (blue-violet) region, and strong in the longer-wave (yellow-red) region of the spectrum. Light from a ruby laser has its energy all concentrated in a very narrow region (around 694 nm) that typically appears deep red to the eye.

Light from the sun or a light bulb, of course, may be used to illuminate objects, which in turn reflect some of the light into the eye. This is called *irradiance* and is measured in energy units of watts per square meter. The symbol H is used for this dimension. Because a given source generally provides different amounts of energy at each wavelength λ, an instrument known as a spectroradiometer has been developed for measuring H at each value of λ. The resulting relationship of irradiance to wavelength is known as the $H(\lambda)$ distribution of light falling on the surface of an object. Carrying the process one step further, a reflectometer can be used to determine the proportion R of light reflected by the surface of an object at each wavelength. Examples of reflectance distributions determined for various surfaces are shown in Figure 10.1 of Chapter 10. If we know both the irradiance distribution $H(\lambda)$,

and the reflectance distribution $R(\lambda)$, we can designate the product $H(\lambda)R(\lambda)$, as a physical description of the surface as a stimulus for the eye. Thus an object is a strong stimulus if it receives an adequate amount of light from the source, and if its surface reflects a large proportion of the light into the eye of the observer. Conversely, an object is a weak stimulus if it is poorly illuminated or if it absorbs most of the light and its surface reflects only a small proportion of the light into the eye. However there is one more very significant factor that determines the physical effect of light on the receptors, namely the sensitivity of the eye for the particular wavelengths that the object sends back to the eye.

Spectral Sensitivity

The various wavelengths of light differ enormously in the extent to which they stim-

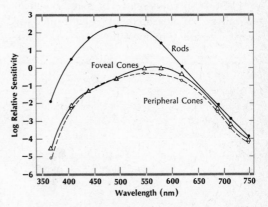

Figure 9.2. The sensitivity of the eye to various wavelengths of light throughout the visible spectrum. The ordinate gives sensitivity, defined as reciprocal of absolute threshold, on a logarithmic scale. Note that the receptors for scotopic vision (rods) are much more sensitive than those for photopic vision (cones), especially for wavelengths below 600 nm. Each curve describes the sensitivity distribution or visibility V as a function of wavelength λ. The rod curve closely resembles the absorption spectrum of the rod photopigment, rhodopsin. The cone curve, however, represents the summed sensitivities of cones containing the various photopic pigments. (Adapted from Wald, 1945.)

ulate the eye. Figure 9.2 presents spectral sensitivity curves (that is, curves showing the relative sensitivity of the eye for each wavelength of light) under scotopic (night vision) and photopic (day vision) conditions. If we call L the luminance or stimulating effect of a given surface illuminated by light, we may deduce from these curves that L depends not only upon the irradiance distribution $H(\lambda)$ of the source of light and the reflectance distribution $R(\lambda)$ of the surface, but also upon the sensitivity distribution $V(\lambda)$ of the eye to the range of wavelengths present in the reflected light. Symbolically,

$$L = H(\lambda)R(\lambda)V(\lambda)$$

Photometry

Calculations of the kind just mentioned are complex and tedious, but they must be used to make the most precise physical specifications of a stimulus field. For many practical purposes the measurement of light intensity can be greatly simplified, however, by the use

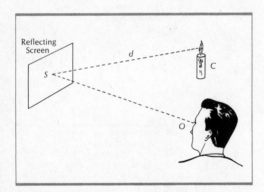

Figure 9.3. A surface S is strongly illuminated by a source of light C if it is close to the source, but it is weakly illuminated if it is far away. Specifically, the illuminance on S in this diagram varies directly with the candlepower, and inversely with the square of the distance, that is, $E = C/d^2$. The luminance L of a screen S, as seen by an observer at O depends on the illuminance times the reflectance R of the screen; thus $L = CR/d^2$. Note that the luminance remains the same regardless of the distance of the observer from the surface. See text for details.

of direct photometry. The original standard for photometric measurement was a candle, manufactured under specified conditions, and used as a source of light. Consider Figure 9.3, in which such a candle is placed at a distance (d) from a white screen (S) that is known to reflect a certain proportion (R) of the light falling upon it. This incident light, known as the illuminance (E) on the screen, is then said to have a value, in footcandles, equal to the candlepower (C) of the source divided by the square of the distance (d) in feet from source to screen. In other words,

$$E = \frac{C}{d^2} \text{ footcandles}$$

Lighting engineers have developed standard levels of illuminance for various visual tasks. A library installation should provide readers with a level above 10 footcandles, for example, whereas street lighting may require less than 1 footcandle. Photoelectric footcandle meters are available to make measurements of this kind.

The appearance of the screen at S to an observer at O depends not only on E, the illuminance of the light falling upon it, but also on R, the reflectance of the screen in the direction of O. If R is defined as the ratio of the light reflected to the light incident on the screen, then L, the luminance of the screen in units called footlamberts, is given by the equation

$$L = ER = \frac{CR}{d^2} \text{ footlamberts}$$

As an example, we may calculate the luminance of a surface that reflects 60 percent of the light reaching it from a 50 candlepower source at a distance of 1.2 feet. Thus

$$L = \frac{50(.60)}{(1.2)^2} = 20.8 \text{ footlamberts}$$

In the practice of photometry, standard tungsten lamps of known candlepower and standard surfaces of measured reflectance are available for laboratory use. In fact, compact

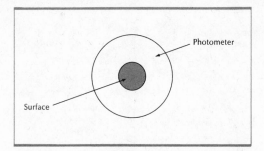

Figure 9.4. The appearance of the photometer field. To measure the luminance of a surface, the observer first points the photometer directly at it so that a portion of the surface fills the central viewing field. He then adjusts the measuring field of the instrument by turning an intensity control until there is a brightness match between the two fields of the instrument. He reads the dial of the control to find the luminance.

instruments (light spot photometers) containing such elements are now available to produce a split visual field of the type shown in Figure 9.4. If we wish to measure the luminance of any particular surface in a visual field, we look directly through the instrument until we can see the surface in question in the central portion of the field. We can then adjust a surrounding part of the field to a brightness that matches the surface in question, using the controls on the instrument for this purpose. The luminance is given directly on the scale that is coupled with these controls. A precision of 1 or 2 percent is possible under the most favorable condition, one in which the two fields have the same color. The method becomes highly unreliable, however, when the observer attempts to match the brightness between a white measuring field, for example, and a red viewing field. For this purpose it may be necessary to use heterochromatic flicker photometry (see p. 312).

In the modern practice of photometry, a glowing platinum source of specified size and temperature has replaced the old standard candle. Furthermore, photoelectric receiving surfaces have been developed that have sensitivity characteristics similar to those of the average human eye at photopic (medium to

high) levels of luminance. Thus light meters, equipped with such photocells, are now used almost exclusively to measure luminance for the practical purposes of industries such as those concerned with lighting, photography, and dyeing.

We have gone into some detail describing the measurement of luminance because, for experimental psychologists, this is the typical way of specifying the intensity dimension of a visual stimulus or a visual environment.

Note that illuminance is a measure that is influenced by distance from the source of light to the surface illuminated (see Figure 9.3). Luminance, however, is independent of the distance from the surface to the eye of the observer. That is why a movie screen, for example, looks equally bright when seen from the back row as from the front row in a theatre. Thus photometry, within the limits imposed by the size of field in the instrument, can be carried out at any convenient distance from the stimulus. This independence from the effects of distance is of course true of the camera as well as the eye; exposure times and lens openings need to be adjusted for the luminance of the object to be photographed but not for the distance from object to camera.

Note also that luminance has been defined physically in footlamberts. The English standard footlambert has been specified in terms of the candlepower of the light source, the distance in feet from source to surface, and the reflectance of the surface. Corresponding metric terms in common use in various countries are based on the millilambert (1 millilambert [mL] = .929 footlambert [ftL] = 3.183 candles per square meter [c/m^2] = 10 apostilbs).

The psychological term that is related to luminance is *brightness*, but we must not make the mistake of assuming that brightness is directly related to or solely dependent on luminance. Brightness, as we see below, is influenced by many factors including the state of the adaptation of the eye, contrast effects, exposure time, and perceptual constancy (see

TABLE 9.1 LUMINANCE VALUES FOR TYPICAL VISUAL STIMULI

	Scale of luminance (mL)	
Sun's surface at noon	10^{10}	
	10^9	Damaging
	10^8	
Tungsten filament	10^7	
	10^6	
	10^5	
White paper in sunlight	10^4	Photopic
	10^3	
	10^2	
Comfortable reading	10	
	1	Mixed
	10^{-1}	
White paper in moonlight	10^{-2}	
	10^{-3}	Scotopic
White paper in starlight	10^{-4}	
	10^{-5}	
Absolute RL	10^{-6}	

Source: Riggs, 1965b

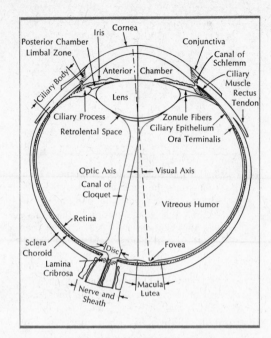

Figure 9.5. Horizontal section of right human eye. Note that two different positions are shown for the posterior surface of the lens. This is because the lens bulges while accommodating for near objects. (Walls, 1942.)

Chapters 12 and 13). However, scaling procedures can be used to attempt a direct estimate of subjective brightness (see Chapter 3). Table 9.1 gives an idea of the wide range of useful luminances over which the eye can function.

For special purposes, still other specifications are sometimes used to describe stimulus intensity. If we consider the stimulus as a patch of light falling on the retina at the back of the eye, we may wish, for example, to note that this light is reduced in proportion to the size of the pupil of the eye. Accordingly, a measure of retinal illuminance, the *troland*, has been arrived at, such that retinal illuminance, E_r in trolands, is given by the expression $E_r = AL$ where L is luminance in c/m² of the visual stimulus at which the subject is looking, and A is the area of his pupil in units of square millimeters. Take the example of a person who is looking at a stimulus field of 25 c/m², or 7.3 ftL, with eyes having a pupillary radius of 2 mm. The area of his pupil is 4π square millimeters and his retinal illuminance is specified by the equation $E_r = 4\pi(25) = 314$ trolands.

VISUAL ANATOMY

The Eyes

A diagram of a human eye is shown in Figure 9.5. Each eye is about 25 mm in diameter and weighs about 7g. The transparent cornea in front and the tough, fibrous sclera surrounding the rest of the eye serve to protect it from injury and to maintain its shape. The choroid is a middle layer of dark material, richly supplied with blood vessels. The retina is a thin and delicate inner layer containing the photoreceptors and an elaborate network of interconnecting nervous tissue.

The eye, as an optical instrument, is somewhat analogous to a camera. Rays of light from the visual field are focused by the eye in such a way that a fairly accurate, inverted image of the field is formed on the retina at the back of the eye. Most of this optical effect results from the curvature of the cornea, but fine adjustments can be made in focus for far

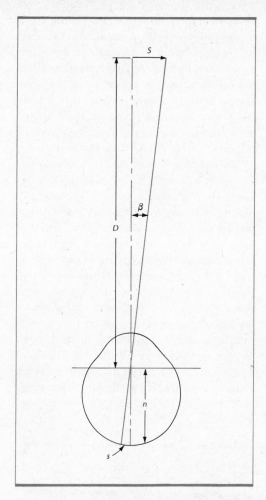

Figure 9.6. Diagram to illustrate the size of a retinal image. (Riggs, 1965c.)

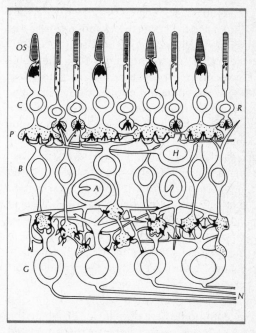

Figure 9.7. Generalized diagram of the retina. See text for details. (After Dowling & Boycott, 1966.)

and near objects. In a camera, focusing is done by moving the lens, but in the human eye it is accomplished by changing the shape of the lens (see Chapter 11). The anterior chamber and posterior chamber on either side of the lens are filled with transparent material (the aqueous and vitreous humors, respectively). The iris is a pigmented structure the central aperture of which, the pupil, contracts and dilates in a manner analogous to the changes in the diaphragm of a camera.

The optical characteristics of the eye are complex, but fairly exact calculations of retinal image size can be made by the use of a schematic eye such as is shown in Figure 9.6.

For simplicity, we draw lines from any points in space crossing each other at a point known as the nodal point of the eye. An object such as the one shown at S in Figure 9.6 is said to subtend a visual angle β at the eye such that $\tan \beta = S/D$ where S is the length or width of the object and D is its distance from the nodal point of the eye. The nodal point is at a distance n of about 17 mm from the image formed on the retina at the back of the eye. The angular size of the retinal image of object S is the same as the visual angle β subtended by that object. Therefore $\tan \beta = s/17$, and the linear size s of the retinal image of S can be calculated, for all small angles, from the equation

$$s = 17 \tan \beta = \frac{17S}{D}$$

The Retina

A schematic view of the retina is presented in Figure 9.7. (Note that in this magnified view the front of the eye lies below.) Light reaches the retina by coming up through the vitreous humor and traversing the various retinal layers before finally reaching the visual receptors, the rods (R) and the cones (C). The outer segments (OS) of the rod receptors are known to contain a photosensitive pigment known as rhodopsin, or visual purple. The rhodopsin is not freely dispersed throughout the segment, however. Instead, it appears organized into hundreds of layers or disks that are oriented transversely to the elongated structure of the rod. It now appears certain that the absorption of a single quantum of light by a molecule of rhodopsin in one of these layers is sufficient to cause a change in the physical structure of that molecule. The change, in turn, acts as a trigger for some sort of signal (chemical, electrical, or both) to travel from the outer segment of the rod receptor to its base or pedicle (P), where the excitation is passed along to the associated neural structures of the bipolar layer of the retina. The bipolars (B) in turn excite the ganglion cells (G), and this causes nerve impulses to travel out of the eye along the optic nerve fibers (N), which are in fact the axons of the ganglion cells of the retina. The optic nerve fibers from every part of the retina travel along its inner surface and emerge from the eye, as shown in Figure 9.5, at the point known as the blind spot, or optic disk. Within that small region of the retina, there indeed are no rod or cone receptors, so that no visual response can originate from this region.

The rod receptors of the eye function most efficiently at low levels of illumination. They are thus responsible for our scotopic, or nighttime vision. In daylight the cone receptors are most responsible for vision. The typical cone is shorter and thicker than a rod, but it is similar to a rod in having a layered structure in its outer segment. These outer segments of the cones also contain photosensitive pigments and, because color vision is mediated by cone receptors, we may assume that there are at least three different types of photopigment (see Chapter 10). Therefore a cone containing one of the pigments would be most sensitive to wavelengths in the range best absorbed by that pigment. Signals from

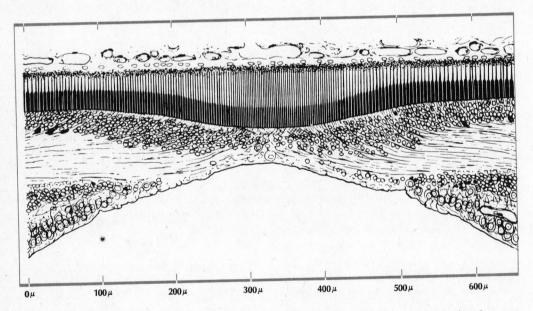

Figure 9.8. Central fovea of the human retina. The whole diagram includes .65 mm of retinal surface, corresponding to a visual angle of about 2°. Only .1 mm (a visual angle of about 20 minutes) is included in the region of the most slender cone receptors and thinnest neural tissue. (Polyak, 1957.)

the cones are passed along through the bipolar and ganglion cell layers to optic nerve fibers.

The horizontal cells (*H*), also shown in Figure 9.7, provide lateral connections among the receptors, whereas amacrine cells (*A*) interconnect bipolars from one region of the retina to another. As we see below, many visual functions appear to be enhanced by the action of such lateral interconnections at the retinal level.

The human retina is by no means uniform in its structural appearance from one region to another. At its very center, or fovea (see Figure 9.5) there are no rod receptors. The cone outer segments in the fovea are unusually long and slender and very densely packed together, as is shown in Figure 9.8. Note that the neural elements (cone nuclei, bipolar and ganglion cells) appear to be swept aside in this region, thus providing direct access of the light to these receptors. It is significant that this relatively small region (about 2° in diameter) is the only portion of the retina with

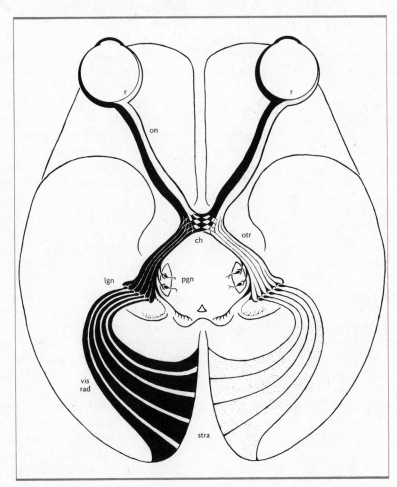

Figure 9.9. Diagram of primary pathways in the human visual system. The optic nerve (*on*) from each retina (*r*) decussates at the chiasma (*ch*) in such a way that each optic tract (*otr*) contains fibers representing one half of the visual field. Each tract terminates in the corresponding lateral geniculate nucleus (*lgn*) from which the visual radiations (*vis rad*) proceed to the striate area (*stra*) in the cortex of the occipital lobe. Some optic tract fibers terminate, however, in the pretectal or pregeniculate (pgn) nucleus (see p. 283). (After Polyak, 1957.)

which we can see very clearly. Look at a single letter on this page and notice that if you do not move your eyes you see very few other letters clearly. The rest of the page is blurred and indistinct. Outside the fovea, rods become mixed with cones, and still farther out in the periphery rods predominate and relatively few cones are present. In the extreme periphery (see Figure 9.5) there are fewer and fewer receptors; the retina finally ends at the *ora terminalis.*

The retina of each eye has more than 100 million rod receptors and fewer than 10 million cones. Considering the entire retina, the total number of bipolar cells is much smaller than the number of receptors. Furthermore the number of ganglion cells is still smaller, being less than 1 million.

The proportions just cited do not hold in the fovea, however. There, the cones are richly supplied with bipolars and ganglion cells. Presumably this fact not only entitles each cone to a more or less direct representation by one fiber of the optic nerve, but also allows signals from individual cones to be influenced by those from cones nearby. Horizontal and amacrine cells are presumably the agents for these interactions within the retina. They are believed to play an important role in the retinal processing of information on color and form (see Chapters 10 and 12).

The peripheral retina is quite differently organized. Bipolar and ganglion cells are sparsely distributed, so that hundreds of rod and cone receptors must excite a given optic nerve fiber. Thus color and form information are not well received in the periphery. The pooling of excitation has one outstanding advantage, however. It permits us to detect the presence or movement of large objects that we are not looking at directly, even under nighttime conditions of low illumination (see p. 285). The optic disk (in Figure 9.5) contains no visual receptors and is thus often called the "blind spot" of each eye. Note that it is the region in which the optic nerve fibers make their way out of the eyeball.

Visual Pathways

Figure 9.9 presents a simplified diagram of the primary visual pathways. The details of structure and function may be found in recent books (Adler, 1959; Brindley, 1960; Granit, 1962). Following is a brief summary of typical features of the organization of the primate visual system including that of man. (1) There is an approximately point-for-point representation of the visual field on each retina, in the various layers of the lateral geniculate body, and in the visual cortex. (2) There is a partial decussation of optic nerve fibers at the optic chiasm such that fibers from the nasal half of each retina cross over to the opposite geniculate and cortical centers, whereas fibers from the temporal do not. This means that the left hemisphere represents the left half-retina of each eye (that is, the right half of the visual field) whereas the right hemisphere represents the right half-retina (left visual field). (3) The "cortical map" of the visual field is a distorted one in that a relatively large proportion of it corresponds to the foveal region, whereas peripheral regions are but poorly represented. (4) The lateral geniculate body has a laminar arrangement such that three layers on the left lateral geniculate receive the axons of ganglion cells from the left hemi-retina of the left eye, whereas the other three layers represent the left hemi-retina of the right eye. In the right lateral geniculate, of course, the situation is reversed. The exact functional significance of the laminar structure is not known, although recent evidence indicates that the encoding of color and pattern may differ from one layer to another. (5) The primary visual projection area (known as the striate area, or area 17) of the cortex has a combination of a laminar and a columnar organization (see below). Again the various layers appear to be specialized for certain types of visual function. Of major significance is the fact that any given column of cells (that is, cells that are found at various depths along a line running perpendicular to the surface) seem to respond selectively to

TABLE 9.2 PHOTOPIC AND SCOTOPIC VISION OF THE HUMAN EYE

	Photopic	*Scotopic*
Receptor	Cones (ca. 7 million)	Rods (ca. 120 million)
Retinal location	Concentrated at center, fewer in periphery	General in periphery, none in fovea
Neural processing	Discriminative	Summative
Peak wavelength	555 nm	505 nm
Luminance level	Daylight (1 to 10^7 mL)	Night (10^{-6} to 1 mL)
Color vision	Normally trichromatic	Achromatic
Dark adaptation	Rapid (ca. 7 min)	Slow (ca. 40 min)
Spatial resolution	High acuity	Low acuity
Temporal resolution	Fast reacting	Slower reacting

one particular slant or light pattern appearing in a particular region of the visual field. (6) Binocular vision is made possible by the fact that any given column of cortical cells receives axons from cells in the lateral geniculate body that are activated by stimulation of corresponding retinal points in each of the two eyes. (7) There are higher regions of the occipital cortex (known as associative areas 18 and 19) that receive their innervation from area 17 and are presumed to mediate perceptual functions as well as to permit integration with other sensory and motor systems. (8) The parietal and temporal lobes contain centers for visual symbols and language. (9) Outside the primary visual pathways are (a) optic tract fibers that go to the pretectal region rather than the lateral geniculate, and are concerned with regulation of the pupil (see Chapter 11); (b) interhemispheric fibers of the corpus callosum that may perhaps relate to binocular functions such as stereoscopic vision; (c) connections of the primary centers with the cerebellum, having to do with visuo-vestibular coordination and regulation of balance; and (d) connections with the reticular formation or other structures relating to activation or attention.

PHOTOPIC AND SCOTOPIC VISION

We can see from the discussion above that the human retina contains two kinds of photoreceptor, the rods and the cones. We note that the two differ importantly in their distribution and in their functional

properties. The duplex nature of vision was clearly pointed out over a century ago (Schultze, 1866). Perhaps the easiest way to summarize the "duplicity theory," as it has come to be called, is to say that cone vision provides acute vision at daytime (photopic) levels of luminance, whereas rod vision provides a high degree of light sensitivity that is essential for seeing at night when light levels are low (scotopic). Nocturnal animals have more rods and relatively few cones in their retinas, and some (deep sea fish, some snakes and bats) are believed to lack cones entirely. Diurnal animals are well provided with cones, and a few species (among the lizards, snakes, birds, and squirrels) lack rods.

Man shares with most other animals the advantages of both photopic and scotopic vision. He is basically a diurnal creature, however (his night life has flourished only in recent times, from the fact that he is able, with bright lights, to turn night into day). Table 9.2 summarizes the properties of human photopic and scotopic vision.

LIGHT AND DARK ADAPTATION

As Table 9.1 shows, the human eye is able to function over a luminance range of more than 13 log units. At any given moment, however, we are seldom confronted with visual stimuli of more than 2 log units, for at any one time, we normally rely on a single source (for example, the sun, moon, or artificial lighting) that illuminates objects which reflect from about 2 to 90 percent of the light falling on them. Few of us must go very often from one light environment rapidly into a very different one, as in going from sunlight into a darkened theatre, tunnel, or mine. When we must, however, the experience takes us out of the immediate dynamic range of visual sensitivity; in other words, we are momentarily blind. Even more disagreeable is the opposite experience of emerging suddenly from darkness into daylight. In this case we normally close the eyes or use dark glasses to allow the eyes to become gradually adapted to the change in light level, after which the eyes can again function efficiently within a new dynamic range of intensities.

Light adaptation is often found to be nearly complete in a minute or two, but dark adaptation may take a half-hour or longer, depending on the previous level of the exposure of the eyes to light. For an understanding of adaptation we need to have experimental data on the exact course it takes, together with measurements of the underlying physiological processes.

Dark-adaptation Curves

In a typical dark-adaptation experiment, the subject is first asked to achieve a high level of light adaptation by fixing his eyes for several minutes on a point at the center of a large bright screen or uniform field of white

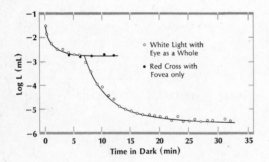

Figure 9.10. The course of dark adaptation in the human eye. On the ordinate is a logarithmic scale of luminance for a test target at the absolute threshold of vision, and on the abscissa is time after exposure of the eye to a high-intensity field of light. (After Hecht, 1934.)

light having a luminance of several hundred footlamberts. The adapting light is then turned off, and the course of dark adaptation is then followed using a test light of variable luminance. The test procedure is to find the absolute threshold as a function of time in the dark, using one of the standard psychophysical methods outlined in Chapter 2.

Figure 9.10 illustrates the course of dark adaptation measured by the method just outlined. Note that a test field of white light must, in this case, be 4 log units (10,000 times) more intense at the beginning of dark adaptation than at the end in order for the subject to report he has seen it. Note also that this curve exhibits two portions, with a "kink" in between. The first, or photopic, portion is due to the cones, as evidenced by the fact that it is the only part of the curve that is shown when the rod-free fovea alone is tested. The second part, after the kink, results from the activity of large numbers of rods; this takes the eye down into scotopic levels of luminance.

The use of a red test light in dark-adaptation experiments deserves some comment. Figure 9.2 shows that rods are scarcely any more sensitive than cones to long wavelengths of light. It is for this reason that a red test light shows no further drop in threshold (Figure 9.10) beyond the photopic portion. The relatively poor sensitivity of rods to red light has also led to the use of red light (Miles, 1953) in situations where it is essential to protect the rods from light adaptation. For example, military men on night lookout duty may be required to wear red goggles or to use red light illumination whenever they must examine charts and instruments immediately before going on watch at night.

After prolonged adaptation to darkness, our vision becomes so sensitive that, under the most favorable conditions, we can see a flash that contains only about a hundred quanta of light. Hecht, Shlaer, and Pirenne (1942) have calculated that a large percentage of these quanta are lost by the various ocular media because of scatter or reflection, among other factors, so that only about 5 to 14 quanta are actually absorbed by the retinal rods. Probability considerations show that this must mean that a single quantum of light is absorbed by a single molecule of the photosensitive material, rhodopsin, in each of 5 to 14 rod receptors. In other words, each receptor is functioning at the upper theoretical limit of its own sensitivity, and the simultaneous excitation of several such receptors is necessary for a flash to be seen. It can be shown, furthermore, that with so small a number of quanta involved a supposedly constant series of flashes will actually show a considerable statistical variation in the number of quanta absorbed by the receptors. Thus a part, at least, of the variability of the absolute visual threshold must be attributed to an irreducible variability in the stimulus itself. Indeed, according to Hecht's calculations (based upon small-number, random Poisson distributions) virtually all of the variability is thus accounted for, and we have an additional reason for stating that the receptor system is performing up to the theoretical limit of its capacity.

Scotopic Vision

It is well worth spending an hour or two in the dark in order to experience some of the consequences of completely scotopic vision. One of the most striking effects is the blindness of the central fovea. That is, a very dim test light or star disappears if we look at it directly, because the fovea contains no rod receptors. We can see dim objects much more effectively if we look at them off-center; that is, if we stare a little to the right or left of the object in order to focus it on the region a few degrees outside the fovea where the rods are found to reach their highest density. Off-center viewing is a trick that is easily mastered by amateur astronomers, men on night lookout duty, and others who must take full advantage of the scotopic visual system.

Another effect of night vision is the appearance of the so-called "photochromatic interval." This is easily understood by reference to Figure 9.2. The interval in question is the vertical separation between the photopic and scotopic sensitivity curves. At any given wavelength, such as 450 nm, scotopic vision is much more sensitive than photopic. Thus even a very dim light will exceed the threshold of the dark-adapted rod receptors, but the light must be raised to a much higher level in order to reach the threshold of the cones. During the interval between the two thresholds the light is seen as colorless, but once the cone threshold is reached, the light assumes the appropriate chromatic appearance. The colorless photochromatic interval holds over most of the spectrum, but, in agreement with Figure 9.2, it becomes vanishingly small for the higher wavelengths of light. Thus light of 650 nm or above, if it is seen at all, is seen as red.

Another consequence of Figure 9.2 is the *Purkinje shift*. This effect may be seen most easily by shining a very weak spectrum at the dark-adapted eye, in which all the wavelengths of light are present with approximately equal energy. At the lowest energy levels, the subject will see only a restricted part of the spectrum centered around 505 nm, as a dim colorless field, in accordance with the scotopic curve of Figure 9.2. At higher levels, however, more and more of the spectrum is seen, the various hues are discriminated, and the wavelength providing a maximum brightness shifts from 505 to 555 nm. In other words, the Purkinje shift is the change in wavelength of maximum effectiveness that occurs in going from scotopic to photopic levels of luminance.

While in a fully dark-adapted state we can also readily see certain unique visual phenomena. An example is the "blue-arcs" that are seen with off-center viewing of a rectangular patch of red light. To get the effect, a projector can be used to place a patch of red light about 3° high and 1° wide on a screen in front of the eye. Covering the left eye, fixate with the right on a point about 2° to the right of this rectangle of light. Notice the bluish streaks that appear to emerge from the top and bottom of the rectangle, pass above and below the center of fixation, and curve toward one another in the darkness on the right. Troland (1920) has noted that these arcs appear to follow the course of the optic nerve fibers as they traverse the retina on their way to the blind spot. The blue arcs are explained as an electrical excitation of retinal units that underlie these fibers. This is presumably done by "leakage" to the receptors, or to retinal neural cells, of the activity set up in these fibers by the red stimulus field; however the bluish color and other aspects of the phenomenon have never been adequately explained (Alpern & Dudley, 1966).

Another example of phenomena seen with scotopic vision is that of the "Purkinje tree." This lets you see the outline of your own retinal blood vessels, the ones that supply the neural structures of the retina. More or less sharp shadows of these vessels fall on the rods and cones when a small point source of light is placed in front of the eye. The effect is clearest when you take a small source, such as a flashlight, and shine it into your eye from one side. Moving the flashlight rapidly around in a small arc gives you a vivid picture of the "tree" whose twigs and branches represent the blood vessels of various sizes lying between the vitreous humor and the retina. Notice that the trunk of the tree is at the blind spot, where the blood vessels enter the eye. Notice also the absence of vessels in the central region of the fovea.

It is interesting that we do not notice the blood vessel shadows under ordinary viewing conditions even though they are present all the time. One reason we do not notice them is that they are not present in the region of our clearest vision. Another reason is that they are not sharply outlined except with the use of a point source of light that is off to the side of a uniform dark field. We must also note that these shadows constitute a "stabilized image" on the retina. (We review the evidence later, on pages 306 and 374, that images of this kind tend to disappear from view, due to the fact that they are unaffected

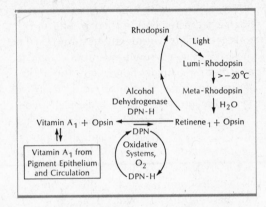

Figure 9.11. Diagram of the molecular basis for responses to light and regeneration of pigment in the rod outer segments. (Wald, 1951.)

by eye movements.) Furthermore, we have become habituated to the continued presence of the images of the blood vessels over the years and do not notice them, any more than we notice the presence of the blind spot in each eye.

Physiological Basis for Visual Adaptation

We have seen that adaptation can be made to a wide range of light levels and that the eye becomes extraordinarily sensitive to dim lights after prolonged dark adaptation. We must now ask whether the adaptation takes place in the brain or in the eye and whether it is due to neuroregulatory processes or to purely photochemical ones.

Dark and light adaptation have a photochemical basis that is well established, especially with respect to the rod receptors. Rhodopsin, the photosensitive substance the molecules of which are arranged in the layers of the rod outer segments, can be bleached by the action of light. Figure 9.11 is a diagram from Wald (1951) that illustrates some of the products of this bleaching at the various stages of this process. The diagram also makes clear the fact that rhodopsin can be restored if the products of the bleaching can use vitamin A. For this reason it is tempting to conclude that light adaptation is equivalent to lowering the concentration of rhodopsin by bleaching it with light, whereas dark adaptation is achieved by removing the light and allowing the restorative processes to raise it again to a high level. Any given level of adaptation would then represent a steady state or balance between the bleaching and restorative reactions, and visual excitation would occur in proportion as the balance was upset, in any given photoreceptor, by increments or decrements in the amount of light falling upon it. Selig Hecht (1937) has given the most extensive and systematic expression to this account of vision as it might apply not only to light and dark adaptation, but also to flicker, acuity, brightness discrimination, and other visual functions.

The classic view, that light and dark adaptation depend exclusively on bleaching and regeneration of the visual pigment, can no longer be entertained. As long ago as 1938, Granit, Holmberg, and Zewi showed that extensive changes in visual threshold can

occur as a result of adaptation even when there is very little change in concentration of visual pigment. Crawford (1947) and Baker (1953) have shown that very large threshold changes are presumably neural, rather than chemical in origin, because they are found to occur within an interval of less than 100 μsec after the adapting light is turned on or off. Rushton (1963) has formulated the hypothesis of retinal "pools." According to this hypothesis, adaptation is regulated by a neural feedback action taking place when high intensities of light cause large numbers of receptors to convey signals to a neural regulatory center or pool. These signals are particularly strong when the eye is being stimulated by a high-intensity light; under this condition the photochemical events shown in Figure 9.11 proceed vigorously. However the signals do not cease when the light is turned off. Instead, they continue to be generated by the receptors and delivered to the neural pool. Thus they maintain a relatively

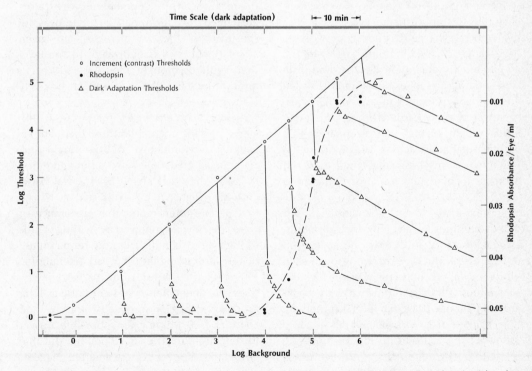

Figure 9.12. Graphical display of the rapid and slow components of dark adaptation, showing the dependence of the latter on the bleaching of rhodopsin. See text for details. (Dowling, 1967.)

high state of activity in the pool that acts to suppress or inhibit responses to test lights until the restorative processes, shown in Figure 9.11, force the receptors to reach their dark-adapted level of equilibrium and thereby stop feeding signals back to the neural pool.

Quantitative data in line with the neural feedback hypothesis of adaptation are shown in Figure 9.12 of Dowling (1967). This is a complicated diagram, but it presents an interesting analysis and deserves careful study. It relates measurements of light and dark adaptation to the concentration of the photopigment (rhodopsin) in the eye of the rat. Considering light adaptation first, we may note the relation between log threshold and log background luminance. We see that there is a nearly straight-line relationship that holds over a range of 6 log units. The open circles are for increment threshold (ΔI) determinations at the various light levels; these thresholds, measured by a technique of electrical recording from the eyeball (the ERG described on pp. 307–308), are notable for demonstrating an approximate agreement with the Weber Law (see Chapter 2) over a very wide range. The dashed-line curve, in the middle of the figure, indicates the rhodopsin concentration (relative concentrations scaled on the right ordinate), measured by photochemical analysis carried out at the same levels of light adaptation. It is apparent that no measurable bleaching of rhodopsin is present over the 4 log unit range from full darkness to moderate levels of background light.

Turning finally to dark adaptation, we see that data on this are given by the Δ symbols, evaluated against the time scale at the top of Figure 9.12. The curve drawn through each set of Δ symbols shows the way in which the visual threshold falls, starting when the background light of a particular level is turned off. It is evident that dark adaptation is rapid following the exposure to low or moderate levels of background light. With high levels of light adaptation, however, significant quantities of rhodopsin are bleached, and the recovery during dark adaptation is very slow.

Dowling's experiments are of particular significance because the various types of measurement (photopigment concentration, increment thresholds at various light levels, and test thresholds taken during dark adaptation) were all conducted on the same species, namely the rat, in which the main pigment is known to be rhodopsin. Experiments by Rushton (1965), using a technique of measuring the absorption of light by receptors in the human eye, have confirmed the relationship of pigment density to visual thresholds determined psychophysically. Johnson and Riggs (1951), using electrical response measurements in the human eye, noted the rapid threshold drop in early dark adaptation, the slow drop following intense light adaptation, and the marked elevation of threshold by relatively weak levels of light adaptation. Barlow (1964) has used the terms "noise" and "dark light" to refer to the signals reaching the neural centers in the human retina from the receptors. Thus a number of investigators are agreed that, during dark adaptation, as the sensitivity of the eye increases, any given adaptational level is equivalent to the level that would be brought about by a real background light of the appropriate intensity (Crawford, 1947).

Several consequences follow from the view of dark adaptation described above. First, as we suddenly go from bright surroundings into darkness, we should continue to "see" the "dark light" as if a real background of light were still present. It is true that people often report the appearance of vivid after-images followed by swirling clouds of "self-light" coming from the retina immediately after going into the dark (Helmholtz, 1909–1911, tr. 1924–1925; Jung, 1961b), but why does this phenomenon not continue as long as dark adaptation proceeds? Barlow and Sparrock (1964) have given a possible answer to this question. They have pointed out that any such after-effect is like an after-image or a stabilized retinal image (see p. 306) in that it disappears quickly and does not reappear unless it is "revived" by some change in the prevailing level of light on the receptors. Indeed they have been able to demonstrate a quantitatively similar effect on visual thresholds if the subject looks at a test light against a background of either the "dark light" that is the after-effect of previous exposure to light, or a stabilized image of real light. In both cases the image has "disappeared" but continues to provide a visually effective background.

A second consequence of the neural "pool" hypothesis is that light falling on one set of visual receptors should produce a generalized state of light adaptation that affects the responses of receptors outside the region directly stimulated by the adapting light. In other words, the visual threshold should rise for neighboring receptors that share the same neural pool. This has indeed been found to occur in experiments made by Lipetz (1961) on the frog and Rushton and Westheimer (1962) on the human eye. Stripes of light falling on the retina caused a marked elevation in threshold for test lights falling on the previously unstimulated receptors lying between the stripes. These effects are much greater than would be caused by light scattering alone.

Finally, the neural-pool hypothesis should be supported by physiological evidence that photoreceptor changes alone are not sufficient to account for changes in light and dark adaptation. Evidence of this kind has already been cited with reference to data on concentration of the photopigment that is found in the receptors. In addition, Dowling (1967) has obtained histological evidence, and evidence from electrical recording, that lead to the conclusion that the main site of visual adaptation is in the bipolar cells of the retina. Dowling's explanation may account in part for the fact that the photopic portion of the human dark-adaptation curve is a small one (Figure 9.10). Not much is known about the bleaching or recovery processes in cone pigments. However, even if they were to behave like rhodopsin, we might expect differences in their rates of dark adaptation. Many more rod receptors than cones typically converge upon a single bipolar; Dowling believes that bipolars are the site of the neural pool, and the opportunity for a strong "dark light" signal may not exist for those bipolars supplied by a relatively small number of cone receptors as it might for those supplied by a much larger number of rods.

SPATIAL ASPECTS OF VISION

So far in this chapter we have considered the way in which light acts upon the retina to initiate the process of seeing. However we have not yet considered one of the main functions of seeing, namely to present us with a spatial representation of the outside world. The chapters on perception will consider the broader aspects of this problem, especially as it relates to the perception of visual depth and the recognition of sizes and shapes of objects. Before doing this, however, we should become acquainted with the more basic mechanisms that transfer to the eye and the rest of the visual system the spatial properties of the visual scene.

The Visual Projection System

We have seen that a more or less accurate optical image is focused upon the retina. Therefore a point-for-point representation of the outer world is impressed on the layer of receptor cells on each retina, each layer of the lateral geniculate bodies, and various layers of the primary visual cortex. We remember, too, that other areas of the brain provide linkages between the main projection system and other systems that control eye movements, pupillary responses, joint activity with the vestibular and other senses, and the general level of activation. With these structural systems in mind we may now turn to such questions as, what kinds of spatial interaction take place between separate points? How accurately is each point localized in relation to other points? How fine is the "grain" of the picture in terms of our discrimination of fine details? What processing of information may occur to enhance the significant features of the visual scene and suppress less significant aspects?

Spatial Interaction

The retina, having an extended photosensitive surface on which an optical image is formed, has been compared to the film of a camera. However, there is abundant evidence that the retina does much more than convert patterns of light into corresponding patterns of optic nerve impulses. Consider, for example, what happens when two small patches of light fall on adjacent groups of receptors. The result may be one of spatial summation, in which small patches of dim light might not be seen when turned on separately but can be seen, when turned on simultaneously, as a single large spot of light. This has been amply shown to be the case for points close to one another in the periphery of the human eye (Graham, 1934), where each optic nerve fiber must pool the excitation it receives from an area containing hundreds of rod receptors. The opposite type of interaction, that of spatial inhibition, is clearly present also. For example, strong stimulation of one region may inhibit the responses of adjacent regions so that they appear less bright, and the contrast between them is enhanced.

Spatial summation Of particular interest here is the case of the absolute threshold for vision. In the earlier description of dark adaptation we found that only a few quanta of light are required to stimulate the eye under the most favorable conditions. One of the conditions is that each quantum be absorbed by a rod receptor within a small enough region of the peripheral retina so that complete spatial summation can occur. This is the situation described by Ricco's Law, or the law of reciprocity of area and intensity of light. In its simplest form, the law states that the absolute threshold for vision is a critical energy of light (E_c), representing the

product of luminance (L) and area (A), or

$$E_c = kAL$$

where k is a constant the value of which depends on the units in which energy, area, and luminance are expressed. Experimental determinations (Abney, 1897; Granit, 1930; Graham, 1934; Graham, Brown, & Mote, 1939) have shown that the area of complete summation as described by the Ricco formula in the periphery may be limited to areas smaller than about 20 minutes of arc in diameter. Much larger areas, however (10° or more in diameter), contribute to partial summation. In other

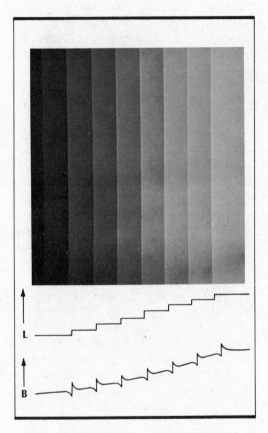

Figure 9.13. Simultaneous brightness contrast. Each strip is actually of uniform luminance (L), as shown in the accompanying graph, but the distribution of perceived brightness (B) is such that the portion of each strip lying near a darker strip appears to be lighter, and vice versa.

words, areas up to that size continue to play a part in the visual threshold, and only for still larger areas is the threshold solely determined by intensity.

The functional significance of spatial summation is that, on a dark night, very dim shapes can be seen if they are rather large; similarly, in daylight, we are aware of the presence of large objects such as automobiles on a cross street that appear to the side of us even when we continue to look straight ahead.

A retinal basis for spatial summation was shown in the pioneer experiments of Adrian and Matthews (1928) on the frequency and latency of nerve impulses in the eye of the conger eel, in the work on single optic nerve fibers in the frog by Hartline (1940a, b), and in the cat by Granit (1947), Kuffler (1952), and Barlow, FitzHugh, & Kuffler (1957). Optic nerve impulses were produced more readily by large patches of light than by small; by patches close together rather than far apart; and by several small patches rather than a single one of the same total area. Interaction effects of this kind were most readily apparent in the fully dark-adapted eye; larger responses were recorded from weak, large-area stimuli than from small-area stimuli of the same luminance. Furthermore, the latency of the response grew shorter as the size of the area illuminated was increased. These facts are consistent with the concept of a receptive field (Hartline, 1940b), the receptive field being the retinal region that includes all the receptors capable of producing a response in a given optic nerve fiber. Neural convergence occurs as the stimulus is passed from the receptors to nerve fibers; the degree of convergence can be enhanced by the application of strychnine, a drug that is known to facilitate synaptic transmission.

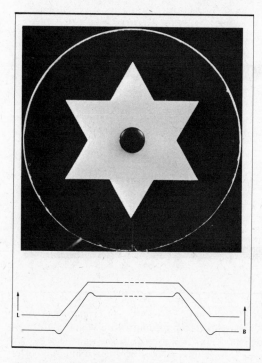 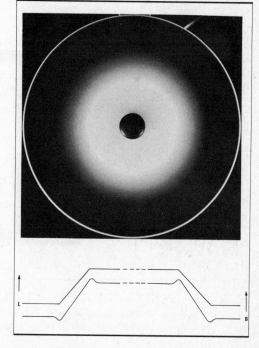

Figure 9.14. *Left:* Star pattern on color wheel used for generating a gradient pattern of luminance. Rapid rotation of the wheel produces the bright and dark Mach bands shown in the right-hand figure. The accompanying graphs show distributions of luminance (*L*) and perceived brightness (*B*) across the horizontal diameter of the color wheel disk (disregarding the black hub of the wheel).

Spatial inhibition Interaction of an inhibitory type is most clearly evident when a relatively high-intensity light is focused at one point on the retina; this acts to depress the activity in a neighboring region. Consider, for example, the series of gray strips in Figure 9.13. The portion of each strip that lies close to a border with a brighter strip looks darker than other portions even though each strip is physically uniform in its composition. Simultaneous contrast and spatial phenomena of greater complexity (see Chapter 13) are undoubtedly dependent in part on the inhibitory effect of strongly excited regions upon less strongly excited ones.

Another example of spatial inhibitory effects is provided by the Mach band phenomenon. This is the subjective appearance of a bright or dark band within a pattern of light that contains no corresponding physical increment or decrement of luminance. A simple procedure for inducing the effect is shown in Figure 9.14. A star-shaped pattern of white paper is placed over a large dark disk and rotated rapidly on a standard color wheel. The resulting physical distribution of light, as shown by line *L* in the accompanying graph, is a solid dark outer ring, a solid white inner ring, and an intermediate zone, produced by the points of the star, in which there is a

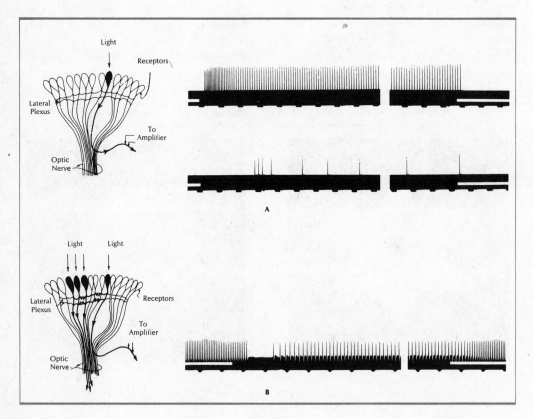

Figure 9.15. Oscillographic records of action potentials in single optic nerve fibers of *Limulus,* the horseshoe crab. A. Response to illumination of a single visual receptor unit with a bright intensity of light (upper record) and with an intensity 4 log units lower (lower record). The signal of exposure to light blackens out the white line above the $\frac{1}{5}$ second time marks. Each record interrupted for about 7 seconds. Records are from Hartline, Wagner, and MacNichol (1952). B. Inhibition of the activity of a steadily illuminated receptor unit produced by illumination of a number of neighboring receptor units. In this record, the blackening of the white line signals the illumination of these neighboring units. The record is from Hartline, Wagner, and Ratliff (1956). (Ratliff, 1965.)

steady change from dark to white. The subjective appearance of the rotating disk is more complex, however. As is shown by line *B* on the graph, it includes a thin, extra-dark ring at the inner edge of the solid dark region and a thin, extra-light ring at the outer edge of the solid bright region.

What causes the dark and light bands? Mach himself (see Ratliff, 1965) pointed out the fact that they occur most readily in regions in which the second derivative of the spatial distribution of luminance has a high value. Such regions are indeed the ones in which the rings mentioned above are seen (see Figure 9.14). The dark outer region of the star has a first derivative (rate of change of luminance over distance) that is zero; the inner white region also has a first derivative of zero. The intermediate zone, however, has a steady change from dark to white. Thus there is an abrupt transition at each edge of this zone, in which the second derivative (change in the rate of change of luminance) is quite large; these are the locations of the two Mach bands.

Mach also speculated on the physiological basis for the bands, believing this to lie in spatial inhibitory effects. However no means were available, at the time he lived, to test this assumption, although a model for explaining spatial inhibition effects now has been provided from the results of experiments on the compound eye of *Limulus*, the horseshoe crab. A single fiber can be dissected free from the rest of the optic nerve (Hartline & Graham, 1932) and records made of its activity (such as that appearing in Figure 9.15). These records illustrate the fact that intensity of excitation is coded as frequency of nerve impulses. This frequency, however, depends not only upon the intensity of light falling on the receptor unit to which the fiber is directly connected, but also upon the activity of neighboring units. In fact. as Figure 9.15 shows, every unit exerts a spatial inhibition over the activity of its neighbors. The effect of this inhibition is to depress the responses of weakly illuminated units more

than those of strongly illuminated ones. An anatomical basis for these inhibitory effects has been found by Hartline, Ratliff, and Miller (1961) in the fact that a plexus of interconnecting neurons lies in the region where the optic nerve fibers emerge from the receptor units.

Ratliff (1962) has shown that the experiments with *Limulus* may serve to explain certain human visual phenomena, if we assume that inhibitory effects take place through the lateral interconnections that are known to be present in the vertebrate retina. This is particularly well illustrated in the Mach band effect. The white inner region in Figure 9.14 illuminates the retina uniformly, so that each retinal region is subjected to direct excitation plus spatial inhibition from neighboring areas. At the outer edge of this white region, however, there is an abrupt drop in the luminance distribution going out into the middle region. At this point, therefore, less spatial inhibition is present. Thus the immediately adjacent portion of the light gray area appears as a bright band, even though no

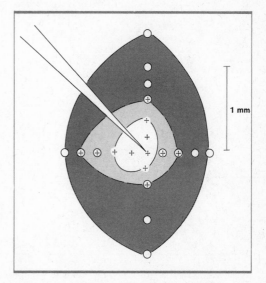

Figure 9.16. Example of a receptive field in a cat retina. A microelectrode placed in contact with a ganglion cell records impulses when a light is turned on at + or off at ○. (Kuffler, 1953.)

physical increase in light intensity can possibly be present. By similar reasoning it is shown that the dark band, appearing even darker than the outer region of uniform darkness, occurs at a point where spatial inhibition is being produced by the higher luminance that is present in the intermediate zone.

Excitatory-inhibitory interactions In the eyes of vertebrates, there appears to be a constant interplay between excitatory and inhibitory neural processes (Granit, 1947). The

basis for this lies in the fact that nerve impulses result not only from the action of light on the receptors, but from its cessation as well. Figure 9.16 shows, for example, the receptive field of a ganglion cell in the retina of a cat. This receptive field is defined as including all the receptors that communicate through bipolar cells with the particular ganglion cell in question. A microelectrode in contact with this ganglion cell records nerve impulses when light falls on retinal receptors situated at one of the points marked "+." No response is recorded when light falls

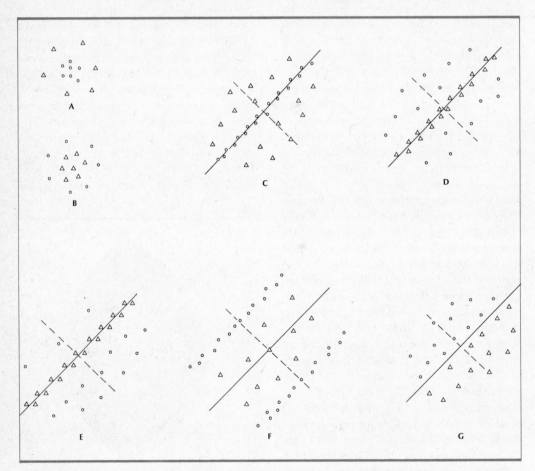

Figure 9.17. Examples of receptive fields of "simple" cells in the lateral geniculate and cortex of the cat. A. *On*-center geniculate receptive field; B. *Off*-center geniculate field; C–G. Various arrangements of "simple" cortical receptive fields: "○" indicates points in the visual field that produce excitatory (*on*) responses in the cell; "△" indicates points in the field that produce inhibitory (*off*) responses. Receptive-field axes are shown by continuous lines through field centers. In the figure these are all oblique, but each arrangement occurs in all orientations. (Hubel & Wiesel, 1962.)

on a spot marked "○" but turning the light off at that spot produces nerve impulses. Furthermore, the "+" and "○" regions inhibit one another; a light directed at a "+" point produces responses that are abolished when a second light is directed at a "○" point. Responses occur each time the light is turned either on or off in the spots marked "⊕." Other ganglion cells are found with the opposite characteristics, namely with *off-sensitivity* at the center and *on-sensitivity* at the outer part of the receptive field. Furthermore, the regions sensitive to the light being on or off inhibit one another; a large patch of light turned on or off over the whole receptive field may therefore stimulate large numbers of receptors but produce little or no response in the ganglion cell to which they are connected. A most effective stimulus is one in which the bright portions of the patch of light fall on regions sensitive to the light's being on at the same time that dark portions fall on regions of the receptive field sensitive to its being off. This, then, is a means of enhancing intensity discrimination; that is, giving the animal a strong visual signal from objects exhibiting a difference in brightness from their backgrounds. Edges and borders, in other words, are emphasized over more uniform visual fields.

A further accentuation of edge and border effects is shown at higher levels in the visual pathways. Hubel and Wiesel (1962) have found that, as in the retina, a single neuron of the lateral geniculate body may respond to the light's being turned on or off at the points defining a concentric pattern (see Figure 9.17A, B). Cortical neurons, most fully explored in the cat, do not show this concentric pattern to a light's being turned on or off. Instead, receptive fields of the kind shown in Figure 9.17C–G are found. These emphasize straight-line borders between the excitatory and inhibitory regions, with various cortical cells showing all possible orientations of the line. It is clear that such an arrangement gives further emphasis to thin lines and sharp borders in the visual field. Furthermore, a line

or edge moving at right angles to its axis of orientation was found to be particularly effective. There is also some specialization, from cell to cell, in the most effective rate and direction of this transverse movement.

Cells of the type just described are called "simple" cortical cells by Hubel and Wiesel. "Complex" and "hypercomplex" cells have also been found, the latter in "associative" areas of the visual cortex. Complex cells are still more specialized, with regard to axis of orientation, than are simple cells. Furthermore, the complex cell has a large receptive field, covering a region of 5 or 10 degrees in width. Thus some complex cells respond to light traveling along lines of a particular orientation, without regard to their specific location within this large receptive field.

A columnar organization of the visual cortex has been found as a result of the Hubel and Wiesel experiments. A microelectrode driven into the cortex to various depths perpendicular to the surface was found to encounter various simple and complex cells with the same axis of orientation. Thus a column of such cells, within a diameter of about 0.5 mm, could be called a functional unit, even though it included cells from six structural layers of the cortex. Furthermore, most of the cells could be excited from either eye, provided that stimuli having the appropriate axis of orientation fell on corresponding points of the two retinas.

There is much evidence that the spatial interactions described above for the cat may hold rather widely for other animals. In lower animals, however, the higher visual centers may not be sufficiently well developed to mediate such activity, and specialization may occur at an earlier (retinal) level. In the octopus, for example, both orientation and direction of movement are preferentially established for single optic nerve fibers (Tomita et al., 1968). Lettvin et al. (1959) attribute to the ganglion cells of the frog a preferential responding to at least five types of stimulus pattern. The goldfish (Wagner, MacNichol, & Wolbarsht, 1960; Cronly-Dillon, 1964; Daw,

1967), the ground squirrel (Michael, 1966), and the pigeon (Maturana & Frenk, 1963) are animals exhibiting highly developed cone vision with elaborate specialization of function in cells of the retina and optic tectum.

Binocular Interaction

The fact that the same cortical cells are activated by stimulation of either eye alone raises many interesting questions. A seemingly simple case is that of binocular summation at the level of the absolute threshold. We have seen that about 100 quanta of 505 nm light are required, under the most favorable conditions, barely to stimulate the dark-adapted eye. If binocular summation were complete, one might expect to reach the same result by delivering 50 quanta to each eye. This is clearly not the case, as many experiments have shown (see Pirenne, 1948; Graham, 1965). However it turns out that there is some advantage to be gained in the use of two eyes, for in this case threshold is reached when fewer than 100 quanta are delivered simultaneously to each of the two eyes. We must not jump to the conclusion, however, that this finding proves that binocular summation is taking place somewhere within the visual pathways. Instead it seems to be true that most of the advantage in using two eyes is a statistical one. In fact, two eyes are better than one even when they are not in the same head!

The statistical advantage of "binocular" vision can easily be seen from the following considerations. Let us say that when one eye is momentarily exposed to a given patch of light about 100 quanta enter the eye and the probability of detecting the flash is 50 percent. The probability of its not being detected is also 50 percent. If the same is true for an exposure of the other eye to the same patch of light, then the combined probability that the light will not be detected by either eye is 50 percent × 50 percent = 25 percent. In other words, the statistical probability that either or both of the two eyes will see the light is 75 percent. We may thus reduce the

number of quanta delivered to each eye until we reach the "binocular" threshold condition in which there will be a 50 percent probability that the flash will be detected. In other words, the RL for light is lower when two eyes are used to view a given patch of light than when one alone is used, and this is true whether the detection of the light is reported by one person using both eyes or by two people using one eye apiece.

An experiment by Matin (1962) leads to the conclusion that the binocular probability of seeing is greater than one would expect from the statistical considerations alone that were made above. This the author attributes to true neural summation in a pathway common to the two eyes. The effect is not a large one and comes about only under conditions in which corresponding retinal locations in the two eyes are used and certain statistical requirements are satisfied.

It is certainly true that there is less summation from the responses of the two eyes than there is from the responses of the two ears. Does this mean that there is little advantage in having two eyes instead of one? It is true that persons blind in one eye appear

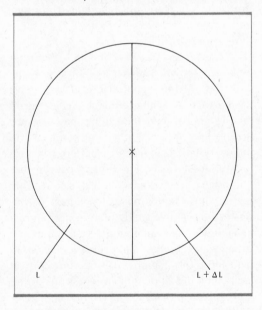

Figure 9.18. Bipartite field for use in determining the increment threshold.

to get along quite well, even to the extent of judging visual directions and distances. However the following points should be kept in mind. (1) Higher animals all have two eyes; lower forms may have six or more. One obvious advantage of having two or more eyes for survival is the fact that the animal can still see if one eye is damaged or destroyed. (2) The field of view is greater (in some animals indeed there is 360° coverage) if one eye is located on each side of the head. (3) Man and a few other animals have true binocular vision in the sense that the visual fields of the two eyes are superimposed in the projection areas of the brain.

Some of the resulting functions of binocular vision are discussed later notably in connection with eye movements (conjugate and vergent, pp. 375–384), stereoscopic depth discrimination (pp. 482–494), and binocular fusion and rivalry (pp. 488–489).

INTENSITY DISCRIMINATION

We can see from the discussion above that the visual system is well equipped to discriminate the edges and borders of various objects that fall within the visual field. The basis for this is intensity discrimination, one of the important functions studied by the methods of psychophysics. A convenient way of studying intensity discrimination is to make use of a bipartite field such as appears in Figure 9.18. The large circular field is presented, having luminance L. While the subject is fixating at the center of the field, a flash of light of luminance ΔL is added to one half of the field. By varying the value of ΔL it is possible to find an increment threshold, ΔL_c, namely the value for which the subject reports that he sees the added flash about 50 percent of the time.[1] The value of ΔL_c represents the difference limen, and $\Delta L_c/L$ is the

[1]A more sophisticated way of doing the experiment would be to use a forced choice procedure, that is, to add the light in random order to the left side or the right side of the field, and to determine the value of ΔL_c for which the subject correctly judges the side about 75 percent of the time (see Chapter 2).

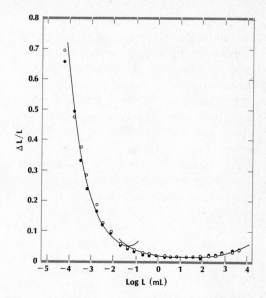

Figure 9.19. Intensity discrimination as a function of luminance. Data from König (open circles) and Brodhun, 1889 (solid circles). Separate curves have been fitted to the high-and low-luminance portions. (After Hecht, 1934.)

Weber ratio. Experiments by König and Brodhun (1889); Hecht, Peskin, and Patt (1938); and Graham and Kemp (1938) have shown that the Weber ratio is not constant, but depends upon numerous parameters such as the size and duration of the increment patch and, most importantly, the value of L, the background intensity (see Figure 9.19). Intensity discrimination is poor in the scotopic range, but the Weber ratio approaches the extraordinarily low value of .01 under the most favorable photopic conditions.

The accuracy of photopic intensity discrimination permits its use in photometry, as is described in connection with Figure 9.4. Accuracy of this kind is only possible, however, with repeated observations by skilled observers, using fields that do not differ greatly in hue or saturation. Flicker photometry (see pp. 312–313) can better be used when qualitative differences in hue and saturation are large. Incidentally, meteorologists have adopted a value of 2 percent as standard for $\Delta L/L$ observations in the field. The meteorological range, for example, is defined as that distance through the atmosphere for which the luminance of a large dark mass (such as a mountain) is 2 percent lower than the luminance of a large bright background (such as the sky).

We may speak of the *contrast* between supra-threshold differences in intensity between two fields. Contrast is conveniently defined by the ratio $\Delta L/(L + \Delta L)$, where ΔL is the intensity difference and $L + \Delta L$ is the intensity of the brighter field. It is clear that this contrast ratio approaches unity for maximum intensity differences, whereas a value of about .01 to .02 is found under favorable conditions as the intensity difference threshold is approached.

VISUAL ACUITY

We have reviewed some of the principles underlying our ability to register spatial aspects of the visual scene. We now turn to the topic of visual acuity, by which is meant the precision with which we can see fine details of the scene. With good acuity we can, for example, see separate stars in the night sky, read signs along a roadway, or identify distant aircraft.

Specification of Acuity

Visual acuity is given a quantitative basis by determining the smallest test object that can be seen by the observer. The familiar eye-test chart, for example, provides letters of various sizes to be read by an observer from a standard distance. In terms of the diagram in Figure 9.6, the width S of lines composing the letters on each line of the chart is reduced until a threshold is reached such that the letters are no longer correctly identified. At this point we may designate the angular threshold β in minutes of arc subtended by S at the eye of the observer. A conventional statement of acuity is then given as the reciprocal of β; for example, a visual acuity of 1.00 designates the ability to see letters having a line width of 1 minute of arc at the standard distance, usually 20 ft. An alternative state-

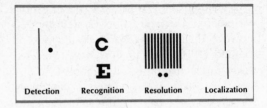

Figure 9.20. Four types of acuity test. (Riggs, 1965c.)

ment of acuity, based on the same standard, is the ratio between the standard viewing distance and the distance at which the smallest test object would subtend an angle of 1 minute of arc. Thus the eye is said to have an acuity of 20/40 or 50 percent if the observer, at a distance of 20 ft from the chart, can only see letters that would subtend an angle of 1 minute of arc at a distance of 40 ft. Persons with very good vision may have acuity ratings as high as 200 percent, or 20/10. In some states a person is called "legally blind" if his best acuity is as low as 5 percent, or 20/400.

Types of Acuity Task

Although the eye chart is a useful device for clinical purposes, it represents only one particular kind of acuity task. The various forms of acuity may conveniently be designated as those involving the detection, recognition, resolution, or localization of the test object. Figure 9.20 gives samples of these various aspects of acuity.

Detection To detect an object, the observer simply judges its presence or absence in a visual field. It can be shown that this judgment is a form of intensity discrimination, for the effect of such a test object as a dark line or dot (Figure 9.20) is to cause a change ΔL in the luminance of one region of the visual field. Observers are extraordinarily good at the detection of a single dark line, perhaps in part because of the action of cortical cells with straight-line axes of orientation (as in Figure 9.17). The threshold width of such a line is about 0.5 second of arc (Hecht & Mintz, 1939).

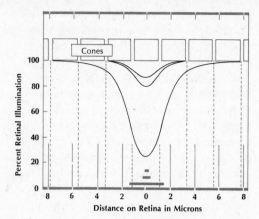

Figure 9.21. Patterns of retinal illumination produced by three widths of black line viewed against a bright field. Actual line widths in units of micrometers (1 $\mu = 10^{-6}$ meter) are shown by solid lines at the base of the figure. Blocks at the top of the figure represent the spacing of the finest cone receptors at the center of the fovea (see Figure 9.8, p. 280). (Hecht & Mintz, 1939.)

The optical phenomenon of diffraction must be considered in relation to problems of detection. Diffraction is an effect due to interference of light waves entering the eye through different parts of the pupil. Because of diffraction, a single point of light is focused on the retina not as a point but as a pattern consisting of a central disk of light surrounded by a series of dark and light rings. The image of a fine line has a width, on the retina, that is typically greater than 30 seconds of arc, no matter how fine the original line used in the test object is. Calculations based on the physical diffraction of light (Byram, 1944) reveal that the retinal image of such a fine line is degraded into a band that is less than 5 percent darker than the surrounding uniform field (Figure 9.21). In other words the line is detected on the basis of intensity discrimination that is nearly as fine as that which is measured with the ideal situation of a bipartite field.

Recognition Figure 9.20 illustrates the task of recognizing a letter E, such as that which appears in a standard eye chart (Snel-

len, 1862; Cowan, 1928) and a broken ring of the kind used by Landolt (1889). The task involves not only brightness discrimination, but some degree of resolution, and localization as well. It may therefore be considered a sort of overall procedure for testing acuity, particularly convenient in the clinical practice of ophthalmologists and optometrists.

Resolution By resolution is meant the ability to discriminate a separation between elements of a visual pattern. Resolution may be measured by presenting a subject with two black dots and determining when he can see them as two rather than one (Figure 9.20) (which is a task similar to that used to measure two-point resolution in the sense of touch). The multiple-line grating pattern is perhaps the most widely used device for testing optical performance, not only that of vision but also of instruments such as the camera or telescope. At best, the eye can resolve a grating in which the line widths are about 35 to 40 seconds of arc (Shlaer, 1937), that is, about 70 to 80 times as wide as a single line that can be detected. This kind of performance is only attained at high levels of intensity with light and dark lines of high contrast.

Modulation transfer functions Engineers have developed methods for measuring the overall efficiency of an optical instrument. The basic principle is to evaluate the image formed by the instrument in comparison with the original test pattern. A camera or telescope, for example, forms a nearly perfect image of a coarse grating. Thus the contrast between the bright and dark lines of the grating is nearly the same in the image as in the original pattern. When tested with a fine grating, however, the optical system forms an image of lower contrast than the original. If an extremely fine grating is used, the performance may become so poor that it fails altogether to transfer the pattern of the original test object to the optical image. The difference in the contrast maintained in the image by the instrument and the contrast that exists in the test pattern may be measured and is referred to as modulation transfer. The fineness of the test pattern is expressed in units of spatial frequency, such as the number of bright lines per angular degree subtended by the test pattern at the location of the

instrument. It is then possible to construct, for any instrument, a modulation transfer function (MTF) in which the contrast ratio is plotted as a function of spatial frequency.

To adapt the MTF principle to tests of human visual acuity, test gratings with lines of differing thickness and differing contrast are employed. One can then determine the contrast thresholds of the eye to detect each line of the various gratings. An example of visual contrast data is shown in Figure 9.22. Thus when the lines of the grating are wide, grating resolution can occur even when there is little contrast between the lines. When the lines of the grating are very fine, however, there must be a much greater contrast between them before they can be resolved. As we see below, the effects of optical aberrations and diffraction are such that the retinal image of a fine (high-frequency) grating has a much lower degree of contrast than does the grating itself. Thus diffraction also accounts for the great discrepancy that we have just noted in the threshold widths of line for single-line and multiple-line (grating) tests of visual acuity.

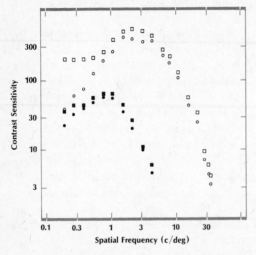

Figure 9.22. Visual acuity defined in terms of contrast sensitivity for bright and dark lines of grating test objects. The ordinate is the contrast sensitivity, defined as the reciprocal of the contrast thresholds determined for subject FWC, where contrast is defined as the modulation (m) of light, that is,

$$m = \frac{L_{\max} - L_{\min}}{2L_{av}}$$

This definition, based as it is on the maximum, minimum, and average values of luminance in the grating, differs slightly from the earlier definition of contrast given on page 298. The abscissa specifies the fineness of the grating, expressed as the frequency in cycles (or number of dark lines) per degree of visual angle. Data are for square-wave (□,■) gratings, such as the one appearing in Figure 9.20, and for sine-wave gratings (○,●) having an average luminance of 160 mL (□,○) and .016 mL (■,●). Compare the effects of luminance with those shown in Figure 9.24. Note also the approximate equivalence of square-wave and sine-wave gratings at all moderate to high spatial frequencies. (Campbell & Robson, 1968.)

Localization The relative positions of two lines in space may be judged by the use of the vernier offset test figure shown in Figure 9.20. The task is one of distinguishing whether the upper vertical line is to the right or left of the lower, and the barely discriminable offset is found to be about 2 seconds of arc (Wright, 1942; Berry, 1948). It is evident from vernier acuity data that the observer not only sees very fine details in the visual scene but also is capable of extremely fine discrimination of the relative positions of objects. Binocular displacements of this kind form the basis for stereoscopic depth discrimination, a topic presented in detail in Chapter 13.

Basic Determiners of Acuity

Important factors to consider in relation to visual acuity are the fineness of the mosaic of retinal receptors, the size of the pupil, the luminance and contrast of the test object, the exposure time of the test object, and the effects of eye movements.

The retinal mosaic   We have seen that the cone receptors at the center of the human fovea are slender and tightly packed together in a mosaic such as that displayed in Figure 9.8. The distance between cones on the retina is about 2.2 μ and represents a visual angle of about 23 seconds of arc. We may well ask whether this value, small as it is, places a limit on visual acuity. Helmholtz (1909–1911) argued that the lines of a grating could only be resolved if its bright lines were far enough apart so that an unstimulated row of cones could lie between them. Present evidence from a variety of sources suggests, however, that no such simple relationship holds. Indeed, it now seems that acuity would not be greatly improved if the eye were equipped with an even finer receptor mosaic.

We have seen that the eye can detect a single line even when its width is only 0.5 seconds of arc (a small fraction of the inter-cone distance). This is possible because the retinal image of the line is so spread out by diffraction that it causes only a slight darkening to occur on a large number of cone receptors. In this case, then, we may conclude that there would be no advantage in having receptors of smaller diameter.

There may appear to be a problem in accounting for the fact that fine lines appear subjectively to be straight and sharp. Perhaps this is not really a problem, for we may see lines that are physically straight and sharp that way even though an intervening stage in our perception of them may involve a blurred and irregular pattern of stimulation on relatively coarse retinal receptors. For the task of localization, a rather similar situation may hold. A vernier offset of 2 seconds of arc can be observed on the basis of signals from receptors the centers of which are separated by more than 10 times that distance. We know that a large number of receptors must take part, in order for such localization to be

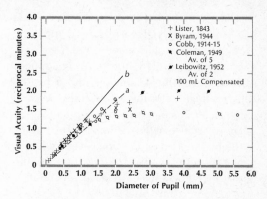

Figure 9.23. The effect of pupil diameter on visual acuity. Lines *a* and *b* are for the predictions made by Rayleigh and Dawes, respectively, with regard to the effects of diffraction of light. (Riggs, 1965c.)

effective. Hering (1899) realized that an "averaging process" might act to fill the gaps between separate receptor elements, and this idea was elaborated into a "retinal mean local sign" hypothesis by Andersen and Weymouth (1923), taking account of the possible effects of diffraction and eye movements. Just as, in statistics, a mean can be determined quite accurately for a large number of relatively variable individual measurements, so a line may appear to have sharpness and a definite location in spite of the irregularity and fuzziness of its image on the retina. For tasks of recognition and resolution, we can show (see below) that visual acuity is approximately as high as would be predicted from the known effects of diffraction in degrading the retinal image. We must therefore conclude that the receptor mosaic is already fine enough so that adequate spatial signaling can occur, and therefore no great improvement in acuity would result if a still finer mosaic were present.

Size of pupil   A number of experimental determinations have been made of acuity with various pupillary diameters. Figure 9.23 shows some of the data. Artificial pupils have been placed before the eye to obtain diameters less than 2 mm, and mydriatic drugs have been used to obtain large pupils in some of these experiments. It is clear from the data that acuity is fairly linearly related to pupillary diameter up to a value of about 1 mm. A small improvement occurs if the pupil is opened to somewhat larger diameters, but a nearly constant high value of acuity holds over a range of 2.5 to 5 mm, which is approximately the normal range of the diameter of the pupils for high to moderate photopic levels of luminance. In other words, the diameter of the pupil does not appear to have much of a practical effect on visual acuity.

It may be of interest, however, to inquire into the reasons why acuity bears the relation it does to size of pupil. The nearly constant level of acuity with normal variations in the pupil can in fact be attributed to a balance between favorable and unfavorable consequences of increasing the pupillary aperture. Favorable factors are those of allowing more light to enter the eye and reducing the effects of the diffraction of light. Unfavorable are the effects of optical aberrations, the effects of which are much more serious as the effective diameter of the optical system of the eye is increased.

If the optics of the eye were perfect, diffraction alone would result in a linear increase of acuity with pupillary diameter. This is because the size of a diffraction pattern is inversely related to the diameter of the pupil. This is the major limiting factor for acuity with pupillary diameter of 1 mm or less, as shown by the linear portion of the data at the left of Figure 9.23.

Because the eye is not a perfect optical instrument, it suffers from optical aberrations of various kinds. They all have in common the fact that rays of light emanating from a single point, but entering the eye through different parts of the pupil, are not brought to one point on the retina, causing distortion of the image. The distortion becomes worse as the diameter of the pupil increases; this is probably the main reason why the acuity values in Figure 9.23 do not continue to rise along a straight line throughout the graph.

Perhaps it is surprising, in view of the seriousness of optical aberrations, that acuity does not decline sharply with large increases in pupillary diameter. A possible explanation lies in the Stiles-Crawford effect. Stiles and Crawford (1933) discovered that light rays entering the eye through the center of the pupil (see Figure 9.5) stimulate the cone receptors much more efficiently than do rays entering the eye through the edges of the pupil. They were able to show that the effect is due to a directional sensitivity of the individual receptors. We have seen that the foveal cones are long and slender (Figure 9.8). Also, each cone is typically oriented in the direction of the center of the pupil; thus a ray of light reaching it from that direction is funneled straight through its base and into the outer segment containing the photosensitive pigment of the cone. Rays from the edges of the pupil hit the cone at such an angle that they are less likely to reach the outer segment where they could have an effect. Thus a large-sized pupil has far less influence on acuity than it might have if it were not for the directional sensitivity of the cones. We may therefore regard the Stiles-Crawford effect as maintaining good acuity with large pupillary apertures, in the face of the serious aberrations that are present for rays passing through outer portions of the pupil.

Rod receptors do not appear to show the same directional sensitivity as the cones. Hence, for scotopic vision, the eye receives the full benefit of a dilated pupil at the lowest light levels. The normal pupil exhibits an area change of about 16 to 1, going from a 2 mm diameter at high intensities of light to an 8 mm diameter in complete darkness; this factor contributes to the increased sensitivity of the eye that takes place during dark adaptation, but the contribution of the pupil is small by comparison with the photochemical and neural factors that we have already found to provide a much greater change of sensitivity.

Light intensity One of the most well-known facts about acuity is that it is affected by the intensity of light. By starlight we can

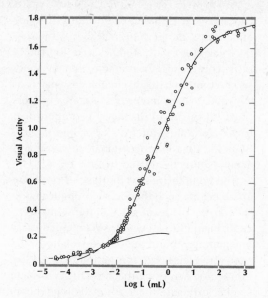

Figure 9.24. Visual acuity as a function of luminance. Separate curves have been fitted to the rod (low-luminance) and cone (high-luminance) portions of the data. (Hecht, 1934.)

see the white page of a book, but not the writing on it; note that this is in the low scotopic luminance range of about .0001 mL (see Table 9.1). Although we can begin to discern separate letters by moonlight, at .01 mL, reading the text does not become comfortable until photopic vision fully predominates, at about 10 mL. Acuity continues to improve as light intensity is further increased, especially when test objects of low contrast are involved.

Figure 9.24 shows the dependence of acuity on intensity, over a wide range of experimental values. In the scotopic range (below .01 millilambert) acuity is poor; it rises only slightly as the intensity of stimulation is increased. This is consistent with the fact that scotopic vision is extrafoveal. The rod receptors, though sensitive to very dim light, are relatively far apart and, as we have seen, combine over a wide region to signal their activity to only a relatively small number of optic nerve fibers. Figure 9.24 shows that acuity improves rapidly as the intensity of the light is increased to the point that photopic

vision can be relied upon and the fovea comes into play. This is easily understood in terms of the fineness in the central fovea of the retinal mosaic and the fact that each cone has ample representation in the fibers of the optic nerve (Polyak, 1941; Vilter, 1949). Less easily interpreted is the fact that acuity continues to rise as intensity is raised far beyond the range of optimal intensity discrimination (compare Figures 9.18 and 9.24). This must mean that stimuli of small dimensions, such as those used for acuity test objects, can be fully discriminated only at intensity levels above those for large test fields such as those used to measure intensity discrimination. One can perhaps assume that optimal discrimination of either type requires the achievement of differentiation of large numbers of excitatory and inhibitory signals; with small test objects this requirement can only be met at high intensity levels, since the number of input channels is limited; larger objects can meet it by supplying fewer signals over each channel, since a larger number of channels are available. Whether or not this hypothesis has any merit, we find it to be consistent with some data of Graham and Bartlett (1940). They show that intensity discrimination in the fovea remains fairly constant over a wide intensity range except for their smallest stimulus patch (of 2 min arc radius), for which intensity discrimination continues to improve as higher and higher intensities are used.

Exposure time   In a later consideration of temporal aspects of vision, we note that a fundamental law of photochemistry, the Bunsen-Roscoe Law, is obeyed if the eye is exposed to light for short periods of time. The data of Sperling and Jolliffe (1965) show, in line with several earlier studies, that the energy of the light necessary for the detection of a small bright disk is constant for all short times (t) of exposure, where energy is the product of time and luminance (L) in agreement with the Bunsen-Roscoe Law. Detection of thin-line targets is similarly in agreement with the law (Niven & Brown,

1944; Bouman, 1953; Keesey, 1960). In each of these studies, however, a critical duration t_c is found above which the law no longer applies. Finally, at very long durations, intensity alone determines the threshold for detection. Values of t_c ranging from .01 sec (Martin, Day, & Kaniowski, 1950) to over .2 sec are found, depending on intensity level and acuity task.

Spatial factors also influence the dependence of acuity on exposure time. In fact, the total energy of light in a test stimulus is governed not only by intensity and exposure time, but also by the area, A, of the test object. For all small area and time values reciprocity extends to the area dimension so that the threshold energy E_c is given by the relation

$$E_c = A \cdot L \cdot t$$

This relationship holds generally for a variety of test objects, as is illustrated in studies by Blackwell (1946), Long (1951), and Davy (1952).

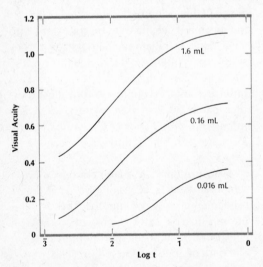

Figure 9.25. Visual acuity as a function of log exposure time (t in seconds). Grating test objects were used and the acuity was defined as a reciprocal of the width of line (minutes of arc of visual angle). Three different luminance values, 1.6, .16, and .016 mL, were used respectively for top, middle and bottom curves. (Graham & Cook, 1937.)

Riggs (1965c) has pointed out that linear dimensions, rather than area, specify the spatial magnitudes of stimuli used for acuity tests. This means, for example, that an acuity score computed for a circular test patch at a given constant intensity (with area proportional to square of diameter) is proportional to $t^{1/2}$ for values of $t < t_c$. For line targets, however, area is proportional to width, and acuity is directly related to t for $t < t_c$.

The complexities of the task of resolving an object are such that no such simple analysis can be made of all the steps involved. Graham and Cook (1937), using high-contrast line gratings, found the sigmoid relationships shown in Figure 9.25 for the influence of log t on acuity. Acuity approaches a high constant level as exposure times are made long; however if the eye is exposed to a light stimulus for a short period of time, acuity becomes as strongly dependent on log t as on log L (compare Figure 9.24).

Schober and Hilz (1965) and Nachmias (1967) have included square-wave grating targets of varying contrast in their studies of resolution in relation to exposure time. This has permitted them to derive threshold contrast functions, as in Figure 9.22, for various values of exposure time.

It is tempting to draw the conclusion (no doubt oversimplified) that one good look at a test target is sufficient for seeing it with maximum acuity. The duration of the best "look" must be greater than t_c, but it need not be longer than one or two tenths of a second at daylight levels of luminance.

Eye movements   In Chapter 11 it is made clear that one of the chief functions of eye movements is to direct the gaze onto objects that are of significance in the visual field. The image of an object is thus brought to the center of the fovea. The observer then attempts to keep his eyes fixed on the object, that is, to keep the image at this optimal location long enough to see it with good acuity, which we have just concluded is an interval of .1 or .2 seconds.

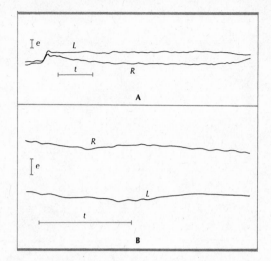

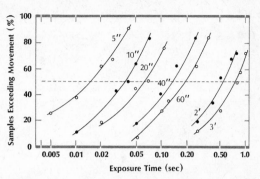

Figure 9.27. Sample data on the extent of involuntary eye movements during various exposure intervals. The ordinate scale is for the percentage of records exhibiting an amount of movement designated beside each curve. The abscissa is the length of record sample (that is, the time interval over which the extent of eye movement was determined). (Riggs, Armington, & Ratliff, 1954.)

Figure 9.26. Involuntary eye movements during attempted steady fixation. Upper records (A) show one "flick" or saccadic movement, well coordinated in the two eyes, and numerous uncoordinated, rapid tremor motions, as well as a slow drift of the eye. Lower records (B) show an enlarged section of A. The length of the line e represents 100 seconds of angular rotation of the eye; length of t is 0.1 second of time. Record L is from the left eye; R is from the right. (Riggs & Ratliff, 1951.)

We must now ask some more questions: Can the eye be held still during this fixational pause, or are there involuntary movements even when steady fixation is attempted? If such movements exist, how large are they and what effect do they have on acuity?

The eye movement records of Ratliff and Riggs (1950), Ditchburn and Ginsborg (1953), Riggs, Armington, and Ratliff (1954), Krauskopf, Cornsweet, and Riggs (1960), Rashbass and Westheimer (1961), and Robinson (1963) are of particular relevance here. In each case, the experimenter attached a tightly fitting contact lens to the eye that supports a mirror or other device that can be used to indicate the extent of the movements of the eye (see Chapter 11). Furthermore, the observer is given a clear fixation point and told to try to keep his eyes fixed on it. The eyes, however, are by no means motionless, as may be seen from the records shown in Figure 9.26. A

sampling of measurements on such records gives the information displayed in Figure 9.27. These measurements show, for example, that the retinal image may be considered stationary only for .02 second. During .1 second exposures the image occasionally exhibits a total excursion of 1 minute of arc or more, but typically the image shifts less than half that much. Considered in relation to the data on acuity versus exposure time, given in the preceding section, we therefore have the question: Is acuity importantly affected by image motions of about a half minute of arc?

Various "dynamic" theories of acuity (Andersen & Weymouth, 1923; Marshall & Talbot, 1942) have pointed out that small eye movements permit a given portion of the retinal image to be scanned by the individual cone receptors. They have assumed that such scanning may sharpen the perception of a border or point in much the same way that the moving fingertips of blind people scan the raised pattern of letters in Braille. An opposite assumption is made if we say that the eye, like a camera, must be perfectly steady if blurring due to the motion of the image of the test object is to be prevented. How can we test visual acuity in the absence

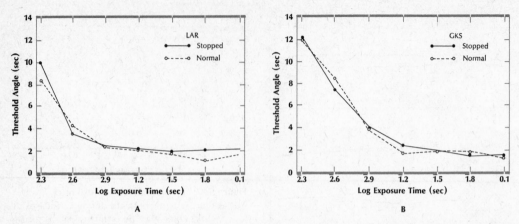

Figure 9.28. Threshold curves for the detection of single black lines under normal viewing conditions and under conditions in which retinal image motion is stopped. (Keesey, 1960.)

of image motion? Can we find a way to clamp the eyeball, or paralyze the eye muscles? Perhaps; but a less hazardous solution to the problem has been developed by applying optical techniques (Ditchburn & Ginsborg, 1952; Riggs & Ratliff, 1952) for producing a *stabilized retinal image*. (These techniques are described in detail in Chapter 11.) They depend for their accuracy on a careful attention to experimental details such as the quality of the optics, clearness of the fixation point, and the careful fitting of a contact lens to support a mirror on the eye. When these conditions are met, the remaining errors of stabilization of the image are not of great visual significance (Riggs & Schick, 1968). It therefore becomes possible to test visual acuity in the absence of image motion.

A direct comparison of acuity with and without motions of the retinal image was made by Keesey (1960). She studied three types of acuity (single-line detection, grating resolution, and vernier offset localization) for exposure times ranging from .02 to 1.28 seconds. A sample of the data is shown in Figure 9.28, where it may be seen that the acuity thresholds are nearly the same whether normal image motion is taking place or whether it is stopped by the technique of optical stabilization. The evidence of these experiments is clearly against any improvement in acuity as a result of scanning of a moving image.

Stereoscopic acuity was found by Shortess and Krauskopf (1961) to be unaffected, also, by normal image motion over a wide range of exposure times.

It is true that the test objects used in the above experiments were all of high contrast, and the possibility exists that vision for low-contrast borders may somehow be improved by image motion. It must also be remembered that image motion is required for the prolonged maintenance of vision; the stabilized image condition results in a sort of functional blindness in which patterns fade and eventually disappear from view (Riggs et al., 1953; see Chapter 11). But we may conclude, on present evidence, that eye movements during a fixational pause are normally too small to have any significant effect on visual acuity as it is usually measured.

TEMPORAL ASPECTS OF VISION

The time dimensions of single and multiple visual stimuli are effective perceptually, and measurements of latent times for visual responses are useful indices of the underlying sensory processes.

Temporal Summation

We have already seen that, in the case of visual acuity, the detectability of a stimulus patch of small area (A), luminance (L), and duration (t) is proportional to the total energy (E) of the light. Thus

$$E_c = A \cdot L \cdot t$$

where E_c is the critical amount of light needed, for example, for a detection probability of 50 percent. (This is the statement of the Bunsen-Roscoe Law mentioned above.) The equation has been shown to hold for a wide variety of visual functions in addition to acuity, for exposure times shorter than t_c, a value known as the critical duration of the flash. The value of t_c may be as short as a few milliseconds if the object being looked at is well illuminated, or it may be as long as several hundred milliseconds if it is not so well illuminated. In any case, the significance of the equation is that it defines a state of complete temporal summation or integration. In summary, within the time t_c the degree of stimulation of the eye is directly proportional to the duration of the stimulus.

Above t_c temporal summation falls off. Stimulus strength still rises with some further increase in t, but finally a duration is reached beyond which there is no further effect of time. At supra-threshold levels, summation holds only for very short flashes. Curiously enough, however, moderately short flashes of light may seem brighter than do longer flashes of the same luminance. This is the Broca-Sulzer effect (1902) discussed by Stainton (1928), Baumgardt and Ségal (1947), Bartley, Paczewitz, and Valsi (1957), Boynton (1961), and Hurvich and Jameson (1966). It furnishes a partial explanation for the fact that a flickering stimulus is particularly effective at rates where the separate flashes are of a duration yielding high brightnesses according to the Broca-Sulzer experiments (see below).

Latency Measurements

The initial effect of light, namely the molecular change that the quanta produce in the photopigment, occurs without measurable latency. Estimates of the time it takes to produce photoproducts (see Figure 9.11) are in the microsecond range. Delays of several milliseconds are presumably associated, how-

ever, with processes that take place in the receptor cell after the photoproducts are formed, whereby the photoproducts act in some way to trigger the signal that is passed along to the bipolar cells. Electrical signs of these events have been recorded. Thus an "early receptor potential" (ERP) is recorded when the retina is exposed to the direct rays of an electronic flash discharge tube (Brown & Murakami, 1964; Cone, 1964). This response, occurring without measurable latency, can be elicited even from an isolated retina that has been removed from the eye and consequently been deprived of its oxygen supply and thereby has lost its neural responses (Goldstein, 1967). Similar potentials can be produced, in chloroplasts taken from plant leaves, by intense flashes of light (Ebrey, 1967). In the eye, therefore, the ERP is presumed to reflect the molecular changes occurring in the outer segment of the receptor.

The electroretinogram (ERG) is a response that is relatively easy to record from any eye

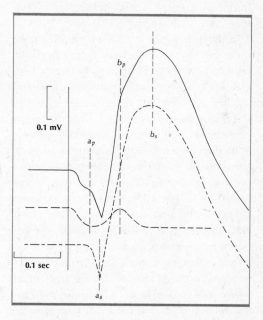

Figure 9.29. Analysis of the photopic (dash line) and scotopic (dot-dash line) components of the electroretinogram of the human eye. The a wave has photopic (a_p) and scotopic (a_s) components, and the b wave similarly has b_p and b_s components. (Armington, Johnson, & Riggs, 1952.)

that is in good metabolic condition (see Granit, 1947, 1955, and 1962; Riggs, 1965a). The ERG can be recorded from a human eye with a contact lens electrode (Riggs, 1941). Figure 9.29 shows an analysis of the human ERG in which an initial a-wave appears with a very short latency, followed by a b-wave that is slower and of opposite polarity. There is considerable evidence to support an early hypothesis of Granit (1947) that the time relations of the a-wave are those of electrical activity in the receptor layer of the retina, whereas the b-waves, which occur later, are the signs of activity at the level of the bipolars. Photopic and scotopic portions of the waves were identified by Adrian (1945, 1946) and later investigators of the human ERG. Modern refinements in technique have permitted the separation of photopic and scotopic ERG activity (Riggs, Johnson, & Schick, 1964, 1966) and have therefore made possible the application of ERG recording to study such photopic functions as spectral sensitivity (Johnson, Riggs, & Schick, 1966), color contrast, and visual acuity.

Judging from the a-wave of the ERG made in response to a moderately bright flash, photopic (cone) receptor activity begins with a latency of only a few milliseconds and reaches a peak in less than 50 msec after the onset of a flash. The scotopic (rod) receptor latency may be 30 msec or longer. Responses at the bipolar level, judging from the b-wave, are some 60 to 100 msec slower than those originating at the receptor level; this is presumably the time consumed by the synaptic delay. At the level of the occipital cortex, electrodes such as those used to record electroencephalograms may be used to pick up potential waves evoked by the activity of neurons in the geniculocalcarine tract or in the various cortical layers. Electrodes used for the recording of human electroencephalograms (EEG) can be used (see Chapter 4) to pick up these responses for latency determinations. Complex wave forms appear that are primarily photopic in origin, with early and late components typically peaking within

about 50 to 150 msec after the onset of moderately strong flash stimulation of the eye (Adrian, 1946).

Experiments on animals have revealed that a major part of the electrical activity of retina and cortex occurs not in the form of nerve impulses (all-or-none spikes) but rather in the form of relatively slow changes (graded membrane potentials) in and around the neurone (see Chapter 4). In the vertebrate retina, for example, microelectrodes have been used to penetrate single cone receptors (Tomita et al., 1967). No evidence is found that the cones are able to generate nerve impulse spikes. Instead the inner portion of each receptor exhibits a generator potential, that is, a change in membrane potential that varies with the intensity of the stimulating light. In other experiments (MacNichol & Svaetichin, 1958) microelectrodes near but outside of receptor cells have been used to record "S-potentials" (see Chapter 10) resulting from the pooled activity of many receptors. These, too, are graded potentials and some of them depend for their size upon the intensity of the stimulus. Others exhibit opposite polarities for contrasting wavelengths of the light. In still other experiments single bipolar and amacrine cells (Werblen, 1968; Kaneko & Hashimoto, 1969) have likewise yielded graded potentials with or without the production of spikes. Finally, the ganglion cells accept the many incoming graded potential forms of response from bipolar and amacrine cells and convert them into true nerve impulses. These are the optic nerve impulses, which travel from the eye to the brain.

One is tempted to compare the retina to an electronic transducer system in which the input signal activates a pattern of 130,000,000 photoreceptor units that feed analog (graded potential) signals into many millions of elements that make up the networks of a miniature computer. The computer analyzes and differentiates these analog signals, enhancing certain of their spatial and temporal properties. Finally, at the output stage, the processed

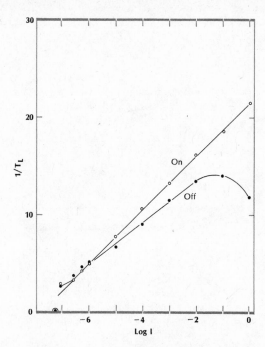

Figure 9.30. The dependence of latency on stimulus intensity in the responses of a single optic nerve fiber of the frog. Reciprocal latencies of on and off responses are plotted as functions of log intensity. (Hartline, 1938.)

analog signals are encoded into digital (nerve impulse) form for efficient transmission along the output cable (optic nerve) to the brain. All of this processing takes place in a sheet of tissue weighing less than a hundredth of an ounce!

Dependence of latency on stimulus parameters The time between the onset of a stimulus and the response recorded from the visual system (the latent time or latency) typically is found to be short if the intensity of the stimulus is high. (Figure 9.30 provides an illustration of the inverse relationship between latent time and log intensity in a single optic nerve fiber of the frog.) The latent time of the response is also inversely related, within limits, to the size of the area stimulated and the duration of the stimulus. Clearly, then, the measurement of latency provides an alternative or supplementary procedure to those psychophysical threshold

procedures used to evaluate the effectiveness of a visual stimulus. In fact it is often true, in the electrical recording of visual responses, that latency measurements are more reliable than measurements of amplitudes of response potential waves or frequencies of nerve impulses.

The simple reaction time of human subjects (see Chapter 4) is one form of latency measure, and like the others, it is inversely related to stimulus intensity. Visual reaction times are commonly reported to reach a minimum of about 150 msec for bright flashes of light, whereas strong cutaneous or auditory stimuli yield reaction times that are 30 to 40 msec shorter. From our analysis of the latencies of response at the various levels in the visual pathways, we may conclude that a significant part of the delay occurs as a result of the processing of signals in the retina. This conclusion is confirmed by experiments such as those of Bartley and Bishop (1933) in the rabbit, and Malis and Kruger (1956) in the cat on direct electrical stimulation of the optic tract. They found that cortical response potential waves have latencies of only a few milliseconds. It is evidently true that the superb spatial analysis that takes place in the eye has been achieved at the cost of many milliseconds' delay in the eliciting of visual responses.

An interesting interaction between spatial and temporal signals to the eye is demonstrated by the so-called "Pulfrich pendulum effect." To cause the effect, one eye is covered with a neutral density filter that allows between 10 and 30 percent of the light to pass through. The other eye is left uncovered. A pendulum is then observed binocularly under good illumination as it swings left and right in a vertical plane. The result is that the observer sees the pendulum as swinging in an elliptical path that seems to carry it nearer and farther from him. The explanation offered by Pulfrich (1922), and further explored by Lit (1949), for the effect is that the weaker stimulation of the covered eye results in a delay, with respect to the other eye, of visual signals indicating the position of the pendulum. Thus the uncovered eye sees the pendulum occupying a position at the middle of its swing, for example, at the same time that the covered eye sees it occupying a slightly earlier position. The disparity in the two eyes is therefore interpreted as a spatial one, even though it is actually a disparity in time. Like any spatial disparity it is interpreted as a change in stereoscopic distance (see Chapter 13); hence the pendulum appears to come closer at the middle of its swing in one direction, and to go farther away when the direction is reversed.

Multiple Flashes

We may recall at this point that a large proportion of the research in vision has been concerned either with more or less continuous illumination of the visual field, or with the presentation of a field illuminated by a single flash. There remains, however, a substantial body of work on the effects of multiple stimulation of the eye. We speak now of various two-flash situations in which the effects of the two flashes interact with one another, or of intermittent light stimuli that commonly result in the perception of flicker.

Two-flash situations Typically, research involving two flashes of light has been concerned with the masking effect that the second flash has upon the response to the first. The term "metacontrast" has been used to denote the situation in which the brightness of a flash is reduced by a second flash that is delivered to an adjacent region of the visual field (Alpern, 1953). The degree of suppression has been shown to vary with the intensity of the second flash and with the time interval that separates the two.

The term "visual masking" is used for a situation in which a test flash falls within the same region that is illuminated by a conditioning flash of light. (A more detailed discussion of two-flash experiments is given in Chapter 12).

An experiment of Crawford (1947) is of

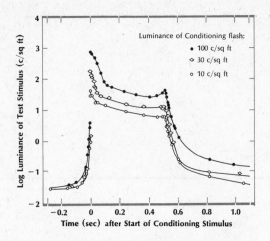

Figure 9.31. Threshold determinations before, during, and after a conditioning flash of light. The ordinate is log luminance threshold for the detection of the test flash. The abscissa is the time relative to the 0.5 second duration of the conditioning flash. (Crawford, 1947.)

particular interest here because it furnishes information about short-term light and dark adaptation. Figure 9.31 presents some of the data. A conditioning stimulus begins at time 0 on the baseline of that figure and remains on for 0.5 sec. A test flash of 0.01 sec duration is presented at various times before, during, and after the conditioning stimulus. On the ordinate is a logarithmic scale of luminance threshold values for the test flash. The various curves show the way in which the threshold value of the test flash is raised by the action of the conditioning stimulus. Paradoxically, the test flash threshold appears to rise *prior* to the onset of the conditioning stimulus. This may be explained, however, by the fact that the conditioning stimulus is so intense that it produces a sensory-neural effect of much shorter latency than that of the weak test flash. Thus the stronger response catches up with the weaker and masks it, even when it was begun at an earlier time. The curves also reveal a large and rapid drop in threshold that takes place at the onset of light adaptation and again at the onset of dark adaptation. These effects have been studied in some detail by Baker (1949, 1963) and by Boynton

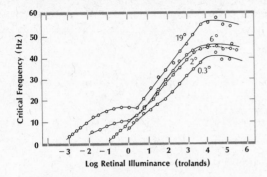

Figure 9.32. The dependence of the critical frequency at fusion on light intensity. (Hecht & Smith, 1936.)

and colleagues (1953, 1954) in the human eye and by Riggs and Graham (1940) in single ommatidia from the eye of *Limulus.*

Flicker: stimulus variables   Modern techniques of stimulus control permit an almost limitless variation in temporal pattern of flashes delivered to the eye. Early experiments were conducted on the temporal resolution for intermittent stimulation, in which the major stimulus variables were the frequency (number of flashes per second), intensity, wavelength composition, and duration of the flashes. The critical response variable was the judgment of "flicker" or "fusion." Flicker is perceived for all low rates of intermittence; fusion is perceived as the frequency is raised to some threshold value known as the *cff,* or critical frequency at fusion. At or above this frequency the light is indistinguishable from a steady light having the equivalent mean luminance L_m, as defined by the Talbot-Plateau Law, as follows:

$$L_m = L_1\left(\frac{t_1}{t_1 + t_d}\right)$$

where L_m is the average over time of the luminance of the flickering field, L_1 is the luminance of each separate flash, t_1 is the duration of each separate flash, and t_d is the duration of the dark interval between flashes.

The dependence of *cff* on luminance is illustrated by the data of Figure 9.32. It is clear from this figure that there are two different portions of the curve if the stimuli are large enough to stimulate both foveal and peripheral regions of the retina. The low-intensity portion of the curve is contributed by the rods. Human photopic resolution rises, at high luminance levels, to approximately 60 flashes per second. Over a middle range of luminances, *cff* rises linearly with log luminance. This is in accordance with the Ferry-Porter Law (see de Lange, 1954; Kelly, 1961), namely that *cff* = *k* log *L* + *C*, where *k* and *C* are constants. At extremely high levels of luminance the Ferry-Porter Law breaks down, and *cff* reaches a plateau or even exhibits a slight decline.

A very extensive literature (see Landis, 1953; Brown, 1965) exists with respect to *cff* under various experimental conditions. Human psychophysical data have been accumulated for the dependence of *cff* on the area of stimulus field, the region of the retina that is stimulated, wavelength composition of the light, and many other stimulus variables. In addition, there have been numerous behavioral and physiological studies of animal vision in which some of the same variables have been explored. Some animals and insects usually active in the daytime are found to have a *cff* well above 120 flashes per second (Autrum, 1958; Devoe, 1962; Kuiper & Leutscher-Hazelhoff, 1965), but nocturnal animals characteristically have a low *cff* (Dodt & Wirth, 1953). In both animal and human subjects, electrical recording at various levels of the visual pathway has shown that the eye itself may respond at higher frequencies than the *cff* determined by behavioral or psychophysical techniques. This leads to the conclusion that temporal resolution is often limited by the brain rather than the eye.

In agreement with the conclusion made above, many studies have shown that *cff* may be used as an index of the physiological functioning of the central nervous system. Fatigue, anoxia, and effects of drugs, state of arousal, and age of the observer are among the factors that have been shown to influence the human *cff* (see Brown, 1965).

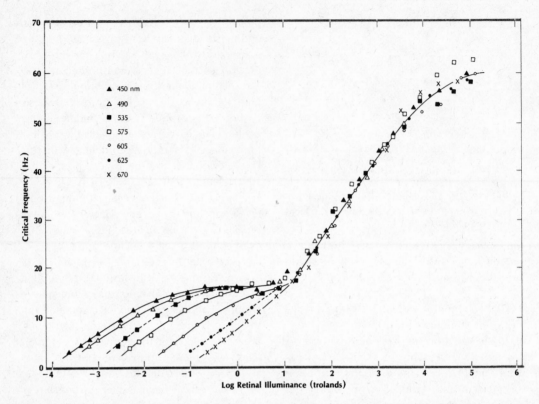

Figure 9.33. The dependence of the critical frequency at fusion on wavelength and the intensity of light. (Hecht & Shlaer, 1936.)

Flicker: wavelength effects Figure 9.33 shows some data of Hecht and Shlaer (1936) in which the *cff* has been determined using light from seven regions of the spectrum. The scale of retinal illuminance was based on a procedure for matching the heterochromatic brightness, carried out at a photopic level of luminance, with comparison fields such as those presented in Figure 9.4. From the figure it is apparent that there is good agreement among the data for various wavelengths, showing that *cff* is primarily dependent on luminance rather than wavelength. The linear portion of the upper curve displays the range over which *cff* is proportional to log luminance, in agreement with the Ferry-Porter Law.

Since the brightness matching was done at photopic levels for Figure 9.33, it is not surprising to find that the various wavelengths have widely differing effectiveness in

the low scotopic range. This is in accord with the Purkinje shift (p. 285) whereby the eye becomes relatively much more sensitive, at scotopic levels, to the short wavelengths of light than to the long. Accordingly, we see an extensive rod-receptor portion of each curve except for the data at the longer wavelengths where, as Figure 9.2 has already shown, the rod and cone receptor sensitivities have nearly the same absolute value. In other words, the 670 nm curve may be taken as an indication of cone sensitivity throughout its entire length, while the 450 nm curve most clearly defines the *cff* function for rods in the portion lying below the level of about 10 trolands.

Flicker: photometry In an earlier section on photometry, we observe that the luminance of a visual field could be measured by the use of a photometer designed to permit a match between the brightness of the unknown field and that of a standard field of adjustable luminance provided by the instrument. The method breaks down, however, when the two fields are very different in color because the observer is unable to find any intensity of the standard white field produced by the instrument that makes it resemble the appearance of an unknown that is red, for example, or blue. A solution to this problem of heterochromatic photometry may be provided using a flicker technique.

A flicker photometer consists of a motor-driven shutter device that presents the observer with a small circular patch first of a standard white and then of a color. At a low rate of alternation the subject sees first one and then the other as separate flashes of light; the white standard is still clearly distinguishable from the color. At a rate of about 15 cycles, however (that is, 30 alternations per second from one to the other) the color difference is markedly reduced even though the flicker rate is still far below the *cff*. Now the observer is asked to manipulate the luminance control of the standard until the flicker is reduced to a minimum. This he can usually do with considerable precision because the large color difference between the alternate flashes is almost completely eliminated. Heterochromatic flicker photometry, then, permits us to establish a luminance level that is more or less equivalent for lights of any wavelength throughout the spectrum.

No firm theoretical basis exists for saying that lights equated by the procedure described above are of the same brightness. In fact, some studies have shown small differences in matches made by the flicker technique and those made by other procedures. In practice, however, flicker photometry is a most valuable aid to the quantitative study of color vision. It may also reinforce the conclusion of many color vision experts (see Chapter 10) that chromatic signals are somehow generated separately from brightness signals in the visual system. In any case, the evidence from flicker photometry is that chro-

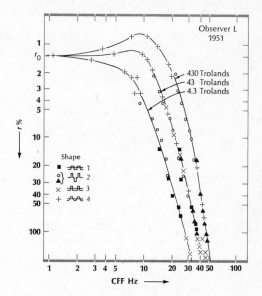

Figure 9.34. Flicker fusion curves defined in terms of the "ripple ratio" at the various frequencies. Note that 4 wave forms were used, as shown in the insert, and that similar functions were found with each of them. (de Lange, 1958.)

matic differences disappear at a lower rate of alternation than do differences in brightness.

Flicker: modulation transfer functions   So far in our consideration of flicker we have confined our discussion to the classic procedure of using rectangular flashes of light, that is, flashes obtained by the use of some sort of shutter that turns the light completely on and off. As early as 1922, however, Ives obtained data on the perception of flicker in response to various nonrectangular wave forms of periodic light stimuli. He came to the conclusion, confirmed by later investigators, that *cff* depends primarily on the frequency rather than the wave form of the stimulating flashes.

Modern work on flicker has greatly benefited from the use of temporal modulation transfer functions (MTF) that are analogous to the spatial MTF that we have already considered on page 299. The application to flicker is illustrated by Figure 9.34, taken from the work of de Lange (1958). The insert in this figure depicts the wave forms employed in these experiments, each one being a plot of luminance (ordinate) versus time (abscissa). In each case, a steady field of light is made alternately brighter or dimmer by some device, other than a simple shutter, that can produce any desired temporal sequence of intensity changes. The intensity variation can range all the way from the classic case of total on and off to small increments and decrements superimposed on the average level of luminance. (The term *amplitude modulation,* borrowed from the field of electronic engineering, is used to designate the change in light intensity.) In Figure 9.34, the ordinate scale designates the degree of modulation in terms of *r*, the *ripple ratio.* This is the ratio of the fundamental wave component of the fluctuation of light, at each frequency, to the mean light intensity. It is therefore analogous in regard to flicker, but not precisely equal, to the Weber ratio $\Delta L/L$ that is used in experiments on brightness discrimination. The abscissa in Figure 9.34 is a logarithmic scale of critical frequency at fusion.

Notice that *r* in Figure 9.34 has a value of about 1.35 percent for very low frequencies of flicker, where the stimulus may be thought of as a series of minimal flashes added to a steady background. This value is in the range of the Weber ratios of 1 to 2 percent that we encountered in Figures 9.19 and 9.22 for brightness discrimination and acuity data.

As the frequency is increased, it is necessary to provide greater and greater amplitudes of modulation in order for the observer to detect the flicker. The value of *r* rises to a level of 100 percent or more for various wave shapes including that of simple on–off flashes of light with no background (shape No. 1 in the insert of the figure). Notice that

the highest ripple ratios permit the *cff* to rise to a value of 30 to 50 flashes per second (see Figure 9.33) depending on retinal illuminance. The curves in Figure 9.34 are photopic temporal resolution threshold functions. They provide a convenient summary of the temporal resolution of the eye, just as its spatial resolution has been displayed by the analogous functions displayed in Figure 9.22 above.

An interesting feature of the temporal resolution curves in Figure 9.34 is the maximum temporal resolution with fluctuation rates of about 8 to 10 cycles per second with sufficiently high intensities of light. This finding is related to the phenomenon of *brightness enhancement* (Brücke, 1864; Ebbecke, 1920; Bartley, 1938), wherein a steady field of light is compared with a light flickering at 10 Hz. The flickering field is usually judged to be brighter even when the average amount of light per second has been made the same for the two fields. Enhanced response has also been demonstrated in single retinal and cortical cells of the cat (Grüsser & Creutzfeldt, 1957) over a similar frequency range. At present the interpretation of brightness enhancement is not clear. Bartley (1939) has called attention to the fact that alpha waves of the EEG occur in the range of 8 to 10 Hz. He has accordingly suggested that enhancement occurs with flashes at this rate because they can most easily evoke responses at a frequency that is already built into a rhythmic spontaneous pattern of activity in the cortex. We must remember, however, that on-off responses represent a major portion of nerve impulse activity at the precortical levels of the ganglion cells and lateral geniculate body, and optic nerve impulse experiments (Enroth, 1952) have shown that intermittent flashes at low to moderate frequencies are strongly effective stimuli.

Robert M. Boynton

COLOR VISION

10

Color vision is a subject that is not the concern of psychologists alone. Among the many other groups interested in it are physicists, physiologists, paint manufacturers, artists, and interior decorators. Such widespread concern over color seems basically attributable to its aesthetic and commercial importance in our daily lives. Color adds immeasurable beauty to our visual world; it can be used to create "atmosphere," and, in the commercial world, to identify and help sell products. (For good reason the Eastman Kodak Company has spent a good deal of money to ensure that the quality of "Kodak yellow" is controlled within very strict and well-defined limits.)

Color creates mood. It is, for example, generally agreed that reds and yellows are "warm" whereas blues are "cool"; it has been demonstrated that people will set a thermostat higher in a blue room than they will in a yellow one, as if to attempt a thermal compensation for coolness that is visually induced.

The richness of chromatic metaphor in our language is great (green with envy, blue note, yellow streak down his back, and so on); it would seem that color experiences, like sensations of taste and smell, are emotionally charged.

In a recent study, Helson and Lansford (1970) studied color preference by placing 125 colored test stimuli against 25 different backgrounds in many hundreds of combinations, and irradiating these with various light sources. His is one of the very few rigor-

315

ous studies of this sort of problem. He has found that, to assure pleasingness, white is the safest background, certain fluorescent light sources are best avoided, and a color preferred against one background may appear unpleasant against another. He also found that women prefer the "warm" colors (red, orange, and yellow) while men prefer the cool. It is important and significant that a beginning has now been made to put the matter of color preference on a firm experimental basis.

Unfortunately, data from many studies, where global judgments of color preference have been obtained, seem meaningless. In the first place, because color is perceptually attached to objects we do not necessarily have a favorite color that transcends all circumstances: red may be fine for fire engines, but not for the living room wall. Secondly, colors typically exist in more than one part of visual space at a time. The appearance of a color depends upon its surroundings, and so do color preferences. Interior decorators know well that certain colors go together and that others do not. Elaborate descriptive schemes have been worked out to supplement modest rules of thumb, these to help artists, homemakers and architects create environments that are chromatically pleasing.

Because this is a chapter in a textbook of *experimental* psychology we will not deal further with the various fascinating topics just mentioned. Perhaps at some future date, a really solid chapter can be put together in which experimental studies of the affective side of color could be cited and integrated into a theoretical framework capable of accounting for some of the data. But the amount of research on the subjective aspects of color perception is so small, and much of it is of such poor scientific quality, that a good theory cannot now be proposed. This does not therefore seem to be the time to make the attempt. Instead, attention will be focused here upon measurable aspects of the subject of color perception.

In addition to adding beauty to the world,

color also improves visibility. For example, certain types of color-defective individuals cannot find a red ball lying in green grass. The ball is immediately obvious to the normal observer, who would suffer in a way similar to the color-defective person only if the ball were painted green to match the grass. Concerning the discrimination of color, there have been very many good experiments—too many in fact for all of them to be included in one chapter, or even one book. Fortunately the field has advanced far enough that a number of important logical and theoretical concepts can be derived. For this reason, there will be more emphasis upon principles, and somewhat less on raw data than may be the case in other chapters of this book.

Although we are concentrating on the measurable aspects of color vision, the experience of color is really subjective. Such experience lies wholly within the observer. Fortunately these sensations do not occur willy-nilly but are related in definable ways to the characteristics of light sources and reflecting surfaces outside us—surfaces to which the color is so compellingly referred in the process of perception that the color seems to be solely a property of the surface itself. However, color is not exclusively a property of the perceived object; nor is the basis for its meaningful perception wholly within the observer. Rather, color relates both to physical events outside and within the eye, as well as to a subjective state, with the anatomical structure and neurochemical activity of the visual nervous system linking the two.

A guiding principle for the organization of this chapter has been a conviction that it is absolutely necessary to keep the physical, physiological, and psychological aspects of color conceptually separated. A second principle, already referred to, is to stress the discriminative aspects of color, a subject that rests upon a firm scientific footing. Even with this restriction, we shall not include here the entirety of what is encompassed by the expression "color vision." A definition of color given by D. B. Judd in Stevens' (1951) *Hand-*

book of *Experimental Psychology* states that color consists of "characteristics of light other than spatial and temporal inhomogeneities." Such exclusion specifically fails to rule out brightness differences. Therefore, if two stimuli look different because one is brighter than the other (even if both appear white) then there is by this definition a color difference between them. This definition is not idiosyncratic with Judd, but expresses also a point of view taken by official organizations such as the Optical Society of America, and the International Commission on Illumination. It is also consistent with the use of the concept "color constancy" in perceptual psychophysics, since many experiments dealing with this class of phenomena are actually concerned only with brightness considerations.

Now this is not what color means to the layman. If he were to pay a premium for color television and then receive only a black-and-white image, his irritation would not be reduced by assurances that, in a technical sense, there *are* color differences in the picture. What mainly would be missing, of course, is *hue:* sensations to which we attach the familiar "color" names of red, green, blue, and so forth. It is this hued aspect of color vision which is to be emphasized in this chapter. In order to be perfectly clear about this, the term "chromatic" will be used instead of "color" when the intent is to exclude from consideration that class of visual discriminations which are based upon brightness differences alone.

REQUIREMENTS FOR CHROMATIC VISION

Continuous Spectral Energy Distribution in the Light Source

Because the perception of surfaces and objects is paramount in vision, and most objects are not themselves luminous, we now discuss chromatic vision of surfaces that reflect light. Most people have had the experience of looking at surfaces under a sodium-vapor lamp, which emits almost all of its energy in a very narrow part of the visible

spectrum which appears yellow. If we pay careful attention to what we see in such a circumstance, we will be forced to agree that there is no chromatic vision at all, other than that which may be mediated by memory. To prove this, place an issue of a popular magazine under a sodium-vapor lamp and try to decide whether the advertisements are in color, or in black and white. Again, excluding memory color, this turns out to be impossible.

From the simple demonstration described above we can conclude that although monochromatic light is sufficient for brightness discrimination to take place, chromatic discrimination is not possible when surfaces are illuminated by such a light source. Hues can best be discriminated when objects are illuminated by a source of light that emits a continuous and balanced spectrum. Since the sun is a source of this type, it is perhaps not too much of a leap of faith to suppose that the evolution of chromatic vision has been partly in response to the availability of sunlight throughout evolutionary history.

Incandescent lamps produce the best man-made continuous spectra. When tungsten, which is the most widely used lamp filament, is heated, a perfectly continuous spectrum is produced, meaning that there are no gaps or discontinuities in the function relating emittance to wavelength (see Figure 9.1, p. 274). The relative emission at each wavelength depends upon the temperature of the heated tungsten, being relatively strong in the long visible wavelengths at low temperatures, with short wavelengths contributing relatively more at high levels. Visually, this produces a change in the color of the light from reddish to bluish as temperature is increased.

Some loss in the quality of chromatic vision will result whenever part of the spectrum is missing, or if a part of the spectrum is very low in energy with respect to the remainder. Suppose that a surface reflects light at only one wavelength and completely absorbs all others. A light source that produces a spectrum lacking only that particular wavelength would consequently fail to reveal the chromatic character of the surface, which would look black. In real life, neither surfaces nor sources are anywhere nearly as selective as this, but the problem definitely exists in less exaggerated form, the most common example arising from the use of fluorescent lights. The original ones, marketed in the 1930s, were markedly deficient in long-wavelength light (the "cool white" lamps of today continue to have this deficiency). The result is a relative darkening of surfaces that would appear reddish under light from a tungsten filament or in daylight. Consequently, such sources are particularly uncomplimentary of human complexions and misrender the color of roast beef, which looks well-done even if nearly raw.

Fluorescent sources do not stand alone in their lack of spectral continuity and evenness. Many others, such as gas-discharge tubes (for example, mercury-vapor lamps widely used in street lighting) also tend to emit spectral "lines." That is, the energy tends to be concentrated in certain parts of the spectrum. Curiously, for reasons that are made clear later in this chapter (p. 355), it is possible to produce an acceptable looking "white" light from a source that emits as few as two very narrow spectral lines, provided that they are carefully chosen and their relative intensities are suitably adjusted. However this source in general does not produce the same chromatic appearance of surfaces that it illuminates as does a matching illuminant having a continuous and balanced spectral distribution. This can be understood by imagining a hypothetical surface that reflects all wavelengths excepting the two that happen to be in the source, or which reflects these wavelengths very unequally.

Some degree of chromatic vision is theoretically possible as long as the source is other than "completely" monochromatic. However, no source—not even a laser, which comes closest—is *completely* monochromatic. Complete monochromasy would imply that all emitted quanta must be of *exactly* the same energy, and this never is the case. In practice, a spectral band as narrow as 5 to 10 nanometers (nm) usually cannot mediate chromatic vision. Such bands are in consequence widely used in vision research, where they are usually—though inexactly—spoken of as "monochromatic," numerically specified in terms of the midpoint of the waveband.

Selective Spectral Reflectance of Surfaces

The appearance of a surface depends to a very important extent upon the way that it reflects light. To a remarkable degree, the color of a surface, as it is viewed subjectively, is not much affected by wide variations in the nature of the illuminant. Much of this type of *color constancy* can be eliminated by viewing the surface through a telescope or reduction screen, causing it to appear as an aperture color having properties that are not relatable either to the illuminant used, nor to the characteristics of the reflecting surface. We can imagine the visual world as being built up from bits and pieces of such areas of aperture color, from which our complex percepts about objects in visual space are derived. (An examination of problems on this higher level of complexity will be given in Chapter 12.)

The property of a surface that is most highly correlated with its perceived color is *diffuse reflectance*. Diffusely reflected light is scattered back from a surface in all possible directions. A perfectly diffuse surface is one that would have the same luminance in all directions and therefore would look equally bright no matter where the observer is positioned with respect to it. A *specularly reflecting* surface, in contrast, is one that reflects incident light in such a manner that the angle of reflection is the same as the angle of incidence. Although no surface can be characterized as being either completely specular or completely diffuse, many surfaces can be approximately so described. For example, a piece of blotting paper comes close to being a perfectly diffuse surface, whereas a plane mirror is almost completely specular.

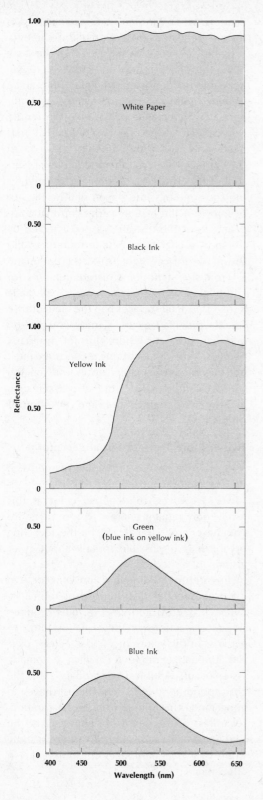

Most surfaces exhibit both specular and diffuse reflection at the same time. The highly polished surface of a new automobile is a good example. In this case, the gloss of the surface is revealed by its specular reflection. Reflected images of objects can be seen in the surface, due to the specular component of its reflectance. However the color of the automobile is determined almost entirely by the diffuse component of reflectance, best seen by looking at the surface at an angle calculated to avoid the specularly reflected component. Another method is to use an extremely large and diffuse source of illumination: even the glossiest surface will look relatively dull under this kind of lighting (see Evans, 1948, for color photographs of this phenomenon).

One of the principal differences between specular and diffuse reflection, apart from directionality, is that specularly reflecting surfaces usually reflect light nonselectively as a function of wavelength. Thus the light of a yellow bulb on a parking lot, reflected from a surface of an automobile, will appear yellow regardless of whether it is reflected from the surface of a red car, a green car, or a black car. If the observer held a reduction screen so that he could see mainly the specularly reflected light from the car, it would be impossible for him to tell what the color of the car really was.

Diffuse reflection, in contrast, is often quite selective with wavelength. In Figure 10.1 are shown spectral reflectance curves of surfaces that appear to most observers, under diffuse white light producing equal energy at all wavelengths, to be yellow, green, blue, white, and black. Each of these curves shows the proportion of incident light, at each

Figure 10.1. Spectral reflection curves of white paper, untreated (top) and covered by inks of various hues as indicated. Each graph shows the percentage of diffusely reflected light measured at each of the wavelengths indicated by the vertical bars. (Adapted from Pirenne, 1948.)

wavelength, which is diffusely reflected to the eye of the viewer.

The proximal optical stimulus for vision is of course the retinal image. All information about the chromatic characteristics of objects in the outside world must be contained in this image; it therefore will profit us to consider at this point the nature of that image relative to the objects that are represented in it.

As is explained in Chapter 9, each object in visual space is imaged on the retina by the optics of the eye. If we consider a given surface of the object, the geometrical distribution of light in the retinal image will approximate the shape of that surface. The chromatic character of that surface is represented in the image by the spectral distribution of the light contained therein. Our problem now is to understand the dependence of this distribution upon the following factors:

(1) the spectral irradiance $H(\lambda)$ of the surface by the light source,
(2) the spectral reflectance $R(\lambda)$ of the surface,
(3) the spectral transmittance $\tau(\lambda)$ of the anterior portions of the eye.

$H'(\lambda)$, representing the spectral irradiance of the retina, is related to these three quantities by the following expression:

$$H'(\lambda) = KH(\lambda)R(\lambda)\tau(\lambda)$$

The equation says that at a given wavelength (λ) the amount of retinal irradiance H' is proportional to the irradiance H of an external object by a light source multiplied by the percentage of light (R) reflected from the object in the direction of the eye at that wavelength, multiplied by the percentage of the light (τ) that is transmitted through the media of the eye before reaching the retina. The constant K does not depend upon wavelength, but rather upon the choice of units used in making the calculation, as well as the dimensions of the eye, which determine the size of the retinal image relative to an external object at a given distance.

When many wavelengths are produced by a light source, as is often the case, the speci-

fication of $H'(\lambda)$ must be made for each through repeated application of the equation.

If we view any two surfaces with the same $H'(\lambda)$ through a reduction screen, they will appear to be identical. The same value can be obtained with many combinations of irradiance and reflectance. If we take the reduction screen away, the two areas will not necessarily appear the same, for the color of the surfaces is also affected by their surroundings. Thus, for example, the brighter the surroundings, the darker will be the appearance of the test area. The chromatic appearance of the test area is also affected by the spectral character of the surroundings, and the nature of the light from the illuminant.

From the standpoint of requirements for chromatic vision, the main point to be made here is this: If all surfaces had the same diffuse spectral reflectance curves, there would be no basis for chromatic vision. Thus for chromatic perception of surfaces to be made, there must not only be a reasonably continuous spectral source of illumination, but also a selective and differential absorption and reflection of the light.

Two or More Types of Visual Receptor

So far, we have dealt explicitly only with optical factors outside and inside the observer. However, there is no color at this level—only radiant energy. Not until the incoming energy is analyzed by the receiving organism is it possible to talk about color vision.

In order for chromatic vision to occur, two differing spectral distributions of retinal irradiance, $xH_1'(\lambda)$ and $yH_2'(\lambda)$, must produce different reactions in the visual system, regardless of the values of x and y, at least over the luminance range for which chromatic vision occurs. A subjective corollary is that the corresponding two patches must have an appearance that differs in hue or saturation, regardless of the relative brightnesses of the two fields. For each value of x, there is some value of y that minimizes the difference in appearance.

Logically, there are two possibilities whereby the visual receptors could respond differentially to the spectral character of monochromatic inputs. One possibility is that, although the cone receptors are all alike, the output of each is in some way "tagged," so that it differs in some qualitative way depending upon the wavelength of the light that falls upon it. The simplest receptor of this kind might respond positively to one part of the spectrum, negatively to another. The other possibility is that the quality of the output of any given receptor is entirely nonspecific so far as wavelength is concerned, but that the eye contains at least two classes of receptor that differ in their spectral sensitivities. Thus the relative activation of the two systems would vary depending upon wavelength.

The evidence in favor of the second kind of scheme is overwhelming, as is made evident in the discussion on page 322, and further on pages 350–353. The requisite number of different types of cone receptor turns out to be at least three. (The first scheme, which requires some kind of "tagged" response by the single receptor, has been seriously proposed from time to time, but we shall see that there is no direct evidence whatever to support it.)

Scotopic vision, already defined and described in Chapter 9, provides an excellent example by which we can appreciate the inherent achromatic character of visual experience when it is mediated by receptors all of which have the same spectral sensitivity. What is required is that we look carefully at surfaces at the low illumination levels where only the rods function. There is no chromatic vision. We can test this with the magazine advertisements mentioned above in connection with perception mediated by high levels of sodium-vapor light, with exactly the same negative result. The reason for this is simply that there is no way for a rod to "know about" (that is, respond differentially to) the wavelength of the light that stimulated it.

If the relative intensities of any two lights at scotopic levels are suitably adjusted, they may be made to match exactly because they cause the same rate of light absorption in the rod photoreceptors. This is proof that there is no "tagged" receptor response to be utilized by the scotopic system.

Differentiation of Signal Transmission

A further requirement for chromatic vision is that the messages transmitted to the brain, based upon chromatically separated signals, somehow preserve information about the signal strengths of the component receptor systems. The early thinking about this matter, as embodied in various extensions of the so-called Young-Helmholtz theory of color vision, indicated that signals emanating from each type of receptor might be transmitted by separate pathways all the way from receptor to brain. Such a simple notion is attractive, and dies hard. It is not logically necessary, however, that the three systems of signals be kept separate; modern communication theory shows that in certain cases a higher degree of reliability of transmission, and/or a more efficient use of available channel capacity, can be achieved by the mixing of signals in certain seemingly complicated ways. Of particular importance is the transmission of signals that reflect differences between the outputs of two systems. Evidence that such difference signals are important in human chromatic vision is given later in this chapter (p. 325).

Qualitatively Different Sensations

One additional logical requirement for chromatic vision is that different sensations from different colors can somehow be aroused by the neural messages which transmit the results of receptor activity from the eye. The expression of these differences should be in terms of the whole gamut of chromatic and achromatic sensations, including red, green, yellow, white, black, and certain combinations of these.

Also it is possible to conceive of a visual system that can differentiate between colors at the receptor level and can transmit all the proper signals to the brain, but which nevertheless produces only one quality of sensation in the brain and thus fails to mediate chromatic vision.

It is not possible to describe the various sensations of chromatic vision adequately with words, any more than tastes and odors can be so described. There is, for example, no conceivable way to describe, to a completely color blind individual, what hue sensations are like. Nevertheless it is worthwhile to attempt to measure these sensations, using techniques of psychological scaling; we cannot ignore the need for these chromatically distinct sensations as one of the logical requirements of chromatic discrimination, fully as necessary as any of the four more objective requirements previously described.

THE PHOTOCHEMICAL AND NEUROPHYSIOLOGICAL BASIS OF CHROMATIC VISION

Three Pigments

The initial non-optical event in the visual process is the absorption of light by the visual photopigments contained within the outer segments of photoreceptors located in the retina of the eye. For more than 100 years, there has been strong presumptive evidence to suggest that three classes of photopigment, each with a different spectral sensitivity, must be present in the photoreceptors as the basis of chromatic discrimination. The hypothesis seemed necessary to account for basic facts of color mixture and chromatic adaptation, to be described later in this chapter. These psychophysical experiments also gave strong suggestions concerning what the spectral sensitivity curves of these three pigments should look like.

For a very long time, however, the best efforts of histologists and chemists failed to reveal the three different photopigments hypothesized above, even though the rod pigment, *rhodopsin,* had been extracted in the nineteenth century, and many of its properties had been examined since that time.

Within the last 15 years, the existence of separate classes of cone pigment has definitely been established by two kinds of physical experiment. The first utilizes a technique known as *retinal densitometry.* A beam of light is directed into the eye; some of this light passes through the media of the eye, including the retina, and is diffusely reflected from surfaces behind the retina. A small percentage of this reflected light emerges through the pupil and is delivered to a sensitive photomultiplier tube. The percentages of light absorbed or reflected by most of the eye media are constant, but the percentage absorbed in the double passage through the retina will vary slightly depending upon the concentration of visual photopigments in the receptors illuminated, being relatively high when the eye is dark adapted, and lower when some of the photopigment has been bleached by the action of absorbed light. Such changes are greatest at the wavelength corresponding to the maximum of the spectral sensitivity curve of the pigment being bleached, with proportionally more light being required to produce the same amount of bleaching at other wavelengths. Such measurements define the *action spectrum* of a pigment.

By taking such measurements at a number of wavelengths when the eye is sucessively light- and dark-adapted, it is possible to determine differences in reflectance caused by the bleaching light. The only reasonable cause of such a *difference spectrum* is the bleaching of photopigments of the retinal receptors, for other structures are unlikely to be affected by the bleaching light.

By applying this method to the peripheral retina, which is rich in rod receptors, a difference spectrum which corresponds to the action spectrum of rhodopsin is obtained (Campbell & Rushton, 1955). Because so much is known about rhodopsin, this is an important control experiment. When the method is applied to the fovea of the retina, where cones predominate, a photopic difference spectrum is obtained which is selectively affected by the wavelength of a bleaching light, as would be expected if two or more photopigments were contained in the reflecting area. Moreover, color-defective subjects known as *protanopes* (see p. 363) who are believed to lack all or most of the long-wave-sensitive ("red") pigment show a difference spectrum corresponding to that of the "green" pigment as inferred from the data of normal subjects (Rushton, 1958).

This is a difficult technique to apply to cone vision, for at least the following reasons: (a) only a very small percentage of the incident light is reflected back out through the pupil; (b) only a very small percentage change occurs in this already small amount as a consequence of bleaching. It is not possible to establish the exact shape of the pigment sensitivity curves for each of the pigments by the method described above, but two main peaks have been localized—one at about 530 nm, the other somewhere around 580 nm.

The other physical technique is still more recent, and no less difficult. The technique, known as microspectrophotometry, allows measurement of light passing through a single cell (Liebman, 1962; Marks, Dobelle, & MacNichol, 1964; Wald, 1964). A collection of cone cells is gathered on a microscope cover slip and two equivalent beams of light are directed at them through two optical systems to form tiny images in the slide plane. One image is aimed squarely within a cone outer segment. The other is aimed outside of the cone on the slide itself. The object of the experiment is to measure absorption of light in the outer segment of the cone, using the outside beam for comparison and as a control. This technique is made difficult because the measuring beam must not be too intense, lest it bleach away the pigment that is being measured. The beam with the required intensity level presents a signal so weak that measurements approach the limits of modern technology, close to theoretical limits as well. The most successful experiments have been made with goldfish cones, the latter being huge in comparison to primate ones. The results indicate that there are definitely three classes of photopigment. For the very small number of primate cones so far measured, peak sensitivities are approximately at 445, 535, and 570 nm.

As a result of the experiments that have been made with retinal densitometry and microspectrophotometry, there can no longer be any doubt about the existence of three or more classes of photopigment in cones. However these experiments have not yet provided hard evidence to indicate exact spectral sensitivities of the photopigments, nor do they provide unequivocal information about the distribution of these pigments within cone types. The evidence to date suggests that a single cone contains only one type of pigment, rather than a mixture.

Opponent-colors Transformation

Red and green cannot be seen in the same place in the visual field at the same time. When mixed together (see p. 349), red and green lights will, if suitably balanced, yield a cancellation of both the red and green sensations, leaving a residual yellow. Blue and yellow bear a similar relation to one another in that they also do not coexist, and when mixed the result is a white that contains not a trace of either component.

Opponent-colors theory was originally based upon such observations as those described above. The German physiologist, Ewald Hering, (1905, 1964) speculated that perhaps a single receptor could act in either of two ways, sometimes to signal red for example, at other times green. This view was challenged by the trichromatic theorists who stressed a viewpoint similar to that stated in the previous section, according to which the response of a single receptor must be nonspecific with respect to the wavelength that produces it. The additional assumption that the trichromatic theorists tended to make was that three separate channels take signals from the location of the photopigment to the visual area of the brain. (See Brindley [1960], for an excellent, brief historical review of this subject.)

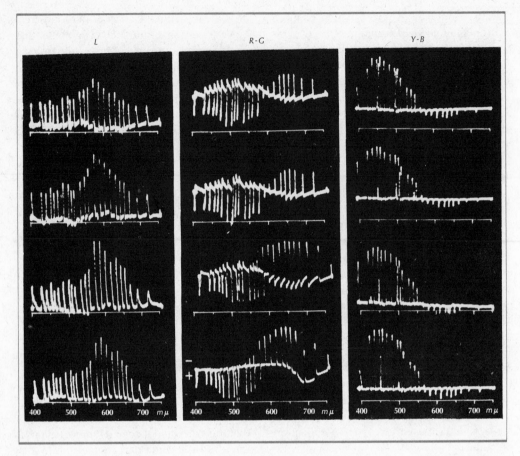

Figure 10.2. Potentials recorded near, but not actually in, the cones of fish (Svaetichin, 1956). Stimuli were 200 msec in duration, and of equal energy, concentrated in the spectral region shown. Some electrode placements give rise to luminosity (L) responses as shown in column 1; others give rise to responses that vary in sign depending upon wavelength as shown in columns 2 and 3. When the neutral wavelength is relatively long, these are called responses from "R-G" units; when it is relatively short, they are called responses from "Y-B" units.

Since the early days of this controversy, a number of writers (Judd, 1951; Hurvich & Jameson, 1955) have correctly pointed out that there is no essential conflict between trichromatic and opponent-colors ideas. The resolution of the contradiction may be made by supposing that the first stage of chromatic vision is trichromatic, but that signals are then recoded into opponent-colors form. There is now a good deal of hard evidence to support this viewpoint, which we review briefly.

It is possible to record electrical activity in the visual system by means of microelectrodes. While attempting to record from single receptors, Svaetichin (1956) discovered responses in the eye of the fish which had very peculiar properties as a function of wavelength. These responses appeared with little latency and remained at maximal strength as long as the stimulating light was left on, returning to the baseline as soon as the light was extinguished. Furthermore—and this is the most important point to be noted here—the electrical *sign* of the response was sometimes found to be wavelength-dependent. An example of this is shown in Figure 10.2. Here the stimulating wavelength was rapidly varied across the spectrum with each light left on for 200 msec, long enough to obtain a maximum response. The time scale has been very much compressed so that the individual responses look like spikes. Although light of the same energy was used at each wavelength tested, note that, for the "R-G" unit, the sign of the response is negative for wavelengths below about 580 nm, whereas it is positive for longer wavelengths. A maximum negative response is reached at about 500 nm, with a maximum positive response being recorded about 650 nm. There is a neutral point at about 580 nm, where no response is recorded, excepting small transients which do not appear on this record.

Svaetichin thought at first that these responses were coming from single cones in the eye of the fish, but further work by MacNichol and himself (1958) proved that this was not so. In this later work, they used a dye-marking technique whereby the exact placement of the microelectrode could be determined histologically at the conclusion of the electrophysiological experiment. It was found that to record this type of response the recording electrode had to be placed very near, but not actually in the receptors. The importance of this finding is the following: If opponent-colors responses actually did come from the receptor, then either the photopigment in the receptor is capable of producing "tagged" responses as a function of wavelength (negative for some, positive for others), or the receptor must contain at least two photopigments that produce responses of opposite sign after they absorb light.

The conclusion of Svaetichin and Mac-Nichol, that the bivalent response does not come directly from the receptor, has been buttressed very recently by Tomita (1966). Tomita also has recorded many responses of the Svaetichin-MacNichol variety and has proposed that these be called "C-responses" (for "color"). He has also succeeded in recording responses from within single cones from a fish eye by using a technique with which the retinal preparation is vibrated onto the delicate recording electrode in a manner

that permits intracellular insertion on some lucky occasions. The data from these experiments indicate that the bioelectric responses from individual cones are all of the same sign, varying only in size as a function of the wavelength and intensity of the stimulating light. Different types of cone have been identified by this technique, for each is sensitive to different wavelengths of light. Tomita et al. (1967) have reported that of the first 114 cones they sampled from the eye of a carp, nearly all fell into three classes as defined by maximum spectral sensitivity, which strongly supports the trichromatic theory at the receptor level.

It appears then that the opponent responses recorded originally by Svaetichin result from an interaction between receptor responses. It is far from certain, however, that C-responses are involved in any simple way with the direct chain of events in the visual pathways, which begins with receptors and ends with activity in the visual part of the brain. However this may be, it is nevertheless clear that opponent-color computation is carried out somehow in the primate retina; this is indicated by opponent responses that have been recorded from the lateral geniculate body, a principal relay station between the eye and brain. Here the long neurons of the retinal ganglion cells, which make up the optic tract and optic nerve, synapse with the optic radiation fibers that connect directly to the visual cortex.

In a long series of important experiments on primates, DeValois (1965) has recorded electrical activity from single units in the lateral geniculate body in response to chromatic input. These units exhibit a resting level of activity (spikes per unit time), in the absence of light stimulation, during which firing is rather irregular, and the spike rate is intermediate to low. After the eye is stimulated by light, the response pattern changes. In some cells that were sampled, short wavelengths produce a vigorous response when the stimulus is begun (increased firing rate), which subsides at the termination of the stimulus. Long wavelengths produce a decrease in the spontaneous firing rate, and exhibit another response (increased firing rate) when the light stimulus is turned off. Such a single unit seems to be carrying information of two qualitatively different kinds. The wavelength of stimulation is encoded, within limits, as either an increase or a decrease in firing rate, depending upon whether the light stimulus is of short or long wavelength. (In an approximately equal number of units, the relations are reversed.) Now it is not likely that a particular unit can tell the difference between two short wavelengths (for example, 420 nm and 440 nm), or between two long ones. However DeValois' work shows that, among a sampling of units, the crossover point, where a zero response occurs (separating the opponent effects of long versus short wavelengths) is not always found at the same wavelength. According to the opponent-colors theory, only two classes of mechanisms are required, each with a different crossover point. Although DeValois has found a considerable spread in these values, he has found that they do tend to fall, statistically, into the required two groups.

We are left, then, with the following picture to account for the encoding and transmission of at least some visual information of a chromatic nature: (1) three types of photopic visual photopigments, each contained more or less exclusively within a given type of receptor; (2) an exquisite organization of the receptor types, such that an opponent interaction occurs somehow between the outputs of selective receptor types; (3) the conversion of these intermediate difference signals into a neural message, encoded in terms of a modulation of a resting (dark) level of activity, either upward or downward, depending upon the balance of the opponent activity between receptors. It seems highly probable that some receptor pairs are concerned with the encoding of information about red and green, with the outputs of cones sensitive to long waves and short waves opposing each other and leading to a difference signal that is capable of increasing or decreasing the resting activity level of the nerve fibers to which they connect. Modulation of this activity in one direction leads to some kind of (unspecified) activity in the visual areas of the brain that is correlated with the experience of "red", whereas modulation in the other direction signals "green." Because such modulation cannot occur upward and downward at the same time, impulses transmitted over such pathways signal "red," "green," or "neither" depending upon the balance between receptor outputs. This balance determines the direction of the ensuing nerve fiber modulation in one direction or the other. An analogous argument can be made for the yellow-blue system.

It has not been proved that all activity related to chromatic vision is encoded and transmitted in this opponent-colors fashion. The possibility remains that some chromatic input may be delivered to the brain without such prior interaction.

Nonopponent Spectral Sensitivity Curves

It is frequently observed, in experiments like those just described, that some units exhibit a response the electrical sign of which does not change with wavelength. This was already noted for the case of the single receptor unit, where all responses were found by Tomita to be negative. However the same is found to be true if electrodes are placed elsewhere in the retina or in the lateral geniculate nucleus where opponent-sign responses are also found.

By implication, if a given electrode placement yields responses that do not vary in sign with wavelength, a given response should be achievable with any choice of wavelength, so long as a suitable intensity adjustment is permitted. The substitution of one wavelength for another in this way has been called *silent substitution*, and it is one of several methods that may be used to show whether a given system is mediating chromatic or achromatic information (see p. 345).

If silent substitution is possible, the spectral sensitivity of a given unit may be determined by finding the stimulus radiance required at each wavelength to produce any convenient criterion response. This type of examination has been made at both the retinal and geniculate levels. The resulting spectral sensitivity curve of the geniculate body from primates is identical, within experimental error, to the photopic luminosity curve of these animals as determined by behavioral procedures (DeValois, 1965). A similar interpretation has been made of nonopponent retinal responses from the eye of a fish. By implication, then, these systems seem to be concerned solely with luminosity (brightness) information. A conclusion that has been reached by many workers is that such a nonspecific brightness system coexists with the chromatic ones; that if the chromatic systems were turned off (as can in fact be achieved by balancing the chromatic systems by the use of a "white" light), only achromatic vision would remain. (This point of view is consistent with the discovery by Weale [1953] that there are a few rare individuals who possess perfectly normal photopic vision, except that chromatic vision is entirely lacking.)

If brightness is mediated by a unitary system, luminances of lights of different color should be additive, a condition known as *Abney's Law*. Imagine the following experiment to test the law. On opposite sides of a split field, place red and green lights and adjust the green until it matches the red for brightness, ignoring differences in hue and saturation insofar as possible. Now add an amount of green light to both sides of the field, equal in luminance to that of the original green side. This produces twice the original amount of green on the one side, and a red-green mixture on the other, which will probably look orange. If this experiment were done at scotopic levels, or in an eye in which only one class of mechanism were active, both halves of the field would look exactly alike throughout the experiment. With the complication of chromatic vision, where systems

are being stimulated that give rise to unequal chromatic appearance, it becomes an empirical question whether the achromatic (brightness) component of the complex sensation will behave similarly. The result of this type of experiment is that the match does not hold exactly. In general, when some cancellation of hue occurs (as in the orange half), the brightness will be a bit less than it would be if the same hues are added (the green half). Chromatic cancellation, evidently is associated with some brightness cancellation as well. These experiments have been well summarized by LeGrand (1957).

If, in contrast, the same type of experiment as that described above is repeated using flicker photometry as a criterion (see Chapter 9), a photopic sensitivity curve can be deduced that does not seem to be affected by what is going on in chromatic parts of the visual system, inasmuch as Abney's Law holds precisely. A similar result, indicating complete additivity, has been reported by Boynton and Kaiser (1968) in an experiment where subjects minimized the distinctness of the border between heterochromatic fields, ignoring the fact that the more saturated field appeared brighter.

These experiments provide further evidence to support the idea of independent achromatic and chromatic mechanisms. That they are independent has seemed so apparent to some writers that they have proposed separate cone receptors, which supposedly exist for the purpose of handling achromatic information. The direct evidence from microspectrophotometry provides no support for this view. It appears then that the same three receptor types must serve a dual function, that in all probability their outputs are utilized in more than one way, so that summation as well as cancellation of receptor outputs may occur. It will be recalled in this connection that Tomita finds that all receptor potentials are of the same sign; thus an opponent color signal must be generated by reversing the sign of responses from one type of receptor before adding the outputs of the two types together.

There is no reason why the outputs having the same sign cannot also be added together and delivered to the achromatic system.

The Processing of Chromatic Information at Higher Levels of the Visual System

According to any doctrine of psychophysical parallelism, there must be some pattern of activity in the brain that differs when one sees a red rather than a green of equal brightness. The purpose of this short section is to note that no experimental evidence exists on this point. Those few investigators who have looked at the activity of the brain in response to a spectrally selective input have generally contented themselves with attempts to measure spectral sensitivity curves. Without further testing, it is not possible to know whether such curves represent the output of a single class of retinal mechanism (which seems unlikely), or whether they reflect the result of complex interactions (more likely). Further, it is not known whether chromatic information is encoded in terms of which units in the brain are activated (place theory), or the way that they are activated (pattern theory) or both. The place theory would predict that microelectrode stimulation of single units in the visual cortex of conscious humans would lead to different chromatic and/or achromatic experiences depending upon electrode placement. Because color is fairly precisely localized in the visual area of the brain, the place theory alluded to here would be applicable only at the submicroscopic level to allow the blending of different cell activities within approximately the same area. There are many difficult questions for which solutions can be found only after a great deal more work has been completed using microelectrodes on the visual cortex and other brain areas.

A WORKING MODEL OF HUMAN CHROMATIC VISION

In this section, a model is presented that attempts to describe, in a quantitative way, some aspects of the functioning of the human color vision system. It is intended to help in the organization and interpretation of facts to be presented in later sections. It has been extracted from several color theories (especially those of Judd, 1950; Walls and Mathews, 1952; Hurvich and Jameson, 1955; and Boynton, 1960). It is as consistent as possible with the known anatomical, photochemical, and physiological facts, but should not be taken too literally. One fault of the description is the fact that the model goes beyond the direct evidence in some cases. Furthermore, the actual state of affairs in the human visual system is known to be very much more complicated than the model suggests. The model is intended to account only for the appearance of stimuli of intermediate size and duration that are presented at the point of fixation in an otherwise dark field.

Some very important problems, such as chromatic adaptation and induction, are not dealt with here; these will be discussed later as they relate to the model, and we shall then see what kinds of addition to the model must be introduced to account for them.

Photopigment Stage

The physical evidence of microspectrophotometry and retinal densitometry, discussed in the preceding section, indicates that there are three different kinds of photopigment, one of each kind located in the outer segments of one of three different types of retinal cones. (Rushton has given the pigments the names *erythrolabe, chlorolabe,* and *cyanolabe,* meaning [roughly] red-absorbing, green-absorbing, and blue-absorbing, respectively.) These physical experiments show that the absorption peaks of the three pigments occur at approximately 570, 535, and 445 nm in the spectrum. To the spectral absorption curves of these we shall attach the symbols α, β, and γ.

The physical experiments that have been performed to date do not define the lower parts of the spectral absorption curves of these pigments very accurately. This is unfortunate because human color vision, par-

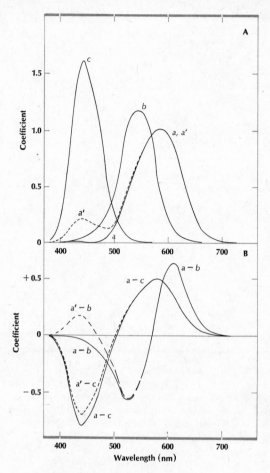

Figure 10.3. A. Fundamental response curves of Thomson and Wright (1953). B. Opponent-color functions calculated from the data of Thomson and Wright: $a' = a + 0.131c$.

ticularly as revealed in color-mixture experiments (to be described below) is critically dependent on light absorbed in small amounts at wavelengths corresponding to the tails of these curves.

When the complication arising from light absorbed in the media of the eye is taken into account, the spectral absorption curves of the cone pigments should be consistent with the many curves derived from color-mixture data obtained from studies made of the human eye (see p. 352). For convenience, we introduce, in Figure 10.3A, the spectral absorption curves of Thomson and Wright (1953): the peaks of these curves agree well with the physical data, and the shapes agree with color-mixture data. (It is interesting to note that these curves were derived, some years before any direct physical data on cone pigments were available, for the purpose of accounting for certain types of color defect to be described later in this chapter.)

Receptor Stage

Photopigments are contained within the outer segments of the cone receptors. Current evidence suggests, as noted in the previous section, that each of these three types of cone pigment is uniquely contained in one of the three types of cone receptor. Assuming this, we may call the cones that contain the blue-sensitive pigment "blue" cones and speak similarly of "green" and "red" cone receptors. These may be symbolized by the capital letters B, G, and R respectively. Two statements of caution are in order regarding this symbolization. First, sensations do not arise directly in the receptors, so that it is not necessarily true that unique stimulation of, say, an R cone would give rise to a sensation of red (such unique stimulation is impossible anyhow, for all real lights cause absorption in more than one type of cone). Secondly, an R cone does not appear red if you look at it. Indeed, the density of photopigments in the cones leads to selective absorption that is so slight that all cones look alike, being more-or-less colorless when directly viewed under the microscope. However if absorption by the various cones could be intensified, a red cone would not appear red because the part of the spectrum in which red falls would be selectively absorbed by the pigment; it would in fact appear blue-green. We must be careful always to bear in mind that chromatic vision does not arise until the higher centers of the visual system have been activated; the absorption of light in visual photopigments constitutes only the first stage of a complex chain of events between light input and the sensory end result. Thus, although we talk about red, green, and blue cones and sometimes also about red, green, and blue lights,

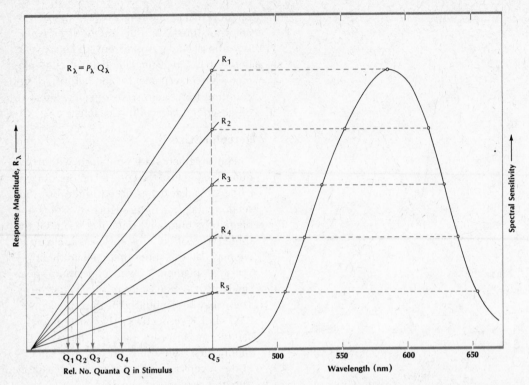

Figure 10.4. *Left:* Functions showing how response magnitude R_λ grows linearly with the number of incident quanta, at a rate which depends upon the probability of quantum absorption p_λ. Spectral sensitivity is defined on a quantum basis. *Right:* Spectral sensitivity of a hypothetical receptor, obtained from response magnitude produced by introducing an equal number of incident quanta at various wavelengths.

such talk is very loose. It does have a mnemonic value, however, so long as we do not lose sight of the fact that visual sensations reside neither in light quanta, visual photopigments, nor cone receptors.

Recently, an electrophysiological response called the "early receptor potential" (ERP) has been measured, which is linearly related to the energy contained in the light stimulus (Brown et al., 1965; Cone, 1965). We may therefore assume, with some justification, that each quantum of light that is absorbed by a receptor gives rise to a tiny element of response. Moreover, these responses appear to summate so that there is a linear relation between the number of quanta absorbed and the magnitude of the initial response of a receptor to a brief flash of light. There is an upper limit to this linearity of response, which

is caused by the bleaching of photopigments by very bright lights; we will not worry about this but will deal only with the normal range of color vision, which takes place at intensity levels below this.

Consider now the action of light upon a single receptor. On the right-hand side of Figure 10.4 is a curve representing the magnitude of response from a cone as a function of wavelength, for a spectrum containing equal numbers of incident quanta at each wavelength. Because response is a linear function of the number of quanta absorbed, this curve is identical in shape to the quantal action spectrum of the pigment contained within the receptor. The latter is obtained by finding how many quanta Q_λ at each wavelength are required to elicit a response R_λ of some particular size. This relation may be clarified by reference to the left-hand side of Figure 10.4. Here we have a set of functions, one for each of five pairs of wavelengths, showing how response magnitude increases with increasing stimulus energy. They are all linear functions, but they have very different slopes. The slope depends upon the probability p_λ that a quantum of light will be absorbed by the receptor under some fixed conditions of delivery to the eye. We may write:

$$R_1 = p_1 Q_1$$
$$R_2 = p_2 Q_2$$
$$R_3 = p_3 Q_3 \qquad (1)$$
$$R_4 = p_4 Q_4$$
$$R_5 = p_5 Q_5$$

from which it is indicated that in order to generate a response of some fixed size R it is necessary that $p_1 Q_1 = p_2 Q_2 = p_3 Q_3 = p_4 Q_4 = p_5 Q_5$. Thus the quantum values Q_1 through Q_5 must be reciprocally related to the probabilities p_1 through p_5, respectively, in order for all responses to be equal.

When a stimulus is presented that contains a mixture of light of different wavelengths, the resulting response may be calculated by simple summation. If Q_1 quanta at wavelength λ_1 are delivered to the receptor along with Q_2 quanta at wavelength λ_2, the total response, R_{total}, is given by the equation,

$$R_{total} = R_1 + R_2 = p_1 Q_1 + p_2 Q_2 \qquad (2)$$

and in the general case of two or more mixed spectral radiations,

$$R_{total} = \Sigma p_\lambda Q_\lambda \qquad (3)$$

For the more common case of a continuous spectrum, Equation 3 may be written as a definite integral:

$$R_{total} = \int p_\lambda Q_\lambda d\lambda \qquad (4)$$

where $Q_\lambda d\lambda$ represents the number of quanta contained in the interval λ to $\lambda + d\lambda$, and the limits of the integration include the wavelengths of the visible spectrum, usually taken as from 380 to 720 nm.

We define the response magnitude from the R receptor as having a units, and those

from the G and B receptors as having b and c units respectively. Because each type of receptor has a different spectral absorption characteristic, subscripts will be used to keep them conceptually separated. We shall use $p_{R\lambda}, p_{G\lambda}$ and $p_{B\lambda}$ to represent the probabilities that a quantum of light of wavelength λ will be absorbed in each of the three receptor types under fixed conditions of stimulation of the eye. Accordingly, the three equations required to specify the responses generated in the three types of cones are:

$$a = \int p_{R\lambda} Q_\lambda \, d\lambda$$
$$b = \int p_{G\lambda} Q_\lambda \, d\lambda \qquad (5)$$
$$c = \int p_{B\lambda} Q_\lambda \, d\lambda$$

For convenience, response units are defined so that the constant of proportionality is unity for each equation; in other words, if one quantum is absorbed, it produces a response a, b, or c that has a magnitude of one unit by definition. Also, for simplicity, the sign of

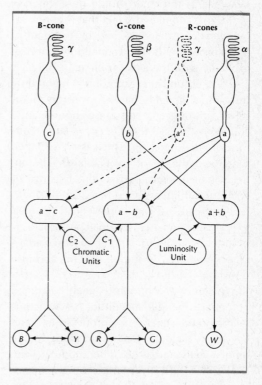

Figure 10.5. Schematic diagram of a model of chromatic visual information processing.

the response is taken to be positive, even though Tomita's experiments indicate that receptor potentials in the fish are negative under his particular conditions of recording, where increasing negativity implies increasing polarization of the cell.

Retinal Interaction Stage

Figure 10.5 shows a schematic diagram of the model under discussion. The outputs of the red, green, and blue cones just discussed are indicated by a, b, and c in the foot of each receptor. These signals become the input to the next stage.

The outputs of the R and G cones summate linearly at a luminosity unit L. Bear in mind here, and for the chromatic interactions to be discussed shortly, that in reality there are many overlapping units forming summation pools, each connected to hundreds or thousands of cones of the appropriate type. This would lead to the expectation that the appearance of the color should be a function of the area stimulated, a fact that is borne out by everyday experience and by the data of many experiments. This model does not deal explicitly with the area problem.

Another fundamental problem ignored by this simple model is that the receptors themselves introduce a response nonlinearity. Following the ERP, there occurs a *late receptor potential* (late RP) which is an **S**-shaped function of the *logarithm* of radiance. The late RP evidence indicates that the linearity of receptor output, assumed here, is unlikely to be exactly true. It can, however, be assumed to hold approximately for small perturbations of intensity around a particular level of adaptation, as well as for stimuli near the absolute thresholds of the cones.

Near the receptor, the L signal is a graded potential, one the magnitude of which is related to the sum of the outputs from R and G cones. This output is passed along by the bipolar cells and is used to modulate the resting level of activity in the ganglion cells, the axons of which make up the optic nerve

fibers that carry information to the lateral geniculate nucleus. There are probably many L units converging upon each ganglion cell, there may be reciprocal overlap, and there are almost certainly inhibitory connections at two or more levels of this system that our model ignores; indeed, no anatomical structures, excepting the cones, are to be implied by Figure 10.5. The main job of the L-system is to maintain or even enhance information pertaining to spatial detail in the light distribution making up the retinal image, but it also must transmit information about the amount of white light in the stimulus.

The output from one stage of a system may be divided and sent to more than one type of structure in the next stage of the nervous system. Here we assume that a second branch of the output from the R cone is delivered to a chromatic cell C_1. A branch of the output from the G cone is also delivered to C_1. The output of C_1 is simply the difference of the two input signals, $a - b$. Therefore, if the outputs from the R and G cones are equal, a zero signal will result from C_1. The output therefore reflects the *imbalance* between the relative stimulation of R and G cones.

In the ganglion cells, information from C_1 is used to modulate nerve impulse frequency in the optic nerve fibers. In the absence of output from C_1, these impulses occur at an intermediate resting frequency. The meaning of this frequency to the brain is "neither red nor green." Positive output from C_1 increases the resting frequency and negative output decreases it.[1] The first of these means "red," the second, "green." In this way, the activity

---

[1] We ignore here the electrophysiological evidence of DeValois that approximately half of the chromatic units he studied behave in opposite fashion. To include this fact in the model, additional chromatic units C_1' and C_2' should be drawn in, each receiving inputs in the same way as do C_1 and C_2, respectively. However the C_1' difference signal would be $b - a$ instead of $a - b$, and the C_2' difference signal would become $c - a$. Two more chromatic pathways would have to be added, to deliver the outputs of C_1' and C_2' to the cortical units. These additions to the model would not alter its quantitative characteristics; therefore they are deliberately omitted to keep the model as simple as possible. The reader is again cautioned, as he was at the beginning of this section, not to take the model too literally.

in the R–G optic nerve fibers can signal either red or green to the brain at different times, but never both at once. This is why we never see red and green at the same place at the same time.

So far, we have defined a dichromatic system, one that could produce a chromatic world of reds and greens only. There are indeed color-defective observers (see p. 362) whose color vision is well described by those parts of the model covered so far. For them, the saturation of a perceived stimulus is related to the relative signal strength of W to that of R or G. The greater the modulation of the resting activity in directions meaning "red" or "green" relative to that occurring in the "white" fibers, the more saturation the stimulus should appear to have.

When the R- and G-cone systems are in equal balance, the resulting sensation for the normal observer is not white, as the simple dichromatic system would require. It is yellow, because the $a - c$ system, which signals yellow and blue, is unbalanced in the yellow direction at the wavelength which produces an $a - b$ signal of zero.

By reference to the pigment-sensitivity curves in Figure 10.3A, we see that under this condition the value of c, the output from the B cone, is very small. Therefore, the value of $a - c$ is large and positive under this condition. (The difference signal, C_2, is shown in Figure 10.3B.)

The C_2 system is analogous to the C_1 system. It is assumed that when a exceeds c, the modulation of optic nerve fibers resulting therefrom signals "yellow" to the brain; when the reverse is true, the signal means "blue." Thus, when the outputs of the R and G cones are equal, $a - b = 0$, meaning that there are no red and no green sensations, but $a - c$ has a large positive value, which signals yellow. Any stimulus that produces a value $a - b = 0$, with a value of $a - c > 0$ will appear uniquely yellow—that is, a yellow which is neither reddish nor greenish in appearance.

For most spectral stimuli, there will be nonzero contributions from both the C_1 and C_2 systems. When this happens, the result will be the simultaneous activity of brain units: either B or Y units on the one hand, together with either R or G units on the other. This dual activity is assumed to produce composite sensations of four possible types. For example, a stimulus at 590 nm produces a nearly equal response from the C_1 and C_2 systems, both positive, associated with sensations of red and yellow, respectively. The result is a subjective mixture of red and yellow, or orange. In order to make the difference curves, shown in Figure 10.3B, consistent with the appearance of the spectrum (see p. 347), the difference signal produced by the C_2 system, shown in Figure 10.3B, is plotted as $(\frac{1}{2})$ $(a - c)$ in order to account for the fact that the long-wave spectrum appears yellowish-red, not reddish-yellow.

Unique green should appear in the spectrum where the $a - c$ signal equals zero, in the neighborhood of 505 nm. It is found experimentally that unique blue[2] appears in the spectrum in the neighborhood of 460 to 470 nm. The model as so far set forth would not predict this, nor would it account for the reappearance of red (the secondary component of the reddish-blue usually called "violet") in the extreme short-wave end of the visible spectrum.

In order to account for the additional phenomena described above, it is necessary to assume that the $a - b$ signal, which accounts for an excess of green over red to the short-wave side of unique yellow, for some reason becomes zero again at the wavelength of unique blue and then shows a positive value at the short-wave end of the spectrum. A possible mechanism for this is shown in the diagram of Figure 10.5. Here, a minority of the R cones (shown as dotted) contain the γ pigment normally found in the B cone. Because these units are sensitive to short waves,

[2]See p. 346 for definition of this term.

they can account for the excess of *a* over *b* and for the existence of unique blue in the spectrum (as well as for certain other phenomena to be discussed later). The curves in Figure 10.3B labeled *a'* − *b* and *a'* − *c*, make this correction.

Sensation Stage

The final stage of the model indicates the sensations produced by the information-processing networks prior to this final stage, starting with the pigment-containing photoreceptors. Because blue-yellow and red-green are impossible combinations, due to the fact that they share common transmission lines, they cannot exist in the same place in the visual field at the same time. Blue or yellow may coexist with red or green, a matrix of four possible combinations. Any of these may coexist with white, to yield sensations having variable *saturation*. The more intense the subjective chromatic content relative to the achromatic, the more saturated the stimulus is said to be.

This completes the formal exposition of the limited model. As outlined here, it can be set up and dealt with by analog or digital computer. It is consistent with a large body of experimental facts and will be useful for helping to organize these facts in subsequent sections.

CHROMATIC ADAPTATION

Two Effects: Changes in Chromatic Appearance and Changes in Sensitivity

The balances among the chromatic mechanisms of the eye are very delicate and easily can be upset. For example, when the eye is deliberately exposed to intense chromatic fields of light, the phenomenon called *chromatic adaptation* takes place. It has been shown to occur electrophysiologically (Armington & Biersdorf, 1956; Svaetichin & MacNichol, 1958; DeValois, Jacobs, & Jones, 1963; DeValois, Jacobs, & Abramov, 1964), and it has been studied in psychophysical experiments to be described below.

The term "chromatic adaptation" has often been used also to describe or explain the apparent change in the chromatic appearance of light fields when they are presented to the eye following adaptation to chromatic stimuli. This phenomenon can easily be demonstrated by the following experiment, which the reader can do without leaving his chair and without using special equipment. Cover one eye tightly with the hand and stare for a minute or two at any large, bright surface, whether chromatic or white. Following this, alternately view various areas of the visual field, first by shutting one eye and then the other. For a time, considerable differences in chromatic appearance will be noticeable between one eye and the other. (For some people, such differences exist even when the eyes are equally adapted.)

The concept of chromatic adaptation applies also to a second type of experiment wherein sensitivity rather than color appearance is measured (Stiles & Crawford, 1934; Wyszecki & Stiles, 1967). In a typical experiment, the spectral sensitivity of the eye will be measured first in the neutrally adapted state, then following adaptation to colored light. The reciprocal of the energy required for threshold visibility is the most common psychophysical criterion, whereas that required to elicit a criterion height of an electrophysiological response, such as the electroretinogram, has also been used.

Changes in Appearance Described

Visualize a stimulus that appears yellow under the conditions to which the model described above (p. 328) applies—a stimulus presented as a small flash of light at the point of fixation in an otherwise dark visual field. Suppose now that the observer looks away from a series of such yellow flashes—presented, say, once per second—in order to fixate a large, intense red field. Now he looks back at the test flashes, which have not physically been changed. Instead of appearing yellow, the flashes will now appear green. As time goes on, the eye will recover from the adaptive effects of the red field; the yellow content of the test flashes will gradually increase relative to the green, and after a few minutes the flashes will again appear yellow as they did before the adapting field was viewed. The converse experiment can also be made: exposure to a bright green will afterwards alter the appearance of the test toward red. In both cases, there will also be a reduction in brightness and changes in saturation.

Changes in Appearance Related to the Model Described Above

Let us consider the experiment just described in terms of the model described above. The yellow test flashes, prior to adaptation, produce a signal $a - b$ of zero, meaning that there is no output from the C_1 unit, and thus we have sensations of neither red nor green. At the same time, such a stimulus produces a positive value of $a - c$, a positive output from C_2, and an optic nerve fiber signal that means "yellow" when received and interpreted in the visual brain.

Now the adapting field is presented. It produces, while present, a strong excess of a over b, and of a over c, leading to a strong yellowish-red sensation. However we are not interested here in the *appearance* of the adapting field, only in its after-effects upon the test stimulus. So we turn the adapting field off, and once again introduce the yellow test flash.

Prior to adaptation, the test flash presumably appeared yellow because it stimulated the R and G cones equally; this was the basis for the zero value of $a - b$. Afterward, it appears green. This means that the modulation of the red-green optic nerve fibers is for some reason changed to signal green. Unless the adaptive stimulus somehow altered the state of the nerve fibers directly, the change in sensation implies that the output of the C_1 units, formerly zero, has now swung in the negative (green) direction in response to test flashes that were previously neutral so far as red and green were concerned. Why should this be?

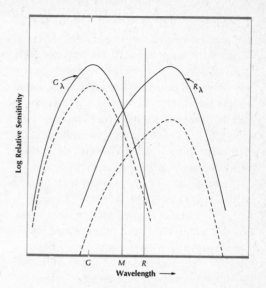

Figure 10.6. Selective chromatic adaptation produced by action of an adapting stimulus of wavelength *R*.

The Receptor Desensitization Hypothesis

The hypothesis most often advanced to explain the changes just described is that the sensitivity of the R cones has been selectively reduced by the stimulus that adapts the eye to bright red; although the adapting stimulus is active upon both the R and G cones, its principal action is upon the former. An attempt to illustrate this is made in Figure 10.6. Prior to adaptation, the yellow test flash at wavelength *M* produced equal stimulation of the red and green cones. The stimulus adapting the eye to red then produced a greater action upon the R cone than the G; as a result the height of the R curve is reduced to a lower position, as is shown by the dotted curve. The G curve is reduced also, but to a lesser degree. In this figure, the curves have all been plotted on a logarithmic ordinate. Because there is reason to believe that the action of an adapting stimulus upon a receptor should be to reduce sensitivity at each wavelength by a constant *ratio*, the ratio shows up as a constant difference on a log plot, which allows us to show the adaptive effect by manipulating the heights of the curves without changing their shapes. This important idea was first explicitly put forth by von Kries (1924), and is known as the *von Kries Coefficient Law*.

With the heights of the curves selectively altered, as shown by the dotted lines, the test flash, which prior to adaptation appeared yellow because it stimulated R and G cones equally, now stimulates the G cones more strongly. The result is a negative output at C_1, and a sensation of green. We may call this idea the *receptor desensitization hypothesis*.

Two questions may be raised with respect to the hypothesis: first, is it true? Second, to the extent that it is true, what is the mechanism of adaptation, or in other words, why is the sensitivity of a system reduced because of prior exposure to an adapting stimulus?

The answer to the first question is that the hypothesis is not exactly true; at best it is incomplete. Very careful experiments have been made using a dichoptic matching technique, where (for example) a yellow test light in the dark-adapted eye is matched to a trichromatic mixture light (see p. 350) presented to the chromatically adapted eye of the same observer. The details of the predictions that the hypothesis makes are beyond the scope of this chapter, but the main idea is this: Assuming that adaptation is solely the result of such a receptor desensitization, it is possible on the basis of such experiments to deduce the spectral sensitivities of the receptors. However, such analyses lead to the conclusion that the shape of the spectral sensitivity curves of at least one of the three types of cone must be altered dramatically—depending upon the wavelength of the adapting field. Now it is very unlikely that this conclusion is correct because there are other conflicting experimental data and purely physical reasons for believing that no such alteration in the shape of any single cone's sensitivity curve can take place. Let us therefore examine the receptor desensitization hypothesis a bit more closely to see what else might be wrong with it.

Implicit in the hypothesis, and in all calculations based upon it, is the following notion. Prior to adaptation, the three types of cone emit signals *a, b,* and *c,* respectively. After adaptation, these outputs are altered; signal *a* is selectively reduced, and so on. However these alterations can be compensated by increasing the inputs to the three types of cone, so that the signals *a, b,* and *c* are restored to the same values they had before adaptation. This is done by selectively increasing the amount of red light in a mixture of inputs involving red, green, and blue stimuli. The hypothesis assumes that when this is done, the sensation produced by the test flash will now be the same as it was for the original stimulus prior to adaptation. It is this assumption that appears to be incorrect.

It appears, on the contrary, that the adaptive process also produces temporary changes in the state of the system beyond the receptor level, so that equal values of *a, b,* and *c,* adjusted following adaptation to the same values they had before, produce unequal effects in subsequent stages, and thus unequal sensations. In order to produce equal sensations, unequal values of *a, b,* and *c* (compared to the preadaptation conditions) must be employed.

There is further experimental evidence to support the idea that the basis of chromatic adaptation is not confined to changes in receptor sensitivity. DeValois and Walraven have shown (1967) that strong adaptation of one eye definitely alters the chromatic appearance of a stimulus presented to the opposite eye, indicating that part of the adaptive effect occurs not in the receptors, nor even in the retina, but in the brain. Boynton and Das (1966) have shown that there is "cross talk" in the adaptive circuitry. Light absorbed, for example, by R cones cannot be limited in its adaptive effect to modifying the R cone sensitivity, but it must alter the sensitivity of other parts of the system as well.

The experiment of DeValois and Walraven has revealed another important fact, that is, that the adaptive effect of a red light that falls on the area of the fovea involved in the test is not primarily, as had been supposed, due to fatigue of the red system by direct action. Rather it appears that the action is mediated by the parts of the adapting field that *sur-*

round the test area. The excess of red activity in the surrounding area induces a relative reduction of the sensitivity to red into the central area. Such effects go beyond the scope included by the model described above (p. 328) and therefore cannot be dealt with explicitly. To do so, the model would need to be complicated by specifically taking lateral interaction effects into account. (A reasonably successful attempt to do this has been made by Hurvich and Jameson [1960].)

Changes in Sensitivity

Let us now consider two examples of changes in the sensitivity of the eye to various colored lights. The first is based on a psychophysical study by Boynton, Kandel, and Onley (1959). This type of study was first done by Stiles and Crawford (1934) and most recently by Wald (1964). First, the spectral sensitivity

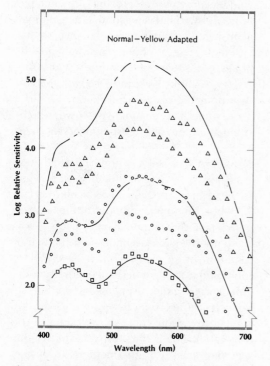

Figure 10.7. Log relative spectral sensitivity as a function of wavelength for foveal flashes. The uppermost curve is for the dark-adapted eye. Lower points, from top to bottom, are for adaptation to a flash of yellow light of 0.8, 2.5, 8.0, 25.0, and 80 mL. (Boynton, Kandel, & Onley, 1959.)

of the eye is measured in the dark-adapted state, by finding the energy required, at each of a number of wavelengths, for threshold visibility at the fovea, where there are only cones. (The reciprocals of these energies are plotted on a log ordinate in Figure 10.7.) The curve of the energies resembles the photopic luminosity function (see Chapter 9). However, if the eye is adapted to yellow light, the shape of the curve is greatly altered. In particular, note the clear emergence of a secondary maximum in the blue end of the spectrum. This particular experiment was repeated using three other chromatic adapting stimuli at various intensity levels, and with color-defective as well as normal subjects. It was found by trial and error that three underlying functions could be found which, when summated, could account fairly well for the experimental data.

Although it was believed at the time of the experiment that the sensitivity curves might be those of the receptors, apparently this is not the case, for the curve indicating the sensitivity of the eye to red in particular does not agree at all with the more modern direct physical evidence. It peaks too far in the long wavelengths, and is too narrow. It may be that the curves represent the peaks of the difference functions of the chromatic units, C_1 and C_2.

Many experiments of the same general type as that described above have been done by taking electro-retinograms from human subjects (see Chapter 9) as a criterion. Most of these, until recently, produced curves that were dominated by results from rod sensitivity and which tended to show little selective chromatic adaptation.

The joint contribution of rods and cones to the perception of color is made clear by many other such studies. For example, it is now possible, through the use of flashing stimuli, average response computers, and appropriate background fields, to eliminate the contribution of the rods to perception completely, but so far the contributions of separate cone systems have not been clearly revealed as humps on the spectral sensitivity curve. A recent experiment by Riggs (1967) used a test field of alternating colored bars. The colors could be changed readily at frequencies too high for the rods to follow. The results suggest that the outputs of the separate cone types summate linearly in the electroretinogram. However they do not seem to be selectively adaptable to a high degree, which suggests that the ERG potentials are recorded at a level of the visual system prior to the site of some of the adaptive mechanisms. (Some additional considerations with respect to chromatic adaptation are dealt with on page 341 of this chapter.)

CRITERIA FOR PROVING THAT ANIMALS AND MAN HAVE CHROMATIC VISION

It is natural to believe that others perceive as we do, and therefore to assume that those aspects of a stimulus configuration that appear most obvious to us are the ones that appear most obvious to the subject of an experiment, even though the subject might be an animal. For example, if a cat is trained to go to a blue dish and to avoid a red one, the uncritical bystander probably will accept this as evidence that the cat has chromatic vision. Actually, the experiment proves nothing of the kind. Although it may be true that the cat *does* have chromatic vision, it is also possible that the two dishes might appear to be chromatically identical to the cat. If so, the cat will base its discrimination upon whatever cues are available. Assuming that cues of position, olfaction, shape of dish, and other factors are controlled, it will seize upon any perceived difference in brightness between the stimuli and respond on this basis. Further, differences in brightness might dominate the cat's perception even though it can perceive chromatic differences.

For an experimenter with normal color vision, brightness differences may seem unimportant in comparison with the vivid chromatic ones that he perceives; moreover, the two stimuli may be equally bright *for him* and

may well have been selected to be so. However it is naive to suppose that equal brightness for man necessarily means equal brightness for the cat.

This chapter is not meant to be a repository for results of experiments concerned with chromatic vision in animals. Many have been done; most of them have had serious methodological flaws. Our purpose here is to summarize methods that can be used to prove or disprove the existence of chromatic vision in man and infra-human subjects, with particular stress upon the logical foundations of these methods.

At the outset, it should be emphasized that the study of color vision is a very difficult subject, for it is logically impossible to prove that chromatic vision does not take place. There are two reasons for this. The first concerns the impossibility—as a statistician would express it—of proving the null hypothesis, by which is meant that a result may be obscured by experimental variance, so that with more data or better experimental techniques, a positive result could show up. This has, for example, been the case with the cat, for whom the disproof of chromatic vision at one time had seemingly been well established. But more recent experiments (Sechzer & Brown, 1964), definitely show that the cat *does* have chromatic vision, although it is weak and the cat seems little disposed to use it. A second reason why it is difficult to prove that color discrimination does not take place is the fact that although chromatic vision might not seem to exist under some particular condition of an experiment, it nevertheless could show itself under some other condition. For example, experiments on human subjects carried out at scotopic levels of luminance would not show evidence of chromatic vision in the short-wave part of the spectrum even if all the methods to be described in this section were tried repeatedly. However, evidence that there is chromatic vision would be easy to obtain by any method carried out at higher luminances. Thus, even when evidence against chromatic vision seems overwhelming, later experiments might be carried out that would prove that chromatic vision is possible. Thus in practice, as negative results continue to accrue for a given species, from many laboratories and by many methods, we come to accept the fact that the species cannot see color, at least very well. This is true, for example, in the case of the dog, although the results from some future study, indicating that the contrary holds, could upset the entire conception for the species.

Five methods will now be reviewed.

Direct Viewing of a Bipartite Field

The first criterion for showing that an organism has chromatic vision has already been discussed in a previous section: this is to show that the two halves of a bipartite (split) field continue to be discriminated over a wide energy range. Even here it is necessary to be very careful. Suppose, for example, that a given animal were entirely blind to long-wave light. If it were, the entire intensity range of such a light, going from that which appears very dark to that which appears dazzlingly red-bright for the normal human, would be completely below the threshold of perception for the animal; thus, even though what might seem to the normal human experimenter to be an inordinately wide range of variation in red intensity were used, the discrimination that the subject might make would be based only upon the perception of visible light, produced by shorter wavelengths compared to darkness in response to longer ones. The only certain solution to this problem is somehow to measure the luminosity function of the subject before beginning the chromatic discrimination experiments. This has been done in many excellent studies, where the luminosity curves obtained are of interest and value in their own right.

Metameric Matching of Bipartite Fields

There are many pairs of lights that are physically different that nevertheless appear identical to an observer. These are called *metamers,* and they will be discussed in detail later (p. 354). Here we consider the probable basis for the phenomenon and its relevance to the question of testing for chromatic vision.

The probable reason that two different lights appear to be the same is that both produce the same amount or rate of light absorption in each of the three classes of visual photopigment. Because a total equivalence of response is established early in the visual nervous system, the equivalence must hold throughout all higher levels as well. Thus the receptor outputs, the opponent colors responses, the optic nerve fiber modulation, the activity of the visual areas of the brain, and the sensations produced by such equivalent action must all be identical.

For a normal subject, a monochromatic yellow light (see p. 346) can be matched by mixing monochromatic red and green lights. We call these "L" and "S" (for long wave and short wave) to remind ourselves that it is wavelength and not hue that is the property of light. In terms of our model (p. 328), yellow will be produced whenever the outputs of the red and green cones are equal ($a = b$). Refer now to Figure 10.3, where the sensitivities of R and G cones are shown. If we have a variable wavelength M (for "medium"), yellow will be produced when M is such that $p_{RM}Q_M = p_{GM}Q_M$. This relation holds only at one wavelength—namely the crossover point of the two curves.

If a mixture of S and L lights is used, their quantum energies[3] can be adjusted so that $a = b$. This relation is expressible as:

$$p_{RL}Q_L + p_{RS}Q_S = p_{GL}Q_L + p_{GS}Q_S \quad (6)$$

[3]For brief stimulus flashes, the appearance of a stimulus depends upon the total number of light quanta absorbed during the time of the flash, without regard to how the quanta are distributed during the period of their presentation. The discussion to follow should be considered as related to such a flash mode of presentation. For stimuli that are continuously presented, it is the *rate* of quantum absorption (quantum intensity) that is important. With the substitution of *I* for *Q* in Equations 1, 2, and 3 the argument to be presented here would apply to the case of continuous stimulus presentation.

Given that a particular amount of red light Q_L is specified, there is a unique solution to the equation, meaning that there is some green light Q_S that will satisfy it and thus produce yellow. Solving Equation 6 shows what this value is

$$Q_S = Q_L \cdot \frac{(p_{RL} - p_{GL})}{(p_{GS} - p_{RS})} \qquad (7)$$

Equation 7 may be stated in these words: A given long-wave stimulus of quantum energy Q_L produces an excess absorption in the R receptor compared to the G, represented by the numerator of the fraction in the right-hand side of the equation. At the same time, a short-wave stimulus of energy Q_S produces an excess absorption in the G receptor compared with the R, represented by the denominator of the fraction. The quantum energy of Q_L required to make the match depends upon the value of the fraction. If it is greater than unity, there is too much absorption in

the R receptor for the equation to hold unless Q_L is reduced to compensate. If the fraction is less than unity, the Q_L must be made greater than Q_S for the equation to hold.

A third way to look at the equation is by the graphical example in Figure 10.8, in which L is a wavelength closer to the crossover point than is wavelength S; thus the difference between the two curves is small. For stimulus S, this difference is larger. In order to obtain the balance required for yellow, the quantum energy of Q_L must be relatively increased to compensate the smaller difference on the right side.

It can be understood from study of Figure 10.8 that Q_M can be increased or decreased to produce the same *absolute* amount of stimulation of the R and G receptor, as that produced by any *absolute* amounts of Q_S and Q_L that themselves produce equal stimulation of R and G. Conversely, to match a monochromatic yellow of energy Q_M, the proper mixture of Q_S and Q_L can be varied in total energy without altering their proportion.

Suppose now that one of the two receptors were missing. Let us assume, for example, that only G remains. It should be clear from Figure 10.8 that, whatever Q_S and Q_L, equal stimulation of the G receptor by the two lights will be possible simply by increasing the energy of one component or reducing that of the other. In more formal terms, this situation corresponds to the simple equation that states that

$$p_{GL}Q_L = p_{GS}Q_S \qquad (8)$$

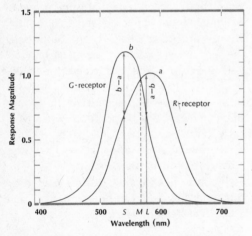

Figure 10.8. Response magnitude curves for the R and G receptors, reproduced from Figure 10.3. Wavelength *M*, near 570 nanometers, produces equal stimulation of the two receptors, and a signal $a - b = 0$. Two flanking wavelengths, *S* and *L*, are also shown. *S* leads to a large value of $b - a$, *L* to a smaller value of $a - b$. If mixed, these stimuli would produce an excess of *b* over *a*. By keeping the wavelengths the same, but increasing the energy of stimulus *L* until $a - b$ equals $b - a$, the zero signal can be recovered.

All of the discussion above may have seemed like a long digression, but it is really necessary to understand why the technique of color mixing can be used to diagnose chromatic vision. The reason is that a person with normal color vision, one who has both R and G cones in his eye, is able to match any energy of a monochromatic yellow with a mixture yellow only if he is allowed to vary two stimulus dimensions.

A commercially available instrument is

commonly used for the purpose of studying chromatic vision, called an *anomaloscope*. A split field is used, on one side of which a monochromatic yellow is projected (actually slightly reddish, but this does not matter), the energy of which can be made to seem either brighter or dimmer, as a knob is turned. On the other side of the split field that the instrument provides, a mixture of red and green monochromatic lights is provided. A second knob can be turned to vary their ratio without altering the brightness of the mixture very much (for a normal observer). That is, as light is subtracted from one component, a compensating amount is added to the other. Turning this knob allows the observer to vary the field from red, through yellow, to green in continuous fashion (imagine running across Figure 10.8 from right to left). For the subject who can see color normally, there will be only one setting of the second knob that will produce a yellow that matches the hue of the monochromatic yellow, and only one setting of the first knob that will produce a brightness of the monochromatic yellow that will match that of the mixture yellow. For the observer who cannot see color normally, who, for example, may be lacking either the R or the G receptor, there are very many settings of the two knobs that will produce mixtures each of different brightness. He will however make a unique (brightness) match if one of the knobs is set and he is told to vary only the other. If the monochromatic yellow is fixed in energy and he is allowed to vary the mixture ratio, the subject who cannot see color normally will require a large amount of Q_L relative to Q_S if the R receptor is missing; the converse would be true if the G receptor were missing.

Before leaving the mixture experiment, one additional point should be made. These experiments do not tell anything directly about what colors look like to an observer. They reveal, as we noted at the outset, that equivalent states exist which probably have their basis in the most peripheral stage of the visual system. These equivalences are passed along

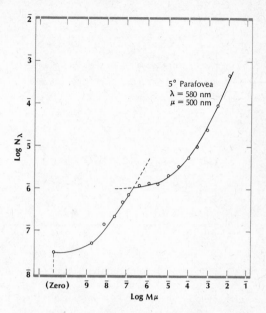

Figure 10.9. Log increment threshold, N_λ versus log field radiance, M_μ for extrafoveal vision. Values are expressed in ergs/sec. deg². Note the rod-cone "break" that occurs where log background radiance is about −6.5. (Stiles, 1959.)

through various stages to the brain, finally to produce equivalent sensations that permit the match to be made. However the matches tell us nothing whatsoever about what these sensations are.

Demonstration of Selective Chromatic Adaptation

The bottom branch of the curve shown in Figure 10.9 is a so-called "threshold versus radiance" (tvr) curve (Stiles, 1959) of the kind that is found in an eye that contains only rods, or in which rods function over a wide range. To determine the curve experimentally, a subject is presented a background field subtending 10° of visual angle, upon which a 1° test flash is superimposed for 60 msec. The concentric fields are centered 5° extrafoveally. If the background is very dimly lit, the radiance required for the flash just to be perceived is the same as that required when the test flash is projected against a zero background (darkness). As the background is made brighter,

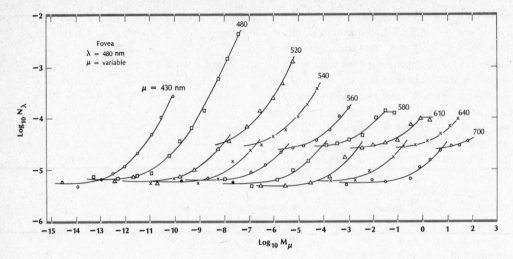

Figure 10.10. Log increment threshold, N_λ versus field radiance M_μ for foveal vision. With test and adapting stimuli both 480 nm, there is no break in the curve. With test stimulus at 480 nm, and as the adapting field is shifted to longer wavelengths there is a pronounced break, which in this case reveals a shift from one photopic mechanism to another. Units same as in Figure 10.9; test stimulus is 1° square, exposed for 63 msec. Horizontal placement of curves is arbitrary. (Stiles, 1953.)

its effectiveness in raising the threshold for perceiving the test flash is at first very slight, and the curve rises gently from the baseline. Its slope gradually increases, so that it rises faster and faster. When the background has been made about 3 log units brighter than it was when the curve began to rise, the curve reaches a slope of 45°, meaning that Weber's Law holds, for the ratio of ΔN (the test radiance) to M (the adapting field) is a constant.

For the scotopic eye, the shape of the tvr curve is independent of the wavelengths of the test and adapting stimuli. Changes in the wavelength (λ) of the test merely cause the curve to shift up and down; changes in the wavelength (μ) of the adapting field cause a shift in the horizontal direction. The curve will have its lowest and leftmost position if wavelengths λ and μ are both set at 505 nm, the wavelength of peak sensitivity for rod vision. The curve will displace itself to the right of this for all other adapting wavelengths, and above this for all other test wavelengths.

For the conditions shown in Figure 10.9, the tvr curve, instead of continuing its upward rise with unit slope, levels off and then rises slowly again before re-achieving unit slope. This is taken as evidence that more than one

mechanism[4] must be at work. The sensitivity of the eye depends, to a first approximation, only upon that mechanism which is most sensitive. At low background radiance, this is of course the rod system unless the test stimulus is confined to the fovea. At higher radiances, one of the cone systems will take over. This produces a rod-cone "break," very evident in Figure 10.9, quite analogous to that already described in Chapter 9, where increasing time in the dark following preadaptation gave the rod system a chance to take over from the cone system which earlier had been more sensitive.

It is possible to obtain "breaks" in the tvr curve at photopic levels using foveal stimuli revealing a changeover from one cone mechanism to another. An example of this is shown in Figure 10.10. The position of the breaks depends upon the particular choice of wavelengths that is made for the test and adapting stimuli. The tvr curve thus has a shape that depends upon stimulus wavelength, and the

[4] The term "mechanism" has been used by Stiles to stress that he is not necessarily referring to pigments or receptors, but to systems containing many of both. A "mechanism," as described by Stiles' technique, has many of the properties of types of cones and may be considered in this way, although inexactly.

eye may be said to have exhibited *selective chromatic adaptation,* in the sense that a given adapting field is shown by the method to have a greater effect on perception when one system of rods or cones is functioning rather than another. Otherwise the breaks in the curve could not occur.

The principle of selective chromatic adaptation is illustrated in another way in Figure 10.6. That is, lowering the sensitivity curve of the G cone at a certain test wavelength is equivalent to raising the tvr curve using the tvr curve method. This is the link between the two approaches.[5] Stiles has deduced the spectral sensitivity of foveal mechanisms by finding the radiance of the adapting field necessary to raise the threshold of a test flash, believed to stimulate uniquely a given mechanism, by a criterion tenfold amount. Of five sensitivity curves obtained by this method, three can be selected which more or less resemble curves of the R, G, and B cones derived by other methods. However there are certain quantitative differences, and it is puzzling that five, rather than just three curves are needed to describe the data.

For purposes of testing color vision, the method of Stiles is too time-consuming to be practical. For this reason, a short-cut method has been developed (Boynton & Wagner, 1961; Boynton et al., 1965) which takes advantage of the fact that, if selective chromatic adaptation has occurred, test flashes should

be more easily seen against backgrounds that differ chromatically than against those that are the same. There is a problem here, one which revolves (as usual) around control of intensity. For example, a red test flash will be harder to see against a very bright green background than against a dim red one. The solution to the problem is to use test and background stimuli in a matrix of four possible combinations that produce a set of four thresholds. An example is given in Table 10.1. The symbols in the matrix represent the logarithmic threshold values for the conditions shown, measured in any convenient units. If the homochromatic condition r_R (red on red) and the heterochromatic condition r_G (red on green) are measured in the same units and for the same test wavelength, the difference between them will be a logarithmic value which corresponds to a dimensionless ratio of the two. Typically, though not always, we can see the combination of red on green more readily.

The heterochromatic threshold reduction factor (HTRF) is defined as the mean of two such differences, one for each wavelength of test stimulus:

$$\text{HTRF} = \tfrac{1}{2}[(r_R - r_G) + (g_G - g_R)] \qquad (9)$$

It can be shown that, if this value is reliably greater than zero, selective chromatic adaptation has occurred. The quantitative value shows the factor by which thresholds are lowered specifically as a result of chromatic differences, below what they are for homochromatic conditions.

This test has been applied successfully to human observers (Boynton & Wagner, 1961). It has proved to be useful to detect color-deficient subjects. For example, "red-green blind" subjects (see p. 362) yield HTRF scores of zero when red and green lights are used. Macaque monkeys (Monjan, 1964) show, as do human subjects, a value of about 0.3 (about a factor of 2) for red and green lights of moderate luminance.

It should be noted that the methods used to measure thresholds, unlike all others noted in this section, do not depend upon the

TABLE 10.1 THE FOUR CONDITIONS REQUIRED TO DETERMINE THE HETEROCHROMATIC THRESHOLD-REDUCTION FACTOR (HTRF); THRESHOLDS FOR THE FOUR CONDITIONS ARE EXPRESSED IN LOGARITHMIC UNITS.

		Background Stimulus	
		R	G
Test	r	r_R	r_G
Stimulus	g	g_R	g_G

[5] From tvr curves for various combinations of test and adapting field wavelength curves like those in Figure 10.6 can be derived immediately; conversely tvr curves for different adapting field radiances, can be obtained. The approach is the same; only the method of displaying various aspects of the results is different.

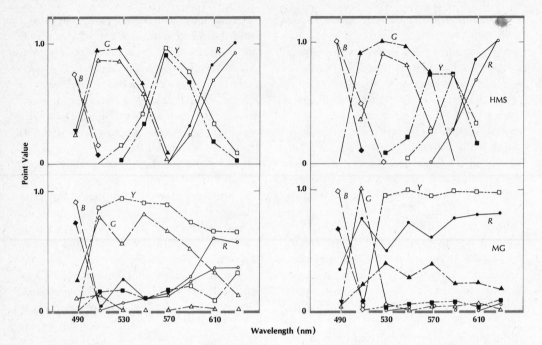

Figure 10.11. Results of a color naming experiment for one normal subject (HMS) and one color-defective subject (MG, a protanope). Filled symbols are for low-luminance stimuli, open symbols are for high-luminance stimuli; stimuli appear equally bright to the subject at a given luminance level. High luminance level matches 1000 trolands of white light, low luminance level, 125. The graph at the left is for dark surround, that at the right is for a white surround of luminance 1000 trolands.

chromatic appearance of the stimuli. The subject is asked only to report the presence or absence of stimuli, not what they look like. It should be noted once again that an organism can indicate that it can tell the difference between one color and another, yet not have true chromatic vision. It is possible also to imagine an eye that shows no adaptation at all, chromatic or otherwise, but which still could exhibit chromatic vision. The methods just described are best considered as revealing the presence or absence of receptor mechanisms that potentially can mediate chromatic vision.

Demonstration of the
Reliable Use of Color Names

Outside of the laboratory, people do not spend much time in making color matches, or in demonstrating selective chromatic adaptation with methods like those just described. Most color defective observers first learn of their defect when they attempt to attach *color names* to surfaces, only to find that their efforts yield surprise or even laughter from others. Indeed, if we did not learn to use color vocabularies, it is doubtful that the defective observer would ever learn about his anomaly, since there would be no direct way for him to know what he was missing in the rich normal realm of chromatic sensations.

It is possible to study this commonplace practice of color naming in the laboratory, where it is found that there are very reliable relations between wavelength and color naming, provided that the naming of colors is restricted in certain ways. (The study will be described in detail later, on p. 367.) Sample results from a color-naming experiment for one protanope (a subject suffering defective differentiation of red and green; see p. 364) and one normal subject are shown in Figure 10.11. The exact meaning of these curves will be explained later on page 367, but here it is necessary only to understand that the curves provide an estimate of the amounts of red, green, yellow, and blue that the subject says he sees in stimulus flashes that are presented against a dark surround. Note that the color-defective subject calls all long-wave stimuli "red" when they are dim and "yellow" when they are bright, almost without regard to wavelength. The normal subject shows very little dependence on the intensity of the light; his estimates depend primarily upon the wavelength of the stimulus. Any such dependence, if intensity is controlled, is evidence of chromatic vision. Figure 10.11 shows a slight amount of chromatic vision remaining in the color defective observer.

Stimulus Substitution Methods

We have saved for last a method which is one of the best; at least it is the most sensitive, although technically the most difficult. In the first parts of this section, the notions of color differences and color matches were introduced using the bipartite field, in which the stimuli are compared simultaneously side by side. Such a comparison can also be made successively in time. Imagine that the area of each color used in the bipartite fields is enlarged to fill the full test field. If the fields are slowly alternated with one another, a slow flicker will appear due to the chromatic and achromatic differences between the successive components; luminance adjustment of one component may reduce the appearance of flicker, but it will not eliminate it. Indeed, the point of minimum flicker is used to define photometric equivalence by the method of flicker photometry.

For an observer lacking chromatic vision (including the normal human subject under scotopic conditions) a stimulus having any arbitrary spectral distribution may be substituted for any other spectral stimulus, with the result that, if their relative intensities are suitably adjusted, a steady light should be perceived. For suitable conditions, in an observer who has chromatic vision, no such null

point should be achievable, excepting the special case of the metameric match, where the results should agree with those obtained by matching steadily-presented bipartite fields. In practice, the null condition is a very hard condition to achieve—so hard in fact that the method has very seldom been used on human observers. The difficulty is mainly technical and concerns the need for perfect substitution in time of one stimulus for another, for the eye is extremely sensitive to small timing errors. Also, inhomogeneities in the retinal area covered by the alternated test field tend to be smoothed out by the perceptual apparatus during maintained viewing but are much more apparent when short flashes are used. The problem of precise stimulus substitution may be made somewhat easier by using sinusoidal rather than rectangular pulses of flickering light. In experiments using sinusoids, an interesting effect has sometimes been found: in order to minimize flicker, under low-intensity photopic conditions when the wavelengths of the components differ, a phase adjustment of one component must be made with respect to the other. This requirement may reflect differences in response times of the underlying chromatic systems.

THE RELATION BETWEEN WAVELENGTH OF MONOCHROMATIC RADIATION AND COLOR SENSATION

When Newton first dispersed sunlight into a spectrum (1672), he indicated that he saw seven bands of color from short wavelengths toward long: he called these violet-purple, indigo, blue, green, yellow, orange, and red. All but indigo and orange were held to be "primary;" these two (and gradations, such as between blue and green), "derived." The names that he used were arbitrary, but this is still a fairly good description of how a balanced spectrum of moderate intensity looks to persons with normal vision.

The appearance of color depends upon the influence of light fields surrounding the color being examined. Because the spectrum is continuous, it is not possible for us to judge the appearance of an arbitrary section of it without having our perception influenced by the surrounding parts of the spectrum. Thus it is better to present one narrow waveband at a time for a controlled duration and to a particular retinal region. Unless the influence of the surrounding areas is specifically under investigation, it is perhaps best to leave these areas dark.

The normal human subject can judge the dominant hue of a narrow waveband with remarkable reliability. (If this were not so, the use of chromatic signal lights, upon which our very lives depend, would be impossible.) But one hue shades off into the next as wavelength is varied; also the exact hue perceived depends upon many other variables. Our purpose in this section is to look in detail into the relation between the physics of wavelength and the psychology of hue, and then to consider this relation in terms of the model described on page 328.

Sensations are private experiences; about the only way we can get at them is through the use of words. Even so, the common use of color language by two people does not prove that each sees the same colors. No such proof is possible. Each of us must therefore rely upon his own experience with chromatic sensations in order to appreciate what is being discussed here.

Fundamental Hues and Unique Wavelengths

It is often productive to reduce a problem to the smallest number of variables that we can and still describe it adequately. In this spirit, many people have argued that only four color names are needed to describe the chromatic character of bright colors viewed in a dark surround. For a full description, the achromatic term, white, must be added, but we shall ignore this complication for the time being.

The four basic color names are red, yellow, green, and blue. Each of these names is held to describe a unique sensation. This means for example that a yellow can be produced which is uniquely yellow in the sense that there is no reddishness, greenness, or blueness about it; it cannot be conceived as being made up of a mixture of any of the other sensations. (The fact, to be discussed later, that red and green *lights* can be mixed to produce a yellow light, is irrelevant here. We are talking now about blends of sensations, not of mixtures of lights.)

There are other hues to which color names have been given, which do not meet the criterion of uniqueness. The most widely used of these names is probably orange, with purple not far behind. Orange does not qualify as a unique hue because—to most people at least—it can be appreciated as being made up subjectively of a mixture of red and yellow. That is, the red and yellow components of orange can be seen admixed in the same patch of light and their ratio can be judged accordingly, as being reddish, yellowish, or an equal mixture of each. The same can be said for the simultaneous red and blue component of a purple or violet sensation, and of blue-green and green-yellow blends.

Of considerable interest is the fact that not all possible combinations of the four unique hues can exist in one place at the same time.

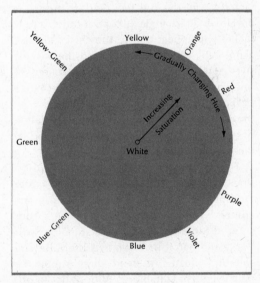

Figure 10.12. Psychological color circle.

For example, mixtures of red and green cannot be seen; we never experience or talk of a "reddish green" or a "greenish red." The same opponent relation exists between yellow and blue, though perhaps it is a little less apparent. The mixtures of chromatic sensations that do or do not occur can be conveniently represented on a diagram such as that of Figure 10.12, which is a "psychological color circle." The hue sensations that lie opposite one another on this diagram are opponent in the sense that they cannot coexist in the same patch of light; adjacent ones can. Intuitively we feel that white should be in the center of the diagram and we place it there. White can mix with any chromatic sensation, simple or complex. Psychological color diagrams such as this have been in use for a very long time, and are based upon pure introspection.

Hue versus Wavelength

Let us now return to the fundamental issue of hue versus wavelength. A convenient way to examine this is by an experiment in which

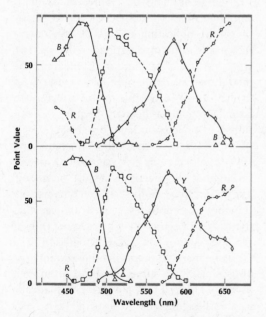

Figure 10.13. Appearance of the spectrum, as gauged by a color-naming technique. (Boynton & Gordon, 1965.)

the subject is restricted to using the names describing the four unique hues to describe a secondary color. In one experiment (Boynton & Gordon, 1965) subjects were instructed to judge spectral hues, one stimulus at a time, and to indicate what they saw with one name (if a unique hue were perceived) or two names (with the name given first describing the dominant component). For example, a reddish orange would be described as red-yellow in that order. A total value of 3 was assigned to each response. When a unique response was given all three points were assigned to it. In the more common double-response case, the first was assigned a weight of two, the second, one. In this way a distribution of response values was built up. The result for one subject is shown in Figure 10.13.

Figure 10.13 provides a good description of the appearance of the spectrum. Consider the upper part of the figure, for stimuli of 100 trolands. The very short wavelengths are reddish blue (violet). Unique blue occurs at about 474 nm, where blue is always the first response, but red and green are given with equal probability as the second response. A balanced blue-green occurs at 496 nm where the blue and green functions cross, and unique green occurs at 513 nm. Following a balanced yellow-green at 565 nm, unique yellow is achieved at 585 nm. This becomes orange at 612 nm where the red and yellow curves cross. The extreme long-wave end of the spectrum still appears as a slightly yellowish red; this is accentuated by raising the luminance to 1000 trolands, as is done in the bottom part of the figure.

Influence of Various Parameters upon the Hue-wavelength Relation

The relation between wavelength and hue is not precisely fixed, even with a dark surrounding field; it depends in detail upon what the exact conditions of the experiment are.

Many experiments, including those of the kinds just described but not limited to these, lead to the following generalizations:

1. As *luminance* is increased, responses of

yellow and blue are made increasingly often relative to those of red and green, although the position of the unique hues in the spectrum is not markedly affected. (This is related to a change in hue with intensity, known as the Bezold-Brücke hue shift.) In particular, the violet end of the spectrum becomes less reddish until at very high luminances the red component disappears; the red end of the spectrum becomes more yellowish. These features can be seen in Figure 10.13. At extremely high luminances under prolonged observation, long-wave stimuli become yellow in appearance—all trace of red disappears.

2. As *area* is increased, responses of yellow and blue increase relative to red and green. Very small areas produce the converse effect; responses of yellow and blue are markedly reduced, particularly in the central fovea, leading to a condition approximating tritanopia (see p. 365).

3. One of the effects of *time* has been alluded to above: prolonged viewing leads to adaptive effects that produce drastic changes in appearance. The effect of very short exposures is similar to that obtained from very dim stimuli of somewhat longer exposure; chromatic appearance depends upon the product of luminance and time for stimuli of about 50 msec duration and shorter (Kaiser, 1968). Small and/or dim stimuli tend to appear white, particularly in the region of the spectrum around 580 nm that normally appears yellow, and also in the region of 400nm.

4. The *region of the retina* stimulated has a powerful effect upon chromatic appearance. Other things being equal, increasing eccentricity of the stimulus relative to the point of fixation leads to relative ascendance of yellow and blue chromatic responses and a reduction of red and green ones (Boynton et al., 1964). Many monochromatic stimuli will be seen as white in the far periphery. Indeed, a safe generalization may be made that yellow sensations tend to be replaced by white ones as viewing conditions are made difficult, whether by reducing luminance, time, or area,

or if the stimulus is perceived in the far periphery of the visual field. The poor quality of chromatic vision in the periphery can be compensated for to a considerable degree by increasing the area and/or the luminance of a stimulus.

5. Chromatic vision is most vivid for large stimulus fields at moderate luminances. Very low luminances lead toward achromatic, scotopic vision whereas very high luminances lead to a "washing out" of chromatic vision with the result that all sensations tend toward white. (The reader is referred to an excellent review by Burnham, Hanes, and Bartleson [1963] for a more detailed description of the effects described above, and for many more detailed and specific references.)

Physiological Bases of These Relations

For stimuli of moderate luminance, duration, and area, centrally fixated, the model discussed on page 328 provides an obvious basis for the chromatic appearance of the spectrum, which depends upon the signs and relative strengths of signals derived from the C_1 (red-green) and C_2 (yellow-blue) units. Although the model does not deal with any of the complicating effects of area, luminance, and duration described in this section, we can point to the kinds of extension in the model that would be necessary to do so. An explicit effort to do this quantitatively with a similar model has been made quite successfully by Hurvich and Jameson (1955).

The linkage of the red with green, and yellow with blue as subsystems, is apparent throughout the phenomena just discussed. These two subsystems seem to come and go together as conditions vary. It appears that the C_1 (red-green) system has a lower threshold and requires less spatial integration from inputs of many receptors in order to function. Thus, small,weak stimuli are most often seen as red or green, if they are seen chromatically at all. That they should also be seen fairly often as white is reasonable; a small sampling of absorbed quanta, even if biased toward wavelengths that would normally be per-

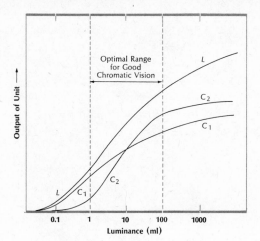

Figure 10.14. Schema to illustrate the shift in dominance of the yellow-blue system (C_1) relative to the red-green (C_2) as stimulus luminance is increased.

ceived as red or green, will sometimes fail statistically to produce the normal imbalance.

It seems clear that, as luminance is raised or area is increased, the effectiveness of the yellow-blue system increases faster than that of the red-green system. Probably the C_1 system also becomes saturated first; that is, the signal from C_1 levels off while the signal from the C_2 system continues to grow.

The L unit, signalling luminosity, has a low threshold, on the same order as that of the C_1 unit, but reaches a much higher level before saturation occurs.[6]

An effort to schematize the notions described above has been made in Figure 10.14, where a qualitative picture of rising output has been given for each of the units as the luminance increases logarithmically.

Saturation

The point of view put forth here is that chromatic and achromatic sensations depend upon signals coming over the pathways leading from the C_1 (red-green), C_2 (yellow-blue) and L (luminosity) pathways. *Saturation* depends upon the relative chromatic-to-achromatic contributions; it is an estimate of the

[6]Note that this use of the term "saturation" is entirely different from that of the next section.

proportion of *chromaticness* in the total sensation. Spectral colors are not equally saturated; saturation is greatest at those wavelengths where the achromatic systems are least active relative to the chromatic ones. This is particularly true at the short-wave end of the spectrum, where the B receptor contributes vigorously to the blue-yellow imbalance, but nothing at all to luminance. The most desaturated stimulus is a white, produced by a balanced spectrum that leads to zero output for C_1 and C_2 together, or any other stimulus producing the same result (see p. 357).

MIXTURES OF RADIATIONS

In order to gain a grasp of fundamentals, we have so far concentrated our attention upon the reaction of the visual system to monochromatic lights. However vision is mainly mediated by surfaces which reflect light continuously throughout the visible spectrum, as is indicated in Figure 10.1. Therefore we must now deal with the problem of how the visual system responds to mixtures of radiant energy that contain such continuous distributions of wavelengths.

Recall that one of the requirements for chromatic vision is that the eye must contain more than one type of visual photopigment. Because all information about the wavelength of light is lost when absorption occurs in the photopigment, any two wavelengths can, if suitably adjusted for intensity, produce identical effects upon any single type of pigment. Therefore, the action of a mixture of wavelengths upon a single pigment comes from the sum of the individual components of the mixture. For example, if 10,000 quanta are absorbed from a flash of light at 600 nm, 5,000 from a flash at 500 nm, and 15,000 from one at 400 nm, a mixture of all three lights would lead to the absorption of 30,000 quanta. However *any* mixture of light leading to the absorption of 30,000 quanta would produce exactly the same effect; for example, the original amount at 400 nm plus 3 times the original amount at 500 nm; or, for another example, 6 times the original amount at 500 nm.

Because the human eye, under photopic conditions, contains not just one, but three different pigments with overlapping spectral sensitivities, the initial basis for chromatic vision lies in the relative absorption of light by each of these three types of pigment. If two physically different stimuli produce the same absorption in all three types of photopigment, it follows that these stimuli should look exactly alike in all respects.

The Basic Colorimetric Experiment and Its Interpretation on the Three-Pigment Hypothesis

We now describe an experiment that is fundamental to *colorimetry,* a science that deals with the specification and measurement of color within a system based upon the experimental operation of *color matching.* The object of the experiment, and the calculations which stem from it, is to attempt a specification of all possible visual stimuli in terms of only three variables. Experimentally, these variables relate to the amounts of three so-called *primary stimuli* which, when mixed together, exactly match the color being specified.

Curiously, although colorimetry is said to specify color, the observer in the basic experiment is not required to judge color appearance. (Color matching has been a favorite visual experiment of the physicist, who often prefers to use the observer only as a null detector.)

In order to carry out the basic experiment, a *colorimeter* is required. First, a means must be provided to produce a *test stimulus* that the subject will try to match. In the experiments that we deal with here, we have chosen to use monochromatic lights as test stimuli, but this need not be so. (Some colorimeters are used to match the color of nonmonochromatic surfaces in the real world.) In our experiment the test stimulus is made to fill one half of a bipartite field uniformly; let us assume that it is the upper half (see Figure

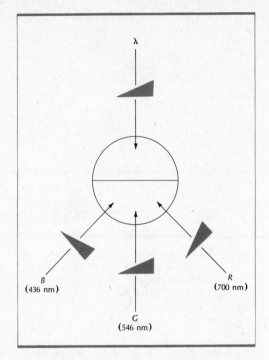

Figure 10.15. Schematic arrangement of stimuli for the color-mixing experiment. A test stimulus (λ) is delivered to the top of a split field, while a mixture of three primaries, B, G, and R, is delivered to the bottom. All are adjustable in intensity by means of neutral wedges. An arrangement must also be provided so that any one of the primaries can, in turn, be added to the test stimulus in the top field.

10.15). Next, a means for obtaining the three primary stimuli must be provided as well as a means for mixing them. (The primary stimuli are likewise monochromatic in the experiment to be described here but, like the test, they need not be.) Mixing is achieved by superposing the three lights on the matching side of the bipartite field uniformly (the bottom half in Figure 10.15). Although it is common to talk of such lights as being "additively mixed," there is in fact no interaction among the light quanta. The situation is analogous to a mixture of sand grains of various sizes which, when poured onto a scale, have a certain weight. Mixture in the eye is a function of the cone receptors that capture the light quanta of various energy values and develop a response that depends upon the rate at which each species of quanta is caught.

Additionally, there must be a means in the apparatus for varying the luminance of the test stimulus, and of each of the three components in the mixture. In Figure 10.15 we have indicated three monochromators, each of which is capable of putting out monochromatic light of any desired wavelength. A *neutral density wedge* is placed in the beam coming from each; this is a variable filter that absorbs light differentially from one end to the other. Some devices of this kind literally are wedge shaped; they absorb more light in the thick positions than in the thin, so that luminance can be varied by sliding the wedge across the beam. For exact work, the bipartite field should be of such good optical quality that the dividing line between its halves should disappear when a perfect match is achieved.

A test wavelength is selected and is placed in the top half of the field at a luminance that is comfortably within the range for good chromatic vision, say about 10 millilamberts. Next the three primary wavelengths are selected, keeping in mind the only requirement that no two of the primaries, when mixed, should match the third. We find that this requirement can only be met when the three are widely separated. Thus we may be sure that each of the three primaries is absorbed preferentially by a different one of the three types of photopigment. Let us select, from an infinity of possibilities, 436, 546, and 700 nanometer wavelengths as blue, green, and red primaries for the experiment. (This particular set was recommended by the International Commission on Illumination [CIE] many years ago, as real reference stimuli in terms of which the properties of the representative eye should be expressed.)

In the remainder of this section we discuss the color matching of an ideal observer, based upon a set of average data selected and slightly smoothed by the CIE in 1931. There are, of course, individual differences even among normal subjects, but the standard data are representative of typical subjects working with centrally-fixated fields subtending about 2° of visual angle.

Three knobs, each connected to one of the neutral wedges in the mixture beams of the optical system, allow the observer to adjust the luminances of the primary components; accordingly, he makes his matches by the method of adjustment. In effect, he acts as an analog computer, finding by trial and error the values of three unknown quantities that yield three simultaneous equations; these equate the amounts of light absorbed in each of the three types of cone photopigment stimulated by the mixture field with those absorbed from the test.

To illustrate the method, we consider only two of the many test stimuli that must be matched in order to build up a full set of color mixture curves. When the test is an orange light of wavelength 600 nm, the observer will discover that he must turn off the blue primary completely in order to make a match. His remaining task is to adjust the amounts of the red and green primaries to achieve an orange field that matches the test field. This is a less difficult match than one requiring all three primaries, yet the subject may experience certain difficulties. For example, if he concentrates on a hue match, he may achieve it only to find that a border remains because of a brightness difference. Both components must then again be adjusted, in which case the hue equality may be thrown off, and so on.

Making a match of blue-green at 500 nm presents a different problem. The observer will discover that the red primary is of no use in the mixture field—any amount of red only makes the match worse. However this time, varying the remaining blue and green primaries presents the complication that, although a match for hue is achievable, the mixture field is always less saturated than the test field. An understanding of why this happens can be grasped by referring once again to Figure 10.3A. A wavelength at 490 nm activates the B and G cones about equally, but it also activates the R cone, although only about 25 percent as much as either of these. However, this activation of the R cone produces some desaturation for two reasons: (1) it reduces the magnitude of the negative values of the C_1 and C_2 signals, reducing the strength of the green and blue signals respectively; (2) it adds to the luminance signal, which increases the white component of the sensation. (If absorption by the R cone could somehow be eliminated, the blue-green sensation provided by the test field would be more saturated than it normally is. This in fact can be accomplished to a degree by prior adaptation to red light.)

When stimuli of mixed colors are used for the test, the blue primary at 436 nm predominately stimulates the B cones. This contributes nothing to luminosity, but it is good for saturation. Because of the great overlap of the sensitivity curves of the R and G cones, the primary at 546 nm stimulates the R cones about 75 percent as much as the G cones. If the B and G cones are again stimulated approximately equally to achieve a hue match, this time by adjusting the components in the mixture, the stimulation of the R cone, due to the green primary, will be about 75 percent that of B or G, compared with the 25 percent produced by the spectral test stimulus. For the reasons stated above, this additional stimulation of the R cone leads to a further decrease in saturation. The match is impossible.

Although it might seem at this point that the mixture experiment is doomed, a solution to the problem is at hand: it is to move the red primary to the same side of the field as the test stimulus. This maneuver allows the subject to desaturate the test stimulus until it matches the mixture field. We will see later that the amount of red light added to the "wrong" side of the field can be legitimately treated as a negative quantity.

A problem that has been ignored so far concerns the units in which the amounts of the three primaries are to be measured. Luminance units normally are not used, al-

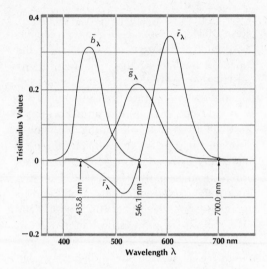

Figure 10.16. Color-matching functions (tristimulus values for an equal energy spectrum) in the primary system where R = 700 nm, G = 546.1 nm, and B = 435.8 nm. (Wyszecki & Stiles, 1967.)

though they could be. Instead, new units are chosen so that when equal amounts of red, green, and blue primaries are mixed, they produce a white (for which an additional experimental operation is required). An amount of white is set into the test field, the subject makes his match, and the settings of the three wedges are marked to indicate that these are so-called *unit trichromatic amounts*. All other quantities are related to these. For example, if the wedge controlling the red primary is adjusted to transmit twice as much light as for the unit setting, the new amount is specified as 2 trichromatic units of the red primary. In making the match, it makes little difference what the absolute amount of white light is, but its spectral distribution is critical, for there are many distributions that will pass for white. The particular white resulting from an equal-energy spectrum, although this is difficult to achieve experimentally, will be assumed here.

The color matching experiment is now continued for each of a large number of test wavelengths throughout the visible spectrum, with the result shown in Figure 10.16. It is not easy to see from the figure that very small positive amounts of the red primary and very small negative amounts of green are present in the short-wave end of the spectrum, to the left of the blue primary at 436 nm. Also, a very small negative amount of the blue primary is necessary to match some colors—more so when large fields are used—throughout the long-wave end of the spectrum. To carry out the full experiment therefore requires apparatus in which any of the three primaries may be shifted to the "wrong" side of the matching field as necessary.

Color Equation

The results of a color match using three spectral primaries may be described by an equation:

$$c(C) + r(R) \equiv g(G) + b(B) \qquad (10)$$

Equation 10 should be read as follows: c units of the test color (C) plus r units of the red primary (R), additively mixed to one half of the field, exactly matches ($\equiv$) g units of the green primary (G) plus b units of the blue primary (B), additively mixed to the other half of the field.

For a test wavelength of 490 nm, the equation reads

$$0.082 \ (C) + 0.058 \ (R) \\ \equiv 0.057 \ (G) + 0.083 \ (B) \qquad (11)$$

This is an empirical statement about an experimental operation, not a formal statement of mathematics. The plus sign is borrowed to indicate colorimetric addition by superposition of lights; the symbol "$\equiv$" is deliberately used to make it clear that an experimental match is implied, rather than a mathematical equality. Nevertheless, if the analogous mathematical statement is written and is manipulated in accordance with the rules of algebra, it is found experimentally (within fairly wide limits) that such calculations predict the results of new color matches when translated back into the experimental analog.

As an example, suppose we multiply Equation 11 by a constant factor of 2. It will then read

$$0.164 \ (C) + 0.116 \ (R) \\ \equiv 0.114 \ (G) + 0.166 \ (B) \qquad (12)$$

After manipulating our wedges to produce these trichromatic amounts, we can then check to see whether there is still a match between the two halves of the field. There will be. Or we could add a given quantity to both sides of the match—let us call the quantity X. Then, mathematically,

$$0.082 \ (C) + 0.058 \ (R) + X \\ \equiv 0.057 \ (G) + 0.083 \ (B) + X \qquad (13)$$

An easy way to check this out is to add a uniform light to the entire field—perhaps reflected off a glass plate in front of the colorimeter. The match will remain.

Generally, the additive, multiplicative, associative, and distributive laws of algebra all work, so that we can predict color matching behavior using the powerful tool of algebra. This is consistent with the model of color vision that has been presented in this chapter, and in fact constitutes one of the primary reasons for believing that equal absorptions in photopigments are responsible for color matches.

There are some algebraic manipulations that cannot be exactly duplicated in the laboratory, namely those that require negative amounts of light. However if a positive quantity is added to the opposite side of the field, as previously explained, the predicted color match will hold.

The values $\bar{r}$, $\bar{g}$, and $\bar{b}$ shown in Figure 10.16 are known as *distribution coefficients* and the curves are called *color mixture functions*. The values have been adjusted so that the area under each of the three functions is 1.0.

In order to provide a colorimetric specification of any stimulus light, it is necessary to evaluate its effectiveness with respect to each of the three color mixture functions. (This is directly related to its effectiveness upon each of the three types of cone photopigment.) For this purpose, the concept of the *tristimulus value* is introduced. There are three of these, defined as follows:

$$R = \int N_\lambda \bar{r} d\lambda$$
$$G = \int N_\lambda \bar{g} d\lambda \qquad (14)$$
$$B = \int N_\lambda \bar{b} d\lambda$$

Here N_λ is the radiance distribution in the stimulus; N must be measured in physical energy units for every wavelength λ throughout the visible range of the spectrum. If we have two stimuli such that $R_1 = R_2$, $G_1 = G_2$, and $B_1 = B_2$, even though physically different values of N had to be used to produce them, they will match for the standard observer. Such matches are called *metameric* and the matching pairs are called *metamers*. (Physical matches are called *isomers*.)

The Chromaticity Diagram

Tristimulus values can have any magnitude, depending upon the radiance levels of the stimuli. Everyday experience tells us that if we double the amount of light (as for example by adding a second light bulb to a lamp) the color appearance of a surface illuminated by the lights changes very little. Because hue and saturation are approximately independent of luminance, it would be convenient to develop a two-variable scheme that deals with relations among trichromatic units, while at the same time factoring luminance out of the system. This is done by specifying *chromaticity coordinates*, defined as follows:

$$r = \frac{R}{R + G + B}$$
$$g = \frac{G}{R + G + B} \qquad (15)$$
$$b = \frac{B}{R + G + B}$$

Tristimulus values, R, G, and B, show the absolute amounts of the three primaries required to make the match being specified. The chromaticity coordinates tell us the ratio of each of the three trichromatic amounts to the sum of the three. (Their sum must total unity and therefore any two of them will provide a complete specification. In practice, a plot of g versus r is most often used.)

A *chromaticity diagram* for this set of pri-

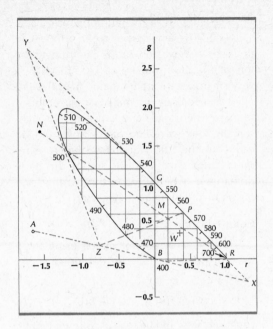

Figure 10.17. Chromaticity diagram based on the spectral primaries of Figure 10.16. X, Y, and Z represent the primaries of the CIE system, as represented in the RGB chromaticity space. (LeGrand, 1957.)

maries is shown in Figure 10.17 in which each spectral stimulus plots as a point. For example if $\lambda = 490$ (for which the tristimulus values were specified in Equation 11), the following chromaticity coordinates are produced:

$$r = \frac{-.058}{.082} = -0.715$$
$$g = \frac{.057}{.082} = +0.700 \qquad (16)$$
$$b = \frac{.083}{.082} = +1.015$$

Other spectral stimuli, calculated and plotted in the same way, form a *spectral locus* connected by a continuous curve that includes all possible intermediate wavelengths.

The diagram in Figure 10.17 has a number of useful properties, the most important of which is that all mixtures of any two stimuli represented on the diagram fall on a straight line connecting the two components of the mixture. The location of the mixture point on this line depends upon the relative number

TABLE 10.2 RELATIONS AMONG LUMINANCE AND TRICHROMATIC UNITS FOR THREE PRIMARY WAVELENGTHS USED IN A COLOR MIXTURE EXPERIMENT

Primary hue	Primary wavelength (nm)	Relative number of trichromatic units	Luminance in mL per relative trichromatic unit	Trichromatic units per luminance unit
Red	700	10	1.00	1.00
Green	546	10	4.59	0.217
Blue	436	10	0.06	16.7
		Sum 30	5.65	17.917

of trichromatic units contained in each of the component stimuli. These may be obtained by the use of equation (14). If these are equal, the mixture point is midway between the two component stimuli on the chromaticity diagram. If one stimulus contains twice the number of trichromatic units as the other, the mixture point will be located two-thirds of the distance from the weaker toward the stronger stimulus, still on the same straight line. If the ratio is 9 to 1, the mixture point will be nine-tenths of the way toward the stronger stimulus, and so on. This has been called the "center-of-gravity" principle. It should be emphasized that if the component stimulus intensities are specified in luminance or radiance units, the center-of-gravity principle cannot be applied, although the mixture point will nevertheless plot somewhere on the line connecting the two stimuli being mixed.

Because the spectrum locus is everywhere convex (although negligibly so for the long wavelengths), it can be seen at a glance that all mixtures of monochromatic lights must fall inside the spectrum locus on the chromaticity chart. Equal-energy white must be located at $r = g = b = 0.333$ because of the manner in which the trichromatic units were defined. Any metamer that matches equal-energy white will plot at the same point.

Any given point on the diagram represents all possible metamers which plot at that point. Excepting the spectral primaries of the system, a color that plots anywhere in the diagram may be obtained in many different ways. Taking the white point as an example,

consider a straight line drawn through it which intersects the spectrum locus at approximately 480 and 580 nm (see Figure 10.17). By rotating this line, all other pairs of spectral stimuli that can produce white can be immediately ascertained. These pairs are said to be *complementary* with respect to this equal-energy white. White could also be made by mixing three stimuli, as is shown in Figure 10.17. (We already know that white can be made from a continuous, equal-energy spectrum.)

The spectral locus does not close upon itself, but leaves a gap between its two ends. Mixtures of spectral stimuli chosen from the extremes of the visible spectrum define a straight line of *extraspectral purples*.

The Relation between Chromaticity and Luminance

The luminances of the three spectral primaries (700, 546, and 436 nm) required to produce equal trichromatic amounts, and thus to match an equal-energy white, are decidedly unequal. Table 10.2 shows this relationship.

From Table 10.2, it can be seen that, if three primaries are mixed together in equal luminance amounts, there would be about 17 times as many trichromatic units of blue as red in the mixture, and an amazing 77 times as many units of blue as green! The resulting mixture would be decidedly blue in appearance, scarcely distinguishable from the blue primary.

If the luminances of the primaries are known, and if Abney's Law is assumed, it should be possible to compute the luminance of any stimulus whatsoever by first matching it with a mixture of the three primaries, and then summing the luminances of the primaries. For example, the stimulus that would be achieved by a mixture of the primary stimuli listed in Table 10.2 would match an equal-energy white and would have a luminance of 56.5 mL. If the tiny amount of blue light (0.6 mL) were removed, the mixture would become yellow in appearance, but its luminance would be reduced by only about 1 percent—hardly a perceptible amount. Thus blue light, which contributes very little to luminance, has powerful coloring powers.

All real light stimuli must have a positive luminance, although we have seen that stimuli can be imagined that have negative amounts. If we could actually produce these, it would be possible to create a series of mixture stimuli having zero luminance. For example, suppose that we could somehow subtract red light from a mixture of 10 trichromatic units of blue and 10 of green. The luminance sum of the blue and green components is 45.9 plus 0.6 = 46.5 mL; to duplicate this luminance with red light would require 4.65 times the 10 mL needed for the 10 trichromatic units, corresponding to 46.5 trichromatic units. From this we can compute the tristimulus values:

$$R = -46.5$$
$$G = 10$$
$$B = 10$$

and the chromaticity coordinates

$$r = -1.755 \qquad g = b = 0.378$$

If we were to increase the energy of the stimulus by any factor, the result would still be a stimulus of zero luminance.

The pair of chromaticity coordinates that we have just calculated falls upon a locus of such points having zero luminance, which Shrödinger (1920) called the *alychne*. In the g versus r chromaticity diagram of Figure 10.17, the alychne is shown as the dotted line

connecting points labeled X and Z; the value that we have just computed is at A on an extension of this line.

The CIE System of Imaginary Primaries

The chromaticity system for specifying color, worked out by Maxwell (although in a triangular coordinate system) more than 100 years ago, proved so useful that an international standardizing organization, the Commission Internationale de l'Eclairage (CIE) in 1931 established an international system. A major point to be decided upon was the choice of primaries, for an infinity of chromaticity charts can be prepared, depending upon the colors that are taken as primaries. Whatever the choice, the red primary on an r versus g chart will plot at $r = 1.0$, $g = 0$, the green primary will plot at $r = 0$, $g = 1.0$, and the blue primary at $r = g = 0$ (note that this is the case in Figure 10.17). It works out that the spectral locus defined by one system of primaries is a projective transformation of that defined by any other system of primaries, a projection which places the three primaries in a relation that forms a right triangle with equal sides adjacent to the right angle.

A straight line in one chromaticity chart will transform into a straight line in another chart based on different primaries, but the lengths of such lines relative to one another will change from chart to chart, as will also their angular relations to one another.

In developing the CIE system, a decision was made to utilize a set of imaginary primaries. In essence, this amounts to an extrapolation in the mathematical domain beyond what can be realized physically. Probably the easiest way to visualize what was done is in terms of the chromaticity diagram of Figure 10.17. This diagram, it will be recalled, is based upon a set of real primaries.

The imaginary primaries that were chosen are shown in Figure 10.17 as the points X, Y, and Z. In this diagram, note that the angle YZX is not a right angle, X does not plot at an abscissa value of 1.0, Y does not plot at

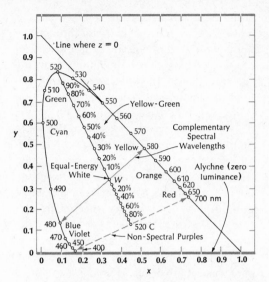

Figure 10.18. Chromaticity diagram based upon the imaginary primaries of the CIE system. (Boynton, 1966.)

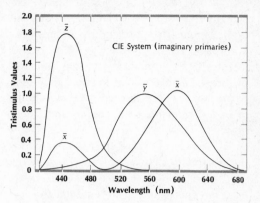

Figure 10.19. Color-matching functions (tristimulus values for an equal-energy spectrum) in the primary system of the CIE. (Boynton, 1966.)

an ordinate value of 1.0, and Z is not at the origin. These positions are accomplished in the diagram of Figure 10.18, which is the appropriate transformation to produce a chromaticity diagram specified in terms of the imaginary primaries X, Y, and Z indicated in the original chromaticity space of Figure 10.17. In both projections, X, Y, and Z are well outside the spectral locus; this is what makes them imaginary. They were deliberately chosen this way so that the chromaticity co-ordinates of all real stimuli would have positive values. In other words, the entire domain of real colors in the transformed diagram falls in the all-positive quadrant.

There are, of course, many sets of three points in the diagram of Figure 10.17 that could accomplish this objective. The ones that were selected have several advantages. In the first place, the lines connecting them just barely graze the spectral locus. This means that there is little waste space near the axes of the transformed diagram. The line X–Y, furthermore, is coincident with the locus of long-wave spectral stimuli from about 550 nm onward. Second, the line X–Z was chosen to

fall on the *alychne*, the zero-luminance line previously discussed. A consequence of this is that both the X and Z primaries in this imaginary system have zero luminance. Calculations pertaining to luminance can therefore be based upon the Y primary alone. To finish the job, the line between Y and Z was drawn to be almost, but not quite, tangent to the spectral locus in the neighborhood of 500 nm.

It will be recalled that the chromaticity diagram in Figure 10.17 was based upon the set of color mixture curves of Figure 10.16. It is possible to go the other way: Given the location of three primaries, such as X, Y, and Z in Figure 10.17, and the luminance of each, a set of color mixture curves can be derived which correspond to these. This has been done for the CIE primaries, and these curves, called $\bar{x}$, $\bar{y}$, and $\bar{z}$, are shown in Figure 10.19. As would be expected, all values are positive. Values of $\bar{z}$ are zero beyond 560 nm. This corresponds to the fact that these stimuli fall on the line where $z = 0$ in the chromaticity chart. Values of $\bar{x}$ form a double-humped curve as a function of wavelength. It reaches close to zero near 500 nm, where the spectral locus of the chromaticity diagram nearly touches the ordinate. The left-hand hump of $\bar{x}$ corresponds to the bending of the spectral locus away from the ordinate in the chromaticity chart as the wavelength is shortened from 500 nm. The $\bar{y}$ function is exactly proportional to the V_λ function discussed in Chapter 9, the luminous efficiency function of the standard observer in the CIE system. As previously noted, this results from a choice of X and Z primaries which puts both of them on the alychne.

The curves of Figure 10.19 are known as the distribution curves for an equal-energy spectrum in the CIE system. These are widely used in order to calculate chromaticities in a standard way, given that the physical characteristics of a stimulus to be evaluated are known; and to predict which stimuli will match other ones.

Suppose that we have two physical samples and we wish to know whether they match. To find out, we determine the tristimulus values X, Y, and Z in the CIE system, defined as follows (see Equation 14):

$$X_1 = \int N_\lambda \bar{x}\, d\lambda$$
$$Y_1 = \int N_\lambda \bar{y}\, d\lambda \qquad (17)$$
$$Z_1 = \int N_\lambda \bar{z}\, d\lambda$$

We do the same for the other sample to obtain X_2, Y_2, and Z_2. If $Y_1 = Y_2$, the two samples have the same luminance, but may not match for hue and/or saturation. If additionally $X_1 = X_2$ and $Z_1 = Z_2$, the two samples will match in all respects.

To determine chromaticity in the CIE system, calculate

$$x = \frac{X}{X + Y + Z}$$
$$y = \frac{Y}{X + Y + Z} \qquad (18)$$

and plot the result in the standard diagram.

The development of the CIE system has been described here by graphical means. (For a discussion of the corresponding algebra, see LeGrand [1957] or Graham [1965] or Wyszecki and Stiles [1967].)

An alternative scheme for specifying chromaticity may be made in terms of *dominant wavelength* and *excitation purity*. To determine the dominant wavelength of a sample, draw a line from the white point through the point which represents the chromaticity of the sample, extending it until it intersects the spectrum locus. This intersection point defines the dominant wavelength. Excitation purity is defined (see Figure 10.18) as the distance of the sample point from the white point, expressed as a percentage of the distance all the way from the white point through the sample point to the spectrum locus. For samples lying between the white point and the line of extraspectral purples (see above) excitation purity is similarly defined as a percentage of the distance from the white point to the purple line. The dominant wavelength of such a sample is specified

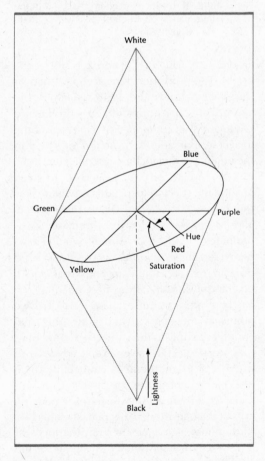

Figure 10.20. Psychological color solid. (After Judd & Wyszecki, 1952.)

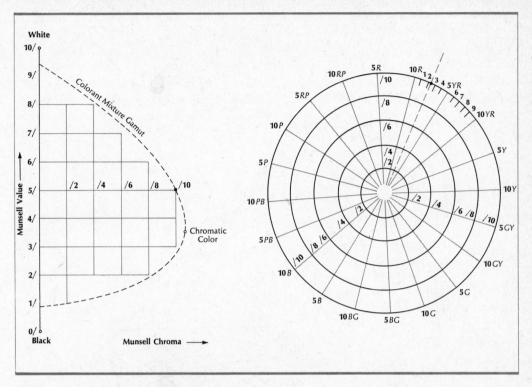

Figure 10.21. Munsell system of color specification. Diagram at the left is for a particular Munsell hue, the one at the right is for a particular Munsell value. If the diagram at the left is for Munsell hue 2.5YR, then the color 2.5YR 5/10 is specified as shown in each part of the diagram. (Wyszecki & Stiles, 1967.)

by the complementary spectral wavelength, followed by a lower-case *c*; for example, $\lambda = 540\ c$.

The Appearance of Mixture Colors: Psychological Color Diagrams and Their Relation to the Chromaticity Diagram

If an individual is given a large collection of chips of colored paper and is asked to arrange them in some reasonable and continuous way, he is likely to order them in a fashion schematized by the psychological color solid depicted in Figure 10.20. The vertical dimension of this solid is a lightness-darkness dimension, which we shall not deal with further here because of the decision to restrict the discussion to chromatic vision and to colors seen against a dark surround. A slice across the diagram yields the familiar color circles previously referred to, with white in the middle, and hues spread around it in the

same order as seen in the spectrum. There is one addition: The circle has been completed in the purple region, which is quite legitimate in this purely psychological diagram, where there is no need to be tied down to what happens to appear in the physical spectrum.

Systems of color specification have been developed, and from these experiments of the kind just described have been carried out. The one most widely known in the United States has led to the publication of the *Munsell Book of Colors,* in which hundreds upon hundreds of color samples are arranged according to their "hue, value, and chroma." (*Value* and *chroma* correspond to lightness and saturation.) Figure 10.21 shows the specification scheme used. To illustrate, taking an example used by Wyszecki and Stiles (1967), "The notation 2.5 YR 5/10 indicates a Munsell hue of 2.5 yellow-red, a Munsell value of 5/

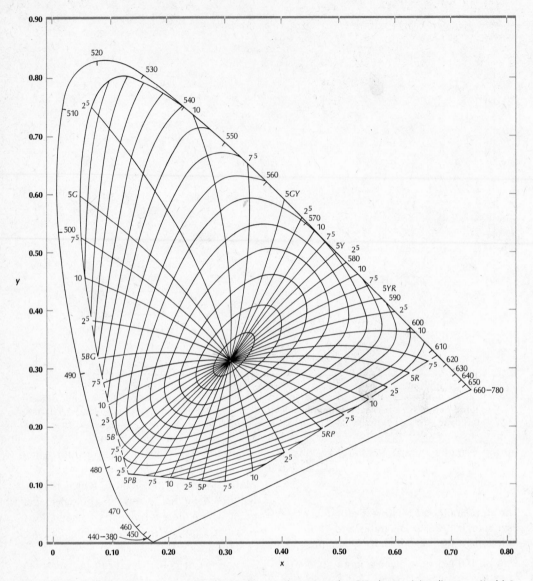

Figure 10.22. Chromaticities of Munsell colors, value 5/, shown on the CIE chromaticity diagram. (Judd & Wyszecki, 1963.)

(which is equally separated from black and white), and a Munsell chroma of /10 (which means 10 steps away from gray (N5/ of the same Munsell value)."

The chromaticity coefficients of all Munsell samples have been calculated (Newhall, Nickerson, & Judd, 1943); this allows the Munsell samples to be plotted on the CIE chromaticity diagram. These plots for Value 5 are shown in Figure 10.22. They reveal the following features:

(1) Because the equal chroma lines emerging from the white point to the spectrum locus are in general curved, stimuli of the same dominant wavelength but variable excitation purity will have a variable hue. For example, if long-wave red at 700 nm is gradually added to equal-energy white, it will first appear as a desaturated bluish red, later as a saturated yellowish red.

(2) The spacings of the closed contours surrounding the white point, each of which

defines a given chroma (saturation) are un-equal, being a function of hue. There are many more chroma steps per unit chromaticity change in the lower left-hand part of the diagram than elsewhere.

(3) Real samples of color approach the spectrum locus in the red-yellow-orange part of the spectrum but not elsewhere. This is the result of two factors: (a) Long-wave pigments that reflect light have characteristics such as those shown in Figure 10.1. They reflect very little light at the short wavelengths, and thus avoid desaturation. (b) To a first approximation, only the R and G cones are activated by the long wavelengths that are reflected, so that mixture colors of stimuli containing these wavelengths fall very near to the spectrum locus. Saturated blue-greens, in contrast, are impossible to obtain from reflecting surfaces for analogous reasons: (1) As shown in Figure 10.1, blue-green pigments do not cut out the irrelevant part of the spectrum so sharply as do red ones. (2) The mixture functions of the eye are such that they would produce desaturation in a broad

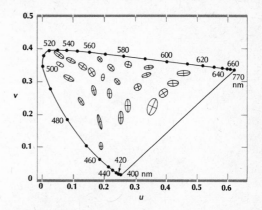

Figure 10.24. MacAdam ellipses plotted in the 1960 CIE-UCS diagram. The new coordinates, u and v, are defined in terms of the standard ones, x and y, as follows: $u = (4x)/(-2x + 12y + 3)$; $v = (6y)/(-2x + 12y + 3)$. (Wyszecki & Stiles, 1967.)

spectral band even if such a sharp cutoff existed.

Many experiments have been made to investigate the lack of uniformity encountered in the CIE chromaticity diagram by other means. Notable among these are the experiments of Brown and MacAdam (1949) and of Brown (1957) in which the dispersion of color matches at various sample points in chromaticity space was carefully measured. The result is a series of ellipses such as those shown in Figure 10.23. Each of these represents 10 times the standard deviation of the match to a stimulus having a chromaticity located at the point in the center. Where the ellipses are small, very small chromaticity changes are discriminable; where they are large, only very large changes are discriminable. This figure should be compared with Figure 10.22, based on the Munsell scheme. Although the one involves a discrimination experiment, and the other a direct color-ordering experiment, the basic agreement between them is obvious.

The CIE in 1960 adopted a transformation of the chromaticity chart that produces MacAdam ellipses of more nearly uniform size. This is shown in Figure 10.24.

MacAdam (1944) has shown that no linear transformation exists that will create perfect uniformity. Farnsworth (1957) worked out an

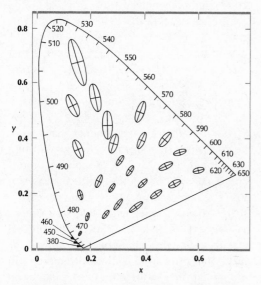

Figure 10.23. MacAdam ellipses. These are plotted as 10 times the standard deviation of attempted isomeric matches, by method of adjustment, approaching the match point in the directions indicated. (Wyszecki & Stiles, 1967.)

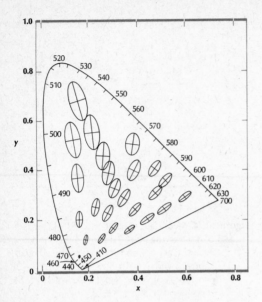

Figure 10.25. Discrimination ellipses derived by Stiles, based upon his line-element theory. These should be compared with the MacAdam ellipses of Figure 10.23. (Wyszecki & Stiles, 1967.)

arbitrary nonlinear projection which creates an acceptable uniformity but which lacks all of the other useful properties of a chromaticity diagram. (Many other nonlinear transformations also have been attempted.)

Because color matching experiments do not require judgments of color appearance, or even of color differences, there is no a priori reason why a chromaticity diagram derived from such experiments should provide any reasonable description whatever of chromatic experience. That it does suggests that there are explicit relations between chromatic stimuli and chromatic sensations. Whereas the model discussed on page 328 gives an idea of what some of these relations are, it is a very simple one and does not attempt to deal explicitly with the problem of nonuniformity. Stiles (Wyszecki & Stiles, 1967) has produced a theory that accounts for the nonuniformity of the chromaticity diagram to a remarkable degree (Figure 10.25). His theory is far too complicated to describe here, but one very important feature of it may

be pointed out. It is an elaboration of a "line element" scheme first proposed by Helmholtz: ". . . with . . . three mechanisms in operation, the smallest perceptible difference is obtained by combining the fractional deviations for the three mechanisms in the same way as independent errors are compounded, using the square root of a sum-of-squares relation" (Wyszecki & Stiles, 1967).

ABNORMAL CHROMATIC VISION

In this section we are concerned with what is known in the vernacular as "color blindness." A better expression would be "chromatic deficiency," for if the term "color" is used in its technical sense (see p. 317), one who is considered to be "color blind" would be completely lacking any form of vision.

Only a handful of people have been turned up who are chromatically blind, that is, who possess only black and white vision. Chromatically *defective* people, in contrast, are very common: about 8 percent of the male population is afflicted, along with perhaps 3 females in every 10,000. The disproportionately large percentage of males is accounted for by the fact that the defect is inherited by way of a defect in the *x*-chromosome. A male, having only one *x*, is color deficient if that *x* is defective. A female, having two *x* chromosomes, is color deficient only if both are defective; the normal one predominates if she has one of each.

Color-matching experiments have provided the principal basis for the classification of color defect. A chief proponent of this approach has been the British physicist, W. D. Wright, whose 1946 volume called *Researches on Normal and Defective Colour Vision* remains today an excellent source of classification criteria and of data on the subject. The physicists' viewpoint appears in modified form in Judd's (1951) chapter in Stevens, *Handbook of Experimental Psychology,* and again in its extreme form in an impressive recent compendium on *Color Science* by Wyszecki and Stiles (1967) which has already been referred to in several places in this chapter.

A limitation of the physicist's approach is that he pays little attention to what the subject actually sees. A vociferous advocate of a more subjective point of view is Arthur Linksz, an ophthalmologist who in his *Essay on Color Vision and Clinical Color-Vision Tests* (1964) is sharply critical of the physical approach and its seeming obsession with difficult mathematical trichromatic concepts. Linksz feels that such concepts ignore a mountain of evidence which seems to support a more direct appeal to sensory experience as it is approached from an opponent-colors viewpoint.

So let the student beware: this is indeed a controversial subject. Color blindness seems to fascinate everyone, even those who have little interest otherwise in vision; it is controversial because of its relation to color theory (itself a controversial subject), because laymen have a tendency to introduce controversy into technical matters, and also because color-defective individuals often do not fit neatly into the pigeonholes that the physically oriented workers have so neatly constructed for them. For every rule, there seem to be exceptions.

The approach to be taken here, to describe defects in color perception, is eclectic. The generally accepted, but clearly oversimplified classification scheme of the physicist will be given; but it would be less than honest to let the subject rest at that point. Therefore, at the end of the section, a few comments will be added to indicate what some of the exceptions are to the statements that have been made.

Color Matching Behavior of Chromatically-Defective Observers

About a quarter of those who are chromatically deficient exhibit the interesting property that they are dichromatic color mixers. Whereas the normal subject, as previously explained, needs three primaries to make a color match, the *dichromat* needs but two,

and this fact defines his condition. For almost all of them, either one of the longwave primaries, the red or the green, can be dispensed with.

On page 341, the *anomaloscope* was described, and the principle of its operation explained. The dichromat evidently has only one longwave-sensitive receptor; both the red and green primary stimuli activate it more than they do the B cone and therefore these cannot be used as independent primaries. When using the anomaloscope, or when making a full trichromatic match, the dichromat finds that there are many combinations of settings of the red and green primaries that will produce the same visual result; thus the matches are not unique. By depriving him of one of the primaries, his unique matching behavior can be examined; the result of this experiment can be plotted on a one-dimensional chromaticity diagram.

It is important to note that, although the dichromat makes matches unacceptable to the normal trichromat, the dichromat will in general accept all matches made by the normal subject. This is theoretically important because it suggests that the dichromat is suffering from a *reduced* form of normal color vision; that which he does have seems to be normal. If the dichromat is made to judge the color matches made by a trichromat, we can plot lines of confusion (called *isochromatic lines*) for the dichromat upon the chromaticity diagram of the normal subject.

The two common forms of dichromatism are known as *protanopia* and *deuteranopia;* those who have these defects are called *protanopes* and *deuteranopes*. The protanope is distinguished by a large insensitivity to stimuli in the long-wave end of the spectrum, requiring five to ten times as much energy to perceive a level of brightness apparently equal to what the normal subject sees. The deuteranope's perception of luminosity, as measured by brightness matching methods, is essentially normal.

Luminosity curves, being arbitrarily set at 1.0 at the value of peak sensitivity, tell us nothing about the differences between normal and defective subjects on an absolute basis. For this purpose, foveal threshold determinations are better, for the absolute radiance levels required are measured throughout the spectrum and can be compared.

In recent studies, Hsia and Graham (1957)

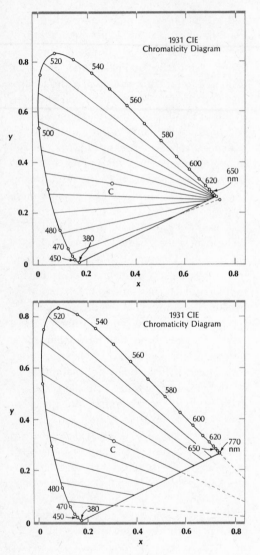

Figure 10.26. Confusion lines for protanopes (top) and deuteranopes (bottom) shown on a standard CIE chromaticity diagram. Any two stimuli the chromaticities of which fall along one of these lines cannot be discriminated by these color-defective observers. (After Wright, 1946.)

worked with 11 dichromats using the threshold method; Wald and Brown (1965) worked with 31. Both agree that the protanope lacks sensitivity in the red end of the spectrum, with average values indicating a loss of sensitivity of a bit more than a factor of 6. Both agree that deuteranopes lack sensitivity to the middle part of the spectrum. Although Hsia and Graham do not show it, Wald and Brown report that deuteranopes are more sensitive than normals to the red end of the spectrum (by a factor of nearly 2) whereas protanopes are more sensitive than normals to the middle of the spectrum (by a factor of nearly 3).

The chromaticity plots of the confusion lines of the protanope and the deuteranope are shown in Figure 10.26. The fact that in each case one of these lines passes through the white point (C) and intersects the spectrum locus suggests that there should be a point in the spectrum that looks white for both classes of observers. This has been confirmed in independent experiments where spectral stimuli have been examined; the deuteranope's neutral point is at a slightly longer wavelength, as would be predicted from the direction of the isochromatic line which for the deuteranope has a steeper slope than it does for the protanope.

The fact that the confusion lines of the protanope seem to converge in the red corner has been interpreted to imply a missing receptor (the point where these lines intersect is known as the *copunctal point* and from it the spectral sensitivity of the missing mechanisms can be derived). Although the deuteranope's confusion lines do not seem to converge as clearly, this is partly a matter of the particular projection of the CIE diagram; they do seem to be converging toward a point outside the diagram, and this can be interpreted to indicate that the deuteranope lacks green receptors.

In terms of the model described on page 328, we may speculate that the protanope lacks R cones containing the red pigment α. If by some genetic mistake, these cones were

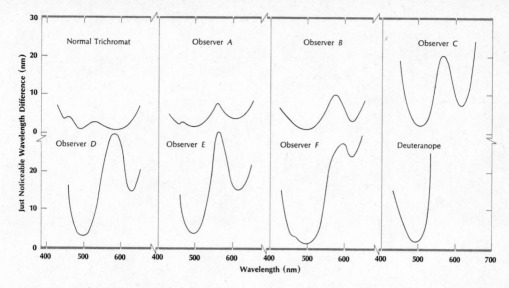

Figure 10.27. Wavelength discrimination functions for subjects ranging from normal (upper left) to the full dichromat (lower right).

to contain the green β pigment instead, this would produce a perpetual zero signal at C_1. The extra β substance would cause an abnormally high sensitivity in the middle part of the spectrum, whereas the loss of α accounts for the sensitivity loss at long wavelengths.

If we assume that the deuteranope lacks the β substance, and that his G cones are filled with the red-sensitive α pigment instead, the basic facts of deuteranopia are accounted for.

A third type of dichromatism exists called *tritanopia,* which is very rare. This seems adequately explained by postulating a loss of B cones.

The largest group of color defective subjects are known as *anomalous trichromats.* As the name implies, they require three controls on the colorimeter in order to make color matches. Their most distinguishing characteristic is that their matches differ from those of a normal subject. If their matches were based upon the use of the same cone photopigments as those possessed by the normal subject, this would be impossible; it is therefore necessary to postulate that at least one of their three pigments has an abnormal spectral sensitivity. The bulk of the evidence

suggests that it is the red-sensitive pigment that is different.

In addition to making atypical matches, anomalous observers usually show visual discrimination of chromatic differences that is poorer than normal. A good way to show this is by measuring their *wavelength discrimination.* A particular wavelength λ is projected into one half of a bipartite matching field, and the other half is adjusted to some other wavelength. The subject is then asked to set a wavelength on each side of the standard which is just barely discriminable. If he attempts to make a match and his dispersions are recorded, this should be recognized as a special case of Brown and MacAdam's method, although it is not possible to generate an ellipse near the spectrum locus.

Results of the wavelength discrimination experiment for a sampling of normal, dichromatic, and anomalous observers are shown in Figure 10.27. Individual differences in this type of experiment are considerable. For the anomalous observers, wavelength discrimination functions range all the way from almost normal to essentially dichromatic in appearance. (Wright [1946] suggests this as a criterion of degree of defect.)

TABLE 10.3 SALIENT PROPERTIES OF COLOR DEFECTIVES

Characteristic	Protanomalous	Deuteranomalous	Protanope	Deuteranope	Tritanope	Rod-Monochromat
Chromaticness discrimination through the spectrum	Materially reduced from red to yellowish-green but to a varying degree in different cases		Absent from the red to about 520 nm	Absent from the red to about 530 nm	Absent in the greenish-blue to blue (445 to 480 nm)	No chromaticness discrimination
Neutral point, that is, wavelength of spectral stimulus that matches white	None	None	494 nm (495.5 nm) Pitt (1935)	499 nm (500.4 nm) Pitt (1935)	(a) 570 nm (b) 400 nm	All wavelengths
Shortening of the red, that is, reduced luminous efficiency of long wavelengths	Yes	No	Yes	No	No	Yes
Wavelength of the maximum of the relative luminous efficiency curve	540 nm	560 nm	540 nm	560 nm	555 nm	507 nm
CIE chromaticity of the confusion point (dichromats only)	—	—	$x_{pc} = 0.747$ $y_{pc} = 0.253$	$x_{dc} = 1.080$ $y_{dc} = -0.080$	$x_{tc} = 0.171$ $y_{tc} = 0$	—
Percentage frequency of occurrence among males among females	1.0 0.02	4.9 0.38	1.0 0.02	1.1 0.01	0.002 0.001	0.003 0.002

From Wyszecki and Stiles (1967)

Anomalous subjects also fall into protan and deutan groupings; they are known as protanomalous if they exhibit a lack of sensitivity for long wavelengths, as evaluated by brightness matching, and as deuteranomalous if they do not. Foveal threshold experiments for anomalous subjects have been done by Wald and Brown (1965).

It is conceivable that the red-sensitive pigment of the anomalous subject constitutes the pigment contained in the second type of R cone in the normal, shown in dotted lines in Figure 10.5. It will be recalled that the reason for introducing this complication was to account for the resurgence, for the normal subject, of red sensations at very short wavelengths, in the violet part of the spectrum. All photopigment absorption curves exhibit a secondary maximum at short wavelengths; for the regular α, β, and γ pigments, this is obliterated by the absorption of ultraviolet light by the eye media. If there were another red-sensitive pigment, with a peak sensitivity at about 625, its secondary short-wave peak would fall within the short-wave end of the visible spectrum and produce a visible effect (Ingling, 1969).

A summary of some of the characteristics of defective chromatic vision is given in Table 10.3, from Wyszecki and Stiles (1967).

At the outset of this section, it was promised that the explanations to be offered of defective chromatic vision would be too pat. One additional experiment will be cited to illustrate this (other complications are spelled out by Linksz, 1964).

In an experiment conducted by Scheibner and Boynton (1968), the color-naming technique was applied to 3 protanopes and 5 deuteranopes. The results for one of the protanopes have already been shown in Figure 10.11, which should be consulted again. In this experiment, the 8 spectral stimuli employed were all equated for brightness for each subject by direct match with a yellow at 580 nm, with the yellow stimulus set at 1000 trolands. Three other sets of stimuli were also used, at 500, 250, and 125 trolands. These were

randomly presented, and color naming functions built up by the procedure already described on page 347. Although there were individual differences, no subject exhibited an absolute lack of discrimination in the long-wave end of the spectrum, where all matching experiments and all color theory dictate that a complete confusion should exist. A reasonable conclusion to draw is that there is some red-sensitive α pigment present in the R cones of the protanope, or that there are a few R cones that contain the normal complement of pigment. Either way, the potential exists for a feeble imbalance at the C_1 chromatic unit. Thus the protanopic loss of red-green discrimination is not complete.

THE EFFECT OF SURROUND FIELDS UPON A CENTRALLY VIEWED TEST AREA

We have so far ignored in this chapter most of what would fall under the heading of *color perception*, as distinct from *chromatic vision*. Because color perception will be covered in Chapter 12, we avoid a treatment of object perception, but deal instead only with a few features of a singularly important topic, the effect of a surround field upon the chromatic characteristics of a centrally viewed test area.

Persistence of Color Matches

Over a considerable range, the introduction of a surround field or, for that matter, a change in the state of adaptation of the eye otherwise produced, will not affect a color match. Such a surround field will dramatically alter the *appearance* of both halves of the test field, but equally so on both sides. Thus a red surround will make a central yellow appear green, but all metamers of the original yellow will be affected alike.

It can be shown that this is a logical consequence of the assumption that the shapes of the absorption spectra of the three cone pigments, when plotted on a logarithmic ordinate, do not change with chromatic induction. As previously noted in the discussion of chromatic adaptation, their heights may be altered, and additional adaptive changes may occur further along in the visual system. However all such changes must be mediated initially by what is absorbed in the retinal photoreceptors, so that unless their absorption curves change shape, color matches must hold true. The failure of the color match to change with changes in surround and/or adaptation is known as the *persistence of color matches.*

Like most generalizations, the discussion above has its limits. Color matches do indeed break down under intense conditions of adaptation, although there is some dispute concerning the luminance levels necessary to produce the breakdown. (The data of Brindley [1953] have shown the effect very clearly.) To explain the effect, it is necessary to suppose that the spectral sensitivity of at least one of the receptors has been changed. This could be caused either by a fourth pigment which, for one reason or another, does not contribute sufficiently to prevent trichromatic color mixing but which is bleached relatively little by bright lights. Or it could be the result of a significant change in the density of one of the three regular pigments. Ingling (1969) has marshalled five converging lines of evidence to favor the view that the red receptor contains a small amount of a fourth pigment, which has its peak sensitivity in the neighborhood of 610 nm.

The Dark Colors

When the surround field is brighter than the test area, it induces blackness or grayness into the test area (Evans, 1964). For test areas on the order of one degree of visual angle, subjective black is reached when the test area has a luminance that is 20 percent or so of that of the surround; further reductions in luminance produce no further increase in blackness.

If the test area is already receiving a chromatic stimulus, say an orange one, the effect of a brighter achromatic surround is to induce blackness into the test area; this causes the dark orange that we call "brown." There is no brown in the spectrum—it is solely the result of the induction process and cannot appear in the simple, bright field. "Navy blue" is another example of a color induced by a brighter surround field; especially with large test areas, the blue content can be seen despite an astonishingly high black content. "Maroon" is the term given for reds that are similarly darkened. The effect described above is critically important, for it adds tremendous variation to our color perceptions of real objects.

Another effect of the induction of grayness into the central test area is to increase the saturation of the test stimulus. For this and probably other reasons, surface colors may appear much more saturated in the complex context in which they are normally viewed than would a stimulus of exactly the same chromaticity if viewed with a dark surround.

It has long been suspected (Hering was quite explicit about it) that induction effects revealed lateral interaction effects in the retina. The experiment of DeValois and Walraven (see p. 336) is one of the more recent to confirm this along with electrophysiological evidence. Furthermore, the dramatic experiments of Land (see Chapter 12) have illustrated just how profound these effects can be. Thus, a great many experiments have already been completed on the subject of chromatic induction (see for example the review of Judd, 1960), and it seems likely that this will be a rich area for psychological investigation in the future.

Mathew Alpern

EFFECTOR MECHANISMS
IN VISION

11

You have seen that vision involves much more than focusing a sharp optical image on a sensitive retina. But even sharp retinal images are formed only after complex sequences of physiological (and psychological) events take place, which culminate in muscle contractions in the eye. In this chapter, some of the effector mechanisms necessary for seeing are described. Others equally important (for example, the secretion of tears and blinking) are not touched upon at all. An experimental psychology of tear secretion does not yet exist (though it is difficult to understand why). One for blinking has an appreciable literature, but it is largely related to experiments on fatigue and on learning, and therefore more appropriately discussed elsewhere.

INTRODUCTION

Of all the oculomotor mechanisms, the one most exhaustively probed by psychologists has been that of eye movements. This is scarcely surprising, for their study is one of the most accessible ways of analyzing visual behavior in a wide variety of animals. Even man reveals many of his inner secrets in the pattern of his eye movements, a fact appreciated very well by oriental merchants, poets, and policemen at least as long ago as it was by psychologists.

Unlike the photographic film to which we so frequently

compare it, the retina does not have the same spatial sensitivity (visual acuity) throughout. We have already noted, in Chapter 9, that the very center of the retina (the fovea) includes a very small region, a little more than a tenth of a millimeter in diameter (see Figure 9.7) where visual acuity is very high. The visual acuity falls off very quickly the farther away from the fovea the image is made. In the area where the first rods appear, the acuity is already reduced by 50 percent. Eight degrees from the foveal center, the acuity is only 15 percent of the maximum value, and it continues to decrease the farther one progresses into the periphery. Such a photographic film in a perfectly motionless camera would reproduce a "picture" with very sharp detail only in its very center, with less and less detail conveyed the farther away from the center the image falls. The great mass of the picture would be hopelessly blurred.

Such an arrangement is quite unsuitable for the very complex visual requirements of our modern world. It is made remarkably effective, however, merely because of six highly responsive muscles (among the fastest in the human body) attached to each eyeball. These muscles originate in the bony wall of the orbit and are so attached to the globe that upon contraction they rotate the eye around its center (or nearly so). In this way, that part of the retina with the highest acuity can be pointed at different objects in the field of view in rapid succession.

If you were asked what your experience is as you view the world, you would probably describe neither the sequence of eye movements nor the blur of the rest of the visual world around the fixation point. On the contrary, you have the *illusion* of spatial solidity with continuous perception of the entire visual field, all parts of which appear equally sharp and distinct. This is one of many mysteries of the process of vision with moving eyes. How are sharp images of all the successive fixation points fitted together to build this picture of one continuous solid space? How does it happen that all of the fuzzy streaks

of the entire retinal image during the movements and the blurred patterns of that part of the retinal image away from the fixation point are usually not perceived at all?

Of these questions, some await the genius of some future generation either for insightful answers (perhaps by a reader of these pages) or for recognition of the fact that they are not capable of solution. Others are just now beginning to generate the thinking and research from which the answers may be found. We will discuss what is known about them presently.

Muscles

There are six extraocular muscles attached to each globe at various positions. Four of these (the rectus muscles) originate posteriorly at the apex of the orbit and insert into the sclera in the anterior part of the globe, from 5.5 to 7.7 mm back from the junction of the cornea and the sclera. The medial rectus muscle attaches nasally, the lateral rectus temporally, the superior and inferior rectus above and below, respectively. In addition, there are two oblique muscles which effectively originate at the nasal anterior corners of the orbit, one above, the other below the globe. These, the superior and inferior oblique muscles, pass back in each case beneath the relevant rectus muscle and attach to the posterior temporal globe (above in the case of the superior, below in the case of the inferior oblique).

Because of the relations among the muscles described above, individual muscles make distinctively different contributions to globe rotation when the eye is in various positions. However a detailed "switching circuit" in the brain stem produces coordination among these muscles so that signals from higher centers are accurately translated into eye movements. In practice, therefore, it is unnecessary for psychologists to analyze what contributions different muscles make to a given globe rotation, although this is a routine problem for a surgeon confronted with a paralysis of one or more of the eye muscles.

METHODS OF MEASURING EYE MOVEMENTS

The analysis of eye movements is a time-honored pursuit of psychologists. For over 60 years the emphasis has been on the development of better objective methods for indicating eye position. Nevertheless, for many questions very simple methods are often quite satisfactory. The easiest is merely to watch the observer's eyes. An expert eye watcher can detect movements as small as 0.5°, but if you are a beginner, it will take practice before you are that sensitive. Of course, your head will protrude into the observer's field of view, but a judiciously positioned mirror or a small peephole cut in the center of the visual display may suffice to overcome this difficulty in many situations. You can, by this means, make rough estimates of where and how frequently the eyes make different kinds of shifts of gaze; but, if you are interested in more quantitative details, you will have to do something different. Just what depends upon the feature of the shift of gaze you are most interested in measuring precisely. A detailed discussion of many of these methods is available in earlier editions of this book, in a historical review by Carmichael and Dearborn (1947), and in a more recent review (Alpern, 1962). The following contains only a very brief description of the older methods and a summary of some more recent developments.

Afterimages

Assume, for the moment, that accuracy is of prime importance and that you have little or no interest in the time characteristics of the movement as such. The easiest solution is a subjective method, which consists of looking at a bright line (or point) of light long enough to impress a strong afterimage on the foveal cones, after which the light is turned off. It is well known that shifting gaze is accompanied by a movement of the afterimage. You can measure where the foveal cones are pointing by aligning the projected afterimage with a pointer, the position of which can then be exactly measured with a meter stick. The extent to which the eyes miss any supposed fixation point can be readily determined, assuming that fixation was exact when the afterimage was impressed.

Variations in the technique described above include using various devices for entoptic[1] perception of the fovea, but these are somewhat less satisfactory because they appear only for a few moments and must therefore be periodically reinforced. One modification of this method is to produce afterimages during the eye movement with a high-intensity, stationary, flickering light. The string of afterimages so produced across the retina allows us to estimate not only the duration of the movement but also precisely where the globe was pointing during the moment each of the afterimages was impressed. If more details about time characteristics of the movement are required, however, it is difficult to obtain them by subjective methods.

Objective Methods Without Attachments to the Eye

There is really no completely satisfactory method of measuring eye movements larger than 8° objectively and accurately. The principal difficulty, shared by almost all methods free of globe attachments, is that they do not successfully distinguish between pure rotations that one hopes to record and translational shifts of the globe in the orbit or of the head. These shifts appear as artifacts on the record because they look like eye movements, yet they do not indicate a shift of the retinal image with respect to the fovea. Although there is unequivocal evidence that such translational shifts accompany many eye rotations, it is still far from clear what the relation between the magnitude of the translational shift and the amount of eye rotation is. One disturbing consequence of this is that all systems that require calibration curves for estimating exact eye position may be completely invalid when a different kind of eye

[1] Lying in or originating from the eyeball, rather than the outside world.

movement is used for study than was employed for calibration. (This problem is one of the major difficulties with most of the following methods.)

Electro-oculography   There is a small but steady difference in electric potential between the cornea and the retina, which can be recorded by ordinary electrodes placed in pairs on the skin around the orbital rim. As the eye rotates, it moves the electrically positive cornea closer to one electrode and further from its partner at the opposite orbital rim (Schott, 1922; Mowrer, Ruch, & Miller, 1936; Hoffman, Wellman, & Carmichael, 1939). As used ordinarily, the paired electrodes are placed at the inner and outer orbital margins (for study of horizontal rotations) and above and below (for study of vertical rotations) or in all four locations (to study vertical and horizontal movements of both eyes). If all four electrode pairs are used, at least four separate channels are required. The potential differences between the electrodes of each pair must be suitably amplified and recorded, usually with a pen recorder, although a slow-sweep oscilloscope trace may also be used. The amplifiers should be stable, low-noise, and directly coupled if a continuous record of eye position is to be made. Also a means of reducing the potential difference to zero— "zero suppression or bias control"—is desirable to place the record on the zero line when the eye is looking straight ahead. (Care must be taken, by using nonpolarizable electrodes, that potential changes while the eye is steady are not too large.) "Drift" introduced by changes in the galvanic skin responses and other sources of potential may, nonetheless, continue to be annoying; blinks always show up on the records.

The corneal–retinal potential changes with the state of light and dark adaptation of the subject, and therefore periodic recalibration must be made. Byford (1963), moreover, has found certain other nonlinearities that limit the suitability of electro-oculography to study eye movement. He found that in the absence of an independent index there is apparently no way of determining when some nonlinearity is present or its extent at any given time. In spite of its limitations, the method is useful in the laboratory, especially because it allows us to measure eye movements when the lids are closed. (Particularly interesting information comes from electro-oculographic records during sleep which may be associated with dreaming [Dement & Kleitman, 1957].)[2] Electro-oculography also provides an easy way to record nystagmus in both man and animals.

Photographic methods   Modern objective recording of eye position was begun by Dodge at about the turn of the century. The method consists of photographing the image of a small light source reflected by the anterior surface of the cornea (as though it were a convex mirror with a radius of about 8 mm). Dodge (1907) employed a film continuously moving vertically so that horizontal eye movements were recorded as lines normal to the direction of film travel and fixations as lines parallel to the direction of film travel. Photographic improvements made possible a device which records the movements of both eyes: the ophthalmograph developed by American Optical Company in 1937. This device, based on the Dodge principle of recording, gives good records of the horizontal movements of the two eyes during reading. It is therefore useful in analyzing certain reading difficulties associated with faulty patterns of coordination and fixation.

Motion picture photography, instead of a continuously moving film, can also be used. Eye position is recorded from changes in position of distinct markings of the iris or a conjunctival blood vessel or a piece of white paraffin placed on the anesthetized cornea.

Modern variations of the techniques described above include a device not only for recording the movements of the eyes but also for superimposing them on the subject's visual field. Two closed-circuit television cam-

[2] A "rapid eye movement" (REM) stage of sleep has been identified and explored in this way.

eras are used to provide one composite picture. One television camera gives an image of the subject's visual world, and the other camera superimposes on this same display, but on a second screen, a bright patch from the corneal reflection of a small light which acts as an eye marker to indicate where the eye is looking. The key details being chosen by the eyes at any moment from the complicated picture being viewed are constantly being identified by the eye marker dancing across the screen. The second television screen, which displays both the eye marker and the scene, can in turn be photographed or recorded on video tape and a permanent record made (Mackworth & Mackworth, 1958).

Another variation of the method just described is to mount a small movie camera on a helmet placed on the subject's head. The camera photographs on the same film the corneal reflection of a small light and the field of view immediately in front of the subject. This is a useful way to study eye movement patterns in the field, as when the subject is flying an airplane, driving an automobile, or directing traffic.

Electro-optical methods Lately photoelectric detection methods have been used to study eye movements. In the simplest form an image of an illuminated portion of the junction between the sclera and the iris is focused onto a photomultiplier tube (Smith & Warter, 1960). Because the white sclera is a highly reflective surface and the iris is not, the amount of light focused onto the photomultiplier tube will depend upon the horizontal rotation of the globe. After the voltage has been amplified from the output, it can be used as a measure of eye rotation. In a more sophisticated study, the difference in the diffuse reflectance of the iris and sclera is also recorded by a photomultiplier tube (Rashbass, 1960). The source of light in this case is, however, an oscilloscope spot, and the output of the photomultiplier tube is used to move this oscilloscope spot in such

a way that its image remains at the margin of the iris at all times, even in the presence of eye rotations. The amount of deflector voltage required to do this is a measure of the eye position and can be displayed on the vertical plates of a second cathode-ray oscilloscope, the horizontal plates of which display time.

Recording eye rotations free of translational shifts All of the methods outlined above have the common difficulty that they do not distinguish between rotations and translational shifts of the globe within the orbit.[3] To isolate the factor of eye rotation, Rashbass and Westheimer (1961a) employed two photocells to record the light reflected back from the eye as a scanning light was moved towards the nose from the sclera onto the cornea. During a single scan, the output of one cell undergoes a change when the image crosses from the sclera to the cornea and the output of the other detects the instant a specular reflection of the image from the cornea is formed exactly in its field of view. The time interval of the two changes in the summed output of the two cells is a measure of the rotational eye position. The time interval is isolated electronically, and a signal relative to eye position is produced. Translational shifts are about five times less likely to produce artifacts in the record than if the limbus position alone is recorded and about ten times less so than if the corneal reflex alone is used. The response is linear up to about 8°, but the records of much larger movements become quite nonlinear.

Cornsweet (1958) has devised a method which also avoids the difficulty of separating eye rotations from translations. A spot of light is focused on the retina and made to scan the optic nerve head repeatedly. The light reflected from this spot is focused on a photo-

[3] Translation moves both the retina (particularly the fovea) and the retinal image by the same amount, and therefore translation has little effect on the perception of objects at typical distances from the eye. Rotation, in contrast, moves the fovea with respect to the retinal image; this is what counts in producing visual movement.

multiplier tube connected to the vertical plates of a cathode-ray oscilloscope. The horizontal oscilloscope sweep is synchronized with the scanning spot. Each time the spot passes over a blood vessel on the optic nerve, a deflection appears on the oscilloscope. The distance between the beginning of the scan and this deflection measures the optical position of the retina with respect to a stationary external stimulus. Changes in this distance represent eye rotations.

Objective Methods with Attachments to the Eye

Early objective studies of eye movements involved attaching reflective devices of one sort or another to the eye. In more recent studies either a close-fitting, individually molded, scleral contact lens or a special suction cup cap (Yarbus, 1967) is used. Contact lenses will slip unless they fit very precisely; thus some recent investigators have attached a suction device to the lens so that a negative pressure up to 40 mm Hg holds the lens snugly on the eye. The amount the contact lens slips can be measured by methods outlined by Barlow (1963).

To measure eye rotation, an optical or electrical device must be attached to the contact lens or suction cup cap.

Mirror The reflective device with by far the slightest encumbrance is a small mirror imbedded in the contact lens (Ratliff & Riggs, 1950). A well-fitted lens of this kind can follow globe rotation with slippage of less than $\frac{1}{2}$ minute of arc for all small rotations of the eye (Riggs & Schick, 1968). A light beam can be reflected off the surface of this mirror and focused on a photographic plate or moving film. If the eye (and therefore the mirror) rotates through an angle θ, the light beam will rotate through an angle 2θ. Three mirrors may be employed—one for vertical, one for horizontal, and a third for torsional movements (Fender, 1955). Alternatively, a more elaborate data analysis method can be used in which both vertical and horizontal movements can

be inferred, using a single mirror (Nachmias, 1959).

Coil of wire Recently, experimenters have cemented about ten turns of fine wire in slots in the portion of the contact lens covering the sclera (Robinson, 1963). The subject is exposed to an alternating magnetic field, and the voltage generated in the coil of wire as the eye rotates can be recorded as a measure of the amount of eye rotation. With two uniform alternating magnetic fields, three d.c. voltages (respectively proportional to the horizontal, the vertical, and the torsional components of gaze) can be recorded simultaneously with a sensitivity of 15 seconds of arc.

Stabilizing the Retinal Image

A device which can measure eye movements can sometimes (with further modification) also be used to convert the information it provides about eye rotation into a form which allows the experimenter to control the objects viewed in such a way that they maintain a fixed relation to the rotations of the eye. One particularly informative relation (but by no means the only one) is to have the retinal image of the object move exactly with the eye so that, irrespective of how the eye rotates, the same small group of receptors is always stimulated. A retinal image that achieves this is said to be stabilized. If the output of the eye movement recorder is a voltage, the object being looked at must be one whose position can be made to be voltage-sensitive. A spot on a cathode-ray oscilloscope is one very useful object of this kind. If optical methods are being relied upon, the mirror on the contact lens which rotates with the eye can be used as part of the optical beam that presents the image to be viewed by the eye (Riggs et al., 1953). When this is done, the optical arrangement must provide a compensating path which corrects for the fact that as the eye rotates through an angle θ the light beam reflects through an angle 2θ. Ditchburn and Ginsborg

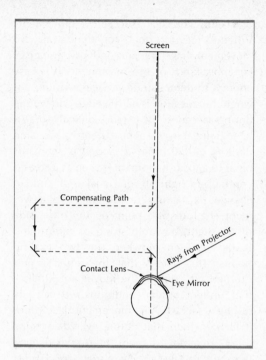

Figure 11.1. Diagram of the method for counteracting the effects of eye movements in order to stabilize the image on the retina. The viewing (compensating) path is effectively double the length of the projection path from the eye mirror to the screen. The compensating path includes an arrangement for providing fixation at the center of a bright annular field. (Riggs et al., 1953.)

(1952), Riggs & Ratliff (1952), Cornsweet (1956), Clowes and Ditchburn (1959), and Keesey (1960) have described various optical systems for achieving this result.

Figure 11.1 illustrates the method employed by Riggs et al. (1953). Light from the target is reflected off the mirror attached to the contact lens and focused on a screen coated with magnesium oxide. With the aid of the additional mirrors in the compensating path, the beam of light used by the eye in viewing this screen is effectively double the distance from the mirror on the contact lens to the screen. As the eye rotates through an angle θ the image on the screen moves through a distance 2θ. However the image, as viewed by the eye, appears to be twice as

far away and hence moves only through an angle θ.

When the test object is viewed for an indefinitely long period, however, stabilization of the image produces a very curious phenomenon. The target borders gradually fade away until the entire object disappears; a temporary blindness takes place. First observed by Riggs and Ratliff (1952), Ditchburn and Ginsborg (1952), Riggs et al. (1953) and Yarbus (1957b), this effect has since been studied with many different targets by Pritchard, Heron, and Hebb (1960), and Yarbus (1967). The descriptions of the appearance of stabilized images vary widely with different investigators due, in part, to differences in the degree of stabilization achieved (Barlow, 1963) and in part to variations in the vividness and novelty of the stimulus field (Riggs & Schick, 1968; see also pp. 305–306.)

VARIETY OF EYE MOVEMENTS

Although eye movements can be classified in a number of different ways, the most meaningful classification is based on whether or not the relation of the lines of sight of the two eyes remains constant or changes during the movement. The first kind of movement is called a *version* (or a conjugate movement); the second is called a *vergence* (disjunctive movement).

Version Movements

Version movements are those in which the angle of intersection of the lines of sight of the two eyes remains constant during the movement. Even cursory examination of an eye movement record shows that they can clearly be divided into two types: saccadic movements and pursuit movements.

Saccadic movements During a saccadic eye movement, there is a sudden parallel change in the fixation of both eyes from one point in space to another. This movement can be studied most easily by instructing the subject to hold fixation point A and to shift fixation to a light (which is suddenly turned on at point B) the moment it appears. West-heimer (1954a) showed that the decision concerning the magnitude of the movement is taken before the movement begins and that the movement then follows an inevitable course. Rashbass (1961) found that small displacements of the fixation target less than 0.25° were not immediately followed by a saccade, and he interpreted this result as showing that there was a small dead zone in the error-correction system of the retina within which target displacements could not evoke a saccade. Cornsweet (1956), in contrast, found no such evidence, after studying the small "microsaccades" of steady fixation. Cornsweet found that whenever the eye drifted even a few minutes of arc away from some "optimal" position, the probability that a saccade in the correct direction would occur was significantly greater than if the eye were held exactly on the target. Whether or not these experimental results are contradictory depends upon the extent to which the "voluntary" saccades evoked by large displacements of the object being looked at utilize the same error-monitoring system as the "involuntary" microsaccades of steady fixation.

The latent period of a saccade varies between 180 and 250 msec, although smaller intervals of time than this have been obtained, especially when the subject has prior knowledge of the position of, and/or the moment when, the fixation light will be turned on. The longer values, measured while unpredictable stimuli are being used, are probably more meaningful estimates of the delay in tracking (Saslow, 1967).

The saccadic eye movement is very fast and lasts about $\frac{1}{10}$ of a second for a 40° saccade. Contrary to a popular misconception, the duration is itself a linearly increasing function of the amplitude, increasing about 2 msec for each degree of movement. The peak velocity of the eye also increases with the amplitude of the movement, and for a 90° movement may become as large as 830° per second.

Vision during saccadic movements

Whether or not one sees during an eye movement has long puzzled psychologists. For most kinds of eye movements it is easy enough to demonstrate very clear vision; but when the question is narrowed to "do we see during saccades?" it is more difficult to answer. If in a dark room a neon glow lamp flashing at 120 times a second is seen just nasal to a fixation point, it is seen as a steady, continuous light. If one makes a sudden change in fixation—a saccadic eye movement—to look at a point on the other side of the light, a whole string of interrupted lights are seen between the two fixation points. This shows that the retina is not "turned off" during the movement—that is, that under certain conditions we can see during a saccadic eye movement. How does it happen then that during everyday seeing in a normal environment the fuzzy streaking that the images of the visual world must evoke on the retina is not often noticed? One answer is that it takes time to see. The extremely high velocity of saccadic movements produces a situation in which the intensity of retinal excitation at any given point at any given moment is very weak. This is, however, by no means the whole answer. That this is so may be demonstrated by impressing an afterimage on your fovea and then observing it in the visual field as you move your eyes, say, during optokinetic nystagmus (see below). During the slow phase of the nystagmus the afterimage is clearly visible, but during the quick (saccadic) returns it is not.

Difficulty in carrying out quantitative experiments on the problem discussed above is created because there must be an accurate check on whether the eye is indeed executing a movement or whether it is pausing briefly during the movement. Moreover, we must distinguish between reduced vision due to some "inhibitory" effect of the eye and/or brain and the reduced vision produced by optical smear of the retinal image. Therefore, the target to be detected during the movement should not differ appreciably from that presented to the fixating eye in either sharpness, intensity, duration, or the region of the retina that it excites. This is readily achieved if light flashes of 20 to 50 μsec duration are produced using a system in which the eye movement itself triggers the flash. Using this method and three different visual tasks (flash detection, grating resolution, and word recognition) Volkmann (1962) found that, though vision was never "blanked out" when the eye was moving, thresholds were about three times as high as they were when the eye was not moving (see also p. 46.) The time course of this impairment was similarly studied by Latour (1962). He noted the percentage of flashes that were perceived at various time intervals before, during, and after

eye movement. His results are shown in Figure 11.2. Because his method does not permit us to stimulate exactly the same region of the retina before, during, and after the movement the generality of the results illustrated here is somewhat less than those obtained by Volkmann. Nevertheless, these results show as a first approximation the time course of the impairment in vision obtained when the eye shifts its gaze. Later experiments by Volkmann, Schick, and Riggs (1968) have served to confirm the phenomenon of visual inhibition and the time course followed by the process in relation to an eye movement.

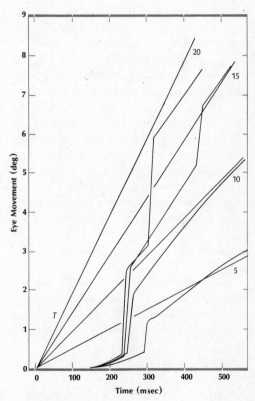

Figure 11.3. Eye movement responses to a smooth target motion of constant velocity of 5, 10, 15, and 20 degrees per second. Each response is the segmental mean of 10 responses of the most common type. The sloping straight lines (T) through the origin represent the target position; the other lines, eye position. (After Robinson, 1965.)

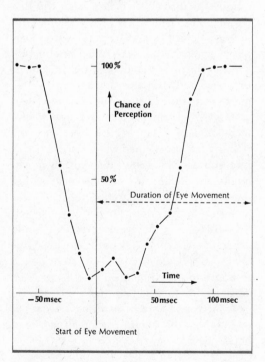

Figure 11.2. The percentage of flashes reported as seen when presented at various times before, during, and after the start of a rapid change of fixation between two lights. The test light is midway between two fixation lights that were alternately flashed on and off at an irregular rate. (Latour, 1962.)

Pursuit movements When a subject is confronted with the task of holding his eyes on a moving target, the eyes do not behave in the same way as they do when a subject is required to shift his gaze from one fixed point in space to another. The simplest situation that can be presented is one in which the fixation point is made to start moving with an unpredictable (but constant) velocity in an unpredictable direction. Typical responses of the eyes to four different velocities of this kind of moving stimulus, measured by Robinson (1965), are illustrated in Figure 11.3. In this figure, the sloping straight lines passing through zero show the target position, the other lines indicate the eye position. For any given target velocity two obviously different eye velocities are discernible. A variety of evidence shows that the higher velocity movement is a saccade and has essentially the same characteristics as those in which the eyes shift gaze between two fixed points. The movements with the slower velocities are known as *pursuit movements*. Because of their slow velocity, they are also called *smooth movements* to distinguish them from the "jerky" saccades. Eye following of a given target is much more variable than is the case given a simple saccade between two fixed points. Thus, the illustrated responses are characteristic only of the majority of responses.

Variations occur not only in the moment during the smooth movement that the saccade is made but also in the amplitude as well as in the number of saccades. In a minority of responses, the velocity of the target and eyes will exactly match (provided the target velocity is smaller than 30° per second, according to Westheimer, 1954b); but in the typical response there is a velocity overshoot in the early part of the movement before the eye and target velocity become matched. This overshoot overcomes the viscous nature of the tissues supporting the globe so that the eye reaches its steady-state velocity much quicker than it would otherwise. The amount of this overshoot varies considerably, some of

the variation being related to target velocity. In Fig. 11.3 the velocity overshoot is pronounced at 5° per second but has disappeared at 15° per second. At 20° per second the eye is already approaching velocity saturation.

We have already seen that the stimulus for a saccade is target displacement. Rashbass (1961) found that the major stimulus for the smooth pursuit movement was a steadily moving target and that the pursuit movement maintains the image stationary on the retina irrespective of position errors. If the target is suddenly shifted in one direction and then begins moving with uniform velocity in the opposite direction, a slow smooth pursuit movement can be induced which does not have any saccade superimposed upon it. Robinson (1965) found that the optimal conditions for this effect occur when the displacement (in degrees) is 0.15 to 0.2 times the uniform velocity (in degrees per second). A displacement of this sort is called a *step-ramp*. It evokes a pure smooth pursuit movement uninterrupted by any saccades. The remarkable feature of such a movement is that, as the eye commences its response to the target *velocity*, it moves away from the *position* the target occupied when the eye began its response. This shows that pursuit movements are elicited by target velocity rather than by target position. The pursuit movements in this experiment do, however, match the positions of the eye and target at some finite time after the eyes begin moving. Otherwise a saccade occurs. The latency of a response to a step-ramp—151 ± 19 msec—is considerably longer than that of a response in which no displacement has occurred, proving that the step displacement has been detected.

Independence of pursuit and tracking movements Are saccades and smooth tracking movements different modes of action of the same neurological apparatus or are different pathways involved? Although we know nothing of the details of the connections in the nervous system that regulate these two kinds of movement, a growing body of indirect evidence suggests that the pathways are quite independent. We have already seen that the stimuli that produce each type of movement are different. Furthermore, electromyography of the eye muscles shows that the electrophysiological characteristics of the muscle responses are easily distinguishable. Thus to make a saccade, the globe is rotated by a high-frequency burst in the agonist muscle and complete inhibition of firing in the antagonist muscle. However to make a smooth pursuit movement the eye is rotated by high-frequency bursts in both agonist and antagonist muscles; there is only a slight difference in the tension in these two muscles as they rotate the globe. In addition, the saccade has a longer latent period than does the pursuit movement. A saccade might occur in the absence of a stimulus, but a pursuit movement usually does not (Yarbus, 1967). Also the peak velocity of the eye during a saccade is some 50 times greater than that during a pursuit movement.

Many of the distinctions between saccades and tracking movements can be characterized by the statement that a saccade is ballistic while the tracking movements are what Stetson and McDill (1923) and Hartson (1939) called *slow tension movements*. A ballistic movement acts as a discrete sampled data system, that is, one in which error-detecting activities are carried out at intervals that are interspersed by periods of insensitivity during which no error-detecting activity is carried out.

Westheimer (1954b) has described an experiment in which a target is moved to one side and then back to its original position after, say, 40 msec. The eye responds by making a following saccade at 200 msec, despite the fact that the movement is at that time wholly inappropriate and takes the eye away from the target. This first movement is then followed 200 msec later by a return to the starting point. The fact that the duration of the inappropriate eye fixation is precisely the duration of the reaction time and not the

appreciably shorter duration of the pulse argues for a sampled data system and not for one in which commands for saccades, once initiated, cannot be canceled. Wheeless, Boynton, and Cohen (1966) have obtained a less clear-cut result when they varied the duration of the pulse. The fact that reaction times to steps in their experiments were significantly longer than for the pulses suggests their subjects were not tracking normally.

How do pursuit movements behave in the analogous situation? Robinson (1965) varied the time interval between step target displacements in two successive step-ramps, either 150, 100, or 75 msec apart. The responses in each case consisted of two distinct smooth pursuit movements which, although delayed in time by the latency, were spaced from each other by 150, 100, and 75 msec respectively, thus indicating that there is no interval in data sampling longer than 75 msec. Smaller intervals produce such small eye movements that the records are not easy to interpret. If smooth pursuit movement is based on a sampled system, it must be one that samples at a rate greater than 13 times per second. Clearly, the simplest hypothesis is that sampling made by a system producing pursuit movements is continuous. In this respect it resembles the accommodation and the fusional vergence systems of the eye.

The difference between saccadic and smooth pursuit movements is clearly brought out by altering the normal relationship between eye rotation and the movement of images across the retina. Riggs and Tulunay (1959), Fender and Nye (1961) and Robinson (1965) have developed methods for doing this. Robinson started with a stabilized retinal image, that is, an image that moves with the eye as the eye rotates. (This is the "open loop" case in which any given rotation of the eye results in a corresponding displacement of the retinal image so that no motion occurs between image and receptors.) He used a small point as an image and aimed it at the center of the fovea. Thus, there was little need for a corrective saccade to occur (Cornsweet,

1956). Then the experimenter upset this situation by displacing the image 2° at a time to one side of the fovea. This displacement caused a series of 2° saccades as the subject attempted to catch up with the target as it receded from him as rapidly as he pursued it. This Tantalus-like target motion will lead the subject's eye, in its vain pursuit, right off the edge of the projection screen.

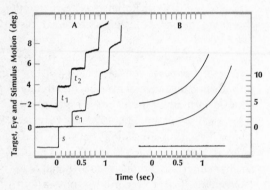

Figure 11.4. The eye movements obtained under positive visual feedback so that the position of the target outpaces the eye position. In each figure, the bottom trace represents the position of the stimulus, controlled by the experimenter; the middle trace represents the eye position; and the top trace represents the position of the target with respect to the eye. In part A the eye is at position zero (fixating on stimulus target) until the moment when the experimenter quickly displaces the stimulus by 2° as shown at s. This causes a corresponding 2° shift t_1 in the position of the target with respect to the center of fixation. Thus t_1 is followed, after a reaction time of about .25 sec, by a saccade e_1, which feeds into the target a displacement t_2 that is slightly larger than e_1 and so on, each eye movement pursuing a target displacement following a reaction time such as is expected in a discrete sampling control system. Part B shows the smooth pursuit system responding by itself to this vain chase when the initial retinal disparity is so small that no saccade is stimulated. Note that the behavior is like a continuous control system with slight positive feedback. The eye movements have a smooth, growing time course with no detectable discrete velocity changes. (Data from Robinson, 1965.)

When the saccadic system engages in this vain pursuit, the result is a staircase pattern of eye movements such as that given in Figure 11.4A, taken from an experiment made by Robinson (1965). This result is typical of a sampled data system.

In the case illustrated in Figure 11.4A, the retinal image was made to move just slightly so that the target not only just kept up with the eye (as with a stabilized image) but actually outpaced it slightly, resulting in the simultaneous development of a growing pursuit velocity between the successive saccades. Figure 11.4B shows how the smooth system by itself responds to this vain chase when the initial retinal disparity is less than 0.1° so that the saccadic system is not stimulated. You can experience a somewhat analogous effect by first producing an afterimage which is just slightly eccentric to the fovea, and then attempting to fixate on it. Thus, Figure 11.4B demonstrates that the smooth pursuit system alone appears to behave like a continuous control system, and under these experimental conditions produces a smooth growing time course with no detectable discrete velocity changes.

There is, moreover, good evidence from experiments made using various drugs that the neural control mechanisms of pursuit and saccadic eye movements are independent. Rashbass (1961) found that barbiturate intoxication produces a pronounced dissociation

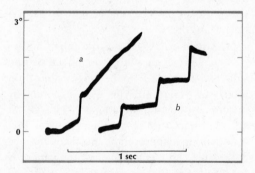

Figure 11.5. Tracking eye movement responses to a target moving with constant velocity (a) before and (b) after administration of a mild barbiturate. (Data from Rashbass, 1961.)

of these two kinds of movements. Figure 11.5 shows eye movements made while tracking a target moving with uniform velocity (3.5° per second) before and after the intravenous administration of sodium thiopentone. The first noticeable effect the drug had was to cause an increase in the number of saccadic movements that occur during the first second of tracking. As the effect of drug increased, the frequency of saccades increased at the expense of smooth movements, until after 8 minutes no smooth tracking could be detected. Similar degradations show if the eye is made to track targets moving sinusoidally after sodium thiopentone has been given to a subject. The behavior of the eye while a subject is tracking sinusoidally moving targets under the influence of barbiturates is very similar to the effect observed when patients with a disease known as myotonic dystrophy try to undertake this task (von Noorden, Thompson, & Van Allen, 1964).

The version movements of the eye that we have just considered result from stimuli that can be presented to the retina of one eye alone. A large variety of animals—even those with eyes on the sides of the head and, consequently, with visual fields that do not overlap—probably display the same kinds of movement, although experimental analysis of versions by behavioral methods on animals is a largely untapped field. Versions have the same characteristics whether one eye is occluded or both are open. There is no change in the angle that the lines of sight make with each other during the course of the movement.

Vergence Movements

In higher primates including man, the eyes, of course, have migrated to the front of the head and the visual fields of the two eyes overlap. One consequence of this is that a second variety of eye movement is required (vergences) to help keep both eyes fixed on the same object. That the vergence system works under normal circumstances can be demonstrated by pressing on one eye through

the lower eyelid. If you manage to keep both eyes open, you will have double vision—diplopia—because the eyeball you are pressing on is shifted and the objects in the visual field that stimulate the foveas of the two eyes (as well as other "corresponding retinal points") are different. The technical way of describing this state of affairs is to say that the egocentric localizations of the visual fields of the two eyes differ.

Considering the large variety of factors that can influence the direction in which each eye is pointing, it would be surprising if with only the version system functioning the lines of sight of both eyes exactly intersected at the object being looked at. Moreover, even if by chance the lines of sight did coincide at a given distance from the eye when only the version system was operating, it should be evident that the lines of sight could not then coincide for objects either nearer to or farther away from the observer. To deal with these changing situations, the vergence system has evolved, according to which the angles that the lines of sight make with each other change during the movement. If you look at a pencil and then move it nearer and nearer to your nose along an extension of the median (saggital) body plane, the eyes converge. As you move the pencil away from you, your eyes diverge. (See also pp. 297, 482–494.)

Binocular coordination Clearly then, in ordinary viewing, not only is the globe rotated to point its most sensitive central cones at different parts of the visual field in rapid succession, but the rotations of the two globes are exquisitely synchronized. The neurophysiological investigations of the basis of such control have not yet been carried out in detail, but we know that a muscle, or muscle group, of one eye is "yoked" together with a corresponding muscle, or muscle group, of the other eye; and in any given yoked pair the innervations are always such that the two eyes respond precisely together and to the same extent. In the case of a version, as we have already seen, a simple movement of both eyes to the right, for example, will occur even when one eye is covered. The uncovered eye, after a short latent period, moves quickly to the right to take up its new fixation point, but the eye under the cover moves after the identical latent period just as quickly—and exactly the same amount—as if it too were seeing.

Movement to the right is a result of contraction of both the lateral rectus of the right eye and the medial rectus of the left. This is one example of a yoked muscle pair. In a convergence movement, on the other hand, the yoked muscle pair is the medial rectus of each eye. Thus, depending on the movement, a given muscle can be yoked to either of two muscles of the other eye which are themselves antagonistic. The point is the two

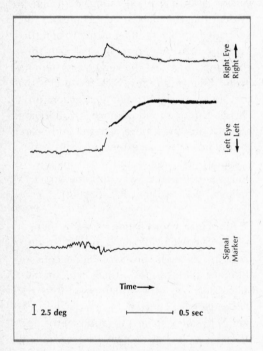

Figure 11.6. Record of the eye movements (by electro-oculography) obtained in binocular fixation from a distant target to one 20 cm from the eye. The near target was carefully aligned on the line of sight of the right eye monocularly. Note that both eyes make two paired movements, a rapid shift to the right and slow convergence onto the target. (Data from Alpern & Ellen, 1956.)

eyes move together. In fact, it is very difficult (but not impossible) to arrange conditions in such a way that only one eye moves, even when that would be the simplest (and most efficient) consequence. For example, close the left eye and bring a near object like the tip of a pencil along the line of sight of the right eye, fixating a distant object. Open the left eye and fixate the distant object binocularly. Since the pencil tip is already along the line of sight of the right eye, it is evident that in order now to shift binocular fixation onto the pencil tip only the left eye needs to move. In fact, it is impossible to shift binocular gaze from the distant to the near object without moving both eyes together.

The movement of the eyes from the distant object to the pencil tip is broken into two parts: a rapid shift of gaze of both eyes to the right (in which the medial rectus of the left eye is yoked to the lateral rectus of the right) and a somewhat slower convergence movement (in which the two medial rectus muscles are yoked together). Because of the differences of time characteristic in the two components, recordings of eye movements during such an experiment clearly reveal this phenomenon (Alpern & Ellen, 1956; Westheimer & Mitchell, 1956; Riggs & Niehl, 1960). Figure 11.6 illustrates a typical record. The bottom line is from a voice microphone, and the irregular deflections on it are caused by the verbal command to look from the far to the near target. The two upper records are of the left (middle line) and right eye. The amplitude of the movement of the right eye is a little less than half of that of the left eye in this record, probably because both component movements begin simultaneously so that for the right eye a fraction of the movement is neutralized even before it can occur. For the left eye (which turns continuously to the right) the two components add together, of course, so that both components are revealed in their entirety.

The details of the control system that allows our eyes to move in this way have not yet been worked out. One theory holds that the eye muscles themselves have two varieties of subunits: slow fibers (perhaps under control of the autonomic nervous system) that are responsible for the vergence, and faster twitch fibers responsible for versions, including the extremely rapid saccades.

Varieties of vergence movements Convergence and divergence are only two examples of vergence movements. Because the eyes may be slightly misaligned by nature, either vertically or with the vertical meridian of one eye not parallel with that of the other, vergence systems exist to correct for both of these kinds of misalignment. (We will say no more about them, but the interested reader will find a thorough discussion of them in Alpern [1962].) The more usual misalignments are those in the horizontal plane.

Insofar as it is now known, the various vergence movements do not differ from one another in time characteristics, for the reaction times of all are about 160 msec. The eyes very quickly achieve maximum velocity and then asymptotically settle into their new positions. The total duration of the movement may be as long as 0.8 to 1.6 sec. The maximum velocity is a simple, linearly increasing function of the amplitude of the movement. Velocities of the order of 20° per second have been reported for movements of 6.6°.

In terms of the absolute value of its velocity, a vergence movement resembles the pursuit movement. However in terms of the way its velocity changes with movement amplitude, it more nearly resembles saccadic eye movements.

Horizontal vergence movements may occur under various conditions. *Fusional* vergences are movements that result when there is a disparity in the egocentric localization of the visual fields of the two eyes with respect to each other. We have already seen that they are nature's way of compensating for minor misalignments of the line of sight of one eye compared to that of its fellow. *Accommodative* vergence is the vergence movement associated with a change in the accommodative

response of the eyes. If you cover one eye and focus sharply on a pencil point as it is brought in along the line of sight of the uncovered eye, the eye underneath the cover converges more and more as the accommodation increases. In addition, vergence movements seem to be evoked by a variety of stimulus variables, including how close the target is to the eyes (independent of changes in accommodation) and to what extent we can evoke "an illusion of nearness" with the target. (This latter may include a number of still poorly defined stimulus parameters, including—among others—familiar, actual, and perceived size.)

Most quantitative data about vergence movements have been obtained on fusional vergence and on accommodative vergence. Rashbass and Westheimer (1961a) have studied horizontal fusional movements under normal viewing conditions as well as under those in which, despite the movements, the disparity in egocentric localization of the two eyes remained fixed. They found that fusional movements are another example of a continuous data sampling process. The movements can be altered during their progress, and information about disparity is continuously sampled during the reaction time as well as during the movements. When the apparatus was arranged in such a way that the movements had no influence on target disparity, any fixed disparity evoked movements that maintained a constant velocity. The velocity was dependent on the amplitude of the disparity. When measuring the phase relation between a sine wave disparity and the movements it evokes, it was found that the control system makes some estimate of what future disparity is to be and that rate of change of disparity is one important factor in this estimate.

Accommodative vergences are related not only to the changes in accommodation of the eyes but also to constriction of the pupil. These three phenomena comprise the *near-focus response*. It is caused principally by changes in the accommodation stimulus, but changes in accommodation response, uncorrelated with changes in the stimulus causing the accommodation, also produce accommodative vergence changes as well as (presumably) pupil size changes.

A variety of evidence supports the view that there are linear relations among the innervations of the accommodation response, the eye rotation, and the pupil constriction. The rate of change of accommodative vergence with a unit of change in accommodation response (within the range where these two are linearly related) is known as AC/A (that is, the ratio of the accommodative convergence to accommodation). AC/A is a quantitative description of the near response of any given individual, which is remarkably stable and insensitive to change either because of age, practice, or drugs (alcohol, amphetamine, and barbiturates are exceptions to this rule) but which is quite different in one individual compared to another. AC/A seems to be correlated with success (or failure) in a variety of different occupations from electronic and camera assemblers to telephone typists and baseball pitchers (Davis & Jobe, 1957). We know nothing about the factors responsible for individual differences in AC/A.

Reflex Movements

In discussing eye movements so far we have made the implicit assumption that the bony structures to which the other ends of the eye muscles are attached remained rigidly fixed with respect to the body and to gravity. In fact, almost all the data described were obtained in a laboratory arrangement designed to hold head and body perfectly still. The best way of doing this is to make impressions of the subject's forehead and teeth in dental wax, and then mount these impressions on a rigid frame to which the subject may be fitted during the experiment. Because in everyday life the head and body move freely about, the characteristics of eye movements discussed above have to be put in the framework of this movement.

Two distinctly different patterns of be-

havior should be distinguished. In the first, both head and eyes move to pick up the fixation of a new object of regard; the angular distance between the old and the new fixation points is covered partly by the head and partly by the eyes. In contrast, the eyes can move in a direction opposite to that the head may be taking to maintain fixation on one and the same object during the course of the head displacements. In the first kind of movement, the head (as well as the eye) movement is directed by the visual feedback from the retina, but the second kind of eye movement is directed, at least in part, by signals initiated elsewhere in the body. To study these latter kinds of eye movement best in the laboratory, the psychologist may find it appropriate to eliminate all visual feedback by performing the experiments in the dark (or with both eyes tightly patched); just as to study eye movements discussed until now it was convenient to hold the head and body fixed with a forehead rest and biting board. Movements of the eyes which can occur in the absence of retinal feedback have been classified in the literature under the name "reflex" (though we exclude from this category eye movements initiated by "voluntary" events, such as verbal commands, however difficult they may be to define operationally). You should remember that while we are seeing under ordinary circumstances these reflex movements are carried on simultaneously with—indeed, superimposed on—eye movements associated by a variety of signals arising in the retinas.

The end organs that are sensitive to movements of the head from verticality are the hair cells in the macula of the saccule and utricle of the vestibular apparatus of the inner ear. These hair cells have small cilia (steriocilia) projecting into the otoliths (literally "ear stones"—in fact, small crystals of calcium carbonate). Under the influence of changes in position of the head with respect to the earth's gravitational field, the otoliths bend the steriocilia and stimulate the hair cells. Such excitation of the hair cells results in reflex deviation of the eyes. For example, flexing the neck back so that the face points to the sky moves the eyes down. Tilting the head so that the right ear is on the right shoulder causes the right eye to move up higher than the left and to rotate around its line of sight so that the top of the vertical meridian of the cornea moves toward the nose while the left eye rotates so that the top of its vertical corneal meridian moves temporally. In each case, the eye movements tend to maintain the eyeball in the *status quo ante*.

Although the otoliths may of themselves produce these movements, they are by no means uniquely essential. Evidence suggests that stimulation of the proprioceptor end organs in the muscles of the head, neck, and body also produces such effects.

The reflex eye movements are among the most important sources of oculomotor adjustments in lower vertebrates, particularly teleosts. In higher vertebrates they become less and less so as the variety of visual behavior expands. The basic patterns remain, but they become overlaid by the more complicated visually evoked responses already described.

The statokinetic oculomotor reflexes are initiated by the hair cells in the crista ampullaris of the three (on each side) semicircular canals (Magnus, 1924). These cells respond to shearing forces induced by angular acceleration of the head. The oculomotor response, like those induced by stimulation of the utricle and saccule, tends to maintain the eyeball in the *status quo ante*. The easiest way of stimulating hair cells in the crista is to produce a pressure differential in the two halves of a given set of semicircular canals by rotating the head with an angular acceleration about an axis perpendicular to the plane of those canals. During the time that the head is accelerated, the eyes move slowly in the opposite direction to the rotation of the head. When, however, the eyes reach the extreme limit of the field of fixation, they make a quick return to the front before resuming once

more the slow rotation in the direction opposite to the head. Thus, a sequence of rhythmical slow and fast eye movements (known as *nystagmus*) is initiated. If the head is abruptly stopped, shearing forces on the hair cells of the crista in the opposite direction persist for several seconds, even minutes. These cause an after-nystagmus which is opposite in direction to that obtained during the rotation. We specify the direction of the nystagmus by the direction of its quick phase (because when looking at the eyes the saccade is much easier to identify). The rotation nystagmus therefore is in the same direction, the after-nystagmus in the opposite direction, to that of the rotation of the head.

There are a number of ways to produce shearing forces in one or the other of the cristae. A chair which rotates around an axis normal to the floor is commonly used to demonstrate the effect. The subject sits in the chair with his head tilted so that this axis is also normal to the plane of one of the three sets of semicircular canals. By suitable tilting of the head either a horizontal, a vertical, or a rotational nystagmus can easily be produced. Another method consists of placing the head in a position such that the plane of one set of canals is vertical and then injecting cold water into one of the auditory canals. This sets up convection currents (which produce shearing forces mainly, if not exclusively, in the canal in the vertical position) and hence nystagmus.

Although observation of nystagmus is the most common way we study eye responses to stimulation of semicircular canals in the laboratory or in the clinic, nystagmus is rarely found in daily use of the eyes by healthy, normal people. Most accelerations to which the head is subject in the everyday world produce only mild and short duration shearing forces in the crista ampullaris compared to those used to obtain the nystagmus in the laboratory. To these, a slow adjustment of the eyes is the only oculomotor response that is made to semicircular canal excitation.

The majority of the population probably never experiences any very severe accelerations unless they deliberately rotate themselves in a parlor game, although the high-speed complexity of modern life makes this statement apply to an ever-decreasing percentage of the population. As interplanetary travel becomes habitual and the associated severe acceleration to which the head and body must be subjected to transcend the earth's gravitational field becomes common-place, the experiences of future generations in this respect are going to be quite different from our own. We know virtually nothing about how this repeated and rather severe excitation of these reflex mechanisms may influence the more usual variety of oculomotor performance. We might profitably undertake an investigation of this question by an exhaustive analysis of the characteristics of the eye movements of professional ice skaters or others whose work involves severe acceleration forces applied to the head.

EYE MOVEMENTS AND SEEING IN THE FIELD

We have now analyzed in various, quite artificial laboratory situations the repertoire of eye movements used in carrying on the ordinary work of the world. Naturally, we do not make these various movements in isolation as they have been studied in the laboratory. All of them—vergences and versions, reflex and retinal-induced responses—are intermingled. To analyze how this is done, let us look in some detail at the behavior of the eyes in three very simple tasks which become, however, progressively more complex.

Steady Fixation

You might expect that the simplest of all visual tasks is to maintain fixation on a single point. In fact, it is found that even if you try as hard as you can, it is impossible to maintain the eyes perfectly motionless. During even the steadiest of fixations, the eyes are constantly making extremely fine movements

known collectively as *physiological nystagmus*. Our best measurements of physiological nystagmus have been made with a mirror mounted on a very tight-fitting contact lens. A light beam reflected off the mirror can be photographed for study of movements in the horizontal plane (Ratliff & Riggs, 1950), or by a bit more elaboration of the optics (and more sophisticated treatment of the data) both horizontal and vertical measurements may be obtained (Nachmias, 1959).

Physiological nystagmus is composed of three different kinds of movement, two of which may be only miniature replications of the varieties of version movement already described. The third, only poorly understood, is quite unique to physiological nystagmus. This is a high-frequency tremor having a median amplitude of about 17 seconds of arc. Frequencies from below 30 to above 100 cycles have been reported by various authors, and amplitudes have ranged from near zero to above 1 minute of arc. The other two varieties of movements are: (1) slow drifts occurring in an amplitude range of about 5 minutes of arc and having an average velocity of 1 minute per second, and (2) rapid binocu-

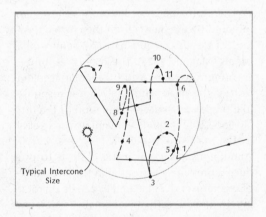

Figure 11.7. Movement of the image of a point object on the retina. The large circle has a radius of 5 minutes of arc. Slow drifts are represented by the dotted, saccades by the solid, lines. The numbered dots indicate the order in which movements are made and are spaced at equal time intervals of $\frac{1}{5}$ of a second. (Ditchburn, 1955.)

lar flicks (or saccades) from 1 to 20 minutes in amplitude, which have a velocity of about 10° per second and occur rather unpredictably. It has been suggested (Cornsweet, 1956) that the saccades act to correct for the drifts which deviate the eyes from some optimum position of fixation. Nachmias (1959) concludes that not only the saccades, but in some degree the drifts as well, serve a corrective function.

The way the drifts and saccades influence the position of the retinal image of a point is illustrated schematically in Figure 11.7, which is due to Ditchburn (1955). The tremor disturbance corresponds to a movement of about 1 to 3 μ on the retina or about the dimension of a single foveal cone (these, however, are not shown in Figure 11.7). The large circle has a radius of about 5 minutes of arc. The dotted lines represent the slow drifts; the solid lines, the rapid saccades. The numbered dots indicate the order in which movements are made and are spaced at equal time intervals 0.2 second apart. On this occasion, all the movements are within the 5-minute radius circle, but records made over longer periods would reveal movements confined to a circle about twice this size. The area, which includes the position of the eye during about 50 percent of the time, is typically an ellipse with a major (horizontal) diameter of around 10 minutes of arc.

It has been suggested that physiological nystagmus plays an important role in improving visual acuity. This appears not to be the case. Ratliff (1952) measured visual acuity during various stages of eye movements, recording the latter with a mirror on a contact lens. Drifts greater than 20 seconds of arc he found were a hindrance, rather than a help, to visual acuity. Keesey (1960) made a systematic study of various forms of visual acuity, comparing the stabilized image condition (see p. 374) with the normal viewing condition in which the physiological nystagmus movements were present. Similar results were obtained in the presence or absence of such movements. These observations strongly sug-

gest that physiological nystagmus plays no role in improving visual acuity (see p. 306).

The brief discussion above shows that the normal movements of physiological nystagmus, although they do not improve visual acuity, have an important function in the visual perception of form. The details of this function and the experiments that relate to them are more appropriately discussed in the chapter on visual perception. For the present, it will suffice to say that continued vision of high-contrast visual forms under steady fixation can occur only because of the eye movements of physiological nystagmus.

Shifts of Gaze

The second degree of complexity in the everyday use of the eyes that we discuss is a simple shift of gaze from an object in one part of the visual field to that in another. If the two points are at the same distance from the observer but have different visual directions, the movement comprises a simple saccade; if the two points have a common visual direction but are at different distances, the movement is a simple vergence movement. What happens if the two points have neither a common visual direction nor a common distance from the observer? The answer seems to be quite simply that the two movements seem to go on virtually simultaneously and apparently quite independently. This kind of movement was studied by Yarbus (1957a, 1967) and by Riggs and Niehl (1960). Because the saccadic movement has a velocity about 20 times that of the vergence movement, it is easy to follow the two kinds of movement even in a single shift of gaze. Yarbus found that the vergence change began a bit sooner and that about 20 percent of the vergence is completed before the saccade appears. During the saccade, the vergence change continues unabated; but, because of the difference in velocity of the saccade and of the vergence, only about 6.5 percent of the vergence is completed between the beginning and the end of the saccadic movement. At the end of a single saccade, the entire shift in visual direction has been achieved and the movement is completed by the unabated continuation of the remaining 73.5 percent of the vergence change. The same basic pattern is found whether one shifts from a far to a near object or in the opposite direction.

Yarbus' study shows a clear separation in the pattern of response of the vergence and version mechanisms when the latter is a simple saccade. Does this same independence persist when the version is a pursuit movement? Rashbass and Westheimer (1961b) asked this question and answered it by recording both the version (tracking) and vergence responses as the stimulus for each was independently manipulated. Both sine wave and square wave stimulus presentations were made. They found that the mean eye position

follows the mean target position according to the characteristics of visual tracking and, simultaneously, the eye vergence response follows the target vergence according to the characteristics of vergence movements. No interaction between the mechanisms was observed. Each can accept and respond to stimuli irrespective of whether the other is being stimulated, is preparing to respond, is

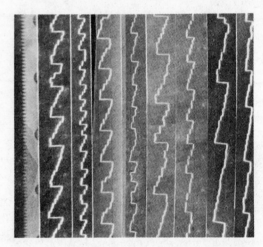

Figure 11.9. Actual photographic records of eye movements obtained by Dearborn (1906). The records are to be read upwards. The short, heavy vertical lines are the fixations, and the lighter oblique lines (almost horizontal) are saccadic eye movements, the long ones to the left carrying the eye from the end of one line to the beginning of the next, and the little ones to the right carrying it from point to point in the reading of a line. Regressive movements can be seen in most of the records.

The records are from four educated adults who differed greatly in reading speed. Each subject is represented by two records, the first from reading material printed in long lines and the second from his reading short newspaper lines. In reading newspaper lines, the complete records, when measured, give the following averages:

Subject	Fixations per line	Average duration of a fixation (msec)
1	3.8	161
2	3.9	216
3	5.5	255
4	5.4	402

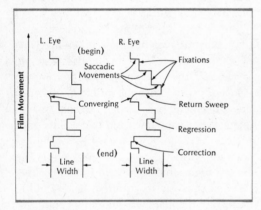

Figure 11.8. Schematic representation of the record of eye movements obtained during reading. Because the film moves upward, the record progresses downward. The length of the vertical lines gives the duration of fixations; that of the horizontal lines, the extent of lateral eye movements. Beginning at the top, the record shows four fixations and three saccadic movements in reading the first line of print. The eyes diverge slightly during the first return sweep and slowly converge to the correct position at the beginning of the second line. There is a regressive movement along this line. The return sweep onto the third line failed to bring the beginning of that line into clear view, and so a corrective movement occurs there. The record was cut off after the next fixation.

responding, or is suffering overload. All target movements were resolved into a vergence and a side-to-side component even when a resolution into right and left eye components would be simpler. This last observation of Rashbass and Westheimer not only confirms the inference we drew from the results illustrated in Figure 11.6 but extends its generality to visual tracking behavior as well.

Eye Movements During Reading

We conclude the discussion of eye movements by considering an even more complex task, namely reading. Now, no doubt, many students may find this, too, much too simple a task. They are interested in much more complicated questions: What do the quarterback's eye movements tell his opponents about the plan of the forthcoming play? How do a guilty man's eye movement responses to incriminating questions differ from those to innocent questions? What characterizes the eye movements to the view of an attractive advertising display as distinct from an ordinary one? And so on. The answers to questions of this sort for the most part still need to be worked out.

The characteristics of eye movements during reading were studied extensively in the first part of the twentieth century (very little new information has been added in the last twenty years). Consequently, previous editions of this text covered this subject more extensively, and those who desire to study the subject in detail should consult them. What follows is an abbreviated summary of this work.

Javal (1879) noted that reading did not consist of smooth tracking of successive rows of letters one after the other. On the contrary, he found that the eyes executed a series of saccadic jumps interspersed by fixations at several different points along each line. These movements have now been extensively studied by photography, using the ophthalmograph. A schematic ophthalmograph record is illustrated in Figure 11.8, which emphasizes certain features. Once the reader is familiar with the phenomena illustrated and explained there, he can find them in the actual records. For example, Figure 11.9 includes several records made by Dearborn over sixty years ago from one eye. They are thus monocular, but because the two eyes work so closely together binocular records would not be very much more informative. Almost all of the features shown in the schematic record can be found in several of Dearborn's photo-

TABLE 11.1 EYE MOVEMENTS IN READING, ACCORDING TO SCHOOL GRADE[a]

School grade	Fixations per line of print	Mean duration of fixation (msec)	Regressive movements per line
I B	18.6	660	5.1
I A	15.5	432	4.0
II	10.7	364	2.3
III	8.9	316	1.8
IV	7.3	268	1.4
V	6.9	252	1.3
VI	7.3	236	1.6
VII	6.8	240	1.5
High school I	7.2	244	1.0
High school II	5.8	248	0.7
High school III	5.5	224	0.7
High school IV	6.4	248	0.7
College	5.9	252	0.5

[a] A sample of 8 to 19 children from each grade, of about medium reading ability, had their eyes photographed while reading, and the mean for each grade is given. From Buswell (1922).

graphs. The average reader shows pretty good coordination of his eyes. They follow the horizontal line pretty well with little vertical movement.

Development of Reading Skill

Reading is a complex skill, and like all skills it develops gradually, improving in both precision and speed. Pencil and paper tests are useful in measuring progress, but eye movement records are of value in analyzing the details of what is happening. By comparing samples of students at various grade levels (see Table 11.1) we see that improvement is made in three ways. In the first place, there is a steady decrease in the number of fixations per line. This holds true even though the reading material increases in difficulty at each grade. Thus, the college student is taking in at least three times as much reading matter per fixation as is the beginning reader. Second, the fixations grow shorter as academic level increases; the advanced reader takes in the material faster. Finally, there is a very marked decrease in regressive movements. This means greater regularity in progressing along the lines of print. It is natural to conclude that the ideal reader would have no regressive movements. Actually, a few regressive movements show that the reader is alert to what he is reading, that he goes back to clear up an obscurity (Buswell, 1937; Bayle, 1942). Sometimes the regressive movement should be blamed on the author rather than on the reader!

Fixations

All reading is done during the fixation pauses, for there is no clear-cut vision during the intervening saccadic movements. Thus, the number and duration of the fixation pauses are two indexes frequently used by psychologists to appraise the quality of reading performance. However, it should always be kept in mind that these are by no means the only relevant variables. The nature of the reading material, as well as the kind of reading

the subject ordinarily does, is also important. There is no single rate or style of reading that is appropriate to all types of reading material. The really good reader is the one who adjusts his speed and, indeed, his whole pattern of reading to that required by whatever reading material he is reading at the moment.

The duration of the fixations, as distinguished from their number, is not closely dependent on the difficulty of the material, at least as far as the mode is concerned (Buswell, 1922; Robinson, 1933). Good college freshmen will average around 210 msec, whereas their slower classmates run around 260 msec (Walker, 1933; Anderson, 1937). These fixations are considerably longer than the exposure needed for perception of dots or letters; the usual tachistoscopic exposure is about 100 msec, depending on the illuminance. All of these facts may suggest that the number and duration of fixations, and hence the speed of reading, are limited by central—rather than by peripheral—factors; that is, the subject moves his eyes only as fast as he can absorb the material.

The saccadic movements themselves take very little of the total time. They average around 22 msec for the short jumps and 40 msec for the return sweeps. If we read a line of print with four fixations, there will be three short jumps and one long return, totaling about 100 msec of actual movement. The four fixations will total about 900 msec, indicating that about 90 percent of the total reading time is spent in fixation pauses (Dearborn, 1906; Schmidt, 1917). During slower reading, with longer pauses and larger numbers of pauses per line, the total fixation time may be as high as 95 percent (Tinker, 1936). A poor reader may also fail to progress evenly across the line and down the page; he may exhibit irregular and frequent returns to portions of the material that have already been read. As a matter of fact, the perceptual processes may well be going on during the saccadic movements; we may remember that retinal stimulation is typically discontinuous and is not effective with the moving eye. Reading, in contrast, may well be a continuous process in that the perceptual development of meaning goes on steadily. Perhaps we can think of it as a continuous production process, a machine into which the raw material is tossed by the shovelful. The output will be continuous as long as there is some raw material in the works. This analogy has another similarity to reading—the rate of input will usually be limited by the rate at which the machine processes the raw material. In a similar fashion, the eye movements adjust to the rate at which the subject is digesting the sensory input. The most efficient reader, in short, is the one who can execute the largest number of fixation pauses per minute and the smallest number per line of print.

ACCOMMODATION

The effector mechanisms so far discussed involved the *extraocular* muscles. There are two systems of effector mechanisms related to the *intraocular* muscles: *accommodation*, brought about by contraction of the ciliary muscle, and changes in *pupil* size brought about by changes in the length of the iris muscles.

The eye, like any optical system, can only be sharply focused at one given distance at any given moment of time. Objects at other distances give rise to greater or lesser degrees of defocused images, depending upon how far they are from the plane of sharp focus and (among other things) on the width of the pupil. The eye has a rather remarkable ability to shift its plane of sharp focus by increasing (or decreasing) its refracting power. It does this quickly by changing the length of the ciliary muscle (a band of smooth muscle—capable of graded contractions—which completely surrounds the lens). Contraction of the ciliary muscle relaxes the tensions on the connective tissue fibers that support the lens, and the lens substance becomes molded by its elastic capsule to assume a more convex, that is more highly refracting form (see the diagram of the eye in Figure 9.5). When the

eye is looking at an object far away, the ciliary muscle is relaxed, supporting fibers are taut, and the lens has a less convex spherical shape and therefore a decreased refracting power for the eye as a whole. Although these details are well understood, we know very little about the essential stimulus that releases the sequence of neurophysiological events culminating in this response. Retinal blur, and chromatic and spherical aberration in connection with the fine oscillatory movements of physiological nystagmus, have all been suggested. There is evidence suggesting that each may be sufficient and that no single one is necessary. We only know that the eye controls its focus on an object with a fair degree of accuracy. Focus will change within a reaction time as the distance of the object from the eye is changed and nearly always in the right direction. Apparently the "error" signal—whatever it is—is continuously monitored.

Of all the control systems associated with the effector mechanisms of the eye, the accommodation mechanism is the one the least well understood. We know its reaction time—about 0.36 ± 0.09 second for far-to-near accommodation and about 0.02 second more in the opposite direction (Campbell & Westheimer, 1960). Its precision is a good deal

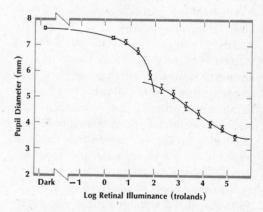

Figure 11.10. Diameter of the pupil as a function of the amount of light stimulating the retina. The plotted points are the means ($\pm$ one standard error of the mean) of the results of 16 experimental repetitions on a single observer. (ten Doesschate & Alpern, 1967.)

poorer than the systems for saccadic and tracking eye movements. However the depth of focus of the eye is sufficient under many conditions that the eye accommodation may fail to keep up with changes in the distance of the fixated object without appreciable blur. (In earlier literature we read of the "lazy lag" of accommodation.)

One potentially informative way of studying accommodation would be to "change the gain in the feedback loop," that is, to examine the accommodation responses obtained when the normal relation between accommodation and clear focus of the retinal image is altered.

PUPIL SIZE

The pupil of the eye gets smaller and smaller as the amount of light reaching the retina gets larger and larger. The exact relationship is shown in Figure 11.10 according to measurements of ten Doesschate and Alpern (1967). If both eyes are equally illuminated, the pupil is consistently smaller (0.4 to 0.7 mm) than the results illustrated in this figure (which were obtained with only one retina illuminated).

The pupil contraction regulates the amount of light that reaches the retina, and it is therefore a textbook example of a biological control system—one of the earliest studied. This regulatory mechanism has been studied both in the "closed loop" (that is normal fashion) and with the "feedback loop opened" (that is, by not allowing the changes in pupil size to influence how much light reaches the retina). These experiments are fascinating in that they demonstrate how the methods of analyzing automatic feedback control systems can be quantitatively applied to biological phenomena. However they are also somewhat disappointing. The limitations of the theory of linear control systems put severe constraints on the variety of responses that can be quantified by these methods, for most biological phenomena are highly nonlinear. Unfortunately the theory of the non-

linear automatic control system is much less well developed and lacks the elegance and the simplicity of the theory of linear systems.

One way of illustrating the nonlinearity of the pupil reflex is the demonstration (Clynes, 1962) that the pupil contracts whether the retina is exposed to a light flash or to a dark flash (a linear system would contract to a light flash and dilate to a dark flash). For the details of the application of the theory of servomechanisms to the human pupil, the reader should examine a paper by Stark (1959) and one by Clynes (1962). In any event, the pupil regulation is highly overrated as a method of controlling the adaptation state of the eye; the retina and the nervous system have developed much more powerful ways of doing this (see Chapter 9).

Although whatever it does when it regulates the amount of light reaching the retina is of trivial importance as a regulator of the adaptation state, the light reflex is a fascinating way of analyzing the sensory mechanisms of the retina.

It might be supposed that for a function of such little moment only an insignificant fraction of retinal photosensitive cells would be capable of exciting a pupil response. Everything we know about the action of the light reflex, on the contrary, suggests that both rods and cones—and, indeed in all likelihood, all rods and all cones—are capable of exciting a pupil contraction. Given sufficiently large fields and sufficiently sensitive detecting methods, the absolute thresholds for rod vision and for photopupillary motility are similar or even identical (Alpern, McCready, and Barr, 1963).

The action spectrum of the light reflex at high light levels is a weighted mean of the logarithm of the rod and cone spectral sensitivities, with both mechanisms given about equal weight. The response of the pupil to light indicates the eye does not easily differentiate between light focused within the geometric retinal image of the test target and light scattered entoptically within the eye, because light focused on the head of the human optic nerve will evoke a somewhat more vigorous response than will light on the surrounding (and hence, sensitive) retina. Thus, to evoke a pupil response by exciting the foveal cones and these alone, the small centrally fixed test flash must be superimposed in the center of a large (at least 15°) and bright blue background. (The background sufficiently adapts the surrounding rods so that the small amount of added light scattered from the test is not capable of exciting them further.) Under such conditions, the action spectrum of the light reflex is the same as that of the psychophysical (foveal) luminosity curve (Alpern & Campbell, 1962). The way the rod and cone signals combine to form suprathreshold pupillary responses at light levels above the cone threshold has yet to be worked out in detail.

Another way of reducing the size of the pupil is to shift the gaze from a distant to a near object, that is to increase accommodation. The miosis (that is, small pupil) associated with increased accommodation and increased accommodative vergence has already been described in the section on vergence movements. Very slight changes in pupil size also occur with fusional movements in about 50 percent of the observers so far examined, but the effect is small. Increased positive fusional convergence evokes almost a 0.087 mm decrease in pupil diameter for each degree of movement. The response to accommodative vergence may be as much as 2.5 times as large as this and occurs in all observers so far examined (Alpern, Mason, & Jardinico, 1961).

THE INFLUENCE OF PSYCHOLOGICAL VARIABLES ON THE INTRAOCULAR MUSCLES

The intraocular muscles that control accommodation and pupil size are smooth muscles. Like all smooth muscles, they are innervated by branches of the autonomic nervous system. Not unnaturally it may be anticipated that relevant psychological variables that can be expected to influence the autonomic nervous system should prove to be associated with changes in pupil size and accommodation. The matter has been studied only a little if at all in a quantitative way insofar as accommodation is concerned, but recently psychologists have become interested in how the pupil size varies when psychological variables are manipulated. It is very easy to photograph the pupil (with either infrared or ordinary panchromatic film), and when the negatives are magnified to about 10 times the size of the eye, the pupil diameter can easily be measured with a precision of 0.01 mm. Working in this way, Hess (1965) found some evidence that the pupil dilates in association with stimuli thought to be "pleasurable" and constricts to those thought to be "unpleasant." Similarly, while a student is trying to solve a simple arithmetic problem, the pupil seems to dilate and to constrict after the subject reports the solution. The greater the difficulty of the problem, the wider the dilation and subsequent constriction. This has led Kahneman and Beatty (1966) to the idea that pupil dilation is "an indicator of the amount of effort involved in the storing of information for (subsequent) report." Hess also found that intellectually interesting material seemed to be associated with a wide pupil. Evidently, the pupil response can be used to study interest, emotion, and thought processes, as well as attitudes.

The same is probably true of accommodation, but because changes in the refraction of the eye are much more difficult to measure, we know next to nothing about this. Enterprising optometrists (Pheiffer, 1955) have from time to time studied subjects with a retinoscope while they were reading or carrying out other tasks. This technique (so-called book retinoscopy) is a relatively crude one, and the length of time required for any single measurement precludes accurate time resolution of these changes, smaller than a few seconds at best. Nevertheless, there is the suggestion from such work that interest in reading matter and problem solving both produce changes in accommodation. Accurate analysis of such effects awaits the application of a highly sensitive infrared recording optometer by some curious psychologist. Even if the elegant recording devices currently available are used (Campbell & Robson, 1959), the task is difficult, but the potential rewards may in fact be considerably greater than those that can be reaped from studying pupil size changes, which are easier to measure.

Julian Hochberg

PERCEPTION

I. COLOR AND SHAPE

12

The world as we perceive it consists of tridimensional objects, stationary or moving, at various distances in space. Our perception of the world depends on—is *mediated by*—our sense organs. Of these, the most important by far is the eye, in which light waves reflected from (or produced by) the objects around us are focused to form an optical image on the retina, the sensitive tissue at the rear of the eye (p. 278).

The preceding chapters on vision, color vision, and effector mechanisms in vision were concerned with the reception and processing of stimulus information that reaches us through our eyes. These chapters had in common a concern for the physiological bases of vision and for quantitative treatments of such topics as visual sensitivity, color discrimination, and muscular adaptations of the eye to the inspection of visual patterns.

In turning our attention now to visual perception we go far beyond the preceding analyses of sensory events. We concern ourselves with the world of real objects, not only with the images formed by those objects on the retina of the eye. We try to understand how such objects can be perceived as solid visual shapes with characteristic properties of color, size, distance, and movement. For answers to these questions, we must often turn to the broad psychological fields of learning, maturation, thinking, and motivation, proceeding well beyond the processing that occurs in the eye and the visual pathways.

The retinal image is very different from any normal description of the environment. There are no objects in the image, only juxtaposed regions of color. The image is in two dimensions, whereas the environment is in three dimensions. The retinal image of an object changes in size and shape as the observer views the object from different distances and angles, even though the object itself is unchanging. In color, too, the image changes as the object's illumination is changed, whereas the object retains its own characteristic reflectance. Nevertheless, the retinal image must somehow provide good information about such object properties as distances, sizes, shapes, and reflectances, for the observer does see them readily and often quite accurately. It is in trying to discover how the observer extracts and uses the retinal information about object properties that many of the general problems of visual perception arise.

Objects' appearances vary in an immense number of ways. They can appear to be animate or inanimate, light or dark, large or small, threatening or friendly. Most experimental research has centered around 4 of the ways in which objects can differ—their colors, their shapes, their sizes, and their locations (and motions) in space—because these attributes seem to be relatively simple to account for in terms of what is known about the specific nerve energies of the visual sensory system (p. 279), because they seem to be fundamental in understanding how we perceive the world, and because they are relatively easy to study. We shall survey the experimental problems of how we see objects' colors and shapes in this chapter; in the next chapter, we shall consider how we see objects' locations, sizes and motions in space.

PROBLEMS IN THE PERCEPTION OF OBJECT COLORS

Our views of the world normally contain regions of color the appearance of which can differ in many ways. As used in the study of visual perception, "color" includes the attributes of lightness and darkness, hue, and saturation. We have seen in Chapter 9 that a great deal of research has been devoted to explaining how these changes in appearance depend on changes in stimulation. In addition, an expanse of color can be described as looking filmlike and insubstantial, or like a hard surface; it can appear bulky and three-dimensional or it can appear flat and two-dimensional; it can look transparent or opaque, luminous or nonluminous, lustrous or nonlustrous (Katz, 1911, 1935). On the contrary, the appearance of a small homogeneous patch of light viewed in an otherwise dark field varies in only 3 ways: in its hue, its saturation, and its brightness (p. 359). Because we can (theoretically) replace any view of the world whatsoever by a picture that will be indistinguishable from the view itself but that is composed of such small homogeneous patches of light, such stimuli offer a simple starting point for the study of the perception of color. In fact, many of the problems of visual perception originated with the historically influential viewpoint called *structuralism* (p. 402), in which the appearances of homogeneous patches of light were considered to be the elementary units of experience, or *sensations,* of which our perceptions of objects and scenes are assembled. If we attempt to explain the appearance of objects' colors in terms of what we know about the appearance of a small patch of light, 3 sets of problems arise.

The first 2 problems, *color constancy* and *color contrast,* arise because an object's apparent hue or lightness is usually not what we would expect it to be from knowing the light that the object reflects to the eye. The third problem, that of *surface color,* arises because objects' surfaces appear to differ from each other not only in their hue, saturation, and brightness but also in additional ways (they may look more or less lustrous, hard, rough, and so on).

THE PROBLEM OF COLOR CONSTANCY

Early Background

Reflectance is a physical property of substances: the property of absorbing some of the incident light and reflecting the remainder. The reflectance R of a gray surface is equivalent to the ratio of the luminance L to the incident light or illuminance E. Thus, $R = L/E$, or, as pointed out in Chapter 9, $L = ER$. Absolute black would reflect no light under any illumination, but such perfectly black surfaces do not exist. A good black will have a reflectance as low as 3 percent, whereas good whites run about 80 percent.

We know that increasing the amount of light on any part of the retina generally increases the perceived lightness of that region (see pp. 276–278). Yet it is a fact of common observation that coal looks black even in sunlight, and chalk looks white even in shadow, and in these conditions the eye may receive much stronger light from the coal than from the chalk. Thus, even when the illumination of an object's retinal image changes, casual observation seems to show that *the object's color appears to remain relatively constant.*

Interest in the problem of color constancy dates from those early giants of physiological optics, Helmholtz and Hering, who laid out the 2 main kinds of explanation of color constancy, posing between them the central issues of color perception (and perhaps of perceptual inquiry in general).

As Helmholtz first said in 1866 (1962 ed., p. 408):

> Colors are mainly important for us as properties of objects and as means of identifying objects. In visual observation we constantly aim to reach a judgment of the object colors and to eliminate differences of illumination. . . . Seeing the same object under . . . different illuminations, we learn to get a correct idea of the object colors in spite of differences of illumination . . . and since our interest lies entirely in the constant object color, we become unconscious of the sensations on which our judgment rests.

That is, Helmholtz is saying that the light that is reflected to the retina from some object acts as the stimulus to produce a given sensation of brightness but that we usually also have indications of what illumination is falling on the object, and we have learned to allow for the effects of different hues and intensities of illumination without being aware of this correction process. It is *as though* we arrive at our judgments of color by making an inference (unconsciously) about the reflecting properties of the object, an inference based on the brightness of the sensation that we experience and on the various indications of illumination that we have learned to take into account (even though we do not notice them).

Judgment based on unconscious sensations seemed to Hering (1874, 1876, 1879) an unrealistic account of the process of color perception. He pointed to the peripheral factors that compensate for changes of illumination: contraction and dilation of the pupil, retinal adaptation, and contrast. Each of these would tend, normally, to keep the apparent brightness of the object constant, even though the overall illumination on the object and its background increases (see pp. 283–289). Thus, with an increase in illumination, the pupil contracts and lets less light through to the retina. If increased light reaches the retina, the eye adapts to the increase and this adaptation results in a decrease in the retina's sensitivity. Finally, *contrast* has the effect that a bright background darkens the appearance of the object it surrounds. For this reason, if retinal images of object and background do receive more illumination, the increased luminance of the background should result in a greater darkening of the object's appearance, a darkening that will tend to compensate for the increased illumination the object has received. Still, Hering agreed that these peripheral factors were not wholly sufficient to account for all constancy phenomena, and accordingly suggested also a cerebral factor, later elaborated (1907, reprinted 1920) as the concept of "memory color." In his own words, "The color in which we have oftenest seen an external thing impresses itself indelibly on our memory and becomes a fixed characteristic of the memory image. What the layman calls the real color of a thing is a color which has become firmly attached to the thing in his memory; I might call it the memory color of the thing." This "approximate color constancy of seen objects," Hering urged, was one of the most remarkable and important facts in the whole realm of physiological optics.

We shall consider evidence and arguments for these two positions. While we shall see good reason to modify both, we will be able neither to accept nor to reject either of them completely.

Katz (1911), who did a great deal of the early work on the effect of changes in illumination on objects' appearances, argued that neither memory color nor Hering's peripheral factors seemed to provide an adequate explanation of the perception of object colors. However, neither did he accept Helmholtz' notion of a two-stage process, namely sensation followed by judgment. Katz maintained that the correlate of luminance is the experience of *insistence* (the degree to which a color attracts attention), not lightness. Our experiences of the surface color and the illumination of a patch of a given luminance

are inseparably coupled, so that with each impression of illuminance we will perceive a different object color (Katz, 1930; see also Gelb, 1929). A white in one illumination is not the same experience as a white in another illumination. For Katz, the problem is therefore not how illumination is taken into account by an act of judgment, but how a color in one illumination comes to be identified as being the same as some color in another.

Since then, "color constancy," along with "size constancy" and "shape constancy" (pp. 506, 515), has become a familiar psychological term. What it refers to is illustrated in Figure 12.1.

The Measurement of Constancy

The factor of reflectance Suppose the observer is to make a color match between a standard gray surface that is receiving an illumination of E_{St} and a variable gray surface (that is, whose reflectance can be changed) viewed under a different illumination, E_V (Figure 12.1). Let the standard have a reflectance, R_{St}, of 40 percent, and an illumination, E_{St}, of 10 foot-candles. Let the variable receive an illumination E_V of 50 ft-c. What reflectance value of the variable gray R_V will an observer choose to match the standard? A priori, it would seem that an observer could choose either of 2 different reflectances that might be regarded as correct. One "match" is a luminance match. Remember that luminance $L = ER$ (see Chapter 9, p. 276). The gray that would equal the luminance of the standard has a reflectance $R_{VL} = 8$ percent (because 8 percent of 50 ft-c = 40 percent of 10 ft-c = 4 ft-L of luminance in each case). However, the "object's color" may also refer to its *reflectance* (or *albedo*). Therefore, the other possible basis for a "match" is given by a reflectance of the variable which equals that of the standard, or $R_{VA} = R_{St}$. Here, $R_{VA} = 40$ percent.

In actual fact, an observer usually chooses neither R_{VA} nor R_{VL}, but instead chooses a third value, which we may take to lie on a continuum between 2 poles, one conforming to stimulus luminance, the other correspond-

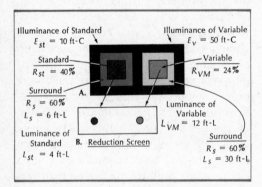

Figure 12.1. A. A simple constancy experiment: the standard and variable are viewed under different levels of illumination. B. Standard and variable are viewed through a reduction screen. See text.

ing to object reflectance:

R_{VL}	R_{VM}	R_{VA}
8 percent	24 percent	40 percent

Brunswik (1929) introduced a method of expressing the results of such a matching procedure as a ratio. He defined perceptual constancy as the ratio

$$\frac{R_{VM} - R_{VL}}{R_{St} - R_{VL}}$$

If the observer were to make a perfect reflectance match, then $R_{VM} = R_{St} = 40$ percent, and the Brunswik ratio = (40 percent − 8 percent)/(40 percent − 8 percent) = 1.0 (that is, the observer achieves perfect constancy). In the case illustrated by Figure 12.1, $R_{VM} = 24$ percent, and the Brunswik ratio = 50 percent. The Brunswik ratio is not the only way of representing the relationship between these measures, of course; several other indices of lightness constancy are described in Woodworth and Schlosberg (1954, page 436; see also Leibowitz, 1956; Landauer, 1962).

It is easy to demonstrate that under *some* circumstances the match between 2 objects is made solely on the basis of their luminances, namely when we use a *reduction screen* (or approximate its use). A reduction screen is a very simple device that merits separate discussion.

The reduction screen or hole screen If you look through a tube or a small hole at a uniformly colored surface, the "surface" vanishes and a mere expanse of color is seen through the hole. This simple piece of apparatus is called the *hole screen* or *reduction screen*. What is seen in an aperture, most appropriately called *aperture color,* appears self-luminous, or internally lit, whereas a surface color appears to be illuminated by an external source. Aperture color ranges from dim to bright, from zero to the maximum brightness. Surface color varies in what is best called *lightness;* in the achromatic series it can also be called *whiteness,* ranging from black through the shades of gray to the

definite upper limit of pure white. Both surface color and aperture color can also vary in hue and saturation.

The hole screen allows the light reflected from a surface to reach the eye but it conceals the surroundings. Clues that the subject might be able to use to discover what the illumination is are thus removed from the field of view. When viewed in a reduction screen, two spots look equally bright only when the stimuli are of equal luminance. Thus, the reduction screen affords a convenient means of matching two stimuli, or of determining their relative brightness, saturation, and hue. When the screen is removed, and the objects are viewed in the unobstructed situation, the subject usually compares the two objects more in terms of their reflectances. Let us survey the experimental results of such experiments in color constancy, and then consider some theories about what these facts imply about the nature of perceptual processes.

Color Constancy Under Normal and Abnormal Conditions of Illumination

Consider a typical experiment by Burzlaff (1931): The observer viewed a set of 48 gray

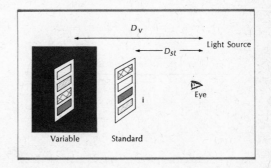

Figure 12.2. Standard and variable at different distances from the light source. Burzlaff (1931) used charts of 48 patches of gray as standard and variable; he obtained Brunswik ratios higher than .90. Brunswik (1929), using one square of gray each for standard and variable, obtained ratios ranging from about .25 to about .65 for adults, and from about .12 to about .50 for young children (ages 3–5).

papers, ranging from the best white to the best black obtainable, placed in irregular order on a large medium-gray cardboard which was set near a window and illuminated by diffuse daylight. A set of identically colored papers, placed in regular graded order from black to white, mounted on a similar piece of medium gray cardboard, was set far back in the room, where it received only $\frac{1}{20}$ of the light that illuminated the irregular set (Fig. 12.2). The subject stood near the window, with his back to it, viewing both charts with the dark rear wall of the room as background. With one gray paper on the near chart designated as the standard, the subject compared each gray in the far chart with the standard, judging whether the variable was the same, lighter, or darker than the standard.

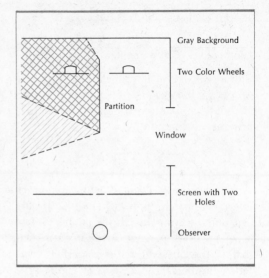

Figure 12.4. The partition between the two color wheels places the left-hand one in shadow. Brunswik ratios for two observers were .31 and .26 for short views; with long inspection periods, they tended more toward luminance matches. (After Katz, 1930.)

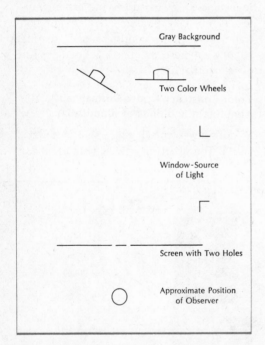

Figure 12.3. Setup for varying angle of incidence. The color wheel on the left had an all white disk. When viewed through the two holes in the reduction screen, the wheel on the right matched the one on the left when the former had a 13 percent white sector and an 87 percent black sector. With a direct view, the two wheels were matched when the right one was 45 percent white and 55 percent black (Katz, 1930). The Brunswik ratio is then .36.

Repeating the procedure with several of the standards, and computing the PSEs according to the method of constant stimuli (p. 23), Burzlaff found that the subject matched a given gray on one chart with a gray of almost the same reflectance on the other chart, in spite of the very different illuminations on the two charts. Thus, despite the fact that the light reflected from any particular gray to the eye was only $\frac{1}{20}$ as much in the dim as in the bright illumination, the object color was judged to be nearly the same (see Figure 12.2). The diminution of stimulation had *some* effect, for errors were mostly in one direction; it took a somewhat lighter shade in the dim light to match a given shade in the bright light. The actual match was thus a compromise between a match of object reflectance and a match of luminance but was much closer, in this experiment, to the former, giving us a good example of color constancy (or perhaps we should say *reflectance constancy*).

Color constancy with nonuniform illumination The issue of color constancy arises whenever illuminance is changed from one part of the visual field to another (or from one time to another). Several such situations are listed below, and illustrated in Figures 12.2 through 12.6.

One object is at a greater distance from the light source than another (Figure 12.2).

One object is at a more oblique angle to the direction of light than the other, so that the same illuminance is spread over a larger area (Figure 12.3).

One object is viewed through a filter, or other light-reducing device, that covers all or part of the view. For example, Katz used such a device to reduce the overall amount of light coming from a white disk and its surroundings to $\frac{1}{4}$, $\frac{1}{12}$, $\frac{1}{36}$, and $\frac{1}{120}$ of the light coming from a variable color wheel, which was viewed directly. Brunswik ratios were .107, .215, .218, and .224, respectively.

One object is in light, the other in shadow (Figure 12.4) or the 2 objects to be matched are otherwise placed in separately illuminated fields.

The lighting of the entire field of view is different from normal lighting in some respect. The page of this book reflects a much yellower light to the eye under incandescent light than in broad daylight, but it still looks white in both cases.

In all of the circumstances described above, Brunswik ratios are usually greater than 0.0 and less than 1.0. The apparent color of an object viewed under different illuminations is a function not only of its luminance, but of its reflectance as well.

We can readily understand how the subject might match 2 grays as being equal in appearance when the same amount of light reaches his eye from each of them. After all, there are physical light detectors that would respond in just those terms. However, the experiments on color constancy show that the matches subjects make generally are influenced by the objects' reflectances. Because there is no known receptor mechanism that can detect reflectances, a great deal of attention has been devoted to trying to discover the basis of these matches. What information

is there in the retinal image to explain this ability?

If we consider only the luminance L of the local patch of color reflected to the eye by an object whose reflectance is R and which receives illumination E, we see that in order to solve the equation, $R = L/E$, for R, we need to know the value of E. If we view the ability to judge objects' reflectances as the ability to solve the equation for R given L, we see that the subject also must have some indication of E. What information is there in the retinal image concerning E? Does the subject really use this information to solve the equation for R?

Achievement explanations of color constancy   Color constancy is an "achievement" (Brunswik, 1952) in this sense: The ability to recognize that the coal is really black, even though it is sending more light to the eye than is the white piece of paper, is *adaptive:* it probably helps one get along in the world. If this ability to judge reflectance rests on anything like the ability to solve the equation, $R = L/E$, for R, given L, then the achievement of color constancy implies the ability to take the illumination E into account, on the basis of whatever indications of E may be available in the retinal image. Because it is hard to see how this ability to take all of the illumination cues into account could be innate (could be built into the organism's nervous system at birth), it seemed reasonable to many psychologists to argue that color constancy is due to the subject's having learned to use the illumination cues (see Helmholtz' explanation, p. 397).

There are, of course, other mechanisms for color constancy that we might postulate, mechanisms that might well be innate, but we shall defer consideration of those mechanisms to a later section (p. 412).

Registering the illumination, E; clues, cues, and unconscious inference   The subject might solve the equation, $R = L/E$, in 2 ways. First, he might perceive the illumination and use that as his guide in deciding what the reflectance is. Second, the subject's visual nervous system might process the information about L and E without his being able to judge either of them separately with any degree of accuracy.

As common observation tells us, it is certainly not true that the subject consciously notices the clues to the illumination and consciously deduces from these the nature and magnitude of E. For this reason, Woodworth (1938) proposed that we use the more neutral word, "cue," rather than "clue" for such processes, implying by this that the subject responds to indications of illumination in a well-rehearsed automatic fashion, initiating inference-like processes even though he might be unable to say either what the cues are, or what the subsequent processes of "taking illumination into account" might be. A similar view underlay Katz's (1935) approach to color perception (see p. 398). It is really not all that different from Helmholtz' explanation—that the visual system acts *as though unnoticed* sensations are used as the basis for *unconscious* inferences. It does avoid some of the connotations suggested by Helmholtz' formulation, and it has become standard usage in the study of perception to use the word "cue" to refer to aspects of the sensory stimulus pattern that can *at least potentially* convey information about some aspect of the physical world, and which the observer may or may not be able to report or notice.

Both kinds of explanation assume that the luminance of any patch of light is in fact the starting point from which the subject arrives at the apparent reflectance or object color. As a corollary, both approaches must assume that the subject obtains information about the illumination E from the retinal image (or from some other source of knowledge) and that the apparent color that is produced by L is modified to take E into account. This assumption is inherited from an extremely simple general psychological system, often called *structuralism*, which we should consider briefly here inasmuch as most of the problems with which these chapters are concerned arose in the context of that system.

Theories of Color Constancy

The structuralist theory and its implications: sensations, learned illumination cues, and unconscious inference; can illumination be perceived?   The simplest system for analyzing the world of visual perception into simple and fundamental sensory events would be something like the following:

We know that we can reduce all possible patterns of stimulation on the retina to various combinations of small, homogeneous patches of light. We also know that we can match the appearance of any such small patch of light with another dot of light that varies only with respect to the physical energy at each wavelength in the spectrum. We know further that if such a dot of light is viewed against a homogeneous background, and the spectral energy distribution is varied systematically, we see a dot whose appearance also varies systematically (Chapter 10). In terms of the sensory physiology of the eye, it seems reasonable to assume that the visual nervous system analyzes the world in just this way: that the retina consists of a mosaic of receptors, some of which respond maximally to one wavelength, some of which respond maximally to another; that at least ideally each receptor responds to physical stimulation falling on it independently of what the other receptors around it may be doing; and, finally, that a characteristic elementary sensory experience would result from (or accompany) each elementary receptor response.

According to this scheme, we would have 3 sets of analytic units: (1) The elementary physical variables of stimulation (wavelength and intensity distribution). (2) The elementary sensory receptors that are presumably responsive to those physical energies. (3) The simple irreducible experiences of color, called *sensations,* that presumably result from—or accompany—the receptors' activities.

How might we apply this system of analysis to the perception of objects and events? We could assume that the appearance of a particular spot would remain unchanged, regardless of what stimulation was exciting its neighboring receptors. That is, in effect, we could assume that sensations are unchanged by the various combinations into which they enter. We could then extend this analysis to the perception of objects, quite simply: The appearance of any part of an object or scene is (by this theory) the same as the appearance which that colored spot would have when it is observed in isolation. By implication, a finite number of color sensations would, in their different possible combinations, account for all of the immense diversity of different objects and object properties that we perceive in the world.

The attempt to explain the perceived world in terms of such fundamental sensory experiences runs through the thinking of Helmholtz (1866) and Wundt (1902), and is most explicitly pursued by Titchener (1902). It offers a clear, simple and consistent program for psychological research, for relating psychology to the neighboring disciplines of physiology and physics, and for the prediction and explanation of the world we perceive. However, this apparent simplicity is misleading. Color sensations do *not* seem to be independent of the combinations in which they occur. As soon as we turn to the perception of complex and nonhomogeneous scenes, we find that an object's apparent color is not determined simply by the stimulation falling within its retinal image. The fact of color constancy shows us this quite clearly: The assumption that the same retinal stimulation produces the same color experience, regardless of what else is happening, is clearly incomplete, at best; for the subject often reports that two objects have the same apparent color when the 2 objects have equal reflectances in the physical world (that is, $R_1 = R_2$), not when the stimuli each projects to the retina are of equal luminance ($L_1 = L_2$).

This discrepancy might be explained, of course, as originating from a great deal of perceptual learning. Thus, Helmholtz argued (see p. 397) that we learn that objects' reflectances R are usually permanent, even though the illuminance E changes; that we learn to detect the various indications, or cues, as to what illumination is falling on any object; and that we learn how to take the effects of the illumination into account in order to arrive at the perception of reflectance.

The implications of this theory are these: the value of luminance of some focal region L_f can in fact be correctly sensed regardless of changes in adjacent stimulation, L_a; the illuminance E can be estimated on the basis of its various indications (retinal or otherwise) and can be correctly taken into account in deriving R from L; and these abilities to detect and use E are learned.

Let us consider the experimental status of these various implications.

Can we, in fact, perceive E? There is a problem here. We must know the object color or reflectance in order to deduce the illuminance from the reflected light, whereas we must know the illumination in order to deduce the object color from the reflected light. That is, if all we know is L, we must have R in order to solve the equation $R = L/E$ for E, whereas we must have E in order to solve for R. Hering raised this logical question in 1907. One possible answer is this: In normal scenes, the illumination on a particular object might be gathered from stimuli received from surrounding objects (Kardos, 1929). Moreover, whereas indirect vision indicates little of the object color, it offers the subject a total impression of the general illumination.[1] However, such estimates of general illumination are not enough; parts of the environment often differ in lighting from the overall background, and if those local differences are not "taken into account," reflectance R must be misjudged. Consider a patch of shadow. Taken by itself, it might be perceived as a region of lowered illuminance E, but it might also be seen as a patch of lower reflectance. What indications are there in the retinal image

[1] Katz (1935) suggested that the experience of the overall *insistence* (see p. 398) of the whole field of view might be the basis for judging illumination, and that this might be studied quantitatively by the use of the homogeneous visual field. As we shall see (p. 426), however, the homogeneous visual field, or *Ganzfeld*, changes its appearance through adaptation so readily that it is not really suited for this purpose.

that the shadowed region is of lower illuminance?

One cue that a region is in shadow is the *penumbra* or half-shadow along the edges of the region, and an analogous fringe borders on an area of raised illumination. Another indication of shading is given by the three-dimensional arrangement. Thus, if the three-dimensional form of a box is clearly perceived, we might then decide that its darker side is in shadow rather than painted black. If we look beyond the local patch itself, at the *surrounding pattern of stimulation,* such illumination cues can usually be found in the retinal image.

To decide whether or not such indications of illumination indeed affect our object-color perception, we can do two things. First, we can conceal the indications of illumination; this should lead the observer to mistake changes in *E* for changes in *R*. Second, we can try to provide false information about *E;* this should change judgments about *R* appropriately.

Experiments with concealed illumination conditions are diagrammed in Figures 12.5 and 12.6. In a classic experiment, Gelb (1929) pre-

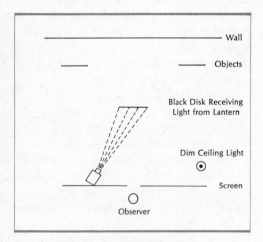

Figure 12.5. Gelb's concealed illumination experiment. The lantern at the left is invisible to the observer, and its light is confined to the black disk. The wall and all objects in the room receive the rather dim light from the ceiling lamp. See text.

sented a background consisting of a wall and several objects illuminated by a rather dim ceiling light (Figure 12.5). In the foreground a textureless black velvet disk received the bright light of a concealed lantern. No penumbra was visible on the disk or on the background. The subject reported seeing a white disk standing in the general illumination (white in the dim light instead of black in the bright light). This represents a complete failure of color constancy. However, the instant a small bit of white paper was held in the bright light, just in front of the disk, the disk was seen to be black. We might say that the bit of white paper was the cue to the extra illumination on the disk. When the white paper was removed, however, the disk returned to its former appearance. We might have expected, from our formula, that once the subject was made aware of the extra illumination of the disk and of its true object color, he would maintain this awareness after the white paper was removed. So he did, no doubt, intellectually; but neither his intellectual knowledge about illumination, nor his knowledge of the true object color was sufficient to maintain color constancy in the absence of the actual white stimulus. We shall see that unequivocal knowledge of the true situation similarly often fails to influence perceptions of size, shape, and distance when we come to discuss experiments with those attributes.

Unqualified claims that perception is the result of knowledge, that is, that we see what we know to be true, are misleading at the very least.

With similar procedures based on concealed illumination, Henneman (1935) showed that if the black disk were replaced by a white one, and only the white disk was placed in the spotlight, the white disk appeared to be *luminous.* This is what we would expect in terms of "taking illumination into account." Because the disk sent more light to the eye than could be accounted for by the dim ceiling light, which was the only visible source of illumination, the disk itself appeared

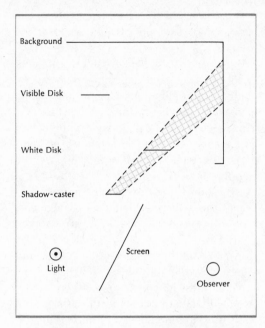

Figure 12.6. The Kardos concealed shadow experiment. The only visible object shaded by the shadow-caster is the white disk, which stands entirely in full shadow. The subject sees this disk as black or gray. Screening the shadow-caster is unnecessary, for even if the subject sees it he gets no suggestion that it is shading the white disk. See p. 404.

to be a source of light; that is, L/E appeared to be greater than 1.00.

Conversely, as shown in Figure 12.6, Kardos (1934) illuminated a field of objects with good light, except for one disk of white paper that was placed in the shadow made by a concealed shadow-caster which covered *only the disk* with shadow. If there is no penumbra (or any other indication of shadow) on the disk, the subject reports a *black* disk standing in good light. Move the shadow a little to the side so that its edge is visible on the disk, and the disk at once appears to be white in shadow instead of black in good light. MacLeod (1932) showed that putting a false shadow on the background made an object in front of it appear lighter and, the larger the background shadow was made, the lighter colored the object appeared.

Thus, by concealing the cues that would

normally show that an object is receiving illumination different from that of its surroundings, or by introducing false cues, the experimenter can influence the subject's perception of object color, much as one would expect from the equation, $R = L/E$.

In all of the experiments that we have described, however, the stimulus conditions have been changed (as by the insertion of the white card in the Gelb experiment) to provide illumination cues. Such experiments can, therefore, show at most that *the stimulus conditions that normally accompany changes in illumination can result also in changes in judgments of surface color*. The experiments cannot show that these stimulus conditions have the effects that they do *because* they are cues or clues, that is, *because* they give the subject information about the illumination which he then takes into account. As we shall see, there are other explanations that can be applied to each of the experiments that we have described. More convincing evidence of the subject's ability to use illumination cues would be direct research on the accuracy with which he makes judgments concerning *illumination* under different conditions. We have as yet only a very little systematic evidence related to this critical point, aside from the information that such judgments can be made (Katz, 1935).

Beck (1959, 1961) had subjects match the illumination falling on a comparison surface to that which appeared to fall on a standard surface, both being viewed in an otherwise dark room. He first explained to the subjects the distinction between a surface's lightness and its illumination. Each pair of surfaces to be compared had texture patterns causing different *average* reflectances; for example, gray with white speckles on one, black with white speckles on the other; gray with white dots on one, black with white dots on the other, and so on. Subjects did make consistent judgments of illumination, setting the illuminance of the comparison surface close to that of the standard. For example, a set of white and gray stripes was used as the standard, receiving an illuminance of 2.88 ft-c, and a set of black and white stripes was used for the comparison, the illuminance of which was varied. The median setting at which subjects judged both surfaces to have the same illuminance was 1.89 ft-c. If both surfaces had appeared to be equally illuminated when the average light that they actually reflected to the eye was equal, the variable illuminance should have been set to 10.4 ft-c. With these alternatives in mind (that is, a retinal match of 10.4 or an illuminance match of 2.88), we can compute an "illumination constancy ratio" $(E_M - E_L)/(E_{st} - E_L)$, by analogy with the Brunswik ratio for brightness constancy. From Beck's data, the illumination constancy is thus $(1.89 - 10.4)/(2.88 - 10.4) = 1.1$.

To what variables are the subjects responding in such illumination-matching experiments? In experiments similar to that described above, Beck (1961) used surfaces with a much finer texture, or *microstructure* (such as fine stippled surfaces, flannel cloth, wood, and so on), rather than clearly discernable patterns of 2 different uniform reflectances. With the stippled and cloth surfaces, illumination constancy was low (Beck's data yield constancy ratios of about 0.10), but when white backgrounds were added to the field of view, the illumination constancy increased considerably (now ranging from 0.4 to 0.8). Beck concludes that subjects' judgments are, in general, close to what we would expect if 2 surfaces were judged to be equally illuminated when equal amounts of light were reflected from their lightest clearly discernible regions.[2]

We can now ask how well judgments of both E and R fit the equation, $R = L/E$, because Beck also had his subjects judge the surfaces' apparent lightnesses. He set the surfaces to the median value at which each sub-

ject had previously judged them to be equally illuminated. The subject then matched the surfaces for lightness against a chart (which was separately illuminated) consisting of pieces of gray paper of various reflectances. If judgments of lightness were made by taking perceived illumination into account, lightness constancy should be poor where illumination judgments were poor. In fact, however, lightness judgments of some of the surfaces (the stipple surfaces, with no white surrounds) were found to produce almost perfect constancy, even though illumination judgments using those surfaces had been very poor.

The discrepancy between illumination constancy and lightness constancy does not necessarily rule out the Helmholtzian theory that lightness judgments depend on unconscious illumination judgments. Perhaps subjects use different cues to form their unconscious judgments of illumination when they explicitly try to match the lightnesses of two surfaces than those they use when they explicitly try to match the illumination of surfaces. After all, the subject has had a lifetime of experience with trying to make correct judgments about reflectance, but he has rarely, if ever, had to concern himself with making explicit responses to illumination as such.

Color constancy in children and animals If color constancy were a learned judgmental ability, it might be less well developed in creatures with less perceptual experience and of less developed intellect. To test such reasoning, color constancy has been studied with human children of different ages to see whether perceptual achievement improves as a function of years of experience, and with animals of different evolutionary level.

Although age differences in color constancy have been found with human subjects in some conditions and not in others (Brunswik, 1929; Burzlaff, 1931; Beck, 1966), it seems clear that at least under *some* judging conditions, if a child is old enough to serve as a

[2] Several subjects, who did not fit this generalization, overestimated the illumination for those surfaces that had the greatest difference in reflectance between parts of the pattern. Perhaps these subjects used the degree of brightness difference as a basis for judging the amount of illumination, a possibility that is particularly interesting in terms of Hering's theory of brightness perception, which we discuss shortly (p. 411).

subject at all, he will display color constancy not substantially inferior to that of the adult. Such experiments are not really conclusive, however, because one may argue that even the very young child has had a very large amount of perceptual experience.

Experiments with animals have, in general, shown their color constancy to be as good as (or better than) that of humans. Locke (1935) tested the ability of rhesus monkeys and of human adults to discriminate a white field from a black field that was separated from it by a partition; the white field was sometimes to the right of the black field and sometimes to the left. The monkeys received a raisin when they reached into the white field. Once the discrimination habit was established, extra light was projected on the black field to raise its luminance above that of the white one. With humans, Brunswik ratios (p. 399) ranged from 0.10 to 0.23; with monkeys, from 0.47 to 0.65.

Burkamp (1923) trained fish to seek their food in troughs of a certain color and then tested them to discover whether they could pick this color from among an assemblage of grays and other colors even when the illumination was altered. The fish displayed excellent constancy: Increasing the light did not make them go to the darker shades, nor did colored light send them to the grays or to other colors, not used in training.

Though these results from children and animals indicate that no exalted intellectual process is necessary to "correct for illumination so as to see object colors," they do not show that no learning is involved, inasmuch as both children and animals have had perceptual experience before the experimental tests were performed. In order to avoid a training period in which perceptual learning might occur, Gogel and Hess (1951) raised chicks in darkness from the time they were hatched until the time they were tested, and then the chicks were tested to determine whether their innate preference for pecking at lighter grain was affected by local differences in the way the grain was illuminated.

The birds picked the lighter grains even when those grains had the lower luminance, because they were under lower illumination.

Regardless of whether learning *contributes* to color constancy, therefore, we must seriously consider the possibility that in at least some creatures there is an *innate* mechanism that permits some minimum amount of "correction for illumination" to occur. Let us now consider a mechanism that might result in color constancy, but which does not use the illumination cues as sources of information about illumination, and which therefore might be innately given in the nature of the sensory nervous system.

Contrast theories of constancy; simultaneous contrast So far, we have considered explanations of lightness constancy that start with the assumption that an observer first makes some response to the light that the object reflects to his eye and that he then modifies this impression by taking the apparent illumination E into account. This kind of explanation implies that the effects that a stimulus produces in the nervous system are independent of the effects of stimuli that impinge on other parts of the retina, until they are modified by higher processes, and that the observer can correctly identify a given stimulus (whether consciously or unconsciously) regardless of its context. Now, subjects can in fact match 2 stimuli with considerable accuracy and precision when the 2 are presented as small homogeneous targets or test patches side by side on a homogeneous background (Chapter 9). However, if the wavelength or intensity of the field surrounding one such spot is made to be different from that surrounding the other, subjects cannot, in general, judge correctly when both spots are the same, even when neither an object nor a source of illumination is clearly represented in the field of view. This is the familiar phenomenon of *simultaneous contrast*, which is discussed in more detail in Chapter 9. Like *lightness constancy*, contrast refers to a discrepancy between the value of

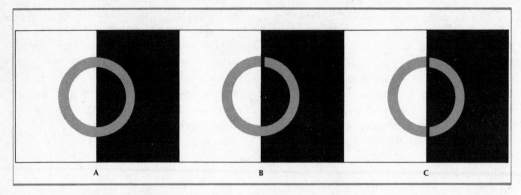

Figure 12.7. Contour and contrast. A. The gray ring appears to be relatively homogeneous at the division between the black and white surrounds. B, C. The gradient of lightness difference between the two halves of the gray ring becomes much more noticeable with the addition of a contour. The configuration of the test region also affects the detectability of the contrast effect (Berman & Leibowitz, 1965; see text). The phenomenon seems to be a relatively local one, and not due to the assimilation of the entire gray region to a single lightness (compare the top and bottom of B).

the local stimulus intensity and the value of the subject's judgment that we would presume to be based on it. Here, however, unlike the case with constancy, the discrepancy seems at first glance not an *achievement,* but rather a *failure* to respond properly to the environment, an "illusion." As a phenomenon, it challenges the assumption that the subject can identify the local stimulus regardless of the context in which it appears.

As a sensory phenomenon, simultaneous contrast usually works to exaggerate the differences between 2 stimuli, speaking loosely. As specific examples of simultaneous contrast, suppose that 2 small identical gray squares or test patches are placed on a variety of different backgrounds or surrounds. The test patch that is surrounded by (or adjacent to) a white background will look darker than one with a black surround; a square with a yellow surround will look bluer than one with a neutral surround; a square with a green surround will look more red, and so on.

An opposite effect, however, may sometimes be observed. This effect is known as *assimilation.* It can be seen in halftone prints and TV screens. Under these conditions, small or narrow regions of color are "diluted" rather than exaggerated, which is what occurs in simultaneous contrast (Newhall, 1942; Burn-

ham, 1953; Helson, 1963). Moreover, even where the conditions are otherwise such that simultaneous contrast should occur, a contour must separate the 2 test patches if the effect is to be clearly observed. Thus, Wundt (Osgood, 1953) noted that a gray test patch placed across the division between a white and a black surround looks uniform in lightness even though we would expect the part in the white surround to look darker. Koffka (1915) and Benussi (1916) are responsible for versions of the demonstration in Figure 12.7. In Figure 12.7A, the gray ring usually appears

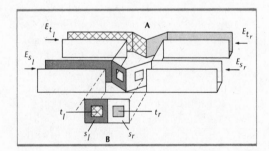

Figure 12.8. A. Apparatus used by Hess and Pretori (1894) to study simultaneous contrast (after Hurvich & Jameson, 1966). The luminance of each of four fields was independently controlled by varying the illuminance each received. B. The appearance of the four fields.

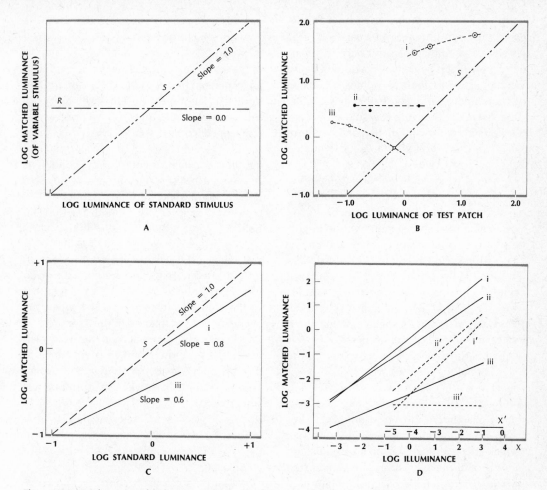

Figure 12.9. Brightness and lightness matches as a function of L_t/L_s.

A. Two theoretical curves representing the values by which an observer might match the appearance of a target and a comparison stimulus. The abscissa shows the luminance to which the target is set. The luminance of the field surrounding the target is varied proportionally, at the same time, so that the ratio, L_t/L_s, is kept fixed. The ordinate represents the values to which a subject might set a comparison stimulus so that it appears equal to the target. If the surround had no effect on the target's appearance, so that for each increase in target luminance, L_t, the luminance must be increased by an equal amount, the subject's judgments would fall on the curve marked S, which has a slope of 1.0. In a constancy experiment, this would have a Brunswik ratio of 0.0 (see p. 399). If the contrast induced by the surroundings, L_s, darkened the appearance of the target by an amount equal to the simultaneous increase in the target's luminance (so that for a given ratio of L_t/L_s the target's appearance remained unchanged), the subject's judgments would fall on the curve marked R, which has a slope of 0.0. In a constancy experiment, these results would yield a Brunswik ratio of 1.0.

In the graphs at B, C, and D, curves marked *i, ii* and *iii* represent high, intermediate, and low ratios of L_t/L_s, respectively. Notice that in each case the slopes obtained with the high ratios of L_t/L_s (in which target luminance is high compared to surround luminance) approach 1.0 most closely.

B. Brightness matches made to test patches at different luminances. For each curve (*i, ii, iii*), the luminance of the surround was varied with that of the target to keep a constant ratio of L_t/L_s. (After Jameson & Hurvich, 1961).

C. Hsia (1943) had subjects match the apparent whiteness of standard and variable discs that were presented in separately illuminated booths. Although the rear walls against which the disks uniform in color; in Figure 12.7C the half that has the white surround looks darker. Koffka (1935) proposed that this is so because a part of the field that is perceived as a unified figure will be made to look as homogeneous as possible, and that a figure that has 2 clear subdivisions, like a figure 8, would show contrast effects even without the dividing contour. This prediction was later substantiated by Berman and Leibowitz (1965).

Under a wide range of conditions, however, we can expect simultaneous contrast to occur. How might we measure such effects?

Consider the classic experiment on brightness contrast carried out by Hess and Pretori (1894; as described by Hering, 1907). Right and left test fields, t_r and t_l (Figure 12.8) were set to one luminance, and the two surrounds were set to another luminance. Then the luminance of t_r was changed, so that it no longer looked equal in brightness to the left test patch. The subject's task was to restore the luminance of the right test field to its original appearance (that is, to make t_r again look like t_l). The adjustment was done, however, not by changing the patch's luminance, but by changing the luminance of its surround. To make both test fields again look equal, the luminance of the right surround was adjusted until its contrast effects exactly compensated for the change, ΔL_t, that had been made in the luminance of the right test field.

For certain conditions, these contrast effects follow an extremely simple quantitative relationship: As long as the luminance ratio of the test patch and its surround is kept constant, the test patch maintains the same apparent brightness. Under these conditions, although the apparent brightness of the test patch is not proportional to L_t alone (because it is also being affected by its surround), it *is* proportional to the ratio L_t/L_s. That is, for each increment in L_t (the test luminance), an increase in the surround that maintains the ratio L_t/L_s at some constant level will keep the apparent brightness of the test patch unchanged (curve R, Figure 12.9A). This simple function would explain the occurrence of lightness constancy in most of the conditions that we have discussed in the previous section, a point that we shall elaborate in a moment. However, this simple relationship holds only in a certain range of initial values of L_t and L_s. With higher initial values of L_t and lower values of L_s, a greater change in the surround is needed to counteract a given luminance change ΔL_t in the test patch; that is, the contrast effect of L_s is less when the background is darker and the test field is brighter. If the luminance of the test patch is made much lower and the luminance of the surround is made much higher, a smaller increase in the luminance of the surround will suffice to counteract a given increase ΔL_t in the luminance of the test patch; again the ratio of L_t/L_s that is needed to keep the test patch at the same apparent brightness is not a constant.

Other variables affect contrast per se, such as the separation between the fields (Leibowitz, Mote, & Thurlow, 1953; Fry & Alpern, 1953), their sizes (Diamond, 1955; Kinney, 1962), configurations (Benary, 1924; Mikesell & Bentley, 1930) and many additional factors that influence the response that the visual system makes to a given stimulus (see Chapter 9). Because experiments on brightness contrast have not usually been carried out

---

appeared were black in both booths, the reflectance of the side walls could be changed. Note that curve *i*, which represents the highest level of L_t/L_s that Hsia used, has a slope closer to 1.0 than does curve *iii*, which represents his lowest level of L_t/L_s. (Adapted from Graham & Brown, 1965.)

D. Data from experiments by Leibowitz and his colleagues, using a setup similar to that of Hsia (Figure 12.9C). The solid lines are from Leibowitz, Myers, and Chinetti (1955); the abscissa (*X*) represents the illuminance of the booth containing the standard. The dotted lines are from an experiment by Leibowitz and Chinetti (1957), in which a very short exposure was used (.0002 sec); the abscissa here (*X'*) represents the relative illuminance. Compare with the observation in Figure 12.4 (p. 400) about the effects of viewing time.

under identical conditions, their findings are not always comparable. Those data that are most relevant to the problems of object-color perception, however, and to the issue of lightness constancy, seem to be reasonably well established. *First,* a more luminous region will lower the brightness matches that a subject will make to a less luminous region that is placed nearby, but the less luminous region will induce little or no enhancement of the brightness of the more luminous region (Diamond, 1953; Heinemann, 1955, 1961; Horeman, 1965). *Second,* the amount by which the more luminous region darkens the less luminous region is not simply governed by some effect exerted by the former on the latter; it is a nonlinear function of *both* luminances (Hess & Pretori, 1894). Very similar results to those of Hess and Pretori were obtained by Jameson and Hurvich (1961) using a very different procedure. Jameson and Hurvich used a field containing 5 neighboring test patches at once, for only 3 of which are the results represented in Figure 12.9B. The graph shows what happens to the apparent brightness of a test patch as we increase its luminance L_t and also increase the luminance of the surround, proportionally, at the same time, so as to keep the ratio L_t/L_s constant. For *i,* the ratio of L_t/L_s is high; for *ii,* it is intermediate; for *iii,* it is low. If the apparent brightness of the test patch simply increased with each increase in its luminance, successive judgments would fall on the line marked *s,* where the slope is 1.0. This does not happen. In a middle range, *ii,* the apparent brightness of the test patch does remain constant even though its luminance is increasing. At higher ranges, however, its apparent brightness will increase (*i*) and, at lower ranges, (*iii*), the apparent brightness of the test patch actually decreases as its luminance is increased!

This apparently paradoxical phenomenon, which has been obtained with different procedures by Jameson and Hurvich (1961) and by Stevens and Stevens (1960), may be easier to envision in terms of the following example.

In a totally dark room, everything looks featureless and gray, according to Hering (see below). If we increase the illumination slightly, we can then barely make out a white object as being somewhat lighter, and a dark object as being somewhat darker than the surrounding gloom. As we increase the illumination more, we also increase the separation of dark and light, until the dark object is clearly black and the light object is clearly white. The dark object has become darker because the contrast induced by its surroundings darkened it more than it was brightened by the additional light that it reflected. The apparent brightness of a patch of light is thus highly dependent on the context in which it appears, so much so that the effects of context can make it look darker with each increase in the light that reaches the retina!

How are we to account for these contrast phenomena? Once again, the major opposing explanations were offered most forcefully by Hering and Helmholtz.

According to Hering (1874, 1876), and to several of his predecessors (Brewster, 1833; Müller, 1834–1840; Plateau, 1834), contrast is a retinal phenomenon. The activity of one retinal area induces an opposed activity in the form of a complementary chemical reaction in the adjacent area. When no light at all reaches the eye, only gray is seen. Light in one part of the retinal image makes that part appear bright, and makes the adjacent regions appear dark as part of the same process; as the stimulation increases, the bright region both becomes brighter and induces the adjacent regions to appear darker. This would provide a purely peripheral mechanism to explain contrast, a mechanism that would presumably be innate. There is now a great deal of evidence that just such a process—or a very similar one involving lateral inhibitory connections between adjacent parts of the sensory system—does in fact work at the boundaries between 2 differently stimulated retinal regions (see Chapter 9). Horeman (1965) has recently shown that the effects of an inducing field on a less luminous target occur at retinal or immediately postretinal levels of the nervous system. Diamond (1960) and Jameson and Hurvich (1961, 1964) have recently offered quantitative theories that attempt to predict the interactions between fields of different luminance. The latter theory is particularly simple, and provides a good fit not only to a fair amount of data concerning brightness contrast, but to color contrast phenomena as well.

Against such peripheral explanations as those mentioned above, Helmholtz' theory is sometimes said to attribute the contrast effect to an error of judgment, but this account of his theory is scarcely adequate. His general principle is that clearly perceived differences (whether in hearing, vision, and so on) are enhanced or exaggerated. In the perception of colors, Helmholtz argued that the subject accepts the average color of the field of view temporarily as the *norm* and identifies it as "white" (or as the color of the illumination rather than of objects' surfaces), and makes the appropriate adjustments in arriving at his perceptions of other colors. In yellow illumination, for example, a pale yellow surface appears white or neutral and a neutral gray stimulus "therefore" appears to be tinged with blue, the complementary color. Quite similar to Helmholtz' emphasis on the average color of the field are the conceptions of Gelb (1932), Koffka (1932, 1935), Judd (1941), and Helson (1943, 1964), who think that the viewer takes the general level of the field as a neutral point and that particular bits of the field have apparent color according to their divergence from this level. These writers, however, avoid Helmholtz' intellectualistic phraseology and his references to "illusions of judgment." Helson's *adaptation level theory* comprises a recent attempt to make this approach at once general, objective, and quantitative.

It is not clear at this time that all of the phenomena that contribute to contrast effects are to be subsumed under one set of mechanisms, whether central or peripheral in nature. However, one conclusion seems clear: Sub-

jects do not respond in the same way to a stimulus of a given luminance when the luminances of neighboring regions of stimulation are changed. The phenomena of lightness constancy that were discussed in the previous section referred to judgments of the reflectances of objects made under different conditions of illumination, conditions of illumination that are apparent to the subject. The phenomena of simultaneous brightness contrast that we have outlined here refer to textureless patches of light under conditions of illumination that are not evident to the observer. Even under these latter "impoverished" conditions, as we have just seen, the apparent brightness of a patch of light is not determined by the stimulus that it projects to the retina; it is complexly determined by the luminance of the region itself, by the luminances of the adjacent regions, and by the sizes of and distances between regions of different luminance.

Sensory theories of color constancy; adaptation, hue contrast, and hue constancy: the effects of field diversity   In the previous section, we considered the Helmholtzian theory that object-color perception depends on a process something like solving the equation $R = L/E$. Let us call this a *cognitive theory* of object-color perception, for it depends on the subject's knowledge (in some sense of the term) about the conditions under which he is receiving the local stimulation. In order for such an hypothesis to be meaningful, we would have to be able to show (directly or indirectly) that the subject can detect cues to illuminance E with sufficient precision to account for his judgments of R. The evidence we have considered to this point certainly is not encouraging. There is also a very strong secondary implication that such illumination cues must be learned and that therefore lightness constancy must also be learned; we have seen that there is little support for this implication. Finally, there is also the assumption that the subject can, at least in principle, respond to or "register" (whether consciously or unconsciously) the light that falls on each region of his retinal image, regardless of the luminances in neighboring regions. The phenomena of brightness contrast certainly do not support this assumption. At one point, it seemed as though the contrast phenomena could themselves be explained cognitively, as a sort of degenerate case of lightness constancy (see p. 412), but because we now know that at least some of the induction effects are sensory in nature (Horeman, 1965), they are at best an encumbrance to a cognitive theory. Although we cannot completely reject the cognitive type of explanation, we must seriously consider *sensory explanations of color constancy,* explanations that attempt to treat lightness constancy and brightness contrast as manifestations of the same sensory mechanisms.

As we have seen, Hering had argued that brightness contrast arises as a function of the way in which the retina responds to light and that this sensory phenomenon would explain at least some of the facts of lightness constancy. The way in which contrast would account for lightness constancy is most readily illustrated by examining Wallach's (1948) proposal to explain perception of the color of objects by a very simple formula: 2 objects will appear equally light when the ratios of their luminances to those of their surrounds are equal. Consider 2 test objects of luminance L_{t1} and L_{t2} seen against surrounds of luminance L_{s1} and L_{s2}, respectively. Wallach states that the objects will appear equally light under conditions in which the ratios of their luminances to those of their surrounds are equal, that is, $L_{t1}/L_{s1} = L_{t2}/L_{s2}$. In the special case in which the objects that are being matched are presented against the same background, Wallach's formula would, of course, assure perfect lightness constancy, because, regardless of the changes in illumination, the *ratios* of luminance presented to the eye by 2 objects of different reflectance would remain unchanged. In this case $L_{t1} = R_{t1}E$, $L_{t2} = R_{t2}E$ and $L_{t1}/L_{t2} = R_{t1}/R_{t2}$. In fact, for any object of reflectance R_t against

any background whose reflectance is R_s, the light reflected to the eye from the object and the background will be in the ratio $L_t/L_s = R_t/R_s$, regardless of the illumination. Furthermore, no matter how the illumination is changed, the stimulus ratio L_t/L_s will also remain constant as long as the relevant reflectances remain constant. If the subject's visual system were to respond directly to that ratio, as a sensory phenomenon, we need not invent higher cognitive processes that would require him to solve the equation $R = L/E$.

In fact, the conditions described above suggest a way in which the problems of color constancy and color contrast become problems no longer. If we simply assert that the stimulus for perceived lightness is not the luminance L_t of the test object but is rather the ratio of that value to the luminance of the adjacent region, L_t/L_s, all inquiries concerning the cues to illumination described above (p. 404), and concerning unconscious inference, memory colors, and the distinction between sensation and perception, may become unnecessary.

The horizontal line R in Figure 12.9A describes this relationship. The apparent color of the test patch remains unchanged even though its luminance L_t is increased. In fact, as we have seen, research on brightness contrast has shown that just this kind of result occurs under some conditions (Hess & Pretori, 1894; Wallach, 1948; Heinemann, 1955; see Freeman, 1967, for a comprehensive review of this point). Where this relationship occurs, lightness constancy should in fact result from the operation of brightness contrast, regardless of whether or not illumination cues are present.

Test patches do *not* always look equally light when the ratios of their luminances to the luminances of their surrounds are equal. In curve *i* in Figure 12.9B, we see that the brightness of the test patch does not remain constant but increases with increasing luminance, and in curve *iii*, the brightness decreases with increasing luminance, even though in both cases the ratio L_t/L_s is constant for each curve. Wallach's proposal holds for only a restricted range of L_t/L_s ratios, for the data of simultaneous contrast. Therefore, if simultaneous contrast is important in lightness constancy, we should expect corresponding departures from constancy in experiments on object-color perception. When ratios of L_t/L_s are high, matches made to the test patch should come closer to luminance matches, and the Brunswik ratio should come closer to 0.0. That is, if the background is dark compared to the object, lightness constancy should be poorer.

There are several experiments that have given this general form of result. In Hsia's (1943) experiment (Figure 12.9C), subjects looked alternately at gray disks set in separately illuminated chambers. The disks were seen against a distant black background, which separated them visually from the illuminated walls and floors of the chambers. Hsia varied the illumination of one chamber, and the subject tried to adjust the luminance of the disk in the second chamber until both disks seemed equally light. If the results are separated into matches made when the ratio of L_t/L_s was high (as when the object's luminance is greater than that of the booth's walls) from those in which L_t/L_s was low, the responses fall closer to a straight luminance match (curve *i*). If a darker standard and more reflective surroundings are used, the matches are somewhat closer to constancy (curve *iii*). More clear-cut evidence that under these conditions constancy decreases when the relative reflectance of the surroundings is decreased was obtained by Leibowitz, Myers, and Chinetti (1955) and Leibowitz and Chinetti (1957). In these experiments, which were similar to Hsia's except that backgrounds differing in reflectance (white, gray, and black) were placed so that they immediately surrounded gray test objects and a much wider range of illuminations was used, the more reflective (white) backgrounds produced matches close to constancy (Figure 12.9D), whereas the less reflective gray and black backgrounds produced less constancy.

Thus, the object's appearance changed more with changes in its illumination when the background was dark than when it was light. (Note particularly the dotted curves, *i*, *ii*, and *iii*, which were obtained by Leibowitz and Chinetti in response to very brief exposures.) Other studies, such as those of Kozaki (1963, 1965) and Warren and Poulton (1966), have also found that constancy is better with light than with dark backgrounds. (These latter researchers found that, under their conditions, it made a difference whether or not the test object or the background was more reflective, but the *degree* by which the two differed had no significant effect.)

So at least some of the expected departures from perfect constancy do occur, in at least a qualitative way. However, this does not mean that we can in fact use the data and models of brightness contrast to predict the data on lightness constancy with any degree of precision. This is so for 2 reasons. First, there are some discrepancies between the data of brightness contrast and those produced by experiments with lightness constancy. For example, although brightness contrast experiments fail, in general (see p. 411), to show any enhancement of a more luminous target by a less luminous surround, some constancy experiments have shown clear enhancement of the object's lightness (Kozaki, 1963; Leibowitz, Myers, & Chinetti, 1955). Second, the procedures of the lightness constancy experiments usually differ in several important ways from those used in the brightness contrast research.

Contrast and constancy experiments usually differ in these ways: (1) Whereas test patches and surrounds are small and homogeneously luminous in contrast experiments, in constancy experiments the objects and their backgrounds are usually large and microtextured, and the background scenes are often quite inhomogeneous. (2) The subjects' task is more complex in the constancy experiments than it is in the contrast experiments. In the latter, the subject need only respond to *any* difference in appearance between comparison and standard test patches, while in the former he must, in addition, decide whether the 2 objects have the same reflectance, regardless of whether they look alike in other respects (in other words, there may be *multiple criteria* on which the subject must base his choice). (3) In the constancy experiments, the comparison and test fields are often considerably separated in space, and appear in surroundings that are of different overall luminance. Therefore, the other mechanisms that help adjust the eye to lighting differences (such as pupillary dilation and retinal adaptation) should contribute their effects to the final judgment.

Some of the discrepancies between brightness contrast and lightness constancy data might plausibly be accounted for in terms of all of the procedural differences mentioned above. In order to evaluate such contrast explanations of lightness constancy, therefore, we should consider not whether their success in precise quantitative prediction is better than that of the cognitive theories (which do not really make such predictions, anyway), but whether we can explain away those examples of constancy that seem to be inexplicable on purely sensory grounds, even as gross qualitative phenomena. Before we attempt to do so, we should consider another factor, adaptation, and the theory of *adaptation level*. This theory, although it is not a contrast theory like those considered above, is not a cognitive theory, either, for it attempts to predict perception of the color of an object from measurable aspects of the visual stimulation.

Adaptation to the intensity of the light entering the eye is a familiar and clear example of the eye's adjustment to the illumination (increasing the eye's sensitivity by a factor of over 10,000 after about half an hour in darkness). In Hering's original explanation of lightness constancy, it will be remembered, adaptation was 1 of the 3 main sensory mechanisms that would enable the visual system to make the same response to a scene even though the illumination changes. Also,

the eye adapts to hue, of course: When you first enter a room lit by colored illumination (or put on tinted sunglasses), objects that were white now have the hue of the illuminant; after a while, however, the tint becomes unnoticeable, and the objects appear as they do in normal illumination.

To Hering, adaptation was a physiological mechanism. Helmholtz, in contrast, had proposed that the color of a region is judged by the way in which that region's luminance deviates from the average luminance of the field, which the subject assumes to be the overall illumination. Let us see what the facts are.

Helson (1938) had subjects sit in a light-tight booth, flooded with nearly homogeneous light, all of one wavelength. The walls and the table were covered with paper of a uniform color. The illumination might be either red, green, blue or yellow; the paper lining the booth might be white, gray, or black, with reflectances of 80, 23, or 3 percent, respectively. Consider a session in which the booth was lined with gray paper and flooded with red light. When the subject first entered, everything looked quite red; or at least red-illuminated. After 5 minutes of adaptation to the illumination, the subject judged a set of 19 gray samples, all non-selective reflectors; under normal illumination, the grays were presented in equal-appearing steps running from white to black. The subject's task was to rate the samples in terms of hue, lightness, and saturation, using notation of the Munsell scale (p. 359), with which he had previously practiced in daylight. Samples that had about the same reflectance as the gray walls and background were judged to be gray, of medium brightness. Brighter samples were judged to be red, and the more their reflectance, the greater their apparent saturation. Samples that were darker than the walls were seen as green or blue-green (the afterimage complement of the red illuminant), and the lower the reflectance, the more saturated the blue-green appeared. The lightness ratings of the grays were about the same throughout as in daylight. When, in another session, the walls were covered with white instead of gray paper, the eyes received stronger red stimulation; that is, a higher *adaptation level* was established, in Helson's terms. With this higher level, only the 2 lightest grays appeared red, the next 2 appeared neutral, and the rest appeared blue-green or blue. When the walls were all black, all except the darkest samples appeared red. Experiments with similar results were performed by Helson and Jeffers (1940) and by Judd (1940).

How can we explain these findings? In each case, an adaptation level was established by the prevailing reflectance. Grays near that level appeared neutral, brighter grays appeared to be of the same hue as the illuminant, and darker grays took on the afterimage complement of that hue. When white paper was used to line the walls, the reflectance of the walls was high, the adaptation level was high, and therefore only a few samples appeared red; conversely, when reflectance of the walls was low and, hence, the adaptation level was low, most samples were above the adaptation level, and appeared red. It is tempting to explain the phenomenon cognitively, saying that the subject takes the illumination into account, and "subtracts" the assumed illumination from the level of luminance of any object, thereby inferring its reflectance. However, we should also note what happens in the *Ganzfeld* (see p. 426), in which no objects or cues to illumination exist: When the eye is exposed to an overall homogeneous visual field of some hue, say red, the color soon fades to something approaching a mid-gray, and appears to stay that way unless some change occurs (Hochberg, Triebel, & Seaman, 1951; Cohen 1958). If the light increases in brightness, it will again appear red; if a shadow is imposed, it appears blue-green (Hochberg, Triebel, & Seaman, 1951). The visual system has adapted to the incident light, which has now become homogeneously neutral in appearance, but in this case the explanation cannot be that the subject has separated out what he considers

to be the illumination from what he considers to be surface color: In the *Ganzfeld* no surface color appears, only a space-filling fog (see p. 426). So we can accept Helmholtz' general line of analysis here only if we discard the intellectual connotations suggested by his terms: The conditions of stimulation, rather than any knowledge about surfaces and sources, bring about adaptation.

"Adaptation level" sounds like a physiological concept, something that might correspond to the momentary concentration of photoreceptive substances in the retina (p. 286). Helson (1948, 1964) has since worked out a formula for computing what the adaptation level is. His formula is to be applied not only to the effects of the walls and the stimuli used in the 1938 experiment, but for all manner of judgment situations, ranging from color constancy and contrast to lifted weights (and even to social attitudes). Thus his concept should be viewed more as a matter of judgment scales (Chapter 3) than as a matter of identifiable physiological processes. If we restrict our attention here to color perception, the explanation based on adaptation level does not differ in its gross outlines from the contrast theories of constancy that we have just been considering. There are some differences in prediction; for example, although both contrast and constancy are reduced when targets are more luminous than their surrounds, as we have seen on page 414, Helson (1943) predicts and finds good lightness constancy even when the background is less reflective than the object, as long as the standard and comparison objects are "anchored" by having backgrounds of the same reflectance. Regardless of such differences, the similarity of the theory of adaptation level to one based on contrast, as an explanation of constancy, is much greater than its differences, and we will not try here to separate adaptation level effects from contrast effects. It is not crucial to the present question whether the adaptation mechanism is a matter of central scaling, of changes in retinal sensitivities, or both. It is clear, of course, that adaptation has produced *incorrect* color judgments in the conditions we have discussed thus far. Of greater significance, however, is the fact that a shift of the adaptation level could account for the fact that we tend to see the hues of surfaces correctly even when the wavelength of the illuminant changes.

Hue contrast, or simultaneous color contrast, is very similar in principle to lightness contrast: A region of the visual field of one color induces the complement of that color in an adjacent region (see Chapter 10), without need for an appreciable adaptation period. Thus, a gray patch on a yellow background will look bluish, on a red background it will look greenish, and a yellow patch on a green background will have an orange appearance. To Hering, of course, such contrast was a sensory phenomenon, susceptible to psychophysical analysis and explanation without invoking any cognitive factors. In fact, the quantitative Jameson-Hurvich model, based on Hering's opponent-process theory, has been extended to include hue contrast as well as brightness contrast (1964). Also, like brightness contrast, hue contrast will help explain the constancy of the perception of the color of an object under changing illumination. Let us see how color adaptation and color contrast would work to bring about the perception of true surface color.

When the illumination is confined to a single narrow band of the spectrum, we have very little ability to perceive the true surface color. However, even a small admixture of white light greatly improves the perception of surface colors (Helson & Jeffers, 1940). Consider a green object in a gray surround, both of them receiving yellow light (Wallach & Galloway, 1946). The object reflects yellow-green light to the eye, but the gray surround also reflects some yellow light. The yellow in the surroundings tends to raise the adaptation level for yellow, and to push the yellow-green away from yellow and towards the complementary, blue. That is, the yellow illuminant falling on the object tends to dis-

color the greenish object toward yellow; the yellow illuminant falling on the background tends to induce the complementary of the yellow illuminant, blue, in the object. If the induced blue were equal to the discoloring effect of the yellow illuminant, the resulting apparent hue of the object would remain unchanged even though the hue of the illuminant had changed from white to yellow. More striking are the well-known demonstrations by Land (1954, 1964): If a slide of various colored objects, photographed through a red filter, is projected (through a red filter) in precise superposition with another slide of the same objects that was photographed through a green filter and projected in white (unfiltered) light, subjects see other colors (greens and yellows for example) on the screen, as well as reds. This is a very impressive form of color constancy, considering that only one "color" (the red record) and one "colorless" slide (the white-light projection) is used. We might interpret such findings as evidence for the efficacy of memory color (see pp. 398, 424), except that reversing the 2 records reverses the apparent colors of the objects as well.

In one sense, of course, all of these "colored shadows" are demonstrations of false color perception because the patches of light and shade on the screen, viewed separately, would be seen as varying shades of red, pink or gray. In another sense, however, the constancy is so remarkable that we can argue that the essential stimuli required for perceiving the color of objects have been retained, despite the apparent paucity of the information being given the subject.

In order to account for these phenomena, Land has been developing a theory in which specific wavelengths are not important in determining a region's hue. At present, however, it seems possible to accommodate Land's findings within the more classical theories about how simultaneous contrast occurs in the visual system, and such explanations have indeed been offered (Hurvich & Jameson, 1960; Judd, 1960; Walls, 1960).

However, the surprising efficacy of Land's demonstrations emphasizes the importance of the interactions that occur between regions that receive different stimulation, and the possibility that most of the phenomena of color constancy can follow directly from the nature of such interactions.

The sensory explanations of the perception of objects' colors, then, seem able to account for most of the facts of lightness and hue constancy, at least in principle. In actual research on the constancies, the stimulation consists of complex fields, to which the subject's response is not an immediate match, but involves memory, labeling, and so on (p. 423). Thus, the potential precision of the sensory theories of brightness contrast cannot be directly tested by the much less precise data of the experiments on lightness constancy. The difference between the qualitative cognitive theories and the more quantitative sensory theories is not a trivial one, however, because very different tasks confront the psychologist, depending on which theory he adopts. If some general cognitive principles are involved in the process of turning meaningless sensations into meaningful perceptions of the color of objects, what we learn about color perception will tell us something about cognitive processes in general. This makes problems of color perception the clear concern of the psychologist. On the other hand, if most or all of the perceptual phenomena occur because of the way in which the relatively peripheral sensory nervous system responds to patterns of stimulation to begin with, the phenomena of color contrast and of color constancy may reduce almost to data of sensory physiology, specific to the visual system. This would leave the psychologist with a clearer field of inquiry, which no longer includes the classic problems of color constancy and contrast, but it would also leave the psychologist with one less window into the nature of general cognition.

Sensory explanations of the perception of objects' colors, regardless of the precise nature of the luminance-brightness relationship they postulate, challenge the cognitive explanations in one major respect. The former assume that the stimulation that falls on the observer's eye is what determines the colors he perceives, after we take his state of adaptation, and so on, into account. The latter do not. This would seem to permit a qualitative confrontation between Hering and Helmholtz to be undertaken, centering on whether or not the distribution of stimulus energies controls the perception of color. Let us next consider what information we have on this point.

Is Perceived Object-Color Stimulus-Determined?

The processes that are responsible for perceived color may be "judgmental" in the Helmholtzian sense, or "physiological" in Hering's sense. In either case they have to start with what is given to the eye. Anything more than the most general sort of "explanation" will have to be able to predict quantitatively what will be seen in response to particular patterns of stimulation.

We can believe, with Helmholtz, that we perceive surface colors as we do because of what we have learned from our experiences with the world, yet still believe that those experiences are themselves lawfully related to measurable aspects of stimulation. After all, the relationships within the physical world are subject to rigorous physical laws (for example, that $R = L/E$), and we would expect most people to learn similar things from their experiences with the physical world (for example, that $R = L/E$, and the various cues about E). However, a theory that explains color constancy as being the result of some process of taking illumination into account has this implication: If we can change the subject's assumption about E without changing the array of luminances in his retinal image, his judgment of R should also change. The cognitive position therefore would not be at all embarrassed by finding that the stimulus does not completely determine the object's apparent color (although, because of the great deal of perceptual learning that has occurred by even a very early age, a Helmholtzian would not be surprised if in fact few such cases of stimulus indeterminacy could be found). To any sensory theory of lightness constancy, on the contrary, to which knowledge of the illumination is irrelevant, a finding that different judgments of lightness are made by subjects, even when the stimulus array remains unchanged, would at first glance seem to pose a very serious challenge. Let us therefore consider what evidence we have on this point.

There have been 2 lines of research concerned with the attempt to change the subject's assumptions about the scene he faces while keeping the stimulus array unchanged. One of these studied the effects of apparent illumination on apparent lightness (some of these have been described above; see p. 404). The other has studied the effect of *memory color*. We consider each of these lines of research in turn.

The effects of space, form and apparent illumination on perceived color We have already reviewed a number of experiments that seemed to show that the subject takes illumination cues into account in order to arrive at his judgments of reflectance. On closer examination, those experiments fail to support a cognitive theory unequivocally. The cues are themselves components in the distributions of luminance in the stimulus array, and even a sensory theory would expect such components to affect the apparent lightness of the test object, *regardless of the fact that they may also be called "illumination cues."* Consider the Gelb experiment (p. 404). In that case, a black disk appeared to be white when it alone was illuminated in an otherwise dark room. As soon as a small piece of white paper was placed in front of the disk so that the paper also received the spotlight's illumination, the black disk appeared dark or black. At first glance, this appears to be due to the fact that the white paper revealed the true state of illumination, which the subject could then discount.

Against this cognitive explanation, however, are the following considerations.

First, each time the white piece of paper was removed, the disk lost its black appearance and again appeared white: sheer knowledge that the black disk is illuminated by a spotlight, and that it is really black, is not enough to make it look black unless the white paper is actually present. This alone discredits the casual version of the cognitive theory that still pervades college textbooks on psychology: Although it may in some sense be true that "what we know affects what we see," none of the terms in this phrase can mean what they do in common usage.

Second, we have not really left the stimulus unchanged when the piece of white paper was introduced because the white paper would itself be expected to darken the disk by contrast. The white paper is small relative to the black disk, however, and we know that induced brightness contrast decreases when the size of the inducing field is decreased (see Chapter 10). For this reason, it has been argued (Osgood, 1953, p. 283) that although such a small bit of white can act as a cue to the illumination, it must be too small to induce any contrast in the disk. On the contrary Stewart (1959) has shown that the disk's appearance does not simply change from white (with no "cue" present) to black (with the white "cue" present), as we would expect it to in terms of the cognitive theory's explanation of the Gelb effect. In a setup that was essentially similar to Gelb's (see Figure 12.5), Stewart placed small white disks of varying size (0.5, 1.0, 2.0 in.) at different distances from the center of the black disk (which was 12 inches in diameter). The black disk looked darker when the white object was made larger and brought closer to the center of the black disk. Moreover, the darkening effects produced by the white object were not uniform over the entire surface of the black disk but were reported to be greatest in the immediate neighborhood of the white object.

Thus, the Gelb effect can be altered by the same stimulus factors that affect brightness contrast, and it seems evident that contrast contributes to the effect. There are probably other factors at work in the Gelb experiment as well. In Stewart's experiment, there may be some size of the white disk (less than 0.5 in.) below which further size decrements do not reduce the Gelb effect. However, this still would not mean that the apparent lightness is determined by cognitive rather than by sensory factors; even a very small patch of white introduced into Gelb's setup has changed the stimulus display that confronts the eye. For example, the *range* of stimulation in the room has been changed with the introduction of the white paper, and Koffka (1932, 1935) and Judd (1941), proposed (in otherwise quite different theories) that what luminance the subject will see as white, and what he will see as black, is determined by that range.

In short, then, the Gelb experiment may mean the opposite of what it first seems to: It may show that knowledge of illumination is *in*effective in changing apparent reflectance.

However, there is another method for manipulating the apparent illumination, this time in such a way as to keep the stimulus array effectively unchanged. We can use an ambiguous spatial arrangement—that is, one in which the object can readily be seen in either of 2 very different positions relative to the source of the illumination. For example, imagine a cube, one of whose faces, 1, receives full illumination while the other face, 2, is in partial shadow. Both sides have the same reflectance, say $R = 50$ percent. Let side 1 receive illumination $E = 100$ ft-c, while side 2 receives 60 ft-c. Then side 1 has a luminance of $L_1 = RE_1 = 50$ percent $\times 100 = 50$ ft-L, and side 2 has a luminance of $L_2 = RE_2 = 50$ percent $\times 60 = 30$ ft-L. If the subject should solve the formula $R = L/E$, with adequate cues to the relative illumination that each face receives, he would correctly take the 2 sides to have equal reflectances. Suppose however that his depth perception is in error, and that he takes side 1 to lie in the same

plane as side 2. The sides would then appear to receive the same illumination, and if he solved the equation for R with that appearance as his starting point, he would then erroneously decide that the 2 sides had unequal reflectances: $R_1 = L_1/E_1 = 50/100 = 50$ percent, $R_2 = L_2/E_2 = 30/100 = 30$ percent.

There are a few demonstrations and experiments with just such results (Mach, 1914; Katona, 1935). Evans (1948) used apparatus similar to that of Hess and Pretori (Figure 12.8, p. 408) to present 2 sets of background and test fields. The depth cues were sufficiently ambiguous so that the subject could see the 2 background fields as being adjacent parts of a single plane surface, with test and comparison fields t_r and t_l located behind that plane; alternatively, the subject could interpret the view as that of the 2 sides of a cube, with 1 face receiving more illumination than the other, and with t_r and t_l as squares of paper pasted on the cube's faces. The subject was instructed to adopt each interpretation. The 2 different instructions produced very different results when the subject was instructed to match test fields t_r and t_l. Instructions were *not* directly about the illumination, it should be noted, but about which of two *spatial* arrangements the subject should consider.

Similarly, Hochberg and Beck (1954) devised an arrangement to mislead the subject about the target's orientation to the light. Viewed monocularly, the target, which was a trapezoid standing upright on a table, looked like a rectangle lying flat on the table. Good "illumination cues" were offered by large white cubes placed on the black table near the gray target X. The subject was asked to match the apparent color of X by referring to a set of gray papers in the background. The apparent slant of X with respect to the direction of illumination was changed by introducing various depth cues (by switching to binocular vision; by waving a black or a white stick behind the target; or by moving the target from side to side with a wire). Several different depth cues were used because each cue is a change in stimulus conditions, regardless of the fact that it offers information about depth (for example, the total field of view may appear brighter with binocular than with monocular viewing—Katz, 1935). When it appears upright, X should also appear to receive less light than when it appears to lie flat (because its surface would then be receiving only parallel or glancing illumination), so that, in solving for R, the target, when apparently upright, should appear lighter than when it appeared to be flat on the table. Subjects did indeed judge the target to look slightly lighter in that condition. Again, Beck (1965), with a different arrangement, found that the 2 sides of a folded figure, one side of which receives more light than another, look appropriately unequal in lightness when the subject is restricted to monocular viewing and the 2 sides look coplanar, but they look equally light when binocular cues as to their spatial arrangement are provided. We should note, however, that such results have not always been obtained (Epstein, 1961), so that the conditions that produce them are not now clear.

We might interpret these findings as demonstrations that, at least in some cases, "exactly the same stimulation" will produce different apparent surface lightnesses and, therefore, as evidence that surface color is not always stimulus determined. They do show that, but do they therefore clearly support the Helmholtzian view that the perceived illumination is taken into account in arriving at perceived color, and do they clearly oppose those theories that consider color constancy to be an automatic and stimulus-determined consequence of the luminance relationships within the retinal image? No, they do not. In order to see why not, we shall have to consider (1) the limitations on what is meant by an "identical stimulus display" (which, because of possible differences in eye movements, does not mean that the subject has actually received the same set of retinal images under two different instructional conditions); (2) the effects of the object's

surface texture; and (3) the possible implications of the fact that the observer usually must match the standard and variable stimuli when they are widely separated in space.

The possible role of eye movements and of differential attention in constancy experiments In the experiments we have just described, the stimulus displays that confront the observer are indeed identical, or essentially identical, in the different experimental conditions. We do not know, however, that the subject makes the same eye movements when he views what he considers to be different spatial arrangements. Hering had noted long ago (1907) that when the eye makes successive fixations in a field of diverse luminances, the apparent lightness of a given patch will depend on the previous stimulation to which that retinal region has been exposed. Flock, Wilson, and Poizner (1966) have asked a subject to match a standard in one part of the visual field by looking at a set of comparison grays in another region. If he is instructed to do so by following a visual path that takes his eye through a set of grays having a low luminance level, he picks a darker comparison figure as matching the standard than he does when his eye traverses an intervening region of high luminance patches. With the setup used by Hochberg and Beck (p. 420), we might expect the subject to compare the target X and the vertical faces of the cubes when X looks upright, for he will assume that those surfaces are receiving the same illumination as the target; when X looks flat on the table, however, the subject may compare it to the upper faces of the cubes. If he moves his eyes back and forth between those surfaces that he is comparing, the effects of successive adaptation would be different when the subject makes different assumptions about the target's orientation. (Even if eye movements do not occur in accordance with this speculation, the subject might still pay attention to different features of the neighboring cubes to anchor his judgments about X before shifting his gaze to the set of comparison grays to make his lightness match.)

The effects of texture and other inhomogeneities on object color   In the Gelb experiment, a rotating black velvet disk, illuminated by a spotlight, appeared to be white until a piece of white paper was placed next to it, and then it looked black. *However, merely stopping the rotation also made the disk look black.* Why is there this difference between a rotating and stationary disk?

A paper, cloth, or wood surface usually has a fine but definite grain or "microstructure." In the case of the velvet disk, small particles of dust and fibres of the velvet reflect more light than the rest of the disk, and provide a visible microstructure. The rotation of a color wheel blurs or washes out the grain of the paper; when the rotation stops, the microstructure becomes visible. Even though the overall luminance of the disk remained the same in Gelb's experiment, whether or not the disk was spinning, the visibility of the microstructure changed the judgments the subjects made of the disk's lightness. Other observers have noted that there is a relationship between a surface's visible texture and its apparent lightness (Katz, 1935; Judd, 1952).

Why should microtexture improve constancy? In terms of a cognitive theory, it has been argued that the presence of microstructure permits the subject to separate surface color from illumination (Katz, 1935, pp. 90f, 275f; Woodworth & Schlosberg, 1954, p. 435). The few quantitative experiments that have been performed relevant to this question, however, do not support this cognitive interpretation. Beck (1964) performed a series of studies on perceived lightness in which the target was either a smooth matte black paper, or a glossy black tile, whose average or overall luminances were equated. The apparent lightness of the glossy surface remained more constant with changes in illumination than did that of the matte surface. The matte surface is uniform, whereas some parts of a glossy surface reflect more light to the eye

than do others. It follows, therefore, that when both surfaces were equated for overall luminance, parts of the glossy surface must have been darker than the matte surface. The glossy tile was in fact judged to appear darker, even though the overall luminances of both surfaces were equal. In another experiment, when the reflections on the glossy tile were restricted to one part of the tile, and the rest of the tile was kept uniformly equal in luminance to the matte paper, the 2 surfaces were judged to be equally light, even though the glossy surface now had a higher overall luminance. When judging inhomogeneous surfaces, therefore, it seems that subjects do not respond to the average luminance as reflected over the whole surface but make their matches on the basis of some particular selected regions of the surface. In this case, they apparently attempted to avoid the reflections.

The highlights and shadows on a textured surface will therefore affect the surface's apparent lightness in at least 2 ways. First, of course, any small highlight darkens parts of the surface adjacent to it, by contrast. That is, the presence of microstructure results in internal contrast, quite apart from the contrast that is produced by the surround. In fact, the apparent lightnesses of surfaces containing distributed highlights remain more independent of changes in the luminance of the surrounding field than do those of the reflective matte target (Beck, 1964, pp. 56, 60). Second, because subjects seem to base their judgments of lightness on local regions rather than on some average taken across the entire surface, their choice of which regions are selected for this purpose will affect their judgment of lightness. Although there is no experimental evidence to this point, it seems probable that this selection depends on which regions they take to be representative of the "normal" reflectance of the surface and on which regions they take to be "accidental" reflections, highlights and shadows. This, in turn, may be determined by what they assume to be the nature of the surface and its uniformity of color; that is, it may be determined by its perceived *surface quality* (see p. 426) and by what they assume to be the arrangement of the illumination (see Beck, 1965). However, this is very different from the theory that the subject uses the microstructure to take illumination into account in solving the equation $R = L/E$. In fact, because judgments about illumination are probably based on the points of maximum luminance, or the highlights (Beck, 1961, 1962; see p. 406) and because textured surfaces can be manipulated so that the highlights can be varied in luminance independently of the rest of the surface, judgments of illumination and of reflectance can probably be made to be quite independent of each other.

There are thus usually several different criteria on which subjects can base their judgments. They can say, for example, that the standard and variable appear to be equal when the standard's highlights match those of the variable, or they can decide that both are equal when the contrast between the targets and their surroundings seems to be the same. Indeed, the color matches that subjects make can be caused to vary by changing the instructions that they are given (MacLeod, 1932; Henneman, 1935; Katz, 1935; Landauer & Roger, 1964). The fact is that in the constancy experiments, as they have been traditionally performed, we have no explicit knowledge about the criteria by which the subject reaches his decisions about whether or not 2 objects are the same color. Until some techniques are found with which to separate the various criteria available to the subject in the constancy experiments in general, the extent to which apparent lightness is stimulus determined, and in fact, the precise amount of color constancy that has to be explained, remains difficult to evaluate.[3]

Naming and Remembering Colors in the Constancy Experiment

Time errors   In the typical constancy experiment, the subject has to decide whether or not 2 objects that receive different illuminations have the same reflectance. To do this, he usually compares objects that are widely separated in space. This means that he must compare his impression of the object at which he is looking with his memory of what the other object looked like. This introduces a new source of error (the *time error,* see Chapter 2), and it may also provide an opportunity for the subject's attitude and knowledge to influence his psychophysical judgment. Having made some decision about an object's surface color, the subject may remember the decision itself, when he turns to consider the comparison stimulus, rather than the complex visual appearance of the object's surface. Brown and Lenneberg (1954) found that the recognizability of a color, which the subject saw in isolation and then had to identify after a long delay (about 3 minutes) by pointing it out from among a chart of many other colors, was correlated with the *codability* of the color (that is, with how well people agree in naming it). Differences in instruction, or in interpretation of what he is looking at, may perhaps affect the subject's psychophysical judgment by affecting the way in which he categorizes or commits to memory one or both of the stimuli he is comparing, even with considerably shorter delays.

The possibility that the subject may label and remember differently objects that would have looked equally light if he could have

---

[3]Additional demonstrations that factors other than the luminance distributions in the visual field can affect lightness judgments have recently received attention. Thus, Gogel and Mershon (1969) found that the stimulus conditions (specifically, binocular disparity—see Chapter 13, p. 481) which make a test patch and its surround appear to be at different distances from the subject also reduce the

contrast effects that are obtained, even though the two regions remain laterally adjacent and unchanged in their luminances. Again, Coren (1969) showed that a stronger contrast effect is obtained in a test region when it is seen as *figure* (see p. 432) than when it is seen as ground, confirming earlier demonstrations to that point (Benary, 1924; Mikesell & Bentley, 1930; Wertheimer, described in Koffka, 1935, p. 136). The extent to which such demonstrations embarass any theory which holds that the perception of color is stimulus determined, and the degree to which they can be accommodated by the kinds of explanations discussed in pages 421–423, remain to be seen.

compared them simultaneously thus offers still another explanation of why the same stimulus display can elicit different psychophysical judgments under different instructions. It also brings us to a second line of research that *seems* to show that factors that are not contained in the stimulus display can influence the appearance of objects' colors, namely, the work on *memory color*.

Effects of memory and memory color In addition to the sensory mechanisms that contribute to color constancy, Hering (see p. 398) proposed a nonsensory factor. He held that what we call the real color of any object is the color that we have most often seen on that object, a color that is indelibly impressed on our memory image of it.

Such *memory colors* could only be of limited use in maintaining color constancy, even in the case of familiar objects, because our memory colors are, in general, significantly different from the natural colors of the objects we are remembering. When subjects are asked to match the remembered colors of objects from an array of color chips, they tend to pick chips of greater saturation and lightness (Newhall, Burnham, & Clark, 1957; Bartleson, 1960). However, that still leaves open the question of the extent to which memory colors can influence our perceptions of objects at which we are currently looking.

Duncker (1939) showed subjects two pieces of the same green material, one cut into the shape of a leaf and the other into the shape of a donkey. Both cutouts were viewed under red illumination; although the light was not monochromatic, subjects reported that the green material appeared gray when it was presented to them in the form of a *circular* cutout. A variable color wheel, viewed under normal illumination, was used to match the appearance of either the leaf or the donkey. We would expect that the leaf would appear greener than the donkey, if memory color contributes to the apparent color of the cutouts in this situation, and that is what happened. The color wheel was taken

as matching the donkey when it had a 29° green sector, and as matching the leaf when it had a 60° green sector. Do these results show an absence of stimulus determination of apparent color?

There are 2 reasons why these results don't necessarily rule out stimulus determination. First, because the standard stimulus (donkey or leaf) and the variable stimulus (color wheel) could not be viewed simultaneously; and second, because the stimuli were not in fact identical, but were of different shape, and the shape should have effects on the amount of contrast that would be induced in the figure (by the red illumination on the surrounding field), regardless of the shape's meaning.

Bruner, Postman, and Rodrigues (1951) performed a variation of Duncker's experiment, with a wider variety of shapes and with several conditions of viewing. When the standard cutouts and the variable color wheel were separated from each other (by 80° of visual angle), so that the subject could not see both simultaneously, those standards that should have displayed a memory color did so. When the standard and variable were adjacent to each other, no effects attributable to memory color were obtained. We cannot take these results, therefore, or Duncker's either, to mean that memory colors affect the *perception* of object color, for the effects only appeared when the variable color wheel was matched to the subject's *memory* of the cutout. The results may merely show that a familiar object's characteristic color affects the way we remember it (Hochberg, 1956), not the way we see it. Bolles, Hulicka, and Hanly (1959) pointed out an additional problem with such experiments, in that the standards and variable were such that an exact match could not be made. In an experiment similar to Duncker's, which also precluded an exact match, Duncker's results were confirmed. However, when a black and a white sector were added to the variable color wheel, so that a good match could be achieved, the difference between the donkey and the leaf

disappeared. These results support the contention that memory color does not change
the actual appearance of a stimulus: when he
is unable to make an exact psychophysical
match, the subject will resolve the impossible
task by making the most reasonable mis-
match, namely one that is close to the object's
characteristic color.

Harper (1953) introduced a procedure that
appeared to be free from both of these flaws.
He placed the test figures in front of a differential color mixer, and varied the degree of
the redness of the figures. The subject's task
was to report when the figure became "indistinguishable" from the background. The test
figures were all cut out from the same orange
paper, three being shapes of red-associated
objects (apple, heart, lobster), and three being
neutral shapes (oval, triangle, letter Y). The
stimuli were introduced with comments
about their color (such as "a reddish apple,"
or "a yellowish-orange oval") that would identify to the subject the appropriate memory
color. Harper found that 71° of red were required to match the nonmeaningful figures,
and 134° were needed for the meaningful
ones. If the stimuli really became indistinguishable from their backgrounds, and if the
effects of memory color on the distinguisha-
bilities of the forms can be unequivocally
demonstrated by this kind of procedure, it
would be a striking fact indeed, for the processes of contour formation that separate
figure from ground are usually thought to
depend at least in part on peripheral mechanisms that respond to objective stimulus
differences in the retinal image.

Fisher, Hull, and Holtz (1956), using Harper's procedure, found that subjects made no
difference in their responses to a cross that
was labeled as a "red cross" symbol, and the
same figure when it was rotated 45° and
called a "letter X." Moreover, in a recent
replication and improvement of Harper's experiment by Delk and Fillenbaum (1965),
differential instructions as to what the cutouts
represented had no effects. It did make a
significant difference in the subjects' matches,

however, whether the cutouts were red-
associated figures (heart, apple, lips), neutral
shapes (oval, circle, and ellipse), or shapes
associated with some other color (horse, bell,
mushroom). Although all shapes were cut out
of the same red-orange paper, and all were
of approximately the same area, significantly
more red had to be mixed in with the background color in order for subjects to decide
that the red-associated figures and the background were of the same color. The cutouts
differed among themselves in their shapes, of
course, so we might argue that it was the
differences in contour per se, not past associations, that influenced the color judgments,
but their data make this argument implausi-
ble. We still have to ask, however, whether
subjects really *saw* a difference in the colors
of the cutouts, or whether they were acting
in accordance with some sort of *response bias*
(see Chapter 2, p. 36). No provision was
made to show that the subjects *really could
not distinguish* the figures at those settings
at which they declared that the cutouts
matched their backgrounds. Perhaps a *signal-
detection* procedure is in order, which would
attempt to separate subjects' *criteria* from
their *sensitivity* (see Chapter 2, p. 41).
However, this last point is one which, as we
have seen (see p. 423), really applies to much
of the research on color perception.

In summary: to the question of whether
color perception is stimulus-determined, we
can answer with a qualified "no." Apparent
spatial orientation, attention, memory—all of
these cause the subjects to make different
judgments in response to one and the same
stimulus display. However, it is still possible
to maintain a sensory theory which views
color constancy as a special case of induced
contrast and to explain away these nonsensory effects as *judgmental* phenomena superimposed on the sensory ones.

Does this reject the cognitive theory?
Again, a qualified "no"; it may only mean that
both Hering and Helmholtz were right, in that
the starting point on which judgmental processes are based is itself already corrected (to

some degree) for illumination changes, by the nature of the contrast-induction mechanism. This means that what the subject "really perceives" is not a simple matter that can be decided merely by asking him. We shall consider this point in more detail, and confront other conflicts between sensory and cognitive theories of perception, when we consider the problems of space and form perception.

For now, let us turn briefly to some of those aspects of apparent color besides hue, saturation and lightness, that we have so far barely mentioned.

OBJECT COLORS AND THE VARIETIES OF SURFACE QUALITY

So far, we have been asking questions only about objects' lightness and hue. These have mostly been questions that can be answered by manipulating the wavelength or intensity of homogeneous fields of light, and they have therefore been relatively easy to instrument. However, the colors we see in the world may vary in other ways. For example, the same yellow hue may be part of an object's surface, or an attribute of the light that illuminates it; the yellow may appear to be the color of the wine that fills a glass, or it may be the color of the glass that holds the fluid (Hering). These are perceptual qualities that cannot be studied, in general, with single patches of light, but which depend on the *pattern* of light at the eye.

Most of the attempts to list and describe the distinguishable types of color appearance rest at an introspective, phenomenal level. That is, these were, in general, studies in which an observer tried to describe what a particular area of color looked like without paying any attention to his knowledge (or to his guesses) about the stimulus, and without any bias as to what the patch *should* look like. An important distinction between modes of color naming, made by Katz (1911, 1935), who was trying to decide how colors appear to the naive observer, is the difference between *surface color* and *film color*. For example, a

uniform surface viewed through a hole or a reduction screen does not appear to be a surface at all, but rather a mere dimensionless expanse of color which fills the hole (see *aperture color*, p. 399). In an early examination of film color, Martin (1923) decided that this mode of appearance is neither bidimensional nor tridimensional but simply without dimensions in the geometrical sense. Her subjects called the stimulus a film color most frequently when the aperture was small (about 2 cm), and called the stimulus a surface most frequently with larger apertures (30 cm). Metzger (1930), who produced the first *Ganzfeld*, or homogeneous visual field, by placing the subject before a specially curved smooth plaster wall, found that some microstructure (see p. 422) was needed in order to perceive a definitely localized surface under those conditions. If the illumination of the *Ganzfeld* was reduced so that subjects could not focus clearly on the wall's texture, they reported that they saw a bulky, space-filling fog, instead of a definite surface (see Avant, 1965, for a review of *Ganzfeld* research). Outside of the *Ganzfeld*, however, texture is *not* essential in order for a colored area to look like a surface. For example, Fry (1931)

Figure 12.10. Two elementary dimensions of surface quality: glossy–matte, rough–smooth. A, matte, rough; B, glossy, rough; C, matte, smooth; D, glossy, smooth. (After a proposal by Evans, 1951.)

reported that if a rotating color wheel was perfectly uniform in luminance over its entire surface, it appeared to be hard and smooth, but that with even a small gradation of luminance over its surface, the disk tended to be perceived as a soft and bulky color, one that seemed to occupy a volume of space and that varied from fluffy to misty depending on the gradient of luminance.

Given a definite surface, clearly localized in space, there are still several distinctly different appearances it can have. Thus, surfaces can vary from *glossy* (or shiny) to *matte* (or dull); from *rough* to *smooth;* and from *opaque* to *transparent* (Judd, 1951; Evans, 1959). Some of the stimulus conditions that produce these different appearances are easy to identify. In Figure 12.10 (which is modeled after Evans, 1951), a rough matte, a rough glossy, a smooth matte, and a smooth glossy surface are portrayed at A, B, C, and D, respectively. A glossy surface is one which reflects light regularly in localized images (see Bixby, 1926; Hunter, 1937; Judd, 1951); a rough surface is one which has a marked distribution of local shadows cast by glancing light (that is, by illumination that is neither diffuse nor perpendicular to the surface).

A transparent surface is, of course, one that we can see through to some degree, and that means that we see two colors at the same place in space: the color of the surface, and the color that we see behind (or through) the surface. *Bulky color* or volume color implies some degree of transparency, and we have seen that Fry (1931) observed that a smooth gradient of luminance appears to be bulky if the surface is interpreted as being homogeneously illuminated. However, such gradients are certainly *not necessary* in order for a region to appear transparent; a perfectly uniform patch of color (A, C, in Figure 12.18) may or may not appear transparent, depending on the pattern in which it is embedded (Fuchs, 1923; Metelli, 1967).

In each of these surface qualities, the relationship between stimulation and appearance is an ambiguous one. Thus, in Figure 12.10D

the object might not be glossy at all, but might have a white streak painted on it; in Figure 12.18C, the gray rectangle at *i* might have black patches on it. In fact, of course, there really are no object surfaces—glossy, transparent, or otherwise—in Figure 12.10, there is only an inhomogeneous array of pigments on the surface of the page. Why do we see a single surface of uniform reflectance, but with the appropriate surface quality? The perception of the color and quality of an object's surface clearly involves the perception of space and form, and we return to this question about surface quality in the course of discussing these topics.

PROBLEMS IN THE PERCEPTION OF OBJECT SHAPE

Up to this point, we have had little to say about spatial relations in the visual field, or about distances, directions, sizes, and shapes. These characteristics of an object usually appear to be just as directly *seen* as are its color and brightness. It is not as easy to find the stimuli that are responsible for our observations of these properties, however, nor to discern the structures of the retina and of the visual nervous system whose actions are the bases of our experiences. For many years, it was hoped that it would be possible to explain these properties as elaborations or additions that occur after the simpler sensations of brightness and color arise from the direct action of light on the visual nervous system. It has therefore become customary to speak of "perception" of shape, rather than of shape "sensations."

The theory, in its very simplest form, was the Structuralist Theory that underlay the views shared by such physiologists and psychologists as Helmholtz, Wundt, and Titchener (see Boring, 1942; Hochberg, 1962; also pp. 396, 402, 527). According to this view we have a mosaic of independent visual receptors whose responses produce *sensations* (simple elementary experiences) of color. These receptors provide all that we have in the way of *specific nerve energies* (see p. 118) for vision; therefore all visual experience consists only of the sensations that they produce, plus whatever memories have become strongly associated with those sensations as the result of a great deal of experience with the physical world. Thus, the surface looks glossy and smooth in Figure 12.10 not because the visual system responds to "gloss" as such, but because that pattern of lightnesses brings to mind the appropriate tactual memories of what such surfaces feel like. Similarly, a circle looks like a circle because that pattern brings to mind the memories of what eye movements would be needed to follow its contour around (that is, to "trace" its outline with the center of vision, the fovea of the eye), together with the memories of curvature felt by the hand in touching a circular object, and so forth. In short, as far as this theory is concerned, we have discussed *purely visual* experience completely when we have analyzed the distribution of brightness and color within the visual field.

The structuralist approach has been vigorously challenged on several grounds. Historically, the primary challenge came from *Gestalt theory,* a viewpoint shared by such psychologists as Wertheimer, Koffka, and Köhler. They maintained that the basic design of the nervous system was such that it responded to shapes and forms directly, not to individual patches of light. Instead of individual receptors the individual responses of which produced the elementary color sensations, the Gestalt picture of the nervous system rested on broad electrical processes, initiated (but not completely determined) by the *configuration* of the light at the eye. These electrical processes, subject to their own internal laws of organization, were held to be the events in the nervous system to which our perceptions are *isomorphic,* or correspond in form. Much pioneer work on shape and form perception was undertaken by Gestalt psychologists, both to demonstrate various points that they were trying to make against the analytical approach of the structuralists,

and to discover the *laws of organization* of the underlying brain processes.

The stock questions that arose around the opposition of the Structuralist and Gestalt approaches (such as whether or not the elements of experience can be used to explain the properties of the whole, or whether shape perception is innate and not learned) have by no means been resolved, but they have been largely submerged and transformed by new programs and by the sheer pressure of continued research that has often obscured the original purposes of inquiry. A comprehensive review of Gestalt work on shape perception can be found in Koffka (1935) and Metzger (1953). A more eclectic survey was written by Hake in 1957.

BOUNDARIES OF SHAPE: CONTOURS, EDGES AND FIGURES

Contours

To start with, shapes are areas of the visual field that are set off from the rest of the field by a visible *contour.* Thus, if 2 regions of the field differ in luminance, a brightness-difference contour appears to separate the field into regions having different shapes. If the 2 regions appear equal in brightness, and differ only in their hue, the corresponding difference in wavelength does not in general result in clear shape perceptions (Leibman, 1927).[4] Moreover, if the luminance of one region shades off gradually into that of another, the shapes of both are indefinite, so the perception of shape would seem to require a sharp enough contour between regions that differ in luminance.

What produces contour? Mach pointed out in 1865 (see Ratliff, 1965) that a contour occurs with a relatively *abrupt change of gradient:* mathematically, it is a change of a change, that is to say, it is the second deriva-

[4] Bishop (1966) reported that contours can be detected between small regions differing only in hue; he does not say, however, whether the regions were separately matched in apparent brightness for each observer, so the issue is still open.

Figure 12.11. Experiment on the development of contour. See text. (Werner, 1935.)

tive of luminance, not the first (d^2L/ds^2, not dL/ds). It belongs in the same class of phenomena as marginal or simultaneous contrast. The neural basis for simultaneous contrast effects has been discussed under the topic of spatial inhibition in Chapter 9, page 292. Because of these effects, the outlines of objects appear sharper and more distinct than they are in the retinal image.

It looks, therefore, as though brightness-difference contours have a sort of unity, in the way in which they are handled by the nervous system, over and above the fact that a particular group of cells in the retinal mosaic is being stimulated. Perceptual research appears to support this view. For example, Fry and Bartley (1953) used threshold methods to study the effect of one contour on another. They determined the minimum luminance-difference necessary to make a contour become visible and found that a contour exerts an inhibitory influence on neighboring parallel contours and exerts a reinforcing influence upon another contour that it approaches at right angles.

Masking contours A phenomenon discovered by Werner (1935) may offer a powerful tool for the study of the processes by which contours are perceived and of their function in the perception of shape. Werner exposed two patterns (Figure 12.11 A, B) successively in the same part of the field. If the presentation of the pattern in A was followed, after a "vacant" (gray) interval of 150 msec by the pattern in B, the black square was not seen at all. The masking figure (A) and the

test figure (B) do not have to be seen by the same eye to obtain these results (Werner, 1940; Kolers & Rosner, 1960). When the sequence was reversed, both squares were seen.

Why was the black square not perceived in the first sequence? Werner proposed that when the pattern in B followed that in A, the latter was obliterated because its contour had insufficient time to establish itself before being wiped out by the opposed luminance-difference of the pattern in B. When the pattern in B was presented first, however, its double contour was too strong to be obliterated. The extent to which the "obliteration" really depends on interactions between contour processes remains to be determined, however, for there are other similar cases in which the explanation based on contour obliteration is not clearly applicable.

There is a wide range of conditions under which the visibility of a test stimulus T is decreased by the presence of a masking stimulus M. Recent reviews of visual masking have been written by Raab (1963) and by Kahneman (1968) (see also Chapter 9). Either or both of the stimuli may be homogeneous patches of light, or patterns with contours; they may be presented simultaneously, or one may follow the other so that some time elapses between the onset of one stimulus and the onset of the other; the retinal image of one may cover that of the other, or their images may fall on disparate retinal regions.

When both stimuli are presented simultaneously in time and do not overlap in space, the darkening of one by the other is, of course, the phenomenon we have already described as *contrast* (pp. 407–412). If the 2 stimuli do not coincide either spatially or temporally, and T precedes M, this backward masking is called *metacontrast;* if M precedes T, the resultant forward masking is called *paracontrast* (Stigler, 1910), although the term metacontrast is often also used for both forward and backward masking. In metacontrast, as in contrast, the brightness of T is reduced by a stimulus M that is presented to an adjacent area (Stigler, 1910; Alpern, 1952, 1953), but under many conditions, T is not only darkened—it disappears entirely (Alpern, 1952; Fehrer & Biederman, 1962; Fehrer & Raab, 1962; Fehrer & Smith, 1962; Kahneman, 1967, 1968). This is, of course, very much like the phenomenon described by Werner, in that one shape has been suppressed or obliterated by the successive presentation of another one.

Backward masking has also been found to "erase" briefly presented letters and digits, even when the masking stimulus is a pattern which does not contain contours that are adjacent and parallel to those of the test stimulus (such as a ring, Averbach and Coriell, 1961; or a pattern of irregular line elements, Sperling, 1963). Eriksen and his co-workers (Eriksen & Hoffman, 1963; Eriksen & Lappin, 1964; Eriksen & Steffy, 1964) have argued that at least some of these masking and erasure phenomena are due simply to the fact that the luminance of the white field of the masking stimulus is added to that of the test field, if both fields are presented at a short enough intervening interval. The extra "veil" of luminance added by the masking field would make the test pattern more difficult to see because it lowers the contrast ratio between the black and white regions of the stimulus.

Such luminance summation should reduce the test pattern's visibility regardless of whether the test pattern is submitted before or after the mask. Moreover, because the summation should decrease as the interval between the stimuli increases, the masking effect should be at its maximum when T and M are simultaneous, decreasing as the interval between T and M increases. Just such results were found by Eriksen and Collins (1964, 1965), Eriksen, Collins, and Greenspoon (1967), and by Schiller and Smith (1966). On the contrary, other investigators have found masking to be maximal not when the two stimuli were presented simultaneously, but rather after a period of around 50 msec had elapsed between the onset of one and the onset of the other (Averbach & Coriell, 1961;

Mayzner et al., 1964; Weisstein & Haber, 1965). This had also been found using figures like those of Werner (Werner, 1940; Kolers & Rosner, 1960; Kolers, 1962).

To some degree the discrepancies mentioned above may result from differences in experimental conditions. They may also be due to differences in *criterion*—a problem that we shall encounter repeatedly: How can we be sure whether or not the subject *saw* the test stimulus? The question of whether the subject saw the stimulus would seem to be a simple one to answer, but he has to report about a very brief presentation at which he cannot look a second time, and what he decides in retrospect is subject to influences that might bias his answers. Various objective measures may be substituted for the subject's report on what he sees. For example, two masking patterns may be used, and the subject given a forced choice as to whether the test pattern appeared with one or with the other. With this method, if complete masking occurs, the subject should be reduced to chance guesses (Heckenmueller & Dember, 1965). Alternatively, the subject may have to choose which of several letters have been used as the test stimulus (Eriksen and his colleagues; Mayzner et al., 1965; Weisstein & Haber, 1965). But not all measures agree with each other. For example, if subjects are required to respond as quickly as possible when the test stimulus is presented in a backward masking experiment, their reaction times are unaffected by the backward masking (Fehrer & Raab, 1963). This is so even when the subjects report that they do not see the targets at all, and when their guesses about the target's presence or absence are near chance (Fehrer & Biederman, 1962).[5]

[5] The fact that subjects report that they do not see the test stimulus does not mean that the sequence T-M looks just like the masking stimulus presented by itself. When 2 masking stimuli flank the test stimulus, for example, the latter are seen as being in motion away from the center, and it is to this that subjects may then respond. The relationship between the conditions under which metacontrast suppression occurs with some patterns, and those under which apparent motion is produced (Chapter 13), has been pointed out by Fehrer and her coworkers (Fehrer & Raab, 1962; Fehrer & Smith, 1962; Fehrer, 1965, 1966), and

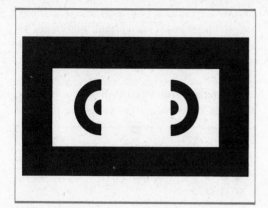

Figure 12.12. Subjective contour. Note the appearance of a vertical white stripe bounded by straight lines at the right and left where it is separated from the semicircular figures. (Schumann, 1904.)

Whether luminance-summation contributes to masking phenomena or not, there are also masking effects that seem to arise from the inhibitory effects of one contour on another. Thus Robinson (1966), using disk patterns as stimuli, showed that if stimulus *b* masked a previously presented test stimulus *a*, *b* could itself be masked by a third stimulus *c*, which in turn masked the masking stimulus *b* and restored visibility to *a*. This has since been replicated, using letters as test stimuli, by Dember and Purcell (1967). Contours also display characteristically inhibitory effects when the two eyes receive different patterns of stimulation (see Ch. 13, page 487).

Subjective contours We have seen that one powerful method for producing definite shapes is by producing a luminance difference

Kahneman (1968). Kahneman suggests that, under the conditions in which masking follows a U-shaped function (that is, in which masking is maximal with a 50 msec interval between the onsets of the two stimuli), the temporal and spatial arrangements would normally result in the perception of movement; with the particular patterns that are used in the masking experiments, however, the resulting movement would be physically impossible (for example, square A expands and becomes outline B, in Figure 12.11). Because the events thus briefly perceived make no sense, they are "lost or suppressed" (see p. 444). Other processes, such as lateral inhibition, also operate in the masking experiments, and contribute the monotonic function that has been obtained in the other experiments to which we have referred.

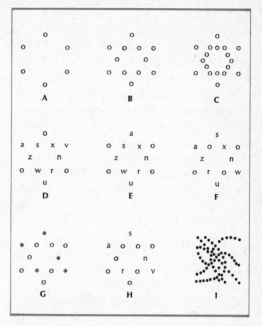

Figure 12.13. Dot figures illustrating the factors of nearness, sameness, continuation, and good figure. The hexagon so clearly visible in A is somewhat obscured in B by the additional dots, but reappears in C as a leftover group when the addition of still more dots in close proximity to each other brings out the interior hexagon. In D, E, and F the sameness of certain items favors grouping them, and the leftovers readily fall into a complementary group, when they make a regular figure, or when, as in G, they are similar; whereas in H, where the leftover items are dissimilar and irregularly arranged, they do not get together readily. I shows the factor of homogeneous continuation, in that the dots are readily seen as lying along straight lines or fairly definite curves.

between two regions. However, there are other ways of producing contours, and hence shapes, that do not involve luminance differences in the same way.

One classic example of "subjective contour" is shown in Figure 12.12, in which the contour is "filled in" or completed across an objectively homogeneous portion of the field. Another is given by the dot-figures in Figure 12.13. Here, you may simply see a set of dots scattered on the page, or the dots may appear to be so grouped as to set off one region of the field from another, depending on factors that we will discuss below (p. 433).

Perhaps most striking are the contours that can be produced by means of binocular vision using 2 displays, neither of which, when viewed separately, shows anything but a random texture. The method for producing such displays, which was devised by Bela Julesz in 1960 for studying stereoscopic depth perception, is described in Chapter 13, p. 483. It has been used to study equal-brightness contours and the shapes that they produce (White, 1962; Lawson & Gulick, 1967; Hochberg, 1968), and to test whether a particular feature of form perception depends on retinal processes or on those of some higher level (Hochberg, 1968; see p. 471, footnote 15).

These contours, and the others shown in Figure 12.13, depend on luminance differences in the retinal image in the sense that each element or dot in the field has luminance-difference contours. Except in this indirect sense, however, we see that luminance-difference contours on the retina are not *necessary* for shape perception.

Figure and Ground

This distinction, first brought out clearly by Rubin (1915, 1921), is fundamental to the

understanding of shape and form perception. Let us first consider certain highlights of Rubin's observations, and then some of the issues that center around this distinction.

The figure-ground attributes   Some of the striking differences between figure and

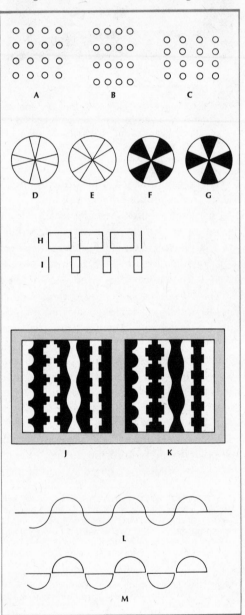

Figure 12.15. Demonstrations of Gestalt organization. See text.

Figure 12.14. Figure and ground. See text and Figure 12.24, page 441.

ground were classified by Rubin as follows. (1) The figure has shape, while the ground is relatively shapeless. For example, in Figure 12.14 you do not see the vase *qua* vase when the black regions are the figures. (2) The ground seems to extend behind the figure's edge. (3) Thus, the figure has some of the character of a *thing,* whereas the ground appears like unformed material. (4) The figure usually tends to appear in front, the ground behind. (5) The figure is more impressive, more apt to suggest meaning, and better remembered.

The first and last points are particularly important. To the limited extent that they are true, an area that is not a figure becomes, in effect, invisible, and even though it is "objectively" present in the world and in the retinal image, it does not provide a stimulus to which the subject can respond.

The determinants of figure-ground organization In Figures 12.13 and 12.15A–C various aggregates of dots appear to group together to form recognizable shapes. Wertheimer (1923), the founder of the Gestalt school of psychology, used such patterns of dots and simple line drawings (Figure 12.15D–G) to study the factors that determine how the dots are grouped into recognizable figures and that determine which of two areas will be the figure and which will be the ground. Some of these determinants are listed below.

1. *Proximity.* Dots near each other readily group to form contours (Figure 12.13C). In Figure 12.15A the small circles are equally spaced; at B, they are closer horizontally, and we see a pattern of rows; at C, they are closer vertically, and we see columns.

2. *Area.* As a closed region is made smaller, it tends more strongly to be seen as a figure (Figure 12.15D as compared to E), a factor that is obviously closely related to *proximity.*

3. *Orientation.* In at least some kinds of pattern, alignment with the main axes of space seems to be a determining factor. Thus,

Rubin (1921) found that a cross made up of vertical and horizontal limbs (Figure 12.15F) is more likely to be seen as figure than one with oblique limbs (Figure 12.15G).

4. *Closedness.* Regions that are marked off by closed contours tend to be seen as figure more than do those with open or incomplete contours; in Figure 12.15H, the vertical lines belong to horizontal rectangular shapes, whereas in Figure 12.15I, the same lines belong to the upright rectangles, even though in the former case they must overcome the law of *proximity* to do so.

5. *Symmetry.* The more symmetrical a region's shape, the more strongly it tends to be seen as figure; in Figure 12.15J, we tend to see white columns on a black background, but black columns on a white ground in Figure 12.15K (Bahnsen, 1928).

All of the factors listed above refer to features of the physical stimulus pattern, although they are not all equally easy to define objectively, or to submit to experimental test.

Area, proximity, orientation—these are readily varied and measured. Using 6-sector and 8-sector patterns like those in Figure 12.15D–G and varying the width (angle), orientation, contrast, and so on, of one set of sectors relative to the others, Graham (1929), Goldhamer (1934), Oyama and Torii (1955), Künnapas (1957), and Oyama (1960) have shown that objective, quantitative measures of figural dominance can be devised to reflect the subjective and qualitative observations on which these laws had originally been based.

In such ambiguous patterns (Figure 12.15), the figure-ground organization reverses spontaneously while the subject gazes at it, apparently with no effort on his part. A commonly used measure of figural dominance is the relative duration with which the subject reports each shape's appearance (say, by pressing a separate switch when he sees each alternative).

Assuming that suitable response measures are used, these first 5 factors seem to offer ready translation from the intuitive and qual-

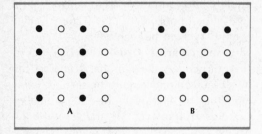

Figure 12.16. Grouping by lightness similarity.

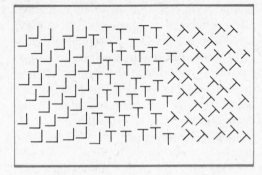

Figure 12.17. Grouping by shape similarity. (Beck, 1966.)

itative form in which they were originally presented, into more quantitative and objective measures. Certainly, a variable such as "proximity" seems like a straightforward physical measure, and we would think that the only problem is to obtain a valid measure of how it affects organization.[6]

The remaining factors—*similarity, good continuation,* and so on—also seem to be features of the physical stimulus display, but

they have not yet been expressed in satisfactory physical measures.

6. *Similarity.* Dots tend to form groups according to their lightnesses (Figure 12.16A, B), and we can set this factor against that of proximity to assess their relative strengths (Rush, 1937; Hochberg & Silverstein, 1956; Hochberg & Hardy, 1960). This is a very easy kind of similarity to state and to measure. However, similarity of *shape* also appears to affect grouping (Figure 12.13D–H), and how can we measure that?

The problem is not a simple one and has not yet been satisfactorily solved. The displays in Figure 12.17 are part of a series used by Beck (1966) to study the effect of the similarity of shape on perceptual grouping. Each display was made up of 3 sections, and the subject was asked to indicate at which of the 2 boundaries the most natural break occurs. Unfortunately, subjects' judgments of how marked the division between any 2 sets of elements looked to be had little relationship to how other subjects rated the similarity in appearance of those 2 sets of elements.

7. *"Common fate."* Dots that move simultaneously in the same direction form a single group. Perhaps the strongest factor of all, common fate may be closely related to (or derived from) *motion parallax,* an important factor in depth perception (p. 505).

8. *Good continuation.* The group of dots follows a uniform direction in Figure 12.13I. We see the particular figure-ground arrange-

---

[6] The task may not be quite that simple, however. Rock and Brosgole (1964) had subjects view an array of dots that was slanted in depth, so that in the retinal image the dots were closer together in one direction (because of perspective foreshortening; see p. 499), whereas both in the physical array and in the way in which subjects perceived the array (because of *shape constancy,* p. 515), they were actually closer together in the other direction. In this experiment, grouping occurred in accordance with *perceived* proximity, rather than with retinal proximity. This seems to imply that attempts to base our predictions about organization on the measured features of the visual field are foredoomed because *perceived* stimulus features, not physically measurable ones, govern perceptual organization. To the contrary, Attneave and Olson (1966), found that the impression of slant in patterns made up of an array of small elements depended on the way in which those elements were grouped into lines, and it was retinal proximity that determined how those elements formed into groups. Helson (1966) attributes the results of the experiment by Rock and Brosgole to an "anchoring effect" produced by the initial grouping, and Bell and Bevan (1968) have indeed shown that anchoring effects can modify the operation of several of the Gestalt organizing principles. For example, when a matrix of dots that is distinctly organized into rows (as in Figure 12.15B) is presented very frequently in the midst of a series of matrices which vary in their spacing, matrices that are normally ambiguous (that is, matrices that can be perceived either as rows or as columns) are perceived as columns. Instead of simply measuring the physical stimulus, therefore, we may have to determine the *effective* stimulus. The effective stimulus would be the difference between the actual level of the variable in the stimulus that is being presented to the subject, and the *adaptation level* (see p. 416) that is computed from the set of patterns to which the subject has been exposed previously. This issue is still therefore open, and we can (with this qualification) consider these first 5 determinants of organization to be susceptible to physical measurement.

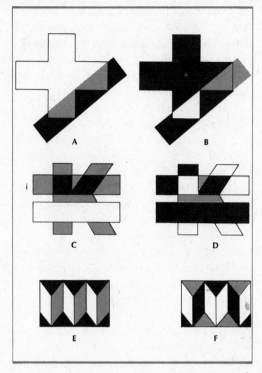

Figure 12.18. Figural organization is as uniform as possible. (A and C are adapted from Fuchs, 1923). In which member of each pair are two overlapping shapes most readily seen?

ment which makes the fewest changes or interruptions in straight or smoothly curving lines or contours. Figure 12.15L is almost always seen as a sine wave superimposed on a line, instead of a set of closed shapes, as shown at *M* (which is what we would expect to see in terms of the law of *closedness*).

9. *Homogeneity or simplicity.* In each example in Figure 12.18, we have alternative ways of seeing: an inhomogeneously colored surface, at some uniform distance and under uniform illumination, is one alternative; a homogeneously colored surface, its parts at varying distances and receiving (or reflecting) nonuniform illumination, is another alternative. In each case, the alternative that *is* seen is the arrangement of edges and distances that will conform to the most homogeneous set of object attributes that is consistent with the stimulus pattern.

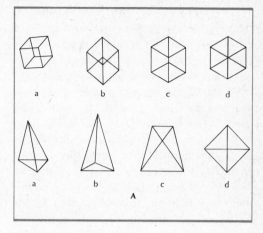

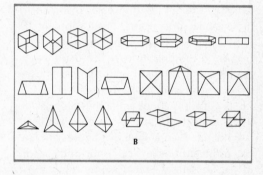

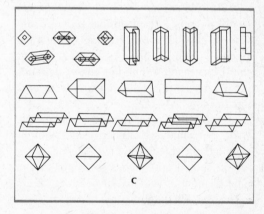

Figure 12.19. A. Plane projections of cube and tetrahedron. (Kopfermann, 1930.) B, C. See text. (Hochberg & Brooks, 1960.)

A related set of examples comes from the work with so-called "reversible-perspective pictures" by Kopfermann (1930). She used ambiguous drawings (Figure 12.19), each of which can readily be perceived in either of

3 very different ways (that is, as flat 2-dimensional arrangements or as either 1 of 2 tridimensional objects). She demonstrated that, in general, whether the subject sees the figure as tridimensional or flat depends on how "good" the figure is in 2 dimensions. If it is compact and symmetrical, with good continuation between lines that would have to be broken apart in order to see the figure as tridimensional (for example, Figure 12.19A, d), there is little urge toward the tridimensional appearance. As you examine the sequences that run from a to d in Figure 12.19A notice how tridimensionality decreases and simplicity (as a two-dimensional organization) increases. Within each row, the tridimensional organization is essentially the same (that is, a cube in the top row, a tetrahedron in the bottom row). The strength of the two-dimensional organization seems to increase as its simplicity increases.

Speculations about brain physiology aside, this epitomizes the promise offered by Gestalt psychology. Even ambiguous figures are lawful. Tridimensional space is not built up out of flat sensations (see Chapter 13, p. 503); instead, tridimensionality and flat shape are part of a single organizational process, and whether any line is perceived as being a flat edge or as being a corner between 2 surfaces (that is, as being a dihedral angle) depends on which version results in a simpler overall organization.

The difficulty, of course, is in deciding what is "simplest," "good," or "homogeneous." In the following few pages, we outline several approaches to this problem, none of them as yet very successful.

The first few determinants of organization (pp. 433–435) could each be stated in terms of obvious and measurable physical variables. In the case of "simplicity", however, we do not even know which of the many geometrical features, varying within a to d in Figure 12.19A, are relevant to the fact that d looks flatter than a.

One picture of some object (Figure 12.19A, d) looks more two-dimensional than another

(a) presumably because it is more "good" or "simple" as a two-dimensional pattern. By determining what measurable features of the patterns are higher for a than for d, we may discover the stimulus bases for the quality of figural "goodness" or "simplicity." Hochberg and Brooks (1960) therefore took the following 3 steps to obtain an objective definition of "goodness" or "simplicity." First, each member of the families of pictures in Figure 12.19B was rated by subjects as to its position on a scale running from "apparently flat" to "apparently tridimensional." Second, very many of the physical characteristics of each picture *as a two-dimensional pattern* were measured, and these measures were then analyzed to find the smallest number of physical features that would predict the subjects' ratings. Two-dimensional simplicity decreased as the number of angles, the number of line segments, and angular variability were increased.[7]

The third step was to test whether the measure of simplicity would be correlated with ratings of the apparent tridimensionality that subjects gave to a new set of reversible-perspective pictures (Figure 12.19C). Correlations were high, meaning that the measure did predict subjects' ratings. The selection of pictures was neither random, however, nor governed by explicit rules, and in consequence we cannot estimate how generalizable the measure is; that is, we cannot tell how well it would predict subjects' ratings of other sets of pictures.

The research described above was undertaken with the hope that the complexity of any figural organization (that is, the inverse of its "simplicity" or its "goodness") could be defined objectively in terms of the *amount*

[7] The measure of two-dimensional complexity arrived at with these figures was $C =$ (the total number of angles + the number of different angles/total number of angles + 2 × the number of separate continuous line segments). Populations of reversible-perspective figures can be generated and randomly sampled according to explicit rules (see Figure 12.28, p. 447), but results obtained with such samples can still only be generalized to those populations. This difficulty also applies to the other attempts that have been made to replace the Gestalt principles of organization with more objective formulations (pp. 445–448).

of information needed to specify that organization. In a rough way, this formulation will fit most of the Gestalt phenomena. Hochberg and MacAlister (1953) had proposed that it could be applied to the kinds of measures of organization that we have been describing, while Attneave (1954) had independently proposed that stimulus information (in the more formal sense of *information theory* measures) could be substituted for the intuitive Gestalt terms. We discuss Attneave's informational approach when we consider shape recognition (p. 445).

Summarizing the determinants of organization We have mentioned several factors that appear to determine figure-ground organization (there are others that we have not described). Musatti (1931) combined these principles into one comprehensive law of *homogeneity:* homogeneity as to place (proximity), as to quality (similarity), and so on. Similar generalizations have been offered by others. For example, Koffka, in talking about *symmetry,* says that the figure-ground organization will, other things being equal, be such as to produce shapes as simple as possible (1935, p. 195); that is, we perceive according to some kind of *minimum principle* (Werner & Wapner, 1952; Hochberg, 1957).

Along a somewhat different line, James (1890) has said that we see that which is definite and probable. This position was developed more explicitly by Brunswik (1934, 1952, 1956; see pp. 502f.), who proposed the following relationship to hold between stimulation and perception: The tendency to see a given arrangement of objects and surfaces in response to a particular pattern of stimulation is a function of the frequency with which the observer has received that pattern of stimulation from that physical arrangement. That is, perceptions reflect the probabilities with which situations occur in the environment.

Both of these kinds of formulation (minimum principle and an environmental-probability principle) have in common this

virtue: They each summarize a number of very different kinds of observation within a single rubric that not only has intuitive appeal but also seems to suggest underlying explanatory mechanisms. However, they share a drawback in that neither is really specific enough to be of much use in predicting just which shape we will recognize in a given instance. Otherwise, the two kinds of summary statement suggest very different kinds of underlying process.

The minimum principle suggests some underlying physiological process corresponding to the figural organization, a process that can readjust its internal relationships to balance local stresses. This is the *Gestalt* view, in which the effect of any local luminance-difference contour depends on what is happening in the rest of the central nervous system. In other words, the entire system is stimulated by the entire visual field, so that the response to the whole stimulus pattern is not simply the sum of the responses that occur when part of the stimulus is presented separately. In order to apply this approach, we have to be able to identify what comprises a "whole" process, and we have to discover some set of rules by which to predict, from objective measures of the stimulus pattern, what the simplest organization will be.

The environmental-probability principle suggests an explanation based on learning. It is hard to imagine that there are receptors in the visual nervous system that are sensitive to faces or vases, or that there are specific nerve energies for Maltese crosses (Figure 12.15D). Instead, we need merely assert that such perceived shapes are not determined by the sensory processes, taken by themselves, but are elaborated by the effects of our previous experiences with the environment. In short, we see those shapes that our personal history has made most familiar to us. In order to apply this approach, we would have to know what the various shapes are with which each observer has had experience and the relative frequency of those experiences (for example, face or vase in Figure 12.14). In addition, we would have to know the relationship between the frequency with which the subject was exposed to a shape, and the consequent strength of perceptual learning. That is, we would have to know the subject's acquired repertoire of shapes and his relative readiness to use each of them.

The reader will recognize that the 2 alternative formulas that attempt to summarize the determinants of organization are very much like the alternative sensory and cognitive explanations of color constancy and contrast (p. 412). With these alternative approaches to explaining the "laws of organization" in mind, let us mention 2 more factors that appear to operate in determining figure-ground organization, but which refer directly to the expectations and past experience of the observer. These factors are what we may call *nonstimulus determinants of organization,* because neither the subject's attitude nor his past experiences comprises part of the stimulus display in any meaningful sense of these words. Hence it is to the effects of such determinants that we should turn in attempting to evaluate "sensory" and "cognitive" explanations of figure-ground selection.

10. Conformity with the observer's set or Einstellung. *Einstellung* is a German word that means a directed readiness for (or expectation of) a particular perceptual event. Wertheimer distinguished 2 kinds of *Einstellung:* "Subjective" *Einstellung* allows the observer to set himself to see a certain grouping and to do so even though the laws of organization do not particularly favor that grouping, or even if they oppose it. "Objective" *Einstellung* means essentially *figural perseveration,* that is, the tendency to continue seeing a given figural organization even after the conditions no longer favor it. For example, if we were to start out with the matrix of clearly horizontal rows in Figure 12.15B, and decrease the vertical spacing by imperceptible steps, while at the same time increasing the horizontal spacing, objective *Einstellung* would carry us through the point of equal spacing (Figure 12.15A). That is, we would still

Figure 12.20. Rubin's nonsense shapes. Type of field presented with instructions calling sometimes for taking the enclosed portion as figure, and sometimes for taking the enclosing portion as figure. (Rubin, 1921.)

continue to see horizontal rows even though we otherwise would not have done so with that spacing.

More research has been done on a closely related form of figural persistence. Rubin (1915; see Woodworth, 1938, p. 631) showed a first series of 9 green nonsense figures on black backgrounds. A subject was given 4 exposures of each, with instructions to see the green area as figure, the black as ground (Figure 12.20). This was followed by a second series of 9 similar patterns, but now the instructions were to see the enclosing black areas as figure. After a 30- to 45-minute interval, the subjects were shown a set of 27 patterns consisting of the first 2 sets and 9 new patterns, presented in shuffled, mixed order. They were asked to remain passive as to which part (black or green) should be seen as figure, but to report which part was the figure and whether the field was recognized as one previously seen. Subjects tended to see the same figure on the second exposure as they had in the original series: 64 percent of the figures were reported in the same way as they would have been seen in accordance with the instructions on their previous presentations, 33.5 percent were seen with the reversed organization, and 2.5 percent were seen in both ways. Rubin considered these

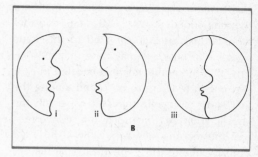

Figure 12.21. Ambiguous figures. A. It can be seen as either a young woman or an old one. (Boring, 1930.) B. Profiles (*i, ii*) and a composite (*iii*). (Schafer & Murphy, 1943.)

results to indicate a carrying over of the same figure-ground organization from one viewing of a pattern to another viewing.

Although the reliability of Rubin's results, and his interpretation of them, have since been questioned on several grounds (see Epstein, 1967), the existence of some such effect seems clear enough. Leeper (1935) showed that subjects who had previously

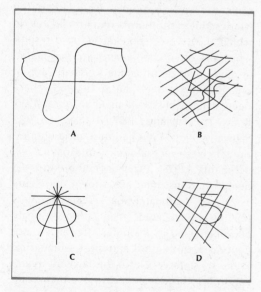

Figure 12.22. The numerals concealed at A and C are revealed at B and D. (Adapted from Köhler, 1929.)

seen an unambiguous version of Boring's ambiguous "wife"-"mother-in-law" pattern (Figure 12.21A), could at first only recognize the version they had previously seen. Again, Epstein and Rock (1960) and Epstein and De Shazo (1961) showed their subjects several unambiguous versions of the Shafer-Murphy faces (Figure 12.21B). The subjects then received brief (tachistoscopic) presentations of the ambiguous composites in each of which 2 of the unambiguous faces were combined. There was a strong tendency for subjects to recognize the particular shape they had most recently been shown.

11. Past experience (familiarity). A series-ofwordslikethisone, which can be separated and read even though neither the configuration nor the spacing would otherwise lead to the appropriate grouping, is one illustration of this factor. Wertheimer urges that this factor of familiarity must not be too readily invoked, and as we can see in the demonstrations in Figure 12.22, the various quite familiar numbers at A and C are there quite well concealed. The numbers are clearly visible at B and D. The fact that they are concealed at A, C cannot be ascribed to "confusion" that is caused by the added lines there because the same shapes are embedded among even more lines at B and D, yet are clearly visible. So much for the simplest form of the *familiarity theory* that we introduced on page 439. The whole patterns in which the shapes are concealed at A, C are certainly no more familiar than the hidden shapes themselves, yet we see the wholes, not the embedded shapes. We shall consider more formal research directed to this issue shortly. For now, we may note that the reasons that the numbers are concealed in A, C and not in B, D are to be found among the first 9 laws of organization (and especially the law of *good continuation*) and, conversely, that the reasons they are visible at B, D are similarly due to those organizational factors, rather than to their familiarity. To prove the reality of the experience factor in any specific case, we must first show that the stimulus factors (and the *Einstellung* variable) do not account for the obtained grouping.

Under some conditions, the association of reward or punishment with one of the two shapes that share a common contour (such as Figures 12.21B *i* and *ii*) affects which shape is identified when the subject is shown an ambiguous pattern (Figure 12.21B *iii*), at an exposure that is too brief for a figure–ground reversal to occur. In general, subjects report seeing the punished shape less often than the nonpunished or rewarded shape (Schafer & Murphy, 1943; Jackson, 1954; Ayllon & Sommer, 1956; Sommer, 1957). Perhaps a partial identification of the punished shape elicits a disruptive emotional response that interferes with the subject's memory of the brief exposure (Hochberg, Haber, & Ryan, 1955; Hochberg & Brooks, 1958; Solley & Murphy, 1960; see also the discussion of tachistoscopic recognition on p. 444). In addition, the subject may really pick up some cues by which he can identify both alternatives, better than by chance guessing, but he may have a response bias (see p. 443) in favor of the rewarded or nonpunished shape (Wallach, 1949; Smith & Hochberg, 1954). In any case, the effects of such differential experience have not always been obtained (Rock & Fleck, 1950; Solley & Long, 1958), and the conditions

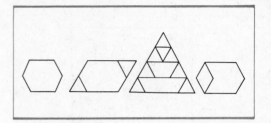

Figure 12.23. A figure hidden in more complex figures. The hidden figure (hexagon) is both familiar and "good." (Gottschaldt, 1926, 1929.)

of their occurrence are not clear. Research on this issue has recently been surveyed by Solley and Murphy (1960) and by Epstein (1967).

In the demonstrations shown in Figure 12.22, familiarity was pitted against good continuation, and the latter won. Gottschaldt (1926) attempted a more formal confrontation between practice or familiarity, on the one hand, and the configurational laws of organization (pp. 433f.), on the other. He showed that simple shapes, like the hexagon in Figure 12.23, with which subjects had received over 500 prior presentations, were not noticed when the subjects were later asked to describe the more complex figures in which they were embedded. These results, which are often cited as proving that figure-ground organization is due to innate laws of organization rather than to learning, have been extensively challenged (Moore, 1930; Braly, 1933; Djang, 1937; Hanawalt, 1942; Schwartz, 1961). Even had they gone unquestioned, however, neither Gottschaldt's experiments (1926, 1929), nor the kinds of demonstrations that are shown in Figure 12.22, can legitimately be enlisted to show that the laws of figural organization are innate and unaffected by learning. After all, we can conceal even the best and most symmetrical figure by suitable use of the laws of organization, yet this does not disprove the advantage of good and symmetrical figures in ordinary perception. Similarly, the fact that we can conceal even the most familiar figures does not disprove the importance of experience in ordinary perception.

Moreover, although the embedding patterns in Figures 12.22 and 12.23 are not familiar ones in the sense that we are likely to have seen each *overall* design before, the *parts* that do the embedding (the uninterrupted lines, the repeated angles, and so on) may be highly familiar units. In other words, some of the factors that we have treated under the heading of "stimulus organization" may in fact be the result of perceptual learning, and may express a more fundamental kind of "familiarity"—a familiarity with edges and corners—than is tapped by particular shapes or symbols.

Possible fundamental explanations for the figure-ground distinction: figural contours and objects' edges The demonstrations that we have surveyed to this point have suggested that there are laws of figure-ground organization, but have not explained the figure-ground phenomenon. According to Gestalt theory, the laws of organization reflect the self-adjusting nature of the underlying brain processes, but very few attempts have been made to be any more specific about those processes. The few attempts that have been made (pp. 459, 468) have little or nothing to say about figure-ground organization and its laws, nor even about why the ground's shape is less recognizable than that of the figure. If we try to explain the figure-ground distinction in terms of some kind of perceptual learning, the case looks more promising (although still highly sketchy). Consider the properties of figure and ground, on the one hand, and the physical properties of a real object, on the other. The figure has a definite shape, while the ground is formless, and seems to extend somewhat behind the figure's contour. The contour seems to belong only to 1 of the 2 areas that it separates, in the sense that the other area seems to extend behind it. Now consider an actual object (say, the silhouette of a vase as represented by the Rubin pattern, Figure 12.24A). If you move your eye across the object's edge (i), there is an abrupt increase in distance d to the next surface (if there is another surface beyond the edge). Accommodation and convergence (see Chapter 11) will remain appropriate to provide a clear image as long as your gaze moves from one point to another within the bounds set by the object's edge. That is, the object has a surface shape that is determinate and fixed to one side. Past that edge, only empty air or unfocused blur would, in general, meet the gaze. Also, we should remember that saccadic eye movements are scheduled in advance of their execution, so that moving your

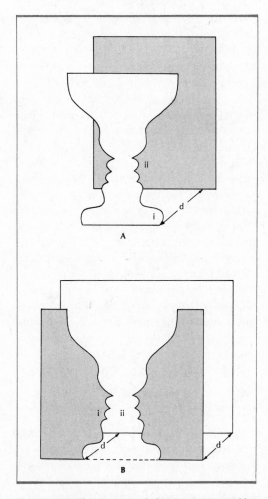

Figure 12.24. The two sets of objects represented by Fig. 12.14 (p. 432). See text. (Adapted from Hochberg, 1962.)

fovea from one point on a surface to another must be guided, in general, by some "expectation" based on peripheral vision of what the fovea will confront (see Chapter 11, p. 375). In addition, each change in the head's viewing position should cause the object's edge to change the part of the background that it hides from view. The extension of the latter is therefore in fact indeterminate, whereas the parts of the object's surface are not similarly subject to such temporary occlusions (see Hochberg, 1962, in press; Gibson et al., 1969; Kaplan, 1969; Chapter 13, p. 504). There is thus a very good fit between the perceptual properties of figure and ground, on the one hand, and object and background, on the other. It is easy to believe, then, that the figure-ground properties are learned; that they are "expectancies" about the consequences of eye and head movements; and that those expectancies arise in response to contours that normally are produced by object edges but that are in these examples (Figures 12.14, 12.15, 12.21–12.23) produced by print on paper. That is, the main features of the figure-ground phenomenon might be the result of carrying over the perceptual habits formed in looking at objects to the perception of lines on paper.

There are also clear differences, of course, between an object's edge and a figure's outline: The latter bounds 2 equally solid regions at an equal distance from the eye, and in line drawings it does so by a ribbon of pigment. These differences are so considerable that pictures have often been regarded as being more or less arbitrary sets of symbols, which we have learned to associate with objects (see Gibson, 1954; Gombrich, 1960; Hochberg, 1962; for diversely biased discussions of the nature of pictures). If pictures and lines are arbitrarily learned symbols, the determinants of figure-ground organization may merely reflect those arbitrary artistic conventions. However, it is doubtful that such is the case. For one thing, a child who had been raised with no opportunity to associate pictures with objects (or with their names), and who had in fact seen very few

pictures at all, under any circumstances, could nevertheless correctly identify the line drawings of familiar objects (Hochberg & Brooks, 1962). Furthermore, the protective coloration of animals that renders them invisible to other predatory animals seems to express the same principles of masking and organization that conceal familiar shapes from human eyes (Metzger, 1953), and surely the predators have not been exposed to our artistic conventions. To the extent that the determinants of organization are learned, it must be chiefly by way of commerce with objects in the real world.

In this vein, Brunswik and Kamiya (1953) attempted to show that contours that are close together in the visual field tend to belong to the same physical object. If they do, then the Law of Proximity (Figures 12.13, 12.15) might be the result of past experience in an ecology in which visual proximity is a useful *cue* (that is, an indication) of connectedness. Brunswik and Kamiya sampled pairs of adjacent contours from a set of still pictures, each contour pair being classified as to proximity on the one hand, and as to physical connectedness or disconnectedness on the other. There was a low but statistically significant correlation between the 2 variables, showing that there might be some basis for learning the Law of Proximity. This experiment may be criticized in that the sample of contours did not allow us to generalize about the environments to which subjects have habitually been exposed (Hochberg, 1966b), but it remains the only attempt at explaining one of the determinants of organization in a specific and testable manner.

THE PHYSICAL DETERMINANTS OF SHAPE

So far, we have talked about the factors that determine which of 2 shapes that are bounded by a common contour will be seen, but not about *what* shapes are seen. Unfortunately, the questions that arise in this connection are not only very difficult to answer; they are extremely difficult to ask. The last decade has seen much thought and work devoted to some of these problems, but the area remains less well developed than many others with which these chapters deal.

Psychophysics of Shapes

We can describe any stimulus configuration as precisely as we wish in terms of analytic geometry. It would seem, therefore, that we should be able to set up a psychophysics of shape, amassing a body of knowledge that would enable us to predict what shape we will see in response to any stimulus display that confronts the eye. However, this proposition becomes vastly more complicated at second glance, as soon as we start to formulate specific questions that we can ask about how the appearance of a shape is related to the physical stimulus pattern. In what ways can we profitably vary patterns to study apparent shape? In what ways can we measure the resulting changes in shape perception?

Speculating about what the underlying organizational tendencies of the visual system might be, Gestaltists thought that the circle would be the simplest of all physiological configurations and that, the more complex a stimulus pattern might be, the less readily the cortical processes (and the perceived shape) would conform to it (Koffka, 1935; Köhler, 1940). Weakening the strength of the stimulus at the retina might permit the "internal forces" to operate more freely. The stimulus could be weakened by various means: by viewing it with the periphery of the eye; by lowering the luminance or shortening the duration of the stimulus presentation; or, in extreme form, by removing the stimulus entirely and allowing the organizing forces to work on the memory trace of the stimulus. These considerations led to the subsequent research on shape-recognition thresholds in which "stimulus strength" was the independent variable.

Thresholds of Shape Recognition

Early observations (reviewed by Koffka, 1935) led to the generalization that decreasing the "effectiveness" of any given configuration results in simpler and more regular perceived shapes. Since then, however, the validity of this generalization has been restricted almost to the vanishing point. It was found, for example, that stimulus configurations viewed in the periphery of the visual field are not seen as better forms; instead, they are labile, uncertain, and vague (Zigler et al., 1930; Drury, 1933). In other experiments, Helson and Fehrer (1932) determined the lowest luminances at which various geometrical figures were seen as definite shapes, that is, their luminance thresholds. Their results were so inconsistent with different measures and for different subjects that no generalization about the relative ease of seeing their various figures was possible. Hochberg, Gleitman, and MacBride (1948) proposed that figural "goodness" varies inversely with the ratio of a figure's perimeter to its area, P/A, and that the absolute luminance thresholds should thus increase with increasing P/A if the patterns were presented to central vision for brief periods in an ascending order (see Chapter 2, p. 15). Under these conditions, the predicted differences were obtained with a few simple . shapes (Hochberg, Gleitman, & MacBride, 1948; Bitterman, Krauskopf, & Hochberg, 1954), but this proposed objective definition of "goodness" turned out to be inadequate when tested with a wide range of patterns (Krauskopf, Duryea, & Bitterman, 1954). Moreover, as Casperson (1950) pointed out, such threshold differences may reflect differences in subjects' readiness to label and report the different shapes rather than differences in what they perceive. This is the problem of *response bias,* which is particularly important in the method of impoverishment that has been most widely used in recent years, namely the method of *tachistoscopic* presentation.

In tachistoscopic experiments, a visual field is exposed for a period of time that is usually too brief to permit the subject to move his eyes or to permit him to respond while the stimulus is still being displayed; for example, the exposure might last 100 msec. After the exposure is terminated, the subject must say what he saw. By increasing the exposure duration until the stimulus is correctly named, a threshold can be obtained. There is now an immense body of literature on tachistoscopic recognition thresholds, obtained, for the most part, using words, numbers or letters as stimuli. Recent reviews are available by Pierce (1963) and Natsoulas (1965). Several characteristics of this method have become clear, in recent years, specific to the method but also revealing more general aspects of the perceptual process. Although the *span of apprehension* in a tachistoscopic experiment seldom goes higher than 6 to 9 items, Sperling (1960, 1963) and Averbach and Coriell (1961) showed that for some brief period after the stimulus was terminated, subjects could be directed to report any one of a much larger matrix of items (such as numbers or letters; see also Eriksen & Lappin, 1967; Keele & Chase, 1967). This demonstrates persistence of the visual information as an "afterimage" or what Neisser (1967) calls an *icon:* If the subject can be instructed to describe what he sees at any portion of the matrix, after the stimulus display is no longer physically present, the entire matrix of items must still be available to him in some form. But even with such persistence (which can be reduced by post-exposure masking; see p. 430), the duration of the effective visual stimulus is less than the time usually needed to scan it and to encode the briefly presented information into some more lasting form, say, to frame the verbal responses with which the subject will report what he saw. The order in which the subject encodes the material is not fixed. For example, Harris and Haber (1963) and Sperling (1963) have shown that subjects tended to encode first what they were asked to report about, and that by the time they came to encoding the features that had not been specifically requested, the immediate (unencoded) memory of the stimulus display was too degraded to be of much use. The primary characteristic of the tachistoscopic experiment thus appears to be that it forces the subject to encode some restricted portion of a stimulus display that fades before his

encoding is complete, and then to make his response on the basis of a memory that he cannot refresh, whose validity he cannot check, and whose detail he cannot extend because the stimulus is no longer present.

Tachistoscopic thresholds should therefore depend on the encoding responses that the subject is ready to make and on the order in which he is prepared to make them. In support of the first point, there is ample evidence that tachistoscopic recognition thresholds are lower for those shapes or words with which the subject is more familiar (Henle, 1942; Solomon & Howes, 1951; Solomon & Postman, 1952); in support of the second point, there is the fact that subjects who are habituated to reading from left to right have lower tachistoscopic thresholds for material displayed in the left part of the field (Anderson & Crosland, 1933; Mishkin & Forgays, 1952; Forgays, 1953; Orbach, 1953; Heron, 1957; Terrace, 1959; Bryden & Rainey, 1963; Harcum & Filion, 1963). Such differences are probably due more to differential readiness to encode the briefly glimpsed pattern than to any differences in sensitivity. Thus, the right-hand differences probably occur because the subject encodes the fading icon in his habitual reading order (Heron, 1957; Sampson & Spong, 1961; Freeburne & Goldman, 1969). Perhaps familiar patterns have lower tachistoscopic thresholds than unfamiliar ones primarily when tasks are used that require the subject to remember and name the stimulus, and have less or no advantage in tasks that do not rely on a naming response. Thus, although Henle (1942) found that mirror images of letters require longer exposures in order to be recognized than do normally oriented letters, Hayes, Robinson, and Brown (1961) found that the thresholds for judging whether or not two patterns are the same were no higher for reversed letters or for letters that are infrequently used than they were for letters that were normally oriented and frequently used (see also Goldiamond & Hawkins, 1958).

This matter of *response bias* (see Chapter

2) also arises in connection with the other techniques that have been used for measuring shape thresholds (Zigler et al., 1930; Krauskopf, Duryea, & Bitterman, 1954; Soltz & Wertheimer, 1959; Pierce, 1963), but the fact that in the tachistoscopic experiment the subject is always confined to describing his memory of the stimulus makes it particularly difficult to determine which tachistoscopic effects, if any, are phenomena of sensory reception, and which are phenomena of memory.[8]

As we noted above, Gestaltists suggested that the same laws of organization would be displayed even more strongly by the memory of the shape than by its percept: The "memory trace" of a good figure would be more stable than that of a poor one, and poor ones either move in the direction of better figures or are lost. The area of *memory for form* is a well worked one in its own right, and is discussed in Chapter 17. Here, let us consider the possibility that by removing the stimulus entirely, we also remove those features that are specific (and, so to speak, accidental or irrelevant) in each method of impoverishment. It might thus be that the "laws of organization" are best revealed by differences in ease of recognizing remembered shapes. To test this possibility, we need objective measures of goodness of organization. The Gestalt "predictions" (such as that a circle with a gap will undergo a change in memory so that the gap gets smaller) were not really made according to formal principles that would permit clear hypotheses and have not in general been substantiated (see Holmes,

1968). Various related attempts have been made to provide such formal principles (see p. 436). As we noted before (p. 437), Attneave (1954) had proposed that the various Gestalt laws are merely expressions of a more general principle that can be stated quantitatively in terms of *information theory* (Attneave, 1959). Consider a matrix of cells, like graph paper. Any scene at all can in principle be duplicated by such a mosaic of cells, if they are sufficiently fine-grained and appropriately colored. If we know that all of the cells are black, there is no uncertainty about how any given cell that we look at will be colored, and it therefore carries no information. *Information theory* offers a mathematical means of stating the uncertainty in such a stimulus display: If each cell's color is independent of any other cell's color, and all colors are equally likely for each cell, the matrix is maximally uncertain. The more cells about which the subject is uncertain, the more information he has to remember, and the various Gestalt laws might make good patterns easier to remember merely because their geometrical order is one way of reducing the overall independence (and uncertainty) of those patterns.

Attneave (1955) chose *symmetry* as the law with which to test this approach and asked whether subjects can remember symmetrical patterns better than irregular ones simply because the former contain less information.

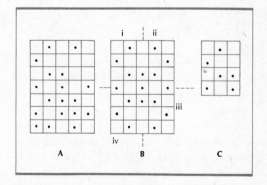

Figure 12.25. Samples of patterns for studying information and memory for shape. (Attneave, 1955.) See text.

[8] This does not mean that we cannot hope to separate the effects of memory and of verbal response readiness from the effects of more immediate perceptual processes. It does mean that we cannot simply accept subjects' reports of what they see as a direct indication of the latter. Various attempts have been made to separate effects on the response from effects on perception (Neisser, 1954; Eriksen, 1958), and a phenomenon recently reported by Haber and Hershenson (1965) and Dainoff and Haber (1967) may make it possible to study differences in tachistoscopic shape perception with less interference from the subjects' verbal expectations. With repeated presentations at the same exposure duration, subjects report an increasing *clarity* of the stimulus material, a change that cannot be attributed to differences in verbal response readiness because the subjects know what the word is before each presentation of the material.

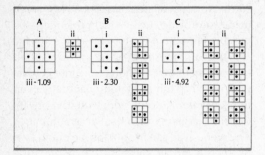

Figure 12.26. Samples of stimuli and their rated goodness. For each stimulus pattern A*i*, B*i*, C*i*, the subset that would be produced by rotation and reflection is shown at *ii*. Subjects' mean goodness ratings are given at *iii*. See text. (Garner & Clement, 1963; Handel & Garner, 1965).

Figure 12.25B, for example, has less information than Figure 12.25A because each of the dots in the parts marked *ii* to *iv* can be predicted from those in the part marked *i*. A critical question is whether symmetrical patterns (Figure 12.25B) remain easier to remember even when they are compared to assymmetrical patterns that have the *same* information (because they have fewer cells; Figure 12.25C). Three measures were used to determine how well subjects could reproduce or identify these patterns from memory, and all of these measures showed that symmetrical patterns were remembered no better (and in fact were worse) than were assymmetrical patterns having the same information content.

With a different information-theoretic approach, Garner (1962, 1966) proposes that "goodness" does not depend on the characteristics of the individual stimulus; in fact, the characteristics that are needed to specify any stimulus themselves depend on the set of alternatives from which that stimulus must be differentiated. A pattern's goodness varies inversely with the number of other equivalent patterns with which the subject classes that stimulus (and which he infers from that stimulus). For example, 5 dots can be arranged in a 3 × 3 matrix (Figure 12.26) to form a total set of 126 different patterns, but the subject

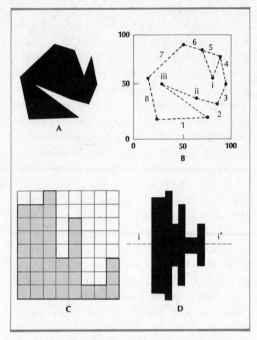

Figure 12.27. Generating populations of patterns. A. A nonsense-figure produced by the method of Attneave and Arnoult (1956). For these figures, *complexity* is a subjective attribute, to be determined empirically from subjects' judgments. B. For details on several methods of generating such figures, see Attneave and Arnoult. As an example, the coordinates for each of the points in Figure 27B may be drawn by pairs from a table of random numbers. The outer points are joined to form the polygon shown by the dashed line. The inner points *i–iii* are joined to the sides (by the dotted lines), again by reference to some arbitrary source such as a random number table. Patterns like these have been the most widely used and studied of the "nonsense shapes." See text, page 449. C. "Metric figures" were constructed by Fitts and his colleagues by assigning a height to each column of the matrix according to various sampling rules. With any given matrix size, the sampling rules determine the number, *N*, of different patterns that can be constructed. For these figures, Fitts and his colleagues defined *complexity* as the number, *N*. Sampling rules that call for a random assignment of heights to the matrix generate the largest *N*. Any limitations or constraints that make the assignment of heights nonrandom reduces *N*, and therefore reduces the complexity of the metric figures that are

treats each pattern as a member of some smaller subset, and the fewer the members of that subset the greater the pattern's goodness. The size of a subset is closely related to the number of different patterns that can be obtained by rotating and reflecting the stimulus. For Figure 12.26A that number is 1.0; for Figure 12.26B*ii*, it is 4; for Figure 12.26C it is 8. With stimuli generated in this fashion, subjects' ratings of "goodness" were predicted well above chance by this measure (Garner & Clement, 1963; Handel & Garner, 1965); the ratings also predict both the ways in which subjects sort the patterns into groups (Garner & Clement, 1963) and what the set of patterns is that any stimulus suggests to subjects (Handel & Garner, 1965).

Such attempts at providing explicit measures of the stimulus (or of the stimulus set) with which we can predict how well subjects remember and discriminate different patterns do not, however, permit us to take up the original task of using impoverished stimuli to discover the determinants of figural organization. First, there is the problem of measuring stimulus information. Various researchers have designed artificial stimuli to make informational measurement relatively easy (see Figures 12.25, 12.26, 12.27 for examples). Unfortunately, however, such stimuli have little in common with those with which the problems of organization were studied, or with those of normal experience. The importance of such properties as *symmetry* or *goodness* for the study of perception lay in their possible value for predicting figural organization (pp. 433–437), and the measures of stimulus information have not been tested in this regard. In fact, it is not clear that those measures can be applied to the problems of figural organization. Perhaps other methods can be devised with which to generate artificial stimuli that will permit information measures to be taken but which will also be more

generated. D. A symmetrical pattern generated from C by reflection around *i–i'*. (Fitts et al., 1956.)

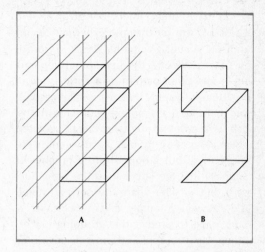

Figure 12.28. A method for generating arbitrary objects. The approach illustrated in Figure 12.27 need not be restricted to flat patterns. For example, one can generate reversible-perspective figures by adding modular surfaces to each others' edges in a three-dimensional matrix, following various arbitrary or random sampling rules. At A: A reversible-perspective figure and its matrix. B. One of the objects represented by A.

relevant to the problems of figural organization; an example of one possible method is shown in Figure 12.28.

Second, there is a difficult problem in determining how much of the stimulus display is actually used by the subject in such experiments. In any recognition or discrimination experiment in which the subject responds to some limited set of stimuli, he can readily select some subset of the features of any stimulus, and respond only to those. If, for example, his task is to decide whether each member of a set of stimuli is a T or an I, the subject need only look for the crossbar at the top in order to class the stimulus one way or the other; he does not even have to see anything else about each stimulus. Similarly, the fact that one part of a pattern is predictable from another (as in Figure 12.25B) does not ensure that the subject will make use of that relationship to obtain the most economical encoding of the stimulus (Attneave, 1955), nor is the subset of alternatives that a subject infers for a given pattern necessarily the set that the experimenter intended (Clement & Varnadoe, 1967). The problem of what the effective perceptual elements are, in any given pattern, is a critical one in any attempt to apply informational measures. Even in the case of simple sequential patterns, such as a series of digits, subjects treat the sequence not as though each event were independent but grouped into a number of "chunks" that are larger than the individual event but smaller than the series (Miller, 1956). Recent attempts (Vitz, 1968; Vitz & Todd, 1969) to predict this grouping or "recoding," and to apply information measures to the recoded elements, seem to be successful at predicting the judged complexities and relative ease of recall for such simple patterns. Nevertheless, this is still very far from being able to apply information measures to the study of two-dimensional shapes and three-dimensional forms.

This leads us to question whether the stimulus measures are really the appropriate independent variables here. For example, Glanzer and his colleagues (Glanzer & Clark, 1963a,b, 1964; Glanzer, Taub, & Murphy, 1968) have shown that the accuracy with which subjects can reproduce or recognize shapes, as measured by a variety of methods, is better predicted from the length of the verbalizations with which subjects describe those shapes, than from information measures taken on the stimuli. Glanzer and Clark propose the *verbal-loop hypothesis*. This is the hypothesis that the differences in recognizability between stimuli are to be accounted for in terms of a *covert verbalization* by which the subject encodes and remembers the stimulus. Hence it is to the characteristics of such verbal encoding that we must ascribe the organizational phenomena. As we saw in our discussion of tachistoscopic recognition, encoding (whether verbal or otherwise) plays a large part in recognition threshold experiments. It may be of course that the lengths of subjects' descriptions, and their recognition errors, reflect a common underlying fig-

ural organization. Glanzer and Clark (1963a) recognize this possibility, and argue that it is unparsimonious, but it is not clear how the nontachistoscopic examples of organization that we discussed on pages 433–436 can depend on covert verbalization to any significant degree. In any case, however, this variable, verbalization length, may turn out to be superior to stimulus information measures, not only because it has been shown to be more predictive in these experiments, but because it can be applied to configurations for which it is difficult or impossible to obtain informational measures. Furthermore, it should remain applicable in those cases in which the subject attends only to selected features of the stimulus.

What Glanzer and Clark have proposed is that the important determinant of shape recognition is the subject's set of verbal responses to any configuration, not the configuration itself. Like any response measure, the verbalization measure has the drawback of not being known before the experiment is performed. A psychophysics of shape would then depend for its predictive power on our ability to decide in advance how people will make such responses to various configurations, and we shall now consider research directed to this question.

Response Dimensions of Shape

Some shapes have specific names, but many more do not. If no name fits exactly, the subject can apply the name that is closest and then add the necessary correction (Woodworth, 1938; Attneave, 1957, 1962). Such qualities as *angular, curved, compact* seem to refer to reasonably measurable geometrical properties, whereas other terms, like *soft, placid, exciting,* may seem harder to pin down to specific physical variables. In any case, the sporadic research that has been done on this topic suffers from an inability to indicate where the patterns that are used in the experiment come from; that is, the results are not generalizable to other stimuli.

Attneave and Arnoult (1956) have offered a convenient means of generating a population of meaningless (nonsense) figures, populations having known statistical parameters, from which random samples of figures could be drawn that would be equivalent in their physical properties (Figure 12.27A,B shows one such figure and indicates the method of generating them). With such populations of stimuli, whatever facts are found out about subjects' responses to the physical variables of one randomly drawn sample of patterns can be tested against another similarly drawn sample.

The configurations are generated according to rules that permit controlled physical variations along certain physical dimensions (for example, number of sides); varying one measure normally changes other physical measures as well (for example, smallest interior angle; total perimeter length). Brown and Owen (1967) have measured and made available a number of these concomitant variations for a total of 1000 configurations, with 200 samples at each of 4,8,12,16, and 20 independent sides.

Figures generated according to the Attneave-Arnoult procedures have been used to study both shape discrimination and paired-associates learning. A population of nonsense shapes has been produced that have known "meaningfulness" as measured by verbal associations (Vanderplas, Sanderson, & Vanderplas, 1965). The area has been reviewed recently by Michels and Zusne (1965). Several studies have pursued the initial purpose of determining the physical correlates of the response dimensions of shape (Attneave & Arnoult, 1956; Arnoult, 1957).

Attneave (1957) found that a weighted combination of the following variables accounted for about 90 percent of subjects' judgments of the *complexity* of a sample of nonsense shapes: the number of sides, symmetry, angular variability, and P^2/A (where P = perimeter and A = area of the figure; see p. 443). Attneave did not attempt to use this measure of complexity as an independent variable [for example, as complexity measures have been used to predict apparent tridimensionality (p. 436) or luminance thresholds (p. 443)]. It is interesting that a dimension of *complexity* has also emerged (with 3 others) in a recent study of similarity judgments among random shapes (Stenson, 1966), again with P^2/A a major physical factor in that judgment. Stenson's other dimensions (that appeared to underlie the judged similarities among 20 Attneave-Arnoult shapes) were *curvature, curvature-dispersion,* and *straight-length dispersion.*

Whether results obtained with such stimuli can be generalized to other (and more meaningful) stimuli remains, as Attneave and Arnoult (1956) are aware, an unresolved problem of unknown magnitude. In any experiment on shape categorization, how a subject names or classifies a given pattern depends not only on that pattern, but on the entire set of stimuli being considered (see p. 446). The criteria by which a subject decides to call a stimulus pattern by one name rather than another, and how these criteria change as a function of the distinctions that the subject is required to make, are problems that we cannot review here. The reader is referred to Hake, Rodwan, and Weintraub (1966); Imai and Garner (1965); and Forsyth and Brown (1967). However, the difficulties of deciding what shape a subject sees from the names with which he describes them, and of deciding what it means when 2 configurations are given the same name, should be kept in mind in reading the following discussion of *transposition.*

Transposed and transformed shapes Although the same pattern falling on different parts of the retina (either because the stimulus object or the observer's eye has moved) stimulates very different retinal receptors, to casual observation the shape seems to be unchanged. Similarly, a large square and a small one fall on completely different sets of receptors, yet look alike. This, of course, was one of the major Gestaltist objections to the mosaic theory (p. 427), and is often referred to as *the* Gestalt problem in attempts to specify the machinery of the visual system. With really familiar items, like letters or other named shapes, the issue can be sidestepped, for it is plausible to say that we have learned to make the same responses to different patterns (thus, we make the same overt response to *CAT,* to *cat,* and to either of these displaced to any other locus on the retina even though we see the differences). However, it also seems to some degree to be true that we can recognize unfamiliar, unnamed shapes as being the same when they appear in 2 different retinal locations. Several models of neural function have been devised that would explain how such transposition might be achieved (Lashley, 1942; Deutsch, 1955; Dodwell, 1961, 1964; Uhr, 1963).

When we examine the problem more closely, we see that it is not yet clear what it is that we have to explain. Wallach and Austin (1954) have presented evidence that patterns falling on different parts of the retina are not completely equivalent. Subjects were told that their experiment was one on the peripheral recognition of familiar shapes. Nine silhouettes (whale, tree, car, and so on), varying in size from 3° to 4.6°, were presented singly in 1 of 4 positions, each 2.6° from the fixation point, for a 0.4-second exposure. Subjects were to name the objects. The last silhouette was a pattern which, when it is viewed with its long axis horizontal, is usually recognized as a dog, while with its axis vertical it is recognized as a chef. Inclined 45°, as it was in the final presentation, this pattern is fairly ambiguous. Both the chef version and the dog version were included among the first 9 shapes. For some subjects, the ambiguous version was shown on the position that had previously been occupied by the chef version; for others it was shown on the position previously occupied by the dog version. The ambiguous version was predominantly recognized as that figure (chef or dog) which had previously occupied the same retinal position. There is, thus, at least this limit to the equivalence of the same shape in different locations and different orientations: Recognition on subsequent presentations is, to some extent, specific to both orientation and locus.

Implicit in the description of the experiment of Wallach and Austin is the fact that a change in the orientation with which a pattern falls on the retina may result in a change in the shape that is perceived. The ease and accuracy with which certain shapes

are recognized certainly depends on the orientation of the stimulus pattern. Inverting or reversing a letter of the alphabet, or a map of a continent, or the picture of a face, interferes with its recognition (Gibson & Robinson, 1935; Hochberg & Galper, 1967). We might well argue that such differences are due to the meaningful responses that are made to those patterns, not to shape perception per se. Then, however, we would have to concede that there must be some basis by which the meaningful responses are tied to retinal orientation.

It is often held that children recognize a figure when it is upside down as readily as when it is right side up; and therefore that the differences that adults display in responding to figures in different orientations are due to learning about specific objects. There is little evidence to support the first assertion. If anything, the contrary seems to be true. Younger children give fewer descriptions of the contents of inverted pictures than of upright ones (Hunton, 1955) and recognize significantly more pictures presented with a tachistoscope when these are upright than when they are in other orientations, whereas older children recognize the figures equally well in all positions (Ghent, 1960). Similarly, the fact that young children perform poorly on learning tasks that require them to discriminate between the right and left mirror-images of a shape (Rudel & Teuber, 1963) does not mean that they perceive a shape and its mirror image as being identical. In fact, if all they have to do is report whether two shapes are the same or different, they perform quite well (Rosenblith, 1965; Robinson & Higgens, 1967).

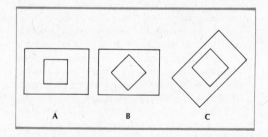

Figure 12.29. Framework and shape. See text.

The effect of orientation on shape recognition may itself be a Gestalt phenomenon, however. The square has become a diamond in Figure 12.29B for example, not necessarily because of the retinal rotation per se; the effect may be due to the pattern's change in relation to the spatial framework that is provided by the page on which it is printed. Any perceived shape would really be a shape-in-relation-to-the-framework, in this view, and the shape that is perceived would change when that relationship changes (Gibson & Robinson, 1935; Koffka, 1935). In Figure 12.29C, the pattern regains much of its appearance as a square (Kopfermann, 1930; in Koffka, 1935, pp. 184 ff.). Using unfamiliar (nonsense) shapes, Rock and his colleagues (Rock, 1956; Rock & Heimer, 1957; Rock & Leaman, 1963) found that the shapes' recognizabilities were not substantially affected by changes in their retinal orientations. On the other hand, changing the shapes' *apparent* orientations (i.e., which part of a pattern appeared to be its "top" with respect to a visual frame of reference, with respect to gravity, and so on), while keeping retinal orientations constant, strongly affected their recognizabilities. This does not mean that patterns were responded to as shapes-in-relation-to-a-visual-framework, however, inasmuch as Rock and Heimer (1957) found that subjects who were merely given verbal information about what the figures' orientations were, recognized the shapes better than did uninformed subjects. The generality of this last point has been questioned by Braine (1965), who argued that the uninformed subjects had been misled because they had automatically assumed that the patterns were in their normal orientation. She showed that subjects who had been told the exact orientation in which briefly presented drawings (horse, elephant, tree, and so on) would appear, recognized them no better than did subjects who were merely informed that the patterns would be disoriented. It remains true, however, that a shape's apparent orientation can be defined in terms of the axis along

which it appears to point, around which symmetry is judged, and with which the shape's recognizability is correlated. So defined, the apparent orientation of a pattern is at least partially independent of its orientation in the retinal image. Thus, as its apparent orientation changes, any stimulus pattern may be perceived as taking on any of several different shapes (Attneave, 1968).

However, the transposition problem as it was raised at the beginning of this section is difficult to state and test with any precision. Even configurations that have not been seen before nevertheless have parts or features that may be very familiar (p. 441), and the subjects may be responding to such features, rather than to entire configurations. Those theories about the nervous system that try to explain transposition may be undertaking an unnecessarily stringent task. Let us consider whether the Gestalt arguments really rule out the possibility that there are units of perception smaller than the entire configuration.

Elementary shapes and features Structuralism sought, in essence, to explain the perception of shapes in terms of 2 different components, namely the elementary point sensations and the associations based on past experience (p. 428). Gestalt theory set the entire figure (with its internal forces of organization, p. 428) as the unit of response. As Hebb has argued very effectively (1949), some middle ground between these extreme

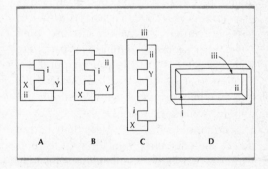

Figure 12.30. Continuous lines serving as inconsistent edges. See text.

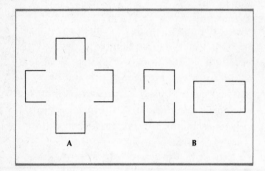

Figure 12.31. Different shapes, same elements.

positions now seems more reasonable than either. Let us here consider some demonstrations that suggest that there are at least 2 components to shape perception, rather than a single process: One component may be designated as the elementary shape feature (which is restricted in extent and sensory in quality). The other component is an integrative *schema* or *map,* which can be much larger than even the contents of the entire retinal image at any moment, and which is less sensory and more conceptual in quality.

First, consider Figure 12.30, which shows a number of shapes in which a contour changes its function from one point to another. In Figure 12.30A, angle *i* is seen predominantly as obtuse (that is, Y is figure), and angle *ii* is a right angle (that is, X is figure). In Figure 12.30B, although the pattern in the immediate vicinity remains as in A, angle *i* looks like a right angle (that is, X is figure). We might say that the overall configuration has determined the function of the contour at *i*. However, in Figure 12.30C, D, as the distances between corners *i, ii,* and *iii* increase, their effect on *i* seems to diminish. What these figures suggest is that the figure-ground distinction (that is, the way a contour faces) is not determined for the entire contour, but only for some local extent.

Second, note that it is clear that we can detect and enumerate similarities of features within very different configurations (as long as the contours continue to face the same way). In Figure 12.31, it is easy to see that the

same corners and edges appear in different locations in the two shapes, A and B. Thus it seems plausible to argue that we can recognize elementary features and that these are larger than points but smaller than most figures. Whence would such elementary shapes derive?

Hebb's (1949) speculations provided a very influential theoretical outline of how such units might result from perceptual learning. Because of the way that the world is constructed, some patterns of stimulation are likely to be encountered repeatedly. In essence, this theory proposes that neural groupings (called *cell-assemblies*) will develop in the associative cortex of the brain. These groupings presumably respond as units, each of which is sensitive to some frequently encountered pattern of sensory stimulation, such as a corner or a particular slope of a line in vision, a vowel sound in hearing, a pressure pattern in touch, and so forth.

This theory, although simply stated, is much more complicated when it is made specific and when questions of frequency, timing, and neural interconnection are really spelled out. The attempts to simulate such a model by use of electronic computers have not proved too encouraging (Rochester et al., 1956; see Uhr, 1963). However, receptive fields in the nervous systems of cats, monkeys, and other animals (see Chapter 9) include neural structures which are sensitive to lines and corners of a particular slope, wherever they fall over fairly large regions of the retina. This means that the cell-assemblies would not have to be learned from scratch.

As we have seen, a given contour on the retina does not specify a single elementary shape response but 2 mutually exclusive ones (Figures 12.14, 12.15). Why would we acquire 2 mutually exclusive response systems to the same stimulus? This is the heart of the figure-ground phenomenon, and no theory of shape recognition that fails to offer an explanation for it has accomplished very much. Let us see how a system similar to Hebb's might handle it.

Consider that the eye seldom maintains its fixation for long, but is poised to move again, usually well within a second's time (Chapter 11, p. 386). Because we receive little or no information that guides the eye while it is in motion, its movements must be largely programmed or preset before it starts to move. As we saw earlier (p. 428), shape perception has frequently been explained as being the knowledge of the movements (and especially the eye movements) needed to trace the contour, or to fixate each of its points (Titchener, 1902; Helmholtz, 1910; Washburn, 1916; Taylor, 1962; Festinger et al., 1967). Even without subscribing completely to such proposals, we would expect that the visuomotor system will have acquired a set of plans or programs that will enable the eye to fixate any point on any highly familiar shape's contours. Such an "efferent readiness" (the term is from Festinger et al., 1967), would include a readiness to adjust the eyes to increased depth after moving from *i* to *ii*, with the arrangements of surfaces in Figure 12.24A (page 441), and a readiness for the reverse adjustment, in Figure 12.24B. A layout like that in Figure 12.24A will usually be accompanied by various depth cues (see Chapter 13), or indications of the surface's distance, and those cues would determine what adjustive movements the eye would make. The preparations to move from *i* to *ii* in Figure 12.24A will be the reverse of those in Figure 12.24B, so that the cell-assemblies responsive to the retinal image produced by those 2 sets of surfaces will be mutually exclusive. Now, when we provide the eye with a pattern like that of Figure 12.14 (p. 432), which has no depth cues, the pattern is common to both cell assemblies—the one that has been developed in response to the arrangement of Figure 12.24A and that for Figure 12.24B. Hence, the 2 possible responses, and hence the figure-ground phenomenon (Hochberg, 1970a, b).

Two major questions come immediately to mind, once we accept the possibility that such elementary subshapes may really act as

Figure 12.32. Fragmentation of stabilized images. (After Pritchard, 1961.)

units of shape perception. First, how can we determine a subject's repertory of such elements? Second, how are these elements combined?

We have no well-developed procedures for discovering what such elementary features might be, at present. One possible procedure is based on the long-known fact that if one stares at a pattern steadily, the shape becomes invisible and fades from view (Chapter 9, p. 306). Hebb has proposed that cell-assemblies (and sets of cell-assemblies that share a high proportion of cells in common) tend to act as units, and that, if this is true, under prolonged fixation a shape will tend to reveal the "joints" between its parts by the way it breaks up as it fades. In general, shapes viewed under image stabilization (p. 374) tend to break up in ways that support this. Pritchard, Heron, and Hebb (1960) and Pritchard (1961) studied ways in which several patterns fragmented when they were viewed as stabilized retinal images and found shapes to appear and disappear as meaningful parts rather than in random fragments. For example, if any part of the HB pattern in Figure 12.32A remained, it was usually one of the meaningful segments shown in Figure 12.32B. A similar kind of fragmentation also seems to occur with voluntary fixation of patterns (that is, segments tend to be meaningful, and identical parts tend to appear and to disappear together) whether the observer fixates a luminous figure under low illumination (McKinney, 1963) or at higher illumination levels (Craig & Lichtenstein, 1953; Clarke & Belcher, 1962; Evans & Piggins, 1963). The shape fragments that are reported in these experiments are influenced by learning, as was demonstrated by Donderi and Kane (1965), who found that different stimulus figures to which subjects had learned to make the same response disappeared together more frequently than if the subjects had not learned to give a common response to them.

In reviewing the research on tachistoscopic recognition of shape, we saw that it is difficult to decide whether the effects of meaning or familiarity are attributable to the initial sensory processing, or are due to the set of responses available for recall and report (p. 444). The same problem arises concerning the fragmentation findings, and for similar reasons. As Schuck and Leahy (1966) point out, both retinal stabilization and voluntary fixation often produce rapidly changing apparent shapes, and the subject may be less able to remember and to report fragments that are not easily described. Schuck, Brock, and Becker (1964) showed that assigning simple verbal labels by which subjects could report line segments affected the reports of disappearance. Similarly, Schuck and Leahy (1966) showed that 29 out of 34 subjects who were asked to *describe* the appearance of a fixated luminous HB (Figure 12.32A) reported at least 1 meaningful disappearance (that is, 1 of the segments shown in Figure 12.32B). To the contrary, only 12 out of 34 subjects who were asked to *trace* the fragmented shape on an outline HB figure indicated at least one meaningful disappearance.

This issue is still in question. Tees and More (1967) exposed their subjects repeatedly to a particular 2-digit number (for example, 32) *without requiring them to make any response to that number.* They then presented the subjects with a luminous display containing the 2 numbers (for example, 332) and found that those 2 digits appeared and disappeared together more frequently than was the case when subjects had not received prior exposure to them. It is not clear why mere exposure to a particular set of digits would change the availability of *response* labels.

The units suggested by the fragmentation phenomena may yield valid visual effects and yet may not be general building blocks in the sense of providing the bases of shape recognition, discrimination, and so on. Other techniques can probably be devised that are more closely related to the purposes that such units should serve. For example, Lichtenstein (1961) and MacFarland (1965) have used a procedure in which the parts of a pattern were presented in rapid succession, instead of simultaneously. The subjects' task was to judge when all parts of the shape appeared to be shown at the same time. This technique might be adapted to find out whether breaking a pattern apart in some places and then presenting the pieces successively makes it harder to recognize a shape than breaking it in other places, that is, whether the subject can perceive shapes more readily when some parts of the configuration are available to him as undivided units than when they are not (see Hochberg, 1968). In any case, such elementary units clearly could not account for the whole of shape perception: They are at once too large and too small. They are too large because we can distinguish patterns on the basis of differences between them, down to the limits of our acuity; they are too small because we can distinguish patterns, all of the elements of which are the same but which present those elements in different spatial orders (see for example Figure 12.31A, B).

Schematic maps Up to this point, we have been considering the retina as though it were a homogeneous mosaic of photoreceptors, and of course it is nothing like that. The acuity falls off very rapidly away from the central fovea (see Chapter 9), so that if a pattern is transposed from one region of the retina to another, the relative acuity of the receptive regions on which its various parts fall is likely to be changed. Similarly, fixating one corner of a large pattern places the other corners so far into the periphery that their detail cannot be discerned. In order to see each corner of a large cross clearly, the eye

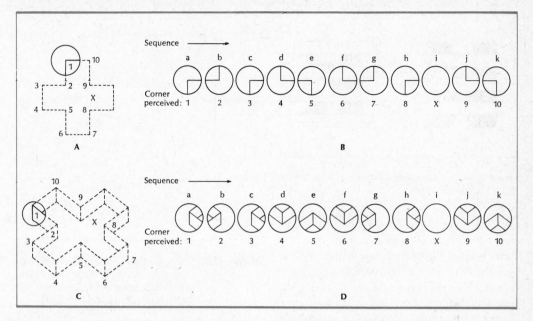

Figure 12.33. Shapes (A, C) presented by successive views (B, D). See text. (After Hochberg, 1968.)

must make at least 4 separate fixations, so that more than a second in time must elapse between the time the first and last corner are fixated. How do we recognize that the shape is a cross, and not one of the other figures that can be built up out of these corners? In some manner, our perceptual system must be able to register and store the relative location of each corner.

The schemas or maps that contain the information of where one has to fixate in order to see some feature are a form of *postretinal storage*. Parks (1965) proposed that postretinal storage could be demonstrated and studied by moving a pattern behind a stationary slit so that its parts appear successively in the same place. Under the proper conditions, the whole shape is recognizable, even though only a narrow region is exposed at any moment. To Parks, this demonstrates the existence of postretinal visual storage. This phenomenon, which was first noted by Zollner (see Helmholtz, 1866), can be at least partially attributed to eye movements that spread the entire pattern out on adjacent regions of the retina. Explanation of this

phenomenon in terms of such eye movements (Helmholtz, 1866) has been repeatedly challenged (Vierordt, 1868; Rothschild, 1922; Hecht, 1924; Parks, 1965; see Anstis and Atkinson, 1967, for a review of this literature), but it now seems to account for many of the features that Parks described, for example, the compression of the perceived shape that is characteristically reported, and the fact that the entire figure appears to be visible simultaneously (Anstis & Atkinson, 1967; Haber & Nathanson, 1968). However, this factor only provides a source of retinally tied storage that contaminates the study of postretinal storage; the latter is also demonstrated by successive viewing of a figure through an aperture. Thus, if one of the outline patterns shown in Figure 12.33A, C is moved around behind a hole at a reasonably slow pace (about 500–1000 msec. between the corners of Fig. 12.33A, or between the bends of Figure 12.33C), adult subjects can recognize the shapes (Hochberg, 1968). Such storage is unlikely to be due exclusively to any tracking of the pattern by eye movements. Indeed, the patterns shown in Figure 12.33A, C are so large

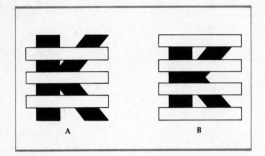

Figure 12.34. The same shape presented by different views. See text.

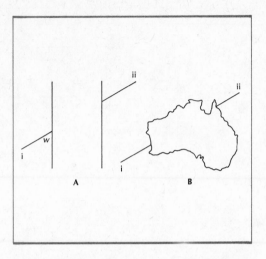

Figure 12.35. The Poggendorf illusion. The diagonals *i–ii* are really aligned. A. With straight-line interruptions. B. With an irregular interruption. (Adapted from Hotopf, 1966.)

that, were the eye to pursue one of the corners even after it disappeared from view, the other end of the pattern would fall too far into the periphery to be seen clearly.

What mechanisms might account for such postretinal storage? Schematic maps are not sensory: When the same shape is recognized in Figure 12.34A, B we do not really see the hidden portions. Similarly, in the aperture viewing of Figure 12.33 (p. 455), there is no real sensory quality either to the shape or its background where these are occluded by the mask. It is as though the *concept* of a cross (perhaps, in the form of a program or plan of the eye movements that would have to be made to trace it out, or to change fixation from one point on it to another, see p. 453), always underlies the perception of this familiar shape, but is only made evident when the sensory overlay in which it is normally clothed has been removed (Hochberg, 1968). A very similar view underlies Neisser's concept of "figural synthesis" (Neisser, 1967). This is thus far only speculation. What should be clear now is that the question of *what* shape is actually *seen* in response to a given retinal configuration is not a simple question with a single answer.

ILLUSIONS AND AFTEREFFECTS

The Geometrical Illusions

Regular vs. irregular patterns If we confine our attention to simple aspects of a given shape, such as its apparent length or curva-

ture, we can often determine with reasonable confidence how that aspect changes with changes in stimulation. When we can do this, we usually find that the relationship of apparent shape to retinal configuration is beyond our present abilities to formulate in general terms or to explain within a single theory. Specific instances in which the apparent curvature or length of a perceived line are not predictable from the curvature or length of its stimulus pattern have long been called the "geometrical illusions," but this does not mean that they occur only with regular lines and patterns; they can also be demonstrated with quite irregular drawings (see Figure 12.35; Hotopf, 1966), and with real objects in normal environments (Chapanis & Mankin, 1967; Zanforlin, 1967). Any theories that dismiss the illusions as being due to the peculiarities of lines on paper (see Gibson) or that explain them as false expectations of rectangularity based on Western man's continuous exposure to a geometrical and "carpentered" world (Segal, Campbell, & Herskovitz, 1963, 1966) are placing unwarranted restrictions on their generality of occurrence. The geometrical character of the traditional illusions is most reasonably re-

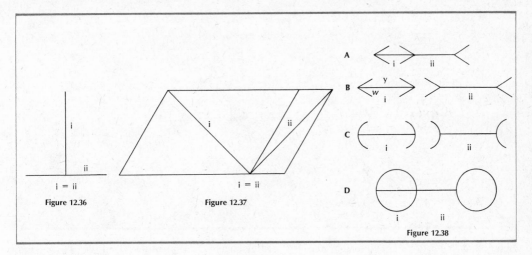

Figure 12.36. Vertical-horizontal illusion.   **Figure 12.37.** Sander parallelogram.   **Figure 12.38.** Variations of the Müller-Lyer illusion. D. is from Zanforlin (1967).

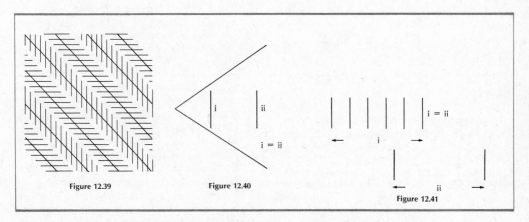

Figure 12.39. Zöllner illusion.   **Figure 12.40.** Ponzo illusion.   **Figure 12.41.** Filled-space illusion.

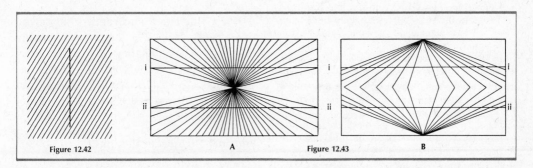

Figure 12.42. The single line is vertical.   **Figure 12.43.** Hering and Wundt illusions. Lines *i* and *ii* are parallel.

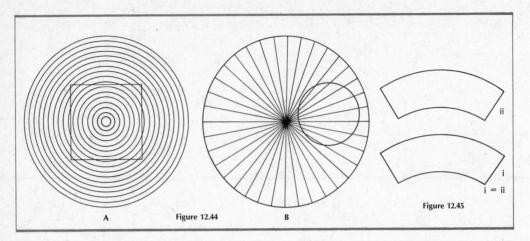

A   Figure 12.44   B   Figure 12.45

Figure 12.44. Ehrenstein and Orbison illusions. The inscribed figures are perfectly symmetrical.   **Figure 12.45.** The upper and lower areas are equal.

garded as a convenient way in which to make the distortions more easily noticeable than they are in ordinary configurations (Hotopf, 1966).

The illusions are important, therefore, because they may provide clues for our understanding of the processes of shape perception in general.

Measurement of the shape illusions under varying conditions   Quantitative methods used to evaluate the extent of illusions have usually been the adjustment method (p. 20) or the method of constant stimuli, with a fair amount of data accrued by both methods (Thiéry, 1895, Heymans, 1896, 1897; Judd et al., 1899, 1902, 1905). Little application has yet been made of the methods of detection theory (p. 39). Quantitative studies of how the illusions vary with changes in pattern bring out effects that might otherwise have gone unnoticed; for example, Finger and Spelt (1947), showed that the usual **T** form of the vertical-horizontal illusion (Figure 12.36) is contaminated by effects due to the bisected cross-bar and that the illusion is markedly smaller in the form of an **L.** Parametric studies of the horizontal-vertical illusion were performed by Künnapas (1957); of the Sander parallelogram (Figure 12.37) by Ipsen (1926); of the Müller-Lyer figure and its variants by Heymans (1896), who found the illusion to be proportional to the cosine of the angles, w (Figure 12.38), and by Judd (1899), who found that all spatial relations in the immediate neighborhood of the Müller-Lyer figure were distorted,

not only the main lines; of the Poggendorf illusion (Figure 12.35), by Burmeister (1896), who found that the apparent displacement of the 2 diagonal lines, *i-ii,* followed the formula $v = k\ u \cot w$; of the Zöllner pattern (Figure 12.39), by Heymans (1896), who found the maximum effect when angle w was 30°; of the Ponzo illusion (Figure 12.40), by Sickles (1942); and of Oppel's or Kundt's illusion (Figure 12.41) by Knox (1893), by Lewis (1912), and by Spiegel (1937), all of whom found that there was a maximum number of subdivisions (for each line length) at which the greatest overestimation of the subdivided line occurred. Hofman and Bielschowsky (1909) measured how the orientation of a field of lines affected the apparent slant of a line superimposed on the field (Figure 12.42), a study the data of which should be relevant not only to such illusions of angle as the Hering (Figure 12.43A), Wundt (Figure 12.43B), and Ehrenstein and Orbison patterns (Figure 12.44), but to some of the aftereffects that we discuss on page 466, as well.

These studies are not an end in themselves, of course, but take their importance from the quantitative data that they offer to any theory which is itself definite enough to deal with such facts. As we shall see, few theories can really avail themselves of these resources at present.

Principal Theories of Illusions

The illusions have received a great deal of attention, over the years, and many of them are known by special names. Instead of attempting a full account of the illusions, we state the principal theories that have been suggested to explain them, and give a selection of illusory figures (Figures 12.35 through 12.45) on which the reader can try out these theories.

The eye-movement theory   In its simplest form, the eye-movement theory assumes that the impression of length is obtained by moving the eye along from one end of a pattern to the other. This would account for the horizontal-vertical illusion (Figure 12.36) by assuming that the vertical movements require greater effort than horizontal movements over the same distance, and therefore seem longer. In the Müller-Lyer figure (Figure 12.38A), the outward lines in one part might cause eye movements to exceed the length of the included line, whereas in the other part of the figure, the inward pointing lines might act to prevent the eyes from moving so far. The major objection to this theory is that the illusion can be obtained in tachistoscopic presentations, which produce exposures too short to permit the eye to move.

Photographic recordings of eye movements made during examination of the Müller-Lyer illusion show some relationship between the eye movement and the differences in pattern to each side of the illusion but nothing which provides an explanation of the former in terms of the latter (Judd, 1905; Yarbus, 1967).

A less-direct form of this theory assumes only that a *tendency* toward such movement is set up by the stimulus pattern itself, even when no movement can occur, and that this tendency is sufficient to give rise to the impression of length. This kind of theory is not a satisfactory explanation unless we can specify further what such movement tendencies should be and how they are affected by the stimulus pattern. Coren and Festinger (1967) have offered a first step toward such a theory, which we consider later on in another context (p. 467).

The empathy theory   Lipps (1897) sought to explain the esthetic effects of architecture on the assumption that the observer responds emotionally in terms of his own actions. A vertical line, in resisting gravity, suggests more effort and thus appears longer than an equally long horizontal line. The right part of the Müller-Lyer pattern in Figure 12.38 suggests expansion, the left, limitation, and therefore the right appears longer. Although there may be circumstances in which this theory might be developed into a predictive one, especially in regard to the expressive arts, it does not really accommodate any of the detailed knowledge of the illusions.

Field factors   According to Gestalt theory, illusions are merely cases in which the entire field affects the appearance of any part. Few specific field theories about the illusions have been offered. Of these, the most general is that of Orbison (1939). Following a proposal made earlier by Brown and Voth (1937) in connection with apparent motion (p. 527n), Orbison suggested that forces of attraction might operate between lines in the visual field, and that these would be in conflict with forces of constraint (which would operate to keep the lines fixed in their retinal locations). The 2 sets of forces in concert would generate such illusions as those of Wundt and Hering, and the special figures that were designed to test this theory by Orbison (1939). In any field of lines (Figures 12.43, 12.44) there will be loci of equilibrium at which the forces of attraction and constraint would be equal, and any other lines that are added to the field would be distorted toward the loci of equilibrium. Thus, in Figure 12.44A the radii are the loci of equilibrium, and the sides of the square are accordingly distorted toward those loci. Berliner and Berliner (1948) argued that a more specific and precise explanation of these kinds of illusion can be given by assuming that any line (straight or curved) changes direction wherever it crosses another line at some angle w, with the change in direction being proportional to the quantity $c \sin 4 w$

(see Webster, 1948, however). In any case, neither this formula nor Orbison's balance of forces gives clear predictions for the other classes of illusion.

A general characteristic of most of these illusions is that acute angles look larger than they are and obtuse angles look smaller. This is an observation of long standing, and many theories have been offered to explain it, one of which we consider next.

The perspective or constancy theory The perspective theory incorporates a general class of theories that imply that the apparent length of lines on paper is affected by the perspective read into the figure and that similar confusions can arise by the mistaken use of cues in the real world, too. Thus a short vertical line in a drawing may represent a relatively long horizontal line extending away from the observer, thus explaining the horizontal-vertical illusion (Figure 12.36). In the Müller-Lyer pattern, the obliques "suggest" perspective, and in terms of the laws of perspective, the horizontal line on the right should, if it appears further away, also appear to represent a line that is longer than the one on the left.

Because, in one form or another, the explanation given above is the most popular explanation of the illusions, at present, let us spell out the general argument in more detail.

Whenever converging lines are present in the retinal image, they are more likely than not to have been projected there by lines that are really not converging, but are extended into distance. We therefore take the left side of the pattern in the Müller-Lyer figure (Figure 12.38A) to be nearer than the right side. The 2 lengths, at *i* and at *ii*, are equal on the page, however, and will also provide images of equal length on the retina of the viewer's eye. In order for this to be so, if *i* is actually nearer than *ii*, *i* must really be shorter than *ii*. Thus, the same mechanisms that enable us to take distance into account and to perceive that an object's size remains constant as it approaches and its retinal image becomes larger

(see *size constancy,* Chapter 13) are reflected in the illusions. The illusions are merely mistaken applications of the distance cues.

This theory has been applied to most of the illusions at one time or another (Thiéry, 1896; Tausch, 1954; von Holzt, 1957; Green & Hoyle, 1963; Gregory, 1963; Segall, Campbell, & Herskovits, 1963). In favor of this theory are the facts of intercultural differences (Rivers, 1901, 1905). Segall, Campbell, and Herskovits (1963, 1966) obtained responses to several illusions from samples of European, African, and other cultures, finding that Europeans showed greater errors on the Müller-Lyer pattern and on the Sander parallelogram (Figure 12.37), whereas most non-European groups showed greater errors on the horizontal-vertical illusion. Their explanation is this: (1) Whenever persons living in "carpentered" or rectangular environments are confronted by lines meeting in nonrectangular junctions, they will perceive the figures in perspective, interpreting them as two-dimensional representations of tridimensional objects having rectangular junctions (hence the tendency to overestimate acute angles and underestimate obtuse angles, mentioned above). (2) Because the horizontal-vertical illusion reflects a tendency to counteract the foreshortening of lines that extend into space away from the observer, people living in open, spacious environments will be more susceptible to the illusion than those dwelling in urban (or rain-forest) surroundings.

The following arguments can be made against the perspective theory. First, there is a question of fact concerning the importance of a "carpentered" environment in determining susceptibility to the various illusions. Jahoda (1966) also found British subjects' judgments to be significantly more susceptible to the Müller-Lyer pattern than were natives of Ghana. The latter subjects, however, had been drawn partly from one population who inhabited open country and lived in round houses devoid of furnishings and partly from another population who lived in dense rain forest and in rectangular dwellings with car-

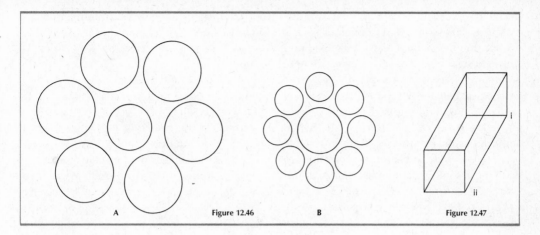

A   Figure 12.46   B   Figure 12.47

Figure 12.46. The inner circles of A and B are equal. p. 462.

Figure 12.47. A version of the Necker cube. See text,

pentered furnishings. The 2 groups of Ghanaians failed to show the expected differences in their responses to the illusions. Cultural differences in the measured effects of the illusions may not be due to expectations of rectangularity, therefore, but to other as-yet unknown determinants. These may include differences in perceptual attitudes (p. 464) or they may even depend on sensory differences. For example, Pollack and Silvar (1967) found that subjects whose central region of the retina (the *fundus oculi;* see Chapter 9) is more darkly pigmented showed less of an illusion when they viewed part of the Müller-Lyer pattern briefly under bluish light, than did subjects with lighter pigmentation. Moreover, optical pigmentation differs with race (Ishak, 1952; Pollack & Silvar, 1967; Silvar & Pollack, 1967). It seems quite unlikely that pigmentation differences account for much of the intercultural difference. But with so many other possible sources of difference, it seems premature to conclude that susceptibility to the geometrical illusions reflects the subjects' familiarity with carpentered environments. Moreover, as Zanforlin (1967) points out, even birds display illusions (Warden & Barr, 1929; Winslow, 1933), and their nests are not normally rectangular.

Second: There are illusions whose detailed effects can be explained in terms of other principles (see Figures 12.41, 12.46, 12.47, and p. 459), but which are not as well predicted by size-constancy or perspective explanations (Berliner, 1948; see also Hotopf, 1966; Virsu, 1967).

Third: The illusions to which the perspective theory seems most immediately addressed can themselves be otherwise explained. Thus, Künnapas (1957) attributes the horizontal-vertical illusion to the fact that the shape of our visual field is oval, so that the vertical line is overestimated because it is nearer to the boundary of the field of view. The Müller-Lyer illusion, it has been argued, occurs because the observer confuses the area included between the arrowheads with the length that he is being asked to judge. In some ways, in fact, this explanation seems more readily applicable. Consider, for example, the variations shown in Figure 12.38C and D (C was originally presented by Müller-Lyer in 1889; D is taken from Zanforlin, 1967): What depth cues, perspective or otherwise, contribute to the effects displayed by C and D?

Fourth: There is a question of what it might mean to say that "side *i* looks smaller *because* it looks nearer." This implies a relationship between perceived size and perceived distance that is similar to the possible relationship between perceived reflectance and perceived illumination $(R = L/E)$ that we discussed in pages 401–406. Evidence of such a relationship between perceived size and perceived distance will be discussed at length in the next chapter. We can give one example here of such evidence, particularly relevant to the case of the illusions. For many observers, line *i* in Figure 12.47 looks longer when line *ii* looks nearer, and when the reversible solid changes its apparent organization so that line *i* looks nearer, then line *ii* looks longer (Sanford, 1897; Hotopf, 1966; Hochberg, 1968; Mefferd & Wieland, 1968). These data are uncertain, however, because Gregory reports no size change (1966). According to perspective theory, pretty much the same thing happens in the case of the geometrical illusions caused by the Müller-Lyer pattern, and to this extent the effects in Figure 12.47 buttress the perspective theory. However, there is this clear difference between Figures 12.47 and 12.38: in the former, lines *i* and *ii* actually seem in some sense to lie at different distances (even though you know that they are really in the plane of the paper), whereas in the latter the 2 lines seem to lie in the same plane. How can we say that the difference in apparent length is caused by the difference in apparent distance, in Figure 12.38, when there is no difference in apparent distance?

Helmholtz' concept of *unconscious inference* (introduced on page 397) is at its most appealing when it deals with problems of size and distance perception, as we see in the next chapter. In essence, it notes that it often seems *as though* what we perceive results from calculations that were made about objects and about their dispositions in space on the basis of the sensory information that our eyes receive, even though we are aware neither of making the calculations nor of receiving the sensory information. That is, there are 2 levels of processing sensory information, only one of which can be consciously reported, but both of which seem to obey the same or roughly similar laws. In the case of the Müller-Lyer pattern, we might say that we have reached conclusions about the lengths

of the lines by unconscious inferences based on the unconscious (and mistaken) impressions of distance produced by the perspective cues.

This was rephrased in less mentalistic terms by Tolman and Brunswik (1935) and by Tausch (1954). If our visual systems have learned, in the course of normal perceptual commerce with objects in space, to allow for the distorting effects of perspective by setting up counterdistortions (for example, to judge objects at the narrow end of converging perspectives to be larger, at the wide end, smaller), then a two-dimensional configuration that contains depth cues that will trigger off the counterdistorting process will itself be distorted. Gregory (1963, 1967) has labeled 2 processes: (1) *primary scaling* (or *depth cue scaling*), in which the perceptual system automatically corrects size judgments in accordance with whatever distance cues are present, regardless of whether or not those distance cues also produce perceived depth. (2) *secondary scaling* (or *hypothesis scaling*), in which apparent distance determines apparent size. In the case of the illusions, only primary scaling is at work because the various cues available to normal vision serve to localize all of the lines as being in the plane of the paper. Secondary scaling was demonstrated in Figure 12.47 where the changes in apparent length were presumably due to changes in apparent distance. Many questions remain to be answered before we can really evaluate this class of explanation.

Why do some patterns, like those in Figure 12.47, produce apparent depth (and, therefore, secondary scaling), despite the indications given to the eye that all of the lines really rest in the plane of the paper, whereas the illusions in Figures 12.35 through 12.45 remain flat and produce only size change (primary scaling)? Also, if the patterns in Figure 12.38A, B are not seen in depth, how do we know that depth cues are present? Gregory (1963, 1966) had subjects, using 1 eye only, look at luminous versions of the illusion in a dark box, so that such indications of flatness as binocular disparity or surface texture (see Chapter 13, pp. 481f.) would not contradict the perspective cues. He reports that when subjects were instructed to set a binocularly viewed spot of light at the same apparent distance from them as the various parts of the pattern, the binocularly viewed spot (the real distance of which was clear to the subject at all times) was in fact set further away when the subject was matching side *ii* than when he was matching side *i*, and that the magnitude of this apparent depth distance varied in the same way as the magnitude of the illusion varied under normal viewing conditions. Experiments with other illusions under similar conditions have not obtained reliable depth responses, however (Green & Hoyle, 1963; Hotopf, 1966), and, in any case, the fact that some patterns *can* produce apparent depth under certain conditions does not prove that that is *why* they produce size distortions under other conditions. The conditions that determine whether primary or secondary scaling will occur; an independent and quantitative method of identifying the depth cues; a statement of the amount of distortion to be attributed to each cue, separately and in interaction—all of these are needed if the "misapplied constancy" theory is to constitute a serious advance over the old perspective and "unconscious inference" theories.

In summary, the perspective or constancy theories seem plausibly to explain many of the illusions, at least partially and qualitatively. There are illusions to which they do not seem immediately relevant, however, and we shall see that there are other explanations that apply equally well to the illusions to which the perspective theories are relevant.

Contrast and confusion theories   The fact that a subject can judge line lengths does not mean that he is necessarily responding to length as such: the areas of the regions divided by the line are also varying in one-to-one correspondence with the line's length, and he might, for example, be responding to the areas. The way in which the Müller-Lyer illusion varies with the angle (p. 458) is con-

sistent with the interpretation that the subject cannot narrow his attention down to the main lines, but is responding also to the areas included between the fins. However, using only half of the traditional pattern (*i* in Figure 12.38B), Erlebacher and Sekuler (1969) have shown that it is the distance *y* between the ends of the fins that is important: if *y* is held constant (by adjusting the lengths of the fins) while the angle *w* is varied, the illusion ceases to vary with the angle. In other words, the subject may base his length judgments on some compromise between 2 of the cues that are available to him for making "equals" judgments, namely the length of the main line and that of the gap *y* between the fins. This is much like what happens when he makes a judgment in an experiment on color constancy (p. 398), size constancy (p. 509), and so on (see Brunswik, 1956).

The "confusion" theory is similar in some respects to the explanation in terms of *confluence* that was originally proposed by Müller-Lyer. Helmholtz' explanation of many of the geometrical illusions was in terms of *contrast; confluence* (or *confluxion*) is essentially negative contrast. In this connection, the term *contrast* means that perceived differences between similar stimuli, or between those that do not appear to be clearly separate, are diminished. In the case of the geometrical illusions, any parts of a pattern that extend close to other parts, or that are only slightly smaller than the other stimuli to which they are being compared, are overestimated, by confluence. Parts of a pattern that are not close to other parts, or that are compared to other stimuli that are considerably larger than they are (within limits, see Ebbinghaus, 1913), will be underestimated (Virsu, 1967).

Are Illusions Determined by Stimulation?

At present, it seems premature to accept a single explanation for all or any of the illusions, a single "correction," which, when applied to our physical measures of the stimulus configuration, will enable us to predict what shapes will be perceived. In fact, to the de-

TABLE 12.1 ATTITUDE AND OBJECTIVE CONDITIONS FAVORING TOTAL AND PART-ISOLATING PERCEPTION

Main lines of Müller-Lyer	white	white	dark gray
Oblique lines	white	dark gray	white
Background	black	black	black
Average illusion under			
whole-perceiving attitude	4.95	2.20	7.66
part-isolating attitude	1.02	− .50	3.20

Each figure in the table is the average of 20–30 measurements, all on a single subject, but confirmed by results from other subjects. From Benussi, 1904.

gree that nonstimulus factors, such as the subjects' attitudes and the effects of practice, affect the existence and magnitude of illusions, attempts to predict the appearance of these patterns in terms of physical measures alone must be inadequate. Moreover, any theory of the illusion must encompass such effects, if they exist. Let us consider, therefore, the results of research on the roles that attitudes and practice play in the geometrical illusions.

Experimentally controlled attitudes of observation Benussi's subjects (1904) were instructed to observe the Müller-Lyer pattern in one case with a "whole-perceiving" attitude and in another case, with a "part-isolating" attitude. The illusion was greater when the subjects approached the experiment with the whole-perceiving than the part-isolating attitude (see also Brunswik). As the objective conditions made the isolation of the horizontal lines easy or difficult, the

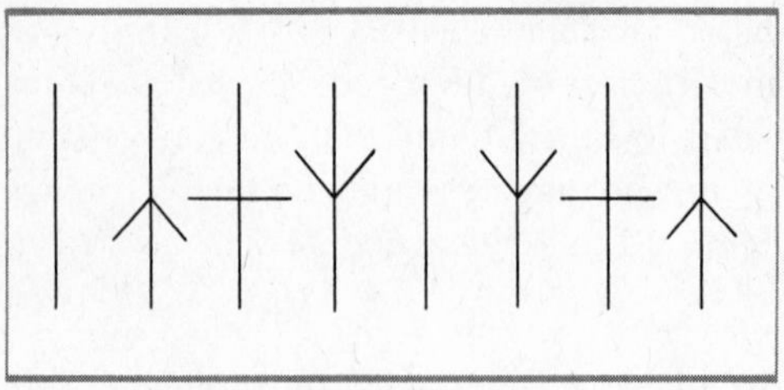

Figure 12.48. Successive positions of the Müller-Lyer element, shown in rapid succession, and giving an appearance of up and down movement of the point of intersection along with the apparent movement of the side lines. (Benussi, 1912.)

illusion itself diminished and increased, respectively, and so did the effectiveness of instructions to overcome it (Table 12.1). In a particularly interesting version of this attitudinal experiment, Benussi (1912) presented the Müller-Lyer figure in rapid succession as in the diagram in Figure 12.48, producing an apparent motion of the "arms." If subjects attend strictly to the lines, and regard the crossing point only as a pivot, the crossing point does not move when the arms do; however, if attention is directed to the changing shape of the total figure, the midpoint seems to glide along the vertical line, upward when the side lines move up and downward when the side lines move down.

It seems plausible at this point to account for the effects of different attitudes in terms of differences in the weight that subjects give to line versus arrowheads (or area) in making their judgments. Because these differential effects of attitude are quite large, even within a culture (Brunswik, 1956), it is difficult to assess how much of the variation in these illusions that has been found between cultures (see p. 460) may be due to differences in attitude and how much to perceptual learning. Changes in attitude may also account for some part of the phenomena we discuss next.

The practice experiments in illusions It has long been known that continued experience with 1 pattern diminishes the amount of the illusion it produces (Heymans, 1896), and several systematic studies of these practice effects have been performed.

Decrements in the magnitude of the illusions due to practice have been studied with the Müller-Lyer pattern (Judd, 1902, 1905; Lewis, 1908; Köhler & Fishback, 1950; Selkin & Wertheimer, 1957; Day, 1962), in the Poggendorf (Cameron & Steele, 1905), in the horizontal-vertical illusion (Seashore et al., 1908), and the Zoellner pattern (Judd & Courten, 1905). In general, the illusions all diminished very greatly, but only if the pattern was in the original position. If the figure were reversed right and left, the illusion returned in full strength, and in some subjects was exaggerated. However, in others the illusion was overcome by a relatively small amount of further practice. The illusion produced by the original figure was revived if the subject stood off and looked at it casually as a whole. Eye movement photographs showed that the subject was by no means passively receptive in viewing the figure. He explored it rather minutely, especially the part with the inward-slanting arrowheads (Judd, 1905). This minute examination of the figure diminished toward the end of practice.

What can account for the decrease in the illusions due to practice? No reinforcement of correct judgments, nor correction of errors, is overtly involved in these experiments. Why then does the illusion decrease with continued inspection? Three major explanations have been suggested.

One plausible explanation is that the subject gradually shifts to an analytic attitude during the practice of judging the illusion (Judd, 1905; Day, 1962), and restricts his attention to the horizontal lines by the use of techniques that are probably adapted to the specific left-right arrangement of the figure with which he is practicing.[9] More challenging explanations have been offered by Köhler and Fishback (1950), based on the assumption of a central "satiation" process, and by Coren

[9]When a subject moves his finger over a raised version of the Müller-Lyer pattern, an illusion is obtained that is similar to the visual one. Rudel and Teuber (1963) found that decrements in the illusion caused by practice obtained with this illusion of active touch—this *haptic* illusion—would transfer to a visual Müller-Lyer illusion, and vice versa. That is, practice with either modality resulted in a decrement not only in the version with which practice had been made (that is, visual or haptic), but in the other version as well. If the decrement is due to a restriction of attention to the horizontal lines, some degree of this restriction of attention would be expected to transfer from visual to haptic judgments, and *vice versa*.

and Festinger (1967), based on a correction of initially erroneous eye movements; we examine both of these explanations in the context of the figural aftereffects, which we consider next.

Shape Adaptation and Figural Aftereffects

The effects of practice on perceived shape have been studied for many years, with increasing diligence and very diverse goals in the last two decades. The aim of most of the research was to test what appeared to be a broad and powerful (if physiologically unorthodox and unconvincing) theory about the isomorphic Gestalt brain processes. The aftereffects thus took on their importance from the breadth of the perceptual theory that they seemed to test, that is, the Köhler-Wallach theory of figural aftereffects. From the beginning, however, many of the same phenomena were studied for quite a different reason, namely to test theories about how the different senses (particularly those of vision, kinesthesis, and proprioception) combine in the perception of space.

Shape adaptation and the learned bases of perceived direction In fact, the study of the effects of practice on shape perception really starts with the question of the relationship between touch and action on the one hand, and the perception of *visual direction* on the other. As we saw on page 427, one might think of a shape as being a set of local signs that identify the two-dimensional spatial location of each retinal element in a stimulus configuration. Wundt (1902) offered the following facts as evidence that the specific two-dimensional spatial meaning of each retinal element is not innate and fixed but rather is learned and changeable. When a subject is first made to wear prismatic glasses, straight lines appear bent and objects' shapes are thus distorted, due to the deformation that the prisms produce in the retinal image. These disturbances gradually disappear if the glasses are worn for some time. After the glasses are removed, distortions appear in the opposite direction even though the retinal image is now again undistorted. Why do these changes occur? Presumably because when a line is curved on the retina but is straight in the physical world, the observer's actions (and his resulting sensations of touch and kinesthesis) inform him of the discrepancy, and a curved configuration of retinal elements now comes to signify the actions by which we define an object's straightness.[10]

The nature of this perceptual learning of the spatial coordinates will concern us again in the next chapter. Before we consider the matter settled, however, let us ponder the issues raised by the following experiments.

Adaptation and aftereffects to curved and tilted lines In the course of research with prisms, Gibson (1933) noticed that adaptation occurred even without any action on the part of the observer. If the subject inspects a slightly curved line in a vertical position for a few minutes, by the end of the inspection period the line appears less curved than it did at first, and if a straight vertical line is then shown in the same place in the visual field, it appears to be curved in the opposite direction. Similar observations had been made by Verhoeff (1925). The loss of apparent curvature (that is, *the adaptation*) in the curved line being looked at during the inspection period was equal to the opposite apparent curvature (the *negative aftereffect*) that a straight line appeared to have when it was shown to the subject just after the inspection period. (This was measured by having the subject adjust a flexible rod to appear straight.) The aftereffect, strong at first, faded out gradually. The same kinds of aftereffect occur whether the curves are vertical, horizontal, or obliquely presented. Similar effects

[10]In fact, because of the optics of the eye, and of the constraints of the muscle system that moves it, straight lines in the environment do not, in general, project straight lines in the retinal image, even in normal (undistorted) viewing. It seems likely, therefore, that whether a given configuration at some point on the retina results in an impression of straightness or curvature is always determined by what our actions with objects, that are really straight in physical space, have taught us about the meaning of that configuration (see Chapter 13, p. 543; also, Helmholtz, 1866; Lamb, 1918; Roberts & Suppes, 1967).

have been found for lines tilted from the vertical or horizontal. These lose their tilt during prolonged inspection, after which a true vertical appears to tilt in the opposite direction (Vernon, 1934; Gibson, 1937; Gibson & Radner, 1937). We concern ourselves with these tilt effects again in the next chapter. For now, consider the implications of the curvature aftereffects described by Gibson. The aftereffect seemed to be limited to lines that have the same general direction and that are in the same retinal region as was stimulated by the inspection line. (This last restriction has since been shown to be invalid in the case of tilted lines [Morant and Mikaelian, 1960].)

This phenomenon seems to imply exactly the opposite explanation from that given by Wundt (1902); here, the line that is curved on the retina is in reality also curved in physical space. Why should continued inspection then teach the observer to see *unveridically*, that is, to see a curved line as straight? Gibson proposed that shape itself is a sensory response, like temperature or hue or brightness, and that it is merely showing the sensory

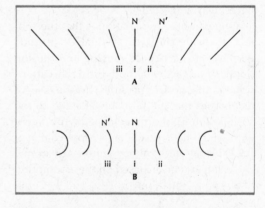

Figure 12.49. Gibson's normalization theory of aftereffects. A. The slant dimension. B. The curvature dimension. After exposure to a line (*ii*), that line tends to be perceived as the neutral point (*N*) on the dimension in question. Because the entire scale of psychophysical correspondence between the physical and perceived dimensions is displaced, the stimulus that was previously seen as neutral (*i*) now has the same appearance that some non-neutral stimulus (*iii*) had before the shift occurred. (Adapted from Gibson, 1950.)

adaptation that is common to such responses (see Chapters 5 and 9). He suggests that a visual line or border has two variable qualities in addition to that of length, namely its place on a continuum that runs from *left-slant* to *right-slant* (Figure 12.49A) and from *convex* to *concave* (Figure 12.49B). These qualities presumably change in the same way as do blue-gray-yellow and warm-neutral-cold during and after prolonged stimulation. That is, adaptation and aftereffects of curvature and tilt result because the neutral point has shifted (Figure 12.49), and what we might call *normalization* of the inspected shape has occurred.

If such normalization occurs with curved lines on the retina seen without distorting prisms, we should expect it to occur as well when the curvature is produced by prisms. Wundt's example would then become a case of adaptation to shape as such, not a proof that visual direction is subject to relearning. We next examine 2 alternative explanations of the curvature adaptation and aftereffects that do not invoke "normalization," but we should note that in any case Held and Rekosh (1963) have found adaptation to distortion of curvature, with prisms, that simply cannot be due to the normalization of curved lines. Indeed, in their procedure, the subject sees no lines at all, either straight or curved: he sees only a random array of spheres (p. 542). Under these conditions, adaptation depends on the subject's being active while wearing prisms, so that Wundt's argument (that the subject can relearn "straightness") remains defensible.

One alternative explanation for the Gibson effect questions the original interpretation, namely that practice leads to illusory perception. Coren and Festinger (1967) showed that the curvature of a line segment is initially *overestimated,* that is, that there is an initial illusion, and that the "normalization" that occurs with continued inspection brings the subject's judgment closer to the actual curvature, not away from it. This is just the kind of practice decrement that we have seen to be characteristic of many of the geometrical

illusions (p. 464). Why should such correction of perceptual error occur when the subject has no way of knowing that he is wrong? The Coren and Festinger explanation is an ingenious one: If the curvature is overestimated (or for that matter, if the lengths are incorrectly estimated in the Müller-Lyer pattern in Figure 12.38) and if eye movements that are made from one point on the pattern to another are guided by these mistaken estimates, such saccades (p. 453) will consistently be found to be in error at their terminal fixation, until suitable recalibration of visual direction is achieved and curvature is correctly seen. The question of why the illusions occur in the first place, and why they are not already corrected by this hypothesized process, long before the subject comes to the experiment, then remains to be answered. Coren and Festinger adopt the perspective theory (that curves act in *primary scaling* [p. 462] as though they were tilted in depth), but in any case, their explanation of the shape aftereffect brings us back to the illusions.[11]

The second explanation for the Gibson effect is the "satiation" theory, an explanation

[11] Festinger, White, and Allyn (1968) have in fact shown that subjects' eye movements tend to overshoot the ends of *ii* in Figure 12.38B, and to undershoot the ends of *i*, when they first start to scan the pattern. These errors decrease as scanning continues. Because Festinger and his colleagues maintain that any contour's perceived location in the visual field is given by the eye movements that the subject is prepared to make in order to fixate the contour, the practice decrement in the illusion simply reflects the correction of the scanning errors. McLaughlin, DeSisto, and Kelly (1969) have challenged this interpretation because of the fact that subjects who are experimentally trained to make a 5° eyemovement in order to fixate a target that was presented 10° in the periphery (the target being shifted to a location at 5° after the subject initates the eye movement) fail to show any effects of this training in the way in which they point at the target with their (unseen) hands (McLaughlin et al., 1968). This argument is not conclusive because it tells us only that hand movements and eye movements are not necessarily guided in the same way by the same visual display. It does not tell us what the display looks like (see Chapter 13, p. 537). In any case, however, it now seems plausible that the decrement occurs because the subjects' eye movements provide information about the illusion. However, Bolles (1969) has shown that the illusion is still about 20 percent in initial viewing when the figure is only 0.5° in extent and falls entirely within the fovea. It would be interesting, therefore, to know whether decrements occur with such small figures, inasmuch as the scanning errors involved could not be more than 0.1°, which is within the range in which the eye normally cannot make and hold fixations very well (see Chapter 11, p. 387).

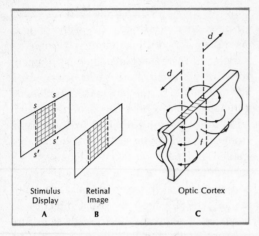

Figure 12.50. The Köhler-Wallach satiation theory of aftereffects. A region of different luminance in the stimulus display, A, produces a region of different bioelectric activity in the optic cortex of the brain, C, causing current flow between the figural region, *f*, and the adjacent tissue. As the current flow continues, the resistance of the adjacent tissue rises, and this process of satiation forces the current further from the original contours. When the stimulus is removed, the persistent satiation will divert the current flow associated with subsequently-viewed stimulus patterns away from that region, as shown by the arrows at *d*.

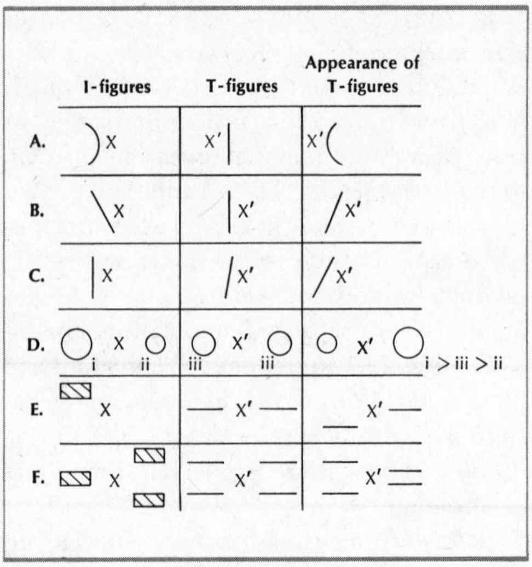

that will also eventually lead us back in a different way to the illusions. This theory has generated a great deal of research in its own right, and offers a very different picture of how shape perception occurs.

The satiation theory of the figural aftereffects   Köhler had proposed in 1920 that electrical fields and currents in the visual cortex of the brain are the basis of form perception (see Figure 12.50; also Köhler, 1920, 1940). Both the Gibson effect (in which the same peripheral stimulation comes to produce a changed shape) and the phenomenon of figural reversal (in which different regions of the field alternate as figure even though the stimulus pattern remains unchanged [see p. 433]) seemed to Köhler to be readily explained in terms of such electrical currents (Köhler, 1940; Köhler & Wallach, 1944).

Figure 12.51. Figural aftereffects. The patterns in the first column are *inspection figures,* with fixation points at *X;* the second column shows *test figures* with fixation points at *X;* and the third shows the direction of the aftereffect (exaggerated in magnitude).

These currents would be generated by potential differences between different parts of the visual cortex, potential differences that are in turn produced by differences in excitation of different parts of the retina. Current flow produces *satiation* (an increased resistance to further current flow) in the tissue in the area adjacent to the boundary or contour (Köhler & Wallach, 1944). As satiation increases, current flow is diverted to less satiated regions, so that satiation spreads progressively. In a reversible figure (p. 432), reversal occurs when satiation reaches some level and, as the new region satiates in turn, reversal continues (Köhler, 1944).

Köhler and Wallach (1944) expanded this explanation to include Gibson's results with a broad class of phenomena they called *figural aftereffects.* In general, the subject fixates some point, *X,* on an inspection (*I*) figure, for a few minutes, and then fixates a point *X'* on the test (*T*) figure (Figure 12.51). The satiation of the tissue surrounding the projection of the *I* figure would force the currents generated by any subsequent *T* figure into the less-satiated region. As a consequence of this displacement of figural currents, the perceived locations of the contours change.[12] The contours of the *T* figure are in general displaced away from the regions that were previously satiated by the contours of the *I* figure. The amount that the *T* figure is displaced increases to a maximum at some short distance away from the *I* figure, and then decreases with a further increase in the distance (this is called the "distance paradox"). A survey of *I* figures, *T* figures, and the appearance of the latter after satiation, is given in Figure 12.51. The aftereffects in Figures 12.51C look very much like the normalization effects of Gibson, and of Gibson and Radner, except that they do not seem to follow from normalization (because *I* is already vertical, it should not affect the neutral point; see Figure 12.49), and they do seem to fit the rubric of contour displacement. The normalization effects might thus simply be instances of the figural aftereffects produced by satiation.

One effect of prolonged viewing remains to be explained by satiation theory, namely the decrement in the geometrical illusions due to practice. Köhler and Fishback (1950) propose that, in the Müller-Lyer pattern, satiation would build up more rapidly within the **V** than in front of its point. The resulting contour displacement would push the **V** outward, in effect. Thus, in the example shown in Figure 12.38B, the space between the points of the 2 **V**s on the right would be decreased by prolonged inspection, while the space between those on the left would be increased. They demonstrated that the reduction was not due to the subjects' practice in *comparing* the 2 parts of the Müller-Lyer figure with each other, for only one part of the figure was exposed at a time (except during a few test trials), and this separate

inspection procedure seemed to destroy the illusion as quickly as when many simultaneous comparisons of the 2 halves were made. It must therefore be the steady inspection per se, and not the comparison process, that destroys the illusion. Note that the satiation theory only attempts to explain the practice decrement, not the illusion itself.

The *satiation theory* had the appeal of covering a wide range of phenomena: In addition to figure-ground reversal and figural aftereffects, it also seemed to make predictions about shape recognition thresholds (p. 443) and about practice effects in the geometrical illusions. It also seemed to show the kind of nonlocal action (action at a distance, or lateral effects) that Gestalt theory demanded (p. 428). This explanation seemed in some respects to be a real first step in exploring the brain processes that Gestalt theory assumed to underlie all perceptual phenomena and with which it hoped to replace the specific nerve energies of the structuralist theory (p. 428). A great many studies on the figural aftereffects (FAE) have been performed, both in the visual modality and in other senses (for example, by presenting *I* objects and *T* objects for the fingers to explore), and we would lose the sense of the purpose of exploring these effects if we attempted to review them in any representative fashion. We shall merely list some areas of inquiry, and otherwise refer the reader to critical reviews by Sagara & Oyama, 1957; McEwen, 1958; Spitz, 1958; Day, Pollack, & Seagrim, 1959.

The size of the FAE depends on the distance between *I* and *T* contours, first increasing and then decreasing with distance (Köhler & Wallach, 1944; Sagara & Oyama, 1957). It increases rapidly as the duration of the inspection period is increased up to 1 minute, then tends to level off. In general, the effect decreases as the interval between the *I* and *T* figure increases (Bales & Follansbee, 1935), after passing through a maximum shortly after the presentation of the *I* figure is terminated (Hammer, 1949; Ikeda & Obonai, 1953; Fehrer & Ganchrow, 1963; Farnè, 1965). The shorter the duration of the presentation of the *T* figure, the greater the aftereffect (Parducci & Brookshire, 1956; Farne, 1965); in fact, Farnè re-

---

[12]Strictly speaking, the cortical locations of the contours are not presumed to move; instead, the density of the "interrelationship" between 2 cortical regions determines their apparent nearness (Köhler & Wallach, 1944), and satiation was thought to change the density distribution in the cortex.

ports that subjects who do not perceive an after-effect with the usual viewing times of 30 seconds to 2 minutes, observe strong aftereffects with exposures of 0.12 second. The FAE increases with an increase in the difference between the luminances of the *I* figure and of its background (Nozawa, 1953; Hochberg & Triebel, 1955; Pollack, 1958; Yoshida, 1960; Graham, 1961; Day, 1962; Gibb, Freeman, & Adam, 1966) and decreases with an increased difference between the *T*-figure and its background (Gibb et al., 1966). It is not affected by the luminance of the *I* figure if the luminance difference is kept at a constant proportion of the luminance (Graham, 1961). Individual differences in FAE (and their relationship to other perceptual measures, such as the ability to detect embedded figures or to set a rod to the vertical when it is surrounded by a tilted framework; see Witkin et al., 1954; and Chapter 13, p. 539n) have been investigated with various purposes, often in hopes of finding general individual differences in cortical functioning (see Immergluck, 1966a, b). Because naïve subjects who have not been specifically set to expect FAEs may not even notice them (Dodwell & Gaze, 1965; Gaze & Dodwell, 1965), we cannot tell whether individual differences in reporting FAE reflect differences in the occurrence of the figural aftereffect as such (and in the underlying physiological processes) or differences in the set with which those subjects approach the perceptual task.

Criticisms of the satiation theory The satiation theory must be criticized on several grounds. While it cannot yet be discarded in its entirety, it is now evident that it cannot be retained intact, either as to substance or promise.

First, objections to the physiological explanation have been raised by Smith (1948), Hebb (1949), and most seriously by Lashley, Chow, and Semmes (1951). The latter made explicit the very serious anatomical difficulties that the theory faces (for example, the necessity for an appropriate current to flow across the various distances in the cortex, where there are gross separations). They also showed that after gold foil and gold pins were inserted into monkeys' occipital surfaces to produce tne short-circuits or other rearrangements of figural currents that we would expect from the satiation theory, no impair-

ment of pattern vision was found. Similar conclusions follow from the research of Sperry and Miner (1955) and Sperry, Miner, and Meyers (1955). Various rebuttals may be attempted, but the fact is that each additional bit of information we acquire about the structure of the visual cortex (see Chapter 9) makes the figural current-flow theory less plausible.

We might nevertheless retain the satiation theory, not as an hypothesis about real physiological events, but as a model which seems to account for various perceptual phenomena. However, the satiation theory fails in this respect, too: Consider, in turn, its ability to predict the full range of figural aftereffects; the phenomena of figure-ground reversal; the normalization phenomena; and the practice decrement in the illusions.

Figural aftereffects in visual depth and in other modalities Figural aftereffects occur not only with flat figures, as in Figure 12.51, but in depth as well (Köhler & Emery, 1947; Fernberger, 1948). After subjects have fixated an *I* figure at some distance from them, a subsequently viewed *T* figure that is slightly farther away is displaced so as to appear still farther, and one that is slightly nearer than the *I* figure is displaced still nearer.[13] The electrical model simply cannot be taken seriously in this context. Furthermore, very similar FAEs occur in other modalities that do not permit this kind of cortical projection. These are FAEs which the satiation model cannot explain; see Köhler (1958). Thus one must question the value of the model: too many classes of phenomena are beyond its powers to explain, even though they are very similar to the phenomena for which it does seem able to account.

---

[13] The conditions used by Köhler and Emery may have produced the aftereffects in depth solely as a result of FAEs in the frontal plane (Farnè, 1965a; Osgood & Heyer, 1952). For example, when the *T*-figure was presented nearer than an *I*-figure of the same size, the contours of the *T*-figure would fall outside those of the *I*-figure and cause the latter to appear smaller and hence further than it really was. This kind of explanation is less readily applied to a set of experiments in which the *I*-figures were textured surfaces, viewed at a slant, through windows that concealed the surfaces' edges. Following inspection of such slanted surfaces, *T*-surfaces in the frontal plane appeared to be oppositely slanted (Bergman & Gibson, 1959; Farnè & Giaminoni, 1968).

Figural reversal and perspective reversal If reversal results from the satiation of cortical regions corresponding to each perceptual organization, figural reversal should increase as viewing time is increased, according to Köhler's theory, but results do not clearly support this prediction. Prior inspection of 1 of the 2 figural alternatives should reduce the proportion of the time during which that alternative is seen when the reversible figure is subsequently viewed, and something like that in fact occurs with flat patterns (Hochberg, 1950). On the other hand, a very similar phenomenon occurs in three dimensions: *ambiguous perspective pictures* (such as the "wire objects" in Figure 12.19) also are reversed spontaneously while the subject regards them. With such stimuli, prolonged exposure to one of the alternatives similarly affects subsequent reversals (Carlson, 1953; Howard, 1961; Orbach, Ehrlich, & Heath, 1963). It is unlikely that the electrical theory of satiation could explain such phenomena. We have seen (p. 468) that *I* and *T* patterns must fall on the same retinal regions in order to obtain the aftereffects, but the processes that are responsible for perspective reversal continue to occur even when the patterns are displaced to different regions of the retina and cortex (Orbach, Ehrlich, & Vainstein, 1963; Kolers, 1964), and reversals occur even while the pattern is in the process of being displaced from one region to another (Kolers, 1964). Some form of "fatigue" or other cumulative process may be involved in perceptual reversal, but it does not seem to derive in any specific way from the electrical-satiation model.

Normalization phenomena It remains an open question whether or not the Gibson effect can be completely subsumed under the contour-displacement rubric. Most of the research that is relevant to this issue has been concerned with tilt, not with curvature, and we discuss it in the next chapter (p. 538), merely noting here that it now appears that *both* contour displacement and normalization seem to be demonstrable as tilt aftereffects.

Practice decrement Decrement in the Müller-Lyer illusion due to practice has, as we have noted before (p. 465) also been obtained with haptically inspected stimuli (Rudel & Teuber, 1963), and the electrical-satiation model makes no provision for intermodal transfer. Moreover, the Köhler-Fishback stimulus subtended a visual angle of 3°, whereas Judd's was 26° (p. 465). Although the difference in size may account for the fact that the illusion was de-

creased much more rapidly with the former, we cannot be sure that satiation alone could ever produce a sufficiently strong decrement to account for the reduction of the illusion, in a figure that large, by contour-displacement alone.[14]

The electrical theory of satiation proposed by Köhler and his colleagues does not, in short, provide the general and inclusive explanation of adaptation, aftereffects, and perceptual reversal that it once seemed to offer. Even if this theory had proved to be more successful in dealing with the aftereffects, it still failed even to make a start on the very problems with which Gestalt psychologists had most cogently confronted structuralist explanations of shape perception: The electrical satiation theory deals only with events at specific places on the retina, and in fact the figural aftereffects are determined mostly or entirely by the pattern of retinal stimulation.[15] The problems of transposition, of organization, of the constancy of shape and of size—all of these must be removed to some secondary stage of processing, to some part of the nervous system other than the part that handles the shape and its aftereffects. This picture is not appreciably closer to what the Gestalt theorists held that a systematic theory of perception should be like than were the theories of Wundt and Helmholtz.

Let us briefly consider the alternatives to

[14] Inasmuch as the illusions can be presented without luminance-difference contours (for example, by means of the binocularly produced edge: described on page 432 [Hochberg, 1966; Pappert, 1961] and by the successive-aperture viewing procedures described on page 455), and inasmuch as we would expect to obtain little or no satiation or figural aftereffects without luminance-difference contours (Hochberg & Triebel, 1955), such procedures should permit us to estimate how much of the decrement due to practice, if any, can be attributed to satiation.

[15] For example, if 2 objects of the same physical size are viewed at different distances, and their retinal images are therefore of different sizes, their apparent sizes do not differ as much as their retinal sizes do (see size constancy, p. 509). If we take the Gestalt principle of *isomorphism* seriously (p. 428), both the electrical brain processes and the resulting satiation effects should be reflected by the objects' apparent sizes. Nevertheless, if retinal size is varied independently of physical size by changing the relative distance of *I* and *T* figures from the observer, it is the retinal size that determines what aftereffects will result (Prentice, 1950; Hochberg & Bitterman, 1951; Terwilliger, 1961).

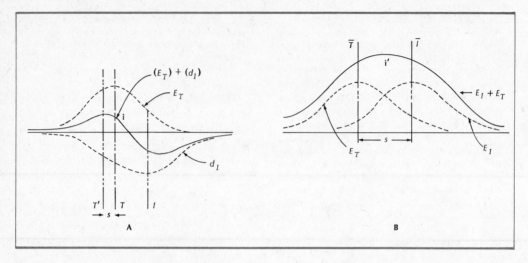

Figure 12.52. Osgood-Heyer theory of the aftereffects. A. The cortical distributions of excitation that would be produced by the T-figure alone is shown by E_T. Because the depression left by the I-figure (shown by d_I) is subtracted from this, the resultant distribution (shown by $i = E_T + d_I$) is displaced so that its peak falls at T' instead of at T. The aftereffect is s. B. Deutsch (1956) pointed out that this would imply that two simultaneously presented contours, separated by the amount s, should not be distinguishable. See text.

the satiation theory, bearing in mind that what made the figural aftereffects most interesting was that they were offered as evidence for a general theory of perception and that none of the alternative theories really fits that description.

Alternatives to the electrical satiation theory These fall into 3 general classes. First, there is the eye-movement and excitation-spread theory proposed by Osgood and Heyer (1952). This theory maintains that each contour that confronts the eye is projected to the optic cortex in a normal distribution of excitation (Figure 12.52A). The cortical projection is spread out partly because rapid involuntary eye movements occur which move the contour around on the retina (see Chapter 11, p. 386) and partly because of the way the nervous system proliferates connections between the retina and the cortex. The contour itself is perceived at the *peak* (I) of the cortical distribution. Prolonged inspection of an I figure leaves a region of fatigue or depressed excitability in the cortex. This depression subtracts from the distribution of excitation that is later produced by

the T figure, and thereby displaces its peak away from that of the I figure's distribution.

An empirical criticism of this theory can be made concerning the function it ascribes to eye movements. Eye-movement fluctuation is certainly not essential to obtaining FAE: FAEs (like those of Figure 12.51D) can be obtained with stimuli that are fixed in their retinal locations (Hochberg & Hay, 1956; Krauskopf, 1960; Ganz, 1964). Similarly, Farnè's report (1964) that stronger FAEs are obtained with I and T figures exposed at 0.12 second (during which no substantial eye movements can occur) than are obtained with longer exposures is inconsistent with an explanation that depends on eye movements. Moreover, Krauskopf (1954) found contour displacements of almost 13 minutes of arc (visual angle), using a display similar to Figure 12.51F with briefly exposed T figures. As he pointed out, eye-movement fluctuation could only be expected to account for something less than 4 minutes of visual angle.

In addition, Deutsch (1956) found a theoretical flaw. Figure 12.52A illustrates the peak shift caused by summation of the I figure's excitation and the depression left by the T

figure, according to the Osgood-Heyer theory. However, if the contour occurs at the distribution peak, and the distributions overlap each other enough to cause a peak shift, as in Figure 12.52A, they also overlap so much that if the I and T figures had been presented not successively but simultaneously, as in Figure 12.52B, the summing of their distributions of excitation would produce only 1 peak (i'), not 2. This means that only 1 contour would be seen. The minimum separation that can be detected between lines is about 1 minute of arc, (see p. 299), yet much larger FAE displacements can be obtained, over much larger separations between I and T figures: Krauskopf (1954) obtained displacements of 12.6 minutes over a distance of 15.8 minutes, and Heinemann and Marill (1954) obtained what they take to be FAEs over a distance of about 240 minutes. On the other hand, George (1962) showed that subjects cannot distinguish the separation between lines that are as much as 24 minutes of arc apart (at places 13° and 20° away from the fixation point) under "fatigue" conditions like the prolonged fixations usually used in FAE experiments, so that the Osgood and Heyer theory might be salvaged by adding this amendment: Under fatigue conditions, excitation distributions spread much farther from the contour. However, this still leaves unsolved problems. For example, how does the subject resolve the single line itself, and how does he detect that it has been displaced by an amount that is (under these "fatigue" conditions) smaller than the spatial distances he can distinguish between lines? And how are FAEs obtained with short exposures?

Recently, several attempts have been made to explain both the FAE contour displacements and at least some of the geometrical illusions, in terms of *lateral inhibition*—the mechanism by which the excitation of one neural region depresses the activity of adjacent regions (Chapter 9, p. 292). Various models have been proposed by Day (1962), Deutsch, (1964), and Ganz (1965, 1966a, b).

Ganz has offered the most complete and detailed theory of this kind. The FAEs are examples of shape contrast (a proposal made also by Freeman, 1964); that is, they are a class of geometrical illusions that occur as a result of the interaction between the T figure and the afterimage of the I figure. Both Gibson (1933) and Köhler and Wallach (1944) thought that the FAE could not be due to afterimages or to retinal fatigue because the FAE occurs when the I figure is viewed by one eye and the T figure is viewed by the other. This conclusion is questionable, however (Day, 1958), because afterimages themselves show interocular transfer (Hansen, 1954). In fact, Terwilliger (1963) demonstrated that afterimages in one eye interact with stimuli presented to the other eye: In the familiar demonstration of the relationship between size and distance (Emmert's Law; see Chapter 13) the apparent size of an afterimage that is produced by a bright light is found to vary directly with the distance from the subject of any surface at which he looks after receiving the afterimage. Terwilliger showed that it makes no difference whether the subject looks at that surface with the eye in which the afterimage was entered, or with the other eye. If an afterimage of the I figure interacts with the subsequently viewed T figure, so that the displacements are due to a simultaneous rather than a successive interaction between the 2 patterns, the FAEs reduce to a class of the geometrical illusions (Verhoeff, 1925; Ganz, 1965, 1966a, b; Howard & Templeton, 1966).

This is not to say that the FAEs amount simply to the simultaneous viewing of I and T figures. For one thing, whatever the effects are that produce afterimages, the latter are not always noticeable, even though the effects that underlie them may persist. For another, the eye is in continual motion during both the inspection and the test periods. These movements will decide the distribution of the afterimage left by the I figure and will therefore determine the interaction of that distribution with the T figure. To the degree that different attitudes toward the I figure (for example, whether the pattern is a B or a 13) affect these eye movements, differences in

FAE would be expected, and the fact that such differences occur (Story, 1959) therefore does not constitute an insuperable difficulty for this theory.

An afterimage decays with a characteristic course that is a function of the intensity of stimulation; its onset has definite temporal characteristics, and the FAE must show intensity and onset and decay effects that are consonant with these characteristics if afterimages are to be implicated in the aftereffects. These constraints raise specific and quantitative questions, which Ganz has attempted to answer specifically and quantitatively (1966). For the moment, the case seems well made, as far as it goes. It should be noted, however, that the adequacy of this theory has been challenged on the grounds that the geometrical illusions and the FAEs do not vary in the same way as a function of the subject's age (Pollack, 1967), and it is true that the relation between the simultaneous illusions and successive displacement effects generated by the various illusion patterns has not been systematically explored.

AN OVERVIEW

In this chapter we have reviewed efforts to explain the perception of the colors and shapes of objects. An early and influential approach was one which attempted to explain and predict the appearance of any object or scene in terms of the appearances of each of the small homogeneous patches of stimulation into which the retinal image can be analyzed and to which the visual system was thought to be directly sensitive. That is, the explanation of visual perception started with what we might call the "elementary sensory mosaic." This approach generated a set of classical problems. In general, these problems arose because subjects' judgments about objects' attributes were discrepant with what the mosaic explanation would lead one to expect. With respect to object color, the major problems are those of *color constancy* and *contrast.* With respect to shape, the major

problems of this kind are those of *transposition, figure-ground organization,* the *illusions,* and *shape constancy* (which we discuss in the next chapter). Additional problems arise because of difficulties in identifying the appropriate stimulus and response measures: the problems associated with the attempt to establish a psychophysics of shape perception.

Three general kinds of solution to these problems can be distinguished from each other. (1) A cognitive explanation can be made in which the observer corrects the aggregate of appearances of the sensory mosaic in accordance with his knowledge of the objective physical stimulus situation. That knowledge is presumably based on characteristic features of the stimulus pattern, called *cues,* which the subject's past experiences have taught him to interpret even though he may not be aware of those features. (2) A sensory explanation can be made that seeks to show that the discrepancy occurs because the visual system responds directly to some variable in the stimulation other than the elements of the sensory mosaic. (3) An organizational theory can be proposed in which the entire visual system responds to the entire configuration of sensory stimulation, so that there is no necessary consistent relationship between the characteristics of stimulation at one region of the retinal image and the appearance of the corresponding part of the visual field. The appearance of any portion of the stimulus pattern thus rests on a number of proposed determinants of organization, or on a more general *minimum principle* (that we perceive the simplest arrangement consistent with the pattern of stimulation).

None of these general solutions can be fully accepted nor fully rejected at present. In the set of problems that we have considered, the distinctions between them are often hard to maintain. We shall encounter similar problems and pursue the same general solutions further when we consider the perception of space, motion, and orientation in the next chapter.

Julian Hochberg

PERCEPTION

II. SPACE AND MOVEMENT

13

FORMULATING THE PROBLEMS OF VISUAL DEPTH

Artists, philosophers, and psychologists have long been challenged by the everyday fact of three-dimensional seeing. The problem is set by the very structure of the eye, which forms an optical image on a two-dimensional surface, the *retina*. Such a mechanism can indicate the *direction* from which a beam of light comes, but not, in any obvious way, the distance that extends from the eye to some visible object. The difficulty is made clear by Figure 13.1. That points A_1 and B_1 lie at different directions in space is easily detected by the fact that their retinal images a and b fall on different parts of the retina. But how can the subject possibly tell, of points A_1, A_2, A_3, which is nearest and which is farthest from his eye?

The Use of Depth Cues

Laboratory studies of visual depth and distance perception are often concerned with the stimulus variables that make this possible, the signs or cues (p. 402) of an object's distance. How shall we discover and evaluate these cues? Why not ask the subject to tell us what cues he is using when he judges one object to be more distant than another? The trouble is that he usually cannot tell. He may even assert that he needs no cues,

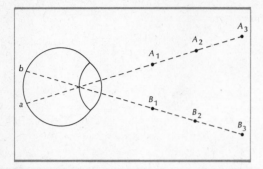

Figure 13.1. The problem of depth perception. The images from all points on a given line, as A_1, A_2, A_3, fall on the retinal point, a. Hence, the retinal point can indicate only the direction of an object, not its distance from the eye.

for he sees the distance of the object directly (he is mistaken here, as our previous analysis has shown). In fact, the training of an artist used to consist, in large part, of learning the rules for portraying depth, which are actually the depth cues themselves.

The depth cues were first studied to help artists portray depth and distance on a flat canvas. Leonardo da Vinci (1452–1519) advised the following experiment:

Go into the country, select objects situated at distances of 100, 200 yards, etc. . . . place a sheet of glass firmly in front of you, keep the eye fixed in location, and trace the outline of a tree on the glass. . . . Now move the glass to the side just enough to allow the tree to be seen beside

its tracing, and color your drawing to duplicate the color and relief of the object. . . . Follow the same procedure in painting the second and third trees situated at the greater distances. Preserve these paintings on glass as aids and teachers in your work.

Leonardo took note of practically all of the depth and distance cues that can be utilized by the painter. Let us set out the depth and distance cues in a single context:

Figure 13.2A is a side view of a scene. Figure 13.2B is a tracing of the scene shown in part A, drawn on the "picture plane" of glass (P) held between the eye and the scene. An examination of the tracings on the picture plane shows us the cues that might be employed by the painter; some of these are listed below, and discussed briefly. Figure 13.2C is the *retinal image*, which is the point of contact between the visual world and the nervous system.

These illustrations help us make the distinction between *proximal* and *distal stimulus variables*. In Figure 13.2A the various spatial arrangements comprise the *distal* stimulation: objects' physical sizes, shapes, distances, and slants. (In general, we shall use the word *distance* to mean the absolute spatial extent between the observer and the object; *depth* will refer to the relative spatial extent between two points in space, for example, between *4* and *5* in Figure 13.2A). In Figure 13.2B

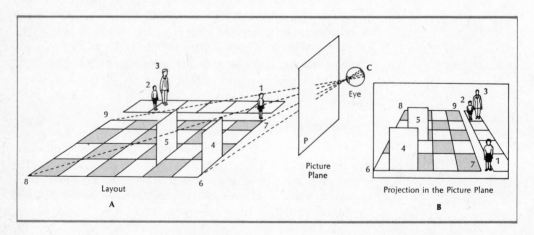

Figure 13.2. Distal layout and its projection in the picture plane and retinal image.

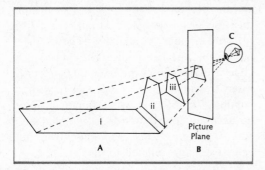

Figure 13.3. Different spatial layouts at *A* all project the same two-dimensional patterns in the picture plane *B* and on the retina *C*.

the tracing (a distal stimulus) provides the eye with the same proximal stimulus pattern as does the layout at A. Note that mathematically the proximal stimulus pattern must be ambiguous because, in each case, as in Figure 13.2A and B (and in any intermediate arrangements, such as the various alternatives at *i*, *ii*, and *iii* in Figure 13.3A), very different *distal* layouts may produce identical visual images on the retina C.

The "tracing" in Figure 13.2B shows us a number of familiar depth and distance cues: *linear perspective* (the fact that the lines converge, so that the distance between *8* and *9* is smaller than between *6* and *7*); *interposition* or covering that occurs because *4* is nearer than, and in front of, *5*; size, the fact that the image of the boy at *1* is about twice as tall as that of the boy at *2*; *texture gradient,* the steady rate of increase of the density in the image of the texture, running from less dense at the bottom (*6–7*) to more dense at the top (*8–9*) of the picture.

Apparent Size and Apparent Distance

Many of these cues follow from the geometry that relates size and distance, as shown in Figure 13.4 (see also Figure 9.6, Chapter 9). There, S is the size (length or width) of the object, D is the distance of the object, while s is the size of the retinal image and n is the distance from the optical nodal point of the eye to the retina. Then $s/n = S/D$ and, because n depends on the size of the eyeball and is constant, $s = n(S/D)$. In other words, the size of the retinal image is proportional to the ratio of object size to distance, and this ratio for all small angles is the tangent of the visual angle subtended by the object (see p. 279). Relative size, linear perspective, and so on, may all be reduced to the same general formula. For example, on a railroad track, the ties are a series of objects of equal size. Because S is constant and D increases, each railroad tie must subtend successively smaller visual angles. Although the retinal size changes with changes in distance, the *apparent* or *judged* size tends to remain constant. It is as though the distance were being "taken into account" in judging size.

In this chapter, we shall examine the following: first, the distance cues and their effects; the perception of movement, and of a stationary world; and finally, we survey what is known about the dependence of space perception on past experience.

NONVISUAL CUES OF DEPTH AND DISTANCE

Accommodation

The motor aspects of accommodation and convergence are treated in Chapter 11. Here we discuss them as cues for the judgment of distance.

Berkeley (1709) had pointed out 2 possible muscular cues to the perception of depth, namely convergence and accommodation. The conception was that the subject adjusted his accommodation and convergence until he had a sharp and single image of the object,

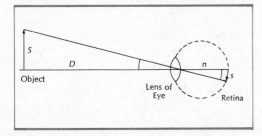

Figure 13.4. The geometry of visual size and depth. See text.

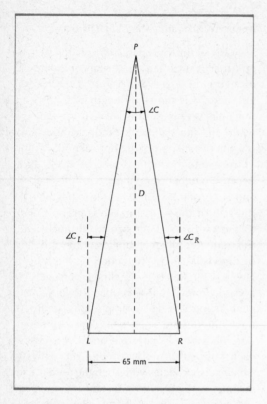

Figure 13.5. The angle of convergence and the distance of the fixated object. *P* is the object; *L* and *R* are the eye positions, assumed to be 65 mm apart (interpupillary distance). In converging upon *P* the left eye turns inward by the angle C_L, the right eye by the angle C_R, and the sum of these angles (which are equal if the observer is facing directly toward the object) is the total convergence and equals the angle *C*. Given the distance *D*, $\angle C$ can be computed; or given this angle the distance can be computed. The computation can use this formula: $\tan \angle C/2 = 32.5/D$, 32.5 mm being half the interocular distance. However, it is more convenient and sufficiently accurate for most purposes to treat the interocular distance, *LR*, as the arc of a circle, with *D* in millimeters as the radius, so that $\angle C = 65/D$, when expressed in radian units. A radian = approximately 57.3°, and more exactly 206,265 angular sec. So we have the following formulas:

(1) Given *D* in mm, to find $\angle C$ in sec,

$$\angle C = \frac{65}{D} \times 206{,}265 = \frac{13{,}407{,}225}{D} \text{ sec}$$

(2) Given $\angle C$ in sec, to find *D* in mm,

and then he judged the object's distance on the basis of the sensation of muscular strain from the eye muscles. Can these cues actually be used in distance perception? In order to attack the question experimentally, it is necessary to eliminate the *visual cues* (p. 480), if possible, to discover what impressions of distance are contributed by accommodation and convergence. This requirement turns out to be extremely difficult to meet.

In order to obtain a clear picture of an object, a camera must be focused for the distance of the object, and the same is true of the eye, which focuses on an object by changing the convexity of the lens. This adjustment, called *accommodation,* is accomplished by the ciliary muscle. If the object is relatively distant (more than 2 yards or so), the muscle is relaxed; as the object comes nearer and nearer, the muscle contracts more and more, causing the lens to become more and more convex. Here then is a possible depth cue: the degree of contraction of the ciliary muscle, signaled to the brain by kinesthetic impulses. However, the fact that we ordinarily shift focus from one near object to another without any trial and error shows that other cues have been used first.

Whether accommodation has any actual value as a depth or distance cue can only be determined by experiments in which all other cues of distance are excluded.

$$D = \frac{13{,}407{,}225}{C} \text{ mm}$$

For example, when single vision is secured by a total convergence of 10°, the distance of the object $= \dfrac{13{,}407{,}225}{36{,}000} = 372$ mm (about 15 in.).

In experimental work, *D* is the primary measurement and the angle *C* is computed from *D*. Here are a few corresponding values:

D in mm	$\angle C$ in sec =	approx.
100	134,072	36°
300	44,691	12°
600	22,345	6°
1,000	13,407	3.7°
10,000	1,341	0.37°
50,000	268	0.07°

In the Wundt experiment the subject looked through a short tube into a room at the far end of which was a smooth illuminated wall: nothing else was visible except the middle section of a single thread that was seen as a straight black line. The thread's distance was changed between trials. After some practice, the subject achieved a monocular threshold for detecting a change in the thread's distance of about 7 percent. The threshold with binocular viewing was about 2 percent. Wundt (1862) took the monocular threshold to represent the use of accommodation alone, assuming that (1) convergence is absent in monocular viewing, and (2) all visual cues had been eliminated in both viewing conditions.

With respect to the first assumption, Hillebrand (1894) argued that the sensations provided by convergence might have been the depth cue that was really used, because the eyes attempt to converge upon the object that is fixated even when only monocular vision is employed. With respect to the second assumption, several alternative depth cues remain. For example, the subject might fixate the background and the thread would in consequence produce double images, the separation of which would vary with the distance of the thread from the background (p. 481). In addition, there might be more detailed vision of irregularities on the thread in nearer positions.

Hillebrand and others after him (Peter, 1915; Bappert, 1923; see Woodworth, 1938, pp. 665–674) varied the experimental conditions in an effort to clear up some of these possibilities. Recently, Heinemann, Tulving, and Nachmias (1959) found that subjects who were required to make a successive discrimination as to which of 2 identical disks was nearer, using no cue other than accommodation, actually failed to reach even a chance level of success. They may have been confused because the disks changed in apparent size as accommodation varied (p. 480).

Künnapas (1968) found that subjects were unable to judge the distances of phosphorescent disks, viewed monocularly in a room which was otherwise completely dark, if the sizes of the disks were so varied that their retinal images had a constant size at all distances and the subjects were left with only accommodation as a depth cue. Seventy years of research of this kind leave us with the conclusion that accommodation is, at best, a pretty weak cue to distance even at short distances.

Convergence

Imagine that an observer faces an object at P in Figure 13.5 and converges his eyes to obtain single vision by bringing the image of the object to the fovea of each eye. The fixed interocular distance provides a base line, and the amounts of convergence of the right and left eyes, or the sum of these amounts, which is the convergence angle C (Figure 13.5) permits the distance to be determined by trigonometry. Not that the subject will know the interocular distance in centimeters or C in degrees. However, the interocular distance is a quantity to which he must be thoroughly habituated. This distance, taken together with the record in his nervous system of what degree of convergence his eyes have been ordered to assume, furnishes a possible distance cue. Even if this cue were too imprecise to give the absolute distance D, it might enable the subject to tell which of 2 points was farther away.

The mirror stereoscope (p. 482) makes it easy to vary convergence; we merely move the pictures laterally in their holders. The expectation would be that increasing convergence would make the pictured object seem nearer. There should also be a secondary effect: If we apply here the rule suggested earlier, we may predict that decreasing the apparent distance while holding retinal size constant should make the object appear smaller. Wheatstone tried this experiment in 1852, and Judd repeated it with different apparatus in 1897. Both found the expected secondary effect, that is, the decrease of apparent size with increased convergence, retinal size presumably remaining constant. However, the judgments of distance were confused and equivocal. Since then, there have been several further demonstrations that apparent size decreases as convergence increases (Frank, 1930; Hermans, 1954; Adams, 1955).

Because changes in both accommodation and pupil size probably accompany convergence change, and because these in turn may alter the size of the object's retinal image (Brown, 1954), Heinemann, Tulving, and Nachmias (1959) had subjects compare the apparent size of featureless disks, at different distances, under 3 viewing conditions: (1) with monocular viewing (in which accommodation alone provided information about depth, but in which convergence accompanied the accommodation); (2) with binocular viewing, in which both eyes fixated a small point of light at the distance of the disk, but only one eye received the image of the disk (here, information for accommodation and convergence were both potentially available); (3) with conditions the same as in the second condition, except that accommodative information was excluded by use of an artificial pupil (see Chapter 11) and by drugs. At all distances the object subtended 1°. In all conditions, a small but very reliable decrease in apparent size occurred with decreasing distance: notice that this was also true of the first condition, which, as we saw above, did not reveal reliable distance discriminations.

As for convergence as a distance cue, some subjects show some ability to judge the distance of an object to which the eyes are converged, holding accommodation and image size constant (Swenson, 1932; Grant, 1942; Gogel, 1961). At best, however, as with accommodation, convergence itself can only furnish secondary cues of an object's distance, for the correct adjustment of the eyes must first be achieved in response to some other cue. Of the cues that are present *before* the correct ocular response is made, the double images that result from imperfect convergence cannot be eliminated from these experiments by anything that the experimenter can do; they can only be eliminated when the subject adjusts his convergence for

the correct distance, and this he must do on the basis of visual information. Let us consider what visual information he has.

BINOCULAR VISUAL CUES

Let us refer once more to the situation of Figure 13.5 in which the observer looks at the point *P*. He does so by the use of a combination of saccadic and vergent eye movements (see Chapter 11) such that an image of *P* is brought to the foveal center of each retina. These foveal centers are *corresponding points* in the anatomical sense that they are linked by fibers of the optic tract to a common locus in the visual projection areas of the cortex (see Chapter 9). Phenomenally, too, the object

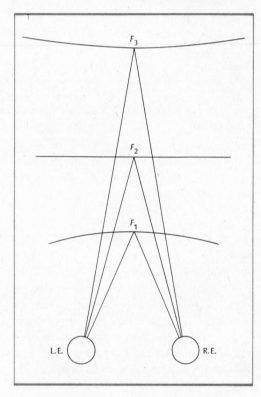

Figure 13.6. The empirical horopter. If the eyes are converged on a rod at F_1, a rod at any other point on the curve passing through F_1 will be seen as single; rods nearer to, or further from, the observer will be seen as double. The actual shape of the horopter changes with fixation distance, as shown by the curves through F_2 and F_3. (Ogle, 1950.)

at P is seen as single rather than double. This is the phenomenon of *binocular fusion* in which the object seems to be located at a single point in space even though two eyes are used for viewing it. In more general terms, the existence of corresponding points is by no means confined to the foveal region. In the discussion that follows, we shall examine the perceptual consequences of corresponding and noncorresponding points as they relate to single and double images received under various conditions of binocular viewing.

Double Images

If a near and a far object are both straight in front and you fixate the near object (F_1 in Figure 13.6) then a far object (F_2 or F_3) is seen by the right eye as lying to the right of F_1 and by the left eye as lying to the left. If you fixate

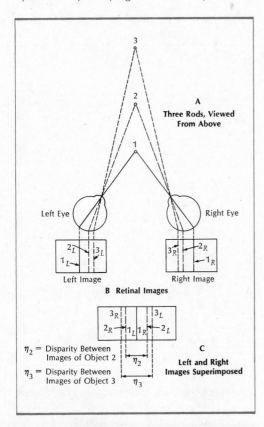

Figure 13.7. Depth and binocular disparity. A. A spatial layout of three rods, viewed from above. B. The images each eye receives. C. The two images superimposed.

the far object, F_3, thus getting double images of the near ones, the right eye sees F_2 or F_1 as lying to the left of F_3 and the left eye sees it to the right.

If you get the latter type of double images (called *crossed disparity*), you can decrease the distance or disparity between them and produce single vision by converging your eyes (see Figure 13.7); this may be used as a cue that the object is nearer than the initial fixation point.

The significance of double images as possible depth cues was noted very early (Hering, 1861–1864) but has often been overlooked since. Some persons cannot notice them at all, and they are certainly not normally observed to the full extent to which they must be present in the combined field of view. While this is no argument against their functional importance, it is hard to see how their contribution could be clearly demonstrated inasmuch as there is no way of eliminating them from binocular vision to find out how much depth perception would be left without them. The *horopter* is the locus of those points in space that, for a given degree of convergence, produce images that fall on corresponding points in the two eyes as shown in Figure 13.6. Geometrically, as Johannes Müller discussed it in 1826, when the eyes are horizontally positioned in the head, the horopter is a circle which passes through the fixated point F and through the centers of rotation of the 2 eyes. However, if we determine the empirical shape of the horopter, by having the subject maintain fixation on one rod while he adjusts other rods until they all look single, it turns out to be quite different, and its actual shape varies with the fixation distance as shown in Figure 13.6. Detailed discussion of the various theoretical horopters, and of empirical measurement procedures and results, may be found in Carr (1935) and Ogle (1950).

Binocular Disparity

Objects that are nearer or further than the horopter project their retinal images on noncorresponding or "disparate" areas of the 2 retinas. *Binocular disparity* is a measurable quantity, which increases with the difference in depth as shown in Figure 13.7. In angular measure, disparity is equal to the convergence angle of the nearer point minus the convergence angle of the farther point; that is, it is equal to the change in convergence in shifting from either point to the other (see Figure 13.5). Because disparity is usually studied in the context of stereoscopy, it is frequently measured pictorially in a projection of the retinal images on a picture plane, as is illustrated in Figure 13.7C; here we are working with the tangents of the convergence angles instead of with these angles measured in degrees. Regardless of how it is measured, however, retinal disparity is a possible depth cue to the distance at which any point lies, nearer or farther than the horopter. As we see in the next section, although there is considerable question about how our visual systems extract the information, there is no question at all about the fact that we can make effective use of this depth cue.

STEREOSCOPIC VISION

The Stereoscope

It was the physicist Charles Wheatstone whose discovery of stereoscopic vision and invention of the stereoscope in 1833 inaugurated the modern era of experimentation on space perception. (For much of this history, see Boring, 1942, pp. 263–311.) Using a diagram similar to the one in Figure 13.7, Wheatstone pointed out in 1838 that the 2 eyes get different views of three-dimensional objects that are located fairly near the observer. The combination of these disparate views, he conjectured, might produce the vivid depth effect of binocular vision. He tested this hypothesis by drawing the view of an object that each eye would receive separately and then presenting each drawing to the appropriate eye. In order to do this with small pictures held close to the eyes, accommodation has to be strong while convergence is relaxed, a trick which is difficult for most people to learn.

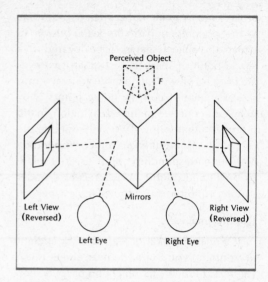

Figure 13.8. Diagram of a mirror stereoscope. The eyes are converged for the distance of the imaginary object at *F*.

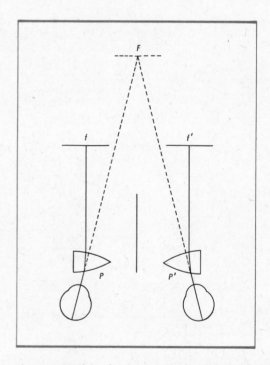

Figure 13.9. Plan of a prism stereoscope. A cardboard slide presents the two views, *f* and *f'*, the rays from which are bent by the prisms *P* and *P'* so as to reach the eyes as if from *F*, the point in space on which the eyes are converged.

Wheatstone therefore invented a device (Figure 13.8) that presents the pictures at the same distance as the objects represented, and that keeps accommodation and convergence in harmony. The 2 retinal images are then those that would be received from the actual object.

The mirror stereoscope is too bulky for any but research and demonstration purposes. More convenient is the *prism* or *lenticular* stereoscope (Figure 13.9) which is usually associated with the name of Brewster (1856), though Wheatstone also developed it independently. This is the gadget that was to be found in almost every home around the turn of the century. Its prisms take the place of the mirrors of Figure 13.8, deflecting the lines of sight outward just enough to center them on right and left pictures mounted on a card and

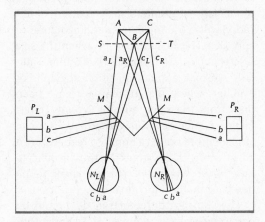

Figure 13.10. The optics of the mirror stereoscope. The eyes are to converge and accommodate as they would in viewing the actual object, here a wedge *ABC*, and the two retinal images are to be the same as in viewing a projection of the wedge on the plane *ST* through the convergence point. With the eyes fixated on the near edge *B*, single foveal vision is obtained of *B*, but there is some (uncrossed) disparity for *A* and also for *C*. This disparity, as present in the projection plane *ST*, is copied in the two drawings to be placed at P_L and P_R and viewed through the mirrors *M* and *M*. If the disparity is not too great, the double images are evidently fused, for the observer sees a single wedge in depth.

placed straight in front of their respective eyes. A thin wooden partition or separator limits each eye to its own picture. The prism is usually ground with a slight convex lens component, so that the picture will be sharp at about 6 inches from the eye, even with accommodation completely relaxed. A large collection of carefully prepared photographic slides was available for these prism stereoscopes, and people could see the Grand Canyon, Niagara Falls, and London Bridge in surprisingly realistic fashion, all in their own parlors.

Binocular disparity in the 2 views, which results from the difference in location of the 2 eyes (approximately 65 mm in interocular distance), is normally horizontal rather than vertical. Only a small amount of vertical disparity can be tolerated. Stereograms can be prepared geometrically by the method illustrated in Figure 13.10; photographically by taking 2 photographs from different positions, separated by the interocular distance (or more in order to increase the depth effect). A particularly useful form of stereogram for laboratory use was recently devised by Julesz (1960, 1964). The stereograms are prepared by a computer, which prints out 2 identical patterns of dots in a random display (or with any other statistical property desired); in one of the patterns an entire region *i* is displaced horizontally relative to the original pattern. Because the original pattern is random, the displacement of region *i* cannot be detected simply by looking at the altered monocular pattern. When the original is viewed by one eye and the altered pattern is viewed by the other, however, the displaced region then becomes visible, floating in space at a different distance than the rest of the pattern. None of the edges that appear to act as contours between surfaces that are seen at different apparent distances in the binocular view are visible when the subject looks with either eye separately. Although such stereograms normally offer cues of convergence (Bridgman, 1964), they are otherwise ideal instruments for the study of the effects of disparity alone on

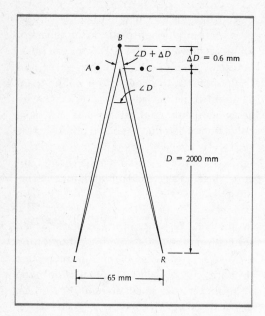

Figure 13.11. The Helmholtz three-needle experiment. The dots *A, B, C* represent vertical needles, mounted on little blocks that are placed on a level table. Only the needle shafts are visible to the observer, who is represented by the nodal points of his eyes, *L* and *R*. The needles are only a few millimeters apart laterally. The observer must judge whether *B* is lined up accurately with *A* and *C* so that all three are equally far away from him, or whether *B* is a little nearer or farther away. His average error is primarily measured in millimeters (ΔD), but such a measure cannot be compared directly with one taken with a different distance, *D*, from the observer to the plane of the needles, *A* and *C*. A better measure is the *angle of disparity,* or angular measure of disparity, which (see p. 482) is the convergence angle for the nearer object minus that for the farther object. In the figure, then, the angle of disparity equals the angle marked $\angle D$ minus the angle marked $\angle D + \Delta D$. A method for computing these angles has been explained under Figure 13.5 and will be applied here to a result of Bourdon (1902), who found one observer successfully discriminating an offset of 0.6 mm at a distance of 2 m (2,000 mm), as indicated on the figure. We have:

$$\angle D = \frac{13,407,225}{2000} = 6,703.6 \text{ sec}$$

stereopsis because there are no other visual depth cues that contribute to the appearance of depth under these conditions.

Let us survey first the accuracy with which depth differences can be discriminated stereoscopically; second, the main theoretical accounts of the nature of stereopsis; and third, the way in which stereopsis contributes to the perception of objects in space.

Accuracy of Stereoscopic Space Perception

Several equivalent terms are in use: depth or stereoscopic acuity, stereoacuity, stereopsis. Sensitivity to slight disparity is almost incredibly keen; this makes the stereoscope a useful device for comparing 2 very similar objects. For example, a 10 dollar bill that is suspected of being counterfeit can be viewed by the right eye, while a genuine one is viewed by the left. When the 2 are fused binocularly, size differences in pattern or lettering will cause the corresponding figures to appear nearer or farther even when the size discrepancies are as small as .005 mm. Similarly we may evaluate microphotographs of 2 bullets which may or may not have been fired from the same gun, or 2 photographs taken of some camouflaged artillery from an airplane from points a hundred feet apart—in all of these cases, stereodepth will indicate differences which are far too small to be detected by the individual eye.

How small a difference in depth can be perceived in binocular vision? Given an object at a standard distance *D* from the observer, what is the difference in distance ΔD of a comparison object that just can be perceived? The fundamental *three-needle experiment* devised by Helmholtz (1856–1866)

$$\angle D + \Delta D = \frac{13,407,225}{2000.6} = 6,701.6 \text{ sec}$$

Angle of disparity = 2.0 sec

We usually consider 1° as a pretty small angle, but in this performance an angle of only 1/1800 of a degree was perceptually utilized.

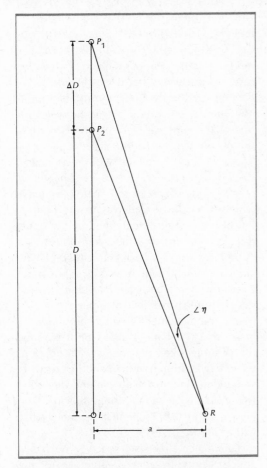

Figure 13.12. Diagram to illustrate the angle of disparity, $\angle\eta$, for points P_1 and P_2 at different distances from the eyes.

and illustrated in Figure 13.11 permits us to measure ΔD and to convert this value into units of visual angle, that is, to compute the smallest amount of disparity that can function as a cue of depth.

Plane geometry can be used to make this conversion, as is shown in Figure 13.12. In this basic diagram the calculations are simplified by the fact that only 2 lines are used and that these far and near lines, at P_1 and P_2, are lined up with the left eye and in a direction perpendicular to the line between the left eye and the right. It is therefore true of the right triangles, P_1LR and P_2LR that $\angle\eta = \angle LP_2R - \angle LP_1R$. If P_1 is a point that is just discriminably farther than P_2 from the observer, then ΔD is the difference threshold at distance D. Then $\angle\eta$ represents the stereoscopic disparity threshold.

Now tan $\angle LP_1R = a/(D + \Delta D)$, and tan $\angle LP_2R = a/D$. Since $\angle\eta = \angle LP_2R - \angle LP_1R$ and since these are all very small angles it is approximately true that they are linearly related to their tangents. Hence tan $\angle\eta = \tan \angle LP_2R -$ tan $\angle LP_1R = a/D - a/(D + \Delta D) = a\Delta D/D(D + \Delta D)$. It is also approximately true, since ΔD is very small compared to D, that tan $\angle\eta = a\Delta D/D^2$. Applying this formula to the results of Bourdon, illustrated in Figure 13.11, we see that tan $\angle\eta = 65(.6)/2000)^2 = .00001$ approximately. Now the tangent of one degree is about .018; hence $\eta =$ approximately $1/1800$ degree, or 2 seconds of arc. A stereoscopic acuity as fine as this can be obtained only under the best of experimental conditions.

Without pushing the determination to its limit, Helmholtz found that his disparity threshold was certainly less than ±60 seconds of visual angle. Later determinations show that the average threshold is much smaller than even this small amount. A widely used, rather crudely made substitute for the three-needle apparatus is called the *Howard-Dolman apparatus,* devised by Howard in 1919 and taken over as a screening test to eliminate aviation candidates who might have "poor depth perception." Two black vertical rods are mounted side by side on separate blocks that move on parallel tracks so that either rod can be moved forward or away from the subject. All the subject sees is 2 black rods; in the simplest case, his task is to adjust the comparison rod (by pulling on cords) until it looks to be at the same distance as the standard rod set at 20 feet (6.1 m). This is the *method of adjustment* (see Chapter 2) in which the differential threshold for distance ΔD is taken to be .6745 σ_D, where σ_D is the *SD* of the distribution of obtained distances to the comparison rod. In the original experiment, Howard used the method of constant stimuli (see Chapter 2), requiring a judgment of "nearer" or "farther" at each fixed distance and taking as the ΔD threshold half the interpolated distance from the 25 percent to the 75 percent point. Out of 106 subjects, the best 14 had thresholds ΔD of about 5.5 mm corresponding to an angular disparity η of about 2 sec arc.

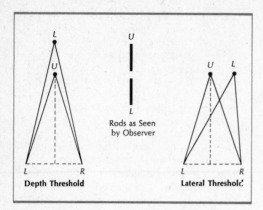

Figure 13.13. Diagram of the observer's task in an experiment comparing depth acuity with lateral (vernier) acuity. The observer saw the two vertical rods, *U* and *L*, as shown in the center. At the right and left are horizontal cross sections suggesting the displacement of the lower rod to one side or the other for determination of the lateral threshold, and forward or back for determination of the depth threshold. (After Berry, 1948.)

In a supplementary experiment with 9 subjects, Howard obtained average binocular thresholds of 14.4 mm as compared to monocular thresholds of 285 mm in the same task. This is a ratio of 20 to 1 in favor of binocular vision. Later experiments that controlled for monocular cues (such as the fact that the width of the image of the further rod will be narrower than that of the near one) have produced substantially the same results (Woodburne, 1934; Matsubayashi, 1937; Hirsch, Horowitz, & Weymouth, 1948); as has research with stereoscopic, as distinguished from "real" depth (Berry, 1948), getting about 2 sec thresholds. Stereoacuity can therefore be at least as sensitive as any other acuity we have. Individual differences are large, however, and some subjects in any unselected population will have little or no stereoscopic vision.

At its best, then, stereoacuity can certainly give exquisitely precise judgments of depth. It is matched only by 2 other kinds of acuity, so similar in both their nature and their magnitude that this may tell us something about the mechanisms that underlie stereoacuity. Berry (1948), using the equipment shown in Figure 13.13, kept the upper rod fixed at a distance of 4.6 m (about 15 feet),

while the lower rod could be displaced either laterally or in depth. The subject's task in one case was to judge whether the lower rod was *right* or *left* of the upper rod and, in the other case, to judge whether it was in *front* or in *back,* using the method of constant stimuli. The vertical separation or gap between the tips of the rods was set, in various parts of the experiment, to various fixed values from 0.5 to 22 mm. The lateral acuity was what is known as *vernier acuity* (see Chapter 9, p. 300), the subject's task being to judge whether the lower rod was to the right or left of the straight line defined by the upper rod. The 2 forms of acuity were both found to be very good, and about equally good, with angular displacement thresholds (η) of about 2 sec. The third comparable level of acuity is that required to detect movement parallax, that is, the movement of one contour relative to another (Graham et al., 1948). It is found that a subject can detect that one object is further away from him than another about as well by moving his head from one viewpoint to another as he can by using binocular stereopsis, as in fact Tschermak-Seysenegg had earlier reported (1939).

Luminance affects stereoacuity much as it affects acuity in general: stereoacuity improves (the threshold becomes smaller) as luminance increases (Mueller & Lloyd, 1948). The familiar rod-cone break (see Chapter 9, p. 303) occurs in the graph of the decrease in acuity; thus some binocular depth discrimination appears even at scotopic levels of illumination (see Berry, Riggs, & Duncan, 1950).

Stereoacuity is highest when the target line (the line whose relative nearness or farness is being judged) is near the reference line, and it falls off regularly as the lateral separation between the 2 lines increases (Matsubayashi, 1937; Graham et al., 1949). These results seem reasonable, for the relative distance of 2 objects ought best to be perceived when they lie nearly in the same line of sight, but no explicit theory has been worked out. Indeed, as we shall see, the theory of binocular stere-

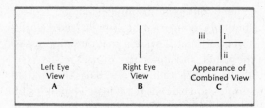

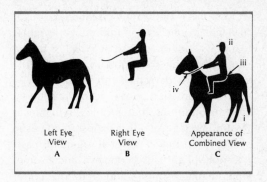

Figure 13.14 (left) and 13.15 (right). Stereograms demonstrating local contralateral suppression at contours. See text. Rivalry occurs at C*i* of Figure 13.14 and C*iii, iv* of Figure 13.15. Otherwise, where one eye's view contains a contour and the other view does not, the contour prevails.

opsis is still, itself, in a rudimentary and speculative state.

Theories of Stereopsis

Each of our eyes usually receives a somewhat different view of the world, but this difference does not normally produce double vision; instead, as we have seen, it produces stereoscopic space perception. The putting together of signals from the 2 eyes to form a single perceptual experience is often so perfectly achieved that the observer is not aware whether, at a given moment, he is using both eyes, his right eye alone or his left eye alone. In some cases, however, the effect can be one of "double vision" or *binocular rivalry*. This can be illustrated by using a stereoscope to present a view to one eye that is markedly different from that of the other. When rivalry occurs, at one moment one eye is dominant for part or even all of the field, so that the view it receives seems to suppress the corresponding portion of the other eye's view. At the next moment, the other eye becomes dominant, and its view prevails. However, rivalry is not commonly noticed outside of the laboratory.

Two distinct questions emerge from these observations: First, by what rules do we see singly instead of doubly? Second, by what rules do we convert binocular disparity into depth?

We really know very little about either of these questions, or about the relationship between them, and all that will be attempted here is to outline the major alternatives.

Combining the monocular fields Panum offered the following 4 rules in 1858.

1. Rivalry of contours. Where one contour intersects a contour in the other eye's view, there is rivalry in the combined view: at point *i* in Figure 13.14C you see one or the other line, but not both.

2. Prevalence of contours. If a contour in one eye competes with a uniform field in the other, the contour is seen nearly all the time (*iii, iv* in Figure 13.15C). Note that the contour seems to carry some of its immediate background into the combined view.

3. Binocular mixture of colors. Mixing colors binocularly is reported under some conditions (see Chapter 10).

4. Mosaic composition of binocular field. Where contours in the 2 monocular fields do not overlap, they simply appear concurrently in the combined view (*ii, iii* in Figure 13.14C; *i, ii* in Figure 13.15C).

With these in mind, let us consider more general rules, according to one or more of which the 2 eye's views combine.

Summation This would be equivalent to a simple superposition of the 2 retinal images, so that a horizontal line in one eye and a vertical line in the other would unite to form a cross; and a moderately bright spot of light that falls in one eye should appear brighter if another spot of light, somewhat less bright, is added to the corresponding point in the other eye. As detection thresholds show, a kind of summation does indeed occur under certain conditions, that is, at low luminances (Matin, 1963) or at short exposures (Erikson et al., 1966), but it is not the general case. If a spot of light falls in one eye, and a somewhat dimmer spot is added to the corresponding point in the other eye, in the combined view the spot does not increase in brightness due to the increment it has received—it gets darker. This is known as *Fechner's paradox* (see Helmholtz, 1866) and suggests an averaging, rather than a summation. For a review of research in this area, see Levelt (1965). However, stereopsis depends on contours (or on texture elements that have contours; see page 432), not on expanses of color, and here the summation model fails more dramatically. Consider how each contour that intersects or comes close to another contour that originates in the other eye's view fails to summate in the combined views (Figures 13.14, 13.15). Instead, each contour seems to carry with it a halo of its background, suppressing in its immediate vicinity the contribution that would have been made there by the contralateral eye.

Suppression There may be several very different kinds of suppression, not all of which involve the same mechanisms. The simplest way of avoiding double vision with two eyes would be to suppress one of them. This was a very early proposal (Porta, 1593). A nearly complete suppression of vision in one eye does in fact occur in some cases of strabismus, but it will clearly not account for most of the phenomena (p. 487) that Panum observed in normal subjects. Nor can binocular suppression explain the findings by Crovitz (1964) and by Crovitz and Lipscomb (1963) that short exposures cause the view on the nasal halves of the retinas to suppress the view on the temporal halves. More to the point of Panum's demonstrations are the various theories of suppression in which a contour in one eye suppresses a corresponding region in the other eye (Verhoeff, 1935; Asher, 1953; Kaufman, 1963; Hochberg, 1964a,b). Where different contours fall on corresponding points in the 2 eyes (see Figures 13.14, 13.15), it is evident that one suppresses the other and *binocular rivalry* occurs (see above, p. 487). Kaufman (1963) has shown that suppression extends for at least 14 minutes of arc around each such rivalrous intersection (and it can be spread further by eye movements). Perhaps the simplest assumption would be that a zone of contralateral suppression (about $\frac{1}{4}$ of a degree wide) surrounds any contour, all of the time, not just when the 2 eyes' views are different (Hochberg, 1964b). Any combined view would then consist of a mosaic made up of bits and pieces of contours from each eye's view (unless contours in one view were spaced so densely and made so strong that their overlapping suppressive fields would completely suppress the other eye's view), but the existence of the suppressive zones that surround each contour would only be manifested when the two views differ (for example, see Figures 13.14, and 13.15). Note that in such a theory of suppression 2 points that originate in different eyes should both be visible in the combined view if they are separated by more than $\frac{1}{4}$ of a degree, but only one should be seen if they are separated by less than that.

Fusion That single vision may be due to fusion is the most widely accepted theory. If 2 points that are perceived in different eyes fall closer together than about $\frac{1}{4}$ of a degree in the combined view, they fall within limits known as *Panum's area,* and "fusion" occurs: only one dot is seen.

This theory is not clearly different from the suppression theory; in terms of the latter, "fusion" would merely mean that 2 eyes' views are so similar that their piecemeal alternation is not discernable as such. The question of whether suppression has occurred during apparent fusion has been explored by Fox and his colleagues. They made the discov-

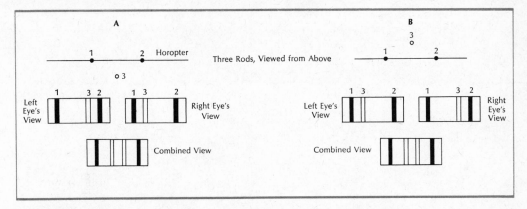

Figure 13.16. The combined view obtained with two rods on the horopter, one off. A. Crossed disparity for the images of rod 3. B. Uncrossed disparity for the images of rod 3. See text.

ery that, in a manifest case of rivalry, a test stimulus that is added to a part of one eye's view while that view is being suppressed is less often perceived than when that view is dominant (Fox & Check, 1966a,b). No interference with test-stimulus recognition was obtained when 2 views containing few contours were "fused" (Fox & Check, 1966a), but interference with test-stimulus recognition was obtained during "fusion" of 2 identical patterns having a high contour density, similar to the interference that occurs during manifest rivalry with dissimilar binocular patterns (Fox & McIntyre, 1967). This is what we would expect if contralateral suppression were generated around each eye's view of a contour in small fields which can summate when they overlap (Hochberg, 1964a,b).

The theory of fusion is not easy to separate from the suppression theory. Because it makes no specific predictions about rivalry, it is relatively unparsimonious with respect to how the two monocular views form a singular binocular field. The fusion theory gains its strongest support in the discussion of the nature of stereopsis, and we shall return to it in that context.

The Nature of Binocular Disparity and Stereopsis

Wheatstone's rule for predicting the stereoscopic effect is a simple one. If the 2 half-views that are paired in a *stereogram* (that is, the pair of views that is to be combined binocularly) are the views of a single solid object as seen by the separate eyes, then the depth effect of the combined binocular view will correspond to that object. Thus, with the 2 half-views shown in Figure 13.16, the combined view will look like 3 rods in depth. Notice that the disparity between the 2 views in Figure 13.16A and in Figure 13.16B is the same in size but opposite in direction; Figure 13.16A has "crossed disparity," Figure 13.16B has "uncrossed disparity." In order to interpret disparity correctly, therefore, the visual system must register which eye each contour in the combined view comes from, an ability that is not reflected directly in awareness. In general, you can only tell which eye is receiving which contour in Figures 13.14, 13.15, and 13.16 by finding secondary clues (for example, by noticing which contour vanishes when you close your right eye, or which one can be occluded by the left side of your nose). As such secondary clues are reduced, it becomes increasingly harder to make that discrimination (Smith, 1945; Pickersgill, 1961). It seems plausible that if secondary clues were eliminated entirely, the ability would be completely lost. The mechanism responsible for producing stereopsis, however, must keep track of this information. Let us sketch some of the suggested mechanisms.

Hering (1861) proposed that each retinal

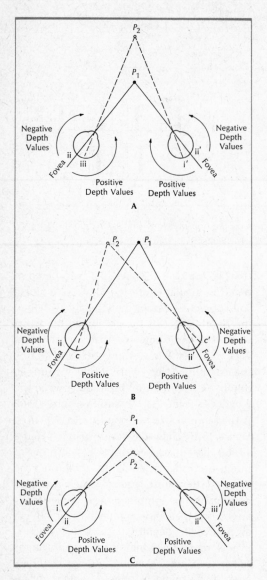

Figure 13.17. Hering's theory of depth-signs. See text.

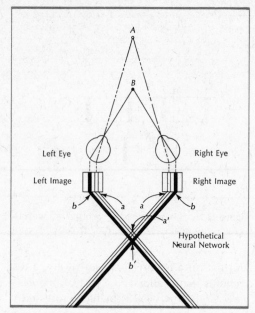

Figure 13.18. One version of a fusion network theory of stereopsis. See text.

i' in Figure 13.17A, or i and iii' in Figure 13.17C). If object P_1 is fixated (Figure 13.17A), its image falls on each eye's fovea (ii and ii'). P_2 appears farther away than P_1 because iii and i' both have positive depth values. In Figure 13.17B, P_2 falls on corresponding points c and c'. These are opposite in sign, and therefore P_2 lies on the horopter with P_1 and the two points seem equally distant. In Figure 13.17C, points i and iii' are both negative, so P_2 looks nearer than P_1.

Hering proposed that these retinal signs innately provide for stereoscopic depth perception. Against this, Helmholtz argued that this model would predict that if we masked the nasal hemiretinas while looking at a wall, that wall would appear to meet at an angle, which simply does not occur.

An alternative model, related, but not identical, is shown in Figure 13.18. This explanation (which was proposed at various times by Boring, 1933; Charnwood, 1951; Linksz, 1952; Dodwell & Engel, 1963; and is reviewed briefly by Kaufman, 1965) shows a hypothetical network in the brain by means of which

point furnishes sensations of light, color, and direction (that is, its position in 2 dimensions) plus a sensation of *depth*. By this theory, these depth sensations are positive (meaning "farther") in the nasal halves of the retinas, negative ("nearer") in the temporal halves. Furthermore, they are identical but opposite in sign at corresponding points (c and c', in Figure 13.17B), identical and of the same sign at symmetrically placed retinal points (iii and

```
patxkrviejlsximudkybfaxkltbdugxlknydjlcx
psfrdcjlgsbmydchksvyfcjkoutrdvgmsckhbkfm
utfvnjfxiyjdmeskmrjxugslmgbdxkhrvugsvkgh
ufbsjlbdfvgruojgdxcvlmhsbcuyrjxklyhbrhjv
lugdxjnrdsulmrcgyxsjhipfsnvwfwyerxiplkmh
gsunxqphedcijmsagckpnyvxrfgenudzkubfxhjn
lumvhdzrtfcynmigkncezyhikmrptcghjfbexdit
lhcrsxkybjrvgjurdxuhvkgrsjnxcuokldbvrxyj
lmtvhdubfhubfxkunhdryjkibdenkyhvfjybdcxg
lmhecshatfbdesupjkinmbghydxesxwzfdghnvrf
jdhgbcxrdsjhbdxukrdhncsiklrvshbfrchudzlm
xlfutgrslnuvcbkfhtdxokmrhbdgcrsklmycidwj
```

A

```
patxkrbiejlsximudkybfaxkltbdugxlknydjlcx
psfrdcjlgsbmydchksvyfcjkoutrdvgmsckhbkfm
utfvnjfxiyjdmeskmrjxugslmgbdxkhrvugsvkgh
ufbsjlbdfvgwruojgdxcvlmhsbcurjxklyhbrhjv
lugdxjnrdsuolmrcgyxsjhipfsnvfwyerxiplkmh
gsunxqphedculjmsagckpnyvxrfgnudzkubfxhjn
lumvhdzrtfcsynmigkncezyhikmrtcghjfbexdit
lhcrsxkybjrdvgjurdxuhvkgrsjncuokldbvrxyj
lmtvhdubfhujbfxkunhdryjkibdekyhvfjybdcxg
lmhecshatfbdesupjkinmbghydxesxwzfdghnvrf
jdhgbcxrdsjhbdxukrdhncsiklrvshbfrchudzlm
xlfutgrslnuvcbkfhtdxokmrhbdgcrsklmycidwj
```

B

```
patxkrviejlsximudkybfaxkltbdugxlknydjlcx
psfrdcjlgsbmydchksvyfcjkoutrdvgmsckhbkfm
utfvnjfxiyjdmeskmrjxugslmgbdxkhrvugsvkgh
ufbsjlbdfvgruojgdxcvlmhsbcuyrjxklyhbrhjv
lugdxjnrdsulmrcgyxsjhipfsnvwfwyerxiplkmh
gsunxqphedcijmsagckpnyvxrfgenudzkubfxhjn
lumvhdzrtfcynmigkncezyhikmrptcghjfbexdit
lhcrsxkybjrvgjurdxuhvkgrsjnxcuokldbvrxyj
lmtvhdubfhubfxkunhdryjkibdenkyhvfjybdcxg
lmhecshatfbdesupjkinmbghydxesxwzfdghnvrf
jdhgbcxrdsjhbdxukrdhncsiklrvshbfrchudzlm
xlfutgrslnuvcbkfhtdxokmrhbdgcrsklmycidwj
```

C

```
patxkrbiejlsximudkybfaxkltbdugxlknydjlcx
psfrdcjlgsbmydchksvyfcjkoutrdvgmsckhbkfm
utfvnjfxiyjdmeskmrjxugslmgbdxkhrvugsvkgh
ufbsjlbdfvgwruojgdxcvlmhsbcurjxklyhbrhjv
lugdxjnrdsuolmrcgyxsjhipfsnvfwyerxiplkmh
gsunxqphedculjmsagckpnyvxrfgnudzkubfxhjn
lumvhdzrtfcsynmigkncezyhikmrtcghjfbexdit
lhcrsxkybjrdvgjurdxuhvkgrsjncuokldbvrxyj
lmtvhdubfhujbfxkunhdryjkibdekyhvfjybdcxg
lmhecshatfbdesupjkinmbghydxesxwzfdghnvrf
jdhgbcxrdsjhbdxukrdhncsiklrvshbfrchudzlm
xlfutgrslnuvcbkfhtdxokmrhbdgcrsklmycidwj
```

D

Figure 13.19. Stereograms in typescript. A, B. Rivalry can be detected during stereoscopic fusion. (Kaufman, 1965) C, D. An ambiguous stereogram. See text. (Kaufman & Pitblado, 1965.)

images falling in the 2 eyes can be brought to fuse at one place in the nervous system even if they fall at disparate places on the retina. Lines from a, a can fuse only at the point a' where their respective neurons intersect. Similarly, lines from b, b can fuse only at b'. In this network, the geometry of the spatial relations that give rise to the disparity in the first place, outside the head, is simply reconstructed inside the head.

The following arguments can be made against such models of binocular fusion, models which are essentially point-by-point in nature.

1. Fusion is not necessary for depth perception. Even when disparities are so large that double images are seen, the appropriate depth is perceived (Hering, 1861; Ogle, 1953). This is not a serious objection, inasmuch as this might comprise a separate class of binocular space perception, depending on a different mechanism. If we start hypothesizing mechanisms that can derive information about

depth from the characteristics of nonfused disparate images, however, then the fusion theory loses some of its special ability to explain stereopsis.[1]

2. The images may not really be fused in stereoscopic "fusion." Stereograms may be prepared with their half-views printed in complementary colors which result in clear rivalry in the combined view (that is, if the left view is red and the right is green, the combined view may display an alternating patchwork of red and green), a fact which does not prevent depth from being perceived

[1] A suppression theory can be extended to accommodate stereopsis by relating the latter to binocular rivalry (see Washburn, 1933; Hochberg, 1964). Eye dominance could then provide a cue as to which is the crossed and which the uncrossed image (Woodworth, 1938, p. 664), and so could changes in convergence that would sort out double images according to their distances from the horopter. The fact that correct judgments of depth can be obtained from the afterimages of very brief exposures (Dove, 1841; Karpinska, 1910; Washburn, 1933; Ogle & Reiher, 1962), and with stabilized retinal images (Shortess & Krauskopf, 1961), however, makes this last explanation necessarily incomplete because convergence changes could not contribute to the depth judgments made in such conditions.

in the combined view (Treisman, 1962; Kaufman, 1964). In fact, in an old method of stereoscopy, the 2 half-views are printed one over the other in complementary colors, and the 2 intermixed scenes (called an *anaglyph*) are sorted out by having each eye look through a filter of the appropriate hue. Moreover, even where there is no obvious rivalry, Asher (1953) claims that alternating suppression, rather than fusion, is usually experienced.

Such observations are very difficult to make with confidence. Kaufman (1965), replacing the dots in the matrix stereograms of Julesz (see p. 483) with letters, has introduced a valuable tool for this purpose. Figure 13.19A,B shows matrices of letters, identical except that the area outlined by the dotted line has been shifted over one column. As with Julesz' patterns, a square of letters is seen at some depth different from the surround: here, the central region appears behind the surround. In some of these letter stereograms, stereopsis occurs even though very dissimilar shapes are superposed; rivalry then also occurs, in which at each moment one or the other eye's view can be discerned.

At least for most of the time (after the initial fraction of a second, and at luminances well above threshold; see page 488), observation seems to support a model of stereopsis that is based on suppression at least as well as one that is based on fusion.

3. *The nature of binocular disparity.* What is the disparity of the 2 half-views in Figure 13.19C and D? The stereogram there is the same as in A and B, except that the luminances of the letters in the inner regions have been modulated to produce a pattern. The pattern has been shifted one letter to the *right* in the left half-view. In Figure 13.19A and B, responding to the displacement of the letters, subjects report that the inner region appears in depth *behind* the surround. In Figure 13.19 C and D, subjects responding to the displacement of the brightness of the pattern , report that the inner region appears to be *in front of* the surroundings (Kaufman & Pitblado, 1965), even though the letters themselves are displaced with the opposite

disparity. After a while, subjects reverse their response, the surroundings appear to be in front of the inner region, and the stereogram acts like one of the reversible-perspective patterns in Figure 12.19). Kaufman and Pitblado suggest that disparities in the patterns of relative brightnesses are the effective stimuli for binocular stereopsis. Pastore (1932), Koffka (1935), Werner (1937), Woodworth (1938), Linschoten (1956), and Wallach and Lindauer (1962) have suggested that the disparity that is effective for stereopsis is a disparity between *patterns* that are similar in some fashion. The precise nature and limits of the similarity remain to be defined, but a definition of disparity in terms of points alone is clearly insufficient.

Disparity and stereoscopic space The physical space in which we move our eyes and body follows familiar geometrical laws. If the spatial meaning of various convergence angles, and of the various binocular disparities that can occur with each, were faithfully learned as a result of our experiences in physical space, we would expect that the same geometry would be reflected in our judgments about objects and their locations. It should then be possible, for example, to map the relationship between the angles of convergence of the 2 eyes needed to fixate a point of light, on the one hand, and the apparent spatial location of that light in relation to the observer and to any other point of light, on the other hand.

In fact, judgments about apparent space that are based on binocular depth cues are not consistent with physical Euclidean space. Figure 13.6, for example, showed that a horopter that is determined on the basis of subjective judgments has a different shape from the circle that is predicted from purely geometrical considerations. As another example, if a subject is asked to arrange a set of lights in an otherwise dark room so that they appear to line up in 2 parallel rows symmetrically placed around the median plane (straight ahead), and he is also asked to arrange 2 rows of lights so that the distances

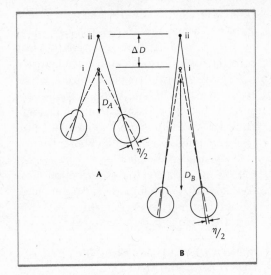

Figure 13.20. Disparity, depth, and distance. The disparity produced by a given depth, ΔD, between two points (i, ii) depends on their distance from the viewer, D. In fact, for large values of D, $\eta = k\,\Delta D/D^2$. See text.

between points of each pair that lie in the same frontal plane are equal, the 2 tasks do not produce equivalent results (Hillebrand, 1902; Blumenfeld, 1913). These inconsistencies need not be unlawful. In fact, Luneberg (1947, 1950) proposed on these and other grounds that visual space is non-Euclidean. The Luneberg theory has been revised and extended by Blank (1953, 1957, 1959) and some of its experimental implications concerning distance matching, aligning, and so on, in binocular space have been tested by Hardy and his colleagues (1953), Zajacskowska (1956), Shipley (1957, 1959), and Foley (1964, 1967).

As a third example, let us consider the apparent depth that is produced by a given disparity. The depth, ΔD, between points i and ii in Figure 13.20 is reflected in the binocular disparity η. As some consideration of Figures 13.12 and 13.20 will show, the relationship between η and ΔD is determined by the object's distance D. However, although the size (s) of the object's retinal image is linearly related to the inverse of the object's distance D (that is, as shown in Figure 13.4, $s = nS/D$), the disparity (η) is related inversely to the square of that distance. This follows from the facts (see p. 485) that very small angles are linearly related to their tangents, and that $\tan\angle\eta = a\Delta D/D^2$.

Let us assume that a subject perceives distance correctly. If he is also to respond correctly to some binocular disparity η, therefore, the apparent depth that he perceives ($\Delta D'$) should be proportional to the square of the perceived distance. Thus, $\Delta D' = k(D')^2$, where $\Delta D'$ is the apparent depth interval between points i and ii and D' is apparent distance. In various forms, this theory has been held by von Kries (1925), Fry (1950), Ogle (1953), and Wallach and Zuckerman (1963).

In order to alter the apparent distance D' of an object without changing its retinal image, Wallach and Zuckerman (1963) had subjects judge the depth and size of an object while looking through a set of mirrors that required them to converge for half the actual distance. They reasoned that because size decreases with D and depth decreases with D^2, the subject should judge the size to be half what it would be under normal viewing conditions, and the depth to be a quarter. The results turned out to be in reasonably close agreement with the prediction. The same disparity η produced different apparent depths, $\Delta D'$, depending on the distance D to which the convergence (and accommodation) were adjusted. Thus, convergence seems to serve as a cue for the $\Delta D'$ judgment even though it does not do so reliably for distance D' itself (see p. 480). According to these findings, the relationship between disparity and apparent depth reflects the geometry of the physical world.

On the other hand, Gogel (1960a,b,c) had shown experimentally that when normal distance cues are available to indicate the object's distance D, the disparity η must increase linearly with distance if the object's apparent depth $\Delta D'$ is to remain the same. This implies, of course, that $\Delta D'/D'$ is constant, for some fixed disparity, a result also obtained by Foley (1967).

Gogel's thesis is that the apparent depth that is produced by a given disparity depends on how large the parts of the visual field that are adjacent to it appear to be. More specifically, the apparent depth produced by a given disparity is proportional to the perceived *frontal size per unit visual angle* (Gogel, 1960a,b,c). Thus, the perceived size of an adjacent object becomes the "yardstick," or standard, which translates the disparity into a perceived depth, and any cue that causes the subject to change the way he perceives the size of the yardstick will change the perceived depth he attributes to any given disparity, as well (Gogel, 1960c, 1964).

The discrepancy with the earlier data (for example, Wallach & Zuckerman, 1963) remains to be resolved. The differences may in part reflect differences in the mixture of depth cues available in different experimental situations. Jameson and Hurvich (1959), summarizing an earlier investigation by Holway and his colleagues, report that depth discriminations on the basis of retinal disparity alone followed the function $\Delta D = kD^2$. In "commonplace conditions" which afforded additional cues (accommodation, image size, and so on), however, $\Delta D = kD^{1.25}$; very similar data were recently obtained by Vincent and his colleagues (1969).

Increased and reversed disparity If the disparity produced by a given depth is increased by increasing the distance between the 2 views over that which would have been provided by normal interocular distances, the binocular effect is extended to faraway objects. In this form, the mirror stereoscope becomes a *telestereoscope.* (For a mathematical analysis, see Riggs et al., 1947.)

Wallach, Moore, and Davidson (1963) have shown that after viewing a rotating three-dimensional object through a telestereoscope for only 10 minutes, the normal relationship between binocular disparity (η) and apparent depth ($\Delta D'$) was changed appreciably, the depth associated with a given disparity decreasing by as much as 20 percent. In subsequent experiments, Wallach and Karsh (1963a,b) found evidence suggesting strongly that the factor that changed the spatial meaning of the disparity was the monocular depth cue provided by the rotation, the *kinetic depth effect,* which we discuss on page 505.

If the views perceived by the right and left eye are interchanged in the stereoscope, we obtain a *pseudoscopic* or reversed depth effect because the directions of the disparities have been reversed. This experiment is instructive in that some pictures will reverse their depth with such a reversal of disparity and some will not. Such reversal rarely suc-

ceeds with pictures of concrete objects, like a chair or a human face (see p. 502).

In short, although binocular stereopsis may seem at first to explain our perceptions of objects and space, it cannot be the whole story. Two kinds of sensory information about space remain to be considered: the pictorial cues, and the information about space provided by motion of object and observer. It is well known that people blind in one eye are capable of ordinary space perception. This fact emphasizes the importance of the pictorial and motion cues in comparison with binocular stereopsis.

MONOCULAR VISUAL CUES OF DEPTH AND DISTANCE

The pictorial cues are effective in monocular as well as binocular vision. They are all ambiguous by their nature (p. 477), but they are frequently good indicators of depth and distance. Let us first consider the efficacy of those pictorial cues that have received the most study and then review the assumption that they are learned by association with the primary cues.

Size If you know the real (*distal*) size of a visible object, and you know the size of the retinal image it subtends at the eye (that is, its *proximal size*), you have a good potential indication of its distance. In Figure 13.4, if S is the size of the object, D is its distance, n is the nodal distance of the eyeball, while s is the size of the retinal image, then $D = nS/s$. There are indeed many demonstrations that proximal size can affect distance judgments, but there are several distinctions that must be drawn with respect to both the definition of the stimulus and the nature of the response.

In Figure 13.2B, the boy at *1* presents a larger proximal stimulus than the boy at *2*. There are 2 cues here that should be distinguished.

Relative size The proximal stimulus for boy *1* is larger than that for boy *2*. This cue can be defined in terms of stimulus measurements alone: Of 2 similar shapes, presented simultaneously or in close succession, the one with the larger proximal stimulus will appear to be nearer. There is considerable evidence that apparent relative distance or depth is influenced by relative size (that is, that the larger of two objects looks nearer) and that, as its retinal image grows larger, the object appears to approach (Hillebrand, 1894; Calavrezo, 1934; Ittelson, 1951b; Hochberg & Hochberg, 1952; Gogel, Hartman, & Harker, 1957; Epstein, 1961).

Familiar or assumed size   If we know the boy's real or distal size, and we can register his proximal or retinal size, then we can tell what his absolute distance is. Boy 1 would thus look nearer than boy 2 because boy 1 is seen as being at distance D_1', boy 2 is seen as being at distance D_2', and $D_1' < D_2'$. By this analysis, the proximal size differences are important only because the observer's visual system assumes that they correspond to objects that have the same distal size. Thus, if we compare man 3 with boy 1, the same apparent difference in distance should arise because, even though the proximal sizes of 1 and 3 are equal, their familiar distal sizes are unequal, and quite different apparent distances (D_1' and D_2', respectively) will be associated by past experiences with their proximal stimuli.

This cue is particularly important to the study of space perception because it is the only one which, *by its very definition*, requires past experience to be invoked, past experience with a particular object, rather than past experience in the sense of learning some rule. Hochberg and Hochberg (1952) argued that the cue of *familiar size* should therefore be disentangled from that of *relative size*, and evaluated separately.

Two types of experiment offer evidence for the efficacy of the familiar size cue: (1) experiments in which stimuli were constructed that were identical in appearance to some familiar object (for example, a playing card) but of an enlarged or reduced physical size; and (2) experiments in which subjects were given different instructions as to the nature of an otherwise ambiguous stimulus. We shall briefly discuss each type.

In an experiment by Ittelson (1951), each of 3 playing cards (1 was normal in size, 1 was twice normal, and 1 was half the normal in size) was presented singly to the subject under complete *reduction conditions* (that is, it was viewed monocularly, with none of the usual monocular or binocular distance cues available). The distance judgment was made by setting a target to the apparent distance of the playing card; the target, however, was viewed with full binocular vision, with all the usual distance cues present. The results for 5 subjects gave almost precisely the results expected:

Card	Predicted D (ft)	Obtained D (ft)
Normal	7.5	7.5
Half-size	15.0	15.0
Double-size	3.8	4.6

There has been considerable controversy about the generality of the results in the table. Gogel, Hartman, and Harker (1953) had subjects throw a dart (without seeing the results of that action) at either a normal or a double-sized playing card, located either 10 or 20 feet from them in a reduced-cue situation. Epstein (1961) used procedures closer to those of Ittelson. Neither experiment showed results similar to those reported by Ittelson; instead, both found only effects of relative size on relative distance.

In contrast, Epstein (1963) did confirm the Ittelson familiar-size hypothesis, by the use of realistic photographs of coins (dime, quarter, or half-dollar). All photographs were made to have the same physical size regardless of the size of the coin, and all were presented at the same distance so as to present the same proximal size, that is, the same-sized retinal image. Subjects viewed each photograph separately under reduced-cue conditions. Distance matches were obtained by having the subject adjust the distance of a cigarette pack, that was visible with good depth cues, to the distance of the photograph. Gogel (1964) argued that these results might simply reflect relative judgments made between the known size of cigarette packs and the known size of coins, so Epstein (1965) repeated the experiment, but provided no visual comparison. Instead, the subject was made to indicate the apparent distance by telling the experimenter to "stop" when the appropriate length of rope had been pulled through his hand.

The familiar-size hypothesis was again confirmed. Moreover, Epstein and Baratz (1964) found that when a pair of pictures of coins was viewed under reduced conditions, the picture which represented a coin of larger physical size was judged as more distant even when the 2 were identical in actual and in proximal size. Gogel has since shown (1968) that the apparent distance of a familiar object is readily influenced by previous conditions, and that this phenomenon may have affected the outcome of the experiment by Gogel, Hartman, and Harker.

It seems that realistic representations of familiar objects do indeed affect the distance judgments made by subjects who have been instructed to judge distance relationships, in the absence of the usual depth cues, under some circumstances (see also Dinnerstein, 1967; Gogel & Mertens, 1967; Ono, 1969). The circumstances and mechanisms remain to be specified, but the following considerations may be relevant to this point.

Hastorf (1950) found that when subjects were shown a disk of light under reduced conditions, and were told that it was a ping-pong ball, they judged it to be at a closer distance than when they were told that it was a billiard ball. This was so despite the fact that two-thirds of the subjects saw that the disk was not really a ball, and despite the fact that some unspecified number realized that 2 different names had been given to the same stimulus. In another experiment, Baird (1963) showed subjects rectangular strips of light, one at a time, under reduced conditions. Each strip was shown at a distance of 25 feet and varied in length from 6 to 24 inches. The subjects were told, however, that the strips were all the same size as a foot ruler, and were asked to give verbal estimates of the distances of each strip. Estimates differed significantly as a function of the length of the strip, the means of the estimates coming very close to what the distances would have had to be if the strips really had been 1 foot long.

Hastorf's results, and Baird's, seem to show quite clearly that, in the absence of definite distance cues, subjects can decide on a distance that is appropriate to the size that they are told (or decide) to assume some stimulus to be. The incidental observations from Hastorf's experiment show, however, that the subjects do not have to *perceive* (or even to believe) that the stimulus is actually the size they are assuming it to be. This raises the question of whether under such circumstances we can safely accept a sub-

ject's distance judgments as representing his *perceptions* of tridimensional space. As an illustration of the distinction between *relative size* and *familiar size,* Hochberg and Hochberg (1952) had shown that drawings that differ in relative size affected the relative durations with which each face of a reversible perspective figure appeared to be nearer. On the other hand, drawings of a man and boy that differed only in familiar size had no such effect. Ono (1969) has since shown that if subjects are asked questions that direct their attention to the maturity and immaturity of the man and boy, respectively, the familiar size patterns that were otherwise ineffective now do affect the appearance of the reversible pattern, which would certainly seem to reflect changes in the subjects' perceptions of depth and not merely changes in their judgments.

In a recent experiment directed to a somewhat different question—whether knowledge about distance affects the perception of distance—Gruber and Dinnerstein (1965) showed subjects 2 luminous squares in an otherwise dark corridor. One square was 24 feet and the other, 48 feet from the subject, but because the farther one was twice the physical size of the near one, they presented the same proximal size to the subject. In the dark, the subject saw only 2 luminous squares at the same distance. When the corridor was illuminated, he could clearly see the squares' physical distances, sizes, and the apparatus by which they were presented. When the corridor was again darkened, however, most subjects reported with surprise that the squares came together again in about 10 seconds, that is, that their relative depth faded away. Thus, subjects' first-hand knowledge of the true sizes and distances left their perceptions of depth unaffected, but it did modify their absolute distance judgments.[2] Perhaps a clear experience of tridimensionality or of apparent depth depends on relative size differences (or on other indications of depth that may be present), whereas the magnitude of the distances that are associated with that apparent depth (or with completely indeterminate spatial location, as in the experi-

[2] These experiments by Gruber and Dinnerstein reopen the distinction made earlier (p. 476) between relative and absolute apparent distance, inasmuch as the latter was affected by providing the subjects with knowledge about the viewing situation and the former was not. It may be that the judgment of absolute distance is much more labile than that of relative distance, more subject to alternative assumptions. However, it may also be that absolute distance is not really perceived at all, in the absence of a ground plane stretching between the observer and the object and in the absence of motion perspective (see pp. 501, 504) and that the observer assigns some arbitrary distance label to one of the objects and judges the other distances relative to that one.

Figure 13.21. Convexities and concavities on a plane surface, with light coming from one direction. Turn the picture over. (After v. Fieandt, 1938.)

ments of Hastorf and Baird), and the biases (see p. 438) with which the subject views a figure having reversible depth (as in the experiments of Dinnerstein and Ono) can be set by known or familiar size (Dinnerstein, 1967; Gogel & Mertens, 1967; Ono, 1969).

The Gruber and Dinnerstein experiment (like the Gelb experiment that we discussed in Chapter 12) shows that it is possible to get subjects to report appearances that are at variance with their knowledge. It would be very useful to extend a method like this one, with suitable payoff procedures (see p. 37) to the other experiments in which we are dubious about whether subjects' judgments reflect their perceptions.

Shadows

Another indication of depth and relief, much used by the painter, is the shading on a rounded or angular surface. Also the shadow cast by one object upon another can show

which object is further away, provided the source or direction of the light is clearly revealed. Little formal research has been done with this cue, either to define or to test it (see, however, pp. 420, 502).

In the simple example in Figure 13.21, the light seems to come from above, as it usually does. This assumption of overhead lighting seems to be just as strong in young children as in adults (von Fieandt, 1938). This does not mean that it is innate: Hess (1950) has shown that young chicks, 7 weeks of age, who were reared from the time of hatching in cages that were lit from below, through the wire-mesh floor, would then peck at photographs which showed wheat grains lit from below. Control animals reared with overhead lighting would peck only at pictures of grains lit from above. These findings suggest that this cue had been learned from the conditions in which they had

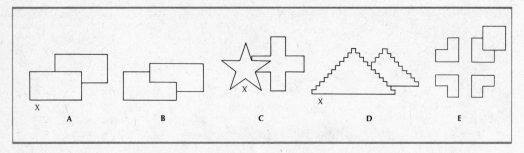

Figure 13.22. Interposition. Helmholtz proposed that the object that does not change direction at the intersection looks nearer. A. An example with consistent cues. B. An example with inconsistent cues.
C, D, E. Examples that do not fit Helmholtz' proposal. See text. (A and B from Ratoosh, 1949; C
and D from Chapanis & McCleary, 1953; E from Dinnerstein & Wertheimer, 1957.)

been reared. However, a second experiment
with samples of chicks tested at 1 to 6 weeks
of age was less successful and seemed to
show that adjustment to lighting from below
was quite difficult, as if overhead lighting
were after all more in accordance with the nature of chicks. As we have noted, the question
of whether some degree of ability to use the
cue is innate or learned can be raised in connection with every one of the depth cues except the one of familiar size; but experimental
evidence is very hard to obtain with human
subjects because so much spatial learning
may occur in the first few months of life.

Aerial Perspective

The distant mountains are blue in the clear
country air, and the buildings a few blocks
away are gray when seen through the smog of
the city. The study of atmospheric optics (see
Minnaert, 1940; Eldridge & Johnson, 1958;
Duntley & Culver, 1963) has provided the basic
physical data and certain generalizations in
regard to attentuation and scattering of light.
These effects give us a distance cue known
as "aerial perspective," that may play an important role over relatively long distances, but
neither systematic statement of this cue, nor
research on its effectiveness, has been pursued.

Interposition or Covering

The impossibility of seeing around a corner
is certainly one of the elementary facts of
visual experience, and one which the little

child must learn very early in his career. He
learns that one object may be hidden behind
another, that the hidden one is farther away,
and that he can often get to see the hidden
object by moving to the right or left. So, by
the combined principles of interposition and
of motion parallax (which we discuss on
p. 504), he can make the acquaintance of the
other depth cues.

When a farther object is only partly
covered by a nearer one, their common
contour may give a pretty good indication of
which one is in front, even without any
movement on the observer's part and with no
familiarity with their shapes. Helmholtz
pointed out that the contour line of the covering object usually does not change its direction where it joins the covered object, a
fact which might be used to discern which
object is nearer even in the absence of any
other cues. Ratoosh (1949) proposed that this
might be formalized by saying that the continuity of the contour's first derivative at the
point of intersection is the feature that determines an object's relative distance, but the
examples in Figure 13.22C,D,E show that this
is inadequate. In Figure 13.22A and B are 2
examples from Ratoosh, showing objects with
unambiguous (a) and ambiguous (b) combinations of intersections; in Figure 13.22C, D,
and E are patterns, taken from Chapanis and
McCleary (1953), and from Dinnerstein and
Wertheimer (1957), in which the interposition
cue cannot be fitted into this formulation
(because both contours change direction, as

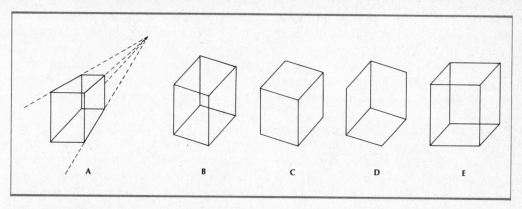

Figure 13.23. The same object in different perspectives. A. Polar projection; B–E. parallel projection. B–D are in isometric perspective; E is in oblique perspective.

in Figure 13.22C or because the formula leads to a false prediction about which object looks nearer). The figure which looked nearer is always labeled *X*. Some overall factor of "simplicity" may be at work here (see p. 435), as well as the local features of the intersection.

Linear Perspective

As an object approaches the eye, the angle that it subtends, its proximal size in the picture plane, and the image that it projects to the retina, all increase as shown in Figure 13.2. The most familiar type of perspective is generated by *polar projection,* with one or more vanishing points at the horizon, as in Figures 13.2 and 13.23A. However, the eye is willing to accept *parallel projections* of various kinds as well, as seen in Figure 13.23B,E. In the latter case, although there is a transformation that compresses the surfaces which are not in the frontal plane, there is no convergence. Such drawings are ambiguous; as you look at them for a while, the depth reverses direction. The solid that you first saw in Figure 13.23B facing one way (say, as in Figure 13.23C) changes the relationship of all of its parts and faces the other way (Figure 13.23D); see p. 519. *Reversible-perspective patterns* provide a research tool in the psychological laboratory, and they have recently attracted the attention of graphic artists (Seitz, 1965). However, such perspective ambiguity is probably not characteristic of nature: As objects increase in size

and their distance decreases, the degree of convergence between near and far edges increases, and the projection of each surface in the picture plane becomes less ambiguous. In fact, when subjects compare the slants of plane rectangles of different sizes, they consistently judge the larger rectangle to have the greater slant (Stavrianos, 1945; Freeman, 1966a). The slants of smaller rectangles are more difficult to judge because the amount of convergence they display is less (Freeman, 1966a,b).

The fact that linear perspective would normally produce foreshortening and convergence in a perspective view of an object means that Figure 13.23B has inconsistent perspective: The object cannot both be seen as a cube (that is, as having equal sides and angles) and still be consistent with the rules of perspective. Attneave and Frost (1969) had subjects view monocularly a number of drawings of cubes having different degrees of inconsistent perspective. The slant in the third dimension that each edge appeared to have was measured by asking the subject to align a rod, which he viewed binocularly, so that it appeared to continue the slant of that edge in space. Given the angles at which the lines met in the drawing, there was only one set of slants that satisfied the condition that all angles and all line lengths and slopes in the perceived object should be maximally homogeneous. The subject's alignments were extremely close to the predicted slant values, lending support to the *minimum principle* that was discussed before in connection with such patterns (Chapter 12, pp. 435, 437). Of particular interest here is the fact that as perspective consistency increased, the apparent extension into the third dimension also increased.

After Western artists discovered the rules of perspective, they followed them to portray depth and distance as faithfully and as compellingly as possible. More recently, with increasing interest in the picture's surface, as such, attempts have been made to explore the effects of using inconsistent and partly in-

verted perspectives to reduce the apparent depth, and to provide incongruities for the viewer to resolve. There is some evidence that the kinds of sketchy perspective that can be used to communicate spatial information to the Western viewer, trained in the interpretation of pictures, do not work with all cultures. Hudson (1960) found that African natives responded to the representations of people and animals as though they were all in the same plane, ignoring the spatial layout portrayed in the pictures. Similar results were obtained by Mundy-Castle (1966) and by Kilbride and Robbins (1968). Because the depth

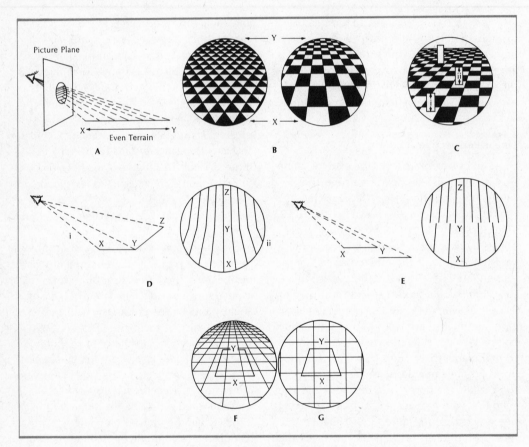

Figure 13.24. Texture density gradients as a possible source of information about the spatial layout. Gibson (1950) has pointed out that terrain that has a statistically homogeneous texture (B) presents the eye with a gradient that is correlated with the slant of the surface. C. Even though objects *i* and *ii* subtend equal visual angles, *ii* covers more units of texture than does *i*, so the observer has been given an indication that *ii* is larger than *i*. D. A change in the slant of the terrain results in a change in the gradient. E. An abrupt change in distance (a "cliff") results in an abrupt change in density. F. *X* and *Y* cover equal amounts of texture, so the pattern is shown to be a rectangle. G. The side *X* covers more texture than does *Y*, so the pattern is shown to be a trapezoid.

was only represented by means of a few sketchy lines of linear perspective, however, we cannot be sure what these results mean; certainly, we cannot assume that subjects who have had little or no experience with pictures will be unable to recognize pictured objects and scenes regardless of the type of picture that is used (see Hochberg & Brooks, 1962, p. 442). The efficacy of more informative perspective displays, such as those in Figure 13.24, has not been tested with pictorially naive viewers.

The effect of linear perspective on the apparent slant of a surface or outline pattern has recently been studied by Clark, Smith, & Rabe (1956), Weinstein (1957), Smith (1959), and Freeman (1966). The effect of perspective on pictorial size constancy was studied by Sonoda (1961), and its effect on represented distance was investigated by Smith, Smith, and Hubbard (1958).

Gradients

When psychologists speak of cues of depth and distance, they are usually thinking of the distance of an isolated object, or of the relative distance (depth) between two objects. In their experiments they are likely to conceal the floors, walls and ceiling of the room in which the objects are located because, with these in plain view, the subject has no difficulty in seeing the distance of any object.

Gibson (1950) calls attention to the importance of such surfaces as the floor or ground over which we walk or creep or drive or fly. He argues that if there is any regular marking or visible texture in the floor, this texture undergoes a perspective transformation such that in the retinal image, or in the *optic array* of light that confronts the eye, there is a *gradient* of texture density. By this he means that there is a specific rate of change in the density of the texture's projection to the eye that is directly correlated with the way objects and surfaces are arranged in the world.

Because any one spatial arrangement of objects and distances can produce the same texture-density gradients under very different

illuminations and with very different textures (Figure 13.24B), Gibson proposed that it is the gradient which is the appropriate stimulus variable to consider, not the points of retinal stimulation, nor the lines in a drawn stimulus. That is, he suggested that a texture gradient is just as truly a stimulus to which the visual system can respond as are the wavelengths and luminances of each part of the retinal image. These gradients in the retinal image are directly correlated with objective arrangements on the one hand and presumably with the subject's perceptions of those arrangements on the other. Thus, he proposed, an all-embracing perception of the immediate environment, and of the surfaces and objects within it, is likely to be achieved before, rather than after, each of the points or shapes into which the scene can be analyzed by a sophisticated observer can be noticed. As the displays in Figure 13.24 show, the gradient of texture-density carries information about the sizes (familiar or otherwise) and distances of objects standing on the surface (C); about the occurrence of a dihedral angle (fold or crease) between surfaces (D); or about the existence of an edge or a cliff between surfaces (E). Even the perception of shape might be accounted for in these terms. In Figure 13.24F, for example, the rear edge of the geometrical figure is the same number of texture-units wide as is the front edge, so that the display may be read as a "square-at-a slant." In Figure 13.24G the top of the figure is a smaller number of texture-units wide than is the bottom, the texture gradient itself is zero (signifying "no slant"), and the figure may be read as "trapezoid-in-the-frontal-plane."

Of these possibilities, the most intensively studied has been that of surface slant, using both regular and irregular textures, with and without outlines. In general, slants have tended to be underestimated when texture is the only cue the subject has to rely on (Gibson, 1950a; Clark, Smith, & Rabe, 1956; Gruber & Clark, 1956; Flock, 1964b). The slants of rectangles, moreover, are judged as well or better without any textures on their surfaces (Clark, Smith, & Rabe, 1955; Freeman, 1966).

Such experiments are difficult to interpret, however, because Gibson has not specified when a texture-density gradient is above threshold, so that we cannot tell whether the gradients involved in those experiments were adequate and comparable to the perspective cues inherent in the outline of a slanted rectangle. Flock (1962, 1964a, b, 1965) has recently undertaken to provide such measures and to reduce the complex pattern of textural stimulation to a single predictive index for slant.

Smith and Smith (1957, 1961) had subjects judge the degree of curvature of a cylinder the ends of which were covered and the surface covering of which could be changed. When the ends were covered, a variety of textures yielded little or no indication of curvature; the same thing was true of some combinations of cues. Texture, linear perspective, convergence, shading, and binocular disparity, all present together, were sufficient for the curvature to be perceived. So was the combination that consisted of seeing the edges (which were insufficient in the absence of other cues) in conjunction with cues that were not sufficient to indicate curvature by themselves. Although texture-density gradients provide *potentially* usable information, it is clear that they are not necessarily used effectively when they are the only cues available (see also Gibson, Purdy, & Lawrence, 1955; Beck, 1960). Gibson no longer rests much of his attempt to devise a psychophysics of space perception on this variable (1966a), as we see shortly (p. 504). However, texture does contribute something to combinations of other cues and can easily be manipulated in demonstrations like those in Figure 13.24. This suggests that it would be worthwhile to devise measures of this visual source of spatial information and to test the limits of its efficacy.

Interaction of Cues

Outside of the laboratory, several cues are nearly always fed into the visual system at once. Normally, they are in agreement, but they will usually differ in the precision with which the observer can use them, and they

may occasionally be in conflict. How will they interact?

In some cases, cues seem to combine their effects quite simply. Thus, Jameson and Hurvich (1959; see p. 494) report that subjects' sensitivity to a difference in distance, ΔD, when all cues were available, was close to the arithmetic sum of the sensitivities obtained with each cue alone. That is, $(1/\Delta D) = (1/\Delta D_1 + 1/\Delta D_2 + 1/\Delta D_3 \ldots)$. However, we do not know how general this simple form of cooperation may be. Schriever (1925) used drawings and photographs of solid objects presented in a stereoscope. When the only cue present was binocular disparity, the stereograms produced a good appearance of depth when viewed stereoscopically and a good appearance of reversed depth when viewed pseudoscopically (that is, with the views to each eye interchanged). Other cues were then added. Linear perspective was insufficient as a cue to cause an appearance of depth against disparity: a reversed view of a skeleton cube figure drawn in perspective was seen not as a cube, but as a truncated pyramid with the small end nearer the observer. When the cue of shading was added to that of perspective and both together pitted against binocular disparity, the appearance was unstable, though disparity prevailed in general. However, when interposition (p. 498) was introduced, it could not be overcome by contrary disparity.

The outcome of such experiments on the interaction of cues depends on how we select the cues and the conditions in which we combine them. The way in which we handle this question may itself reveal a theoretical precommitment.

Representative sampling of the kinds of scene to which the organism is normally exposed, is required by the logic of an *empiricist position*. As Brunswik argued effectively (1952, 1956), inasmuch as each cue is ambiguous, it will cause us to interpret what we see incorrectly some of the time. It is a matter of probabilities, and we should expect any cue to be relied on by the subject in proportion to the relative frequency with which it

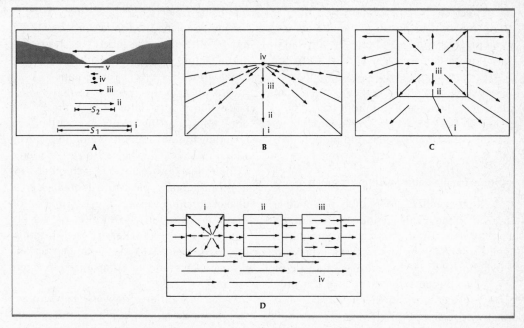

Figure 13.25. Motion perspective and optical flow. These diagrams illustrate the way in which the motion of the observer results in regular transformations of the distribution of points in the visual field in ways that are correlated with the layout and motions of objects in space. If the observer moves his eyes, head, or body, the entire image moves uniformly. In A, the observer is moving to the left and looking in the middle distance, at *iv*. Note that the arrows, which indicate the velocity with which points in the picture plane are moving relative to each other, are distributed in a smooth gradient from *i* to *iv*. B. Locomotion toward the horizon, *iv*. C. Locomotion toward point of contact with a wall, at *iii*. D. The observer is moving to the left, over the ground, *iv*. Object *i* is approaching the observer, object *ii* is upright and stationary on the ground, and object *iii* is moving to the left, but not as fast as the observer is moving. (Adapted from Gibson, 1950a.)

has been right in his past experience. If we wish to estimate the efficacy of any cue or combination of cues, therefore, or to estimate how accurately the organism can judge size, distance, and so on, we should do experiments in which the cues are present in the same combinations as they are in the situations to which the organism has been habitually exposed. That is, our experimental conditions should include *ecologically representative samples*. Only in that way will we be able to predict what the organism will do in some other (similar) situation, and be able to assess the relative contribution to be expected from the various cues in combination.

To the Gestalt psychologist, "cues" do not exist as such. Instead, either as a result of the kinds of rules that we learn about the world, or because of the way in which our perceptual processes are innately organized (see pp. 435, 437), we will see depth when the overall organization favors it. The pictorial "cues" just happen to be features that are common to many patterns that favor a tridimensional organization.[3] They cannot simply be added together, nor can they be exhaustively listed.

To Gibson, as to the Gestalt psychologists, the "cues" are an irrelevancy: the relevant variables are the stimulus gradients and other invariant features of stimulation that confront

[3]Consider the cues that were labeled in Figure 13.2B; they are shown combined in a simple picture. Each one can be seen as a flat pattern (for example, *6, 7, 8, 9* can be seen as a trapezoid in the plane of the paper, *5* can be seen as an inverted **L** adjacent to a square, *4*), or each can be seen as the three-dimensional arrangements shown in Figure 13.2A. Note that in each case, the version in Figure 13.2A is somewhat simpler (in terms of number of different angles or line lengths, and so on; see Chapter 12, p. 436) than that in Figure 13.2B.

the normal moving observer (1954, 1957, 1961). These variables of proximal stimulation are, to all practical purposes, perfectly correlated with the distances, sizes, and so forth, of distal events, and therefore provide information that is essentially certain, rather than probable.[4] The force of this proposal can only be felt in the context of a discussion about the cues of motion parallax and motion perspective.

Motion Parallax and Motion Perspective

Motion parallax and motion perspective depend on the relative motion of parts of the field of view. These cues cannot, of course, be incorporated into still pictures. Even with moving pictures we cannot make full use of these cues because the cues arise not only when objects move in the world, but also when we ourselves move about the world in our sensory exploration of it. This factor of sensory exploration may well be the primary source of visual information about space. In Helmholtz' words, "It is only by voluntarily bringing our organs of sense in various relations to the objects that we learn to be sure as to our judgments [of them]. . . . If the objects had simply been passed in review before our eyes . . . probably we should never have found our way about amid such an optical phantasmagoria."

Parallax in general is the change in the visual field resulting from a change in the observer's position. As your head or body moves (or as you are moved in a vehicle), the projections of objects in the picture plane all move about. If you fixate an object in the middle distance (point *iv*, in Figure 13.25A) while you move to the left, the images of all

the nearer objects will move to the right in the picture plane (*i*). The farther objects will move with you to the left (*v*), each velocity in the picture plane being a smoothly graded function of the object's real distance.

Not only do the objects at different distances move with different velocities in the optic array, but the points in each surface, including the very important ground plane on which most objects appear to rest, undergo a differential flow relative to each other. This flow of the points of texture contains a great deal of potentially useful, precise information about the position and motion of the observer. Some of the details of such information have been worked out by Gibson and his coworkers, and are summarized in Figure 13.25A–D.

When the observer moves relative to any textured surface, the resulting motion perspective could, in principle, offer the observer information about slants and distances (Figure 13.25A) and about relative velocities (Figure 13.25D), provided only that the subject can decode the information and that he assumes that the surfaces are themselves rigid and not being deformed at different rates to mimic the flow of motion perspective. In terms of any of the analyses of space that we have been considering up to this point, the scene in the proximal stimulus is one of meaningless confusion, and it is the strength of Gibson's proposal that he attempts to reduce this apparent confusion to simplicity. What Gibson proposes is that space perception is not achieved by restoring the third dimension to the flat proximal stimulus, mediated by the shapes that we see in the latter (such as the shapes that comprise perspective, interposition, and the other cues). Instead, the visual system might respond directly to some features of the continuous transformations due to motion that are confronting the eye, features that are invariant throughout those transformations as long as the distal world itself is invariant, and that therefore contain information about the world.

Figure 13.25 shows the kinds of information available with various kinds of motion.

---

[4] There is good reason to doubt, as we shall see (p. 517) that observers utilize all of this potential information. Furthermore, to the extent that environments differ in the availability of such information, some kind of *ecological sampling*, in Brunswik's sense, will be needed before Gibson's hypotheses can be fully tested or used (Hochberg & Smith, 1955). However, a fundamental difference remains between Gibson's theory and any theory that rests on depth cues. Gibson has shown how one can propose a psychophysics of space perception in which the only use of statistics is to handle errors, not to evaluate the probability that a cue will be a correct indication of distal arrangements.

Analyses of the *optical expansion pattern* and *motion perspective* have been undertaken by Gibson, Olum, and Rosenblatt (1955) and by Purdy (1958); of the rotations and translations of a rigid object, by Hay (1966); and of the occlusion of texture at an object's edge, by Gibson et al. (1969) and Kaplan (1969).

The radical nature of this proposal, and the potential importance of its implications, can hardly be overstated. If Gibson is right, we must replace all previous assumptions about what are the adequate units of stimulation to which we respond (Gibson, 1950, 1960), about what has to be learned in the course of perceptual development, and about how it is learned (Gibson & Gibson, 1957).

Actual research has been very exploratory; at least some of the kinds of transformation shown in Figure 13.25 are indeed seen by subjects as the theory would predict. In other cases, the information is apparently not appropriately used.

> In some of the experiments by Gibson and his coworkers, an object or a sheet of clear plastic (with texture or shapes on it) was placed on a turntable, between a point source of light and a translucent screen, so that the light cast the pattern's shadow on the screen. From the other side of the screen, subjects viewed the shadow cast by the pattern. Gibson and Gibson (1957) showed subjects both regular and irregular shapes and textures, rotating the turntable back and forth through an arc of from 15° to 70°, so that the shadows underwent a continuous transformation on the screen. Subjects saw the shadows as being constant shapes at a changing slant, and could make good slant judgments (something that subjects could not do when viewing static shadows of the same objects). Flock (1964, 1965) has extended this experiment, supporting Gibson's supposition that accurate perception of the slant of a moving surface is independent of the particular texture used (within the limits that were tested).

> Using a very different method of generating patterns of movement (namely, motion pictures of displays of moving dots, programmed one frame at a time by a computer), Green (1959) and Braunstein (1962) presented subjects with the continuous transformations that would be produced by plane and by spherical surfaces undergoing various rotations or translations: Both found that subjects were able to identify the nature of the surface and its movements.

In a subsequent experiment (Braunstein, 1968), the normal correlation between gradients of texture and gradients of velocity was artificially reduced, and the velocity gradients were found to determine the subjects' judgments of slant much more than did the texture gradients.

There is thus some support for the view that our visual system can extract some kinds of information about surface slant and motion from the transformations of textural elements alone. However, we should note that several experiments have also been performed in which the subjects simply failed to use some or all of the information potentially present in such displays (Gibson & Carel, 1952; Smith & Smith, 1961, 1963; see Epstein and Park, 1964; Kaufman, 1968). Moreover, although there has been some demonstration that even very young animals will respond to an expanding pattern as though it were an approaching object (Schiff, Caviness, & Gibson, 1962; Schiff, 1965), the extent to which the optical flow patterns (Figure 13.25) can actually be used by subjects as a source of information about depth remains to be tested.

There is older work to the same point discussed above: that patterns which look flat when they are stationary will spring into three dimensions when they are moved (see Braunstein, 1962, for a review). The *kinetic depth effect* (KDE), as studied by Wallach and his coworkers, and to which we have referred earlier (p. 494), rested on the same phenomenon. An irregular wire outline figure is placed on a turntable between a screen and a light (with the light far enough away so that its rays are essentially parallel). While the figure is at rest, its shadow looks two dimensional. When the object is rotated around its vertical axis, the shadows snap immediately into three dimensions. At least, this is true for forms meeting certain criteria: the rotations of the figure must result in shadows that change simultaneously in both length and direction. Again, however, there are limits as to how much of the potential information present in such continuous perspective transformations can actually be used, as we see in the next section (p. 517), when we discuss a famous illusion that occurs in perceiving the shape, slant, and motion of a rotating figure.

OBJECTS IN SPACE

What can we infer when a subject reports that he *perceives* depth or distance? That is, what does his report imply beyond the mere fact of this assertion? As we have seen, such reports are hard to interpret, and it is only when further implications can be stated in at least a programmatic fashion that anything is gained by talking about "perception" (see pp. 512, 515; also Garner, Hake, & Eriksen, 1956; Hochberg, 1956, 1968; Natsoulas, 1967). For one thing, we would expect that various of our activities in our environment (reaching, throwing, jumping, among others) would all be appropriate to that report, to the degree that such behaviors are accurate (and to the degree that they do not themselves change the percept). That is, a "perceived distance" refers to some model of spatial arrangement which guides the subject's spatial behaviors, a model which may or may not correspond to the physical reality that confronts the subject and which must be inferred from his spatial behaviors and from what the subject says he sees. In a gross way, it seems clear enough that our spatial behavior is guided by some sort of spatial schema or map of the world that exists only in the subject's nervous system (see pp. 454, 533ff.), and such activities as dart throwing (p. 495), reaching (p. 534), pointing (p. 537), and jumping (p. 548) have been used as measures of a subject's space perception. Unfortunately, these measures do not always agree, either with each other or with the subject's reports, and it is not always easy to infer a consistent underlying percept that we can impute to the subject (pp. 533, 550; see Smith & Smith, 1966).

Second, the concept of "perceived distance" has also been used to explain other attributes or events we perceive. We have considered parallel examples of such "perceptual causation" in connection with color constancy (p. 397) and with the illusions (p. 460). In the former case, the classic example was Helmholtz' suggestion that we take perceived illumination into account when we judge reflectance. Similarly, it has long been argued (p. 477) that we must take an object's distance into account, in order to judge its size, and if for some reason we see it as being farther away than it really is, it will then appear larger; or, conversely, if the object

appears nearer than it really is, it looks smaller (Helmholtz, 1866). That is, it is the perceived distance, not the physical distance, that presumably affects the size that will be perceived in response to any given retinal image, and in this sense the perceived distance is one of the determinants of the perceived size. To Helmholtz, this relation between size and distance was something that could only be acquired by experience, and therefore children should be expected to make mistakes in its use. This is one reason for psychologists' interest in the course of size constancy as a function of age.

The relationship between size and distance is physically a very simple one. The size s of the retinal image that is subtended by some object of physical size S, varies inversely with the distance of the object from the eye. That is, s is proportional to S/D. Therefore, for some fixed retinal image, the ratio of size to distance is constant: $S/D = k$ (see p. 477). If this relationship between size and distance were reflected in the observer's perceptual system, the same thing would be true for apparent size S' and apparent distance D', namely that $S'/D' = k$. This has been called the *size-distance invariance hypothesis* (Kilpatrick & Ittelson, 1953). However, we should note that this is only an hypothesis, and that judgments of size and judgments of distance need not be related to each other except to the extent that the stimulus variables on which judgments of size are based, and those on which judgments of distance are based, are normally closely coupled to each other in the physical world (Gruber, 1954; Epstein, 1961; Rump, 1961; Smith & Smith, 1966).

Closely related to the size-distance relationship are those of slant and shape, and of motion and distance. All of the objects (*i-iii*) in Figure 13.3 (p. 477) project the same shape to the eye, and, on the basis of retinal shape alone, the rectangle at *i* may be taken for one of the trapezoids. If the different distances of the near and far edges are accurately taken into account, however, then both the edges should appear to be of equal length, so that the rectangle's shape would be correctly perceived if slant and shape were coupled perceptually as they are physically. Conversely, even if the rectangle were set at different slants to the line of sight, and its proximal stimulus varied with such change, the apparent shape would remain constant if slant were correctly taken into account. Similarly, if points *i* and *ii* in Figure 13.25A move with the same velocity $S_1/t = S_2/t$, the near one will have moved further in the proximal stimulus ($s_1 > s_2$). To the degree that distance is correctly taken into account, and the 2 distances traversed appear equal, we should expect the 2 velocities to appear equal.

Within the explanation presented above, therefore, an entire network of perceptual attributes depends on (and thereby defines what we mean by) perceived distance. To the extent that these other perceptual attributes are in fact predictable from perceived distance, it is important to be able to measure (or to infer) what distances the subject does perceive while looking at some scene.

The physical relationship is so simple that the existence of such relationships between the perceptual variables has been widely accepted as explaining size constancy, shape constancy, and so on (see Epstein, Park, & Casey, 1961; Epstein & Park, 1963, for recent reviews). Let us note, however, that such relationships between perceptual attributes are neither logically required, nor as yet well established by experimental research.

In the discussion of color perception we saw that, as an alternative to Helmholtz' theory that we take illumination into account when judging the lightness of any part of the visual field, we could attempt to explain lightness constancy by assuming that the stimulus for lightness is a *relationship* between local luminances. Similar alternatives exist with respect to the perception of size, shape, and so on. We thus try to account for the phenomena of size constancy by taking the stimulus for an object's apparent size to be some relationship within the retinal image rather than the retinal image size *s* itself. Let us consider 2 such theories, which we will call *relational* or *stimulus-determined theories of size perception.*

Relational Theories of Size Perception

Objects are generally seen standing on the ground, their distance from the observer being defined by the point on the texture-density gradient at which they intersect the ground. The texture-density gradient may indeed provide information about the object's real distance. However, the ground's texture may provide information about the object's *size,* as well. If, as Gibson suggests, our perceptions of the sizes of objects are a function of the amount of environmental texture the object hides (see Figure 13.24C), that variable of stimulation would remain constant for a given object size, regardless of the distance from which the object is viewed. That is, as the object's distance increases, the number of texture elements that it covers remains constant or invariant; to the extent that the overall gradient of the texture defines the scale of the texture in any region (see p. 501), the object will look to be the same size despite the marked differences in its proximal size. We might call this the *texture-scale size cue.*

Similarly, shape constancy follows this analysis, without any need for "taking slant into account" (see Figure 13.24F and p. 501).

Note that in this theory there is no *necessary* psychological relationship between perceived size and perceived distance. To the extent that distance perception and size perception are both determined by the information in the texture gradient, and to the extent that the texture is in fact homogeneously distributed over the surface of the ground, correct size judgments and correct distance judgments will both be made, regardless of whether or not there is any *internal* (psychological) coupling between the perceived variables. Any degrading of the stimulus display that destroys the texture density gradient will remove both the information about distance and the information about size, and, for this reason, the fact that size constancy and shape constancy both are lost when the depth cues are removed offers no proof that those constancies rest on taking distance into account.

A somewhat similar hypothesis about a relational stimulus for apparent size was offered and tested by Rock and Ebenholtz (1959). Wallach (1948) had proposed that the stimulus for perceiving a particular gray is the ratio of light intensities of neighboring retinal areas (p. 413), and J. F. Brown (1931) had proposed that perceived motion depends not on the rate of displacement in the retinal image but on the rate of displacement relative to the frame of reference in which the movement appears (p. 520). In analogy to these, Rock and Ebenholtz suggested that the stimulus correlate for an object's apparent size is the ratio of its image size to the image size of some neighboring object which serves as a frame of reference. To test this hypothesis, subjects viewed luminous patterns in an otherwise dark room. Each pattern consisted of a rod surrounded by a rectangular frame; subjects were required to report when the lines appeared equal. With the standard a 3-inch line in a 4-inch rectangle, the average setting of the variable line in a 12-inch rectangle at which the subjects reported that it appeared equal in length to the standard was between 6.0 and 7.2 inches—more than twice as long as the standard.[5]

How do these relational theories of size perception differ from the size-distance theory? The former theories propose that an object's apparent size is a direct response to some specific and measurable feature of the pattern of sensory stimulation. That feature (for example, the relationship between retinal size and the adjacent texture scale) is one which is normally in good correspondence to objects' physical sizes, regardless of how the objects' distances may vary. The latter theory

assumes that the visual system makes a response to the size of the retinal image, and then modifies that response by taking distance into account, using any available sources of information about distance.

Regardless of whether either or both of these particular relational-size theories is correct, they represent a class of explanation that is very different from the size-distance theory. The distinction between the 2 explanations here is analogous to the distinction between the sensory and cognitive theories of the perception of lightness that we considered at some length in the previous chapter (see pp. 412–425).

Can we see retinal size? The size-distance theory takes the size of the object's retinal image s as the starting point for size perception, and we might expect, therefore, that subjects would be able to judge s at least as well as S. In fact, as we shall see, when all depth cues are removed, subjects perceive 2 objects as being the same size when the objects subtend equal visual angles (see p. 509). However, this may mean only that in the absence of any cues, subjects assume that the standard and variable are both at some completely arbitrary but specific distance, and make their match in terms of the apparent object sizes that are appropriate to that distance (Gilinsky, 1951; Woodworth & Schlosberg, 1954; Wallach & McKenna, 1960; Epstein, Park, & Casey, 1961; Gogel & Newton, 1969). Note that this explanation assumes a perceptual coupling between size and distance—the size-distance invariance hypothesis (p. 506). The hypothesis that subjects can *not* respond to retinal size as such was supported by the results of an experiment by Wallach and McKenna (1960). They showed that most subjects found it virtually impossible to match a normally viewed variable (which was viewed in the light, with distance cues present) to a standard stimulus, which was viewed under *reduction conditions* (that is, with distance cues removed by presenting the stimuli monocularly and in an otherwise dark room). These results are not surprising if the stimulus

[5]Earlier experiments by Obonai (1954) and Künnapas (1955) were performed with similar displays in order to study context effects in the geometrical illusions (pp. 456–463); these experiments found much smaller effects. They had been performed under full illumination, however, and therefore there was probably a common frame of reference for both rectangles, which would presumably reduce or could even eliminate the relational size effect.

for size is relational rather than absolute. On the other hand, Rock and McDermott (1964) found that when both the standard and variable stimuli (which were both luminous equilateral triangles) were presented in an otherwise dark room, and the standard was viewed under completely reduced conditions, subjects could match it reliably with a variable stimulus that subtended the same visual angle. This was so regardless of whether the variable stimulus itself was viewed under completely reduced conditions or with binocular depth cues. When both the standard and the variable are viewed without any *visual* context, therefore, subjects can judge when their retinal images are equal (see also p. 512).

Moreover, even when size judgments are made under daylight conditions, with all depth cues available, subjects who are instructed to match the standard to the variable in terms of visual angle generally succeed in coming quite close to doing so. (Holaday,

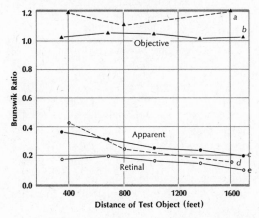

Figure 13.26. Size constancy as a function of instructions. Subjects made size matches of test objects that were located at different distances from them, and each point on the graph shows the Brunswik ratios calculated from those judgments. Lines *a, b* were obtained under instructions to make objective matches; lines *d, e* were obtained under instructions to make retinal matches; line *c* was obtained under instructions to match the apparent size of the test object. (Lines *b, c, e* from Leibowitz & Harvey, 1967; lines *a, d,* calculated from data of Gilinsky, 1955.)

1933; Gilinsky, 1955; Jenkin & Hyman, 1959; Carlson, 1960, 1962). Figure 13.26 shows how the Brunswik ratios (which we defined in connection with lightness constancy on p. 399 and which are used here as estimates of the percentage of size constancy) vary with distance, under different instructions.[6] The ratios have been computed from the data of Gilinsky (1955), who used triangles as stimuli, and from a graph presented by Leibowitz and Harvey (1967), who used human beings as stimuli. Both experiments were performed out of doors and involved unusually large ranges of distance.

In the closely related case of shape-constancy experiments, in which the standard and variable objects are presented at different slants to the line of sight, instructions have similar effects. If subjects are given instructions to match standard and variable objects, their Brunswik ratios are high; under instructions to match their retinal projections, Brunswik ratios are low (Klimpfinger, 1933; Gottheil & Bitterman, 1951; Epstein, Bontrager, & Park, 1962; Lichte & Borreson, 1967). Thus, subjects can respond at least partially (although not completely) in terms of their retinal images even when depth cues are present.

We really do not need formal experiments to prove the point, however. It is evident that railroad tracks *do* seem to converge to the horizon; that far-off trees *do* look smaller, in some sense, than near ones; that billboards near the highway *do* move faster across the visual field than those that are far back from the road. Thus it is clear that we can see things somewhat as they are in the retinal image.

How can we interpret these facts? Suppose that it had turned out that subjects could *not* make proximal matches. Would this have disproved the Helmholtzian theory? Not at

[6] Here, the Brunswik ratio would be given by the expression $(S' - s)/(S - s)$, where S' is the match that is actually obtained between standard and variable, S is the setting of the variable that is physically equal to the standard, and s is the setting of the variable that subtends the same visual angle (Figure 13.4), as does the standard. A ratio of 1.0 would mean that perfect constancy had been achieved.

all, because Helmholtz (1866) was not arguing that retinal size is consciously reportable: ". . . we are not in the habit of observing our sensations accurately, except as they are useful in enabling us to recognize external objects" (1962 ed., p. 6), and the uncorrected experience of size, in Helmholtz' view, is an unnoticed sensation on the basis of which unconscious inference-like processes operate to produce a conscious judgment of object size.

On the other hand, does the fact that subjects can respond in terms of their proximal stimulus distributions, albeit in a limited fashion, disprove the relational theories? No, because there is no reason why the proponents of such relational theories cannot also admit that there may be several different criteria on which subjects can decide to base their size judgments. "Size" is a word that subjects have learned in the context of a number of very different visual tasks, and there are probably several quite different aspects of perceptual experience to which they can refer in making their judgments. Surely, the railroad tracks occupy a smaller proportion of the total visual field at the horizon than they do at the bottom of the visual field. Even a young subject must have had ample opportunity to learn that in some sense the distance between the railroad tracks does indeed become smaller as they ascend the visual field, and that in some sense the shape of a rectangle viewed at a slant is a trapezoid. Gibson has called these kinds of experience—the pattern of perceptual responses that are more in correspondence with proximal than with distal stimulation—the *visual field*, as opposed to the *visual world*. He takes the latter to be the body of perceptual experiences on which behavior is really based and the former to be a quite different domain (see the debate between Boring, 1952a,b, and Gibson, 1952). To Gibson, then, the visual field is in no sense the basis of the visual world; it is a separate set of experiences that can at best intrude into our perception of the true physical layout (1966, p. 306). But is the visual field really all that useless, and are its effects merely an "intrusion"? If so, it is hard to see why the subject ever identifies proximal size as "size" and maintains any ability to respond to it.

In fact, the relationships within the visual field must guide our activities in the spatial environment, too. To move your eye from 6 to 7 in Figure 13.2B takes a longer excursion of the eye than to move it from 8 to 9; to turn your head so that your nose no longer obscures some object requires a greater rotation when the object is near than far. When 2 objects are at the same distance, "size" as measured by absolute retinal image size coincides with size as measured by relational criteria. When the 2 objects are at different distances, object-oriented behaviors and image-oriented behaviors no longer coincide. The subject may have quite different sensory criteria for judging equality according to each meaning, and unless the experimental conditions can explicitly separate these meanings for him, his actual decision may be some unstable compromise between them.

In any case, the answer to the question of whether we can respond to the retinal image seems to be a qualified "yes", but this fact does not really support the Helmholtzian theory or oppose the relational one. What it does suggest is the need to study object perception with tools like those of signal detection methodology (p. 34) or with reaction-time procedures (see p. 47) that will help to separate the various criteria that subjects may use.

Size-Distance Invariance

If retinal size is fixed, so is the ratio of S/D that will produce it (Figure 13.4). We have already considered (p. 506) the hypothesis that the ratio of perceived size to perceived distance S'/D' is also fixed, for a given image size. For a recent review of evidence concerning this relationship, see Epstein, Park and Casey (1961). At first glance, the evidence for such a relationship is encouraging, and we have seen that it has been used to account for such powerful effects as the geometrical illusions (p. 462), as well as the constancies. So closely related to it that both are often used interchangeably is *Emmert's Law,* which offers a good example both of the implications and difficulties of this hypothesis.

Emmert's Law refers to the fact noted by Emmert in 1881 (Boring, 1942) that an afterimage actually looks bigger if it is projected on a more distant surface, the judged size of the image being proportional to the distance of that surface. As a matter of fact, any physical measure of the projected size of the afterimage must increase with distance because the affected area on the retina has a fixed retinal size *s,* and the proportion that it covers of the measuring surface is simply proportional to the distance *D.* This is true, of course, regardless of whether or not there are any distance cues. However, the change in the *apparent* size of the afterimage as a function of distance does depend on the presence of such cues (Helson, 1936; Edwards, 1953; Hastorf & Kennedy, 1957), and it therefore appeared reasonable to propose that the apparent change in the size of an afterimage results from the same mechanisms that produce size constancy. Specifically, perhaps the apparent size of an afterimage is proportional to the apparent distance of the surface on which it is projected: this would then make Emmert's Law a case of the size-distance invariance relationship.

The relationship between Emmert's Law and size perception in general has been discussed by Boring (1940, 1942), Edwards (1950), and Boring and Edwards (1951); the identification of Emmert's Law and size constancy was questioned by Young (1950, 1951) and Crookes (1959). Distinctions between *S* and *D,* on the one hand, and *S'* and *D',* on the other hand, have not always been kept clear, and there are unresolved measurement problems (for reviews, see Epstein, Park, & Casey, 1961; Onizawa, 1954).

In any case, however, as long as the changes in the apparent distance of the afterimage are produced by varying the distance of the surface against which the afterimage is being judged, the relational determinants of size (and perhaps the effects of binocular convergence, see p. 480) may be responsible for the change in the apparent size of the afterimage, independent of any change in apparent distance.

Let us therefore consider a classical case in which the apparent size of an object undergoes a change, even though the size of its retinal image remains constant and is not projected on a real textured surface.

The moon illusion Most readers will have noticed a phenomenon that has been known and puzzled over for centuries, namely that the moon appears to be much larger when it is low in the sky. It has been shown repeatedly that this is not due to any simple physical effect such as the greater atmospheric scattering or refraction of light when the moon is near the horizon. In fact, the illusion has been demonstrated without the moon at all, so such physical explanations are irrelevant when an artificial image of the moon is presented to the eye against different regions of the sky (Kaufman & Rock, 1962; Rock & Kaufman, 1962), or when an afterimage of fixed retinal size is projected near the horizon or at a 45° elevation (Reimann, 1902; King & Gruber, 1953). It has been thought since Ptolemy that the effect was somehow dependent on apparent distance (Boring, 1942).

Boring and his associates (1943) worked on the top of a high building, using both the real and mirrored moons. In some cases, they could make the real moon seem to move from zenith to horizon, or vice versa, by mirrors mounted on long supports. Subjects matched the moon's size by means of a nearby disk of variable size. Their final conclusion was that the illusion was largely dependent on the direction of the eyes in relation to the head. If the subject lies on his back, he chooses a larger variable stimulus to match the size of the moon at the zenith, and a smaller one to match the moon at the horizon. The obvious explanation would seem to be that turning the eyes upwards tends to give a slight reflex divergence of the eyes that would increase the strain to maintain convergence which would, in turn, serve as a cue to decreased distance. If the moon were judged to be nearer at the zenith than at the horizon, it would seem smaller at the zenith, by the size-distance invariance hypothesis, because retinal size is unchanged.

However, the illusion produced by eye direction is small whereas the moon illusion is a large phenomenon, and other factors contribute to it. Kaufman and Rock used two artificial moons optically introduced at different places in the visual field. Under their conditions, eye elevation had no effect, but the presence of terrain adjacent to the horizon was important in causing an increase of from 30 to 100 percent in the apparent size of the moon. Presumably this was so because the distance cues in the terrain made the horizon appear more remote than the zenith sky (Kaufman & Rock, 1962; see also King & Gruber, 1962). The size increase occurs because when the moon is low its proximity to the horizon makes it appear equidistant with the horizon (Gogel, 1965).

There are 2 troubles with these size-distance explanations of the moon illusion. The first is that the illusion may not result from changes in the apparent distance of the moon, but may be a relational size effect produced by the terrain at the horizon. Second, and more troublesome for the size-distance invariance hypothesis: the subject usually reports that the moon *looks* farther away at the zenith, instead of closer. Perhaps size-distance invariance determines the apparent size of the moon in an automatic fashion, but the distance judgment that is the basis of this process is not directly available to introspection. Then the size judgments that the subject has made (once he has encoded them into some stable form; see p. 423) might serve as the basis for another judgment of distance, which may be opposite to the distance judgment that was first arrived at and on which the size judgment was based (Woodworth & Schlosberg, 1954; Kaufman & Rock, 1962a,b).

Inherent in the idea of "allowing for distance," in judging size, is the assumption that some internal representation of distance, D', is a mediating variable. That is, in solving the equation $S'/D' = k$, the effective variable is

D' itself, rather than any of the various stimulus patterns by which the observer arrives at his estimate of D. Yet in each of our 2 classical examples, Emmert's Law and the moon illusion, the size may change because the patterns of stimulation act as relational size determinants (p. 507), not because they provide depth cues. The same objection applies to the many demonstrations, which we next examine, showing that depth cues are necessary to size constancy.

Size constancy depends on the presence of depth cues, as a number of experiments show. Consider a series of experiments performed by Holway and Boring (1941). The

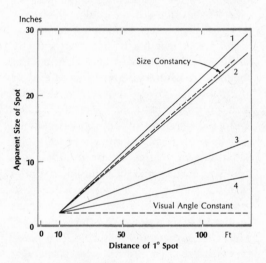

Figure 13.27. Perceived size as a function of depth cues. The standard was a disk of light, displayed at various distances from the observer. Its actual size was increased as the distance was increased to yield a constant retinal angle. The observer varied the comparison disk until it appeared to be the same size as the standard; the distance of the comparison was held constant at 10 ft. There was good size constancy under conditions 1 and 2, which employed binocular and monocular vision, respectively. In 3 some depth cues were removed by use of an artificial pupil, reducing the constancy. Further reduction of cues by the use of drapes to kill reflections (4) forced the observer to make matches almost entirely in terms of visual angle. (Holway & Boring, 1941.)

subject stood at the intersection of 2 long corridors, stretching out like the arms of an L. In one corridor was a variable stimulus, a disk of light that was adjustable in size, placed 10 feet from the subject. At various distances (10 to 120 feet) down the other arm of the L, a standard disk was exposed, its size so chosen that it always subtended exactly 1 degree of visual angle. The subject's task was to set the size of the comparison stimulus so that it looked as large as the standard. The size constancy line (in Figure 13.27) shows the settings that would represent perfect matching of physical size, since an angle of 1° subtends about $8\frac{1}{2}$ inches at 40 feet, 17 inches at 80 feet, and so on. Using normal binocular vision, the subject's results are shown in line 1; they actually overshoot constancy slightly. Line 2 shows the results using monocular observation. When a reduction screen (p. 399) was introduced to reduce depth cues further, the settings fell (to line 3). Some depth cues remained available from faint reflections in the doors that lined the corridor. When these were minimized by black drapes, the settings (line 4) approached still closer to those determined by visual angle. In a later experiment, Lichten and Lurie (1950) reduced these depth cues still further by the use of screens that prevented the subject from seeing anything but the targets. Under these conditions there remained no trace of size constancy.

In more recent experiments in which distance cues were eliminated or reduced (Chalmers, 1952; Hastorf & Way, 1952; Zeigler & Leibowitz, 1957; Rock & McDermott, 1962), similar results were obtained; stimuli were judged to be equal when they subtended equal visual angles. These results might reasonably be taken to mean that the subject can judge the size of an unknown object only to the extent that he has reliable cues as to the object's distance. However, as we have seen, this is not the only plausible interpretation of such results, because impairing vision and removing depth cues not only interferes with the perception of distance, but also eliminates features of stimulation that may be relational

determinants of apparent size, irrespective of the fact that these features may also be depth cues.

How can we change the apparent distance D' of an object without introducing any of the stimulus features which may determine apparent size directly?

When we discussed the "primary" or nonvisual distance cues (p. 479), we noted that as convergence and/or accommodation increased, the apparent size of an object decreased, even though the proximal stimulus remained unchanged (Wheatstone, 1852; Judd, 1897; Hermans, 1954; Bleything, 1957; Roelofs & Zeeman, 1957; Heinemann, Tulving, & Nachmias, 1959; Rock & McDermott, 1962). Inasmuch as convergence normally increases as D decreases, convergence is a potential depth cue, and this decrease in apparent size is what we would expect from the equation $S'/D' = k$. The changes in apparent size, here, which are well attested, cannot be ascribed to the presence of any visual relational determinants, like those proposed by Gibson and by Rock and Ebenholtz (pp. 501, 508), inasmuch as the size s of the retinal image has remained unchanged.

However, this does not necessarily mean that the primary distance cues first produce some response of a perceived distance D' and that this perceived distance then determines a perceived size s'. Of the authors cited, only Roelofs and Zeeman, and Bleything obtained changes in apparent distance that were at all commensurate with the changes in apparent size. In some cases subjects judged that objects that were objectively nearer were further away (Heinemann, Tulving, & Nachmias, 1959). This discrepancy between S' and D' is not a trivial matter, for it makes it difficult to state formally what we mean by "taking distance into account."

Nor is this discrepancy peculiar to the use of the "primary cues." Gruber (1954) had the same subjects make both size and distance judgments, at each of 6 distances (ranging from 200 to 450 cm) and found that while they overestimated the relative size of the standard object, they underestimated its relative distance. Jenkin and Hyman (1959) obtained a similar inverted relationship between estimates of size S and estimates of distance D (in feet) when subjects were instructed to make objective size matches. But surprisingly enough they obtained appropriate size and distance judgments when subjects were instructed to make *analytic* matches (that is, to judge in terms of retinal images).

On the other hand, Blessing and Landauer (1967) instructed their subjects to make objective size and distance judgments of targets that were presented with false perspective cues in order to vary apparent distance; judgments made under these conditions provided a very good fit to the size-distance invariance hypothesis. Coltheart (1969) had subjects view an illuminated triangle with no depth cues in a dark room, and gave them cut-out triangles of different sizes to hold, as haptic information about the visual targets. When subjects were given larger triangles to hold they judged that the targets were at a greater distance (although the distance was significantly underestimated); when both the visual target and the haptic target were doubled in size, the apparent distance of the target remained constant, which is what we would expect under these conditions in terms of the size-distance invariance hypothesis. More indirectly, Künnapas (1968) found that the relation between D' and D varies as a function of the available depth cues in very much the same way as judgments of size varied in the experiment by Holway and Boring.

Nevertheless, subjects often overestimate the size of objects as their physical distance is increased (Holway & Boring, 1941; Chalmers, 1952; Gilinsky, 1955; Jenkin, 1957, 1959), although, using human beings as the stimuli, Leibowitz and Harvey (1967) did not find such overestimation. If we take such judgments to be measures of perceived size S', we must question the efficacy of the relational determinants of size, for these should remain constant regardless of distance. Moreover, if the size-distance invariance hypothesis is to be maintained, we would expect to find that perceived distance D' should also be overestimated as the real distance D is increased; the data do not clearly support this prediction. Gilinsky (1951) had subjects indicate the midpoint of each of 14 distances (ranging from 8 to 200 feet), under normal viewing conditions, and found that subjects set the further sections of each such division too large when comparing them with the nearer ones; that is, far physical distances were *underestimated* in comparison to near ones. Smith (1958) and Harway (1963) found similar results, whereas Purdy and Gibson (1955)

found few errors at all. Only in indoor viewing have greater physical distances been overestimated compared to lesser ones (Teghtsoonian & Teghtsoonian, 1969; Künnapas, 1960; Luria, Kinney, & Weissman, 1967).

In short, the overestimation of size with increasing distance cannot be explained by saying that apparent distance increases faster than physical distance, *if we accept subjects' distance estimates as our definition of D'*. There is little reason to do so. Many criteria are available on which the subject can base his response, and with no special training to narrow his use of those criteria, we should not expect that his judgment directly reflects any one of them. In the present case, for example, Carlson (1960) has proposed that the phenomenon of overestimating size occurs because, when the subject is trying to judge actual physical size, he brings to bear all his beliefs about the size-distance relationships, including the belief that an object near by must look larger than one further away in order for the 2 to be equal in physical size. Thus, in terms of this explanation, having arrived at an apparent size that has automatically taken distance into account, he may apply a conscious correction for distance in arriving at his size judgment and thus end up with an erroneous size match. This is the same explanation that was offered earlier for the failure of the hypothesis of the size-distance invariance to predict judgments based on the primary cues (p. 513) and to explain the paradoxes involved in the moon illusion (p. 512). It is an interesting kind of explanation, reminiscent of the Helmholtzian one in this respect: One level of perceived size (what the subject sees before he makes his misguided correction) serves as the basis for a second level of response (the judgments actually made). Presumably these different levels of "perceiving size" differ in ways that the subject could learn to detect under suitable training conditions, and differ also in the speed with which the judgments can be made (permitting, perhaps, their separation by suitable methods of measuring reaction-time).

Certainly, however, indirect methods will be needed to decide the values of S' to put in the formula when solving for D' and vice versa.

Shape Constancy and Shape-Slant Invariance

If an object with a constant physical configuration is viewed from different slants to the line of sight, it produces retinal images of different configurations (Figure 13.3). In the usual experiments to study the judgments of the shape of an object, a subject tries to match the shape of an object (the standard) that is presented to him at one slant, by choosing from among a set of objects having different configurations (the variables), which are viewed at another slant, the one object of the set that has the same apparent shape. The match that he makes under normal viewing conditions usually is intermediate between one in which the 2 objects have the same physical configuration, and one in which their retinal images have the same configurations.

Brunswik or Thouless ratios are often employed to measure the degree to which constancy is "achieved" (although there are inadequacies with these measures here as in the other constancies (see pp. 399, 509; Epstein & Park, 1963).

The first explanation that suggests itself for shape constancy, as for any of the constancies (see pp. 398, 495), is that we know what shape any object really has because of our previous experiences with it. However, most research has found no clear influence of familiarity on shape constancy (Thouless, 1931; Langdon, 1953; Nelson & Bartley, 1956).

Borreson and Lichte (1962) have recently shown that a familiarization session with nonsense shapes (like those of Attneave and Arnoult in Chapter 12, p. 446) that were subsequently used in an experiment, increased the Brunswik ratios that were obtained with one group of subjects. However, the shapes were shown at varying orientations in another familiarization session, yet this specific experience with what these irregular and quite unfamiliar shapes looked like at various slants had no significant effects on the constancy ratios. Perhaps a wider range of experiences would have produced different results. On the other hand, Hake and Myers (1969) have shown that the effects of familiarization that were obtained may be an artifact of the method that was used, and in any case, even with no familiarization at all, average Brunswik ratios for the different shapes that were used varied from 0.19 to 0.77, or 77 percent of constancy in the latter case. Thus, shape constancy does not necessarily arise from one's memory of the true shape, although familiarity can contribute to it.

Alternatively, we could explain shape-constancy rather simply in this way. Using depth cues, the subject sees that one edge of the shape is further away than the other; then he automatically makes allowance for this increased distance when he judges the sizes of the near and far edges. Indeed, when viewing conditions are made worse or impoverished (for example, by viewing the shapes monocularly instead of binocularly, by eliminating views of the background, by reducing exposure time and intensity, by removing texture, and so on), so that cues as to the object's orientation are likely to be reduced or obliterated, shape constancy decreases as well (Thouless, 1931; Eissler, 1933; Stavrianos, 1945; Langdon, 1951, 1953; Leibowitz, Mitchell, & Angris, 1954; Leibowitz & Bourne, 1956; Nelson & Bartley, 1956; Leibowitz, Bussey, & McGuire, 1957). However, slant cues (or depth cues) are themselves often patterns of stimulation which influence the perception of shapes, regardless of their possible function as depth cues (see Figure 13.24). As with size and color, therefore, we cannot simply assume that because shape judgments are more like the distal than like the proximal patterns when the slant cues are present, this is due to anything like "taking slant into account."

If shape constancy depended on slant being taken into account, we might at first thought expect that shape constancy could be no better than the accuracy with which subjects make judgments of the object's slant.

Stavrianos (1945) performed a series of experiments in which judgments of both slant and shape were obtained, using rectangles and el-lipses under 3 conditions of observation. In gen-eral, subjects made relatively accurate judgments of the shape of objects under conditions in which they made inaccurate judgments of the slant. We can, of course, argue that the subjects are not responding to the same cues with equal attention when they are making their judgments of shape and slant. As we noted above, the attitudes (objective, retinal, or apparent) with which sub-jects are instructed to make their matches of the shapes of the objects have marked effects. Sub-jects instructed to make an analytical or retinal match obtain lower constancy ratios, similar to those obtained with partial removal of the depth cues (Klimpfinger, 1933; Gottheil & Bitterman, 1951; Epstein, Bontrager, & Parks, 1962; Lichte & Borreson, 1967), and although some of the earlier studies could not be unequivocally interpreted to this point, the results now seem to be quite conclusive. Certainly, the fact that a change in instructions can produce a reliable change in the nature of the shape matches that subjects make, and can result in judgments that approach (but do not reach) correspondence to the retinal image, is evidence that there are at least 2 different sets of criteria on which subjects can base their judgments of shapes viewed at some slant.

However, it may also be true that at least some criteria of apparent slant and apparent shape are psychologically coupled to each other. Koffka (1935) proposed that perceived slant and perceived shape are in an invariant relationship, similar to the size-distance relationship we have discussed above (p. 506; see also Chapter 12, p. 460). More specifically, Beck and Gibson (1955) hypothesized that a given retinal projection de-termines a family of "apparent-shapes-at-ap-parent-slants." This shape-slant invariance hy-pothesis does not imply that slant is taken into account to arrive at a shape judgment. It does imply that when different judgments of slant and of shape can be obtained with the same retinal image, the judgments of slant and of shape will be correlated with each other. Although Flock (1964) did not find a systematic relationship be-tween shape and slant judgments, other experi-ments have yielded judgments of slant and shape that are at least roughly correlated (Stavrianos, 1945; Winnick & Rogoff, 1965). To test the slant-shape invariance hypothesis, however, we must be sure that the slant cues are not acting as re-lational determiners of shape (see p. 501), rather than as information about the object's slant. In one experiment, Beck and Gibson (1955) pre-sented subjects with a textureless triangle at a

45° slant to a textured vertical background; the subjects viewed the triangle monocularly, keep-ing their heads motionless. The subjects saw the triangle as being in the plane of the vertical background. Two comparison figures were mounted flat on the same background, one having the same objective shape as the standard, the other having the same projective shape (that is, producing a similar image on the retina). Under these viewing conditions, all subjects chose the latter. When binocular vision was permitted, however, the standard triangle was seen to be slanted out from its background; and now 77 percent of the subjects chose the com-parison triangle which was objectively equal to the standard. A modified replication and ex-tension of this experiment, performed by Epstein, Bontrager, and Park (1962), also indicated that subjects made a change toward an objective match when binocular viewing was permitted, although their judgments of slant and shape did not fit each other very well. Kaiser (1967) recently refined and extended this procedure, using 3 trapezoids at different slants to the observer (15°, 45°, and 65°). Each trapezoid was so proportioned that they all projected the same retinal pattern. Subjects were provided with a variable shape, which was viewed in the upright position; the subjects were instructed to adjust the shape to match the judged objective shape of the slanted object. They also rotated a half-black, half-white disk (a procedure previously used by Flock, 1964) to match the object's slant. They were permitted to adjust these variables until they were satisfied with both. Viewing was done under both mo-nocular and binocular conditions, and the way in which the subjects' matches of shape changed between the 2 conditions was compared with the way in which their slant matches changed. Changes in the apparent shape of the trapezoid, as measured by the ratio of height to base, were highly correlated with changes in apparent slant ($r = +.90$); changes in the ratio of top to base were also significantly correlated with changes in slant but somewhat less so ($r = +.68$). In this experiment, therefore, the slant-shape invariance hypothesis was confirmed.

In any case, all 3 studies showed that binocu-lar depth cues which affect perceived slant also affect shape judgments. It is not easy to see how the binocular depth cues could comprise rela-tional size and shape determinants in the sense that we are using this term (see p. 507). There-fore, there does indeed seem to be some cou-pling between the apparent slant and apparent shape.

Earlier evidence to this point can be obtained

from the experiments of Langdon (1951, 1953, 1955a,b). In one experiment (1951), the standard was a luminous wire circle, and the comparison stimulus was one of 15 luminous ellipses presented in the frontal-parallel plane, both being viewed in an otherwise completely dark room. The circle was rotated around its vertical axis, and the subject's task was to indicate when in the course of its rotation the shape of the rotating circle matched one of the stationary ellipses. In general, the 2 were chosen as being equal when the proximal stimulus projected by the circle was actually narrower than the ellipse. That is, shape constancy was obtained as a result of the spatial information provided by the rotary motion, and by the consequent *motion perspective* (p. 503). Langdon obtained similar results with various modifications of this procedure (1953, 1955a,b), and although he concluded that a simple slant-shape formula is inapplicable (because of marked irregularities in the way that the degree of constancy varied with slant), this is another example of a stimulus variable that cannot plausibly be considered to be a relational shape determinant but which affects judgments of shape by way of the information about slant that it can provide to the visual system.

There thus seems to be evidence to support the existence of a relationship between the stimulus conditions that provide information about slant and the shape that is perceived under those conditions. However, there is little or no support for the proposition that the information must first manifest itself as *perceived* slant before it can work its effects. Indeed, taking the present body of evidence into account, it is not even necessary that the information about slant be reflected in any perception of slant; although not all subjects in Langdon's (1951) experiment experienced tridimensionality as a result of the rotation imparted to the circular standard, this did not appear to interfere with the degree of constancy that they achieved.

Does the achievement of shape constancy imply that the retinal image was corrected by "taking slant into account," supporting the Helmholtzian position? Not necessarily: To Gibson, information about the object's shape is potentially available in those features that remain invariant in the transformations that

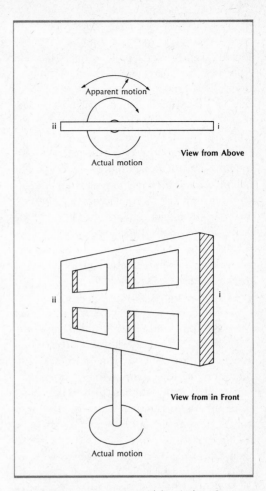

Figure 13.28. Ames' "trapezoidal" window. See text.

its projection undergoes in the optic array (p. 504), and it is only the departures from constancy that require explanation. Let us consider this further in the context of an illusion which seems to show an extremely striking departure from constancy despite the fact that the proximal shape undergoes a continuous rotary transformation.

Perspective reversal

The Ames trapezoidal window produces a phenomenon that has received a great deal of attention in recent years. The subject stands about 20 feet from an object that looks like a window sash mounted on a vertical rod, as an axis (Figure 13.28). The rod is rotated slowly, but the subject does not see the rotation correctly. Instead, the sash seems to oscillate back and forth through an arc of 90° to 100°. The sash is actually a trapezoid, cut from flat cardboard, shaped and painted to resemble a solid window drawn in perspective. A little thought shows that the sash will tend to appear slanted even in frontal-parallel view and that it will seem to swing from this slant to the opposite one as it rotates. Inasmuch as oscillation rather than rotation is perceived, and the longer end always appears to be nearer, we see that the rotary motion has not only failed to reveal the object's true shape; during half of the oscillation, the apparent motion is opposite to the true motion. Of course, the demonstration must be viewed from a fair distance to eliminate contradictory cues from accommodation, convergence, and other sources (one of which we discuss shortly), but the illusion is surprisingly strong. Objects like a card, a ball, or a tube, when attached to the window, appear to make full rotations (as they are actually doing, of course); this makes them appear to pass clear through the "oscillating" sash. If the trapezoidal pattern is replaced by a rectangle, oscillation ceases, and the full rotation is seen. Construction details are given by Ames (1951) and Ittelson (1952).

To Ames, the subject's past experience with rectangular windows was responsible for the phenomenon, and the importance of past experience of some sort is also suggested by cross-cultural differences in the illusion, that were found by Allport and Pettigrew (1957). It has been shown, however, that the pattern need not be a simulated window (Pastore, 1952; Canestrari, 1956), nor even a trapezoid. The illusion of reversal can be obtained with a circle, an ellipse, and a "nonsense figure," none of which contains any linear perspective (Day & Power, 1963, 1965). Various alternative theories have been offered by Pastore (1952); Canestrari (1956); Graham (1963); Day and Power (1965); Guastella (1966); Cook, Mefferd, and Wieland (1967); and Braunstein and Payne (1968). For our present purposes, there are 3 questions to be answered:

1. *Why does the rotary motion fail to be perceived continuously and veridically?* Graham (1963) pointed out that the differential angular velocity between any 2 points on the figure's surface is the same whether that part of the window is approaching or receding, so that the direction of rotation is ambiguous (see also Day & Power, 1965). This is geometrically true, of course, only in the case of parallel projection, such as is approximated when the distance from which the object is viewed is large relative to its size (Hershberger, 1967; see also p. 499). Otherwise, retinal projection is polar projection, and the 2 directions of motion should not give equivalent angular velocities in the optic array. In fact, Zegers (1965) has shown that the reversal rate increases as the viewing distance is increased and the trapezoid size decreased. Braunstein and Payne (1968) find that with parallel projection the rectangle as well as the trapezoid appears to reverse direction, whereas with polar projection, both shapes seem to rotate correctly and continuously.

In short, failure to see the correct motion may occur only when the rotation cues are subliminal. Although Gibson has not seriously addressed himself to the problem of thresholds in connection with the information available in perspective transformations, this is clearly a matter that will have to be taken into account (see pp. 502, 505).

2. *Why does the rectangle appear to rotate as it really does when the trapezoid does not do so, at intermediate ranges of motion perspective?* Perhaps because we are more sensitive to perspective changes in right angles (as Braunstein and Payne suggest), although how this hypothesis might be phrased when we are dealing with continuous perspective transformations has not been specifically spelled out. Perhaps because we respond to the implied linear perspective of the figure (as Pastore, 1952, and Graham, 1963, suggest) when motion perspective is a relatively weak cue. Lending support to the latter interpretation, Canestrari and Farnè (1969) have shown

that the depth cues of interposition (p. 498) and the texture-density gradient (p. 501) also cause continuous rotation to look like oscillation.

Furthermore, Cross and Cross (1969) pointed out that the picture thickness of the Ames window comprises a depth cue that is consistent with oscillatory motion and is inconsistent with rotation; when this cue was removed or reduced, subjects reported a smaller number of reversals.

3. *Why does reversal occur?* The fact that the cues to motion are ambiguous does not explain why the direction of rotation appears to reverse. It seems likely that this problem is related to the other reversal phenomena (pp. 433, 499; see Cook, Mefferd, & Wieland, 1967), and must await a general solution.

As a brief survey of the reversal phenomena, let us note the following points.

Perspective reversal is not restricted to pictures, but will occur while viewing wire objects those pictures represent (Howard, 1961; Cormack & Upchurch, 1969; Price, 1969). Binocular viewing and rotation of the object reduce the reversal rate (Cormack & Upchurch, 1969). Reversal rate for pictured objects appears to be lower with more complex or more difficult forms (Gordon, 1903; Porter, 1938; Ammons, 1954), and the rate generally increases as a result of practice with a given figure (Ammons, Ulrich, & Ammons, 1959; Smith, Imparato, & Exner, 1968). However, a drop in reversal rate also has been reported after more extended observation. (Bruner, Postman, & Mosteller, 1950). Using a rotating reversible object, Price (1969) found that the version that was initially perceived decreased in its duration over the first several reversals (thus increasing the reversal rate) and then became very variable in duration; but the alternative phase remained relatively constant in duration throughout.

The occurrence of the reversals still cannot be explained. At least two components are involved in the reversal of perspective in pictures. One of them seems to be regular and independent of the size of the stimulus, while the other component appears to slow down the first one, has different effects on large than on small figures, and seems to be related to shifts in fixation (Washburn, Mallay, & Naylor, 1931). Washburn and Gillette (1933) showed that although subjects can best control the appearance of an outline cube when they are free to move their fixation point from one region to another, reversals also occur and can be controlled to some degree even when the retinal image is stabilized by viewing it as an afterimage. Moreover, were eye movements responsible for reversals, we should expect adjacent figures to reverse simultaneously and, although neighboring (or nested) outline cubes may reverse at the same time (Adams & Haire, 1959), they may also do so independently (Washburn & Gillette, 1933) as do rotating reversible objects (Mulholland, 1956; Howard, 1961). Changes in fixation are therefore not necessary either to obtain reversals or to control them. The success with which the subject can hold any alternative has been held to be a function of its relative simplicity (defined in terms of the motor actions it suggests) and of the frequency with which the object that it represents is encountered in ordinary life (Washburn, Reagan, & Thurston, 1934).

It is relatively easy to observe reversals in the direction of apparent rotation, or gross changes in the orientation of the object. With each reversal in apparent movement, however, there is associated a large number of more subtle changes in apparent depth relationships and in what Mefferd (1968) has termed "endogeneously-supplied visual attributes of depth." The visual system appears to fit erroneous assumptions about the object's three-dimensional orientation to the changing stimulus patterns that arise as the object rotates. These changes are difficult to study systematically, but are very important to an understanding of the kind of perceptual coupling (pp. 506, 516) that we have been discussing in this chapter.

PERCEPTION OF VISUAL MOVEMENT

Just as the image that falls on the retina is ambiguous as an indicator of the size and distance of the object that projects it, the retinal image is also ambiguous as to the locations and motions of objects in space. An object whose image is tilted on the retina may be tilted in space, or it may be upright and the observer may be tilted. An object whose retinal image is in motion may be moving in space, or the observer may be moving. In order to perceive the location and motion of an object correctly, therefore, the observer must somehow take his bodily positions and movements into account.

There are several sensory systems that respond to the internal state of our joints and muscles, and to the pull of gravity. The information that these systems can provide about the position and motion of the body and of its parts is supplemented by records that are kept in the nervous system concerning the motor impulses that have been sent to move those parts and to change their positions. These sensory systems are discussed in Chapter 11. We shall not attempt to consider them separately here. Instead, we shall usually refer to them indiscriminately as the *position sense,* or as *proprioception.*

Real Movement

Movement is perceived when the image of an object remains stationary on the retina while the eye pursues the object. We may suppose, therefore, that the perception of movement results from sensing the eye movements made while tracking the object. Movement is also perceived, however, when the eye is stationary, and the object's image moves across the retina; in fact, motion in the periphery of the image is what usually initiates eye movements in the pursuit of a moving object. Movement is *not* perceived when the retinal image moves as a result of saccadic eye movements (Chapter 11). We shall also see that movement is perceived under certain conditions in which the eye and its retinal image are both stationary. It is clear that several different processes lead to the same "final common percept" of movement (Kolers, 1963) and that the perception of movement is complexly determined.

Thresholds of displacement   Consider an object, the retinal image of which is displaced some distance *s* in some interval of time *t*. The minimum velocity (ds/dt) that can be detected is called the *velocity threshold.* The minimum distance over which movement can

be detected is the *displacement threshold.* Because the luminance, duration, uniformity of motion, size of the field over which movement occurs, and the number of moving targets can all be varied, in addition to velocity and displacement, many kinds of thresholds can be studied in the perception of real movement. Threshold research has recently been surveyed by Graham (1965) and by Spigel (1965). In the following discussion, the notation min/sec refers to angular velocity at the eye, that is, to minutes of visual angle of displacement divided by seconds of time. A higher ratio threshold means that a faster movement is needed in order for the movement to be detected than does a lower ratio.

The velocity threshold while fixating a moving stimulus is about 1 to 2 min/sec, when some parts of the visual field are stationary, and about 10 to 20 min/sec when only the moving stimulus is presented (Aubert, 1886; Bourdon, 1902; Grim, 1911). Brown and Conklin (1954) found a threshold of 18 min/sec at an exposure of 0.5 sec in an otherwise homogeneous visual field; with increasing durations, the threshold decreased to a limiting value of 9 min/sec at 16 sec duration. The velocity threshold is higher in peripheral than in central vision (Aubert, 1886); it varies as a function of luminance (Brown, 1955; Leibowitz, 1955a); and it varies with duration up to about 0.3 sec (Brown, 1955). As the velocity of a moving target increases, visual acuity decreases, probably due to failure of the eye to match the motion of the target (Ludvigh, 1948, 1949, 1955, 1965). Smith and Gulick (1956, 1957, 1962) found that although the contour of a small moving square could not be clearly seen at velocities exceeding about 13°/sec, if the stimulus was presented in a fixed position prior to movement, the maximum velocity at which the contours could then be clearly distinguished increased, to an upper limit of about 40°/sec.

The threshold for detecting that 2 stimuli have different velocities was found to be 1 to 2 min/sec by Aubert, and about 30 sec/sec by Graham and his colleagues (1948). Brown (1931) exposed a repetitive pattern of moving targets (for example, a band of small squares on a white background) behind windows of variable size, and found that if the linear dimensions of such a field of movement are increased, the stimulus velocity must also be increased in the same proportion if the motions of the 2 fields are to appear of equal velocity. This "transposition effect" might bring about "velocity constancy," in normal viewing conditions, because the ratio of the retinal displacement rate to the extent of the retinal displacement would remain constant, regardless of the distance of the target from the observer.[7] Smith and Sherlock (1957), however, have shown that subjects in such experiments may be judging the frequency with which moving targets cross the boundaries of the aperture, not the targets' velocities. Perhaps this kind of judgment would also contribute to velocity constancy in normal viewing conditions, in which the ground provides a uniform gradient of texture the elements of which are occluded by the edges of moving objects.

The fact that the velocity threshold is about 10 times as great to perceive a single moving object as it is when a stationary reference stimulus is present suggests that different processes are involved in judging relative and absolute (or *egocentric*) movement. Exner (1875) had proposed that at moderate velocities, displacements are directly sensed as movement, whereas at lower velocities the observer judges that an object is in motion by noting its change in position. Leibowitz (1955b) suggested that at short exposures (.25 sec) only the velocity-sensitive component would operate and that therefore only at longer exposures (16 sec) would velocity thresholds be improved by the presence of a stationary framework. A similar distinction was made by Gregory (1964). Leibowitz' experimental data supported his prediction. Shaffer and Wallach (1966) have reported, however, that displacement thresholds are lower with a framework than without one at all durations, even with exposures as short as 0.011 sec. This finding does not necessarily refute Leibowitz' proposal because Shaffer and Wallach used a framework which closely

surrounded the target, and, at the short exposures, subjects may have used the assymmetrical location within the framework as their criterion for deciding that movement had occurred. In any case, their findings clearly support the hypothesis that the visual system is sensitive to the retinal displacement of a single target, inasmuch as a moving spot can be seen to move even when there is no stationary reference framework at all and when the exposure was too brief for any eye movement to occur, for example, 0.05 sec. This same point is made in a different context by the results of recent research on an old illusion of movement.

Movement aftereffects   After looking at a nearby waterfall for a time, look at the bank and you will see the trees swim upward. (For a history of the "waterfall illusion" see Boring [1942].) One plausible explanation was that downward eye movements made in pursuing the water persist when the eyes turn to the bank (Addams, 1834; Helmholtz, 1866). However, a similar aftereffect is obtained after you watch a spiral rotating on a color wheel. If the spiral appears to shrink or recede during

[7]If 2 objects are at different distances from the observer, D_1 and D_2, and they move through the same physical distance, $(S_1 = S_2)$ at the same rate $(dS_1/t = dS_2/t)$, the motions of the retinal images of the 2 objects will be unequal: $s_1/D_1 \neq s_2/D_2$ (see p. 504). Consequently, the rates of their retinal displacements will also be unequal: $ds/dt \neq ds_2/dt$. However, the ratios $(ds_1/dt)/s_1$ and $(ds_2/dt)/s_2$ will be equal, and if it is on these ratios that perceived velocity depends, the 2 objects should appear to move at the same rate, even though their retinal images are moving at different rates.

Figure 13.29. A spiral to be rotated for the reverse aftereffect. (Sanford, 1898.)

rotation (Figure 13.29), it will appear to expand or approach when the rotation is suddenly stopped. It is hard to imagine eye movements that would make an object seem to expand in all directions at once. Perhaps the retina or the visual cortex becomes adjusted to the continued movement and does not recover immediately from this adjustment when the movement in the retinal image ceases (see Wohlgemuth, 1911; Boring, 1942; Woodworth and Schlosberg, 1954, for reviews of such theories). Sutherland (1961) has offered the following more specific explanation: Neural cells which respond to displacement in a single direction in the retinal image have been found in the visual cortex of the cat (Chapter 9). If these exist also in man, and if the effect of prolonged viewing of displacement in one direction is to lower the normal firing rate of the cells which respond to that direction as compared to those which respond to the opposite displacement, this imbalance in the normal firing rate may produce the movement aftereffects.

Supporting this hypothesis, Sekuler and Ganz (1963) showed that after prolonged inspection of stripes moving in one direction, subjects have a higher luminance threshold for stripes moving in that direction than for stripes moving in the opposite direction. In a second experiment, they showed quite clearly that the movement aftereffects occur with conditions of image stabilization (see Chapter 9). These results are consistent with an explanation of the aftereffect in terms of neural units that are sensitive to the direction of displacement in the retinal image. In any case, the second experiment demonstrates that the waterfall illusion can be produced by retinal displacement alone, without eye movements. This point was further supported by Anstis and Gregory (1964), who found that when subjects were instructed to follow, with their eyes, a fixation point that could be moved independently of a set of moving stripes, the aftereffect was determined by the direction of the retinal displacement, not by the direction of eye movements. We shall see,

however, that there are other movement aftereffects to which eye movements do indeed contribute (p. 545).

Sequential patterns of movement The mere fact that a relative displacement is suprathreshold tells us little about what movement is perceived. Consider 2 objects, 1 of which is stationary and 1 of which is moving. The change in the distance between 2 objects' retinal images, considered by itself, is ambiguous. Physically, either one or both of the objects could be in motion and still produce the same retinal image. If you are seated in a smoothly moving train, looking out the window at another train, and proprioceptive information about your own movement is slight, it is a common experience to be uncertain as to which train is moving. Duncker (1938) has shown that there are visual factors that often decide how the relative movement will be distributed between 2 objects, only 1 of which is really moving. The object which is really moving may appear to be completely stationary, and the object which is really stationary will then carry the relative movement. These effects are called *induced movement*. The phenomenon can readily be observed on a cloudy night, in which the moon appears to sail slowly across the sky through apparently stationary clouds.

The smaller of 2 objects generally appears to move, especially if it is enclosed by the larger one. If one of the objects is fixated, that one appears to move (Duncker, 1929). Eye movements are not necessary for induced movement to occur (Shaffer & Wallach, 1966), but that does not mean that eye movements do not normally contribute to it. The objects that we expect from our past experiences to be mobile—cars, planes, people—will appear to move more than the neutral objects that are in fact moving (Duncker, 1929; Comalli, Werner, & Wapner, 1957; Jensen, 1960; Brosgole & Whalen, 1967); however, Brosgole and Whalen (1967) report that enclosing the stationary object in a moving framework obliterates the difference. If the object that is really being displaced is to appear stationary, its absolute velocity may have to fall below the threshold for *egocentric* or "subject-relative" movement

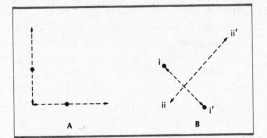

Figure 13.30. Dots moving with the motion shown at A, appear to move as at B. See text. (Johansson, 1950.)

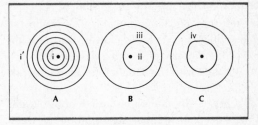

Figure 13.31. Circular patterns mounted on a rotating turntable give rise to illusory motion perception. In all cases, the center of the turntable is marked by the black dot. See text. A. After Benussi (in Musatti, 1924). B, C. After Wallach, Weisz & Adams (1956).

(Wallach, 1959). However, even with more rapid displacements, the physical movements may not be correctly perceived.

Thus, Johansson (1950) found that 2 dots which move toward and away from each other in a homogeneous white field, as shown in Figure 13.30A, are seen to move toward and away from each other on the diagonal *i–i'*; less noticeably, the entire path of movement, *i–i'*, itself appears to move up and down on the diagonal shown at *ii–ii'*. Note that this construction fits the purely visual information as well as the real movement does. For example, if the eyes were following the path marked *ii–ii'*, the diagonal at *i–i'* would in fact represent the movement in the proximal stimulus. Johansson does not give his displacements in visual angles, but by making reasonable assumptions about his viewing distances, the velocity of each dot falls between 1°/sec and 3°/sec, well above the absolute velocity thresholds given above. The visual system has extracted a motion that is common to all parts (*ii = ii'*, in this case), and this motion itself has become the framework against which the residual movement is seen.

The fact that a relative displacement is above threshold, therefore, does not tell us unequivocally what movement will be perceived, because the apparent path of movement is affected by the overall configuration. The situation is similar to that of shape perception (p. 437): Intuitively, it seems that some general principle determines the apparent movement, but none of the general principles or rules that had been proposed in the context of shape perception is specific enough to predict the actual movement illusions that occur.

As an example of such illusory movements, consider the effects that occur when patterns are displayed on a rotating turntable. Musatti (1924) reported that an ellipse that is mounted eccentrically on the turntable tends to appear fluid, and to display amoebalike movements. Benussi (Musatti, 1924) found that eccentrically arranged rings (Figure 13.31A), viewed monocularly, appear to rise up out of the plane of the turntable, forming a three-dimensional cone. Wallach, Weisz, and Adams (1956) have shown similar effects with patterns that look flat when the turntable is stationary but that rise when the turntable revolves. They explain these phenomena as special cases of the kinetic depth effect (p. 505) by the following reasoning. First, they report an exceedingly curious illusion of another kind: that a featureless circle, drawn or pasted on a rotating turntable, does not appear to revolve with the surface. Instead, it seems to undergo just those compound movements that will maintain its orientation. For example, the eccentrically mounted circle in Figure 13.31B seems to revolve not only around the turntable's center, but around its own center, *ii*, as well, in order to keep the imaginary point, *iii*, toward the top of the page. In fact, if a deformed circle is mounted as in Figure 13.31C, it seems to remain fixed in orientation and the bulge, *iv*, travels in a wave around it. If each point on the circle retains its identity in this sense, then in the Benussi figure, points *i* and *i'* are corresponding points on the inner and outer circles. Because the distances between these points change in both length and direction as the pattern revolves, they provide the conditions for depth to be seen in accordance with the rules of the kinetic depth effect.

The phenomena described above were produced at rotation rates of about 20 to 60 revolutions per minute. If luminous patterns rotating at slower rates (for example, 5 to 8 rpm) are viewed in darkness, the range of alternative movements is increased (Mefferd & Wieland, 1967). Even if a naive subject has first seen the object correctly when it was stationary, the illusory movements soon appear when the pattern is rotated.[8]

As with the geometrical illusions (Chapter 12), it is unwarranted to assume that such illusions of movement are confined to these simple patterns and that they therefore reveal nothing about the perception of movement in general. As with the geometrical illusions, also, they cannot now be accounted for by any single explanation. They certainly do not accord with any general rubric of "Gestalt simplicity" (see p. 437). Just as there seem to be different processes contributing to the perception of movement, there may be a number of different sets of rules that govern perceived movement, and the successful formulation of such rules may await the analysis of the perception of movement into its separable components.

Some of the components involved in the perception of movement may involve relatively peripheral mechanisms, such as neural units that respond to specific displacements in the retinal image (p. 522). Other components may depend more on the way the subject encodes and remembers a sequence of events than on any direct sensory response: The fact that movements which take a con-

siderable period of time to run their course can be recognized and compared with each other implies some mechanism of retention by which an entire temporal event can be registered and remembered. Like the experiments on tachistoscopic recognition (p. 444) and on the fragmentation of shapes with stabilized images (p. 454), experiments on movement may call on the subject's memory, on the repertory of temporal events or *schematic sequences* (Hochberg, 1968) with which the subject is familiar. He can use these to identify and store the successive elementary displacements to which the eye

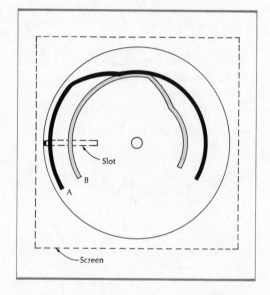

Figure 13.32. Disk for giving kinetic impressions. Through the slot square portions of the stripes *A* and *B* are seen, while the disk rotates in the counterclockwise direction behind the screen. As long as stripe *A* remains at the same distance from the center, the square seen through the slot remains still; but when stripe *A* approaches center the visible part of it approaches *B*. When *A* has reached *B*, *A* becomes stationary and *B* begins to move. The stripes are $\frac{1}{5}$ in. wide, the same as the slot, which is 6 in. long; the subject is 5 ft away. *A* and *B* are 1.6 in. apart at the start, and the speed of the apparent movement is 12 in./sec. These measurements were varied. (Michotte, 1946.)

---

[8] The "coupling" of perceptual attributes (p. 506) is marked, in these cases. If slant is perceived, at least some degrees of slant-shape invariance (p. 516) is displayed; if slant is not perceived, the figures look accordingly nonrigid. There seems to be little doubt that the subjects "really see" the illusory movements reported, in this sense (Mefferd & Wieiand, 1967).

Apparent Movement

Action and causation We have a few words with which we can identify movements in physical terms, such as "smooth," "abrupt," "erratic"; and we can describe simple movements in terms of their geometrical shapes. These are clearly not the only categories we have with which to identify and remember patterns of displacement. There are many more complex movements to which we are continually exposed in the form of animate and inanimate actions, and to which we make well-practiced responses. Most of these go unclassified and unstudied. Let us merely note here that they seem to be susceptible to disciplined analysis and study. Heider and Simmel (1944) devised an animated cartoon in which triangles and a circle follow complex paths of movement that observers find very difficult to describe in physical terms but which are easy to remember and describe in social terms. The psychophysical relationships involved in such "social perception" have not been further studied. In contrast, the bases for perceiving physical causation have been extensively explored by Michotte (1946) using the apparatus shown in Figure 13.32. As objects, he used small squares seen through a horizontal slot in a screen. When the objects are first shown to the subject, A and B are a short distance apart and both are stationary; then A moves rapidly toward B but stops when it reaches B, and B immediately moves away in the same direction. The observer has a very clear impression of causation, A acting on B and propelling it forward. If A moves along with B, instead of stopping when it reaches B, the impression is that A carries B along. It is interesting to note that slight discontinuities can be tolerated, but when these tolerances are exceeded, the impression received is that of 2 separate events instead of a single causal process. "Causation" seems to be a clear example of a schematic sequence by which a number of successive displacements can be responded to as a single unit.

The simplest example of responding to 2 successive physical events as a single unit is probably the phenomenon of stroboscopic movement, which we shall consider next in some detail.

Stroboscopic movement On the motion picture screen, or on the TV screen, there is of course no actual motion of the figures. The motion picture camera has taken a series of snapshots separated by brief intervals of time, and the projector casts these still views and blank intervals on the screen. The fact that apparent visual motion could be effected under such conditions became known in 1833 with the invention of the stroboscope, a device for illuminating a moving object with intermittent light. The apparent movement is accordingly also called *stroboscopic movement*.

The history of research on stroboscopic movement has been reviewed by Boring (1942). The psychological study of this effect received its major impetus from Wertheimer's paper in 1912. He had a subject look at 2 short vertical lines, 1 cm apart and at reading distance; they were exposed one after the other with a blank interval between them. If the blank interval was about 200 msec or more, the appearance corresponded to the reality: 2 stationary lines, one presented after the other. If the interval was about 30 msec or less, the 2 lines seemed to be presented simultaneously. If the blank interval was adjusted between these limits, various kinds of movement were seen, the kind depending on the arrangement of the lines and on the duration of the interval. There are thus several thresholds that can be measured. The 2 major thresholds are that between succession and movement, and that between movement and simultaneity. The thresholds are in general quite variable and dependent on many factors.

Several kinds of apparent movement have been named. *Optimal movement* is produced with a blank interval of about 60 msec in Wertheimer's arrangement. In this condition, the line clearly appears to move from one place to another. If the intervals are made somewhat longer, *partial movement* seems to occur. Of major interest is what Wertheimer called *phi movement,* or *pure movement.* This is apparent movement between two places even though no object appears to move.

> The following additional names have been offered to distinguish different kinds of apparent movement. In *alpha movement* an object appears to change size (Kenkel, 1913). In *beta* an object appears to move from one place to another (Kenkel, 1913); this is equivalent to Wertheimer's optimal movement. In *gamma movement* (Kenkel, 1913) an apparent expansion and contraction occurs when the stimulus object's luminance is increased and decreased, respectively. In *delta movement* the direction of movement is reversed when the second stimulus is more luminous than the first one (Korte, 1915). *Bow movement* does not follow the shortest path connecting the 2 stimuli; this usually occurs when an obstructing stimulus is introduced between the first and second stimulus; the apparent movement may then curve around the obstruction via the third dimension (Benussi, 1916).
>
> Korte (1915) varied the most obvious stimulus factors, and his results are sometimes called *Korte's Laws.* These relate the threshold values critical to obtaining beta movement in terms of the following variables: the spatial separation of the 2 stimuli, their luminances, the exposure times of the 2 stimuli, and the duration of the interval between them. (Korte's Laws are reviewed in Neff [1936] and Graham [1965].) In summary, these laws mean that it is more difficult to see apparent movement when the illumination is very low, or when the time gap is very short, or when the space gap is very wide. If the space gap is increased, you must increase the time gap to get apparent movement. Subsequent work by Neuhaus (1930) and Sgro (1963) over a larger range of these variables has extended and revised Korte's data.

Although the variables of luminance, distance, and duration are important, and are easy to measure and to specify, they are as insufficient to the prediction of stroboscopic movement in general as they are to real movement. Configurational factors also affect what apparent movement, if any, will be seen,

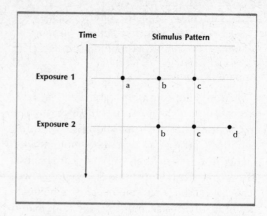

Figure 13.33. The factor of identity in stroboscopic movement. See text. (After Ternus, 1926.)

and as we have noted before, we are not yet prepared to make useful generalizations, wherever configuration is a major factor in perception. Let us simply examine some of the ways in which configuration affects the organization of apparent movement.

> In order for stroboscopic movement to be perceived, the visual system must respond to the second stimulus as being the same object as the first stimulus and must treat the 2 presentations as being at different places in space. In the simplest experiment described above, a single object appears to maintain its identity and change its locus. Ternus (1926) showed that if the 3 spots *a, b, c* in Figure 13.33 comprise the first exposure, followed by 3 spots *b, c, d* for the second exposure, the common points *b* and *c* do not appear twice if beta movement occurs. Instead, *a* moves to *b, b* moves to *c* and *c* moves to *d.* Points *b* and *c* have changed their identity, even though they fall on the same retinal locus. If the common points are not interrupted by the blank period, they retain their identity; as long as the blank period intervenes, however, the identity that a point appears to maintain is determined not by whether it falls on the same retinal region, but where it fits in the overall pattern. The path of the apparent movement tends to be the one which will preserve the identity of 2 successively viewed patterns. The conditions for phenomenal identity are not now clear, but they would seem to be extremely important to the phenomenon of apparent movement, and to the path that the apparent movement takes. When the 2 stimuli are alike, a simple sliding movement along a straight or curved path will usually be seen (Hall, Earle, &

Crookes, 1952), but rotations and translatory movements through the third dimension will occur when these offer simpler "solutions" (see p. 503n), as when an inverted V is followed by a V right-side up and slightly lower in the field. Many examples of three-dimensional apparent movement have been published by Steinig (1929), Fernberger (1934), and Orlansky (1940). The more dissimilar the 2 alternating figures, the more difficult it is to see them as a single figure which is moving and changing form or color as it moves, and the longer the blank interval that is needed to obtain apparent movement (Orlansky, 1940). The interval is therefore not merely a function of spatial separation between the 2 stimuli. Moreover, "spatial separation" is itself not simply a matter of distance in the visual image. When Corbin (1942) measured the time interval required to see movement as a function of the separation between the first and second stimulus, he obtained the same time thresholds whether the 2 stimuli were in the frontal plane or in a plane that was slanted 60° away from the observer, even though the retinal separations were only half as great in the latter case as in the former.

According to structuralist analysis (p. 427), movement is not a simple sensory phenomenon, but a complex perceptual experience compounded of the successive sensations that would normally be provided by a stimulus moving over the retina (Titchener, 1902) or by the eye in pursuing a moving object (Helmholtz, 1866). To Wertheimer, the so-called "phi phenomenon" was of great theoretical importance because it showed that the intervening sensations are unnecessary to the perception of movement. Wertheimer showed also that eye movements are unnecessary to create the effect of stroboscopic movement, inasmuch as 2 movements in opposite directions are seen when 2 suitable pairs of lines are presented. Guilford and Helson (1929) later showed, by eye movement photography, that no significant relation existed between the eye movements and the reports of apparent movement. Nor does the subject need to *infer* movement from an apparent change in position: Experiments have shown that apparent movement is perceived as unequivocally as real movement (Stratton, 1911; Wertheimer, 1925; De Silva,

1929) when 2 dots are shown the observer 1 of which really moves while the other undergoes optimal stroboscopic movement.

Wertheimer therefore held with Exner (1875), Mach, and others (see Boring, 1942) that movement is as direct an experience as is brightness or hue, an experience mediated by its own physiological mechanism rather than by experiences of changes in position. What might that mechanism be? Exner (1875) proposed that the retina is actually stimulated in the region lying between the initial and terminal positions, but against this theory is the fact that apparent movement occurs even if the first stimulus is applied to one eye and the second stimulus to the other. Wertheimer proposed a theory somewhat like Exner's, but he proposed that the hypothetical movement occurs neurally in the visual cortex instead of in the retina. The cortical excitation aroused by the first stimulus could spread and be attracted toward the region excited by the second stimulus, and the movement of excitation along the cortex could give a sensation of movement, a sort of streak.[9] This was the forerunner of the doctrine of *isomorphism*, with which Gestalt psychologists attempted to provide the equivalent of "specific nerve energies" for organized processes like shape and form (pp. 428, 436f.). Against this theory are the following facts. (1) In lower animals, the visual cortex may be removed without interfering with the pursuit movements of the animal's head and eyes that are normally produced by a field of moving stripes, even when those stripes are stroboscopically il-

[9] Brown and Voth (1937) performed a series of experiments to test this "attraction" theory. They exposed lights successively at the corners of a square. If there are long intervals between stimuli, simple succession occurs. As the interval is shortened, so that each light is presented close enough in time to the preceding light to attract it, simple beta movement occurs, and the light is seen to move around the corners of the square. An analysis of the vectors working on each apparent position of the light shows that the path should become circular as the interstimulus interval decreases further, so that lights further apart in space become closer in time and exert cohesive forces on each position. In fact the path does become circular, falling well within the 4 corners of the square. If the interstimulus interval is further reduced, the circle becomes larger again and eventually, of course, the 4 lights are all seen simultaneously.

luminated (Smith, 1940). (2) Although in man, at least, there is a stronger tendency for apparent movement to occur between points whose projections fall in the same cerebral hemisphere than between points that fall in different hemispheres (Gengerelli, 1948), the fact that apparent movement is perceived at all between the 2 hemispheres makes Wertheimer's theory inadequate (Smith, 1948). (3) Apparent movement may occur when the successive presentations fall on the *same* retinal region. Thus, Duncker (1929) caused an objectively stationary dot to appear to move back and forth by presenting it within a rectangular framework for exposures of half a second, the rectangle being displaced to one side or the other on alternate exposures. Perhaps in this experiment the observer's eye followed the center of the rectangle, so that the dot was really projected on disparate retinal locations from one exposure to the next. The results of an experiment by Rock and Ebenholtz (1962) could not be explained in this way. They had subjects look back and forth between 2 places that were physically separated in space. A light flashed at each place as they looked at it. Although the same retinal area—the fovea—was stimulated at each flash, 6 of the 10 subjects reported seeing movement from one position to the other. (4) The existence of tridimensional apparent movements (p. 527) and the fact that objective separation rather than retinal separation determines the time interval needed to produce stroboscopic movement (Corbin, 1942), both seem incompatible with a theory of spreading excitation in the visual cortex.

As Woodworth and Schlosberg said in 1954, we seem left without any acceptable theory to explain apparent movement. It is probably unwarranted to try to lump together under one explanation all the different conditions in which reports of apparent movement are obtained, for the latter may be based on diverse criteria and on very different mechanisms under the different conditions of stimulation. Even though stroboscopic and continuous (real) motion in the stimulus field may produce equally convincing appearances of movement, this does not mean that they do so in the same way. In fact, the visual process must be different for the 2 conditions, if only at the retinal level. Kolers (1963) has shown, for example, that when a target is briefly presented in the path of an objectively moving line, the luminance threshold for detecting the target increases, but this does not happen when the line only appears to move (beta movement).

We have seen that quite different criteria and processes may elicit a judgment that real movement has occurred (pp. 520f.); for example, there may be a direct response mediated by local retinal displacement (Exner, 1875; Leibowitz, 1955a); a response based on relative displacement (p. 521); and a response based on pursuit movements by the eye. Similarly, different processes may contribute to stroboscopic movement. The sort of apparent movement that seems to depend on a change in the egocentric location rather than on retinal displacement may be based on different criteria than is beta or phi movement. In the experiment of Rock and Ebenholtz (1962), the subject looked at successive flashes that were about 7 inches apart at a viewing distance of about 22 inches, or some 17° of visual angle, whereas De Silva (1929, 1935) reported that continuous optimal movement could not be obtained under more ordinary conditions of viewing when the targets appeared successively with separations greater than 4.5°.

In another experiment in the same series, Rock and Ebenholtz (1962) flashed a light successively at the *same* place in space, but this time the subjects moved their eyes from one direction to another in such a way that different parts of the retina were stimulated alternately. No apparent movement was reported in this case. The experimenters concluded that this was so because the light was perceived as being at the same egocentric location even though different retinal regions were stimulated. As we shall see shortly, however, this may reflect a different mechanism; a displacement of the retinal image may simply not result in apparent movement when it occurs in association with a saccadic eye movement. Before we examine this possibility, we consider the more general issue that it implies, namely the question of how we see an object as being stationary in space even when its retinal image is displaced.

PERCEIVING A STATIONARY WORLD

There are 2 questions that arise when we view stationary objects. The first arises from the fact that when we fixate a stationary object in the absence of a well-structured visual field, that object appears to move due to what is called the *autokinetic effect*. The second arises from the fact that when we change our fixation point from one direction to another, the retinal image is displaced but the world appears to remain stationary.

The Autokinetic Phenomenon

Put the subject in a perfectly dark room, and then turn on a pinpoint of light. In a short time, most subjects will report that the point of light is moving or drifting. The phenomenon has a long history, dating back at least to von Humbolt's observation in 1799 that stars seen through a telescope appear to drift about (Howard & Templeton, 1966). Aubert rediscovered it and named it the *autokinetic* (self-moving) phenomenon in 1887. A review of the early literature may be found in Guilford (1928); more recent research and theories are reviewed by Howard and Templeton (1966).

Various measures of autokinetic movement have been attempted, such as drawing it (Guilford & Dallenbach, 1928), having the subject actually control the light to bring it back to the starting point (Bridges & Bitterman, 1954), or having the subject try to touch the point of light (Sandström, 1951). The validity of each of these methods is difficult to assess.

Two general explanations for the phenomenon have received most recent atten-

tion, one in terms of eye movements and the other in terms of changes in muscle tonus. Let us consider the explanation based on eye movement first.

Explanations based on eye movements Movements of the eye, made while looking at a stationary distal stimulus, cause movements in the retinal image. Normally, we move our eyes about a great deal, but stationary objects nevertheless appear stationary. However, those eye movements are intentional. Unintentional eye movements, such as can be produced by moving the eye passively by pressing on it through the eyelid, do cause the visual field to appear to move (Helmholtz, 1866). Hoppe suggested in 1879 that involuntary eye movements are responsible for the displacement of the retinal image, which, in turn, results in what we now call *autokinetic movement*. Eye-movement photography (Guilford & Dallenbach, 1928) has not found eye movements to be correlated with autokinetic movement, but the methods used may have been inadequate for the purpose (Skolnik, 1940). Matin and MacKinnon (1964) used image stabilization techniques (see Chapter 9, p. 306) to reduce the displacement in the retinal image that would result from any horizontal eye movements that the subject might make. A normal, unstabilized view of the point of light (35 min in diameter) could be instantaneously substituted for the stabilized view. The subject indicated the direction of autokinetic movement by pressing switches. A much smaller number of horizontal movements was reported under the stabilized condition as compared to the normal viewing condition. This suggests that involuntary eye movements normally contribute to the autokinetic phenomenon.

But how can a point appear to move away from where it first appeared to be, namely straight ahead, yet remain clearly fixated? Something more than involuntary eye movements would also seem to be involved.

Explanations based on muscle tension The eye can change its apparent position even though it has not in fact moved, and remains fixated straight ahead. Subjects often report that their eyes pursue the target as it moves, even though the target really remains fixed (Carr, 1910; Adams, 1912; DeSisto & McLaughlin, 1968). Normally, of course, if the eye moves but a point of light continues to fall on the same part of the retina (for example, the fovea), the point of light will appear to move to a new location. Bruell and Albee (1955) propose that such a perceived change in location occurs *if and only if* the change in tension of the oculomotor muscles, that causes the eye movement, has been voluntarily initiated. If because of postural reflexes (see Chapter 4, p. 103) or because of fatigue, the eye is subjected to tension that would turn it to one side, say the left, a voluntary signal to increase the muscle tension in the opposite direction would be needed to maintain fixation. Because only that voluntary signal would have an effect on the perceived direction, this would be equivalent to having turned the eye to the right; because the object remains fixated on the fovea, it in turn would appear to have moved to the right. The following facts suggest that something like this does occur.[10]

Fixating a stimulus with the eyes held in one direction, which might be expected to fatigue one set of eye muscles, affects the direction of subsequent autokinetic movements (Carr, 1910; Gregory, 1959; Gregory & Zangwill, 1963). Adams (1912) and Luchins (1954) reported that if the subject's head is held so that the light must be fixated eccentrically, autokinetic movement increased in the direction to which the eyes were turned, and Battersby and his coworkers (1956) obtained similar results by turning the head and trunk to one side.

The kind of explanation given above is plausible only if we do not have very good proprioceptive information about the whereabouts of our eyes. There is now considerable

evidence strongly suggesting that that is indeed the case (Ludvigh, 1952; Merton, 1961; Matin & Kibler, 1966). For example, Matin and his colleagues (1966) presented subjects with a fixation target in an otherwise dark room; then they removed the target and had the subjects attempt to maintain their fixation in the same position during a 3-second interval in total darkness. After the 3 seconds had elapsed, a test flash was presented in various horizontal locations, and the subject had to say whether it appeared to the right or to the left of the previously viewed fixation target. Throughout this period, eye movements were monitored by using a technique involving contact lenses (Chapter 11, p. 374). Large involuntary eye movements were found to occur while the subject was trying to hold his fixation in darkness. When the test flash was presented, the subject's judgment of whether the flash was to the right or to the left of the fixation point was determined by whether it was to the right or to the left of wherever the fovea happened to be: no account was taken, apparently, of the fact that the eye had moved from its original position. This is, of course, in contrast with what we have previously said about the effects of *voluntary* eye movement, namely that an object appears to remain stable or stationary when voluntary eye movements are made, even though the retinal image of the object is displaced. Let us now consider how such stability might be achieved.

Stability of the World during Saccadic Eye Movements

The eye normally moves its fixation point several times a second, yet the objects in the world appear to remain fixed in space. This stability may be arrived at by a compensation procedure, in which a record is kept of the direction and amount that the eye is ordered to move, and this record (variously called the sense of innervation, by Helmholtz, 1866; the efferent copy, by von Holst, 1954; and the corollary discharge, by Teuber, 1960) is compared to the subsequent movement in the

[10] In order to evaluate such theories, we need more specific bases than have yet been offered for deciding which movements are voluntary and which are involuntary.

retinal image.[11] If the movements of the retinal image are exactly those that would be produced by the eye movements alone, no movement of the objects would be seen. We shall see that something roughly like this does occur with head movements. It is not now clear to what extent this kind of compensation actually occurs with saccadic eye movements, which are by far the most important source of movement in man's retinal image. But let us briefly consider some of the factors involved.

As we have seen (p. 521), we are far more sensitive to relative than to absolute displacements in the retinal image. When a saccade occurs, the entire visual image is displaced, so that the parts of the visual field have remained in an unmoving relationship to each other. Perhaps this is why the world remains stable despite the saccades (Duncker, 1929; Koffka, 1935; Gibson, 1954). Against this argument, however, we can show that apparent movement does occur even when the entire image is displaced, or when the eye muscles are ordered to execute a saccade but the eye movement itself is prevented from occurring.

One old example is the apparent movement of the scene that occurs when the eyeball is moved passively by pressure through the eyelid (p. 529). Presumably this happens because no efferent copy is subtracted from the retinal movement. It is not clear how comparable this example is to a saccadic displacement, however, because the velocity of the image in this condition is relatively low, whereas retinal displacement during a saccade might be too rapid to affect the hypothetical velocity-sensitive neural units (p. 522). The range of velocities within which passive movement of the eye produces apparent movement of the scene is not now known.

At the other extreme are cases in which the image remains stationary on the retina, yet movement is perceived as though a saccade had occurred. Thus, if the eye is immobilized by paralysis of the muscles or by mechanical means and the subject then tries to turn his gaze to one side, the entire scene appears to move in that direction (Helmholtz, 1866; Brindley & Merton, 1960). Some thought will show that in both cases this is what we would expect to happen if the saccade had been executed and no corresponding *reafference* (that is, no visual consequence of the eye movement) had occurred.

These arguments are not completely conclusive, however. They do suggest very strongly that voluntary saccadic eye movements normally cause a change in the apparent direction signified by any given place on the retina and that this change in apparent direction can result in apparent movement. However, this does not necessarily imply that the subtraction of such a change in direction is the reason why actual retinal displacement fails to produce apparent movement when such displacement results from saccadic eye movements. This logical point must be noted because there is some evidence that there may not be any need for compensation, at least for small saccadic displacements. Wallach and Lewis (1965), using an optical device that changed the amount that the retinal image was displaced by any saccade, showed that subjects failed to notice displacements that differed from the displacement that the saccade should have produced. Similarly, in an experiment by Sperling and Speelman (1965), in which the onset of a subject's saccade electronically caused a displacement of the stimulus, subjects failed to notice displacements of as much as 2°. Moreover, if a light is presented to the eye during a voluntary saccade, in a room that is otherwise completely dark, the apparent location of the light shows that only a very small amount of compensation for the eye movement has occurred (Matin, Matin, & Pearce, 1969).

In short, it is not clear at this time how much of the stability of the visual world

[11] Information about the position of the eyes is now thought to come only from these efferent records and from the changes in visual stimulation that result from eye movements (see Chapter 11).

during saccadic eye movements is due to a compensatory mechanism and how much is due to the integrative processes by which successive views are fitted together into a single picture of the world. Almost every motion picture made over the last 30 years has cut back and forth from one camera viewpoint to another, and the observer usually has a good picture of the stable world within which actors move about even though no efferent copies or corollary discharges provide him with compensatory proprioceptive information (see the discussion of "maps" in Chapter 12, p. 454).

A stronger case can be made for the importance of compensatory processes that allow a stationary object to be perceived as stationary despite the movements of its retinal image that occur when the head and body are moving. The relevant experiments involve rearrangements of the relationship between head movement and the resulting movement of the retinal image, and we consider those experiments in the context of optical rearrangement (p. 544f.).

Comparison of Normal and Rearranged Vision

Visual and nonvisual localization of objects Purely visual information about where an object is located in space must, by itself, be ambiguous. We must therefore also use non-visual (proprioceptive) information about the disposition of our eyes, head, and body if our perception of the object's location is to be certain, and if our actions directed toward it are to be successfully executed. The study of how the visual and nonvisual sources of spatial information are fitted together calls quite naturally for experiments that disturb the normal relationship that exists between them. Various optical devices can alter or rearrange the retinal image that is produced by a given visual display and a given arrangement of the eyes, head, and body. These devices therefore have provided an important research tool in the study of perceived loca-

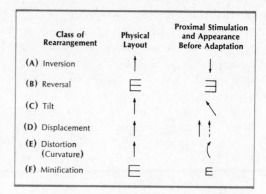

Figure 13.34. Classes of optical rearrangement.

tion, and of the perceptuomotor behaviors associated with this field of inquiry.

Experiments on rearranged vision If the spatial arrangement that we perceive in response to a particular retinal image is the result of what our tactual and kinesthetic experiences with objects in space have taught us (as the classical empiricist position would have it, pp. 465, 477), it may be possible to change our visual perceptions by changing the tactual experiences associated with that retinal image. We may do this by placing some optical device, like a prism or a mirror, in the path of the light entering the eye, to alter the retinal image that is produced by any arrangement of objects in space. Thus, mirrors and lenses can be used to invert, reverse, displace, tilt, curve, break, or "minify" the retinal image that is produced by a given display (Figure 13.34). Inasmuch as the physical arrangement of objects remains unchanged with respect to the observer's body and limbs, the rearranged retinal images will initially mislead any visually guided attempts that we make to touch those objects, and this in turn causes the observer to relearn the spatial meaning of his retinal images.

The hypothesis is that active movement and tactual experience with the world, while wearing devices that produce visual rearrangement, will result in a change in visual appearance that brings the latter into agreement with where things are localized by the sense of touch. We shall examine several attempts at adaptation to rearranged vision with this hypothesis in mind. A trickle of research on adaptation to rearranged vision, going back to 1866 (see Howard & Templeton, 1966), has become a torrent in the last decade, too diverse and unwieldy to review adequately here. Critical reviews by Smith and Smith (1962), Harris (1965), Howard and Templeton (1966), Rock (1966), Epstein (1967), and Taub and Berman (1968) cover much of the recent work.

Stratton (1896, 1897) wore inverting lenses to determine whether the top and bottom of the retinal image are inherently seen as down and up in the visual world, respectively (Figure 13.34A). In that case, he argued, the world would continue to appear inverted no matter how long he wore the lenses. Initially, of course, the world did appear upside down, but Stratton reported that after several days it occasionally appeared "right side up." This result led many psychologists (Carr, 1925, for example) to conclude that adaptation to wearing the prisms had resulted in a change in Stratton's visual perceptions, as such. Since then, Ewert (1930), Peterson and Peterson (1938), and Snyder and Pronko (1952) repeated Stratton's experiment; the latter two used procedures similar to those Stratton used, and obtained improvements in their abilities to behave in tasks that involved vision, but found no clear signs of change in the way the world looked. Thus, when Snyder was asked whether things looked upside down, he replied that although he had been unaware of it until the question was asked, things did look upside down when compared to the way they had looked before he put the glasses on.

A series of investigations by Kohler (1951, 1953, 1964) repeated and extended the rearrangement-adaptation experiments. In general, Kohler's results seemed strongly to support Stratton's conclusion. When rearranging spectacles are first put on, says Kohler, the world seems strange in various ways. Faces look unfamiliar; walking people seem to move mechanically, so that the up-and-down component, normally not noticed, becomes very apparent; and as the subject's head moves, the normally stationary world appears to swing about wildly. Behaviorally, of course, the subject is almost incapacitated.

If he is wearing reversing spectacles, for example, and he wants to touch an object that is objectively to his right, he will reach out toward his left. After some adaptation has occurred, the subject can negotiate streets, can "fence" with the experimenter, can ride a bicycle, and so on. Despite such effective motor performance, however, the visual world remains reversed in appearance. Adaptation does occur eventually in the sense that the world becomes more stable and does not swing around with each head movement, even while the subject performs complicated behavior (bicycling, among other activities). However, visual adaptation in other respects (uprightness as opposed to invertedness, correct left-right orientation as opposed to reversed appearance, and so on) seems to proceed in a curiously piecemeal fashion, judging from subjects' reports. Thus Kohler reports that some parts of the visual field are perceived correctly while other parts remain reversed; vehicles are correctly perceived as driving on the "right" side of the road, but their license numbers are seen as mirror images (1964, p. 155; see also Taylor, 1962). Finally, after many weeks, the subject achieves impressions that are, Kohler claims, almost completely "correct," even when he is viewing letters or numbers. That is, the process of adaptation does not seem to be in any sense a matter of learning to invert (or reverse) the whole visual field at once. This is certainly a bizarre phenomenon, and an explanation of it by Harris (1965) will be important in our further discussion of rearrangement-adaptation. The final stage in these experiments should be noted first, however. This is reached after adaptation has occurred,

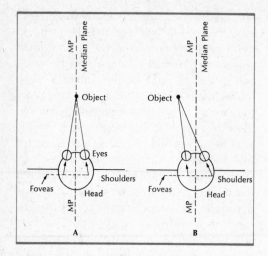

Figure 13.35. Eye movement and the *apparent straight ahead.* See text.

and the spectacles are removed. The visual field now appears rearranged to the unencumbered gaze, rearranged in a way that is complementary to the effects of the adaptation-producing optical devices. For example, after having adapted to reversing prisms (Figure 13.34B), Kohler reports that when these were removed, the subject saw the whole room as though it were reversed. As Rock points out (1966), such aftereffects are impressive evidence that changes have occurred in the *perceptual* system, inasmuch as the subject has no intellectual reason to believe that a correction of any sort is necessary when the device is no longer before his eyes.

Most of the behavioral aspects of the adaptation phenomena described by Kohler have since been replicated, using various kinds of rearrangement. However, it is not at all clear that *visual* perception has been relearned in the service of touch, kinesthesis, and proprioception, as is often inferred. We consider several of these phenomena in more detail.

Perception of "straight ahead" and adaptation to displacement If the eyes, head and trunk are all aligned as in Figure 13.35A, and some object lies in the median plane *MP*, the image falls on the fovea of each retina, and the object appears to be straight ahead. If the

eyes are turned so that the object's image no longer falls on the fovea, some account must be taken of the eyes' rotation if the subject is to continue to see the object as being straight ahead with respect to his body.

The proprioceptive information about the relative position of eye, head, and trunk are not all taken into account with unfailing accuracy. Thus, if the eyes are kept turned to the right, the position at which some object will be judged to be straight ahead (the *apparent straight ahead*) also shifts to the right (Fischer, 1915; Goldstein & Riese, 1923; Werner, Wapner, & Bruell, 1953). Moreover, if a luminous pattern or a pair of spots of light is viewed in the dark, with the leftmost edge of the pattern lying on the *MP* (that is, objectively straight ahead), the pattern appears to be displaced to the left and the apparent straight ahead is now somewhere to the right of the *MP* (Dietzel, 1924; Roelofs, 1935; Akishige, 1951). The apparent straight ahead is therefore shifted toward the pattern's center, and in fact the amount of the shift increases with the width of the pattern (Bruell & Albee, 1955).

Active and passive experience What happens when we change the relationship between proprioception and vision? In 1866, Helmholtz reported that when he looked at an object while wearing prisms which deflected the visual image to the left (as in Figure 13.34D), and then closed his eyes and reached for the object, he initially made a leftwards error. (His eyes were closed during this test so that his reaching would not be guided by continuous vision of his hand approaching the object.) This error was quickly corrected by reaching for the object several times with one hand while he watched that hand through the prism. After having learned to do this, if he removed the prisms, gazed steadily at the object, and then closed his eyes and tried to touch it, he missed the object by reaching too far to the right. Let us reconsider Figure 13.35 in terms of what it implies concerning visually guided actions.

If the eyes, head, and trunk are all aligned as in Figure 13.35A, and the object lies in the median plane *MP*, the image falls on the fovea of the retina, and the hand will touch the object when extended toward the *MP*. However, this does not mean, of course, that any time an object's image is on the fovea that the hand must reach to the median plane to touch it. If the object is displaced to one side, and the eyes or head are turned so that the image still falls on the fovea (Figure 13.35B), the motor system must bring the hand to a position that is no longer on *MP*. Movements that are directed towards objects in space must be guided by some sensorimotor mechanism that combines the information in the retinal image with the information about the relative positions or motions of eye, head and trunk.

In 1961, Held proposed that many kinds of adaptation to rearrangement result from changes in these sensorimotor mechanisms, changes that establish a new correlation between the efferent neural commands that produce the subject's actions, on the one hand, and the visual changes that result from those actions, or *reafference* (von Holst, 1954; see pp. 530f.), on the other hand. For this kind of adaptation to occur, therefore, the subject must engage in active (voluntary) movement while he is wearing the distorting devices and must simultaneously receive the changes in retinal image that result from his movement. Because Held and his colleagues (Held & Bossom, 1961; Held & Freedman, 1963; Held & Hein, 1963; Held & Bauer, 1967) propose that the same process may operate both in the infant's development of these sensorimotor mechanisms and in the adult's adaptation to rearrangement, study of the latter may tell us how the mechanisms that maintain spatially oriented behaviors develop in the first place.

Held's proposal is not the classical empiricist theory. Although active movement is necessary to the kinds of adaptation that he postulates, and although he assumes that the characteristics of such sensorimotor changes

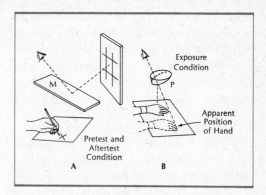

Figure 13.36. Prism adaptation experiment. See text. (After Held & Gottlieb, 1958.)

reveal the nature of the processes by which the infant first acquires the ability to perform the spatial behavior in question, Held does not maintain that *all* spatial behaviors are learned, nor that *all* visual adaptation requires active movement. In fact, he and his colleagues have gone to considerable pains in the attempt to remove from their data the effects of those kinds of adaptation that can occur without active movement and without reafference.

Held and his colleagues have used more objective and sensitive versions of Helmholtz' procedure, measuring the effects of the adaptation or exposure period (B, in Figure 13.36) on perceptuomotor tasks that are administered to the subject before and after adaptation (A in Figure 13.36). For example (Held & Gottlieb, 1958), the subject looks into the mirror M during a pretest and again during an aftertest session. The mirror hides his hand with which he is to mark the apparent location of the target that he sees reflected in the mirror. During the adaptation period, the mirror is removed, and the subject views his arm through the prism P. Held and Hein (1958) found that subjects who moved their arms voluntarily while watching them through a prism that produced a lateral displacement (Figure 13.34D) subsequently displayed a considerable degree of adaptation, whereas subjects whose arms were moved for them during the exposure period displayed no adaptation. Subjects' actions and the visual consequences of the actions must be virtually simultaneous if prism adaptation is to occur; a delay of even 0.3 sec between the hand movement and the visual feedback from it prevents adaptation from occurring (Held, Efstathiou, & Greene, 1966).[12]

Using different adaptation and test procedures, Held and Bossom (1961) had a subject walk around while wearing displacing prisms. Subsequently his head was placed in a cylindrical drum, the inner surface of which bore a vertical line, and he was asked to position himself so that the vertical line appeared to be straight ahead. This test revealed a lateral displacement of approximately the predicted amount and direction. Most importantly, however, subjects who had been passively transported over the same path in a wheelchair, so that they were in the same visual environment but were undergoing only *passive* movement, did not obtain the same aftereffects. However, we cannot as yet conclude that active movement and reafference were *necessary*, in a direct sense, for this adaptation to occur, nor that the adaptation that was obtained resulted from recorrelation of the sensorimotor mechanisms.

First, we should note that there are several experiments in which passive subjects adapted to displacement, sometimes as strongly as did active ones (Wertheimer & Arena, 1959; Weinstein et al., 1964; Pick & Hay, 1965; Singer & Day, 1966), and there is some evidence to suggest that if the subject receives adequate information that the visual field is displaced, adaptation will occur even in the absence of any movement. Thus, passive inspection of one's feet through displacing prisms produced some adaptation (presumably because of the information provided by the discrepancy between the felt and seen locations of the feet), as measured subsequently by a pointing task (Wallach, Kravitz, & Lindauer, 1963). Similarly, Howard, Craske, and Templeton (1965) showed that prodding the subject's lips with a rod, which was made to appear in a displaced position by use of mirrors, also produced adaptation when measured by a pointing task. In other words, it is possible that what is important about active movement is not the action per se, but rather the greater information about the nature of the visual rearrangement that such movement makes available (see p. 540; for further discussion of this viewpoint, see Rock, 1966).

Why did the passive subjects show no adaptation in the experiment of Held and Hein? Perhaps the felt position of a passive hand does not offer the required information that the visual field is displaced. In fact, Hay, Pick, and Ikeda (1965) found that as soon as subjects looked at their hands through a prism, *visual capture* occurred, and the felt position of their hands coincided with the position at which their hands appeared to be in the visual field, not with their actual position in space. There is considerable evidence of this kind to indicate that vision dominates proprioception when the 2 modalities are brought into conflict (Gibson, 1933; Nielsen, 1963; Rock and Victor, 1964; Over, 1966; Rock, 1966; Rock and Harris, 1967). Perhaps, in the experiments of Held and his colleagues, the discrepancy between vision and proprioception made itself felt only when the subject found that an arm movement that normally brought the hand to the median plane in space, for example, and to the fovea of the eye, now failed to do so.

This brings us to the second point, namely that the adaptation that is obtained in these experiments may not result from a recorrelation of sensorimotor mechanisms, but from relatively restricted changes in one modality or the other. The subject has to perform visually guided actions while wearing prisms that change the normal relationship between vision, on the one hand, and action and proprio-

---

[12] This experiment was performed by having the subject move a rod that controlled the motion of the luminous line on an oscilloscope. The line was superimposed on the position of the hand, which was hidden from the direct sight of the subject, by a mirror, and the delay was introduced by means of audio tape recorders. Video tape recorders were first used to study the effects of delays in visual feedback by Smith, McGrary, and Smith (1960); a discussion of such research is to be found in Smith and Smith (1962).

ception, on the other hand. The discrepancy would indeed be resolved if the visual appearance associated with a particular retinal image changed so that it agreed with the information provided by proprioception; this is what one might expect from the classical empiricist viewpoint. Harmony would also be restored, however, if proprioception and the motor system accommodated themselves to vision.[13] Walls (1951a,b,c) pointed out that Stratton's findings were at least as well explained by the second of these alternatives as by the first, and the data obtained by Held and his colleagues have been similarly interpreted as being due to changes in proprioception (McFarland, 1962; Harris, 1963, 1965; Hochberg, 1963; Hamilton, 1964; Hay & Pick, 1964).

Thus, in a review of research on adaptation, Harris (1965) finds most of the data to be consistent with the view that such adaptation consists of changes in the felt position of the subject's arm, head, or eyes. If the adaptation consisted of changes in the visually perceived location of objects a hand-pointing test should reveal those changes regardless of which hand is used. In several experiments, however, in which subjects watched one hand through a displacing prism while pointing with that hand at targets or while moving it back and forth, evidence of adaptation was obtained only when the subject was tested with the hand that had been used during practice (Scholl, 1926; Harris, 1963; Hamilton, 1964). This supports the view that the felt position of the hand, rather than the apparent visual position of the target, is changed by the adaptation. That is, when his arm is really pointing in one direction (for example, straight ahead), the subject feels that it is pointing in another direction (for example, 10° to the right). Additional support for this interpretation was given by the finding that subjects showed the effects of adaptation by

making errors of position when they pointed with their adapted hands at targets even when they could see neither the hand nor the target: this occurred when, with eyes closed, they pointed at a sound-emitting target, at their nonadapted hand, or "straight ahead" (Scholl, 1926; Harris, 1963; Hay & Pick, 1963; McLaughlin & Rifkin, 1965). They also made the appropriate errors in judging the distance between their adapted and their nonadapted hands, while blindfolded (Harris, 1965).

The absence of intermanual transfer occurs only under certain conditions.[14] Thus, in the experiment described by Helmholtz, in which he watched one of his hands while wearing prisms, the effect of adaptation was shown by the other hand as well, even though he had kept it out of sight during the adaptation period. He concluded, therefore, that it was not the felt position of his hand that had changed, but rather his judgment about the direction of his gaze, because a change in the latter should affect all of his visually guided behaviors. In fact, although a subject who is instructed to look straight ahead before adaptation does so without appreciable error, photographic records show that after adaptation his response to the same instruction is to rotate his eyes in the direction of the displacement (Kalil & Freedman, 1966; Craske, 1967; McLaughlin & Webster, 1967). This fact could account for part of the adaptation to displacing prisms, and changes in the felt

[13] It is now generally believed (Chapter 11) that the muscles of the oculomotor system provide no proprioceptive information. Instead, "proprioception" and "felt position" here refer to the calibration of the nonvisual systems that guide and execute spatial behaviors, including movements of the head and eyes.

[14] The conditions for obtaining much or little adaptation with the unexposed arm are not clear at present. Harris (1963) and Hamilton (1964) thought that intermanual transfer was due to a change in felt head position, and that this occurred only when the subject was free to move his head during adaptation. In fact, with unrestricted movements, adaptation effects have been obtained with both arms even if *neither* had been visible through the prisms (Bossom & Held, 1957), and subjects described an object as appearing straight ahead when it was actually displaced to one side (Held & Bossom, 1961; Kohler, 1964). But this does not vitiate Harris' thesis: The fact that *some* conditions can be found under which intermanual transfer does not occur suffices to cast doubt on any interpretation of adaptation as a change in vision per se. Those cases in which intermanual transfer does occur may be attributed to changes in judged head or eye position. For example, prism-adaptation can also result in changes in the judgment of the direction in which the eye is pointed, even when the head has been kept fixed during adaptation (Kalil & Freedman, 1966; Craske, 1967; McLaughlin & Webster, 1967), and this, as we shall see, should also result in intermanual transfer.

positions of other parts of the body might well account for the remainder. In fact, Hay and Pick (1966) have obtained separate measures that indicate that the proprioceptive change in the arm, and a change in felt direction of gaze (or eye posture) develop concurrently, but at different rates, during protracted adaptation to displacement by prisms.

The proprioceptive-change hypothesis has not gone unchallenged. The hypothesis predicts that if only one hand is adapted, it will point incorrectly no matter what the task is, and with the same size and direction of error in all cases. This result has been obtained, as we noted above, in pointing at visible targets, at sound-emitting targets, and "straight ahead." Efstathiou, Bauer, Greene, and Held (1967) have described two exceptions, however: They found the error to be smaller when the subject pointed at his unadapted hand, and they found that no significant error was made when the blindfolded subject was asked to mark the remembered locations of four pins for which he had learned to reach, while blindfolded, before adapting. The authors interpret these findings as follows: Proprioception or felt position of the hand has not changed. Instead, what has changed is the correlation between the direction of the hand movement that the subject makes when he wishes to touch any target, and the direction in which his head would face if he were to orient it toward that target.[15]

It is not clear, however, to what extent this interpretation really conflicts with the explanation based on a change in the felt position. "Felt position" cannot be directly observed; it has to be inferred from subjects' behaviors. There may be several criteria for deciding "felt position," only one of which (the relationship between head and hand, for example) is involved in the adaptation that occurred in these experiments. The 2 explanations may yet turn out to be supplementary (or even equivalent), rather than being irreconcilable.

What is important to us here is that in one explanation the motor-proprioceptive system of one arm has changed, and in the other, it is the correlation between the motor-proprioceptive system of the arm and that of the head, in judging visual direction, that has altered. Neither explanation predicates a change in vision itself.

Perception of "upright" and adaptation to tilt A line that is upright with respect to gravity may be tilted in the visual field, and vice versa, depending on the subject's posture and position. Thus, the subject must use information about the orientation both of his head and of the line in his retinal image if he is to judge correctly whether the line is vertical. Howard and Templeton (1966) have recently reviewed research on spatial orientation; here we are concerned only with certain kinds of conflict between visual and proprioceptive information and with the adaptation that results when the relationship between the image's retinal orientation and the subject's posture is changed.

As with the "straight ahead," the compensation for changes in posture is not perfectly maintained. Thus, Aubert (1861) noted that after he tilted his head to one side for a few seconds while looking at a luminous line in an otherwise dark room, the line appeared to be tilted in the opposite direction. Aubert concluded that this occurred because we come to underestimate the tilt of the head after it has been held for some time in the tilted position.[16]

---

[15]By this theory, the direction in which a subject reaches for a target is determined by the actual or potential orientation of his head toward that target. Adaptation to displacement changes the set of reaching movements of the adapted arm that go with a given orientation of the head. In the "remembered locations" task, the subject presumably guides his hand by the arm's proprioception alone, without orienting his head, and so no adaptation effects appear. In pointing at the unexposed hand, if the subject guided his pointing solely by the relationships between each hand and his head, the fact that the correlation between head-hand orientation had been changed for one hand and not for the other would result in a displacement in pointing. But because the subject can also match up the positions of the two hands on the basis of their felt positions (which the authors say remain unchanged), the total effect of adaptation is less in this task than in pointing at a visual target.

[16]We saw that displacement adaptation is in part attributable to changes in the position at which the eyes are felt

Unlike the "straight ahead," we normally have good visual indications of the upright, as in vertical trees and walls, horizontal lakes and floors. We can therefore often rely on vision alone in judging uprightness, taking little account of proprioception. In fact, Koffka (1935) maintained that the main lines of the visual field determine the directions of the apparent vertical and horizontal. When the visual framework is tilted with respect to gravity, and is therefore brought into conflict with proprioception, the visual indications often do determine what is judged to be vertical.[17] Thus, Wertheimer (1912) reported that when he looked into a tilted mirror to see a room in which he was standing, the room soon "righted itself" and looked upright or less tilted.

In more formal versions of this experiment, Asch and Witkin (1948a, b) had subjects judge when a pivoted rod was set vertically in terms of the room in which they were standing. The rod was in a model room which itself was tilted. Using a simpler apparatus, Witkin and Asch (1948b) placed a pivoted rod inside a tilted square frame, and with nothing but the rod and frame in view, the subject had to judge when the rod was vertical. In both experiments, the subject's chair could also be tilted. In general, tilting the visual framework affected subjects' judgments of when the line was vertical more than did tilting the chair. Subsequent research has generally confirmed the finding that the visual framework affects the judgment of uprightness (Curran & Lane, 1962; Mann, 1952), but not all research has done so (Gibson & Mowrer, 1938; Boring, 1952), and subjects vary greatly in their sus-

ceptibility to the effects of the visual framework.[18]

Even if the effects of the framework were more complete and more reliable than they are, the framework could not be considered the *necessary* determinant of apparent tilt. Subjects can adjust a luminous line to the vertical in an otherwise dark room without any framework (Neal, 1926), and they can even make a reliable judgment of whether a line is parallel to their bodies when they are lying supine (Rock, 1954). There is thus a relationship between an object's orientation in the retinal image and its apparent uprightness (or its alignment with the subject's body). This relationship can readily be changed by means of prisms that rotate or tilt the visual field, as in Figure 13.34C, providing another means of studying adaptation to rearrangement.

Thus, Mikaelian and Held (1964) had subjects wear prisms that tilted the visual field 20° during the exposure conditions. Before and after wearing the prisms, the subjects had to set a luminous line, viewed in an otherwise dark room, to an apparently vertical position. Two conditions of exposure were used. Subjects who were passively wheeled along a corridor displayed very little adaptation to tilt (1.9°). In the active condition, in which subjects walked back and forth in the same hallway, an adaptation effect of 6.8° was found after an hour of exposure, and 3 selected subjects achieved full compensation (approximately 20°) after an additional 2 hours. Unselected subjects stop short of complete adaptation, with little additional increment occurring after the first hour (Ebenholtz, 1966). The amount of the adaptation to tilt that is obtained under such conditions is a surprisingly simple linear function of the degree of optical tilt that is produced by the adapting prism (Morant & Beller, 1965; Ebenholtz, 1966), and is less when measured with the eye that was covered during adaptation (Ebenholtz, 1966).

The fact that the passive subjects of Mikaelian and Held showed any tilt-adaptation at all raises the same set of issues that we discussed in connection with displacement-adaptation. Because

---

to be looking straight ahead (p. 537). Ogle (1950) suggested that rotation of the eyes about the visual axis (torsion) might account for tilt normalization, but Howard and Templeton (1964b) measured eye torsion photographically under conditions in which tilt adaptation occurred and found no measurable torsion.

[17] In the amusement parks, rooms are sometimes set up in which balls appear to roll uphill (of course, it is the entire room that is tilted), or artificial scenery swings back and forth outside the windows so that the room itself seems to rock, and the people in it feel the appropriate (but illusory) kinesthetic sensations and dizziness.

[18] In fact, individual differences have been used as a measure of "field dependence," a personality variable that has emerged from research correlating performance on these visual orientation tasks with other perceptual and personality tests (Witkin et al., 1954).

Held and his colleagues are primarily concerned with those kinds of adaptation which result from a change in the sensorimotor mechanisms, they have tried to eliminate or to measure separately any adaptation that is due to changes solely in vision or solely in proprioception. Thus, because we know that adaptation to tilt occurs even when a motionless subject views a tilted line (Gibson, 1933; see Chapter 12, p. 466), the Gibson "normalization" effect would be expected to produce some adaptation to the vertical lines in the room, which would be tilted in the subject's retinal image because of the prisms he is wearing. Furthermore, as Mack (1967) has suggested, the "righting" effect of a tilted visual framework noted by Wertheimer and discussed above (p. 539) may also contribute to the adaptation. Mikaelian and Held (1964) therefore went on to eliminate these components by repeating their experiment in a room in which all the subject could see was a set of luminous spheres set in a random arrangement that contained no straight lines. In fact, the random stimulus field gave no clue as to the nature of the rearrangement produced by the prisms, as long as the observer remained motionless. If subjects moved actively during the inspection period, they subsequently displayed adaptation effects of about 2°, 2 selected subjects giving effects of about 5°. Subjects who were wheeled around passively during the exposure period showed no adaptation effects, so that tilt adaptation appears to depend on active movement under these conditions. As in the case of displacement-adaptation (p. 536), however, what might be important about the active movement is the information about the nature of the rearrangement that it offers. Thus, for example, a streaming movement of the spheres across the visual field of the subject who has been passively moved may offer few cues as to the nature of the prism that he is wearing, whereas the active subject would be able to learn, for example, that each horizontal rotation of his head to the left results not in the usual horizontal movement of the visual field to the right, but in a skewed (tilted) movement over the retina (see Held & Bossom, 1961; Rock, 1966).

As to the nature of tilt adaptation, we have seen that there are at least 2 possible components (normalization and frame effects) that do not require active movement. The third component, which was isolated by Mikaelian and Held in their experiments with luminous spheres, may reflect changes in the sensorimotor mechanisms, as Held proposes.

Or the visual appearance that results from a given retinal image may have changed, as the classical empiricist explanation suggests. However, it is just as plausible to assume that a line that appears upright on the retina continues to appear upright with respect to the subject's head, but that his head or body now feels tilted, when it is really upright; that is, that proprioception rather than vision has changed (McFarland, 1962; Hochberg, 1963). The general dominance of vision over proprioception in the perception of the upright (p. 539) makes this last alternative as likely as the others. There is at present no direct evidence to this point.

One may ask whether all of this discussion of proprioceptive change is not irrelevant, anyway, because Stratton and Kohler both reported that the appearance of the world actually changed as a result of adaptation. True, Stratton and Kohler do say, in some places, that the world's visual appearance changed in the course of adaptation, but, as we have seen in connection with problems connected with the perception of color and of shape (pp. 426, 451), perceptual reports cannot in general be taken at face value. Closer examination of Stratton's and Kohler's descriptions of their experiences lends plausibility to the view that it is touch and proprioception that have changed, not vision. For detailed analyses of their reports, see Walls (1951) and Harris (1965). If it seems odd to question these observers' own conclusions about their own experiences, note that they showed considerable uncertainty about the matter themselves.

Left-right and adaptation to reversal   Little is known about the discrimination of right from left. Children can discriminate right from left on their own persons by six years of age, but they cannot discriminate right from left on other people until later (Piaget, 1926; Swanson & Benton, 1955). Piaget considers this difference to be a "development away from egocentric thought." Howard and Templeton (1966) point out, however, that one

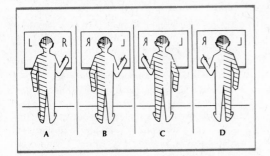

Figure 13.37. A subject's perceptions during the course of adaptation to reversed vision according to the proprioceptive-change hypothesis. In all cases perception of letters is visual; perception for the subject's head and body is proprioceptive. A. The actual physical arrangement. B. The subject's perceptions when he first puts on reversing goggles. C. The subject's perceptions at an intermediate stage of adaptation, with only his arms adapted. D. The subject's perceptions at an advanced stage of adaptation. (Harris, 1965.)

always has the same relation to one's own body, but not to other peoples' bodies, so that the constancy of the former makes the discrimination a much simpler task.

Unlike devices that tilt the visual field, which will normally offer good visual indications to the subject that the field has been tilted (p. 539), an optical device that reverses right for left will present little indication of that reversal to a passive subject. An active subject, of course, obtains visual feedback that reveals the nature of the optical rearrangement. As we have seen (p. 533), Kohler reports that active subjects undergo a curious "piecemeal" adaptation to reversing prisms. Let us now consider Harris' explanation of how this piecemeal adaptation would be accounted for if it is proprioception and not vision that is changing. Imagine a subject looking at the blackboard in Figure 13.37A. When he first puts on reversing prisms, he feels his right hand to be near the side of the blackboard that he sees on the right-hand side of the visual field, namely the side with the reversed *L* on it (Figure 13.37B). If he now looks at his hand, adaptation begins. When

he moves his hand to the right, he sees it moving to the left, and he soon begins to *feel* it to be moving to the left. In fact, this reversal of his proprioceptive perceptions may even make him write letters backwards while blindfolded, as Harris and Harris found (summarized by Rock & Harris, 1967). Similarly, because his right hand looks nearer to the reversed *R* on the blackboard than to the *L,* that hand *feels* nearer to the reversed *R* than to the *L*: that is, felt location of the limb comes to match its seen location, as in the experiments on displacement. When the subject is asked at this stage which end of the blackboard appears to be on his right, he should answer that the side with the reversed *R* does, if he asks himself which side is nearest his right hand (which has changed its felt location). During this stage of adaptation, the reversed writing on the blackboard is illegible, so that we get what looks to the experimenter like piecemeal visual adaptation. In time, the subject also learns to read writing that is reversed, as he would do even without mirrors or prisms, if he were continually confronted by mirror writing. It is easy to see, therefore, why Kohler might conclude that "mirrorwise seeing" had been established as a result of the adaptation, even if the change were primarily proprioceptive and not visual.

The explanation based on proprioceptive change must still be considered a tentative one. For one thing, we have seen that there are displacement-adaptation effects that do not seem to fit it (see Efstathiou et al., p. 538). For another, adaptation to curvature distortion of the retinal image presents a critical problem for a proprioceptive-change hypothesis.

Adaptation to curvature and distortion It is relatively easy to say, of a change in the relationship between vision and proprioception, that proprioception has changed. If the adaptation consists of a rearrangement of relationships within the visual field, however, it would be more difficult to escape the conclusion that it is vision that has changed

(Hochberg, 1963). Adaptation to curvature may provide such a case.

If a subject wears a prism which distorts the visual field in such a way that straight lines initially appear curved, adaptation will occur, and the lines come to look straighter (p. 465). After the prisms are removed, straight lines look curved in the opposite direction (Wundt, 1902; Kohler, 1964; Pick & Hay, 1964). This adaptation might be due, at least in part, to the normalization effect that Gibson (1933) had shown to occur with curved lines (p. 466). To avoid any Gibson normalization effect, Held and Rekosh (1963) used a method similar to that of the second experiment of Mikaelian and Held (1964). Each subject wore prisms while he was exposed to a visual field that was filled with an irregular array of spots. Before and after the exposure period, the subjects adjusted a line of varying curvature until it looked straight. One group of subjects, who had walked around during the exposure period, showed a curvature aftereffect; that is, the line had to be curved in the opposite direction to the distortion produced by the prism in order to look straight. Another group of subjects, who had been moved around in a wheel chair during the exposure period, showed no aftereffect. This demonstrates the existence of a curvature aftereffect which cannot be attributed to a line-normalization phenomenon, for no lines were visible in the field during the exposure period.

Another demonstration that curvature aftereffects can occur without normalization is given in an experiment by Festinger and his colleagues (1967). Taylor (1962) had reported that curvature aftereffects could be obtained after adaptation with a prism that was mounted on a contact lens (that is, on a lens that rides on the front of the eye; see Chapter 11, p. 374). Festinger and his colleagues had their subjects view an apparently straight line while wearing such a distorting contact lens. The optical effect of the prism was such as to make objectively straight lines appear curved, so that the line that the subjects were inspecting had to be objectively curved in order for it to appear straight. The subjects were instructed to look back and forth along the apparently straight line; head movements were pre-

vented by means of a clamping device. Despite the fact that the line appeared to be straight, of course, the subject's eye would actually have to execute a set of saccadic movements that corresponded to the objective curvature of the line if the line were to be kept on the fovea. These subjects displayed a curvature aftereffect when they removed the contact lens. Inasmuch as the line had been adjusted to compensate for the curvature produced by the prism during the adaptation period, these aftereffects cannot be attributed to normalization.

In the Held-Rekosh experiment, which used prism spectacles, active movements of the head or body were needed to obtain the curvature aftereffects, if only because without such movements the subject had little or no evidence of the optical rearrangement: The eye movements needed to bring one or another part of the retinal image to the fovea are not changed by prism spectacles. With the prisms mounted on contact lenses, as they were in the experiment of Festinger and his coworkers, the relationship between retinal image and eye movements has been rearranged: For example, a curved path of eye movements is needed to scan a line that produces a straight retinal image. Under these conditions, head movements are unnecessary for the aftereffects to occur. Thus, in both experiments, active movements were needed to obtain the aftereffects, but in the second case, movement of the eyes was sufficient.

Not all active movement results in adaptation, however. Festinger and his colleagues (1967) and Burnham (1968) performed a series of experiments to show that only those actions that require the subject to learn to make a new set of movements in response to the pattern of retinal stimulation will produce the curvature aftereffect. In these experiments, subjects wore prism spectacles while shooting (with light beams) at a moving target. The target bore a photocell, and gave an audible signal when the light beam hit it. Adaptation and aftereffects were obtained in the case of subjects who could see neither their hands nor the light beam (because it was infrared light, in that condition). Other subjects shot at the target with visible light beams and could therefore perform the task by purely visual aiming. These subjects showed no adaptation. Only those subjects who were forced to learn to make new pointing arm movements in response to the rearranged retinal image showed adaptation when they were subsequently tested, even though all subjects executed similar overt movements.[19]

It is difficult, but not impossible, to attempt an explanation of curvature adaptation in terms of nonvisual change. For example, Harris (1965) has suggested that perhaps after adaptation the subject feels that his eyes have followed a straight line when they have actually moved along a curve. This would make the change a proprioceptive one, and from this explanation we would expect that the curvature aftereffects would not be obtained if the subject had to make his curvature judgments without moving his eyes. Alternatively, we may note that the visual property of apparent straightness is not uniquely tied to a particular property of the retinal image: A line which appears to be straight when it is fixated with the eyes in one position of the head appears to be curved when fixated with the eyes in another position (Helmholtz, 1866; see Chapter 12, p. 466n). We might argue that in the curvature adaptation experiments the purely visual appearances remain unchanged but that there is a change in the criterion for "straightness," for a given position of the eyes.

It may seem like quibbling to argue in this way about whether the change that occurs in the course of curvature-adaptation is visual or not. There are effects of adaptation to rearrangement that seem unassailably visual, and we consider these next.

Visual changes in adaptation to rearranged vision When prisms are used to achieve optical rearrangement, color fringes are produced at each contour between regions of different luminances in the field of view, and these fringes result in both adaptation and

aftereffects (Hay, Pick, & Rosser, 1964; Kohler, 1964) that must be classed as visual. They do not seem to involve any need for active movement. It seems reasonable to regard them as a different kind of phenomenon from those we have been discussing, an adaptation phenomenon involving relatively peripheral mechanisms such as receptive fields (McCollough, 1965). In any case, they provide no clear implications for the explanation of space perception.

More to the present point is the work on adaptation to minification by Rock and his colleagues. In our earlier discussion of apparent size (p. 509), we saw that there was some evidence that subjects can respond to the absolute size, s, of the retinal image. As Rock points out (1966), if we could respond only to *relationships* within the visual field, any change in the overall size of the retinal image which leaves those relationships unchanged should have no effect on apparent size. Nevertheless, reducing the size of the entire field of view by looking at objects reflected in a convex mirror makes them look smaller, even if one's field of view is restricted to the minified scene. This implies that the visual system maintains some memory or *trace* of the retinal image size that was produced by each object in the scene, at its distance from the eye, before the minifying device was employed. Rock argues that the changes that occur during adaptation in general are in the subject's memories or traces of those features of the retinal image that correspond to the object-property in question (straightness, uprightness, size, and so forth). This is similar to the classical empiricist explanation of perception (see pp. 466, 532, 546). To Rock, however, the primary source of information about the object properties is visual, not kinesthetic. The sight of one's own body, or of familiar objects which have a known shape and size, would therefore be sufficient to bring about adaptation, and active movement would not in principle be necessary to obtain adaptation.

Rock (1965) and his collaborators had sub-

---

[19]Festinger, like Taylor (1962), supports a local sign theory in which the consciousness of any line or shape in the visual field *is* the readiness to perform the movements needed to point the eyes (or the arm) at any point on it (see Chapter 12, p. 467), so to him the distinction between vision and proprioception would be an empty one in this case.

jects view a 12-inch line in a lighted room from a distance of two feet. The subjects then had to match that length from memory, using a luminous line of variable length that they viewed in an otherwise dark room. This comprised the pretest. They were then exposed to a scene whose reflection they viewed in a convex (minifying) mirror. Their view was restricted to their head, trunk, arms, hands, and various objects on a table. After the exposure conditions, they used the luminous line, viewed in darkness, to match their memories of the original 12-inch standard. Subjects who had been in a control condition, in which a plane mirror was used, showed no difference between the pretest and aftertest. Subjects who had viewed a minified image, reflected by a convex mirror, showed a significant decrease in the length of the line that matched their memory of the standard. There was no difference between subjects who had watched the scene while they drew, played checkers, and so on, and those who simply looked at the scene. Thus, we may conclude that active movement is not necessary for adaptation to minification.

But we should reconsider what is meant by the distinction between active and passive adaptation. As was suggested earlier, in the discussion on whether and why subjects are able to respond to retinal size per se (p. 510), the angular size subtended by any part of the visual field has adaptive significance in guiding eye movements, and may be associated with a saccade of corresponding magnitude. Minification increases the proportion of any seen object's extent that is traversed by a given saccade, and the judged size of that saccadic movement might change in consequence of experience with minified images. That is, the essential activity in adaptation to minification may consist of eye movements made in scanning the scene.

As in our similar discussion of curvature-adaptation, this is merely speculation, but in our final example we shall see experimental evidence that a recorrelation between eye movements and apparent motion in the vis-

ual field can be established in the course of adaptation to rearrangement.

Adaptation to rearranged visual effects of head movement When optical rearranging devices, such as prisms, are first put on, the world appears to swing around wildly. Let us first see why this should happen. Consider an object at some distance from the observer, and 10° to the right of the median plane when he keeps his eyes straight ahead. If the observer turns his head 10° to the right, without wearing any rearranging devices, that object now lies in the median plane and is imaged on his fovea when he looks straight ahead. If he is wearing reversing spectacles, however, after turning to the right the image will now fall still further to the left of the fovea. The direction of retinal movement produced by any head movement has been changed by the prisms, and the eye movements that would normally compensate for the head movement (Chapter 11, p. 384) will no longer do so. Wallach and Kravitz (1965a,b) and Posin (described by Rock, 1966) independently used very similar procedures to demonstrate that adaptation does indeed occur to these rearranged relationships between body movements and retinal image movements, as Stratton and Kohler reported.

As their test condition, Wallach and Kravitz had the subject wear headgear so arranged that it projected a visual target to a curved screen. The subject sat before this screen in an otherwise dark room, and rotated his head. A variable-ratio transmission device was used to vary the relationship between the amount of head rotation that was made and the amount of target movement that this rotation produced. The subject's task was to say whether the target was stationary. In the pretest, the mean setting chosen was one in which the target was in fact stationary. The subject was then given an adapting condition, in which his head movement resulted in a different rate of retinal image movement than normally occurs. Specifically, the subjects were required to wear minifying spectacles for

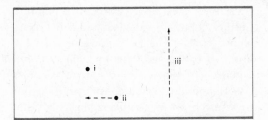

Figure 13.38. Stimulus movement (*ii*) contingent on head movement (*iii*). See text. (After Hay, 1968.)

6 hours, which reduced the rate of image displacement caused by head movement. In the post-test, the amount of movement of the target that the subjects judged to be stationary when the head was moving had changed as a result of exposure to the adapting condition. Both Wallach and Kravitz (1965b) and Posin (Rock, 1966) found such adaptation to occur both with active movement by the subject, and when the subject was moved around by the experimenter.

But what does passive movement mean in this case? Even when the experimenter rotates the subject, compensatory movements of his eyes occur, movements that normally operate to keep the image stable on the retina when the head or body is rotated (Chapter 11, p. 385). Perhaps the major effect of the adaptation to rearranged head-image movements consists of a recorrelation between the direction and magnitude of a head movement, on the one hand, and the compensatory eye movements that it elicits, on the other. Experiments by Hay (1968) suggest that a very similar kind of recorrelation can occur quite rapidly. In his experiments, the subject viewed two spots of light in an otherwise dark room. A bite-board apparatus both registered the subject's head movements, and constrained them to a vertical plane. One of the 2 spots was stationary (Figure 13.38 *i*). The other (*ii*) was moved horizontally each time the subject moved his head vertically, by means of an electronic coupling of spot *ii* with the bite board. In one adapting condition, the subjects were instructed to keep spot *ii*

fixated while they moved their heads. This required them to learn to execute diagonal eye movements correlated with their vertical head movements. During the course of this adaptation, spot *ii* came to appear stationary while spot *i* seemed to make a diagonal movement across the field. In a second adapting condition, the subjects merely fixated the stationary spot, *i*, while they moved their heads vertically. This required them to make only the usual vertical eye movements that are required to compensate for vertical head movements. After adaptation, a test condition was employed in which both spots were held stationary, and the subject moved his head vertically. For subjects who adapted to the first condition, *both* spots now appeared to move in the direction *opposite* to that in which the stationary spot *i* had appeared to move during the adaptation period. For subjects adapted to the second condition, no such aftereffect was obtained. Thus, in the first condition, the subjects seem to have learned to make a set of diagonal eye movements during vertical head movements, in order to compensate for the head movements and keep the spot fixated. This is what we have said may be occurring quite generally in prism-adaptation experiments. Also, as was true in the prism-adaptation experiments, there are at least 2 different kinds of movement aftereffect. The aftereffect that Hay reported seems to depend on the recorrelation of compensatory eye movements and head movements; it obviously requires the subject to make active movements if adaptation is to occur. On the contrary, the aftereffects due to retinal displacement (p. 521), like the "waterfall illusion," can occur with a passive observer and even with stabilized retinal images.

In summary, some forms of adaptation to rearranged vision clearly may occur without active movement. Other forms of such adaptation do require active movement, but a good case can be made for supposing that the changes that occur involve the spatial calibration of the proprioceptive and motor systems, not the visual system. This distinction tends to dissolve, however, when eye movements are closely involved in the visual task, as they so often are. However, the classical interpretation of adaptation to visual arrangement as the re-education of vision to agree with proprioception is certainly not supported. In fact, where vision and proprioception are brought into immediate conflict, proprioception seems to change in order to agree with vision and not vice versa (see p. 536). If visual space is in fact originally learned by early associations between visual and proprioceptive-kinesthetic experiences, as the classical empiricist position maintained, that will have to be demonstrated by research on the origins of space perception, not by the evidence thus far provided by experiments on rearranged vision.

ON THE NATURE-NURTURE QUESTION IN SPACE PERCEPTION

Spatial Perception with Minimal Experience

The question of whether our abilities to perceive the spatial aspects of our environment are completely the result of learning, or whether any of them may be innate, dominated the study of perception from its inception, and remains a challenging issue today, despite some three centuries of controversy.

The issue has been important to different disciplines—to philosophy, to physiology, to art, to psychology—for very different reasons, and the diverse purposes for which this general question was asked cannot always be equally well served by a given answer (Hochberg, 1962). For example, a common assertion in art theory is that if the depth cues required to understand a picture are all learned symbols, then all are arbitrary and subject to change by artistic convention and education. However, this does not follow at all: Instead, we may learn the depth cues during our first few months of visual experience, and they might thereafter be completely

resistant to relearning. A common assumption of sensory physiologists is that if a depth cue is innate, it will be more powerful than any acquired or learned basis for judging depth with which it may be brought into conflict (see Helmholtz, 1896); a considerable amount of research on perceptual change has been motivated by this assumption. Again, however, it does not follow of necessity that what is innate must be stronger than what is learned.

Studies of infants   The most direct experimental attack on the question of whether visual space perception *must* be learned by association with tactual-kinesthetic-proprioceptive experience, as the empiricist position would have it, is to ask whether any degree of this ability can be found in subjects who have had no opportunity whatsoever to form such associations.[20]

Severe methodological difficulties beset such research. We can ask newborn infants only indirectly about what their spatial perceptions may be; that is, only by setting up behavioral tests of depth discrimination. In the higher animals and in man, coordinated motor behavior is very poorly developed at birth, so that few behavioral tests are then available. Nor can we use human infants in control experiments that would deprive them of normal sensorimotor development.

Although eye movements are not well coordinated and the eye's focusing ability is quite limited in earliest infancy (Haynes,

[20] The reasoning that seems to demand an empiricist explanation of space perception, by logic alone, is easily set aside. If space perception were indeed completely learned, the effects of that learning must consist of acquiring particular structures in the nervous system (say, some changes in the synapses in the neural network). At least some of these neural structures might have been acquired during some millions of years of evolutionary selection rather than during the few months or years of an individual's infancy. Thus the baby might be born with all the neural connections he needs for at least some aspects of space perception. Therefore, the question is really one for experimental inquiry, not for logical analysis. However, note that what gave this question its clear theoretical importance was not whether the course of experience with the world modifies or affects spatial behaviors and perception: It was the nature of the underlying general psychological theory of which the empiricist assertion was a part (pp. 428, 437).

White, & Held, 1965; see Hershenson, 1967 for a recent review), some eye-movement behaviors seem to be guided by the spatial features of stimulation shortly after birth. In a unique experiment, Wertheimer (1961) started testing an infant (who had been delivered by natural childbirth and hence was in an undrugged state) 3 minutes after birth. As the infant lay on her back, clicks were sounded next to the right ear or next to the left ear. On most of the trials on which movements occurred, the eyes moved in the direction of the click. Thus, some appropriate visuomotor behavior was elicited by spatially separated auditory stimuli, suggesting strongly that in some degree the discrimination of direction is innate.

Fantz (1961), Hershenson (1964), Hershenson, Munsinger, and Kessen (1965), and Salapatek and Kessen (1966), have demonstrated that different spatial distributions of visual stimulation can evoke different sets of eye movements in infants considerably older than the one used by Wertheimer (see Hershenson, 1967; E. Gibson, 1969). They presented their subjects with patterned visual displays and observed, directly or via motion-picture photography, where the infant appeared to be fixating. The rationale for these studies is that if the subject could not discriminate one stimulus from another, he would have no basis for turning his eye toward one rather than toward the other. Inasmuch as infants' eye movements do appear to be reliably affected by the configuration of the stimulus display, we may attribute to the infants some minimum amount of "pattern vision" (that is, of responses that are controlled by the spatial characteristics of the stimulus, not merely by its overall wavelength and intensity). To go further than that, and to say that we can tell that infants perceive depth because they look more often at a sphere than at a disk (Fantz, 1961) is not yet warranted, inasmuch as it may merely be two-dimensional pattern differences to which they are responding in these cases as well. But is it not true in every case that 2 stimulus displays that

differ in 3 dimensions will necessarily differ as two-dimensional patterns, as well? And if that is so, how can we ever be sure that the infant's response is not simply being given to the two-dimensional differences in pattern?

These questions are simply an extreme form of "How do we know what the subject perceives," which we have encountered before (pp. 426, 505, 540). We can simply note here that, so long as there are features to which the infant might be responding (such as the complexity of a pattern), which are known to attract his gaze even when they are not associated with depth, it seems premature to attribute fixation of those features to "depth perception." To talk profitably about space perception depends on being able to predict the organism's behavior better from the characteristics of objects in space than from the retinal image that falls in the subject's eye. For example, demonstrating the extent to which an infant appears to draw upon his perception of distance to achieve size constancy (pp. 506–510), to reach for objects, and to avoid places, would provide more justification for talking about depth perception.

A major problem, of course, is that the higher organism's response repertory is extremely meager at birth. Perhaps the usefulness of that repertory can be increased by techniques of operant conditioning (p. 595); for example, Bower (1964) reports that infants 70 to 85 days old could be conditioned to perform small head movements in response to the presentation of a 12-inch cube. They showed more generalization to the same cube at 3 times the original distance than to a much larger cube that maintained the original visual angle at the greater distance. Thus, they seemed to be responding to object size, rather than to retinal image size.

The classic solution to this problem, however, is to use older subjects who have been reared under special conditions, such as total darkness, which prevent them from having had any opportunity to associate tactual-kinesthetic experience with the visual stimuli on which they will be tested. Ideally, the subject should be allowed to mature sufficiently to display a full range of responses, but he should not be allowed to attach those responses to any pattern of visual stimulation. The first exposure to visual stimulation would then elicit only those responses (if any) that are innately tied to that pattern.

Dark-rearing can obviously not be carried out with human infants. Fortunately (for the experimenter) certain forms of partial blindness occur very early in life that (fortunately for the child) can often be cured later; these offer the experimenter a substitute for dark-rearing. Although many sight-restoring operations have been performed (Senden, 1932; London, 1960), postoperative visual disturbances (Senden, 1932; Dennis, 1934; Wertheimer, 1951), crudeness of testing, and the fact that varying amounts of visual experience have been available to the preoperative subjects, despite the fact that they were technically blind, make it difficult to draw any firm conclusions from such research. In general, some minimal amount of direction, depth, and even shape recognition seems to have been in evidence (Senden, 1932; Gregory & Wallace, 1963; Ueda, 1967), but it is not safe to build any theoretical structures on these data.

Studies of animals reared in darkness
Animals have been raised in the dark successfully, but the results are difficult to interpret. Negative results (that is, absence of any evidence of innate spatial responses) are inconclusive, inasmuch as the visual nervous system and the perceptuomotor guidance systems may both deteriorate rapidly unless used fairly soon after birth (see Riesen, 1947; Chow & Nissen, 1955; Wiesel & Hubel, 1961, 1963). Moreover, abnormal habits of performance acquired during visual deprivation may interfere with subsequent use of the visual information. For example, Held and Hein (1963) designed an elegant experiment to show the necessity of visuomotor experience for the development of depth discrim-

ination in the cat (which, as we shall see, does not seem to show innate spatial abilities after dark-rearing). They paired kittens in a "carousel" so that an active member wheeled his passive partner around for one hour each day. Both animals were otherwise reared in darkness and both were thus exposed to equal amounts of moving, contoured light. The passive cats showed marked disabilities when confronted with the visual cliff (see below), and in other tasks that require visuomotor coordination and that seem to implicate depth perception. However, we must not infer from these results that the passive cat necessarily has inferior spatial discrimination. An animal (and especially a kitten) that has received visual stimulation only while its limbs were confined, may have started to make movements in response to that stimulation, but, being frustrated by the constraints then felt, may simply have learned not to respond to such stimulation.

In any case, positive findings (that is, evidence of innate spatial responses) are somewhat easier to interpret, although they have their own hazards.[21] Experiments on a variety of species of animals have yielded positive results. (For a recent review, see Walk, 1966.)

Thus, when chicks that had been raised in darkness since they were hatched are taken into light for the first time, and are placed on platforms of varying height, they display more hesitation in jumping from high platforms than from low ones (Spalding, 1873; Thorndike, 1899; Kurke, 1955). To the extent that the chicks' reluctance to jump is a function of the visual depth cues, their performance must reflect innate depth discrimination. Additional experiments have

[21] The mechanism underlying the innate depth discrimination might have little to do with what we normally think of as depth perception. For example, it might be that some species of animals will not locomote when unfocused images fall on their retinas. In that case, when as infants, with poor accommodation for distance vision, they are confronted by the kind of "visual cliff" that we describe below, they might "freeze" while trying to resolve the blurred images. If this mechanism were responsible for the avoidance of the deep side of such a cliff, flooding the scene with a great deal of light would reduce the size of their pupils, increase the sharpness of focus of the deep side, and eliminate the avoidance behavior.

made use of a "visual cliff" consisting of a horizontal sheet of heavy glass at some height above the floor. A visual pattern, such as a checkerboard design, is attached to the underside of one half of the glass sheet. On the "cliff" side, the same pattern is laid on the floor. Walk, Gibson, and Tighe (1957) and Walk and Gibson (1961) used this device to show that dark-reared rats and light-reared rats both avoided the cliff side when they were placed on the centerboard. This finding was confirmed with additional controls by Neally and Edwards (1960), who also showed that blinded animals failed to distinguish between the cliff side and the shallow side. This evidence of innate depth discrimination in rats is in line with results obtained with some other species. Thus, chicks show innate depth discrimination (Spalding, 1873; Thorndike, 1899; Gibson & Walk, 1960; Tallarico, 1961) and so may monkeys (Fantz, 1961, 1965; Rosenblum & Cross, 1963) and rabbits (Walk, 1966). Kittens, which normally discriminate depth by 4 weeks of age, do not discriminate on the visual cliff if they have been reared in the dark for that period (Gibson & Walk, 1960), nor do they show other depth-discriminatory behavior (Riesen & Aarons, 1959; Gibson & Walk, 1960), but that may at least in part be due to the fact that prolonged dark-rearing itself interferes destructively with performance on the visual cliff even with species that otherwise display innate depth discrimination (Nealy & Riley, 1963; Walk, Trychin, & Karmel, 1965).

The fact that some species show innate depth discrimination and some do not is interesting from a comparative standpoint. It may be a mistake to think of "space perception," or even of depth discrimination, as a unitary ability. Between species, as we have seen, differences in depth discrimination are gross and can be affected further by dark-rearing. In addition, it has been shown that differences in rearing environments can change the way in which animals behave on the visual cliff within a species (Kaess & Wilson, 1964; Lemmon & Patterson, 1964; Tallarico & Farrell, 1964; Carr & McGuigan, 1965).

However, the fact that differences in environment can effect differences in depth discrimination does not mean that the spatial meaning of visual stimulation is arbitrary, acquired merely by association with tactual-kinesthetic experiences of the world. Hess (1956) found evidence for innate directional cues in experiments with chicks that had been hatched in darkness and had been fitted with hoods containing prisms that displaced the visual field 7° laterally. He observed their initial pecks at a small target and at individual kernels of grain. The main finding was that the average peck was about 7° off target. The initial pecks were deflected as we would expect if their spatial localization were innate. Hess's chicks appeared to show no adaptation to the prisms, but Rossi (1968) has found slight but reliable amounts of such adaptation, together with an aftereffect in the direction opposed to the displacement produced by the prisms. These experiments provide a clear example of a behavior which seems to be innate yet which is subject to adaptation and "relearning."

Developmental Studies

Differences in spatial performance are found not only between members of different species but in the same subject at different ages. As with species differences, these may help us to sort out component abilities that are difficult to separate in adult behavior. However, it is unjustified to infer, from the fact that the performance of some spatial task improves with age, that the underlying perceptual ability was initially learned rather than innate: The fact that an ability continues to improve with age does not imply that it was at one time completely absent. Furthermore, what data we have on the relationship between the sensory systems are not encouraging for the simple empiricist hypothesis that space perception is learned by the association of specific visual patterns with tactual-kinesthetic experiences in space. That hypothesis was the motivation for most research on the development of the constancies, and it will no longer serve that purpose. More specific theories which predict patterns of improvement and of change with age are now needed, and several have been proposed and tested for the various constancies and illusions (Piaget et al., 1942, 1961; Wapner &

Werner, 1957; Pollock et al., 1963, 1967). Developmental studies have recently been reviewed by E. J. Gibson and Olum (1960), Wohlwill (1960), E. J. Gibson (1963, 1969), and by Tanaka (1967), Shinno (1967), and Ueda (1967). The pattern of results is quite complex because whether or not differences between subjects of different ages are found at all is a function of the task. A review of the development of space perception would in consequence be too involved to attempt here. Nevertheless, there are several points that we should note here.

Although age differences have been found in such measures of space perception as size constancy (Beyrl, 1926; Piaget & Lambercier, 1943; Zeigler & Leibowitz, 1957; Tanaka, 1967), these differences only appear with certain tasks and under certain testing conditions. We cannot, therefore, assume that these experiments measure a single homogeneously improving perceptual ability, the development of which would be manifested equally well by all behaviors that depend on space perception: We cannot assume, for example, because a child grossly underestimates the size of a stimulus in a size-constancy experiment, that he will also be unable to throw a ball accurately at that target (Smith & Smith, 1966; Tanaka, 1967). The fact that some perceptual measures change with age, moreover, may mean only that the motivation and the problem-solving strategies with which the subject approaches the experimental task have changed. For example, because the magnitudes of the geometrical illusions change as a function of age, some increasing

and others decreasing at different age levels (Gibson, 1969, pp. 407–409), several attempts have been made to use these developmental differences to sort out separate processes that might underlie the illusions (Pollack & Chaplin, 1963). Such theories suggest cumulative and nonreversible changes. An intriguing demonstration by Parrish, Lundy, and Leibowitz (1968), showed that adults, who had been hypnotically instructed that they were two years old, performed like children on the Ponzo and Poggendorf illusions (pp. 456, 457). This suggests instead that reversible factors (as in attentiveness, judgment attitude, and so on) may underlie some of the age changes.

If the various spatial behaviors were completely independent of each other, and if the effects of the various depth cues on those behaviors were also independent, there would be little systematic interest in measuring any of them; nor would there be much reason to retain the word "perception" in the psychologists' vocabulary. The term is not that empty, however, and there are sets of spatial behaviors that seem to be related to each other as measures of some common underlying perception of space, as we have seen (pp. 499, 505, 511–519). However, the fact that many measures are uncorrelated means that if research on individual and developmental differences is to be profitable past the bare point of testing the Berkeleyan theory of space perception (p. 477), it must rest on other assumptions about what stimulus information, what tasks, and what response measures are related to each other and to our purposes of inquiry.

INDICES

BIBLIOGRAPHIC

INDEX

Aarons, L., see Riesen, A. H., 1959.

Abbey, D. S. Cross-modality matching of numerosity and pitch. *Canadian Journal of Psychology*, 1962, *16*, 283–290. **86**

Abbott, D. W., & Price, L. E. Stimulus generalization of the conditioned eyelid response to structurally similar nonsense syllables. *Journal of Experimental Psychology*, 1964, *68*, 368–371. **1047**

Abelson, R. P., & Sermat, V. Multidimensional scaling of facial expression. *Journal of Experimental Psychology*, 1962, *63*, 546–554. **57**

Abney, W. de W. The sensitiveness of the retina to light and colour. *Philosophical Transactions of the Royal Society* (London), Ser. A, 1897, *190A*, 155–193. **290**

Abplanalp, P. L., see Hoffman, H. S., 1964.

Abraham, F., see Gormezano, I., 1961.

Abrahams, H., Krakauer, D., & Dallenbach, K. M. Gustatory adaptation to salt. *American Journal of Psychology*, 1937, *49*, 462–469. **184**

Abramov, I., see DeValois, R. L., 1964.

Abrevay, E. L., see Mayzner, M. S., 1964.

Adachi, A. Neurophysiological study on taste effectiveness of seasoning. *Journal of the Physiological Society of Japan*, 1964, *26*, 347–355. **188**

Adachi, A., Funakoshi, M., & Kawamura, Y. Neurophysiological studies on taste effectiveness of chemical taste enhancers. In T. Hayashi (Ed.), *Olfaction and taste*. Vol. II. New York: Pergamon Press, 1967. Pp. 411–413. **188**

Adam, J., see Gibb, M., 1966.

Adams, G., see Brackbill, Y., 1967.

Adams, H. F. The autokinetic sensations. *Psychological Review Monograph Supplement*, 1912, *14*, 1–45. **530**

Adams, J. A. A source of decrement in psychomotor performance. *Journal of Experimental Psychology*, 1955, *49*, 390–394. **575**

Adams, J. A. *Human memory*. New York: McGraw-Hill, 1967. **1131**

Adams, L., see Rock, I., 1965.

Adams, O. S. Stereogram decentration and stereobase as factors influencing the apparent size of stereoscopic pictures. *American Journal of Psychology*, 1955, *68*, 54–68. **480**

Adams, P. A., & Haire, M. The effect of orientation on the reversal of one cube inscribed in another. *American Journal of Psychology*, 1959, *72*, 296–299. **519**

Adams, P. A., see also Postman, L., 1955, 1956; Wallach, H., 1956.

Adams, R. An account of a peculiar optical phenomenon seen after having looked at a moving body. *Philosophical Magazine*, 1834, *5*, 373f. Cited in E. G. Boring. *Sensation and perception in the history of experimental psychology*. New York: Appleton, 1942. **521**

Adelman, H. M., & Maatsch, J. L. Resistance to extinction as a function of the type of response elicited by frustration. *Journal of Experimental Psychology*, 1955, *50*, 61–65. **573**

Adey, W. R., see Wendt, R. H., 1963.

Adler, F. H. *Physiology of the eye: Clinical application.* (3rd ed.) St. Louis: Mosby, 1959. **282**

Adler, S., see Mayzner, M. S., 1964.

Adolph, E. F. Urges to eat and drink in rats. *American Journal of Physiology*, 1947, *151*, 110–125. **812**

Adrian, E. D. Olfactory reactions in the brain of the hedgehog. *Journal of Physiology*, 1942, *100*, 459–473. **201**

Adrian, E. D. Electric responses of the human eye. *Journal of Physiology*, 1945, *104*, 84–104. **308**

Adrian, E. D. Rod and cone components in the electric response of the eye. *Journal of Physiology*, 1946, *105*, 24–37. **308**

Adrian, E. D. Sensory discrimination with some recent

evidence from the olfactory organ. *British Medical Bulletin,* 1950, *6,* 330-333. **218**

Adrian, E. D. The mechanism of olfactory stimulation in the mammal. *Advances in Science,* 1953, *9,* 417-420. **202, 216, 218**

Adrian, E. D. Basis of sensation: Some recent studies of olfaction (Banting memorial lecture). *British Medical Journal,* 1954, *1,* 287-290. **216**

Adrian, E. D. & Matthews, R. The action of light on the eye: III. The interaction of retinal neurones. *Journal of Physiology,* 1928, *65,* 273-298. **291**

Adrignolo, A. J., *see* Mayzner, M. S., 1967.

Aiken, E. G., *see* Mowrer, O. H., 1954.

Ajmone-Marsan, C., *see* Jasper, H. H., 1955.

Akesson, C., *see* Ekman, G., 1964.

Akishige, Y. Experimental researches on the structure of the perceptual space. *Bulletin of the Faculty of Literature, Kyushu Univ.,* 1951, *281,* 288. **534**

Albee, G. W., *see* Bruell, J. H., 1955.

Alberts, E., & Ehrenfreund, D. Transposition in children as a function of age. *Journal of Experimental Psychology,* 1951, *41,* 30-38. **765**

Albrecht, J. J., *see* Inglett, G. E., 1965.

Allen, C., *see* Wickens, D. D., 1963.

Allen, F., & Weinberg, M. The gustatory sensory reflex. *Quarterly Journal of Experimental Psychology,* 1925, *15,* 385-420. **178**

Allison, A. C. The structure of the olfactory bulb and its relation to the olfactory pathways in the rabbit and the rat. *Journal of Comparative Neurology,* 1953, *98,* 309-348.(a) **197**

Allison, A. C. The morphology of the olfactory system in vertebrates. *Biological Review,* 1953, *28,* 195-244. (b) **196**

Allison, J., Larson, D., & Jensen, D. D. Acquired fear, brightness preference, and one-way shuttlebox performance. *Psychonomic Science,* 1967, *8,* 269-270. **803**

Allison, V. C., & Katz, S. H. An investigation of stenches and odors for industrial purposes. *Journal of Industrial Engineering and Chemistry,* 1919, *11,* 336-338. **199, 201, 203, 204**

Allport, G. W., & Pettigrew, T. G. Cultural influence on the perception of movement: The trapezoidal illusion among Zulus. *Journal of Abnormal and Social Psychology,* 1957, *55,* 104-113. **518**

Allyn, M. R., *see* Festinger, L., 1968.

Alpern, M. Metacontrast: Historical introduction. *American Journal of Optometry,* 1952, *29,* 631-646. **429, 430**

Alpern, M. Metacontrast. *Journal of the Optical Society of America,* 1953, *43,* 648-657. **310, 429**

Alpern, M. *The eye.* In H. Davson (Ed.), *Muscular mechanisms,* New York: Academic Press, 1962. Vol. 3, pp. 3-229. **371, 383**

Alpern, M., & Campbell, F. W. The spectral sensitivity of the consensual light reflex. *Journal of Physiology,* 1962, *164,* 478-507. **393**

Alpern, M., & Dudley, D. The blue arcs of the retina. *Journal of General Physiology,* 1966, *49,* 405-421. **286**

Alpern, M., & Ellen, P. A quantitative analysis of the horizontal movements of the eyes in the experiment of Johannes Mueller. *American Journal of Ophthalmology,* 1956, *42,* 289-303. **382**

Alpern, M., McCready, D. W. J., & Barr, L. M. The dependence of the photopupil response on flash duration and intensity. *Journal of General Physiology,* 1963, *47,* 265-278. **392**

Alpern, M., Mason, G. L., & Jardinico, R. E. Vergence and accommodation: V. *American Journal of Ophthalmology,* 1961, *52,* 762-767. **393**

Alpern, M., *see also* Fry, G. A., 1952; ten Doesschate, J., 1967.

Alrutz, S. Untersuchungen über die Temperatursinne. *Zeitschrift für Psychologie,* 1908, *47,* 161. **148**

Alston, J. H. The spatial condition of the fusion of warmth and cold in heat. *American Journal of Psychology,* 1920, *31,* 303-312. **148**

Amatsu, M., *see* Ishiko, N., 1967.

Amerine, M. A., Pangborn, R. M., & Roessler, E. B. *Principles of sensory evaluation of food,* New York: Academic Press, 1965. **171, 187**

Ames, A. Visual perception and the rotating trapezoidal window. *Psychological Monographs,* 1951, No. 324. **518**

Ammons, C. H., Worchel, P., & Dallenbach, K. M. "Facial vision": Perception of obstacles out of doors by blindfolded and blindfolded-deafened subjects. *American Journal of Psychology,* 1953, *66,* 519-53. **270**

Ammons, C. H., *see also* Ammons, R. B., 1959.

Ammons, H., & Irion, A. L. A note on the Ballard reminiscence phenomenon. *Journal of Experimental Psychology,* 1954, *48,* 184-186. **1121**

Ammons, R. B. Acquisition of motor skill: I. Quantitative analysis and theoretical formulation. *Psychological Review,* 1948, *54,* 263-281. **575, 1034, 1039**

Ammons, R. B. Experimental factors in visual form perception: I. Review and formulation of problems. *Journal of Genetic Psychology,* 1954, *84,* 3-25. **519**

Ammons, R. B., Ulrich, P., & Ammons, C. H. Voluntary control of depth in a two-dimensional drawing. *Proceedings of the Montana Academy of Science,* 1959, *19,* 160-168. **519**

Amoore, J. E. The stereochemical theory of olfaction: 1. Identification of the seven primary odours. *Proceedings of the Scientific Section of the Toilet Goods Association,* 1962, *37* (suppl.), 1-12. (a) **213**

Amoore, J. E. The stereochemical theory of olfaction: 2. Elucidation of the stereochemical properties of the olfactory receptor sites. *Proceedings of the Scientific Section of the Toilet Goods Association,* 1962, *37* (suppl.), 13-23. (b) **213**

Amoore, J. E. Psychophysics of odor. *Cold Spring Harbor Symposia in Quantitative Biology,* 1965, *30,* 623-637. **214**

Amoore, J. E., Johnston, J. W. Jr., & Rubin, M. The stereochemical theory of odor. *Scientific American,* 1964, *210,* 42-49. **214**

Amsel, A. Selective association and the anticipatory goal response mechanism as explanatory concepts in learning theory. *Journal of Experimental Psychology,* 1949, *39,* 785-799. **801**

Amsel, A. The role of frustrative nonreward in noncontinuous reward situations. *Psychological Bulletin,* 1958, *55,* 102-119. **576, 695, 810**

Amsel, A. Frustrative nonreward in partial reinforcement and discrimination learning: Some recent history and a theoretical extension. *Psychological Review,* 1962, *69,* 306-328. **810**

Amsel, A. Partial reinforcement effects on vigor and persistence: Advances in frustration theory derived from a variety of within-subjects experiments. In K. W. Spence & J. T. Spence (Eds.), *The psychology of learning and motivation.* New York: Academic Press, 1967. Vol. 1, pp. 1-65. **622, 810**

Amsel, A., & Hancock, W. Motivational properties of frustration: III. Relation of frustration effect to antedating goal factors. *Journal of Experimental Psychology,* 1957, *53,* 126-131. **810**

Amsel, A., & Penick, E. C. The influence of early experience on the frustration effect. *Journal of Experimental Psychology,* 1962, *63,* 167-176. **810**

Amsel, A., & Roussel, J. Motivational properties of frustration: I. Effect on a running response of the addition of frustration to the motivational complex. *Journal of Experimental Psychology,* 1952, *43,* 363-368. **809**

Amsel, A., & Work, M. S. The role of learned factors in "spontaneous" activity. *Journal of Comparative and Physiological Psychology,* 1961, *54,* 527-532. **822**

Amsel, A., Work, M. S., & Penick, E. C. Activity during and between periods of stimulus change related to feeding. *Journal of Comparative and Physiological Psychology*, 1962, *55*, 1114–1117. **822**

Amsel, A., see also Peckham, R. H., Jr., 1964.

Anand, B. K. Nervous regulation of food intake. *Physiological Reviews*, 1961, *41*, 677–708. **812**

Anastasio, E. J., see Sgro, J. A., 1967.

Andersen, E. E., and Weymouth, F. W. Visual perception and the retinal mosaic: I. Retinal mean local sign—an explanation of the fineness of binocular perception of distance. *American Journal of Physiology*, 1923, *64*, 561–594. **301, 305**

Andersen, H. T., Funakoshi, M., & Zotterman, Y. Electrophysiological responses to sugars and their depression by salt. In Y. Zotterman (Ed.), *Olfaction and taste.* Vol. 1. New York: Pergamon, 1963, 177–192. **186**

Anderson, D. C., see Brown, J. S., 1966; Pearl, J. 1964

Anderson, I., & Crosland, H. A method of measuring the effect of primacy of report in the range of experiment. *American Journal of Psychology*, 1933, *45*, 701–712. **444**

Anderson, I. H. Studies in the eye-movements of good and poor readers. *Psychological Monographs*, No. 215, 1937. **390**

Anderson, J. F., see Rose, J. E., 1967.

Anderson, K. The effects of shifts in sucrose concentration on bar press rates of monkeys. Unpublished doctoral dissertation, Brown University, 1965. **639**

Anderson, L., see Osgood, C. E., 1957.

Anderson, N., see Turnage, T., 1965.

Anderson, N. H. An analysis of sequential dependencies. In R. R. Bush & W. K. Estes (Eds.), *Studies in mathematical learning theory.* Stanford: Stanford University Press, 1959. Pp. 248–264. **922**

Anderson, N. H. Effect of first-order conditional probability in a two-choice learning situation. *Journal of Experimental Psychology*, 1960, *59*, 73–93. **922**

Anderson, N. H. An evaluation of stimulus sampling theory: Comments on Professor Estes' paper. In A. W. Melton (Ed.). *Categories of human learning.* New York: Academic Press, 1964. Pp. 129–144. **922, 934**

Anderson, N. H. Test of a prediction of stimulus sampling theory in probability learning. *Journal of Experimental Psychology*, 1966, *71*, 499–510. **930**

Anderson, N. H., & Grant, D. A. A test of a statistical learning theory model for two-choice behavior with double stimulus events. *Journal of Experimental Psychology*, 1957, *54*, 305–317. **933**

Anderson, N. H., & Grant, D. A. Correction and reanalysis. *Journal of Experimental Psychology*, 1958, *56*, 453–454. **933**

Anderson, N. H., see also Coons, E. E., 1960.

Anderson, N. S., see Fitts, P. M., 1956.

Anderson, O. D. see Liddell, H. S., 1934.

Anderson, R. E., see McLaughlin, S. C., 1968.

Anger, D. The dependence of interresponse times upon the relative reinforcement of different interresponse times. *Journal of Experimental Psychology*, 1956, *52*, 145–161. **606**

Anger, D. The role of temporal discriminations in the reinforcement of Sidman avoidance behavior. *Journal of the Experimental Analysis of Behavior*, 1963, 6 (suppl.), 447–506. **731, 732**

Angrist, B., see Leibowitz, H., 1954.

Annau, Z., & Kamin, L. J. The conditioned emotional response as a function of intensity of the US. *Journal of Comparative and Physiological Psychology*, 1961, *54*, 428–432. **713, 714**

Anstis, S. M., & Atkinson, J. Distortions in moving figures viewed through a stationary slit. *American Journal of Psychology*, 1967, *80*, 572–585. **455**

Anstis, S. M., & Gregory, R. K. The after-effect of seen motion: The role of retinal stimulation and of eye movements. *Quarterly Journal of Experimental Psychology*, 1964, *17*, 173–174. **522**

Antonitis, J. J., see Kish, G. B., 1956.

Arbuckle, T., see Tulving, E., 1963, 1966.

Archer, E. J. A re-evaluation of the meaningfulness of all possible CVC trigrams. *Psychological Monographs*, 1960, *74*. **852, 853, 982**

Archer, E. J. The psychological nature of concepts. In H. J. Klausmeier & C. W. Harris (Eds.), *Analysis of concept learning.* New York: Academic Press, 1966. Pp. 37–50. **942, 944**

Archer, E. J., & Underwood, B. J. Retroactive inhibition of verbal associations as a multiple function of temporal point of interpolation and degree of interpolated learning. *Journal of Experimental Psychology*, 1951, *42*, 283–290. **1100**

Arena, A. J., see Wertheimer, M., 1959.

Armington, J. C., & Biersdorf, W. R. Flicker and color adaptation in the human electroretinogram. *Journal of the Optical Society of America*, 1956, *46*, 393–400. **334**

Armington, J. C., Johnson, E. P., & Riggs, L. A. The scotopic A-wave in the electrical response of the human retina. *Journal of Physiology*, 1952, *118*, 289–298. **307**

Armington, J. C., see also Riggs, L. A., 1954.

Armstrong, D., Dry, R. M. L., Keele, C. A., & Markham, J. W. Method for studying chemical excitants of cutaneous pain in man. *Journal of Physiology*, 1951, 115, 59–61. **156**

Armus, H. L., Carlson, K. R., Guinan, J. F., & Crowell, R. A. Effect of a secondary reinforcement stimulus on the auditory startle response. *Psychological Reports*, 1964, *14*, 535–540. **808**

Armus, H. L., & Sniadowski-Dolinsky, D. Startle decrement and secondary reinforcement stimulation. *Psychonomic Science*, 1966, *4*, 175–176. **808**

Arnold, E. M. M., see Keehn, J. D., 1960.

Arnold, W. J., see Koronakis, C., 1957.

Arnoult, M. D. Stimulus predifferentiation: Some generalizations and hypotheses. *Psychological Bulletin*, 1957, *54*, 339–350. **1062**

Arnoult, M. D., see also Attneave, F., 1956; Vincent, R. J., 1969.

Arthur, R. P., & Shelley, W. B. The peripheral mechanism of itch in man. In G. E. W. Wolsteinholme & M. O'Connor (Eds.), *Pain and itch, nervous mechanisms.* Boston, Mass.: Little Brown, 1959. Pp. 84–97. **166**

Asch, S. E., & Ebenholtz, S. M. The process of free recall: Evidence for non-associative factors in acquisition and retention. *Journal of Psychology*, 1962, *54*, 3–31. **1095, 1101, 1102**

Asch, S. E., & Witkin, H. A. Studies in space orientation: I. Perception of the upright with displaced visual fields; II. Perception of the upright with displaced visual fields and with body tilted. *Journal of Experimental Psychology*, 1948, *38*, 325–337, 455–477. **539**

Asch, S. E., see also Witkin, H. A., 1948.

Asher, H. Suppression theory of binocular vision. *British Journal of Opthalmology*, 1953, *37*, 37–49. **488, 492**

Ashton, E. H., see Moulton, D., 1960.

Asratyan, E. A. Some aspects of the elaboration of conditioned connections and formation of their properties. In J. F. Delafresnaye (Ed.), *Brain mechanisms and learning: A symposium.* Oxford: Blackwell, 1961. **564**

Atkinson, J., see Anstis, S. M., 1967.

Atkinson, R. C. An analysis of the effect of non-reinforced trials in terms of statistical learning theory. *Journal of Experimental Psychology*, 1956, *52*, 28–32. **933**

Atkinson, R. C. A theory of stimulus discrimination learning. In K. J. Arrow, S. Karlin, & P. Suppes (Eds.), *Mathematical methods in the social sciences,* Stanford: Stanford University Press, 1960. Pp. 221–241. **948**

Atkinson, R. C. The observing response in discrimination learning. *Journal of Experimental Psychology,* 1961, *62,* 253–262. **1001**

Atkinson, R. C. A variable sensitivity theory of signal detection. *Psychological Review,* 1961, *68,* 301–304. **41, 44**

Atkinson, R. C., Bogartz, W. H., & Turner, R. N. Discrimination learning with probabilistic reinforcement schedules. *Journal of Experimental Psychology,* 1959, *57,* 349–350. **926**

Atkinson, R. C., Bower, G. H., & Crothers, E. J. *An introduction to mathematical learning theory.* New York: Wiley, 1965. **906, 911, 922, 953**

Atkinson, R. C., & Crothers, E. J. A comparison of paired-associate learning models having different acquisition and retention axioms. *Journal of Mathematical Psychology,* 1964, *1,* 285–315. **997, 998**

Atkinson, R. C., & Estes, W. K. Stimulus sampling theory. In R. D. Luce, R. R. Bush, & E. Galanter (Eds.), *Handbook of mathematical psychology,* Vol. II. New York: Wiley, 1963. Pp. 121–268. **911, 922, 927, 928, 995, 1002**

Atkinson, R. C., & Shiffrin, R. M. *Mathematical models for memory and learning.* Technical Report No. 79, Institute for Mathematical Studies in the Social Sciences, Stanford University, 1965. **1109**

Atkinson, R. C., *see also* Calfee, R. C., 1965; Estes, W. K., 1957; Myers, J. L., 1964; Popper, J., 1958; Suppes, P., 1960.

Attneave, F. A method of graded dichotomies for scaling of judgments. *Psychological Review,* 1949, *56,* 334–340. **58**

Attneave, F. Psychological probability as a function of experienced frequency. *Journal of Experimental Psychology,* 1953, *46,* 81–86. **897**

Attneave, F. Some informational aspects of visual perception. *Psychological Review,* 1954, *61,* 183–193. **437, 445**

Attneave, F. Symmetry, information and memory for patterns. *American Journal of Psychology,* 1955, *68,* 209–22. **445, 447**

Attneave, F. Physical determinants of the judged complexity of shapes. *Journal of Experimental Psychology,* 1957, *53,* 221–227. **448, 449**

Attneave, F. Transfer of experience with a class-schema to identification-learning of patterns and shapes. *Journal of Experimental Psychology,* 1957, *54,* 81–88. **449**

Attneave, F. *Applications of information theory to psychology.* New York: Holt, Rinehart and Winston, 1959. **445**

Attneave, F. Perception and related areas. In S. Koch (Ed.), *Psychology: A study of a science.* Vol. 4. New York: McGraw-Hill, 1962. **247, 448**

Attneave, F. Triangles as ambiguous figures. *American Journal of Psychology,* 1968, *81,* 447–453. **451**

Attneave, F., & Arnoult, M. D. The quantitative study of shape and pattern perception. *Psychological Bulletin,* 1956, *53,* 452–471. **446, 449**

Attneave, F., & Frost, R. The discrimination of perceived tridimensional orientation by minimum criteria. *Perception and Psychophysics,* 1969, *6,* 391–396. **499**

Attneave, F., & Olson, R. K. Inferences about visual mechanisms from monocular depth effects. *Psychonomic Science,* 1966, *4,* 133–134. **434n**

Atwater, S. K. Proactive inhibition and associative facilitation as affected by degree of prior learning. *Journal of Experimental Psychology,* 1953, *46,* 400–404. **1103**

Aubert, H. Eine scheinbare bedeutende Drehung von Objekten bei Neigung des Kopfesnach rechts oder links. *Virchow's Archiv,* 1861, *20,* 381–393. As described in Howard & Templeton, 1966. **538**

Aubert, H. Die Bewegungsempfindung. *Archiv für die Gesamte Physiologie,* 1886, *39,* 347–370. **520**

Austin, G. A., *see* Bruner, J. S., 1956.

Austin, P., *see* Wallach, H., 1954.

Autrum, H. Electrophysiological analysis of the visual systems in insects. *Experimental Cell Research,* 1958, Suppl. 5, 426–439. **311**

Avant, L. L. Vision in the Ganzfeld. *Psychological Bulletin,* 1965, *64,* 246–258. **426**

Averbach, E., & Coriell, A. S. Short-term memory in vision. *Bell System Technical Journal,* 1961, *40,* 309–328. **430, 444**

Aylesworth, M., *see* Warden, C. J., 1927.

Ayllon, T., & Sommer, R. Autism, emphasis and figure ground perception. *Journal of Psychology,* 1956, *41,* 163–176. **440**

Ayres, J. J. B. Conditioned suppression and the information hypothesis. *Journal of Comparative and Physiological Psychology,* 1966, *62,* 21–25. **676**

Azrin, N. H. Some effects of two intermittent schedules of immediate and non-immediate punishment. *Journal of Psychology,* 1956, *42,* 3–21. **737**

Azrin, N. H. A technique for delivering shock to pigeons. *Journal of the Experimental Analysis of Behavior,* 1959, *2,* 161–163. **706**

Azrin, N. H., & Holz, W. C. Punishment during fixed-interval reinforcement. *Journal of the Experimental Analysis of Behavior,* 1961, *4,* 343–347. **734, 735**

Azrin, N. H., & Holz, W. C. Punishment. In W. K. Honig (Ed.), *Operant behavior: Areas of research and application.* New York: Appleton, 1966. Pp. 380–447. **734**

Azrin, N. H., Hopwood, J., & Powell, J. A rat chamber and electrode procedure for avoidance conditioning. *Journal of the Experimental Analysis of Behavior,* 1967, *10,* 291–298. **706**

Azrin, N. H., *see also* Hake, D. R., 1965.

Bach, H. Determination of threshold values of olfaction. *Gesundheits-Ingenieur,* 1937, *60,* 222–225. Cited by R. W. Moncrieff, *The chemical senses,* New York: Wiley, 1944. **201**

Backer, R., *see* Sheffield, F. D., 1951.

Bacon, W. E., *see* Hulse, S. H., 1960.

Baddeley, A. D. Semantic and acoustic similarity in short-term memory. *Nature,* 1964, *204,* 1116–1117. **1117**

Baddeley, A. D. The influence of acoustic and semantic similarity on long-term memory for word sequences. *Quarterly Journal of Experimental Psychology,* 1966, *18,* 302–309. (a) **1117**

Baddeley, A. D. Short-term memory for word sequences as a function of acoustic, semantic and formal similarity. *Quarterly Journal of Experimental Psychology,* 1966, *18,* 362–368. (b) **1117**

Baddeley, A. D., & Dale, H. C. A. The effect of semantic similarity on retroactive interference in long- and short-term memory. *Journal of Verbal Learning and Verbal Behavior,* 1966, *5,* 417–420. **1119**

Badia, P. R., *see* Ehrenfreund, D., 1962.

Bahnson, P. Eine Untersuchung uber Symmetrie und Asymmetrie bei visuellen Wahrnehmungen. *Zeitschrift für Psychologie,* 1928, *108,* 129–154. **433**

Bahrick, H. P., & Bahrick, P. O. A re-examination of the interrelations among measures of retention. *Quarterly Journal of Experimental Psychology,* 1964, *16,* 318–324. **893**

Bahrick, P. O., *see* Bahrick, H. P., 1964.

Bailey, D. E., *see* Bolles, R. C., 1956.

Baird, J. C. Retinal and assumed size cues as determinants of size and distance perception. *Journal of Experimental Psychology,* 1963, *66,* 155–162. **496**

Baker, H. D. The course of foveal light adaptation measured by the threshold intensity increment. *Journal of the Optical Society of America,* 1949, *39,* 172–179. **310**

Baker, H. D. The instantaneous threshold and early dark

adaptation. *Journal of the Optical Society of America,* 1953, *43,* 798-803. **287**

Baker, H. D. Initial stages of light and dark adaptation. *Journal of the Optical Society of America,* 1963, *53,* 98-103. **310**

Baker, K. E., see Gagné, R. M., 1950; Graham, C. H., 1948.

Baker, L. M., & Elliott, D. N. Controlled and free association-times with identical stimulus- and response-words. *American Journal of Psychology,* 1948, *61,* 535-539. **868**

Bales, J. F., & Follansbee, G. L. The after-effect of the perception of curved lines. *Journal of Experimental Psychology,* 1935, *18,* 499-503. **469**

Ballard, P. B. Oblivescence and reminiscence. *British Journal of Psychology Monograph Supplements,* 1913, No. 2. **1121**

Bamber, D., see Festinger, L., 1967.

Banerji, R. B. The description list of concepts. *Communications of the ACM,* 1962, *5,* 426-432. **938**

Banister, H. Three experiments on the localization of tones. *British Journal of Psychology,* 1926, *16,* 265-292. **266**

Banks, R. K. Persistence to continuous punishment following intermittent punishment training. *Journal of Experimental Psychology,* 1966, *71,* 373-377. **737**

Banuazizi, A., see Miller, N. E., 1968.

Bappert, J. Neue untersuchungen zum Problem des Verhältnisses von Akkomodation und Konvergenz zur Wahrnehmung der Tiefe. *Zeitschrift für Psychologie,* 1923, *90,* 167-203. **479**

Baradi, A. F., & Bourne, G. H. Localization of gustatory and olfactory enzymes in the rabbit, and the problems of taste and smell. *Nature,* 1951, *168,* 977-979. **189, 220**

Baratz, S. S., see Epstein, W., 1964.

Barclay, A., see Goulet, L. R., 1965.

Bare, J. K., see Pfaffmann, C., 1950.

Barker, A. N., see Hull, C. L., 1951.

Barlow, H. B. Slippage of contact lenses and other artifacts in relation to fading and regeneration of supposedly stable retinal images. *Quarterly Journal of Experimental Psychology,* 1963, *15,* 36-51. **374, 375**

Barlow, H. B., FitzHugh, R., & Kuffler, S. W. Change of organization in the receptive fields of the cat's retina during dark adaptation. *Journal of Physiology,* 1957, *137,* 327-337. **291**

Barlow, H. B., & Sparrock, J. M. B. The role of afterimages in dark adaptation. *Science,* 1964, *144,* 1309-1314. **288**

Barnes, J. M., & Underwood, B. J. "Fate" of first-list associations in transfer theory. *Journal of Experimental Psychology,* 1959, *58,* 97-105. **1011, 1058, 1062, 1086, 1089, 1092, 1093**

Barney, H. L., & Dunn, H. K. Speech analysis: Speech synthesis. In L. Kaiser (Ed.), *Manual of phonetics.* Amsterdam: North-Holland Publ. Co., 1957. **252**

Barney, H. L., see also Peterson, G. E., 1952.

Baron, A., see Warren, J. M., 1956.

Baron, M. R., see Newman, F. L., 1965.

Barr, J., see Warden, C. J., 1929.

Barr, L. M., see Alpern, M., 1963.

Barrett, R. J., Peyser, C. S., & McHose, J. H. Effects of complete and incomplete reward reduction on a subsequent response. *Psychonomic Science,* 1965, *3,* 277-278. **810**

Barrientos, G., see Wike, E. L., 1958.

Bartleson, C. J. Memory colors of familiar objects. *Journal of the Optical Society of America,* 1960, *50,* 73-77. **424**

Bartleson, C. J., see also Burnham, R. W., 1963.

Bartlett, F. C. *Remembering.* Cambridge: Cambridge University Press, 1932. **552**

Bartlett, N. R., see Graham, C. H., 1940.

Bartley, S. H. Subjective brightness in relation to flash rate and the light-dark ratio. *Journal of Experimental Psychology,* 1938, *23,* 313-319. **314**

Bartley, S. H. Some factors in brightness discrimination. *Psychological Review,* 1939, *46,* 337-358. **314**

Bartley, S. H., & Bishop, G. H. The cortical response to stimulation of the optic nerve in the rabbit. *American Journal of Physiology,* 1933, *103,* 159-172. **309**

Bartley, S. H., Paczewitz, G., & Valsi, E. Brightness enhancement and the stimulus cycle. *Journal of Psychology,* 1957, *43,* 187-192. **307**

Bartley, S. H., see also Fry, G. A., 1953; Nelson, T. M., 1956.

Bartolovic, B. Internal regulation of gustatory sensitivity. *Acta Instituti Psychologici Universitatis Zagrebensis,* 1964, *45,* 73-80. **189**

Bartoshuk, A. K. Electromyographic gradients as indicants of motivation. *Canadian Journal of Psychology,* 1955, *9,* 215-230. **833**

Bartoshuk, A. K. EMG gradients and EEG amplitude during motivated listening. *Canadian Journal of Psychology,* 1956, *10,* 156-164. **833**

Bartoshuk, A. K. Electromyographic reactions to strong auditory stimulation as a function of alpha amplitude. *Journal of Comparative and Physiological Psychology,* 1959, *52,* 540-545. **834**

Bartoshuk, A. K. Human neonatal cardiac acceleration to sound: Habituation and dishabituation. *Perceptual and Motor Skills,* 1962, *15,* 15-27. (a) **591**

Bartoshuk, A. K. Response decrement with repeated elicitation of human neonatal cardiac acceleration to sound. *Journal of Comparative and Physiological Psychology,* 1962, *55,* 9-13. (b) **591, 834**

Bartoshuk, A. K. Human neonatal cardiac responses to sound: A power function. *Psychonomic Science,* 1964, *1,* 151-152. **840**

Bartoshuk, L. M. Water taste in man. *Perception and Psychophysics,* 1968. **184, 186**

Bartoshuk, L. M., Dateo, G. P., Vandenbelt, D. J., Buttrick, R. D., & Long, L. Effects of *Gymnema sylvestre* and *Synsepalum dulcificum* on taste in man. In C. Pfaffmann (Ed.), *Olfaction and taste.* Vol. III. New York: Rockefeller University Press, 1969. **177**

Bartoshuk, L. M., McBurney, D. H., & Pfaffmann, C. Taste of sodium chloride solutions after adaptation to sodium chloride: Implications for the "water taste." *Science,* 1964, *143,* 967-968. **81, 184**

Bartoshuk, L. M., & Pfaffmann, C. Effects of pre-treatment on the water taste response in cat and rat. *Federation Proceedings,* 1965, 24 (abstract). **186**

Bartoshuk, L. M., see also Pfaffmann, C., 1969.

Bass, M. J., & Hull, C. L. Irradiation of a tactile conditioned reflex in man. *Journal of Comparative Psychology,* 1934, *17,* 47-65. **601**

Bassett, I. G., & Eastmond, E. J. Echo location: Measurement of pitch versus distance for sounds reflected from a flat surface. *Journal of the Acoustical Society of America,* 1964, *36,* 911-916. **271**

Bastian, J. Associative factors in verbal transfer. *Journal of Experimental Psychology,* 1961, *62,* 70-79. **1058, 1084**

Bateson, P. P. G. Changes in chicks' responses to novel moving objects over the sensitive period for imprinting. *Animal Behaviour,* 1964, *12,* 479-489. (a) **584**

Bateson, P. P. G. Effect of similarity between rearing and testing conditions on chicks' following and avoidance responses. *Journal of Comparative and Physiological Psychology,* 1964, *57,* 100-103. (b) **587**

Bateson, P. P. G. The characteristics and context of imprinting. *Biological Reviews,* 1966, *41,* 177-220. **583, 588, 700**

Bateson, P. P. G., & Reese, E. Reinforcing properties of conspicuous objects before imprinting has occurred. *Psychonomic Science,* 1968, *10,* 379-380. **587**

Battersby, W. S., Kahn, R. L., Pollack, M., & Bender, M. B.,

Effects of visual, vestibular, and somatosensori-motor deficit on autokinetic perception. *Journal of Experimental Psychology,* 1956, *52,* 398–410. **530**

Battig, W. F. Scaled difficulty of nonsense-syllable pairs consisting of syllables of equal association value. *Psychological Reports,* 1959, *5,* 126. **899**

Battig, W. F. Comparison of two methods of scaling nonsense-syllable pairs for ease of learning. *Psychological Reports,* 1960, *6,* 363–366. **899**

Battig, W. F. Procedural problems in paired-associate learning research. *Psychonomic Monograph Supplements,* 1965, *1,* 12. **855, 856**

Battig, W. F. Paired-associate learning. In T. R. Dixon & D. L. Horton (Eds.), *Verbal behavior and general behavior theory.* Englewood Cliffs, N.J.: Prentice-Hall, 1968. **855, 1126**

Bauer, F. J., & Lawrence, D. H. Influence of similarity of choice-point and goal cues on discrimination learning. *Journal of Comparative and Physiological Psychology,* 1953, *46,* 241–252. **783**

Bauer, J., see Efstathiou, A., 1967.

Bauer, J. A., see Held, R., 1967.

Baumeister, A., Hawkins, W. F., & Cromwell, R. L. Need state and activity level. *Psychological Bulletin,* 1964, *61,* 438–453. **821**

Baumgardt, E., & Ségal, J. Facilitation et inhibition, paramètres de la fonction visuelle. *Année psychologique,* 1947, *43–44,* 54–102. **307**

Bayle, E. The nature and causes of regressive movements in reading. *Journal of Experimental Education,* 1942, *11,* 16–36. **390**

Bazett, H. C. Temperature sense in man. In *Temperature, its measurement, and control in science and industry.* New York: Reinhold, 1941. Pp. 489–501. **153**

Beatty, J., see Kahneman, D., 1966.

Beauchamp, R. D., see Church, R. M., 1967.

Beck, E. C., see Brown, H. M., 1966.

Beck, J. Stimulus correlates for the judged illumination of a surface. *Journal of Experimental Psychology,* 1959, *58,* 267–274. **405**

Beck, J. Texture-gradients and judgments of slant and recession. *American Journal of Psychology,* 1960, *73,* 411–416. **502**

Beck, J. Judgments of surface illumination and lightness. *Journal of Experimental Psychology,* 1961, *61,* 368–375. **405, 406, 423**

Beck, J. Supplementary report: An examination of an aspect of the Gelb effect. *Journal of Experimental Psychology,* 1962, *64,* 199–200. **423**

Beck, J. The effect of gloss on perceived lightness. *American Journal of Psychology,* 1964, *77,* 54–63. **422**

Beck, J. Apparent spatial position and the perception of lightness. *Journal of Experimental Psychology,* 1965, *69,* 170–179. **421**

Beck, J. Age differences in lightness perception. *Psychonomic Science,* 1966, *4,* 201–202. (a) **406**

Beck, J. Effect of orientation and of shape similarity on perceptual grouping. *Perception and Psychophysics,* 1966, *1,* 300–302. (b) **434**

Beck, J., & Gibson, J. J. The relation of apparent shape to apparent slant in the perception of objects. *Journal of Experimental Psychology,* 1955, *50,* 125–133. **516**

Beck, J., & Shaw, W. A. The scaling of pitch by the method of magnitude estimation. *American Journal of Psychology,* 1961, *74,* 242–251. **244**

Beck, J., & Shaw, W. A. Single estimates of pitch magnitude. *Journal of the Acoustical Society of America,* 1963, *35,* 1722–1724. **244**

Beck, J., see also Hochberg, J., 1954.

Beck, L. H., Kruger, L., & Calabresi, P. The observations on olfactory intensity: I. Training procedure, methods, and data for two aliphatic homologous series. *Annals of the New York Academy of Science,* 1954, *58,* 225–238. **197, 200**

Beck, L. H., & Miles, W. R. Some theoretical and experimental relationships between infrared absorption and olfaction. *Science,* 1947, *106,* 511. **220**

Beck, R. C. The rat's adaptation to a 23.5-hour water-deprivation schedule. *Journal of Comparative and Physiological Psychology,* 1962, *55,* 646–648. **819**

Becker, L. A., see Schuck, J. R., 1964.

Becker, R. F., King, J. E., & Markee, J. E. Studies on olfactory discrimination in dogs: II. Discriminatory behavior in a free environment. *Journal of Comparative and Physiological Psychology,* 1962, *55,* 773–780. **202**

Beebe-Center, J. G. The variability of affective judgments upon odors. *Journal of Experimental Psychology,* 1931, *14,* 91–93. **215**

Beebe-Center, J. G., & Waddell, D. A general psychological scale of taste. *Journal of Psychology,* 1948, *26,* 517–524. **175**

Beecher, H. K. Relationship of significance of wound to the pain experienced. *Journal of the American Medical Association,* 1956, *161,* 1609–1613. **155**

Beecher, H. K. *Measurement of subjective responses.* New York: Oxford University Press, 1959. **155, 163, 164**

Beecher, H. K. Pain: One mystery solved. *Science,* 1966, *151,* 840–841. **155**

Beecher, H. K., see also Smith, G. M., 1966.

Beecroft, R. S. Verbal learning and retention as a function of the number of competing associations. *Journal of Experimental Psychology,* 1956, *51,* 216–220. **1126**

Beer, B., Hodos, W., & Matthews, T. J. Rate of intracranial self-stimulation as a function of reinforcement magnitude and density. *Psychonomic Science,* 1964, *1,* 321–322. **649, 650**

Beer, B., & Trumble, G. Timing behavior as a function of amount of reinforcement. *Psychonomic Science,* 1965, *2,* 71–72. **695**

Beer, B., & Valenstein, E. S. Discrimination of tones during reinforcing brain stimulation. *Science,* 1960, *132,* 297–298. **659**

Beer B., see also Steiner, S. S., 1968; Valenstein, E. S., 1961, 1964.

Beets, M. G. J. A molecular approach to olfaction. In E. J. Ariens (Ed.), *Molecular pharmacology.* Vol. II. New York: Academic Press, 1964, 3–51. **220**

Beez, V., see Di Lollo, V., 1966.

Behar, V., see Goulet, L. R., 1966.

Behrend, E. R., & Bitterman, M. E. Avoidance-conditioning in the goldfish: Exploratory studies of the CS–US interval. *American Journal of Psychology,* 1962, *75,* 18–34. **729**

Behrend, E. R., see also Gonzalez, R. C., 1965.

Beidler, L. M. Properties of chemoreceptors of tongue of rat. *Journal of Neurophysiology,* 1953, *16,* 595–607. **187**

Beidler, L. M. A theory of taste stimulation. *Journal of General Physiology,* 1954, *38,* 133–139. **189**

Beidler, L. M. Facts and theory on the mechanism of taste and odor perception. In J. H. Mitchell, Jr. (Ed.), *Chemistry of natural food flavors.* Chicago: Quartermaster Food Container Institute for the Armed Forces, 1957. Pp. 7–47. **211, 218**

Beidler, L. M. Effect of odor flow rate on olfactory response. *Federation Proceedings,* 1958, *17,* 13. **207**

Beidler, L. M. Physiology of olfaction and gustation. *Annals of Otolaryngology, Rhinology, and Laryngology,* 1960, *69,* 398–409. **205**

Beidler, L. M. Taste receptor stimulation. In J. A. V. Butler, H. E. Huxley, & R. E. Zirkle (Eds.), *Progress in biophysics and biophysical chemistry.* Vol. 12. New York: Pergamon Press, 1961. Pp. 107–151. **186, 189**

Beidler, L. M. Dynamics of taste cells. In Y. Zotterman (Ed.),

Olfaction and taste. Vol. 1. New York: Pergamon Press, 1963. Pp. 133–145. **172**

Beidler, L. M. Comparison of gustatory receptors, olfactory receptors, and free nerve endings. In *Cold Spring Harbor Symposia on Quantitative Biology*, 1965, *30*, 191–200. **171**

Beidler, L. M., & Smallman, R. L. Renewal of cells within taste buds. *Journal of Cell Biology*, 1965, *27*, 263–272. **172**

Beidler, L. M., & Tucker, D. Olfactory and trigeminal nerve responses to odors. *Federation Proceedings*, 1956, *15*, 14. **205, 211**

Beidler, L. M., *see also* Kimura, K., 1961; Moulton, D. G., 1967; Tateda, H., 1964.

Beier, E. M., *see* Logan, F. A., 1956.

Békésy, G. von, *see* von Békésy, G.

Bélanger, D., & Feldman, S. M. Effects of water deprivation upon heart rate and instrumental activity in the rat. *Journal of Comparative and Physiological Psychology*, 1962, *55*, 220–225. **827, 828, 834**

Bélanger, D., *see also* Ducharme, R., 1961; Malmo, R. B., 1967.

Belcher, S. J., *see* Clarke, F. J., 1962.

Bell, R. A., & Bevan, W. The influence of anchors upon the operation of certain Gestalt organizing principles. *Journal of Experimental Psychology*, 1968, *78*, 67–678. **434n**

Beller, H. K., *see* Morant, R. B., 1965.

Belloni, M., *see* Brown, J. S., 1963.

Benary, W. Beobachtungen zu einein Experiment uber Helligkeitskontrast. *Psychologische Forschung*, 1924, *5*, 131–142. **410, 423n**

Bender, M. B., *see* Battersby, W. S., 1956.

Benjamin, F. B. Release of intracellular potassium as a factor in pain production. In D. R. Kenshalo (Ed.), *The skin senses*, Springfield, Ill.: Charles C Thomas, 1968, pp. 466–479. **160, 162**

Benjamin, R. M., & Burton, H. Projection of taste nerve afferents to anterior opercular–insular cortex in squirrel monkey (*Saimiri sciureus*). *Brain Research*, 1968, *7*, 221–231. **172**

Benjamin, R. M., Halpern, B. P., Moulton, D. G., & Mozell, M. M. The chemical senses. *Annals of the New York Academy of Sciences*, 1965, *16*, 381–416. **190, 220**

Benjamin, R. M., & Thompson, R. F. Differential effects of cortical lesions in infant and adult cats on roughness discrimination. *Experimental Neurology*, 1959, *1*, 305–321. **845**

Benjamin, R. M., *see also* Oakley, B., 1966.

Benson, R. W., *see* Hirsh, I. J., 1952.

Benson, W. M., *see* Young, R. K., 1963.

Bentley, M., *see* Mikesell, W. H., 1930.

Benton, A. L., *see* Swanson, R., 1955.

Benussi, V. Stroboskopische Scheinbewegungen und geometrischoptische Gestaltausscheinungen. *Archiv für die Gesamte Psychologie*, 1912, *24*, 31–62. **464**

Benussi, V. Versuche zur Analyse taktil erweckter Scheinbewegungen. *Archiv für die Gesamte Psychologie*, 1916, *36*, 59–135. Cited in Boring, E. C. *Sensation and perception in the history of experimental psychology.* New York: Appleton, 1942. **408, 526**

Benussi, V. Zur Psychologie der Gestalterfassens. In A. Meinong (Ed.), *Untersuch Gegenstands theorie*, 1904. Pp. 303–448. **464**

Beranek, L. L. Criteria for office quieting based on questionnaire rating studies. *Journal of the Acoustical Society of America*, 1956, *28*, 833–852. **258**

Beranek, L. L. Revised criteria for noise in buildings. *Noise Control*, 1957, *3*, 19–27. **258**

Berg, H. W., Pangborn, R. M., Roessler, E. B., & Webb, A. D. Influence of hunger on olfactory acuity. *Nature*, 1963, *197*, 108. **208**

Bergeijk, W. A. van, *see* van Bergeijk, W. A.

Bergman, G., & Spence, K. W. The logic of psychophysical measurements. *Psychological Review*, 1944, *51*, 1–24. **246**

Bergman, R., & Gibson, J. J. The negative aftereffect of a surface slanted in the third dimension. *American Journal of Psychology*, 1959, *72*, 364–374. **470n**

Berkeley, G. *An essay towards a new theory of vision.* Dublin: Jeremy Pepyat, 1709. Reprinted New York: Dutton, 1922. **477**

Berkley, M. A. Discrimination of rewards as a function of contrast in rewarded stimuli. *Journal of Experimental Psychology*, 1963, *66*, 371–376. **630**

Berkley, M. A., *see also* Kling, J. W., 1968; Su, Jiuan, 1966.

Berko, J., *see* Brown, R. W., 1960.

Berkowitz, H., *see* Bousfield, W. A., 1960.

Berkun, M., *see* Kagan, J., 1954.

Berliner, A. *Lectures on visual psychology.* Chicago: Professional Press, 1948. **461**

Berliner, A., & Berliner, S. The distortion of straight and curved lines in geometrical fields. *American Journal of Psychology*, 1948, *61*, 153–166. **459**

Berliner, S., *see* Berliner, A., 1948.

Berlyne, D. E. *Conflict, arousal and curiosity.* New York: McGraw-Hill, 1960. **841**

Berlyne, D. E. Curiosity and exploration. *Science*, 1966, *153*, 25–33. **841**

Berlyne, D. E. Arousal and reinforcement. In D. Levine (Ed.), *Nebraska symposium on motivation.* Lincoln: University of Nebraska Press, 1967. Pp. 1–110. **673, 841, 845**

Berlyne, D. E., & McDonnell, P. Effects of stimulus complexity and incongruity on duration of EEG desynchronization. *Electroencephalography and Clinical Neurophysiology*, 1965, *18*, 156–161. **841**

Berman, A. J., *see* Taub, E., in press.

Berman, P. W., & Liebowitz, H. W. Some effects of contour on simultaneous brightness contrast. *Journal of Experimental Psychology*, 1965, *69*, 251–256. **408, 410**

Bernbach, H. A. A forgetting model for paired-associate learning. *Journal of Mathematical Psychology*, 1965, *2*, 128–144. **1000**

Bernbach, H. A. Stimulus learning and recognition in paired-associate learning. *Journal of Experimental Psychology*, 1967, *75*, 513–519. **1048**

Bernstein, S., *see* Thurlow, W. R., 1957.

Berry, J. H., *see* Worchel, P., 1952.

Berry, R. N. Quantitative relations among vernier, real depth, and stereoscopic depth acuities. *Journal of Experimental Psychology*, 1948, *38*, 708–721. **300, 486**

Berry, R. N., Riggs, L. A., & Duncan, C. P. The relation of vernier and depth discrimination to field brightness. *Journal of Experimental Psychology*, 1950, *40*, 349–354. **486**

Bersh, P. J. The influence of two variables upon the establishment of a secondary reinforcer for operant responses. *Journal of Experimental Psychology*, 1951, *41*, 62–73. **666**

Bershansky, I. The areal and punctiform integration of warmth and pressure. *American Journal of Psychology*, 1922, *33*, 584–587. **166**

Besch, N. F., & Reynolds, W. F. Associative interference in verbal paired-associate learning. *Journal of Experimental Psychology*, 1958, *55*, 554–558. **1055, 1064**

Besch, N. F., Thompson, W. E., & Wetzel, A. B. Studies in associative interference. *Journal of Experimental Psychology*, 1962, *63*, 342–352. **1065**

Bevan, W. An adaptation-level interpretation of reinforcement. *Perceptual and Motor Skills*, 1966, *23*, 511–531. **634**

Bevan, W., *see also* Bell, R. A., 1968.

Beyrl, R. Ueber die Grossenauffassung bei Kindern. *Zeitschrift für Psychologie*, 1926, *100*, 344–371. **550**

Bhatt, B. J., *see* Thurlow, W. R., 1965.

Bicknell, E., *see* Calvin, J. S., 1953.

Bidder, T. G., *see* Rowland, V., 1960.

Biddulph, R., *see* Shower, E. G., 1931.

Biederman, I., *see* Fehrer, E., 1962.

Bielschowsky, A., *see* Hoffman, F. B., 1909.

Biersdorf, W. R., *see* Armington, J. C., 1956.

Bigelow, N. H., *see* Harrison, I. B., 1943.

Bilger, R. C. Intensive determinants of remote masking. *Journal of the Acoustical Society of America*, 1958, *30*, 817-824. **239**

Bilger, R. C. Remote masking in the absence of intra-aural muscles. *Journal of the Acoustical Society of America*, 1966, *39*, 103-108. **240**

Bilger, R. C., & Hirsh, I. J. Masking of tones by bands of noise. *Journal of the Acoustical Society of America*, 1956, *28*, 623-630. **239**

Bilger, R. C., *see also* Deatherage, B. H., 1957.

Bilodeau, E. A., & Howell, D. C. Free association norms by discrete and continued methods. Technical Report No. 1 for Contract Nonr-475(10) between Tulane University and the Office of Naval Research, 1965. **861**

Bilodeau, I. McD. Information feedback. In E. A. Bilodeau (Ed.), *Acquisition of skill.* New York: Academic Press, 1966. **687**

Bilodeau, I. McD., & Schlosberg, H. Similarity in stimulating conditions as a variable in retroactive inhibition. *Journal of Experimental Psychology*, 1951, *41*, 199-204. **1084**

Binder, A., & Estes, W. K. Transfer of response in visual recognition situations as a function of frequency variables. *Psychological Monographs*, 1966, *80.* **1005**

Binder, A., & Feldman, S. E. The effects of experimentally controlled experience upon recognition responses. *Psychological Monographs*, 1960, *74.* **954, 1004, 1005**

Bindra, D. Stimulus change, reactions to novelty, and response decrement. *Psychological Review*, 1959, *66*, 96-103. **818**

Bindra, D. Components of general activity and the analysis of behavior. *Psychological Review*, 1961, *68*, 205-215. **818, 822**

Bindra, D. Neuropsychological interpretation of the effects of drive and incentive-motivation on general activity and instrumental behavior. *Psychological Review*, 1968, *75*, 1-22. **809**

Bindra, D., & Palfai, T. The nature of positive and negative incentive-motivational effects on general activity. *Journal of Comparative and Physiological Psychology*, 1967, *63*, 288-297. **808, 818, 823**

Bindra, D., *see also* Baum, M., 1968.

Binet, A., & Henri, V. La psychologie individuelle. *L'Année Psychologique*, 1896, *2*, 411-465. **598**

Binford, J. R., & Gettys, C. Nonstationarity in paired-associate learning as indicated by a second guess procedure. *Journal of Mathematical Psychology*, 1965, *2*, 190-195. **1010**

Birch, D., Burnstein, E., & Clarke, R. A. Response strength as a function of hours of food deprivation under a controlled maintenance schedule. *Journal of Comparative and Physiological Psychology*, 1958, *51*, 350-354. **830, 831**

Birdsall, T. G., *see* Swets, J. A., 1961.

Birge, Jane S. Verbal responses in transfer. Doctoral dissertation. New Haven: Yale University Press, 1941. **780**

Birnbaum, I. M. Long-term retention of first-list associations in the A-B, A-C paradigm. *Journal of Verbal Learning and Verbal Behavior*, 1965, *4*, 515-520. **1098, 1099**

Birnbaum, I. M. Unlearning in two directions. *Journal of Experimental Psychology*, 1966, *72*, 61-67. **1095**

Birnbaum, I. M. Unlearning as a function of second-list dominance. *Journal of Verbal Learning and Verbal Behavior*, 1968, *7*, 257-259. **1087, 1098**

Bishop, G. H. Relation of pain sensory threshold to form of mechanical stimulator. *Journal of Neurophysiology*, 1949, *12*, 51-57. **160**

Bishop, G. H. The relation of nerve fiber size to modality of sensation. In W. Montagna (Ed.), *Advances in biology of skin*: Vol. 1, *Cutaneous innervation.* New York: Pergamon, 1960. Pp. 99-111. **162**

Bishop, G. H., *see also* Bartley, S. H., 1933; Heinbecker, P., 1933.

Bishop, H. P. Separation thresholds for colored bars with and without luminance contrast. *Psychonomic Science*, 1966, *4*, 223-224. **428*n***

Bishop, H. P. Separation thresholds for bar targets presented with color contrast only. *Psychonomic Science*, 1966, *6*, 293-294. **428*n***

Bitterman, M. E. Toward a comparative psychology of learning. *American Psychologist*, 1960, *15*, 704-712. **603**

Bitterman, M. E. Classical conditioning in the goldfish as a function of the CS-US interval. *Journal of Comparative and Physiological Psychology*, 1964, *58*, 359-366. **559, 578**

Bitterman, M. E. The CS-US interval in classical and avoidance conditioning. In W. F. Prokasy, (Ed.), *Classical conditioning.* New York: Appleton, 1965. **559, 729**

Bitterman, M. E., Krauskopf, J., & Hochberg, J. E. Threshold for visual form: A diffusion model. *American Journal of Psychology*, 1954, *67*, 205-219. **443**

Bitterman, M. E., Tyler, D. W., & Elam, C. B. Simultaneous and successive discrimination under identical stimulation conditions. *American Journal of Psychology*, 1955, *68*, 237-248. **775**

Bitterman, M. E., & Wodinsky, J. Simultaneous and successive discrimination. *Psychological Review*, 1953, *60*, 371-376. **774**

Bitterman, M. E., *see also* Behrend, E. R., 1962; Bridges, C. C., 1954; Crum, J., 1951; Deatherage, B. H., 1952; Gonzalez, R. C., 1962, 1965; Hochberg, J., 1951; Krauskopf, J., 1954; Lowes, G., 1967; Stevenson, H. W., 1955; Weise, P., 1951.

Bixby, F. L. A phenomenological study of luster. *Journal of General Psychology*, 1926, *1*, 136. **427**

Björkman, M., & Ekman, G. *Experimental psykologiska metoder.* Stockholm: Almqvist & Wiksell, 1962. **79**

Black, A. H. The extinction of avoidance responses under curare. *Journal of Comparative and Physiological Psychology*, 1958, *51*, 519-524. **732**

Black, A. H. Heart rate changes during avoidance learning in dogs. *Canadian Journal of Psychology*, 1959, *13*, 229-242. **726**

Black, A. H. Cardiac conditioning in curarized dogs: The relationship between heart rate and skeletal behaviour. In W. F. Prokasy (Ed.), *Classical conditioning.* New York: Appleton, 1965. Pp. 20-47. **711**

Black, A. H., Carlson, N. J., & Solomon, R. L. Exploratory studies of the conditioning of autonomic responses in curarized dogs. *Psychological Monographs*, 1962, *76.* **711**

Black, A. H. & Lang, W. M. Cardiac conditioning and skeletal responding in curarized dogs. *Psychological Review*, 1964, *71*, 80-85. **711**

Black, A. H., *see also* Church, R. M., 1958; deToledo, L., 1966; Kamin, L. J., 1963.

Black, J. W. Multiple-choice intelligibility tests. *Journal of Speech and Hearing Disorders*, 1957, *22*, 213-235. **255**

Black, R. W. On the combination of drive and incentive motivation. *Psychological Review*, 1965, *72*, 310-317. **807**

Black, R. W. Shifts in magnitude of reward and contrast effects in instrumental and selective learning: A reinterpretation. *Psychological Review*, 1968, *75*, 114-126. **638*n***

Black, W. C., *see* Perez-Cruet, J., 1963.

Blackwell, H. R. Contrast thresholds of the human eye. *Journal of the Optical Society of America*, 1946, *36*, 624-643. **304**

Blackwell, H. R. Psychophysical thresholds: Experimental studies of methods of measurements. *Bulletin of the Engineering Research Institute, University of Michigan*, No. 36, 1953. **19, 20**

Blanchard, D. C., *see* Blanchard, R. J., 1966.

Blanchard, R. J., & Blanchard, D. C. Food deprivation and reactivity to shock. *Psychonomic Science*, 1966, *4*, 317-318. **710**

Blank, A. A. The Luneburg theory of binocular visual space. *Journal of the Optical Society of America*, 1953, *43*, 717-727. **493**

Blank, A. A. The geometry of vision. *British Journal of Physiological Optics* (3), 1957, *14*, 154-169, 222-235. **493**

Blank, A. A. The Luneburg theory of binocular space perception. In S. Koch (Ed.), *Psychology: A study of a science.* Study I. Vol. 1. New York: McGraw-Hill, 1959. **493**

Blank, A. A., *see also* Hardy, L. H., 1953.

Blankenship, A. B., *see* Whitely, P. L., 1936.

Blatt, M. H., *see* Mayzner, M. S., 1965.

Blattner, K. C., *see* Peterson, M. J., 1963, 1964.

Blessing, W. W., Landauer, A. A., & Coltheart, M. The effect of false perspective cues on distance- and size-judgments: An examination of the invariance hypothesis. *American Journal of Psychology*, 1967, *60*, 250-256. **514**

Bleything, W. B. Factors influencing stereoscopic localization. *American Journal of Optometry*, 1957, *34*, 416-429. **513**

Bliss, J. *see* Dunn, S., 1958.

Blodgett, H. C. The effect of the introduction of reward upon the maze performance of rats. *University of California Publications in Psychology*, 1929, *4*, 113-134. **795**

Blodgett, H. C., *see also* Jeffress, L., 1956, 1962.

Blomquist, A. J., *see* Benjamin, R. M., 1968.

Bloom, G. Studies on the olfactory epithelium of the frog and the toad with the aid of light and electron microscopy. *Zeitschrift für Zellforschung der Mikroskopische Anatomie: Abtung Histochemie*, 1954, *41*, 89-100. **195**

Bloom, W., *see* Thompson, T. I., 1966.

Bloomfield, T. M. Some temporal properties of behavioral contrast. *Journal of the Experimental Analysis of Behavior*, 1967, *10*, 159-164. **641**

Blough, D. S. A method for obtaining psychophysical thresholds from the pigeon. *Journal of the Experimental Analysis of Behavior*, 1958, *1*, 31-43. **20, 756**

Blough, D. S. Animal psychophysics. *Scientific American*, 1961, *205*, 113-122. **756**

Blough, D. S. Delayed matching in the pigeon. *Journal of the Experimental Analysis of Behavior*, 1959, *2*, 151-160. **788, 789**

Blough, D. S. Definition and measurement in generalization research. In D. I. Mostofsky (Ed.), *Stimulus generalization.* Stanford: Stanford University Press, 1965. Pp. 30-37. **760**

Blough, D. S. The study of animal sensory processes by operant methods. In W. K. Honig (Ed.), *Operant behavior: Areas of research and application.* New York: Appleton, 1966. **607, 694, 753**

Blough, D., & Millward, R. Operant conditioning and verbal learning. *Annual Review of Psychology*, 1965, *16*, 63-94. **1001n**

Blum, H. B., *see* Fabian, F. W., 1943.

Blumenfeld, W. Untersuchungen über die scheinbare Grösse im Schraume. *Zeitschrift für Psychologie*, 1913, *65*, 241-404. **493**

Bocca, E., & Calearo, C. Central hearing processes. In J. Jerger (Ed.), *Modern developments in audiology*, New York: Academic Press, 1963. **235**

Boch, R. D., and Jones, L. V. *The measurement and prediction of judgment and choice.* San Francisco: Holden-Day, 1968. **54**

Boe, E., *see* Holborn, S., 1965.

Boe, E. E. Extinction as a function of intensity of punishment, amount of training, and reinforcement of a competing response. *Canadian Journal of Psychology*, 1964, *18*, 328-342. **738**

Boe, E. E., & Church, R. M. Permanent effects of punishment during extinction. *Journal of Comparative and Physiological Psychology*, 1967, *63*, 486-492. **738**

Boeder, P., *see* Hardy, L. H., 1953.

Bogart, L. M., *see* McBurney, D. H., 1962, 1967.

Bogartz, W. H., *see* Atkinson, R. C., 1959; Maltzman, I., 1958.

Bolles, R. C. The usefulness of the drive concept. In M. R. Jones (Ed.), *Nebraska symposium on motivation.* Lincoln, Nebraska: University of Nebraska Press, 1958. Pp. 1-33. **795n**

Bolles, R. C. Group and individual performance as a function of intensity and kind of deprivation. *Journal of Comparative and Physiological Psychology*, 1959, *52*, 579-585. **821**

Bolles, R. C. Generalization of deprivation-produced stimuli. *Psychological Reports*, 1961, *9*, 623-626. **831**

Bolles, R. C. The readiness to eat and drink: The effect of deprivation conditions. *Journal of Comparative and Physiological Psychology*, 1962, *55*, 230-234. **814, 816**

Bolles, R. C. A failure to find evidence of the estrus cycle in the rat's activity level. *Psychological Reports*, 1963, *12*, 530. **825**

Bolles, R. C. Readiness to eat: Effects of age, sex, and weight loss. *Journal of Comparative and Physiological Psychology*, 1965, *60*, 88-92. **813, 816**

Bolles, R. C. *Theory of motivation.* New York: Harper & Row, 1967. **793n, 795n, 801, 802n, 803, 807, 812, 816**

Bolles, R. C. The role of eye movements in the Müller-Lyer illusion. *Perception and Psychophysics*, 1969, *6*, 175-176. **476n**

Bolles, R. C., & de Lorge, J. The rat's adjustment to a-diurnal feeding cycles. *Journal of Comparative and Physiological Psychology*, 1962, *55*, 760-762. **820**

Bolles, R. C., Hulicka, I. M., & Hanly, B. Color judgment as a function of stimulus conditions and memory color. *Canadian Journal of Psychology*, 1959, *13*, 175-185. **424**

Bolles, R. C., & Rapp, H. M. Readiness to eat and drink: Effect of stimulus conditions. *Journal of Comparative and Physiological Psychology*, 1965, *60*, 93-97. **818**

Bolles, R. C., Rapp, H. M., & White, G. C. Failure of sexual activity to reinforce female rats. *Journal of Comparative and Physiological Psychology*, 1968, *65*, 311-313. **693**

Bolles, R. C., & Stokes, L. W. Rat's anticipation of diurnal and a-diurnal feeding. *Journal of Comparative and Physiological Psychology*, 1965, *60*, 290-294. **820**

Bolles, R. C., & Younger, M. S. The effect of hunger on the threshold of behavioral arousal. *Psychonomic Science*, 1967, *7*, 243-244. **823**

Boneau, C. A., & Cole, J. L. Decision theory, the pigeon, and the psychophysical function. *Psychological Review*, 1967, *74*, 123-135. **757**

Bontrager, H., *see* Epstein, W., 1962.

Borer, K. T. Disappearance of preferences and aversions for sapid solutions in rats ingesting untasted fluids. *Journal of Comparative and Physiological Psychology*, 1968, *65*, 213-221. **797**

Borg, G., Diamant, H., Oakley, B., Ström, L., & Zotterman, Y. A comparative study of neural and psychophysical responses to gustatory stimuli. In T. Hayashi (Ed.), *Olfaction and taste.* Vol. II. New York: Pergamon, 1967. Pp. 253–264. **175, 185**

Boring, E. G. Urban's tables and the method of constant stimuli. *American Journal of Psychology,* 1917, *28,* 280–293. **33**

Boring, E. G. A new ambiguous figure. *American Journal of Psychology,* 1930, *42,* 444–445. **439**

Boring, E. G. *The physical dimensions of consciousness.* New York: Century, 1933. **490**

Boring, E. G. Size-constancy and Emmert's law. *American Journal of Psychology,* 1940, *53,* 293–295. **511**

Boring, E. G. *Sensation and perception in the history of experimental psychology.* New York: Appleton, 1942. **65, 118, 250, 427, 482, 511, 521, 522, 525, 527**

Boring, E. G. The moon illusion. *American Journal of Physics,* 1943, *11,* 55–60. **511**

Boring, E. G. *A history of experimental psychology.* (2nd ed.) New York: Appleton, 1950. **793n, 794**

Boring, E. C., & Edwards, W. What is Emmert's law? *American Journal of Psychology,* 1951, *64,* 416–422. **511**

Boring, E. G. Visual perception and invariance. *Psychological Review,* 1952, *59,* 141–148. (a) **510, 539**

Boring, E. G. The Gibsonian visual field. *Psychological Review,* 1952, *59,* 246–247. (b) **510**

Boring, E. G., Langfeld, H. S., & Weld, H. P. *Foundations of psychology.* New York: Wiley, 1948. **243**

Boring, E. G., *see also* Holway, A. H., 1941.

Born, D., *see* Wickens, D. D., 1963.

Bornstein, R., *see* Grier, J. B., 1966.

Borresen, C. R., & Lichte, W. H. Shape constancy: Dependence upon stimulus familiarity. *Journal of Experimental Psychology,* 1962, *63,* 91–97. **515**

Borresen, C. R., *see also* Lichte, W. H., 1967.

Borst, J. M., *see* Cooper, F. S., 1952.

Bosley, J., *see* Stone, H., 1965.

Bosley, J. J., *see* De Soto, C. B., 1962.

Bossom, J., & Held, R. Shifts in egocentric localization following prolonged displacement of the retinal image. *American Psychologist,* 1957, *12,* 454 (abstract). **537n**

Bossom, J., *see also* Held, R., 1961.

Bouman, M. A. Visual thresholds for line-shaped targets. *Journal of the Optical Society of America,* 1953, *43,* 209–211. **303**

Bourdon, B. *La perception visuelle de l'espace.* Paris: Schleicher, 1902. **520**

Bourne, G. H. (Ed.), *The structure and function in muscle.* Vol. 1, *Structure.* New York: Academic Press, 1960. **91**

Bourne, G. H., *see also* Baradi, A. F., 1951.

Bourne, L. E., Jr. Effects of delay of information feedback and task complexity on the identification of concepts. *Journal of Experimental Psychology,* 1957, *54,* 201–207. **973, 975**

Bourne, L. E., Jr. Learning and utilization of conceptual rules. In B. Kleinmuntz (Ed.), *Concepts and the structure of memory.* New York: Wiley, 1967. Pp. 1–32. **966**

Bourne, L. E., Jr., & Bunderson, T. V. Effects of delay of informative feedback and length of postfeedback interval on concept identification. *Journal of Experimental Psychology,* 1963, *65,* 1–5. **973, 975**

Bourne, L. E., Jr., Goldstein, S., & Link, W. E. Concept learning as a function of availability of previously presented information. *Journal of Experimental Psychology,* 1964, *67,* 439–448. **972**

Bourne, L. E., Jr., Guy, D. E., Dodd, D. H., & Justesen, D. R. Concept identification: The effects of varying length in informational components of the intertrial interval. *Journal of Experimental Psychology,* 1965, *69,* 624–629. **973, 974**

Bourne, L. E., & Restle, F. Mathematical theory of concept

identification. *Psychological Review,* 1959, *66,* 278–296. **949, 957, 973, 1001**

Bourne, L. E. Jr., *see also* Dodd, D. H., 1967; Haygood, R., 1965; Leibowitz, H., 1956.

Bousfield, W. A. The occurrence of clustering in the recall of randomly arranged associates. *Journal of General Psychology,* 1953, *49,* 229–240. **891**

Bousfield, W. A., & Elliott, M. H. The effect of fasting on the eating behavior of rats. *Journal of Genetic Psychology,* 1934, *45,* 227–237. **814, 820**

Bousfield, W. A., Steward, J. R., & Cowan, T. R. The use of free associational norms for the prediction of clustering. Tech. Rep. No. 36, Contract Nonr-631(00), Office of Naval Research and University of Connecticut, 1961. **881**

Bousfield, W. A., Whitmarsh, G. A., & Berkowitz, H. Partial response identities in associative clustering. *Journal of General Psychology,* 1960, *63,* 233–238. **880**

Bousfield, W. A., Whitmarsh, G. A., & Danick, J. J. Partial response identity in verbal generalization. *Psychological Reports,* 1958, *4,* 703–713. **880**

Bousfield, W. A. *see also* Cohen, B. H., 1957.

Bower, G. H. Partial and correlated reward in escape learning. *Journal of Experimental Psychology,* 1960, *59,* 126–130. **723, 724**

Bower, G. H. Application of a model to paired-associate learning. *Psychometrika,* 1961, *26,* 255–281. **990**

Bower, G. H. A contrast effect in differential conditioning. *Journal of Experimental Psychology,* 1961, *62,* 196–199. **638, 639**

Bower, G. H. Correlated delay of reinforcement. *Journal of Comparative and Physiological Psychology,* 1961, *54,* 196–203. **843**

Bower, G. H. An association model for response and training variables in paired-associate learning. *Psychological Review,* 1962, *69,* 34–53. **994**

Bower, G. H. The influence of graded reductions in reward and prior frustrating events upon the magnitude of the frustration effect. *Journal of Comparative and Physiological Psychology,* 1962, *55,* 582–587. **810**

Bower, G. H., Fowler, H., & Trapold, M. A. Escape learning as a function of amount of shock reduction. *Journal of Experimental Psychology,* 1959, *58,* 482–484. **721**

Bower, G. H., & Miller, N. E. Rewarding and punishing effects from stimulating the same place in the rat's brain. *Journal of Comparative and Physiological Psychology,* 1958, *51,* 669–674. **647**

Bower, G. H., & Theios, J. A learning model for discrete performance levels. In R. C. Atkinson (Ed.), *Studies in mathematical psychology.* Stanford: Stanford University Press, 1964. Pp. 1–31. **996**

Bower, G. H., & Trabasso, D. Reversals prior to solutions in concept identification. *Journal of Experimental Psychology,* 1963, *66,* 409–418. **954, 974**

Bower, G. H., & Trabasso, T. R. Concept identification. In R. C. Atkinson (Ed.), *Studies in mathematical psychology.* Stanford: Stanford University Press, 1964. Pp. 32–94. **949, 950, 951, 953**

Bower, G. H., *see also* Atkinson, R. C., 1965; Hilgard, E. R., 1966; Trabasso, T., 1964, 1966.

Bower, T. G. R. Discrimination of depth in premotor infants. *Psychonomic Science.,* 1964, *1,* 368. **547**

Bowers, C., *see* Davis, H., 1967.

Boycott, B. B., *see* Dowling, J. E., 1966.

Boynton, R. M. Theory of color vision. *Journal of the Optical Society of America,* 1960, *50,* 929–944. **328**

Boynton, R. M. Some temporal factors in vision. In W. A. Rosenblith (Ed.), *Sensory communication.* New York: Wiley, 1961. Pp. 739–756. **307**

Boynton, R. M. Vision. In J. Sidowski (Ed.), *Experimental methods and instrumentation in psychology.* New York: McGraw-Hill, 1966. **357**

Boynton, R. M., Bush, W. R., & Enoch, J. M. Rapid changes in foveal sensitivity resulting from direct and indirect adapting stimuli. *Journal of the Optical Society of America,* 1954, *44,* 56–60. **310**

Boynton, R. M., & Das, S. R. Visual adaptation: Increased efficiency resulting from spectrally-distributed mixtures of stimuli. *Science,* 1966, *154,* 1581–1583. **336**

Boynton, R. M., & Gordon, J. Bezold-Brucke hue shift measured by color-naming technique. *Journal of the Optical Society of America,* 1965, *55,* 78–86. **347**

Boynton, R. M., & Kaiser, P. Vision: The additivity law made to work for heterochromatic photometry with bipartite fields. *Science,* 1968, *161,* 366–368. **327**

Boynton, R. M., Kandel, G., & Onley, J. W. Rapid chromatic adaptation of normal and dichromatic observers. *Journal of the Optical Society of America,* 1959, *49,* 654–666. **337**

Boynton, R. M., Schafer, W., & Neun, M. E. Hue-wavelength relation measured by color-naming method for three retinal locations. *Science,* 1964, *146,* 666–668. **348**

Boynton, R. M., Scheibner, H., Yates, T., & Rinalducci, E. Theory and experiments concerning the heterochromatic threshold-reduction factor (HTRF). *Journal of the Optical Society of America,* 1965, *55,* 1672–1685. **343**

Boynton, R. M., & Triedman, M. H. A psychophysical and electrophysiological study of light adaptation. *Journal of Experimental Psychology,* 1953, *46,* 125–134. **310**

Boynton, R. M., & Wagner, M. Two-color threshold as test of color vision. *Journal of the Optical Society of America,* 1961, *51,* 429–440. **343**

Boynton, R. M., *see also* Scheibner, H., 1968; Wheeless, L. L., Jr., 1966.

Brackbill, Y., Adams, G., & Reaney, T. P. A parametric study of the delay-retention effect. *Psychological Reports,* 1967, *20,* 433–434. **687**

Braden, I., *see* Jones, A., 1961.

Brady, J. V., *see* Hunt, H. F., 1955; Perez-Cruet, J., 1963; Stein, L., 1958.

Braine, L. G. Disorientation of forms: An examination of Rock's theory. *Psychonomic Science,* 1965, *3,* 541–542. **451**

Braly, K. W. The influence of past experience on visual perception. *Journal of Experimental Psychology,* 1933, *16,* 613–643. **440**

Brand, H., Woods, P. J., & Sakoda, J. N. Anticipation of reward as a function of partial reinforcement. *Journal of Experimental Psychology.* 1956, *52,* 18–22. **932**

Braunstein, M. L. The perception of depth through motion. *Psychological Bulletin,* 1962, *59,* 422–433. **505**

Braunstein, M. L. Motion and texture as sources of slant information. *Journal of Experimental Psychology,* 1968, *78,* 247–253. **505**

Braunstein, M. L., & Payne, J. W. Perspective and the rotating trapezoid. *Journal of the Optical Society of America,* 1968, *58,* 399–403. **518**

Bray, C. W., *see* Wever, E. G., 1930.

Brearley, E. A., & Kenshalo, D. R. Behavioral measurements of the sensitivity of cat's upper lip to warm and cool stimuli. *Journal of Comparative and Physiological Psychology,* 1970, *70,* 1–4. **150**

Brefer, L. *see* Maltzman, I., 1958.

Breland, K., & Breland, M. The misbehavior of organisms. *American Psychologist,* 1961, *16,* 681–684. **746**

Breland, M., *see* Breland, K., 1961.

Brelsford, J. Jr., *see* Theios, H. J., 1966.

Bremer, F. Neurogenic factors influencing the evoked potentials of the cerebral cortex. In W. A. Rosenblith (Ed.), *Sensory communication.* New York: Wiley, 1961. **233**

Breneman, E. J., *see* Bartleson, C. J., 1967.

Bressler, J. Judgments in absolute units as a psychophysi-cal method. *Archives of Psychology* (New York), 1933, *152.* **30**

Brethower, D. R., & Reynolds, G. S. A facilitative effect of punishment on unpunished behavior. *Journal of the Experimental Analysis of Behavior,* 1962, *5,* 191–199. **779**

Brewster, D. Ueber Schwingungen in der Netzhaut, erregt durch die Wirkung leuchtender Punkte und Linien. *Poggendorff, Annalen der Physiologie und Chemie,* 1833, *27,* 490–497. **411**

Bridges, C. C., & Bitterman, M. E. The measurement of autokinetic movement. *American Journal of Psychology,* 1954, *67,* 525–529. **529**

Bridgman, C. S. Analysis of a recently discovered stereoscopic effect. *American Journal of Psychology,* 1964, *77,* 138–143. **483**

Briggs, G. E. Acquisition, extinction and recovery functions in retroactive inhibition. *Journal of Experimental Psychology,* 1954, *47,* 285–293. **1092, 1099**

Briggs, G. E. Retroactive inhibition as a function of degree of original and interpolated learning. *Journal of Experimental Psychology,* 1957, *53,* 60–67. **1085, 1086**

Briggs, G. E., Thompson, R. F., & Brogden, W. J. Retention functions in reproductive inhibition. *Journal of Experimental Psychology,* 1954, *48,* 419–423. **1092, 1099**

Brimer, C. J. Inhibition and disinhibition of an operant response. *Bulletin of the Maritime Psychological Association,* 1964, *13,* 40–45. **714**

Brimer, C. J., & Kamin, L. J. Disinhibition, habituation, sensitization, and the conditioned emotional response. *Journal of Comparative and Physiological Psychology,* 1963, *56,* 508–516. **714**

Brimer, C. J., *see also* Kamin, L. J., 1963.

Brindley, G. S. The effects on colour vision of adaptation to very bright lights. *Journal of Physiology,* 1953, *122,* 332–350. **368**

Brindley, G. [S.] *Physiology of the retina and the visual pathway.* London: Edward Arnold, 1960. **323**

Brindley, G. S., & Merton, P. A. The absence of position sense in the human eye. *Journal of Physiology,* 1960, *153,* 127–130. **531**

Britt, S. H. Retroactive inhibition: A review of the literature. *Psychological Bulletin,* 1936, *32,* 381–440. **1080, 1088**

Broadbent, D. E. Failures of attention in selective listening. *Journal of Experimental Psychology,* 1952, *44,* 428–433. **259**

Broadbent, D. E. *Perception and communication.* New York: Pergamon, 1958. **236, 258, 259, 997, 998**

Broadbent, D. E. Flow of information within the organism. *Journal of Verbal Learning and Verbal Behavior,* 1963, *2,* 34–39. **998, 1114**

Broadhurst, P. L. Emotionality and the Yerkes-Dodson Law. *Journal of Experimental Psychology,* 1957, *54,* 345–352. **799, 830**

Brobeck, J. R. Regulation of feeding and drinking. In J. Field, H. W. Magoun, and V. E. Hall (Eds.), *Handbook of physiology.* Vol. II. Washington, D.C.: American Physiological Society, 1960. Pp. 1197–1206. **796**

Broca, A., & Sulzer, D. La sensation lumineuse en fonction du temps. *Comptes Rendus de Séances de l'Académie des Sciences,* Paris, 1902, *134,* 831–834; 1903, *137,* 944–946. **307**

Brock, T. C., *see* Schuck, J. R., 1964.

Brodhun, E., *see* König, A., 1889.

Brody, N. Anxiety and the variability of word associates. *Journal of Abnormal and Social Psychology,* 1964, *68,* 331–334. **876**

Brogden, W. J. Sensory preconditioning. *Journal of Experimental Psychology,* 1939, *25,* 323–332. **564**

Brogden, W. J., *see also* Briggs, G. E., 1954; Culler, E., 1935; Hoffeld, D. R., 1960.

Bromer, J. A., see Harlow, H. F., 1938.

Brooks, V., see Hochberg, J., 1958, 1960, 1962.

Brookshire, K., see Parducci, A., 1956.

Brookshire, K. H., see Moran, J. M., 1959.

Brosgole, L., & Whalen, P. M. The effect of meaning on the allocation of visually induced movement. *Perception and Psychophysics*, 1967, *2*, 275–277. **522**

Brosgole, L., see also Rock, I., 1964.

Brown, B. L., see Richardson, J., 1966.

Brown, B. R., see Vincent, R. J., 1969.

Brown, C. S., see Brown, J. S., 1966.

Brown, D. L., see Owens, J. A., 1968.

Brown, D. R., & Owen, D. H. The metrics of visual form: Methodological dyspepsia. *Psychological Bulletin*, 1967, *68*, 243–259. **449**

Brown, D. R., see also Forsyth, G. A., 1967.

Brown, E., see Fisher, G. L., 1965.

Brown, H. M., Dustman, R. E., & Beck, E. C. Sensitization in planaria. *Physiology and Behavior*, 1966, *1*, 305–308. **556**

Brown, H. O., see Smith, S. M., 1947.

Brown, J. Some tests of the decay theory of immediate memory. *Quarterly Journal of Experimental Psychology*. 1958, *10*, 12–21. **1110, 1114**

Brown, J. F. The visual perception of velocity. *Psychologische Forschung* 1931, *14*, 199–232. **508**

Brown, J. F. The thresholds for visual movement. *Psychologische Forschung.*, 1931, *14*, 249–269. **520**

Brown, J. F., & Voth, A. C. The path of seen movement as a function of the vector field. *American Journal of Psychology*, 1937, *49*, 543–563. **459, 527n**

Brown, J. L. The effect of drive on learning with secondary reinforcement. *Journal of Comparative and Physiological Psychology*, 1956, *49*, 254–260. **668**

Brown, J. L. Flicker and intermittent stimulation. In C. H. Graham (Ed.). *Vision and visual perception*. New York: Wiley, 1965. Pp. 251–320. **311**

Brown, J. L., see also Graham, C. H., 1965; Sechzer, J. A., 1964.

Brown, J. S. *The motivation of behavior*. New York: McGraw-Hill, 1961. **795, 796, 799, 800, 801, 809, 811, 816, 842**

Brown, J. S. Factors affecting self-punitive locomotor behavior. In B. A. Campbell & R. M. Church (Eds.), *Punishment*. New York: Appleton, 1969. **725**

Brown, J. S., Anderson, D. C., & Brown, C. S. Conflict as a function of food-deprivation time during approach training, avoidance training, and conflict tests. *Journal of Experimental Psychology*, 1966, *72*, 390–400. **809**

Brown, J. S., & Belloni, M. Performance as a function of deprivation time following periodic feeding in an isolated environment. *Journal of Comparative and Physiological Psychology*, 1963, *56*, 105–110. **830**

Brown, J. S., & Farber, I. E. Secondary motivational systems. *Annual Review of Psychology*, 1968, *19*, 99–134. **794n, 795, 798, 803, 804, 805, 807, 808, 811**

Brown, J. S., Kalish, H. I., & Farber, I. E. Conditioned fear as revealed by magnitude of startle response to an auditory stimulus. *Journal of Experimental Psychology*, 1951, *41*, 317–328. **803, 804**

Brown, J. S., Martin, R. C., & Morrow, M. W. Self-punitive behavior in the rat: Facilitative effects of punishment on resistance to extinction. *Journal of Comparative and Physiological Psychology*, 1964, *57*, 127–133. **725**

Brown, K. T. An optical illusion of spontaneous fluctuations in apparent size. *American Journal of Psychology*, 1954, *67*, 533–538. **480**

Brown, K. T., & Murakami, M. A new receptor potential of the monkey retina with no detectable latency. *Nature*, 1964, *201*, 626–628. **307**

Brown, K. T., Watanabe, K., and Murakami, M. Early and late receptors potentials of monkey cones and rods. *Cold Spring Harbor Symposia on Quantitative Biology*, 1965, *30*, 457–482. **330**

Brown, L., see Hayes, W. J., 1961; Jenkins, J. J., 1965.

Brown, L. K., Jenkins, J. J., & Lavik, J. Response transfer as a function of verbal associative strength. *Journal of Experimental Psychology*, 1966, *71*, 138–142. **1048**

Brown, L. T., see Robinson, J. S., 1964.

Brown, P. K., see Wald, G., 1965.

Brown, R. H. Velocity discrimination and the intensity–time relation. *Journal of the Optical Society of America*, 1955, *45*, 189–192. **520**

Brown, R. H., & Conklin, J. E. The lower threshold of visible movement as a function of exposure time. *American Journal of Psychology*, 1954, *67*, 104–110. **520**

Brown, R. H., see also Graham, C. H., 1939; Niven, J. I., 1944.

Brown, R. W., & Berko, J. Word-association and the acquisition of grammar. *Child Development*, 1960, *31*, 8–14. **874**

Brown, R. W., & Lenneberg, E. H. A study in language and cognition. *Journal of Abnormal and Social Psychology*, 1954, *49*, 454–462. **423**

Brown, W. To what extent is memory measured by a single recall? *Journal of Experimental Psychology*, 1923, *6*, 377–385. **5n**

Brown, W. L., see Crum, J., 1951.

Brown, W. P. Emotional indicators in word association. *British Journal of Psychology*, 1965, *56*, 401–412. **864**

Brown, W. P. The Yerkes–Dodson law repealed. *Psychological Reports*, 1965, *17*, 663–666. **830**

Brown, W. R. J. Color discrimination of twelve observers. *Journal of the Optical Society of America*, 1957, *47*, 137. **361**

Brown, W. R. J., & MacAdam, D. L. Visual sensitivities to combined chromaticity and luminance differences. *Journal of the Optical Society of America*, 1949, *39*, 808. **361**

Bruce, D., & Cofer, C. N. 1967. An examination of recognition and free recall as measures of acquisition and long-term retention. *Journal of Experimental Psychology*, 1967, *75*, 283–289. **893**

Bruce, H. M., see Parkes, A. S., 1961.

Bruce, R. W. Conditions of transfer of training. *Journal of Experimental Psychology*, 1933, *16*, 343–361. **1045, 1055, 1063, 1068**

Brücke, E. Über den Nutzeffect intermittierender Netzhautreizungen. *S.-B. K Akad. Wiss., Wien, math.-nat. Kl.*, 1864, *49*, II, 128–153. **314**

Bruell, J. H., & Albee, G. W. Notes towards a motor theory of visual egocentric localization. *Psychological Review*, 1955, *62*, 391–399. **530, 534**

Bruell, J. H., see also Werner, H., 1953.

Brugge, J. F., Dubrovsky, N., & Rose, J. E. Some discharge characteristics of single neurons in cat's auditory cortex. *Science*, 1964, *146*, 433–434. **265**

Brugge, J. F., see also Rose, J. E., 1967.

Bruner, J. S., Goodnow, J. J., & Austin, G. A. *A study of thinking*. New York: Wiley, 1956. **943, 947, 961, 963, 970**

Bruner, J. S., Miller, G. A., & Zimmerman, C. Discriminative skill and discriminative matching in perceptual recognition. *Journal of Experimental Psychology*, 1955, *49*, 187–192. **256**

Bruner, J., Postman, L., & Mosteller, F. A note on the measurement of reversals of perspective. *Psychometrika*, 1950, *15*, 63-72. **519**

Bruner, J. S., Postman, L., & Rodrigues, J. Expectations and the perception of color. *American Journal of Psychology*, 1951, *64*, 216-227. **424**

Bruner, J., & Tauc, L. Habituation at the synaptic level in *Aplysia. Nature*, 1966, *210*, 37-39. **592**

Bruner, J., *see also* Kehoe, J. S., 1966.

Brunswik, E. Zur Entwicklung der Albedowahrnehmung. *Zeitschrift für Psychologie*, 1929, *109*, 40-115. **399, 406**

Brunswik, E. *Wahrnehmung und Gegenstandswelt: Grundlegung einer Psychologie vom Gegenstand her*. Leipzig: Deuticke, 1934. **437**

Brunswik, E. The conceptual framework of psychology. In *International Encyclopedia of Unified Science*. Vol. 1, No. 10. Chicago: University of Chicago Press, 1952. **401, 437, 502**

Brunswik, E. *Perception and the representative design of psychological experiments*. (2nd ed.) Berkeley: University of California Press, 1956, **437, 463, 464, 502**

Brunswik, E., & Kamiya, J. Ecological cue-validity of "proximity" and other Gestalt factors. *American Journal of Psychology*, 1953, *66*, 20-32. **442**

Brunswik, E., *see also* Tolman, E. C., 1935.

Brush, E. S., *see* Brush, F. R., 1955; Solomon, R. L., 1956.

Brush, F. R. The effects of shock intensity on the acquisition and extinction of an avoidance response in dogs. *Journal of Comparative and Physiological Psychology*, 1957, *50*, 547-552. **729**

Brush, F. R. An efficient, inexpensive relay grid scrambler for multiple boxes. *Journal of the Experimental Analysis of Behavior*, 1967, *10*, 393-394. **706**

Brush, F. R., Brush, E. S., & Solomon, R. L. Traumatic avoidance learning: The effects of CS-US interval with a delayed-conditioning procedure. *Journal of Comparative and Physiological Psychology*, 1955, *48*, 285-293. **729**

Brush, F. R., *see also* Church, R. M., 1956.

Brust-Carmona, H., *see* Hernandez-Peon, R., 1961.

Bryan, J. D., *see* Young, R. K., 1963.

Bryan, J. S., *see* Nelson, P. G., 1966.

Bryden, M., & Rainey, C. Left-right differences in tachistocopic recognition. *Journal of Experimental Psychology*, 1963, *66*, 568-571. **444**

Buchsbaum, W. H., *see* Mayzner, M. S., 1965.

Buddulph, R., *see* Shower, E. G., 1931.

Budin, W., *see* Flavell, J. H., 1958.

Bugelski, B. R. Extinction with and without sub-goal reinforcement. *Journal of Comparative Psychology*, 1938, *26*, 121-133. **662, 673**

Bugelski, B. R. *The psychology of learning*. New York: Holt, Rinehart and Winston, 1956. **673**

Bugelski, B. R. In defense of remote associations. *Psychological Review*, 1965, *72*, 169-174. **1015**

Bugelski, B. R., & Cadwallader, T. C. A reappraisal of the transfer and retro-action surface. *Journal of Experimental Psychology*, 1956, *52*, 360-366. **1051, 1056, 1083**

Bugelski, B. R., & Scharlock, D. P. An experimental demonstration of unconscious mediated association. *Journal of Experimental Psychology*, 1952, *44*, 334-338. **781, 1071**

Buining, E., *see* Zwislocki, J., 1967.

Bujas, Z. Kontrast- und Hemmungserscheinungen bei disparaten simultanen Geschmacksreizen. *Acta Instituti Psychologica Universitatis Zagrebensis*, 1937, *2*, 3-12. **183**

Bujas, Z. Beobachtungen über den Restitutions Vorgang beim Geschmackssinn. *Acta Instituti Psychologici Universitatis Zagrebensis*, 1939, *3*, 3-14. **185**

Bujas, Z. L'adaptation gustative et son mécanisme. *Acta Instituti Psychologici Universitatis Zagrebensis*, 1953, *17*, 1-11. **184**

Bujas, Z., & Ostojčić, A. La sensibilité gustative en fonction de la surface excitée. *Acta Instituti Psychologici Universitatis Zagrebensis*, 1941, *13*, 1-20. **175**

Bunch, M. E. The amount of transfer in rational learning as a function of time. *Journal of Comparative Psychology*, 1936, *22*, 325-337. **1037**

Bunderson, T. V., *see* Bourne, L. E., Jr., 1963.

Burgeat, M., *see* Hirsh, I. J., 1958.

Burger, J. F. Front-back discrimination of the hearing system. *Acustica*, 1958, *8*, 301-302. **266, 267**

Burger, J. F., *see also* Lochner, J. P. A., 1961.

Burgess, P. R., & Perl, E. R. Myelinated afferent fibers responding specifically to noxious stimulation of the skin. *Journal of Physiology*, 1967, *190*, 541-562. **162, 165**

Burkamp, W. Versuche über das Farbenwiedererkennen der Fische. *Zeitschrift für Sinnesphysik*, 1923, *55*, 133-170. **407**

Burke, C. J. Application of a linear model to two-person interactions. In R. R. Bush & W. K. Estes (Eds.), *Studies in mathematical learning theory*. Stanford: Stanford University Press, 1959. Pp. 180-203. **934**

Burke, C. J. Some two-person interactions. In K. J. Arrow, S. Karlin, & P. Suppes (Eds.), *Mathematical methods in the social sciences, 1959*. Stanford: Stanford University Press, 1960, 242-253. **934**

Burke, C. J. Two-person interactive learning: A progress report. In J. H. Criswell, H. Solomon, & P. Suppes (Eds.), *Mathematical methods in small group processes*. Stanford: Stanford University Press, 1962. Pp. 49-68. **934**

Burke, C. J., & Estes, W. K. A component model for stimulus variables in discrimination learning. *Psychometrika*, 1957, *22*, 133-145. **924, 934**

Burke, C. J., Estes, W. K., & Hellyer, S. Rate of verbal conditioning in relation to stimulus variability. *Journal of Experimental Psychology*, 1954, *48*, 153-161. **930**

Burke, C. J., *see also* Estes, W. K., 1953, 1955, 1957; Friedman, M. P., 1964.

Burmeister, E. Beitrag zur experimentellen Bestimmung geometrisch-optischer Taeuschungen. *Zeitschrift für Psychologie und Physiologie de Sinnes*, 1896, *12*, 355-394. **458**

Burnett, N. G., & Dallenbach, K. M. The experience of heat. *American Journal of Psychology*, 1927, *38*, 418-431. **148**

Burnham, C. A. Adaptation to prismatically induced curvature with invisible arm movements. *Psychonomic Science*, 1968, *10*, 273-274. **542**

Burnham, C. A., *see also* Festinger, L., 1967.

Burnham, R. W. Bezold's color-mixture effect. *American Journal of Psychology*, 1953, *66*, 377-385. **408**

Burnham, R. W., Hanes, R. M., & Bartleson, C. J. *Color: A guide to basic facts and concepts*. New York: Wiley, 1963. **348**

Burnham, R. W., *see also* Newhall, S. M., 1957.

Burns, S., *see* Postman, L., 1968.

Burnstein, E., *see* Birch, D., 1958.

Burrill, D. Y., *see* Goetzl, F. R., 1943.

Burton, H., *see* Benjamin, R. M., 1968.

Burzlaff, W. Methodologische Beitrage zum Problem der Farbenkonstanz. *Zeitschrift für Psychologie*, 1931, *119*, 177-235. **399, 406**

Bush, R. R., Galanter, E., & Luce, R. D. Characterization and classification of choice experiments. In R. D. Luce, R. R. Bush, & E. Galanter (Eds.), *Handbook of mathematical psychology*. Vol. I. New York: Wiley, 1963. Pp. 77-102. **907**

Bush, R. R., & Mosteller, F. A model for stimulus generalization and discrimination. *Psychological Review*, 1951, *58*, 413–423. **948, 1001**

Bush, R. R., & Mosteller, F. *Stochastic models for learning.* New York: Wiley, 1955. **911, 912n, 919n, 922**

Bush, R. R., *see also* Luce, R. D., 1963.

Bush, W. R., *see* Boynton, R. M., 1954.

Buss, A. *The psychology of aggression.* New York: Wiley, 1961. **900**

Buss, A. H. A study of concept formation as a function of reinforcement and stimulus generalization. *Journal of Experimental Psychology*, 1950, *40*, 494–503. **786**

Bussey, T., *see* Leibowitz, H., 1957.

Buswell, G. T. Fundamental reading habits: A study of their development. *Education Monographs* (Supplement), 1922, *21*. **389, 390**

Buswell, G. T. How adults read. *Education Monographs* (Supplement), 1937, *45*. **390**

Butler, B., *see* Seward, J. P., 1957.

Butler, R. A. The effect of deprivation of visual incentives on visual exploration motivation in monkeys. *Journal of Comparative and Physiological Psychology*, 1957, *50*, 177–179. **840**

Butler, R. A. Some effects of unilateral auditory masking upon the localization of sound in space. *Journal of the Acoustical Society of America*, 1962, *34*, 1100–1107. **263**

Butler, R. A. Investigative behavior. In A. M. Schrier, H. F. Harlow, & F. Stollnitz (Eds.), *Behavior of nonhuman primates.* Vol. II. New York: Academic Press, 1965. **673**

Butler, R. A., & Naunton, R. F. Role of stimulus frequency and duration in the phenomenon of localization shifts. *Journal of the Acoustical Society of America*, 1964, *36*, 917–922. **263, 266**

Butler, R. A., *see also* Roffler, S. K., 1968.

Buttrick, R. D., *see* Bartoshuk, L. M., 1969.

Buxton, C. E. The status of research on reminiscence. *Psychological Bulletin*, 1943, *40*, 313–340. **1122**

Byford, G. H. Non-linear relations between the corneal-retinal potential and horizontal eye movements. *Journal of Physiology*, 1963, *168*, 14P. **372**

Byram, G. M. The physical and photochemical basis of visual resolving power: I. The distribution of illumination in retinal images. *Journal of the Optical Society of America*, 1944, *34*, 571–591. **299**

Cadwallader, T. C., *see* Bugelski, B. R., 1956.

Cahill, H., & Hovland, C. I. The role of memory in the acquisition of concepts. *Journal of Experimental Psychology*, 1960, *59*, 137–144. **971**

Cain, W. S. An analysis of the odor properties of the linear aliphatic alcohols by direct psychophysical scaling. Unpublished M.S. thesis, Brown University, 1966. **85**

Cain, W. S. Olfactory adaptation and direct scaling of odor intensity, Unpublished doctoral dissertation, Brown University, 1968. **75, 210n**

Cairns, R. B. Development, maintenance, and extinction of social attachment behavior in sheep. *Journal of Comparative and Physiological Psychology*, 1966, *62*, 298–306. **581**

Cairns, R. B., & Johnson, D. L. The development of interspecies social attachments. *Psychonomic Science*, 1965, *2*, 337–338. **581**

Calabresi, P., *see* Beck, L. H., 1954.

Calavrezo, C. Über den Einfluss von Grössenanderungen auf die scheinbare Tiefe. *Psychologische Forschung*, 1934, *19*, 311–365. **495**

Calearo, C., *see* Bocca, E., 1963.

Calfee, R. C., & Atkinson, R. C. Paired-associate models and the effects of list length. *Journal of Mathematical Psychology*, 1965, *2*, 254–265. **999, 1009**

Calvin, J. S., Bicknell, E., & Sperling, D. S. Establishment of a conditioned drive based upon the hunger drive. *Journal of Comparative and Physiological Psychology*, 1953, *46*, 173–175. **805**

Camerer, W. Ueber die Abhängigkeit des Geschmacksinns von der gereizten Stelle der Mundhöhle. *Zeitschrift für Biologie*, 1870, *6*, 440–452. **175**

Cameron, E. H., & Steele, W. M. The Poggendorf illusion. *Psychological Review, Monograph Supplement*, 1905, *7*, 83–111. **465**

Camp, D. S., Raymond, G. A., & Church, R. M. Temporal relationship between response and punishment. *Journal of Experimental Psychology*, 1967, *74*, 114–123. **737**

Campbell, B. A. The reinforcement difference limen (RDL) function for shock reduction. *Journal of Experimental Psychology*, 1956, *52*, 258–262. **722**

Campbell, B. A. Theory and research on the effects of water deprivation on random activity in the rat. In M. J. Wayner (Ed.), *Thirst.* Oxford: Pergamon, 1964. Pp. 317–334. **816**

Campbell, B. A., & Cicala, G. A. Studies of water deprivation in rats as a function of age. *Journal of Comparative and Physiological Psychology*, 1962, *55*, 763–768. **813, 814, 817, 822**

Campbell, B. A., & Kraeling, D. Response strength as a function of drive level and amount of drive reduction. *Journal of Experimental Psychology*. 1953, *45*, 97–101. **721, 722**

Campbell, B. A., & Lynch, G. S. Influence of hunger and thirst on the relationship between spontaneous activity and body temperature. *Journal of Comparative and Physiological Psychology*, 1968, *65*, 492–498. **824**

Campbell, B. A., & Masterson, F. A. Psychophysics of punishment. In B. A. Campbell, & R. M. Church (Eds.), *Punishment.* New York: Appleton, 1969. **705, 706**

Campbell, B. A., & Misanin, J. R. Basic drives. *Annual Review of Psychology*, 1969, *20*, 57–84. **794n**

Campbell, B. A., & Pickleman, J. R. The imprinting object as a reinforcing stimulus. *Journal of Comparative and Physiological Psychology*, 1961, *54*, 592–596. **581**

Campbell, B. A., & Sheffield, F. D. Relation of random activity to food deprivation. *Journal of Comparative and Physiological Psychology*, 1953, *46*, 320–322. **822**

Campbell, B. A., Smith, N. F., Misanin, J. R., & Jaynes, J. Species differences in activity during hunger and thirst. *Journal of Comparative and Physiological Psychology*, 1966, *61*, 123–127. **821, 824**

Campbell, B. A., & Teghtsoonian, R. Electrical and behavioral effects of different types of shock stimuli on the rat. *Journal of Comparative and Physiological Psychology*, 1958, *51*, 185–192. **705**

Campbell, B. A., Teghtsoonian, R., & Williams, R. A. Activity, weight loss, and survival time of food-deprived rats as a function of age. *Journal of Comparative and Physiological Psychology*, 1961, *54*, 216–219. **813, 822**

Campbell, B. A., *see also* Sheffield, F. D., 1954; Teghtsoonian, R., 1960; Williams, R. A., 1961.

Campbell, B. J., *see* Cong, E. R., 1958.

Campbell, D., *see* Kamin, L., 1959.

Campbell, D. T., *see* Segall, M. H., 1963, 1966.

Campbell, F. W., & Robson, J. G. High-speed infrared optometer. *Journal of the Optical Society of America*, 1959, *49*, 268–272. **394**

Campbell, F. W., & Robson, J. G. Application of Fourier analysis to the visibility of gratings. *Journal of Physiology*, 1968, *197*, 553–568. **300**

Campbell, F. W., & Rushton, W. A. H. Measurement of the scotopic pigment in the living human eye. *Journal of Physiology*, 1955, *130*, 131–147. **322**

Campbell, F. W., & Westheimer, G. Dynamics of accommodation responses of the human eye. *Journal of Physiology*, 1960, *151*, 285–295. **391**

Campbell, F. W., *see also* Alpern, M., 1962.

Campbell, R. A., & Small, A. M., Jr. Effect of practice and feedback on frequency discrimination. *Journal of the Acoustical Society of America,* 1963, *35,* 1511-1514. **249**

Campbell, R. A., *see also* Small, A. M. Jr., 1961.

Campbell, S. L., *see* Dinsmoor, J. A., 1956; Skinner, B. F., 1947.

Campbell, T. C., Lewis, N. A., & Hunt, W. A. Context effects with judgmental language that is absolute, extensive, and extra-experimentally anchored. *Journal of Experimental Psychology,* 1958, *55,* 220-228. **60**

Canestrari, R., & Farné, M. Depth cues and apparent oscillatory motion. *Perceptual and Motor Skills,* 1969, *29,* 508-510. **518**

Cantor, G. N. The effects of three types of pretraining on discrimination learning in children. *Journal of Experimental Psychology,* 1955, *49,* 339-342. **781**

Capaldi, E. J. A sequential hypothesis of instrumental learning. In K. W. Spence & J. T. Spence (Eds.), *The psychology of learning and motivation.* Vol. 1. New York: Academic Press, 1967. Pp. 67-156. **622, 633n, 681**

Capaldi, E. J., & Lynch, D. Repeated shifts in reward magnitude: Evidence in favor of an associational and absolute (noncontextual) interpretation. *Journal of Experimental Psychology,* 1967, *75,* 226-235. **634**

Capretta, P. J., *see* Smith, M. P., 1956.

Card, G. W., *see* Stellwagen, W. T., 1965.

Carel, W., *see* Gibson, J. J., 1952.

Carhart, K., *see* Olsen, W. O., 1966.

Carhart, R., Tilman, T. W., & Johnson, K. R. Release of masking for speech through interaural time delay. *Journal of the Acoustical Society of America,* 1967, *42,* 124-138. **258**

Carlin, S., Ward, W. D., Gershon, A., & Ingraham, R. Sound stimulation and its effect on dental sensation threshold. *Science,* 1962, *138,* 1258-1259. **164**

Carlson, J. Pseudomediation effects with no intertrial intervals. *Psychonomic Science,* 1966, *5,* 77-78. **1077**

Carlson, K. R., *see* Armus, H. L., 1964.

Carlson, N. J., *see* Black, A. H., 1962.

Carlson, V. R. Satiation in reversible perspective figure. *Journal of Experimental Psychology,* 1953, *45,* 442-448. **471**

Carlson, V. R. Overestimation in size constancy judgments. *American Journal of Psychology,* 1960, *73,* 199-213. **509, 514**

Carlson, V. R. Size constancy judgments and perceptual compromise. *Journal of Experimental Psychology,* 1962, *63,* 68-73. **509**

Carlson, W., *see* Eriksen, C. W., 1966.

Carmichael, L., & Dearborn, W. F. *Reading and visual fatigue.* Boston: Houghton Mifflin, 1947. **371**

Carmichael, L., *see also* Warren, H. C., 1930.

Caron, A. J., Unger, S. M., & Parloff, M. B. A test of Moltzman's theory of originality training. *Journal of Verbal Learning and Verbal Behavior,* 1963, *1,* 436-442. **867**

Carpenter, J. A. Species differences in taste preferences. *Journal of Comparative and Physiological Psychology,* 1956, *49,* 139-144. **190**

Carr, H. A. The autokinetic sensation. *Psychological Review,* 1910, *17,* 42-75. **533**

Carr, H. A. *Psychology: A study of mental activity.* New York: Longmans, Green, 1925. **533**

Carr, W. J. The effect of adrenalectomy upon the NaCl taste threshold in rat. *Journal of Comparative and Physiological Psychology,* 1952, *45,* 377-380. **176**

Carr, W. J., & Caul, W. F. The effect of castration in rats upon the discrimination of sex odours. *Animal Behaviour,* 1962, *10,* 20-27. **210**

Carr, W. J., & McGuigan, D. I. The stimulus basis and

modification of visual cliff performance in the rat. *Animal Behaviour,* 1965, *13,* 25-29. **549**

Carroll, J. B., Kjeldergaard, P. M., & Carton, A. S. Number of opposites versus number of primaries as a response measure in free-association tests. *Journal of Verbal Learning and Verbal Behavior,* 1962, *1,* 22-30. **871, 873**

Carter, E. A., *see* Seashore, E. C., 1908.

Carter, S., *see* Gelfan, S., 1967.

Carterette, E. C., *see* Egan, J. P., 1954.

Carterette, T. S. An application of stimulus sampling theory to summated generalization. *Journal of Experimental Psychology,* 1961, *62,* 448-455. **929**

Carton, A. S., *see* Carroll, J. B., 1962.

Casella, C., *see* Rapuzzi, G., 1965.

Casey, A., *see* Epstein, W., 1961.

Casey, K. L., *see* Melzack, R., 1968.

Casey, M., *see* Young, R. J., 1964.

Cason, H. The conditioned eyelid reaction. *Journal of Experimental Psychology,* 1922, *5,* 153-196. **562**

Casperson, R. C. The visual discrimination of geometric forms. *Journal of Experimental Psychology,* 1950, *40,* 668-681. **443**

Castaneda, A. Effects of stress on complex learning and performance. *Journal of Experimental Psychology,* 1956, *52,* 9-12. **790**

Castaneda, A. Supplementary report: Differential position habits and anxiety in children as determinants of performance in learning. *Journal of Experimental Psychology,* 1961, *61,* 257-258. **790, 791**

Castaneda, A., & Lipsitt, L. P. Relation of stress and differential position habits to performance in motor learning. *Journal of Experimental Psychology,* 1959, *57,* 25-30. **790**

Castaneda, A., & Palermo, D. S. Psychomotor performance as a function of amount of training and stress. *Journal of Experimental Psychology,* 1955, *50,* 175-179. **790**

Castaneda, A., Palermo, D. S., & McCandless, B. R. Complex learning and performance as a function of anxiety in children and task difficulty. *Child Development,* 1956, *27,* 327-332. **790**

Castaneda, A., *see also* Lipsitt, L. P., 1959.

Catania, A. C. Concurrent operants. In Honig, W. K. (Ed.), *Operant behavior: Areas of research and application.* New York: Appleton, 1966. **752**

Catania, A. C., *see also* Lane, H. L., 1961.

Cattell, J. McK. A statistical study of American men of science. *Science,* 1906, *24,* 658-665, 699-707, 732-742. Reprinted in *James McKeen Cattell: Man of science: 1860-1944.* Vol. 1. Lancaster, Pa.: Science Press, 1947. **62**

Cattell, J. McK. Statistics of American psychologists. *American Journal of Psychology,* 1903, *14,* 310-328. Reprinted in *James McKeen Cattell: Man of Science: 1860-1944.* Vol. 1. Lancaster, Pa.: Science Press, 1947. **61**

Cattell, J. McK., & Hoagland, H. Response of tactile receptors to intermittent stimulation. *Journal of Physiology,* 1931, *72,* 392-404. **165**

Cattell, J. McK., *see also* Fullerton, G. S., 1892.

Caul, W. F., *see* Carr, W. J., 1962.

Cauna, N. Light and electron microscopal structure of sensory end-organs of human skins. In D. R. Kenshalo (Ed.), *The skin senses.* Springfield, Ill.: Charles C Thomas, 1968. Pp. 15-37. **129**

Caviness, J., *see* Schiff, W., 1962.

Ceraso, J., & Henderson, A. Unavailability and associative loss in RI and PI. *Journal of Experimental Psychology,* 1965, *70,* 300-303. **1099, 1105**

Ceraso, J., & Henderson, A. Unavailability and associative loss in RI and PI: Second try. *Journal of Experimental Psychology,* 1966, *72,* 314-316. **1099, 1105**

Ceraso, J., *see also* Slamecka, N. J., 1960.

Cermak, L. S., *see* Wickens, D. D., 1967.

Chalmers, E. L. Monocular and binocular cues in the perception of size and distance. *American Journal of Psychology*, 1952, *65*, 415–423. **513, 514**

Chang, J. J., *see* Shepard, R. N., 1963.

Chapanis, A., & McCleary, R. A. Interposition as a cue for the perception of relative distance. *Journal of General Psychology*, 1953, *48*, 113–132. **498**

Chapanis, A., & Mankin, D. A. The vertical-horizontal illusion in a visually-rich environment. *Perception and Psychophysics*, 1967, *2*, 249–255. **456**

Chaplin, M. R., *see* Pollack, R. H., 1963.

Chapman, R. M., & Levy, N. Hunger drive and reinforcing effects of novel stimuli. *Journal of Comparative and Physiological Psychology*, 1957, *50*, 233–238. **673**

Chapman, W. P., & Jones, C. M. Variations in cutaneous and visceral pain sensitivity in normal subjects. *Journal of Clinical Investigation*, 1944, *23*, 81–91. **156**

Charnwood, J. R. B. *Essay on binocular vision.* London: Hatton, 1951. Pp. 106–108. **490**

Chase, H. H., *see* Keen, R. E., 1965.

Chase, W. G., *see* Keele, S. W., 1967.

Check, R., *see* Fox, R., 1966a, b.

Cheng, N. Y. Retroactive effect and degree of similarity. *Journal of Experimental Psychology*, 1929, *12*, 444–449. **1082**

Cherry, C., *see* Leakey, D. M., 1958.

Cherry, E. C. Some experiments on the recognition of speech, with one and two ears. *Journal of the Acoustical Society of America*, 1953, *25*, 975–979. **259**

Cherry, E. C., & Sayers, B. McA. On the mechanism of binaural fusion. *Journal of the Acoustical Society of America*, 1959, *31*, 535. **263**

Cheung, C. C., & Goulet, L. R. Retroactive inhibition of R-S associations in the A-B, B-C, C-B paradigms. *Journal of Experimental Psychology*, 1968, *76*, 321–322. **1096**

Chinetti, P., *see* Leibowitz, H., 1955, 1956, 1957.

Chinn, R. McC., *see* Riopelle, A. J.

Chistovitch, L. A., & Ivanova, V. A. Mutual masking of short sound pulses. *Biophysics*, 1959, *4*, 46–56. **241**

Cho, C., *see* Meyer, D. R., 1960.

Chomsky, N., *Syntactic structure.* The Hague: Mouton, 1957. **904**

Chomsky, N. *Aspects of the theory of syntax.* Cambridge, Mass.: The MIT Press, 1966. **904n**

Chorover, S. L., *see* Mendelson, J., 1965.

Chow, K. L., & Nissen, H. W. Interocular transfer of learning in visually naive and experienced infant chimpanzees. *Journal of Comparative and Physiological Psychology*, 1955, *48*, 229–237. **548**

Chow, K. L., *see also* Lashley, K. S., 1951.

Church, A. A. *Introduction to mathematical logic.* Princeton: Princeton University Press, 1958. **943**

Church, R. M. The varied effects of punishment on behavior. *Psychological Review*, 1963, *70*, 369–402. **734**

Church, R. M. Response suppression. In B. A. Campbell, & R. M. Church (Eds.). *Punishment.* New York: Appleton, 1969. **713, 734, 737**

Church, R. M., & Black, A. H. Latency of the conditioned heart rate as a function of the CS-US interval. *Journal of Comparative and Physiological Psychology*, 1958, *51*, 478–482. **711, 729**

Church, R. M., Brush, F. R., & Solomon, R. L. Traumatic avoidance learning: The effects of CS-US interval with a delayed-conditioning prodecure in a free-responding situation. *Journal of Comparative and Physiological Psychology*, 1956, *49*, 301–308. **729**

Church, R. M., LoLordo, V., Overmier, J. B., Solomon, R. L., & Turner, H. Cardiac responses to shock in curarized dogs: Effects of shock intensity and duration, warning signal, and prior experience with shock. *Journal of Comparative and Physiological Psychology*, 1966, *62*, 1–7. **711**

Church, R. M., Raymond, G. A., & Beauchamp, R. D. Response

suppression as a function of intensity and duration of a punishment. *Journal of Comparative and Physiological Psychology*, 1967, *63*, 39–44. **735, 736**

Church, R. M., & Solomon, R. L. Traumatic avoidance learning: The effects of delay of shock termination. *Psychological Reports*, 1956, *2*, 357–368. **727**

Church, R. M., *see also* Camp, D. S., 1967.

Cicala, G. A., *see also* Campbell, B. A., 1962.

Cieutat, V. J., Stockwell, F. E., & Noble, C. E., The interaction of ability and amount of practice with stimulus and response meaningfulness (*m*, *m'*) in paired-associate learning. *Journal of Experimental Psychology*, 1958, *56*, 193–202. **856**

Cisek, J. G., *see* Harvey, F. K., 1963.

Clack, T. D. Aural harmonics: Preliminary time-intensity relationships using the tone-on-tone masking technique. *Journal of the Acoustical Society of America*, 1968, *43*, 283–288. **238**

Clark, J. R., *see* Newhall, S. M., 1957.

Clark, L. L, Lansford, T. G., & Dallenbach, K. M. Repetition and associative learning. *American Journal of Psychology*, 1960, *73*, 22–40. **987**

Clark, R. A., *see* Birch, D., 1958.

Clark, W. C., Smith, A. H., & Rabe, A. Retinal gradient of outline as a stimulus for slant. *Canadian Journal of Psychology*, 1955, *9*, 247–253. **501**

Clark, W. C., Smith, A. H., & Rabe, A. The interaction of surface texture, outline gradient, and ground in the perception of slant. *Canadian Journal of Psychology*, 1956, *10*, 1–8. **501**

Clark, W. C., *see also* Gruber, H. E., 1956.

Clark, W. H., *see* Glanzer, M., 1963, 1964.

Clarke, F. J., & Belcher, S. J. On the localization of Troxler's effect in the visual pathway. *Vision Research*, 1962, *2*, 53–68. **453**

Clarke, R. H., *see* Horsley, V., 1908.

Clayton, F. L., & Savin, H. B. Strength of a secondary reinforcer following continuous or variable ratio primary reinforcement. *Psychological Reports*, 1960, *6*, 99–106. **663**

Clayton, K. N., *see* Knott, P. D., 1966.

Clement, D. E., & Varnadoe, K. W. Pattern uncertainty and the discrimination of visual patterns. *Perception and Psychophysics*, 1967, *2*, 427–431. **448**

Clement, D. E., *see also* Garner, W. R., 1963.

Clemente, C. D., Sterman, M. B., & Wyrwicka, W. Post-reinforcement EEG synchronization during alimentary behavior. *Electroencephalography and Clinical Neurophysiology*, 1964, *16*, 355–365. **838**

Clemente, C. D., *see also* Roth, S. R., 1967; Wyrwicka, W., 1962.

Clifton, C., Jr. Some determinants of the effectiveness of priming word associations. *Journal of Verbal Learning and Verbal Behavior*, 1966, *6*, 161–171. **872**

Clowes, M. B., & Ditchburn, R. W. An improved apparatus for producing a stabilized retinal image. *Optica Acta*, 1959, *6*, 252–265. **375**

Clynes, M. The non-linear biological dynamics of unidirectional rate sensitivity illustrated by analog computer analysis, pupillary reflex to light and sound, and heart rate behavior. *Annals of the New York Academy of Science*, 1962, *98*, 806–845. **392**

Cockrell, J. T. Operant behavior in relation to the concentration of a nonnutritive sweet substance used as a reinforcement. Unpublished doctoral dissertation, Indiana University, 1952. **627, 629**

Cofer, C. N. Associative commonality and rated similarity of certain words from Haagen's list. *Psychological Reports*, 1957, *3*, 603–606. **890**

Cofer, C. N. Comparison of word associations obtained by the methods of discrete single word and continued association. *Psychological Reports*, 1958, *4*, 507-510. **872, 877**

Cofer, C. N. Motivation. *Annual Review of Psychology*, 1959, *10*, 173-202. **794n**

Cofer, C. N. On some factors in the organizational characteristics of free recall. *American Psychologist*, 1965, *20*, 261-272. **890**

Cofer, C. N. Some evidence for coding processes derived from clustering in free recall. *Journal of Verbal Learning and Verbal Behavior*, 1966, *5*, 188-192. **891**

Cofer, C. N. Does conceptual organization influence the amount retained in immediate free recall? In B. Kleinmuntz (Ed.), *Concepts and the structure of memory*. New York: Wiley, 1967. (a) **883, 887, 891**

Cofer, C. N. Conditions for the use of verbal associations. *Psychological Bulletin*, 1967, *68*, 1-12. (b) **871, 872**

Cofer, C. N. Some data on controlled association. *Journal of Verbal Learning and Verbal Behavior*, 1967, 6, 601-608. (c) **870**

Cofer, C. N., & Foley, J. P., Jr. Mediated generalization and the interpretation of verbal behavior: I. Prolegomena. *Psychological Review*, 1942, *49*, 513-540. **1071**

Cofer, C. N., *see also* Bruce, D., 1967; Havron, M. D., 1957; Jenkins, P. M., 1957; Marshall, G. R., 1963.

Cofoid, D. A., & Honig, W. K. Stimulus generalization of imprinting. *Science*, 1961, *134*, 1692-1694. **582, 700**

Cohen, A. Further investigation of the effects of intensity upon the pitch of pure tones. *Journal of the Acoustical Society of America*, 1961, *33*, 1363-1375. **244**

Cohen, A., *see also* Mayzner, M. S., 1967.

Cohen, B. H., Bousfield, W. A., & Whitmarsh, G. A. Cultural norms for verbal items in 43 categories. Technical Report No. 22, Contract Nonr 631(00), Office of Naval Research and University of Connecticut, 1957. **879, 891**

Cohen, B. H., & Hut, P. A. Learning of responses to stimulus classes and to specific stimuli. *Journal of Experimental Psychology*, 1963, *66*, 274-280. **892**

Cohen, G. H., *see* Wheeless, L. L., Jr., 1966.

Cohen, W. Color perception in the chromatic Ganzfeld. *American Journal of Psychology*, 1958, *71*, 390-394. **416**

Cohn, J. Experimentelle Untersuchungen über die Gefühlsbetonung der Farben, Helligkeiten, und ihrer Combinationen. *Philosophische Studien*, 1894, *10*, 562-603. **51**

Coke, E. U., *see* Rothkopf, E. Z. 1961a, b.

Colavita, F., *see* Peterson, M. J., 1964.

Colburn, H. S., & Durlach, N. I. Time-intensity relations in binaural unmasking. *Journal of the Acoustical Society of America*, 1965, *38*, 93-103. **243**

Cole, J. L., *see* Boneau, C. A., 1967.

Cole, N., *see* Friedman, M. P., 1964.

Coleman, E. B. The association hierarchy as an indicator of extraexperimental interference. *Journal of Verbal Learning and Verbal Behavior*, 1963, *2*, 417-421. **889**

Coleman, E. B. The association hierarchy as a measure of extra-experimental transfer. *Journal of Psychology*, 1964, *57*, 403-417. **889**

Coleman, P. Failure to localize the source distance of an unfamiliar sound. *Journal of the Acoustical Society of America*, 1962, *34*, 345-346. **269**

Coleman, P. An analysis of cues to auditory depth perception in free space. *Psychological Bulletin*, 1963, *60*, 302-315. **269**

Collias, N. E. The analysis of socialization in sheep and goats. *Ecology*, 1956, *37*, 228-239. **581**

Collier, G. Some properties of saccharin as a reinforcer. *Journal of Experimental Psychology*, 1962, *64*, 184-191. **626, 627, 630**

Collier, G. Thirst as a determinant of reinforcement. In M. I. Wayner (Ed.), *Thirst*. Oxford: Pergamon, 1964. Pp. 287-303. **814, 816, 819**

Collier, G., & Marx, M. H. Changes in performance as a function of shifts in the magnitude of reinforcement. *Journal of Experimental Psychology*, 1959, *57*, 305-309. **633, 634, 635, 637, 638**

Collier, G., & Myers, L. The loci of reinforcement. *Journal of Experimental Psychology*, 1961, *61*, 57-66. **626**

Collier, G., & Novell, K. Saccharin as a sugar surrogate. *Journal of Comparative and Physiological Psychology*, 1967, *64*, 404-408. **630**

Collier, G., & Siskel, M., Jr. Performance as a joint function of amount of reinforcement and inter-reinforcement interval. *Journal of Experimental Psychology*, 1959, *57*, 115-120. **626**

Collier, G., & Willis, F. N. Deprivation and reinforcement. *Journal of Experimental Psychology*, 1961, *62*, 377-384. **626**

Collier, G., *see also* Premack, D., 1957.

Collins, J. F., *see* Eriksen, C. W., 1964, 1965.

Collins, W. F., Nulsen, F. E., & Randt, C. T. Relation of peripheral nerve fiber size and sensation in man. *Archives of Neurology*, 1960, *3*, 381-385. **156, 162**

Coltheart, M. The influence of haptic size information upon visual judgments of absolute distance. *Perception and Psychophysics*, 1969, *5*, 143-144. **514**

Coltheart, M., *see also* Blessing, W. W., 1967.

Comrey, A. L. A proposed method for absolute scaling. *Psychmetrika*, 1950, *15*, 317-325. **71**

Conant, M. V., & Trabasso, T. Conjunctive and disjunctive concept formation under equal-information conditions. *Journal of Experimental Psychology*, 1964, *67*, 250-255. **963**

Cone, R. A. Early receptor potential of the vertebrate retina. *Nature*, 1964, *204*, 736-739. **307**

Cone, R. A. Early receptor potential of the vertebrate eye. *Cold Spring Harbor Symposia on Quantitative Biology*, 1965, *30*, 483-493. **330**

Conklin, J. E., *see* Brown, R. H., 1954.

Conrad, D. G., *see* Sidman, M., 1957.

Conrad, R. Acoustic confusions in immediate memory. *British Journal of Psychology*, 1964, *55*, 75-84. **1115**

Conrad, R. Interference or decay over short retention intervals? *Journal of Verbal Learning and Verbal Behavior*, 1967, 6, 49-54. **1116**

Conrad, R., & Hull, A. Information, acoustic confusion and memory span. *British Journal of Psychology*, 1964, *55*, 429-432. **1115**

Cook, B., *see* Zigler, M. J., 1930.

Cook, C., *see* Graham, C. H., 1937.

Cook, S. W., *see* Raskin, E., 1937.

Cook, T. H., Mefford, R. B., Jr., & Wieland, B. A. Apparent reversals of orientation (perspective reversals) in depth as determinants of apparent reversals of rotary motion. *Perceptual and Motor Skills*, 1967, *24*, 691-702. **518, 519**

Coombs, C. H. *A theory of data*. New York: Wiley, 1964. **63**

Coons, E. E., Anderson, N. H., & Myers, A. K. Disappearance of avoidance responding during continued training. *Journal of Comparative and Physiological Psychology*, 1960, *53*, 290-292. **730**

Cooper, F. S., DeLattre, P. C., Liberman, A. M., Boret, J. M., & Gerstman, L. J. Some experiments on speech perception. *Journal of the Acoustical Society of America*, 1952, *24*, 597-606. **253**

Cooper, F. S., *see also* Harris, E. S., 1958; Liberman, A. M., 1954, 1958, 1962, 1967.

Copelan, E., *see* Riopelle, A. J., 1954.

Corbin, H. H. The perception of grouping and apparent movement in visual depth. *Archives of Psychology* (New York), 1942, *273*. **527, 528**

Corbit, J. D. Osmotic thirst: Theoretical and experimental

analysis. *Journal of Comparative and Physiological Psychology*, 1969, *67*, 3–14. **816**

Corbit, J. D., & Stellar, E. Palatability, food intake, and obesity in normal and hyperphagic rats. *Journal of Comparative and Physiological Psychology*, 1964, *58*, 63–67. **817**

Coren, S. Brightness contrast as function of figure-ground relations. *Journal of Experimental Psychology*, 1969, *80*, 517–524. **423n**

Coren, S., & Festinger, L. An alternative view of the "Gibson normalization effect." *Perception and Psychophysics*, 1967, *2*, 621–626. **459, 465, 467**

Coriell, A. S., *see* Averbach, E., 1961.

Corliss, E. L. R., & Winzer, G. E. Study of methods for estimating loudness. *Journal of the Acoustical Society of America*, 1965, *38*, 424–428. **249**

Cormack, R. H., & Upchurch, R. L. Necker cube reversibility and perspective duration as a function of rotation and retinal disparity. *Psychonomic Science*, 1969, *15*, 305–307. **519**

Cornsweet, J. C., *see* Riggs, L. A., 1953.

Cornsweet, T. N. Determination of the stimuli for involuntary drifts and saccadic eye movements. *Journal of the Optical Society of America*, 1956, *46*, 987–993. **375, 376, 380, 387**

Cornsweet, T. N. A new technique for the measurement of small eye movements. *Journal of the Optical Society of America*, 1958, *48*, 808–811. **373**

Cornsweet, T. N. The staircase-method in psychophysics. *American Journal of Psychology*, 1962, *75*, 485–491. **20**

Cornsweet, T. N., *see also* Krauskopf, J., 1960; Riggs, L. A., 1953.

Corso, J. F. The neural quantum theory of sensory discrimination. *Psychological Bulletin*, 1956, *53*, 371–393. **34**

Corso, J. F. Absolute thresholds for tones of low frequency. *American Journal of Psychology*, 1958, *71*, 367–374. **233**

Corso, J. F. Bone conduction thresholds for sonic and ultrasonic frequencies. *Journal of the Acoustical Society of America*, 1963, *35*, 1738–1743. **233**

Corso, J. F. *The experimental psychology of sensory behavior.* New York: Holt, Rinehart and Winston, 1967. **233**

Cortesina, G., *see* Rossi, G., 1965.

Costiloe, J. P., *see* Schneider, R. A., 1958.

Cotzin, M., & Dallenbach, K. M. "Facial vision": The role of pitch and loudness in the perception of obstacles by the blind. *American Journal of Psychology*, 1950, *63*, 483–515. **271**

Cotzin, M., *see also* Supa, M., 1944.

Courten, H. C., *see* Judd, C. H., 1905.

Cowan, A. Test cards for determination of visual acuity. *Archives of Ophthalmology*, 1928, *57*, 283–295. **299**

Cowan, P. A., *see* Mandler, G., 1964.

Cowan, T. R., *see* Bousfield, W. A., 1961.

Cowles, J. T. Food-tokens as incentives for learning by chimpanzees. *Comparative Psychology Monographs*, 1937, *14*, No. 71. **665**

Craig, E. A., & Lichtenstein, M. Visibility–invisibility cycles as a function of stimulus orientation. *American Journal of Psychology*, 1953, *66*, 554–563. **453**

Cramer, P. Successful mediated priming via associative bonds. *Psychological Reports*, 1964, *15*, 235–238. **871**

Cramer, P. Recovery of a discrete memory. *Journal of Personal and Social Psychology*, 1965, *1*, 326–332. (a) **886**

Cramer, P. Response entropy as a function of the affective quality of the stimulus. *Psychonomic Science*, 1965, *3*, 347–348. (b) **864, 866**

Cramer, P. Mediated transfer via natural language association. *Journal of Verbal Learning and Verbal Behavior*, 1967, *6*, 512–519. **1078**

Cramer, P. *Word association.* New York: Academic Press. 1968. **861, 863n, 864, 865, 866**

Craske, B., *see* Howard, I. P., 1965.

Crawford, B. H. Visual adaptation in relation to brief conditioning stimuli. *Proceedings of the Royal Society* (London), Ser. B, 1947, *134B*, 283–300. **287, 288, 310**

Crawford, B. H., *see also* Stiles, W. S., 1933, 1934.

Crawford, J., Hunt, E., & Peak, G. One-trial learning of disjunctive concepts. *Journal of Verbal Learning and Verbal Behavior*, 1967, *6*, 207–212. **958, 963**

Crawford, J. L., & Vanderplas, J. M. An experiment on the mediation of transfer in paired-associate learning. *Journal of Psychology*, 1959, *47*, 87–98. **1075**

Creelman, C. D., *see* Garner, W. R., 1967.

Crespi, L. Quantitative variation of incentive and performance in the white rat. *American Journal of Psychology*, 1942, *15*, 467–517. **617, 631, 634, 635, 795**

Crespi, L. Amount of reinforcement and level of performance. *Psychological Review*, 1944, *51*, 341–357. **634, 635, 795**

Creutzfeldt, O., *see* Grüsser, O.-J., 1957.

Crisler, G., *see* Kleitman, N., 1927.

Crocker, E. C. Odor in flavor. *American Perfumer*, 1947, *50*, 164–165. **213**

Cromwell, R. L., *see* Baumeister, A., 1964.

Cronly-Dillon, J. R. Units sensitive to direction of movement in goldfish optic tectum. *Nature*, 1964, *203*, 214–215. **295**

Cronly-Dillon, J. R., *see also* Wall, P. D., 1960.

Crookes, T. G. The apparent size of after-images. *American Journal of Psychology*, 1959, *72*, 547–553. **511**

Crookes, T. G., *see also* Hall, K. R. L., 1952.

Crosby, E. C., Humphrey, T., & Lauer, E. W. *Correlative anatomy of the nervous system.* New York: Macmillan, 1962. **90**

Cross, H. A., *see* Rosenblum, L. A., 1963.

Cross, J., & Cross, J. The misperception of rotary motion. *Perception and Psychophysics*, 1969, *5*, 94–96. **519**

Crothers, E. J., *see also* Atkinson, R. C., 1964, 1965; Estes, W. K., 1960.

Crovitz, H. F. Köllner effect and suppression of the view of an eye. *Science*, 1964, *146*, 1329–1330. **488**

Crovitz, H. F., & Lipscomb, D. B. Dominance of the temporal visual fields at a short duration of stimulation. *American Journal of Psychology*, 1963, *76*, 631–637. **488**

Crowell, R. A., *see* Armus, H. L., 1964.

Crowley, M. E., *see* Gagné, R. M., 1948.

Crowne, D. P., *see* Horton, D. L.

Crum, J., Brown, W. L., & Bitterman, M. E. The effect of partial and delayed reinforcement on resistance to extinction. *American Journal of Psychology*, 1951, *64*, 228–237. **685**

Culbertson, J. L. The effects of brief delays of reinforcement on the acquisition and extinction of visual brightness discriminations using brain stimulation as a reinforcer. Doctoral dissertation, Brown University, 1968. Dis. Abstracts No. 69-9950, *30*, Issue 1. **683, 685, 686**

Culbertson, J. L. Effects of brief reinforcement delays on acquisition and extinction of brightness discriminations in rats. *Journal of Comparative and Physiological Psychology*, 1970, *70*, 317–325. **680, 682**

Culbertson, J. L., Kling, J. W., & Berkley, M. A. Extinction responding following ICS and food reinforcement, *Psychonomic Science*, 1966, *5*, 127–128. **653**

Culler, E., Finch, G., Girden, E., & Brogden, W. Measurements of acuity by the conditioned-response technique. *Journal of General Psychology*, 1935, *12*, 223–227. **566**

Cunningham, M., Jr., *see* Grover, D. E., 1967.

Curran, C. R., & Lane, H. L. On the relations among some factors that contribute to estimates of verticality. *Journal of Experimental Psychology*, 1962, *64*, 295–299. **539**

Curran, J. F., *see* Grant, D. A., 1953.

Dadson, R. S., *see* Robinson, D. W., 1956.

Dainoff, M., & Haber, R. N. How much help do repeated

presentations give to recognition processes? *Perception and Psychophysics*, 1967, *2*, 131–136. **445***n*

Dale, H. C. A., *see* Baddeley, A. D., 1966.

Dallenbach, J. W., & Dallenbach, K. M. The effects of bitter-adaptation on sensitivity to the other taste qualities. *American Journal of Psychology*, 1943, *56*, 21–31. **182, 186**

Dallenbach, K. The temperature spots and end-organs. *American Journal of Psychology*, 1927, *39*, 402–427. **120**

Dallenbach, K. M. Pain: History and present status. *American Journal of Psychology*, 1939, *52*, 331–347. **157**

Dallenbach, K. M. The staircase-method critically examined. *American Journal of Psychology*, 1966, *79*, 654–656. **20**

Dallenbach, K. M., *see also* Abrahams, H., 1937; Ammons, C. H., 1953; Burnett, N. G., 1927; Clark, L. L., 1960; Cotzin, M., 1950; Dallenbach, J. W., 1943; Edes, B., 1936; Ferrall, S. C., 1930; Foster, D., 1950; Guilford, J. P., 1928; Jenkins, J. G., 1924; Krakauer, D., 1937; Lowenstein, E., 1930; Stone, L. J., 1934; Supa, M., 1944; Worchel, P., 1947.

Dallett, J. M. In defense of remote associations. *Psychological Review*, 1965, *72*, 164–168. **1015**

Dallett, K. M. The transfer surface re-examined. *Journal of Verbal Learning and Verbal Behavior*, 1962, *1*, 91–94. (a) **1051, 1056, 1063**

Dallett, K. M. The role of response similarity in proactive inhibition. *Journal of Experimental Psychology*, 1962, *64*, 364–372. (b) **1104**

Dallett, K. M. Practice effects in free and ordered recall. *Journal of Experimental Psychology*, 1963, *66*, 65–71. **1044**

Dallett, K. M. Proactive and retroactive inhibition in the *A–B, A–B'* paradigm. *Journal of Experimental Psychology*, 1964, *68*, 190–200. **1103, 1104**

Dallett, K. M. A transfer surface for paradigms in which second-list *S–R* pairings do not correspond to first-list pairings. *Journal of Verbal Learning and Verbal Behavior*, 1965, *4*, 528–534. **1055, 1056**

Dallett, K. M. Effects of within-list and between-list acoustic similarity on the learning and retention of paired associates. *Journal of Experimental Psychology*, 1966, *72*, 667–677. **1126**

D'Amato, M. R. Transfer of secondary reinforcement across the hunger and thirst drives. *Journal of Experimental Psychology*, 1955, *49*, 352–356. (a) **668**

D'Amato, M. R. Secondary reinforcement and magnitude of primary reinforcement. *Journal of Comparative and Physiological Psychology*, 1955, *48*, 378–380. (b) **666**

D'Amato, M. R., & Fazzaro, J. Discriminated lever-press avoidance learning as a function of type and intensity of shock. *Journal of Comparative and Physiological Psychology*, 1966, *61*, 313–315. **729**

D'Amato, M. R., Fazzaro, J., & Etkin, M. Discriminated bar-press avoidance maintenance and extinction in rats as a function of shock intensity. *Journal of Comparative and Physiological Psychology*, 1967, *63*, 351–354. **729**

Damianopoulos, E. N., *see* Sqislocki, J., 1967.

Danick, J. J., *see* Bousfield, W. A., 1958.

Darian-Smith, I., *see* Mountcastle, V. B., 1967.

Darwin, C. *Expression of the emotions in man and animal.* London: Murray, 1872. Reprinted by The University of Chicago Press, 1965, with an introduction by Konrad Lorenz. **55**

Das, S. R., *see* Boynton, R. M., 1966.

Dastoli, F. R., & Price, S. Sweet-sensitive protein from bovine taste buds: Isolation and assay. *Science*, 1966, *154*, 905–907. **189**

Dateo, G. P., *see* Bartoshuk, L. M., 1969.

David, E. E., Guttman, N., & van Bergeijk, W. A. On the mechanism of binaural fusion. *Journal of the Acoustical Society of America*, 1958, *30*, 801–802. **263, 266**

David, E. E., Guttman, N., & van Bergeijk, W. A. Binaural interaction of high-frequency complex stimuli. *Journal of the Acoustical Society of America*, 1959, *31*, 774. **263**

David, E. E., *see also* Guttman, N., 1960; van Bergeijk, W. A., 1960.

Davidson, E. H. Some determinants of verbal association times. Doctoral dissertation, Pennsylvania State University, 1965. **862, 869**

Davidson, L., *see* Wallach, H., 1963.

Davies, J. T. A theory of the quality of odours. *Journal of Theoretical Biology*, 1965, *8*, 1–7. **222**

Davis, C. J., & Jobe, F. W. Further studies on the A.C.A. ratio as measured on the ortho-rater. *American Journal of Optometry*, 1957, *34*, 16–25. **384**

Davis, H. Chapter 4 in C. M. Harris (Ed.), *Handbook of noise control.* New York: McGraw-Hill, 1957. **229**

Davis, H. Mechanisms of excitation of auditory nerve impulses. In G. L. Rasmussen & W. F. Windle (Eds.), *Neural mechanisms of the auditory and vestibular systems.* Springfield, Ill.: Charles C Thomas, 1960. **230**

Davis, H., Hirsh, S. K., Shelnutt, J., & Bowers, C. Further validation of evoked response audiometry. *Journal of Speech and Hearing Research*, 1967, *10*, 717–732. **235**

Davis, H., & Krantz, F. W. International audiometric zero. *Journal of the Acoustical Society of America*, 1964, *36*, 1450–1454. **233, 235**

Davis, H., & Silverman, S. R. *Hearing and deafness.* New York: Holt, Rinehart and Winston, 1960. **226, 228, 235, 254, 255, 256**

Davis, H., & Zerlin, S. Acoustic relations of the human vertex potential. *Journal of the Acoustical Society of America*, 1966, *39*, 109–116. **235**

Davis, H., *see also* Deatherage, B. H., 1957; Galambos, R., 1943, 1944; Hirsh, I. J., 1952; Stevens, S. S., 1938; Tasaki, I., 1952, 1954; Teas, D. C., 1962.

Davis, J. D., *see* Grice, G. R., 1957.

Davy, E. Intensity–time relation for multiple flashes of light in the peripheral retina. *Journal of the Optical Society of America*, 1952, *42*, 937–941. **304**

Daw, N. W. Goldfish retina: Organization for simultaneous color contrast, *Science*, 1967, *158*, 942–944. **295**

Day, D. J., *see* Martin, L. C., 1950.

Day, R. H. Application of the statistical theory to form perception. *Psychological Review*, 1956, *63*, 139–148.

Day, R. H. On interocular transfer and the central origin of visual after-effects. *American Journal of Psychology*, 1958, *71*, 784–789. **473**

Day, R. H. Excitatory and inhibitory processes as the basis of contour shift and negative aftereffect. *Psychologia*, 1962, *5*, 185–193. **470, 473**

Day, R. H. Effects of repeated trials and prolonged fixations on error in the Müller-Lyer. *Psychological Monographs*, 1962, *76.* **465**

Day, R. H., Pollack, R. H., & Seagrim, G. N. Figural aftereffects: A critical review. *Austalian Journal of Psychology*, 1959, *11*, 15–45. **469**

Day, R. H., & Power, R. P. Frequency of apparent reversal of rotary motion in depth as a function of shape and pattern. *Australian Journal of Psychology*, 1963, *15*, 162–174. **518**

Day, R. H., & Power, R. P. Apparent reversal (oscillation) of rotary motion in depth: An investigation and a general theory. *Psychological Review*, 1965, *72*, 117–127. **518**

Day, R. H., *see also* Ganz, L., 1965; Singer, G., 1966.

Dean, M. G., & Kausler, D. H. Degree of first-list learning and stimulus meaningfulness as related to transfer in the *A–B, C–B* paradigm. *Journal of Verbal Learning and Verbal Behavior*, 1964, *3*, 330–334. **1061, 1063, 1068**

Dean, S. J., *see* Martin, R. B., 1964.

Dearborn, W. F. The psychology of reading. *Archives of Philosophy, Psychology and Scientific Methods*, 1906, *4.* **388, 390**

Dearborn, W. F. The general effects of special practice in memory. *Psychological Bulletin*, 1909, *6*, 44. **1031**

Dearborn, W. F., *see also* Carmichael, L., 1947.

Deatherage, B. H., Bilger, R. C., & Eldredge, D. H. Remote masking in selected frequency regions. *Journal of the Acoustical Society of America*, 1957, *29*, 512-514. **239**

Deatherage, B. H., Davis, H., & Eldredge, D. H. Physiological evidence for masking of low frequencies by high. *Journal of the Acoustical Society of America*, 1957, *29*, 132-137. **239**

Deatherage, B. H., & Hirsh, I. J. Auditory localization of clicks. *Journal of the Acoustical Society of America*, 1959, *31*, 486-492. **262, 266**

Deatherage, B. H., *see also* Jeffress, L., 1962.

Deaux, E. B., *see* Patten, R. L., 1966.

de Boer, E. *On the "residue" in hearing.* 'S-Gravenhage, The Netherlands: Excelsior, 1956. **245**

Decker, L., *see* Pollack, I., 1959.

Decker, T., *see* Kenshalo, D. R., 1967.

Deese, J. Influence of inter-item associative strength upon immediate free recall. *Psychological Reports*, 1959, *5*, 305-312. (a) **879, 887, 1129**

Deese, J. On the prediction of occurrence of particular verbal intrusions in immediate recall. *Journal of Experimental Psychology*, 1959, *58*, 17-22. (b) **887**

Deese, J. Frequency of usage and number of words in free recall: The role of association. *Psychological Reports*, 1960, *7*, 337-344. **854, 886, 896, 1129**

Deese, J. From the isolated verbal unit to connected discourse. In C. N. Cofer (Ed.), *Verbal learning and verbal behavior.* New York: McGraw-Hill, 1961. Pp. 11-31. **848, 878, 901, 903**

Deese, J. Form class and the determinants of association. *Journal of Verbal Learning and Verbal Behavior*, 1962, *1*, 79-84. **863, 866, 874**

Deese, J. On the structure of associative meaning. *Psychological Review*, 1962, *69*, 161-175. **1129**

Deese, J. *The structure of associations in language and thought.* Baltimore: The Johns Hopkins University Press, 1965. **848, 850, 877, 878, 880, 882, 883, 885**

Deese, J., & Marder, V. J. The pattern of errors in delayed recall of serial learning after interpolation. *American Journal of Psychology*, 1957, *70*, 594-599. **1091**

de Lange, H. Relationship between critical flicker frequency and a set of low-frequency characteristics of the eye. *Journal of the Optical Society of America*, 1954, *44*, 380-389. **311**

de Lange, H. Research into the dynamic nature of the human fovea-cortex systems with intermittent and modulated light: I. Attenuation characteristics with white and colored light. *Journal of the Optical Society of America*, 1958, *48*, 777-784. **313**

DeLattre, P. C., *see* Cooper, F. S., 1952; Harris, E. S., 1958; Liberman, A. M., 1954, 1958.

Delgado, J. M. R., Roberts, W. W., & Miller, N. E. Learning motivated by electrical stimulation of the brain. *American Journal of Physiology*, 1954, *179*, 587-593. **643, 706**

Delk, J. L., & Fillenbaum, S. Differences in perceived color as a function of characteristic color. *American Journal of Psychology*, 1965, *78*, 290-293. **425**

De Lorenzo, A. J. Electron microscopic observations of the olfactory mucosa and olfactory nerve. *Journal of Biophysics, Biochemistry and Cytology*, 1957, *3*, 839-850. **195, 196, 197**

de Lorge, J., *see* Bolles, R. C., 1962.

Dember, W. N., & Purcell, D. G. Recovery of masked visual targets by inhibition of the masking stimulus. *Science*, 1967, *157*, 1335-1336. **431**

Dember, W. N., *see also* Heckernmueller, E., 1965.

Dement, W., & Kleitman, N. Cyclic variations in EEG during sleep and their relation to eye movements, body motility and dreaming. *Electroencephalography and Clinical Neurophysiology*, 1957, *9*, 673-690. **372**

Dennis, W. Congenital cataract and unlearned behavior. *Journal of Genetic Psychology*, 1934, *44*, 340-351. **548**

Dennis, W. *Readings in the history of psychology.* New York: Appleton, 1948. **118**

Denny, M. R., *see* Weisman, R. G., 1966.

Derks, P. L. The generality of the "conditioning axiom" in human binary prediction. *Journal of Experimental Psychology*, 1962, *63*, 538-545. **921**

Derks, P. L. Effect of run length on the "gambler's fallacy." *Journal of Experimental Psychology*, 1963, *65*, 213-214. **921**

De Shazo, D., *see* Epstein, W., 1961.

De Silva, H. R. An analysis of the visual perception of movement. *British Journal of Psychology*, 1929, *19*, 268-305. **527, 528**

De Silva, H. R. The perception of movement. In E. G. Boring, H. S. Langfeld, & H. P. Weld (Eds.), *Psychology.* New York: Wiley, 1935. **528**

De Sisto, M. J., & McLaughlin, S. C. Change in judgment of direction of gaze after autokinetic perception. *Psychonomic Science*, 1968, *10*, 221-222. **530**

De Sisto, M. J., *see also* McLaughlin, S. C., 1969.

Desmedt, J. E. Neurophysiological mechanisms controlling acoustic output. In G. Rasmussen & W. A. Windle (Eds.), *Neural mechanisms of the auditory and vestibular systems.* Springfield, Ill.: Charles C Thomas, 1960. **233**

Desmedt, J. E. Auditory-evoked potentials from cochlea to cortex as influenced by activation of the efferent olivo-cochlear bundle. *Journal of the Acoustical Society of America*, 1962, *34*, 1478-1496. **233**

De Soto, C. B., & Bosley, J. J. The cognitive structure of a social structure. *Journal of Abnormal and Social Psychology*, 1962, *64*, 303-307. **889**

Detambel, M. H. A test of a model for multiple-choice behavior. *Journal of Experimental Psychology*, 1955, *49*, 97-104. **932**

Dethier, V. G., *see* Pfaffmann, C., 1954.

de Toledo, L. & Black, A. H. Heart rate: Changes during conditioned suppression in rats. *Science*, 1966, *152*, 1404-1406. **713**

Deutsch, D., *see* Deutsch, J. A., 1966.

Deutsch, J. A. A theory of shape recognition. *British Journal of Psychology*, 1955, *46*, 30-37. **450**

Deutsch, J. A. The statistical theory of figural aftereffects and acuity. *British Journal of Psychology*, 1956, *57*, 208-215. **472**

Deutsch, J. A. Neurophysiological contrast phenomena and figural aftereffects. *Psychological Review*, 1964, *71*, 19-26. **473**

Deutsch, J. A., & Deutsch, D. Attention: Some theoretical considerations. *Psychological Review*, 1963, *70*, 80-90. **769**

Deutsch, J. A., & Deutsch, D. *Physiological psychology.* Homewood, Ill.: Dorsey Press, 1966. **658**

Deutsch, J. A., & Howarth, C. I. Some tests of a theory of intracranial self-stimulation. *Psychological Review*, 1963, *70*, 444-460. **659**

Deutsch, J. A., & Jones, A. D. Diluted water: An explanation of the rat's preference for saline. *Journal of Comparative and Physiological Psychology*, 1960, *53*, 122-127. **190**

DeValois, R. Behavioral and electrophysiological studies of primate vision. In *Contributions to sensory psychology.* New York: Academic Press, 1965. **325, 327**

DeValois, R. L., Jacobs, G. H., & Abramov, I. Responses of single cells in visual system to shifts in the wavelength of light. *Science*, 1964, *146*, 1184-1186. **334**

DeValois, R. L., Jacobs, G. H., & Jones, A. E. Responses of single cells in primate red-green color vision system. *Optik*, 1963, *20*, 87. **334**

DeValois, R. L., & Walraven, J. Monocular and binocular aftereffects of chromatic adaptation. *Science*, 1967, *155*, 463. **336**

DeVito, J. L., & Smith, O. A., Jr. Effects of temperature and food deprivation on the random activity of *Macaca Mulatta*. *Journal of Comparative and Physiological Psychology*, 1959, *52*, 29-32. **824**

DeVoe, R. D. Linear superposition of retinal action potentials to predict electrical flicker responses from the eye of the wolf spider, *Lycosa baltimoriana* (Keyserling). *Journal of General Physiology*, 1962, *46*, 75-96. **311**

DeWardener, H. E., & Herxheimer, A. The effect of a high water intake on salt consumption, taste thresholds and salivary secretion in man. *Journal of Physiology*, 1957, *139*, 53-63. **189**

Dews, P. B. Free-operant behavior under conditions of delayed reinforcement: I. CRF-type schedules. *Journal of the Experimental Analysis of Behavior*, 1960, *3*, 221-234. **684**

Diamant, H., Funakoshi, M. Ström, L., & Zotterman, Y. Electrophysiological studies on human taste nerves. In Y. Zotterman (Ed.), *Olfaction and taste*. Vol. 1. New York: Pergamon, 1963. Pp. 193-203. **174, 175**

Diamant, H., see also Borg, G., 1967.

Diamond, A. L. Foveal simultaneous brightness contrast as a function of inducing and test-field luminances. *Journal of Experimental Psychology*, 1953, *45*, 304-315. **411**

Diamond, A. L. Foveal simultaneous contrast as a function of inducing-field area. *Journal of Experimental Psychology*, 1955, *50*, 144-152. **410**

Diamond, A. L. A Theory of depression and enhancement in the brightness response. *Psychological Review*, 1960, *67*, 168-199. **412**

Diamond, I. T., see Masterton, R. B., 1968.

Di Cara, L. V., & Miller, N. E. Changes in heart rate instrumentally learned by curarized rats as avoidance responses. *Journal of Comparative and Physiological Psychology*, 1968, *65*, 8-12. **839**

Dicken, C. F. Connotative meaning as a determinant of stimulus generalization. *Psychological Monographs*, 1961, *75*, No. 505. **1048**

Dietzel, H. Untersuchungen uber die optische Lokalisation der Mediane. *Zeitschrift für Biologie*, 1924, *80*, 289-316. **534**

Di Lollo, V. Runway performance in relation to runway-goal-box similarity and changes in incentive amount. *Journal of Comparative and Physiological Psychology*, 1964, *58*, 327-329. **633, 634, 635**

Di Lollo, V., & Beez, V. Negative contrast effect as a function of magnitude of reward decrement. *Psychonomic Science*, 1966, *5*, 99-100. **634, 635**

Dingman, H. F., see Guilford, J. P., 1954, 1955.

Dinner, J. E., & Duncan, C. P. Warm-up in retention as a function of degree of verbal learning. *Journal of Experimental Psychology*, 1959, *57*, 257-261. **1040**

Dinnerstein, A. J. Image size and instructions in the perception of depth. *Journal of Experimental Psychology*, 1967, *75*, 525-528. **496, 497**

Dinnerstein, A. J., see also Gruber, H. E., 1965.

Dinnerstein, D. & Wertheimer, M. Some determinants of phenomenal overlapping. *American Journal of Psychology*, 1957, *70*, 21-37. **498**

Dinsmoor, J. A. A quantitative comparison of the discriminative and reinforcing functions of a stimulus. *Journal of Experimental Psychology*, 1950, *40*, 458-472. **674**

Dinsmoor, J. A. Punishment: I. The avoidance hypothesis. *Psychological Review*, 1954, *61*, 34-46. **734**

Dinsmoor, J. A., & Campbell, S. L. Escape-from-shock training following exposure to inescapable shock. *Psychological Reports*, 1956, *2*, 43-49. **723**

Ditchburn, R. W. Eye movements in relation to retinal action. *Optica Acta*, 1955, *1*, 171-176. **387**

Ditchburn, R. W., & Fender, D. H. The stabilized retinal image. *Optica Acta*, 1955, *2*, 128-133. **386**

Ditchburn, R. W., & Ginsborg, B. L. Vision with a stabilized retinal image. *Nature*, 1952, *170*, 36-37. **305, 306, 374, 375**

Ditchburn, R. W., see also Clowes, M. B., 1959.

Ditrichs, R., see Martin, R. B., 1966.

Dittmar, D. G., see Grant, D. A., 1940.

Dixon, W. F., & Massey, F. J. *Introduction to statistical analysis*. New York: McGraw-Hill, 1956. Pp. 279-286. **20**

Djang, S. S. The role of past experience in the visual apprehension of masked forms. *Journal of Experimental Psychology*, 1937, *20*, 25-59. **440**

Dobelle, W. H., see Marks, W. B., 1964.

Dodd, D. H., and Bourne, L. E., Jr. *A direct test of some assumptions of a hypothesis-testing model of concept identification*. Program on Cognitive Processes Report No. 101. Institute of Behavioral Science, University of Colorado, 1967. **957, 970**

Dodd, D. H., see also Bourne, L. E. Jr., 1965.

Dodge, R. An experimental study of visual fixation. *Psychological Review*, Monograph Supplement, 1907, *8*, 4, 1-95. **372**

Dodge, S. H., see Walk, R. D., 1962.

Dodson, J. D., see Yerkes, R. M., 1908.

Dodt, E., & Wirth, A. Differentiation between rods and cones by flicker electroretinography in pigeon and guinea pig. *Acta physiologica Scandinavica*, 1953, *30*, 80-89. **311**

Dodwell, P. C. Coding and learning in shape discrimination. *Psychological Review*, 1961, *68*, 373-382. **450**

Dodwell, P. C. A coupling system for coding and learning shape discrimination. *Psychological Review*, 1964, *71*, 148-159. **450**

Dodwell, P. C., & Engel, G. R. A theory of binocular fusion. *Nature*, 1963, *198*, 39-40. **490**

Dodwell, P. C., & Gaze, L. The role of experience without set in figural after-effects. *Psychonomic Science*, 1965, *2*, 277-278. **470**

Dodwell, P. C., see also Gaze, L., 1965.

Doerr, H. O., & Hokanson, J. E. Food deprivation, performance, and heart rate in the rat. *Journal of Comparative and Physiological Psychology*, 1968, *65*, 227-231. **836**

Doetsch, G. S., see Erickson, R. P., 1965.

Dolan, T. R., & Robinson, D. E. Explanation of masking-level differences that result from interaural intensive disparities of noise. *Journal of the Acoustical Society of America*, 1967, *42*, 977-981. **243**

Dollard, J., & Miller, N. E. *Personality and psychotherapy*. New York: McGraw-Hill, 1950. **780**

Dollard, J., see also Miller, N. E., 1941.

Dominowski, R. L. Role of memory in concept learning. *Psychological Bulletin*, 1965, *63*, 271-280. **975**

Donderi, D. C., & Kane, E. Perceptual learning produced by common responses to different stimuli. *Canadian Journal of Psychology*, 1965, *19*, 15-30. **454**

Doty, R. W. Electrical stimulation of the brain in behavioral context. *Annual Review of Psychology*, 1969, *20*, 289-320. **564**

Douglas, W. W., & Ritchie, J. M. Mammalian nonmyelinated nerve fibers. *Physiological Review*, 1962, *42*, 297-334. **162**

Dove, H. W. Die Combination der Eindrücke beider Ohren

und beider Augen zu einem Eindruck. *Berliner preussische Akademie Wissenschaften,* 1841, 251–252. Cited in C. Osgood, *Method and theory in experimental psychology,* New York: Oxford University Press, 1953, 270. **491n**

Döving, K. B. Studies on the responses of bulbar neurons of frog to different odour stimuli. *Revue de Laryngologie* (Bordeaux), 1965, *86,* 845–854. **216**

Döving, K. B. An electrophysiological study of odour similarities of homologous substances. *Journal of Physiology,* 1966, *186,* 97–109. (a) **216**

Döving, K. B. Analysis of odour similarities from electrophysiological data. *Acta Physiologica Scandinavica,* 1966, *68,* 404–418. (b) **216**

Dowling, B., see Inglett, G. E., 1965.

Dowling, J. E. The site of visual adaptation. *Science,* 1967, *155,* 273–279. **287, 288, 289**

Dowling, J. E., & Boycott, B. B. Organization of the primate retina: Electron microscopy. *Proceedings of the Royal Society* (London), Ser. B, 1966, *166,* 80–111. **279**

Draguns, J., see Flavell, J. H., 1958.

Draper, D. O., see Pollio, H. R., 1966.

Dravnieks, A. Physicochemical basis of olfaction. *Annals of the New York Academy of Science,* 1964, *116,* 429–439. **220**

Dreher, J. J., see Moser, H. M., 1955.

Drury, M. B. Progressive changes in non-foveal perception of line patterns. *American Journal of Psychology,* 1933, *45,* 628–646. **443**

Dry, R. M. L., see Armstrong, D., 1951.

Dubrovsky, N., see Brugge, J. F., 1964.

Ducharme, R. Activité physique et déactivation: Baisse du rhythme cardiaquè au cours de l'activité instrumentale. *Canadian Journal of Psychology,* 1966, *20,* 445–454. (a) **835**

Ducharme, R. Effect of internal and external cues on the heart rate of the rat. *Canadian Journal of Psychology,* 1966, *20,* 97–104. (b) **829, 835, 836**

Ducharme, R., & Bélanger, D. Influence d'une stimulation électrique sur le niveau d'activation et la performance. *Canadian Journal of Psychology,* 1961, *15,* 61–68. **828, 829, 835**

Duda, W. L., see Rochester, H., 1956.

Dudley, D., see Alpern, M., 1966.

Duffy, E. *Activation and behavior.* New York: Wiley, 1962. **831**

Duffy, E., & Lacey, O. L. Adaptation in energy mobilization: Changes in general level of palmar conductance. *Journal of Experimental Psychology,* 1946, *36,* 437–452. **834**

Dufort, R. H. Adjustment of the rat to 23-, 47-, and 71-hour water-deprivation schedules. *Psychological Reports,* 1963, *13,* 243–250. (a) **819**

Dufort, R. H. Weight loss in rats continuously deprived of food, water, and both food and water. *Psychological Reports,* 1963, *12,* 307–312. (b) **816**

Dufort, R. H. Additional evidence on the rat's adjustment to the 71-hour water-deprivation schedule. *Psychological Reports,* 1964, *15,* 518. (a) **819**

Dufort, R. H. The rat's adjustment to 23-, 47-, and 71-hour food-deprivation schedules. *Psychological Reports,* 1964, *14,* 663–669. (b) **815, 818, 819, 820**

Dufort, R. H., & Wright, J. H. Food intake as a function of duration of food deprivation. *Journal of Psychology,* 1962, *53,* 465–468. **815**

Dufort, R. H., see also Kimble, G. A., 1955.

Dufresne, C. Influence de la privation de nourriture sur le rhythme cardiaque et l'activité instrumentale. Unpublished master's thesis, Université de Montréal, 1961. **828, 829, 835**

Duncan, C. P. Transfer after training with single versus multiple tasks. *Journal of Experimental Psychology,* 1958, *55,* 63–72. **1042**

Duncan, C. P. Descriptions of learning to learn in human subjects. *American Journal of Psychology,* 1960, *73,* 108–114. **1041**

Duncan, C. P., see also Berry, R. N., 1950; Dinner, J. E., 1959; Loess, H. B., 1952; Porter, L. W., 1953; Rockway, M. R., 1952.

Duncan, D. G., see Kenshalo, D. R., 1967.

Duncker, K. Uber induzierte Bewegung. *Psychologische Forschung,* 1929, *12,* 180–259. **522, 528, 531**

Duncker, K. Induced motion. In W. D. Ellis (Ed.), *A source book of Gestalt psychology.* New York: Harcourt, Brace, 1938, Pp. 161–172. **522**

Duncker, K. The influence of past experience upon perceptual properties. *American Journal of Psychology,* 1939, *52,* 255–265. **424**

Dunham, P. J. Contrasted conditions of reinforcement: A selective critique. *Psychological Bulletin,* 1968, *69,* 295–315. **638n**

Dunham, P. J., & Kilps, B. Shifts in magnitude of reinforcement: Confounded factors or contrast effects? *Journal of Experimental Psychology,* 1969, *79,* 373–374. **634, 638n**

Dunn, H. K., see Barney, H. L., 1957.

Dunn, S., Bliss, J., & Siipola, E. Effects of impulsivity, introversion, and individual values upon association under free conditions. *Journal of Personality,* 1958, *26,* 61–76. **875**

Durlach, N. I. Equalization and cancellation theory of binaural masking-level difference. *Journal of the Acoustical Society of America,* 1963, *35,* 1206–1218. **242**

Durlach, N. I., see also Colburn, H. S., 1965.

Duryea, R. A., see Krauskopf, J., 1954.

Dustman, R. E., see Brown, H. M., 1966.

Dyal, J. A., see Sgro, J. A., 1967.

Dyson, G. M. The scientific basis of odour. *Chemistry and Industry,* 1938, *57,* 647–651. **220**

Dzendolet, E. A structure common to sweet-evoking compounds. *Perception and Psychophysics,* 1968, *3,* 65–68. **179**

Dzendolet, E., & Meiselman, H. L. Cation and anion contributions to gustatory quality of simple salts. *Perception and Psychophysics,* 1967, *2,* 601–604. (a) **178**

Dzendolet, E., & Meiselman, L. Gustatory quality changes as a function of solution concentration. *Perception and Psychophysics,* 1967, *2,* 29–33. (b) **179**

Eady, H., see Klumpp, R. G., 1956.

Earhard, B., & Earhard, M. Role of interference factors in three-stage mediation paradigms. *Journal of Experimental Psychology,* 1967, *73,* 526–531. **1075, 1077**

Earhard, B., & Mandler, G. Mediated associations, paradigms, controls, and mechanisms. *Canadian Journal of Psychology,* 1965, *19,* 346–378. (a) **1071, 1076**

Earhard, B., & Mandler, G. Pseudomediation: A reply and more data. *Psychonomic Science,* 1965, *3,* 137–138. (b) **1075, 1076, 1077**

Earhard, B., see also Mandler, G., 1964.

Earhard, M., see Earhard, B., 1967.

Earle, A. E., see Hall, K. R. L., 1952.

Eastmond, E. J., see Bassett, I. G., 1964.

Eayrs, J. T., see Moulton, D., 1960.

Ebbecke, U. Über das Sehen im Flimmerlicht. *Pflüger's Archiv für die Gesamte Physiologie des Menschen und der Tiere,* 1920, *185,* 196–223. **314**

Ebbecke, U. Über die Temperaturempfindungen in ihrer Abhängigheit von der Hautdurchbluting und von den Reflexzentren. *Pflüger's Archiv fur die Gesamte Physiologie des Menschen und der Tiere,* 1917, *169,* 395–462. **153**

Ebbinghaus, H. *Memory: A contribution to experimental psychology:* 1885. (H. A. Ruger & C. E. Bussenius, Tr.) New York: Teachers College, Columbia University, 1913. **980, 982, 1013**

Ebbinghaus, H. *Über das Gedächtnis.* Leipzig: Duncker & Humbolt, 1885. (H. A. Ruger & C. E. Bussenius, Tr.) New York: Teachers College, 1913. Reissued, New York: Dover, 1964. **592, 598, 601, 847, 848, 854, 1107**

Ebbinghaus, H. *Grundzüge der Psychologie,* Vol. II. Leipzig: Dürr, E., Fortges, 1913. **463**

Ebeling, E., see Ritchie, B. F., 1950.

Ebenholtz, S., see Rock, I., 1959, 1962.

Ebenholtz, S. M. Position mediated transfer between serial learning and a spatial discrimination task. *Journal of Experimental Psychology,* 1963, *65,* 603–608. (a) **1012**

Ebenholtz, S. M. Serial learning: Position learning and sequential associations. *Journal of Experimental Psychology,* 1963, *66,* 353–362. (b) **1012, 1013**

Ebenholtz, S. M. Adaptation to a rotated visual field as a function of degree of optical tilt and exposure time. *Journal of Experimental Psychology,* 1966, *72,* 629–634. **539**

Ebenholtz, S. M., see also Asch, S. E., 1962.

Ebert, E., & Meumann, E. Über einige Grundfragen der Psychologie der Übungsphenomene im Bereiche des Gedächtnisses. *Archiv für die Gesamte Psychologie,* 1905, *4,* 1–232. **1030**

Ebrey, T. G. Fast light-evoked potential from leaves. *Science,* 1967, *155,* 1556–1557. **307**

Eckert, B., & Lewis, M. Competition between drives for intracranial stimulation and sodium chloride by adrenalectomized NaCl deprived rats. *Journal of Comparative and Physiological Psychology,* 1967, *64,* 349–352. **651**

Edes, B., & Dallenbach, K. M. The adaptation of pain aroused by cold. *American Journal of Psychology,* 1936, *48,* 307–315. **159**

Edwards, B. J., see Nealey, S. M., 1960.

Edwards, W. Emmert's law and Euclid's optics. *American Journal of Psychology,* 1950, *63,* 607–612. **511**

Edwards, W. Apparent size of after-images under conditions of reduction. *American Journal of Psychology,* 1953, *66,* 449–455. **511**

Edwards, W. Reward probability, amount, and information as determiners of sequential two-alternative decisions. *Journal of Experimental Psychology,* 1956, *52,* 177–188. **918**

Edwards, W. Probability learning in 1000 trials. *Journal of Experimental Psychology,* 1961, *962,* 385–394. **918, 920, 921**

Edwards, W., see also Boring, E. G., 1951; Lindman, H., 1961.

Efstathiou, A., Bauer, J., Greene, M., & Held, R. Altered reaching following adaptation to optical displacement of the hand. *Journal of Experimental Psychology,* 1967, *73,* 113–120. **538**

Efstathiou, A., see also Held, R., 1966.

Egan, J. P. Articulation testing methods. *The Laryngoscope,* 1948, *58,* 955–991. **254, 255**

Egan, J. P. Hearing. In C. P. Stone (Ed.), *Annual review of psychology.* Vol. 5. Stanford: Annual Reviews, Inc., 1954. **240**

Egan, J. P. Masking-level differences as a function of interaural disparities in intensity of signal and noise. *Journal of the Acoustical Society of America,* 1965, *38,* 1043–1049. **243**

Egan, J. P., Carterette, E. C., & Thwing, E. J. Some factors affecting multichannel listening. *Journal of the Acoustical Society of America,* 1954, *26,* 774–782. **259**

Egan, J. P., & Hake, H. W. On the masking pattern of a simple auditory stimulus. *Journal of the Acoustical Society of America,* 1950, *22,* 622–630. **238, 239**

Egan, J. P., & Wiener, F. M. On the intelligibility of bands of speech in noise. *Journal of the Acoustical Society of America,* 1946, *18,* 435–441. **257**

Egbert, L. D., see Smith, G. M., 1966.

Egger, M. D., & Miller, N. E. Secondary reinforcement in rats as a function of information value and reliability of the stimulus. *Journal of Experimental Psychology,* 1962, *64,* 97–104. **556, 675, 676**

Egger, M. D., & Miller, N. E. When is a reward reinforcing?: An experimental study of the information hypothesis. *Journal of Comparative and Physiological Psychology,* 1963, *56,* 132–137. **556, 676**

Ehmann, E. D., see Erickson, J. R., 1966.

Ehmer, R. H. Masking by tones vs. noise bands. *Journal of the Acoustical Society of America,* 1959, *31,* 1253–1256. **239**

Ehrenfreund, D. An experimental test of the continuity theory of discrimination with pattern vision. *Journal of Comparative Psychology,* 1948, *41,* 408–422. **749, 766**

Ehrenfreund, D. The relationship between weight loss during deprivation and food consumption. *Journal of Comparative and Physiological Psychology,* 1959, *52,* 123–125. **812**

Ehrenfreund, D. The motivational effect of a continuous weight loss schedule. *Psychological Reports,* 1960, *6,* 339–345. **819**

Ehrenfreund, D., & Badia, P. R. Response strength as a function of drive level and pre- and post-shift incentive magnitude. *Journal of Experimental Psychology,* 1962, *63,* 468–471. **633, 634**

Ehrenfreund, D., see also Alberts, E., 1951.

Ehrlich, D., see Orbach, J., 1963.

Eijkman, E. G., see Vendrik, A. J. H., 1968.

Eimas, P. D., see Shepp, B. E., 1964.

Eisenberger, R., Karpman, M., & Trattner, J. What is the necessary and sufficient condition for reinforcement in the contingency situation? *Journal of Experimental Psychology,* 1967, *74,* 342–350. **624**

Eisenstein, E. M., and Cohen, M. J. Learning in an isolated prothoracic insect ganglion. *Animal Behaviour,* 1965, *13,* 104–108. **578**

Eisler, H. On the problem of category scales in psychophysics. *Scandinavian Journal of Psychology,* 1962, *3,* 81–87. (a) **83**

Eisler, H. Empirical test of a model relating magnitude and category scales. *Scandinavian Journal of Psychology,* 1962, *3,* 88–96. (b) **83**

Eisler, H., see also Ekman, G., 1960.

Eisman, B. S. Attitude formation: The development of a color-preference response through mediated generalization. *Journal of Abnormal and Social Psychology,* 1955, *50,* 321–326. **781**

Eisman, E., Effects of deprivation and consummatory activity on heart rate. *Journal of Comparative and Physiological Psychology,* 1966, *62,* 71–75. **836, 838**

Eissler, K. Die Gestaltkonstanz der Sehdinge bei Variation der Objekte und ihrer Einwirkungsweise auf den Wahrnehmenden. *Archiv für die Gesamte Psychologie,* 1933, *88,* 487–550. **515**

Ekman, G. Discriminal sensitivity on the subjective continuum. *Acta psychologica,* 1956, *12,* 15–18. **83**

Ekman, G. Two generalized ratio scaling methods. *Journal of Psychology,* 1958, *45,* 287–295. **68, 71, 72**

Ekman, G. Weber's law and related functions. *Journal of Psychology,* 1959, *47,* 343–352. **18, 80, 81, 83**

Ekman, G. A methodological note on scales of gustatory intensity. *Scandinavian Journal of Psychology,* 1961, *2,* 185–190. **80, 81, 175**

Ekman, G. A simple method for fitting psychophysical power functions. *Journal of Psychology,* 1961, *51,* 343–350. **68**

Ekman, G. Measurement of moral judgment. *Perceptual and Motor Skills,* 1962, *15,* 3–9. **82**

Ekman, G. Is the power law a special case of Fechner's law? *Perceptual and Motor Skills,* 1964, *19,* 730. **85, 86n**

Ekman, G., & Akesson, C. Saltiness, sweetness and preference: A study of quantitative relations in individual subjects. *Reports from the Psychological Laboratories, The University of Stockholm,* 1964, *177,* 1-13. **175**

Ekman, G., Eisler, H., & Künnapas, T. Brightness of monocular light as measured by the method of magnitude production. *Acta Psychologica,* 1960, *17,* 392-397. **67**

Ekman, G., & Künnapas, T. Scales of aesthetic value. *Perceptual and Motor Skills,* 1962, *14,* 19-26. (a) **82**

Ekman, G., & Künnapas, T. Scales of aesthetic value by "direct" and "indirect" methods. *Scandinavian Journal of Psychology,* 1962, *3,* 33-39. (b) **82**

Ekman, G., & Künnapas, T. A further study of direct and indirect scaling methods. *Scandinavian Journal of Psychology,* 1963, *4,* 77-88. (a) **82**

Ekman, G., & Künnapas, T. Scales of conservatism. *Perceptual and Motor Skills,* 1963, *16,* 329-334. (b) **82**

Ekman, G., & Sjöberg, L. Scaling. *Annual Review of Psychology,* 1965, *16,* 451-474.

Ekman, G., see also Björkman, M., 1962.

Ekstrand, B. R. Backward associations. *Psychological Bulletin,* 1966, *65,* 60-64. **1060**

Ekstrand, B. R. Effect of sleep on memory. *Journal of Experimental Psychology,* 1967, *75,* 64-72. **1123**

Ekstrand, B. R., & Underwood, B. J. Free learning and recall as a function of unit-sequence and letter-sequence interference. *Journal of Verbal Learning and Verbal Behavior,* 1965, *4,* 390-396. **1128**

Ekstrand, B. R., Wallace, W. P., & Underwood, B. J. A frequency theory of verbal-discrimination learning. *Psychological Review,* 1966, *13,* 566-578. **854, 887, 898**

Ekstrand, B. R., see also Underwood, B. J., 1964, 1966, 1967a, b, 1968a, b.

Elam, C. B., see Bitterman, M. E., 1955.

Eldert, K., see Kirsh, I. J., 1952.

Eldredge, D. H., see Deatherage, B. H., 1957; Kryter, K. D., 1966; Tasaki, I., 1954; Teas, D. C., 1962.

Eldridge, R. G., & Johnson, J. C. Diffuse transmission through real atmospheres. *Journal of the Optical Society of America,* 1958, *48,* 463-468. **498**

Elfner, L. F., see Thurlow, W. R., 1959, 1961.

Elfner, L. L. Systematic shifts in the judgments of octaves of high frequencies. *Journal of the Acoustical Society of America,* 1964, *36,* 270-276. **243**

Ellen, P. The compulsive nature of abnormal fixations. *Journal of Comparative and Physiological Psychology,* 1956, *49,* 309-317. **791**

Ellen, P., see also Alpern, M., 1956; Feldman, R. S., 1951; Maier, N. R. F., 1951.

Ellington, N. R., & Kausler, D. H. "Fate" of List 1 associations in transfer theory. *Journal of Experimental Psychology,* 1965, *69,* 207-208. **1095**

Elliot, O., see Stanley, W. C., 1962.

Elliot, P. B. Tables of d'. In J. A. Swets (Ed.), *Signal detection and recognition by human observers.* New York: Wiley, 1964, 651-658. **42**

Elliott, D. N., see Baker, L. M., 1948.

Elliott, L. L. Backward masking: Monotic and dichotic conditions. *Journal of the Acoustical Society of America,* 1962, *34,* 1108-1115. (a) **241**

Elliott, L. L. Backward and forward masking of probe tones of different frequencies. *Journal of the Acoustical Society of America,* 1962, *34,* 1116-1117. (b) **241**

Elliott, M. H. The effect of change of reward on the maze performance of rats. *University of California Publications in Psychology,* 1928, *4,* 19-30. **617**

Elliott, M. H. Some determining factors in maze performance. *American Journal of Psychology,* 1930, *42,* 315-317. **617**

Elliott, M. H., see also Bousfield, W. A., 1934.

Ellis, N. R. Object-quality discrimination learning sets in mental defectives. *Journal of Comparative and Physiological Psychology,* 1958, *51,* 79-81. **768**

Ellis, W. D. (Ed.) *A source book of Gestalt psychology.* London: Routledge, 1938. **764**

Emmerich, D., see Restle, F., 1966.

Emmers, R., see also Benjamin, R. M., 1968; Wayner, M. J. Jr., 1959.

Emery, D. A., see Köhler, W., 1947.

Engel, G. R., see Dodwell, P. C., 1963.

Engen, T. Effect of practice and instruction on olfactory threshold. *Perceptual and Motor Skills,* 1960, *10,* 195-198. **18, 207**

Engen, T. Direct scaling of odor intensity. *Reports from the Psychological Laboratories, The University of Stockholm,* 1961, *106.* **70, 204, 205**

Engen, T. The psychological similarity of the odors of the aliphatic alcohols. *Reports from the Psychological Laboratories, The University of Stockholm,* 1962, *127.* **215, 216**

Engen, T. Cross adaptation to aliphatic alcohols. *American Journal of Psychology,* 1963, *76,* 96-102. **215**

Engen, T. Psychophysical scaling of odor intensity and quality. *Annals of the New York Academy of Science,* 1964, *116,* 504-516. **200, 205**

Engen, T., Bartoshuk, L., & McBurney, D. H. The effect of food deprivation on the detection of sucrose in distilled water. Unpublished experiment, Brown University, 1964. **36, 43**

Engen, T. & Levy, N. The influence of context on constant-sum loudness-judgments. *American Journal of Psychology,* 1958, *71,* 731-736. **73**

Engen, T., Levy, N., and Schlosberg, H. The dimensional analysis of a new series of facial expressions. *Journal of Experimental Psychology,* 1958, *55,* 454-458. **56, 57**

Engen, T., & Lindström, C. O. Psychophysical scales of the odor intensity of amyl acetate. *Scandinavian Journal of Psychology,* 1963, *4,* 23-28. **75**

Engen, T., & Lipsitt, L. P. Decrement and recovery of responses to olfactory stimuli in the human neonate. *Journal of Comparative and Physiological Psychology,* 1965, *59,* 312-316. **590**

Engen, T., & McBurney, D. H. Magnitude and category scales of the pleasantness of odors. *Journal of Experimental Psychology,* 1964, *68,* 435-440. **64, 216**

Engen, T., & Pfaffmann, C. Absolute judgments of odor intensity. *Journal of Experimental Psychology,* 1959, *58,* 23-26. **199, 205**

Engen, T., & Tulunay, Ü. Some sources of error in half-heaviness judgments. *Journal of Experimental Psychology,* 1956, *54,* 208-212. **67, 70**

Enoch, J. M., see Boynton, R. M., 1954.

Enroth, C. The mechanism of flicker and fusion studied on single retinal elements in the dark-adapted eye of the cat. *Acta Physiologica Scandinavica,* 1952, *27,* Suppl. 100, 1-67. **314**

Entwisle, D. R. *Word associations of young children.* Baltimore: Johns Hopkins University Press, 1966. **861**

Entwisle, D. R., Forsyth, D. F., & Muus, R. The syntactic-paradigmatic shift in children's word associations. *Journal of Verbal Learning and Verbal Behavior,* 1964, *3,* 19-29. **874**

Epley, J. M., see Simmons, F. B., 1965.

Epstein, A. N. Reciprocal changes in feeding behavior produced by intra-hypothalamus chemical injections. *American Journal of Physiology,* 1960, *199,* 969-974. **651**

Epstein, A. N., & Teitelbaum, P. Regulation of food intake in the absence of taste, smell, and other oropharyngeal sensations. *Journal of Comparative and Physiological Psychology,* 1962, 753-759. **621n, 797**

Epstein, A. N., see also Teitelbaum, P., 1962, 1963.

Epstein, W. The influence of syntactical structure on learning. *American Journal of Psychology,* 1961, *74,* 80-85. **903**

Epstein, W. The known-size-apparent-distance hypothesis. *American Journal of Psychology*, 1961, 74, 333–346. **495, 506**

Epstein, W. Phenomenal orientation and perceived achromatic color. *Journal of Psychology*, 1961, 52, 51–53. **421**

Epstein, W. Backward association as a function of meaningfulness. *Journal of General Psychology*, 1962, 67, 11–20. (a) **857**

Epstein, W. A further study of the influence of syntactic structure on learning. *American Journal of Psychology*, 1962, 75, 121–126. (b) **903**

Epstein, W. The influence of assumed size on apparent distance. *American Journal of Psychology*, 1963, 76, 257–265. **495**

Epstein, W. Nonrelational judgment of size and distance. *American Journal of Psychology*, 1965, 78, 120–123. **495**

Epstein, W. *Varieties of perceptual learning.* New York: McGraw-Hill, 1967. **439, 440**

Epstein, W., & Baratz, S. S. Relative size in isolation as a stimulus for relative perceived distance. *Journal of Experimental Psychology*, 1964, 67, 507–513. **496**

Epstein, W., Bontrager, H., & Park, J. The induction of nonveridical slant and the perception of shape. *Journal of Experimental Psychology*, 1962, 63, 472–479. **509, 516**

Epstein, W., & DeShazo, D. Recency as a function of perceptual oscillation. *American Journal of Psychology*, 1961, 74, 215–223. **439**

Epstein, W., & Park, J. N. Shape constancy: Functional relationships and theoretical formulations. *Psychological Bulletin*, 1963, 60, 265–288. **507, 515**

Epstein, W., & Park, J. Examination of Gibson's psychophysical hypothesis. *Psychological Bulletin*, 1964, 62, 180–196. **505**

Epstein, W., Park, J., & Casey, A. The current status of the size-distance hypothesis. *Psychological Bulletin*, 1961, 58, 491–514. **507, 508, 510, 511**

Epstein, W., & Rock, I. Set as an artifact of recency. *American Journal of Psychology*, 1960, 73, 214–228. **439**

Erickson, J. R., & Zajkowski, M. M. Learning several concept-identification problems concurrently: A test of the sampling-with-replacement assumption. *Journal of Experimental Psychology*, 1967, 74, 212–218. **974**

Erickson, J. R., Zajkowski, M. M., & Ehmann, E. D. All-or-none assumptions in concept identification. *Journal of Experimental Psychology*, 1966, 72, 690–697. **957, 974**

Erickson, R. P. Sensory neural patterns and gustation. In Y. Zotterman (Ed.), *Olfaction and taste.* Vol. 1. New York: Pergamon Press, 1963. Pp. 205–213. **180**

Erickson, R. P., Doetsch, G. S., & Marshall, D. A. The gustatory neural response function. *Journal of General Physiology*, 1965, 49, 247–263. **180**

Erickson, R. P., *see also* Harper, H. W., 1966; Pfaffmann, C., 1961.

Erickson, T., *see* Penfield, W., 1941.

Eriksen, C. W. Unconscious processes. In M. R. Jones (Ed.), *Nebraska symposium on motivation: 1958.* Lincoln, Nebraska: University of Nebraska Press, 1958. **445n**

Eriksen, C. W., & Collins, J. F. Backward masking in vision. *Psychonomic Science*, 1964, 1, 101–102. **430**

Eriksen, C. W., Collins, J. F., Greenspoon, T. S. An analysis of certain factors responsible for nonmonotonic backward masking functions. *Journal of Experimental Psychology*, 1967, 75, 500–507. **430**

Eriksen, C. W., & Collins, J. F. Reinterpretation of one form of backward and forward masking in visual perception. *Journal of Experimental Psychology*, 1965, 70, 343–351. **430**

Eriksen, C. W., Greenspoon, T. S., Lappin, J., & Carlson, W. A. Binocular summation in the perception of form at brief durations. *Perception & Psychophysics*, 1966, 1, 415–419. **488**

Eriksen, C. W., & Hoffman, M. Form recognition at brief durations as a function of adapting field and interval between stimulations. *Journal of Experimental Psychology*, 1963, 66, 485–499. **430**

Eriksen, C. W., & Lappin, J. Luminance summation–contrast reduction as a basis for certain forward and backward masking effect. *Psychonomic Science*, 1964, 1, 313–314. **430**

Eriksen, C. W., & Lappin, J. S. Selective attention and very short-term recognition memory for nonsense forms. *Journal of Experimental Psychology*, 1967, 73, 358–364. **444**

Eriksen, C. W., & Steffy, R. A. Short-term memory and retroactive interference in visual perception. *Journal of Experimental Psychology*, 1964, 68, 423–434. **430**

Eriksen, C. W., *see also* Garner, W. R., 1956.

Erlebacher, A., & Sekuler, R. Explanation of the Müller-Lyer illusion: Confusion theory examined. *Journal of Experimental Psychology*, 1969, 80, 462–467. **463**

Erlebacher, A., *see also* Richardson, J., 1958.

Erulkar, S. A., *see* Nelson, P. G., 1966.

Ervin, S. M. Changes with age in the verbal determinants of word-association. *American Journal of Psychology*, 1961, 74, 361–372. **874**

Estes, W. K. An experimental study of punishment. *Psychological Monographs*, 1944, 57, Whole No. 263. **737, 738**

Estes, W. K. Toward a statistical theory of learning. *Psychological Review*, 1950, 57, 94–107. **908**

Estes, W. K. Statistical theory of distributional phenomena in learning. *Psychological Review*, 1955, 62, 369–377. **929**

Estes, W. K. The problem of inference from curves based on group data. *Psychological Bulletin*, 1956, 53, 134–140. **609, 917**

Estes, W. K. Stimulus-response theory of drive. In M. R. Jones (Ed.), *Nebraska symposium on motivation.* Lincoln, Nebraska: University of Nebraska Press, 1958. **801**

Estes, W. K. Component and pattern models with Markovian interpretations. In R. R. Bush & W. K. Estes (Eds.), *Studies in mathematical learning theory.* Stanford: Stanford University Press, 1959. Pp. 9–52. (a) **927, 990, 995, 1002**

Estes, W. K. The statistical approach to learning theory. In S. Koch (Ed.), *Psychology: A study of a science.* Vol. 2. New York: McGraw-Hill, 1959. Pp. 380–491. (b) **909, 910, 929**

Estes, W. K. Learning theory and the new "mental chemistry." *Psychological Review*, 1960, 67, 207–233. **987**

Estes, W. K. New developments in statistical behavior theory: Differential tests of axioms for associative learning. *Psychometrika*, 1961, 26, 73–84. **987, 988**

Estes, W. K. All-or-none processes in learning and retention. *American Psychologist*, 1964, 19, 16–25. (a) **987**

Estes, W. K. Probability learning. In A. W. Melton (Ed.), *Categories of human learning.* New York: Academic Press, 1964. Pp. 89–128. (b) **919, 922**

Estes, W. K. Transfer of verbal discriminations based on differential reward magnitudes. *Journal of Experimental Psychology*, 1966, 72, 276–283. **641**

Estes, W. K. Outline of a theory of punishment. In B. A. Campbell & R. M. Church (Eds.), *Punishment.* New York: Appleton, 1969. **738**

Estes, W. K., & Burke, C. J. A theory of stimulus variability in learning *Psychological Review*, 1953, 60, 276–286. **924**

Estes, W. K., & Burke, C. J. Application of a statistical model to simple discrimination learning in human subjects. *Journal of Experimental Psychology*, 1955, 50, 81–88. **930**

Estes, W. K., Burke, C. J., Atkinson, R. C., & Frankmann, J. B. Probabilistic discrimination learning. *Journal of Experimental Psychology*, 1957, 54, 233–239. **927**

Estes, W. K., & Hopkins, B. L. Acquisition and transfer in pattern-vs.-component discrimination learning. *Journal of Experimental Psychology*, 1961, *61*, 322-328. **927, 1002, 1003**

Estes, W. K., Hopkins, B. L., & Crothers, E. J. All-or-none and conservation effects in the learning and retention of paired-associates. *Journal of Experimental Psychology*, 1960, *60*, 329-339. **987, 989**

Estes, W. K., & Skinner, B. F. Some quantitative properties of anxiety. *Journal of Experimental Psychology*, 1941, *29*, 390-400. **712, 713**

Estes, W. K., & Straughan, J. H. Analysis of a verbal conditioning situation in terms of statistical learning theory. *Journal of Experimental Psychology*, 1954, *47*, 225-234. **908**

Estes, W. K., & Suppes, P. Foundations of linear models. In R. R. Bush & W. K. Estes (Eds.), *Studies in mathematical learning theory*. Stanford: Stanford University Press, 1959. Pp. 137-179. **911, 919, 922**

Estes, W. K., *see also* Atkinson, R. C., 1963; Binder, A., 1966; Burke, C. J., 1954, 1957; Friedman, M. P., 1964.

Etkin, M., *see* D'Amato, M. R., 1967.

Evans, C. R., & Piggins, D. J. A comparison of the behavior of geometrical shapes when viewed under conditions of steady fixation and with apparatus for producing a stabilized retinal image. *British Journal of Physiological Optics*, 1963, *20*, 1-13. **453**

Evans, D. R. Chemical structure and stimulation by carbohydrates. In Y. Zotterman (Ed.), *Olfaction and taste*. Vol. I. New York: Pergamon, 1963, Pp. 165-176. **190**

Evans, D. R., & Mellon, D. Stimulation of a primary taste receptor by salts. *Journal of General Physiology*, 1962, *45*, 651-661. **189**

Evans, E. F., *see* Whitefield, I. C., 1965.

Evans, R. M. *An introduction to color*. New York: Wiley, 1948. **319, 420**

Evans, R. M. Psychological aspects of color and illumination. *Illuminating Engineering* (New York) 1951, *46*, 176-184. **426, 427**

Evans, R. M. Variables of perceived color. *Journal of the Optical Society of America*, 1964, *54*, 1467-1473. **368**

Evarts, E. V. Relation of pyramidal tract activity to force exerted during voluntary movement. *Journal of Neurophysiology*, 1968, *31*, 14-27. **113**

Everett, N. B. *Functional neuroanatomy*. (5th ed.) Philadelphia: Lea & Febiger, 1965. **128**

Ewert, P. H. A study of the effect of inverted retinal stimulation upon spatially coordinated behavior. *Genetic Psychology Monographs*, 1930, *7*, 177-363. **533**

Exner, J. E., *see also* Smith, O. W., 1968.

Eysenck, M. D. An experimental and statistical study of olfactory preferences. *Journal of Experimental Psychology*, 1944, *34*, 246-252. **216**

Eyzaguirre, C., *see* Kuffler, S. W., 1955-56.

Fabian, F. W., & Blum, H. B. Relative taste potency of some basic food constituents and their competitive and compensatory action. *Food Research*, 1943, *8*, 179-193. **187**

Fagot, R. F., & Stewart, M. R. An experimental comparison of stimulus and response translated power functions for brightness. *Perception and Psychophysics*, 1968, *3*, 297-305. **81**

Fairbanks, G. Test for phonemic differentiation: The rhyme test. *Journal of the Acoustical Society of America*, 1958, *30*, 596-600. **255**

Fairbanks, G., & Kodman, F., Jr. Word intelligibility as a function of time compression. *Journal of the Acoustical Society of America*, 1957, *29*, 636-641. **257**

Fantino, E., & Herrnstein, R. J. Secondary reinforcement and number of primary reinforcements. *Journal of the Experimental Analysis of Behavior*, 1968, *11*, 9-14. **667**

Fantz, R. L. A method for studying depth perception in infants under six months of age. *Psychological Record*, 1961, *11*, 27-32. **547, 549**

Fantz, R. L. The origin of form perception. *Scientific American*, 1961, *204*, 66-72. **549**

Fantz, R. L. Ontogeny of perception. In A. M. Schrier, H. F. Harlow, & F. Stollnitz (Eds.), *Behavior of nonhuman primates: Modern research trends*. Vol. 2. New York: Academic Press, 1965. **549**

Farber, I. E. Response fixation under anxiety and non-anxiety conditions. *Journal of Experimental Psychology*, 1948, *38*, 111-131. **791**

Farber, I. E., *see also* Brown, J. S., 1951, 1968.

Farné, M. Ulteriore contributo allo studio degli stimoli marginali. (Another contribution to the study of marginal stimuli.) *Archivo di Psicologia, Neurologia e Psichiatria*, 1964, *25*, 444-463. **472**

Farné, M. Grado do discernibilita dello stimolo e comportamento percettivo. (Degree of stimulus discriminability and perceptual behavior.) *Archivo di Psicologia, Neurologia e Psichiatria*, 1965, *26*, 566-576. **469, 470n**

Farné, M., *see also* Canestrari, R., 1969.

Farnsworth, D. A temporal factor in colour discrimination. In *Visual problems of colour*. London: HM Stationery Office, 1958. **361**

Farnum, E. C., *see* Seashore, E. C., 1908.

Farrell, W. M., *see* Tallarico, R. B., 1964.

Frazzaro, J., *see* D'Amato, M. R., 1966, 1967.

Fechner, G. T. *Elemente der Psychophysik*. Leipzig: Breitkopf and Härterl, 1860. English translation of Vol. 1 by H. E. Adler (D. H. Howes and E. G. Boring, Eds.). New York: Holt, Rinehart and Winston, 1966. **11, 49, 82**

Feddersen, W. E., Sandel, T. T., Teas, D. C., & Jeffress, L. A. Localization of high frequency tones. *Journal of the Acoustical Society of America*, 1957, *29*, 989-991. **260**

Fedderson, W. E., *see also* Sandel, T. T., 1955.

Fehr, F. S., *see* Hahn, W. W., 1964.

Fehrer, E. Effects of amount of reinforcement and of pre- and post-reinforcement delays on learning and extinction. *Journal of Experimental Psychology*, 1956, *52*, 167-176. **619, 620**

Fehrer, E. Contribution of perceptual segregation to the relationship between stimulus similarity and backward masking. *Perceptual and Motor Skills*, 1965, *21*, 27-33. **430**

Fehrer, E. Effect of stimulus similarity on retroactive masking. *Journal of Experimental Psychology*, 1966, *71*, 612-615. **430**

Fehrer, E., & Biederman, I. A comparison of reaction and verbal report in the detection of masked stimuli. *Journal of Experimental Psychology*, 1962, *64*, 126-130. **430**

Fehrer, E., & Ganchrow, D. Effects of exposure variables on figural after-effects under tachistoscopic presentation. *Journal of Experimental Psychology*, 1963, *66*, 506-513. **469**

Fehrer, E., & Raab, D. Reaction time to stimuli masked by metacontrast. *Journal of Experimental Psychology*, 1962, *63*, 143-147. **430**

Fehrer, E. & Smith, E. Effect of luminance ratio on masking. *Perceptual and Motor Skills*, 1962, *14*, 243-253. **430**

Fehrer. E. V., *see also* Helson, H., 1932.

Feigenbaum, E. A. *An information processing theory of verbal learning*. Report P-1817. Santa Monica. The RAND Corporation, 1959. **1008, 1016**

Feigenbaum, E. A. The simulation of verbal learning. In E. A. Feigenbaum & J. Feldman (Eds.), *Computers and thought*. New York: McGraw-Hill, 1963. Pp. 297-309. **1008**

Feigenbaum, E. A., & Simon, H. A. Comment: The distinctiveness of stimuli. *Psychological Review*, 1961, *68*, 285-288. **1008, 1017**

Feigenbaum, E. A., & Simon, H. A. A theory of the serial

position effect. *British Journal of Psychology*, 1962, *53*, 307-320. **1008, 1013, 1016**

Feigenbaum, E. A., & Simon, H. A. Brief notes on the EPAM theory of verbal learning. In C. N. Cofer & B. S. Musgrave (Eds.), *Verbal behavior and learning: Problems and processes*. New York: McGraw-Hill, 1963. Pp. 333-335. **1008**

Feigenbaum, E. A., *see also* Simon, H. A., 1964.

Feinberg, L. D., *see* Flavell, J. H., 1958.

Feirstein, A. R., & Miller, N. E. Learning to resist pain and fear: Effects of electric shock before versus after reaching goal. *Journal of Comparative and Physiological Psychology*, 1963, *56*, 797-800. **706, 737**

Feldman, J. An analysis of prediction behavior in a two-choice situation. In E. A. Feigenbaum & J. Feldman (Eds.), *Computers and thought*. New York: McGraw-Hill, 1963. **907**

Feldman, J., & Hanna, J. F. The structure of responses to a sequence of binary events. *Journal of Mathematical Psychology*, 1966, *3*, 371-387. **936**

Feldman, R. S. An automatically controlled Lashley discrimination mechanism. *American Journal of Psychology*, 1948, *61*, 414-419. **749, 750**

Feldman, R. S., & Ellen, P. Frustration and fixation. (Film.) Pennsylvania State College: Psychological Cinema Register, 16 mm sound, 1951. **791**

Feldman, R. S., *see also* Zwislocki, J., 1956.

Feldman, S., *see* Laffal, J., 1962-63.

Feldman, S. E., *see* Binder, A., 1960.

Feldman, S. M., & Underwood, B. J. Stimulus recall following paired-associate learning. *Journal of Experimental Psychology*, 1957, *53*, 11-15. **893**

Feldman, S. M., *see also* Belanger, D., 1962.

Feller, W. *An introduction to probability theory and its applications*. (2nd ed.) New York: Wiley, 1957. **995**

Fender, D. H. Torsional motions of the eyeball. *British Journal of Ophthalmology*, 1955, *39*, 65-72. **374**

Fender, D. H., & Nye, P. W. An investigation of the mechanisms of eye movement control. *Kybernetik*, 1961, *1*, 81-88. **379**

Fender, D. H., *see also* Ditchburn, R. W., 1955.

Ferguson, C. V., *see* Langmuir, I., 1944.

Fernberger, S. W. New phenomena of apparent visual movement. *American Journal of Psychology*, 1934, *46*, 309-314. **527**

Fernberger, S. W. The figural after-effect in the third dimension of visual space. *American Journal of Psychology*, 1948, *61*, 291-293. **470**

Ferrall, S. C., & Dallenbach, K. M. The analysis and synthesis of burning heat. *American Journal of Psychology*, 1930, *42*, 72-82. **148**

Ferster, C. B. Sustained behavior under delayed reinforcement. *Journal of Experimental Psychology*, 1953, *48*, 218-224. **684**

Ferster, C. B. The use of the free operant in the analysis of behavior. *Psychological Bulletin*, 1953, *50*, 263-274. **747**

Ferster, C. B., & Skinner, B. F. *Schedules of reinforcement*. New York: Appleton, 1957. **604, 605, 607, 608, 665, 697, 698**

Festinger, L., Ono, H., Burnham, C. A., & Bamber, D. Efference and the conscious experience of perception. *Journal of Experimental Psychology Monograph*, 1967. Whole No. 637. **453, 542**

Festinger, L., White, C. W., & Allyn, M. R. Eye movements and decrement in the Müller-Lyer illusion. *Perception and Psychophysics*, 1968, *3*, 376-382. **467n**

Festinger, L., *see also* Coren, S., 1967.

Fex, J. Auditory activity in centrifugal and centripetal cochlear fibers in cat. *Acta Physiologica Scandinavia*, Suppl. 189, 1962, *55*, 1-68. **233**

Ficks, L., *see* Pollack, I., 1954.

Filion, R. D. C., *see* Harcum, E. R., 1963.

Fillenbaum, S., & Jones, L. V. Grammatical contingencies in word association. *Journal of Verbal Learning and Verbal Behavior*, 1965, *4*, 248-255. **874**

Fillenbaum, S., *see also* Delk, J. L., 1965.

Finch, G., *see also* Culler, E., 1935.

Findley, J. D. Preference and switching under concurrent scheduling. *Journal of the Experimental Analysis of Behavior*, 1958, *1*, 123-145. **641**

Finger, F. W. Quantitative studies of "conflict:" I. Variations in latency and strength of the rat's response in a discrimination-jumping situation. *Journal of Comparative Psychology*, 1941, *31*, 97-127. **749**

Finger, F. W. Estrous activity as a function of measuring device. *Journal of Comparative and Physiological Psychology*, 1961, *54*, 524-526. **825**

Finger, F. W., Reid, L. S., & Weasner, M. H. Activity changes as a function of reinforcement under low drive. *Journal of Comparative and Physiological Psychology*, 1960, *53*, 385-387. **823**

Finger, F. W., & Spelt, D. K. The illustration of the horizontal-vertical illusion. *Journal of Experimental Psychology*, 1947, *37*, 243-250. **458**

Finger, F. W., *see also* Reid, L. S., 1955.

Fink, E., *see* Weisberg, P., 1966.

Fink, J. B., & Patton, R. M. Decrement of a learned drinking response accompanying changes in several stimulus characteristics. *Journal of Comparative and Physiological Psychology*, 1953, *46*, 23-27. **818**

Finn, J., *see* Johnson, T. J., 1965.

Fischer, B. Der Einfluss der Blickrichtung und Änderung der Kopfstellung (Halsreflex) auf die Bárányshen Zeigversuch. *Jahrbach der Psychiatrie und Neurologie*, 1915, *35*, 155-158. **534**

Fischer, G. J. Discrimination and successive spatial reversal learning in chicks that fail to imprint vs. ones that imprint strongly. *Perceptual and Motor Skills*, 1966, *23*, 579-584. **585**

Fischer, R. Genetics and gustatory chemoreception in man and other primates. In M. R. Kare & O. Maller (Eds.), *The chemical senses and nutrition*. Baltimore: Johns Hopkins Press, 1967. Pp. 61-81. **182**

Fischer, R., & Griffin, F. Pharmacogenetic aspects of gustation. *Arzneimittel-Forschung (Drug Research)*, 1964, *14*, 673-686. **182, 190**

Fishback, J., *see* Köhler, W., 1950.

Fisher, G. L. Saline preference in rats determined by contingent licking. *Journal of the Experimental Analysis of Behavior*, 1965, *8*, 295-303. **190**

Fisher, G. L., Pfaffmann, C., & Brown, E. Dulcin and saccharin taste in squirrel monkeys, rats, and man. *Science*, 1965, *150*, 506-507. **628**

Fisher, G. L., *see also* Pfaffmann, C., 1967.

Fisher, L., *see* Weinstein, S., 1964.

Fisher, R. A. *The design of experiments*. Edinburgh: Oliver & Boyd, 1935. **599**

Fisher, S. C., Hull, C., & Holtz, P. Past experience and perception: Memory color. *Amer. J. Psychol.*, 1956, *69*, 546-560. **425**

Fiske, D. W., & Maddi, S. R. (Eds.), *Functions of varied experience*. Homewood, Ill.: Dorsey Press, 1961. **841**

Fitch, F. B., *see* Hull, C. L., 1940.

Fitts, P. M. Perceptual-motor skill learning. In A. W. Melton (Ed.), *Categories of human learning*. New York: Academic Press, 1964, Pp. 243-285. **979**

Fitts, P. M., & Leonard, J. A. *Stimulus correlates of visual pattern recognition: A probability approach*. Columbus: Ohio State University Press, 1957.

Fitts, P. M., Meyer, W., Rappoport, M., Anderson, N. S., & Leonard, J. A. Stimulus correlates of visual pattern recognition: A probability approach. *Journal of Experimental Psychology*, 1956, *51*, 1-11. **447n**

FitzHugh, R., see Barlow, H. B., 1957.

Flanagan, J. L. Speech analysis, synthesis, and perception. New York: Academic Press, 1956. **229, 231, 251, 252, 253**

Flaugher, R. L., see Nunnally, J. C., 1963.

Flavell, J. H. Meaning and meaning similarity: II. The semantic differential and co-occurrence as predictors of judged similarity in meaning. Journal of General Psychology, 1961, 54, 321-335. **901**

Flavell, J. H., Draguns, J., Feinberg, L. D., & Budin, W. A microgenetic approach to word association. Journal of Abnormal and Social Psychology, 1958, 57, 1-7. **863**

Flavell, J. H., & Johnson, B. A. Meaning and meaning similarity: III. Latency and number of similarities as predictors of judged similarity in meaning. Journal of General Psychology, 1961, 64, 337-348. **901**

Fleck F., see Rock, I., 1950.

Fleshler, M., see Hoffman, H. S., 1961, 1962, 1964.

Fletcher, H. Speech and hearing. Princeton, N.J.: Van Nostrand, 1929. **257**

Fletcher, H. Loudness, pitch and timbre of musical tones and their relation to the intensity, the frequency, and the overtone structure. Journal of the Acoustical Society of America, 1934, 6, 59-69. **244, 245**

Fletcher, H. Auditory patterns. Review of Modern Physics, 1940, 12, 47-65. **240**

Fletcher, H. The pitch, loudness, and quality of musical tones. American Journal of Physics, 1946, 14, 215-225. **226**

Fletcher, H. Speech and hearing in communication. Princeton, N.J.: Van Nostrand, 1953. **250, 254, 256, 257**

Fletcher, J. L., & Riopelle, A. Protective effect of the acoustic reflex for impulsive noises. Journal of the Acoustical Society of America, 1960, 32, 401. **236**

Flock, H. R. A possible optical basis for monocular slant perception. Psychological Review, 1964, 71, 380-391. (a) **501, 502, 505, 516**

Flock, H. R. Three theoretical views of slant perception. Psychological Bulletin, 1964, 62, 110-121. (b) **501, 502, 505, 516**

Flock, H. R. Optical texture and linear perspective as stimuli for slant perception. Psychological Review, 1965, 72, 505-514. **502, 505**

Flock, H. R., Wilson, A., & Poizner, S. Lightness matching for different visual routes through a compound scene. Perception and Psychophysics, 1966, 1, 382-384. **421**

Flom, M. C., Weymouth, F. W., & Kahneman, D. Visual resolution and contour interaction. Journal of the Optical Society of America, 1963, 53, 1026-1032.

Foley, J. M. Desarguesian property in visual space. Journal of the Optical Society of America, 1964, 54, 684-692. **493**

Foley, J. M. Binocular disparity and perceived relative distance: An examination of two hypotheses. Vision Research, 1967, 7, 655-670. **493**

Foley, J. P., Jr., & MacMillan, Z. L. Mediated generalization and the interpretation of verbal behavior: V. "Free association" as related to differences in professional training. Journal of Experimental Psychology, 1943, 33, 299-310. **875**

Foley, J. P., Jr., see also Cofer, C. N., 1942.

Folgmann, E. E. E. An experimental study of composer-preferences of four outstanding orchestras. Journal of Experimental Psychology, 1933, 16, 709-724. **53**

Follansbee, G. L., see Bales, J. F., 1935.

Forgays, D. Retinal locus as a factor in recognition of visually perceived words. American Journal of Psychology, 1953, 65, 555-562. **444**

Forgays, D. G., see Mishkin, M., 1952.

Forsyth, D. F., see Entwisle, D. R., 1964.

Forsyth, G. A., & Brown, D. R. Stimulus correlates of tachisto-scopic discrimination-recognition performance: Compactness, jaggedness and areal asymmetry. Perception & Psychophysics, 1967, 2, 597-600. **449**

Fort, J. G., see Myers, J. L., 1963.

Foss, D. J., see Jenkins, J. J., 1965.

Foster, D., Scofield, E. H., & Dallenbach, K. M. An olfactorium. American Journal of Psychology, 1950, 63, 431-440. **201**

Foster, H., see Gagné, R. M., 1948, 1949, 1950.

Fowler, H. Curiosity and exploratory behavior, New York: Macmillan, 1965. **673, 841**

Fowler, H. Satiation and curiosity: Constructs for a drive and incentive-motivational theory of exploration. In K. W. Spence & J. T. Spence (Eds.), The psychology of learning and motivation. Vol. 1. New York: Academic Press, 1967. Pp. 157-227. **841**

Fowler, H., & Miller, N. E. Facilitation and inhibition of runway performance by hind- and forepaw shock of various intensities. Journal of Comparative and Physiological Psychology, 1963, 56, 801-805. **734**

Fowler, H., & Trapold, M. A. Escape performance as a function of delay of reinforcement. Journal of Experimental Psychology, 1962, 63, 464-467. **722**

Fowler, H., & Wischner, G. J. Discrimination performance as affected by problem difficulty and shock for either the correct or incorrect response. Journal of Experimental Psychology, 1965, 69, 413-418. **740**

Fowler, H., & Wischner, G. J. The varied functions of punishment in discrimination learning. In B. A. Campbell & R. M. Church (Eds.), Punishment. New York: Appleton, 1969. **740**

Fowler, H., see also Bower, G. H., 1959; Trapold, M. A., 1960; Wischner, G. J., 1963.

Fox, R., & Check, R. Binocular fusion: A test of the suppression theory. Perception and Psychophysics, 1966, 1, 331-334. (a) **489**

Fox, R., & Check, R. Forced-choice form recognition during binocular rivalry. Psychonomic Science, 1966, 6, 471-472. (b) **489**

Fox, R., & McIntyre, C. Suppression during binocular fusion of complex targets. Psychonomic Science, 1967, 8, 143-144. **489**

Fox, R., see also Harrison, K., 1966.

Fox, R. E., & King, R. A. The effects of reinforcement scheduling on the strength of a secondary reinforcer. Journal of Comparative and Physiological Psychology, 1961, 54, 266-269. **670**

Fox, S. S. Self-maintained sensory input and sensory deprivation in monkeys: A behavioral and neuropharmacological study. Journal of Comparative and Physiological Psychology, 1962, 55, 438-444. **840**

Fox, S. S., see also Wendt, R. H., 1963.

Fraenkel, G. S., & Gunn, D. L. The orientation of animals. Oxford: Clarendon, 1940. **745**

Frank, H. Ueber den Einfluss inadaquäter Konvergenz und Akkommodation auf die Sehgrosse. Psychologische Forschung, 1930, 13, 135-144. **480**

Frank, M. K., see Pfaffmann, C., 1967.

Frankmann, J. B., see Estes, W. K., 1957.

Frankmann, R. W., see Suppes, P., 1961, 1964.

Fraser, J., see Postman, L., 1968.

Fraser-Rowell, C. H., see Horn, G., 1968.

Freeburne, C. M., & Goldman, R. D. Left-right differences in tachistoscopic recognition as a function of order of report, expectancy and training. Journal of Experimental Psychology, 1969, 79, 570-572. **444**

Freedman, J. L., see Mednick, S. A., 1960.

Freedman, S., see Held, R., 1963.

Freedman, S. J., see Kalil, R. E., 1966.

Freeman, I., see Bigg, M., 1966.

Freeman, R. B. Figural after-effects: Displacement or contrast? *American Journal of Psychology*, 1964, *77*, 607–613. **473**

Freeman, R. B., Jr. Absolute threshold for visual slant: The effect of stimulus size and retinal perspective. *Journal of Experimental Psychology*, 1966, *71*, 170–176. **501**

Freeman, R. B., Jr. Effect of size on visual slant. *Journal of Experimental Psychology*, 1966, *71*, 96–103. (a) **499**

Freeman, R. B., Jr. Function of cues in the perceptual learning of visual slant: An experimental and theoretical analysis. *Psychological Monographs*, 1966, *80*. (Whole No. 610). (b) **499**

Freeman, R. B., Jr. Optical texture versus retinal perspective: A reply to Flock. *Psychological Review*, 1966, *73*, 365–371. (c) **502, 505**

Freeman, R. B., Jr. Contrast interpretation of brightness constancy. *Psychological Bulletin*, 1967, *67*, 165–187. **413**

Freibergs, V., & Tulving, E. The effect of practice on utilization of information from positive and negative instances in concept formation. *Canadian Journal of Psychology*, 1961, *15*, 101–106. **964**

Frenk, S., see Maturana, H. R., 1963.

Frey, M. von, see von Frey, M.

Frey, R. E., see Mayzner, M. S., 1964.

Friedel, R. T., see Mayzner, M. S., 1965.

Friedman, M. Transfer effects and response strategies in pattern-vs-component discrimination learning. *Journal of Experimental Psychology*, 1966, *71*, 420–428. **1004**

Friedman, M., Trabasso, T., & Mosberg, L. Tests of a mixed model for paired-associate learning with overlapping stimuli. *Journal of Mathematical Psychology*, 1967, *4*, 316–334. **1004**

Friedman, M. J., & Reynolds, J. H. Retroactive inhibition as a function of response-class similarity. *Journal of Experimental Psychology*, 1967, *74*, 351–355. **1097**

Friedman, M. P., Burke, C. J., Cole, N., Keller, L., Millward, R. B., & Estes, W. K. Two-choice behavior under extended training with shifting probabilities of reinforcement. In R. C. Atkinson (Ed.), *Studies in mathematical psychology*. Stanford: Stanford University Press, 1964. Pp. 250–316. **918, 919, 930, 934**

Friedman, M. P., & Gelfand, H. Transfer effects in discrimination learning. *Journal of Mathematical Psychology*, 1964, *1*, 204–214. **1004**

Friedman, M. P., see also Furchtgott, E., 1960.

Frincke, G., see Johnson, R. C., 1960, 1961.

Frings, H. Sweet taste in the cat and the taste-spectrum. *Experientia*, 1951, *7*, 424–426. **190**

Frishkopf, L. S., see Simmons, F. B., 1965.

Frommer, G. P. Gustatory afferent responses in the thalamus. In M. R. Kare & B. P. Halpern (Eds.), *Physiological and behavioral aspects of taste*. Chicago: University of Chicago Press, 1961. Pp. 50–65. **182**

Frommer, G. P., see also Pfaffmann, C., 1961.

Frost, R., see Attneave, F., 1969.

Fry, G. A. The stimulus correlate of bulky color. *American Journal of Psychology*, 1931, *43*, 618. **426, 427**

Fry, G. A. Visual perception of space. *American Journal of Optometry*, 1950, *27*, 531–553. **493**

Fuchs, W. Experimentelle Untersuchungen über die Änderung von Farben unter dem Einfluss von Gestalten. *Zeitschrift für Psychologie*, 1923, *92*, 249–325. **427**

Fuchs, W. Experimentelle Untersuchungen über das simultane Hintereinander auf derselben Sehrichtung. *Zeitschrift für Psychologie*, 1923, *91*, 145–235. **435**

Fullerton, G. S., & Cattell, J. McK., On the perception of small differences. *Philosophy Series* #2. Philadelphia: University of Pennsylvania Press, 1892. **30, 33**

Funakoshi, M., see Adachi, A., 1967; Andersen, H. T., 1963; Diamant, H., 1963.

Furchtgott, E., & Friedman, M. P. The effects of hunger on taste and odor RLs. *Journal of Comparative and Physiological Psychology*, 1960, *53*, 576–581. **208**

Furchtgott, E., & Rubin, R. The effect of magnitude of reward on maze learning in the white rat. *Journal of Comparative and Physiological Psychology*, 1953, *46*, 9–12. **637**

Furukawa, H., see Ikeda, S., 1962.

Fuster, J. M. Effects of stimulation of brain stem on tachistoscopic perception. *Science*, 1958, *127*, 150. **841, 842**

Fuster, J. M., & Uyeda, A. A. Facilitation of tachistoscopic performance by stimulation of midbrain tegmental points in the monkey. *Experimental Neurology*, 1962, *6*, 384–406. **841, 842**

Gaensler, E. A. Quantitative determination of the visceral pain threshold in man: Characteristics of visceral pain, effect of inflammation and analgesics on the threshold, and relationship of analgesia to visceral spasm. *Journal of Clinical Investigation*, 1951, *30*, 406–420. **156**

Gage, F. H., see Shaxby, J. H., 1932.

Gagné, R. M., Baker, K. E., & Foster, H. On the relation between similarity and transfer of training in the learning of discriminative motor tasks. *Psychological Review*, 1950, *57*, 67–79. **1055**

Gagné, R. M., & Foster, H. Transfer of training from practice on components in a motor skill. *Journal of Experimental Psychology*, 1949, *39*, 47–68. **1026**

Gagné, R. M., Foster, H., & Crowley, M. E. The measurement of transfer of training. *Psychological Bulletin*, 1948, *45*, 97–130. **1026**

Galambos, R. Studies of the auditory system with implanted electrodes. In G. Rasmussen & W. F. Windle (Eds.), *Neural mechanisms of the auditory and vestibular systems*. Springfield, Ill.: Charles C Thomas, 1960. **232**

Galambos, R., & Davis, H. The response of single auditory-nerve fibers to acoustic stimulation. *Journal of Neurophysiology*, 1943, *6*, 39–57. **230, 231**

Galambos, R., & Davis, H. Inhibition in activity of single auditory nerve fibers by acoustic stimulation. *Journal of Neurophysiology*, 1944, *7*, 287–303. **239**

Galambos, R., Schwartzkopff, J., & Rupert, A. Microelectrode study of superior olivary nuclei. *American Journal of Physiology*, 1959, *197*, 527–536. **264**

Galambos, R., see also Griffin, D. R., 1941; Hubel, D. H., 1959; Morgan, C. T., 1951; Weitzman, E. D., 1961.

Galanter, E. H. Contemporary psychophysics. In *New directions in psychology*. New York: Holt, Rinehart, and Winston, 1962. **84**

Galanter, E., & Holman, G. L. Some invariances of the isosensitivity function and their implication for the utility function of money. *Journal of Experimental Psychology*, 1967, *73*, 333–339. **38**

Galanter, E., & Smith, W. A. S. Some experiments on a simple thought problem. *American Journal of Psychology*, 1958, *71*, 359–366. **907**

Galanter, E., see also Bish, R. R., 1963; Linker, E., 1964; Luce, R. D., 1963; Miller, G. A., 1960; Stevens, S. S., 1957.

Gales, R. S., see Thompson, P. O., 1961.

Gallegos, E. S., see Kenshalo, D. R., 1967.

Galloway, A., see Wallach, H., 1946.

Gallup, H. F. Originality in free and controlled association responses. *Psychological Reports*, 1963, *13*, 923–929. **867**

Gallup, H. F., see also Maltzman, I., 1964.

Galper, R. E., see Hochberg, J., 1967.

Galton, F. Psychometric experiments. *Brain*, 1879–1880, *2*, 149–162. **848, 859, 873**

Galton, F. *Inquiries into human faculty and its development*. London: Macmillan, 1883. **55, 598**

Gambino, B., & Myers, J. L. Effect of mean and variability

of event run length on two-choice learning. *Journal of Experimental Psychology,* 1966, *72,* 904-908. **921**

Ganchrow, D., see Fehrer, E., 1963.

Gandelman, R., Panksepp, J., & Trowill, J. The effect of lever retraction on resistance to extinction of a response rewarded with electrical stimulation of the brain. *Psychonomic Science,* 1968, *10,* 5-6. **654**

Ganong, W. F., see Martini, L., 1966.

Gantt, W. H. Cardiovascular component of the conditional reflex to pain, food, and other stimuli. *Physiological Reviews,* 1960, *40,* Supplement No. 4, 266-291. **711**

Gantt, W. H. Pavlov's systems. In B. B. Wolman (Ed.), *Scientific psychology.* New York: Basic Books, 1965. **554**

Gantt, W. H. Conditioned or conditional, reflex or response? *Conditional Reflex,* 1966, *1,* 69-73. **555n**

Ganz, L. Is the figural aftereffect an *aftereffect? Psychological Bulletin,* 1966, *66,* 151-165. (a) **473, 474**

Ganz, L. The mechanism of figural aftereffect. *Psychological Review,* 1966, *73,* 128-150. (b) **473, 474**

Ganz, L. Lateral inhibition and the location of visual contours: An analysis of figural aftereffects. *Vision Research,* 1965, *4,* 465-481. **472, 473**

Ganz, L., & Day, R. H. An analysis of the satiation–fatigue mechanism of figural aftereffects. *American Journal of Psychology,* 1965, *78,* 345-361. **472, 473**

Ganz, L., see also Sekuler, R. W., 1963.

Gardner, E. Spinal cord and brain stem pathways for afferents from joints. In A. V. S. de Reuch & J. Knight (Eds.), *Myotatic, kinesthetic and vestibular mechanisms.* London: J. & A. Churchill, 1967. Pp. 56-76. **129**

Gardner, J., see Jones, A., 1964.

Gardner, M. B. Historical background of the Haas and/or precedence effect. *Journal of the Acoustical Society of America,* 1968, *43,* 1243-1248. **268**

Gardner, M. B., see also Steinberg, J. C., 1937.

Gardner, W. J., Licklider, J. C. R., & Weisz, A. Z. Suppression of pain by sound. *Science,* 1960, *132,* 32-33. **164**

Garmezano, I. Yoked comparisons of classical and instrumental conditioning of the eyelid response; and an addendum on "voluntary responders." In W. F. Prokasy (Ed.), *Classical conditioning.* New York: Appleton, 1965. **557**

Garner, W. R. Auditory thresholds of short tones as a function of repetition rates. *Journal of the Acoustical Society of America,* 1947, *19,* 600-608. (a) **234**

Garner, W. R. The effect of frequency spectrum on temporal integration of energy in the ear. *Journal of the Acoustical Society of America,* 1947, *19,* 808-815. (b) **234**

Garner, W. R. Hearing. In C. P. Stone (Ed.), *Annual review of psychology,* Vol. 3, Palo Alto, Calif.: Annual Reviews, 1952. **246**

Garner, W. R. A technique and a scale of loudness measurement. *Journal of the Acoustical Society of America,* 1954, *26,* 73-88. (a) **84, 247, 248**

Garner, W. R. Context effects and the validity of loudness scales. *Journal of Experimental Psychology,* 1954, *48,* 218-224. (b) **84**

Garner, W. R. *Uncertainty and structure as psychological concepts.* New York: Wiley, 1962. **256, 446**

Garner, W. R. To perceive is to know. *American Psychologist,* 1966, *21,* 11-19. **446**

Garner, W. R., & Clement, D. E. Goodness of pattern and pattern uncertainty. *Journal of Verbal Learning and Verbal Behavior,* 1963, *2,* 446-452. **446, 447**

Garner, W. R., & Creelman, C. D. Problems and methods of psychological scaling. In H. Helson & W. Bevan (Eds.), *Contemporary approaches to psychology.* Princeton, N.J.: Van Nostrand, 1967. **49**

Garner, W. R., & Hake, H. W. The amount of information in absolute judgments. *Psychological Review,* 1951, *58,* 446-459. **58**

Garner, W. R., Hake, H. W. & Eriksen, C. W. Operationism and the concept of perception. *Psychological Review,* 1956, *63,* 149-159. **506**

Garner, W. R., & Miller, G. A. The masked threshold of pure tones as a function of duration. *Journal of Experimental Psychology,* 1947, *37,* 293-303. **234**

Garner, W. R., see also Handel, S., 1965; Imai, S., 1965; Morgan, C. T., 1951.

Garskof, B. E. Relation between single word association and continued association response hierarchies. *Psychological Reports,* 1965, *16,* 307-309. **877**

Garskof, B. E. Unlearning as a function of degree of interpolated learning and method of testing in the A–B, A–C and A–B, C–D paradigms. *Journal of Experimental Psychology,* 1968, *76,* 579-583. **1096**

Garskof, B. E., & Houston, J. P. Measurement of verbal relatedness: An idiographic approach. *Psychological Review,* 1963, *70,* 277-278. **881**

Garskof, B. E., & Marshall, G. R. Relationship between two measures of verbal relatedness: Preliminary report. *Psychological Reports,* 1965, *16,* 17-18. **881**

Garskof, B. E., & Sandak, J. M. Unlearning in recognition memory. *Psychonomic Science.* 1964, *1,* 197-198. **1096**

Garskof, B. E., see also Sandak, J. M., 1967.

Garvey, W. D. The intelligibility of speeded speech. *Journal of Experimental Psychology,* 1953, *45,* 102-108. **257**

Gasser, H. S. Pain producing impulses in peripheral nerves. *Proceedings of the Association for Research in Nervous and Mental Disease,* 1943, *23,* 154-165. **160**

Gasser, H. S. Olfactory nerve fibers. *Journal of General Physiology,* 1956, *39,* 473-496. **197**

Gaze, L., & Dodwell, P. C. The role of induced set in figural after-effects. *Psychonomic Science,* 1965, *2,* 275-276. **470**

Gaze, L., see also Dodwell, P. C., 1965.

Geisler, C. D., see Rose, J. E., 1966.

Gelb, A: Die "Farbenkonstanz" der Sehdinge. *Handb. norm. path. Phys.,* 1929, *12,* 594-678. **398, 404**

Gelb, A. Die Erscheinungen des simultanen Kontrastes und der Eindruck der Feldbeleuchtung. *Zeitschrift für Psychologie,* 1932, *127,* 42-59. **412**

Geldard, F. A. The perception of mechanical vibration: I. History of a controversy. *Journal of General Psychology,* 1940, *22,* 243-269. (a) **134**

Geldard, F. A. The perception of mechanical vibration: II. The response of pressure receptors. *Journal of General Psychology,* 1940, *22,* 271-280. (b) **134**

Geldard, F. A. The perception of mechanical vibration: III. The frequency function. *Journal of General Psychology,* 1940, *22,* 281-289. (c) **134**

Geldard, F. A. The perception of mechanical vibration: IV. Is there a separate "vibratory sense"? *Journal of General Psychology,* 1940, *22,* 291-308. (d) **134**

Geldard, F. A. *The human senses.* New York: Wiley, 1953. **134, 165**

Gelfan, S., & Carter, S. Muscle sense in man. *Experimental Neurology,* 1967, *18,* 469-473. **129**

Gelfand, H., see Friedman, M. P., 1964.

Gellerman, L. W. Form discrimination in chimpanzees and two-year-old children: I. Form (triangularity) *per se. Journal of Genetic Psychology,* 1933, *42,* 3. (a) **750**

Gellerman, L. W. Form discrimination in chimpanzees and two-year-old children: II. Form versus background. *Journal of Genetic Psychology,* 1933, *42,* 28. (b) **750**

Gengerelli, A. Apparent movement in relation to homonymous and heteronymous stimulation of the cerebral hemispheres. *Journal of Experimental Psychology,* 1948, *38,* 592-599. **528**

Gentile, A., see Peterson, L. R., 1965.

George, F. H. Acuity and the statistical theory of figural after-effect. *Journal of Experimental Psychology,* 1962, *63,* 423-425. **473**

Gerebtzoff, M. A. L'olfaction, structure de l'organe olfactif et méchanisme de l'olfaction. *Journal de Physiologie (Paris)*, 1953, *45*, 247-283. **220**

Gerjuoy, H., see Wynne, R. D., 1965.

Gerjuoy, I. R. Discrimination learning as a function of the similarity of the stimulus names. *Child Development*, 1964, *35*, 677-684. **781**

Gershon, A., see Carlin, S., 1962.

Gerstman, L. J., see Cooper, F. S., 1952; Liberman, A. M., 1954.

Gertz, E. Psychophysische Untersuchungen über die Adaptation im Gebiet der Temperatursinne und über ihren Einfluß auf die Reiz-und Unterschiedsschwellen: I. *Hälfte Zeitschrift fur Sinnesphysiologie*, 1921, *52*, 1-51. **142**

Gesteland, R. C., Lettvin, J. Y., & Pitts, W. H. Chemical transmission in the nose of the frog. *Journal of Physiology (London)* 1965, *181*, 525-559. **214, 217, 221**

Gesteland, R. J., see also Lettvin, J., 1965.

Gettys, C., see Binford, J. R., 1965.

Ghent, L. The relation of experience to the development of hunger. *Canadian Journal of Psychology*, 1951, *5*, 77-81. **818**

Ghent, L. Some effects of deprivation on eating and drinking behavior. *Journal of Comparative and Physiological Psychology*, 1957, *50*, 172-176. **818**

Ghent, L. Recognition by children of realistic figures presented in various orientations. *Canadian Journal of Psychology*, 1960, *14*, 249-256. **450**

Gibb, M., Freeman, I., & Adam, J. Effects of luminance contrast factors upon figural aftereffects induced by short fixation periods. *Perceptual and Motor Skills*, 1966, *22*, 535-541. **470**

Gibson, E. J. A systematic application of the concepts of generalization and differentiation to verbal learning. *Psychological Review*, 1940, *47*, 196-229. **980, 981, 984, 990, 1007, 1048, 1060**

Gibson, E. J. Retroactive inhibition as a function of degree of generalization between tasks. *Journal of Experimental Psychology*, 1941, *28*, 93-115. **1049, 1050, 1051, 1054, 1055, 1083**

Gibson, E. J. Intra-list generalization as a factor in verbal learning. *Journal of Experimental Psychology*, 1942, *30*, 185-200. **1049, 1125**

Gibson, E. J. Improvement in perceptual judgment as a function of controlled practice and training. *Psychological Bulletin*, 1953, *50*, 401-431. **44**

Gibson, E. J. Perceptual learning. *Annual Review of Psychology*, 1963, *14*, 29-56. **550**

Gibson, E. J. *Principles of perceptual learning and development.* New York: Appleton, 1969. **547, 550**

Gibson, E. J., & Olum, V. Experimental methods of studying perception in children. In P. H. Mussen (Ed.), *Handbook of research methods in child development.* New York: Wiley, 1960. Pp. 311-373. **550**

Gibson, E. J., & Walk, R. D. The effect of prolonged exposure to visually presented patterns on learning to discriminate them. *Journal of Comparative and Physiological Psychology*, 1956, *49*, 239-242. **580**

Gibson, E. J., & Walk, R. D. The "visual cliff." *Scientific American*, 1960, *202*, 64-71. **549**

Gibson, E. J., Walk, R. D., Pick, H. L., & Tighe, T. J. The effect of prolonged exposure to visual patterns on learning to discriminate similar and different patterns. *Journal of Comparative and Physiological Psychology*, 1958, *51*, 584-587. **580**

Gibson, E. J., Walk, R. D., & Tighe, T. J. Enhancement and deprivation of visual stimulation during rearing as factors in visual discrimination learning. *Journal of Comparative and Physiological Psychology*, 1959, *52*, 74-81. **580, 700**

Gibson, E. J., see also Gibson, J. J., 1957; Purdy, J., 1955; Walk, R. D., 1957, 1961.

Gibson, J. J. Adaptation, after-effect and contrast in perception of curved lines. *Journal of Experimental Psychology*, 1933, *16*, 1-31. **466, 473, 536, 540, 542, 552**

Gibson, J. J. Adaptation, after-effect and contrast in the perception of tilted lines: II. Simultaneous contrast and the areal restriction of the after-effect. *Journal of Experimental Psychology*, 1937, *20*, 553-569. **466**

Gibson, J. J. The perception of visual surfaces. *American Journal of Psychology*, 1950, *63*, 367-384. **501, 503, 505**

Gibson, J. J. *The perception of the visual world.* Boston: Houghton Mifflin, 1950. **466**

Gibson, J. J. The visual field and the visual world: A reply to Professor Boring. *Psychological Review*, 1952, *59*, 149-151. **510**

Gibson, J. J. A theory of pictorial perception. *A-V Communications Review*, 1954, *1*, 3-23. **442**

Gibson, J. J. The visual perception of objective motion and subjective movement. *Psychological Review*, 1954, *61*, 304-314. **504, 531**

Gibson, J. J. Optimal motions and transformations as stimuli for visual perception. *Psychological Review*, 1957, *64*, 288-295. **504**

Gibson, J. J. The concept of the stimulus in psychology. *American Psychologist*, 1960, *15*, 694-703. **505**

Gibson, J. J. *The senses considered as perceptual systems.* Boston: Houghton Mifflin, 1966. **502, 510**

Gibson, J. J., & Carel, W. Does motion perspective independently produce the impression of a receding surface? *Journal of Experimental Psychology*, 1952, *44*, 16-18. **505**

Gibson, J. J., & Gibson, E. J. Continuous perspective transformations and the perception of rigid motion. *Journal of Experimental Psychology*, 1957, *54*, 129-138. **505**

Gibson, J. J., Kaplan, G. A., Reynolds, H. V., & Wheeler, K. The change from visible to invisible: A study of optical transitions. *Perception and Psychophysics*, 1969, *5*, 113-116. **442**

Gibson, J. J., & Mowrer, O. H. Determinants of the perceived vertical and horizontal. *Psychological Review*, 1938, *45*, 300-324. **539**

Gibson, J. J., Olum, P. & Rosenblatt, F. Parallax and perspective during aircraft landings. *American Journal of Psychology*, 1955, *68*, 372-385. **505**

Gibson, J. J., Purdy, J., & Lawrence, L. A method of controlling stimulation for the study of space perception: The optical tunnel. *Journal of Experimental Psychology*, 1955, *50*, 1-14. **502**

Gibson, J. J., & Radner, M. Adaptation, aftereffect and contrast in the perception of tilted lines: I. Quantitative studies. *J. exp. Psychol.*, 1937, *20*, 453-467. **466**

Gibson, J. J., & Robinson, D. Orientation in visual perception: The recognition of familiar plane forms in differing orientations. *Psychological Monographs*, 1935, *46*, 39-47. **450, 451**

Gibson, J. J., see also Beck, J., 1955; Bergman, R., 1959; Schiff, W., 1962.

Gibson, R. H. Electrical stimulation of pain and touch. In D. R. Kenshalo (Ed.), *The skin senses.* Springfield, Ill.: Charles C Thomas, 1968. Pp. 223-261. **137**

Gibson, W. E., Reid, L. D., Sakai, M., & Porter, P. B. Intracranial reinforcement compared with sugar-water reinforcement. *Science*, 1965, *148*, 1357-1359. **654**

Gilinsky, A. S. Perceived size and distance in visual space. *Psychological Review*, 1951, *58*, 460-482. **508, 514**

Gilinsky, A. S. The effect of attitude upon the perception of size. *American Journal of Psychology*, 1955, *68*, 173-192. **509, 514**

Gill, M., see Rapaport, D., 1946.

Gillette, A., see Washburn, M. F., 1933.

Ginsberg, R., see Suppes, P., 1963.

Ginsberg, S., see Schulz, R., 1965.

Ginsborg, B. L., see Ditchburn, R. W., 1952, 1953.

Girden, E., see Culler, E., 1935.

Glanz, J., see Zwislocki, J., 1967.

Glanzer, M. Grammatical category: A rote learning and word association analysis. *Journal of Verbal Learning and Verbal Behavior,* 1962, *1,* 31–41. **903**

Glanzer, M., & Clark, W. H. Accuracy of perceptual recall: An analysis of organization. *Journal of Verbal Learning and Verbal Behavior,* 1963, *1,* 289–299. (a) **448**

Glanzer, M., & Clark, W. H. The verbal loop hypothesis: Binary numbers. *Journal of Verbal Learning and Verbal Behavior,* 1963, *2,* 301–309. (b) **448**

Glanzer, M., & Clark, W. The verbal loop hypothesis: Conventional figures. *American Journal of Psychology,* 1964, *77,* 621–626. **448**

Glanzer, M., Taub, T., & Murphy, R. An evaluation of three theories of figural organization. In press, 1968. **448**

Glaser, E. M. *The physiological basis of habituation.* London: Oxford University Press, 1966. **589**

Glaser, N. M., see Maier, N. R. F., 1940.

Glaze, J. A. The association value of nonsense syllables. *Journal of Genetic Psychology,* 1928, *35,* 255–267. **852, 859, 982**

Gleitman, H., Nachmias, J., & Neisser, U. The S–R reinforcement theory of extinction. *Psychological Review,* 1954, *61,* 23–33. **575**

Gleitman, H., see also Gonzalez, R. C., 1962; Hochberg, J. E., 1948.

Glickman, S. E., & Hartz, K. E. Exploratory behavior in several species of rodents. *Journal of Comparative and Physiological Psychology,* 1964, *58,* 101–104. **824**

Glickman, S. E., & Schiff, B. B. A biological theory of reinforcement. *Psychological Review,* 1967, *74,* 81–109. **658**

Glorig, A., see Nixon, J. C., 1961; Ward, W. D., 1959.

Goad, D., see Underwood, B. J., 1951.

Goetzl, F. R., Burrill, D. Y., & Ivy, A. C. A critical analysis of algesimetric methods with suggestions for a useful procedure. *Quarterly Bulletin, Northwestern University Medical School,* 1943, *17,* 280–291. **156**

Goff, G. D. Differential discrimination of frequency of cutaneous mechanical vibration. *Journal of Experimental Psychology,* 1967, *74,* 294–299. **136**

Goff, W. R. Measurement of absolute olfactory sensitivity in rats. *American Journal of Psychology,* 1961, *74,* 384–393. **200, 203, 204**

Goff, W. R., see also Rosner, B. S., 1967.

Gogel, W. C. Perceived frontal size as a determiner of perceived binocular depth. *Journal of Psychology,* 1960, *50,* 119–131. (a) **493**

Gogel, W. C. The perception of shape from binocular disparity cues. *Journal of Psychology,* 1960, *50,* 179–192. (b) **493**

Gogel, W. C. The perception of a depth interval with binocular disparity cues. *Journal of Psychology,* 1960, *50,* 257–269. (c) **493, 494**

Gogel, W. C. Size cues to visually perceived distance. *Psychological Bulletin,* 1964, *62,* 217–235. **495**

Gogel, W. C. Equidistance tendency and its consequences. *Psychological Bulletin,* 1965, *64,* 153–163. **512**

Gogel, W. C. The effect of set on perceived egocentric distance. *Acta Psychologica,* 1968, *28,* 283–292. **496**

Gogel, W. C., Gregg, J. M., & Wainwright, A. *Convergence as a cue to absolute distance.* U.S. Army Medical Research Laboratory (Fort Knox, Kentucky), Report No. 467, 1961, 1–16. **480**

Gogel, W. C., Hartman, B. O., & Harker, G. S. The retinal size of a familiar object as a determiner of apparent distance. *Psychological Monographs,* 1957, *71,* 1–16. **495**

Gogel, W. C., & Hess, E. H. A study of color constancy in the newly hatched chick by means of an innate color preference (Abst.). *American Journal of Psychology,* 1951, *6,* 282. **407**

Gogel, W. C., & Mershon, D. H. Depth adjacency in simultaneous contrast. *Perception and Psychophysics,* 1969, *5,* 13–17. **423***n*

Gogel, W. C., & Mertens, H. W. Perceived size and distance of familiar objects. *Perceptual and Motor Skills,* 1967, *25,* 213–225. **496, 497**

Gogel, W. C., & Newton, R. E. Perception of off-sized objects. *Perception and Psychophysics,* 1969, *5,* 7–9. **508**

Goggin, J. Retroactive and proactive inhibition in the short-term retention of paired associates. *Journal of Verbal Learning and Verbal Behavior,* 1966, *5,* 526–535. **1117**

Goggin, J. First-list recall as a function of second-list learning method. *Journal of Verbal Learning and Verbal Behavior,* 1967, *6,* 423–427. **1097**

Goggin, J., see also Postman, L., 1966.

Gold, C., see Mandler, G., 1964.

Goldberg, J., see Rock, I., 1966.

Goldberg, J. M., see Rose, J. E., 1963.

Goldberg, S. *Introduction to difference equations.* New York: Wiley, 1958. **912**

Gol'dburt, S. N. Persistence of auditory processes within micro-intervals of time (new data on retroactive masking). *Biophysics,* 1961, *6,* 76–81. **241**

Goldhamer, H. The influence of area, position and brightness in the visual perception of a reversible configuration. *American Journal of Psychology,* 1934, *46,* 189–206. **433**

Goldiamond, I. Indicators of perception: I. Subliminal perception, subception, unconscious perception; an analysis in terms of psychophysical indicator methodology. *Psychological Bulletin,* 1958, *55,* 373–411.

Goldiamond, I., & Hawkins, W. T. Vexierversuch: The log relationship between word-frequency and recognition obtained in the absence of stimulus words. *Journal of Experimental Psychology,* 1958, *56,* 457–463. **444**

Goldman, R. D., see Freeburne, C. M., 1969.

Goldstein, E. see Reynolds, W. F., 1964.

Goldstein, E. B. Early receptor potential of the isolated frog (*Rana pipiens*) retina. *Vision Research,* 1967, *7,* 837–845. **307**

Goldstein, J. L. Auditory nonlinearity. *Journal of the Acoustical Society of America,* 1967, *41,* 676–689. **237, 239**

Goldstein, K., & Riese, W. Über induzierte Veränderungen des Tonus (Halsreflexe, Labyrinthreflexe und ähnliche Erscheinungen): III. Blickrichtung und Zeigeversuch. *Klinische Wissenschraft,* 1923, *2,* 2338–2340. **534**

Goldstein, M. D., see Keesey, R. E., 1968.

Goldstein, S., see Bourne, L. E. Jr., 1964.

Gollub, L. R., see Kelleher, R. T., 1962.

Gombrich, E. H. *Art and illusion: A study in the psychology of pictorial representation.* New York: Pantheon, 1960. **442**

Gonzalez, R. C., Behrend, E. R., & Bitterman, M. E. Partial reinforcement in the fish: Experiments with spaced trials and partial delay. *American Journal of Psychology,* 1965, *78,* 198–207. **608**

Gonzalez, R. C., Gleitman, H., & Bitterman, M. E. Some observations on the depression effect. *Journal of Comparative and Physiological Psychology,* 1962, *55,* 578–581. **634, 635**

Goodell, H., see Hardy, J. D., 1940, 1947, 1951; Schumacher, G. A., 1940.

Goodenough, F. The use of free association in the objective measurement of personality. In Q. McNemar & M. A. Merrill (Eds.), *Studies in personality.* New York: McGraw-Hill, 1942. Pp. 87–103. **873**

Goodenough, F. Semantic choice and personality structure. *Science,* 1946, *104,* 451–456. **873**

Goodman, L. S., see Smith, S. M., 1947.

Goodnow, J. J. Determinance of choice-distribution in two-choice situations. *American Journal of Psychology,* 1955, *68,* 106–116. **907, 934**

Goodnow, J. J., see also Bruner, J. S., 1956.

Goodrich, K. P., & Zaretsky, H. Running speed as a function of concentration of sucrose incentive during pretraining. *Psychological Reports*, 1962, *11*, 463–468. **634**

Goodwin, P. E., *see* Mayzner, M. S., 1965.

Goodwin, W. R., & Lawrence, D. H. The functional independence of two discrimination habits associated with a constant stimulus situation. *Journal of Comparative and Physiological Psychology*, 1955, *48*, 437–443. **783**

Gordon, J., *see* Boynton, R. M., 1965.

Gordon, K. Meaning in memory and attention. *Psychological Review*, 1903, *10*, 280–283. **519**

Gormezano, I., & Abraham, F. Intermittent reinforcement, non-reversal shifts, and neutralization in concept formation. *Journal of Experimental Psychology*, 1961, *61*, 1–6. **948**

Goss, A. Verbal mediating responses in concept formation. *Psychological Review*, 1961, *68*, 248–274. **948**

Goss, A. E. Early behaviorism and verbal mediating responses. *American Psychologist*, 1961, *16*, 285–298. **1071**

Goss, A. E. Comments on Professor Noble's paper. In C. N. Cofer & B. S. Musgrave (Eds.), *Verbal behavior and learning: Problems and processes.* New York: McGraw-Hill, 1963. Pp. 119–155. **856**

Goss, A. E., & Nodine, C. F. *Paired-associates learning: The role of meaningfulness, similarity and familiarization.* New York: Academic Press, 1965. **853, 856, 857, 894, 896, 898, 900, 901**

Gottheil, E., & Bitterman, M. E. The measurement of shape-constancy. *American Journal of Psychology*, 1951, *64*, 406–408. **509, 516**

Gottlieb, N., *see* Held, R., 1958.

Gottschaldt, K. Über den Einfluss der Erfahrung auf die Wahrnehmung von Figuren: 1. *Psychologische Forschung*, 1926, *8*, 261–317. **440**

Gottschaldt, K. Über den Einfluss der Erfahrung auf die Wahrnehmung von Figuren: 11. *Psychologische Forschung*, 1929, *12*, 1–87. **440**

Goulet, L. R. Interlist response meaningfulness and transfer effects under the *A–B, A–C* paradigm. *Journal of Experimental Psychology*, 1965, *70*, 264–269. **1062**

Goulet, L. R. Retroaction and the "fate" of the mediator in three stage mediation paradigms. *Journal of Verbal Learning and Verbal Behavior*, 1966, *5*, 172–176. **1077**

Goulet, L. R. Degree of learning and transfer of training. *Psychonomic Science*, 1967, *8*, 245–246. **1069**

Goulet, L. R., & Barclay, A. Comparison of paired-associate transfer effects between the *A–B, C–A* and *B–C* transfer paradigms. *Journal of Experimental Psychology*, 1965, *70*, 537–539. **1064**

Goulet, L. R., & Behar, V. Bidirectional paired-associate learning and transfer effects in the *A–B, C–B* and *A–B, A–C* paradigms. *Psychonomic Science*, 1966, *6*, 299–300. **1063**

Goulet, L. R., Meltzer, R., & O'Shaunessy, K. Further data on degree of learning and transfer of training. *Psychonomic Science*, 1967, *9*, 469–470. **1069**

Goulet, L. R., & Postman, L. An experimental evaluation of the pseudomediation hypothesis. *Psychonomic Science*, 1966, *4*, 163–164. **1077**

Goulet, L. R., *see also* Cheung, C. C., 1968.

Gourevitch, G. Auditory masking in the rat. *Journal of the Acoustical Society of America*, 1965, *37*, 439–443. **555n**

Gourevitch, G., & Hack, M. H. Audibility in the rat. *Journal of Comparative and Physiological Psychology*, 1966, *62*, 289–291. **555n**

Gousec, T. The peak shift in stimulus generalization: Equivalent effects of errors and non-contingent shock. *Journal of the Experimental Analysis of Behavior*, 1968, *11*, 239–249. **779**

Graham, C. A. Area, color and brightness difference in a reversible configuration. *Journal of General Psychology*, 1929, *2*, 470–481. **433**

Graham, C. H. Vision: III. Some neural correlations. In C. Murchison (Ed.), *Handbook of general experimental psychology.* Worcester, Mass.: Clark University Press, 1934. Pp. 829–879. **290**

Graham, C. H. On some aspects of real and apparent visual movement. *Journal of the Optical Society of America*, 1963, *53*, 1019–1025. **518**

Graham, C. H. (Ed.) *Vision and visual perception.* New York: Wiley, 1965. **84, 296, 358, 520, 526**

Graham, C. H., Baker, K. E., Hecht, M., & Lloyd, V. V. Factors influencing thresholds for monocular movement parallax. *Journal of Experimental Psychology*, 1948, *38*, 205–223. **486, 520**

Graham, C. H., & Bartlett, N. R. The relation of size of stimulus and intensity in the human eye: III. The influence of area on foveal intensity discrimination. *Journal of Experimental Psychology*, 1940, *27*, 149–159. **303**

Graham, C. H., & Brown, J. L. Color contrast and color appearances: Brightness constancy and color constancy. In C. H. Graham (Ed.), *Vision and visual perception.* New York: Wiley, 1965. **410**

Graham, C. H., Brown, R. H., & Mote, F. A. The relative size of stimulus and intensity in the human eye: I. *Journal of Experimental Psychology*, 1939, *24*, 555–573. **290**

Graham, C. H., & Cook, C. Visual acuity as a function of intensity and exposure time. *American Journal of Psychology*, 1937, *49*, 654–691. **304**

Graham, C. H., & Kemp, E. H. Brightness discrimination as a function of the duration of the increment in intensity. *Journal of General Physiology*, 1938, *21*, 635–650. **297**

Graham, C. H., Riggs, L. A., Mueller, C. G., & Solomon, R. L. Precision of stereoscopic settings as influenced by distance of target from a fiducial line. *Journal of Psychology*, 1949, *27*, 203–207. **486**

Graham, C. H., *see also* Hartline, H. K., 1932; Hsia, Y., 1957; Riggs, L. A., 1940, 1947.

Graham, E. H. Figural after-effects as functions of contrast, area, and luminance of the inspection figure. *Psychologia*, 1961, *4*, 201–208. **470**

Graham, F. K. *see* Keen, R. E., 1965.

Granath, L. P., *see* Herget, C. M., 1941.

Grandine, L., & Harlow, H. F. Generalization of the characteristics of a single learned stimulus by monkeys. *Journal of Comparative and Physiological Psychology*, 1948, *41*, 327–338. **772**

Granger, L., Ducharme, R., & Bélanger, D. Effects of water deprivation upon heart rate and running speed of the white rat in a straight alley. *Psychophysiology*, 1969, *5*, 638–643. **827**

Granit, R. Comparative studies on the peripheral and central retina: I. On interaction between distant areas in the human eye. *American Journal of Physiology*, 1930, *94*, 41–50. **290**

Granit, R. *Sensory mechanisms of the retina.* New York: Oxford University Press, 1947. **291, 294, 308**

Granit, R. *Receptors and sensory perception.* New Haven: Yale University Press, 1955. **81, 108, 308**

Granit, R. The visual pathway. In H. Davson (Ed.), *The eye.* Vol. 2. New York: Academic Press, 1962. Pp. 537–763. **282, 308**

Granit, R., Holmberg, T., & Zewi, M. On the mode of action of visual purple on the rod cell. *Journal of Physiology*, 1938, *94*, 430–440. **287**

Grant, D. A. Perceptual vs. analytical responses to the number concept of a Weigl-type card sorting task. *Journal of Experimental Psychology*, 1951, *41*, 23–29. **961**

Grant, D. A. Classical and operant conditioning. In A. W. Melton (Ed.), *Categories of human learning.* New York: Academic Press, 1964. **564**

Grant, D. A., & Curran, J. F. Relative difficulty of number, form, and color concepts of a Weigl-type problem using unsystematic number cards. *Journal of Experimental Psychology*, 1953, *43*, 408–413. **961**

Grant, D. A., & Dittmer, D. G. An experimental investigation of Pavlov's cortical irradiation hypothesis. *Journal of Experimental Psychology*, 1940, *26*, 299–310. **564**

Grant, D. A., Jones, O. R., & Tallantis, B. The relative difficulty of number, form, and color concepts of a Weigl-type problem. *Journal of Experimental Psychology*, 1949, *39*, 552–557. **961**

Grant, D. A., & Norris, E. B. Eyelid conditioning as influenced by the presence of sensitized beta-responses. *Journal of Experimental Psychology*, 1947, *37*, 423–433. **556, 557, 565**

Grant, D. A., *see also* Anderson, N. H., 1957, 1958; Hake, H. W., 1951; Hartman, T. F., 1962; Norris, E. B., 1948.

Grant, V. W. Accommodation and convergence in visual space perception. *Journal of Experimental Psychology*, 1942, *31*, 89–104. **480**

Green, B. F. Kinetic depth-effect. In *Psychology Group 58: Quarterly Progress Report.* Cambridge, Mass.: Massachusetts Institute of Technology, Lincoln Laboratory, March 1959. **505**

Green, D. M. Detection of auditory sinusoids of uncertain frequency. *Journal of the Acoustical Society of America*, 1961, *33*, 897–903. **250**

Green, D. M., Henning, G. B. Audition. In P. H. Mussen & M. R. Rosenzweig (Eds.), *Annual Review of Psychology*, Vol. 20. Palo Alto, Calif.: Annual Reviews, 1969. **243**

Green, D. M., & Swets, J. A. *Signal detection theory and psychophysics.* New York: Wiley, 1966. **42, 240**

Green, H. C., *see* Potter, R. K., 1947.

Green, R. T., & Hoyle, E. M. The Poggendorf illusion as a constancy phenomenon. *Nature*, 1963, *200*, 611–612. **460, 463**

Greenbaum, H. B., *see* Stevens, S. S., 1966.

Greenberg, R., & Underwood, B. J. Retention as a function of stage of practice. *Journal of Experimental Psychology*, 1950, *40*, 452–457. **1041, 1104, 1106**

Greenbloom, R., & Kimble, G. A. Extinction of R-S associations and performance on recall trials without immediate feedback. *Journal of Verbal Learning and Verbal Behavior*, 1965, *4*, 341–347. **1095**

Greenbloom, R., *see also* Postman, L., 1967.

Greene, L. C., & Hardy, J. D. Spatial summation of pain. *Journal of Applied Physiology*, 1958, *13*, 457–464. **160**

Greene, L. C., & Hardy, J. D. Adaptation to thermal pain in the skin. *Journal of Applied Physiology*, 1962, *17*, 693–696. **159**

Greene, M., *see* Efstathiou, A., 1967; Held, R., 1966.

Greenhouse, P., *see* Neimark, E., 1965.

Greeno, J. G. Effects of nonreinforced trials in two-choice learning with noncontingent reinforcement. *Journal of Experimental Psychology*, 1962, *64*, 373–379. **933**

Greeno, J. G. Paired-associate learning with massed and distributed repetition of items. *Journal of Experimental Psychology*, 1964, *67*, 286–295. **999, 1009**

Greeno, J. G. Paired-associate learning with short-term retention: Mathematical analysis and data regarding identification of parameters. *Journal of Mathematical Psychology*, 1967, *4*, 430–472. **999**

Greeno, J. G., & Scandura, J. M. All-or-none transfer based on verbally mediated concepts. *Journal of Mathematical Psychology*, 1966, *3*, 388–411. **946, 1007, 1010**

Greeno, J. G., *see also* James, C. T., 1967; La Berge, D. L., 1962.

Greenspoon, J. The reinforcing effect of two spoken sounds on the frequency of two responses. *American Journal of Psychology*, 1955, *68*, 409–416. **908n**

Greenspoon, J., & Ranyard, R. Stimulus conditions and retroactive inhibition. *Journal of Experimental Psychology*, 1957, *53*, 55–59. **1084**

Greenspoon, T. S., *see* Eriksen, C. W., et al., 1967.

Greenwood, D. Critical band width and the frequency coordinates of the basilar membrane. *Journal of the Acoustical Society of America*, 1961, *33*, 1344–1356. **240**

Greenwood, D. D., *see* Rose, J. E., 1963.

Gregg, J. M., *see* Gogel, W. C., 1961.

Gregg, L. W., & Simon, H. A. Process models and stochastic theories of simple concept formation. *Journal of Mathematical Psychology*, 1967, *4*, 246–276. **978**

Gregory, R. L. Distortion of visual space as inappropriate constancy scaling. *Nature*, 1963, *199*, 678–680. **460, 462**

Gregory, R. L. Eye movements and the stability of the visual world. *Bulletin of the British Psychological Society*, 1959, *38*, 23A. See also *Nature*, 1958, *182*, 1214–1216. **530**

Gregory, R. L. Human perception. *British Medical Bulletin*, 1964, *20*, 21–26. **521**

Gregory, R. L. Visual illusions. In B. M. Foss (Ed.), *New horizons in psychology.* Harmondsworth, England: Penguin Books, 1966. **462**

Gregory, R. L. Comments on the inappropriate constancy scaling theory of the illusions and its implications. *Quarterly Journal of Experimental Psychology*, 1967, *19*, 291–223. **462**

Gregory, R. L., & Wallace, J. G., *Recovery from early blindness. Experimental Psychology Society Monograph 2,* Cambridge: Heffer, 1963. **548**

Gregory, R. L., & Zangwill, O. L. The origin of the autokinetic effect. *Quarterly Journal of Experimental Psychology*, 1963, *15*, 252–261. **530**

Gregory, R. L., *see also* Anstis, S. M., 1964.

Grether, W. F. Pseudo-conditioning without paired stimulation encountered in attempted backward conditioning. *Journal of Comparative Psychology*, 1938, *25*, 91–96. **578**

Grice, G. R. The relation of secondary reinforcement to delayed reward in visual discrimination learning. *Journal of Experimental Psychology*, 1948, *38*, 1–16. (a) **679, 680, 684, 689, 783**

Grice, G. R. An experimental test of the expectation theory of learning. *Journal of Comparative and Physiological Psychology*, 1948, *41*, 137–143. (b) **669, 772**

Grice, G. R., & Davis, J. D. Effect of irrelevant thirst motivation on a response learned with food reward. *Journal of Experimental Psychology*, 1957, *53*, 347–352. **669**

Grice, G. R., & Hunter, J. J. Stimulus intensity effects depend upon the type of experimental design. *Psychological Review*, 1964, *71*, 247–256. **600**

Grice, G. R., & Reynolds, B. Effect of varying amount of rest on conventional and bilateral transfer "reminiscence." *Journal of Experimental Psychology*, 1952, *44*, 247–252. **575**

Grier, J. B., & Bornstein, R. Probability matching in concept identification. *Journal of Experimental Psychology*, 1966, *71*, 339–342. **958**

Griffin, D. R. *Echoes of bats and man.* Garden City, N.Y.: Doubleday, 1959. **270**

Griffin, D. R., & Galambos, R. The sensory basis of obstacle avoidance by flying bats. *Journal of Experimental Zoology*, 1941, *86*, 481–506. **269**

Griffin, F., *see* Fisher, R., 1964.

Grim, K. Über die Genauigkeit der Wahrnehmung und Ausführung von Augenbewegungen. *Zeitschrift für Sinnesphysiologie*, 1911, *45*, 9–26. **520**

Grindley, G. C. Experiments on the influence of amount of reward on learning in young chickens. *British Journal of Psychology*, 1929, *20*, 173–180. **617**

Grindley, G. C. The formation of a simple habit in guinea pigs. *British Journal of Psychology*, 1932, *23*, 127–147. **697**

Grinnell, A. D. The neurophysiology of audition in bats: Intensity and frequency parameters. *Journal of Physiology*, 1963, *167*, 38–66. **270**

Grinnell, A. D., & McCue, J. J. G. Neurophysiological investigations of the bat *Myotis lucifugus*, stimulated by frequency-modulated acoustical pulses. *Nature*, 1963, *198*, 453–455. **232**

Groen, G., see Suppes, P., 1966.

Gropper, M. S., see Richardson, J., 1964.

Grosland, H., see Anderson, I., 1933.

Gross, K., & Stern, J. A. Habituation of orienting responses as a function of "instructional set." *Conditional Reflex*, 1967, *2*, 23–36. **555n**

Gross, N. B., see Rose, J. E., 1966; Thurlow, W. R., 1951.

Grossman, S. P. Acquisition and performance of avoidance responses during chemical stimulation of the midbrain reticular formation. *Journal of Comparative and Physiological Psychology*, 1966, *61*, 42–49. **843**

Grossman, S. P. *A textbook of physiological psychology*. New York: Wiley, 1967. **812**

Grover, D. E., Horton, D. L., & Cunningham, M., Jr. Mediated facilitation and interference in a four-stage paradigm. *Journal of Verbal Learning and Verbal Behavior*, 1967, *6*, 42–46. **1076**

Gruber, H., see King, W., 1962.

Gruber, H. E. The relation of perceived size to perceived distance. *American Journal of Psychology*, 1954, *67*, 411–426. **506, 513**

Gruber, H. E., & Clark, W. C. Perception of slanted surfaces. *Perceptual and Motor Skills*, 1956, *6*, 97–106. **501**

Gruber, H. E., & Dinnerstein, A. J. The role of knowledge in distance perception. *American Journal of Psychology*, 1965, *78*, 575–581. **496**

Grüsser, O.-J., and Creutzfeldt, O. Eine neurophysiologische Grundlage des Brücke-Bartley-Effektes: Maxima der Impulsfrequenz retinaler und corticaler Neurone bei Flimmerlicht mittlerer Frequenzen. *Pflüger's Archiv der Gesamte Physiologie*, 1957, *263*, 668–681. **314**

Guastella, M. J. New theory of apparent movement. *Journal of the Optical Society of America*, 1966, *56*, 960–966. **518**

Guilford, J. P. Autokinesis and the streaming phenomenon. *American Journal of Psychology*, 1928, *40*, 401–417. **529**

Guilford, J. P. The computation of psychological values from judgments in absolute categories. *Journal of Experimental Psychology*, 1938, *22*, 32–42. **58**

Guilford, J. P. *Psychometric methods*. (ed. 2) New York: McGraw-Hill, 1954. **16, 24, 32, 33, 34, 53, 57, 58, 62**

Guilford, J. P., & Dallenbach, K. M. A study of the autokinetic sensation. *American Journal of Psychology*, 1928, *40*, 83–91. **529**

Guilford, J. P., & Dingman, H. F. A validation study of ratio-judgment methods. *American Journal of Psychology*, 1954, *67*, 395–410. **72**

Guilford, J. P., & Dingman, H. F. A modification of the method of equal-appearing intervals. *American Journal of Psychology*, 1955, *68*, 450–454. **65**

Guilford, J. P., & Helson, H. Eye-movements and the phi-phenomenon. *American Journal of Psychology*, 1929, *41*, 595–606. **527**

Guinan, J. F., see Armus, H. L., 1964.

Guirao, N., see Stevens, S. S., 1962; Stevens, J. C., 1964.

Gulick, W. L., see Lawson, R. B., 1967; Smith, W. M., 1956, 1957, 1962.

Gulliksen, H. Transfer of response in human subjects. *Journal of Experimental Psychology*, 1932, *15*, 496–516. **1047**

Gunn, D. L., see Fraenkel, G. S., 1940.

Gunther, M. Instinct and the nursing couple. *Lancet*, 1955, 575–578. **582**

Gustafson, L. M., see Irion, A. L., 1952.

Guthrie, E. R. *The psychology of learning*. New York: Harper, 1935. **560, 567, 571, 908**

Guthrie, E. R. *The psychology of learning*. (Rev. ed.) New York: Harper, 1952. **560, 567, 571, 734**

Guthrie, E. R. Association by contiguity. In S. Koch (Ed.), *Psychology: A study of a science*. Vol. 2. New York: McGraw-Hill, 1959. **560, 908, 912**

Guthrie, E. R., see also Smith, S., 1921.

Guttman, L. Chapters 2, 3, 6, 8, and 9 in S. A. Stouffer et al. (Eds.), *Measurement and prediction*. Princeton: Princeton University Press, 1950. **63**

Guttman, N. Operant conditioning, extinction, and periodic reinforcement in relation to concentration of sucrose as a reinforcing agent. *Journal of Experimental Psychology*, 1953, *46*, 213–224. **600, 624, 625, 627, 629, 630**

Guttman, N. Equal-reinforcement values for sucrose and glucose solutions as compared with equal-sweetness values. *Journal of Experimental Psychology*, 1954, *47*, 358–361. **627**

Guttman, N., van Bergeijk, W. A., & David, E. E. Monaural temporal masking investigated by binaural interaction. *Journal of the Acoustical Society of America*, 1960, *32*, 1329–1336. **268**

Guttman, N., & Kalish, H. I. Discriminability and stimulus generalization. *Journal of Experimental Psychology*, 1956, *51*, 79–88. **753, 760, 761**

Guttman, N., see also David, E. E., 1958, 1959; Simmons, F. B., 1965.

Guy, D. E., see Bourne, L. E. Jr., 1965.

Gwinn, G. T. The effects of punishment on acts motivated by fear. *Journal of Experimental Psychology*, 1949, *39*, 260–269. **725**

Haagen, C. H. *Learning and retention as a function of the synonymity of original and interpolated tasks*. Doctoral dissertation, University of Iowa, 1943. **1084**

Haagen, C. H. Synonymity, vividness, familiarity, and association value ratings of 400 pairs of common adjectives. *Journal of Psychology*, 1949, *27*, 453–463. **890, 900, 1052, 1057**

Haas, E. L., see Warden, C. J., 1927.

Haas, von H. Über den Einfluss eines Einfachechos auf die Horsamkeit von Sprache. *Acustica*, 1951, *1*, 49–58. **268**

Haber, R. N., & Hershensen, M. The effects of repeated brief exposures on the growth of a percept. *Journal of Experimental Psychology*, 1965, *69*, 40–46. **445n**

Haber, R. N., & Nathanson, L. Post-retinal storage? Some further observations on Parks' camel as seen through the eye of a needle. *Perception and Psychophysics*, 1968, *3*, 349–355. **455**

Haber, R. N., see also Dainoff, M., 1967; Harris, C. S., 1963; Weisstein, N., 1965.

Haber, S., see Hochberg, J., 1955.

Hack, M. H. Signal detection in the rat. *Science*, 1963, 758–759. **757**

Hack, M. H., see also Gourevitch, G., 1966.

Hagen, E., Knoche, H., Sinclair, D., & Weddell, G. The role of specialized nerve terminals in cutaneous sensibility. *Proceedings of the Royal Society; Series B: Biological Sciences*, 1953, *141*, 279–287. **122, 125, 154**

Hagstrom, E. C., see Pfaffmann, C., 1955.

Hahn, H. Die Adaptation des Geschmackssinnes. *Zeitschrift für Sinnesphysiologie*, 1934, *65*, 105–145. **183, 184, 552**

Hahn, H. *Beiträge zur Reizphysiologie*. Heidelberg: Scherer Verlag, 1949. **186**

Hahn, J. F. Cutaneous vibratory thresholds for square wave electrical pulses. *Science*, 1958, *127*, 879–880. **136, 137**

Hahn, J. F. Vibrotactile adaptation and recovery measured by two methods. *Journal of Experimental Psychology*, 1966, *71*, 655–658. **136**

Hahn, W. W., Stern, J. A., & Fehr, F. S. Generalizability of heart rate as a measure of drive state. *Journal of Compar-*

ative and Physiological Psychology, 1964, *58*, 305–309. **836**

Hahn, W. W., Stern, J. A., & McDonald, D. G. Effects of water deprivation and bar pressing activity on heart rate of the male albino rat. *Journal of Comparative and Physiological Psychology*, 1962, *55*, 786–790. **836**

Haibt, L. H., *see* Rochester, H., 1956.

Haider, M., *see* Spong, P., 1965.

Haire, M., *see* Adams, P. A., 1959.

Hake, D. R., & Azrin, N. H. Conditioned punishment. *Journal of the Experimental Analysis of Behavior*, 1965, *8*, 279–293. **665, 719**

Hake, H. W. *Contributions of psychology to the study of pattern vision.* WADC Technical Report 57-621. Wright Air Development Center, Aero Medical Laboratory. Project No. 7192-71598, 1957. Pp. 1–118. **428**

Hake, H. W., Grant, D. A. & Hornseth, J. P. Resistance to extinction and the pattern of reinforcement: III. The effect of trial patterning in verbal "conditioning." *Journal of Experimental Psychology*, 1951, *41*, 221–225. **908**

Hake, H. W., & Hyman, R. Perception of the statistical structure of a random series of binary symbols. *Journal of Experimental Psychology*, 1953, *45*, 64–74. **934**

Hake, H. W., & Myers, A. E. Familiarity and shape constancy. *Journal of Experimental Psychology*, 1969, *80*, 205–214. **515**

Hake, H. W., Rodwan, A. & Weintraub, D. Noise reduction in perception. In Kenneth R. Hammond (Ed.), *The psychology of Egon Brunswik*, New York: Holt, Rinehart and Winston, 1966. **449**

Hake, H. W., *see also* Egan, J. P., 1950; Garner, W. R., 1951, 1956.

Hakes, D., *see* James, C. T., 1965.

Hall, J. F. Studies in secondary reinforcement: I. Secondary reinforcement as a function of the frequency of primary reinforcement. *Journal of Comparative and Physiological Psychology*, 1951, *44*, 246–251. (a) **667**

Hall, J. F. Studies in secondary reinforcement: II. Secondary reinforcement as a function of the strength of drive during primary reinforcement. *Journal of Comparative and Physiological Psychology*, 1951, *44*, 462–466. (b) **668**

Hall, J. F. Learning as a function of word-frequency. *American Journal of Psychology*, 1954, *67*, 138–140. **895**

Hall, J. F. Activity as a function of a restricted drinking schedule. *Journal of Comparative and Physiological Psychology*, 1955, *48*, 265–266.

Hall, J. F., & Ugelow, A. Free association time as a function of word frequency. *Canadian Journal of Psychology*, 1957, *11*, 29–32. **865**

Hall, J. F., *see also* Treichler, F. R., 1962.

Hall, J. L., II. Binaural interaction in the accessory superior-olivary nucleus of the cat. *Journal of the Acoustical Society of America*, 1965, *37*, 814–823. **265**

Hall, K. R. L., Earle, A. E., & Crookes, T. G. A pendulum phenomenon in the visual perception of apparent movement. *Quarterly Journal of Experimental Psychology*, 1952, *4*, 109–120. **527**

Hall, M., *see* Hull, C. L., 1940.

Hall, R. D. An integration of discrete-trial and free-operant conditioning techniques. Doctoral dissertation, Brown University, 1960. Ann Arbor, Mich.: University Microfilms No. 62-5747. **619**

Hall, R. D., & Kling, J. W. Amount of consummatory activity and performance in a modified T maze. *Journal of Comparative and Physiological Psychology*, 1960, *53*, 165–168. **623**

Halpern, B. P. Chemical coding in taste-temporal patterns. In Y. Zotterman (Ed.), *Olfaction and taste*. Vol. I. New York: Pergamon, 1963. Pp. 275–284. **182**

Halpern, B. P. Chemotopic coding for sucrose and quinine hydrochloride in the nucleus of the fasciculus solitarius.

In T. Hayashi (Ed.), *Olfaction and taste*. Vol. 2. New York: Pergamon, 1967. Pp. 549–562. (a) **182**

Halpern, B. P. Some relationships between electrophysiology and behavior in taste. In M. R. Kare & O. Maller (Eds.), *The chemical senses and nutrition*. Baltimore: Johns Hopkins Press, 1967. Pp. 213–241. (b) **186, 187**

Halpern, B. P., & Nelson, L. M. Bulbar gustatory responses to anterior and to posterior tongue stimulation in the rat. *American Journal of Physiology*, 1965, *209*, 105–110. **182**

Halpern, B. P., *see also* Benjamin, R. M., 1965; Pfaffmann, C., 1961.

Halverson, H. M. Binaural localization of tones as dependent upon differences of phase and intensity. *American Journal of Psychology*, 1922, *33*, 178–212. **266**

Ham, M., *see* Underwood, B. J., 1962.

Hamilton, A., *see* Kenshalo, D. R., 1967.

Hamilton, C. E. The relationship between length of interval separating two learning tasks and performance on the second task. *Journal of Experimental Psychology*, 1950, *40*, 613–621. **1034, 1036**

Hamilton, C. R. Intermanual transfer of adaptation to prisms. *American Journal of Psychology*, 1964, *77*, 457–462. **537**

Hamilton, E. L. The effect of delayed incentive on the hunger drive in the white rat. *Genetic Psychology Monographs*, 1929, *5*, 133–207. **678**

Hamilton, H., *see* Saltz, E., 1967.

Hamilton, R. J. Retroactive facilitation as a function of degree of generalization between tasks. *Journal of Experimental Psychology*, 1943, *32*, 363–376. **1050, 1051, 1053, 1083**

Hamilton, W. J., III, *see* Marler, P. R., 1966.

Hammer, E. R. Temporal factor in figural after-effects. *American Journal of Psychology*, 1949, *62*, 337–354. **469**

Hammer, L. R. Saccharin and sucrose intake in rats: Long- and short-term tests. *Psychonomic Science*, 1967, *8*, 367–368. **630**

Hammock, J. T., *see* Long, E. R., 1958.

Hanawalt, N. G. The effect of practice upon the perception of simple designs masked by more complex figures. *Journal of Experimental Psychology*, 1942, *31*, 134–148. **440**

Hancock, W., *see* Amsel, A., 1957.

Handel, S., & Garner, W. R. The structure of visual pattern associates and pattern goodness. *Perception and Psychophysics*, 1965, *1*, 33–38. **446, 447**

Hanes, R. M. A scale of subjective brightness. *Journal of Experimental Psychology*, 1949, *39*, 438–452. **67, 70**

Hanes, R. M., *see also* Burnham, R. W., 1963.

Hanly, B., *see* Bolles, R. C., 1959.

Hanna, J. F., *see* Feldman, J., 1966.

Hansen, A. K. "After-image transfer test" in anomalous retinal correspondence. *Archives of Opthalmology*. 1954, *52*, 369–374. **473**

Hanson, H. M. Effects of discrimination training on stimulus generalization. *Journal of Experimental Psychology*, 1959, *58*, 321–334. **765, 778**

Hara, S. Interrelationship among stimulus intensity, stimulated area and reaction time in the human gustatory sensation. *Bulletin of the Tokyo Medical and Dental University*, 1955, *2*, 147–158. **175**

Harcum, E. R. Verbal transfer of overlearned forward and backward associations. *American Journal of Psychology*, 1953, *66*, 622–625. **1063, 1064, 1068**

Harcum, E. R., & Filion, R. D. C. Effects of stimulus reversals on lateral dominance in word recognition. *Perceptual and Motor Skills*, 1963, *17*, 779–794. **444**

Harden, L. M. A quantitative study of the similarity factor in retroactive inhibition. *Journal of General Psychology*, 1929, *2*, 421–432. **1081**

Hardy, D., *see* Hochberg, J., 1960.

Hardy, J. D., Goodell, H., & Wolff, H. G. Influence of skin

temperature on pain threshold. *Science*, 1951, *114*, 149–150. **150, 158**

Hardy, J. D., & Oppel, T. W. Studies in temperature sensation: III. The sensitivity of the body to heat and spatial summation of the end-organ responses. *Journal of Clinical Investigation*, 1937, *16*, 533–540. **143, 146, 147**

Hardy, J. D., & Oppel, T. W. Studies in temperature sensation: IV. The stimulation of cold by radiation. *Journal of Clinical Investigation*, 1938, *17*, 771–777. **143, 146**

Hardy, J. D., Stolwijk, J. A. J., & Hoffman, D. Pain following step increase in skin temperature. In D. R. Kenshalo (Ed.), *The skin senses*. Springfield, Ill.: Charles C Thomas, 1968. Pp. 444–457. **159, 162**

Hardy, J. D., Wolff, H. G., & Goodell, H. Studies on pain: A new method for measuring pain threshold: Observations on spatial summation of pain. *Journal of Clinical Investigation*, 1940, *19*, 649–657. **156, 157**

Hardy, J. D., Wolff, H. G., & Goodell, H. Studies on pain: Discrimination of differences in intensity of a pain stimulus as a basis for a scale of pain intensity. *Journal of Clinical Investigation*, 1947, *26*, 1152–1158. **158**

Hardy, J. D., *see also* Greene, L. C., 1958, 1962; Hendler, E., 1960; Herget, C. M., 1941, 1942; Lipkin, M., 1954; Schumacher, G. A., 1940; Wolf, S., 1941.

Hardy, L. H., Rand, G., Rittler, M. C., Blank, A. A. & Boeder, P. *The geometry of binocular space perception*. New York: Knapp Memorial Laboratories, Institute of Ophthalmology, Columbia University College of Physicians and Surgeons, 1953. **493**

Harford, R. A., *see* Hefferline, R. F., 1959.

Harker, G. S., *see* Gogel, W. C., 1957.

Harlow, H. F. The formation of learning sets. *Psychological Review*, 1949, *56*, 51–65. **750, 768**

Harlow, H. F. Analysis of discrimination learning by monkeys. *Journal of Experimental Psychology*, 1950, *40*, 26–39. **773**

Harlow, H. F. Mice, monkeys, men, and motives. *Psychological Review*, 1953, *60*, 23–32. (a) **840**

Harlow, H. F. Motivation as a factor in the acquisition of new responses. In *Current theory and research in motivation: A symposium*. Lincoln, Nebraska: University of Nebraska Press, 1953. Pp. 24–49. (b) **840**

Harlow, H. F. The nature of love. *American Psychologist*, 1958, *13*, 673–685. **585**

Harlow, H. F. Learning set and error factor theory. In S. Koch (Ed.), *Psychology: A study of a science*. New York: McGraw-Hill, 1959. Vol. 2. Pp. 492–537. **766, 768, 773**

Harlow, H. F. Love in infant monkeys. *Scientific American*, 1959, *200*, 68–74. **585**

Harlow, H. F. The development of affectional patterns in infant monkeys. In B. M. Foss (Ed.), *Determinants of infant behavior*. Vol. I., London: Methuen, 1961. **585**

Harlow, H. F., & Bromer, J. A. A test-apparatus for monkeys. *Psychological Record*, 1938, *19*, 434. **750**

Harlow, H. F., & Harlow, M. K. Learning to think. *Scientific American*, 1949. **768**

Harlow, H. F., & Harlow, M. K. Social deprivation in monkeys. *Scientific American*, 1962, *207*, 137–146. **585**

Harlow, H. F., & Harlow, M. K. The affectional systems. In A. M. Schrier, H. F. Harlow, & F. Stollnitz (Eds.), *Behavior of non-human primates*. New York: Academic Press, 1965. Pp. 287–333. **122**

Harlow, H. F., Harlow, M. K., Rueping, R., & Mason, W. A. Performance of infant rhesus monkeys on discrimination learning, delayed response, and discrimination learning set. *Journal of Comparative and Physiological Psychology*, 1960, *53*, 113–121. **768**

Harlow, H. F., *see also* Grandine, L., 1948; Schrier, A. M., 1956.

Harlow, M. K., *see* Harlow, H. F., 1949.

Harmon, L. D., *see* Simmons, F. B., 1965.

Harper, H. W., Jay, J. R., & Erickson, R. P. Chemically evoked sensations from single human taste papillae. *Physiology and Behavior*, 1966, *1*, 319–325. **175, 178**

Harper, R. On odour classification. *Journal of Food Technology*, 1966, *1*, 167–176. **213**

Harper, R. S. The perceptual modification of colored figures. *American Journal of Psychology*, 1953, *66*, 86–89. **425**

Harper, R. S., & Stevens, S. S. A psychological scale of weight and a formula for its derivation. *American Journal of Psychology*, 1948, *61*, 343–351. **67, 68**

Harriman, A. E., & MacLeod, R. B. Discriminative thresholds of salt for normal and adrenalectomized rats. *American Journal of Psychology*, 1953, *66*, 465–471. **176**

Harrington, G. M., & Kohler, G. R. Sensory deprivation and sensory reinforcement with shock. *Psychological Reports*, 1966, *18*, 803–808. **616**

Harris, C., *see* Rock, I., 1967.

Harris, C. S. Adaptation to displaced vision: Visual, motor or proprioceptive change? *Science*, 1963, *140*, 812–813. **537**

Harris, C. S. Perceptual adaptation to inverted, reversed and displaced vision. *Psychological Review*, 1965, *72*, 419–444. **533, 537, 540, 541, 543**

Harris, C. S., & Haber, R. N. Selective attention and coding in visual perception. *Journal of Experimental Psychology*, 1963, *65*, 328–333. **444**

Harris, E. S., Hoffman, H. S., Liberman, A. M., Delattre, P. C., & Cooper, F. S. Effect of third formant transitions on the perception of the voiced stop consonants. *Journal of the Acoustical Society of America*, 1958, *30*, 122–126. **253**

Harris, G. Binaural interactions of impulsive stimuli and pure tones. *Journal of the Acoustical Society of America*, 1960, *32*, 685–692. **263, 266**

Harris, G. Periodicity perception using gated noise. *Journal of the Acoustical Society of America*, 1963, *35*, 1225–1233. **245**

Harris, J. D. Pitch discrimination. *Journal of the Acoustical Society of America*, 1952, *24*, 750–755. **29, 249**

Harris, J. D. A brief critical review of loudness recruitment. *Psychological Bulletin*, 1953, *50*, 190–203. **240**

Harris, J. D. Hearing. In P. R. Farnsworth (Ed.), *Annual review of psychology*, Vol. 9. Palo Alto, Calif.: Annual Reviews, 1958. **234**

Harris, J. D. The scaling of pitch intervals. *Journal of the Acoustical Society of America*, 1960, *32*, 1575–1581. **244**

Harris, J. D. Loudness discrimination. *Journal of Speech and Hearing Research*, (Monograph Supplement), 1963, *11*. **249**

Harris, K. S., *see* Liberman, A. M., 1962.

Harrison, I. B., & Bigelow, N. H. Quantitative studies of visceral pain produced by the contraction of ischemic muscle. *Proceedings of the Association for Research in Nervous and Mental Disease*, 1943, *23*, 154–165. **156**

Harrison, R. H., *see* Jenkins, H. M., 1960, 1962.

Hart, G., *see* Miller, N. E., 1948.

Harter, S. Discrimination learning set in children as a function of IQ and MA. *Journal of Experimental Child Psychology*, 1965, *2*, 31–43. **768**

Hartline, H. K. The response of single optic nerve fibers of the vertebrate eye to illumination of the retina. *American Journal of Physiology*, 1938, *121*, 400–415. **203, 309**

Hartline, H. K. The effects of spatial summation in the retina on the excitation of the fibers in the optic nerve. *American Journal of Physiology*, 1940, *130*, 700–711. (a) **291**

Hartline, H. K. The receptive fields of optic nerve fibers. *American Journal of Physiology*, 1940, *130*, 690–699. (b) **291**

Hartline, H. K., & Graham, C. H. Nerve impulses from single receptors in the eye. *Journal of Cellular and Comparative Physiology*, 1932, *1*, 277–295. **293**

Hartline, H. K., Ratliff, F., & Miller, W. H. Inhibitory inter-action in the retina and its significance in vision. In E. Florey (Ed.), *Nervous inhibition.* New York: Pergamon, 1961. Pp. 241–284. **293**

Hartline, H. K., Wagner, H. G., & Ratliff, F. Inhibition in the eye of *Limulus. Journal of General Physiology,* 1956, *39,* 651–673. **292**

Hartman, B. O., *see* Gogel, W. C., 1957.

Hartman, R., *see* Horton, D. L., 1963.

Hartman, T. F. Dynamic transmission, elective generaliza-tion, and semantic conditioning. In W. F. Prokasy (Ed.), *Classical conditioning.* New York: Appleton, 1965. **555**

Hartman, T. F., & Grant, D. A. Differential eyelid condition-ing as a function of the CS–UCS interval. *Journal of Experimental Psychology,* 1962, *64,* 131–136. **558**

Hartman, T. F., *see also* Thurlow, W. R., 1959.

Hartson, L. D. Contrasting approaches to the analysis of skilled movements. *Journal of General Psychology,* 1939, *20,* 276–293. **379**

Hartz, K. E., *see* Glickman, S. E., 1964.

Harvey, F. K., Cisek, J. G., MacLean, D. J., & Schroeder, M. R. Some aspects of stereophony applicable to confer-ence use. *Journal of the Audio English Society,* 1963, *11,* 212–217. **258**

Harvey, L. O. Jr., *see* Leibowitz, H. W., 1967.

Harway, N. I. Judgment of distance in children and adults. *Journal of Experimental Psychology,* 1963, *65,* 385–390. **514**

Hashimoto, H., *see* Kaneko, A., 1969.

Hasler, A. D., *see* Wisby, W. J., 1954.

Hastorf, A. H. The influence of suggestion on the relation between stimulus size and perceived distance. *Journal of Psychology,* 1950, *29,* 195–217. **496**

Hastorf, A. H., & Kennedy, J. L. Emmert's law and size-constancy. *American Journal of Psychology,* 1957, *70,* 114–116. **511**

Hastorf, A. H., & Way, K. S. Apparent size with and without distance cues. *Journal of General Psychology,* 1952, *47,* 181–188. **513**

Hatton, G. I., *see* O'Kelly, L. I., 1965.

Haun, K. W. Measures of association and verbal learning. *Psychological Reports,* 1960, *7,* 451–460. **900**

Havron, M. D., Nordlie, P. G., & Cofer, C. N. Measurement of attitude by a simple word association technique. *Journal of Social Psychology,* 1957, *46,* 81–89. **876**

Hawkins, J. E., Jr., & Stevens, S. S. The masking of pure tones and of speech by white noise. *Journal of the Acoustical Society of America,* 1950, *22,* 6–13. **240, 257**

Hawkins, J. E., *see also* Hudgins, C. V., 1947.

Hawkins, T. D., *see* Pliskoff, S. S., 1964, 1967.

Hawkins, W. F., *see* Baumeister, A., 1964.

Hawkins, W. T., *see* Goldiamond, I., 1958.

Hawley, M., *see* Kryter, K. D., 1963.

Hay, J., *see* Hochberg, J. E., 1956.

Hay, J. C. Optical motions and space perception: An exten-sion of Gibson's analysis. *Psychological Review,* 1966, *73,* 550–565. **505**

Hay, J. C. Visual adaptation to an altered correlation be-tween eye movement and head movement. *Science,* 1968, *160,* 429–430. **545**

Hay, J. C., & Pick, H. L., Jr. Visual and proprioceptive adap-tation to optical displacement of the visual stimulus. *Journal of Experimental Psychology,* 1966, *71,* 150–158. **538**

Hay, J. C., Pick, H. L., Jr., & Ikeda, K. Visual capture produced by prism spectacles. *Psychonomic Science,* 1965, *2,* 215–216. **536**

Hay, J. C., *see also* Pick, H. L. Jr., 1964, 1965, 1966.

Hayes, J. R., *see* Verplanck, W. S., 1953.

Hayes, K. J. The backward learning curve: A method for the study of learning. *Psychological Review,* 1953, *60,* 269–275. **613**

Hayes, S. P. Facial vision or the sense of obstacles. *Perkins Publications,* 1935, *12,* 1–45. **270**

Hayes, S. P. *Contributions to a psychology of blindness.* New York: American Foundation for the Blind, 1941. **270**

Hayes, W. H., *see* Robinson, J. S., 1964.

Hayes, W. J., Robinson, J., & Brown, L. An effect of past experiences on perception: An artifact. *American Psy-chology,* 1961, *16,* 420 (Abstr.). **444**

Haygood, R., & Bourne, L. E. Attribute and rule learning aspects of conceptual behavior. *Psychological Review,* 1965, *72,* 175–195. **939, 965**

Haynes, H., White, B. L., & Held, R. Visual accommodation in human infants. *Science,* 1965, *148,* 528–530. **547**

Hays, W. L. *Statistics for psychologists.* New York: Holt, Rinehart and Winston, 1963. **61, 713**

Heath, H. A., *see* Orbach, J., 1963.

Heath, R. M., *see* McClelland, D. C., 1943.

Hebb, D. L. Distinctive features of learning in the higher animal. In J. F. Delafresnaye (Ed.), *Brain mechanisms and learning.* Oxford: Blackwell, 1961. **998**

Hebb, D. O. On the nature of fear. *Psychological Review,* 1946, *53,* 250–275. **586**

Hebb, D. O. *The organization of behavior,* New York: Wiley, 1949. **451, 452, 470, 763, 818**

Hebb, D. O. Drives and the C.N.S. (conceptual nervous system). *Psychological Review,* 1955, *62,* 243–254. **796, 832, 840, 842**

Hebb, D. O. *A textbook of psychology.* (2nd ed.) Philadel-phia: Saunders, 1966. **832, 840**

Hebb, D. O., *see also* Pritchard, R. M., 1960.

Hecht, H. Die simultane Erfassung der Figuren, *Zeitschrift für Psychologie,* 1924, *94,* 153–194. **455**

Hecht, M., *see* Graham, C. H., 1948.

Hecht, S. Vision: II. The nature of the photoreceptor process. In C. Murchison (Ed.), *A handbook of general experimen-tal psychology.* Worchester, Mass.: Clark University Press, 1934. Pp. 704–828. **284, 297, 303**

Hecht, S. Rods, cones, and the chemical basis of vision. *Physiological Review,* 1937, *17,* 239–290. **287**

Hecht, S., & Mintz, E. U. The visibility of single lines at various illuminations and the retinal basis of visual reso-lution. *Journal of General Physiology,* 1939, *22,* 593–612. **298, 299**

Hecht, S., Peskin, J. C., & Patt, M. Intensity discrimination in the human eye: II. Relationship between $\Delta I/I$ and intensity for different parts of the spectrum. *Journal of General Physiology,* 1938, *22,* 7–19. **297**

Hecht, S., & Shlaer, S. Intermittent stimulation by light: V. The relation between intensity and critical frequency for different parts of the spectrum. *Journal of General Physi-ology,* 1936, *19,* 965–979. **312**

Hecht, S., Shlaer, S., & Pirenne, M. H. Energy, quanta, and vision. *Journal of General Physiology,* 1942, *25,* 819–840. **284**

Hecht, S., & Smith, E. L. Intermittent stimulation by light: VI. Area and the relation between critical frequency and intensity. *Journal of General Physiology,* 1936, *19,* 979–989. **311**

Heckenmueller, E., & Dember, W. N. A forced choice indi-cator for use with Werner's disc-ring pattern in studies of backward masking. *Psychonomic Science,* 1965, *3,* 167–168. **430**

Hecker, M. H. L., *see* House, A. S., 1965.

Hefferline, R. F., Keenan, B., & Harford, R. A. Escape and avoidance conditioning in human subjects without their observation of the response. *Science,* 1959, *130,* 1338–1339. **87, 115**

Heidbreder, E. The attainment of concepts: II. The problem. *Journal of General Psychology,* 1946, *35,* 191–223. **786**

Heidbreder, E. The attainment of concepts: III. The process. *Journal of Psychology,* 1947, *24,* 93–138. **946, 961**

Heider, F., & Simmel, M. An experimental study of apparent

behavior. *American Journal of Psychology*, 1944, *57*, 243–259. **525**

Heimer, W., see Rock, I., 1957, 1959.

Hein, A. V., see Held, R., 1958, 1963.

Heinbecker, P., Bishop, G. H., & O'Leary, J. Pain and touch fibers in peripheral nerves. *Archives of Neurology and Psychiatry*, 1933, *29*, 771–789. **156, 162**

Heine, R. Uber Wiedererkennen und rückwirkende Hemmung. *Zeitschrift für Psychologie*, 1914, *68*, 161–236. **1080**

Heineman, C., see Schlosberg, H., 1950.

Heinemann, E. G. Simultaneous brightness induction as a function of inducing- and test-field luminances. *Journal of Experimental Psychology*, 1955, *50*, 89–96. **411, 413**

Heinemann, E. G. The relation of apparent brightness to the threshold for differences in luminance. *Journal of Experimental Psychology*, 1961, *61*, 389–399. **411**

Heinemann, E. G., & Marill, T. Tilt adaptation and figural after-effects. *Journal of Experimental Psychology*, 1954, *48*, 468–472. **473**

Heinemann, E. G., Tulving, E., & Nachmias, J. The effect of oculomotor adjustments on apparent size. *American Journal of Psychology*, 1959, *72*, 32–45. **479, 480, 513**

Heinemann, S. H., see Mandler, G., 1956.

Heise, G. A., see Miller, G. A., 1951.

Held, R. Exposure-history as a factor in maintaining stability of perception and coordination. *Journal of Nervous and Mental Disorders*, 1961, *132*, 26–32. **535**

Held, R., & Bauer, J. A. Visually guided reaching in infant monkeys after restricted rearing. *Science*, 1967, *155*, 718–720. **535**

Held, R., & Bossom, J. Neonatal deprivation and adult rearrangement: Complementary techniques for analyzing plastic sensory-motor coordinations. *Journal of Comparative and Physiological Psychology*, 1961, *54*, 33–37. **535, 536, 537n, 540**

Held, R., Efstathiou, A., & Greene, M. Adaptation to displaced and delayed visual feedback from the hand. *Journal of Experimental Psychology*, 1966, *72*, 887–891. **536**

Held, R., & Freedman, S. Plasticity in human sensorimotor control. *Science*, 1963, *142*, 455–462. **535**

Held, R., & Gottlieb, N. A technique for studying adaptation to disarranged hand-eye coordination. *Perceptual and Motor Skills*, 1958, *8*, 83–86. **535**

Held, R., & Hein, A. V. Adaptation of disarranged hand-eye coordination contingent upon re-afferent stimulation. *Perceptual and Motor Skills*, 1958, *8*, 87–90. **535**

Held, R., & Hein, A. Movement produced stimulation in the development of visually-guided behavior. *Journal of Comparative and Physiological Psychology*, 1963, *56*, 872–876. **535, 548**

Held, R., & Rekosh, J. Motor-sensory feedback and the geometry of visual space. *Science*, 1963, *141*, 722–723. **467, 542**

Held, R., see also Bossom, J., 1957; Efstathiou, A., 1967; Haynes, H., 1965; Mikaelian, H., 1964.

Hellman, R. P., & Zwislocki, J. Some factors affecting the estimation of loudness. *Journal of the Acoustical Society of America*, 1961, *33*, 687–694. **247**

Hellyer, S., see Burke, C. J., 1954.

Helmholtz, H. von. *Treatise on physiological optics*. Vol. III (trans. from the 3rd German ed., J. P. C. Southall, Ed.) New York: Dover, 1962. **397**

Helmholtz, H. von. *Handbuch der physiologischen Optik*. (3rd ed.) Hamburg & Leipzig: Voss, 1909–1911. First pub. 1856–1866, 2nd ed., 1896. **403, 455, 466n, 484, 488, 506, 510, 521, 527, 529, 530, 531, 534, 543, 546**

Helmholtz, H. von. *Helmholtz's Physiological optics*. Trans. from the 3rd German ed. (1909–1911) by J. P. C. Southall, Ed. Rochester, N.Y.; Optical Society of America, 1924–25. **288, 301, 397**

Helson, H. Size constancy of the projected afterimage.

American Journal of Psychology, 1936, *48*, 638–642. **511**

Helson, H., Fundamental problems in color vision: The principle governing changes in hue, saturation, and lightness of non-selective samples in chromatic illumination. *Journal of Experimental Psychology*, 1938, *23*, 439–476. **415**

Helson, H. Some factors and implications of color constancy. *Journal of the Optical Society of America*, 1943, *33*, 555–567. **412, 416**

Helson, H. Adaptation-level as a basis for a quantitative theory of frames of reference. *Psychological Review*, 1948, *55*, 297–313. **416**

Helson, H. Studies of anomalous contrast and assimilation. *Journal of the Optical Society of America*, 1963, *53*, 179–184. **408**

Helson, H. *Adaptation-level theory: An experimental and systematic approach to behavior.* New York: Harper, 1964. **59, 60, 412, 416**

Helson, H. Some problems in motivation from the point of view of the theory of adaptation level. In D. Levine (Ed.), *Nebraska symposium on motivation, 1966*. Lincoln: University of Nebraska Press, 1966. **434n, 634, 637**

Helson, H., & Fehrer, E. V. The role of form in perception. *American Journal of Psychology*, 1932, *44*, 79–102. **443**

Helson, H., & Jeffers, V. B. Fundamental problems in color vision: II. Hue, lightness, and saturation of selective samples in chromatic illumination. *Journal of Experimental Psychology*, 1940, *26*, 1–27. **416, 417**

Helson, H., & Lansford, T. The role of spectral energy of source and background color in pleasantness of object colors. *Applied Optics*, 1970, *9*, 1513–1562. **315**

Helson, H., see also Guilford, J. P., 1929; Michels, W. C., 1949.

Henderson, A., see Ceraso, J., 1965, 1966.

Hendler, E. & Hardy, J. D. Infrared and microwave effects on skin heating and temperature sensation. *IRE Transactions on Medical Electronics*, 1960, ME-7, 114–152. **140, 154, 158**

Henkin, R. I. The definition of primary and accessory areas of olfaction as the basis for a classification of decreased olfactory acuity. In T. Hayashi (Ed.), *Olfaction and taste*. Vol. II, New York: Pergamon, 1967. Pp. 235–252. **197, 207**

Henkin, R. I., & Powell, G. F. Increased sensitivity of taste and smell in cystic fibrosis. *Science*, 1962, *138*, 1107–1108. **210**

Henkin, R. I., & Solomon, D. H. Salt-taste threshold in adrenal insufficiency in man. *Journal of Clinical Endocrinology and Metabolism*, 1962, *22*, 856–858. **189**

Henle, M. An experimental investigation of past experience as a determinant of form perception. *Journal of Experimental Psychology*, 1942, *30*, 1–22. **444**

Hennelly, E. F., see Langmuir, I., 1944.

Henneman, R. H. A photometric study of the perception of object color. *Archives of Psychology* (New York), 1935, *179*. **404, 423**

Henning, G. B., see Green, D. M., 1969.

Henri, V., see Binet, A., 1896.

Henry, C. E., see Knott, J. R., 1941.

Hensel, H. Temperaturempfindung und intracutane Warmebewegung. *Pflüger's Archiv fur die Gesamte Physiologie des Menschen und der Tiere*, 1950, *252*, 165–215. **142, 144, 145**

Hensel, H. Physiologie der Thermoreception. *Ergebnisse der Physiologie*, 1952, *47*, 166–368. **141**

Hensel, H., & Kenshalo, D. R. Warm receptors in the nasal region of cats. *Journal of Physiology*, 1969, *204*, 99–112. **151**

Hensel, H., Ström, L., & Zotterman, Y. Electrophysiological measurements of depth of thermoreceptors. *Journal of Neurophysiology*, 1951, *14*, 423–439. **140**

Hensel, H. & Witt, I. Spatial temperature gradient and thermoreceptor stimulation. *Journal of Physiology*, 1959, *148*, 180–187. **153**

Hensel, H., & Zotterman, Y. Quantitative Beziehungen zwischen der Entladung einzelner Kaltfasern der Temperatur. *Acta Physiologica Scandinavica*, 1951, *23*, 291-319. **151**

Henson, C. D., see Hubel, D. H., 1959.

Henton, W. W., Smith, J. C. & Tucker, D. Odor discrimination in the pigeon. *Science*, 1966, *153*, 1138-1139. **755**

Herberg, L. J. Seminal ejaculation following positively reinforcing electrical stimulation of the rat hypothalamus. *Journal of Comparative and Physiological Psychology*, 1963, *56*, 679-685. **660**

Herget, C. M., Granath, L. P., & Hardy, J. D. Warmth sense in relation to skin area stimulated. *American Journal of Physiology*, 1941, *135*, 20-26. **147**

Herget, C. M., & Hardy, J. D. Spatial summation of heat. *American Journal of Physiology*, 1942, *135*, 426-429. **148, 149**

Hering, E. *Beitrage zur Physiologie*. Heft 1. Leipzig: Englemann, 1861. Pp. 305f. **481, 489, 491**

Hering, E. Zur Lehre vom Lichtsinn. *Wien Akademie der Wissenschaften. Mathematische-Naturwissenschaftlichte Klasse Sitzungsberichte*, 1874, *69*, 85-104. **397, 411**

Hering, E. Zur Lehre von der Beziehung zwischen Leib und Seele: 1. Uber Fechner's psychophysisches Gesetz. *Wien Akademie der Wissenschaften. Mathematisch-Naturwissenschaftliche. Klasse Sitzungsberichte*, 1876, *72*, 310-348. **377, 411**

Hering, E. Grundzuge einer Théorie des Temperatursinnes. *Wien Akademie der Wissenschaften. Mathematische-Naturwissenschaftliche. Klasse Sitzungsberichte*, 1877, *75*, 101-135. **154**

Hering, E. Der Raumsinn und die Bewegungen des Auges. In L. Hermann (Ed.), *Handbuch der Physiologie*. Vol. 3, Leipzig; Vogel, 1879. Pp. 343-601. **397**

Hering, E. Über die Grenzen der Sehschärfe. *Ber. math.-phys. Kl. Königl. Sächs. ges. Wiss. zu Leipzig*, 1899, 16-24. **301**

Hering, E. Grundzuge der Lehre vom Lichtsinn. In Graefe & Saemisch (Eds.), *Handbuch der gesammten Augenheilkunde*, Vol. III, ch. 13; 1905. 2nd ed., W. Englemann, Ed. Leipzig: J. Springer, 1920. **323**

Hering, E. *Outlines of a theory of the light sense*. Cambridge, Mass.: Harvard University Press, 1964. **323, 397, 410, 421**

Hermans, T. G. The relationship of convergence and elevation changes to judgments of size. *Journal of Experimental Psychology*, 1954, *48*, 204-208. **480, 513**

Heron, W. T. The warming-up effect in learning nonsense syllables. *Journal of Genetic Psychology*, 1928, *35*, 219-228. **1033**

Heron, W. Perception as a function of retinal locus and attention. *American Journal of Psychology*, 1957, *70*, 38-48. **444**

Heron, W. T., & Skinner, B. F. Changes in hunger during starvation. *Psychological Record*, 1937, *1*, 51-60. **826**

Heron, W. see also Pritchard, R. M., 1960.

Herrnstein, R. J. Superstition: A corollary of the principles of operant conditioning. In W. K. Honig (Ed.), *Operant behavior: Areas of research and application*. New York: Appleton, 1966. **675, 692n**

Herrnstein, R. J. & Hineline, P. N. Negative reinforcement as shock-frequency reduction. *Journal of the Experimental Analysis of Behavior*, 1966, *9*, 421-430. **731**

Herrnstein, R. J., see also Fantino, E., 1968; Sidman, M., 1957.

Herron, W., see Pritchard, R. M., 1960.

Hershberger, W. A. Comment on "Apparent reversal (oscillation) of rotary motion in depth." *Psychological Review*, 1967, *74*, 235-238. **518**

Hershenson, M. Visual discrimination in the human newborn. *Journal of Comparative and Physiological Psychology*, 1964, *58*, 270-276. **547**

Hershenson, M. Development of the perception of form. *Psychological Bulletin*, 1967, *67*, 326-336. **547**

Hershenson, M., Munsinger, & Kessen, W. Preference for shapes of intermediate variability in the newborn human. *Science*, 1965, 147, 630-631. **547**

Hershensen, M., see also Haber, R. N., 1965.

Hersher, L., Richmond, J. B., & Moore, A. U. Modifiability of the critical period for the development of maternal behavior in sheep and goats. *Behaviour*, 1963, *20*, 311-320. **584**

Herskovits, M. J., see Segall, M. H., 1963, 1966.

Hertzman, M., see Witkin, H. A., 1954.

Herxheimer, A. see DeWardener, H. E., 1957.

Heslam, R. M., see Malmo, R. B., 1951.

Hess, C., & Pretori, H. Messende Untersuchungen über die Gesetzmässigkeit des simultanen Helligkeits-Contrastes. *Archiv für Ophthalmologie*, 1894, *40*, 1-24. As described in E. Hering, *Outlines of a theory of the light sense* (trans. L. M. Hurvich & D. Jameson). Cambridge, Mass.: Harvard University Press, 1964. **408, 410, 411, 413**

Hess, E. H. Development of the chick's response to light and shade cues of depth. *Journal of Comparative and Physiological Psychology*, 1950, *43*, 112-122. **497**

Hess, E. H. Space perception in the chick. *Scientific American*, 1956, *195*, 71-80. **547**

Hess, E. H. The conditions limiting critical age of imprinting. *Journal of Comparative and Physiological Psychology*, 1959, *52*, 515-518. **583**

Hess, E. H. Attitude and pupil size. *Scientific American*, 1965, *212*, 46-54. **393**

Hess, E. H., see also Gogel, W. C., 1951.

Hess, W. R. *Beiträge zur Physiologie des Hirnstammes. I: Die Methodik der lokalisierten Reizung und Ausschaltung subkortikaler Hirnabschnitte*. Leipzig: Thieme, 1932. **643**

Heuckeroth, O., see Myers, J. L., 1966.

Heyer, A. W., see Osgood, C. E., 1952.

Heymans, G. Quantitative Untersuchungen über das "optische Paradoxon." *Zeitschrift für Psychologie*, 1896, *9*, 221-255. **458, 464**

Higa, M. Interference effects of intralist word relationships in verbal learning. *Journal of Verbal Learning and Verbal Behavior*, 1963, *2*, 170-175. **894**

Higgins, K. E., see Robinson, J. S., 1967.

Hilgard, E. R. The nature of the conditioned response: I. The case for and against stimulus substitution. *Psychological Review*, 1936, *43*, 366-385. **565**

Hilgard, E. R. Methods and procedures in the study of learning. In S. S. Stevens (Ed.), *Handbook of experimental psychology*. New York: Wiley, 1951. Pp. 517-567. **890n**

Hilgard, E. R., & Bower, G. H. *Theories of learning*. (3d Ed.) New York: Appleton, 1966. **554n, 616n, 983**

Hilgard, E. R., & Humphreys, L. G. The effect of supporting and antagonistic voluntary instructions on conditioned discrimination. *Journal of Experimental Psychology*, 1938, *22*, 291-304. **561**

Hilgard, E. R., & Marquis, D. G. *Conditioning and learning*. New York: Appleton, 1940. **563, 565**

Hill, A. L., see Rock, I., 1965.

Hill, J. H., see Stellar, E., 1952.

Hill, W. F. Sources of evaluative reinforcement. *Psychological Bulletin*, 1968, *69*, 132-146. **677**

Hill, W. F., see also Spear, N. E., 1965.

Hillebrand, F. Das Verhältnis von Accommodation und Konvergenz zur Tiefenlokalisation. *Zeitschrift für Psychologie*, 1894, *7*, 97-151. **479, 495**

Hillebrand, F. Theorie der scheinbaren Grösse bei binocularem Sehen. *Denkschr. Acad. Wiss. Wien.*, 1902, *72*, 255-307. **493**

Hillman, B., Hunter, W. S., & Kimble, G. A. The effect of drive level on the maze performance of the white rat.

Journal of Comparative and Physiological Psychology, 1953, *46,* 87–89. **794, 830**

Hillner, K., *see* Peterson, L. R., 1962.

Hilz, R., *see* Schober, H. A. W., 1965.

Hind, J. E. Unit activity in the auditory cortex. In G. Rasmussen & W. F. Windle (Eds.), *Neural mechanisms of the auditory and vestibular systems.* Springfield, Ill.: Charles C Thomas, 1960. **232**

Hind, J. E., *see also* Rose, J. E., 1963, 1966, 1967.

Hinde, R. A. Factors governing the change in strength of a partially inborn response, as shown by the mobbing behaviour of the chaffinch (*Fringilla coelebs*): I. The nature of the response, and an examination of its course. *Proceedings of the Royal Society,* Ser. B, 1954, *142,* 306–331. (a) **589**

Hinde, R. A. Factors governing the change in strength of a partially inborn response, as shown by the mobbing behaviour of the chaffinch (*Fringilla coelebs*): II. The waning of the response. *Proceedings of the Royal Society,* Ser. B, 1954, *142,* 331–358. (b) **589, 590**

Hinde, R. A. Factors governing the change in strength of a partially inborn response, as shown by the mobbing behaviour of the chaffinch (*Fringilla coelebs*): III. Interaction of short-term and long-term incremental and decremental effects. *Proceedings of the Royal Society,* Ser. B, 1961, *153,* 398–420. **589**

Hinde, R. A. *Animal behaviour: A synthesis of ethology and comparative psychology.* New York: McGraw-Hill, 1966. **587, 595, 603, 702, 746, 822**

Hinde, R. A. *Animal behaviour: A synthesis of ethology and comparative psychology.* (ed.2) New York: McGraw-Hill, 1970. **582, 588**

Hinde, R. A. Behavioural habituation. In G. Horn & R. A. Hinde (Eds.), *Short term changes in neural activity and behaviour.* Cambridge: Cambridge University Press, 1970. **591, 745**

Hinde, R. A. Incremental and decremental changes in behaviour. In G. Horn & R. A. Hinde (Eds.), *Short-term changes in neural activity and behaviour.* London: Cambridge University Press, 1970. **591**

Hinde, R. A., Thorpe, W. H., & Vince, M. A. The following responses of young coots and moorhens. *Behaviour,* 1956, *11,* 214–242. **583**

Hineline, P. N., *see* Harrnstein, R. J., 1966.

Hinshaw, J. R., *see* Sinclair, D. C., 1951.

Hintzman, D. L. Some tests of a discrimination net theory: Paired-associate learning as a function of stimulus similarity and number of responses. *Journal of Verbal Learning and Verbal Behavior,* 1967, *6,* 809–816. **1009**

Hintzman, D. L. Explorations with a discrimination model for paired-associate learning. *Journal of Mathematical Psychology,* 1968, *5,* 123–162. **1008**

Hirsch, M. J., Horowitz, M., & Weymouth, F. W. Distance discrimination: III. Effect of rod width on threshold. *Archives of Ophthalmology,* 1948, *39,* 325–332. **486**

Hirsh, I. J. The influence of interaural phase on interaural summation and inhibition. *Journal of the Acoustical Society of America,* 1948, *20,* 536–554. **242**

Hirsh, I. J. The relation between localization and intelligibility. *Journal of the Acoustical Society of America,* 1950, *22,* 196–200. **258**

Hirsh, I. J. Hearing. In C. P. Stone (Ed.), *Annual review of psychology,* Vol. 6. Palo Alto, Calif.: Annual Reviews, 1955. **235**

Hirsh, I. J., & Burgeat, M. Binaural effects in remote masking. *Journal of the Acoustical Society of America,* 1958, *30,* 827–832. **239**

Hirsh, I. J., Davis, H., Silverman, S. R., Reynolds, E. G., Eldert, E., & Benson, R. W. Development of materials for speech audiometry. *Journal of Speech and Hearing Disabilities,* 1952, *17,* 321–337. **254, 255**

Hirsh, I. J., Reynolds, E. G., & Joseph, M. Intelligibility of different speech materials. *Journal of the Acoustical Society of America,* 1954, *26,* 530–538. **256, 257**

Hirsh, I. J., *see also* Bilger, R. C., 1956; Deatherage, B. H., 1959.

Hirsh, S. K., *see* Davis, H., 1967.

Hoagland, H., *see* Cattell, McK., 1931.

Hobhouse, L. T. *Mind in evolution.* New York: Macmillan, 1901. **750**

Hochberg, C. B., & Hochberg, J. E. Familiar size and the perception of depth. *Journal of Psychology,* 1952, *34,* 107–114. **495, 496**

Hochberg, J. Figure-ground reversal as a function of visual satiation. *Journal of Experimental Psychology,* 1950, *40,* 682–686. **471**

Hochberg, J. Perception: Toward a recovery of a definition. *Psychological Review,* 1956, *63,* 400–405. **424, 506**

Hochberg, J. Effects of the *Gestalt* revolution: The Cornell symposium on perception. *Psychological Review,* 1957, *64.* 78–84. **437**

Hochberg, J. Nativism and empiricism in perception. In Leo Postman (Ed.), *Psychology in the making,* New York: Knopf, 1962. **427, 441, 546**

Hochberg, J. The psychophysics of pictorial perception. *A–V Communication Review,* 1962, *10,* 22–54. **441**

Hochberg, J. On the importance of movement-produced stimulation in prism-induced after-effects. *Perceptual and Motor Skills,* 1963, *16,* 544. **537, 540, 542**

Hochberg, J. A theory of the binocular cyclopean field: On the possibility of simulated stereopsis. *Perceptual and Motor Skills,* 1964, *19,* 685. (a) **488, 489**

Hochberg, J. Contralateral suppressive fields of binocular combination. *Psychonomic Science,* 1964, *1,* 157–158. (b) **488, 489, 491***n*

Hochberg, J. Representative sampling and the purposes of perceptual research: Pictures of the world and the world of pictures. In Kenneth R. Hammond (Ed.), *The Psychology of Egon Brunswick.* New York: Holt, Rinehart and Winston, 1966. **471***n*

Hochberg, J. In the mind's eye. In R. N. Haber (Ed.), *Contemporary theory and research in visual perception.* New York: Holt, Rinehart and Winston, 1968. **432, 454, 455, 456, 462, 506, 524**

Hochberg, J. Units of perceptual analysis. In J. Mehler (Ed.), *Handbook of cognitive psychology.* Englewood Cliffs, N. J.: Prentice-Hall, in press. **442, 453**

Hochberg, J. Attention, organization and consciousness. In D. Mostofsky (Ed.), *Attention: Contemporary theory and analysis,* New York: Appleton, 1970. **442, 453**

Hochberg, J., & Beck, J. Apparent spatial arrangement and perceived brightness. *Journal of Experimental Psychology,* 1954, *47,* 263–266. **420**

Hochberg, J., & Bitterman, M. E. Figural after-effects as a function of the retinal size of the inspection figure. *American Journal of Psychology,* 1951, *64,* 99–102. **471***n*

Hochberg, J., & Brooks, V. Effects of previously associated annoying stimuli (auditory) on visual recognition thresholds. *Journal of Experimental Psychology,* 1958, *55,* 490–491. **440**

Hochberg, J., & Brooks, V. The psychophysics of form: Reversible-perspective drawings of spatial objects. *American Journal of Psychology,* 1960, *73,* 337–354. **435, 436**

Hochberg, J., & Brooks, V. Pictorial recognition as an unlearned ability: A study of one child's performance. *American Journal of Psychology,* 1962, *75,* 624–628. **442, 501**

Hochberg, J., & Galper, R. E. Recognition of faces: I. An exploratory study. *Psychonomic Science,* 1967, *9,* 12. **450**

Hochberg, J. E., Gleitman, H., & MacBride, P. D. Visual thresholds as a function of simplicity of form. *Proc. of* the 28th Annual Meeting of the Western Psychological Association. *American Psychologist,* 1948, *3,* 341–342. **443**

Hochberg, J., Haber, S., & Ryan, T. A. "Perceptual defense" as an interference phenomenon. *Perceptual and Motor Skills,* 1955, *5,* 15–17. **440**

Hochberg, J., Hardy, D. Brightness and proximity factors in grouping. *Perceptual and Motor Skills,* 1960, *10,* 22. **434**

Hochberg, J. E., & Hay, J. Figural after-effect, after-image, and physiological nystagmus. *American Journal of Psychology,* 1956, *69,* 480–482. **472**

Hochberg, J., & McAlister, E. A quantitative approach to figural "goodness." *Journal of Experimental Psychology,* 1953, *46,* 361–364. **437**

Hochberg, J., & Silverstein, A. A quantitative index of stimulus similarity: Proximity vs. differences in brightness. *American Journal of Psychology,* 1956, *69,* 456–459. **434**

Hochberg, J., & Smith, O. W. Landing strip markings and the "expansion pattern": I. Program, preliminary analysis and apparatus. *Perceptual and Motor Skills,* 1955, *5,* 81–92. **504n**

Hochberg, J., & Triebel, W. Figural after-effects with colored stimuli. *American Journal of Psychology,* 1955, *68,* 133–135. **470, 471n**

Hochberg, J. E., Triebel, W., & Seaman, G. Color adaptation under conditions of homogeneous stimulation (*Ganzfeld*). *Journal of Experimental Psychology,* 1951, *41,* 153–159. **416**

Hochberg, J. E., *see also* Bitterman, M. E., 1954; Hochberg, C. B., 1952; Smith, D., 1954.

Hockman, C. H. EEG and behavioral effects of food deprivation in the albino rat. *Electroencephalography and Clinical Neurophysiology,* 1964, *17,* 420–427. **837**

Hockman, C. H., & Lipsitt, L. P. Delay-of-reward gradients in discrimination learning with children for two levels of difficulty. *Journal of Comparative and Physiological Psychology,* 1961, *54,* 24–27. **688**

Hodgson, E. S. Chemical senses in the invertebrates. In M. R. Kare & O. Maller (Eds.). *The chemical senses and nutrition.* Baltimore: The Johns Hopkins Press, 1967. Pp. 7–18. **181**

Hodgson, W. R. Audiological report of a patient with left hemispherectomy. *Journal of Speech and Hearing Disabilities,* 1967, *32,* 39–45. **264**

Hodos, W. Progressive ratio as a measure of reward strength. *Science,* 1961, *134,* 943–944. **649, 653**

Hodos, W. Motivational properties of long durations of rewarding brain stimulation. *Journal of Comparative and Physiological Psychology,* 1965, *59,* 219–224. **649**

Hodos, W., & Kalman, G. Effects of increment size and reinforcer volume on progressive ratio performance. *Journal of the Experimental Analysis of Behavior,* 1963, *6,* 387–392. **649**

Hodos, W., & Valenstein, E. S. An evaluation of response rate as a measure of rewarding intracranial stimulation. *Journal of Comparative and Physiological Psychology,* 1962, *55,* 80–84. **650**

Hoffeld, D. R., Kendall, S. B., Thompson, R. F., & Brogden, W. J. Effect of amount of preconditioning training upon magnitude of sensory preconditioning. *Journal of Comparative and Physiological Psychology,* 1960, *59,* 198–204. **564**

Hodos, W., *see also* Beer, B., 1964; Weitzman, E. D., 1961.

Hoebel, B. G., & Teitelbaum, P. Hypothalamic control of feeding and self-stimulation. *Science,* 1962, *135,* 375–377. **798**

Hoffman, D., *see* Hardy, J. D., 1968.

Hofman, F. B., & A. Bielschowsky. Über die Einstellung der scheinbaren Horizontalen und Vertikalen bei Betrachtung eines von schrägen Konturen erfüllten Gesichtsfeldes. *Pflüger's Archiv der gesamte Physiologie,* 1909, *126,* 453–475. **458**

Hoffman, H. S. The stimulus generalization of conditioned suppression. In D. I. Mostofsky (Ed.), *Stimulus generalization.* Stanford: Stanford University Press, 1965. Pp. 715, 356–372. **759**

Hoffman, H. S. A flexible connector for delivering shock to pigeons. *Journal of the Experimental Analysis of Behavior,* 1960, *3,* 330. **706**

Hoffman, H. S. The analysis of discriminated avoidance. In W. K. Honig (Ed.), *Operant behavior: Areas of research and application.* New York: Appleton, 1966. **726**

Hoffman, H. S., & Fleshler, M. Stimulus factors in aversive controls: The generalization of conditioned suppression. *Journal of the Experimental Analysis of Behavior,* 1961, *4,* 371–378. **713**

Hoffman H. S., & Fleshler, M. The course of emotionality in the development of avoidance. *Journal of Experimental Psychology,* 1962, *64,* 288–294. **726**

Hoffman, H. S., Fleshler, M., & Abplanalp, P. L. Startle reaction to electrical shock in the rat. *Journal of Comparative and Physiological Psychology,* 1964, *58,* 132–139. **710**

Hoffman, H. S., Searle, J. L., Toffey, S., & Kuzma, F., Jr. Behavioral control by an imprinted stimulus. *Journal of the Experimental Analysis of Behavior,* 1966, *9,* 177–189. **581, 587**

Hoffman, H. S., *see also* Harris, E. S., 1958.

Hoffman, M., *see* Eriksen, C. W., 1963.

Hoglan, F. A., *see* Inglett, G., 1965.

Hokanson, J. E., *see* Doerr, H. O., 1968.

Holaday, B. E. Die Grössenkonstanz der Sehdinge bei Variation der inneren und äusseren Wahrnehmungsbedingungen. *Archiv der gesamte Psychologie,* 1933, *88,* 419–486. **509**

Holborn, S., & Boe, E. The effect of overlearning on transfer of training. *Quarterly Journal of Experimental Psychology,* 1965, *17,* 178–180. **1067**

Holland, J. H., *see* Rochester, H., 1956.

Hollingworth, H. L., & Poffenberger, A. T. *The sense of taste.* New York: Moffat, Yard, 1917. **177**

Holm, K. G. Die Dauer der Temperaturempfindungen bei konstanter. Reiztemperatur. *Archiv Physiologica Scandinavica,* 1903, *14,* 242–258. **142**

Holman, G. L., *see* Galanter, E., 1967.

Holmberg, T. *see* Granit, R., 1938.

Holmes, C. E., *see* Kenshalo, D. R., 1968.

Holmes, D. S. Search for "closure" in a visually perceived pattern. *Psychological Bulletin,* 1968, *70,* 296–312. **445**

Holst, E. von, *see* von Holst, E.

Holstein, S. B., & Premack, D. On the different effects of random reinforcement and presolution reversal on human concept identification. *Journal of Experimental Psychology,* 1965, *70,* 335–337. **955**

Holtz, P., *see* Fischer, S. C., 1956.

Holway, A. H., & Boring, E. G. Determinants of apparent visual size with distance variant. *American Journal of Psychology,* 1941, *54,* 21–37. **512, 514**

Holz, W. C., *see* Azrin, N. H., 1961, 1966

Homme, L. E. Spontaneous recovery and statistical learning theory. *Journal of Experimental Psychology,* 1956, *51,* 205–212. **570n**

Honig, W. K. Generalization of extinction on the spectral continuum. *Psychological Record,* 1961, *11,* 269–278. **577**

Honig, W. K. Discrimination, generalization, and transfer on the basis of stimulus differences. In D. I. Mostofsky (Ed.), *Stimulus generalization.* Stanford: Stanford University Press, 1965. Pp. 218–254. **763, 765**

Honig, W. K. (Ed.) *Operant behavior: Areas of application and research.* New York: Appleton, 1966. **604, 608**

Honig, W. K. The role of discrimination training in the generalization of punishment. *Journal of the Experimental Analysis of Behavior,* 1966, *9,* 377–384. **762**

Honig, W. K., see also Cofoid, D. A., 1961.

Hopkins, B. L., see Estes, W. K., 1960, 1961.

Hopkins, C. O. Effectiveness of secondary reinforcing stimuli as a function of the quantity and quality of food reinforcement. *Journal of Experimental Psychology*, 1955, *50*, 339-342. **666**

Hoppe, J. I. *Die Scheinbewegung.* Würzburg: A. Stuber, 1879. Cited in J. P. Guilford & K. M. Dallenbach: A study of the autokinetic sensation. *American Journal of Psychology*, 1928, *40*, 83-91. **529**

Hopwood, J., see Azrin, N. H., 1967.

Horeman, H. W. Relations between brightness and luminance under induction. *Vision Research*, 1965, *5*, 331-340. **411, 413**

Horenstein, B. R. Performance of conditioned responses as a function of strength of hunger drive. *Journal of Comparative and Physiological Psychology*, 1951, *44*, 210-224. **815**

Horn, G. Neuronal mechanisms of habituation. *Nature*, 1967, *215*, 707-711. **589, 591**

Horn, G. & Fraser-Rowell, C. H. Medium and long-term changes in the behaviour of visual neurones in the tritocerebrum of locusts. *Journal of Experimental Biology*, 1968, *49*, 143-169. **591**

Hornbostel, E. M. von, & Wertheimer, M. Uber die Warnehmung der Schallrichtung. *Akademie der Wissenschaft am Berlin. Prussische Sitzungsberichte*, 1920, 388-396. **261**

Hornseth, J. P., see Hake, H. W., 1951.

Horowitz, L. M. Free recall and ordering of trigrams. *Journal of Experimental Psychology*, 1961, *62*, 51-57. **893**

Horowitz, L., & Izawa, C. Comparison of serial and paired-associate learning. *Journal of Experimental Psychology*, 1963, *65*, 352-361. **1012**

Horowitz, M., see Hirsch, M. J., 1948.

Horridge, G. A. Learning of leg position by the ventral nerve cord in headless insects. *Proceedings of the Royal Society*, London, 1962, B *157*, 33-52. **578**

Horsley, V., & Clarke, R. H. The structure and function of the cerebellum examined by a new method. *Brain*, 1908, *31*, 45-124. **114**

Horton, D. L. The effects of meaningfulness, awareness and type of design in verbal mediation. *Journal of Verbal Learning and Verbal Behavior*, 1964, *3*, 187-194. **1074**

Horton, D. L. Mediation or pseudomediation: A reply to Earhard and Mandler. *Canadian Journal of Psychology*, 1967, *21*, 471-489. **1071, 1077**

Horton, D. L., & Hartman, R. Verbal mediation as a function of associative directionality and exposure frequency. *Journal of Verbal Learning and Verbal Behavior*, 1963, *1*, 361-364. **1074, 1075**

Horton, D. L., & Kjeldergaard, P. M. An experimental analysis of associative factors in mediated generalization. *Psychological Monographs*, 1961, *75*. **1071, 1072, 1074, 1075, 1078**

Horton, D. L., Marlowe, D., & Crowne, D. P. The effects of instructional set and need for social approval on commonality of word association responses. *Journal of Abnormal and Social Psychology*, 1963, *66*, 67-72. **863, 867**

Horton, D. L., & Wiley, R. E. The effect of mediation on the retention and strength of previously formed associations. *Journal of Verbal Learning and Verbal Behavior*, 1967, *6*, 36-41, (a) **1077**

Horton, D. L., & Wiley, R. E. Mediate association: Facilitation and interference. *Journal of Experimental Psychology*, 1967, *73*, 636-638. (b) **1075, 1077**

Horton, D. L., see also Grover, D. E., 1967.

Horvath, W. J. A stochastic model for word association tests. *Psychological Review*, 1963, *70*, 361-364. **860**

Hotopf, W. H. N. The size-constancy theory of visual illusions. *British Journal of Psychology*, 1966, *57*, 307-318. **456, 458, 461, 462, 463**

House, A. S., Williams, C. E., Hecker, M. H. L., & Kryter, K. D. Articulation testing methods: Consonantal differentiation with a closed response set. *Journal of the Acoustical Society of America*, 1965, *37*, 158-166. **255**

House, B. J., & Zeaman, D. Miniature experiments in the discrimination learning of retardates. In L. P. Lipsitt & C. C. Spiker (Eds.), *Advances in child development and behavior.* Vol. I. New York: Academic Press, 1963. Pp. 313-374. **767, 949**

House, P. J., see Zeaman, D., 1963.

Houston, J. P. Verbal transfer and interlist similarities. *Psychological Review*, 1964, *71*, 412-414. (a) **1055, 1056**

Houston, J. P. Verbal R-S strength following S-R extinction. *Psychonomic Science*, 1964, *1*, 173-174. (b) **1095**

Houston, J. P. A repaired S_1-R_2 and S_2-R_1 transfer surface. *Psychonomic Science*, 1965, *3*, 343-344. **1056**

Houston, J. P. Verbal transfer as a function of S_1-R_2 and S_2-R_1 interlist similarity. *Journal of Experimental Psychology*, 1966, *71*, 232-235. (a) **1056, 1064**

Houston, J. P. Transfer as a function of the similarity between first-list stimuli and second-list responses. *Journal of Verbal Learning and Verbal Behavior*, 1966, *5*, 322-323. (b) **1056, 1064**

Houston, J. P. Stimulus recall and experimental paradigm. *Journal of Experimental Psychology*, 1966, *72*, 619-621. (c) **1095**

Houston, J. P. First-list retention and time and method of recall. *Journal of Experimental Psychology*, 1966, *71*, 839-843. (d) **1099**

Houston, J. P. Proactive inhibition and competition at recall. *Journal of Experimental Psychology*, 1967, *75*, 118-121. (a) **1105**

Houston, J. P. Unlearning of specific associations in the *A-B, C-D* paradigm. *Journal of Experimental Psychology*, 1967, *74*, 254-258. (b) **1061**

Houston, J. P. Retroactive inhibition and point of interpolation. *Journal of Verbal Learning and Verbal Behavior*, 1967, *6*, 84-88. (c) **1100**

Houston, J. P., & Morony, L. Transfer in repaired S_1-R_2 and S_2-R_1 paradigms. *Psychonomic Science*, 1966, *4*, 83-84. **1056**

Houston, J. P., see also Garskoff, B. E., 1963.

Hovland, C. I. "Inhibition of reinforcement" and phenomena of experimental extinction. *Proceedings of the National Academy of Science*, 1936, *22*, 430-433. **573**

Hovland, C. I. The generalization of conditioned responses: I. The sensory generalization of conditioned responses with varying frequencies of tone. *Journal of General Psychology*, 1937, *17*, 125-148. (a) **758**

Hovland, C. I. The generalization of conditioned responses: II. The sensory generalization of conditioned responses with varying intensities of tone. *Journal of General Psychology*, 1937, *17*, 279-291. (b) **758**

Hovland, C. I. A "communication analysis" of concept learning. *Psychological Review*, 1952, *59*, 461-472. **938**

Hovland, C. I., & Riesen, A. H. Magnitude of galvanic and vasomotor response as a function of stimulus intensity. *Journal of General Psychology*, 1940, *23*, 103-121. **839**

Hovland, C. I., & Weiss, W. I. Transmission of information concerning concepts through positive and negative instances. *Journal of Experimental Psychology*, 1953, *45*, 175-182. **964**

Hovland, C. I., see also Cahill, H., 1960; Hull, C. L., 1940; Hunt, E. B., 1960, 1961; Shepard, R. N., 1961.

Hovland, C. J. Experimental studies in rote-learning theory: I. Reminiscence following learning by massed and distributed practice. *Journal of Experimental Psychology*, 1938, *22*, 210-224. **1121**

Howard, I. P. An investigation of a satiation process in the reversible perspective of revolving skeletal shapes.

Quarterly Journal of Experimental Psychology, 1961, *13*, 19-33. **471, 519**

Howard, I. P., Craske, B., & Templeton, W. B. Visuo-motor adaptation to discordant exafferent stimulation. *Journal of Experimental Psychology*, 1965, *70*, 189-191. **536**

Howard, I. P., & Templeton, W. B. Visually-induced eye torsion and tilt adaptation. *Vision Research*, 1964, *4*, 433-437. **539n**

Howard, I. P., & Templeton, W. B. *Human spatial orientation.* New York: Wiley, 1966. **473, 529, 533, 538, 540**

Howard, R. P., *see* Schneider, R. A.

Howarth, C. I., *see* Deutsch, J. A., 1963.

Howe, E. S. Uncertainty and other associative correlates of Osgood's D_4. *Journal of Verbal Learning and Verbal Behavior*, 1965, *4*, 498-509. **861n, 865, 900**

Howe, E. S. Some quantitative free associative correlates of Noble's *m*. *Journal of Verbal Learning and Verbal Behavior*, 1969. **858**

Howe, T. S. Unlearning and competition in List-1 recall. *Journal of Experimental Psychology*, 1967, *75*, 559-565. **1087, 1099**

Howell, D. C., *see* Bilodeau, E. A., 1965.

Howes, D. On the interpretation of word frequency as a variable affecting speed of recognition. *Journal of Experimental Psychology*, 1954, *48*, 106-112. **896**

Howes, D. On the relation between the intelligibility and frequency of occurrence of English words. *Journal of the Acoustical Society of America*, 1957, *29*, 296-305. **255**

Howes, D. On the relation between the probability of a word as an association and in general linguistic usage. *Journal of Abnormal and Social Psychology*, 1957, *54*, 75-85. **862**

Howes, D. A word count of spoken English. *Journal of Verbal Learning and Verbal Behavior*, 1966, *5*, 572-604. **895**

Howes, D., & Osgood, C. E. On the combination of associative probabilities in linguistic contexts. *American Journal of Psychology*, 1954, *67*, 241-258. **871**

Howes, D., & Solomon, R. L. Visual duration thresholds as a function of word probability. *Journal of Experimental Psychology*, 1951, *41*, 401-410. **255**

Howes, D. H., *see also* Solomon, R. L., 1951.

Hoyle, E. M., *see* Green, R. T., 1963.

Hsia, Y. Whiteness constancy as a function of difference in illumination. *Archives of Psychology* (New York), 1943, *284*. **409, 414**

Hsia, Y., & Graham, C. H. Spectral luminosity curves of protanopic, deuteranopic, and normal subjects. *Proceedings of the National Academy of Science*, 1957, *43*, 1011-1019. **364**

Hsü, E. H. A factorial analysis of olfaction. *Psychometrika*, 1946, *11*, 31-42. **216**

Hubbard, D., *see* Smith, O. W., 1958.

Hubel, D. H., Henson, C. D., Rupert, A., & Galambos, R. "Attention" units in the auditory cortex. *Science*, 1959, *129*, 1279-1280. **232**

Hubel, D. H., & Wiesel, T. N. Receptive fields, binocular interaction and functional architecture in the cat's visual cortex. *Journal of Physiology*, 1962, *160*, 106-154. **294, 295**

Hubel, D. H., *see also* Wiesel, T. N., 1963.

Hudgins, C. V., Hawkins, J. E., Karlin, J. E., & Stevens, S. S. The development of recorded auditory tests for measuring loss for speech. *Laryngoscope*, 1947, *57*, 57-89. **254**

Hudson, B. B. One-trial learning in the domestic rat. *Genetic Psychology Monographs*, 1950, *41*, 99-145. **568**

Hudson, W. Pictorial depth perception in subcultural groups in Africa. *Journal of Social Psychology*, 1960, *52*, 183-208. **500**

Huggins, W. H., & Licklider, J. G. R. Place mechanisms in auditory frequency analysis. *Journal of the Acoustical Society of America*, 1951, *23*, 290-299. **231**

Hughes, J. W. The upper frequency limit for the binaural localization of a pure tone by a phase difference. *Proceedings of the Royal Society* (London), Series B, 1940, *128*, 293-305. **262**

Hughes, L. H. Saccharin reinforcement in a T-maze. *Journal of Comparative and Physiological Psychology*, 1957, *50*, 431-435. **627**

Hulicka, I. M., *see* Bolles, R. C., 1959.

Hull, A., *see* Conrad, R., 1964.

Hull, C., *see* Fischer, S. C., 1956.

Hull, C. L. Quantitative aspects of the evolution of concepts. *Psychological Monographs*, 1920, *28*. (Whole No. 123) **785, 786, 945**

Hull, C. L. Knowledge and purpose as habit mechanisms. *Psychological Review*, 1930, *37*, 511-525. **622**

Hull, C. L. The goal gradient hypothesis and maze learning. *Psychological Review*, 1932, *39*, 25-43. **621, 679**

Hull, C. L. Differential habituation to internal stimuli in the albino rat. *Journal of Comparative Psychology*, 1933, *16*, 255-273. **800**

Hull, C. L. The meaningfulness of 320 selected nonsense syllables. *American Journal of Psychology*, 1933, *45*, 730-734. **852**

Hull, C. L. *Principles of behavior: An introduction to behavior theory.* New York: Appleton, 1943. **567, 574, 575, 596, 597, 616, 619n, 635, 679, 681, 689, 690, 741, 760, 765, 801, 804, 812, 826, 1053**

Hull, C. L. *A behavior system.* New Haven: Yale University Press, 1952. **596n, 597, 619n, 622, 680, 770, 802, 805, 812**

Hull, C. L., Hovland, C. I., Ross, R. T., Hall, M., Perkins, B. T., & Fitch, F. B. *Mathematico-deductive theory of rote learning.* New Haven: Yale University Press, 1940. **980**

Hull, C. L., Livingston, J. R., Rouse, R. O., & Barker, A. N. True, sham, and esophageal feeding as reinforcements. *Journal of Comparative and Physiological Psychology*, 1951, *44*, 236-245. **670, 816**

Hull, C. L., *see also* Bass, M. J., 1934; Koch, S., 1954.

Hulse, S. H., Jr. A precision liquid feeding system controlled by licking behavior. *Journal of the Experimental Analysis of Behavior*, 1960, *3*, 1. **623, 639**

Hulse, S. H., Jr. Discrimination of the reward in learning with partial and continuous reinforcement. *Journal of Experimental Psychology*, 1962, *64*, 277-233. **639**

Hulse, S. H., Snyder, H. L., & Bacon, W. E. Instrumental licking behavior as a function of schedule, volume, and concentration of a saccharine reinforcer. *Journal of Experimental Psychology*, 1960, *60*, 359-364. **626**

Humphrey, G. *The nature of learning in its relation to the living system.* London: Kegan Paul, 1933. **591**

Humphrey, G. *Thinking: An introduction to its experimental psychology.* New York: Wiley, 1951. **868**

Humphreys, L. G. Acquisition and extinction of verbal expectations in a situation analogous to conditioning. *Journal of Experimental Psychology*, 1939, *25*, 294-301. **560n**

Humphreys, L. G., *see also* Hilgard, E. R., 1938.

Hunt, C. C., & McIntyre, A. K. Properties of cutaneous touch receptors in cat. *Journal of Physiology*, 1960, *153*, 88-98. (a) **165**

Hunt, C. C., & McIntyre, A. K. An analysis of fibre diameter and receptor characteristics of myelinated cutaneous afferent fibres in cat. *Journal of Physiology*, 1960, *153*, 99-112. (b) **165**

Hunt, E., *see* Crawford, J., 1967.

Hunt, E. B. Memory effects in concept learning. *Journal of Experimental Psychology*, 1961, *62*, 598-604. **960, 971**

Hunt, E. B. *Concept learning: An information processing problem.* New York: Wiley, 1962. **938, 943, 944, 949**

Hunt, E. B. Utilization of memory in concept-learning systems. In B. Kleinmuntz (Ed.), *Concepts in memory.* New York: Wiley, 1967. Pp. 77-106. **978**

Hunt, E. B., & Hovland, C. I. Order of consideration of logical types of concepts. *Journal of Experimental Psychology*, 1960, *59*, 220-225. **963**

Hunt, E. B., & Hovland, C. I. Programming a model of human concept formulation. *Proceedings of the Western Joint Computer Conference*, 1961, 145-155. **942, 977**

Hunt, E. B., Marin, J., & Stone, P. J. *Experiments in induction*. New York: Academic Press, 1966. **938, 967, 976, 978**

Hunt, H. F., & Brady, J. V. Some effects of punishment and intercurrent "anxiety" on a simple operant. *Journal of Comparative and Physiological Psychology*, 1955, *48*, 305-310. **733**

Hunt, J. McV. Motivation inherent in information processing and action. In O. J. Harvey (Ed.), *Motivation and social interaction: Cognitive determinants*. New York: Ronald, 1963. Pp. 35-94. **841**

Hunt, W. A., *see* Campbell, T. C., 1958.

Hunter, I. M. L. An experimental investigation of absolute and relative theories of transpositional behaviour in children. *British Journal of Psychology*, 1952, *43*, 113-128. **765**

Hunter, J. J., *see* Grice, G. R., 1964.

Hunter, R. S. Methods of determining gloss. *Journal of Research of the National Bureau of Standards*, 1937, *18*, 19-39. **427**

Hunter, W. S. The delayed reaction in animals and children. *Behavior Monographs*, 1913, No. 6. **786**

Hunter, W. S. The auditory sensitivity of the white rat. *Journal of Animal Behavior*, 1914, *4*, 215-222. **774**

Hunter, W. S. Delayed reaction in a child. *Psychological Review*, 1917, *24*, 74-87. **786, 788**

Hunter, W. S. Muscle potentials and conditioning in the rat. *Journal of Experimental Psychology*, 1937, *21*, 611-624. **577**

Hunter, W. S., & Bartlett, S. C. Double alternation in young children. *Journal of Experimental Psychology*, 1948, *38*, 558-567. **5n**

Hunter, W. S., *see also* Hillman, B., 1953; McCrary, J. W., 1953; Prosser, C. L., 1936.

Huntington, D. A., *see* Simmons, F. B., 1964.

Hunton, D. The recognition of inverted pictures by children. *Journal of Genetic Psychology*, 1955, *86*, 281-288. **450**

Hurvich, L. M., & Jameson, D. Some quantitative aspects of an opponent-colors theory: II. Brightness, saturation and hue in normal and dichromatic vision. *Journal of the Optical Society of America*, 1955, *45*, 602. **324, 328, 348**

Hurvich, L. M., & Jameson, D. Perceived color, induction effects, and opponent response mechanisms. *Journal of General Physiology*, 1960, *43*, Suppl. No. 2, 63-80. **337, 417**

Hurvich, L. M., & Jameson, D. *The perception of brightness and darkness*. Boston: Allyn and Bacon, 1966. **307, 408**

Hurvich, L. M., *see also* Jameson, D., 1959, 1961, 1964.

Hurvich, M. S., *see* Wishner, J., 1957.

Hut, P. A., *see* Cohen, B. H., 1963.

Hutt, P. J. Rate of bar pressing as a function of quality and quantity of food reward. *Journal of Comparative and Physiological Psychology*, 1954, *47*, 235-239. **630, 631**

Hyman, R., *see* Hake, H. W., 1953; Jenkins, N., 1959.

Iggo, A. An electrophysiological analysis of afferent fibres in primate skin. *Acta Neurovegetativa*, 1963, *Band 24*: 225-240. **133, 153**

Iggo, A. Cutaneous thermoreceptors in primates and subprimates. *Journal of Physiology*, 1969, *200*, 403-430. **151**

Ikeda, S., Furukawa, H., & Yamaguchi, S. An attempt to establish scales of taste: Measurement of delicious taste intensity by Thurstone-Mosteller's method. *Statistical Quality Control* (in Japanese, English summary), 1962, *13*, 76-79.

Ikeda, H. & Obonai, T. The quantitative analysis of figural aftereffects: I. The process of growth and decay of figural

after-effects. *Japanese Journal of Psychology*, 1953, *24*, 179-192. **469**

Ikeda, K., *see also* Hay, J. C., 1965.

Imai, S., & Garner, W. R. Discriminability and preference for attributes in free and constrained classification. *Journal of Experimental Psychology*, 1965, *69*, 596-608. **449**

Immergluck, L. Resistance to an optical illusion: Figural after-effects, and field dependence. *Psychonomic Science*, 1966, *6*, 281-282. **470**

Immergluck, L. Visual figural after-effects and field dependence. *Psychonomic Science*, 1966, *4*, 219-220. **470**

Imparato, N., *see* Smith, O. W., 1968.

Ingham, J. G. Variations in cross-masking with frequency. *Journal of Experimental Psychology*, 1959, *58*, 199-205. **242**

Inglett, G. E., Dowling, B., Albrecht, J. J., & Hoglan, F. A. Taste-modifying properties of miracle fruit (*Synsepalum dulcificum*). *Journal of Agricultural and Food Chemistry*, 1965, *13*, 284-287. **177**

Ingling, C. R. *The spectral sensitivities of receptor systems in human color vision*. Doctoral dissertation, University of Rochester, 1967. **367, 368**

Ingling, C. R. A tetrachromatic hypothesis for human color vision. *Vision Research*, 1969, *9*, 1131-1148. **349**

Ingraham, R., *see* Carlin, S., 1962.

Ipsen, G. Über Gestaltauffassung. Erörterung des Sanderschen Parallelogramms. *Neue Psychologische Studien*, 1926, *1*, 167-278. **458**

Irion, A. L. The relation of "set" to retention. *Psychological Review*, 1948, *55*, 336-341. **1034, 1039**

Irion, A. L. Retention and warming-up effects in paired-associate learning. *Journal of Experimental Psychology*, 1949, *39*, 669-675. **1039**

Irion, A. L. Rote learning. In S. Koch, (Ed.), *Psychology: A study of a science*. Vol. 2. New York: McGraw-Hill. Pp. 538-560. **848, 849**

Irion, A. L. A brief history of research on the acquisition of skill. In E. A. Bilodeau (Ed.), *Acquisition of skill*. New York: Academic Press, 1966. **575**

Irion, A. L., & Gustafson, L. M. "Reminiscence" in bilateral transfer. *Journal of Experimental Psychology*, 1952, *43*, 321-323. **575**

Irion, A. L., & Wham, D. S. Recovery from retention loss as a function of amount of pre-recall warming up. *Journal of Experimental Psychology*, 1951, *41*, 242-246. **1039**

Irion, A. L., *see also* Ammons, H., 1954; McGeoch, J. A., 1952.

Irwin, F. W. Motivation and performance. *Annual Review of Psychology*, 1961, *12*, 217-242. **794n**

Irwin, J. M., *see* Melton, A. W., 1940.

Iscoe, I., *see* Stevenson, H. W., 1955.

Ishak, I. G. H. The spectral chromaticity coordinates for one British and eight Egyptian trichromats. *Journal of the Optical Society of America*, 1952, *42*, 534-539. **461**

Ishiko, N., Amatsu, M., & Sato, Y. Thalamic representation of taste qualities and temperature change in the cat. In T. Hayashi (Ed.), *Olfaction and taste*. Vol. 2. New York: Pergamon, 1967. Pp. 563-572. **182**

Ison, J. R., *see* Rosen, A. J., 1965.

Ittelson, W. H. Size as a cue to distance: Static localization. *American Journal of Psychology*, 1951, *64*, 54-67. **495**

Ittelson, W. H. Size as a cue to distance: Radial motion. *American Journal of Psychology*, 1951, *64*, 188-202. **495**

Ittelson, W. H. *The Ames demonstrations in perception*. Princeton, N. J.: Princeton University Press, 1952. **518**

Ittelson, W. H., *see also* Kilpatrick, F. P., 1953.

Ivanova, V. A., *see* Chistovitch, L. A., 1959.

Ivanov-Smolensky, A. G. On the methods of examining the conditioned food reflexes in children and in mental disorders. *Brain*, 1927, *50*, 138-141. **564**

Iverson, K. E. *A programming language*. New York: Wiley, 1962. **938**

Ives, H. E. Critical frequency relations in scotopic vision. *Journal of the Optical Society of America*, 1922, *6*, 254–268. **313**

Ivy, A. C., *see* Goetzl, F. R., 1943.

Izawa, C. Reinforcement-test sequences in paired-associate learning. *Psychological Reports*, 1966, *18*, 879–919. **987, 990**

Izawa, C. Function of test trial in paired-associate learning. *Journal of Experimental Psychology*, 1967, *75*, 194–209. **987, 990**

Izawa, C., *see also* Horowitz, L., 1963.

Jackson, D. N. A further examination of the role of autism in a visual figure-ground relationship. *Journal of Psychology*, 1954, *38*, 339–357. **440**

Jacobs, G. H., *see* DeValois, R. L., 1963, 1964.

Jacobs, H. L. Observations on the ontogeny of saccharine preference in the neonate rat. *Psychonomic Science*, 1964, *1*, 105–106. **190**

Jacobs, H. L., & K. N. Sharma. Taste versus calories: Sensory and metabolic signals in the regulation of food intake. *Annals of the New York Academy of Sciences*, 1969, *157*, 1084–1125. **190, 817**

Jahoda, G. Geometric illusions and environment: A study in Ghana. *British Journal of Psychology*, 1966, *57*, 193–199. **460**

James, C. T., & Greeno, J. G. Stimulus selection at different stages of paired-associate learning. *Journal of Experimental Psychology*, 1967, *74*, 75–83. **1021**

James, C. T., & Hakes, D. Mediated transfer in a four-stage, stimulus-equivalence paradigm. *Journal of Verbal Learning and Verbal Behavior*, 1965, *4*, 89–93. **1076**

James, L., *see* Peterson, L. R., 1967.

James, W. *Principles of psychology*. New York: Holt, 1890. **437, 596, 1030**

James, W. T., *see* Liddell, H. S., 1934.

Jameson, D., & Hurvich, L. M. Note on factors influencing the relation between stereoscopic acuity and observation distance. *Journal of the Optical Society of America*, 1959, *49*, 639. **494, 502**

Jameson, D., & Hurvich, L. M. Complexities of perceived brightness. *Science*, 1961, *133*, 174–179. **409, 411, 412**

Jameson, D., & Hurvich, L. M. Theory of brightness and color contrast in human vision. *Vision Research*, 1964, *4*, 135–154. **412, 417**

Jameson, D., *see also* Hurvich, L. M., 1955, 1960, 1966.

Jamison, S. M., *see* Peterson, M. J., 1965.

Jane, J. A., *see* Masterton, R. B., 1968.

Jardinico, R. E., *see* Alpern, M., 1961.

Jarvik, M. E. Probability learning and a negative recency effect in the serial anticipation of alternative symbols. *Journal of Experimental Psychology*, 1951, *41*, 291–297. **920, 921**

Jasper, H. H., & Ajmone-Marsan, C. *A stereotaxic atlas of the diencephalon of the cat*. Ottawa: National Research Council of Canada, 1955. **114**

Jasper, H. H., *see also* Penfield, W., 1954; Sharpless, S., 1956.

Javal, L. E. Essai sur la physiologie de la lecture. *Annales D'Oculistique*, 1879, *82*, 242–253. **389**

Jay, J. R., *see* Harper, H. W., 1966.

Jaynes, J. Imprinting: The interaction of learned and innate behavior: I. Development and generalization. *Journal of Comparative and Physiological Psychology*, 1956, *49*, 201–206. **585**

Jaynes, J. Imprinting: The interaction of learned and innate behavior: II. The critical period. *Journal of Comparative and Physiological Psychology*, 1957, *50*, 6–10. **585**

Jaynes, J., *see also* Campbell, B. A., 1966.

Jeffers, V. B., *see* Helson, H., 1940.

Jeffress, L. A. A place theory of sound localization. *Journal of Comparative and Physiological Psychology*, 1948, *41*, 35–39. **265**

Jeffress, L., Blodgett, H. C., Sandel, T. T., & Wood, C. L.: III. Masking of tonal signals. *Journal of the Acoustical Society of America*, 1956, *28*, 416–426. **242**

Jeffress, L., Blodgett, H. C., & Deatherage, B. H. Masking and interaural phase: II. 167 cycles. *Journal of the Acoustical Society of America*, 1962, *34*, 1124–1126. **242, 243**

Jeffress, L. A., & Taylor, R. W. Lateralization vs. localization. *Journal of the Acoustical Society of America*, 1961, *33*, 482–483. **261**

Jeffress, L. A., *see also* Feddersen, W. E., 1957; Robinson, D. E., 1963; Sandel, T. T., 1955.

Jeffrey, W. E. The effects of verbal and non-verbal responses in mediating an instrumental act. *Journal of Experimental Psychology*, 1953, *45*, 327–333. **780, 783**

Jeffrey, W. E., & Kaplan, R. J. Semantic generalization with experimentally induced association. *Journal of Experimental Psychology*, 1957, *54*, 336–338. **1075**

Jenkin, N. Effects of varied distance on short-range size judgments. *Journal of Experimental Psychology*, 1957, *54*, 327–331. **514**

Jenkin, N. A relationship between increments of distance and estimates of objective size. *American Journal of Psychology*, 1959, *72*, 345–363. **514**

Jenkin, N., & Hyman, R. Attitude and distance-estimation as variables in size-matching. *American Journal of Psychology*, 1959, *72*, 68–76. **509, 514**

Jenkins, H. M. The effect of discrimination training on extinction. *Journal of Experimental Psychology*, 1961, *61*, 111–121. **777**

Jenkins, H. M. Measurement of stimulus control during discriminative operant conditioning. *Psychological Bulletin*, 1965, *64*, 365–376. (a) **754n, 779**

Jenkins, H. M., Generalization gradients and the concept of inhibition. In D. I. Mostofsky (Ed.), *Stimulus generalization*. Stanford: Stanford University Press, 1965, Pp. 55–61. (b) **753**

Jenkins, H. M., & Harrison, R. H. Effect of discrimination training on auditory generalization. *Journal of Experimental Psychology*, 1960, *59*, 246–253. **761, 762**

Jenkins, H. M., & Harrison, R. H. Generalization gradients of inhibition following auditory discrimination learning. *Journal of the Experimental Analysis of Behavior*, 1962, *5*, 435–441. **779**

Jenkins, H. M., *see also* Shepard, R. N., 1961.

Jenkins, J. G., & Dallenbach, K. M. Oblivescence during sleep and waking. *American Journal of Psychology*, 1924, *35*, 605–612. **1122**

Jenkins, J. J. Effects on word-association of the set to give popular responses. *Psychological Reports*, 1959, *5*, 94. **868**

Jenkins, J. J. Commonality of association as an indicator of more general patterns of verbal behavior. In T. M. Sebeok (Ed.), *Style in language*. New York: Wiley, 1960. (a) **873**

Jenkins, J. J. Degree of polarization and scores on the principal factors for concepts in the semantic atlas study. *American Journal of Psychology*, 1960, *73*, 274–279. (b) **865, 900**

Jenkins, J. J. Stimulus "fractionation" in paired-associate learning. *Psychological Reports*, 1963, *13*, 409–410. (a) **1047**

Jenkins, J. J. Mediated associations: Paradigms and situations. In C. N. Cofer & B. S. Musgrave (Eds.), *Verbal behavior and learning: Problems and processes*. New York: McGraw-Hill, 1963. Pp. 210–245. (b) **888, 949, 1071, 1074, 1075**

Jenkins, J. J., & Brown, L. The use of interspersed test items in measuring mediated response transfer. *Journal of Verbal Learning and Verbal Behavior*, 1965, *4*, 425–429. **1048**

Jenkins, J. J., & Foss, D. J. An experimental analysis of

pseudomediation. *Psychonomic Science,* 1965, *2,* 99–100. **1077**

Jenkins, J. J., Foss, D., & Odom, P. Associative mediation in paired-associate learning with multiple controls. *Journal of Verbal Learning and Verbal Behavior,* 1965, *4,* 141–147. **1078**

Jenkins, J. J., Mink, W. D., & Russell, W. A. Associative clustering as a function of verbal association strength. *Psychological Reports,* 1958, *4,* 127–136. **887**

Jenkins, J. J., & Palermo, D. S. Further data on changes in word-association norms. *Journal of Personality and Social Psychology,* 1965, *1,* 303–309. **875**

Jenkins, J. J., & Russell, W. A. Systematic changes in word association norms: 1910–1952. *Journal of Abnormal and Social Psychology,* 1960, *60,* 293–304. **875**

Jenkins, J. J., & Russell, W. A. Miscellaneous studies in word association. Technical Report #24, Contract N8ONR-66216, between the Office of Naval Research and the University of Minnesota, undated. **873**

Jenkins, J. J., Russell, W. A., & Suci, G. J. An atlas of semantic profiles for 360 words. *American Journal of Psychology,* 1958, *71,* 688–699. **900**

Jenkins, J. J., Russell, W. A., & Suci, G. J. A table of distances for the semantic atlas. *American Journal of Psychology,* 1959, *72,* 623–625. **901**

Jenkins, J. J., *see also* Brown, L. K., 1966; Palermo, D. S., 1964a, b, 1965a, b; Russell, W. A., 1954.

Jenkins, P. M., & Cofer, C. N. An exploratory study of discrete free association to compound verbal stimuli. *Psychological Reports,* 1957, *3,* 599–602. **871, 880**

Jenkins, T. N., Warner, L. H., & Warden, C. J. Standard apparatus for the study of animal motivation. *Journal of Comparative Psychology,* 1926, *6,* 361–382. **651, 704**

Jenkins, W. L. Studies in thermal sensitivity: VIII. Analytic evidence against the Alrutz theory. *Journal of Experimental Psychology,* 1938, *23,* 417. **148**

Jenkins, W. L., & Karr, A. C. Paradoxical warmth: A sufficient condition for its arousal. *American Journal of Psychology,* 1957, *70,* 640–641. **148**

Jenkins, W. O., & Stanley, J. C., Jr. Partial reinforcement: A review and critique. *Psychological Bulletin,* 1950, *47,* 193–234. **607**

Jennings, P. C., *see* Young, R. K., 1964.

Jensen, A. R. An empirical theory of the serial-position effect. *Journal of Psychology,* 1962, *53,* 127–142. (a) **1013**

Jensen, A. R. Temporal and spatial effects of serial position. *American Journal of Psychology,* 1962, *75,* 390–400. (b) **1013**

Jensen, A. R. Transfer between paired-associate and serial learning. *Journal of Verbal Learning and Verbal Behavior,* 1962, *1,* 269–280. (c) **1012, 1013**

Jensen, A. R. The Von Restorff isolation effect with minimal response learning. *Journal of Experimental Psychology,* 1962, *64,* 123–125. (d) **1013**

Jensen, A. R., & Rohwer, W. D., Jr. What is learned in serial learning? *Journal of Verbal Learning and Verbal Behavior,* 1965, *4,* 62–72. **1012, 1013**

Jensen, D. D. Paramecia, planaria, and pseudo-learning. In *Learning and associated phenomena in invertebrates: Animal Behaviour, Supplement Number 1,* 1965, 9–20. **556**

Jensen, D. D., *see also* Allison, J., 1967.

Jensen, G. D. Effect of past experience upon induced movement. *Perceptual and Motor Skills,* 1960, *11,* 281–288. **522**

Jepson, O. Middle-ear muscle reflexes in man. In J. Jerger (Ed.), *Modern developments in audiology.* New York: Academic Press, 1963. **236**

Jerger, J. *Modern developments in audiology.* New York: Academic Press, 1963. **235**

Jobe, F. W., *see* Davis, C. J., 1957.

Johansson, G. *Configurations in event perception.* Uppsala: Almquist and Wiksells Boktryschkeri AB. 1950. **523**

Johnson, B. A., *see* Flavell, J. H., 1961.

Johnson, D. L., *see* Cairns, R. B., 1965.

Johnson, D. M. Generalization of a scale of values by the averaging of practice effects. *Journal of Experimental Psychology,* 1944, *34,* 425–436. **65**

Johnson, E. P., & Riggs, L. A. Electroretinal and psychophysical dark adaptation curves. *Journal of Experimental Psychology,* 1951, *41,* 139–147. **288**

Johnson, E. P., Riggs, L. A., & Schick, A. M. L. Photopic retinal potentials evoked by phase alternation of a barred pattern. In *Clinical electroretinography* (Supplement to *Vision Research*), 1966, 75–91. **308**

Johnson, E. P., *see also* Armington, J. C., 1952; Riggs, L. A., 1964, 1966.

Johnson, H. M. Visual pattern-discrimination in the vertebrates: I. Problems and methods. *Journal of Animal Behavior,* 1914, *4,* 319. **750**

Johnson, H. M. Visual pattern-discrimination in the vertebrates: III. Effective differences in width of visible striae for the monkey and the chick. *Journal of Animal Behavior,* 1916, *6,* 169. **750**

Johnson, J. C., *see* Eldridge, R. G., 1958.

Johnson, K. R., *see* Carhart, R., 1967.

Johnson, L. M. Similarity of meaning as a factor in retroactive inhibition. *Journal of General Psychology,* 1933, *9,* 377–389. **1054, 1083**

Johnson, N. F. Linguistic models and functional units of language behavior. In S. Rosenberg (Ed.), *Directions in psycholinguistics.* New York: Macmillan, 1965. Pp. 29–65. **904**

Johnson, R. C. Reanalysis of "meaningfulness and verbal learning." *Psychological Review,* 1962, *69,* 233–238. **897, 900**

Johnson, R. C., Frincke, G., & Martin, L. Meaningfulness, frequency, and affective character of words as related to visual duration threshold. *Canadian Journal of Psychology,* 1961, *15,* 199–204. **900**

Johnson, R. C., Thomson, C. W., & Frincke, G. Word values, word frequency, and visual duration thresholds. *Psychological Review,* 1960, *67,* 332–342. **900**

Johnson, R. C., Weiss, R. L., & Zelhart, P. F. Similarities and differences between normal and psychotic subjects in responses to verbal stimuli. *Journal of Abnormal and Social Psychology,* 1964, *68,* 221–226. **900**

Johnson, T. J., Meinke, D. L., Van Mondfrans, A. P., & Finn, J. Word frequency of synonym responses as a function of word frequency of the stimulus and list position of the response. *Psychonomic Science,* 1965, *2,* 235–236. **866**

Johnston, J. W. Jr. An application of the steric odor theory. *Georgetown Medical Bulletin,* 1963, *17,* 40–42. **212**

Johnston, J. W. Jr., *see also* Amoore, J. E., 1964.

Joinson, P. A., & Runquist, W. N. Effects of intralist stimulus similarity and degree of learning on forgetting. *Journal of Verbal Learning and Verbal Behavior,* 1968, *7,* 554–559. **1126**

Jolliffe, C. L., *see* Sperling, H. G., 1965.

Jones, A., Gardner, J., & Thornton, D. W. The persistence of information motivational phenomena over 48- and 96-hour periods of visual deprivation. *Journal of Experimental Research in Personality,* 1967, *2,* 252–259. **840, 841**

Jones, A., Wilkinson, H. J., & Braden, I. Information deprivation as a motivational variable. *Journal of Experimental Psychology,* 1961, *62,* 126–137. **840**

Jones, A. D., *see* Deutsch, J. A., 1960.

Jones, A. E., *see* DeValois, R. L., 1963.

Jones, C. M., *see* Chapman, W. P., 1944.

Jones, F. N. A test of the validity of the Elsberg method of olfactometry. *American Journal of Psychology,* 1953, *66,* 81–85. **199**

Jones, F. N. A comparison of methods of olfactory stimulation: Blasting vs. sniffing. *American Journal of Psychology*, 1955, *68*, 486–488. **199, 200, 201**

Jones, F. N. A forced-choice method of limits. *American Journal of Psychology*, 1956, *69*, 672–673. **19**

Jones, F. N. Scales of subjective intensity for odors of diverse chemical nature. *American Journal of Psychology*, 1958, *71*, 305–310. **205**

Jones, F. N., & Jones, M. H. Modern theories of olfaction: A critical review. *Journal of Psychology*, 1953, *36*, 207–241. **220**

Jones, F. N., Singer, D., & Twelker, P. A. Interactions among the somesthetic senses in judgments of subjective magnitude. *Journal of Experimental Psychology*, 1962, *64*, 105–109. **147**

Jones, F. N., & M. H. Woskow. On the intensity of odor mixtures. *Annals of the New York Academy of Science*, 1964, *116*, 484–494. **212**

Jones, F. N., see also Jones, M. H., 1952.

Jones, J. E. All-or-none vs. incremental learning. *Psychological Review*, 1962, *69*, 156–160. **990, 1000**

Jones, L. V., see Boch, R. D., 1968; Fillenbaum, S., 1965.

Jones, M. C. The elimination of children's fears. *Journal of Experimental Psychology*, 1924, *7*, 382–390. **571**

Jones, M. H. Second pain: Fact or artifact? *Science*, 1956, *124*, 442–443. **156, 160**

Jones, M. H., & Jones, F. N. The critical frequency of taste. *Science*, 1952, *115*, 355–356. **178**

Jones, M. H., see also Jones, F. N., 1953.

Jones, M. R., & Myers, J. L. A comparison of two methods of event randomization in probability learning. *Journal of Experimental Psychology*, 1966, *72*, 909–911. **921**

Jones, O. R., see Grant, D. A., 1949.

Jones, R. B., see Seward, J. P., 1957.

Jonkhees, L. B. W., & Veer, R. A. On directional sound localization in unilateral deafness and its explanation. *Acta Oto-Laryngologica*, 1958, *49*, 119–131. **267**

Jordan, A. E., see Scott, T. R., 1963.

Jørgensen, H. The influence of saccharin on the blood sugar. *Acta Physiologica Scandinavica*, 1950, *20*, 33–37. **797**

Joseph, M., see Hirsh, I. J., 1954.

Judd, C. H. Some facts of binocular vision. *Psychological Review*, 1897, *4*, 374–389. **479, 513**

Judd, C. H. A study of geometrical illusions. *Psychological Review*, 1899, *6*, 241–261. **458**

Judd, C. H. Practice and its effects on the perception of illusions. *Psychological Review*, 1902, *9*, 27–39. **465**

Judd, C. H. The Müller-Lyer Illusion. *Psychological Review Monograph Supplement*, 1905, *7*, 55–81. **458, 459, 465**

Judd, C. H., & Courten, H. C. The Zöllner Illusion. *Psychological Review Monograph Supplement*, 1905, *7*, 112–139. **458, 465**

Judd, D. B. Hue saturation and lightness of surface colors with chromatic illumination. *Journal of the Optical Society of America*, 1940, *30*, 2–32. **416**

Judd, D. B. Color systems and their interrelation. *Illuminating Engineering* (New York), 1941, *36*, 336. **412, 420**

Judd, D. B. Basic correlates of the visual stimulus. In Stevens, S. S. (Ed.), *Handbook of experimental psychology*. New York: Wiley, 1951. **324, 328, 362, 427**

Judd, D. B. *Color in business, science and industry*. New York: Wiley, 1952. **422**

Judd, D. B. Appraisal of Land's work on two-primary color projections. *Journal of the Optical Society of America*, 1960, *50*, 254–268. **368, 417**

Judd, D. B., & Wyszecki, G. W. *Color in business, science, and industry*. (2nd ed.) New York: Wiley, 1963. **358, 360**

Judd, D. B., see also Newhall, S. M., 1943.

Judd, R., see Kamin, L., 1959.

Julesz, B. Binocular depth perception without familiarity cues. *Science*, 1964, *145*, 356–362. **483**

Julesz, B. Binocular depth perception of computer-generated patterns. *Bell System Technical Journal*, 1960, *39*, 1125–1161. **432, 483**

Jung, J. Transfer of training as a function of degree of first-list learning. *Journal of Verbal Learning and Verbal Behavior*, 1962, *1*, 197–199. **1036, 1064, 1068**

Jung, J. Effects of response meaningfulness (m) on transfer of training under two different paradigms. *Journal of Experimental Psychology*, 1963, *65*, 377–384. **1062, 1063**

Jung, J. Comments on Mandler's "From association to structure." *Psychological Review*, 1965, *72*, 318–322. **1068**

Jung, J. Experimental studies of factors affecting word associations. *Psychological Bulletin*, 1966, *66*, 125–133. **862, 868, 876**

Jung, R. Neuronal integration in the visual cortex and its significance for visual information. In W. A. Rosenblith (Ed.), *Sensory communication*. New York: Wiley, 1961. Pp. 627–674. **288**

Justesen, D. R., see Bourne, L. E., Jr., 1965.

Kaess, D. W., & Wilson, J. P. Modification of the rat's avoidance of visual depth. *Journal of Comparative and Physiological Psychology*, 1964, *58*, 151–152. **549**

Kagan, J. Differential reward value of incomplete and complete sexual behavior. *Journal of Comparative and Physiological Psychology*, 1955, *48*, 59–64. **669, 798**

Kahn, R. L., see Battersby, W. S., 1956.

Kahneman, D. An onset-onset law for one case of apparent motion and metacontrast. *Perceptual and Motor Skills*, 1967, *2*, 577–584. **430**

Kahneman, D. Method, findings and theory in studies of visual masking. *Psychological Bulletin*, 1968, *70*, 404–425. **429, 430, 431n**

Kahneman, D., & Beatty, J. Pupil diameter: A linear relationship with memory load. *Science*, 1966, *154*, 1583–1585. **393**

Kahneman, D., see also Flom, M. C., 1963.

Kaiser, P. K. Perceived shape and its dependency on perceived slant. *Journal of Experimental Psychology*, 1967, *75*, 345–353. **516**

Kaiser, P. K. Color names of very small fields varying in duration. *Journal of the Optical Society of America*, 1968, *58*, 690–696. **348**

Kaiser, P. K., see also Boynton, R. M.

Kalikow, D. N. Psychofit. Unpublished computer program (Fortran) for the analysis of magnitude estimates, Brown University, 1967. (Expansion of a program by D. W. Panek and J. C. Stevens.) **77**

Kalil, R. E., & Freedman, S. J. Persistence of ocular rotation following compensation for displaced vision. *Perceptual and Motor Skills*, 1966, *22*, 135–139. **537**

Kalish, H. I., see Brown, J. S., 1951; Guttman, N., 1956; Haber, A., 1963.

Kalman, G., see Hodos, W., 1963.

Kalmus, H. The discrimination by the nose of the dog of individual human odours and in particular of the odours of twins. *British Journal of Animal Behaviour*, 1955, *3*, 25–31. **202**

Kamin, L. J. Traumatic avoidance learning: The effects of CS-US interval with a trace-conditioning procedure. *Journal of Comparative and Physiological Psychology*, 1954, *47*, 65–72. **729, 732**

Kamin, L. J. The effects of termination of the CS and avoidance of the US on avoidance learning. *Journal of Comparative and Physiological Psychology*, 1956, *49*, 420–424. **728**

Kamin, L. J. The gradient of delay of secondary reward in avoidance learning tested on avoidance trials only. *Journal of Comparative and Physiological Psychology,* 1957, *50,* 450–456. **728**

Kamin, L. J. CS-termination as a factor in the emergence of anticipatory avoidance. *Psychological Reports,* 1959, *5,* 455–456. (a) **727**

Kamin, L. J. The delay-of-punishment gradient. *Journal of Comparative and Physiological Psychology,* 1959, *52,* 434–437. (b) **737**

Kamin, L. J. Trace conditioning of the conditioned emotional response. *Journal of Comparative and Physiological Psychology,* 1961, *54,* 149–153. **714**

Kamin, L. J. Backward conditioning and the conditioned emotional response. *Journal of Comparative and Physiological Psychology,* 1963, *56,* 517–519. **715**

Kamin, L. J. Temporal and intensity characteristics of the conditioned stimulus. In W. F. Prokasy (Ed.), *Classical conditioning.* New York: Appleton, 1965. Pp. 118–147. **715, 716**

Kamin, L. Predictability, surprise, attention, and conditioning. In B. A. Campbell & R. M. Church (Eds.), *Punishment and aversive behavior.* New York: Appleton, 1969. **556**

Kamin, L. J., Brimer, C. J., & Black, A. H. Conditioned suppression as a monitor of fear of the CS in the course of avoidance training. *Journal of Comparative and Physiological Psychology,* 1963, *56,* 497–501. **726**

Kamin, L., Campbell, D., Judd, R., Ryan, T., & Walker, J. Two determinants of the emergence of anticipatory avoidance. *Journal of Comparative and Physiological Psychology,* 1959, *52,* 202–205. **727**

Kamin, L. J., & Schaub, R. E. Effects of conditioned stimulus intensity on the conditioned emotional response. *Journal of Comparative and Physiological Psychology,* 1963, *56,* 502–507. **715**

Kamin, L. J., see also Annau, Z., 1961; Brimer, C. J., 1963; Solomon, R. L., 1953.

Kamiya, J., see Brunswik, E., 1953.

Kandel, E. R., & Tauc, L. Heterosynaptic facilitation in neurones of the abdominal ganglion of *Aplesia depilans. Journal of Physiology,* 1965, *181,* 1–27. **591**

Kane, E., see Donderi, D. C., 1965.

Kaneko, A., & Hashimoto, H. Electrophysiological study of single neurons in the inner nuclear layer of the carp retina. *Vision Research,* 1969, *9,* 37–55. **308**

Kaniowski, W., see Martin, L. C., 1950.

Kanon, D., see Mayzner, M. S., 1965.

Kanoti, G. A., see Kausler, D. H., 1963.

Kantrow, R. W. An investigation of conditioned feeding responses and concomitant adaptive behavior in young infants. *University of Iowa Studies in Child Welfare,* 1937, *13,* No. 3. **573**

Kanungo, R. Meaning mediation in verbal transfer. *British Journal of Psychology,* 1967, *58,* 205–212. **1083**

Kaplan, G. A. Kinetic disruption of optical texture: The perception of depth at an edge. *Perception and Psychophysics,* 1969, *6,* 193–198. **442**

Kaplan, G. A., see also Gibson, J. J., 1969.

Kaplan, R. J., see Jeffrey, W. E., 1957.

Kaplan, S., see Kleinsmith, L. J., 1964, 1964.

Kaplon, M. D., see Wolfe, J. B., 1941.

Kardos, L. Die "Konstanz" phänomenaler Dingmomente. *Beiträge zur Problemgeschichte Psychologie,* 1929, Buhler Festschrift, 1–77. **403**

Kardos, L. Ding und Schatten. *Zeitschrift für Psychologische Ergebnisse,* 1934, No. 23. **405**

Kare, M. R., see Maller, O., 1967.

Karlin, J. E., see Hudgins, C. V., 1947.

Karmel, B. Z., see Walk, R. D., 1965.

Karpinska, L. von, see von Karpinska, L.

Karpman, B., see Woodrow, H., 1917.

Karpman, M., see Eisenberger, R., 1967.

Karr, A. C., see Jenkins, W. L., 1957.

Karsh, E. B. Effects of number of rewarded trials and intensity of punishment on running speed. *Journal of Comparative and Physiological Psychology,* 1962, *55,* 44–51. **734**

Karsh, E. B. Changes in intensity of punishment: Effect on running behavior of rats. *Science,* 1963, *140,* 1084–1085. **737**

Karsh, E. B. Resistance to punishment resulting from training with delayed, partial, and increasing shock. *Proceedings of the 74th Annual Convention of the American Psychological Association,* 1966, 51–52. **737**

Karsh, E. B., see also Wallach, H., 1963.

Kasschau, R. A., & Pollio, H. R. Response transfer mediated by meaningfully similar and associated stimuli using a separate-list design. *Journal of Experimental Psychology,* 1967, *74,* 146–148. **1048**

Kasschau, R. A., see also McBurney, D. H., 1962, 1967.

Katkin, E. S., & Murray, E. N. Instrumental conditioning of autonomically mediated behavior: Theoretical and methodological issues. *Psychological Bulletin,* 1968, *70,* 52–68. **839**

Katona, G. Color contrast and color constancy. *Journal of Experimental Psychology,* 1935, *18,* 48–63. **420**

Katsuki, Y. Neural mechanism of auditory sensation in cats. In W. A. Rosenblith (Ed.), *Sensory communication.* New York: Wiley, 1961. **231**

Katz, D. Die Erscheinungsweisen der Farben und ihre Beeinflussung durch die individuelle Erfahrung. *Zeitschrift für Psychologische Ergebnisse,* 1911, *7.* **396, 398, 426**

Katz, D. *Der Aufbau der Farbwelt.* (2nd ed.) Leipzig: Barth. *The World of Color.* R. B. MacLeod & C. W. Fox, trans. London: Kegan Paul, 1935. **396, 402, 403, 405, 421, 422, 423, 426**

Katz, L., see Myers, J. L., 1963.

Katz, S. H., see Allison, V. C., 1919.

Katzev, R. Extinguishing avoidance responses as a function of delayed warning signal termination. *Journal of Experimental Psychology,* 1967, *75,* 339–344. **732**

Kaufman, H. G., see Mayzner, M. S., 1964.

Kaufman, L. On the spread of suppression and binocular rivalry. *Vision Research,* 1963, *3,* 401–415. **488**

Kaufman, L. Suppression and fusion in viewing complex stereograms. *American Journal of Psychology,* 1964, *77,* 193–205. **492**

Kaufman, L. Some new stereoscopic phenomena and their implications for the theory of stereopsis. *American Journal of Psychology,* 1965, *78,* 1–20. **490, 491, 492**

Kaufman, L. Research in visual perception for carrier landing: Suppl. 2. Studies on the perception of impact point based on shadowgraph techniques. Report SGD-5265-0031. Prepared by Sperry Rand Corp., Great Neck, New York, for Physiol. Psychol. Branch -ONR for Contract #Nonr 4081 (00). 1968. **505**

Kaufman, L., & Pitblado, C. Further observations on the nature of effective binocular disparities. *American Journal of Psychology,* 1965, *78,* 379–391. **491, 492**

Kaufman, L., & Rock, I. The moon illusion: I. *Science,* 1962, *136,* 953–961. **511, 512**

Kaufman, L., & Rock, I. The moon illusion. *Scientific American,* 1962, *207,* 120–132. **511, 512**

Kaufman, L., see also Rock, I., 1962.

Kaufman, M. E., & Peterson, W. M. Acquisition of a learning set by normal and mentally retarded children. *Journal of Comparative and Physiological Psychology,* 1958, *51,* 619–621. **768**

Kausler, D. H., & Kanoti, G. A. R-S learning and negative transfer effects with a mixed list. *Journal of Experimental Psychology,* 1963, *65,* 201–205. **1063, 1064**

Kausler, D. H., see also Dean, M. G., 1964; Ellington, N. R., 1965; Oliver, K., 1966.

Kavanau, J. L. Compulsory regime and control of environment in animal behaviour: I. Wheel running. *Behaviour*, 1963, *20*, 251–281. **692**

Kawakami, M., *see* Sawyer, C. H., 1959.

Kawamura, Y., *see* Adachi, A., 1967.

Keehn, J. D., & Arnold, E. M. M. Licking rates of albino rats. *Science*, 1960, *132*, 739–741. **814**

Keele, C. A., *see* Armstrong, D., 1951.

Keele, S. W., & Chase, W. G. Short-term visual storage. *Perception and Psychophysics*, 1967, *2*, 383–386. **444**

Keen, R. E., Chase, H. H., & Graham, F. K. Twenty-four hour retention by neonates of an habituated heart rate response. *Psychonomic Science*, 1965, *2*, 265–266. **591**

Keenan, B., *see* Hefferline, R. F., 1959.

Keesey, R. E. The relation between pulse frequency, intensity, and duration and the rate of responding for intracranial stimulation. *Journal of Comparative and Physiological Psychology*, 1962, *55*, 671–678. **599, 645, 646**

Keesey, R. E. Intracranial reward delay and the acquisition rate of a brightness discrimination. *Science*, 1964, *143*, 700–701. (a) **655, 680**

Keesey, R. E. Duration of stimulation and the reward properties of hypothalamic stimulation. *Journal of Comparative and Physiological Psychology*, 1964, *58*, 201–207. (b) **691**

Keesey, R. E., & Goldstein, M. D. Use of progressive fixed-ratio procedures in the assessment of intracranial reinforcement. *Journal of the Experimental Analysis of Behavior*, 1968, *11*, 293–301. **649, 654**

Keesey, R. E., & Kling, J. W. Amount of reinforcement and free operant responding. *Journal of the Experimental Analysis of Behavior*, 1961, *4*, 125–132. **605, 620, 694**

Keesey, R. E., & Lindholm, E. P., Differential rates of discrimination learning reinforced by medial versus lateral hypothalamic stimulation. *Journal of Comparative and Physiological Psychology*, 1969, *68*, 544–551. **700, 701**

Keesey, U. T. Effects of involuntary eye movements on visual acuity. *Journal of the Optical Society of America*, 1960, *50*, 769–774. **303, 306, 375, 387**

Kehoe, J. S., & Bruner, J. Specificité de l'habituation de la voie activitée etudiée au niveau des neurones centraux de l'Aplysie. *Journale de Physiologie* (Paris), 1966, *58*, 542–543. **591**

Keidel, U. O., *see* Keidel, W. D., 1961.

Keidel, W. D., Keidel, U. O., & Wigand, M. E. Adaptation: Loss or gain of sensory information? In W. A. Rosenblith (Ed.), *Sensory communication*. New York: Wiley, 1961. Pp. 319–338. **184**

Keleman, A., *see* Mayzner, M. S., 1965.

Kelleher, R. T. Chaining and conditioned reinforcement. In W. K. Honig (Ed.), *Operant behavior: Areas of research and application*. New York: Appleton, 1966. **671, 672**

Kelleher, R. T., & Gollub, L. R. A review of positive conditioned reinforcement. *Journal of the Experimental Analysis of Behavior*, 1962, *5*, 543–597. **665, 671**

Keller, F. S., & Schoenfeld, W. N. *Principles of psychology*. New York: Appleton, 1950. **674**

Keller, L. Run structure and the learning of periodic sequences. Unpublished doctoral dissertation, Indiana University, 1963. **935, 983**

Keller, L., *see also* Friedman, M. P., 1964.

Kellogg, W. N. An experimental comparison of psychophysical methods. *Archives of Psychology* (New York), 1929, No. 106. **23**

Kellogg, W. N. *Porpoises and sonar*. Chicago: University of Chicago Press, 1961. **270**

Kellogg, W. N. Sonar system of the blind. *Science*, 1962, *137*, 399–404. **271**

Kellogg, W. N., *See also* Spooner, A., 1947.

Kelly, D. H. Visual responses to time-dependent stimuli: I. Amplitude sensitivity measurements. *Journal of the Optical Society of America*, 1961, *51*, 422–429. **311**

Kelly, M. J., *see* McLaughlin, S. C., 1968, 1969.

Kemble, J. D., *see* Lipsitt, L. P., 1959.

Kemeny, J. G. *A philosopher looks at science*. Princeton, N.J.: Van Nostrand, 1959. **917**

Kemp, E. H., *see* Graham, C. H., 1938; Thurlow, W. R., 1951.

Kendall, J. W., Jr., *see* Kimble, G. A., 1953.

Kendall, S. B., *see* Hoffeld, D. R., 1960.

Kendler, H. H. The concept of the concept. In A. W. Melton (Ed.), *Categories of human learning*. New York: Academic Press, 1964. Pp. 212–236. **942**

Kendler, H. H., & Kendler, T. S. Vertical and horizontal processes in problem solving. *Psychological Review*, 1962, *69*, 1–16. **767**

Kendler, H. H., *see also* Kendler, T. S., 1959.

Kendler, T. S. Concept formation. *Annual Review of Psychology*, 1961, *12*, 447–472. **944**

Kendler, T. S., & Kendler, H. H. Reversal and non-reversal shifts in kindergarten children. *Journal of Experimental Psychology*, 1959, *58*, 56–60. **767**

Kendler, T. S., *see also* Kendler, H. H., 1962.

Kenkel, F. Untersuchungen über den Zusammenhang zwischen Erscheinungsgrösse und Erscheinungsbewegung bei einigen sogenannten optischen Täuschungen. *Zeitschrift für Psychologie*, 1913, *67*, 358–447. **526**

Kennedy, J. L., *see* Hastorf, A. H., 1957.

Kennelly, T. W. The role of similarity in retroactive inhibition. *Archives of Psychology*, 1941, *37*. **1081, 1082**

Kenshalo, D. S. Comparison of the thermal sensitivity of the forehead, lip, conjunctiva and cornea. *Journal of Applied Physiology*, 1960, *15*, 987–991. **129, 154, 162**

Kenshalo, D. R. Improved method for the psychophysical study of the temperature sense. *Review of Scientific Instruments*, 1963, *34*, 883–886. **141, 149**

Kenshalo, D. R. The temperature sensitivity of furred skin of cats. *Journal of Physiology*, 1964, *172*, 439–448. **150**

Kenshalo, D. R. Psychophysical studies of temperature sensitivity. In W. D. Neff (Ed.), *Contributions to sensory physiology*. New York: Academic Press, 1970. (a) **142, 144, 147**

Kenshalo, D. R. Cutaneous temperature receptors: Some operating characteristics for a model. In J. D. Hardy (Ed.), *Physiological and behavioral temperature regulation*. Springfield, Ill.: Charles C Thomas, 1970. (b) **154**

Kenshalo, D. R., & Brearley, Elizabeth A. Electrophysiological measurements of the sensitivity of cat's upper lip to warm and cool stimuli. *Journal of Comparative and Physiological Psychology*, 1970, *70*, 5–14. **152**

Kenshalo, D. R., Decker, T., & Hamilton, A. Spatial summation on the forehead, forearm, and back produced by radiant and conducted heat. *Journal of Comparative and Physiological Psychology*, 1967, *63*, 510–515. **146**

Kenshalo, D. R., Duncan, D. G., & Weymark, C. Thresholds for thermal stimulation of the inner thigh, foot pad, and face of cats. *Journal of Comparative and Physiological Psychology*, 1967, *63*, 133–138. **150**

Kenshalo, D. R., & Gallegos, E. S. Multiple temperature-sensitive spots innervated by single nerve fibers. *Science*, 1967, *158*, 1064–1065. **147**

Kenshalo, D. R., Holmes, C. E., & Wood, P. B. Warm and cool thresholds as a function of rate of stimulus temperature change. *Perception and Psychophysics*, 1968, *3*, 81–84. **145**

Kenshalo, D. R., & Nafe, J. P. A quantitative theory of feeling—1960. *Psychological Review*, 1962, *69*, 17–33. **121**

Kenshalo, D. R., & Scott, H. H., Jr. Temporal course of thermal adaptation. *Science*, 1966, *151*, 1095–1096. **142**

Kenshalo, D. R., *see also* Nafe, J. P., 1958; Rice, C. E., 1962.

Kent, G. H., & Rosanoff, A. J. A study of association in insanity. *American Journal of Insanity*, 1910, *67*, 37–96, 317–390. **860, 874**

Keppel, G. Word value and verbal learning. *Journal of Verbal Learning and Verbal Behavior*, 1963, *1*, 353–356. **900**

Keppel, G. Facilitation in short- and long-term retention of paired associates following distributed practice in learning. *Journal of Verbal Learning and Verbal Behavior,* 1964, *3,* 91–111. **1108**

Keppel, G. Problems of method in the study of short-term memory. *Psychological Bulletin,* 1965, *63,* 1–13. **1111, 1112, 1113**

Keppel, G. Association by contiguity: Role of response availability. *Journal of Experimental Psychology,* 1966, *71,* 624–628. **854**

Keppel, G. Unlearning in serial learning. *Journal of Experimental Psychology,* 1966, *71,* 143–149. **1102**

Keppel, G. A reconsideration of the extinction-recovery theory. *Journal of Verbal Learning and Verbal Behavior,* 1967, *6,* 476–486. **1108**

Keppel, G. Retroactive and proactive inhibition. In T. R. Dixon & D. L. Horton (Eds.), *Verbal behavior and general behavior theory.* Englewood Cliffs, N.J.: Prentice-Hall, 1968. **1096**

Keppel, G., & Postman, L. Studies of learning to learn: III. Conditions of improvement in the performance of successive transfer tasks. *Journal of Verbal Learning and Verbal Behavior,* 1966, *5,* 260–267. **1062, 1070**

Keppel, G., Postman, L., & Zavortink, B. Studies of learning to learn: VIII. The influence of massive amounts of training upon the learning and retention of paired-associate lists. *Journal of Verbal Learning and Verbal Behavior,* 1968, *7,* 790–796. **1041, 1106**

Keppel, G., & Rauch, D. S. Unlearning as a function of second-list error instructions. *Journal of Verbal Learning and Verbal Behavior,* 1966, *5,* 50–58. **1097**

Keppel, G., & Underwood, B. J. Retroactive inhibition of R–S associations. *Journal of Experimental Psychology,* 1962, *64,* 400–404. (a) **1095**

Keppel, G., & Underwood, B. J. Proactive inhibition in short-term retention of single items. *Journal of Verbal Learning and Verbal Behavior,* 1962, *1,* 153–161. (b) **1113**

Keppel, G., & Underwood, B. J. Reminiscence in short-term retention of paired-associate lists. *Journal of Verbal Learning and Verbal Behavior,* 1967, *6,* 375–382. **1121**

Keppel, G., *see also* Postman, L., 1965, 1967, 1968; Shuell, T. J., 1967; Underwood, B. J., 1962, 1962, 1962, 1963, 1964; Zavortinck, B., 1968.

Keppel, J., *see* Shuell, P. J., 1967.

Kessen, M. L., *see* Miller, N. E., 1952.

Kessen, W. *see* Hershenson, M., 1965; Salapatek, P., 1966.

Kiang, N. Y. S., *see* Sachs, M. B., 1967.

Kibler, G., *see* Martin, L., 1966.

Kiesow, F. Beiträge zur physiologischen Psychologie des Geschmackssinnes. *Philosophische Studien,* 1894, *10,* 523–561. **183, 186, 187**

Kiesow, F. Beiträge zur physiologischen Psychologie des Geschmackssinnes. *Philosophische Studien,* 1896, *12,* 255–278. **187**

Kiesow, F. Schmeckversuche an einzelnen Papillen. *Philosophische Studien,* 1898, *14,* 591–615. **175, 178, 183**

Kiesow, F., *see also* von Frey, M., 1899.

Kietz, H. Das raumliche Horen. *Acustica,* 1953, *3,* 73–86. **266**

Killbride, P. L., & Robbins, M. C. Linear perspective, pictorial depth perception and education among the Baganda. *Perceptual and Motor Skills,* 1968, *27,* 601–602. **500**

Kilpatrick, F. P., & Ittleson, W. H. The size-distance invariance hypothesis. *Psychological Review,* 1953, *60,* 223–231. **506**

Kilps, B., *see* Dunham, P. J., 1969.

Kimble, G. A. Transfer of work inhibition in motor learning. *Journal of Experimental Psychology,* 1952, *43,* 391–392. **575**

Kimble, G. A. Shock intensity and avoidance learning. *Journal of Comparative and Physiological Psychology,* 1955, *48,* 281–284. **710, 729**

Kimble, G. A. *Hilgard and Marquis' conditioning and learning.* (2nd ed.) New York: Appleton, 1961. **554n, 557, 674, 774, 827, 983, 1100**

Kimble, G. A. Categories of learning and the problem of definition: Comments on Professor Grant's paper. In A. W. Melton (Ed.), *Categories of human learning.* New York: Academic Press, 1964. **565**

Kimble, G. A., & Kendall, J. W., Jr. A comparison of two methods of producing experimental extinction. *Journal of Experimental Psychology,* 1953, *45,* 87–90. **572**

Kimble, G. A., Mann, L. I., & Dufort, R. H. Classical and instrumental eyelid conditioning. *Journal of Experimental Psychology,* 1955, *219,* 407–417. **558**

Kimble, G. A., & Shattel, R. B. The relationship between two kinds of inhibition and the amount of practice. *Journal of Experimental Psychology,* 1952, *44,* 355–359. **574, 575**

Kimble, G. A., *see also* Greenbloom, R., 1965; Hillman, B., 1953; Nicholls, M. F., 1964.

Kimble, J. P., Jr., *see* Moran, L. J., 1964.

Kimura, K., & Beidler, L. M. Microelectrode study of taste receptors of rat and hamster. *Journal of Cellular and Comparative Physiology,* 1961, *58,* 131–139. **173, 180**

Kincaid, W. D., *see* Logan, F. A., 1956.

King, D. J. On the accuracy of written recall: A scaling and factor analytic study. *Psychological Record,* 1960, *10,* 113–122. **902**

King, D. J., & Schultz, D. P. Additional observations on scoring the accuracy of written recall. *Psychological Record,* 1960, *10,* 203–204. **902**

King, D. J., & Yu, K. C. The effect of reducing the variability of length of written recalls on the rank order scale values of the recalls. *Psychological Record,* 1962, *12,* 39–44. **902**

King, J. E., *see* Becker, R. F., 1962.

King, R. A. The effects of training and motivation on the components of a learned instrumental response. Unpublished doctoral dissertation, Duke University, 1959. Cited by Kimble, G. A., 1961. **827**

King, R. A., *see also* Fox, R. E., 1961.

King, W., & Gruber, H. Moon illusion and Emmert's law. *Science,* 1962, *135,* 1125–1126. **512**

King, W. A., *see* Welker, W. I., 1962.

Kinney, J. A. S. Factors affecting induced color. *Vision Research,* 1962, *2,* 503–525. **410**

Kinsbourne, M., & Warrington, E. K. The effect of an aftercoming random pattern on the perception of brief visual stimuli. *Quarterly Journal of Experimental Psychology,* 1962, *14,* 223–234. (a) **463**

Kinsbourne, M., & Warrington, E. K. Further studies on the masking of brief visual stimuli by a random pattern. *Quarterly Journal of Experimental Psychology,* 1962, *14,* 235–245. (b) **463**

Kintsch, W. Runway performance as a function of drive strength and magnitude of reinforcement. *Journal of Comparative and Physiological Psychology,* 1962, *55,* 882–887. **807**

Kintsch, W. All-or-none learning and the role of repetition in paired-associate learning. *Science,* 1963, *140,* 310–312. **987, 996**

Kintsch, W. Habituation of the GSR component of the orienting reflex during paired-associate learning. *Journal of Mathematical Psychology,* 1965, *2,* 330–341. **957**

Kintsch, W., & Wike, E. L. Habit reversal as a function of length of partial delay of reinforcement. *Psychological Reports,* 1957, *3,* 11–14. **685**

Kintsch, W., *see also* Wike, E. L., 1959.

Kirkpatrick, M., *see* Peterson, L. R., 1963.

Kish, G. B. Studies of sensory reinforcement. In W. K. Honig (Ed.), *Operant behavior: Areas of research and application.* New York: Appleton, 1966. **690n**

Kistiakowsky, G. B. On the theory of odors. *Science,* 1950, *112,* 154–155. **220**

Kjeldergaard, P. M. Commonality scores under instructions

to give opposites. *Psychological Reports*, 1962, *11*, 219–220. **868**

Kjeldergaard, P. M. Transfer and mediation in verbal learning. In T. R. Dixon & D. L. Horton (Eds.), *Verbal behavior and general behavior theory*. Englewood Cliffs, N.J.: Prentice-Hall, 1968. **1071, 1075**

Kjeldergaard, P. M., *see also* Carroll, J. B., 1962; Horton, D. L., 1961.

Klee, J. B. The relation of frustration and motivation to the production of abnormal fixations in the rat. *Psychological Monographs*, 1944, *56*, (Whole No. 257). **738**

Klee, J. B., *see also* Maier, N. R. F., 1940, 1941.

Kleiber, M. *The fire of life*. New York: Wiley, 1961. **812**

Kleinsmith, L. J., & Kaplan, S. Paired-associate learning as a function of arousal and interpolated interval. *Journal of Experimental Psychology*, 1963, *65*, 190–193. **1121**

Kleinsmith, L. J., & Kaplan, S. Interaction of arousal and recall interval in nonsense syllable paired-associate learning. *Journal of Experimental Psychology*, 1964, *67*, 124–126. **1121**

Kleitman, N., & Crisler, G. A quantitative study of a salivary conditioned reflex. *American Journal of Physiology*, 1927, *79*, 571–614. **557n**

Kleitman, N., *see also* Dement, W., 1957.

Klemm, O. Untersuchungen uber die Lokalisation von Schallreizen. Uber den Einfluss des binauralen Zeitunterschiedes auf die Localisation. *Archiv für die gesamte Psychologie*, 1920, *40*, 117–146. **261**

Klensch, H. Beitrag zur Frage der Lokalisation des Schalles im Raum. *Pflugers Archiv für die gesamte Physiologie*, 1948, *250*, 492–500. **267**

Klimpfinger, S. Die Entwicklung der Gestaltkonstanz vom Kind zum Erwachsenen. *Archiv für die gesamte Psychologie*, 1933, *88*, 599–629. (a) **509, 516**

Klimpfinger, S. Ueber den Einfluss von intentionaler Einstellung und Üebung auf die Gestaltkonstanz. *Archiv die gesamte Psychologie*, 1933, *88*, 551–599. (b) **509, 516**

Kling, J. W. Generalization of extinction of an instrumental response to stimuli varying in the size dimension. *Journal of Experimental Psychology*, 1952, *44*, 339–346. **577**

Kling, J. W. Speed of running as a function of goal-box behavior. *Journal of Comparative and Physiological Psychology*, 1956, *49*, 474–476. **619, 623**

Kling, J. W., & Berkley, M. A. Electrical brain stimulation and food reinforcement in discrimination and generalization situations. *Journal of Comparative and Physiological Psychology*, 1968, *65*, 507–511. **654, 657, 701**

Kling, J. W., & Matsumiya, Y. Relative reinforcement values of food and intracranial stimulation. *Science*, 1962, *135*, 668–670. **655**

Kling, J. W., & Stevenson, J. G. Habituation and extinction. In G. Horn & R. A. Hinde (Eds.), *Short-term changes in neural activity and behaviour*. Cambridge: Cambridge University Press, 1970. **578**

Kling, J. W., *see also* Hall, R. D., 1960; Keesey, R. E., 1961; Su, J., 1966; Terman, M., 1968.

Klippel, R. A., *see* Konig, J. F. R., 1963.

Klopfer, P. H. Imprinting: A reassessment. *Science*, 1965, *147*, 302–303. **588**

Klumpp, R. G., & Eady, H. Some measurements of interaural time difference thresholds. *Journal of the Acoustical Society of America*, 1956, *28*, 859–860. **266**

Klüver, H. The equivalence of stimuli in the behavior of monkeys. *Journal of Genetic Psychology*, 1931, *39*, 3–27. **750**

Klüver, H. *Behavior mechanisms in monkeys*. Chicago: University of Chicago Press, 1933. **750, 764**

Kniep, E. H., Morgan, W. L., & Young, P. T. Studies in affective psychology. *American Journal of Psychology*, 1931, *43*, 406–421. **215, 216**

Knoche, H., *see* Hagen, E., 1953.

Knott, J. R., & Henry, C. E. The conditioning of the blocking

of the alpha rhythm of the human electroencephalogram. *Journal of Experimental Psychology*, 1941, *28*, 134–144. **591**

Knott, P. D., & Clayton, K. N. Durable secondary reinforcement using brain stimulation as the primary reinforcer. *Journal of Comparative and Physiological Psychology*, 1966, *61*, 151–153. **675**

Knox, H. W. On the quantitative determination of an optical illusion. *American Journal of Psychology*, 1893–1895, *6*, 413–421. **458**

Kobrick, J. L., *see* Hall, J. F., 1952.

Koch, S. Clark L. Hull. In W. K. Estes, S. Koch, K. MacCorquodale, P. E. Meehl, C. G. Mueller, Jr., W. N. Schoenfeld, & W. S. Verplanck (Eds.), *Modern learning theory*. New York: Appleton, 1954. Pp. 1–176. **983**

Koch, S., *see also* Saltzman, I., 1948.

Kock, W. E. Binaural localization and masking. *Journal of the Acoustical Society of America*, 1950, *22*, 801–804. **258**

Kodman, F. Jr., *see* Fairbanks, G., 1957.

Koehler, J., Jr. Role of construction in two-choice verbal conditioning with contingent partial reinforcement. *Journal of Experimental Psychology*, 1961, *62*, 122–125. **932**

Koen, F. Polarization, *m* and emotionality in words. *Journal of Verbal Learning and Verbal Behavior*, 1962, *1*, 183–187. **864, 900**

Koenig, W. Subjective effects in binaural hearing. *Journal of the Acoustical Society of America*, 1950, *22*, 61–62. **267**

Koffka, K. *Zur Analyse der Vorstellungen und ihrer Gesetze*. Leipzig: Quelle, 1912. **852**

Koffka, K. Zur Grundlegung der Wahrmehmungspsychogie: Eine Auseinandersetzung mit V. Benussi. *Zeitschrift für Psychologie*, 1915, *73*, 11–90. **408**

Koffka, K. Some remarks on the theory of colour constancy. *Psychologische Forschung*, 1932, *16*, 329–354. **412, 420**

Koffka, K. *Principles of Gestalt psychology*, New York: Harcourt, Brace, 1935. **410, 412, 420, 423n, 428, 437, 443, 451, 492, 516, 531, 539**

Koh, S. D., & Teitelbaum, P. Absolute behavioral taste thresholds in the rat. *Journal of Comparative and Physiological Psychology*, 1961, *54*, 223–229. **176**

Kohler, G. R., *see* Harrington, G. M., 1966.

Kohler, I. Über Aufbau und Wandlungen der Wahrnehmungswelt. *Osterreichische Akademie der Wissenschaften, Sitzungsberichte, Philosophisch-historische Klasse*, 1951, *227*, 1–118. **533**

Kohler, I. The formation and transformation of the perceptual world (trans. by H. Fiss). *Psychological Issues*, 1964, *3*(4), 1–173. **533, 537n, 542, 543**

Köhler, W. *Die physischen Gestalten in Ruhe und im stationären Zustand*. Braunschweig: Vieweg, 1920. **468**

Köhler, W. *Dynamics in psychology*. New York: Liveright, 1940. **443, 468**

Köhler, W. The present situation in brain psychology. *American Psychologist*, 1958, *13*, 150–154. **470**

Köhler, W., & Emery, D. A. Figural after-effects in the third dimension of visual space. *American Journal of Psychology*, 1947, *60*, 159–201. **470**

Köhler, W., & Fishback, J. The destruction of the Muller-Lyer illusion in repeated trials: (1) An examination of two theories; (2) Satiation patterns and memory traces. *Journal of Experimental Psychology*, 1950, *40*, 267–281; 398–410. **465, 469**

Köhler, W., & Wallach, H. Figural after-effects: An investigation of visual processes. *Proceedings of the American Philosophical Society*, 1944, *88*, 269–357. **468, 469, 473**

Kohts, N. Untersuchungen uber die Erkenntnisfahigkeiten des Schimpansen. (In Russian; German translation of summary) Moscow: Museum Darwinianum, 1923. Pp. 454–492. **750**

Kolb, D., see Siipola, E., 1955.

Kolers, P. A. Intensity and contour effects in visual masking. Vision Research, 1962, 2, 277-294. **430**

Kolers, P. A. Some differences between real and apparent visual movement. Vision Research, 1963, 3, 191-206. **520, 528**

Kolers, P. A. Apparent movement of a Necker cube. American Journal of Psychology, 1964, 77, 220-230. **471**

Kolers, P. A., & Rosner, B. On visual masking (metacontrast): Dichoptic observation. American Journal of Psychology, 1960, 73, 2-21. **429, 430**

Konick, A., see Posner, M. J., 1966.

König, A., & Brodhun, E. Experimentelle Untersuchungen ueber die psychophysische Fundamentalformel in Bezug auf den Gesichtssinn. Sitzungsberichte Preussische Akademie Wissenschaften, Berlin, 1889, 27, 641-644. **297**

König, J. F. R., & Klippel, R. A. The rat brain. Baltimore: Williams and Wilkins, 1963. **643**

Konorski, J. Integrative activity of the brain. Chicago: University of Chicago Press, 1967. **559, 588, 592**

Konorski, J., see also Miller, S., 1928.

Kopfermann, H. Psychologische Untersuchungen über die Wirkung Zweidimensionälar Darstellungen körperlicher Gebilde. Psychologische Forschung, 1930, 13, 293-364. Cited in K. Koffka. Principles of gestalt psychology. New York: Harcourt, Brace, 1935. Pp. 184ff. **435, 451**

Kopp, G. A., see Potter, R. K., 1947.

Koppenaal, R. J. Time changes in strengths of A–B, A–C lists: Spontaneous recovery? Journal of Verbal Learning and Verbal Behavior, 1963, 2, 310-319. **1099, 1105**

Korn, J. H., & Lindley, R. H. Immediate memory for consonants as a function of frequency of occurrence and frequency of appearance. Journal of Experimental Psychology, 1963, 66, 149-154. **897**

Korn, J. H., see also Moyer, K. E., 1964.

Kornhuber, H. H., see Mountcastle, V. B., 1967.

Koronakis, C., & Arnold, W. J. The formation of learning sets in rats. Journal of Comparative and Physiological Psychology, 1957, 50, 11-14. **768**

Korte, A. Kinematoskopische Untersuchungen. Zeitschrift für Psychologie, 1915, 72, 193-296. **526**

Kotovsky, K., see Simon, H. A., 1963.

Kozaki, A. A. A further study in the relationship between brightness constancy and contrast. Japanese Psychological Research, 1963, 5, 129-136. **414**

Kozaki, A. A. The effect of co-existent stimuli on brightness constancy. Japanese Psychological Research, 1965, 7, 138-147. **414**

Kraeling, D., see Campbell, B. A., 1953.

Kraemer, H. C. The average error of a learning model: Estimation and use in testing the fit of models. Psychometrika, 1965, 30, 343-352. **993**

Krakauer, D., & Dallenbach, K. M. Gustatory adaptation to sweet, sour and bitter. American Journal of Psychology, 1937, 49, 469-475. **184**

Krakauer, D., see also Abrahams, H., 1937.

Krantz, F. W., see Davis, H., 1964.

Krauskopf, J. The magnitude of figural after-effects as a function of the duration of the test-period. American Journal of Psychology, 1954, 67, 684-690. **472, 473**

Krauskopf, J. Figural after-effects with a stabilized retinal image. American Journal of Psychology, 1960, 73, 294-297. **472**

Krauskopf, J., Cornsweet, T. N., & Riggs, L. A. Analysis of eye movements during monocular and binocular fixation. Journal of the Optical Society of America, 1960, 50, 572-578. **305**

Krauskopf, J., Duryea, R. A., & Bitterman, M. E. Threshold for visual form: Further experiments. American Journal of Psychology, 1954, 67, 427-440. **443, 445**

Krauskopf, J., see also Bitterman, M. E., 1954; Shortess, G. K., 1961.

Kravitz, J. H., see Wallach, H., 1963, 1965.

Krechevsky, I. "Hypotheses" in rats. Psychological Review, 1932, 39, 516-532. (a) **765, 954**

Krechevsky, I. "Hypotheses" versus "chance" in the pre-solution period in sensory discrimination-learning. University of California Publications in Psychology, 1932, 6, 27-44. (b) **765, 766**

Krechevsky, I. A study of the continuity of the problem-solving process. Psychological Review, 1938, 45, 107-133. **773**

Krechevsky, I., see also Tolman, E. C., 1933.

Kries, J. von, see von Kries, J.

Krueger, W. C. F. The effect of overlearning on retention. Journal of Experimental Psychology, 1929, 12, 71-78. **1124**

Krueger, W. C. F. The relative difficulty of nonsense syllables. Journal of Experimental Psychology, 1934, 17, 145-153. **852**

Kruger, L., see Beck, L. H., 1954; Malis, L. C., 1956.

Kryter, K. D. Effects of ear protective devices on the intelligibility of speech in noise. Journal of the Acoustical Society of America, 1946, 18, 413-417. **254**

Kryter, K. D. The effects of noise on man. Journal of Speech Disabilities (Monograph Supplement), 1950, 1. **236**

Kryter, K. D. Exposure to steady-state noise and impairment of hearing. Journal of the Acoustical Society of America, 1963, 35, 1515-1525. **236**

Kryter, K. D. Psychological reactions to aircraft noise. Science, 1966, 151, 1346-1355. **236**

Kryter, K. D. Concepts of perceived noisiness, their implementation and application. Journal of the Acoustical Society of America, 1968, 43, 344-361. **236**

Kryter, K. D., Licklider, J. C. R., Webster, J. C., & Hawley, M. Speech communication. In C. T. Morgan et al. (Eds.), Human engineering guide to equipment design, New York: McGraw-Hill, 1963. **258**

Kryter, K. D., & Pearsons, K. S. Some effects of spectral content and duration on perceived noise level. Journal of the Acoustical Society of America, 1963, 35, 866-883. **236**

Kryter, K. D., Ward, W. D., Miller, J. D., & Eldredge, D. H. Hazardous exposure to intermittent and steady-state noise. Journal of the Acoustical Society of America, 1966, 39, 451-464. **236**

Kryter, K. D., see also House, A. S., 1965.

Kuenne, M. R. Experimental investigation of the relation of language to transposition behavior in young children. Journal of Experimental Psychology, 1946, 36, 471-490. **419**

Kuffler, S. W. Neurons in the retina: Organization, inhibition and excitation problems. Cold Spring Harbor Symposia on Quantitative Biology, 1952, 17, 281-292. **291**

Kuffler, S. W. Discharge patterns and functional organization of mammalian retina. Journal of Neurophysiology, 1953, 16, 37-68. **293**

Kuffler, S. W., & Eyzaguirre, C. Synaptic inhibition in an isolated nerve cell. Journal of General Physiology, 1955-56, 39, 155-184. **222**

Kuffler, S. W., see also Barlow, H. B., 1957.

Kuiper, J. W., & Leutscher-Hazelhoff, J. T. Linear and non-linear responses from the compound eye of Calliphora erythrocephala. Cold Spring Harbor Symposia on Quantitative Biology, 1965, 30, 419-427. **311**

Kulka, K. Odor control by modification. Annals of the New York Academy of Science, 1964, 116, 676-681. **213**

Künnapas, T. M. Influence of frame size on apparent length of a line. Journal of Experimental Psychology, 1955, 50, 168-170. **508n**

Künnapas, T. Experiments on figural dominance. Journal of Experimental Psychology, 1957, 53, 31-39. **433**

Künnapas, T. M. The vertical-horizontal illusion and the visual field. Journal of Experimental Psychology, 1957, 53, 405-407. **461**

Künnapas, T. Scales for subjective distance. *Scandinavian Journal of Psychology*, 1960, *1*, 187-192. **514**

Künnapas, T. Distance perception as a function of available visual cues. *Journal of Experimental Psychology*, 1968, *77*, 523-579. **479, 514**

Künnapas, T., *see also* Ekman, G., 1960, 1962, 1963.

Kupfermann, I., & Kandel, E. R. Neuronal controls of a behavioral response mediated by the abdominal ganglion of *Aplysia. Science*, 1969, *164*, 847-850. **591**

Kurke, M. I. The role of motor experience in the visual discrimination of depth in the chick. *Journal of Genetic Psychology*, 1955, *86*, 191-196. **548**

Kurtz, K. H. Discrimination of complex stimuli: The relationships of training and test stimuli in transfer of discrimination. *Journal of Experimental Psychology*, 1955, *50*, 283-292. **782, 783**

Kurtz, K. H., & Siegel, A. Conditioned fear and magnitude of startle response: A replication and extension. *Journal of Comparative and Physiological Psychology*, 1966, *62*, 8-14. **803, 804, 808**

Kushnick, S. A., *see* Wischner, G. J., 1963.

Kuzma, F., Jr., *see* Hoffman, H. S., 1966.

Kuznesof, A. W., *see* Routtenberg, A., 1967.

La Berge, D. L. A model with neutral elements. In R. R. Bush & W. K. Estes (Eds.), *Studies in mathematical learning theory.* Stanford: Stanford University Press, 1959. Pp. 53-64. **911*n***

La Berge, D. L. Generalization gradients in a discrimination situation. *Journal of Experimental Psychology*, 1961, *62*, 88-94. **929**

La Berge, D. L., Greeno, J. G., & Peterson, O. F. Nonreinforcement and neutralization of stimuli. *Journal of Experimental Psychology*, 1962, *63*, 207-213. **933**

Lacey, J. I. Somatic response patterning and stress: Some revisions of activation theory. In M. H. Appley & R. Trumbull (Eds.), *Psychological stress: Issues in research.* New York: Appleton, 1967. Pp. 14-37. **833**

Lacey, J. I., *see also* Meyers, W. J., 1963.

Lacey, O. L., *see* Duffy, E., 1946.

Laffal, J. Response faults in word association as a function of response entropy. *Journal of Abnormal and Social Psychology*, 1955, *50*, 265-270. **861*n*, 862, 864, 876**

Laffal, J. *Pathological and normal language.* New York: Atherton, 1965. **861*n*, 872, 877, 878, 885**

Laffal, J., & Feldman, S. The structure of single word and continuous word associations. *Journal of Verbal Learning and Verbal Behavior*, 1962-63, *1*, 54-61. **872**

Lambe, R. *Human binary prediction under two schedules of response-contingent reinforcement.* Doctoral dissertation, Brown University, 1968. **932**

Lambercier, M., *see* Piaget, J., 1943.

Lambert, W. E. Associational fluency as a function of stimulus abstractness. *Canadian Journal of Psychology*, 1955, *9*, 103-106. **858**

Lamoreaux, R. R., *see* Mowrer, O. H., 1946.

Land, V., *see* Peterson, L. R., 1962.

Landauer, A. A., & Rodgers, R. S. Effect of "apparent" instructions on brightness judgments. *Journal of Experimental Psychology*, 1964, *68*, 80-84. **423**

Landauer, A. A., *see also* Blessing, W. W., 1967.

Landgren, S. The response of thalamic and cortical neurons to electrical and physiological stimulation of the cat's tongue. In W. A. Rosenblith (Ed.), *Sensory communication.* New York: Wiley, 1961. Pp. 437-453. **172**

Landis, C. *An annotated bibliography of flicker fusion phenomena, covering the period of 1740-1952.* Armed Forces-National Research Council: June, 1953. **311**

Landis, E. M. Micro-injection studies of capillary blood pressure in human skin. *Heart*, 1930, *15*, 209-228. **162**

Landolt, E. Tableau d'optotypes pour la détermination de l'acuité visuelle. *Societé Français d'Ophthalmologie*, 1889, p. 157. Cited in Cowan, A., 1928. **299**

Lane, C. E., *see* Wegel, R. L., 1924.

Lane, H. The motor theory of speech perception: A critical review. *Psychological Review*, 1965, *72*, 275-309. **254**

Lane, H., *see also* Schneider, B., 1963.

Lane, H. L., Catania, A. C., & Stevens, S. S. Voice level: Autophonic scale, perceived loudness, and effects of sidetone. *Journal of the Acoustical Society of America*, 1961, *33*, 160-167. **77**

Lane, H. L., *see also* Curran, C. R., 1962.

Lang, W. M., *see* Black, A. H., 1964.

Langdon, J. The perception of a changing shape. *Quarterly Journal of Experimental Psychology*, 1951, *3*, 157-165. **515, 517**

Langdon, J. Further studies in the perception of changing shape. *Quarterly Journal of Experimental Psychology*, 1953, *5*, 89-107. **515, 517**

Langdon, J. The perception of three-dimensional solids. *Quarterly Journal of Experimental Psychology*, 1955, *7*, 133-146. (a) **517**

Langdon, J. The role of spatial stimuli in the perception of shape: *Quarterly Journal of Experimental Psychology*, 1955, *7*, 19-27. (b) **517**

Langfeld, H. S., *see* Boring, E. G., 1948.

Langmuir, I., Schaefer, V. J., Ferguson, C. V., & Hennelly, E. F. *A study of binaural perception of the direction of a sound source.* OSRD. Rept. 4079, Publ. 31014 (30 June, 1944). **242**

Lansford, T. G., *see* Clark, L. L., 1960.

Lappin, J., *see* Eriksen, C. W., 1964, 1966, 1967.

Larson, D., *see* Allison, J., 1967.

Lashley, K. S. Visual discrimination of size and form in the albino rat. *Journal of Animal Behavior*, 1912, *2*, 310-331. **784**

Lashley, K. S. The mechanism of vision: I. A method for rapid analysis of pattern vision in the rat. *Journal of Genetic Psychology*, 1930, *37*, 453-460. **749**

Lashley, K. S. The mechanism of vision: XV. Preliminary studies of the rat's capacity for detail vision. *Journal of General Psychology*, 1938, *18*, 123-193. **749, 771, 784**

Lashley, K. S. An examination of the "continuity theory" as applied to discriminative learning. *Journal of General Psychology*, 1942, *26*, 241-265. **771**

Lashley, K. S. The problem of cerebral organization in vision. In H. Klüver (Ed.), *Visual mechanisms and biological symposium*, *7*, 1942. **450**

Lashley, K. S. The problem of serial order in behavior. In L. A. Jeffries (Ed.), *Cerebral mechanisms in behavior.* New York: Wiley, 1951. Pp. 112-136. **698, 1013**

Lashley, K. S., Chow, K. L., & Semmes, J. An examination of the electrical field theory of cerebral integration. *Psychological Review*, 1951, *58*, 123-136. **470**

Lashley, K. S., & Wade, M. The Pavlovian theory of generalization. *Psychological Review*, 1946, *53*, 72-87. **771**

Latour, P. L. Visual threshold during eye movement. *Vision Research*, 1962, *2*, 261-262. **377**

Lavik, J., *see* Brown, L. K., 1966.

Law, S., *see* Neimark, E., 1965.

Lawler, E. E., III. Secondary reinforcement value of stimuli associated with shock reduction. *Quarterly Journal of Experimental Psychology*, 1965, *17*, 57-62. **718**

Lawrence, D. H. Acquired distinctiveness of cues: I. Transfer between discriminations on the basis of familiarity with the stimulus. *Journal of Experimental Psychology*, 1949, *39*, 770-784. **783**

Lawrence, D. H. Acquired distinctiveness of cues: II. Selective association in a constant stimulus situation. *Journal of Experimental Psychology*, 1949, *40*, 175-188. **783**

Lawrence, D. H. The nature of a stimulus: Some relationships between learning and perception. In S. Koch

(Ed.), *Psychology: A study of a science*. Vol. V. New York: McGraw-Hill, 1963. Pp. 179–212. **1001**

Lawrence, D. H., & Mason, W. A. Food intake in the rat as a function of deprivation intervals and feeding rhythms. *Journal of Comparative and Physiological Psychology,* 1955, *48,* 267–271. (a) **820**

Lawrence, D. H., & Mason, W. A. Intake and weight adjustment in rats to changes in feeding schedule. *Journal of Comparative and Physiological Psychology,* 1955, *48,* 43–46. (b) **818, 819**

Lawrence, D. H., & Mason, W. A. Systematic behavior during discrimination reversal and change of dimensions. *Journal of Comparative and Physiological Psychology,* 1955, *48,* 1–7. **783**

Lawrence, D. H., see also Bauer, F. J., 1953.

Lawrence, L., see Gibson, J. J., 1955.

Lawrence, M. Dynamic range of the cochlear transducer. In *Cold Spring Harbor Symposia on Quantitative Biology.* New York: Cold Spring Harbor Laboratory of Quantitative Biology, 1965. **230**

Lawrence, M., see also Wever, E. G., 1954.

Lawson, R. Brightness discrimination performance and secondary reward strength as a function of primary reward amount. *Journal of Comparative and Physiological Psychology,* 1957, *50,* 35–39. **637, 638, 639**

Lawson, R. B., & Gulick, W. L. Stereopsis and anomalous contour. *Vision Research,* 1967, *7,* 271–297. **432**

Lazar, G. Warm-up before recall of paired adjectives. *Journal of Verbal Learning and Verbal Behavior,* 1967, *6,* 321–327. **1040**

Leahy, W. R., see Schuck, J., 1966.

Leakey, D. M., Sayers, B. McA., & Cherry, C. Binaural fusion of low- and high-frequency sounds. *Journal of the Acoustical Society of America,* 1958, *30,* 222. **263**

Leary, R. W. Homogeneous and heterogeneous reward of monkeys. *Journal of Comparative and Physiological Psychology,* 1958, *51,* 706–710. **638, 639**

Leeper, R. The role of motivation in learning: A study of the phenomenon of differential motivational control of the utilization of habits. *Journal of Genetic Psychology,* 1935, *46,* 3–40. **801**

Leeper, R. W. A study of a neglected portion of the field of learning. *Pediatric Seminar and Journal of General Psychology,* 1935, *46,* 41–75. **439**

Leeper, R. Cognitive processes. In S. S. Stevens (Ed.), *Handbook of experimental psychology.* New York: Wiley, 1951, 730–757.

Leeper, R. W. Comments on Dr. Premack's paper. In D. Levine (Ed.) *Nebraska symposium on motivation* Lincoln: University of Nebraska Press, 1965. Pp. 180–188. **624**

LeGouix, J. P., see Tasaki, I., 1952.

LeGrand, Y. *Light, colour and vision.* New York: Dover, 1957. **327, 354, 358**

Le Gros Clark, W. E. The projection of the olfactory epithelium on the olfactory bulb in the rabbit. *Journal of Neurology and Psychiatry,* 1951, *14,* 1–10. **197**

Le Gros Clark, W. E. Inquiries into the anatomical basis of olfactory discrimination. *Proceedings of the Royal Society (London),* Ser. B, 1957, *146,* 299–319. **197**

Le Gros Clark, W. E., & Warwick, R. T. The pattern of olfactory innervation. *Journal of Neurology and Psychiatry,* 1946, *9,* 101–112. **195**

Leibowitz, H. W. Effect of reference lines on the discrimination of movement. *Journal of the Optical Society of America,* 1955, *45,* 829–830. (a) **528**

Leibowitz, H. W. The relation between the rate threshold for the perception of movement and luminance for various durations of exposure. *Journal of Experimental Psychology,* 1955, *49,* 209–214. (b) **520, 521**

Leibowitz, H. W. Relation between the Brunswik and Thouless ratios and functional relations in experimental investigations of perceived shape, size and brightness. *Perceptual and Motor Skills,* 1956, *6,* 65–68. **399**

Leibowitz, H. W., & Bourne, L. E., Jr. Time and intensity as determiners of perceived shape. *Journal of Experimental Psychology,* 1956, *51,* 227–281. **515**

Leibowitz, H. W., Bussey, T., & McGuire, P. Shape and size constancy in photographic reproductions. *Journal of the Optical Society of America,* 1957, *47,* 658–661. **515**

Leibowitz, H. W., & Chinetti, P. Effect of reduced exposure duration on brightness constancy. *Journal of Experimental Psychology,* 1957, *54,* 49–53. **410, 414**

Leibowitz, H. W., & Harvey, L. O., Jr. Size matching as a function of instructions in a naturalistic environment. *Journal of Experimental Psychology,* 1967, *74,* 378–382. **509, 514**

Leibowitz, H. W., Mitchell, E., & Angrist, B. Exposure duration in the perception of shape. *Science,* 1954, *120,* 400. **515**

Leibowitz, H. W., Myers, N. A., & Chinetti, P. The role of simultaneous contrast in brightness constancy. *Journal of Experimental Psychology,* 1955, *50,* 15–18. **410, 414**

Leibowitz, H. W., see also Berman, P. W., 1965; Parrish, M., 1968; Zeigler, H. P., 1957.

Leitenberg, H., see Levine, M., 1964.

Lele, P. P. Relationship between cutaneous thermal thresholds, skin temperature and cross-sectional area of the stimulus. *Journal of Physiology,* 1954, *126,* 191–205. **144**

Lele, P. P., & Weddell, G. Relationship between neurohistology and corneal sensibility. *Brain,* 1956, *79,* 119–154. **154, 162**

Lele, P. P., Weddell, G., & Williams, C. M. The relationship between heat transfer, skin temperature, and cutaneous sensibility. *Journal of Physiology,* 1954, *126,* 206–234. **153, 158**

Le Magnen, J. Étude d'une méthode d'analyse qualitative de l'olfaction. *L'année Psychologique,* 1942–43, *43–44,* 249–264. **200**

Le Magnen, J. Étude des facteurs dynamiques de l'excitation olfactive. *L'année Psychologique,* 1944–45, *45–46,* 77–89. **206, 207**

Le Magnen, J. Étude des phénomènes olfacto-sexuels chez le rat blanc: Variations de l'odeur biologique de la femelle avec son état sexuel et la discrimination de ces odeurs par le mâle adulte. *Comptes Rendus de la Sociétié de Biologie,* 1951, *145,* 854–857. **210**

Le Magnen, J. L'olfaction: Le fonctionnement olfactif et son intervention dans les régulations psychophysiologiques. *Journal de Physiologie* (Paris), 1953, *45,* 285–326. **209, 210**

Lemmon, W. B., & Patterson, G. H., Depth perception in sheep: Effects of interupting the mother–neonate bond. *Science,* 1964, *145,* 835–837. **549**

Lenneberg, E. Understanding language without ability to speak: A case report. *Journal of Abnormal and Social Psychology,* 1962, *65,* 419–425. **254**

Lenneberg, E. H., see also Brown, R. W., 1954.

Leonard, J. A., see Fitts, P. M., 1956, 1957.

Lettvin, J., & Gesteland, R. Speculations on smell. *Cold Spring Harbor Symposia on Quantitative Biology,* 1965, *30,* 217–225. **217, 218**

Lettvin, J. Y., Maturana, H. R., McCulloch, W. S., & Pitts, W. H. What the frog's eye tells the frog's brain. *Proceedings of the Institute of Radio Engineering,* 1959, *47,* 1940–1951. **295**

Lettvin, J. Y., see also Gesteland, R. C., 1965.

Leutscher-Hazelhoff, J. T., see Kuiper, J. W., 1965.

Levelt, W. J. M. *On binocular rivalry.* RVO-TNO edition. Soesterberg, The Netherlands: Institute for Perception, 1965. **488**

Leventhal, T., see Witkin, H. A., 1952.

Levine, M. Cue neutralization: The effects of random reinforcement upon discrimination learning. *Journal of Experimental Psychology*, 1962, *63*, 438–443. **955**

Levine, M. Mediating processes in humans at the outset of discrimination learning. *Psychological Review*, 1963, *70*, 254–276. **958**

Levine, M. Hypothesis behavior by humans during discrimination learning. *Journal of Experimental Psychology*, 1966, *71*, 331–338. **959, 960**

Levine, M., Leitenberg, H., & Richter, M. Blank trials law: Equivalence of positive reinforcement and non-reinforcement. *Psychological Review*, 1964, *71*, 94–103. **959**

Levine, M., Miller, P., & Steinmeyer, C. H. The none-to-all theorem of human discrimination learning. *Journal of Experimental Psychology*, 1967, *73*, 568–573. **960**

Levine, M., *see also* Suppes, P., 1964.

Levine, S., *see* Brush, F. R., 1965, 1966.

Levitt, H., & Rabiner, L. R. Binaural release from masking for speech and gain in intelligibility. *Journal of the Acoustical Society of America*, 1967, *42*, 601–608. **258**

Levy, N., *see* Chapman, R. M., 1957; Engen, T., 1958.

Lewis, C., *see* Wallace, H., 1966.

Lewis, D. *Quantitative methods in psychology.* New York: McGraw-Hill, 1960. **28, 78**

Lewis, D. J. Partial reinforcement: A selective review of the literature since 1950. *Psychological Bulletin*, 1960, *57*, 1–28. **607, 670**

Lewis, D. R. Psychological scales of taste. *Journal of Psychology*, 1948, *26*, 437–446. **174**

Lewis, E. O. The effect of practice on the perception of the Müller-Lyer Illusion. *British Journal of Psychology*, 1908, *2*, 294–306. **465**

Lewis, E. O. The illusion of filled and unfilled space. *British Journal of Psychology*, 1912–1913, *5*, 36–50. **458**

Lewis, H. B., *see* Witkin, H. A., 1954.

Lewis, M., *see* Eckert, B., 1967.

Lewis, N. A., *see* Campbell, T. C., 1958.

Lewis, T., & Pochin, E. E. The double pain response of the human skin to a single stimulus. *Clinical Science*, 1937, *3*, 67–76. **160**

Lewis, W. R., *see* Simmons, F. B., 1964.

Liberman, A. M. Some results of research on speech perception. *Journal of the Acoustical Society of America*, 1957, *29*, 117–123. **253**

Liberman, A. M., Cooper, F. S., Shankweiler, D. P., & Studdert-Kennedy, M. Perception of the speech code. *Psychological Review*, 1967, *74*, 431–461. **253, 254**

Liberman, A. M., Cooper, F. S., Harris, K. S., & MacNeilage, P. F. A motor theory of speech perception. *Proceedings of the Speech Communication Seminar.* Stockholm: Royal Institute of Technology, September 1962. **254**

Liberman, A. M., DeLattre, P. C., & Cooper, F. S. Some cues for the distinction between voiced and voiceless stops in initial position. *Language and Speech*, 1958, *1*, 153–167. **253**

Liberman, A. M., DeLattre, P. C., Cooper, F. S., & Gerstman, L. J. The role of consonant-vowel transitions in the perception of stop and nasal consonants. *Psychological Monographs*, 1954, *68.* **253**

Liberman, A. M., *see also* Cooper, F. S., 1952; Harris, E. S., 1958.

Libet, B. Delayed pain as a peripheral sensory pathway. *Science*, 1957, *126*, 256–257. **161**

Libman, E. Observations on individual sensitiveness to pain with special reference to abdominal disorders. *Journal of the American Medical Association*, 1934, *102*, 335–341. **156**

Licht, L., *see* Maltzman, I., 1960.

Lichte, W. H., & Borreson, C. R. Influence of instructions on degree of shape constancy. *Journal of Experimental Psychology*, 1967, *74*, 538–542. **509, 516**

Lichte, W. H., *see also* Borresen, C. R., 1962.

Lichten, W., & Lurie, S. A new technique for the study of perceived size. *American Journal of Psychology*, 1950, *63*, 280–282. **513**

Lichten, W., *see also* Miller, G. A., 1951.

Lichtenstein, M. Phenomenal simultaneity with irregular timing of components of the visual stimulus. *Perceptual and Motor Skills*, 1961, *12*, 47–60. **454**

Lichtenstein, M., *see also* Craig, E. A., 1953.

Lichtenstein, P. E. Studies of anxiety: I. The production of a feeding inhibition in dogs. *Journal of Comparative and Physiological Psychology*, 1950, *43*, 16–29. **738**

Licklider, J. C. R. The influence of interaural phase relations upon the masking of speech by white noise. *Journal of the Acoustical Society of America*, 1948, *20*, 150–159. **258**

Licklider, J. C. R. Basic correlates of the auditory stimulus. In S. S. Stevens (Ed.), *Handbook of experimental psychology.* New York: Wiley, 1951. **233, 245, 257**

Licklider, J. C. R. Three auditory theories. In S. Koch (Ed.), *Psychology: A study of a science.* Vol. I. New York: McGraw-Hill, 1952. **245, 265**

Licklider, J. C. R., & Miller, G. A. The perception of speech. In S. S. Stevens (Ed.), *Handbook of experimental psychology.* New York: Wiley, 1951. **254, 256, 257**

Licklider, J. C. R., *see also* Gardner, W. J., 1960; Huggins, W. H., 1951; Kryter, K. D., 1963.

Liddell, H. S. A laboratory for the study of conditioned motor reflexes. *American Journal of Psychology*, 1926, *37*, 418–419. **562, 566**

Liddell, H. S., James, W. T., & Anderson, O. D. The comparative physiology of the conditioned motor reflex, based on experiments with the pig, dog, sheep, goat, and rabbit. *Comparative Psychology Monographs*, 1934, No. 51. **566**

Liebman, P. A. *In situ* microspectrophotometric studies on the pigments of single retinal rods. *Biophysics Journal*, 1962, *2*, 161–178. **323**

Liebman, S. Über das Verhalten farbiger Formen bei Helligkeitsgleichheit von Figur und Grund. *Psychologische Forschung*, 1927, *9*, 300–353. **428**

Liljestrand, G., & Zotterman, Y. The water taste in mammals. *Acta Physiologica Scandinavica*, 1954, *32*, 291–303. **186**

Lim, K. S. Cutaneous and visceral pain: Somesthetic chemoreceptors. In D. R. Kenshalo (Ed.), *The skin senses.* Springfield, Ill.: Charles C Thomas, 1968, 458–464. **162**

Limpo, A. J., *see* Reynolds, G. S., 1968.

Lindauer, J., *see* Wallach, H., 1962, 1963.

Lindley, R. H., *see* Korn, J. H., 1963.

Lindman, H., & Edwards, W. Unlearning the Gambler's Fallacy. *Journal of Experimental Psychology*, 1961, *62*, 630–631. **921**

Lindsley, D. B. Emotion. In S. S. Stevens (Ed.), *Handbook of experimental psychology.* New York: Wiley, 1951. Pp. 473–516. **831**

Lindsley, D. B. Psychological phenomena and the electroencephalogram. *Electroencephalography and Clinical Neurophysiology*, 1952, *4*, 443–456. **832**

Lindsley, D. B. Psychophysiology and motivation, In M. R. Jones (Ed.), *Nebraska symposium on motivation.* Lincoln: University of Nebraska Press, 1957. Pp. 44–105. **832, 842**

Lindsley, D. B. The reticular system and perceptual discrimination. In H. H. Jasper, L. D. Proctor, R. S. Knighton, W. C. Noshay, & R. T. Costello (Eds.), *Reticular formation of the brain.* Boston: Little, Brown, 1958, 513–534. **832, 842**

Lindsley, D. B. Attention, consciousness, sleep and wakefulness. In J. Field & H. W. Magoun (Eds.), *Handbook of physiology.* Vol. III. Washington, D. C.: American Physiology Society, 1960, 1553–1593. **832**

Lindsley, D. B. The reticular activating system and perceptual integration. In D. E. Sheer (Ed.), *Electrical stimulation of the brain.* Austin: University of Texas Press, 1961. Pp. 331–349. **842**

Lindsley, D. B., *see also* Spong, P., 1965.

Lindsley, D. F., *see* Wendt, R. H., 1963.

Lindy, J., *see* Routtenberg, A., 1965.

Link, W. E., *see* Bourne, L. E. Jr., 1964.

Linker, E., Moore, M. E., & Galanter, E. Taste thresholds, detection models, and disparate results. *Journal of Experimental Psychology*, 1964, 67, 59–66. **36, 37, 43**

Linker, E., *see also* Moore, M. E., 1965.

Linksz, A. Physiology of the eye. *Vision*, 1952, 2, 380. **490**

Linksz, A. *An essay in color vision and clinical color vision tests.* New York: Grune & Stratton, 1964. **363, 367**

Linschoten, J. *Strukturanalyse der binokularen Teifenwahrenehmung.* New York: Gregory Lounz, 1956. **492**

Lipetz, L. E. Mechanism of light adaptation. *Science*, 1961, 133, 639–640. **289**

Lipkin, M., & Hardy, J. D. Measurement of some thermal properties of human tissues. *Journal of Applied Physiology*, 1954, 7, 212–217. **141, 146**

Lipps, T. *Raumaesthetik und geometrischeoptische Täuschungen.* Leipzig: Barth, 1897. **459**

Lipscomb, D. B., *see* Crovitz, H. F., 1963.

Lipsitt, L. P. Simultaneous and successive discrimination learning in children. *Child Development*, 1961, 32, 337–347. **751, 775**

Lipsitt, L. P. Stimulus generalization and discrimination learning by children. *Perceptual and Motor Skills*, 1962, 14, 11–17. **772**

Lipsitt, L. P. Learning in the first year of life. In L. P. Lipsitt, & C. C. Spiker (Eds.), *Advances in child development and behavior.* New York: Academic Press, 1963. **556**

Lipsitt, L. P., Castaneda, A., & Kemble, J. D. Effects of delayed reward pretraining on discrimination learning. *Child Development*, 1959, 30, 273–278. **556**

Lipsitt, L. P., *see also* Castaneda, A., 1959; Engen, T., 1965; Hockman, C. H., 1961; Wismer, B., 1964.

Liston, J. R., *see* Schulz, R. W., 1968.

Lit, A. The magnitude of the Pulfrich stereo-phenomenon as a function of binocular differences of intensity at various levels of illumination. *American Journal of Psychology*, 1949, 62, 159–181. **309**

Livingston, J. R., *see* Hull, C. L., 1951.

Lloyd, V. V., *see* Graham, C. H., 1948; Mueller, C. G., 1948.

Lochner, J. P. A., & Burger, J. F. The intelligibility of speech under reverberant conditions. *Acustica*, 1961, 11, 195–200. **257**

Lockard, J. S. Choice of a warning signal or no warning signal in an unavoidable shock situation. *Journal of Comparative and Physiological Psychology*, 1963, 56, 526–530. **730**

Locke, N. M. Color constancy in the rhesus monkey and in man. *Archives of Psychology* (New York), 1935, No. 193. **407**

Loeffel, R., *see* Mueller, E. E., 1953.

Loess, H. Proactive inhibition in short-term memory. *Journal of Verbal Learning and Verbal Behavior*, 1964, 3, 362–368. **1113**

Loess, H. Short-term memory, word class and sequence of items. *Journal of Experimental Psychology*, 1967, 74, 556–561. **1116**

Loess, H., & Waugh, N. C. Short-term memory and intertrial interval. *Journal of Verbal Learning and Verbal Behavior*, 1967, 6, 455–460. **1113**

Loess, H. B., & Duncan, C. P. Human discrimination learning with simultaneous and successive presentation of stimuli. *Journal of Experimental Psychology*, 1952, 44, 215–221. **775**

Loewenstein, W. R. The generation of electric activity in a nerve ending. *Annals of the New York Academy of Science*, 1959, 81, 367–387. **129**

Logan, F. A. The role of delay of reinforcement in determining reaction potential. *Journal of Experimental Psychology*, 1952, 43, 393–399. **747**

Logan, F. A. *Incentive: How the conditions of reinforcement affect the performance of rats.* New Haven: Yale University Press, 1960. **602, 616, 639, 640, 695, 723, 843**

Logan, F. A. Continuously negatively correlated amount of reinforcement. *Journal of Comparative and Physiological Psychology*, 1966, 62, 31–34. **843**

Logan, F. A., Beier, E. M., & Kincaid, W. D. Extinction following partial and varied reinforcement. *Journal of Experimental Psychology*, 1956, 52, 65–70. **686**

Logan, F. A., & Wagner, A. R. *Reward and punishment.* Boston: Allyn & Bacon, 1965. **801**

LoLordo, V., *see* Church, R. M., 1966; Rescorla, R. A., 1965.

London, I. D. A Russian report on the postoperative newly seeing. *American Journal of Psychology*, 1960, 73, 478–482. **548**

Long, E. R., Hammock, J. T., May, F., & Campbell, B. J. Intermittent reinforcement of operant behavior in children. *Journal of the Experimental Analysis of Behavior*, 1958, 1, 315–339. **605, 608**

Long, G. E. The effect of duration of onset and cessation of light flash on the intensity–time relation in the peripheral retina. *Journal of the Optical Society of America*, 1951, 41, 743–747. **304**

Long, J., *see* Solley, C. M., 1958.

Long, L. Conceptual relationships in children: The concept of roundness. *Journal of General Psychology*, 1940, 57, 289–315. **785**

Long, L., *see also* Bartoshuk, L. M., 1969.

Longo, V. G., *see* Sadowski, B., 1962.

Lopez, L. J., *see* Thomas, D. R.

LoPopolo, M. H., *see* Mayer, D. R., 1966.

Lore, R. K., *see* Pollio, H. R., 1965.

Lorenz, K. The companion in the bird's world. *Auk*, 1937, 54, 245–273. **581, 582, 583**

Lorge, I., *see* Thorndike, E. L., 1944.

Lovejoy, E. Analysis of the overlearning reversal effect. *Psychological Review*, 1966, 73, 87–103. **1001**

Lovelace, E., *see* Schulz, R., 1964.

Lowell, F., *see* Woodrow, H., 1916a, b.

Lowenstein, E., & Dallenbach, K. M. The critical temperature for heat and for burning heat. *American Journal of Psychology*, 1930, 42, 423–429. **148**

Lowes, G., & Bitterman, M. E. Reward and learning in the goldfish. *Science*, 1967, 157, 455–457. **634**

Lowy, K., *see* Thurlow, W. R., 1951.

Luce, R. D. A threshold theory for simple detection experiments. *Psychological Review*, 1963, 70, 61–79. **45**

Luce, R. D., Bush, R. R., & Galanter, E. *Handbook of mathematical psychology.* New York: Wiley, 1963. **14, 24**

Luce, R. D., & Galanter, E. Psychophysical scaling. In R. D. Luce, R. R. Bush, & E. Galanter (Eds.), *Handbook of mathematical psychology.* New York: Wiley, 1963. **86**

Luce, R. D. & Suppes, P. Preference, utility, & subjective probability. In R. D. Luce, R. R. Bush, & E. Galanter (Eds.), *Handbook of mathematical psychology.* Vol. III. New York: Wiley, 1965. Pp. 249–410. **907, 918**

Luce, R. D., *see also* Bush, R. R., 1963.

Luchins, A. S. The autokinetic effect in central and peripheral vision. *Journal of General Psychology*, 1954, 50, 39–44. **530**

Luciani, L. *Human physiology.* Vol. 4. (F. A. Welby, trans.) London: Macmillan, 1917. **187**

Ludvigh, E. The visibility of moving objects. *Science*, 1948, 108, 63–64. **520**

Ludvigh, E. Visual acuity while one is viewing a moving object. *Archives of Ophthalmology* (Chicago), 1949, 42, 14–22. **520**

Ludvigh, E. Possible role of proprioception in the extraocular muscles. *Archives of Ophthalmology*, (New York), 1952, 48, 436–441. **530**

Ludvigh, E. J. Visual and stereoscopic acuity for moving

objects. *Symposium on Physiological Psychology*, School of Aviation Medicine, Pensacola, Florida; Office of Naval Research, Department of the Navy, 1955. Reprinted in I. M. Spigel, 1965. **520**

Ludvigson, H. W., *see* McHose, J. H., 1965.

Lummis, R. C., *see* Simmons, F. B., 1965.

Lundin, R. W. *Personality: An experimental approach.* New York: Macmillan, 1961. **791**

Lundström, C. O., *see* Engen, T., 1963.

Lundy, R. M., *see* Parrish, M., 1968.

Luneburg, R. K. *Mathematical analysis of binocular vision.* Princeton, N.J.: Princeton University Press, 1947. **493**

Luneburg, R. K. The metric of binocular visual space. *Journal of the Optical Society of America*, 1950, *40*, 627–642. **493**

Lurie, S., *see* Lichten, W., 1950.

Lynch, D., *see* Capaldi, E. J., 1967.

Lynch, G. S., *see* Campbell, B. A., 1968.

Maatsch, J. L., *see* Adelman, H. M., 1955.

MacAdam, D. L. On the geometry of color space. *Journal of the Franklin Institute*, 1944, *238*, 195. **361**

MacAdam, D. L., *see also* Brown, W. R. J., 1949.

McAlister, E., *see* Hochberg, J., 1953.

McAllister, W. R. Eyelid conditioning as a function of the CS–UCS interval. *Journal of Experimental Psychology*, 1953, *45*, 417–422. **558**

MacBride, P. D., *see* Hochberg, J. E., 1948.

McBurney, D. H. Magnitude estimation of the taste of sodium chloride after adaptation to sodium chloride. *Journal of Experimental Psychology*, 1966, *72*, 869–873. **175, 184**

McBurney, D. H. A note on the relation between area and intensity in taste. *Perception and Psychophysics*, 1969, *6*, 250. **175**

McBurney, D. H., Kasschau, R. A., & Bogart, L. M. The effect of adaptation on taste jnds. *Perception and Psychophysics*, 1967, *2*, 175–178. **184**

McBurney, D. H., & Pfaffmann, C. Gustatory adaptation to saliva and sodium chloride. *Journal of Experimental Psychology*, 1963, *65*, 523–529. **184**

McBurney, D. H., *see also* Bartoshuk, L. M., 1964; Engen, T., 1964; Pfaffman, C., 1969; Smith, D. V., 1969.

McCall, R. B. Stimulus change in light-contingent bar pressing. *Journal of Comparative and Physiological Psychology*, 1965, *59*, 258–262. **673**

McCandless, B. R., *see* Castaneda, A., 1956.

MacCaslin, E. F. Successive and simultaneous discrimination as a function of stimulus similarity. *American Journal of Psychology*, 1954, *67*, 308–314. **775**

McClearn, G. E. The inheritance of behavior. In L. Postman (Ed.), *Psychology in the making.* New York: Knopf, 1963. **702**

McCleary, R. A. Taste and post-ingestive factors in specific-hunger behavior. *Journal of Comparative and Physiological Psychology*, 1953, *46*, 411–421. **626**

McCleary, R. A. Response specificity in the behavioral effects of limbic system lesions in the cat. *Journal of Comparative and Physiological Psychology*, 1961, *54*, 605–613. **576n**

McCleary, R. A., *see also* Chapanis, A., 1953.

McClelland, D. C. Studies in serial verbal discrimination learning: I. Reminiscence with two speeds of pair presentation. *Journal of Experimental Psychology*, 1942, *31*, 44–56. **854**

McClelland, D. C., & Heath, R. M. Retroactive inhibition as a function of degree of association of original and interpolated activities. *Journal of Experimental Psychology*, 1943, *33*, 420–430. **1084**

McCollough, C. Color adaptation of edge-detectors in the human visual system. *Science*, 1965, *149*, 1115–1116. **543**

McConnell, C., *see* Stevenson, H. W., 1955.

McConnell, J. V., *see* Thompson, R., 1955.

McCormack, P. D. Backward mediated positive transfer in a paired-associate task. *Journal of Experimental Psychology*, 1961, *61*, 138–141. **1074**

MacCorquodale, K., & Meehl, P. E. Preliminary suggestions as to a formalization of expectancy theory. *Psychological Review*, 1953, *60*, 55–63. **560n**

MacCorquodale, K., & Meehl, P. E. Edward C. Tolman. In Estes, W. K., et al. (Eds.), *Modern learning theory.* New York: Appleton, 1954. **560n**

McCrary, J. W., & Hunter, W. S. Serial position curves in verbal learning. *Science*, 1953, *117*, 131–134. **1015, 1016**

McCrary, J. W., *see also* Smith, W. M., 1960.

McCready, D. W., Jr., *see* Alpern, M., 1963.

McCue, J. J. G., *see* Grinnell, A. D., 1963.

McCulloch, T. L. Performance preferentials of the white rat in force-resisting and spatial dimensions. *Journal of Comparative Psychology*, 1934, *18*, 85–111. **750**

McCulloch, T. L., & Pratt, J. G. A study in the pre-solution period in weight discrimination by white rats. *Journal of Comparative Psychology*, 1934, *18*, 271–290. **750, 766, 954**

McCulloch, W. S., *see* Lettvin, J. Y., 1959.

McDermott, W., *see* Rock, I., 1964.

McDill, J. A., *see* Stetson, R. H., 1923.

McDonald, D. G., *see* Hahn, W. W., 1962.

McDonald, W. T., *see* McGeoch, J. A., 1931.

MacDonnell, M. F., *see* Siegel, P. S., 1954.

McDonnell, P., *see* Berlyne, D. E., 1965.

McEwen, P. Figural after-effects. *British Journal of Psychology* (Monograph supplement), 1958, No. 31. **469**

McFarland, J. H. Visual and proprioceptive changes during visual exposure to a tilted line. *Perceptual and Motor Skills*, 1962, *15*, 322. **537, 540**

McFarland, J. H. Sequential part presentation: A method of studying visual form perception. *British Journal of Psychology*, 1965, *56*, 439–446. **454**

McFarland, W. L., *see* Smith, O. A. Jr., 1961.

McGehee, N. E., & Schulz, R. W. Mediation in paired-associate learning. *Journal of Experimental Psychology*, 1961, *62*, 565–570. **1078, 1079**

McGeoch, G. O., *see* McGeoch, J. A., 1936.

McGeoch, J. A. The influence of degree of learning upon retroactive inhibition. *American Journal of Psychology*, 1929, *41*, 252–262. **1085**

McGeoch, J. A. The influence of associative value upon the difficulty of nonsense-syllable lists. *Journal of Genetic Psychology*, 1930, *37*, 421–426. **854**

McGeoch, J. A. The influence of four different interpolations upon retention. *Journal of Experimental Psychology*, 1931, *14*, 400–413. **1088**

McGeoch, J. A. Forgetting and the law of disuse. *Psychological Review*, 1932, *39*, 352–370. (a) **1022, 1122**

McGeoch, J. A. The influence of degree of interpolated learning upon retroactive inhibition. *American Journal of Psychology*, 1932, *44*, 695–708. (b) **1086**

McGeoch, J. A. Studies in retroactive inhibition: II. Relationships between temporal point of interpolation, length of interval and amount of retroactive inhibition. *Journal of General Psychology*, 1933, *9*, 44–57. **1100**

McGeoch, J. A. Studies in retroactive inhibition: VII. Retroactive inhibition as a function of the length and frequency of presentation of the interpolated lists. *Journal of Experimental Psychology*, 1936, *19*, 674–693. **1088**

McGeoch, J. A. *The psychology of human learning.* New York: Longmans, Green, 1942. **1021, 1083, 1087, 1088**

McGeoch, J. A., & Irion, A. L. *The psychology of human learning.* New York: Longmans, Green, 1952. **907, 980, 985, 1013, 1014, 1034, 1037**

McGeoch, J. A., & McDonald, W. T. Meaningful relation and retroactive inhibition. *American Journal of Psychology*, 1931, *43*, 579–588. **1054, 1082**

McGeoch, J. A., & McGeoch, G. O. Studies in retroactive inhibition: VI. The influence of the relative serial positions of interpolated synonyms. *Journal of Experimental Psychology*, 1936, *18*, 1–23. **1054, 1083**

McGeoch, J. A., McKinney, F., & Peters, H. N. Studies in retroactive inhibition: IX. Retroactive inhibition, reproductive inhibition and reminiscence. *Journal of Experimental Psychology*, 1937, *20*, 131–143. **1088**

McGeoch, J. A., & Underwood, B. J. Tests of the two-factor theory of retroactive inhibition. *Journal of Experimental Psychology*, 1943, *32*, 1–16. **1104**

McGeoch, J. A., see also McKinney, F., 1935.

McGovern, J. B. Extinction of associations in four transfer paradigms. *Psychological Monographs*, 1964, *78*, Whole No. 593. **1064, 1094**

McGuigan, D. I., see Carr, W. J., 1965.

McGuire, P., see Leibowitz, H., 1957.

McGuire, W. J. A multiprocess model for paired-associate learning. *Journal of Experimental Psychology*, 1961, *62*, 335–347. **1007**

McHose, J. H., & Ludvigson, H. W. Role of reward magnitude and incomplete reduction of reward magnitude in the frustration effect. *Journal of Experimental Psychology*, 1965, *70*, 490–495. **810**

McHose, J. H., see also Barrett, R. J., 1965.

Machover, K., see Witkin, H. A., 1954.

McIntyre, A. K., see Hunt, C. C., 1960a, b.

McIntyre, C., see Fox, R., 1967.

MacIntyre, W. J., see Rowland, V., 1960.

Mack, A. The role of movement in perceptual adaptation to a tilted retinal image. *Perception and Psychophysics*, 1967, *2*, 65–68. **540**

McKelvey, R. K. The relationship between training methods and reward variables in brightness discrimination learning. *Journal of Comparative and Physiological Psychology*, 1956, *49*, 485–491. **637**

McKenna, A. E. The experimental approach to pain. *Journal of Applied Physiology*, 1958, *13*, 449–456. **158**

McKenna, V. V., see Wallach, H., 1960.

McKinney, F. Quantitative and qualitative essential elements of transfer. *Journal of Experimental Psychology*, 1933, *16*, 854–864. **1047**

McKinney, F., & McGeoch, J. A. The character and extent of transfer in retroactive inhibition: Disparate serial lists. *American Journal of Psychology*, 1935, *47*, 409–423. **1088**

McKinney, F., see also McGeoch, J. A., 1937.

McKinney, J. P. Disappearance of luminous designs. *Science*, 1963, *140*, 403–404. **453**

MacKinnon, G. E., see Matin, L., 1964.

Mackintosh, N. J. Selective attention in animal discrimination learning. *Psychological Bulletin*, 1965, *64*, 124–150. **773**

Mackworth, J. F., & Mackworth, N. H. Eye fixations recorded on changing visual scenes by the television eye-marker. *Journal of the Optical Society of America*, 1958, *48*, 439–445. **373**

Mackworth, N. H., see Mackworth, J. F., 1958.

McLaughlin, S. C., DeSisto, M. J., & Kelly, M. J. Comment on eye movements and decrement in the Müller-Lyer illusion. *Perception and Psychophysics*, 1969, *5*, 288. **467n**

McLaughlin, S. C., Kelly, M. J., Anderson, R. E., & Wenz, T. G. Localization of a peripheral target during parametric adjustment of saccadic eye movements. *Perception and Psychophysics*, 1968, *4*, 45–48. **467n**

McLaughlin, S. C., & Rifkin, K. I. Change in straight ahead during adaptation to prism. *Psychonomic Science*, 1965, *2*, 107–108. **537**

McLaughlin, S. C., & Webster, R. G. Changes in straight-ahead eye position during adaptation to wedge prisms. *Perception and Psychophysics*, 1967, *2*, 37–44. **537**

McLaughlin, S. C., see also DeSisto, M. J., 1968.

MacLean, D. J., see Harvey, F. K., 1963.

MacLeod, R. B. An experimental investigation of brightness constancy. *Archives of Psychology* (New York), 1932, No. 135. **405, 423**

MacLeod, R. B., see also Harriman, A. E., 1953.

MacMillan, Z. L., see Foley, J. P., Jr., 1943.

MacNeilage, P. F., see Liberman, A. M., 1962.

McNeill, D., see Rosenzweig, M. R., 1962.

MacNichol, E. F., Jr., & Svaetichin, G. Electric responses from the isolated retinas of fishes. *American Journal of Ophthalmology*, 1958, *46*, 26–40. **308, 325**

MacNichol, E. F. Jr., see Hartline, H. K., 1952; Marks, W. B., 1964; Svaetichin, G., 1958; Wagner, H. G., 1960.

McNulty, J. A., see Tulving, E., 1965.

Maddi, S. R., see Fiske, D. W., 1961.

Madsen, C. H. Jr., see Young, P. T., 1963.

Magnus, R. *Körperstellung.* Berlin: J. Springer, 1924. **385**

Maher, W. B., & Wickens, D. D. Effect of differential quantity of reward on acquisition and performance of a maze habit. *Journal of Comparative and Physiological Psychology*, 1954, *47*, 44–46. **637**

Mahut, H. Effects of subcortical electrical stimulation on discrimination learning in cats. *Journal of Comparative and Physiological Psychology*, 1964, *58*, 390–395. **842**

Maier, N. R. F. *Frustration: The study of behavior without a goal.* New York: McGraw-Hill, 1949. **704, 749, 750, 791**

Maier, N. R. F., & Ellen, P. The effects of lactose in the diet on frustration-susceptibility in rats. *Journal of Comparative and Physiological Psychology*, 1951, *44*, 551–556. **750**

Maier, N. R. F., Glaser, N. M., & Klee, J. B. Studies of abnormal behavior in the rat: III. The development of behavior fixations through frustration. *Journal of Experimental Psychology*, 1940, *26*, 521–546. **791**

Maier, N. R. F., & Klee, J. B. Studies of abnormal behavior in the rat: XVII. Guidance versus trial and error in the and their relation to convulsive tendencies. *Journal of Experimental Psychology*, 1941, *29*, 380–389. **791**

Maier, N. R. F., & Klee, J. B. Studies of abnormal behavior in the rat: XVII. Guidance versus trial and error in the alteration of habits and fixations. *Journal of Psychology*, 1945, *19*, 133–163. **791**

Maier, S. F., Seligman, M. E. P., & Solomon, R. L. Pavlovian fear conditioning and learned helplessness: Effects on escape and avoidance behavior of (a) the CS-US contingency and (b) the independence of the US and voluntary responding. In B. A. Campbell & R. M. Church (Eds.), *Punishment and aversive behavior.* New York: Appleton, 1969. **570n, 661n, 710, 717, 724**

Makous, W., Nord, S., Oakley, B., & Pfaffmann, C. The gustatory relay in the medulla. In Y. Zotterman (Ed.), *Olfaction and taste.* Vol. 1. New York: Pergamon, 1963. Pp. 381–393. **182**

Malis, L. C., & Kruger, L. Multiple response and excitability of cat's visual cortex. *Journal of Neurophysiology*, 1956, *19*, 172–186. **309**

Mallay, H., see Washburn, M. F., 1931.

Maller, O., & Kare, M. R. Observations on the sense of taste in the armadillo (*Dasypus novemcinctus*). *Animal Behaviour*, 1967, *15*, 8–10. **190**

Malmo, R. B. Anxiety and behavioral arousal. *Psychological Review*, 1957, *64*, 276–287. **832**

Malmo, R. B. Measurement of drive: An unsolved problem in psychology. In M. R. Jones (Ed.), *Nebraska symposium on motivation.* Lincoln: University of Nebraska Press, 1958. Pp. 229–265. **831, 832, 833, 842**

Malmo, R. B. Activation: A neuropsychological dimension. *Psychological Review*, 1959, *66*, 367–386. **832**

Malmo, R. B. Activation. In A. J. Bachrach (Ed.), *Experimental foundations of clinical psychology.* New York: Basic Books, 1962. Pp. 386–422. **832**

Malmo, R. B. Heart rate reactions and locus of stimulation

within the septal area of the rat. *Science*, 1964, *144*, 1029–1030. **657**

Malmo, R. B. Physiological gradients and behavior. *Psychological Bulletin*, 1965, *64*, 225–234. **833**

Malmo, R. B., & Bélanger, D. Related physiological and behavioral changes: What are their determinants? In S. S. Kety, E. V. Evarts, & H. L. Williams (Eds.), *Sleep and altered states of consciousness*. Baltimore: Williams & Wilkins, 1967. Pp. 288–318. **833, 835**

Malmo, R. B., Shagass, C., & Heslam, R. M. Blood pressure response to repeated brief stress in psychoneurosis: A study of adaptation. *Canadian Journal of Psychology*, 1951, *5*, 167–179. **834**

Maltzman, I. Theoretical conceptions of semantic conditioning and generalization. In T. R. Dixon & D. L. Horton (Eds.), *Verbal behavior and general behavior theory*. Englewood Cliffs, N. J.: Prentice-Hall, 1968. **1048**

Maltzman, I., Bogartz, W., & Breger, L. A procedure for increasing word association originality and its transfer effects. *Journal of Experimental Psychology*, 1958, *56*, 392–398. **867**

Maltzman, I., & Gallup, H. F. Comments on "originality" in free and controlled association responses. *Psychological Reports*, 1964, *14*, 573–574. **867**

Maltzman, I., & Simon, S. A recency effect between word-association lists. *Psychological Reports*, 1959, *5*, 632. **867n**

Maltzman, I., Simon, S., Raskin, D., & Licht, L. Experimental studies in the training of originality. *Psychological Monographs*, 1960, *74*, Whole No. 493. **867**

Mandler, G. Response factors in human learning. *Psychological Review*, 1954, *61*, 235–244. **993**

Mandler, G. Associative frequency and associative prepotency as measures of response to nonsense syllables. *American Journal of Psychology*, 1955, *68*, 662–665. **852**

Mandler, G. Comments on Professor Russell's paper. In C. N. Cofer (Ed.), *Verbal learning and verbal behavior*. New York: McGraw-Hill, 1961. Pp. 123–128. **949**

Mandler, G. From association to structure. *Psychological Review*, 1962, *69*, 415–427. **1067, 1068**

Mandler, G. Comments on Professor Jenkin's paper. In C. N. Cofer & B. S. Musgrave (Eds.), *Verbal behavior and learning: Problems and processes*. New York: McGraw-Hill, 1963. Pp. 245–252. **949**

Mandler, G. Subjects do think. *Psychological Review*, 1965, *72*, 323–326. **1068**

Mandler, G. Organization and memory. In K. W. Spence, & J. T. Spence (Eds.), *The psychology of learning and motivation*. Vol. I. New York: Academic Press, 1967. **892**

Mandler, G. Verbal learning. In G. Mandler, P. Mussen, N. Kogan, & M. A. Wallach (Eds.), *New directions in psychology*. Vol. III. New York: Holt, Rinehart and Winston, 1967. **949**

Mandler, G., Cowan, P. A., & Gold, C. Concept learning and probability matching. *Journal of Experimental Psychology*, 1964, *67*, 514–522. **958**

Mandler, G., & Earhard, B. Pseudomediation: Is chaining an artifact? *Psychonomic Science*, 1964, *1*, 247–248. **1076**

Mandler, G., & Heinemann, S. H. Effect of overlearning of a verbal response on transfer of training. *Journal of Experimental Psychology*, 1956, *57*, 39–46. **1063, 1064, 1067**

Mandler, G., & Parnes, E. W. Frequency and idiosyncrasy of associative responses. *Journal of Abnormal and Social Psychology*, 1957, *55*, 58–65. **873**

Mandler, G., see also Earhard, B., 1965a, b; Mandler, J. M., 1964.

Mandler, J. M., & Mandler, G. *Thinking: From association to gestalt*. New York: Wiley, 1964. **850**

Mangabeira-Albernaz, P. L., see Sherrik, C., 1961.

Mangels, J. W., see Thurlow, W. R., 1967.

Mankin, D. A., see Chapanis, A., 1967.

Mann, C. W. Visual factors in the perception of verticality.

Journal of Experimental Psychology, 1952, *44*, 460–464. **539**

Mann, L. I., see Kimble, G. A., 1955.

Manning, H. M. The effect of varying conditions of hunger and thirst on two responses learned to hunger or thirst alone. *Journal of Comparative and Physiological Psychology*, 1956, *49*, 249–253. **801**

Manning, P., see Washburn, M. F., 1934.

Marbe, K., see Thumb, A., 1901.

Marder, V. J., see Deese, J., 1957.

Margules, D. L., & Olds, J. Identical "feeding" and "rewarding" systems in the lateral hypothalamus of rats. *Science*, 1962, *135*, 374–375. **651, 798**

Marill, T., see Heinemann, E. G., 1954.

Marin, J., see Hunt, E. B., 1966.

Markee, J. E., see Becker, R. F., 1962.

Markham, J. W., see Armstrong, D., 1951.

Markley, R. P., see Vincent, R. J., 1969.

Markowitz, R. A., see Smith, G. M., 1966.

Marks, L. E., & Miller, G. A. The role of semantic and syntactic constraints in the memorization of English sentences. *Journal of Verbal Learning and Verbal Behavior*, 1964, *3*, 1–5. **903**

Marks, L. E., & Stevens, J. C. Individual brightness functions. *Perception and Psychophysics*, 1966, *2*, 7–24. **79**

Marks, W. B., Dobelle, W. H., & MacNichol, E. F., Jr. Visual pigments of single primate cones. *Science*, 1964, *143*, 1181–1183. **323**

Marler, P. Territory and individual distance in the chaffinch *Fringilla coelebs*. *Ibis*, 1956, *98*, 496–501. **693**

Marler, P. R., & Hamilton, W. J., III., *Mechanisms of animal behavior*. New York: Wiley, 1966. **589n**

Marlowe, D., see Horton, D. L., 1963.

Marquis, D. G., & Porter, J. M., Jr. Differential characteristics of conditioned eyelid responses established by reflex and voluntary reinforcement. *Journal of Experimental Psychology*, 1939, *24*, 347–365. **564**

Marquis, D. G., see also Hilgard, E. R., 1940.

Marshall, D. A. A comparative study of neural coding in gustation. *Physiology and Behavior*, 1967. **181**

Marshall, D. A., see also Erickson, R. P., 1965.

Marshall, G. R. The organization of verbal material in free recall: The effects of patterns of associative overlap on clustering. Doctoral dissertation. New York University, 1963. **887, 891**

Marshall, G. R., & Cofer, C. N. Associative indices as measures of word relatedness: A summary and comparison of ten methods. *Journal of Verbal Learning and Verbal Behavior*, 1963, *1*, 408–421. **879, 880, 881, 888**

Marshall, G. R., see also Garskoff, B. E., 1965.

Marshall, W. H., & Talbot, S. A. Recent evidence for neural mechanisms in vision leading to a general theory of sensory acuity. In H. Klüver (Ed.), *Biological symposia*. Vol. 7: *Visual mechanisms*. Lancaster, Pa.: Jacques Cattell, 1942. **305**

Marten, A. E., see Thurlow, W. R., 1963, 1965.

Martin, E. Transfer of verbal paired associates. *Psychological Review*, 1965, *72*, 327–343. **1059, 1061, 1067**

Martin, E. Stimulus recognition in aural paired-associate learning. *Journal of Verbal Learning and Verbal Behavior*, 1967, *6*, 272–276. (a) **1048**

Martin, E. Relation between stimulus recognition and paired-associate learning. *Journal of Experimental Psychology*, 1967, *74*, 500–505. (b) **1048**

Martin, J. G. Associative strength and word frequency in paired-associate learning. *Journal of Verbal Learning and Verbal Behavior*, 1964, *3*, 317–320. **888**

Martin, L., see Johnson, R. C., 1961.

Martin, L. C. The photometric matching field. *Proceedings of the Royal Society*, (London), Ser. A, 1923, *104*, 302–315. **426**

Martin, L. C., Day, D. J., & Kaniowski, W. Visual acuity with brief stimuli. *British Journal of Ophthalmology*, 1950, *34*, 89–104. **304**

Martin, R. B., & Dean, S. J. Implicit and explicit mediation in paired-associate learning. *Journal of Experimental Psychology*, 1964, *68*, 21–27. **1079**

Martin, R. B., Simon, S., & Ditrichs, R. Verbal paired-associate transfer as a function of practice and paradigm shift. *Psychonomic Science*, 1966, *4*, 419–420. **1070**

Martin, R. C., *see* Brown, J. S., 1964.

Martini, L., & Ganong, W. F. (Eds.), *Neuroendocrinology*. New York: Academic Press, 1966. **91**

Maruhashi, J., Mizuguchi, J., & Tasaki, I. Action current in single afferent nerve fibers elicited by stimulation of the skin of the toad and the cat. *Journal of Physiology*, 1952, *117*, 129–151. **165**

Maruyama, N., *see* Katsuki, Y., 1959.

Marx, M. H. Some relations between frustration and drive. In M. R. Jones (Ed.), *Nebraska symposium on motivation*. Lincoln: University of Nebraska Press, 1956. Pp. 92–130. **810**

Marx, M. H., & Pieper, W. A. Acquisition of instrumental response as a function of incentive contrast. *Psychological Reports*, 1962, *10*, 635–638. **638**

Marx, M. H., & Pieper, W. A. Instrumental acquisition and performance on fixed-interval reinforcement as a function of incentive contrast. *Psychological Reports*, 1963, *12*, 255–258. **638**

Marx, M. H., *see also* Collier, G., 1959.

Mason, G. L., *see* Alpern, M., 1961.

Mason, W. A., *see* Lawrence, D. H., 1955.

Masserman, J. H., & Pechtel, C. Neuroses in monkeys: A preliminary report of experimental observations. *Annals of The New York Academy of Science*, 1953, *56*, 253–265. **704**

Massey, F. J., *see* Dixon, W. F., 1956.

Masterson, F. A., *see* Campbell, B. A., 1968.

Masterton, R. B., Jane, J. A., & Diamond, I. T. Role of brain-stem auditory structures in sound localization. *Journal of Neurophysiology*, 1968, *31*, 96–108. **264**

Mateer, F. *Child behavior*. Boston: Badger, 1918. **562**

Mathews, R. W., *see* Walls, G. L., 1952.

Matin, E., *see* Matin, L., 1966, 1969.

Matin, L. Binocular summation at the absolute threshold of peripheral vision. *Journal of the Optical Society of America*, 1962, *52*, 1276–1286. **296**

Matin, L. Binocular summation at the absolute threshold of peripheral vision. *Journal of the Optical Society of America*, 1963, *53*, 1199–1205. **488**

Matin, L., & Kibler, G. Acuity of visual perception of direction in the dark for various positions of the eye in orbit. *Perceptual and Motor Skills*, 1966, *22*, 407–420. **530**

Matin, L., & MacKinnon, G. E. Autokinetic movement: Selective manipulation of directional components by image stabilization. *Science*, 1964, *143*, 147–148. **529**

Matin, L., Matin, E., & Pearce, D. G. Visual perception of direction when voluntary saccades occur: I. Relation of visual direction of a fixation target extinguished before a saccade to a flash presented during the saccade. *Perception and Psychophysics*, 1969, *5*, 65–80. **531**

Matin, L., Pearce, D., Matin, E., & Kibler, G. Visual perception of direction in the dark: Roles of local sign, eye movements, and ocular proprioception. *Vision Research*, 1966, *6*, 453–469. **530**

Matsubayashi, A. Forschung über die Tiefenwahrnehmung: II. *Acta Societatis Ophthalmologica Japonica*, 1937, *41*, 2055–2074. Cited in Graham, C. H., 1965. **486**

Matsumiya, Y. The effects of US intensity and CS-US pattern on conditioned emotional response. *Japanese Psychological Research*, 1960, *2*, 35–42. **579, 719**

Matsumiya, Y., *see also* Kling, J. W., 1962.

Matthews, R., *see* Adrian, E. D., 1928.

Matthews, T. J., *see* Beer, B., 1964.

Maturana, H. R., & Frenk, S. Directional movement and horizontal edge detectors in the pigeon retina. *Science*, 1963, *142*, 977–979. **296**

Maturana, H. R., *see also* Lettvin, J. Y., 1959.

May, F., *see* Long, E. R., 1958.

Mayer, B. Messende Untersuchungen über die Umstimmung des Geschmackswerkzeugs. *Zeitschrift für Sinnesphysiologie*, 1927, *58*, 133–152. **186, 187**

Mayhew, A. J. Interlist changes in subjective organization during free-recall learning. *Journal of Experimental Psychology*, 1967, *74*, 425–430. **1045**

Mayzner, M. S., Abrevay, E. L., Frey, R. E., Kaufman, H. G., & Schoenberg, K. M. Short-term memory in vision: A partial replication of the Averbach and Coriell study. *Psychonomic Science*, 1964, *1*, 225–226. **430**

Mayzner, M. S., Blatt, M. H., Buchsbaum, W. H., Friedel, R. T., Goodwin, P. E., Kanon, D., Keleman, A., & Nilsson, W. D. A U-shaped backward masking function in vision: A partial replication of the Weisstein and Haber study with two ring sizes. *Psychonomic Science*, 1965, *3*, 79–80. **430**

Mayzner, M. S., & Schoenberg, K. M. Single-letter and digram frequency effects in immediate serial recall. *Journal of Verbal Learning and Verbal Behavior*, 1964, *3*, 397–400. **897**

Mayzner, M. S., & Tresselt, M. E. The ranking of letter pairs and single letters to match digram and single-letter frequency counts. *Journal of Verbal Learning and Verbal Behavior*, 1962, *1*, 203–207. **898**

Mayzner, M. S., & Tresselt, M. E. Tables of single-letter and digram frequency counts for various word-length and letter-position combinations. *Psychonomic Science (Monograph Supplement)*, 1965, *1*, No. 2. **896**

Mayzner, M. S., Tresselt, M. E., Adler, S., & Schoenberg, K. M. Correlations between subject generated letter frequencies and observed frequencies in English. *Psychonomic Science*, 1964, *1*, 295–296. **898**

Mayzner, M. S., Tresselt, M. E., & Wolin, B. R. Tables of trigram frequency counts for various word-length and letter-position combinations. *Psychonomic Science (Monograph Supplement)*, 1965, *1*, No. 3. (a) **896**

Mayzner, M. S., Tresselt, M. E., & Wolin, B. R. Tables of tetragram frequency counts for various word-length and letter-position combinations. *Psychonomic Science (Monograph Supplement)*, 1965, *1*, No. 4. (b) **896**

Mayzner, M. S., Tresselt, M. E., & Wolin, B. R. Tables of pentagram frequency counts for various word-length and letter-position combinations. *Psychonomic Science (Monograph Supplement)*, 1965, *1*, No. 5. (c) **896**

Mead, S., *see* Mueller, E. E., 1953.

Mednick, M. T. Mediated generalization and the incubation effect as a function of manifest anxiety. *Journal of Abnormal and Social Psychology*, 1957, *55*, 315–321. **1047**

Mednick, S. A., & Freedman, J. L. Stimulus generalization. *Psychological Bulletin*, 1960, *57*, 170–200. **761**

Meehl, P. E. On the circularity of the law of effect. *Psychological Bulletin*, 1950, *47*, 52–75. **567**

Meehl, P. E., *see also* MacCorquodale, K., 1953, 1954.

Mefferd, R. B. Endogenously-supplied visual attributes of depth. *Perceptual and Motor Skills*, 1968, *27*, 1115–1122. **519**

Mefferd, R. B. Perceptual fluctuations involving orientation and organization. *Perceptual and Motor Skills*, 1968, *27*, 827–834. **519**

Mefferd, R. B., Jr., & Wieland, B. A. Perception of depth in ·rotating objects: 2. Perspective as a determinant of stereokinesis. *Perceptual and Motor Skills*, 1967, *25*, 621–628. **524**

Mefferd, R. B., & Wieland, B. A. Apparent size-apparent

distance relationship in flat stimuli. *Perceptual and Motor Skills*, 1968, 26, 959–966. **462**

Mefferd, R. B., Jr., *see also* Cook, T. H., 1967; Moran, L. J., 1964.

Megibow, M., & Zeigler, H. P. Readiness to eat in the pigeon. *Psychonomic Science*, 1968, 12, 17–18. **816**

Mehler, J. Some effects of grammatical transformations on the recall of English sentences. *Journal of Verbal Learning and Verbal Behavior*, 1963, 3, 346–351. **904**

Meinke, D. L., *see* Johnson, T. J., 1965.

Meiselman, H. L. Adaptation and cross-adaptation of the four gustatory qualities. *Perception and Psychophysics*, 1968, 4, 368–372. **186**

Meiselman, L., *see* Dzendolet, E., 1967a, b.

Meissner, G. Untersuchungen über den Tastsinn. *Zeitschrift für Rationelle Medicin*, 1859, 7, 92–118. **129**

Meissner, P. B., *see* Witkin, H. A., 1954.

Melamed, L. E., *see* Thurlow, W. R., 1967.

Mellon, D., *see* Evans, D. R., 1962.

Melton, A. W. The end-spurt in memorization curves as an artifact of the averaging of individual curves. *Psychological Monographs*, 1936, 47, 119–134. **613, 1025**

Melton, A. W. Comments on Professor Postman's paper. In C. N. Cofer (Ed.), *Verbal learning and verbal behavior*. New York: McGraw-Hill, 1961. **1092, 1097**

Melton, A. W. Comments on Professor Peterson's paper. In C. N. Cofer & B. S. Musgrave (Eds.), *Verbal behavior and learning*. New York: McGraw-Hill, 1963. (a) **1109**

Melton, A. W. Implications of short-term memory for a general theory of memory. *Journal of Verbal Learning and Verbal Behavior*, 1963, 2, 1–21. (b) **997, 998, 1109, 1110, 1111**

Melton, A. W., & Irwin, J. M. The influence of degree of interpolated learning on retroactive inhibition and the overt transfer of specific responses. *American Journal of Psychology*, 1940, 53, 173–203. **1086, 1089**

Melton, A. W., & Von Lackum, W. J. Retroactive and proactive inhibition in retention: Evidence for a two-factor theory of retroactive inhibition. *American Journal of Psychology*, 1941, 54, 157–173. **613, 1041, 1054, 1082, 1103, 1104**

Meltzer, R., *see* Goulet, L. R., 1967.

Melzack, R. Irrational fears in the dog. *Canadian Journal of Psychology*, 1952, 6, 141–147. **586**

Melzack, R., & Casey, K. L. Sensory, motivational, and central control determinants of pain. In D. R. Kenshalo (Ed.), *The skin senses*. Springfield, Ill.: Charles C Thomas, 1968. Pp. 423–443. **155**

Melzack, R., & Wall, P. D. On the nature of cutaneous sensory mechanisms. *Brain*, 1962, 85 (II), 331–356. **119, 121, 167**

Melzack, R., & Wall, P. D. Pain mechanisms: A new theory. *Science*, 1965, 150, 971–979. **165, 167**

Menahem, R., *see* Rosenzweig, M. R., 1962.

Mendelson, J., & Chorover, S. L. Lateral hypothalamic stimulation in satiated rats: T-maze learning for food. *Science*, 1965, 149, 559–561. **798**

Merikle, P. M. Paired-associate transfer as a function of stimulus and response meaningfulness. *Psychological Reports*, 1968, 22, 131–138. **1062, 1063, 1064**

Mershon, D. H., *see* Gogel, W. C., 1969.

Mertens, H. W., *see* Gogel, W. C., 1967.

Merton, P. A. The accuracy of directing the eyes and the hand in the dark. *Journal of Physiology*, 1961, 156, 555–577. **530**

Merton, P. A., *see also* Brindley, G. S., 1960.

Meryman, J. J. Magnitude of startle response as a function of hunger and fear. Unpublished master's thesis, State University of Iowa, 1952. Cited by Brown, 1961. **796**

Meseck, O. R., *see* Russell, W. A., 1959.

Metelli, F. Zur Analyse der phanomenalen Durchtigkeitser-

scheinungen. In *Gestalt und Wirklichkeit: Festgabe für Ferdinand Weinhandl*. Berlin: Duncker und Humboldt, 1967. **427**

Metfessel, M. A proposal for quantitative reporting of comparative judgments. *Journal of Psychology*, 1947, 24, 229–235. **71**

Metzger, W. Optische Unterschungengen am Ganzfelds: II. Zur Phanomenologic des homogenen Ganzfelds. *Psychologische Forschung*, 1930, 13, 6–29. **426**

Metzger, W. *Gesetze des Sehens*. Frankfurt am Main: Kramer, 1953. **428, 442**

Meumann, E., *see* Ebert, E., 1905.

Meyer, D. R. The effects of differential rewards on discrimination reversal learning by monkeys. *Journal of Experimental Psychology*, 1951, 41, 268–274. **636, 637, 638, 639**

Meyer, D. R. Some psychological determinants of sparing and loss following damage to the brain. In H. H. Harlow & C. N. Woolsey (Eds.), *Biological and biochemical bases of behavior*. Madison: University of Wisconsin Press, 1958. Pp. 173–192. **845**

Meyer, D. R., Cho, C., & Wesemann, A. F. On problems of conditioning discriminated lever-press avoidance responses. *Psychological Review*, 1960, 67, 224–228. **730**

Meyer, D. R., LoPopolo, M. H., & Singh, D. Learning and transfer in the monkey as a function of differential levels of incentive. *Journal of Experimental Psychology*, 1966, 72, 284–286. **640**

Meyer, D. R., & Miles, R. C. Intralist-interlist relations in verbal learning. *Journal of Experimental Psychology*, 1953, 45, 109–115. **1043**

Meyer, D. R., Treichler, F. R., & Meyer, P. M. Discrete-trial training techniques and stimulus variables. In A. M. Schrier, H. F. Harlow, & F. Stollnitz (Eds.), *Behavior of nonhuman primates*. Vol. 1. New York: Academic Press, 1965. **750, 751**

Meyer, D. R., *see also* Miles, R. C., 1956.

Meyer, P. M., *see* Meyer, D. R., 1965.

Meyer, W., *see* Fitts, P. M., 1956.

Meyers, R. E., *see* Sperry, R. W., 1955.

Meyers, W. J., Valenstein, E. S., & Lacey, J. I. Heart rate changes after reinforcing brain stimulation in rats. *Science*, 1963, 140, 1233–1235. **657**

Meyers, W. J., *see also* Valenstein, E. S., 1964.

Michael, C. R. Receptive fields of directionally selective units in the optic nerve of the ground squirrel. *Science*, 1966, 152, 1092–1097. **296**

Michels, K. M., & Zusne, L. Metrics of visual form. *Psychological Bulletin*, 1965, 63, 74–86. **449**

Michels, K. M., *see also* Wright, R. H., 1964.

Michels, W. C., & Helson, H. A reformulation of the Fechner law in terms of adaptation-level applied to rating-scale data. *American Journal of Psychology*, 1949, 62, 355–368. **60**

Michelsen, W. J. Procedure for studying olfactory discrimination in pigeons. *Science*, 1959, 130, 630–631. **753, 754**

Michotte, A. *La perception de la causalité*. Louvain: Institut Supérieur de Philosophie, 1946. **524, 525**

Mikaelian, H., & Held, R. Two types of adaptation to an optically rotated visual field. *American Journal of Psychology*, 1964, 77, 257–263. **539, 540, 542**

Mikaelian, H., *see also* Held, R., 1964; Morant, R. B., 1960.

Mikesell, W. H., & Bentley, M. Configuration and brightness contrast. *Journal of Experimental Psychology*, 1930, 13, 1–23. **410, 423n**

Mikulka, P. J., *see* Spear, N. E., 1966.

Milauckas, E. W., *see* Young, R. K., 1963.

Miles, R. C. The relative effectiveness of secondary reinforcers throughout deprivation and habit-strength parameters. *Journal of Comparative and Physiological Psychology*, 1956, 49, 126–130. **666, 668**

Miles, R. C. Learning-set formation in the squirrel monkey. *Journal of Comparative and Physiological Psychology,* 1957, *50,* 356-357. **768**

Miles, R. C., & Meyer, D. R. Learning sets in marmosets. *Journal of Comparative and Physiological Psychology,* 1956, *49,* 219-222. **768**

Miles, R. C., see also Meyer, D. R., 1953.

Miles, W. R. Effectiveness of red light on dark adaptation. *Journal of the Optical Society of America,* 1953, *43,* 435-441. **284**

Miles, W. R., see also Beck, L. H., 1947.

Miller, D., see Zigler, M. J., 1930.

Miller, E. Context in the perception of sentences. *American Journal of Psychology,* 1956, *69,* 653-654. **448**

Miller, G. A. *Language and communication.* New York: McGraw-Hill, 1951. **895**

Miller, G. A. The magical number seven, plus or minus two: Some limits on our capacity for processing information. *Psychological Review,* 1956, *63,* 81-97. **205, 250, 998**

Miller, G. A. Some psychological studies of grammar. *American Psychologist,* 1962, *17,* 748-762. **904**

Miller, G. A., Galanter, E., & Pribram, K. *Plans and the structure of behavior.* New York: Holt, Rinehart and Winston, 1960. **975**

Miller, G. A., Heise, G. A., & Lichten, W. The intelligibility of speech as a function of the context of the test materials. *Journal of Experimental Psychology,* 1951, *41,* 329-335. **254, 256**

Miller, G. A., & Selfridge, J. Verbal context and the recall of meaningful material. *American Journal of Psychology,* 1950, *63,* 176-185. **902**

Miller, G. A., & Taylor, W. G. The perception of repeated bursts of noise. *Journal of the Acoustical Society of America,* 1948, *20,* 171-182. **245**

Miller, G. A., see also Bruner, J. S., 1955; Garner, W. R., 1947; Licklider, J. C. R., 1951; Marks, L. E., 1964.

Miller, J. The effect of facilitating and inhibitory attitudes on eyelid conditioning. Doctoral dissertation, Yale University, 1939. **561**

Miller, J. D., see Kryter, K. D., 1966.

Miller, N. E. A reply to "sign-gestalt or conditioned reflex?" *Psychological Review,* 1935, *42,* 280-292. **621, 780**

Miller, N. E. Studies of fear as an acquirable drive: I. Fear as motivation and fear-reduction as reinforcement in the learning of new responses. *Journal of Experimental Psychology,* 1948, *38,* 89-101. **717, 718, 802, 803, 804**

Miller, N. E. Theory and experiment relating psychoanalytic displacement to stimulus response generalization. *Journal of Abnormal and Social Psychology,* 1948, *43,* 155-178. **780**

Miller, N. E. Learnable drives and rewards. In S. S. Stevens (Ed.), *Handbook of experimental psychology.* New York: Wiley, 1951. Pp. 435-472. **718, 802**

Miller, N. E. Shortcomings of food consumption as a measure of hunger: Results from other behavioral techniques. *Annals of the New York Academy of Sciences,* 1955, *63,* 141-143. **797**

Miller, N. E. Effects of drugs on motivation: The value of using a variety of measures. *Annals of the New York Academy of Sciences,* 1956, *65,* 318-333. **815, 827**

Miller, N. E. Experiments on motivation. *Science,* 1957, *126,* 1271-1278. **690, 800**

Miller, N. E. Liberalization of basic S-R concepts: Extensions to conflict behavior, motivation, and social learning. In S. Koch (Ed.), *Psychology: A study of a science.* Vol. II. New York: McGraw-Hill, 1959. Pp. 196-292. **821**

Miller, N. E. Learning resistance to pain and fear: Effects of overlearning, exposure, and rewarded exposure in context. *Journal of Experimental Psychology,* 1960, *60,* 137-145. **736**

Miller, N. E. Motivational effects of brain stimulation and drugs. *Federation Proceedings,* 1960, *19,* 846-854. **798**

Miller, N. E. Some reflections on the law of effect produce a new alternative to drive reduction. In M. R. Jones (Ed.), *Nebraska symposium on motivation.* Lincoln: University of Nebraska Press, 1963, *11,* 65-112. **660, 690**

Miller, N. E. Learning of visceral and glandular responses. *Science,* 1969, *163,* 434-446. **563, 655**

Miller, N. E., & Banuazizi, A. Instrumental learning by curarized rats of a specific visceral response, intestinal or cardiac. *Journal of Comparative and Physiological Psychology,* 1968, *65,* 1-7. **655, 699, 839**

Miller, N. E., & Dollard, J. *Social learning and imitation.* New Haven: Yale University Press, 1941. **821**

Miller, N. E., & Kessen, M. L. Reward effects of food via stomach fistula compared with those of food via mouth. *Journal of Comparative and Physiological Psychology,* 1952, *45,* 555-564. **621, 797**

Miller, N. E., see also Bower, G. H., 1958; Delgado, J. M. R., 1954, 1954b; DiCara, L. V., 1968; Dollard, J., 1950; Egger, M. D., 1963; Feirstein, A. R., 1963; Fowler, H., 1963; Mowrer, O. H., 1936; Myers, A. K., 1954.

Miller, P., see Levine, M., 1967.

Miller, R. L. Masking effect of periodically pulsed tones as a function of time and frequency. *Journal of the Acoustical Society of America,* 1947, *19,* 798-807. **241**

Miller, S., & Konorski, J. Sur une forme particulière des réflexes conditionels. *Comptes Rendus des Séances de la Société Polonaise de Biologie,* 1928, *49,* 1155-1158. **565n**

Miller, S., see also Weddell, G., 1962.

Miller, T. M., see Shapiro, M. M., 1965.

Miller, W. H., see Hartline, H. K., 1961.

Mills, A. W. On the minimum audible angle. *Journal of the Acoustical Society of America,* 1958, *30,* 237-246. **266, 267**

Mills, A. W. Lateralization of high-frequency tones. *Journal of the Acoustical Society of America,* 1960, *32,* 132-134. **266**

Millward, R. An all-or-none model for noncorrection routines with elimination of incorrect responses. *Journal of Mathematical Psychology,* 1964, *1,* 392-404. (a) **994**

Millward, R. B. Latency in a modified paired-associate learning experiment. *Journal of Verbal Learning and Verbal Behavior,* 1964, *3,* 309-316. (b) **957**

Millward, R. Two learning models for two-choice conditioning experiments involving nonreinforced trials. *Psychological Reports,* 1967, *20,* 1211-1229. **933**

Millward, R. B. Probabilistic reinforcement of reversal and dimensional shifts. *Journal of Mathematical Psychology,* 1968, *5,* 196-223. **955**

Millward, R. B., & Reber, A. S. Event recall in probability learning. Technical Report, No. 2; 1967, Brown University. **936**

Millward, R. B., see also Blough, D., 1965; Friedman, M. P., 1964; Reber, A. S., 1968.

Milner, P. M., see Olds, J., 1954.

Miner, N., see Sperry, R. W., 1955.

Mink, W. D. Semantic generalization as related to word association. *Psychological Reports,* 1963, *12,* 59-67. **1048**

Mink, W. D., see also Jenkins, J. J., 1958.

Minnaert, M. *Light and colour in the open air.* (Tr. H. M. Kremer-Priest; rev. K. E. Brian-Jay.) London: G. Bell, 1940. **498**

Mintz, D. E., see Notterman, J. M., 1962, 1965.

Mintz, E. U., see Hecht, S., 1939.

Miron, M. S., see Shanmugam, A. V., 1966.

Misanin, J. R., see Campbell, B. A., 1966, 1969.

Mishkin, M., & Forgays, D. G. Word recognition as a function of retinal locus. *Journal of Experimental Psychology,* 1952, *43,* 43-48. **444**

Mitchell, A. M., see Westheimer, G. H., 1956.

Mitchell, E., see Leibowitz, H., 1954.

Mittelstaedt, H., see Holst, E. von, 1950.

Mitzuguchi, J., see Maruhashi, J., 1952.

Mogenson, G. J. An attempt to establish secondary reinforcement with rewarding brain stimulation. *Psychological Reports*, 1965, *16*, 163–167. **675**

Mogenson, G. J., & Stevenson, J. A. F. Drinking and self-stimulation with electrical stimulation of the lateral hypothalamus. *Physiology and Behavior*, 1966, *1*, 251–254. **652**

Moll, R. R. Drive and maturation effects in the development of consummatory behavior. *Psychological Reports*, 1964, *15*, 295–302. **820**

Moller, J. A. The effect of food deprivation on heart rate under low environmental stimulation. Canadian Psychological Association, 22nd. annual meeting, Quebec, June, 1963. **836**

Moltz, H. Imprinting: An epigenetic view. *Psychological Review*, 1963, *70*, 123–138. **584, 588**

Moltz, H., Rosenblum, L. A., & Stettner, L. J. Some parameters of imprinting effectiveness. *Journal of Comparative and Physiological Psychology*, 1960, *53*, 297–301. **586**

Moltz, H., & Stettner, L. J. The influence of patterned light deprivation on the critical period for imprinting. *Journal of Comparative and Physiological Psychology*, 1961, *54*, 297–283. **583**

Moncrieff, R. W. Olfactory adaptation and odor-intensity. *American Journal of Psychology*, 1957, *70*, 1–20. **203, 204**

Moncrieff, R. W. *The chemical senses*. Cleveland: CRC Press, 1967. **194, 220**

Moncrieff, R. W. *The chemical senses*. (3rd ed.) London: Leonard Hill, 1967. **177, 178**

Mongeon, C. J., see Simmons, F. B., 1964.

Monjan, A. *Chromatic adaption and the HTRF in the macaque*. Doctoral dissertation, University of Rochester, 1964. **343**

Montagna, W. *The structure and function of skin*. New York: Academic Press, 1962. **122, 125**

Mook, D. G. Oral and postingestional determinants of the intake of various solutions in rats with esophageal fistulas. *Journal of Comparative and Physiological Psychology*, 1963, *56*, 645–659. **621, 627**

Moon, P. *The scientific basis of illuminating engineering*. New York: McGraw-Hill, 1936. **274**

Moore, J. W., see Halpern, J., 1967.

Moore, M. E., Linker, E., & Purcell, M. Taste-sensitivity after eating: A signal detection approach. *American Journal of Psychology*, 1965, *78*, 107–111. **188**

Moore, M. E., see also Linker, E., 1964; Wallach, H., 1963.

Moore, M. G. Gestalt vs. experience. *American Journal of Psychology*, 1930, *42*, 453–455. **440**

Moran, L. J. Generality of word-association response sets. *Psychological Monographs*, 1966, *80*, Whole No. 612. **876**

Moran, L. J., Mefford, R. B., Jr., & Kimble, J. P., Jr. Idiodynamic sets in word association. *Psychological Monographs*, 1964, *78*, Whole No. 579. **876**

Morant, R. B. & Beller, H. K. Adaptation to prismatically rotated visual fields. *Science*, 1965, *148*, 530–531. **539**

Morant, R. B., & Mikaelian, H. H. Interfield tilt after-effects. *Perceptual and Motor Skills*, 1960, *10*, 95–98. **466**

Moray, N. Attention in dichotic listening: Affective cues and the influence of instruction. *Quarterly Journal of Experimental Psychology*, 1959, *11*, 56–60. **259**

More, L. K., see Tees, R. C., 1967.

Morgan, C. T., Galambos, R., & Garner, W. R. Pitch and intensity. *Journal of the Acoustical Society of America*, 1951, *23*, 658–663. **244**

Morgan, C. T., see also Stevens, S. S., 1941.

Morgan, R. I., & Underwood, B. J. Proactive inhibition as a function of response similarity. *Journal of Experimental Psychology*, 1950, *40*, 592–603. **1056, 1057, 1104**

Morgan, W. L., see Kniep, E. H., 1931.

Morgane, P. J. Limbic-hypothalamic-midbrain interaction in thirst and thirst motivated behavior. In M. J. Wayner (Ed.), *Thirst: First international symposium on thirst in the regulation of body water*. New York: Macmillan, 1964. Pp. 429–453. **647**

Morgulis, S., see Yerkes, R. M., 1909.

Morning, N., & Voss, J. F. Mediation of R_1–R_2 in the acquisition of S–R_1, S–R_2 associations. *Journal of Experimental Psychology*, 1964, *67*, 51–71. **1075**

Morony, L., see Houston, J., 1966.

Morrison, G. R. Behavioural response patterns to salt stimuli in the rat. *Canadian Journal of Psychology*, 1967, *21*, 141–152. **180**

Morrison, G. R., & Norrison W. Taste detection in the rat. *Canadian Journal of Psychology*, 1966, *20*, 208–217. **177**

Morrow, M. W., see Brown, J. S., 1964.

Morse, W. H. Intermittent reinforcement. In W. K. Honig (Ed.), *Operant behavior*. New York: Appleton, 1966. **606, 620**

Morse, W. H., & Skinner, B. F. A second type of superstition in the pigeon. *American Journal of Psychology*, 1957, *70*, 308–311. **675**

Mosberg, L., see Friedman, M., 1967.

Moser, H. M., & Dreher, J. J. Effects of training on listeners in intelligibility studies. *Journal of the Acoustical Society of America*, 1955, *27*, 1213–1219. **255**

Mosteller, F., see Bruner, J., 1950; Bush, R. R., 1951, 1955; Smith, G. M., 1966.

Mote, F. A., see Graham, C. H., 1939; Riggs, L. A., 1947.

Moulton, D. G. Studies in olfactory acuity: III. Relative detectability of *n*-aliphatic acetates by the rat. *Quarterly Journal of Experimental Psychology*, 1960, *12*, 203–213. **203, 204**

Moulton, D. G., Ashton, E. H., & Eayrs, J. T. Studies in olfactory acuity: IV. Relative detectability of *n*-aliphatic acids by the dog. *Animal Behaviour*, 1960, *8*, 117–128. **202**

Moulton, D. G., & Beidler, L. M. Structure and function in the peripheral olfactory system. *Physiological Review*, 1967, *47*, 1–52. **195, 220**

Moulton, D. G., & Eayrs, J. T. Studies in olfactory acuity: II. Relative detectability of *n*-aliphatic alcohols by the rat. *Quarterly Journal of Experimental Psychology*, 1960, *12*, 99–109. **199**

Moulton, D. G., see also Benjamin, R. M., 1965.

Mountcastle, V. B., Talbot, W. H., Darian-Smith, I., & Kornhuber, H. H. Neural basis of the sense of flutter-vibration. *Science*, 1967, *155*, 597–600. **138**

Mountcastle, V. B., see also Poggio, G. F., 1960; Rose, J. E., 1959.

Mowrer, O. H. On the dual nature of learning: A re-interpretation of "conditioning" and "problem-solving." *Harvard Educational Review*, 1947, *17*, 102–148. **563, 726**

Mowrer, O. H. Motivation. *Annual Review of Psychology*, 1952, *3*, 419–438. **794n**

Mowrer, O. H., & Aiken, E. G. Contiguity vs. drive-reduction in conditioned fear: Temporal variations in conditioned and unconditioned stimulus. *American Journal of Psychology*, 1954, *67*, 26–38. **579, 718, 719**

Mowrer, O. H., & Lamoreaux, R. R. Fear as an intervening variable in avoidance conditioning. *Journal of Comparative Psychology*, 1946, *39*, 29–50. **727**

Mowrer, O. H., Ruch, T. C., & Miller, N. E. The corneo-retinal potential difference as the basis of the galvanometric record of recording eye movements. *American Journal of Physiology*, 1936, *114*, 423–428. **372**

Mowrer, O. H., & Solomon, L. N. Contiguity vs. drive-reduction in conditioned fear: The proximity and abruptness of drive-reduction. *American Journal of Psychology*, 1954, *67*, 15–25. **719**

Mowrer, O. H., see also Gibson, J. J., 1938; Whiting, J. W. M., 1943.

Moyer, K. E., & Korn, J. H. Effect of UCS intensity on the acquisition and extinction of an avoidance response. *Journal of Experimental Psychology*, 1964, *67*, 352-359. **728, 729**

Mozell, M. M. Electrophysiology of the olfactory bulb. *Journal of Neurophysiology*, 1958, *21*, 183-196. **200, 203, 204**

Mozell, M. M. The spatiotemporal analysis of odorants at the level of the olfactory receptor sheet. *Journal of General Physiology*, 1966, *50*, 25-41. **200, 218, 219**

Mozell, M. M., & Pfaffmann, C. The afferent neural process in odor perception. *Annals of the New York Academy of Science*, 1954, *58*, 96-108. **218**

Mozell, M. M., *see also* Benjamin, R. M., 1965; O'Connell, R. J., 1969.

Mueller, C. G. Frequency of seeing functions for intensity discrimination at various levels of adapting intensity. *Journal of General Psychology*, 1951, *34*, 463-474. **29**

Mueller, C. G., & Lloyd, V. V. Stereoscopic acuity for various levels of illumination. *Proceedings of the National Academy of Science*, 1948, *34*, 223-227. **486**

Graham, C. H., 1949; Riggs, L. A., 1947.

Mueller, E. E., Loeffel, R., & Mead, S. Skin impedance in relation to pain threshold testing by electrical means. *Journal of Applied Physiology*, 1953, *5*, 746-752. **156**

Mueller-Lyer, F. C. Optische Urteilstaeuschungen. *Archiv für Psychologie*, 1889, *Suppl. Bd.*, 263-270. **461**

Muenzinger, K. F. Motivation in learning: I. Electric shock for correct response in the visual discrimination habit. *Journal of Comparative Psychology*, 1934, *17*, 267-277. **739, 784**

Muenzinger, K. F. Vicarious trial and error at a point of choice: I. A general survey of its relation to learning efficiency. *Journal of General Psychology*, 1938, *53*, 75-86. **784**

Muenzinger, K. F., Bernstone, A. H., & Richards, L. Motivation in learning: VIII. Equivalent amounts of electric shock for right and wrong responses in a visual discrimination habit. *Journal of Comparative Psychology*, 1938, *26*, 177-186. **784**

Muenzinger, K. F., & Fletcher, F. M. Motivation in learning: VII. The effect of an enforced delay at the point of choice in the visual discrimination habit. *Journal of Comparative Psychology*, 1937, *23*, 383-392. **784**

Muenzinger, K. F., & Newcomb, H. Motivation in learning: V. The relative effectiveness of jumping a gap and crossing an electric grid in a visual discrimination habit. *Journal of Comparative Psychology*, 1936, *21*, 95-104. **784**

Muenzinger, K. F., & Wood, A. Motivation in learning: IV. The function of punishment as determined by its temporal relation to the act of choice in the visual discrimination habit. *Journal of Comparative Psychology*, 1935, *20*, 95-106. **784**

Mueser, G. E., *see* White, B. H., 1960.

Mulholland, T. B. Motion perceived while viewing rotating stimulus objects. *American Journal of Psychology*, 1956, *69*, 96-99. **519**

Müller, G. E., & Pilzecker, A. Experimentelle Beiträge zur Lehre vom Gedächtniss. *Zeitschrift für Psychologie, Ergbd.* #1, 1900. **1080**

Müller, J. Beiträge zur vergleichenden Physiologie des Gesichtsinnes. Leipzig: Knobloch, 1826. P. 46. **481**

Müller, J. H., Handbuch der Physiologie des Menschen fur Vorlesungen. Coblenz: Holscher, 1834-1840. Trans. from the German by W. Baly under the title, *Elements of physiology*. Philadelphia: Lea & Blanchard, 1843. Vol. II, Pp. 276-393. **411**

Mundy-Castle, A. C. Pictorial depth perception in Ghanaian children. *International Journal of Psychology*, 1966, *1*, 289-301. **500**

Munn, N. L. Handbook of psychological research on the rat. Boston: Houghton Mifflin, 1950. **612, 662n, 821**

Munsinger, *see* Hershenson, M., 1965.

Murakami, M., *see* Brown, K. T., 1964, 1965; Tomita, T., 1967.

Murdock, B. B., Jr. Effects of failure and retroactive inhibition in mediating an instrumental act. *Journal of Experimental Psychology*, 1952, *44*, 156-164. **781**

Murdock, B. B., Jr. "Backward" learning in paired associates. *Journal of Experimental Psychology*, 1956, *51*, 213-215. **1056, 1064**

Murdock, B. B., Jr. Transfer designs and formulas, *Psychological Bulletin*, 1957, *54*, 313-326. **1022, 1026**

Murdock, B. B., Jr. "Backward" associations in transfer and learning. *Journal of Experimental Psychology*, 1958, *55*, 111-114. **1064**

Murdock, B. B., Jr. The immediate retention of unrelated words. *Journal of Experimental Psychology*, 1960, *60*, 222-234. **1044**

Murdock, B. B., Jr. The retention of individual items. *Journal of Experimental Psychology*, 1961, *62*. 618-625. (a) **1110, 1111**

Murdock, B. B., Jr. Short-term retention of single paired associates. *Psychological Reports*, 1961, *8*, 280. (b) **997, 998, 1111, 1112, 1118**

Murdock, B. B., Jr. Short-term retention of single paired associates. *Journal of Experimental Psychology*, 1963, *65*, 433-443. (a) **1111, 1112, 1114, 1118**

Murdock, B. B., Jr. Short-term memory and paired-associate learning. *Journal of Verbal Learning and Verbal Behavior*, 1963, *2*, 320-328. (b) **1111, 1118**

Murdock, B. B., Jr. Interpolated recall in short-term memory. *Journal of Experimental Psychology*, 1963, *66*, 525-532. (c) **1118**

Murdock, B. B., Jr. Proactive inhibition in short-term memory. *Journal of Experimental Psychology*, 1964, *68*, 184-189. **1111, 1114, 1118**

Murdock, B. B., Jr. Distractor and probe techniques in short-term memory. *Canadian Journal of Psychology*, 1967, *21*, 25-36. (a) **1110, 1112**

Murdock, B. B., Jr. Recent developments in short-term memory. *British Journal of Psychology*, 1967, *58*, 421-433. (b) **1116**

Murphy, G. An experimental study of literary *vs.* scientific types. *American Journal of Psychology*, 1917, *28*, 238-262. **875**

Murphy, G., *see also* Schafer, R., 1943; Solley, C. M., 1960.

Murphy, R., *see* Glanzer, M., in press.

Murray, E. N., *see* Katkin, E. S., 1968.

Musatti, C. L. Sui fenomeni stereocinatici. *Archivio Italiano di Psicologia*, 1924, *3*, 105-120. **523**

Mussatti, C. L. Forma e assimilazione. *Archivio Italiano di Psichologia*, 1931, *9*, 61-156. **437**

Muus, R., *see* Entwisle, D. R., 1964.

Myers, A. E., *see* Hake, H. W., 1969.

Myers, A. K. Onset vs. termination of stimulus energy as the CS in avoidance conditioning and pseudoconditioning. *Journal of Comparative and Physiological Psychology*, 1960, *53*, 72-78. **728**

Myers, A. K., & Miller, N. E. Failure to find a learned drive based on hunger: Evidence for learning motivated by "exploration." *Journal of Comparative and Physiological Psychology*, 1954, *47*, 428-436. **804**

Myers, A. K., *see also* Coons, E. E., 1960.

Myers, J. L., & Atkinson, R. C. Choice behavior and reward structure. *Journal of Mathematical Psychology*, 1964, *1*, 170-203. **933**

Myers, J. L., Fort, J. G., Katz, L., & Suydam, M. M. Differential monetary gains and losses and event probabilities in a two-choice situation. *Journal of Experimental Psychology*, 1963, *66*, 521-522. **918**

Myers, J. L., Suydam, M. N., & Heuckeroth, O. Choice

behavior and reward structure: Differential payoff. *Journal of Mathematical Psychology*, 1966, *3*, 458–469. **933**

Myers, J. L., *see also* Gambino, B., 1966; Jones, M. R., 1966.

Myers, L., *see* Collier, G., 1961.

Myers, N. A., *see* Leibowitz, H., 1955.

Nachman, M. Learned aversion to the taste of lithium chloride and generalization to other salts. *Journal of Comparative and Physiological Psychology*, 1963, *56*, 343–349. **180**

Nachman, M., & Pfaffmann, C. Gustatory nerve discharge in normal and sodium-deficient rats. *Journal of Comparative and Physiological Psychology*, 1963, *56*, 1007–1011. **189**

Nachmias, J. Two-dimensional motion of the retinal image during monocular fixation. *Journal of the Optical Society of America*, 1959, *49*, 901–908. **374, 386, 387**

Nachmias, J. Effect of exposure duration on visual contrast sensitivity with square-wave gratings. *Journal of the Optical Society of America*, 1967, *57*, 421–427. **304**

Nachmias, J., *see also* Gleitman, H., 1964; Heinemann, E. G., 1959.

Nafe, J. P. Dermal sensitivity with special reference to the qualities of tickle and itch. *Journal of Genetic Psychology*, 1927, *34*, 14–27. **134**

Nafe, J. P. Pressure, pain, and temperature senses. In C. A. Murchison (Ed.), *A handbook of general experimental psychology*. Worcester, Mass.: Clark University Press, 1934. Pp. 1037–1087. **154**

Nafe, J. P., & Kenshalo, D. R. Stimulation and neural response. *American Journal of Psychology*, 1958, *71*, 199–208. **132**

Nafe, J. P., & Wagoner, K. S. The nature of sensory adaptation. *Journal of General Psychology*, 1941, *25*, 295–321. (a) **130, 131**

Nafe, J. P., & Wagoner, K. S. The nature of pressure adaptation. *Journal of General Psychology*, 1941, *25*, 323–351. (b) **130, 131**

Nafe, J. P., *see also* Kenshalo, D. R., 1962.

Nagel, E. *The structure of science*. New York: Harcourt, Brace, 1961. **906**

Nagge, J. W. An experimental test of the theory of associative interference. *Journal of Experimental Psychology*, 1935, *18*, 663–682. **1084**

Nahinsky, I. D. A duoprocess model for paired-associate learning. *Psychological Reports*, 1964, *14*, 467–471. **994**

Nahinsky, I. D. Statistics and moments-parameter estimates for a duoprocess paired-associate model. *Journal of Mathematical Psychology*, 1967, *4*, 140–150. **994**

Nakajima, S. Effects of chemical injection into the reticular formation of rats. *Journal of Comparative and Physiological Psychology*, 1964, *58*, 10–15. **843**

Nastuk, W. L. (Ed.) *Physical techniques in biological research*. Vol. V, *Electrophysiological methods*, Part A. New York, Academic Press, 1964. **92, 93**

Natsoulas, T. Converging operations for perceptual defense. *Psychological Bulletin*, 1965, *64*, 393–401. **444**

Natsoulas, T., What are perceptual reports about? *Psychological Bulletin*, 1967, *67*, 4, 249–272. **506**

Naunton, R. F., *see* Butler, R. A., 1964.

Naylor, A., *see* Washburn, M. F., 1931.

Neal, E. Visual localization of the vertical. *American Journal of Psychology*, 1926, *37*, 287–291. **539**

Nealey, S. M., & Edwards, B. J. "Depth perception" in rats without pattern vision experience. *Journal of Comparative and Physiological Psychology*, 1960, *53*, 468–469. **549**

Nealey, S. M., & Riley, D. A. Loss and recovery of discrimination of visual depth in dark-reared rats. *American Journal of Psychology*, 1963, *76*, 329–332. **549**

Neff, W. D. Sensory discrimination. In John Field, H. W. Magoun, & V. E. Hall (Eds.) *Handbook of physiology*. Vol III, Sec. I. *Neurophysiology*. Washington, D. C.: American Physiological Society, 1960. Pp. 1447–1470. **118**

Neff, W. D. Neural mechanisms in auditory discrimination. In W. A. Rosenblith (Ed.), *Sensory communication*. New York: Wiley, 1961. **264**

Neff, W. S. A critical investigation of the visual apprehension of movement. *American Journal of Psychology*, 1936, *48*, 1–42. **526**

Neilson, D. R., Jr., *see* Spencer, W. A., 1966.

Neilsen, T. I. Volition: A new experimental approach. *Scandinavian Journal of Psychology*, 1963, *4*, 225–230. **536**

Neimark, E. D. Effects of type of non-reinforcement and number of alternative responses in two verbal conditioning situations. *Journal of Experimental Psychology*, 1956, *52*, 209–220. **933**

Neimark, E., Greenhouse, P., Law, S., & Weinheimer, S. The effect of rehearsal-preventing task upon retention of CVC syllables. *Journal of Verbal Learning and Verbal Behavior*, 1965, *4*, 280–285. **1119**

Neisser, U. An experimental distinction between perceptual process and verbal response. *Journal of Experimental Psychology*, 1954, *47*, 399–402. **445n**

Neisser, U. *Cognitive psychology*. New York: Appleton, 1967. **255, 444, 456**

Neisser, U., & Weene, B. Hierarchies in concept attainment. *Journal of Experimental Psychology*, 1962, *64*, 640–645. **941, 965, 967**

Neisser, U., *see also* Gleitman, H., 1954; Wallach, H., 1953.

Nelson, L. M., *see* Halpern, B. P., 1965.

Nelson, P. G., Erulkar, S. D., & Bryan, J. S. Responses of units of the inferior colliculus to time-varying acoustic stimuli. *Journal of Neurophysiology*, 1966, *24*, 834–860. **232**

Nelson, T. M., & Bartley, S. H. The perception of form in an unstructured field. *Journal of General Psychology*, 1956, *54*, 57–63. **515**

Neuhaus, W. Experimentelle Untersuchung der Scheinbewegung. *Archiv für gesamte Psychologie*, 1930, *75*, 315–458. **526**

Neun, M. E., *see* Boynton, R. M., 1964.

Neuringer, A. J. Many responses per food reward with free food present. *Science*, 1970, *169*, 503–504. **692n**

Newell, A., Shaw, J. G., & Simon, H. A. Elements of a theory of human problem solving. *Psychological Review*, 1958, *65*, 151–166. **976**

Newell, A., & Simon, H. A. The simulation of human thought. In *Current trends in psychological theory*. Pittsburgh: University of Pittsburgh, 1961. Pp. 152–179. **976**

Newell, A., & Simon, H. A. GPS, a program that simulates human thought. In E. A. Feigenbaum & J. Feldman (Eds.), *Computers and thought*. New York: McGraw-Hill, 1963. Pp. 279–293. **976**

Newhall, S. M. The reversal of simultaneous brightness contrast. *Journal of Experimental Psychology*, 1942, *31*, 393–409. **408**

Newhall, S. M., Burnham, R. W., & Clark, J. R. Comparison of successive with simultaneous color matching. *Journal of the Optical Society of America*, 1957, *47*, 43–56. **424**

Newhall, S. M., Nickerson, D., & Judd, D. B. Final report of the O.S.A. subcommittee on spacing of the Munsell colors. *Journal of the Optical Society of America*, 1943, *33*, 385. **360**

Newman, E. B., *see* Stevens, S. S., 1936; Wallach, H., 1949.

Newman, F. L., & Baron, M. R. Stimulus generalization along the dimension of angularity: A comparison of training procedures. *Journal of Comparative and Physiological Psychology*, 1965, *60*, 59–63. **762**

Newton, J. M., & Wickens, D. D. Retroactive inhibition as a function of the temporal position of interpolated learning. *Journal of Experimental Psychology*, 1956, *51*, 149–154. **1037, 1091, 1100**

Nicholls, M. F., & Kimble, G. A. Effect of instructions upon eyelid conditioning. *Journal of Experimental Psychology*, 1964, *67*, 400–402. **561**

Nickerson, D., *see* Newhall, S. M., 1943.

Nicks, D. C. Prediction of sequential two-choice decisions from event runs. *Journal of Experimental Psychology,* 1959, *57,* 105-114. **920, 921**

Nicolaides, S. Early systemic responses to orogastric stimulation in the regulation of food and water balance: Functional and electrophysiological data. *Annals of the New York Academy of Sciences,* 1969, *157,* 1176-1203. **797**

Niehl, E. W., *see* Riggs, L. A., 1960.

Nilsson, W. D., *see* Mayzner, M. S., 1965.

Nissen, H. W., *see* Chow, K. L., 1955.

Niven, J. I., & Brown, R. H. Visual resolution as a function of intensity and exposure time in the human fovea. *Journal of the Optical Society of America,* 1944, *34,* 738-743. **303**

Nixon, J. C., & Glorig, A. Noise-induced permanent threshold shift at 2000 cps and 4000 cps. *Journal of the Acoustical Society of America,* 1961, *33,* 904-908. **236**

Noble, C. E. An analysis of meaning. *Psychological Review,* 1952, *59,* 421-430. (a) **850, 851, 852, 856, 982, 1127**

Noble, C. E. The role of stimulus meaning (*m*) in serial verbal learning. *Journal of Experimental Psychology,* 1952, *43,* 437-446. (b) **854, 899**

Noble, C. E. The meaning-familiarity relationship. *Psychological Review,* 1953, *60,* 89-98. **982**

Noble, C. E. Emotionality (*e*) and meaningfulness. *Psychological Reports,* 1958, *4,* 16. (a) **900**

Noble, C. E. Tables of the *e* and *m* scales. *Psychological Reports,* 1958, *4,* 590. (b) **900**

Noble, C. E. Measurements of association value (a), rated associations (a'), and scaled meaningfulness (*m*') for the 2100 CVC combinations of the English alphabet. *Psychological Reports,* 1961, *8,* 487-521. **853**

Noble, C. E. Meaningfulness and familiarity. In C. N. Cofer & B. S. Musgrave (Eds.), *Verbal behavior and learning: Problems and processes,* New York: McGraw-Hill, 1963. Pp. 76-119. **853, 856, 897, 899**

Noble, C. E., & Parker, G. V. C. The Montana scale of meaningfulness. *Psychological Reports,* 1960, *7,* 325-331. **852, 853**

Noble, C. E., Stockwell, F. E., & Pryer, M. W. Meaningfulness (*m*') and association value in paired-associate syllable learning. *Psychological Reports,* 1957, *3,* 441-452. **852, 853, 857, 982**

Noble, C. E., *see also* Cieutat, V. J., 1958.

Nodine, C. F., *see* Goss, A. E., 1965.

Norcross, K. J. Effects on discrimination performance of similarity of previously acquired stimulus names. *Journal of Experimental Psychology,* 1958, *56,* 305-309. **783**

Norcross, K. J., & Spiker, C. C. The effects of type of stimulus pretraining on discrimination performance in preschool children. *Child Development,* 1957, *28,* 79-84. **782**

Norcross, K. J., & Spiker, C. C. Effects of mediated associations on transfer in paired-associate learning. *Journal of Experimental Psychology,* 1958, *55,* 129-134. **1077**

Nord, S., *see* Makous, W., 1963.

Nordlie, P. G., *see* Havron, M. D., 1957.

Norman, D., *see* Waugh, N. C., 1965.

Norman, D. A., *see* Wickelgren, W. A., 1966.

Norman, M. F. Incremental learning on random trials. *Journal of Mathematical Psychology,* 1964, *1,* 336-350. **997**

Norris, E. B., & Grant, D. A. Eyelid conditioning as affected by verbally induced inhibitory set and counter reinforcement. *American Journal of Psychology,* 1948, *61,* 37-49. **561**

Norris, E. B., *see also* Grant, S. A., 1947.

Norrison, W., *see* Morrison, G. R., 1966.

Notterman, J. M., & Mintz, D. E. Exteroceptive cueing of response force. *Science,* 1962, *135,* 1070-1071. **700**

Notterman, J. M., & Mintz, D. E. *Dynamics of behavior.* New York: Wiley, 1965. **700**

Novell, K., *see* Collier, G., 1967.

Nozawa, S. Zukel no Iizokushi to sono zonko. 1. Gibson koka no Iikkrnyekl Kenkyer (Prolonged inspection of a figure and its after-effects. 1. Experimental study of the Gibson effect.) *Japanese Journal of Psychology,* 1953, *24,* 47-58. **470**

Nulsen, F. E., *see* Collins, W. F., 1960.

Nunnally, J. C., & Flaugher, R. L. Psychological implications of word usage. *Science,* 1963, *140,* 775-781. **875**

Nye, P. W., *see* Fender, D. H., 1961

Oakley, B. Altered temperature and taste responses from cross-regenerated sensory nerves in the rat's tongue. *Journal of Physiology,* 1967, *188,* 353-371. **173**

Oakley, B., & Benjamin, R. M. Neural mechanisms of taste. *Physiological Reviews,* 1966, *46,* 173-211. **180**

Oakley, B., *see also* Borg, G., 1967; Makous, W., 1963.

Obonai, T. Induction effects in estimates of extent. *Journal of Experimental Psychology,* 1954, *47,* 57-60. **508n**

Obonai, T., *see also* Ikeda, H., 1953.

Ochs, S. *Elements of neurophysiology.* New York: Wiley, 1965. **95**

O'Connell, D. N., *see* Wallach, H., 1953.

O'Connell R. Quantitative stimulation of single olfactory receptors. Doctoral dissertation, Department of Physiology, Upstate Medical Center, State University of New York, 1967. **200**

O'Connell, R. J., & Mozell, M. M. Quantitative stimulation of frog olfactory receptors. *Journal of Neurophysiology,* 1969, *32,* 51-63. **200, 217, 218**

O'Connor, J. *Born that way.* Baltimore: Williams & Wilkins, 1928. **874n**

Odom, P., *see* Jenkins, J. J., 1965.

Ogawa, H., *see* Yamashita, S., 1967.

Ogle, K. N. *Researches in binocular vision.* Philadelphia: Saunders, 1950. **480, 481, 539n**

Ogle, K. N. Precision and validity of stereoscopic depth perception from double images. *Journal of the Optical Society of America,* 1953, *43,* 906-913. **491, 493**

Ogle, K., & Reiher, L. Stereoscopic depth perception from after-images. *Vision Research,* 1962, *2,* 439-447. **491n**

Öhrwall, H. Untersuchungen über den Geschmackssinn. *Skandinavisches Archiv für Physiologie,* 1891, *2,* 1-69. **175, 178**

O'Kelly, L. I. The psychophysiology of motivation. *Annual Review of Psychology,* 1963, *14,* 57-92. **794n**

Oldfield, R. C. Continuous recording of sensory thresholds and other psychophysical variables. *Nature,* 1949, *164,* 581. **20**

Olds, J. Physiological mechanisms in reward. In M. R. Jones (Ed.), *Nebraska symposium on motivation.* Lincoln: University of Nebraska Press, 1955. **642, 653**

Olds, J. Pleasure centers in the brain. *Scientific American,* 1956, *193,* 105-116. **642**

Olds, J. Self-stimulation of the brain. *Science,* 1958, *127,* 315-324. (a) **651**

Olds, J. Effects of hunger and male sex hormone on self-stimulation of the brain. *Journal of Comparative and Physiological Psychology,* 1958, *51,* 320-324. (b) **654**

Olds, J. Satiation effects in self-stimulation of the brain. *Journal of Comparative and Physiological Psychology,* 1958, *51,* 675-678. (c) **655**

Olds, J., & Milner, P. M. Positive reinforcement produced by electrical stimulation of septal area and other regions of rat brain. *Journal of Comparative and Physiological Psychology,* 1954, *47,* 419-427. **642**

Olds, J., & Peretz, B. A motivational analysis of the reticular activating system. *Electroencephalography and Clinical Neurophysiology,* 1960, *12,* 445-454. **844**

Olds, J., & Sinclair, J. C. Self-stimulation in the obstruction box. *American Psychologist,* 1957, *12,* 464. **651**

Olds, J., *see also* Margules, D. L., 1962; Olds, M. E., 1963; 1965; Seward, J. P., 1959.

Olds, M. E., & Olds, J. Approach-avoidance analysis of rat

diencephalon. *Journal of Comparative Neurology*, 1963, *120*, 259-295. **647**

Olds, M., & Olds, J. Drives, rewards and the brain. In T. M. Newcomb (Ed.), *New directions in psychology II.* New York: Holt, Rinehart and Winston, 1965. **646, 657, 658**

O'Leary, J., see Heinbecker, P., 1933.

Olivier, K., & Kausler, D. H. Transfer in the *A–B, C–B* paradigm as a function of stimulus class. *Psychonomic Science*, 1966, *5*, 47-48. **1064**

Olsen, W. O., & Carhart, K. Integration of acoustic power at threshold by normal hearers. *Journal of the Acoustical Society of America*, 1966, *40*, 591-599. **234**

Olson, R. K., see Attneave, F., 1966.

Olum, V., see Gibson, E. J., 1960; Gibson, J. J., 1955.

O'Neill, J. J. Recognition of intelligibility text materials in context and isolation. *Journal of Speech and Hearing Disabilities* 1957, *22*, 87-90. **256**

Onizawa, T. Research on the size of the projected afterimage: I. On the method of measurement. *Tohuku Psychologica Folia*, 1954, *14*, 75-78. **511**

Ono, H. Apparent distance as a function of familiar size, *Journal of Experimental Psychology*, 1969, *79*, 109-115. **496, 497**

Ono, H., see also Festinger, L., 1967.

Oppel, T. W., see Hardy, J. D., 1937, 1938.

Orbach, J. Retinal locus as a factor in recognition of visually perceived words. *American Journal of Psychology*, 1953, *65*, 555-562. **444**

Orbach, J., Ehrlich, D., & Heath, H. A. Reversibility of the Necker cube: I. An examination of the concept of "satiation of orientation." *Perceptual and Motor Skills*, 1963, *17*, 439-458. **471**

Orbach, J., Ehrlich, D., & Vainstein, E. Reversibility of the Necker Cube: III. Effects of interpolation on reversal rate of the cube presented repetitively. *Perceptual and Motor Skills*, 1963, *17*, 459-464. **471**

Orbison, W. D. Shape as a function of the vector field. *American Journal of Psychology*, 1939, *52*, 31-45. **459**

Orlansky, J. The effect of similarity and difference in form on apparent visual movement. *Archives of Psychology* (New York), 1940, No. *246.* **527**

Osgood, C. E. Meaningful similarity and interference in learning. *Journal of Experimental Psychology*, 1946, *36*, 277-301. **1052, 1053, 1054, 1057, 1083**

Osgood, C. E. An investigation into the causes of retroactive inhibition. *Journal of Experimental Psychology*, 1948, *38*, 132-154. **1052, 1053, 1054, 1083**

Osgood, C. E. The similarity paradox in human learning: A resolution. *Psychological Review*, 1949, *56*, 132-143. **1052, 1053, 1054**

Osgood, C. E. *Method and theory in experimental psychology.* New York: Oxford, 1953. **408, 419, 773, 877, 895, 1052**

Osgood, C. E., & Anderson, L. Certain relations among experienced contingencies, associative structure, and contingencies in coded messages. *American Journal of Psychology*, 1957, *70*, 411-420. **862**

Osgood, C. E., & Heyer, A. W. A new interpretation of the figural after-effect. *Psychological Review*, 1952, *59*, 98-118. **470n, 472**

Osgood, C. E., see also Howes, D., 1954.

O'Shaunessy, K., see Goulet, L. R., 1967.

Osman, E., & Raab, D. Temporal masking of clicks by noise bursts. *Journal of the Acoustical Society of America*, 1963, *35*, 1939-1941. **241**

Ostojčić, A., see Bujas, Z., 1941.

Ottoson, D. Analysis of the electrical activity of the olfactory epithelium. *Acta Physiologica Scandinavia*, 1956, *35* (suppl. 122), 1-83. **211, 221**

Ottoson, D. Some aspects of the function of the olfactory system. *Pharmacological Review*, 1963, *15*, 1-42. **220**

Ough, C. S., & Stone, H. An olfactometer for rapid and critical odor measurement. *Journal of Food Science*, 1961, *26*, 452-456. **200**

Ough, C. S., see also Stone, H., 1962.

Over, R. An experimentally induced conflict between vision and proprioception. *British Journal of Psychology*, 1966, *57*, 335-341. **536**

Overmier, J. B., & Seligman, M. E. P. Effects of inescapable shock upon subsequent escape and avoidance responding. *Journal of Comparative and Physiological Psychology*, 1967, *63*, 28-33. **708, 724**

Overmier, J. B., see also Church, R. M., 1966.

Owen, D. H., see Brown, D. R., 1967.

Owens, J. A., & Brown, D. L. ICS reinforcement of DRL behavior in the rat. *Psychonomic Science*, 1968, *10*, 309-310. **654**

Oyama, T. Figure-ground dominance as a function of sector angle, brightness, hue, and orientation. *Journal of Experimental Psychology*, 1960, *60*, 299-305. **433**

Oyama, T., & Torii, S. Experimental studies of figure-ground reversal: I. The effects of area, voluntary control and prolonged observation in the continuous presentation. *Japanese Journal of Psychology*, 1955, *26* (Japanese text, 178-188; English summary, 217-218). **433**

Oyama, T., see also Sagara, M., 1957.

Ozier, M., see Tulving, E., 1965.

Paczewitz, G., see Bartley, S. H., 1957.

Page, H. A., see Wyckoff, L. B., 1954.

Paivio, A. Abstractness, imagery, and meaningfulness in paired-associate learning. *Journal of Verbal Learning and Verbal Behavior*, 1965, *4*, 32-38. **858**

Palermo, D. S. Proactive interference and facilitation as a function of amount of training and stress. *Journal of Experimental Psychology*, 1957, *53*, 293-296. **790**

Palermo, D. S. Backward associations in the paired-associate learning of fourth and sixth grade children. *Psychological Reports*. 1961, *9*, 227-233. **1064**

Palermo, D. S. Word associations and children's verbal behavior. In L. P. Lipsitt & C. C. Spiker (Eds.), *Advances in child development and behavior.* Vol. 1. New York: Academic Press, 1963. **873, 874**

Palermo, D. S. Mediated association in the paired-associate learning of children using heterogeneous and homogeneous lists. *Journal of Experimental Psychology*, 1966, *71*, 711-717. **1074, 1077**

Palermo, D. S., & Jenkins, J. J. Word association norms: Grade school through college. Minneapolis: University of Minnesota Press, 1964. (a) **861, 879, 888**

Palermo, D. S., & Jenkins, J. J. Paired-associate learning as a function of the strength of links in the associative chain. *Journal of Verbal Learning and Verbal Behavior*, 1964, *3*, 406-412. (b) **888**

Palermo, D. S., & Jenkins, J. J. Sex differences in word associations. *Journal of General Psychology*, 1965, *72*, 77-84. (a) **873**

Palermo, D. S., & Jenkins, J. J. Changes in the word associations of fourth- and fifth-grade children from 1916 to 1961. *Journal of Verbal Learning and Verbal Behavior*, 1965, *4*, 180-187. (b) **875**

Palermo, D. S., see also Castaneda, A., 1955, 1956; Jenkins, J. J., 1965.

Palfai, T., see Bindra, D., 1967.

Pallie, W., see Weddell, G., 1954, 1955.

Palmer, E., see Weddell, G., 1955.

Pangborn, R. M., see Amerine, M., 1965; Berg, H. W., 1963; Stone, H., 1962.

Panksepp, J., see Gandelman, R., 1968.

Panum, P. L. *Physiologische Untersuchungen über das Sehen mit zwei Augen.* Kiel: Schwers, 1858. **487, 488**

Pappert, S., Centrally produced geometrical illusion. *Nature*, 1961, *191*, 733. **471n**

Peterson, M. J., Colavita, F., Sheahan, D., & Blattner, K. C. Verbal mediating chains and response availability as a function of the acquisition paradigm. *Journal of Verbal Learning and Verbal Behavior*, 1964, *3*, 11–18. **1073, 1074**

Peterson, M. J., & Jamison, S. M. Effects of distribution of practice of the acquisition pairs upon mediating responses and response availability. *Journal of Experimental Psychology*, 1965, *70*, 549–558. **1073**

Peterson, M. J., *see also* Peterson, L. R., 1959, 1962.

Peterson, N. Control of behavior by presentation of an imprinted stimulus. *Science*, 1960, *132*, 1395–1396. **581, 587**

Peterson, N. Effect of monochromatic rearing on control of responding by wavelength. *Science*, 1962, *136*, 774–776. **762**

Peterson, O. F., *see* La Berge, D. L., 1962.

Peterson, W. M., *see* Kaufman, M. E., 1958.

Petraitis, J., *see* Wayner, M. J., 1967.

Pettigrew, T. F., *see* Allport, G. W., 1957.

Peyser, C. S., *see* Barrett, R. J., 1965.

Pfaffmann, C. Gustatory afferent impulses. *Journal of Cellular and Comparative Physiology*, 1941, *17*, 243–258. **180**

Pfaffmann, C. Taste and smell. In S. S. Stevens (Ed.), *Handbook of experimental psychology*. New York: Wiley, 1951. Pp. 1143–1171. **212, 628**

Pfaffmann, C. Gustatory nerve impulses in rat, cat and rabbit. *Journal of Neurophysiology*, 1955, *18*, 429–440. **173, 179, 180**

Pfaffmann, C. The sense of taste. In J. Field, H. W. Magoun, & V. E. Hall (Eds.), *Handbook of physiology*. Vol. I. Washington, D. C.: American Physiological Society, 1959. Pp. 507–533. **174, 179**

Pfaffmann, C. The pleasures of sensation. *Psychological Review*, 1960, *67*, 253–268. **171, 176**

Pfaffmann, C. Taste, its sensory and motivating properties. *American Scientist*, 1964, *52*, 187–206. **189**

Pfaffmann, C., & Bare, J. K. Gustatory nerve discharges in normal and adrenalectomized rats. *Journal of Comparative and Physiological Psychology*, 1950, *43*, 320–324. **189**

Pfaffmann, C., Bartoshuk, L. M., & McBurney, D. H. Taste psychophysics. In L. M. Beidler (Ed.), *Handbook of taste physiology*. New York: Springer-Verlag, 1969. **183**

Pfaffmann, C., Erickson, R. P., Frommer, G. P., & Halpern, B. F. Gustatory discharges in the rat medulla and thalamus. In W. A. Rosenblith (Ed.), *Sensory communication*. New York: Wiley, 1961. Pp. 455–473. **172, 182**

Pfaffmann, C., Fisher, G. L., & Frank, M. K. The sensory and behavioral factors in taste preferences. In T. Hayashi (Ed.), *Olfaction and taste*. Vol. 2. New York: Pergamon, 1967. Pp. 361–381. **176**

Pfaffmann, C., & Hagstrom, E. C. Factors influencing taste sensitivity to sugar. *American Journal of Physiology*, 1955, 183. (Abstract) **189**

Pfaffmann, C., & Powers, J. B. Partial adaptation of taste. *Psychonomic Science*, 1964, *1*, 41–42. **174**

Pfaffmann, C., Young, P. T., Dethier, V. G., Richter, C. P., & Stellar, E. The preparation of solutions for research in chemoreception and food acceptance. *Journal of Comparative and Physiological Psychology*, 1954, *49*, 93–96. **625n**

Pfaffmann, C., *see also* Bartoshuk, L. M., 1964, 1965; Engen, T., 1959; Fisher, G. L., 1965; Makous, W., 1963; McBurney, D. H., 1963; Mozell, M. M., 1954; Nachman, M., 1963; Warren, R. M., 1959; Warren, R. P., 1958.

Pheiffer, C. H. Book retinoscopy. *American Journal of Optometry*, 1955, *32*, 540–545. **393**

Phillips, L. W., *see* Postman, L., 1955, 1961.

Piaget, J. *Judgment and reasoning in the child*. New York: Harcourt, 1926. **540**

Piaget, J., & Lambercier, M. Recherches sur le developpe-ment des perceptions: III. Le problème de la comparaison visuelle en profondeur (constance de la grandeur) et l'erreur systématique de l'étalon. *Archives de Psychologie* (Genève), 1943, *29*, 253–308. **550**

Pick, H. L., Jr., & Hay, J. C. Adaptation to prismatic distortion. *Psychonomic Science*, 1964, *1*, 199–200. **542**

Pick, H. L., Jr., & Hay, J. C. A passive test of the Held re-afference hypothesis. *Perceptual and Motor Skills*, 1965, *20*, 1070–1072. **536**

Pick, H. L., *see also* Gibson, E. J., 1958; Hay, J. C., 1965, 1966.

Pickersgill, M. On knowing with which eye one is seeing. *Quarterly Journal of Experimental Psychology*, 1961, *13*, 168–172. **489**

Pickleman, J. R., *see* Campbell, B. A., 1961.

Pieper, W. A., *see* Marx, M. H., 1963.

Pierce, A. H. *Studies in auditory and visual space perception*. New York: Longmans, Green, 1901. **259**

Pierce, J. Determinants of threshold for form. *Psychological Bulletin*, 1963, *60*, 391–407. **444, 445**

Pierce, J. R., *see* Bergeijk, W. A. van, 1960.

Pieron, H. Nervous pathways of cutaneous pains. *Science*, 1959, *129*, 1547–1548. **161**

Pierrel, R. Taste effects resulting from intermittent electrical stimulation of the tongue. *Journal of Experimental Psychology*, 1955, *49*, 374–380. **178**

Piggins, D. J., *see* Evans, C. R., 1963.

Pilzecker, A., *see* Müller, G. E., 1900.

Pirenne, M. H. *Vision and the eye*. London: Chapman and Hall, 1948. **296, 319**

Pirenne, M. H., *see also* Hecht, S., 1942.

Pitblado, C., *see* Kaufman, L., 1965.

Pitts, W. H., *see* Gesteland, R. C., 1965; Lettvin, J. Y., 1959.

Plateau, J. Ueber das Phänomen der zufälligen Farben. *Poggendorff's Annalen der Physiologie und Chemie*, 1834, *32*, 543–554. **411**

Platt, J. R. Strong inference. *Science*, 1964, *146*, 347. **917**

Platt, S. A., *see* Weisman, R. G., 1966.

Pliskoff, S. S., & Hawkins, T. D. A method for increasing the reinforcement magnitude of intracranial stimulation. *Journal of the Experimental Analysis of Behavior*, 1967, *10*, 281–289. **650, 654**

Pliskoff, S. S., Hawkins, T. D. & Wright, J. E. Some observations on the discriminative stimulus hypothesis and rewarding electrical stimulation of the brain. *Psychological Record*, 1964, *14*, 179–184. **675**

Plomp, R. The ear as a frequency analyzer. *Journal of the Acoustical Society of America*, 1964, *36*, 1628–1636. **250**

Plomp, R. Detectability threshold for combination tones. *Journal of the Acoustical Society of America*, 1965, *37*, 1110–1123. **238**

Pochin, E. E., *see* Lewis, T., 1937.

Podd, M., *see* Spear, N. E., 1966.

Podell, H. A. A quantitative study of convergent association. *Journal of Verbal Learning and Verbal Behavior*, 1963, *2*, 234–241. **872**

Poffenberger, A. T. The influence of improvement in one simple mental process upon other related processes. *Journal of Educational Psychology*, 1915, *6*, 459–474. **1045**

Poffenberger, A. T., *see also* Hollingsworth, H. L., 1917.

Poggio, G. F., & Mountcastle, V. B. A study of the functional contributions of the lemniscal and spinothalamic systems to somatic sensibility: Central nervous mechanisms in pain. *Johns Hopkins Hospital Bulletin*, 1960, *106*, 266–316. **163**

Poizner, S., *see* Flock, H. R., 1966.

Pollack, I. Specification of sound pressure levels. *American Journal of Psychology*, 1949, *62*, 412–417. **226**

Pollack, I. Message uncertainty and message reception. *Journal of the Acoustical Society of America*, 1959, *31*, 1500–1508. **256**

Pollack, I. Ohm's acoustical law and short-term auditory

memory. *Journal of the Acoustical Society of America*, 1964, *36*, 2340-2345. **250**

Pollack, I., & Ficks, L. Information of elementary multidimensional auditory displays. *Journal of the Acoustical Society of America*, 1954, *26*, 155-158. **250**

Pollack, I., Rubenstein, H., & Decker, L. Intelligibility of known and unknown message sets. *Journal of the Acoustical Society of America*, 1959, *31*, 273-279. **255, 256**

Pollack, I., *see also* Sumby, W. H., 1954.

Pollack, M., *see* Battersby, W. S., 1956.

Pollack, R. H. Figural after-effects: Quantitative studies of displacement. *Australian Journal of Psychology*, 1958, *10*, 269-277. **470**

Pollack, R. H. Changes in the effects of fixation upon apparent distance in the third dimension. *Psychonomic Science*, 1967, *8*, 141-142. **474**

Pollack, R. H., & Chaplin, M. R. Perceptual behavior: The necessity for a developmental approach to its study. *Acta Psychologica*, 1963, *21*, 371-376. **550**

Pollack, R. H., & Silvar, S. D. Magnitude of the Müller-Lyer illusion in children as a function of pigmentation of the fundus oculi. *Psychonomic Science*, 1967, *8*, 83-84. **461**

Pollack, R. H., *see also* Day, R. H., 1959; Silvar, S. D., 1967.

Pollio, H. R. A simple matrix analysis of associative structure. *Journal of Verbal Learning and Verbal Behavior*, 1963, *2*, 166-169. (a) **879**

Pollio, H. R. Word association as a function of conditioned meaning. *Journal of Experimental Psychology*, 1963, *66*, 454-460. (b) **865**

Pollio, H. R. Composition of associative structures. *Journal of Experimental Psychology*, 1964, *67*, 199-208. (a) **879**

Pollio, H. R. Some semantic relations among word-associates. *American Journal of Psychology*, 1964, *77*, 249-256. (b) **864**

Pollio, H. R. Oppositional serial structures and paired-associate learning. *Psychological Reports*, 1966, *19*, 643-647. **889**

Pollio, H. R., & Draper, D. O. The effect of a serial structure on paired-associate learning. *Journal of Verbal Learning and Verbal Behavior*, 1966, *5*, 301-308. **889**

Pollio, H. R., & Lore, R. K. The effect of a semantically congruent context on word-association behavior. *Journal of Psychology*, 1965, *61*, 17-26. **865**

Pollio, H. R., *see also* Kasschau, R. A., 1967.

Polson, M., Restle, F., & Polson, P. Association and discrimination in paired-associate learning. *Journal of Experimental Psychology*, 1965, *69*, 47-55. **1006**

Polson, P., *see* Polson, M., 1965.

Polyak, S. L. *The retina*. Chicago: University of Chicago Press, 1941. **303**

Polyak, S. In H. L. Klüver (Ed.), *The vertebrate visual system*. Chicago: University of Chicago Press, 1957. **280, 281, 282**

Popper, J. Mediated generalization. In R. R. Bush & W. K. Estes (Eds.), *Studies in mathematical learning theory*. Stanford: Stanford University Press, 1959. Pp. 94-108. **949**

Popper, J., & Atkinson, R. C. Discrimination learning in a verbal conditioning situation. *Journal of Experimental Psychology*, 1958, *56*, 21-25. **926**

Pores, E. B., *see* Warren, R. M., 1958.

Porter, E. K. H. Factors in the fluctuations of fifteen ambiguous phenomena. *Psychological Record*, 1938, *2*, 231-253. **519**

Porter, J. M., Jr., *see* Marquis, D. G., 1939.

Porter, L. W., & Duncan, C. P. Negative transfer in verbal learning. *Journal of Experimental Psychology*, 1953, *46*, 61-64. **1055, 1064**

Porter, P. B., *see* Gibson, W. E., 1965.

Posner, M. I., & Konick, A. On the role of interference in short-term retention. *Journal of Experimental Psychology*. 1966, *72*, 221-231. **119**

Posner, M. I., & Rossman, E. Effect of size and location of

informational transforms upon short-term retention. *Journal of Experimental Psychology*, 1965, *70*, 496-505. **1119**

Postman, L. The generalization gradient in recognition memory. *Journal of Experimental Psychology*, 1951, *42*, 231-235. **1048**

Postman, L. The present status of interference theory. In C. N. Cofer (Ed.), *Verbal learning and verbal behavior*. New York: McGraw-Hill, 1961. (a) **1089**

Postman, L. Extra-experimental interference and the retention of words. *Journal of Experimental Psychology*, 1961, *61*, 97-110. (b) **854, 857, 886, 896, 1128**

Postman, L. Repetition and paired-associate learning. *American Journal of Psychology*, 1962, *75*, 372-389. **987**

Postman, L. Transfer of training as a function of experimental paradigm and degree of first-list learning. *Journal of Verbal Learning and Verbal Behavior*, 1962, *1*, 109-118. (a) **1036, 1059, 1062, 1063, 1064, 1068**

Postman, L. Retention of first-list associations as a function of the conditions of transfer. *Journal of Experimental Psychology*, 1962, *64*, 380-387. (b) **1062, 1093**

Postman, L. The temporal course of proactive inhibition for serial lists. *Journal of Experimental Psychology*, 1962, *63*, 361-369. (c) **1041, 1104, 1129**

Postman, L. Retention as a function of degree of overlearning. *Science*, 1962, *135*, 666-667. (d) **1124**

Postman, L. The effects of language habits on the acquisition and retention of verbal associations. *Journal of Experimental Psychology*, 1962, *64*, 7-19. (e) **854, 857, 888, 1128**

Postman, L. Does interference theory predict too much forgetting? *Journal of Verbal Learning and Verbal Behavior*, 1963, *2*, 40-48. **1129**

Postman, L. One-trial learning. In C. N. Cofer & B. S. Musgrave (Eds.), *Verbal behavior and learning*. New York: McGraw-Hill, 1963. Pp. 295-321. **987**

Postman, L. Acquisition and retention of consistent associative responses. *Journal of Experimental Psychology*, 1964, *67*, 183-190. **865**

Postman, L. Studies of learning to learn: II. Changes in transfer as a function of practice. *Journal of Verbal Learning and Verbal Behavior*, 1964, *3*, 437-447. (a) **1062, 1064, 1070**

Postman, L. Short-term memory and incidental learning. In A. W. Melton (Ed.), *Categories of human learning*. New York: Academic Press, 1964. (b) **998, 1112**

Postman, L. Unlearning under conditions of successive interpolation. *Journal of Experimental Psychology*, 1965, *70*, 237-245. **1087, 1096, 1098**

Postman, L. Differences between unmixed and mixed transfer designs as a function of paradigm. *Journal of Verbal Learning and Verbal Behavior*, 1966, *5*, 240-248. **1069**

Postman, L. The effect of interitem associative strength on the acquisition and retention of serial lists. *Journal of Verbal Learning and Verbal Behavior*, 1967, *6*, 721-728. **1130**

Postman, L. Association and performance in the analysis of verbal learning. In T. R. Dixon & D. L. Horton (Eds.), *Verbal behavior and general behavior theory*. Englewood Cliffs, N. J.: Prentice-Hall, 1968. (a) **1025**

Postman, L. Studies of learning to learn: VI. General transfer effects in three-stage mediation. *Journal of Verbal Learning and Verbal Behavior*, 1968, *7*, 659-664. (b) **1070**

Postman, L. *Norms of word association*. New York: Academic Press, (in press). **861**

Postman, L., & Adams, P. A. Studies in incidental learning: IV. The interaction of orienting tasks and stimulus materials. *Journal of Experimental Psychology*, 1956, *51*, 329-332. **855**

Postman, L., Adams, P. A., & Phillips, L. W. Studies in incidental learning: II The effects of association value and of the method of testing. *Journal of Experimental Psychology*, 1955, *49*, 1–10. **855**

Postman, L., Fraser, J., & Burns, S. Unit-sequence facilitation in recall. *Journal of Verbal Learning and Verbal Behavior*, 1968, *7*, 217–224. **1130**

Postman, L., & Goggin, J. Whole vs. part learning of paired-associate lists. *Journal of Experimental Psychology*, 1966, *71*, 867–877. **1009**

Postman, L., & Greenbloom, R. Conditions of cue selection in the acquisition of paired-associate lists. *Journal of Experimental Psychology*, 1967, *73*, 91–100. **1047**

Postman, L., & Keppel, G. Retroactive inhibition in free recall. *Journal of Experimental Psychology*, 1967, *74*, 203–211. **1101, 1102**

Postman, L., Keppel, G., & Stark, K. Unlearning as a function of the relationship between successive response classes. *Journal of Experimental Psychology*, 1965, *69*, 111–118. **1097**

Postman, L., Keppel, G., & Zacks, R. Studies of learning to learn: VII. The effects of practice on response integration. *Journal of Verbal Learning and Verbal Behavior*, 1968, *7*, 776–784. **1043**

Postman, L., & Phillips, L. W. Studies in incidental learning: IX. A comparison of the methods of successive and single recalls. *Journal of Experimental Psychology*, 1961, *61*, 236–241. **855**

Postman, L., & Riley, D. A. Degree of learning and interserial interference in retention. *University of California Publications in Psychology*, 1959, *8*, 271–396. **1085, 1086, 1103**

Postman, L., & Schwartz, M. Studies of learning to learn: I. Transfer as a function of method of practice and class of verbal materials. *Journal of Verbal Learning and Verbal Behavior*, 1964, *3*, 37–49. **1042, 1043**

Postman, L., & Stark, K. Proactive inhibition as a function of the conditions of transfer. *Journal of Verbal Learning and Verbal Behavior*, 1964, *3*, 437–447. **1058, 1104**

Postman, L., & Stark, K. Studies of learning to learn: IV. Transfer from serial to paired-associate learning. *Journal of Verbal Learning and Verbal Behavior*, 1967, *6*, 339–353. **1012**

Postman, L., & Stark, K. The role of response availability in transfer and interference. *Journal of Experimental Psychology*, 1969 (in press). **1062, 1065, 1066, 1096**

Postman, L., Stark, K., & Fraser, J. Temporal changes in interference. *Journal of Verbal Learning and Verbal Behavior*, 1968, *7*, 672–694. **1099, 1100, 1101, 1105**

Postman, L., *see also* Bruner, J. S., 1950, 1951; Postman, L., *see* Goulet, L. R., 1966; Keppel, G., 1966, 1968; Rosenzweig, M. R., 1957; Schwinn, E., 1967; Solomon, R. L., 1952; Underwood, B. J., 1960.

Potter, R. K., Kopp, G. A., & Green, H. C. *Visible speech.* Princeton, N.J.: Van Nostrand, 1947. **251**

Poulton, E. C. Listening to overlapping calls. *Journal of Experimental Psychology*, 1956, *52*, 334–339. **258**

Poulton, E. C., *see also* Stevens, S. S., 1956; Warren, R. M., 1966.

Powell, G. F., *see* Henkin, R. I., 1962.

Powell, J., *see* Azrin, N. H., 1967.

Power, R. P., *see* Day, R. H., 1963, 1965.

Powers, J. B., *see* Pfaffmann, C., 1964.

Powley, T. L., & Keesey, R. E. Relationship of body weight to the lateral hypothalamic-feeding syndrome. *Journal of Comparative and Physiological Psychology*, 1970, *70*, 25–36. **651**

Pratt, C. H., *see* Schlosberg, H., 1956.

Pratt, J. G., *see* McCulloch, T. L., 1934.

Premack, D. Toward empirical behavioral laws: I. Positive reinforcement. *Psychological Review*, 1959, *66*, 219–233. **624, 817**

Premack, D. Reversibility of the reinforcement relation. *Science*, 1962, *136*, 255–257. **624, 817, 823**

Premack, D. Reinforcement theory. In D. Levine (Ed.), *Nebraska symposium on motivation.* Lincoln: University of Nebraska Press, 1965. Pp. 123–180. **623, 624, 690, 817, 823**

Premack, D., Collier, G., & Roberts, C. L. Frequency of light-contingent bar pressing as a function of the amount of deprivation of light. *American Psychologist*, 1957, *12*, 411 (abstract). **840**

Premack, D., *see also* Holstein, S. B., 1965; Schaeffer, R. W., 1961.

Prentice, W. C. H. The relation of distance to the apparent size of figural after-effects. *American Journal of Psychology*, 1950, *63*, 589–593. **471n**

Prescott, J. W. Neural timing mechanisms, conditioning and the CS-UCS interval. *Psychophysiology*, 1965, *2*, 125–131. **558n**

Prescott, R. G. W. Diurnal activity cycles and intracranial self-stimulation in the rat. *Journal of Comparative and Physiological Psychology*, 1967, *64*, 346–349. **655n**

Pressman, Y. M., *see* Varga, M. E., 1967.

Pretori, H., *see* Hess, C., 1894.

Prewitt, E. P. Number of preconditioning trials in sensory preconditioning using CER training. *Journal of Comparative and Physiological Psychology*, 1967, *64*, 360–362. **564**

Pribram, K., *see* Miller, G. A., 1960.

Price, A. E., *see* Zeiler, M. D., 1965.

Price, L. E. *see* Abbott, D. W., 1964.

Price, S., *see* Dastoli, F. R., 1966.

Primoff, E. Backward and forward association as an organizing act in serial and in paired-associate learning. *Journal of Psychology*, 1938, *5*, 375–395. **1011, 1013, 1064**

Pritchard, R. M. Stabilized images on the retina. *Scientific American*, 1961, *204*, 72–78. **453**

Pritchard, R. M., Heron, W., & Hebb, D. O. Visual perception approached by the method of stabilized images. *Canadian Journal of Psychology*, 1960, *14*, 67–77. **375, 453**

Pritchatt, D., Avoidance of electric shock by the cockroach. *Animal Behaviour*, 1968, *16*, 178–185. **578**

Pronko, N. H., *see* Snyder, F. W., 1952.

Prosser, C. L., & Hunter, W. S. The extinction of startle responses and spinal reflexes in the white rat. *American Journal of Physiology*, 1936, *117*, 609–618. **577, 591**

Pryer, M. W., *see* Noble, C. E., 1957.

Pubols, B. H., Jr. Delay of reinforcement, response perseveration, and discrimination reversal. *Journal of Experimental Psychology*, 1958, *56*, 32–40. **685, 686**

Pubols, B. H., Jr. Incentive magnitude, learning, and performance in animals. *Psychological Bulletin*, 1960, *57*, 89–115. **635**

Pulfrich, C. Die Stereoskopie im Dienste der isochromen und heterochromen Photometrie. *Naturwissenschaften*, 1922, *10*, 533–564; 569–601; 714–722; 735–743; 751–761. **309**

Purcell, D. G., *see* Dember, W. N., 1967.

Purcell, M., *see* Moore, M. E., 1965.

Purdy, J., & Gibson, E. J. Distance judgment by the method of fractionation. *Journal of Experimental Psychology*, 1955, *50*, 374–380. **514**

Purdy, J., *see also* Gibson, J. J., 1955.

Purdy, W. C. The hypothesis of psychophysical correspondence in space perception. Doctoral dissertation, Cornell University. Ann Arbor: University Microfilms, 1958, No. 58-5594. **505**

Quartermain, D., & Webster, D. Extinction following intracranial reward: The effect of delay between acquisition and extinction. *Science*, 1968, *159*, 1259–1260. **659**

Raab, D. Backward masking. *Psychological Bulletin*, 1963, *60*, 118–129. **241, 429**

Raab, D., *see also* Fehrer, E., 1962; Osman, E., 1963.

Rabe, A., see Clark, W. C., 1955, 1956.

Rabiner, L. R., see Levitt, H., 1967.

Radloff, W. P., see Wilson, G. T. 1967.

Radner, M., see Gibson, J. J., 1937.

Rainey, C., see Bryden, M., 1963.

Rand, G., see Hardy, L. H., 1953.

Randt, C. T., see Collins, W. F., 1960.

Rapaport, D. (Ed.). Organization and pathology of thought. New York: Columbia University Press, 1951. **864**

Rapaport, D., Gill, M., & Schafer, R. Diagnostic psychological testing. Vol. 2. Chicago: Year Book Publishers, 1946. **864**

Rapp, H. M., see Bolles, R. C., 1965, 1968.

Rappoport, M., see Fitts, P. M., 1956.

Rapuzzi, G., & Casella, C. Innervation of the fungiform papillae in the frog tongue. Journal of Neurophysiology, 1965, 28, 154-165. **183**

Rashbass, C. New method for recording eye movements. Journal of the Optical Society of America, 1960, 50, 642-644. **373**

Rashbass, C. The relationship between saccadic and smooth tracking eye movements. Journal of Physiology, 1961, 159, 326-338. **376, 378, 380**

Rashbass, C., & Westheimer, G. H. Disjunctive eye movements. Journal of Physiology, 1961, 159, 149-170. (a) **305, 373, 383**

Rashbass, C., & Westheimer, G. H. Independence of conjugate and disjunctive eye movements. Journal of Physiology, 1961, 159, 361-364. (b) **388**

Raskin, D., see Maltzman, I., 1960.

Raskin, D. C., see Seward, J. P., 1960.

Raskin, E., & Cook, S. W. The strength and direction of associations formed in the learning of nonsense syllables. Journal of Experimental Psychology, 1937, 20, 381-395. **1014**

Rasmussen, A. T. The principal nervous pathways. New York: Macmillan, 1947. **126**

Rasmussen, A. T. see also Penfield, W., 1950.

Rasmussen, G. L. Efferent fibers of the cochlear nerve and cochlear nucleus. In G. L. Rasmussen & W. A. Windle (Eds.), Neural mechanisms of the auditory and vestibular systems. Springfield, Ill.: Charles C Thomas, 1960. **233**

Rasmussen, G. L., & Windle, W. A. Neural mechanisms of the auditory and vestibular systems. Springfield, Ill.: Charles C Thomas, 1960. **231**

Ratliff, F. The role of physiological nystagmus in monocular acuity. Journal of Experimental Psychology, 1952, 43, 163-172. **387**

Ratliff, F. Some interrelations among physics, physiology, and psychology in the study of vision. In S. Koch (Ed.), Psychology: A study of a science. Vol. 4: Biologically oriented fields: Their place in psychology and in biological science. New York: McGraw-Hill, 1962. Pp. 417-482. **293**

Ratliff, F. Mach bands: Quantitative studies on neural networks in the retina. New York: Holden-Day, 1965. **292, 293, 428**

Ratliff, F., & Riggs, L. A. Involuntary motions of the eye during monocular fixation. Journal of Experimental Psychology, 1950, 40, 687-701. **305, 374, 386**

Ratliff, F., see also Hartline, H. K., 1956, 1961; Riggs, L. A., 1951, 1952, 1953, 1954.

Ratoosh, P. On interposition as a cue for the perception of distance. Proceedings of the National Academy of Science, 1949, 35, 257-259. **498**

Rauch, D. S., see Keppel, G., 1966.

Rawlings, I. L., see Thurlow, W. R., 1959.

Ray, O. S., & Stein, L. Generalization of conditioned suppression. Journal of the Experimental Analysis of Behavior, 1959, 2, 357-361. **715**

Raymond, G. A., see Camp, D. S., 1967; Church, R. M., 1967.

Rayner, R., see Watson, J. B., 1920.

Razran, G. H. S. Conditioned responses in animals other than dogs. Psychological Bulletin, 1933, 30, 261-324. **562**

Razran, G. H. S. Conditioned responses: An experimental study and a theoretical analysis. Archives of Psychology, 1935, 191. **561**

Razran, G. A quantitative study of meaning by a conditioned salivary technique (semantic conditioning). Science, 1939, 90, 89-91. **1047**

Razran, G. H. Studies in configural conditioning: II. The effects of subjects' attitudes and task-sets upon configural conditioning. Journal of Experimental Psychology, 1939, 24, 95-105. **562**

Razran, G. Semantic and phonetographic generalization of salivary conditioning to verbal stimuli. Journal of Experimental Psychology, 1949, 39, 642-652. **1047**

Reagan, C., see Washburn, M. F., 1934.

Reaney, T. P., see Brackbill, Y., 1967.

Reber, A. S., & Millward, R. B. Event observation in probability learning. Journal of Experimental Psychology, 1968, 77, 317-327. **918, 932, 933**

Reber, A. S., see also Millward, R. B., 1967.

Reed, H. B. A repetition of Ebert and Meumann's practice experiment in memory. Journal of Experimental Psychology, 1917, 2, 315-346. **1031**

Reed, H. B. Factors influencing learning and retention of concepts: I. Influence of set. Journal of Experimental Psychology, 1946, 36, 71-87. (a) **946**

Reed, H. B. The influence of length of series: III. The origin of concepts. Journal of Experimental Psychology, 1946, 36, 166-181. (b) **946**

Reed, H. B. The influence of complexity of the stimuli: IV. Journal of Experimental Psychology, 1946, 36, 252-261. (c) **946**

Reed, J. D. Spontaneous activity of animals: A review of the literature since 1929. Psychological Bulletin, 1947, 44, 393-412. **821**

Reese, E., see Bateson, P. P. G., 1968.

Reese, H. W. Motor paired associate learning and stimulus pretraining. Child Development, 1960, 31, 505-513. **783**

Reese, H. W. Transposition in the intermediate-size problem by preschool children. Child Development, 1961, 32, 311-315. **765**

Reese, H. W. The perception of stimulus relations. New York: Academic Press, 1968. **765**

Reese, T. S. Olfactory cilia in the frog. Journal of Cellular Biology, 1965, 25, 209-230. **195, 196**

Reese, T. S., & Stevens, S. S. Subjective intensity of coffee odor. American Journal of Psychology, 1960, 73, 424-428. **205**

Reese, T. W. et al. Psychophysical research: Summary report, 1946-1952. Psychophysical Research Unit, Mount Holyoke College, 1953. **73**

Reese, T. W., see also Stevenson, J. G., 1962.

Rehula, R., see Underwood, B. J., 1962.

Reid, L. D., see Gibson, W. E., 1965.

Reid, L. S., & Finger, F. W. The rat's adjustment to 23-hour food deprivation cycles. Journal of Comparative and Physiological Psychology, 1955, 48, 110-113. **818, 819**

Reid, L. A., see Finger, F. W., 1960.

Reiher, L., see Ogle, K., 1962.

Reimann, E. Die scheinbare Vergrösserung der Sonne und des Mondes am Horizont. Zeitschrift für Psychologie, 1902, 30, 1-38, 161-195. **511**

Rekosh, J., see Held, R., 1963.

Remple, R., see Wike, E. L., 1959.

Renner, K. E. Delay of reinforcement: A historical review. Psychological Bulletin, 1964, 61, 341-361. **685**

Renner, K. E. Delay of reinforcement and resistance to extinction: A supplementary report. Psychological Reports, 1965, 16, 197-198. (a) **686**

Renner, K. E. Influence of delay of reinforcement and overlearning on position reversal. *Psychological Reports,* 1965, *16,* 1101–1106. (b) **686**

Renyard, R., *see* Greenspoon, J., 1957.

Rescorla, R. A. Pavlovian conditioning and its proper control procedures. *Psychological Review,* 1967, *74,* 71–80. **717**

Rescorla, R. A., & LoLordo, V. M. Inhibition of avoidance behavior. *Journal of Comparative and Physiological Psychology,* 1965, *59,* 406–412. **709, 716, 717**

Rescorla, R. A., & Solomon, R. L. Two-process learning theory: Relationships between Pavlovian conditioning and instrumental learning. *Psychological Review.* 1967, *74,* 151–182. **569, 726, 809**

Restle, F. A theory of discrimination learning. *Psychological Review,* 1955, *62,* 11–19. (a) **949, 957**

Restle, F. Axioms of a theory of discrimination learning. *Psychometrika,* 1955, *20,* 201–208. (b) **949, 957**

Restle, F. Theory of selective learning with probable reinforcements. *Psychological Review,* 1957, *64,* 182–191. **948, 949, 957**

Restle, F. Toward a quantitative description of learning set data. *Psychological Review,* 1958, *65,* 77–91. **957**

Restle, F. Additivity of cues and transfer in discrimination of consonant clusters. *Journal of Experimental Psychology,* 1959, *57,* 9–14. **957**

Restle, F. *Psychology of judgment and choice: A theoretical essay.* New York: Wiley, 1961. **928, 934, 938, 1005**

Restle, F. The selection of strategies in cue learning. *Psychological Review,* 1962, *69,* 329–343. **949**

Restle, F. Sources of difficulty in learning paired-associates. In R. C. Atkinson (Ed.), *Studies in mathematical psychology.* Stanford: Stanford University Press, 1964. Pp. 116–172. **1005, 1006**

Restle, F. Significance of all-or-none learning. *Psychological Bulletin,* 1965, *64,* 313–325. **989**

Restle, F. Run structure and probability learning: Disproof of Restle's model. *Journal of Experimental Psychology,* 1966, *72,* 382–389. **935, 983**

Restle, F. Grammatical analysis of the prediction of binary events. *Journal of Verbal Learning and Verbal Behavior,* 1967, *6,* 17–25. **935**

Restle, F., & Emmerich, D. Memory in concept attainment: Effects of giving several problems concurrently. *Journal of Experimental Psychology,* 1966, *71,* 794–799. **972, 974**

Restle, F., *see also* Bourne, L. E., 1959; Polson, M., 1965.

Reynolds, B. Extinction of trace conditioned responses as a function of the spacing of trials during acquisition and extinction series. *Journal of Experimental Psychology,* 1945, *35,* 81–95. **570***n*

Reynolds, B. The acquisition of a black-white discrimination habit under two levels of reinforcement. *Journal of Experimental Psychology,* 1949, *39,* 760–769. **637**

Reynolds, B. Acquisition of a simple spatial discrimination as a function of the amount of reinforcement. *Journal of Experimental Psychology,* 1950, *40,* 152–160. **637**

Reynolds, B., *see also* Grice, G. R., 1952.

Reynolds, E. G., *see* Hirsh, I. J., 1952, 1954.

Reynolds, G. S. Attention in the pigeon. *Journal of the Experimental Analysis of Behavior,* 1961, *4,* 203–208. **763, 777**

Reynolds, G. S. Behavioral contrast. *Journal of the Experimental Analysis of Behavior,* 1961, *4,* 57–71. **641**

Reynolds, G. S., & Limpo, A. J. Negative contrast after prolonged discrimination maintenance. *Psychonomic Science,* 1968, *10,* 323–324. **641**

Reynolds, H. V., *see* Gibson, J. J., 1969.

Reynolds, J. H., *see* Friedman, M. J., 1967.

Reynolds, W. F., Pavlik, W. B., & Goldstein, E. Secondary reinforcement effects as a function of reward magnitude training methods. *Psychological Reports,* 1964, *15,* 7–10. **666**

Reynolds, W. F., *see also* Besch, N. F., 1958.

Rice, C. E., & Kenshalo, D. R. Nociceptive threshold measurements in the cat. *Journal of Applied Physiology,* 1962, *17,* 1009–1012. **157**

Richardson, J. The relationship of stimulus similarity and number of responses. *Journal of Experimental Psychology,* 1958, *56,* 478–484. **892**

Richardson, J. Association among stimuli and the learning of verbal concept lists. *Journal of Experimental Psychology,* 1960, *60,* 290–298. **892**

Richardson, J. The learning of concept names mediated by concept examples. *Journal of Verbal Learning and Verbal Behavior,* 1962, *1,* 281–288. **1078**

Richardson, J. Facilitation of mediated transfer by instruction, B–C training and presentation of the mediating response. *Journal of Verbal Learning and Verbal Behavior,* 1966, *5,* 59–67. (a) **1078**

Richardson, J. The effect of B–C presentation and anticipation interval on mediated transfer. *Journal of Verbal Learning and Verbal Behavior,* 1966, *5,* 119–125. (b) **1078, 1079**

Richardson, J. The locus of mediation and the duration of the anticipation interval in a transfer paradigm. *Journal of Verbal Learning and Verbal Behavior,* 1967, *6,* 247–256. (a) **1078, 1079**

Richardson, J. Latencies of implicit verbal responses and the effect of the anticipation interval on mediated transfer. *Journal of Verbal Learning and Verbal Behavior,* 1967, *6,* 819–826. (b) **1058, 1079**

Richardson, J. Transfer and the *A–B* anticipation interval in the *A–B', A–B* paradigm. *Journal of Verbal Learning and Verbal Behavior,* 1967, *6,* 897–902. (c) **1058**

Richardson, J. Implicit verbal chaining as the basis of transfer in paired-associate learning. *Journal of Experimental Psychology,* 1968, *76,* 109–115. (a) **1079**

Richardson, J. Latencies of implicit associative responses and positive transfer in paired-associate learning. *Journal of Verbal Learning and Verbal Behavior,* 1968, *7,* 638–646. (b) **1058, 1077**

Richardson, J., & Brown, B. L. Mediated transfer in paired-associate learning as a function of presentation rate and stimulus meaningfulness. *Journal of Experimental Psychology,* 1966, *72,* 820–828. **1062, 1079**

Richardson, J., & Erlebacher, A. Associative connection between paired verbal items. *Journal of Experimental Psychology,* 1958, *56,* 62–69. **899**

Richardson, J., & Gropper, M. S. Learning during recall trials. *Psychological Reports,* 1964, *15,* 551–560. **1096**

Richardson, J., *see* Underwood, B. J., 1956, 1956a, b, c.

Richter, C. P. Salt taste thresholds of normal and adrenalectomized rats. *Endocrinology,* 1939, *24,* 367–371. **627**

Richter, C. P., *see also* Pfaffmann, C., 1954; Wilkins, L., 1940.

Richter, M., *see* Levine, M., 1964.

Riese, W. *see* Goldstein, K., 1923.

Riesen, A. H. Delayed reward in discrimination learning by chimpanzees. *Comparative Psychology Monographs,* 1940, (No. 77) *15,* 1–53. **784**

Riesen, A. H. The development of visual perception in man and chimpanzee. *Science,* 1947, *106,* 107–108. **548**

Riesen, A. H. Studying perceptual development using the technique of sensory deprivation. *Journal of Nervous and Mental Disease,* 1961, *132,* 21–25. **548**

Riesen, A. H., & Aarons, L. Visual movement and intensity discrimination in cats after early deprivation of pattern vision. *Journal of Comparative and Physiological Psychology,* 1959, *52,* 142–149. **549**

Riesen, A. H., *see also* Hovland, C. I., 1940.

Rifkin, K. I., *see* McLaughlin, S. C., 1965.

Riggs, L. A. Continuous and reproducible records of the electrical activity of the human retina. *Proceedings of the Society for Experimental Biology and Medicine,* 1941, *48,* 204–207. **308**

Riggs, L. A. Electrophysiology of vision. In C. H. Graham

(Ed.), *Vision and visual perception.* New York: Wiley, 1965. Pp. 81-131. (a) **308**

Riggs, L. A. Light as a stimulus for vision. In C. H. Graham (Ed.), *Vision and visual perception.* New York: Wiley, 1965. Pp. 1-38. (b) **274, 278**

Riggs, L. A. Visual acuity. In C. H. Graham (Ed.), *Vision and visual perception.* New York: Wiley, 1965. Pp. 321-349. (c) **279, 298, 301, 304**

Riggs, L. A., Armington, J. C., & Ratliff, F. Motions of the retinal image during fixation. *Journal of the Optical Society of America,* 1954, *44,* 315-321. **305**

Riggs, L. A., & Graham, C. H. Some aspects of light adaptation in a single photo-receptor unit. *Journal of Cellular and Comparative Physiology,* 1940, *16,* 15-23. **311**

Riggs, L. A., Johnson, E. P., & Schick, A. M. L. Electrical responses of the human eye to moving stimulus patterns. *Science,* 1964, *144,* 567. **308**

Riggs, L. A., Johnson, E. P., & Schick, A. M. L. Electrical responses of the human eye to changes in wavelength of stimulating light. *Journal of the Optical Society of America,* 1966, *56,* 1621-1627. **308, 338**

Riggs, L. A., Mueller, C. G., Graham, C. H., & Mote, F. A. Photographic measurements of atmospheric "boil." *Journal of the Optical Society of America,* 1947, *37,* 415-420. **494**

Riggs, L. A., & Niehl, E. W. Eye movements recorded during convergence and divergence. *Journal of the Optical Society of America,* 1960, *50,* 913-920. **382, 387**

Riggs, L. A., & Ratliff, F. Visual acuity and the normal tremor of the eyes. *Science,* 1951, *41,* 139-147. **305**

Riggs, L. A., & Ratliff, F. The effects of counteracting the normal movements of the eye. *Journal of the Optical Society of America,* 1952, *42,* 872-873. **306, 375**

Riggs, L. A. Ratliff, F., Cornsweet, J. C., & Cornsweet, T. N. The disappearance of steadily fixated visual test objects. *Journal of the Optical Society of America,* 1953, *43,* 495-501. **306, 374, 375**

Riggs, L. A., & Schick, A. M. L. Accuracy of retinal image stabilization achieved with a plane mirror on a tightly fitting contact lens. *Vision Research,* 1968, *8,* 159-169. **306, 374, 375**

Riggs, L. A., & Tulunay, S. U. Visual effects of varying the extent of compensation for eye movements. *Journal of the Optical Society of America,* 1959, *49,* 741-745. **379**

Riggs, L. A., *see also* Armington, J. C., 1952; Berry, R. N., 1950; Graham, C. H., 1949; Johnson, E. P., 1951, 1964; Krauskopf, J., 1960; Ratliff, F., 1950.

Riley, D. A. Discrimination learning. In *Contemporary topics in experimental psychology.* Boston: Allyn and Bacon, 1968. **780**

Riley, D. A., *see also* Nealey, S. M., 1963; Postman, L., 1959.

Rinalducci, E., *see* Boynton, R. M., 1965.

Riopelle, A. J. Transfer suppression and learning sets. *Journal of Comparative and Physiological Psychology,* 1953, *46,* 108-114. **768**

Riopelle, A. J., Wunderlich, R. A., & Francisco, E. W. Discrimination of concentric-ring patterns by monkeys. *Journal of Comparative and Physiological Psychology,* 1958, *51,* 622. **768**

Riopelle, A., *see also* Fletcher, J. L., 1960.

Ritchie, B. F., Ebeling, E., & Roth, W. Evidence for continuity in the discrimination of vertical and horizontal patterns. *Journal of Comparative and Physiological Psychology,* 1950, 168-180. **767**

Ritchie, J. M., *see* Douglas, W. W., 1962.

Rittler, M. C., *see* Hardy, L. H., 1953.

Rivers, W. H. R. Vision. In A. C. Haddon (Ed.), *Reports of the Cambridge Anthropological Expedition to the Torres Straits.* Vol. II, Part 1. Cambridge: Cambridge University Press, 1901. **460**

Rivers, W. H. R. Observations on the senses of the Todas. *British Journal of Psychology,* 1905, *1,* 321-396. **460**

Rixon, R. H., *see* Stevenson, J. A. F., 1957.

Robbins, M. C., *see* Kilbride, P. L., 1968.

Roberts, C. L., *see* Premack, D., 1957.

Roberts, F. S., & Suppes, P. Some problems in the geometry of visual perception. *Synthese,* 1967, *17,* 173-201. **466n**

Roberts, W. A. The effects of shifts in magnitude of reward on runway performance in immature and adult rats. *Psychonomic Science,* 1966, *5,* 37-38. **634**

Roberts, W. H. The effect of delayed feeding on white rats in a problem cage. *Journal of Genetic Psychology,* 1930, *37,* 35-58. **678**

Roberts, W. W. Both rewarding and punishing effects from stimulation of hypothalamus of cat with same electrode at same intensity. *Journal of Comparative and Physiological Psychology,* 1958, *51,* 400-407. (a) **798**

Roberts, W. W. Rapid escape learning without avoidance learning motivated by hypothalamic stimulation in cats. *Journal of Comparative and Physiological Psychology,* 1958, *51,* 391-399. (b) **798**

Roberts, W. W. Fear-like behavior elicited from dorsomedial thalamus of cat. *Journal of Comparative and Physiological Psychology,* 1962, *55,* 191-197. **798**

Roberts, W. W., *see also* Delgado, J. M. R., 1954, 1954b.

Robinson, D., *see* Gibson, J. J., 1935.

Robinson, D. A. A method of measuring eye movement using a scleral search coil in a magnetic field. Institute of Electrical and Electronics Engineers, *Transactions on Bio-Medical Electronics,* 1963, *10,* 137-145. **305, 374**

Robinson, D. A. The mechanics of human smooth pursuit eye movements. *Journal of Physiology,* 1965, *180,* 569-591. **377, 378, 379, 380**

Robinson, D. E., & Jeffress, L. A. Effect of varying interaural noise correlation on the detectability of tonal signals. *Journal of the Acoustical Society of America,* 1963, *35,* 1947-1952. **242**

Robinson, D. E., *see also* Dolan, T. R., 1967.

Robinson, D. N. Disinhibition of visually masked stimuli. *Science,* 1966, *154,* 157-158. **431**

Robinson, D. W. The relation between the sone and phon scales of loudness. *Acustica,* 1953, *3,* 344-358. **247**

Robinson, D. W., & Dadson, R. S. A re-determination of the equal loudness relations for pure tones. *British Journal of Applied Physics,* 1956, *7,* 166-181. **246**

Robinson, E. S. Some factors determining the degree of retroactive inhibition. *Psychological Monographs,* 1920, *28,* No. 128. **1081, 1085**

Robinson, E. S. The "similarity" factor in retroaction. *American Journal of Psychology,* 1927, *39,* 297-312. **1081**

Robinson, E. S. *Association theory today.* New York: Century, 1932. **980**

Robinson, F. P. The role of eye movements in reading with an evaluation of the techniques for their improvement. *Iowa State University Aims Program Research,* 1933, *39.* **390**

Robinson, J., *see* Hayes, W. J., 1961.

Robinson, J. S. Stimulus substitution and response learning in the earthworm. *Journal of Comparative and Physiological Psychology,* 1953, *46,* 262-266. **698**

Robinson, J. S., & Higgins, K. S. The young child's ability to see a difference between mirror image forms. *Perceptual and Motor Skills,* 1967, *25,* 893-897. **450**

Robson, J. G., *see* Campbell, F. W., 1959.

Roby, T. B., *see* Sheffield, F. D., 1950, 1954.

Rochester, H., Holland, J. H., Haibt, L. H., & Duda, W. L. Tests on a cell assembly theory of the action of the brain, using a large digital computer. *IRE Transactions on Information Theory,* 1956, *2,* 80-93. **452**

Rock, I. The perception of the egocentric orientation of a line. *Journal of Experimental Psychology,* 1954, *48,* 367-374. **539**

Rock, I. The orientation of forms on the retina and in the

environment. *American Journal of Psychology*, 1956, 69, 513–528. **451**

Rock, I. The role of repetition in associative learning. *American Journal of Psychology*, 1957, 70, 186–193. **986**

Rock, I. Adaptation to a minified image. *Psychonomic Science*, 1965, 2, 105–106. **543**

Rock, I. *The nature of perceptual adaptation.* New York: Basic Books, 1966. **533, 534, 536, 540, 543, 544, 545**

Rock, I., & Brosgole, L. Grouping based on phenomenal proximity. *Journal of Experimental Psychology*, 1964, 67, 531–538. **434n**

Rock, I., & Ebenholtz, S. The relational determination of perceived size. *Psychological Review*, 1959, 66, 387–401. **508**

Rock, I., & Ebenholtz, S. Stroboscopic movement based on change of phenomenal rather than retinal location. *American Journal of Psychology*, 1962, 75, 193–207. **528**

Rock, I., & Fleck, F. A re-examination of the effect of monetary reward and punishment in figure–ground perception. *Journal of Experimental Psychology*, 1950, 40, 766–776. **440**

Rock, I., & Harris, C. Vision and touch. *Scientific American*, 1967, 216, 96–104. **536, 541**

Rock, I., & Heimer, W. The effect of retinal and phenomenal orientation on the perception of form. *American Journal of Psychology*, 1957, 70, 493–511. **451**

Rock, I., & Heimer, W. Further evidence of one-trial associative learning. *American Journal of Psychology*, 1959, 72, 1–16. **986**

Rock, I., & Kaufman, L. The moon illusion: II. *Science*, 1962, 136, 1023–1031. **511**

Rock, I., & McDermott, W. The perception of visual angle. *Acta Psychologica*, 1964, 22, 119–134. **509**

Rock, I., & Victor, J. Vision and touch: An experimentally created conflict between the two senses. *Science*, 1964, 143, 594–596. **536**

Rock, I., *see also* Epstein, W., 1960; Kaufman, L., 1962.

Rockway, M. R., & Duncan, C. P. Pre-recall warming up in verbal retention. *Journal of Experimental Psychology*, 1952, 43, 305–312. **1039**

Rodgers, R. S., *see* Landauer, A. A., 1964.

Rodrigues, J., *see* Bruner, J. S., 1951.

Rodwan, A., *see* Hake, H. W., 1966.

Roelofs, C. O. Die Optische Lokalisation. *Archiv für Augenheilkunde*, 1935, 109, 395–415. **534**

Roelofs, C. O., & Zeeman, W. P. C. Apparent size and apparent distance in binocular and monocular distance. *Ophthalmologica*, 1957, 133, 188–204. **513**

Roessler, E. B., *see* Amerine, M., 1965; Berg, H. W., 1963.

Roffler, S. K., & Butler, R. A. Factors that influence the localization of sound in the vertical plane. *Journal of the Acoustical Society of America*, 1968, 43, 1255–1259. **267**

Rogers, J. V., *see* Walters, G. C., 1963.

Rogers, R., *see* Sherrick, C. E., 1966.

Rogoff, I., *see* Winnick, W. A., 1965.

Rohles, F., *see* Helson, H., 1959.

Rohwer, W. D. Jr., *see* Jensen, A. R., 1965.

Rosanoff, A. J., *see* Kent, G. H., 1910.

Rose, J. Organization of frequency sensitive neurons in the cochlear nuclear complex of the cat. In G. Rasmussen & W. F. Windle (Eds.), *Neural mechanisms of the auditory and vestibular systems*. Springfield, Ill.: Charles C Thomas, 1960. **232**

Rose, J., Brugge, J. F., Anderson, D. J., & Hind, J. E. Phase-locked response to low-frequency tones in single auditory nerve fibers of the squirrel monkey. *Journal of Neurophysiology*, 1967, 30, 769–793. **232**

Rose, J. E., Greenwood, D. D., Goldberg, J. M., & Hind, J. E. Some discharge characteristics of single neurons in the inferior colliculus of the cat: I. Tonotopical organization, relation of spike counts to tone intensity, and firing

patterns of single elements. *Journal of Neurophysiology*, 1963, 26, 294–320. **232**

Rose, J. E., Gross, N. B., Geisler, C. D., & Hind, J. E. Some effects of binaural stimulation on the activity of single neurons in the inferior colliculus of the cat. *Journal of Neurophysiology*, 1966, 29, 288–314. **265**

Rose, J. E., & Mountcastle, V. B. Touch and kinesthesis. In J. Field, H. W. Magoun, & V. E. Hall (Eds.), *Handbook of physiology*. Sec. 1, Vol. I. *Neurophysiology*. American Physiological Society, Washington D. C., 1959. Pp. 387–429. **128**

Rose, J. E., *see also* Brugge, J. F., 1964.

Rose, R. M., & Vitz, P. C. Role of runs in probability learning. *Journal of Experimental Psychology*, 1966, 72, 751–760. **936**

Rosen, E., & Russell, W. A. Frequency-characteristics of successive word-association. *American Journal of Psychology*, 1957, 70, 120–122. **872, 873**

Rosenberg, A. E. Effect of masking on periodic pulses. *Journal of the Acoustical Society of America*, 1965, 38, 747–758. **245**

Rosenblatt, F., *see* Gibson, J. J., 1955.

Rosenblith, J. F. Judgment of simple geometric figures by children. *Perceptual and Motor Skills*, 1965, 21, 947–990. **450**

Rosenblith, W. A., & Stevens, K. N. On the DL for frequency. *Journal of the Acoustical Society of America*, 1953, 25, 980–985. **249**

Rosenblith, W. A., *see also* Bekesy, Georg von, 1951.

Rosenblum, L. A., & Cross, H. A. Performance of neonatal monkeys in the visual-cliff situation. *American Journal of Psychology*, 1963, 76, 318–320. **549**

Rosenblum, L. A., *see also* Moltz, H., 1960.

Rosenthal, R. *Experimental effects in behavioral research.* New York: Appleton, 1966. **562n**

Rosenthal, S. R. Histamine as the chemical mediator for referred pain. In D. R. Kenshalo (Ed.), *The skin senses*. Springfield, Ill.: Charles C Thomas, 1968. Pp. 480–498. **162**

Rosenzweig, M. R. Cortical correlates of auditory localization and of related perceptual phenomena. *Journal of Comparative and Physiological Psychology*, 1954, 47, 269–276. **264**

Rosenzweig, M. R. Etudes sur l'association des mots. *Année Psychologique*, 1957, 57, 23–32. **875**

Rosenzweig, M. R. Comparisons among word-association responses in English, French, German, and Italian. *American Journal of Psychology*, 1961, 74, 347–360. **875**

Rosenzweig, M. R. The mechanisms of hunger and thirst. In L. Postman (Ed.), *Psychology in the making*. New York: Knopf, 1962. Pp. 73–143. **816**

Rosenzweig, M. R. Word associations of French workmen: Comparisons with associations of French students and American workmen and students. *Journal of Verbal Learning and Verbal Behavior*, 1964, 3, 57–69. **875**

Rosenzweig, M. R., & McNeill, D. Uses of the semantic count in experimental studies of verbal behavior. *American Journal of Psychology*, 1962, 75, 492–495. **895n**

Rosenzweig, M. R., & Manahem, R. Age, sexe et niveau d'instruction comme facteurs déterminants dans les associations de mots. *Année Psychologique*, 1962, 62, 45–61. **874**

Rosenzweig, M. R., & Postman, L. Intelligibility as a function of frequency of usage. *Journal of Experimental Psychology*, 1957, 54, 412–422. **255**

Rosenzweig, M. R., *see also* Wallach, H., 1949.

Rosner, B., *see* Kolers, P., 1960.

Rosner, B. S., & Goff, W. R. Electrical responses of the nervous system and subjective scales of intensity. In W. D. Neff (Ed.), *Contributions to sensory physiology*. New York: Academic Press, 1967. **82**

Ross, G. S., *see* Weitzman, E. D., 1961.

Ross, L., & Versace, J. The critical frequency for taste. *American Journal of Psychology*, 1953, *66*, 496–497. **178**

Ross, L. E. Eyelid conditioning as a tool in psychological research: Some problems and prospects. In W. F. Prokasy (Ed.), *Classical conditioning*. New York: Appleton, 1965. **557**

Ross, L. E., *see also* Spence, K. W., 1959.

Ross, R. T., *see* Hull, C. L., 1940.

Ross, S. Matching functions and equal-sensation contours for loudness. *Journal of the Acoustical Society of America*, 1967, *42*, 778–793. **247**

Rossi, P. J. Adaptation and negative aftereffect to lateral optical displacement in newly hatched chicks. *Science*, 1968, *160*, 430–432. **549**

Rossi, G., & Cortesina, G. The efferent innervation of the inner ear: A historical–bibliographical survey. *Laryngoscope*, 1965, *75*, 212–235. **233**

Rossman, E., *see* Posner, M. I., 1965.

Roth, S. R., Sterman, M. B., & Clemente, C. D. Comparison of EEG correlates of reinforcement, internal inhibition and sleep. *Electroencephalography and Clinical Neurophysiology*, 1967, *23*, 509–520. **838**

Roth, W., *see* Ritchie, B. F., 1950.

Rothkopf, E. Z. Two predictors of stimulus equivalence in paired associate learning. *Psychological Reports*, 1960, *7*, 241–250. **880**

Rothkopf, E. Z., & Coke, E. U. The prediction of free recall from word association measures. *Journal of Experimental Psychology*, 1961, *62*, 433–438. (a) **879, 887**

Rothkopf, E. Z., & Coke, E. U. Intralist association data for 99 words of the Kent-Rosanoff word list. *Psychological, Reports*, 1961, *8*, 463–474. (b) **879**

Rothschild, H. Untersuchungen über die sogenannten anorthoskopischen Zerrbilder. *Zeitschrift für Psychologie*, 1922, *90*, 137–166. **455**

Rouanet, H., *see* Suppes, P., 1964.

Rouse, R. O., & Verinis, J. S. Compound verbal stimuli and word association. *Psychological Report*, 1965, *17*, 403–406. **871**

Rouse, R. O., *see also* Hull, C. L., 1951; Schwartz, F., 1961.

Roussel, J. Frustration effect as a function of repeated non-reinforcements and as a function of the consistency of reinforcement prior to the introduction of non-reinforcement. Unpublished master's thesis, Tulane University, 1952. Cited by Amsel, 1958. **810**

Roussel, J., *see also* Amsel, A., 1952.

Routtenberg, A. The two-arousal hypothesis: Reticular formation and limbic system. *Psychological Review*, 1968, *75*, 51–80. **658**

Routtenberg, A., & Kuznesof, A. W. Self-starvation of rats living in activity wheels on a restricted feeding schedule. *Journal of Comparative and Physiological Psychology*, 1967, *64*, 414–421. **653**

Routtenberg, A., & Lindy, J. Effects of the availability of rewarding septal and hypothalamic stimulation on bar pressing for food under conditions of deprivation. *Journal of Comparative and Physiological Psychology*, 1965, *60*, 158–161. **651, 652**

Rowland, V., MacIntyre, W. J., & Bidder, T. G. The production of brain lesions with electric currents: II. Bidirectional currents. *Journal of Neurosurgery*, 1960, *17*, 55–69. **644**

Rozin, P., *see* Smith, R. H., 1967.

Rubin, E. *Synoplevede Figurer*. Copenhagen: Gyldendalske, 1915. **432, 438**

Rubin, E. *Visuell wahrgenommene Figuren*. Copenhagen: Glydendalske, 1921. **432, 438**

Rubin, M., *see* Amoore, J. E., 1964.

Rubin, R., *see* Furchgott, E., 1953.

Rubinstein, H., *see* Pollack, I., 1959.

Ruch, T. C. The nervous system: Sensory functions. In J. F. Fulton (Ed.), *Howell's Textbook of Physiology*. (ed. 15) Philadelphia: Saunders, 1946. **81**

Ruch, T. C. Pathophysiology of pain. In T. C. Ruch, H. D. Patton, J. W. Woodbury, & A. L. Towe (Eds.), *Neurophysiology*. Philadelphia: Saunders, 1965. Pp. 345–363. **161**

Ruch, T. C., & Patton, H. D. (Eds.) *Physiology and biophysics*. Philadelphia: Saunders, 1965. **95**

Ruch, T. C., *see also* Mowrer, O. H., 1936.

Rudel, R. G., & Teuber, H. L. Decrement of visual and haptic Müller-Lyer illusion on repeated trials: A study of cross-modal transfer. *Quarterly Journal of Experimental Psychology*, 1963, *15*, 125–131. **450, 465n, 471**

Rudy, J. W., *see* Patten, R. L., 1967.

Rump, E. E. The relationship between perceived size and perceived distance. *British Journal of Psychology*, 1961, *52*, 111–124. **506**

Rundquist, E. A. Inheritance of spontaneous activity in rats. *Journal of Comparative Psychology*, 1933, *16*, 415–438. **824**

Runge, P. S., *see* Thurlow, W. R., 1967.

Runquist, W. N. Retention of verbal associates as a function of strength. *Journal of Experimental Psychology*, 1957, *54*, 369–374. **1086**

Runquist, W. N. Verbal learning. In J. B. Sidowski (Ed.), *Experimental methods and instrumentation in psychology*. New York: McGraw-Hill, 1966. **853n**

Runquist, W. N., *see* Johnson, P. A., 1968; Underwood, B. J., 1959.

Rupert, A., *see* Galambos, R., 1959; Hubel, D. H., 1959.

Rush, G. P. Visual grouping in relation to age. *Archives of Psychology*, 1937, *31*. **434**

Rushton, W. A. H. Visual pigments in the colour blind. *Nature*, 1958, *182*, 690–692. **323**

Rushton, W. A. H. Increment threshold and dark adaptation. *Journal of the Optical Society of America*, 1963, *3*, 104–109. **287**

Rushton, W. A. H. Cone pigment dynamics in the deuteranope. *Journal of Physiology*, 1965, *176*, 38–45. **288**

Rushton, W. A. H., & Westheimer, G. The effect upon the rod threshold of bleaching neighbouring rods. *Journal of Physiology*, 1962, *164*, 318–329. **289**

Rushton, W. A. H., *see also* Campbell, F. W., 1954.

Russell, W. A. Assessment versus experimental acquisition of verbal habits. In C. N. Cofer (Ed.), *Verbal learning and verbal behavior*. New York: McGraw-Hill, 1961. Pp. 110–123. **850**

Russell, W. A., & Jenkins, J. J. The complete Minnesota norms for responses to 100 words from the Kent-Rosanoff Word Association Test. Tech. Rep. No. 11, Contract N8-Onr 66216, between the Office of Naval Research and the University of Minnesota, 1954. **875**

Russell, W. A., & Meseck, O. R. Der Einfluss der Assoziation auf das Erinnern von Worten in der Deutschen, Französischen, und Englischen Sprache. *Zeitschrift für experimentelle und angewandte Psychologie*, 1959, *6*, 191–211. **875**

Russell, W. A., & Storms, L. H. Implicit verbal chaining in paired associate learning. *Journal of Experimental Psychology*, 1955, *49*, 287–293. **781, 1078**

Russell, W. A., *see also* Jenkins, J. J., 1958, 1959, 1960, undated; Rosen, E., 1957.

Ryan, J. J. Comparison of verbal response transfer mediated by meaningfully similar and associated stimuli. *Journal of Experimental Psychology*, 1960, *60*, 408–415. **1048, 1052**

Ryan, T., *see* Kamin, L., 1959.

Ryan, T. A., *see* Hochberg, J., 1955.

Sachs, M. B., & Kiang, N. Y. S. Two-tone inhibition in auditory-nerve fibers. *Journal of the Acoustical Society of America*, 1967, *43*, 1120–1128. **233, 239**

Sadowski, B., & Longo, V. G. Electroencephalographic and

behavioural correlates of an instrumental reward conditioned response in rabbits. *Electroencephalography and Clinical Neurophysiology,* 1962, *14,* 465-476. **837**

Sadowsky, S. Discrimination learning as a function of stimulus location along an auditory intensity continuum. *Journal of the Experimental Analysis of Behavior,* 1966, *9,* 209-225. **715**

Sadowsky, S. Discriminative responding on associated mixed and multiple schedules as a function of food and ICS reinforcement. *Journal of the Experimental Analysis of Behavior,* 1969, *12,* 933-945. **607, 655, 694, 701**

Sagara, M., & Oyama, T. Experimental studies on figural aftereffects in Japan. *Psychological Bulletin,* 1957, *54,* 327-338. **469**

Sakai, M., *see* Gibson, W. E., 1965.

Sakoda, J. N., *see* Brand, H., 1956.

Salapatek, P., & Kesson, W. Visual scanning of triangles by the human newborn. *Journal of Experimental Child Psychology,* 1966, *3,* 155-167. **547**

Salk, L. Mother's heartbeat as an imprinting stimulus. *Transactions of the New York Academy of Science,* 1962, *24,* 753-763. **582**

Salk, L. Thoughts on the concept of imprinting and its place in early human development. *Canadian Psychiatric Association Journal,* 1966. *11* (Supplement), 295-305. **582**

Saltz, E. Response pretraining: Differentiation or availability? *Journal of Experimental Psychology.* 1961, *62,* 583-587. **1060**

Saltz, E., & Hamilton, H. Spontaneous recovery of List 1 responses in the *A-B, A'-C* paradigm. *Journal of Experimental Psychology,* 1967, *75,* 267-273. **1099**

Saltzman, D., *see* Peterson, L. R., 1962, 1963.

Saltzman, I. J. Maze learning in the absence of primary reinforcement: A study of secondary reinforcement. *Journal of Comparative and Physiological Psychology,* 1949, *42,* 161-173. **663, 664**

Saltzman, I., & Koch, S. The effect of low intensities of hunger on the behavior mediated by a habit of maximum strength. *Journal of Experimental Psychology,* 1948, *38,* 347-370. **826**

Salzen, E. A., & Sluckin, W. The incidence of the following response and the duration of responsiveness in domestic fowl. *Animal Behaviour,* 1959, *7,* 172-179. **585**

Sampson, H., & Spong, P. Binocular fixation and immediate memory. *British Journal of Psychology,* 1961, *52,* 239-248. **444**

Sandak, J. M., & Garskof, B. E. Associative unlearning as a function of degree of interpolated learning. *Psychonomic Science,* 1967, *7,* 215-216. **1096**

Sandak, J. M., *see also* Garskof, B. E., 1964.

Sandel, T. T., Teas, D. C., Feddersen, W. E., & Jeffress, L. A. Localization of sound from single and paired sources. *Journal of the Acoustical Society of America,* 1955, *27,* 842-852. **266**

Sandel, T. T., *see also* Feddersen, W. E., 1957; Jeffress, L., 1956.

Sanderson, W. R., *see* Vanderplas, J. M., 1965.

Sandström, C. I. *Orientation in the present space.* Stockholm: Almquist and Wiksell, 1951. **529**

Sanford, E. C. *A course in experimental psychology. Part I: Sensation and perception.* London: Heath, 1897. **462**

Sanford, E. C. *A course in experimental psychology.* Boston: Heath, 1898. **521**

Saslow, M. G. Latency for saccadic eye movement. *Journal of the Optical Society of America,* 1967, *57,* 1030-1033. **376**

Satinoff, E., *see* Smith, R. H., 1967.

Sato, M. The effect of temperature change on the response of taste receptors. In Y. Zotterman (Ed.), *Olfaction and taste.* Vol. I. New York: Pergamon, 1963. Pp. 151-164. **181**

Sato, M., *see also* Yamashita, S., 1967.

Sato, Y., *see* Ishiko, N., 1967.

Saunders, M. G., *see* Zubek, J. P., 1963.

Savage, C. W. Introspectionist and behaviorist interpretations of ratio scales of perceptual magnitudes. *Psychological Monographs,* 1966, *80,* Whole number 627. **84**

Savin, H. B., *see* Clayton, F. L., 1960.

Sawyer, C. H., & Kawakami, M. Characteristics of behavioral and electroencephalographic after-reactions to copulation and vaginal stimulation in the female rabbit. *Endocrinology,* 1959, *65,* 622-630. **838**

Sayers, B. McA. Acoustic-image lateralization judgments with binaural tones. *Journal of the Acoustical Society of America,* 1964, *36,* 923-926. **261**

Sayers, B. McA., & Toole, F. E. Acoustic-image lateralization judgments with binaural transients. *Journal of the Acoustical Society of America,* 1964, *36,* 1199-1205. **266**

Sayers, B. McA., *see also* Cherry, E. C., 1959; Leakey, D. M., 1958.

Scahill, G. H., *see* Dimmick, F. L., 1925.

Scandura, J. M., *see* Greeno, J. G., 1966.

Schachter, S. Obesity and eating. *Science,* 1968, *161,* 751-756. **817**

Schaefer, V. J., *see* Langmuir, I., 1944.

Schaeffer, R. W., & Premack, D. Licking rates in infant albino rats. *Science,* 1961, *134,* 1980-1981. **814**

Schafer, R., & Murphy, G. The role of autism in a visual figure-ground relationship. *Journal of Experimental Psychology,* 1943, *32,* 335-343. **439, 440**

Schafer, R., *see also* Rapaport, D., 1946.

Schafer, W., *see* Boynton, R. M., 1964.

Scharf, B. Complex sounds and critical bands. *Psychological Bulletin,* 1961, *58,* 205-217. **234, 240**

Scharf, B., & Stevens, J. C. The form of the loudness function near threshold. Vol. 1. *Proceedings of the 3rd International Congress on Acoustics, Stuttgart, 1959.* Amsterdam: Elsevier, 1961. Pp. 80-82. **80**

Scharf, B., *see also* Zwicker, E., 1965.

Scharlock, D. P., *see* Bugelski, B. R., 1952.

Schaub, R. E., *see* Kamin, L. J., 1963.

Scheible, H., & Underwood, B. J. The role of overt errors in serial rote learning. *Journal of Experimental Psychology,* 1954, *47,* 160-162. **1038**

Scheibner, H., *see* Boynton, R. M., 1965.

Scheibner, J. M. O., & Boynton, R. M. Residual red-green discrimination in dichromats. *Journal of the Optical Society of America,* 1968, *58,* 1151-1158. **367**

Schenkel, K. D. Accumulation-theory of binaural masked thresholds. *Journal of the Acoustical Society of America,* 1967, *41,* 20-31. **242**

Schick, A. M. L., *see* Johnson, E. P., 1964; Riggs, L. A., 1964, 1966, 1968.

Schiff, B. B., *see* Glickman, S. E., 1967.

Schiff, W. Perception of impending collision: A study of visually directed avoidance behavior. *Psychological Monographs: General and Applied,* 1965, *79,* 1-26. **505**

Schiff, W., Caviness, J., & Gibson, J. J. Persistent fear responses in rhesus monkeys to the optical stimulus of "looming." *Science,* 1962, *136,* 982-983. **505**

Schiffman, H., *see* Wynne, R. D., 1965.

Schiller, P., & Smith, M. Detection in metacontrast. *Journal of Experimental Psychology,* 1966, *71,* 32-46. **430**

Schlag-Rey, M., *see* Suppes, P., 1966.

Schlosberg, H. A study of the conditioned patellar reflex. *Journal of Experimental Psychology,* 1928, *11,* 468-494. **562, 563, 601**

Schlosberg, H. Conditioned responses in the white rat. *Journal of Genetic Psychology,* 1934, *45,* 303-335. **563, 571**

Schlosberg, H. Conditioned responses in the white rat: II. Conditioned responses based on shock to the foreleg. *Journal of Genetic Psychology,* 1936, *49,* 107-138. **563**

Schlosberg, H. The relationship between success and the laws of conditioning. *Psychological Review*, 1937, *44*, 379–394. **563, 726**

Schlosberg, H. The description of facial expression in terms of two dimensions. *Journal of Experimental Psychology*, 1952, *44*, 229–237. **55**

Schlosberg, H. Three dimensions of emotion. *Psychological Review*, 1954, *61*, 81–88. **55**

Schlosberg, H., & Heineman, C. The relationship between two measures of response strength. *Journal of Experimental Psychology*, 1950, *40*, 235–247. **861**

Schlosberg, H., & Pratt, C. H. The secondary reward value of inaccessible food for hungry and satiated rats. *Journal of Comparative and Physiological Psychology*, 1956, *49*, 149–152. **657, 669, 678n**

Schlosberg, H., *see also* Bilodeau, I. McD., 1951; Engen, T., 1958; White, C. T., 1952; Woodworth, R. S., 1954.

Schmidt, W. A. An experimental study in the psychology of reading. *Educational Monographs* (Supplement), 2, 1917. **390**

Schneider, B., & Lane, H. Ratio scales, category scales, and variability in the production of loudness and softness. *Journal of the Acoustical Society of America*, 1963, *35*, 1953–1961. **248**

Schneider, R. A., Costiloe, J. P., Howard, R. P., & Wolf, S. Olfactory perception thresholds in hypogonadal women: Changes accompanying the administration of androgen and estrogen. *Journal of Clinical Endocrinology*, 1958, *18*, 379–390. **209**

Schneider, R. A., & Wolf, S. Olfactory perception thresholds for "citral" utilizing a new type of olfactorium. *Journal of Applied Physiology*, 1955, *8*, 337–342. **201, 208**

Schneider, R. A., & Wolf, S. Relation of olfactory acuity to nasal membrane function. *Journal of Applied Physiology*, 1960, *15*, 914–920. **209**

Schneiderman, N., *see* Vandercar, D. H., 1967.

Schober, H. A. W., & Hilz, R. Contrast sensitivity of the human eye for square-wave gratings. *Journal of the Optical Society of America*, 1965, *55*, 1086–1091. **304**

Schoeffler, M. S. Probability of response to compounds of discriminated stimuli. *Journal of Experimental Psychology*, 1956, *48*, 323–329. **927**

Schoenberg, K. M., *see* Mayzner, M. S., 1964.

Schoenfeld, W. N., Antonitis, J. J., & Bersh, P. J. A preliminary study of training conditions necessary for secondary reinforcement. *Journal of Experimental Psychology*, 1950, *40*, 40–45. **674**

Schoenfeld, W. N., *see also* Keller, F. S., 1950.

Scholl, K. Das räumliche Zusammenarbeiten von Auge und Hand. *Deutsche Zeitschrift für Nervenheilkunde*, 1926, *92*, 280–303. **537**

Schott, E. Ueber die Registrierung des Nystagmus und anderer Augenbewegungen vermittels des Saitengalvanometers. *Deutsche Archiv für klinische Medizin*, 1922. *140*, 79–90. **372**

Schouten, J. F. The perception of pitch. *Philips Technical Review*, 1940, *5*, 286–294. **245**

Schrier, A. M. Amount of incentive and performance on a black-white discrimination problem. *Journal of Comparative and Physiological Psychology*, 1956, *49*, 123–125. **637, 700**

Schrier, A. M. Comparison of two methods of investigating the effect of amount of reward on performance. *Journal of Comparative and Physiological Psychology*, 1958, *51*, 725–731. **637, 638, 639**

Schrier, A. M. A modified version of the Wisconsin General Test Apparatus. *Journal of Psychology*, 1961, *52*, 193–200. **750**

Schrier, A. M. Response latency of monkeys as a function of amount of reward. *Psychological Reports*, 1961, *8*, 283–289. **635, 638**

Schrier, A. M. Response latency of monkeys as a function of reward amount and trials within test days. *Psychological Reports*, 1962, *10*, 439–444. **638**

Schrier, A. M. Reinforcement variables and response rates of monkeys (*Macaca mulatta*). *Journal of Comparative and Physiological Psychology*, 1965, *59*, 378–384. **626, 630**

Schrier, A. M. Effects of an upward shift in amount of reinforcer on runway performance of rats. *Journal of Comparative and Physiological Psychology*, 1967, *64*, 490–492. **633, 635**

Schrier, A. M., & Harlow, H. F. Effect of amount of incentive on discrimination learning by monkeys. *Journal of Comparative and Physiological Psychology*, 1956, *49*, 117–122. **637, 639, 700**

Schrödinger, E. Theorie der Pigmente von grosster Leuchtkraft. *Annalen der Physik*, 1920, *62*, 603. **356**

Schriever, W. Experimentelle Studien über Stereoskopische Sehen. *Z. Psychol.*, 1925, *96*, 113–170. **502**

Schroeder, M. R., *see* Harvey, F. K., 1963.

Schuck, J. R., Brock, T. C., & Becker, L. A. Luminous figures: Factors affecting the reporting of disappearances. *Science*, 1964, *146*, 1598–1599. **454**

Schuck, J., & Leahy, W. R. A comparison of verbal and non-verbal reports of fragmenting visual images. *Perception and Psychophysics*, 1966, *1*, 191–192. **454**

Schulman, R. M. Paired-associate transfer following early stages of List I learning. *Journal of Experimental Psychology*, 1967, *73*, 589–594. **1069**

Schultz, D. P., *see* King, D. J., 1960.

Schultze, M. Zur Anatomie und Physiologie der Retina. *Archiv für Mikroshopische Anatomie*, 1866, *2*, 175–286 (also Plates 8–15). **283**

Schulz, R., *see* Spence, J., 1965.

Schulz, R. W., Liston, J. R., & Weaver, G. E. The *A–B, B–C, A–C* mediation paradigm: Recall of *A–B* following *A–C* learning. *Journal of Verbal Learning and Verbal Behavior*, 1968, *7*, 602–607. **1077**

Schulz, R. W., & Lovelace, E. Mediation in verbal paired-associate learning: The role of temporal factors. *Psychonomic Science*, 1964, *1*, 95–96. **1058, 1079**

Schulz, R. W., & Thysell, R. The effects of familiarization on meaningfulness. *Journal of Verbal Learning and Verbal Behavior*, 1965, *4*, 409–413. **866**

Schulz, R. W., & Weaver, G. E. The *A–B, B–C, A–C* mediation paradigm: The effects of variation in *A–C* study- and test-interval lengths and strength of *A–B, B–C*. *Journal of Experimental Psychology*, 1968, *76*, 303–311. **1075, 1079**

Schulz, R., Weaver, G., & Ginsberg, S. Mediation with pseudomediation controlled: Chaining is not an artifact! *Psychonomic Science*, 1965, *2*, 169–170. **1077**

Schulz, R. W., *see also* McGhee, N. ⌐., 1961; Spreen, O., 1966; Underwood, B. J., 1959, 1960a, b, 1962.

Schumacher, G. A., Goodell, H., Hardy, J. D., & Wolff, H. G. Uniformity of the pain threshold in man. *Science*, 1940, *92*, 110. **158**

Schwartz, C. B. *Visual discrimination of camouflaged figures.* Unpublished doctoral dissertation, University of California at Berkeley, 1961. **440**

Schwartz, F., & Rouse, R. O. The activation and recovery of associations. *Psychological Issues*, 1961, *3*. **886**

Schwartz, M. Effect of stimulus class on transfer and RI in the *A–B, C–B* paradigm. *Journal of Verbal Learning and Verbal Behavior*, 1968, *7*, 189–195. **1064**

Schwartz, M., *see also* Postman, L., 1964.

Schwartzkopff, J., *see* Galambos, R., 1959.

Schwenn, E., & Postman, L. Studies of learning to learn: V. Gains in performance as a function of warm-up and associative practice. *Journal of Verbal Learning and Verbal Behavior*, 1967, *6*, 565–573. **1038**

Schwenn, E., & Underwood, B. J. Simulated similarity and

mediation time in transfer. *Journal of Verbal Learning and Verbal Behavior*, 1965, *4*, 476-483. **1058, 1079**

Scofield, E. H., *see* Foster, D., 1950.

Scott, E. D., & Wike, E. L. The effect of partially delayed reinforcement and trial-distribution on the extinction of an instrumental response. *American Journal of Psychology*, 1956, *69*, 264-268. **685**

Scott, H. H., Jr., *see* Kenshalo, D. R., 1966.

Scott, J. P. *Animal behavior*. Chicago: University of Chicago Press, 1958. **581**

Seagrim, G. N., *see* Day, R. H., 1959; Pollack, 1959.

Seaman, G., *see* Hochberg, J. E., 1951.

Searle, J. L., *see* Hoffman, H. S., 1966.

Sears, R. R. Effect of optic lobe ablation on the visuo-motor behavior of the goldfish. *Journal of Comparative Psychology*, 1934, *17*, 233-265. **578**

Seashore, E. C., Carter, E. A., Farnum, E. C., & Seis, R. W. The effect of practice on normal illusions. *Psychological Review* (Monograph Supplement), 1908, *9*, 103-104. **465**

Sechzer, J. A., & Brown, J. L. Color discrimination in the cat. *Science*, 1964, *144*, 427-429. **338**

Ségal, J., *see* Baumgardt, E., 1947.

Segall, M. H., Campbell, D. T., & Herskovits, M. J. Cultural differences in the perception of geometric illusions. *Science*, 1963, *139*, 769-771. **456, 460**

Segall, M. H., Campbell, D. T., & Herskovits, M. J. *The influence of culture on visual perception*. Indianapolis, Ind.: Bobbs-Merrill, 1966. **456, 460**

Seidel, R. J. A review of sensory preconditioning. *Psychological Bulletin*, 1959, *56*, 58-73. **564**

Seidel, R. J. The importance of the S-R role of the verbal mediator in mediate association. *Canadian Journal of Psychology*, 1962, *16*, 170-176. **1074**

Seidel, R. J. RTT paradigm: No panacea for theories of associative learning. *Psychological Review*, 1963, *70*, 565-572. **990**

Seis, R. W., *see* Seashore, E. C., 1908.

Seitz, W. C. *The responsive eye*. New York: Museum of Modern Art, 1965. **499**

Sekey, A. Short-term auditory frequency discrimination. *Journal of the Acoustical Society of America*, 1963, *35*, 682-690. **249**

Sekuler, R. W., & Ganz, L. Aftereffect of seen motion with a stabilized retinal image. *Science*, 1963, *139*, 419-420. **522**

Sekuler, R. W., *see also* Erlebacher, A., 1969.

Selfridge, J., *see* Miller, G. A., 1950.

Seligman, M. E. P. CS redundancy and secondary punishment. *Journal of Experimental Psychology*, 1966, *4*, 546-550. **676**

Seligman, M. E. P., *see also* Maier, S. F., 1968, 1969; Overmier, J. B., 1967.

Selkin, J., & Wertheimer, M. Disappearance of the Müller-Lyer Illusion under prolonged inspection. *Perceptual and Motor Skills*, 1957, *7*, 265-266. **465**

Sem-Jacobsen, C. W., & Torkildsen, A. Depth recording and electrical stimulation in the human brain. In E. R. Ramey & D. S. O'Doherty (Eds.), *Electrical studies on the unanesthetized brain*. New York: Hoeber, 1960. Pp. 280-288. **660**

Semmes, J., *see* Lashley, K. S., 1951.

Senden, M. von, *see* von Senden, M.

Sermat, V., *see* Abelson, R. P., 1962.

Sersen, E. A., *see* Warren, R. M., 1958; Weinstein, S., 1964.

Seward, J. P. An experimental test of Guthrie's theory of reinforcement. *Journal of Experimental Psychology*, 1942, *30*, 247-256. **568**

Seward, J. P., & Raskin, D. C. The role of fear in aversive behavior. *Journal of Comparative and Physiological Psychology*, 1960, *53*, 328-335. **725**

Seward, J. P., Uyeda, A. A., & Olds, J. Resistance to extinction

following cranial self-stimulation. *Journal of Comparative and Physiological Psychology*, 1959, *52*, 294-299. **675**

Sgro, F. J. Beta motion thresholds. *Journal of Experimental Psychology*, 1963, *66*, 281-285. **526**

Sgro, J. A., Dyal, J. A., & Anastasio, E. J. Effects of constant delay of reinforcement on acquisition asymptote and resistance to extinction. *Journal of Experimental Psychology*, 1967, *73*, 634-636. **685**

Sgro, J. A., & Weinstock, S. Effects of delay on subsequent running under immediate reinforcement. *Journal of Experimental Psychology*, 1963, *66*, 260-263. **685**

Shaffer, J. P. Effect of different stimulus frequencies on discrimination learning with probabilistic reinforcement. *Journal of Experimental Psychology*, 1963, *65*, 265-269. **926**

Shaffer, M. M., *see* Steiner, S. S., 1968.

Shaffer, O., & Wallach, H. Extent-of-motion thresholds under subject-relative and object-relative conditions. *Perception and Psychophysics*, 1966, *1*, 447-451. **521, 522**

Shagass, C., *see* Malmo, R. B., 1951.

Shanmugam, A. V., & Miron, M. S. Semantic effects in mediated transfer. *Journal of Verbal Learning and Verbal Behavior*, 1966, *5*, 361-368. **1074, 1075**

Shankweiler, D. P., *see* Liberman, A. M., 1967.

Shapiro, M. M. Salivary conditioning in dogs during fixed-interval reinforcement contingent upon lever pressing. *Journal of the Experimental Analysis of Behavior*, 1961, *4*, 361-364. **565**

Shapiro, M. M., & Miller, T. M. On the relationship between conditioned and discriminative stimuli and between instrumental and consummatory responses. In W. F. Prokasy (Ed.), *Classical conditioning*. New York: Appleton, 1965. **565, 622**

Shapiro, S. I. Response latencies in paired-associate learning as a function of free association strength, hierarchy, directionality, and mediation. Doctoral dissertation, Pennsylvania State University, 1966. **888**

Sharma, K. N., *see* Jacobs, H. L., 1968.

Sharma, K. N., *see also* Jacobs, H. L., 1969.

Sharpless, S., & Jasper, H. H. Habituation of the arousal reaction. *Brain*, 1956, *79*, 655-680. **591, 833, 834**

Shatel, R. B., *see* Kimble, G. A., 1952.

Shaw, J. G., *see* Newell, A., 1958.

Shaw, W. A., *see* Beck, J., 1961, 1963.

Shaxby, J. H., & Gage, F. H. The localization of sounds in the median plane. *Medical Research Council Special Report*, Series 166. London, 1932. **262**

Sheahan, D., *see* Peterson, M. J., 1964.

Sheeley, E. C. Temporal integration as a function of frequency. *Journal of the Acoustical Society of America*, 1964, *36*, 1850-1857. **234**

Sheer, D. E. (Ed.). *Electrical stimulation of the brain*. Austin: University of Texas Press, 1961. **644**

Sheffield, F. D. Relations between classical conditioning and instrumental learning. In W. F. Prokasy (Ed.), *Classical conditioning*. New York: Appleton, 1965. 302-322. **567n, 695, 696, 697n**

Sheffield, F. D. A drive-induction theory of reinforcement. In R. N. Haber (Ed.), *Current research in motivation*. New York: Holt, Rinehart and Winston, 1966. Pp. 98-111. **622, 657, 691, 695**

Sheffield, F. D., & Campbell, B. A. The role of experience in the "spontaneous" activity of hungry rats. *Journal of Comparative and Physiological Psychology*, 1954, *47*, 97-100. **808, 822**

Sheffield, F. D., & Roby, T. B. Reward value of a non-nutritive sweet taste. *Journal of Comparative and Physiological Psychology*, 1950, *43*, 471-481. **691, 817**

Sheffield, F. D., Roby, T. B., & Campbell, B. A. Drive reduction versus consummatory behavior as determinants of reinforcement. *Journal of Comparative and Physiological Psychology*, 1954, *47*, 349-355. **797**

Sheffield, F. D., & Temmer, H. W. Relative resistance to extinction of escape training and avoidance training. *Journal of Experimental Psychology*, 1950, *40*, 287–298. **724**

Sheffield, F. D., Wulff, J. J., & Backer, R. Reward value of copulation without sex drive reduction. *Journal of Comparative and Physiological Psychology*, 1951, *44*, 3–8. **691, 797**

Sheffield, F. D., *see also* Campbell, B. A., 1953.

Sheffield, V. F. Extinction as a function of partial reinforcement and distribution of practice. *Journal of Experimental Psychology*, 1949, *39*, 511–526. **576, 695**

Shelden, C. H. Depolarization in the treatment of trigeminal neuralgia: Evaluation of compression and electrical methods; clinical concept of neurophysiological mechanism. In R. S. Knighton & P. R. Dumke (Eds.), *Pain*. Boston: Little, Brown, 1966. Pp. 373–386. **165, 166**

Shelley, W. B., *see* Arthur, R. P., 1959.

Shelnutt, J., *see* Davis, H., 1967.

Shepard, R. N. Comments on Professor Underwood's paper. In C. N. Cofer & B. B. Musgrave (Eds.), *Verbal behavior and learning: Problems and processes.* New York: McGraw-Hill, 1963. Pp. 48–75. **1001**

Shepard, R. N. Attention and the metric structure of the stimulus. *Journal of Mathematical Psychology*, 1964, *1*, 54–87. **1001***n*

Shepard, R. N. Approximation to uniform gradients of generalization by monotone transformations of scale. In D. I. Mostofsky (Ed.), *Stimulus generalization*. Stanford: Stanford University Press, 1965. **761**

Shepard, R. N., & Chang, J. Forced-choice of recognition memory under steady-state conditions. *Journal of Verbal Learning and Verbal Behavior*, 1963, *2*, 93–101. **1119**

Shepard, R. N., & Chang, J. J. Stimulus generalization and classification. *Journal of Experimental Psychology*, 1963, *65*, 94–102. **1001**

Shepard, R. N., Hovland, C. I., & Jenkins, H. M. Learning and memorization of classifications. *Psychological Monographs*, 1961, *75* (whole no. 517). **968, 969, 1001***n*

Shepard, R. N., & Teghtsoonian, M. Retention of information under conditions approaching a steady state. *Journal of Experimental Psychology*, 1961, *62*, 202–222. **1118**

Shepard, W. O. Learning set in preschool children. *Journal of Comparative and Physiological Psychology*, 1957, *50*, 15–17. **768**

Shepp, B., & Zeaman, D. Discrimination learning of size and brightness by retardates. *Journal of Comparative and Physiological Psychology*, 1966, *62*, 55–59. **613**

Shepp, B. E., & Eimas, P. D. Intradimensional and extradimensional shifts in the rat. *Journal of Comparative and Physiological Psychology*, 1964, *57*, 357–361. **751**

Shepp, B. E., & Turrisi, F. D. Learning and transfer of mediating responses in discriminative learning. In N. R. Ellis (Ed.), *International review of research in mental retardation.* Vol. II. New York: Academic Press, 1966. Pp. 85–121. **767**

Sherlock, L., *see* Smith, O. W., 1957.

Sherrick, C. E. Studies of apparent tactile movement. In D. R. Kenshalo (Ed.), *The skin senses.* Springfield, Ill.: Charles C Thomas, 1968. Pp. 331–344. **139**

Sherrick, C. E., & Mangabeira-Albernaz, P. L. Auditory threshold shifts produced by simultaneously pulsed contralateral stimuli. *Journal of the Acoustical Society of America*, 1961, *33*, 1381–1385. **242**

Sherrick, C. E., & Rogers, R. Apparent haptic movement. *Perception and Psychophysics*, 1966, *1*, 175–180. **139**

Sherrington, C. S. The spinal cord. In E. A. (Sharpey-) Schaefer (Ed.), *Text-book of physiology.* Edinburgh: Pentland, 1900. Vol. 2. Cited by Brobeck, J. R., 1960. **796**

Sherrington, C. S. *Integrative action of the nervous system.* New Haven: Yale University Press, 1906. **121**

Shibuya, S., *see* Shibuya, T., 1963.

Shibuya, T. Dissociation of olfactory response and mucosal potential. *Science*, 1964, *143*, 1338–1340. **221**

Shibuya, T., & Shibuya, S. Olfactory epithelium: Unitary responses in the tortoise. *Science*, 1963, *140*, 495–496. **217**

Shibuya, T., *see also* Tucker, D., 1965.

Shiffrin, R. M., *see* Atkinson, R. C., 1965.

Shinno, T. Developmental studies on distance-constancy. In Y. Akishige (Ed.), *Experimental researches on the structure of the perceptual space.* Fukuoka, Japan: Kyushu University, 1967. **550**

Shipley, T. Convergence function in binocular visual space: I. A note on theory. *Journal of the Optical Society of America*, 1957, *47*, 795–803. **493**

Shipley, T. The frontal reference surface of visual space. *Documenta Opthalmologica*, 1959, *13*, 487–516. **493**

Shipley, T. E. Jr., *see* Wishner, J., 1957.

Shipley, W. C. Indirect conditioning. *Journal of General Psychology*, 1935, *12*, 337–357. **1073**

Shlaer, S. The relation between visual acuity and illumination. *Journal of General Physiology*, 1937, *21*, 165–188. **299**

Shlaer, S., *see also* Hecht, S., 1936, 1942.

Shortess, G. K., & Krauskopf, J. Role of involuntary eye movements in stereoscopic acuity. *Journal of the Optical Society of America*, 1961, *51*, 555–559. **306, 491***n*

Shower, E. G., & Biddulph, R. Differential pitch sensitivity of the ear. *Journal of the Acoustical Society of America*, 1931, *3*, 275–287. **18, 249**

Shuell, P. J., & Keppel, J. A further test of the chaining hypothesis of serial learning. *Journal of Verbal Learning and Verbal Behavior*, 1967, *6*, 439–445. **1012**

Shuell, T. J. Retroactive inhibition in free-recall learning of categorized lists. *Journal of Verbal Learning and Verbal Behavior*, 1968, *7*, 797–805. **1102**

Shuell, T. J., & Keppel, G. Retroactive inhibition as a function of learning method. *Journal of Experimental Psychology*, 1967, *75*, 457–463. **1102**

Sickles, W. R. Experimental evidence for the electrical character of visual fields derived from quantitative analysis of the Ponzo Illusion. *Journal of Experimental Psychology*, 1942, *30*, 84–91. **458**

Sidman, M. A note on functional relations obtained from group data. *Psychological Bulletin*, 1952, *49*, 263–269. **609, 917**

Sidman, M. Two temporal parameters of the maintenance of avoidance behavior by the white rat. *Journal of Comparative and Physiological Psychology*, 1953, *46*, 253–261. **730, 731**

Sidman, M. *Tactics of scientific research.* New York: Basic Books, 1960. **598, 600, 620**

Sidman, M. Avoidance behavior. In W. K. Honig (Ed.), *Operant behavior: Areas of research and application.* New York: Appleton, 1966. Pp. 448–498. **730, 731**

Sidman, M., Herrnstein, R. J., & Conrad, D. G. Maintenance of avoidance behavior by unavoidable shocks. *Journal of Comparative and Physiological Psychology*, 1957, *50*, 553–557. **717**

Sidman, M., & Stebbins, W. C. Satiation effects under fixed-ratio schedules of reinforcement. *Journal of Comparative and Physiological Psychology*, 1954, *47*, 114–116. **605, 608**

Sidman, M., *see also* Stein, L., 1958.

Sieck, M. H., *see* Wenzell, B., 1966; Wenzel, B., 1966.

Siegel, A., *see* Kurtz, K. H., 1966.

Siegel, P. S. The relationship between voluntary water intake, body weight loss, and number of hours of water privation in the rat. *Journal of Comparative and Physiological Psychology*, 1947, *40*, 231–238. **813**

Siegel, P. S., & MacDonnell, M. F. A repetition of the Calvin-Bicknell-Sperling study of conditioned drive.

Journal of Comparative and Physiological Psychology, 1954, *47,* 250–252. **805**

Siegel, S. *Nonparametric statistics for the behavioral sciences.* New York: McGraw-Hill, 1956. **61**

Siipola, E., Walker, W. N., & Kolb, D. Task attitudes in word association, projective and nonprojective. *Journal of Personality,* 1955, *23,* 441–459. **863, 875**

Siipola, E., *see also* Dunn, S., 1958.

Silvar, S. D., & Pollack, R. H. Racial differences in pigmentation of the fundus oculi. *Psychonomic Science,* 1967, *7,* 159–160. **461**

Silvar, S. D., *see also* Pollack, R. H., 1967.

Silverman, S. R. Tolerance for pure tones and speech in normal and defective hearing. *Annals of Otolaryngology,* 1947, *56,* 658–677. **254**

Silverman, S. R., *see also* Davis, H., 1960; Hirsh, I. J., 1952.

Silverstein, A. The prediction of individual association hierarchies from cultural frequencies. *American Journal of Psychology,* 1967, *80,* 88–94. **876**

Silverstein, A. Unlearning, spontaneous recovery and the partial-reinforcement effect in paired-associate learning. *Journal of Experimental Psychology,* 1967, *73,* 15–21. **1099**

Silverstein, A., *see also* Hochberg, J., 1956; Paul, C., 1968.

Simmel, M., *see* Heider, F., 1944.

Simmons, F. B., Epley, J. M., Lummis, R. C., Guttman, N., Frishkopf, L. S., Harmon, L. D., & Zwicker, E. Auditory nerve: Electrical stimulation in man. *Science,* 1965, *148,* 104–106. **244, 245**

Simmons, F. B., Mongeon, C. J., Lewis, W. R., & Huntingdon, D. A. Electrical stimulation of acoustical nerve and inferior colliculus. *Archives of Otolaryngology,* 1964, *79,* 559–567. **245**

Simmons, M. W., *see* Weisberg, P., 1966.

Simmons, R. The relative effectiveness of certain incentives in animal learning. *Comparative Psychology Monographs,* 1924, *2,* No. 7. **617, 672**

Simon, H. A., & Feigenbaum, E. A. An information-processing theory of some effects of similarity, familiarization, and meaningfulness in verbal learning. *Journal of Verbal Learning and Verbal Behavior,* 1964, *3,* 385–396. **1008**

Simon, H. A., & Kotovsky, K. Human acquisition of concepts for sequential patterns. *Psychological Review,* 1963, *70,* 534–546. **979**

Simon, H. A., *see also* Feigenbaum, E. A., 1961, 1962, 1963; Gregg, L. W., 1967; Newell, A., 1958, 1961, 1963.

Simon, S., *see* Maltzman, I., 1959, 1960; Martin, R. B., 1966.

Sinclair, D., *see* Hagen, E., 1953.

Sinclair, D. C. Cutaneous sensation and the doctrine of specific energy. *Brain,* 1955, *78,* 584–614. **167**

Sinclair, D. C., & Hinshaw, J. R. Sensory changes in nerve blocks induced by cooling. *Brain,* 1951, *74,* 318–335. **160**

Sinclair, J. C., *see* Olds, J., 1957.

Singer, D., *see* Jones, F. N., 1962.

Singer, G., & Day, R. H. Spatial adaptation and aftereffect with optically transformed vision: Effects of active and passive responding and the relationship between test and exposure responses. *Journal of Experimental Psychology,* 1966, *71,* 725–731. **536**

Singh, D., *see* Meyer, D. S., 1966.

Siqueland, E. R. Basic learning processes: Instrumental conditioning in infants. In H. W. Reese & L. P. Lipsitt (Eds.), *Experimental child psychology: The scientific study of child behavior and development.* New York, Academic Press, 1970. **673**

Siskel, M., Jr., *see* Collier, G., 1959.

Sjöberg, L., *see* Ekman, G., 1965.

Skaggs, E. B. Further studies in retroactive inhibition. *Psychological Monographs,* 1925, *34.* **1081**

Skilling, A. K. Verbal association. Mimeographed report under Cooperative Research Program, U. S. Office of Education Contract N1073, with the University of Michigan,

S. A. and M. T. Mednick, principal investigators, 1962. **863n**

Skinner, B. F. Drive and reflex strength: II. *Journal of General Psychology,* 1932, *6,* 38–48. **602**

Skinner, B. F. Two types of conditioned reflex and a pseudotype. *Journal of General Psychology,* 1935, *12,* 66–77. **563, 565, 594**

Skinner, B. F. Two types of conditioned reflex: A reply to Konorski and Miller. *Journal of General Psychology,* 1937, *16,* 272–279. **699**

Skinner, B. F. *The behavior of organisms.* New York: Appleton, 1938. **102, 565n, 594, 596, 662, 663, 679, 681, 684, 704, 738, 741, 752, 917**

Skinner, B. F. "Superstition" in the pigeon. *Journal of Experimental Psychology,* 1948, *38,* 168–172. **683, 692**

Skinner, B. F. Are theories of learning necessary? *Psychological Review,* 1950, *57,* 193–216. **907**

Skinner, B. F. *Science and human behavior.* New York: Macmillan, 1953. **553, 566n, 616n, 677, 697**

Skinner, B. F. A case history in scientific method. *American Psychologist,* 1956, *11,* 221–233. **602, 603**

Skinner, B. F. Pigeons in a pelican. *American Psychologist,* 1960, *15,* 28–37. **584**

Skinner, B. F. Operant behavior. In W. K. Honig (Ed.), *Operant behavior: Areas of research and application.* New York: Appleton, 1966. **697**

Skinner, B. F., & Campbell, S. L. An automatic shocking-grid apparatus for continuous use. *Journal of Comparative and Physiological Psychology,* 1947, *40,* 305–307. **706**

Skinner, B. F., *see also* Estes, W. K., 1941; Ferster, C. B., 1957; Heron, W. T., 1937; Morse, W. H., 1957.

Sklar, D. L., *see* Ward, W. D., 1959.

Skolnick, A. The role of eye-movements in the autokinetic phenomenon. *Journal of Experimental Psychology,* 1940, *26,* 373–393. **529**

Skude, G. Complexities of human taste variation. *Journal of Heredity,* 1960, *51,* 259–263. **182**

Slamecka, N. J. Retroactive inhibition of connected discourse as a function of practice level. *Journal of Experimental Psychology,* 1960, *59,* 104–108. (a) **1085, 1086**

Slamecka, N. J. Retroactive inhibition of connected discourse as a function of similarity of topic. *Journal of Experimental Psychology,* 1960, *60,* 245–249. (b) **1083**

Slamecka, N. J. Proactive inhibition of connected discourse. *Journal of Experimental Psychology,* 1961, *62,* 295–301. **1103, 1104**

Slamecka, N. J. An inquiry into the doctrine of remote associations. *Psychological Review,* 1964, *71,* 61–77. **1013**

Slamecka, N. J. Supplementary report: A search for spontaneous recovery of verbal associations. *Journal of Verbal Learning and Verbal Behavior,* 1966, *5,* 205–207. **1099**

Slamecka, N. J. Transfer with mixed and unmixed lists as a function of semantic relations. *Journal of Experimental Psychology,* 1967, *73,* 405–410. **1061, 1070**

Slamecka, N. J., & Ceraso, J. Retroactive and proactive inhibition of verbal learning. *Psychological Bulletin,* 1960, *57,* 449–475. **1084**

Sleight, W. G. Memory and formal training. *British Journal of Psychology,* 1911, *4,* 386–457. **1031**

Sluckin, W. *Imprinting and early learning.* Chicago: Aldine, 1965. **584, 587, 588, 746**

Sluckin, W., *see also* Salzen, E. A., 1959.

Small, A. M., Jr. Some parameters influencing the pitch of amplitude modulated signals. *Journal of the Acoustical Society of America,* 1955, *27,* 751–760. **245**

Small, A. M., Jr. Audition. In P. R. Farnsworth (Ed.), *Annual review of psychology.* Vol. 14. Palo Alto, Calif.: Annual Reviews, 1963. (a) **234**

Small, A. M., Jr. Auditory adaptation. In J. Jerger (Ed.), *Modern developments in audiology.* New York: Academic Press, 1963. (b) **235**

Small, A. M., Jr., & Campbell, R. A. Masking of pulsed tones by bands of noise. *Journal of the Acoustical Society of America*, 1961, *33*, 1570–1576. **245**

Small, A. M., Jr., & Thurlow, W. R. Loudness relations in two-component tones. *Journal of the Acoustical Society of America*, 1954, *26*, 381–388. **240**

Small, A. M., Jr., *see also* Campbell, R. A., 1963; Thurlow, W. R., 1955.

Small, W. S. An experimental study of the mental processes of the rat: I. *American Journal of Psychology*, 1899–1900, *11*, 133–164. **598**

Small, W. S. An experimental study of the mental processes of the rat: II. *American Journal of Psychology*, 1900–1901, *12*, 206–239. **598**

Smallman, R. L., *see* Beidler, L. M., 1965.

Smith, A. H. Outline convergence versus closure in the perception of slant. *Perceptual and Motor Skills*, 1959, *9*, 259–266. **501**

Smith, A. H., *see also* Clark, W. C., 1955, 1956.

Smith, D., & Hochberg, J. The effect of "punishment" (electric shock) on figure–ground perception. *Journal of Psychology*, 1954, *37*, 83–87. **440**

Smith, D. V., & McBurney, D. H. Gustatory cross-adaptation: Does a single mechanism code the salty taste? *Journal of Experimental Psychology*, 1969, *80*, 101–105. **186**

Smith, E., *see* Fehrer, E., 1962.

Smith, E. L., *see* Hecht, S., 1936.

Smith, G. M., Egbert, L. D., Markowitz, R. A., Mosteller, F., & Beecher, H. K. An experimental pain method sensitive to morphine in man: The submaximum effort tourniquet technique. *Journal of Pharmacology and Experimental Therapeutics*, 1966, *154*, 324–332. **163**

Smith, J. C., *see* Henton, W. W., 1966.

Smith, K. Conditioning as an artifact. *Psychological Review*, 1954, *61*, 217–225. **711**

Smith, K. R. The satiational theory of the figural after-effect. *American Journal of Psychology*, 1948, *61*, 482–485. **470**

Smith, K. R. Visual apparent movement in the absence of neural interaction. *American Journal of Psychology*, 1948, *61*, 73–78. **528**

Smith, K. U. The neural centers concerned in the mediation of apparent movement vision. *Journal of Experimental Psychology*, 1940, *26*, 443–466. **528**

Smith, K. U. Cybernetic theory and analysis of learning. In E. A. Bilodeau (Ed.), *Acquisition of skill*. New York: Academic Press, 1966. **687**

Smith, K. U., & Smith, W. M. *Perception and motion*. Philadelphia: Saunders, 1962. **533, 536n**

Smith, K. U., *see also* Smith, W. M., 1960.

Smith, M. C., *see* Schiller, P. H., 1966.

Smith, M. P., & Capretta, P. J. Effects of drive level and experience on the reward value of saccharine solutions. *Journal of Comparative and Physiological Psychology*, 1956, *49*, 553–557. **797, 817**

Smith, N. F., *see* Campbell, B. A., 1966.

Smith, O. A., Jr., McFarland, W. L., & Taylor, E. Performance in a shock-avoidance conditioning situation interpreted as pseudoconditioning. *Journal of Comparative and Physiological Psychology*, 1961, *54*, 154–157. **730**

Smith, O. A., Jr., *see also* DeVito, J. L., 1959.

Smith, O. W. Judgments of size and distance in photographs. *American Journal of Psychology*, 1958, *71*, 529–538. **514**

Smith, O. W., Imparato, N., & Exner, J. E. Effects of practice on reversals of incomplete Necker cubes. *Perceptual and Motor Skills*, 1968, *27*, 951–954. **519**

Smith, O. W., & Sherlock, L. A new explanation of the velocity-transposition phenomenon. *American Journal of Psychology*, 1957, *70*, 102–105. **521**

Smith, O. W., & Smith, P. C. Interaction of the effects of cues involved in judgments of curvature. *American Journal of Psychology*, 1957, *70*, 361–375. **502**

Smith, O. W., & Smith, P. C. On motion parallax and per-

ceived depth. *Journal of Experimental Psychology*, 1963, *65*, 107–108. **505**

Smith, O. W., & Smith, P. C. Development studies of spatial judgments by children and adults. *Perceptual and Motor Skills*, 1966, *22*, 3–73. **506, 550**

Smith, O. W., Smith, P. C., & Hubbard, D. Perceived distance as a function of the method of representing perspective. *American Journal of Psychology*, 1958, *71*, 662–674. **501**

Smith, O. W., *see also* Hochberg, J., 1955; Smith, P. C., 1961.

Smith, P. C., & Smith, O. W. Veridical perceptions of cylindricality: A problem of depth discrimination and object identification. *Journal of Experimental Psychology*, 1961, *62*, 145–152. **502**

Smith, P. C., *see also* Smith, O. W., 1957, 1958, 1963, 1966.

Smith, R. H., Satinoff, E., & Rozin, P. Bar pressing for heat versus running in a wheel by food-deprived white rats. *Eastern Psychological Association*, 1967, *36*. (Abstract) **824**

Smith, R. W., *see* Zeaman, D., 1965.

Smith, S. Utrocular, or 'which eye,' discrimination. *Journal of Experimental Psychology*, 1945, *35*, 1–14. **489**

Smith, S., & Guthrie, E. R. *General psychology in terms of behavior*. New York: Appleton, 1921. **562**

Smith, S. M., Brown, H. O., Toman, J. E. P., & Goodman, L. S. The lack of cerebral effects of *d*-tubocurarine. *Anesthesiology*, 1947, *8*, 1–14. **711**

Smith, W. A. S., *see* Galanter, E., 1958.

Smith, W. M., & Gulick, W. L. Visual contour and movement perception. *Science*, 1956, *124*, 316–317. **520**

Smith, W. M., & Gulick, W. L. Dynamic contour perception. *Journal of Experimental Psychology*, 1957, *53*, 145–152. **520**

Smith, W. M., & Gulick, W. L. A statistical theory of dynamic contour perception. *Psychological Review*, 1962, *69*, 91–108. **520**

Smith, W. M., McGrary, J. W., & Smith, K. U. Delayed visual feedback and behavior. *Science*, 1960, *132*, 1013–1014. **536n**

Smith, W. M., & Warter, P. J., Jr. Eye movement and stimulus movement: New photoelectric electromechanical system for recording and measuring tracking motions of the eye. *Journal of the Optical Society of America*, 1960, *50*, 245–250. **373**

Smith, W. M., *see* Smith, K. U., 1962.

Smoke, K. L. An objective study of concept formation. *Psychological Monographs*, 1932, *42*, (Whole no. 191). **946**

Smoke, K. L. Negative instances in concept learning. *Psychological Review*, 1933, *16*, 583–588. **964**

Snellen, H. *Probebuchstaben zur Bestimmung der Sehschärfe*. Utrecht: P. W. van de Weijer, 1862. Cited in Cowan, A., 1928. **299**

Sniadowski-Dolinsky, D., *see* Armus, H. L., 1966.

Snyder, F. W., & Pronko, N. H. *Vision with spatial inversion*. Wichita, Kans.: McCormick-Armstrong, 1952. **533**

Snyder, H. L., *see* Hulse, S. H., 1960.

Sokolov, E. N. Neuronal modes and the orienting reflex. In M. A. B. Brazier (Ed.), *The central nervous system and behavior*. New York: Josiah Macy, Jr., Foundation, 1960. **555, 591**

Solley, C. M., & Long, J. When is "uh huh" reinforcing? *Perceptual and Motor Skills*, 1958, *8*, 277. **440**

Solley, C. M., & Murphy, G. *Development of the perceptual world*. New York: Basic Books, 1960. **440**

Solomon, D. H., *see* Henkin, R. I., 1962.

Solomon, L. N., *see* Mowrer, O. H., 1954.

Solomon, R. I., *see* Church, R. M., 1956.

Solomon, R. L. The influence of work on behavior. *Psychological Bulletin*, 1948, *45*, 1–40. **574**

Solomon, R. L. An extension of control group design. *Psychological Bulletin*, 1949, *46*, 137–150. **1024**

Solomon, R. L. A note on the alternation of guesses. *Journal of Experimental Psychology*, 1949, *39*, 322–326. **604**

Solomon, R. L. The role of effort in the performance of a

distance discrimination. *Journal of Experimental Psychology*, 1949, 39, 73–83. **700**

Solomon, R. L. Punishment. *American Psychologist*, 1964, 19, 239–253. **738n**

Solomon, R. L., & Brush, E. S. Experimentally derived conceptions of anxiety and aversion. In M. R. Jones (Ed.), *Nebraska symposium on motivation.* Vol. 4. Lincoln: University of Nebraska Press, 1956. Pp. 212–305. **726**

Solomon, R. L., & Howes, D. H. Word frequency, personal values and visual duration thresholds. *Psychological Review*, 1951, 58, 256–270. **444**

Solomon, R. L., Kamin, L. J., & Wynne, L. C. Traumatic avoidance learning: The outcome of several extinction procedures with dogs. *Journal of Abnormal and Social Psychology*, 1953, 48, 291–302. **727, 732**

Solomon, R. L., & Postman, L. Frequency of usage as a determinant of recognition thresholds for words. *Journal of Experimental Psychology*, 1952, 43, 195–201. **255, 444**

Solomon, R. L., & Turner, L. H. Discriminative classical conditioning in dogs paralyzed by curare can later control discriminative avoidance responses in the normal state. *Psychological Review*, 1962, 69, 202–219. **728, 818**

Solomon, R. L., & Wynne, L. C. Traumatic avoidance learning: Acquisition in normal dogs. *Psychological Monographs*, 1953, 67, (Whole no. 354). **725, 726**

Solomon, R. L., *see also* Black, A. H., 1962; Brush, F. R., 1955; Church, R. M., 1956, 1966; Graham, C. H., 1949; Howes, D., 1951; Maier, S. F., 1968, 1969; Rescorla, R. A., 1967; Turner, L. H., 1962; Wynne, L. C., 1955.

Soltz, D. F., & Wertheimer, M. The retention of "good" and "bad" figures. *American Journal of Psychology*, 1959, 72, 450–452. **445**

Sommer, R. The effects of rewards and punishments during perceptual organization. *Journal of Personality*, 1957, 25, 550–559. **440**

Sommer, R., *see also* Ayllon, T., 1956.

Sonoda, G. Perceptual constancies observed in plane pictures. In Y. Akishige (Ed.), *Experimental research on the structure of the perceptual space.* Fukuoka, Japan: Kyushu University, 1961. **501**

Spalding, D. A. Instinct with original observations on young animals. *Macmillan's Magazine*, 1873, 27, 282–293. Reprinted in *British Journal of Animal Behaviour*, 1954, 2, 2–11. **548, 549, 581**

Sparrock, J. M. B., *see* Barlow, H. B., 1964.

Spear, N. E. Replication report: Absence of a successive contrast effect on instrumental running behavior after a shift in sucrose concentration. *Psychological Reports*, 1965, 16, 393–394. **634**

Spear, N. E., & Hill, W. F. Adjustment to new reward: Simultaneous- and successive-contrast effects. *Journal of Experimental Psychology*, 1965, 70, 510–519. **640**

Spear, N. E., Mikulka, P. J., & Podd, M. Transfer as a function of time to mediate. *Journal of Experimental Psychology*, 1966, 72, 40–46. **1058**

Spear, N. E., & Spitzner, J. H. Simultaneous and successive contrast effects in selective learning. *Psychological Monographs*, 1966, 80, (Whole no. 618). **640**

Spearman, C. The proof and measurement of association between two things. *American Journal of Psychology*, 1904, 15, 72–101. **61**

Spearman, C. The method of "right and wrong cases" without Gauss' formula. *British Journal of Psychology*, 1908, 2, 227–242. **26**

Speelman, R., *see* Sperling, G., 1965.

Spelt, D. K. The conditioning of the human fetus *in utero. Journal of Experimental Psychology*, 1948, 38, 338–346. **556**

Spelt, D. K., *see also* Finger, F. W., 1947.

Spence, J., & Schulz, R. Negative transfer in paired-associate learning as a function of first-list trials. *Journal of Verbal Learning and Verbal Behavior*, 1965, 4, 397–400. **1036, 1068**

Spence, J. T., *see* Spence, K. W., 1966.

Spence, K. W. The nature of discrimination learning in animals. *Psychological Review*, 1936, 43, 427–449. **576, 596, 770, 774**

Spence, K. W. The differential response in animals to stimuli varying within a single dimension. *Psychological Review*, 1937, 44, 430–444. **596, 751, 760, 764, 770**

Spence, K. W. An experimental test of the continuity and noncontinuity theories of discrimination learning. *Journal of Experimental Psychology*, 1945, 35, 253–266. **766**

Spence, K. W. The role of secondary reinforcement in delayed reward learning. *Psychological Review*, 1947, 54, 1–8. **679, 682**

Spence, K. W. Theoretical interpretations of learning. In S. S. Stevens (Ed.), *Handbook of experimental psychology.* New York: Wiley, 1951. Pp. 690–729. **559, 773, 801, 805**

Spence, K. W. The nature of response in discrimination learning. *Psychological Review*, 1952, 59, 89–93. **774, 775**

Spence, K. W. *Behavior theory and conditioning.* New Haven: Yale University Press, 1956. **596n, 597, 621, 622, 632, 633, 635, 681, 741, 789, 805, 812, 984**

Spence, K. W. A theory of emotionally based drive (D) and its relation to performance in simple learning situations. *American Psychologist*, 1958, 13, 131–141. **789**

Spence, K. W., & Ross, L. E. A methodological study of the form and latency of eyelid responses in conditioning. *Journal of Experimental Psychology*, 1959, 58, 376–381. **557**

Spence, K. W., & Spence, J. T. The motivational components of manifest anxiety: Drive and drive stimuli. In C. D. Spielberger (Ed.), *Anxiety and behavior.* New York: Academic Press, 1966. Pp. 291–326. **790**

Spence, K. W., *see also* Bergman, G., 1944.

Spencer, W. A., Thompson, R. F. & Neilson, D. R., Jr. Response decrement of the flexion reflex in the acute spinal cat and transient restoration by strong stimuli. *Journal of Neurophysiology*, 1966, 29, 221–239. **591**

Sperling, D. S., *see* Calvin, J. S., 1953.

Sperling, G. The information available in brief visual presentations. *Psychological Monographs*, 1960, 74, (Whole No. 498). **444**

Sperling, G. A model for visual memory tasks. *Human Factors*, 1963, 5, 19–31. **430, 444**

Sperling, G., & Speelman, R. Visual spatial localization during object motion, apparent object motion and image motion produced by eye movements. *Program of the 1965 annual meeting of the Optical Society of America, Journal of the Optical Society of America*, 1965, 55, 1576 (abstract). **531**

Sperling, H. G., & Jolliffe, C. L. Intensity-time relationship at threshold for spectral stimuli in human vision. *Journal of the Optical Society of America*, 1965, 55, 191–199. **303**

Sperry, R. W., & Miner, N. Pattern perception following insertion of mica plates into visual cortex. *Journal of Comparative and Physiological Psychology*, 1955, 48, 463–469. **470**

Sperry, R. W., Miner, N., & Meyers, R. E. Visual pattern perception following subpial slicing and tantalum wire implantations in the visual cortex. *Journal of Comparative and Physiological Psychology*, 1955, 48, 50–58. **470**

Spiegel, H. G. Ueber den Einfluss des Zwischenfeldes auf gesehene Abstaende. *Psychologische Forschung*, 1937, 21, 327–383. **458**

Spigel, I. M. *Readings in the study of visually perceived movement.* New York: Harper and Row, 1965. **520**

Spiker, C. C. Experiments with children on the hypotheses of acquired distinctiveness and equivalence of cues. *Child Development*, 1956, 27, 253–263. **751, 788**

Spiker, C. C. Associative transfer in paired-associate verbal learning. *Child Development*, 1960, *31*, 73-87. **1036**

Spiker, C. C. The hypothesis of stimulus interaction and an explanation of stimulus compounding. In L. P. Lipsitt & C. C. Spiker (Eds.), *Advances in child development and behavior*. Vol. 1. New York: Academic Press, 1963. Pp. 233-264. **782**

Spiker, C. C., *see also* Norcross, K. J., 1957, 1958.

Spitz, H. H. The present status of the Köhler-Wallach theory of satiation. *Psychological Bulletin*, 1958, *55*, 1-28. **469**

Spitzner, J. H., *see* Spear, N. E., 1966.

Spong, P., Haider, M., & Lindsley, D. B. Selective attentiveness and cortical evoked responses to visual and auditory stimuli. *Science*, 1965, *148*, 395-397. **233**

Spong, P., *see also* Sampson, H., 1961.

Spooner, A., & Kellogg, W. N. The backward conditioning curve. *American Journal of Psychology*, 1947, *60*, 321-334. **558, 561**

Spragg, S. D. S. Morphine addiction in chimpanzees. *Comparative Psychology Monographs*, 1940, *15*, No. 7. **557n**

Spreen, O., & Schulz, R. W. Parameters of abstraction, meaningfulness, and pronunciability for 329 nouns. *Journal of Verbal Learning and Verbal Behavior*, 1966, *5*, 459-468. **901**

Staats, A. W., & Staats, C. K. Meaning and *m*: Correlated but separate. *Psychological Review*, 1959, *66*, 136-144. **865**

Staats, C. K., *see* Staats, A. W., 1959.

Stainton, W. H. The phenomenon of Broca and Sulzer in foveal vision. *Journal of the Optical Society of America*, 1928, *16*, 26-39. **307**

Staner, B. J. Transfer as a function of simultaneous stimulus and response generalization. Unpublished master's thesis, Northwestern University, 1956. **1052, 1056**

Stanley, J. C., Jr., *see* Jenkins, W. O., 1950.

Stanley, W. C. Extinction as a function of the spacing of extinction trials. *Journal of Experimental Psychology*, 1952, *43*, 249-260. **576, 695**

Stanley, W. C., & Elliot, O. Differential human handling as reinforcing events and as treatments influencing later social behavior in basenji puppies. *Psychological Reports*, 1962, *10*, 775-788. **704**

Stark, K., *see* Postman, L., 1964, 1965, 1967, 1968, 1969.

Stark, L. Stability, oscillations, and noise in the human pupil servomechanism. *Proceedings of the Institute of Radio Engineers*, 1959, *47*, 1925-1939. **392**

Stavrianos, B. K. The relation of shape perception to explicit judgments of inclination. *Archives of Psychology*, 1945, *296*. **499, 515, 516**

Stearns, E. M. Reward value of saline and water for the rat. *Psychonomic Science*, 1965, *2*, 193-194. **190**

Stebbins, W. C. Auditory reaction time and the derivation of equal loudness contours for the monkey. *Journal of the Experimental Analysis of Behavior*, 1966, *9*, 135-142. **757**

Stebbins, W. C., *see also* Sidman, M., 1954.

Steele, W. M., *see* Cameron, E. H., 1905.

Steffy, R. A., *see* Eriksen, C. W., 1964.

Stein, L. Secondary reinforcement established with subcortical stimulation. *Science*, 1958, *127*, 466-467. **655, 674, 675**

Stein, L. Reciprocal action of reward and punishment mechanism. In R. Heath (Ed.), *The role of pleasure in behavior*. New York: Hoeber, 1964. Pp. 113-139. **647**

Stein, L., Sidman, M., & Brady, J. V. Some effects of two temporal variables on conditioned suppression. *Journal of the Experimental Analysis of Behavior*, 1958, *1*, 153-162. **713, 716**

Stein, L., *see also* Ray, O. S., 1959.

Steinberg, J. C., & Gardner, M. B. The dependence of hearing impairment on sound intensity. *Journal of the Acoustical Society of America*, 1937, *9*, 11-23. **240**

Steiner, S. S., Beer, B., & Shaffer, M. M. Escape from self-produced rates of brain-stimulation. *Science*, 1968, *163*, 90-91. **692**

Steiner, W. G. Electrical activity of rat brain as a correlate of primary drive. *Electroencephalography and Clinical Neurophysiology*, 1962, *14*, 233-243. **837**

Steinig, K. Untersuchungen über die Wahrnehmung der Bewegung durch das Auge: IV. *Zeitschrift für Psychologie*, 1929, *109*, 291-336. **527**

Steinmeyer, C. H., *see* Levine, M., 1967.

Stellar, E., & Hill, J. H. The rat's rate of drinking as a function of water deprivation. *Journal of Comparative and Physiological Psychology*, 1952, *45*, 96-102. **622, 813, 814, 818**

Stellar, E., *see also* Corbit, J. D., 1964; Pfaffmann, C., 1954.

Stellwagen, W. T., & Card, G. W. Human learning in multiple T-maze: An investigation of verbal and motor learning modes. *Psychonomic Science*, 1965, *2*, 227-228. **698**

Stenson, H. H. The physical factor structure of random forms and their judged complexity. *Perception and Psychophysics*, 1966, *1*, 303-310. **449**

Sterman, M. B., & Wyrwicka, W. EEG correlates of sleep: Evidence for separate forebrain substrates. *Brain Research*, 1967, *6*, 143-163. **838**

Sterman, M. B., *see also* Clemente, C. D., 1964; Roth, S. R., 1967; Wyrwicka, W., 1962.

Stern, J. A., *see* Gross, K., 1967; Hahn, W. W., 1962, 1964.

Sternbach, R. A. *Pain: A psychophysical analysis*. New York: Academic Press, 1968. **122, 155, 157**

Sternberg, S. Stochastic learning theory. In R. D. Luce, R. R. Bush, & E. Galanter (Eds.), *Handbook of mathematical psychology*. Vol. II. New York: Wiley, 1963. Pp. 9-120. **912n**

Stetson, R. H., & McDill, J. A. Mechanism of the different types of movement with a preliminary report of experimental data. *Psychological Monographs*, 1923, *32*, 18-40. **379**

Stettner, L. J., *see* Moltz, H., 1960.

Stevens, C. F. *Neurophysiology: A primer*. New York: Wiley, 1966. **95**

Stevens, C. F. Synaptic physiology. *Proceedings of the IEEE*, 1968, *56*, 915-930. **90**

Stevens, J. C., & Guirao, N. Individual loudness functions. *Journal of the Acoustical Society of America*, 1964, *36*, 2210-2213. **247**

Stevens, J. C., & Stevens, S. S. Warmth and cold: Dynamics of sensory intensity. *Journal of Experimental Psychology*, 1960, *60*, 183-192. **80**

Stevens, J. C., & Stevens, S. S. Brightness function: Effects of adaptation. *Journal of the Optical Society of America*, 1963, *53*, 375-385. **81**

Stevens, J. C., *see also* Marks, L. E., 1966; Scharf, B., 1959; Stevens, S. S., 1960.

Stevens, K. N., *see* Rosenblith, W. A., 1953.

Stevens, S. S. A scale for the measurement of a psychological magnitude: Loudness. *Psychological Review*, 1936, *43*, 405-416. **67**

Stevens, S. S. (Ed.). *Handbook of experimental psychology*. New York: Wiley, 1951. **17, 48, 316**

Stevens, S. S. Mathematics, measurement, and psychophysics. In S. S. Stevens (Ed.), *Handbook of experimental psychology*. New York: Wiley, 1951. Pp. 1-49. **833**

Stevens, S. S. The measurement of loudness. *Journal of the Acoustical Society of America*, 1955, *27*, 815-829. **247**

Stevens, S. S. On the averaging of data. *Science*, 1955, *121*, 113-116. **65**

Stevens, S. S. Calculation of the loudness of complex noises. *Journal of the Acoustical Society of America*, 1956, *28*, 807-832. (a) **248, 249**

Stevens, S. S. The direct estimation of sensory magnitudes—loudness. *American Journal of Psychology*, 1956, 69, 1–25. (b) **247**

Stevens, S. S. On the psychophysical law. *Psychological Review*, 1957, 64, 153–181. **69, 82, 928**

Stevens, S. S. Problems and methods of psychophysics. *Psychological Bulletin*, 1958, 54, 177–196. **86**

Stevens, S. S. Cross-modality validation of subjective scales for loudness, vibration, and electric shock. *Journal of Experimental Psychology*, 1959, 57, 201–209. **84**

Stevens, S. S. On the new psychophysics. *Scandinavian Journal of Psychology*, 1960, 1, 27–35. **175**

Stevens, S. S. Is there a quantal threshold? In W. A. Rosenblith (Ed.), *Sensory communication*. New York: Wiley, 1961. **34**

Stevens, S. S. The psychophysics of sensory function. In W. A. Rosenblith (Ed.), *Sensory communication*. New York: Wiley, 1961. **79, 247**

Stevens, S. S. The basis of psychophysical judgments. *Journal of the Acoustical Society of America*, 1963, 35, 611–612. **248**

Stevens, S. S. Matching functions between loudness and ten other continua. *Perception and Psychophysics*, 1966, 1, 5–8. **84**

Stevens, S. S., & Davis, H. *Hearing*. New York: Wiley, 1938. **228, 230, 233, 244, 249**

Stevens, S. S., & Galanter, E. H. Ratio scales and category scales for dozen perceptual continua. *Journal of Experimental Psychology*, 1957, 54, 377–411. **65, 82**

Stevens, S. S., & Greenbaum, H. B. Regression effects in psychophysical judgment. *Perception and Psychophysics*, 1966, 1, 439–446. **84**

Stevens, S. S., & Guirao, N. Loudness, reciprocality, and partition scales. *Journal of the Acoustical Society of America*, 1962, 34, 1466–1471. **248**

Stevens, S. S., Morgan, C. T., & Volkmann, J. Theory of neural quantum in the discrimination of loudness and pitch. *American Journal of Psychology*, 1941, 54, 315–35. **33**

Stevens, S. S., & Newman, E. B. The localization of actual sources of sound. *American Journal of Psychology*, 1936, 48, 297–306. **266**

Stevens, S. S., & Poulton, E. C. The estimation of loudness by unpracticed observers. *Journal of Experimental Psychology*, 1956, 51, 71–78. **70**

Stevens, S. S., & Stevens, J. C. Brightness function: Parametric effects of adaptation and contrast. *Journal of the Optical Society of America*, 1960, 50, 1139. **411**

Stevens, S. S., & Volkmann, J. The relation of pitch to frequency, a revised scale. *American Journal of Psychology*, 1940, 53, 329–353. **67, 244**

Stevens, S. S., & Warshofsky, F. *Sound and hearing*. New York: Time, Inc., 1965. **270**

Stevens, S. S., *see also* Harper, R. S., 1948; Hawkins, J. E. Jr., 1950; Hudgins, C. V., 1947; Lane, H. L., 1961; Reese, T. S., 1960; Stevens, J. C., 1960, 1963.

Stevenson, H. W., & Bitterman, M. E. The distance-effect in the transposition of intermediate size by children. *American Journal of Psychology*, 1955, 68, 274–279. **765**

Stevenson, H. W., Iscoe, I., & McConnell, C. A developmental study of transposition. *Journal of Experimental Psychology*, 1955, 49, 278–280. **765**

Stevenson, J. A. F., & Rixon, R. H. Environmental temperature and deprivation of food and water on the spontaneous activity of rats. *Yale Journal of Biology and Medicine*, 1957, 29, 575–584. **824**

Stevenson, J. A. F., *see also* Morgenson, G. J., 1966.

Stevenson, J. G. Reinforcing effects of chaffinch song. *Animal Behaviour*, 1967, 15, 427–432. **693**

Stevenson, J. G. Song as a reinforcer. In R. A. Hinde (Ed.), *Bird vocalizations in relation to current problems in biology and psychology*. Cambridge: Cambridge University Press, 1969. **693**

Stevenson, J. G., & Reese, T. W. The effect of two schedules of primary and conditioned reinforcement. *Journal of the Experimental Analysis of Behavior*, 1962, 5, 505–510. **671**

Steward, J. R., *see* Bousfield, W. A., 1961.

Stewart, E. C. The Gelb effect. *Journal of Experimental Psychology*, 1959, 57, 235–242. **419**

Stewart, M. R., *see* Fagot, R. F., 1968.

Stigler, R. Chronophotische Studien über der Umgebungskontrast. *Pflügers Archiv für die gesamte Physiologie*, 1910, 134, 365–435. **429**

Stiles, W. S. Visual properties studied by subjective measurements on the colour-adapted eye. *British Medical Bulletin*, 1953, 9, 41–49. **342**

Stiles, W. S. Color vision: The approach through increment threshold sensitivity. *Proceedings of the National Academy of Science*, 1959, 45, 100. **341**

Stiles, W. S., & Crawford, B. H. The luminous efficiency of rays entering the eye pupil at different points. *Proceedings of the Royal Society* (London), Ser. B, 1933, 112, 428–450. **302**

Stiles, W. S., & Crawford, B. The luminal brightness increment as a function of wavelength for different conditions of the foveal and parafoveal retina. *Proceedings of the Royal Society* (London), Ser. B, 1934, 113, 496–530. **334, 337**

Stiles, W. S., *see also* Wyszecki, G., 1967.

Stockwell, F. E., *see* Cieutat, V. J., 1958; Noble, C. E., 1957.

Stokes, L. W., *see* Bolles, R. C., 1965.

Stolurow, L. M. Rodent behavior in the presence of barriers: II. The metabolic maintenance method; A technique for caloric drive control and manipulation. *Journal of Genetic Psychology*, 1951, 79, 289–335. **812, 826**

Stolwijk, J. A. J., *see* Hardy, J. D., 1968.

Stone, H. Determination of odor difference limens for three compounds. *Journal of Experimental Psychology*, 1963, 66, 466–473. (a) **202**

Stone, H. Techniques for odor measurement: Olfactometric vs. sniffing. *Journal of Food Science*, 1963, 28, 719–725. (b) **198, 201**

Stone, H. Behavioral aspects of absolute and differential olfactory sensitivity. *Annals of the New York Academy of Science*, 1964, 2, 527–534. **18, 199**

Stone, H., & Bosley, J. Olfactory discrimination and Weber's Law. *Perceptual and Motor Skills*, 1965, 20, 657–665. **202**

Stone, H., Ough C. S., & Pangborn, R. M. Determination of odor difference thresholds. *Journal of Food Science*, 1962, 27, 197–202. **202**

Stone, H., *see also* Ough, C. S., 1961.

Stone, L. J., & Dallenbach, K. M. Adaptation to the pain of radiant heat. *American Journal of Psychology*, 1934, 46, 229–242. **159**

Stone, P. J., *see* Hunt, E. B., 1966.

Storms, L. H. Apparent backward association: A situational effect. *Journal of Experimental Psychology*, 1958, 55, 390–395. **872**

Storms, L. H., *see also* Russell, W. A., 1955.

Story, A. Figural after-effects as a function of the perceived characteristics of the inspection figure. *American Journal of Psychology*, 1959, 72, 46–56. **530**

Strassburger, F., & Wertheimer, M. The discrepancy hypothesis of affect and association values of nonsense syllables. *Psychological Reports*, 1959, 5, 528. **900**

Stratton, G. M. Some preliminary experiments on vision without inversion of the retinal image. *Psychological Review*, 1896, 3, 611–617. **533**

Stratton, G. M. Upright vision and the retinal image. *Psychological Review*, 1897, 4, 182–187. **533**

Stratton, G. M. The psychology of change: How is the perception of movement related to that of succession? *Psychological Review*, 1911, 18, 262–293. **527**

Straughan, J. H., *see* Estes, W. K., 1954.

Ström, L., see Borg, G., 1967; Diamant, H., 1963; Hensel, H., 1951.

Studdert-Kennedy, M., see Liberman, A. M., 1967.

Stuiver, M. *Biophysics of the sense of smell.* Doctoral dissertation, University of Groningen, Netherlands, 1958. **200, 202, 210, 211**

Su, J., Berkley, M. A., Terman, M., & Kling, J. W. Rate of intracranial self-stimulation as a function of stimulus waveform and intensity. *Psychonomic Science*, 1966, *5*, 219-220. **646**

Suci, G. J., see Jenkins, J. J., 1958, 1959.

Sulzer, D., see Broca, A., 1903.

Sumby, W. H., & Pollack, I. Visual contribution to speech intelligibility. *Journal of the Acoustical Society of America*, 1954, *26*, 212-215. **256**

Summers, D. A., see Hammond, K. R., 1965.

Supa, M., Cotzin, M., & Dallenbach, K. M. "Facial vision": The perception of obstacles by the blind. *American Journal of Psychology*, 1944, *57*, 133-183. **270**

Suppes, P. *Introduction to logic.* Princeton, N.J.: Van Nostrand, 1957. **906, 943**

Suppes, P., & Atkinson, R. C. *Markov learning models for multiperson interactions.* Stanford: Stanford University Press, 1960. **934, 990**

Suppes, P. & Frankmann, R. W. Test of stimulus sampling theory for a continuum of responses with unimodal non-contingent determinant reinforcement. *Journal of Experimental Psychology*, 1961, *61*, 122-132. **934**

Suppes, P., & Ginsberg, R. A fundamental property of all-or-none models, binominal distribution of responses prior to conditioning, with application to concept formation in children. *Psychological Review*, 1963, *70*, 139-161. **951, 952, 996**

Suppes, P., Groen, G., & Schlag-Rey, M. A model for response latency in paired-associate learning. *Journal of Mathematical Psychology*, 1966, *3*, 99-128. **957**

Suppes, P., Rouanet, H., Levine, M., & Frankmann, R. W. Empirical comparison of models for a continuum of responses with non-contingent bimodal reinforcement. In R. C. Atkinson (Ed.), *Studies in mathematical psychology.* Stanford: Stanford University Press, 1964. Pp. 358-379. **934**

Suppes, P., & Zinnes, J. L. Stochastic learning theories for a response continuum with nondeterminant reinforcement. *Psychometrika*, 1961, *26*, 373-390. **934**

Suppes, P., & Zinnes, J. L. A continuous-response task with nondeterminant, contingent reinforcement. *Journal of Mathematical Psychology*, 1966, *3*, 197-216. **934**

Suppes, P., see also Estes, W. K., 1959; Luce, R. D., 1965; Roberts, F. S., 1967.

Sutherland, N. S. Figural after-effects and apparent size. *Quarterly Journal of Experimental Psychology*, 1961, *13*, 117-121. **522**

Sutherland, N. S. Stimulus analyzing mechanisms. In *Proceedings of a symposium on the mechanization of thought processes.* Vol. II. London: Her Majesty's Stationery Office, 1959. Pp. 575-609. **1001**

Suydam, M. M., see Myers, J. L., 1963, 1966.

Svaetichin, G. The cone action potential. *Acta Physiologica Scandinavica*, 1956, *39*, 17-46. **324**

Svaetichin, G., & MacNichol, E. F. Retinal mechanisms for chromatic and achromatic vision. *Annals of the New York Academy of Science*, 1958, *74*, 385. **334**

Svaetichin, G., see also MacNichol, E. F., Jr., 1958.

Swanson, R., & Benton A. L. Some aspects of the genetic development of right-left discrimination. *Child Development*, 1955, *26*, 123-133. **540**

Sweet, W. Pain. In J. Field (Ed.), *Handbook of physiology: Neurophysiology.* Sec. 1, Vol. 1. Washington, D.C.: American Physiological Society, 1959. Pp. 459-506. **162**

Sweet, W. H., see also Wall, P. D., 1967; White, J. C., 1955.

Swenson, E. J. *Retroactive inhibition: A review of the literature.* Minneapolis: University of Minnesota Press, 1941. **1088**

Swenson, H. A. The relative influence of accommodation and convergence in the judgment of distance. *Journal of General Psychology*, 1932, *7*, 360-380. **480**

Swets, J. A. Central factors in auditory frequency selectivity. *Psychological Bulletin*, 1963, *60*, 429-440. **240**

Swets, J. A. Is there a sensory threshold? *Science*, 1961, *134*, 168-177. Also in J. A. Swets, *Signal detection and recognition by human observers.* New York: Wiley, 1964. **32**

Swets, J. A., Tanner, W. P., & Birdsall, T. G. Decision processes in perception. *Psychological Review*, 1961, *68*, 301-340. **34**

Swets, J. A., see also Green, D. M., 1966.

Talbot, S. A., see Marshall, W. H., 1942.

Talbot, W. H., see Mountcastle, V. B., 1967.

Tallantis, B., see Grant, D. A., 1949.

Tallarico, R. B. Studies of visual depth perception: III. Choice behavior of newly hatched chicks on a visual cliff. *Perceptual and Motor Skills*, 1961, *12*, 259-262. **549**

Tallarico, R. B., & Farrell, W. M. Studies of visual depth perception: An effect of early experience on chicks on a visual cliff. *Journal of Comparative and Physiological Psychology*, 1964, *57*, 94-96. **549**

Tanaka, K. Developmental studies on size constancy. In Y. Akishige (Ed.), *Experimental researches on the structure of the perceptual space.* Bull. of the Faculty of Literature of Kyushu University, No. 10, Fukuoka, Japan, 1967. **550**

Tanner, W. P., see Swets, J. A., 1961.

Tasaki, I., Davis, H., & Eldredge, D. H. Exploration of cochlear potentials in guinea pig with a microelectrode. *Journal of the Acoustical Society of America*, 1954, *26*, 765-773. **230**

Tasaki, I., Davis, H., & LeGouix, J. P. Space-time pattern of the cochlear microphonics (guinea pig) as recorded by differential electrodes. *Journal of the Acoustical Society of America*, 1952, *24*, 502-519. **230**

Tasaki, I., see also Maruhashi, J., 1952.

Tateda, H., & Beidler, L. M. The receptor potential of the taste cell of the rat. *Journal of General Physiology*, 1964, *47*, 479-486. **180**

Taub, E., & Berman, A. J. Movement and learning in the absence of sensory feedback. In S. J. Freedman (Ed.), *The neuropsychology of spatially oriented behavior.* Homewood, Ill.: Dorsey Press, 1968. **533**

Taub, T., see Glanzer, M., in press.

Tauc, L., see Bruner, J., 1966; Kandel, E. R., 1965.

Tausch, R. Optische Täuschungen als artifizielle Effekte der Gestaltungsprozesse von Grössen und Formenkonstanz in der natürlichen Raumwahrnehmung. *Psychologische Forschung*, 1954, *24*, 299-348. **460, 462**

Taylor, E., see Smith, O. A. Jr., 1961.

Taylor, J. A. Drive theory and manifest anxiety. *Psychological Bulletin*, 1956, *53*, 303-320. **789**

Taylor, J. G. *The behavioral basis of perception.* New Haven: Yale University Press, 1962. **453, 533, 542, 543n**

Taylor, R. W., see Jeffress, L. A., 1961.

Taylor, W. C., see Miller, G. A., 1948.

Teas, D. Lateralization of acoustic transients. *Journal of the Acoustical Society of America*, 1962, *34*, 1460-1465. **263**

Teas, D. C., Eldredge, D. H., & Davis, H. Cochlear responses to acoustic transients: An interpretation of whole-nerve action potentials. *Journal of the Acoustical Society of America*, 1962, *34*, 1438-1459. **230**

Teas, D. C., see also Feddersen, W. E., 1957; Sandel, T. T., 1955.

Tees, R. C., & More, L. K. Effect of amount of perceptual learning upon disappearances observed under reduced

Thorndike, E. L., & Woodworth, R. S. The influence of improvement in one mental function upon the efficiency of other functions. *Psychological Review,* 1901, *8,* 247–261, 384–395, 553–564. **1031**

Thornton, D. W., *see* Jones, A., 1967.

Thornton, G. B., *see* Tulving, E., 1959.

Thorpe, W. H. *Learning and instinct in animals.* 2nd ed. Cambridge: Harvard University Press, 1963. **556, 581, 584, 587, 588, 591, 592, 697**

Thorpe, W. H., *see also* Hinde, R. A., 1956.

Thouless, R. H. Phenomenal regression to the real object. *British Journal of Psychology,* 1931, *21,* 339–359; *22,* 1–30. **515**

Thumb, A., & Marbe, K. *Experimentelle Untersuchungen über die psychologischen Grundlagen der sprachlichen Analogiebildung.* Leipzig: W. Englemann, 1901. **861**

Thune, E. L. The effect of different types of preliminary activities on subsequent learning of paired-associate material. *Journal of Experimental Psychology,* 1950, *40,* 423–438. **1034, 1035**

Thune, L. E. Warm-up effect as a function of level of practice in verbal learning. *Journal of Experimental Psychology,* 1951, *42,* 250–256. **1034, 1036, 1037, 1045**

Thune, L. E., & Underwood, B. J. Retroactive inhibition as a function of degree of interpolated learning. *Journal of Experimental Psychology,* 1943, *32,* 185–200. **1086, 1090**

Thurlow, W. R. Studies in auditory theory: I. Binaural interaction and the perception of pitch. *Journal of Experimental Psychology,* 1943, *32,* 17–36. **244**

Thurlow, W. R. The perception of the pitch of high frequencies. *American Psychologist,* 1946, *1,* 255. **243**

Thurlow, W. R. Perception of low auditory pitch: A multicue, mediation theory. *Psychological Review,* 1963, *70,* 461–470. **246**

Thurlow, W. R. Audition. In P. Farnsworth (Ed.), *Annual review of psychology,* Vol. 16. Palo Alto, Calif.: Annual Reviews, 1965. **243**

Thurlow, W. R., & Bernstein, S. Simultaneous two-tone pitch discrimination. *Journal of the Acoustical Society of America,* 1957, *29,* 515–519. **250**

Thurlow, W. R., & Elfner, L. F. Pure-tone cross-ear localization effects. *Journal of the Acoustical Society of America,* 1959, *31,* 1606–1608. **263, 266**

Thurlow, W. R., & Elfner, L. F. Localization effects with steady thermal noise in one ear and pulsed thermal noise in the other. *Science,* 1961, *134,* 617–618. **263**

Thurlow, W. R., Gross, N. B., Kemp, E. H., & Lowy, K. Microelectrode studies of neural auditory activity of cat: I. Inferior colliculus. *Journal of Neurophysiology,* 1951, *14,* 289–304. **232**

Thurlow, W. R., & Hartman, T. F. The "missing fundamental" and related pitch effects. *Perceptual and Motor Skills,* 1959, *9,* 315–324. **246**

Thurlow, W. R., Mangels, J. W., & Runge, P. S. Head movements during sound localization. *Journal of the Acoustical Society of America,* 1967, *42,* 489–493. **267**

Thurlow, W. R., & Marten, A. E. Perception of steady and intermittent sound with alternating noise-burst stimuli. *Journal of the Acoustical Society of America,* 1962, *34,* 1853–1858. **265**

Thurlow, W. R., Marten, A. E., & Bhatt, B. J. Localization after-effects with pulse-tone and pulse–pulse stimuli. *Journal of the Acoustical Society of America,* 1965, *37,* 837–842. **265, 266**

Thurlow, W. R., & Melamed, L. E. Some new hypotheses on the mediation of loudness judgments. *Perception and Psychophysics,* 1967, *2,* 77–80. **248**

Thurlow, W. R., Parks, T. E. Precedence-suppression effects for two click sources. *Perceptual and Motor Skills,* 1961, *13,* 7–12. **268**

Thurlow, W. R., & Rawlings, I. L. Discrimination of number of simultaneously sounding tones. *Journal of the Acoustical Society of America,* 1959, *31,* 1332–1336. **250**

Thurlow, W. R., & Runge, P. S. Effect of induced head movements on localization of direction of sounds. *Journal of the Acoustical Society of America,* 1967, *42,* 480–488. **267, 268**

Thurlow, W. R., & Small, A. M., Jr. Pitch perception for certain periodic auditory stimuli. *Journal of the Acoustical Society of America,* 1955, *27,* 132–137. **245**

Thurlow, W. R., *see also* Small, A. M. Jr., 1954.

Thurston, E., *see* Washburn, M. F., 1934.

Thurstone, L. L. Psychophysical analysis. *American Journal of Psychology,* 1927, *38,* 368–389. (a). Also in L. L. Thurstone, *The measurement of values.* Chicago: University of Chicago Press, 1959. **51**

Thurstone, L. L. A law of comparative judgment. *Psychological Review,* 1927, *34,* 273–286. (b). Also in L. L. Thurstone, *The measurement of values.* Chicago: University of Chicago Press, 1959. **53**

Thurstone, L. L. The phi-gamma hypothesis. *Journal of Experimental Psychology,* 1928, *9,* 293–305. Also in L. L. Thurstone, *The measurement of values.* Chicago: University of Chicago Press, 1959. **32**

Thwing, E. J., *see* Egan, J. P., 1954.

Thysell, R., *see* Schulz, R. W., 1965.

Tighe, T. J., *see* Gibson, E. J., 1958, 1959; Walk, R. D., 1957.

Tilman, T. W., *see* Carhart, R., 1967.

Tinbergen, N. *The study of instinct.* Oxford: Clarendon Press, 1951. **745**

Tinbergen, N. The curious behavior of the stickleback. *Scientific American,* 1952, *187,* 22–26. **745**

Tinker, M. A. Reliability and validity of eye-movement measures of reading. *Journal of Experimental Psychology,* 1936, *19,* 732–746. **390**

Tinklepaugh, O. L. An experimental study of representative factors in monkeys. *Journal of Comparative Psychology,* 1928, *8,* 197–236. **689**

Titchener, E. B. *An outline of psychology.* New York: Macmillan, 1902. **403, 453, 527**

Titchener, E. B. *Experimental psychology: Vol. II. Quantitative.* New York: Macmillan, 1905. **14, 15**

Titchener, E. B. *Experimental psychology; Vol. II. Quantitative.* Part II. Instructors Manual. New York: Macmillan, 1905. **65, 66, 73**

Tobias, J. V., & Zerlin, S. Lateralization threshold as a function of stimulus duration. *Journal of the Acoustical Society of America,* 1959, *31,* 1591–1594. **263**

Todd, T. C., *see* Vitz, P. C., 1969.

Toffey, S., *see* Hoffman, H. S., 1966.

Tolman, E. C. *Purposive behavior in animals and men.* New York: Appleton, 1932. (Reprinted, University of California Press, 1949). **560n, 597, 662, 679, 681, 697, 741**

Tolman, E. C. Prediction of vicarious trial and error by means of the schematic sowbug. *Psychological Review,* 1939, *46,* 318–336. **749, 784**

Tolman, E. C. Discrimination versus learning and the schematic sowbug. *Psychological Review,* 1941, *48,* 367–382. **784**

Tolman, E. C. Cognitive maps in rats and men. *Psychological Review,* 1948, *55,* 189–208. **568**

Tolman, E. C. Principles of purposive behavior. In S. Koch (Ed.), *Psychology: A study of a science,* Vol 2. New York: McGraw-Hill, 1959. **560n**

Tolman, E. C., & Brunswik, E. The organism and the causal texture of the environment. *Psychological Review,* 1935, *42,* 43–77. **462**

Tolman, E. C., & Krechevsky, I. Means-end readiness and hypothesis: A contribution to comparative psychology. *Psychological Review,* 1933, *40,* 60–70. **765**

Tolman, E. C., & Minium, E. VTE in rats: Overlearning and

difficulty of discrimination. *Journal of Comparative Psychology*, 1942, *34*, 301–306. **784**

Toman, J. E. P., *see* Smith, S. M., 1947.

Tomita, T. Electrophysiological study of mechanisms subserving color coding in the fish retina. *Cold Spring Harbor Symposia on Quantitative Biology*, 1966, *30*, 559–566. **325**

Tomita, T., Kaneko, A., Murakami, M., & Pautler, E. L. Spectral response curves of single cones in the carp. *Vision Research*, 1967, *7*, 519–531. **308, 325**

Tomita, T., et al. Personal communication, 1968. **295**

Tonndorf, J. Harmonic distortion in cochlear models. *Journal of the Acoustical Society of America*, 1958, *30*, 929–937. **239**

Toole, F. E., *see* Sayers, B. McA., 1964.

Torgerson, W. S. *Theory and methods of scaling*. New York: Wiley, 1958. **53, 54, 57, 70, 71, 72**

Torgerson, W. S. Quantitative judgment scales. In H. Gullicksen & S. Messick (Eds.), *Psychological scaling*. New York: Wiley, 1960. **248**

Torgerson, W. S. Distances and ratios in psychophysical scaling. *Acta Psychologica* (Amsterdam), 1961, *19*, 201–205. **248**

Torii, S., *see* Oyama, T., 1955.

Trabasso, D., *see* Bower, G. H., 1963.

Trabasso, T. Additivity of cues in discrimination learning of letter patterns. *Journal of Experimental Psychology*, 1960, *60*, 83–88. **957**

Trabasso, T. Stimulus emphasis and all-or-none learning of concept identification. *Journal of Experimental Psychology*, 1963, *65*, 395–406. **957, 961**

Trabasso, T., & Bower, G. H. Component learning in the four-category concept problem. *Journal of Mathematical Psychology*, 1964, *1*, 143–169. (a) **958, 964, 975**

Trabasso, T., & Bower, G. H. Memory in concept identification. *Psychonomic Science*, 1964, *1*, 133–134. (b) **960, 973**

Trabasso, T., & Bower, G. H. Presolution dimensional shifts in concept identification: A test of the sampling with replacement axiom in all-or-none models. *Journal of Mathematical Psychology*, 1966, *3*, 163–173. **956, 957, 970, 978**

Trabasso, T. R., *see also* Bower, G. H., 1964; Friedman, M., 1967; Wonant, M. V., 1964.

Trapold, M. A. The effect of incentive motivation on an unrelated reflex response. *Journal of Comparative and Physiological Psychology*, 1962, *55*, 1034–1039. **808**

Trapold, M. A., & Fowler, H. Instrumental escape performance as a function of the intensity of noxious stimulation. *Journal of Experimental Psychology*, 1960, *60*, 323–326. **720, 721**

Trapold, M. A., *see also* Bower, G. H., 1959; Fowler, H., 1962.

Trattner, J., *see* Eisenberger, R., 1967.

Travis, A. M., & Woolsey, C. N. Motor performance of monkeys after bilateral partial and total cerebral decortications. *American Journal of Physical Medicine*. 1956, *35*, 273–310. **845**

Treichler, F. R., *see* Meyer, D. R., 1965.

Treisman, A. Contextual cues in selective listening. *Quarterly Journal of Experimental Psychology*, 1960, *12*, 242–248. **259**

Treisman, A. Binocular rivalry and stereoscopic depth perception. *Quarterly Journal of Experimental Psychology*, 1962, *14*, 23–37. **492**

Treisman, A. Monitoring and storage of irrelevant messages in selective attention. *Journal of Verbal Learning and Verbal Behavior*, 1964, *3*, 449–459. **259**

Treisman, M. Sensory scaling and the psychophysical law. *Quarterly Journal of Experimental Psychology*, 1964, *16*, 11–22. (a) **84**

Treisman, M. What do sensory scales measure? *Quarterly Journal of Experimental Psychology*, 1964, *16*, 385–391. (b) **84**

Tresselt, M. E., *see* Mayzner, M. S., 1962, 1964, 1965a, b, c.

Triebel, W., *see* Hochberg, J. E., 1951, 1955.

Triedman, R. H., *see* Boynton, R. M., 1953.

Troland, L. The "all or none law" in visual response. *Journal of the Optical Society of America*, 1920, *4*, 161–186. **286**

Trowill, J., *see* Gandelman, R., 1968.

Trumble, G., *see* Beer, B., 1965.

Trychin, S. Jr., *see* Walk, R. D., 1965.

Tschermak-Seysenegg, A. Über Parallaktoskopie. *Pflügers Archiv für Physiologie*, 1939, *241*, 455–469. **486**

Tucker, D. Physiology of olfaction. *Annual Symposium of American Society of Perfumers*, April 13, 1961. **208**

Tucker, D. Physical variables in the olfactory stimulation process. *Journal of General Physiology*, 1963, *46*, 453–489. (a) **200, 207**

Tucker, D. Olfactory, vomeronasal and trigeminal receptor responses to odorants. In Y. Zotterman (Ed.), *Olfaction and taste*. New York: Pergamon, 1963, 45–69. (b) **207**

Tucker, D., & Shibuya, T. A physiologic and pharmacologic study of olfactory receptors. *Cold Spring Harbor Symposia on Quantitative Biology*, 1965, *30*, 207–215. **194**

Tucker, D., *see also* Beidler, L. M., 1956; Henton, W. W., 1966.

Tulunay, S. U., *see* Riggs, L. A., 1959.

Tulunay, Ü., *see* Engen, T., 1956.

Tulving, E. Subjective organization in free recall of "unrelated" words. *Psychological Review*, 1962, *69*, 344–354. **855, 1043, 1045**

Tulving, E. Theoretical issues in free recall. In T. R. Dixon & D. L. Horton (Eds.), *Verbal behavior and general behavior theory*. Englewood Cliffs, N.J.: Prentice-Hall, 1968. **1043, 1101**

Tulving, E., & Arbuckle, T. Sources of intra-trial interference in immediate recall of paired associates. *Journal of Verbal Learning and Verbal Behavior*, 1963, *1*, 321–324. **1118**

Tulving, E., & Arbuckle, T. Input and output interference in short-term associative memory. *Journal of Experimental Psychology*, 1966, *72*, 145–150. **1118**

Tulving, E., McNulty, J. A., & Ozier, M. Vividness of words and learning to learn in free-recall learning. *Canadian Journal of Psychology*, 1965, *19*, 242–252. **1044, 1045**

Tulving, E., & Thornton, G. B. Interaction between proaction and retroaction in short-term retention. *Canadian Journal of Psychology*, 1959, *13*, 255–265. **1101**

Tulving, E., *see also* Freibergs, V., 1961; Heinemann, E. G., 1959.

Tunturi, A. R. Anatomy and physiology of the auditory cortex. In G. Rasmussen & W. F. Windle (Eds.), *Neural mechanisms of the auditory and vestibular systems*. Springfield, Ill.: Charles C Thomas, 1960. **232**

Turnage, T. W. Unit-sequence interference in short-term memory. *Journal of Verbal Learning and Verbal Behavior*, 1967, *6*, 61–65. **1128**

Turnage, T., & Anderson, N. Letter-frequency and associative probability as determinants of learning and retention. *Journal of Verbal Learning and Verbal Behavior*, 1965, *4*, 463–468. **1129**

Turnbull, W. W. Pitch discrimination as a function of tonal duration. *Journal of Experimental Psychology*, 1944, *34*, 302–316. **249**

Turner, L. H., & Solomon, R. L. Human traumatic avoidance learning: Theory and experiments on the operant-respondent distinction and failures to learn. *Psychological Monographs*, 1962, *76*, (Whole No. 559). **730**

Turner, L. H., *see also* Church, R. M., 1966; Solomon, R. L., 1962.

Turner, R. N., *see* Atkinson, R. C., 1959.

Turrisi, F. D., *see* Shepp, B. E., 1966.

Turvey, M. Analysis of augmented recall in short-term memory following a shift in connotation. *British Journal of Psychology*, 1968, *59*, 2, 131–137. **1117**

Twedt, H. M., & Underwood, B. J. Mixed vs. unmixed lists

in paired-associate learning. *American Journal of Psychology*, 1962, *75*, 353–371. **897**

Underwood, B. J., & Richardson, J. Some verbal materials for the study of concept formation. *Psychological Bulletin*, 1956, *53*, 84–95. (a) **881, 889**

Underwood, B. J., & Richardson, J. Verbal concept learning as a function of instructions and dominance level. *Journal of Experimental Psychology*, 1956, *51*, 229–238. (b) **881, 889**

Underwood, B. J., & Richardson, J. Some verbal materials for the study of concept formation. *Psychological Bulletin*, 1956, *53*, 84–95. **1078**

Underwood, B. J., Runquist, W. N., & Schulz, R. W. Response learning in paired-associate lists as a function of intra-list similarity. *Journal of Experimental Psychology*, 1959, *58*, 70–78. **893, 1007, 1060**

Underwood, B. J., & Schulz, R. W. *Meaningfulness and verbal learning.* Chicago: Lippincott, 1960. (a) **852, 853, 854, 856, 858, 892, 896, 897, 899, 900, 982, 1007, 1050, 1059**

Underwood, B. J., & Schulz, R. W. Response dominance and rate of learning paired-associates. *Journal of General Psychology*, 1960, *62*, 153–158. (b) **889**

Underwood, B. J., *see also* Archer, E. J., 1951; Barnes, J. M., 1959; Ekstrand, B. R., 1965, 1966; Feldman, S. M., 1957; Greenberg, R., 1950; Keppel, G., 1962a, b, 1967; McGeoch, J. A., 1943; Morgan, R. I., 1950; Scheible, H., 1954; Schwenn, E., 1965; Thune, L. E., 1943; Twedt, H. M., 1959.

Unger, S. M., *see* Caron, A. J., 1963.

Upchurch, R. L., *see* Cormack, R. H., 1969.

Uyeda, A. A., *see* Fuster, J. M., 1962; Seward, J. P., 1959.

Vainstein, E., *see* Orbach, J., 1963.

Valenstein, E. S. The anatomical locus of reinforcement. In E. Stellar & J. M. Sprague (Eds.), *Progress in physiological psychology.* Vol. 1. New York: Academic Press, 1966. **644, 647**

Valenstein, E. S., & Beer, B. Unipolar and bipolar electrodes in self-stimulation experiments. *American Journal of Physiology*, 1961, *201*, 1181–1186. **644**

Valenstein, E. S., & Beer, B. Continuous opportunity for reinforcing brain stimulation. *Journal of the Experimental Analysis of Behavior*, 1964, *7*, 183–184. **654**

Valenstein, E. S., & Meyers, W. J. Rate-independent test of reinforcing consequences of brain stimulation. *Journal of Comparative and Physiological Psychology*, 1964, *57*, 52–60. **649, 650**

Valenstein, E. S., & Weber, M. L. Potentiation of insulin coma by saccharin. *Journal of Comparative and Physiological Psychology*, 1965, *60*, 443–446. **797**

Valenstein, E. S., *see also* Beer, B., 1960; Hodos, W., 1962; Meyers, W. J., 1963.

Valsi, E., *see* Bartley, S. H., 1957.

Van Allen, M. W., *see* von Noorden, G. K., 1964.

van Bergeijk, W. A. Variation on a theme of Békésy: A model of binaural interaction. *Journal of the Acoustical Society of America*, 1962, *34*, 1431–1437. **264**

van Bergeijk, W. A., Pierce, J. R., & David, E. E., Jr. *Waves and the ear.* Garden City, New York: Doubleday, 1960. **227**

van Bergeijk, W. A., *see also* Guttman, N., 1960; David, E. E., 1958, 1959.

Vandenbelt, D. J., *see* Bartoshuk, L. M., 1969.

Vandercar, D. H., & Schneiderman, N. Interstimulus interval functions in different response systems during classical discrimination conditioning of rabbits. *Psychonomic Science*, 1967, *9*, 9–10. **558, 559**

Vanderplas, J. M., Sanderson, W. R., & Vanderplas, J. N. Statistical and associational characteristics of 1,100 random shapes. *Perceptual and Motor Skills*, 1965, *21*, 339–348. **449**

Vanderplas, J. M., *see also* Crawford, J. L., 1959.

Vanderplas, J. N., *see* Vanderplas, J. M., 1965.

Van Mondfrans, A. P., *see* Johnson, T. J., 1965.

Van Ormer, E. B. Retention after intervals of sleep and waking. *Archives of Psychology*, 1932, *21*, No. 137. **1123**

Varga, M. E., & Pressman, Y. M. On conditioned connections in the forward and reverse directions. In A. A. Airapetyan et al. (Eds.), *Central and peripheral mechanisms of nervous activity.* Erevan, USSR: Akademiya Nauk Armyanskoi SSR, 1966. (In Russian: English abstract by I. D. London in *Psychological Abstracts*, 1967, *41*, 1518.) **560n**

Varnadoe, K. W., *see* Clement, D. E., 1967.

Veer, R. A., *see* Jonkhees, L. B. W., 1958.

Vendrik, A. J. H., & Eijkman, E. G. Psychophysical properties determined with internal noise. In D. R. Kenshalo (Ed.), *The skin senses.* Springfield, Ill.: Charles C Thomas, 1968. Pp. 178–194. **147**

Vendrik, A. J. H., & Vos, J. J. Comparison of the stimulation of the warmth sense organ by microwave and infrared. *Journal of Applied Physiology*, 1958, *13*, 435–444. **153**

Veness, T. An experiment on slips of the tongue and word association faults. *Language and Speech*, 1962, *5*, 128–137. **866**

Verhoeff, F. H. The theory of binocular perspective. *American Journal of Physiological Optics*, 1925, *6*, 416. **466, 473**

Verhoeff, F. A new theory of binocular vision. *Archives of Ophthalmology*, 1935, *13*, 151–175. **488**

Verinis, J. S., *see* Rouse, R. O., 1965.

Vernon, M. D. The perception of inclined lines. *British Journal of Psychology*, 1934, *25*, 186–196. **466**

Verplanck, W. S. Burrhus F. Skinner. In W. K. Estes et al. (Eds.), *Modern learning theory.* New York: Appleton, 1954. **608**

Verplanck, W. S. The control of the content of conversation: Reinforcement of statements of opinion. *Journal of Abnormal and Social Psychology*, 1955, *51*, 668–676. **908n**

Verplanck, W. S., & Hayes, J. R. Eating and drinking as a function of maintenance schedule. *Journal of Comparative and Physiological Psychology*, 1953, *46*, 327–333. **669, 816**

Verrillo, R. T. Vibrotactile thresholds for hairy skin. *Journal of Experimental Psychology*, 1966, *72*, 47–50. **135**

Verrillo, R. T. A duplex mechanism of mechanoreception. In D. R. Kenshalo (Ed.), *The skin senses.* Springfield, Ill.: Charles C Thomas, 1968. Pp. 139–159. **135, 137**

Versace, J., *see* Ross, L., 1953.

Victor, J., *see* Rock, I., 1964.

Vierordt, K. *Der Zeitsinn nach Versuchen: Scheinbare Verzerrung bewegter Gegenstände.* Tübingen: H. Laupp, 1868.

Vilter, V. Nouvelle conception de relations synaptiques dans la photoperception par les cônes rétiniens. *Comptes Rendus ses Séances de la Société de Biologie* (Paris), 1949, *143*, 338–341. **303**

Vinacke, W. E. The investigation of concept formation. *Psychological Bulletin*, 1951, *48*, 1–31. **786**

Vince, M. A., *see* Hinde, R. A., 1956.

Vincent, R. J., Brown, B. R., Markley, R. P., & Arnoult, M. D. Distance discrimination in a simulated space environment. *Perception and Psychophysics*, 1969, *5*, 235–238. **494**

Vincent, S. B. The function of the vibrissae in the behavior of the white rat. *Behavioral Monographs*, 1912, *5*. **612**

Virsu, V. Contrast and confluxion as components in geometric illusions. *Quarterly Journal of Experimental Psychology*, 1967, *19*, 198–207. **461, 463**

Vitz, P. C., & Todd, T. C. A coded element model of the

perceptual processing of sequential stimuli. *Psychological Review,* 1969, *76,* 433-449. **448**

Vitz, P. C., *see also* Rose, R. M., 1966.

Voeks, V. Formalization and clarification of a theory of learning. *Journal of Psychology,* 1950, *30,* 341-363. **567**

Volkmann, A. Über den Einflusss der Übung auf das Erkennen räumlicher Distanzen. *Berichte Sächsischer Gesellshaft der Wissenschaften, Mathematisch-Physische Klasse,* 1858, *10,* 38-69. **1030**

Volkmann, F. C. Vision during voluntary saccadic eye movements. *Journal of the Optical Society of America,* 1962, *52,* 571-578. **45, 377**

Volkmann, F. C., Schick, A. M. L., & Riggs, L. A. Time course of visual inhibition during voluntary saccades. *Journal of the Optical Society of America,* 1968, *58,* 362-569. **377**

Volkmann, J., *see* Stevens, S. S., 1940, 1941.

von Békésy, G. Über das Fechner'sche Gesetz und seine akustischen Beobachtungsfehler und die Theorie des Hörens. *Annalen der Physik,* 1930, *7,* 329-359. **33**

von Békésy, G. The variation of phase along the basilar membrane with sinusoidal vibration. *Journal of the Acoustical Society of America,* 1947, *19,* 452-460. **230**

von Békésy, G. The moon illusion and similar auditory phenomena. *American Journal of Psychology,* 1949, *62,* 540-552. **269**

von Békésy, G. Gross localization of the place of origin of the cochlear microphonics. *Journal of the Acoustical Society of America,* 1952, *24,* 399-409. (a) **230**

von Békésy, G. Resting potentials inside the cochlear partition of the guinea pig. *Nature,* 1952, *169,* 241-242. (b) **230**

von Békésy, G. Current status of theories of hearing. *Science,* 1956, *123,* 779-783. **229**

von Békésy, G. Similarities between hearing and skin sensations. *Psychological Review,* 1959, *66,* 1-22. **140, 268**

von Békésy, G. In E. G. Wever (Ed.), *Experiments in hearing.* New York: McGraw-Hill, 1960. **237, 238, 261, 265, 268, 269**

von Békésy, G. Hearing theories and complex sounds. *Journal of the Acoustical Society of America,* 1963, *35,* 588-601. **244, 245**

von Békésy, G. Sweetness produced electrically on the tongue and its relation to taste theories. *Journal of Applied Physiology,* 1964, *19,* 1105-1113. **178, 181**

von Békésy, G. Taste theories and the chemical stimulation of single papillae. *Journal of Applied Physiology,* 1966, *21,* 1-9. **172, 175, 178**

von Békésy, G. *Sensory inhibition.* Princeton, N.J.: Princeton University Press, 1967. **231**

von Békésy, G., & Rosenblith, W. A. The mechanical properties of the ear. In S. S. Stevens (Ed.), *Handbook of experimental psychology.* New York: Wiley, 1951. **229**

von Fieandt, K. *Über Sehen von Tiefenbilden bei wechselnder Beleuchtungsrichtung.* Helsinki: Psychological Institute, University of Helsinki, 1938. **497**

von Frey, M. Beiträge zur Sinnesphysiologie der Haut. *Akademie der Wissenschaften Leipzig. Mathematisch-Naturwissenschaftlich Klasse Berichte.* 1895, *47,* 166-184. **120, 121, 148, 155**

von Frey, M., & Kiesow, F. Über die Function der Tastkörperchen. *Zeitschrift für Psychologie,* 1899, *20,* 126-163. **130**

von Frisch, K. *Bees, their vision, chemical senses and language.* Ithaca, New York: Cornell University Press, 1950. **745**

von Helmholtz, H., *see* Helmholtz, H. von

von Holtz, E. Relations between the central nervous system and the peripheral organs. *British Journal of Animal Behaviour,* 1954, *2,* 89-94. **530, 535**

von Holtz, E. Aktive Leistungen der menschlichen Gesischtwahrnehmung. *Stadium Generale,* 1957, *10,* 231-243. **460**

von Karpinska, L. Experimentelle Beiträge zur Analyse der Tiefenwahrnehmung. *Zeitschrift für Psychologie,* 1910, *57,* 1-88. **491n**

von Kries, J. Normal and anomalous color systems. In Helmholtz, H. von, *Treatise on physiological optics,* English translation by J. P. C. Southall. Vol. II. Rochester, New York: Optical Society of America, 1924. Pp. 395-421. **336**

von Kries, J. Notes on perception of depth. 1925. In Helmholtz, H. von, *Treatise on physiological optics* J. P. C. Southall, (Ed.). Vol. 3. New York: Dover, 1962. **493**

von Lackum, W. J., *see* Melton, A. W., 1941.

von Noorden, G. K., Thompson, H. S., Van Allen, M. W. Eye movements in myotonic dystrophy. *Investigations in Ophthalmology,* 1964, *3,* 313-324. **381**

von Senden, M. *Space and sight* (1932) (Transl. P. Heath). London: Methuen, 1960. **548**

von Skramlik, E. *Handbuch der Physiologie der niederen Sinne.* Leipzig: Georg Thieme, 1926. **182, 183, 184**

Vos, J. J., *see* Vendrik, A. J. H., 1958.

Voss, J. F., *see* Morning, N., 1964.

Voth, A. C., *see* Brown, J. F., 1937.

Waddell, D., *see* Beebe-Center, J. G., 1948.

Wade, M., *see* Lashley, K. S., 1946.

Wagner, A. R. The role of reinforcement and nonreinforcement in an "apparent frustration effect." *Journal of Experimental Psychology,* 1959, *57,* 130-136. **576, 810**

Wagner, A. R. Conditioned frustration as a learned drive. *Journal of Experimental Psychology,* 1963, *66,* 142-148. **811**

Wagner, A. R. Frustration and punishment. In R. N. Haber (Ed.), *Current research in motivation.* New York: Holt, Rinehart and Winston, 1966. Pp. 229-239. **811**

Wagner, A. R. Frustrative-nonreward: A variety of punishment? In B. A. Campbell & R. M. Church (Eds.), *Punishment.* New York: Appleton, 1969. **704**

Wagner, A. R., *see also* Logan, F. A., 1965.

Wagner, H. G., MacNichol, E. F., Jr., & Wolbarsht, M. L. The response properties of single ganglion cells in the goldfish retina. *Journal of General Physiology,* 1960, *43,* Suppl. 2, 45-62. **295**

Wagner, H. G., *see also* Hartline, H. K., 1952, 1956.

Wagner, M., *see* Boynton, R. M., 1961.

Wagoner, K. S., *see* Nafe, J. P., 1941a, b.

Wainwright, A., *see* Gogel, W. C., 1961.

Wald, G. Human vision and the spectrum. *Science,* 1945, *101,* 653-658. **275**

Wald, G. The chemistry of rod vision. *Science,* 1951, *113,* 287-291. **286**

Wald, G. The receptors of human color vision. *Science,* 1964, *145,* 1007-1016. **323, 337**

Wald, G., & Brown, P. K. Human color vision and color blindness. *Cold Spring Harbor Symposia on Quantitative Biology,* 1965, *30,* 345-361. **364, 367**

Walk, R. D. The development of depth perception in animals and human infants. *Child Development Monographs,* 1966, *31,* Serial 107, No. 5, 82-108. **548, 549**

Walk, R. D., & Gibson, E. J. A comparative and analytical study of visual depth perception. *Psychological Monographs,* 1961, *75,* (Whole No. 519). **549**

Walk, R. D., Gibson, E. J., & Tighe, T. J. Behavior of light- and dark-reared rats on a visual cliff. *Science,* 1957, *126,* 80-81. **549**

Walk, R. D., Trychin, S. Jr., & Karmel, B. Z. Depth perception in the dark-reared rat as a function of time in the dark. *Psychonomic Science,* 1965, *3,* 9-10. **549**

Walk, R. D., *see* Gibson, E. J., 1956, 1958, 1959, 1960.

Walker, J., *see* Kamin, L., 1959.

Walker, R. Y. The eye-movements of good readers. *Psychological Monographs,* 1933, No. 199. **390**

Walker, W. N. *see* Siipola, E., 1955.

Wall, P. D., & Cronly-Dillon, J. R. Pain, itch, and vibration. *Archives of Neurology*, 1960, *2*, 365–375. **164**

Wall, P. D., & Sweet, W. H. Temporary abolition of pain in man. *Science*, 1967, *155*, 108–109. **165, 166**

Wall, P. D., *see also* Melzack, R., 1962, 1965.

Wallace, J. G., *see* Gregory, R. L., 1963.

Wallace, W. P., *see* Eckstrand, B. R., 1966.

Wallach, H. On sound localization. *Journal of the Acoustical Society of America*, 1939, *10*, 270–274. **268**

Wallach, H. The role of head movements and vestibular and visual cues in sound localization. *Journal of Experimental Psychology*, 1940, *27*, 339–368. **268**

Wallach, H. Brightness constancy and the nature of achromatic colors. *Journal of Experimental Psychology*, 1948, *38*, 310–324. **413, 508**

Wallach, H. Some considerations concerning the relation between perception and cognition. *Journal of Personality*, 1949, *18*, 6–13. **440**

Wallach, H. Perception of motion. *Scientific American*, 1959, *201*, 56–60. **523**

Wallach, H., & Austin, P. Recognition and the localization of visual traces. *American Journal of Psychology*, 1954, *57*, 338–340. **450**

Wallach, H., & Galloway, A. The constancy of colored objects in colored illumination. *Journal of Experimental Psychology*, 1946, *36*, 119–126. **417**

Wallach, H., & Karsh, E. B. The modification of stereoscopic depth-perception and the kinetic depth effect. *American Journal of Psychology*, 1963, *76*, 429–435. (a) **494**

Wallach, H., & Karsh, E. B. Why the modification of stereoscopic depth perception is so rapid. *American Journal of Psychology*, 1963, *76*, 413–420. (b) **494**

Wallach, H., & Kravitz, J. H. The measurement of the constancy of visual direction and its adaptation. *Psychonomic Science*, 1965, *2*, 217–218. (a) **544**

Wallach, H., & Kravitz, J. H. Rapid adaptation in the constancy of visual direction with active and passive rotation. *Psychonomic Science*, 1965, *3*, 165–166. (b) **544, 545**

Wallach, H., Kravitz, J. H., & Lindauer, J. A. passive condition for rapid adaptation to displaced visual direction. *American Journal of Psychology*, 1963, *76*, 568–578. **536**

Wallach, H., & Lewis, C. The effect of abnormal displacement of the retinal image during eye movements. *Perception and Psychophysics*, 1966, *1*, 25–29. **531**

Wallach, H., & Lindauer, J. On the definition of retinal disparity. *Psychologische Beiträge*, 1962, *6*, 521–530. **492**

Wallach, H., & McKenna, V. V. On size-perception in the absence of cues for distance. *American Journal of Psychology*, 1960, *73*, 458–460. **508**

Wallach, H., Moore, M. E., & Davidson, L. Modification of stereoscopic depth-perception. *American Journal of Psychology*, 1963, *76*, 191–204. **494**

Wallach, H., Newman, E. B., & Rosenzweig, M. R. The precedence effect in sound localization. *American Journal of Psychology*, 1949, *62*, 315–336. **268**

Wallach, H., Weisz, A., & Adams, P. A. Circles and derived figures in rotation. *American Journal of Psychology*, 1956, *69*, 48–59. **523**

Wallach, H., & Zuckerman, C. The constancy of stereoscopic depth. *American Journal of Psychology*, 1963, *76*, 404–412. **493, 494**

Wallach, H., *see also* Köhler, W., 1944; Shaffer, O., 1966.

Waller, T. G. Effects of magnitude of reward in spatial and brightness discrimination tasks. *Journal of Comparative and Physiological Psychology*, 1968, *66*, 122–127. **700**

Walls, G. Land! Land! *Psychological Bulletin*, 1960, *57*, 29–48. **417**

Walls, G. L. *The vertebrate eye*. Bloomfield Hills, Mich.: Cranbrook Institute of Science, 1942. **278**

Walls, G. L. The problem of visual direction. *American Journal of Optometry*, 1951, *28*, 55–83, 115–146, 173–212. **537, 540**

Walls, G. L., & Mathews, R. W. *New means of studying color blindness and normal foveal color vision*. Los Angeles: University of California Press, 1952. **328**

Walraven, J., *see* deValois, R. L., 1967.

Walsh, E. G. An investigation of sound localization in patients with neurological abnormalities. *Brain*, 1957, *80*, 222–250. **264**

Walters, G. C., & Rogers, J. V. Aversive stimulation of the rat: Long-term effects on subsequent behavior. *Science*, 1963, *142*, 70–71. **737**

Walters, G. C., *see also* Pearl, J., 1964.

Wampler, R., *see* Peterson, L. R., 1963.

Wang, G. H. Relation between "spontaneous" activity and oestrus cycle in the white rat. *Comparative Psychology Monographs*, 1923, *2* (Whole No. 6). **825**

Wapner, S., & Werner, H. *Perceptual development: An investigation within the framework of sensory-tonic field theory.* Worcester, Mass.: Clark University Press, 1957. **550**

Wapner, S., *see also* Werner, H., 1952, 1953; Witkin, H. A., 1952, 1954.

Ward, H. P. Stimulus factors in self-stimulation. *American Journal of Physiology*, 1959, *196*, 779–782. **646**

Ward, L. B. Reminiscence and rote learning. *Psychological Monographs*, 1937, *49*, No. 220. **1040, 1121**

Ward, W. D. Subjective musical pitch. *Journal of the Acoustical Society of America*, 1954, *26*, 369–380. **243**

Ward, W. D. Auditory fatigue and masking. In J. Jerger (Ed.), *Modern developments in audiology.* New York: Academic Press, 1963. **235**

Ward, W. D. Audition. In P. R. Farnsworth (Ed.), *Annual review of psychology*, Vol. 17. Palo Alto, Calif.: Annual Reviews, 1966. **235**

Ward, W. D. Further observations on contralateral remote masking and related phenomena. *Journal of the Acoustical Society of America*, 1967, *42*, 593–600. **242**

Ward, W. D. Effects of noise on hearing threshold. In W. D. Ward, & J. E. Fricke (Eds.), *Noise as a public health hazard*, ASHA Report #4, American Speech and Hearing Association, Washington, 1969. **236**

Ward, W. D., Glorig, A., & Sklar, D. L. Temporary threshold shift from octave-band noise: Applications to damage-risk criterion. *Journal of the Acoustical Society of America*, 1959, *31*, 522–528. **235**

Ward, W. D., *see also* Carlin, S., 1962; Kryter, K. D., 1966.

Warden, C. J., & Aylesworth, M. The relative value of reward and punishment in the formation of a visual discrimination habit in the white rat. *Journal of Comparative Psychology*, 1927, *7*, 117–127. **739**

Warden, C. J., & Barr, J. The Müller-Lyer illusion in the ring dove *Turtur risorius*. *Journal of Comparative Psychology*, 1929, *9*, 275–292. Cited in Mario Zanforlin, Some observations on Gregory's theory of perceptual illusions. *Quarterly Journal of Experimental Psychology*, 1967, *19*, 193–197. **461**

Warden, C. J., & Haas, E. L. The effect of short intervals of delay in feeding upon speed of maze learning. *Journal of Comparative Psychology*, 1927, *7*, 107–116. **678**

Warden, C. J., Jenkins, T. N., & Warner, L. H. *Comparative psychology: A comprehensive treatise.* Vol. 2: *Plants and invertebrates.* New York: Ronald, 1936. **556**

Warden C. J., *see also* Jenkins, T. N., 1926.

Warner, L. H. The association span of the white rat. *Journal of Genetic Psychology*, 1932, *41*, 57–90. **715, 729**

Warner, L. H., *see also* Jenkins, T. N., 1926; Warden, C. J., 1936.

Warr, P. B. The relative importance of pro-active inhibition and degree of learning in retention of paired associate items. *British Journal of Psychology*, 1964, *55*, 19–30. **1041, 1106**

Warren, H. C. *A history of the association psychology.* New York: Scribner's, 1921. **849**

Warren, J. M. Reversed discrimination as a function of the number of reinforcements during pre-training. *American Journal of Psychology,* 1954, *67,* 720. **768**

Warren, J. M., & Baron, A. The formation of learning sets by cats. *Journal of Comparative and Physiological Psychology,* 1956, *49,* 227-231. **768**

Warren, J. M., & Brookshire, K. H. Stimulus generalization and discrimination learning by primates. *Journal of Experimental Psychology,* 1959, *58,* 348-351. **772**

Warren, R. A., *see* Warren, R. M., 1963.

Warren, R. M. A basis for judgments of sensory intensity. *American Journal of Psychology,* 1958, *71,* 675-687. **244**

Warren, R. M., & Pfaffmann, C. Early experience and taste aversion. *Journal of Comparative and Physiological Psychology,* 1958, *52,* 263-266. **190**

Warren, R. M., & Pfaffmann, C. Suppression of sweet sensitivity by potassium gymnemate. *Journal of Applied Physiology,* 1959, *14,* 40-42. **177**

Warren, R. M., & Poulton, E. C. Lightness of grays: Effects of background reflectance. *Perception and Psychophysics,* 1966, *1,* 145-148. **414**

Warren, R. M., Sersen, E. A., & Pores, E. B. A basis for loudness judgments. *American Journal of Psychology,* 1958, *71,* 700-709. **248**

Warren, R. M., & Warren, R. A. A critique of Stevens' "new psychophysics." *Perceptual and Motor Skills,* 1963, *16,* 797-810. **84**

Warrington, E. K., *see* Kinsbourne, M., 1962.

Warshofsky, F., *see* Stevens, S. S., 1965.

Warter, P. J., Jr., *see* Smith, W. M., 1960.

Warwick, R. T. T., *see* Le Gros Clark, W. E., 1946.

Washburn, M. F. *Movement and mental imagery.* Boston: Houghton Mifflin, 1916. **453**

Washburn, M. F. Retinal rivalry as a neglected factor in stereoscopic vision. *Proceedings of the National Academy of Science,* 1933, *19,* 773-777. **491n**

Washburn, M. F., & Gillette, A. Motor factors in voluntary control of cube perspective fluctuations and retinal rivalry fluctuations. *American Journal of Psychology,* 1933, *45,* 315-319. **519**

Washburn, M. F., Mallay, H., & Naylor, A. The influence of the size of an outline cube on the fluctuations of its perspective. *American Journal of Psychology,* 1931, *43,* 484-489. **519**

Washburn, M. F., Reagan, C., & Thurston, E. The comparative controllability of the fluctuations of simple and complex ambiguous perspective figures. *American Journal of Psychology,* 1934, *46,* 636-638. **519**

Wason, P. C. The processing of positive and negative information. *Quarterly Journal of Experimental Psychology,* 1959, *11,* 92-107. **964**

Wason, P. C. On the failure to eliminate hypotheses in a conceptual task. *Quarterly Journal of Experimental Psychology,* 1960, *12,* 129-140. **964**

Wason, P. C. Response to a primitive and negative binary statement. *British Journal of Psychology,* 1961, *52,* 133-142. **964**

Watanabe, K., *see* Brown, K. T., 1965.

Watanobe, T., *see* Katsuki, Y., 1959.

Waters, J. E. A theoretical and developmental investigation of delayed speech feedback. *Genetic Psychology Monographs,* 1968, *78,* 3-54. **687**

Watson, J. B. The place of the conditioned-reflex in psychology. *Psychological Review,* 1916, *23,* 89-116. **562**

Watson, J. B. The effect of delayed feeding upon learning. *Psychobiology,* 1917, *1,* 51-60. **678**

Watson, J. B. *Psychology from the standpoint of a behaviorist.* Philadelphia: Lippincott, 1919. **562, 689**

Watson, J. B. *Psychological care of infant and child.* New York: Norton, 1928. **562**

Watson, J. B. *Behaviorism.* Chicago: University of Chicago Press, 1930. **621**

Watson, J. B., & Rayner, R. Conditioned emotional reactions. *Journal of Experimental Psychology,* 1920, *3,* 1-14. **562, 704**

Watson, J. B., *see also* Yerkes, R. M., 1911.

Waugh, N. C., & Norman, D. Primary memory. *Psychological Review,* 1965, *72,* 89-104. **1109, 1111**

Waugh, N. C., *see also* Loess, H., 1967.

Way, K. S., *see* Hastorf, A. H., 1952.

Wayner, M. J. Effects of intracarotid injections of hypertonic saline on spinal reflex excitability. In M. J. Wayner (Ed.), *Thirst.* Oxford: Pergamon, 1964, 335-360. **836**

Weale, R. A. Cone-monochromatism. *Journal of Physiology,* 1953, *121,* 548-569. **327**

Weasner, M. H., *see* Finger, F. W., 1960.

Weaver, G. E., *see* Schulz, R. W., 1965, 1968.

Webb, A. D., *see* Berg, H. W., 1963.

Webb, W. B. Drive stimuli as cues. *Psychological Reports,* 1955, *1,* 287-298. **795n**

Webb, W. B., *see also* Wipf, J. L., 1962.

Weber, E. Der Tastsinn und das Gemeingefühl. In Wagner (Ed.), *Handworterbuch der Physiologie,* 1846, *3,* 481-588. **129, 153**

Weber, M. L., *see* Valenstein, E. S., 1965.

Webster, D., *see* Quartermain, D., 1968.

Webster, H. The distortion of straight and curved lines in geometrical fields. *American Journal of Psychology,* 1948, *61,* 573. **460**

Webster, J. C. Speech communications as limited by ambient noise. *Journal of the Acoustical Society of America,* 1965, *37,* 692-699. **258**

Webster, J. C., & Thompson, P. O. Responding to both of two overlapping messages. *Journal of the Acoustical Society of America,* 1954, *26,* 396-402. **258**

Webster, J. C., *see also* Kryter, K. D., 1963; Thompson, P. O., 1961.

Webster, R. G., *see* McLaughlin, S. C., 1967.

Weddell, G. Somesthesis and the chemical senses. *Annual Review of Psychology,* 1955, *6,* 119-136. **154, 167**

Weddell, G., & Miller, S. Cutaneous sensibility. *Annual Review of Physiology,* 1962, *24,* 199-222. **124**

Weddell, G., & Pallie, W. Observations on the neurohistology of cutaneous blood vessels. In G. E. Wolstenholme & J. S. Freeman (Eds.), *Peripheral circulation in man* (A CIBA Foundation Symposium). London: J. & A. Churchill, 1954. Pp. 132-140. **124**

Weddell, G., Palmer, E., & Pallie, W. Nerve endings in mammalian skin. *Biological Review of the Cambridge Philosophical Society,* 1955, *30,* 159-195. **162**

Weddell, G., *see also* Hagen, E., 1953; Lele, P. P., 1954, 1956; Pattle, R. E., 1948.

Weeks, J. R. Experimental narcotics addiction. *Scientific American,* 1964, *210,* 46-52. **557n**

Weene, B., *see* Neisser, U., 1962.

Wegel, R. L., & Lane, C. E. The auditory masking of one pure tone by another and its probable relation to the dynamics of the inner ear. *Physiological Review,* 1924, *23,* 266-285. **239**

Weinberg, M., *see* Allen, F., 1925.

Weingartner, H. Associative structure and serial learning. *Journal of Verbal Learning and Verbal Behavior,* 1963, *2,* 476-478. **886**

Weinheimer, S., *see* Neimark, E., 1965.

Weinstein, S. The perception of depth in the absence of texture-gradient. *American Journal of Psychology,* 1957, *70,* 611-615. **501**

Weinstein, S. Intensive and extensive aspects of tactile sensitivity as a function of body part, sex, and laterality. In D. R. Kenshalo (Ed.), *The skin senses.* Springfield, Ill.: Charles C Thomas, 1968. Pp. 195-222. **133, 134, 138, 139**

Weinstein, S., Sersen, E. A., Fisher, L., & Weisinger, M. Is re-afference necessary for visual adaptation? *Perceptual and Motor Skills,* 1964, *18,* 641–648. **536**

Weinstock, S. Resistance to extinction of a running response following partial reinforcement under widely spaced trials. *Journal of Comparative and Physiological Psychology,* 1964, *47,* 318–322. **573**

Weinstock, S., see also Sgro, J. A., 1963.

Weintraub, D., see Hake, H. W., 1966.

Weisberg, P., & Fink, E. Fixed ratio and extinction performance of infants in the second year of life. *Journal of the Experimental Analysis of Behavior,* 1966, *9,* 105–109. **605, 608**

Weisberg, P., & Simmons, M. W. A modified WGTA for infants in their second year of life. *Journal of Psychology,* 1966, *63,* 99–104. **751**

Weise, P., & Bitterman, M. E. Response selection in discriminative learning. *Psychological Review,* 1951, *58,* 185–195. **774**

Weisinger, M., see Weinstein, S., 1964.

Weisman, R. G., Denny, M. R., Platt, S. A., & Zerbolio, D. J., Jr. Facilitation of extinction by a stimulus associated with long nonshock confinement periods. *Journal of Comparative and Physiological Psychology,* 1966, *62,* 26–30. **573**

Weiss, J. A tail electrode for unrestrained rats. *Journal of the Experimental Analysis of Behavior,* 1967, *10,* 85–86. **706**

Weiss, R. L., see Johnson, R. C., 1964.

Weiss, W. I., see Hovland, C. I., 1953.

Weisstein, N., & Haber, R. N. A U-shaped backward masking function in vision. *Psychonomic Science,* 1965, *2,* 75–76. **430**

Weisz, A., see Wallach, H., 1956; Gardner, W. J., 1960.

Weitz, J. Vibratory sensitivity as a function of skin temperature. *Journal of Experimental Psychology,* 1941, *28,* 21–36. **136**

Weitzman, E. D., Ross, G. S., Hodos, W., & Galambos, R. Behavioral method of study of pain in the monkey. *Science,* 1961, *133,* 37–38. **157**

Welch, G., see Zubek, J. P., 1963.

Welch, L. A preliminary study of the interaction of conflicting concepts of children between the ages of 3 and 5 years. *Psychological Review,* 1938, *2,* 439–459. **786**

Welch, L., & Long, L. The higher structural phases of concept formation of children. *Journal of Psychology,* 1940, *9,* 59–95. **786**

Weld, H. P., see Boring, E. G., 1948.

Wellman, B., see Hoffman, A. C., 1939.

Wells, C., see Diamant, H., 1965.

Wells, F. L. Practice effects in free association. *American Journal of Psychology,* 1911, *22,* 1–13. **866**

Wells, F. L. *Mental tests in clinical practice.* Yonkers, N. Y.: World Book, 1927. **877**

Wells, H. H. The effects of transfer in disjunctive concept formation. *Journal of Experimental Psychology,* 1963, *65,* 63–69. **963**

Wells, H. S. Temperature equilization for the relief of pain: An experimental study of the relation of thermal gradients to pain. *Archives of Physical Medicine and Rehabilitation,* 1947, *28,* 135–139. **156**

Wemple, L., see Zigler, M. J., 1930.

Wendt, G. R. An interpretation of inhibition and conditioned reflexes as competition between reaction systems. *Psychological Review,* 1936, *43,* 258–281. **571**

Wendt, R. H., Lindsley, D. F., Adey, W. R., & Fox S. S. Self-maintained visual stimulation in monkeys after long-term visual deprivation. *Science,* 1963, *139,* 336–338. **840**

Wenz, T. G., see McLaughlin, S. C., 1968.

Wenzel, B., & Sieck, M. H. Olfaction. *Annual Review of Physiology,* 1966, *28,* 381–434. **220**

Werblin, F. S. Functional organization of the vertebrate retina studied by intracellular recording from the retina of the mudpuppy, *Necturus maculosus.* Thesis, Johns Hopkins University, Baltimore, 1968. **308**

Werner, H. Studies on contour. *American Journal of Psychology,* 1935, *47,* 40–64. **429**

Werner, H. Dynamics in binocular depth perception. *Psychological Monographs,* 1937 (Whole No. 218). **492**

Werner, H. Studies on contour strobostereoscopic phenomena. *American Journal of Psychology,* 1940, *53,* 418–422. **429, 430**

Werner, H., & Wapner, S. Toward a general theory of perception. *Psychological Review,* 1952, *59,* 324–338. **437**

Werner, H., Wapner, S., & Bruell, J. H. Experiments on sensory-tonic field theory of perception: VI. Effect of position of head, eyes and of object on position of the apparent median plane. *Journal of Experimental Psychology,* 1953, *46,* 293–299. **534**

Werner, H., see also Wapner, S., 1957.

Wertheimer, M. Experimentelle Studien über das Sehen von Bewegung. *Zeitschrift für Psychologie,* 1912, *61,* 161–265. **525, 539**

Wertheimer, M. Untersuchungen zur Lehre von der Gestalt: II. *Psychologische Forschung,* 1923, *4,* 301–350. Abridged translation by M. Wertheimer: Principles of perceptual organization. In D. C. Beardslee & M. Wertheimer (Eds.), *Readings in perception.* Princeton, N.J.: Van Nostrand, 1958. **433**

Wertheimer, M. Psychomotor coordination of auditory and visual space at birth. *Science,* 1961, *134,* 1692. **547**

Wertheimer, M. *Drei Abhandlungen zur Gestalttheorie.* Erlangen: Philosophischen Akademie, 1925. **527**

Wertheimer, M., & Arena, A. J. Effect of exposure time on adaptation to disarranged hand-eye coordination. *Perceptual and Motor Skills,* 1959, *9,* 159–164. **536**

Wertheimer, M., see also Dinnerstein, D., 1957; Hornbostel, E. M. von, 1920; Selkin, J., 1957; Soltz, D. F., 1959; Strassburger, F., 1959.

Wesemann, A. F., see Meyer, D. R., 1960.

West, M. *A general service list of English words.* London: Longmans, 1953. **863, 895**n

Westheimer, G. H. Mechanism of saccadic eye movements. *Archives of Ophthalmology,* 1954, *52,* 710–724. (a) **376**

Westheimer, G. H. Eye movement responses to a horizontally moving visual stimulus. *Archives of Ophthalmology,* 1954, *52,* 932–943. (b) **378, 379**

Westheimer, G. H., & Mitchell, A. M. Eye movement responses to convergence stimuli. *Archives of Ophthalmology,* 1956, *55,* 848–856. **382**

Westheimer, G., see Campbell, F. W., 1960; Rashbass, C., 1961a, b; Rushton, W. A. H., 1962.

Wetzel, A. B., see Besch, N. F., 1962.

Wever, E. G. Beats and related phenomena resulting from the simultaneous sounding of two tones. *Psychological Review,* 1929, *36,* 402–418, 512–523. **237**

Wever, E. G. *Theory of hearing.* New York: Wiley, 1949. **228, 232, 233, 237, 244, 245**

Wever, E. G. Electrical potentials of the cochlea. *Physiological Review,* 1966, *46,* 102–127. **230**

Wever, E. G., & Bray, C. W. Action currents in the auditory nerve in response to acoustic stimulation. *Proceedings of the National Academy of Science,* 1930, *16,* 344–350. **230, 232**

Wever, E. G., & Lawrence, M. *Physiological acoustics.* Princeton, N.J.: Princeton University Press, 1954. **230, 238**

Wever, E. G., & Zener, K. E. The method of absolute judgment in psychophysics. *Psychological Review,* 1928, *35,* 466–493. **58**

Weymark, C., see Kenshalo, D. R., 1967.

Weymouth, F. W., see Andersen, E. E., 1923; Flom, M. C., 1963; Hirsch, M. J., 1948.

Whalen, P. M., see Brosgole, L., 1967.

Whalen, R. E. Effects of mounting without intromission and intromission without ejaculation on sexual behavior and maze learning. *Journal of Comparative and Physiological Psychology*, 1961, *54*, 409-415. **798**

Wham, D. S., *see* Irion, A. L., 1951.

Wheatstone, C., On some remarkable and hitherto unobserved phenomena of binocular vision: Part 2. *Philosophical Magazine*, 1852, series 4, 504-523. **479, 513**

Wheeler, K., *see* Gibson, J. J., 1969.

Wheeless, L. L., Jr., Boynton, R. M., & Cohen, G. H. Eye-movement responses to step and pulse-step stimuli. *Journal of the Optical Society of America*, 1966, *56*, 956-960. **379**

White, B., *see* Held, R., 1959.

White, B. L., *see* Haynes, H., 1965.

White, B. W. Stimulus conditions affecting a recently discovered stereoscopic effect. *American Journal of Psychology*, 1962, *75*, 411-420. **432**

White, C. T., & Schlosberg, H. Degree of conditioning of the GSR as a function of the period of delay. *Journal of Experimental Psychology*, 1952, *43*, 357-362. **558**

White, C. W., *see* Festinger, L., 1968.

White, G. C., *see* Bolles, R. C., 1968.

White, J. C., & Sweet, W. *Pain: Its mechanisms and neurosurgical control.* Springfield, Ill.: Charles C Thomas, 1955. **162, 164**

White, S. H., & Plum, G. E. Eye movement photography during children's discrimination learning. *Journal of Experimental Child Psychology*, 1965, *1*, 327-338. **784**

Whitely, P. L. The dependence of learning and recall upon prior intellectual activities. *Journal of Experimental Psychology*, 1927, *10*, 489-508. **1102**

Whitely, P. L., & Blankenship, A. B. The influence of certain conditions prior to learning upon subsequent recall. *Journal of Experimental Psychology*, 1936, *19*, 496-504. **1102**

Whitfield, I. C. *An introduction to electronics for physiological workers.* (2nd ed.) New York: Macmillan, 1959. **92**

Whitfield, I. C., & Evans, E. F. Responses of auditory cortical neurons to stimuli of changing frequency. *Journal of Neurophysiology*, 1965, *28*, 655-672. **232**

Whiting, J. W. M., & Mowrer, O. H. Habit progression and regression: A laboratory study of some factors relevant to human socialization. *Journal of Comparative Psychology*, 1943, *36*, 229-253, **740**

Whitmarsh, G. A., *see* Bousfield, W. A., 1958, 1960; Cohen, B. H., 1957.

Wickelgren, W. A. Acoustic similarity and intrusion errors in short-term memory. *Journal of Experimental Psychology*, 1965. *70*, 102-108. (a) **1001n, 1116**

Wickelgren, W. A. Distinctive features and errors in short-term memory for English vowels. *Journal of the Acoustical Society of America*, 1965, *38*, 583-588. (b) **1116**

Wickelgren, W. A. Acoustic similarity and retroactive interference in short-term memory. *Journal of Verbal Learning and Verbal Behavior*, 1965, *4*, 53-61. (c) **1119**

Wickelgren, W. A. Distinctive features and errors in short-term memory for English consonants. *Journal of the Acoustical Society of America*, 1966, *39*, 388-398. (a) **1116**

Wickelgren, W. A. Phonemic similarity and interference in short-term memory for single letters. *Journal of Experimental Psychology*, 1966, *71*, 396-404. (b) **1001n, 1116, 1118, 1119**

Wickelgren, W. A. Short-term recognition memory for single letters and phonemic similarity of retroactive interference. *Quarterly Journal of Experimental Psychology*, 1966, *18*, 55-62. (c) **1119**

Wickelgren, W. A., & Norman, D. A. Strength models and serial position in short-term recognition memory. *Journal of Mathematical Psychology*, 1966, *3*, 316-347. **998**

Wickens, C., *see* Wickens, D. D., 1940.

Wickens, D. D. The centrality of verbal learning. In A. W. Melton (Ed.), *Categories of human learning.* New York: Academic Press, 1964. Pp. 79-87. **979**

Wickens, D. D., Born, D., & Allen, C. Proactive inhibition and item similarity in short-term memory. *Journal of Verbal Learning and Verbal Behavior*, 1963, *2*, 440-445. **1114, 1116**

Wickens, D. D., & Cermak, L. S. Transfer effects of synonyms and antonyms in mixed and unmixed lists. *Journal of Verbal Learning and Verbal Behavior*, 1967, *6*, 832-839. **1070**

Wickens, D. D., & Wickens, C. A study of conditioning in the neonate. *Journal of Experimental Psychology*, 1940, *26*, 94-102. **553**

Wickens, D. D., *see also* Maher, W. B., 1954; Newton, J. M., 1956.

Wieland, B. A., *see* Cook, T. H., 1967; Mefferd, R. B. Jr., 1967, 1968.

Wiener, F. M., *see* Egan, J. P., 1946.

Wiesel, T. N., *see* Hubel, D. H., 1962.

Wigand, M. E., *see* Keidel, W. D., 1961.

Wiggins, J. S. Two determinants of associative reaction time. *Journal of Experimental Psychology*, 1957, *54*, 144-147. **862**

Wike, E. L. *Secondary reinforcement.* New York: Harper, 1966. **670, 671**

Wike, E. L., & Barrientos, G. Secondary reinforcement and multiple drive reduction. *Journal of Comparative and Physiological Psychology*, 1958, *51*, 640-643. **668**

Wike, E. L., & Kintsch, W. Delayed reinforcement and runway performance. *Psychological Review*, 1959, *9*, 179-187. **685**

Wike, E. L., & Remple, R. Delayed reinforcement, selective learning and habit reversal. *Psychological Record*, 1959, *9*, 179-187. **685**

Wike, E. L., *see also* Kintsch, W., 1957; Scott, E. D., 1956.

Wiley, R. E., *see* Horton, D. L., 1967a, b.

Wilkins, L., & Richter, C. P. A great craving for salt by a child with corticoadrenal insufficiency. *Journal of the American Medical Association*, 1940, *114*, 866-868. **188**

Wilkinson, H. J., *see* Jones, A., 1961.

Williams, C. E., *see* House, A. S., 1965.

Williams, C. M., *see* Lele, P. P., 1954.

Williams, D. R. Classical conditioning and incentive motivation. In W. F. Prokasy (Ed.), *Classical conditioning.* New York: Appleton, 1965. **622**

Williams, O. A study of the phenomenon of reminiscence. *Journal of Experimental Psychology*, 1926, *9*, 368-387. **1121**

Williams, R. A. Effects of repeated food deprivations and repeated feeding tests on feeding behavior. *Journal of Comparative and Physiological Psychology*, 1968, *65*, 222-226. **820, 821**

Williams, R. A., & Campbell, B. A. Weight loss and quinine-milk ingestion as measures of "hunger" in infant and adult rats. *Journal of Comparative and Physiological Psychology*, 1961, *54*, 220-222. **815, 817**

Williams, R. A., *see also* Campbell, B. A., 1961.

Willis, F. N., *see* Collier, G., 1961.

Wilson, A., *see* Flock, H. R., 1966.

Wilson, E. O. Chemical communication in the social insects. *Science*, 1965, *149*, 1064-1071. **194**

Wilson, G. T., & Radloff, W. P. Degree of arousal and performance: Effects of reticular stimulation on an operant task. *Psychonomic Science*, 1967, *7*, 13-14. **841**

Wilson, J. P. An auditory after-image. In *Symposium on frequency analysis and periodicity detection in hearing.* Driebergen, The Netherlands, 1969. **246**

Wilson, J. P., *see also* Kaess, D. W., 1964.

Wimer, C. An analysis of semantic stimulus factors in paired-associated learning. *Journal of Verbal Learning and Verbal Behavior*, 1963, *1*, 397-407. **900**

Wimer, R. Osgood's transfer surface: Extension and test.

Journal of Verbal Learning and Verbal Behavior, 1964, *3*, 274–279. **1052, 1056**

Winch, W. H. The transfer of improvement in memory in school children. *British Journal of Psychology,* 1908, *2*, 284–293. **1031**

Winch, W. H. The transfer of improvement in memory in school children. *British Journal of Psychology,* 1910, *3*, 386–405. **1031**

Windle, W. F., *see* Rasmussen, G. L., 1960.

Winkelmann, R. K. The sensory endings in the skin of the cat. *Journal of Comparative Neurology,* 1958, *109*, 221–232. **125**

Winnick, W. A., & Rogoff, I. Role of apparent slant in shape judgments. *Journal of Experimental Psychology,* 1965, *69*, 554–563. **516**

Winograd, E. Escape behavior under different fixed ratios and shock intensities. *Journal of the Experimental Analysis of Behavior,* 1965, *8*, 117–124. **723**

Winograd, E. List differentiation as a function of frequency and retention interval. *Journal of Experimental Psychology,* 1968, *76*, Monograph Supplement No. 2. **1091, 1103**

Winslow, C. N. Visual illusions in the chick. *Archives of Physiology,* 1933, *153*, 1–83. Cited in Zanforlin, M. Some observations of Gregory's theory of perceptual illusions. *Quarterly Journal of Experimental Psychology,* 1967, *19*, 193–197. **461**

Winzer, G. E., *see* Corliss, E. L. R., 1965.

Wipf, J. L., & Webb, W. B. Supplementary report: Proactive inhibition as a function of the method of reproduction. *Journal of Experimental Psychology,* 1962, *64*, 421. **1106**

Wirth, A., *see* Dodt, E., 1953.

Wisby, W. J., & Hasler, A. D. Effect of olfactory occlusion on migrating silver salmon (*O. kisutch*). *Journal of the Fisheries Research Board of Canada,* 1954, *11*, 472–478. **194**

Wischner, G. J. The effect of punishment on discrimination learning in a non-correction situation. *Journal of Experimental Psychology,* 1947, *37*, 271–284. **739**

Wischner, G. J., Fowler, H., & Kushnick, S. A. Effect of strength of punishment for "correct" or "incorrect" responses on visual discrimination performance. *Journal of Experimental Psychology,* 1963, *65*, 131–138. **740**

Wischner, G. J., *see also* Fowler, H., 1965, 1968.

Wishner, J., Shipley, T. E., Jr., & Hurvich, M. S. The serial-position curve as a function of organization. *American Journal of Psychology,* 1957, *70*, 258–262. **1016**

Wismer, B., & Lipsitt, L. P. Verbal mediation in paired-associate learning. *Journal of Experimental Psychology,* 1964, *68*, 441–448. **1077**

Witkin, H. A., & Asch, S. E. Studies in space orientation: III. Perception of the upright in the absence of a visual field. IV. Further experiments on perception of the upright with displaced visual fields. *Journal of Experimental Psychology,* 1948, *38*, 603–614, 762–782. **539**

Witkin, H. A., Lewis, H. B., Hertzman, M., Machover, K., Meissner, P. B., & Wapner, S. *Personality through perception.* New York: Harper, 1954. **470, 539n**

Witkin, H. A., Wapner, S., & Leventhal, T. Sound localization with conflicting visual and auditory cues. *Journal of Experimental Psychology,* 1952, *43*, 58–57. **269**

Witkin, H. A., *see also* Asch, S. E., 1948.

Witmer, L. R. The association value of three-place consonant syllables. *Journal of Genetic Psychology,* 1935, *47*, 337–360. **852, 982**

Witt, I., *see* Hensel, H., 1959.

Witte, R. S. Long-term effects of patterned reward schedules. *Journal of Experimental Psychology,* 1964, *68*, 588–594. **921, 934**

Wodinsky, J., *see* Bitterman, M. E., 1953.

Wohlgemuth, A. On the after-effect of seen movement. *British Journal of Psychology Monographs,* 1911, *1*. **522**

Wohlwill, J. F. Developmental studies of perception. *Psychological Bulletin,* 1960, *57*, 249–288. **550**

Wolbarsht, M. L., *see* Wagner, H. G., 1960.

Wolf, A. V. *Thirst: Physiology of the urge to drink and problems of water lack.* Springfield, Ill.: Charles C Thomas, 1958. **816**

Wolf, S., & Hardy, J. D. Studies on pain: Observations on pain due to local cooling. *Journal of Clinical Investigation,* 1941, *20*, 521–533. **159**

Wolf, S., *see also* Schneider, R. A., 1955, 1960.

Wolfe, J. B. The effect of delayed reward upon learning in the white rat. *Journal of Comparative Psychology,* 1943, *17*, 1–21. **679**

Wolfe, J. B. Effectiveness of token-rewards for chimpanzees. *Comparative Psychology Monographs,* 1936, *12*, No. 60. **665**

Wolfe, J. B., & Kaplon, M. D. Effect of amount of reward and consummative activity on learning in chickens. *Journal of Comparative Psychology,* 1941, *31*, 353–361. **617, 623**

Wolff, H. G., *see* Hardy, J. D., 1940, 1947, 1951; Schumacher, G. A., 1940.

Wolfle, H. M. Conditioning as a function of the interval between the conditioned and the original stimulus. *Journal of General Psychology,* 1932, *7*, 80–103. **558, 561**

Wolin, B. R., *see* Mayzner, M. S., 1965a, b, c.

Wood, C. L., III, *see* Jeffress, L., 1956.

Wood, P. B., *see* Kenshalo, D. R., 1968.

Woodburne, L. S. The effect of a constant visual angle upon the binocular discrimination of depth differences. *American Journal of Psychology,* 1934, *46*, 273–286. **486**

Woodrow, H. The effect of training upon transference. *Journal of Educational Psychology,* 1927, *18*, 159–172. **1032**

Woodrow, H., & Karpman, B. A new olfactometric technique and some results. *Journal of Experimental Psychology,* 1917, *2*, 431–447. **200, 211**

Woodrow, H., & Lowell, F. Children's association frequency tables. *Psychological Monographs,* 1916, *22*, (Whole No. 97). **864, 874**

Woods, P. J. The relationship between probability difference $(\pi_1 - \pi_2)$ and learning rate in a contingent partial reinforcement situation. *Journal of Experimental Psychology,* 1959, *58*, 27–30. **932**

Woods, P. J., *see also* Brand, H., 1956.

Woodworth, R. S. *Dynamic psychology.* New York: Columbia University Press, 1918. **793, 794**

Woodworth, R. S. *Experimental psychology.* New York: Holt, 1938. **402, 438, 448, 491n, 492, 563, 794n, 850, 851n, 864, 877, 980**

Woodworth, R. S. *Dynamics of behavior.* New York: Holt, Rinehart & Winston, 1958. **793n**

Woodworth, R. S., & Schlosberg, H. *Experimental psychology.* New York: Holt, 1954. **212, 213, 399, 422, 508, 512, 522, 528, 558n, 559, 574, 575, 611, 619, 710, 794, 831, 850, 851n, 853n, 859n, 860, 861, 864, 868n, 877, 907, 945, 980**

Woodworth, R. S., *see also* Thorndike, E. L., 1901.

Woolsey, C. N. Organization of cortical auditory system: A review and synthesis. In G. Rasmussen & W. F. Windle (Eds.), *Neural mechanisms of the auditory and vestibular systems.* Springfield, Ill.: Charles C Thomas, 1960. **232**

Woolsey, C. N., *see also* Travis, A. M., 1956.

Worchel, P., & Berry, J. H. The perception of obstacles by the deaf. *Journal of Experimental Psychology,* 1952, *43*, 187–194. **270**

Worchel, P., & Dallenbach, K. M. "Facial vision": Perception of obstacles by the deaf-blind. *American Journal of Psychology,* 1947, *60*, 502–553. **270**

Worchel, P., *see also* Ammons, C. H., 1953.

Work, M. S., *see* Amsel, A., 1961, 1962.

Woskow, M. H., *see* Jones, F. N., 1964.

Wright, H. N. Temporal summation and backward masking. *Journal of the Acoustical Society of America*, 1964, *36*, 927-932. **241**

Wright, J. E., *see* Pliskoff, S. S., 1964.

Wright, J. H. Effects of formal interitem similarity and length of retention interval on proactive inhibition of short-term memory. *Journal of Experimental Psychology*, 1967, *75*, 386-395. **1115**

Wright, J. H., *see also* Dufort, R. H., 1962.

Wright, R. H., & Michels, K. M. Evaluation of far infrared relations to odor by a standards similarity method. *Annals of the New York Academy of Science*, 1964, *116*, 535-551. **220**

Wright, W. D. The functions and performance of the eye. *Journal of the Scientific Institute*, 1942, *19*, 161-165. **300**

Wright, W. D. *Researches in normal and defective colour vision.* London: Henry Kimpton, 1946. **362, 364, 365**

Wright, W. D., *see also* Thomson, L. C., 1953.

Wuest, F. J. *Psychophysical measurements from two theoretical viewpoints.* Unpublished doctoral dissertation, Brown University, 1961. **44**

Wulff, J. J., *see* Sheffield, F. D., 1951.

Wundt, W. *Beiträge zur Theorie der Sinneswahrnehmung.* Leipzig: C. F. Winter, 1862. **479**

Wundt, W. *Outlines of psychology* (4th German ed., transl. by C. H. Judd). Leipzig: Englemann, 1902. **403, 465, 466, 542**

Wyckoff, L. B., Jr. The role of observing responses in discrimination learning. *Psychological Review*, 1952, *59*, 431-442. **769, 948**

Wyckoff, L. B., & Page, H. A. A grid for administering shock. *American Journal of Psychology*, 1954, *67*, 154. **706**

Wyckoff, L. B., *see also* Ziegler, H., 1961.

Wylie, H. H. An experimental study of transfer of response in the white rat. *Behavior Monographs*, 1919, No. 16. **1045**

Wynne, L. C., *see* Solomon, R. L., 1953.

Wynne, R. D., Gerjuoy, H., & Schiffman, H. Association test antonym-response set. *Journal of Verbal Learning and Verbal Behavior*, 1965, *4*, 354-359. **871**

Wyrwicka, W., *see* Clemente, C. D., 1964; Sterman, M. B., 1967.

Wyszecki, G., & Stiles, W. S. *Color science: Concepts and methods, quantitative data and formulas.* New York: Wiley, 1967. **334, 352, 358, 359, 361, 362, 366, 367**

Yamaguchi, H. G. Drive (D) as a function of hours of hunger (h). *Journal of Experimental Psychology*, 1951, *42*, 108-117. **802, 825, 826**

Yamaguchi, H. G. Gradients of drive stimulus (S_D) intensity generalization. *Journal of Experimental Psychology*, 1952, *43*, 298-304. **830**

Yamaguchi, S. The synergistic taste effect of monosodium glutamate and disodium 5'-inosinate. *Journal of Food Science*, 1967, *32*, 473-478. **187**

Yamaguchi, S., *see also* Ikeda, S., 1962.

Yamashita, S., Ogawa, H., & Sato, M. Multimodal sensitivity of taste units in the rat. *Kumamoto Medical Journal*, 1967, *20*, 67-70. **181**

Yarbus, A. L. Motion of the eye on interchanging fixating points at rest in space. *Biophysics*, 1957, *2*, 679-683 (translated from *Biofizika 2*, 698-702). (a) **387**

Yarbus, A. L. The perception of an image fixed with respect to the retina. *Biophysics*, 1957, *2*, 683-690 (translated from *Biofizika 2*, 703-712). (b) **375**

Yarbus, A. L. *Eye movements and vision.* New York: Plenum Press, 1967. **374, 375, 379, 387, 459**

Yates, T., *see* Boynton, R. M., 1965.

Yellott, J. I., Jr. *Some effects of noncontingent success in human probability learning.* Technical Report No. 89, 1965. Stanford, Calif.: Institute for Mathematical Studies in the Social Sciences, Stanford University. **937**

Yensen, R. Some factors affecting taste sensitivity in man: II. Depletion of body salt. *Quarterly Journal of Experimental Psychology*, 1959, *11*, 230-238. **188**

Yensen, R. Taste sensitivity and food deprivation, blood sugar level and composition of meal. *Nature*, 1964, *203*, 327-328. **189**

Yerkes, D. N., *see* Yerkes, R. M., 1928.

Yerkes, R. M. The instincts, habits, and reactions of the frog: I. Associative processes of the green frog. *Harvard Psychology Studies*, 1903, *1*, 579-638. **704**

Yerkes, R. M. *The dancing mouse.* New York: Macmillan, 1907. **748**

Yerkes, R. M. The intelligence of earthworms. *Journal of Animal Behavior*, 1912, *2*, 332-352. **698**

Yerkes, R. M., & Dodson, J. D. The relation of strength of stimulus to rapidity of habit-formation. *Journal of Comparative Neurology and Psychology*, 1908, *18*, 459-482. **704, 829**

Yerkes, R. M., & Morgulis, S. The method of Pawlow in animal psychology. *Psychological Bulletin*, 1909, *6*, 257-273. **562**

Yerkes, R. M., & Watson, J. B. Methods of studying vision in animals. *Behavioral Monographs*, 1911, No. 2. **748**

Yerkes, R. M., & Yerkes, D. N. Concerning memory in the chimpanzee. *Journal of Comparative Psychology*, 1928, *8*, 237-271. **689**

Yoshida, M. Studies of psychometric classification of odors: 5. *Japanese Psychological Research*, 1964, *6*, 145-154. **216**

Yoshida, T. Figural aftereffect as a function of the brightness ratio between the inspection figure and its surrounding field. In *Studies in psychology in commemoration of Professor Matsusaburo Yokoyama's seventy-first birthday.* Tokyo: Keio University, 1960. **470**

Young, F. A. Boring's interpretation of Emmert's law. *American Journal of Psychology*, 1950, *63*, 277-280. **511**

Young, F. A. Concerning Emmert's law. *American Journal of Psychology*, 1951, *64*, 124-128. **511**

Young, P. T. Constancy of affective judgments to odor. *Journal of Experimental Psychology*, 1923, *6*, 182-191. **215**

Young, P. T. The role of head movements in auditory localization. *Journal of Experimental Psychology*, 1931, *14*, 95-124. **267**

Young, P. T., & Madsen, C. H., Jr. Individual isohedons in sucrose-sodium chloride and sucrose-saccharin gustatory areas. *Journal of Comparative and Physiological Psychology*, 1963, *56*, 903-909. **628**

Young, P. T., *see also* Kniep, E. H., 1931; Pfaffman, C., 1954.

Young, R. Paired-associate learning when the same items occur as stimuli and responses. *Journal of Experimental Psychology*, 1961, *61*, 315-318. **1012**

Young, R. K. Retroactive and proactive effects under varying conditions of response similarity. *Journal of Experimental Psychology*, 1955, *50*, 113-119. **1056, 1083, 1104**

Young, R. K. A comparison of two methods of learning serial associations. *American Journal of Psychology*, 1959, *72*, 554-559. **1012, 1023, 1064**

Young, R. K. Tests of three hypotheses about the stimulus in serial learning. *Journal of Experimental Psychology*, 1962, *63*, 307-313. **1012**

Young, R. K., & Casey, M. Transfer from serial to paired-associate learning. *Journal of Experimental Psychology*, 1964, *67*, 594-595. **1012**

Young, R. K., & Jennings, P. C. Backward learning when the same items serve as stimuli and responses. *Journal of Experimental Psychology*, 1964, *68*, 64-70. **1064**

Young, R. K., Milauckas, E. W., & Bryan, J. D. Serial learning as a function of prior paired-associate learning. *American Journal of Psychology*, 1963, *76*, 82-88. **1012**

Young, R. K., Patterson, J., & Benson, W. M. Backward serial learning. *Journal of Verbal Learning and Verbal Behavior*, 1963, *1*, 335-338. **1012**

Younger, M. S., see Bolles, R. C., 1967.

Yu, K. C., see King, D. J., 1962.

Yum, K. S. An experimental test of the law of assimilation. *Journal of Experimental Psychology*, 1931, *14*, 66–82. **1047**

Zachs, R., see Postman, L., 1968.

Zajaczkowska, A. Experimental test of Luneburg's theory: Horopter and alley experiments. *Journal of the Optical Society of America*, 1956, *46*, 514–527. **493**

Zajkowski, M. M., see Erickson, J. R., 1966, 1967.

Zanforlin, M. Some observations on Gregory's theory of perceptual illusions. *Quarterly Journal of Experimental Psychology*, 1967, *29*, 193–197. **456, 457, 461**

Zangwill, O. L., see Gregory, R. L., 1963.

Zaretsky, H., see Goodrich, K. P., 1962.

Zavortink, B. Retroactive inhibition in free-recall learning of conceptually related words as a function of change in context and interlist similarity. Unpublished doctoral dissertation, Univ. of California, Berkeley, 1968. **1085**

Zavortink, B., & Keppel, G. The influence of interpolated MMFR upon relearning in the *A-B, A-C* and *A-B, A-B'* paradigms. *Journal of Verbal Learning and Verbal Behavior*, 1968, *7*, 254–256. (a) **1062**

Zavortink, B., & Keppel, G. Retroactive inhibition in free-recall learning with alphabetical cues. *Journal of Experimental Psychology*, 1968. (b) **1044**

Zavortinck, B., see also Keppel, G., 1968.

Zeaman, D. Response latency as a function of the amount of reinforcement. *Journal of Experimental Psychology*, 1949, *39*, 466–483. **617, 618, 631, 795**

Zeaman, D., & House, P. J. The role of attention in retardate discrimination learning. In N. R. Ellis (Ed.), *Handbook in mental deficiency: Psychological theory and research.* New York: McGraw-Hill, 1963. Pp. 159–233. **949, 1001**

Zeaman, D., & Smith, R. W. Review of some recent findings in human cardiac conditioning. In W. F. Prokasy (Ed.), *Classical conditioning.* New York: Appleton, 1965. **567**

Zeaman, D., see also House, B. J., 1963; Shepp, B., 1966.

Zeeman, W. P. C., see Roelofs, C. O., 1957.

Zegers, R. T. The reversal illusion of the Ames trapezoid. *Transactions of the New York Academy of Sciences*, 1965, *26*, 377–400. **518**

Zeigler, H. P., see Megibow, M., 1968.

Zeigler, H. P., & Leibowitz, H. Apparent visual size as a function of distance for children and adults. *American Journal of Psychology*, 1957, *70*, 106–109. **513, 550**

Zeiler, M. D. The ratio theory of intermediate size discrimination. *Psychological Review*, 1963, *70*, 516–533. **765**

Zeiler, M. D. Stimulus definition and choice. In L. P. Lipsitt & C. C. Spiker (Eds.), *Advances in child development and behavior.* Vol. III. New York: Academic Press, 1967. Pp. 125–156. **765**

Zeiler, M. D., & Price, A. E. Discrimination with variable interval and continuous reinforcement schedules. *Psychonomic Science*, 1965, *3*, 299–300. **768**

Zelhart, P. F., see Johnson, R. C., 1964.

Zener, K. The significance of behavior accompanying conditioned salivary secretion for theories of the conditioned response. *American Journal of Psychology*, 1937, *50*, 384–403. **565**

Zener, K. E., see Wever, E. G., 1928.

Zerbolio, D. J., Jr., see Weisman, R. G., 1966.

Zerlin, S., see Davis, H., 1966; Tobias, J. V., 1959.

Zewi, M., see Granit, R., 1938.

Ziegler, H., & Wyckoff, L. B. Observing responses and discrimination learning. *Quarterly Journal of Experimental Psychology*, 1961, *13*, 129–140. **769**

Zigler, M. J., Cook, B., Miller, D., & Wemple, L. The perception of form in peripheral vision. *American Journal of Psychology*, 1930, *42*, 246–259. **443, 445**

Zimmerman, C., see Bruner, J. S., 1955.

Zimmerman, D. W. Durable secondary reinforcement. *Psychological Review*, 1957, *64*, 373–383. **670**

Zimmerman, D. W. Sustained performance in rats based on secondary reinforcement. *Journal of Comparative and Physiological Psychology*, 1959, *52*, 353–358. **672, 673**

Zimmerman, J. Technique for sustaining behavior with conditioned reinforcement. *Science*, 1963, *142*, 682–684. **665**

Zinnes, J. L., Suppes, P., 1961, 1966.

Zotterman, Y. Studies in the peripheral nervous mechanism of pain. *Acta Medica Scandinavica*, 1933, *80*, 185–242. **160**

Zotterman, Y. The water taste of the frog. *Experientia*, 1950, *6*, 57–58. **186**

Zotterman, Y. Species differences in the water taste. *Acta Physiologica Scandinavica*, 1956, *37*, 60–70. **186, 190**

Zotterman, Y., see also Andersen, H. T., 1963; Borg, G., 1967; Diamant, H., 1963, 1965; Hensel, H., 1951; Liljestrand, G., 1954.

Zubek, J. P., Welch, G., & Saunders, M. G. Electroencephalographic changes during and after 14 days of perceptual deprivation. *Science*, 1963, *139*, 490–492. **841**

Zuckerman, C., see Wallach, H., 1963.

Zusne, L., see Michels, K. M., 1965.

Zwaardemaker, H., *L'odorat.* Paris: Doin, 1925. **211, 212**

Zwicker, E. Der Ungewohnliche Amplitudengang der nichtlinearen Verzerrungen des Ohres. *Acustica*, 1955, *5*, 67–74. **237, 239**

Zwicker, E. "Negative after-image" in hearing. *Journal of the Acoustical Society of America*, 1964, *36*, 2413–2415. **244**

Zwicker, E., & Scharf, B. A model of loudness summation. *Psychological Review*, 1965, *72*, 3–26. **248**

Zwicker, E., see also Simmons, F. B., 1965.

Zwislocki, J. Theory of temporal auditory summation. *Journal of the Acoustical Society of America*, 1960, *32*, 1046–1060. **234**

Zwislocki, J., Damianopoulos, E. N., Buining, E., & Glanz, J. Central masking: Some steady-state and transient effects. *Perception and Psychophysics*, 1967, *2*, 59–64. **242**

Zwislocki, J., & Feldman, R. S. Just noticeable differences in dichotic phase. *Journal of the Acoustical Society of America*, 1956, *28*, 860–864. **266**

Zwislocki, J., see also Hellman, R. P., 1961.

SUBJECT
INDEX

REFERENCE TABLES AND FORMULAS

1. p AND z VALUES
2. FOUR-PLACE LOGARITHMS
3. RANDOM NUMBERS
4. SQUARES, SQUARE ROOTS, AND RECIPROCALS
5. PERCENTILE VALUES OF "STUDENT'S" DISTRIBUTION

FORMULAS USEFUL IN LABORATORY WORK

REFERENCE TABLE 1 *p* AND *z* VALUES

p	.01	.02	.03	.04	.05	.06	.07	.08	.09	.10
z	−2.33	−2.05	−1.88	−1.75	−1.64	−1.55	−1.48	−1.41	−1.34	−1.28
p	.11	.12	.13	.14	.15	.16	.17	.18	.19	.20
z	−1.23	−1.18	−1.13	−1.08	−1.04	− .99	− .95	− .92	− .88	− .84
p	.21	.22	.23	.24	.25	.26	.27	.28	.29	.30
z	− .81	− .77	− .74	− .71	− .67	− .64	− .61	− .58	− .55	− .52
p	.31	.32	.33	.34	.35	.36	.37	.38	.39	.40
z	− .50	− .47	− .44	− .41	− .39	− .36	− .33	− .31	− .28	− .25
p	.41	.42	.43	.44	.45	.46	.47	.48	.49	.50
z	− .23	− .20	− .18	− .15	− .13	− .10	− .08	− .05	− .03	00
p	.51	.52	.53	.54	.55	.56	.57	.58	.59	.60
z	+ .03	+ .05	+ .08	+ .10	+ .13	+ .15	+ .18	+ .20	+ .23	+ .25
p	.61	.62	.63	.64	.65	.66	.67	.68	.69	.70
z	+ .28	+ .31	+ .33	+ .36	+ .39	+ .41	+ .44	+ .47	+ .50	+ .52
p	.71	.72	.73	.74	.75	.76	.77	.78	.79	.80
z	+ .55	+ .58	+ .61	+ .64	+ .67	+ .71	+ .74	+ .77	+ .81	+ .84
p	.81	.82	.83	.84	.85	.86	.87	.88	.89	.90
z	+ .88	+ .92	+ .95	+ .99	+1.04	+1.08	+1.13	+1.18	+1.23	+1.28
p	.91	.92	.93	.94	.95	.96	.97	.98	.99	.995
z	+1.34	+1.41	+1.48	+1.55	+1.64	+1.75	+1.88	+2.05	+2.33	+2.58

REFERENCE TABLE 2   FOUR-PLACE LOGARITHMS

n	0	1	2	3	4	5	6	7	8	9
10	0000	0043	0086	0128	0170	0212	0253	0294	0334	0374
11	0414	0453	0492	0531	0569	0607	0645	0682	0719	0755
12	0792	0828	0864	0899	0934	0969	1004	1038	1072	1106
13	1139	1173	1206	1239	1271	1303	1335	1367	1399	1430
14	1461	1492	1523	1553	1584	1614	1644	1673	1703	1732
15	1761	1790	1818	1847	1875	1903	1931	1959	1987	2014
16	2041	2068	2095	2122	2148	2175	2201	2227	2253	2279
17	2304	2330	2355	2380	2405	2430	2455	2480	2504	2529
18	2553	2577	2601	2625	2648	2672	2695	2718	2742	2765
19	2788	2810	2833	2856	2878	2900	2923	2945	2967	2989
20	3010	3032	3054	3075	3096	3118	3139	3160	3181	3201
21	3222	3243	3263	3284	3304	3324	3345	3365	3385	3404
22	3424	3444	3464	3483	3502	3522	3541	3560	3579	3598
23	3617	3636	3655	3674	3692	3711	3729	3747	3766	3784
24	3802	3820	3838	3856	3874	3892	3909	3927	3945	3962
25	3979	3997	4014	4031	4048	4065	4082	4099	4116	4133
26	4150	4166	4183	4200	4216	4232	4249	4265	4281	4298
27	4314	4330	4346	4362	4378	4393	4409	4425	4440	4456
28	4472	4487	4502	4518	4533	4548	4564	4579	4594	4609
29	4624	4639	4654	4669	4683	4698	4713	4728	4742	4757
30	4771	4786	4800	4814	4829	4843	4857	4871	4886	4900
31	4914	4928	4942	4955	4969	4983	4997	5011	5024	5038
32	5051	5065	5079	5092	5105	5119	5132	5145	5159	5172
33	5185	5198	5211	5224	5237	5250	5263	5276	5289	5302
34	5315	5328	5340	5353	5366	5378	5391	5403	5416	5428
35	5441	5453	5465	5478	5490	5502	5514	5527	5539	5551
36	5563	5575	5587	5599	5611	5623	5635	5647	5658	5670
37	5682	5694	5705	5717	5729	5740	5752	5763	5775	5786
38	5798	5809	5821	5832	5843	5855	5866	5877	5888	5899
39	5911	5922	5933	5944	5955	5966	5977	5988	5999	6010
40	6021	6031	6042	6053	6064	6075	6085	6096	6107	6117
41	6128	6138	6149	6160	6170	6180	6191	6201	6212	6222
42	6232	6243	6253	6263	6274	6284	6294	6304	6314	6325
43	6335	6345	6355	6365	6375	6385	6395	6405	6415	6425
44	6435	6444	6454	6464	6474	6484	6493	6503	6513	6522
45	6532	6542	6551	6561	6571	6580	6590	6599	6609	6618
46	6628	6637	6646	6656	6665	6675	6684	6693	6702	6712
47	6721	6730	6739	6749	6758	6767	6776	6785	6794	6803
48	6812	6821	6830	6839	6848	6857	6866	6875	6884	6893
49	6902	6911	6920	6928	6937	6946	6955	6964	6972	6981
50	6990	6998	7007	7016	7024	7033	7042	7050	7059	7067
51	7076	7084	7093	7101	7110	7118	7126	7135	7143	7152
52	7160	7168	7177	7185	7193	7202	7210	7218	7226	7235
53	7243	7251	7259	7267	7275	7284	7292	7300	7308	7316
54	7324	7332	7340	7348	7356	7364	7372	7380	7388	7396

REFERENCE TABLE 2 FOUR-PLACE LOGARITHMS (*Continued*)

n	0	1	2	3	4	5	6	7	8	9
55	7404	7412	7419	7427	7435	7443	7451	7459	7466	7474
56	7482	7490	7497	7505	7513	7520	7528	7536	7543	7551
57	7559	7566	7574	7582	7589	7597	7604	7612	7619	7627
58	7634	7642	7649	7657	7664	7672	7679	7686	7694	7701
59	7709	7716	7723	7731	7738	7745	7752	7760	7767	7774
60	7782	7789	7796	7803	7810	7818	7825	7832	7839	7846
61	7853	7860	7868	7875	7882	7889	7896	7903	7910	7917
62	7924	7931	7938	7945	7952	7959	7966	7973	7980	7987
63	7993	8000	8007	8014	8021	8028	8035	8041	8048	8055
64	8062	8069	8075	8082	8089	8096	8102	8109	8116	8122
65	8129	8136	8142	8149	8156	8162	8169	8176	8182	8189
66	8195	8202	8209	8215	8222	8228	8235	8241	8248	8254
67	8261	8267	8274	8280	8287	8293	8299	8306	8312	8319
68	8325	8331	8338	8344	8351	8357	8363	8370	8376	8382
69	8388	8395	8401	8407	8414	8420	8426	8432	8439	8445
70	8451	8457	8463	8470	8476	8482	8488	8494	8500	8506
71	8513	8519	8525	8531	8537	8543	8549	8555	8561	8567
72	8573	8579	8585	8591	8597	8603	8609	8615	8621	8627
73	8633	8639	8645	8651	8657	8663	8669	8675	8681	8686
74	8692	8698	8704	8710	8716	8722	8727	8733	8739	8745
75	8751	8756	8762	8768	8774	8779	8785	8791	8797	8802
76	8808	8814	8820	8825	8831	8837	8842	8848	8854	8859
77	8865	8871	8876	8882	8887	8893	8899	8904	8910	8915
78	8921	8927	8932	8938	8943	8949	8954	8960	8965	8971
79	8976	8982	8987	8993	8998	9004	9009	9015	9020	9025
80	9031	9036	9042	9047	9053	9058	9063	9069	9074	9079
81	9085	9090	9096	9101	9106	9112	9117	9122	9128	9133
82	9138	9143	9149	9154	9159	9165	9170	9175	9180	9186
83	9191	9196	9201	9206	9212	9217	9222	9227	9232	9238
84	9243	9248	9253	9258	9263	9269	9274	9279	9284	9289
85	9294	9299	9304	9309	9315	9320	9325	9330	9335	9340
86	9345	9350	9355	9360	9365	9370	9375	9380	9385	9390
87	9395	9400	9405	9410	9415	9420	9425	9430	9435	9440
88	9445	9450	9455	9460	9465	9469	9474	9479	9484	9489
89	9494	9499	9504	9509	9513	9518	9523	9528	9533	9538
90	9542	9547	9552	9557	9562	9566	9571	9576	9581	9586
91	9590	9595	9600	9605	9609	9614	9619	9624	9628	9633
92	9638	9643	9647	9652	9657	9661	9666	9671	9675	9680
93	9685	9689	9694	9699	9703	9708	9713	9717	9722	9727
94	9731	9736	9741	9745	9750	9754	9759	9763	9768	9773
95	9777	9782	9786	9791	9795	9800	9805	9809	9814	9818
96	9823	9827	9832	9836	9841	9845	9850	9854	9859	9863
97	9868	9872	9877	9881	9886	9890	9894	9899	9903	9908
98	9912	9917	9921	9926	9930	9934	9939	9943	9948	9952
99	9956	9961	9965	9969	9974	9978	9983	9987	9991	9996

REFERENCE TABLE 3 RANDOM NUMBERS

Line \ Col.	(1)	(2)	(3)	(4)	(5)	(6)	(7)	(8)	(9)	(10)	(11)	(12)	(13)	(14)
1	10480	15011	01536	02011	81647	91646	69179	14194	62590	36207	20969	99570	91291	90700
2	22368	46573	25595	85393	30995	89198	27982	53402	93965	34095	52666	19174	39615	99505
3	24130	48360	22527	97265	76393	64809	15179	24830	49340	32081	30680	19655	63348	58629
4	42167	93093	06243	61680	07856	16376	39440	53537	71341	57004	00849	74917	97758	16379
5	37570	39975	81837	16656	06121	91782	60468	81305	49684	60672	14110	06927	01263	54613
6	77921	06907	11008	42751	27756	53498	18602	70659	90655	15053	21916	81825	44394	42880
7	99562	72905	56420	69994	98872	31016	71194	18738	44013	48840	63213	21069	10634	12952
8	96301	91977	05463	07972	18876	20922	94595	56869	69014	60045	18425	84903	42508	32307
9	89579	14342	63661	10281	17453	18103	57740	84378	25331	12566	58678	44947	05585	56941
10	85475	36857	53342	53988	53060	59533	38867	62300	08158	17983	16439	11458	18593	64952
11	28918	69578	88231	33276	70997	79936	56865	05859	90106	31595	01547	85590	91610	78188
12	63553	40961	48235	03427	49626	69445	18663	72695	52180	20847	12243	90511	33703	90322
13	09429	93969	52636	92737	88974	33488	36320	17617	30015	08272	84115	27156	30613	74952
14	10365	61129	87529	85689	48237	52267	67689	93394	01511	26358	85104	20285	29975	89868
15	07119	97336	71048	08178	77233	13916	47564	81056	97735	85977	29372	74461	28551	90707
16	51085	12765	51821	51259	77452	16308	60756	92144	49442	53900	70960	63990	75601	40719
17	02368	21382	52404	60268	89368	19885	55322	44819	01188	65255	64835	44919	05944	55157
18	01011	54092	33362	94904	31273	04146	18594	29852	71585	85030	51132	01915	92747	64951
19	52162	53916	46369	58586	23216	14513	83149	98736	23495	64350	94738	17752	35156	35749
20	07056	97628	33787	09998	42698	06691	76988	13602	51851	46104	88916	19509	25625	58104
21	48663	91245	85828	14346	09172	30168	90229	04734	59193	22178	30421	61666	99904	32812
22	54164	58492	22421	74103	47070	25306	76468	26384	58151	06646	21524	15227	96909	44592
23	32639	32363	05597	24200	13363	38005	94342	28728	35806	06912	17012	64161	18296	22851
24	29334	27001	87637	87308	58731	00256	45834	15398	46557	41135	10367	07684	36188	18510
25	02488	33062	28834	07351	19731	92420	60952	61280	50001	67658	32586	86679	50720	94953
26	81525	72295	04839	96423	24878	82651	66566	14778	76797	14780	13300	87074	79666	95725
27	29676	20591	68086	26432	46901	20849	89768	81536	86645	12659	92259	57102	80428	25280
28	00742	57392	39064	66432	84673	40027	32832	61362	98947	96067	64760	64584	96096	98253
29	05366	04213	25669	26422	44407	44048	37937	63904	45766	66134	75470	66520	34693	90449
30	91921	26418	64117	94305	26766	25940	39972	22209	71500	64568	91402	42416	07844	69618
31	00582	04711	87917	77341	42206	35126	74087	99547	81817	42607	43808	76655	62028	76630
32	00725	69884	62797	56170	86324	88072	76222	36086	84637	93161	76038	65855	77919	88006
33	69011	65795	95876	55293	18988	27354	26575	08615	40801	59920	29841	80150	12777	48501
34	25976	57948	29888	88604	67917	48708	18912	82271	65424	69774	33611	54262	85963	03547
35	09763	83473	73577	12908	30883	18317	28290	35797	05998	41688	34952	37888	38917	88050
36	91567	42595	27958	30134	04024	86385	29880	99730	55536	84855	29080	09250	79656	73211
37	17955	56349	90999	49127	20044	59931	06115	20542	18059	02008	73708	83517	36103	42791
38	46503	18584	18845	49618	02304	51038	20655	58727	28168	15475	56942	53389	20562	87338
39	92157	89634	94824	78171	84610	82834	09922	25417	44137	84813	25555	21246	35509	20468
40	14577	62765	35605	81263	39667	47358	56873	56307	61607	49518	89656	20103	77490	18062
41	98427	07523	33362	64270	01638	92477	66969	98420	04880	45585	46565	04102	46880	45709
42	34914	63976	88720	82765	34476	17032	87589	40836	32427	70002	70663	88863	77775	69348
43	70060	28277	39475	46473	23219	53416	94970	25832	69975	94884	19661	72828	00102	66794
44	53976	54914	06990	67245	68350	82948	11398	42878	80287	88267	47363	46634	06541	97809
45	76072	29515	40980	07391	58745	25774	22987	80059	39911	96189	41151	14222	60697	59583
46	90725	52210	83974	29992	65831	38857	50490	83765	55657	14361	31720	57375	56228	41546
47	64364	67412	33339	31926	14883	24413	59744	92351	97473	89286	35931	04110	23726	51900
48	08962	00358	31662	25388	61642	34072	81249	35648	56891	69352	48373	45578	78547	81788
49	95012	68379	93526	70765	10592	04542	76463	54328	02349	17247	28865	14777	62730	92277
50	15664	10493	20492	38391	91132	21999	59516	81652	27195	48223	46751	22923	32261	85653

Taken from the 30-page table of 105,000 random digits prepared by the Bureau of Transport Economics and Statistics of the Interstate Commerce Commission, Washington, D.C.

REFERENCE TABLE 4　SQUARES, SQUARE ROOTS, AND RECIPROCALS

n	n²	√n	√10n	1/n	n	n²	√n	√10n	1/n
1	1	1.000	3.162	1.00000	51	2601	7.141	22.583	.01961
2	4	1.414	4.472	.50000	52	2704	7.211	22.804	.01923
3	9	1.732	5.477	.33333	53	2809	7.280	23.022	.01887
4	16	2.000	6.325	.25000	54	2916	7.348	23.238	.01852
5	25	2.236	7.071	.20000	55	3025	7.416	23.452	.01818
6	36	2.449	7.746	.16667	56	3136	7.483	23.664	.01786
7	49	2.646	8.367	.14286	57	3249	7.550	23.875	.01754
8	64	2.828	8.944	.12500	58	3364	7.616	24.083	.01724
9	81	3.000	9.487	.11111	59	3481	7.681	24.290	.01695
10	100	3.162	10.000	.10000	60	3600	7.746	24.495	.01667
11	121	3.317	10.488	.09091	61	3721	7.810	24.698	.01639
12	144	3.464	10.954	.08333	62	3844	7.874	24.900	.01613
13	169	3.606	11.402	.07692	63	3969	7.937	25.100	.01587
14	196	3.742	11.832	.07143	64	4096	8.000	25.298	.01562
15	225	3.873	12.247	.06667	65	4225	8.062	25.495	.01538
16	256	4.000	12.649	.06250	66	4356	8.124	25.690	.01515
17	289	4.123	13.038	.05882	67	4489	8.185	25.884	.01493
18	324	4.243	13.416	.05556	68	4624	8.246	26.077	.01471
19	361	4.359	13.784	.05263	69	4761	8.307	26.268	.01449
20	400	4.472	14.142	.05000	70	4900	8.367	26.458	.01429
21	441	4.583	14.491	.04762	71	5041	8.426	26.646	.01408
22	484	4.690	14.832	.04545	72	5184	8.485	26.833	.01389
23	529	4.796	15.166	.04348	73	5329	8.544	27.019	.01370
24	576	4.899	15.492	.04167	74	5476	8.602	27.203	.01351
25	625	5.000	15.811	.04000	75	5625	8.660	27.386	.01333
26	676	5.099	16.125	.03846	76	5776	8.718	27.568	.01316
27	729	5.196	16.432	.03704	77	5929	8.775	27.749	.01299
28	784	5.292	16.733	.03571	78	6084	8.832	27.928	.01282
29	841	5.385	17.029	.03448	79	6241	8.888	28.107	.01266
30	900	5.477	17.321	.03333	80	6400	8.944	28.284	.01250
31	961	5.568	17.607	.03226	81	6561	9.000	28.460	.01235
32	1024	5.657	17.889	.03125	82	6724	9.055	28.636	.01220
33	1089	5.745	18.166	.03030	83	6889	9.110	28.810	.01205
34	1156	5.831	18.439	.02941	84	7056	9.165	28.983	.01190
35	1225	5.916	18.708	.02857	85	7225	9.220	29.155	.01176
36	1296	6.000	18.974	.02778	86	7396	9.274	29.326	.01163
37	1369	6.083	19.235	.02703	87	7569	9.327	29.496	.01149
38	1444	6.164	19.494	.02632	88	7744	9.381	29.665	.01136
39	1521	6.245	19.748	.02564	89	7921	9.434	29.833	.01124
40	1600	6.325	20.000	.02500	90	8100	9.487	30.000	.01111
41	1681	6.403	20.248	.02439	91	8281	9.539	30.166	.01099
42	1764	6.481	20.494	.02381	92	8464	9.592	30.332	.01087
43	1849	6.557	20.736	.02326	93	8649	9.644	30.496	.01075
44	1936	6.633	20.976	.02273	94	8836	9.695	30.659	.01064
45	2025	6.708	21.213	.02222	95	9025	9.747	30.822	.01053
46	2116	6.782	21.448	.02174	96	9216	9.798	30.984	.01042
47	2209	6.856	21.679	.02128	97	9409	9.849	31.145	.01031
48	2304	6.928	21.909	.02083	98	9604	9.899	31.305	.01020
49	2401	7.000	22.136	.02041	99	9801	9.950	31.464	.01010
50	2500	7.071	22.361	.02000	100	10000	10.000	31.623	.01000

REFERENCE TABLE 5 PERCENTILE VALUES OF "STUDENT'S" DISTRIBUTION

n	$t_{.75}$	$t_{.90}$	$t_{.95}$	$t_{.99}$	$t_{.995}$
1	1.00	3.08	6.31	31.82	63.66
2	.82	1.89	2.92	6.96	9.92
3	.76	1.64	2.35	4.54	5.84
4	.74	1.53	2.13	3.75	4.60
5	.73	1.48	2.02	3.36	4.03
6	.72	1.44	1.94	3.14	3.71
7	.71	1.42	1.89	3.00	3.50
8	.71	1.40	1.86	2.90	3.36
9	.70	1.38	1.83	2.82	3.25
10	.70	1.37	1.81	2.76	3.17
11	.70	1.36	1.80	2.72	3.11
12	.70	1.36	1.78	2.68	3.05
13	.69	1.35	1.77	2.65	3.01
14	.69	1.34	1.76	2.62	2.98
15	.69	1.34	1.75	2.60	2.95
16	.69	1.34	1.75	2.58	2.92
17	.69	1.33	1.74	2.57	2.90
18	.69	1.33	1.73	2.55	2.88
19	.69	1.33	1.73	2.54	2.86
20	.69	1.32	1.72	2.53	2.85
21	.69	1.32	1.72	2.52	2.83
22	.69	1.32	1.72	2.51	2.82
23	.69	1.32	1.71	2.50	2.81
24	.68	1.32	1.71	2.49	2.80
25	.68	1.32	1.71	2.48	2.79
26	.68	1.32	1.71	2.48	2.78
27	.68	1.31	1.70	2.47	2.77
28	.68	1.31	1.70	2.47	2.76
29	.68	1.31	1.70	2.46	2.76
30	.68	1.31	1.70	2.46	2.75

Reprinted abridged from R. A. Fisher and F. Yates, *Statistical Tables for Biological, Agricultural, and Medical Research*, published by Oliver & Boyd Ltd., Edinburgh, 1963, by permission of the authors and publishers.

FORMULAS USEFUL IN LABORATORY WORK

Length

1 meter (m) = 3.28 feet (ft) = 39.37 inches (in.)
   = 100 centimeters (cm) = 1000 millimeters (mm)
   = 10^6 micrometers (μm), or microns (μ)
   = 10^9 nanometers (nm), or millimicrons (mμ)
   = 10^{10} Ångstrom units (Å)
1 foot = 12 in. = 30.48 cm
1 inch = 2.54 cm

Volume

1 liter (l) = 1.0567 quarts (qt) = 1000 milliliters (ml)
   = 1000.03 cubic centimeters (cc or cm^3)

Weight

1 gram (g) = .0022 pound (lb) = .035274 ounce (oz)
   = 1000 milligrams (mg) = 10^6 micrograms (μg)

Angle

1 degree (°, deg) = 60 minutes (min) = 3600 seconds (sec) = 0.0175 radian (rad)

Photometry

1 millilambert (mL) = 0.929 footlambert (ft L) = 3.183 candles per square meter (c/m^2)
   = 10 apostilbs

Frequency

1 cycle per sec = 1 cps = 1 Hz = 360°/sec = 2 π rad/sec

Time

1 second (sec) = 1000 milliseconds (msec) = 10^6 microseconds (μsec)

Temperature

Degrees centigrade (°C) = 5/9(n°F − 32) = n°K − 273
Degrees fahrenheit (°F) = 9/5n°C + 32
Degrees kelvin (°K) = n°C + 273

π = 3.1416

e = 2.71828